A TREASURY OF
AMERICAN FOLKLORE

A TREASURY OF
AMERICAN
FOLKLORE

STORIES, BALLADS, AND
TRADITIONS OF THE PEOPLE

Edited by

B. A. BOTKIN

with a Foreword by

CARL SANDBURG

AMERICAN LEGACY PRESS

NEW YORK

This edition is published by American Legacy Press,
distributed by Crown Publishers, Inc.,
225 Park Avenue South, New York, New York 10003,
by arrangement with Crown Publishers, Inc.

Manufactured in the United States of America

Library of Congress Cataloging-in-Publication Data

A Treasury of American folklore.

    Includes index.
    1. Folklore—United States. 2. Legends—United
States. 3. United States—Social life and customs.
I. Botkin, Benjamin Albert, 1901–
GR105.T73 1989   398'.0973   88-29634

h g f e d c b a

FOREWORD

WE HAVE heard of the boy and his sister coming home from school to tell their mother, "We learned today we have been talking prose all our lives and we didn't know it." Likewise many of us grown-ups have talked off a lot of folklore in our lives and we didn't know it was folklore—and if we had known it wouldn't have made much difference. You can't stop 'em from telling it even if they politely warn you beforehand, "Stop me if you've heard this." They (or we?) are irrepressible as the tenacious debating opponent of whom A. Lincoln said in 1858 that the only way you could make him quit would be "to stop his mouth with a corn cob."

So here we have nothing less than an encyclopedia of the folklore of America. An encyclopedia is where you get up into box car numbers. There have been small fry collections of folklore we might say, but this one is a big shot. It will pass the time, furnish laughter, provide entertainment. And then besides giving you the company of nice, darnfool yarn spinners, it will give you something of the feel of American history, of the gloom chasers that moved many a good man who fought fire and flood, varmints and vermin, as region after region filled with the settlers and homesteaders who proclaimed, "We are breaking sod for unnumbered millions to come."

And now that the days of those pioneers are passed, we have cities and skyscraping structures of steel and concrete that would have amazed them, motion pictures and radio transmissions that some would have declared "plumb ridiculous," not to mention the tractors which can plow without mules and the storm-proof all-steel buggies and wagons that do better than a mile a minute without a horse to pull.

And this smart later generation of youth has its folklore and our encyclopedia has plenty of specimens of Little Audrey, of Knock Knock, Who's There?, of the little moron who being told he was dead ordered that he should be moved into the living room.

Something rather sweetly modern and quite impossible to see as coming alive out of any former generation is such a story as the editor dug out of "Chicago Industrial Folklore," by Jack Conroy. There it was hiding out in the Manuscripts of the Federal Writers' Project of the Works Progress Administration for the State of Illinois. It tells about Slappy Hooper, the World's Biggest, Fastest and Bestest Sign Painter and is a fresh modern masterpiece worth standing alongside the well-liked antiques which will not fail to be passed along from generation to generation.

A longtime book is this. One reading won't do for it. There are places in it where good fools have such love for other good fools that they must trade the follies and whims of their imaginations, to help forget their troubles, even their tragedies.

Excellent authority tells us that the right laughter is medicine to weary bones. And on many a page here one may find the droll smile or the rocking laughter that moved many a humble and honest struggler on American soil as he studied, with whatever of mind he had, what the present of his country was—and what the future might be.

The people or the folk of the present hour that is and of the future that is to be, many and many of them are seen here in their toil, laughter and struggle, are heard and made known in part in the heaped-up and sprawling materials of this book. It breathes of the human diversity of these United States.

CARL SANDBURG

CONTENTS

II. PSEUDO BAD MEN

III. KILLERS

IV. FREE LANCES

V. MIRACLE MEN

VI. PATRON SAINTS

PART TWO: BOOSTERS AND KNOCKERS

I. TALL TALK

II. THE SKY'S THE LIMIT

III. LOCAL CRACKS AND SLAMS

PART THREE: JESTERS

I. PRANKS AND TRICKS

II. HUMOROUS ANECDOTES AND JESTS

PART FOUR: LIARS

I. YARNS AND TALL TALES

II. FROM THE LIARS' BENCH

PART FIVE: FOLK TALES AND LEGENDS

I. ANIMAL TALES

II. NURSERY TALES

III. WITCH TALES

IV. GHOST TALES

V. DEVIL TALES

VI. QUEER TALES

PART SIX: SONGS AND RHYMES

I. PLAY RHYMES AND CATCH COLLOQUIES

II. SINGING AND PLAY-PARTY GAMES

III. BALLADS AND SONGS

INTRODUCTION

I

WHEN I began to think of a book of American folklore, I thought of all the good songs and stories and all the good talk that would go into it, and of what a richly human and entertaining book it would be. A book of American folklore, I thought, should be as big as this country of ours—as American as Davy Crockett and as universal as Brer Rabbit. For when one thinks of American folklore one thinks not only of the folklore of American life—the traditions that have sprung up on American soil—but also of the literature of folklore— the migratory traditions that have found a home here.

Because folklore is so elemental and folk songs and stories are such good neighbors and pleasant companions, it is hard to understand why American folklore is not more widely known and appreciated. For this the word "folklore" is partly responsible. Folklore is the scholar's word for something that is as simple and natural as singing songs and spinning yarns among the folk who know the nature and the meaning but not the name—and certainly not the scholarship—of folklore. Because the word denotes both the material and its study, and has come to stand more for the study of the thing than for the thing itself, folklore, in fact, seems to have become the possession of the few who study it rather than of the many who make or use it.

The essence of folklore, however, is something that cannot be contained in a definition but that grows upon one with folklore experience. Old songs, old stories, old sayings, old beliefs, customs, and practices—the mindskills and handskills that have been handed down so long that they seem to have a life of their own, a life that cannot be destroyed by print but that constantly has to get back to the spoken word to be renewed; patterned by common experience; varied by individual repetition, inventive or forgetful; and cherished because somehow characteristic or expressive: all this, for want of a better word, is folklore.

Complementary to the "Stop me if you've heard this" aspect of folklore is the trait implied in the comeback: "That's not the way I heard it." For what makes a thing folklore is not only that you

have heard it before yet want to hear it again, because it is different, but also that you want to tell it again in your own way, because it is anybody's property. On the one hand, repeated retelling
establishes confidence in the rightness of what is said and how it
is said. On the other hand, the beauty of a folk lyric, tune, story,
or saying is that, if you don't like it, you can always change it, and,
if *you* don't, someone else will.

But if folklore is old wine in new bottles, it is also new wine in
old bottles. It says not only, "Back where I come from," but also,
"Where do we go from here?" If this book is intended to bring the
reader back to anything, it is not to the "good old days" but to an
enjoyment and understanding of living American folklore for what
it is and what it is worth. This is an experience in which Americans
as compared with other peoples are sadly deficient. Perhaps it is because we are not one people but many peoples in one, and a young
people, who have grown up too close to the machine age. The industrial folk tales and songs in this book are evidence enough that
machinery does not destroy folklore. Rather, in our rapid development from a rural and agricultural to an urban and industrial folk,
we have become estranged from the folklore of the past, which we
cannot help feeling a little self-conscious or antiquarian about, without yet being able to recognize or appreciate the folklore of the
present.

Perhaps the best way to understand the songs and stories in this
book is in terms of a species of living literature which has no fixed
form (in this respect differing from the classics, which it resembles
in permanence and universality of appeal) and which is constantly
shifting back and forth between written and unwritten tradition.
Since print tends to freeze a song or a story, folklore is most alive
or at home out of print, and in its purest form is associated with the
"grapevine" and the bookless world. But that does not make it
synonymous with illiteracy or ignorance, nor is it true that the
educated do not also have their lore, or that lore ceases to be lore
as soon as it is written down or published. Folk literature differs
from the rest of literature only in its history: its author is the
original "forgotten man."

Not only does folklore shift, but it changes as it shifts, between
the top and bottom layers of culture. As it gets nearer to the world
of professional poets and story-tellers, it tends to shape about itself a formal "literary" tradition of its own, as in the great collections of legends and folk tales that have come down to us from
ancient and medieval times and have been pored over by scholars.

But alongside of this more classic folk literature, which has acquired scholarly prestige and which gives and takes erudition, is the humbler and homelier folk literature of everyday life and the common man—today's people's literature (which the older folk literature may once have been). The difference between the two (a difference perhaps only of degree) is the difference, say, between the English and Scottish ballads and the "Dust Bowl Ballads" of Woody Guthrie.

This range of variation within the folklore field is a source of both strength and weakness. For while it enables folklore perpetually to rebuild itself from the ground up, it creates a kind of class-consciousness among folklorists. Thus the British folk-song and folk-dance expert, Cecil J. Sharp, while very much taken with the vigor and beauty of our mountain songs and dances, was unable to see in our cowboy songs anything but the fact that the "cowboy has been despoiled of his inheritance of traditional song" and has "nothing behind him" and nothing but "himself and his daily occupations to sing about, and that in a self-centered, self-conscious way, e.g., 'The cowboy's life is a dreadful life'; 'I'm a poor lonesome cowboy'; 'I'm a lonely bull-whacker,' and so forth."

Further complicating and diversifying the picture is a third quantity, midway between "folk" and "academic"—the "popular." The latter is distinguished by its wider and more passing acceptance, the result of transmission through such "timely" media as stage, press, radio, and films. Yet the so-called lively arts—jazz, vaudeville, burlesque, comic strips, animated cartoons, pulps—often have a folk basis or give rise to new folk creations, such as Mickey Mouse and Donald Duck. Many of the innovations of popular lore are associated with new inventions: e.g., the Ford joke and the gremlins. At the same time many of our modern gags have an ancient and honorable, if somewhat wheezy, lineage. The one about the two Irishmen, the Hebrew, and the baloney ("The Three Dreams") goes back to the twelfth century, while Little Moron jokes are as old as the Turkish Nasreddin.

Also close to folk sources but to be distinguished from folk literature proper is literature about the folk. This ranges from old-timers' reminiscences (one of the best examples of which in this book is Martha L. Smith's "Going to God's Country") and homespun humor and verse to local color and regional stories and sketches, all of which throw light on the folk and folklore backgrounds, culminating in that small body of masterpieces of "folk art" mined out of the collective experience and imagination by writers, known and unknown, who have succeeded in identifying themselves with their folk tradition.

II

It would be possible to get a good idea of American folklore by reading the fifty-seven volumes of the *Journal of American Folklore*. Since, however, writers of all kinds are always making use of folklore in one way or another, sometimes when one least expects it, one can turn up a surprising amount of good folklore simply by going through books, magazines, and newspapers. The present collection is a generous sampling, selected and arranged according to the interpretative principle of relating the material to certain folk motifs, such as hero-worship, boasting, pranking, jesting, "artistic" lying, and the like. By further relating these activities to certain regional and occupational groupings, the book is designed to reveal the cultural pattern of which American folklore is a part.

The term "American folklore" is employed here in the sense that one speaks of American literature, language, humor, etc., as an expression of the land, the people, and their experience. The same images and symbols have permeated all parts of this expression, so that folklore, literature, language, and humor are inseparable. "American folklore" is a much narrower and yet more definite concept than "folklore in America," which includes not only all the Americas but European folklore in America. For practical purposes, because I have had to draw the line somewhere, I have limited myself to folklore in the English idiom in the United States, excluding necessarily the Indian and foreign-language minorities. It is with considerable regret, and not with any intention of overstressing the Anglo-Saxon element, that I have had to dispense with the contrast of these "strips, stripes, and streaks of color." But for the resultant loss of diversity there may be a compensating gain in unity. Even within these limits I have collected a great deal more than I could find room for.

In order to keep the book further in hand, two tests were applied to all selections: readability, with an emphasis on literary and especially narrative interest, and permanence and breadth of appeal. Articles and collections of data being ruled out, customs and beliefs are represented only as they enter into song and story. According to my conception of folklore as the stuff that travels and the stuff that sticks—the basic principle of selection—I have had to leave out much good material valuable as social history rather than as folklore or purely local in interest. At the same time, a certain amount of stuff that travels without sticking or that sticks without traveling has been included as representative of folklore in the making.

In dealing with such a large mass of material from so many different sources and of so many different types and tones, it sometimes becomes difficult to see the woods for the trees. If I have chopped down a few trees here and lopped off a few branches there, it is also to clear a path through the wilderness. If I have preferred a little looseness to too much tightness of selection and arrangement, it is because I believe a smoother flow is achieved thereby and also because I have wanted to give the mass effect of thousands of unknown singers and story-tellers.

To vary the pace and to show both the discrete and the discursive folk imagination at work, short and long pieces have been intermingled in varying proportions. In those cases in which a song or a story might have served more than one purpose, it has been placed where it seems to have the most effect. In the same way, I have chosen versions which seem to me most effective, though the reader will probably think of versions he likes better, possibly because he knows them better. I should like to hear of these, too. Wherever possible and desirable, I have preferred the earlier sources, though there are seldom, if ever, "original" sources for folklore. In the matter of text, I have left spelling, punctuation, etc., alone, in spite of inconsistencies, except where they might get in the way of the reader. Original titles have been retained for complete pieces, but in the case of excerpts no attempt has been made to distinguish between original and added titles.

In the amount and nature of the introductory comment (in solid type) by the editor, two rules have been observed: (1) Where material is already available in other books, as in the various types of folk tales and folk songs, the comment has been kept to a minimum; where the material is fairly fresh, as in the first four parts of the book, more comment has been deemed necessary. (2) The approach has been broadly literary and social rather than strictly folkloristic. All uninitialed footnotes are by the editor.

III

Although for the most part I have preferred to let American folklore speak for itself, in one respect it is necessary to distinguish between folklore as we find it and folklore as we believe it ought to be. Folklore as we find it perpetuates human ignorance, perversity, and depravity along with human wisdom and goodness. Historically we cannot deny or condone this baser side of folklore—

and yet we may understand and condemn it as we condemn other manifestations of human error.

Folklore, like life itself, in Santayana's phrase, is animal in its origins and spiritual in its possible fruit. Much of the animalism, of course, does not appear here except by implication because of the taboos surrounding print. What does come through, however, often in violent contradiction of our modern social standards, is the essential viciousness of many of our folk heroes, stories, and expressions, especially in their treatment of minorities—Indians, Negroes, Mexicans, Chinese, etc.

In stories of anti-social humor and "necktie justice"—"Trimming a Darky's Heel," "Roy Bean and the Chinaman," "Variants of Roy Bean's Sentence"—the narrator inevitably reflects the prejudices belonging to his and his hero's race and class. Such stories stick because they have the tang of life and are a historical comment. They should be preserved not to perpetuate but to reveal and correct the errors and evils they narrate. With this perspective the whole of folklore may become an instrument for understanding and good will.

A word should be said here about the movement that seeks to make folklore the basis of an entire social or art tradition. One can forgive "folksiness" almost everything—its nostalgia, its quaintness, its cuteness—but not its clannishness, which is next to chauvinism, and which speaks of folklore in terms of the "racial heritage" or insists that a particular folk group or body of tradition is "superior" or "pure." On the other hand, it is not necessary to go to the opposite extreme and to deny the importance of folklore and even a healthy provincialism, as one of the ingredients, though not necessarily the most important ingredient, of a well-rounded culture. It is hoped that, while preserving this normal view of folklore, the book may serve as an inspiration and a source-book for writers, teachers, and all others who are concerned with the materials of an American culture.

For the rest, I have tried to let the material flow as it will in shaping itself about our ways of thinking and feeling in America, much as the literature of American folklore may be said to shape itself about the folklore of American life. In this way I have sought to give not only an American view of folklore but a folk's-eye view of America. By going to almost every form and medium of writing about America as well as to the regular folklore publications, I have hoped to give a broader and more living conception of American folklore than is to be gained from any single line of approach.

IV

The source of each selection is indicated in a note at the foot of the page on which the selection begins. Where several selections appear on the same page, the sources are indicated in the same order. These source notes constitute at once a complete list of acknowledgments and a selected bibliography. Special thanks are due to those who have contributed unpublished material, and to the Federal Writers' Project, for which much of this material was originally written.

Grateful acknowledgments are due to the many authors and publishers, selections from whose publications are included in this book. An exhaustive effort has been made to locate all persons having any rights or interests in this material, and to clear reprint permissions. If any required acknowledgments have been omitted or any rights overlooked, it is by accident and forgiveness is desired.

In addition to those who have read or discussed with me various parts of the book at one time or another during the four years in which it took shape, the following have been close to the work as a whole:

Paul R. ("Febold Feboldson") Beath, especially in the first compilation;

Gertrude Botkin, my wife, who shared the labor with me from first to last;

Hugo V. Buonagurio, who made the music drawings;

Crown Publishers, consistently sympathetic in their encouragement and support;

Edmund Fuller, who first suggested the idea and name of A Treasury of American Folklore and saw it through to the end;

Bertha Krantz, his assistant, who handled the permissions and served as a steadying influence;

Charles Seeger, who served as music consultant for the book.

Finally, without the collections of the Library of Congress, with which my work as Fellow in Folklore as well as folk-song archivist has brought me in close contact, this book would not have been possible.

B. A. BOTKIN

Washington, D. C.

*Casy spoke . . . "I know a bunch of stories, but
I only love people."*

—JOHN STEINBECK

PART ONE

HEROES AND BOASTERS

The history of any public character involves not only the facts about him but what the public has taken to be facts.

— J. Frank Dobie

The heroic spirit, as seen in heroic poetry, we are told, is the outcome of a society cut loose from its roots, of a time of migrations, of the shifting of populations.

— John G. Neihardt

Braggin' saves advertisin'.

— Sam Slick

I. BACKWOODS BOASTERS

The Backwoodsman is a soldier from necessity. Mind and body have been disciplined in a practical warfare. He belongs to this continent and to no other. He is an original. He thinks "big"; he talks "big"; and when it is necessary to toe the mark, he acts "big." He is the genius of the New World.
— JAMES K. PAULDING

These are the untamable. America has always been fecund in the production of roughs. — BERNARD DEVOTO

1. THE "IRREPRESSIBLE BACKWOODSMAN"

HERO tales tell us more about a people than perhaps any other tales. For, as admirable or exceptional men, heroes embody the qualities that we most admire or desire in ourselves. So we begin with the heroes as our most potent folk symbols and most reliable touchstones of a people's "choice."

In every age heroes arise from a people's dream of greatness or from homage to the great and near-great. In other times and places heroes received their sanction from religion or mythology as they derived their being or their powers from a world other than our own. Lacking a body of true myth and ritual, Americans conceive of their heroes, save for vague demigods of the Paul Bunyan type, as strictly of this world, however much they may take us out of it.

In modern times, especially in a democracy, hero myths and hero worship have become inextricably mixed. From a universal need of models larger than life or "desire to be ruled by strength and ability," Americans choose or create heroes in their own image. In a complex industrial society, hero-making goes on at various levels, so that every walk of life and almost every occupation have their heroes. Essentially, however, American heroes are of three main types: the poor boy who makes good, the good boy gone wrong, and the kind that is too good or too bad to be true. Thus, on the one hand, the schoolbooks and popular literature of edification draw upon the ranks of leaders—explorers, pioneers, soldiers, statesmen, inventors, and industrialists—for patron saints and tutelary geniuses, to inspire love of country or teach the ethics of success. On the other hand, the dime-novel concealed behind the geography book glorifies the gentlemen on horseback and the demons with the six-shooter. Midway between these two extremes is an American fairyland of strong men and giants who perform the impossible.

A composite picture of the American hero would show him to be a plain, tough, practical fellow, equally good at a bargain or a fight, a star-performer on the job and a hell-raiser off it, and something of a salesman and a showman, with a flair for prodigious stories, jokes, and stunts and a general capacity for putting himself over. Our nearest approach to a national myth, explaining and justifying the many contradictions in our heroes, is the frontier or pioneer myth. This reconciles the primitive virtues of brute strength, courage, and cunning with the economic virtues of thrift, hard work, and perseverance.

The backwoodsman was the first of our tall men, whose words were tall talk and whose deeds were tall tales. Romantic fiction has made much of his fierce, wild courage and independence and his "rough diamond" chivalry as well as of his skill with the rifle. "That murderous weapon," wrote Audubon of the Kentucky hunters, "is the means of procuring them subsistence during all their wild and extensive rambles, and is the source of their principal sports and pleasures." It also brought them into national prominence in the Battle of New Orleans, January 8, 1815. "Tough as a hickory," these "coonskin voters" helped put "Old Hickory" in the White House thirteen years later. In May, 1822, seven years after the battle, before a New Orleans audience of stamping, clapping, whooping flatboatmen and keelboatmen (many of whom had fought under Jackson), Noah Ludlow, the comedian, sang a song which marked the passing of the backwoodsman from history into legend. This was "The Hunters of Kentucky." By this time, too, the backwoodsman had emerged into his later phases. Like Mike Fink, the hunter had become a riverman; and beyond the Mississippi, following his free, wild way of living, he was to revert once more, like Mike Fink, to hunting and trapping.

In pursuit of game, skins, scalps, land, or adventure, the backwoodsman followed the shifting fringe of settlement, marching ahead of civilization or running away from it. As a picaresque type, the footloose adventurer, he illustrates what Lucy Lockwood Hazard calls the "dwindling of the hero," from the godlike or kinglike to the average human and subhuman level.

2. THE LION OF THE WEST

More and more, as the country was settled, the backwoodsman's motto became, in the words of the picaresque Simon Suggs, "It is good for a man to be shifty in a new country." To be shifty in a new country meant beating the other fellow to it. For a society that cannot support a large population puts a premium on outdoing—out-running, out-licking, and out-hollering—one's neighbor. Men with the bark on must also be men of gumption and gusto, who could talk, as well as walk, tall into and out of scrapes, rows, and sprees.

Boasting—the epic brag—has always been part of the trappings of the hero. The strong man of the Beowulf type or the medieval knight would gird himself for combat and inspire confidence in his followers by rehearsing his exploits in big talk. In his "paradise of puffers," however, the backwoods boaster tended to boast in terms of the future rather than of the past, and seemed more interested in making claims than in living up to them. Moreover, since boasting, like bombast, contains in itself the seeds of its own travesty, it became hard to distinguish bragging from windy laughing at bragging and serious from mock or burlesque boasts. From his noise the boaster became known as a roarer or screamer.

Because the qualities of the horse and the alligator seemed most fitting to the animal antics and noises of the ring-tailed roarer, the alligator horse or half-horse, half-alligator became his emblem. "It is an old remark," writes Washington Irving, "that persons of Indian mixture are half civilized, half savage, and half devil—a third half being provided for their particular convenience. It is for similar reasons, and probably with equal truth, that the backwoodsmen of Kentucky are styled half man, half horse, and half alligator, by the settlers on the Mississippi, and held accordingly in great respect and abhorrence." [1] Perhaps the best literary description we have of the strange breed in action is Robert Montgomery Bird's portrayal of the Salt River roarer, [2] Roaring Ralph Stackpole, rascally horse thief and stentorian braggart, in *Nick of the Woods* (1837).

Like the first successful Yankee character—Jonathan, in Royall Tyler's *The Contrast* (1787)—the first full-length portrait of the ring-tailed roarer was a stage creation. This was Colonel Nimrod Wildfire, the hero of James K. Paulding's lost prize-play, *The Lion of the West*, [3] which was produced at the Park Theatre, New York City, on April 25, 1831. The rôle of Colonel Wildfire, "a raw Kentuckian recently elected to Congress," was created by James J. Hackett, the "rising young comedian" and donor of the prize, who was also responsible for the names of the play and the hero. Wildfire was acclaimed as a contribution to the gallery of native American types (along with Hackett's Solomon Swap), and, through two rewritings of the play over a period of twenty years, remained one of the most successful rôles of the actor's career.

The one surviving speech of the play appears in several newspaper, almanac, and jokebook versions, attributed now to Colonel Wildfire and now to the meteoric Davy Crockett, who in 1831 was nearing the end of his second term in Congress. According to Paulding's son and biographer, the playwright disclaimed any intention of a take-off of that "well-known personage," [4] eliciting from him the following reply:

---

[1] *A History of New York*, by Diedrich Knickerbocker (1809), Book VI, Chapter III.

[2] The Salt River roarer was so called from the Kentucky freshwater stream of that name, which was derived from the salt once made on its banks. Because of the difficulty of navigation, the river has also given rise to the phrase for a political or other defeat, *to row* (some one) *up Salt River.* Other explanations of the origin of the phrase are "that refractory slaves used to be punished by hiring them out to row up the river; that the salt-boilers upon it were rough characters; that river pirates infested it; that after Kentucky summer elections, candidates, victor and vanquished alike, went up Salt River for a rest as far as Harrodsburg Springs. The story accepted in Kentucky, and repeated to me by state officials, is that when Henry Clay was candidate for President in 1832, he engaged a Jackson Democrat to row him up the Ohio to Louisville, where he was to speak. The boatman rowed him up Salt River instead, and he did not reach his destination until the day after election, when he learned of his own defeat. An intriguing picture, but one too full of geographic and logical improbabilities to credit." (*Sycamore Shores*, by Clark B. Firestone, 1936, p. 131.)

[3] Wildfire was not Paulding's only attempt to portray backwoods character, for in Ambrose Bushfield, in *Westward Ho!* (1832), he created a burlesque Natty Bumppo.

[4] It has also been suggested that the original of Wildfire may have been Florida's Governor William Pope Duval (father of John C. Duval), who supplied material for several stories by Washington Irving, Paulding's collaborator in the *Salmagundi* papers.

Washington City, 22nd Decr. 1830.

Sir your letter of the 15 Inst was handed to me this day by my friend M^r. Wilde
—the newspaper publications to which you refer I have never seen; and if I
had I should not have taken the reference to myself in exclusion of many who
fill offices and who are as untaught as I am. I thank you however for your
civility in assuring me that you had no reference to my peculiarites. The frank-
ness of your letter induces me to say a declaration from you to that effect was
not necessary to convince me that you were incapable of wounding the feelings
of a strainger and unlettered man who had never injured you—your charecter
for letters and as a gentleman is not altogethar unknown to me.

I have the honor with
great respects &c—
DAVID CROCKETT.[1]

Whatever Paulding's intentions, the actor's interpretation and the
public's acceptance of Wildfire must have profited by the resemblance
between the two lions of the West, even to Crockett's taking a bow at a
performance of the play. Thus the wood-engraving of Crockett on the
cover of the 1837 almanac is virtually indistinguishable from the cut of
Hackett in the rôle of Wildfire.[2] Following the Crockett version of the
Wildfire speech, the author of the *Sketches and Eccentricities of Col. David
Crockett, of West Tennessee* (1833), has this to say of the play:

This scene, with some slight alteration, has been attributed I understand to
an imaginary character, Colonel Wildfire. This I have not seen. But I am
unwilling that the *hard earnings* of Crockett should be given to another.

Such curious coincidences and correspondences illustrate the way in
which folklore becomes mixed with life and literature, and also point to
the fact that many Crockett stories may have had their source in current
anecdotes and been identified with other characters.

3. DAVY CROCKETT

If the prevailing rusticity of American folk heroes may be said to
constitute one of their chief attractions, then none of them is more attractive than Davy Crockett, the prime example of the country boy who made
good. "Crockett was rude and uncouth," writes one of his admirers, "but
honest and heroic. To the homely sense of the backwoodsman, he joined
a spirit as brave and chivalrous as any that followed the banner of the
Black Prince against the infidel."[3] His rise to fame serves as a peg on
which to hang the moral, "You can't keep a good man down."

It is certainly a very curious phase of American and especially of western
character, which is exhibited in the ease and promptness with which the colonel

---

[1] *Literary Life of James K. Paulding*, by William I. Paulding (1867), pp. 218–219.
[2] See the plate facing page 504 in *Annals of the New York Stage*, by George C. D.
Odell, Vol. III (1928).
[3] *Ben Hardin, His Times and Contemporaries*, by Lucius P. Little (1887), p. viii.

passes from one act of the singular drama of his life to another. Yesterday a rough bear-hunter, to-day, a member of the legislature, to-morrow about to become a member of Congress, and the fearless opponent of his old commander. General Jackson.

Such sudden and successful advances in life are scarcely seen except in our own country, where perfect freedom opens a boundless field to enterprise and perseverance.[1]

Although in his own day Crockett's name was a household word for his jokes as well as his achievements, the image of the "Colonel" that endures to-day is not that of a national political figure or the martyr of the Alamo but that of the comic backwoodsman. While historians of the American epic may, with Frank Norris, deplore the fact that "Crockett is the hero only of a 'funny story' about a sagacious coon,"[2] the epic's loss is humor's gain. The transformation of this prototype of the forks-of-the-creek philosopher and grass-roots politician into the archetype of the protean, wandering, legendary, American hero of the Munchausen-Eulenspiegel breed is an important and fascinating chapter in the annals of American hero-making.

In the "gentleman from the cane" the ring-tailed roarer is superimposed upon the comic backwoodsman, who is essentially the droll Yankee with more guts and gusto and less guile, to become the "gamecock of the wilderness." Because of his many-sidedness, his lively, humorous, homespun figure has supplanted the romantic frontiersman of the Daniel Boone type as the "heroic version of the poor-white," and rivals many another American hero. Thus, in his gumption he outdoes his older contemporary, Mike Fink, whom he resembles as game-hog and Indian-fighter but to whose tough guy he plays the smart aleck among backwoods boasters. In his rôle of cracker-box philosopher and story-telling politician, the coonskin Congressman anticipates Lincoln, although with Crockett story-telling was a business rather than an art—the business of being a wag and a good fellow.

While electioneering, the colonel always conciliates every crowd into which he may be thrown by the narration of some anecdote. It is his manner, more than the anecdote, which delights you. . . .

Pursuing this course, he laughs away any prejudice which may exist against him; and having created a favourable impression, enforces his claims by local arguments, showing the bearing which great national questions have upon the interests of the persons whom he wishes to represent. This mode, together with the faculty of being a boon companion to every one he meets, generally enables him to accomplish his object.[3]

The ancedotes of Crockett's Washington adventures show the "irrepressible backwoodsman" playing up to the accepted notion of himself as the rustic wag and wisecracker, a rôle in which he seems to have been the

---

[1] *Life of Colonel David Crockett* (1860), p. 140n.

[2] "A Neglected Epic," *Essays on Authorship* (1902).

[3] *Sketches and Eccentricities of Col. David Crockett, of West Tennessee* (1833), pp. 77, 78.

victim partly of his own ambitior. and good nature and partly of the designs of political friends and foes. Yet in his speeches in Congress, where he served three terms between 1827 and 1835, he is a sincere, plain-spoken champion of the people, with an occasional stroke of hard-hitting sarcasm:

Sirs, I do not consider it good sense to be sitting here passing laws for Andrew Jackson to laugh at; it is not even good nonsense . . . out of those that the President has got about him, I have never seen but one honest countenance since I have been here, and he has just resigned.[1]

In the autobiographical comic prose epics ascribed to him (1833–1836), he becomes "our first Southern humorist." From now on, laughter gains the ascendancy, and horse sense gives way to horseplay. Posthumously, he plays the buffoon in the "Crockett" almanacs (1835–1856), where his heroics are swallowed up in slapstick and hokum. Hoax, legend, myth, and caricature, he thus runs the gamut from the poor but honest farmer who made good by his own wits and go-aheadativeness ("Be sure you are always right, then go ahead") to the demigod who "totes the thunder in his fist and flings the lightning from his fingers." Somewhere between these two extremes the real Crockett has been lost. Even the stock figure of the backwoods bully and boaster yields to the riproaring superman of the jokebooks, whose tedium is relieved by an occasional flash of vernacular prose poetry and comic sublimity, as in "Crockett's Morning Hunt." Folk memories of Crockett linger in occasional hunting yarns of the South.[2]

Throughout the following sketches Crockett is essentially the hunter in pursuit of ever bigger and better game, from varmints and politicians to the challenging elements. Nowhere is backwoods mythology more alive than in Crockett's encounters with his animal friends and foes, in which Crockett is half-varmint and every varmint is half-Crockett.

4. MIKE FINK

In one of the Crockett almanacs we read of a shooting match between Crockett and Mike Fink ("a helliferocious fellow" and "an almighty fine shot"), in which the former lost by default. First, Crockett aimed at a cat sitting on the top rail of Mike's potato patch at a distance of about a hundred and fifty yards, and "the ball cut off both the old tom cat's ears close to his head, and shaved the hair off clean across the skull, as slick as if I'd done it with a razor, and the critter never stirred, nor knew he'd lost his ears till he tried to scratch 'em." Next, Mike aimed at a sow with a litter of pigs around her, "away off furder than the eend of the world" and kept "loading and firing for dear life, till he hadn't left one of them pigs enough tail to make a toothpick on." Then Crockett mended Mike's shot, which had left one of the pigs about an inch of tail, and cut it off as if it "had been drove in with a hammer."

---

[1] Speech on the Fortification Bill, *Register of Debates in Congress*, Part IV of Vol. X, June 19, 1834, p. 4586.

[2] For ten "Crockett" tall tales of hunting and shooting, see Vance Randolph's *Ozark Mountain Folks* (1932).

That made Mike a kinder sorter wrothy, and he sends a ball after his wife as she was going to the spring after a gourd full of water, and knocked half her comb out of her head, without stirring a hair, and calls out to her to stop for me to take a blizzard at what was left on it. The angeliferous critter stood still as a scarecrow in a cornfield, for she'd got used to Mike's tricks by long practice.

"No, no, Mike," sez I, "Davy Crockett's hand would be sure to shake if his iron war pointed within a hundred mile of a shemale, and I give up beat, Mike."

These feats of marksmanship are in the true Mike Fink tradition, which ranged from driving nails with bullets to shooting tin cups and scalp locks from heads. Mike's unique claim to fame among deadshots lay in the fact that most of his shooting wagers were sadistic pranks. For as a bully and cut-up hell-bent for fun Mike had more in common with the pseudo bad men of the West than he had with the river pirates and common ruffians among whom he moved. Unlike the frontier rascals who thought that "even a crime might take on the aspect of a good joke," Mike was one to carry a joke to the point of being a crime. He was quite impartial in his choice of victims, shooting off a Negro's heel because he disliked its shape or forcing his woman to lie down in a pile of leaves to which he set fire, to cure her of looking at other men.

Born of Scotch-Irish parents at old Fort Pitt in 1770, Mike Fink in his youth acquired a reputation as an Indian scout and the best shot in Pittsburgh. As the country filled up and the Indians were pushed across the Lakes and beyond the Mississippi, wrote Morgan Neville, in "The Last of the Boatmen" (1829), many of the scouts, "from a strong attachment to their erratic mode of life, joined the boatmen, then just becoming a distinct class." Among them he soon distinguished himself not only as the "king of the keelboatmen," known as the Snag on the Mississippi and the Snapping Turtle on the Ohio, but also as the "demigod of the rivers," in whom according to Bernard DeVoto, "Casanova, together with Paul Bunyan, merges into Thor." [1]

It was the perpetual fight of the boatmen with the river that made them "reckless savages." Among the various types of river craft the keelboat offered the greatest challenge to the boatman's strength, skill, and endurance.

In ascending the river, it was a continued series of toil, rendered more irksome by the snail like rate, at which they moved. The boat was propelled by poles, against which the shoulder was placed; and the whole strength and skill of the individual was applied in this manner. As the boatmen moved along the running board, with their heads nearly touching the plank on which they walked, the effect produced on the mind of an observer was similar to that on beholding the ox, rocking before an overloaded cart. Their bodies, naked to their waist, for the purpose of moving with greater ease, and of enjoying the breeze of the river, were exposed to the burning suns of summer, and to the rain of autumn. After a hard day's push, they would take their "fillee," or ration of whisky, and having swallowed a miserable supper of meat half burnt, and of bread half

---

[1] *Mark Twain's America* (1932), p. 60.

baked, stretch themselves without covering, on the deck, and slumber till the steersman's call invited them to the morning "fillee." Notwithstanding this, the boatman's life had charms as irresistible as those presented by the splendid illusions of the stage. Sons abandoned the comfortable farms of their fathers, and apprentices fled from the service of their masters. There was a captivation in the idea of "going down the river"; and the youthful boatman who had "pushed a keel" from New Orleans, felt all the pride of a young merchant after his first voyage to an English sea port. From an exclusive association together, they had formed a kind of slang peculiar to themselves; and from the constant exercise of wit, with the "squatters" on shore, and the crews of other boats, they acquired a quickness, and smartness of vulgar retort, that was quite amusing. The frequent battles they were engaged in with the boatmen of different parts of the river, and with the less civilized inhabitants of the lower Ohio, and Mississippi, invested them with that ferocious reputation, which has made them spoken of throughout Europe.[1]

In the same year that Noah Ludlow introduced "The Hunters of Kentucky" to the people of New Orleans, Mike Fink became one of Ashley's men in the service of the Mountain Fur Company. For, as the supremacy of the steamboat was established, the flatboatmen and keelboatmen turned to other fields. Some went to work on the steamboats, others became raftsmen, and still others like Mike Fink joined the trapping and trading expeditions that crossed the Rockies. At Fort Henry in Montana this champion marksman, fighter, drinker, lover, boaster, and jester was "killed in a skrimmage," in which his various types of prowess were called into play.

The Hunters of Kentucky

Ye gentlemen and ladies fair,
  Who grace this famous city,
Just listen, if ye've time to spare,
  While I rehearse a ditty;
And for the opportunity,
  Conceive yourselves quite lucky,
For 'tis not often that you see,
  A hunter from Kentucky.
Oh! Kentucky, the hunters of Kentucky,
  The hunters of Kentucky.

[1] "The Last of the Boatmen," by Morgan Neville, *The Western Souvenir*, for 1829.

From *Melodies, Duets, Trios, Songs, and Ballads, Pastoral, Amatory, Sentimental, Patriotic, Religious, and Miscellaneous*. Together with Metrical Epistles, Tales and Recitations, by Samuel Woodworth, pp. 221–223. New York: James M. Campbell; 1826.

Hunters of Kentucky.

Facsimile from *The Amateur's Song Book*, Boston, 1843.

We are a hardy free-born race,
  Each man to fear a stranger,
Whate'er the game, we join in chase,
  Despising toil and danger;
And if a daring foe annoys,
  Whate'er his strength and forces,
We'll show him that Kentucky boys
  Are "alligator horses."
Oh! Kentucky, the hunters of Kentucky,
  The hunters of Kentucky.

I s'pose you've read it in the prints,
  How Packenham attempted
To make Old Hickory Jackson wince,
  But soon his scheme repented;
For we with rifles ready cock'd,
  Thought such occasion lucky,
And soon around the General flock'd
  The hunters of Kentucky.
      Oh! Kentucky, &c.

You've heard, I s'pose, how New-Orleans
  Is famed for wealth and beauty—
There's girls of every hue, it seems,
  From snowy white to sooty;
So Packenham he made his brags,
  If he in fight was lucky,
He'd have their girls and cotton bags,
  In spite of Old Kentucky.[1]
      Oh! Kentucky, &c.

But JACKSON, he was wide awake,
  And wasn't scared at trifles;
For well he knew what aim we take,
  With our Kentucky rifles;
So he led us down to Cypress swamp,
  The ground was low and mucky;
There stood John Bull, in martial pomp,
  And here was Old Kentucky.
      Oh! Kentucky, &c.

A bank was raised to hide our breast,
  Not that we thought of dying,
But then we always like to rest,
  Unless the game is flying;

---

[1] "It must crimson with a blush every Englishman . . . when he finds it recorded, that an officer, the pride of England, confident of capturing of one of the finest cities in America, gave it as a *countersign*, upon the day his army was to enter it—'BOOTY, AND BEAUTY!!'"—Waldo's *Memoirs of Andrew Jackson* (1820). Cited in *Their Weight in Wildcats*, edited and illustrated by James Daugherty (1936), p. 48.

Behind it stood our little force—
   None wished it to be greater,
For every man was half a horse,
   And half an alligator.
      Oh! Kentucky, &c.

They did not let our patience tire,
   Before they showed their faces—
We did not choose to waste our fire,
   So snugly kept our places;
But when so near we saw them wink,
   We thought it time to stop them;
And 'twould have done you good, I think,
   To see Kentucky pop them.
      Oh! Kentucky, &c.

They found at last 'twas vain to fight
   Where lead was all their booty,
And so they wisely took to flight,
   And left us all the beauty.
And now, if danger e'er annoys,
   Remember what our trade is,
Just send for us Kentucky boys,
   And we'll protect you, Ladies.
      Oh! Kentucky, &c.

Roaring Ralph Stackpole

"CUNNEL," said he, "you're a man in authority, and my superior officer; wharfo' thar' can be no scalping between us. But my name's Tom Dowdle, the rag-man!" he screamed, suddenly skipping into the thickest of the throng, and sounding a note of defiance; "my name's Tom Dowdle, the rag-man, and I'm for any man that insults me! log-leg or leather-breeches, green-shirt or blanket-coat, land-trotter or river-roller,—I'm the man for a massacree!" Then giving himself a twirl upon his foot that would have done credit to a dancing-master, he proceeded to other antic demonstrations of hostility, which when performed in after years on the banks of the Lower Mississippi, by himself and his worthy imitators, were, we suspect, the cause of their receiving the name of the mighty alligator. It is said, by naturalists, of this monstrous reptile, that he delights, when the returning warmth of spring has brought his fellows from their holes, and placed them basking along the banks of a swampy lagoon, to dart into the centre of the expanse, and challenge the whole field to combat. He roars, he blows the water from his nostrils, he lashes it with his tail, he

From *Nick of the Woods, or The Jibbenainosay, A Tale of Kentucky*, by Robert Montgomery Bird, Vol. I, pp. 58–59. Philadelphia: Carey, Lea & Blanchard. 1837.

whirls round and round, churning the water into foam; until, having worked himself into a proper fury, he darts back again to the shore, to seek an antagonist. Had the gallant captain of horse-thieves boasted the blood, as he afterwards did the name, of an "alligator half-breed," he could scarce have conducted himself in a way more worthy of his parentage. He leaped into the centre of the throng, where, having found elbow-room for his purpose, he performed the gyration mentioned before, following it up by other feats expressive of his hostile humor. He flapped his wings and crowed, until every chanticleer in the settlement replied to the note of battle; he snorted and neighed like a horse; he bellowed like a bull; he barked like a dog; he yelled like an Indian; he whined like a panther; he howled like a wolf; until one would have thought he was a living menagerie, comprising within his single body the spirit of every animal noted for its love of conflict. Then, not content with such a display of readiness to fight the field, he darted from the centre of the area allowed him for his exercise, and invited the lookers-on individually to battle. "Whar's your buffalo-bull," he cried, "to cross horns with the roarer of Salt River? Whar's your full-blood colt that can shake a saddle off? H'yar's an old nag can kick off the top of a buck-eye! Whar's your cat of the Knobs? your wolf of the Rolling Prairies? H'yar's the old brown b'ar can claw the bark off a gum-tree! H'yar's a man for you, Tom Bruce! Same to you, Sim Roberts! to you, Jimmy Big-nose! to you, and to you, and to you! Ar'n't I a ring-tailed squealer? Can go down Salt on my back, and swim up the Ohio! Whar's the man to fight Roaring Ralph Stackpole?"

The Lion of the West

THE *Lion of the West* was played on Friday evening, and drew a crowded house, notwithstanding the inclemency of the weather. The principal character in this production is, to use his own elegant language, a *screamer*. Some idea of his peculiarities may be formed from the following slight sketch which he gives of an affair between himself and a raftsman.

"I was ridin' along the Mississippi in my wagon, when I come acrost a feller floatin' down stream, settin' in the starn of his boat fast asleep! Well, I hadn't had a fight for ten days—*felt as tho' I should have to kiver myself up in a salt barrel to keep*—so wolfy about the head and shoulders. So, says I, 'Hulloa, strannger! if you don't take keer your boat will run away with you!' So he looked up at me slantindicler, and I looked down on him slantindicler—he took out a chor o' tobaccer, and says he, 'I don't value you tantamount to *that*!' and then the varmint flapped his wings

From the *Daily Louisville Public Advertiser*, October 17, 1831. Cited in *The Beginnings of American English*, by M. M. Mathews. pp. 116–117. Chicago: University of Chicago Press. 1931.

and crowed like a cock. I ris up, shook my mane, crooked my neck, and neighed like a horse. He run his boat plump, head-foremost ashore. I stopped my wagon and sot my triggers. 'Mister,' says he, 'I can whip my weight in wildcats, and ride straight through a crab-apple orchard on a flash of lightning. Clear meat-ax disposition; the best man, if I a'nt, I wish I may be tetotaciously exfluncted!' "

The two belligerents join issue, and the Colonel goes on to say—

"He was a pretty severe colt, but no part of a priming to such a feller as me. *I put it to him mighty droll*—in ten minutes he yelled Enough! and swore I was a rip-staver! Says I, *'A'nt I the yaller flower of the forest!* and I'm all brimstone but the head, and that's aquafortis!' Says he, *'Stranger, you're a beauty!* and if I only know'd your name, I'd vote for you next election.' Says I, 'My name is Nimrod Wildfire—half horse, half alligator and a touch of the airthquake—that's got the prettiest sister, fastest horse and ugliest dog in the District, and can outrun, outjump, throw down, drag out and whip any man in all Kaintuck.' "

A Vote for Crockett

"I HAD taken old Betsy," said he, "and straggled off to the banks of the Mississippi river; and meeting with no game, I didn't like it. I felt mighty wolfish about the head and ears, and thought I would spile if I wasn't kivured up in salt, for I hadn't had a fight in ten days; and I cum acrost a fellow floatin' down stream settin' in the stern of his boat fast asleep. Said I, 'Hello, stranger! if you don't take keer your boat will run away with you'—and he looked up; and said he, 'I don't value you.' He looked up at me slantendicler, and I looked down upon him slantendicler; and he took out a chaw of turbaccur, and said he, 'I don't value you that.' Said I, 'Cum ashore, I can whip you—I've been trying to git a fight all the mornin' '; and the varmint flapped his wings and crowed like a chicken. I ris up, shook my mane, and neighed like a horse. He run his boat plump head foremost ashore. I stood still and sot my triggurs, that is, took off my shurt, and tied my galluses tight around my waist—and at it we went. He was a right smart coon, but hardly a bait for such a fellur as me. I put it to him mighty droll. In ten minutes he yelled enough, and swore I was a ripstavur. Said I, 'Ain't I the yaller flower of the forest! And I am all brimstone but the head and ears, and that's aquafortis.' Said he, 'Stranger, you are a beauty: and if I know'd your name, I'd vote for you next election.' Said I, 'I'm that same David Crockett. You know what I'm made of. I've got the closest shootin' rifle, the best 'coon dog, the biggest ticlur, and the ruffest racking horse in the district. I can kill more lickur, fool more varmints, and cool out more men than any man you

From *Sketches and Eccentricities of Col. David Crockett, of West Tennessee*, pp. 44–145. New York: Printed and Published by J. & J. Harper. 1833.

can find in all Kentucky.' Said he, 'Good mornin', stranger—I'm satisfied.'
Said I, 'Good mornin', sir; I feel much better since our meetin' "; but after
I got away a piece, I said, 'Hello, friend, don't forget that vote.' "

The Ballad of Davy Crockett

Now, don't you want to know something concernin'
Where it was I come from and where I got my learnin'?
Oh, the world is made of mud out o' the Mississippi River!
The sun's a ball of foxfire, as well you may disciver.

Chorus:
    Take the ladies out at night. They shine so bright
    They make the world light when the moon is out of sight.

And so one day as I was goin' a-spoonin'
I met Colonel Davy, and he was goin' a-coonin'.
Says I, "Where's your gun?" "I ain' got none."
"How you goin' kill a coon when you haven't got a gun?"

From *American Ballads and Folk Songs,* collected and compiled by John A. Lomax
and Alan Lomax, pp. 251–253. Copyright, 1934, by The Macmillan Company. New
York. Adapted from "The Ballad of Davy Crockett," by Julia Beazley, in *Texas and
Southwestern Lore,* Publications of the Texas Folk-Lore Society, Number VI (1927),
edited by J. Frank Dobie, pp. 205–206.

Says he, "Pompcalf, just follow after Davy,
And he'll soon show you how to grin a coon crazy "
I followed on a piece and thar sot a squirrel,
A-settin' on a log and a-eatin' sheep sorrel.

When Davy did that see, he looked around at me,
Saying, "All I want now is a brace agin your knee."
And thar I braced a great big sinner.
He grinned six times hard enough to git his dinner!

The critter on the log didn't seem to mind him—
Jest kep' a-settin' thar and wouldn't look behind him.
Then it was he said, "The critter must be dead.
See the bark a-flyin' all around the critter's head?"

I walked right up the truth to disciver.
Drot! It was a pine knot so hard it made me shiver.
Says he, "Pompcalf, don't you begin to laugh—
I'll pin back your ears, and bite you half in half!"

I flung down my gun and all my ammunition.
Says I, "Davy Crockett, I can cool your ambition!"
He throwed back his head and he blowed like a steamer.
Says he, "Pompcalf, I'm a Tennessee screamer!"

Then we locked horns and we wallered in the thorns.
I never had such a fight since the hour I was born.
We fought a day and a night and then agreed to drop it.
I was purty badly whipped—and so was Davy Crockett.

I looked all around and found my head a-missin'—
He'd bit off my head and I had swallered his'n!
Then we did agree to let each other be;
I was too much for him, and he was too much for me.

"Davy Crockett" is an interesting example of a folklorized negro minstrel song. "Pompey Smash" was a popular song on the minstrel stage before the middle of the nineteenth century. It is included in *The Negro Singer's Own Book* (Philadelphia, n. d.) and in *Lloyd's Ethiopian Song Book* (London, 1847). It has been twice before reported as a transformed folk song: in H. M. Belden's *A Partial List of Song Ballads and Other Popular Poetry Known in Missouri,* No. 59; and in J. H. Cox's *Folk-Songs of the South,* No. 177. But neither of these versions is as complete as the one reported here by Miss Beazley, nor has any folk tune, so far as I know, been heretofore recorded.—L. W. PAYNE, JR.

Nearly a generation ago, before the advent of motor cars and motor boats, I heard some sailors on the Texas coast singing "Davy Crockett." They were old time sailor men, and the ruggedness of the meter of the song in nowise hampered their gusto in singing it. For the music of the song I am indebted to Mrs. Tom C. Rowe, of Houston, who transcribed it, and to Mrs. Melton, who sang it. The words as sung by Mrs. Melton are slightly different from those originally learned by me, but the meter is the same.—J. B.

Telling Stories *vs.* Talking Government Matters

. . .. About this time there was a great squirrel hunt on Duck River, which was among my people. They were to hunt two days; then to meet and count the scalps, and have a big barbecue, and what might be called a tip-top country frolic. The dinner, and a general treat, was all to be paid for by the party having taken the fewest scalps. I joined one side, taking the place of one of the hunters, and got a gun ready for the hunt. I killed a great many squirrels, and when we counted scalps, my party was victorious.

The company had every thing to eat and drink that could be furnished in so new a country, and much fun and good humor prevailed. But before the regular frolic commenced, I mean the dancing, I was called on to make a speech as a candidate; which was a business I was as ignorant of as an outlandish negro.

A public document I had never seen, nor did I know there were such things; and how to begin I couldn't tell. I made many apologies, and tried to get off, for I know'd I had a man to run against who could speak prime, and I know'd, too, that I wasn't able to shuffle and cut with him. He was there, and knowing my ignorance as well as I did myself, he also urged me to make a speech. The truth is, he thought my being a candidate was a mere matter of sport; and didn't think for a moment, that he was in any danger from an ignorant backwoods bear hunter. But I found I couldn't get off, and so I determined just to go ahead, and leave it to chance what I should say. I got up and told the people I reckoned they know'd what I had come for, but if not, I could tell them. I had come for their votes, and if they didn't watch mighty close I'd get them too. But the worst of all was, that I could not tell them anything about government. I tried to speak about something, and I cared very little what, until I choked up as bad as if my mouth had been jamm'd and cramm'd chock full of dry mush. There the people stood, listening all the while, with their eyes, mouths, and ears all open, to catch every word I would speak.

At last I told them I was like a fellow I had heard of not long before. He was beating on the head of an empty barrel near the roadside, when a traveler, who was passing along, asked him what he was doing that for? The fellow replied that there was some cider in that barrel a few days before, and he was trying to see if there was any then, but if there was he couldn't get at it. I told them that there had been a little bit of a speech in me a while ago, but I believed I couldn't get it out. They all roared out in a mighty laugh, and I told some other anecdotes, equally amusing to them, and believing I had them in a first-rate way, I quit and got down, thanking the people for their attention. But I took care to remark that

From *Life of Colonel David Crockett,* Written by Himself, pp. 114–116. Philadelphia: G. G. Evans. 1860.

I was as dry as a powder-horn, and that I thought it was time for us all to wet our whistles a little; and so I put off to the liquor stand, and was followed by the greater part of the crowd.

I felt certain this was necessary, for I knowed my competitor could talk government matters to them as easy as he pleased. He had, however, mighty few left to hear him, as I continued with the crowd, now and then taking a horn, and telling good-humored stories, till he was done speaking.

The Story of a Skow

WHILE in the legislature, there was a bill before it for the creation of a county. The author of it wished to run the boundary line, so as to support his popularity; to this the colonel was opposed, because his interest was affected by it. They were hammering at it for some time; whatever the author of the bill would affect by speaking, the colonel would undo by logrolling; until the matter was drawing to a close, when he rose and made the following speech:

"Mr. Speaker,—Do you know what that man's bill reminds me of? Well, I s'pose you don't, so I'll tell you. Well, Mr. Speaker, when I first come to this country, a blacksmith was a rare thing; but there happened to be one in my neighbourhood; he had no striker, and whenever any of the neighbours wanted any work done, he had to go over and strike till his work was finished. These were hard times, Mr. Speaker, but we had to do the best we could. It happened that one of my neighbours wanted an axe, so he took along with him a piece of iron, and went over to the blacksmith's to strike till his axe was done. The iron was heated, and my neighbour fell to work, and was striking there nearly all day; when the blacksmith concluded the iron wouldn't make an axe, but 'twould make a fine mattock; so my neighbour wanting a mattock, concluded he would go over and strike till his mattock was done; accordingly, he went over the next day, and worked faithfully; but towards night the blacksmith concluded his iron wouldn't make a mattock, but 'twould make a fine ploughshare; so my neighbour wanting a ploughshare, agreed that he would go over the next day and strike till that was done; accordingly, he again went over, and fell hard to work; but towards night the black-smith concluded his iron wouldn't make a ploughshare, but 'twould make a fine *skow;* so my neighbour, tired working, cried, a skow let it be— and the blacksmith taking up the red hot iron, threw it into a trough of water near him, and as it fell in, it sung out *skow*. And this, Mr. Speaker, will be the way with that man's bill for a county; he'll keep you all here doing nothing, and finally his bill will turn out a *skow*, now mind if it don't."

From *Sketches and Eccentricities of Col. David Crockett, of West Tennessee*, pp. 79–80. New York: Printed and published by J. & J. Harper. 1833.

Grinning the Bark off a Tree

THAT Colonel Crockett could avail himself, in electioneering, of the advantages which well applied satire ensures, the following anecdote will sufficiently prove:

In the canvass of the Congressional election of 18—, Mr. ***** was the Colonel's opponent—a gentleman of the most pleasing and conciliating manners—who seldom addressed a person or a company without wearing upon his countenance a peculiarly good humoured smile. The colonel, to counteract the influence of this winning attribute, thus alluded to it in a stump speech:

"Yes, gentlemen, he may get some votes by *grinning,* for he can *outgrin me*—and you know I ain't slow—and to prove to you that I am not, I will tell you an anecdote. I was concerned myself—and I was fooled a little of the wickedest. You all know I love hunting. Well, I discovered a long time ago that a 'coon couldn't stand my grin. I could bring one tumbling down from the highest tree. I never wasted powder and lead, when I wanted one of the creatures. Well, as I was walking out one night, a few hundred yards from my house, looking carelessly about me, I saw a 'coon planted upon one of the highest limbs of an old tree. The night was very *moony* and clear, and old Ratler was with me; but Ratler won't bark at a 'coon—he's a queer dog in that way. So, I thought I'd bring the lark down in the usual way, *by a grin.* I set myself—and, after grinning at the 'coon a reasonable time, found that he didn't come down. I wondered what was the reason—and I took another steady grin at him. Still he was *there.* It made me a little mad; so I felt round and got an old limb about five feet long, and, planting one end upon the ground, I placed my chin upon the other, and took *a rest.* I then grinned my best for about five minutes; but the cursed 'coon hung on. So, finding I could not bring him down by grinning, I determined to have him—for I thought he must be a droll chap. I went over to the house, got my axe, returned to the tree, saw the 'coon still there, and began to cut away. Down it come, and I ran forward; but d—n the 'coon was there to be seen. I found that what I had taken for one, was a large knot upon the branch of the tree and, upon looking at it closely, I saw that *I had grinned all the bark off, and left the knot perfectly smooth.*

"Now, fellow-citizens," continued the Colonel, "you must be convinced that, in the *grinning line,* I myself am not slow—yet, when I look upon my opponent's countenance, I must admit that he is my superior. You must all admit it. Therefore, be wide awake—look sharp—and do not let him grin you out of your votes."

Ibid., pp. 125–127.

The Coon-Skin Trick

WHILE on the subject of election matters, I will just relate a little anecdote about myself, which will show the people to the East how we manage these things on the frontiers. It was when I first run for Congress; I was then in favor of the Hero [Andrew Jackson], for he had chalked out his course so sleek in his letter to the Tennessee legislature that, like Sam Patch, says I, "There can be no mistake in him," and so I went ahead. No one dreamt about the monster and the deposits at that time, and so, as I afterward found, many like myself were taken in by these fair promises, which were worth about as much as a flash in the pan when you have a fair shot at a fat bear.

But I am losing sight of my story. Well, I started off to the Cross Roads dressed in my hunting shirt, and my rifle on my shoulder. Many of our constituents had assembled there to get a taste of the quality of the candidates at orating. Job Snelling, a gander-shanked Yankee, who had been caught somewhere about Plymouth Bay, and been shipped to the West with a cargo of codfish and rum, erected a large shantee, and set up shop for the occasion. A large posse of the voters had assembled before I arrived, and my opponent had already made considerable headway with his speechifying and his treating, when they spied me about a rifle shot from camp, sauntering along as if I was not a party in business. "There comes Crockett," cried one. "Let us hear the colonel," cried another; and so I mounted the stump that had been cut down for the occasion, and began to bushwhack in the most approved style.

I had not been up long before there was such an uproar in the crowd

From *Life of Colonel David Crockett,* Written by Himself, pp. 240–245. Philadelphia: G. G. Evans. 1860.

For a similar trick involving a gopher and its possible connection with the coonskin story, see "Davy Crockett and John Horse: A Possible Origin of the Coonskin Story," by Kenneth W. Porter, *American Literature,* Vol. XV (March, 1943), No. 1, pp. 10–15.

For another kind of coonskin trick, in which the Yankee "skins" the backwoodsman, and the use of coonskins for currency, cf. the following account:

"I was much amused by a story told me about these skins. 'Money was at one time so scarce in Indiana, that racoon skins passed current, being handled from one person to another. But some Yankees (New Englanders) forged these notes, by sewing a racoon's tail to a cat's skin, and thus destroyed the currency.' This, like many other good stories about the Yankees, is no doubt a fiction; and was only intended to perpetuate the dislike of the New Englanders, who nevertheless excel all the settlers in industry, education, civility, and morality." (William Newnham Blane, "An excursion through the United States and Canada, during the years 1822–1823," *Pictures of Illinois One Hundred Years Ago,* edited by Milo Milton Quaife, p. 63. The Lakeside Classics. Chicago: R. R. Donnelly & Sons Company, the Lakeside Press. 1918.)

Counterfeit coonskin currency made by tying coon tails to possum skins is the subject of an anecdote related by Mrs. Anne Royall in *Letters from Alabama* (Washington, 1830), pp. 21–23, and cited in *The Beginnings of American English,* by M. M. Mathews, p. 93.

that I could not hear my own voice, and some of my constituents let me know that they could not listen to me on such a dry subject as the welfare of the nation until they had something to drink, and that I must treat them. Accordingly I jumped down from the rostrum, and led the way to the shantee, followed by my constituents, shouting, "Huzza for Crockett!" and "Crockett forever!"

When we entered the shantee Job was busy dealing out his rum in a style that showed he was making a good day's work of it, and I called for a quart of the best; but the crooked crittur returned no other answer than by pointing to a board over the bar, on which he had chalked in large letters, "*Pay to-day and trust to-morrow.*" Now that idea brought me up all standing; it was a sort of cornering in which there was no back-out, for ready money in the West, in those times, was the shyest thing in all natur, and it was most particularly shy with me on that occasion.

The voters, seeing my predicament, fell off to the other side, and I was left deserted and alone, as the Government will be, when he no longer has any offices to bestow. I saw as plain as day that the tide of popular opinion was against me, and that unless I got some rum speedily I should lose my election as sure as there are snakes in Virginny; and it must be done soon, or even burnt brandy wouldn't save me. So I walked away from the shantee, but in another guess sort from the way I entered it, for on this occasion I had no train after me, and not a voice shouted, "Huzza for Crockett!" Popularity sometimes depends on a very small matter indeed; in this particular it was worth a quart of New England rum, and no more.

Well, knowing that a crisis was at hand, I struck into the woods, with my rifle on my shoulder, my best friend in time of need; and, as good fortune would have it, I had not been out more than a quarter of an hour before I treed a fat coon, and in the pulling of a trigger he lay dead at the foot of the tree. I soon whipped his hairy jacket off his back, and again bent my steps towards the shantee, and walked up to the bar, but not alone, for this time I had half a dozen of my constituents at my heels. I threw down the coon-skin upon the counter, and called for a quart, and Job, though busy dealing out rum, forgot to point at his chalked rules and regulations; for he knew that a coon was as good a legal tender for a quart in the West as a New York shilling any day in the year.

My constituents now flocked about me, and cried, "Huzza for Crockett!" "Crockett forever!" and finding the tide had taken a turn, I told them several yarns to get them in a good humor; and having soon dispatched the value of the coon, I went out and mounted the stump without opposition, and a clear majority of the voters followed me to hear what I had to offer for the good of the nation. Before I was half through one of my constituents moved that they would hear the balance of my speech after they had washed down the first part with some more of Job Snelling's extract of cornstalk and molasses, and the question being put, it was carried unanimously. It wasn't considered necessary to tell the yeas and nays, so we adjourned to the shantee, and on the way I began to reckon that the fate of the nation pretty much depended upon my shooting another coon.

While standing at the bar, feeling sort of bashful while Job's rules and regulations stared me in the face, I cast down my eyes, and discovered one end of the coon-skin sticking between the logs that supported the bar. Job had slung it there in the hurry of business. I gave it a sort of quick jerk, and it followed my hand as natural as if I had been the rightful owner. I slapped it on the counter, and Job, little dreaming that he was barking up the wrong tree, shoved along another bottle, which my constituents quickly disposed of with great good humor, for some of them saw the trick; and then we withdrew to the rostrum to discuss the affairs of the nation.

I don't know how it was, but the voters soon became dry again, and nothing would do but we must adjourn to the shantee; and as luck would have it, the coon-skin was still sticking between the logs, as if Job had flung it there on purpose to tempt me. I was not slow in raising it to the counter, the rum followed, of course, and I wish I may be shot if I didn't, before the day was over, get ten quarts for the same identical skin, and from a fellow, too, who in those parts was considered as sharp as a steel trap and as bright as a pewter button.

This joke secured me my election, for it soon circulated like smoke among my constituents, and they allowed, with one accord, that the man who could get the whip hand of Job Snelling in fair trade, could outwit Old Nick himself, and was the real grit for them in Congress. Job was by no means popular; he boasted of always being wide awake, and that any one who could take him in was free to do so, for he came from a stock that, sleeping or waking, had always one eye open, and the other not more than half closed. The whole family were geniuses. His father was the inventor of wooden nutmegs, by which Job said he might have made a fortune, if he had only taken out a patent and kept the business in his own hands; his mother, Patience, manufactured the first white oak pumpkin seeds of the mammoth kind, and turned a pretty penny the first season; and his aunt Prudence was the first to discover that corn husks, steeped into tobacco water, would make as handsome Spanish wrappers as ever came from Havana, and that oak leaves would answer all the purpose of filling, for no one could discover the difference except the man who smoked them, and then it would be too late to make a stir about it. Job himself bragged of having made some useful discoveries, the most profitable of which was the art of converting mahogany sawdust into cayenne pepper, which he said was a profitable and safe business; for the people have been so long accustomed to having dust thrown in their eyes that there wasn't much danger of being found out.

The way I got to the blind side of the Yankee merchant was pretty generally known before election day, and the result was that my opponent might as well have whistled jigs to a milestone as attempt to beat up for votes in that district. I beat him out and out, quite back into the old year, and there was scarce enough left of him, after the canvass was over, to make a small grease spot. He disappeared without even leaving a mark behind; and such will be the fate of Adam Huntsman, if there is a fair fight and no gouging.

After the election was over, I sent Snelling the price of the rum, but took good care to keep the fact from the knowledge of my constituents. Job refused the money, and sent me word that it did him good to be taken in occasionally, as it served to brighten his ideas; but I afterwards learnt when he found out the trick that had been played upon him, he put all the rum I had ordered in his bill against my opponent, who, being elated with the speeches he had made on the affairs of the nation, could not descend to examine into the particulars of a bill of a vender of rum in the small way.

A Riproarious Fight on the Mississippi River

ONE day as I was sitting in the stern of my broad horn, the old Free and Easy, on the Mississippi, taking a horn of midshipman's grog, with a tin pot in each hand, first a draught of whiskey, and then one of river water, who should float down past me but Joe Snag; he was in a snooze, as fast as a church, with his mouth wide open; he had been ramsquaddled with whiskey for a fortnight, and as it evaporated from his body it looked like the steam from a vent pipe. Knowing the feller would be darned hard to wake, with all this steam on, as he floated past me I hit him a crack over his knob with my big steering oar. He waked in a thundering rage. Says he, halloe stranger, who axed you to crack my lice? Says I, shut up your mouth, or your teeth will get sunburnt. Upon this he crooked up his neck and neighed like a stallion. I clapped my arms and crowed like a cock. Says he, if you are a game chicken I'll pick all the pin feathers off of you. For some time back I had been so wolfy about the head and shoulders that I was obliged to keep kivered up in a salt crib to keep from spiling, for I had not had a fight for as much as ten days. Says I, give us none of your chin music, but set your kickers on land, and I'll give you a severe licking. The fellow now jumped ashore, and he was so tall he could not tell when his feet were cold. He jumped up a rod. Says he, take care how I lite on you, and he gave a real sockdologer that made my very liver and lites turn to jelly. But he found me a real scrouger. I brake three of his ribs, and he knocked out five of my teeth and one eye. He was the severest colt that ever I tried to break. I finally got a bite hold that he could not shake off. We were now parted by some boatmen, and we were so exorsted that it was more than a month before either could have a fight. It seemed to me like a little eternity. And although I didn't come out second best, I took care not to wake up a ring tailed roarer with an oar again.

From Davy Crockett's *Almanack of Wild Sports in the West*, Vol. 1, No. 4, 1838, p. 13. Nashville, Tennessee.

Treeing a Wolf

ONCE thar war a deep snow on the ground, and I sot out to make a call on my friend Luke Twig, as it war a leisure day, and I war goin' to be idle. Luke lived next door to me, only about fifteen mile off, and so i war goin' to foot it. Jest as I got up by Brush Hollow, the snow war as deep as my middle, the wind blowed so hard that I went into a hollow tree to warm myself. I hung kill-devil up and begun to thrash my hands, when a wolf cum along, and looked in. He stared right up in my face, as much as to ax leave to pick a breakfast off of any part of me he wanted. I war so astonished at his imperdence that I stood right still a minit. Then the wolf turned about, and war going off, when the end of his tail stuck through a big knot hole in the tree. I ketched hold and pulled his tail through. He jumped and twitched and tried to get away, and screeched like a dying hawk. I tied his tail into a big knot and fastened it with a strap, so that he couldn't haul it out, and left him thar to amuse himself. I could hear him holler all the way till I got to Luke Twig's house.

Skinning a Bear

ONE day when Oak Wing's sister war going to a baptizing, and had her feed in a bag under her arm, she seed a big bear that had come out from a holler tree, and he looked first at her, then at the feed, as if he didn't know which to eat fust. He kinder poked out his nose, and smelt of the dinner which war sassengers maid of bear's meat and crocodile's liver. She stood a minute an looked at him, in hopes he would feel ashamed of himself an go off; but he then cum up and smelt of her, and then she thort twar time to be stirring. So she threw the dinner down before him, an when he put his nose to it, to take a bite, she threw herself on him, an caught the scuff of his neck in her teeth; an the bear shot ahead, for it felt beautiful, as her teeth war as long an as sharp as nales. He tried to run, an she held on with her teeth, an it stript the skin clear off of him, an left him as naked as he was born, she held on with her teeth till it cum clear off the tale. The bear was seen a week arterwards up in Muskrat Hollow, running without his skin. She made herself a good warm petticoat out of the pesky varmint's hide.

From *Twenty-Five Cents Worth of Nonsense; or The Treasure Box of Unconsidered Trifles*. Philadelphia, New York, and Boston: Fisher & Brothers. [184–?]

From *Mince Pie for the Million*. Philadelphia and New York: Turner & Fisher. 1846.

The Death Hug

WE ARE all smashen huggers in our parts, an arter we once git a reglar natral embrace, it takes us a day to git apart agin, but the all smashinest huggin I ever knowed, was the one that I give a great he barr that squeezed me out of a nap once, as I laid at the root of a big holler black oak. You see the tarnal cowardly crittur had put both his great fore paws around me, and clinched 'em behind my back, and begun huggen me up to him to take a taste o' my Kentucky taller, an the way he curled his tail an wiped his red tongue about was elegantifferously greedy, and his mouth watered for it, like a fresh medder ditch in the spring o' the year, but he war most pressenly disappointed, for he jist woke up about half o' me, and left the t'other half still asleep. I snored a leetle tantalization at him, then grabbed him by the ear with my finger flesh vice, put an arm around his tarnal fat body, and with jist a single squeeze I hugged him in a bar jelly, corked it up in his skin, and took it home for presarves.

A Sensible Varmint

ALMOST every boddy that knows the forrest, understands parfectly well that Davy Crockett never loses powder and ball, havin' ben brort up to blieve it a sin to throw away amminition, and that is the bennefit of a vartuous eddikation. I war out in the forrest won arternoon, and had jist got to a plaice called the grate gap, when I seed a rakkoon setting all alone upon a tree. I klapped the breech of Brown Betty to my sholder, and war jist a going to put a piece of led between his sholders, when he lifted one paw, and sez he, "Is your name Crockett?"

Sez I, "You are rite for wonst, my name is Davy Crockett."

"Then," sez he, "you needn't take no further trubble, for I may as well cum down without another word"; and the cretur wauked rite down from the tree, for he considered himself shot.

I stoops down and pats him on the head, and sez I, "I hope I may be shot myself before I hurt a hare of your head, for I never had sich a kompliment in my life."

"Seeing as how you say that," sez he, "I'll jist walk off for the present, not doubting your word a bit, d'ye see, but lest you should kinder happen to change your mind."

Ibid.

Ibid.

The Fox

ONE day I war out in the forest with kill-devil, and thar war a deep snow on the ground, and I seed a Fox crossing my track, and jumping up in the snow, but couldn't get ahead, tho' he tried hard to get out of my way. So I telled growler to be still and I walked along as if I didn't see him: for Davy Crockett war never the man to take advantage of a feller cretur in distress.

The Tame Bear

THE creturs of the forest is of different kinds, like humans. Some is stupid and some is easy to larn. The most knowing cretur that ever I seed war a barr that my darter Pinetta picked up in the woods. It used to follow her to church, and at last it got so tame, it would cum into the house, and set down in one corner of the fire-place to warm itself. I larned it to smoke a pipe and while it sot in one corner smoking, I sot in the other with my pipe. We couldn't talk to one another; but we would look, and I knowed by the shine of his eye what he wanted to say, though he didn't speak a word. The cretur would set up o'nights when I war out late, and open the door for me. But it war the greatest in churning butter. It did all that business for the family. At last it got so civilized that it caught the hooping cough and died. My wife went to the minister and tried to get him to give the barr a christian burial: but the skunk war so bigotted that he wouldn't do it, and I telled him the barr war a better christian than he ever war.

Crockett Electioneering

ONE day, when I was getting ready to go down into Green Swamp for a mess of rattlesnakes, Luke Wing, Grizzle Newcome, and Batt Wiggle, cum to my house to try to coax me to set up for Congress. I telled them I didn't understand them kind of splunctifications; but they telled me it was sartain the country would be ruined if I didn't go to Congress. So I seed thar war no other way, and so I got ready to go round among the 'lectors, and argufy upon it. I went down to Hay Hollow and ketched a pesky great alligator, and made a bridle for him of painter's hides, and

From *Twenty-Five Cents Worth of Nonsense; or, The Treasure Box of Unconsidered Trifles.* Philadelphia, New York, and Boston: Fisher & Brothers. [184–?]

Ibid.

Ibid.

then I got on his back, and rid up to Bear Cleering, whar thar war a whole heap of fellows talking politicks. I driv rite in among 'em, and my crockodile opened his mouth as wide as Black Cave, and they war all astonished. It did wonders for my election. When he opened his mouth every tooth in his head counted for a voter, and when I driv through 'em, I yelled seven times as loud as a hull drove of injins, and then I crowed till my eyes stuck out two inches. 'Tother candidate begun to think he had a smart chance of losing his 'lections; so he got on the stump to speechify. But I driv my alligator right up to the spot, and he opened his mouth wider than ever, as if he was goin to swallow the feller, and he jumpt off that stump, and run and hollered murder, and was never seen arterward, and so I won the 'lection.

Speech of Crockett during the Canvass of 1829

FRIENDS, FELLOW-CITIZENS, BROTHERS AND SISTERS: On the first Tuesday previous to next Saturday you will be called on to perform one of the most important duties that belong to free white folks—that are a fact. On that day you will be called upon to elect your members to the Senate and House of Representatives in the Congress of the United States, and feeling that in times of great political commotion like these, it becomes you to be well represented, I feel no hesitation in offering myself as a candidate to represent such a high-minded and magnanimous white set.

Friends, fellow-citizens, brothers and sisters: Carroll is a statesman, Jackson is a hero, and Crockett is a *horse!!*

Friends, fellow-citizens, brothers and sisters: They accuse me of adultery; it's a lie—I never ran away with any man's wife, that was not willing, in my life. They accuse me of gambling, it's a lie—for I always plank down the cash.

Friends, fellow-citizens, brothers and sisters: They accuse me of being a drunkard, it's a d—d eternal lie,—for whisky can't make me drunk.

Speech of Colonel Crockett in Congress

"MR. SPEAKER.

Who—Who—Whoop—Bow—Wow—Wow—Yough. I say, Mr. Speaker; I've had a speech in soak this six months, and it has swelled me like a

From *Old Times in West Tennessee*, Reminiscences—Semi-Historic—of Pioneer Life and the Early Emigrant Settlers in the Big Hatchie Country, by a Descendant of One of the First Settlers [Joseph S. Williams], pp. 175–176. Memphis: W. G. Cheeney, Printer and Publisher. 1873. As reported by a correspondent of the *Missouri Republican*.

From *Davy Crockett's Almanac, of Wild Sports in the West, Life in the Backwoods, & Sketches of Texas*, Vol. I, No. 3, 1837, p. 40. Nashville, Tennessee: Published by the heirs of Col. Crockett.

drowned horse; if I don't deliver it I shall burst and smash the windows. The gentleman from Massachusetts [Mr. Everett] talks of summing up the merits of the question, but I'll sum up my own. In one word I'm a screamer, and have got the roughest racking horse, the prettiest sister, the surest rifle and the ugliest dog in the district. I'm a leetle the savagest crittur you ever *did see*. My father can whip any man in Kentucky, and I can lick my father. I can outspeak any man on this floor, and give him two hours start. I can run faster, dive deeper, stay longer under, and come out drier, than any *chap* this side the big *Swamp*. I can outlook a panther and outstare a flash of lightning, tote a steamboat on my back and play at rough and tumble with a lion, and an occasional kick from a *zebra*. To sum up all in one word *I'm a horse*. Goliah was a pretty hard colt but I could choke him. I can take the rag off—frighten the old folks—astonish the natives—and beat the Dutch all to smash—make nothing of sleeping under a blanket of snow—and don't mind being frozen more than a rotten apple.

"Congress allows *lemonade* to the members and has it charged under the head of stationery—I move also that *whiskey* be allowed under the item of *fuel*. For *bitters* I can suck away at a noggin of aquafortis, sweetened with brimstone, stirred with a lightning rod, and skimmed with a hurricane. I've soaked my head and shoulders in Salt River, so much that I'm always corned. I can walk like an ox, run like a fox, swim like an eel, yell like an Indian, fight like a devil, spout like an earthquake, make love like a mad bull, and swallow a nigger whole without choking if you butter his head and pin his ears back."

Crockett's Opinion of a Thunder Storm

FOLKS may talk and crow as much as they can about the roar of Niagara, the growlin o' the sea, and the barkin o' them big iron bull dogs called cannons, but give me a hull team of stormbrewed thunder, an your other natral music is no more than a penny trumpet to the hand organ of a hurrycane. By the great bein above, a reglar round roarin savage peal o' thunder is the greatest treat in all creation! it sets everything but a coward an a darned culprit shouting in the very heart and soul till both on 'em swell so etarnal big with nat'ral glorification that one feels as if he could swoller the entire creation at a gap, hug the hull universe at once, then go to sleep with his entire nater, so full of thunder glory, that he'll wake up with his head an entire electrical machine, and his arms a teetotal thunderbolt. Jist give me a touch o' this sort o' natral music afore I go to sleep, another night; arter I wake up, I feel my bump of veneration for old mammy nater so all mountain big, that I can kneel down

From *Twenty-Five Cents Worth of Nonsense; or, The Treasure Box of Unconsidered Trifles.* Philadelphia, New York, and Boston: Fisher & Brothers. [184–?]

an hug old Mississippi, bust a big rock, an feel strong enough to do the duty of an entire saw mill.

The Colonel Swallows a Thunderbolt

THAR ar a grate menny kinds of larning. I found it out when I went to Kongress. Thar ar your mattymatticks, your jommytrees, your sighentifficks, and your axletrissity. I nose nothin about the other wons, but the axletressity is a screamer. Thar war a feller in Washington that put the thunder and litening into glass bottles, and when a feller had the roomatiz, or the Saint Vitals dance, he would put the axletressity into his corpse jist like pouring whiskey into a powder horn, and it cured him as clean as a barked tree. So I seed how 'twas done; and intarmined whenever ennything aled me to try it, only I didn't keer about the bottles, for I thort I could jist as well take the litening in the raw state as it cum from the clouds. I had been used to drink out of the Mississippy without a cup, and so I could take the litening without the bottles and whirligigs that belongs to an axletressityfying masheen. It fell out that sum two yeers arter I had ben to see this axletrissity, I got a leetle in love with a pesky smart gal in our cleering, and I knowed it war not rite, seeing I war a married man. So I combobbolated on the subject and at last I resisted that I would explunctificate my passions by axletrissity, so it must be done by bringing it rite on the hart and driving the love out of it. So I went out into the forrest one arternoon when thar war a pestiferous thunder gust, I opened my mouth, so that the axletressity might run down and hit my hart, to cure it of love. I stood so for an hour, and then I seed a thunderbolt a cummin, and I dodged my mouth rite under it, and plump it went into my throte. My eyes! it war as if seven buffaloes war kicking in my bowels. My hart spun round amongst my insides like a grindstone going by steem, but the litening went clean through me, and tore the trowsers cleen off as it cum out. I had a sore gizzard for two weeks arterward, and my inwards war so hot that I use to eat raw vittals for a month arterward, and it would be cooked befour it got farely down my throte. I have never felt love since.

Crockett's Morning Hunt

ONE January morning it was so all-screwen-up cold that the forest trees war so stiff that they couldn't shake, and the very day-break froze

From *Mince Pie for the Million*. Philadelphia and New York: Turner & Fisher. 1846.

From *Davy Crockett, American Comic Legend*, selected and edited by Richard M. Dorson, pp. 16–17. Copyright, 1939, by Rockland Editions. New York. Reprinted from the 1854 Crockett Almanac (New York, Cozans).

fast as it war tryin' to dawn. The tinder-box in my cabin would no more ketch fire than a sunk raft at the bottom o' the sea. Seein' that daylight war so far behind time, I thought creation war in a fair way for freezin' fast.

"So," thinks I, "I must strike a leetle fire from my fingers, light my pipe, travel out a few leagues, and see about it."

Then I brought my knuckles together like two thunder clouds, but the sparks froze up afore I could begin to collect 'em—so out I walked, and endeavored to keep myself unfriz by goin' at a hop, step and jump gait, and whistlin' the tune of "fire in the mountains!" as I went along in three double quick time. Well, arter I had walked about twenty-five miles up the peak o' Daybreak Hill, I soon discovered what war the matter. The airth had actually friz fast in her axis, and couldn't turn round; the sun had got jammed between two cakes o' ice under the wheels, an' thar he had bin shinin' and workin' to get loose, till he friz fast in his cold sweat.

"C-r-e-a-t-i-o-n!" thought I, "this are the toughest sort o' suspension, and it mustn't be endured—somethin' must be done, or human creation is done for."

It war then so antedeluvian and premature cold that upper and lower teeth an' tongue war all collapsed together as tight as a friz oyster. I took a fresh twenty pound bear off o' my back that I'd picked up on the road, an' beat the animal agin the ice till the hot ile began to walk out on him at all sides. I then took an' held him over the airth's axes, an' squeezed him till I thaw'd 'em loose, poured about a ton on it over the sun's face, give the airth's cog-wheel one kick backward, till I got the sun loose—whistled "Push along, keep movin'!" an' in about fifteen seconds the airth gin a grunt, and begun movin'—the sun walked up beautiful, salutin' me with sich a wind o' gratitude that it made me sneeze. I lit my pipe by the blaze o' his top-knot, shouldered my bear, an' walked home, introducin' the people to fresh daylight with a piece of sunrise in my pocket, with which I cooked my bear steaks, an' enjoyed one o' the best breakfasts I had tasted for some time. If I didn't, jist wake some mornin' and go with me to the office o' sunrise!

The Shooting of the Cup

A FEW hours brought us to one of those stopping points, known by the name of "wooding places." It was situated immediately above Letart's Falls. The boat, obedient to the wheel of the pilot, made a graceful sweep towards the island above the chute, and rounding to, approached

From "The Last of the Boatmen," by N. [Morgan Neville], in *The Western Souvenir*, A Christmas and New Year's Gift for 1829, edited by James Hall, pp. 110-114. Cincinnati: Published by N. and G. Guilford. [1828?]

the wood pile. As the boat drew near the shore, the escape steam reverberated through the forest and hills, like the chafed bellowing of the caged tiger. The root of a tree, concealed beneath the water, prevented the boat from getting sufficiently near the bank, and it became necessary to use the paddles to take a different position.

"Back out! Mannee! and try it again!" exclaimed a voice from the shore. "Throw your pole wide—and brace off! or you'll run against a snag!"

This was a kind of language long familiar to us on the Ohio. It was a sample of the slang of the keel-boatmen.

The speaker was immediately cheered by a dozen of voices from the deck; and I recognised in him the person of an old acquaintance, familiarly known to me from my boyhood. He was leaning carelessly against a large beech; and, as his left arm negligently pressed a rifle to his side, presented a figure, that Salvator would have chosen from a million, as a model for his wild and gloomy pencil. His stature was upwards of six feet, his proportions perfectly symmetrical, and exhibiting the evidence of Herculean powers. To a stranger, he would have seemed a complete mulatto. Long exposure to the sun and weather on the lower Ohio and Mississippi had changed his skin; and, but for the fine European cast of his countenance, he might have passed for the principal warrior of some powerful tribe. Although at least fifty years of age, his hair was as black as the wing of the raven. Next to his skin he wore a red flannel shirt, covered by a blue capot, ornamented with white fringe. On his feet were moccasins, and a broad leathern belt, from which hung, suspended in a sheath, a large knife, encircled his waist.

As soon as the steam boat became stationary, the cabin passengers jumped on shore. On ascending the bank, the figure I have just described advanced to offer me his hand.

"How are you, Mike?" said I.

"How goes it?" replied the boatman—grasping my hand with a squeeze, that I can compare to nothing, but that of a blacksmith's vise.

"I am glad to see you, Mannee!"—continued he in his abrupt manner. "I am going to shoot at the tin cup for a quart—off hand—and you must be judge."

I understood Mike at once, and on any other occasion, should have remonstrated, and prevented the daring trial of skill. But I was accompanied by a couple of English tourists, who had scarcely ever been beyond the sound of Bow Bells; and who were travelling post over the United States to make up a book of observation, on our manners and customs. There were, also, among the passengers, a few bloods from Philadelphia and Baltimore, who could conceive of nothing equal to Chestnut or Howard streets; and who expressed great disappointment, at not being able to find terrapins and oysters at every village—marvellously lauding the comforts of Rubicum's. My tramontane pride was aroused: and I resolved to give them an opportunity of seeing a Western Lion—for such Mike undoubtedly was—in all his glory. The philanthropist may start, and accuse me of want of humanity. I deny the charge, and refer for apology to one of the best understood principles of human nature.

Mike, followed by several of his crew, led the way to a beech grove, some little distance from the landing. I invited my fellow passengers to witness the scene.—On arriving at the spot, a stout, bull-headed boatman, dressed in a hunting shirt—but fare-footed—in whom I recognised a younger brother of Mike, drew a line with his toe; and stepping off thirty yards—turned round fronting his brother—took a tin cup, which hung from his belt, and placed it on his head. Although I had seen this feat performed before I acknowledge, I felt uneasy, whilst this silent prepara-tion was going on. But I had not much time for reflection; for this second Albert exclaimed—

"Blaze away, Mike! and let's have the quart."

My "compagnons de voyage," as soon as they recovered from the first effect of their astonishment, exhibited a disposition to interfere. But Mike, throwing back his left leg, levelled his rifle at the head of his brother. In this horizontal position the weapon remained for some seconds as immovable, as if the arm which held it, was affected by no pulsation.

"Elevate your piece a little lower, Mike! or you will pay the corn," cried the imperturbable brother.

I know not if the advice was obeyed or not; but the sharp crack of the rifle immediately followed, and the cup flew off thirty or forty yards— rendered unfit for future service. There was a cry of admiration from the strangers, who pressed forward to see if the foolhardy boatman was really safe. He remained as immovable, as if he had been a figure hewn out of stone. He had not even winked, when the ball struck the cup within two inches of his skull.

"Mike has won!" I exclaimed; and my decision was the signal which, according to their rules, permitted him of the target to move from his position. No more sensation was exhibited among the boatmen, than if a common wager had been won. The bet being decided, they hurried back to their boat, giving me and my friends an invitation to partake of "the treat." We declined, and took leave of the thoughtless creatures. In a few minutes afterwards, we observed their "Keel" wheeling into the current, —the gigantic form of Mike, bestriding the large steering oar, and the others arranging themselves in their places in front of the cabin, that extended nearly the whole length of the boat, covering merchandize of immense value. As they left the shore, they gave the Indian yell; and broke out into a sort of unconnected chorus—commencing with—

> "Hard upon the beech oar!—
> She moves too slow!
> All the way to Shawneetown,
> Long while ago."

Mike Fink, the Indian, and the Deer

AT THE early age of seventeen, Mike's character was displayed, by enlisting himself in a corps of Scouts—a body of irregular rangers, which was employed on the North-western frontiers of Pennsylvania, to watch the Indians, and to give notice of any threatened inroad.

At that time, Pittsburgh was on the extreme verge of white population, and the spies, who were constantly employed, generally extended their explorations forty or fifty miles to the west of this post. They went out, singly, lived as did the Indian, and in every respect, became perfectly assimilated in habits, taste, and feeling, with the red men of the desert. A kind of border warfare was kept up, and the scout thought it as praiseworthy to bring in the scalp of a Shawnee, as the skin of a panther. He would remain in the woods for weeks together, using parched corn for bread, and depending on his rifle for his meat—and slept at night in perfect comfort, rolled in his blanket.

In this corps, whilst yet a stripling, Mike acquired a reputation for boldness, and cunning, far beyond his companions. A thousand legends illustrate the fearlessness of his character. There was one, which he told, himself, with much pride, and which made an indelible impression on my boyish memory. He had been out on the hills of Mahoning, when, to use his own words, "he saw signs of Indians being about."—He had discovered the recent print of the moccasin on the grass; and found drops of the fresh blood of a deer on the green bush. He became cautious, skulked for some time in the deepest thickets of hazel and briar; and, for several days, did not discharge his rifle. He subsisted patiently on parched corn and jerk, which he had dried on his first coming into the woods. He gave no alarm to the settlements, because he discovered with perfect certainty, that the enemy consisted of a small hunting party, who were receding from the Allegheny.

As he was creeping along one morning, with the stealthy tread of a cat, his eye fell upon a beautiful buck, browsing on the edge of a barren spot, three hundred yards distant. The temptation was too strong for the woodsman, and he resolved to have a shot at every hazard. Re-priming his gun, and picking his flint, he made his approaches in the usual noiseless manner. At the moment he reached the spot from which he meant to take his aim, he observed a large savage, intent upon the same object, advancing from a direction a little different from his own. Mike shrunk behind a tree, with the quickness of thought, and keeping his eye fixed on the hunter, waited the result with patience. In a few moments, the Indian halted within fifty paces, and levelled his piece at the deer. In the meanwhile, Mike presented his rifle at the body of the savage; and at

---

Ibid., pp. 118–120.

the moment the smoke issued from the gun of the latter, the bullet of Fink passed through the red man's breast. He uttered a yell, and fell dead at the same instant with the deer. Mike re-loaded his rifle, and remained in his covert for some minutes, to ascertain whether there were more enemies at hand. He then stepped up to the prostrate savage, and having satisfied himself that life was extinguished, turned his attention to the buck, and took from the carcase those pieces suited to the process of jerking.

Mike Teaches Peg a Lesson

MIKE, at one time, had a woman who passed for his wife; whether she was truly so, we do not know. But at any rate, the following anecdote is a rare instance of conjugal discipline.

Some time in the latter part of autumn, a few years after the close of the late war with Great Britain, several keelboats landed for the night near the mouth of the Muskingum, among which was that of Mike. After making all fast, Mike was observed, just under the bank, scraping into a heap the dried beech leaves which had been blown there during the day, having just fallen from the effects of the early autumn frosts. To all questions as to what he was doing he returned no answer, but continued at his work until he had piled them up as high as his head. He then separated them, making a sort of an oblong ring, in which he laid down, as if to ascertain whether it was a good bed or not. Getting up, he sauntered on board, hunted up his rifle, made great preparations about his priming, and then called in a very impressive manner upon his wife to follow him. Both proceeded up to the pile of leaves, poor *"Peg"* in a terrible flutter as she had discovered that Mike was in no very amiable humor.

"Get in there and lie down," was the command to Peg, topped off with one of Mike's very choicest oaths. "Now, *Mr.* Fink,"—she always mistered him when his blood was up—"what have I done? I don't know, I'm sure—"

"Get in there and lie down, or I'll shoot you," with another oath, and drawing up his rifle to his shoulder. Poor Peg obeyed, and crawled into the leaf pile, and Mike covered her up with the combustibles. He then took a flour barrel and split the staves into fine pieces, and lighted them

From "The Western Boatmen," in *The Great West: Containing Narratives of the Most Important and Interesting Events in Western History—Remarkable Individual Adventures—Sketches of Frontier Life—Descriptions of Natural Curiosities: To Which Is Appended Historical and Descriptive Sketches of Oregon, New Mexico, Texas, Minnesota, Utah, California, Washington, Nebraska, Kansas, Etc., Etc., Etc.,* by Henry Howe, pp. 277–278. New York: Published by Geo. F. Tuttle; Cincinnati: Published by Henry Howe. 1857. Based on a letter to the editor of Cist's *Cincinnati Miscellany.* Vol. I, 1845, pp. 156–157

at the fire on board the boat, all the time watching the leaf pile, and swearing he would shoot Peg if she moved. So soon as his splinters began to blaze he took them into his hand and deliberately set fire, in four different places, to the leaves that surrounded his wife. In an instant the whole mass was on fire, aided by a fresh wind which was blowing at the time, while Mike was quietly standing by enjoying the fun. Peg, through fear of Mike, stood it as long as she could; but it soon became too hot, and she made a run for the river, her hair and clothing all on fire. In a few seconds she reached the water and plunged in, rejoiced to know she had escaped both fire and rifle so well. "There," said Mike, "that'll' larn you not to be winkin' at them fellers on t'other boat."

The Disgraced Scalp-Lock

. . . AMONG the flat-boatmen there were none that gained the notoriety of *Mike Fink*. His name is still remembered along the whole of the Ohio as a man who excelled his fellows in every thing,—particularly in his rifle-shot, which was acknowledged to be unsurpassed. Probably no man ever lived who could compete with Mike Fink in the latter accomplishment. Strong as Hercules, free from all nervous excitement, possessed of perfect health, and familiar with his weapon from childhood, he raised the rifle to his eye, and, having once taken sight, it was as firmly fixed as if buried in rock. It was Mike's pride, and he rejoiced on all occasions where he could bring it into use, whether it was turned against the beast of prey or the more savage Indian; and in his day these last named were the common foe with whom Mike Fink and his associates had to contend. On the occasion that we would particularly introduce Mike to the reader, he had bound himself for a while to the pursuits of trade, until a voyage from the head-waters of the Ohio, and down the Mississippi, could be completed. Heretofore he had kept himself exclusively to the Ohio, but a liberal reward, and some curiosity, prompted him to extend his business character beyond his ordinary habits and inclinations. In accomplishment of this object, he was lolling carelessly over the big "sweep" that guided the "flat" on which he officiated; the current of the river bore the boat swiftly along, and made his labour light; his eye glanced around him, and he broke forth in ecstasies at what he saw and felt. If there is a

From "The Disgraced Scalp-Lock, or, Incidents on the Western Waters," in *The Mysteries of the Backwoods; or, Sketches of the Southwest: including Character, Scenery, and Rural Sports,* by T. B. Thorpe, pp. 119–136. Philadelphia: Carey & Hart. 1846. Also published as "The Flatboatmen of the West . . ." in *Cincinnati Miscellany, or Antiquities of the West:* and Pioneer History and General and Local Statistics, Compiled from the Western General Advertiser, from April 1st, 1845, to April 1st, 1846, by Charles Cist, Vol. II, pp. 332–334, 342–344. Cincinnati: Robinson & Jones. 1846.

river in the world that merits the name of beautiful, it is the Ohio, when its channel is

"Without o'erflowing, full."

The scenery is everywhere soft; there are no jutting rocks, no steep banks, no high hills; but the clear and swift current laves beautiful and undulating shores, that descend gradually to the water's edge. The foliage is rich and luxuriant, and its outlines in the water are no less distinct than when it is relieved against the sky. Interspersed along its route are islands, as beautiful as ever figured in poetry as the land of the fairies; enchanted spots indeed, that seem to sit so lightly on the water that you almost expect them, as you approach, to vanish into dreams. So late as when Mike Fink disturbed the solitude of the Ohio with his rifle, the canoe of the Indian was hidden in the little recesses along the shore; they moved about in their frail barks like spirits; and clung, in spite of the constant encroachments of civilization, to places which tradition had designated as the happy places of a favoured people.

Wild and uncultivated as Mike appeared, he loved nature, and had a soul that sometimes felt, while admiring it, an exalted enthusiasm. The Ohio was his favourite stream. From where it runs no stronger than a gentle rivulet, to where it mixes with the muddy Mississippi, Mike was as familiar with its meanderings as a child could be with those of a flower-garden. He could not help noticing with sorrow the desecrating hand of improvement as he passed along, and half soliloquizing, and half addressing his companions, he broke forth:—"I knew these parts afore a squatter's axe had blazed a tree; 'twasn't then pulling a —— sweep to get a living; but pulling the trigger's the business. Those were times to see; a man might call himself lucky. What's the use of improvements? When did cutting down trees make deer more plenty? Who ever found wild buffalo or a brave Indian in a city? Where's the fun, the frolicking, the fighting? Gone! Gone! The rifle won't make a man a living now—he must turn nigger and work. If forests continue to be used up, I may yet be smothered in a settlement. Boys, this 'ere life won't do. I'll stick to the broadhorn 'cordin' to contract; but once done with it, I'm off for a frolic. If the Choctaws or Cherokees on the Massassip don't give us a brush as we pass along, I shall grow as poor as a starved wolf in a pitfall. I must, to live peaceably, point my rifle at something more dangerous than varmint. Six months and no fight would spile me worse than a dead horse on a prairie."

Mike ceased speaking. The then beautiful village of Louisville appeared in sight; the labour of landing the boat occupied his attention—the bustle and confusion that followed such an incident ensued, and Mike was his own master by law until his employers ceased trafficking, and again required his services.

At the time we write of, there were a great many renegade Indians who lived about the settlements, and which is still the case in the extreme south-west. These Indians generally are the most degraded of their tribe

—outcasts, who, for crime or dissipation, are no longer allowed to associate with their people; they live by hunting or stealing, and spend their precarious gains in intoxication. Among the throng that crowded on the flat-boat on his arrival, were a number of these unfortunate beings; they were influenced by no other motive than that of loitering round in idle speculation at what was going on. Mike was attracted towards them at sight; and as he too was in the situation that is deemed most favourable to mischief, it struck him that it was a good opportunity to have a little sport at the Indians' expense. Without ceremony, he gave a terrific war-whoop; and then mixing the language of the aborigines and his own together, he went on in savage fashion and bragged of his triumphs and victories on the warpath, with all the seeming earnestness of a real "brave." Nor were taunting words spared to exasperate the poor creatures, who, perfectly helpless, listened to the tales of their own greatness, and their own shame, until wound up to the highest pitch of impotent exasperation. Mike's companions joined in; thoughtless boys caught the spirit of the affair; and the Indians were goaded until they in turn made battle with their tongues. Then commenced a system of running against them, pulling off their blankets, together with a thousand other indignities; finally they made a precipitate retreat ashore, amid the hooting and jeering of an unfeeling crowd, who considered them poor devils destitute of feeling and humanity. Among this crowd of outcasts was a Cherokee, who bore the name of Proud Joe; what his real cognomen was, no one knew, for he was taciturn, haughty—and, in spite of his poverty and his manner of life won the name we have mentioned. His face was expressive of talent, but it was furrowed by the most terrible habits of drunkenness. That he was a superior Indian was admitted; and it was also understood that he was banished from his mountain home, his tribe being then numerous and powerful, for some great crime. He was always looked up to by his companions, and managed, however intoxicated he might be, to sustain a singularly proud bearing, which did not even depart from him while prostrated on the ground. Joe was filthy in his person and habits—in this respect he was behind his fellows; but one ornament of his person was attended to with a care which would have done honour to him if surrounded by his people, and in his native woods. Joe still wore with Indian dignity his scalp-lock; he ornamented it with taste, and cherished it, as report said, that some Indian messenger of vengeance might tear it from his head, as expiatory of his numerous crimes. Mike noticed this peculiarity; and reaching out his hand, plucked from it a hawk's feather, which was attached to the scalp-lock. The Indian glared horribly on Mike as he consummated the insult, snatched the feather from his hand, then shaking his clenched fist in the air, as if calling on Heaven for revenge, retreated with his friends. Mike saw that he had roused the savage's soul, and he marvelled wonderfully that so much resentment should be exhibited; and as an earnest to Proud Joe that the wrong he had done him should not rest unrevenged, he swore that he would cut the scalp-lock off close to his head the first convenient opportunity he got, and then he thought no more about it.

The morning following the arrival of the boat at Louisville was occupied in making preparations to pursue the voyage down the river. Nearly every thing was completed, and Mike had taken his favourite place at the sweep, when looking up the river-bank, he beheld at some distance Joe and his companions, and perceived from their gesticulations that they were making him the subject of conversation.

Mike thought instantly of several ways in which he could show them altogether a fair fight, and then whip them with ease; he also reflected with what extreme satisfaction he would enter into the spirit of the arrangement, and other matters to him equally pleasing, when all the Indians disappeared, save Joe himself, who stood at times reviewing him in moody silence, and then staring round at passing objects. From the peculiarity of Joe's position to Mike, who was below him, his head and upper part of his body relieved boldly against the sky, and in one of his movements he brought his profile face to view. The prominent scalp-lock and its adornments seemed to be more striking than ever, and it again roused the pugnacity of Mike Fink; in an instant he raised his rifle, always loaded and at command, brought it to his eye, and, before he could be prevented, drew sight upon Proud Joe and fired. The ball whistled loud and shrill, and Joe, springing his whole length into the air, fell upon the ground. The cold-blooded murder was noticed by fifty persons at least, and there arose from the crowd an universal cry of horror and indignation at the bloody deed. Mike himself seemed to be much astonished, and in an instant reloaded his rifle, and as a number of white persons rushed towards the boat, Mike threw aside his coat, and, taking his powder horn between his teeth, leaped, rifle in hand, into the Ohio, and commenced swimming for the opposite shore. Some bold spirits determined Mike should not so easily escape, and jumping into the only skiff at command, pulled swiftly after him. Mike watched their movements until they came within a hundred yards of him, then turning in the water, he supported himself by his feet alone, and raised his deadly rifle to his eye. Its muzzle, if it spoke hostilely, was as certain to send a messenger of death through one or more of his pursuers, as if it were lightning, and they knew it; dropping their oars and turning pale, they bid Mike not to fire. Mike waved his hand towards the little village of Louisville, and again pursued his way to the opposite shore.

The time consumed by the firing of Mike's rifle, the pursuit, and the abandonment of it, required less time than we have taken to give the details; and in that time, to the astonishment of the gaping crowd around Joe, they saw him rising with a bewildered air; a moment more and he recovered his senses and stood up—*at his feet lay his scalp-lock!* The ball had cut it clear from his head; the cord around the root of it, in which were placed feathers and other ornaments, held it together; the concussion had merely stunned its owner; farther, he had escaped all bodily harm!

A cry of exultation rose at the last evidence of the skill of Mike Fink—
the exhibition of a shot that established his claim, indisputable, to the
eminence he ever afterwards held—the unrivalled marksman of all the
flat-boatmen of the western ‑vaters. Proud Joe had received many insults.
He looked upon himself as a degraded, worthless being; and the ignominy
heaped upon him he never, except by reply, resented; but this last insult
was like seizing the lion by the mane, or a Roman senator by the beard
—it roused the slumbering demon within, and made him again thirst to
resent his wrongs with an intensity of emotion that can only be felt by
an Indian. His eye glared upon the jeering crowd around like a fiend;
his chest swelled and heaved until it seemed that he must suffocate. No
one noticed this emotion. All were intent upon the exploit that had so
singularly deprived Joe of his war-lock; and, smothering his wrath, he
retreated to his associates with a consuming fire at his vitals. He was a
different man from an hour before; and with that desperate resolution on
which a man stakes his all, he swore by the Great Spirit of his forefathers
that he would be revenged.

An hour after the disappearance of Joe, both he and Mike Fink were
forgotten. The flat-boat, which the latter had deserted, was got under
way, and dashing through the rapids in the river opposite Louisville
wended its course. As is customary when night sets in, the boat was
securely fastened in some little bend or bay in the shore, where it remained
until early morn.

Long before the sun had fairly risen, the boat was again pushed into
the stream, and it passed through a valley presenting the greatest possible
beauty and freshness of landscape the mind can conceive.

It was spring, and a thousand tints of green developed themselves in
the half-formed foliage and bursting buds. The beautiful mallard skimmed
across the water, ignorant of the danger of the white man's approach;
the splendid spoon-bill decked the shallow places near the shore, while
myriads of singing-birds filled the air with their unwritten songs. In the
far reaches down the river, there occasionally might be seen a bear
stepping along the ground as if dainty of its feet, and, snuffing the in-
truder on his wild home, he would retreat into the woods. To enliven all
this, and give the picture the look of humanity, there might also be seen,
struggling with the floating mists, a column of blue smoke that came
from a fire built on a projecting point of land, around which the current
swept rapidly and carried every thing that floated on the river. The eye
of the boatman saw the advantage of the situation which the place
rendered to those on shore, to annoy and attack, and as wandering Indians,
in those days, did not hesitate to rob, there was much speculation as to
what reception the boat would receive from the builders of the fire.

The rifles were all loaded, to be prepared for the worst, and the loss of
Mike Fink lamented, as a prospect of a fight presented itself, where he
could use his terrible rifle. The boat in the mean time swept round the
point; but instead of an enemy, there lay, in a profound sleep, Mike Fink,

with his feet toasting at the fire. His pillow was a huge bear that had been shot on the day previous, while at his sides, and scattered in profusion around him were several deer and wild turkeys. Mike had not been idle. After picking out a place most eligible to notice the passing boat, he had spent his time in hunting, and he was surrounded by trophies of his prowess. The scene that he presented was worthy of the time and the man, and would have thrown Landseer into a delirium of joy, could he have witnessed it. The boat, owing to the swiftness of the current, passed Mike's resting place, although it was pulled strongly to the shore. As Mike's companions came opposite to him, they raised such a shout, half exultation at meeting him, and half to alarm him with the idea that Joe's friends were upon him. Mike, at the sound, sprang to his feet, rifle in hand, and as he looked around, he raised it to his eyes, and by the time he discovered the boat, he was ready to fire. "Down with your shooting-iron, you wild critter," shouted one of the boatmen. Mike dropped the piece, and gave a loud halloo, that echoed among the solitudes like a piece of artillery. The meeting between Mike and his fellows was characteristic. They joked, and jibed him with their rough wit, and he parried it off with a most creditable ingenuity. Mike soon learned the extent of his rifle-shot—he seemed perfectly indifferent to the fact that Proud Joe was not dead. The only sentiment he uttered, was regret that he did not fire at the vagabond's head, and if he hadn't hit it, why he made the first bad shot in twenty years. The dead game was carried on board of the boat, the adventure was forgotten, and every thing resumed the monotony of floating in a flat-boat down the Ohio.

A month or more elapsed, and Mike had progressed several hundred miles down the Mississippi; his journey had been remarkably free from incident; morning, noon, and night presented the same banks, the same muddy water, and he sighed to see some broken land, some high hills, and he railed and swore that he should have been such a fool as to desert his favourite Ohio for a river that produced nothing but alligators, and was never at best half finished.

Occasionally, the plentifulness of game put him in spirits, but it did not last long; he wanted more lasting excitement, and declared himself as perfectly miserable and helpless as a wild-cat without teeth or claws.

In the vicinity of Natchez rises a few abrupt hills, which tower above the surrounding lowlands of the Mississippi like monuments; they are not high, but from their loneliness and rarity they create sensations of pleasure and awe.

Under the shadow of one of these bluffs, Mike and his associates made the customary preparations to pass the night. Mike's enthusiasm knew no bounds at the sight of land again; he said it was as pleasant as "cold water to a fresh wound"; and, as his spirits rose, he went on making the region round about, according to his notions, an agreeable residence.

"The Choctaws live in these diggins," said Mike, "and a cursed time they must have of it. Now if I lived in these parts I'd declare war on 'em just to have something to keep me from growing dull; without some such business I'd be as musty as an old swamp moccasin. I could build a cabin on that ar hill yonder that could, from its location, with my rifle, repulse a whole tribe if they came after me. What a beautiful time I'd have of it! I never was particular about what's called a fair fight; I just ask half a chance, and the odds against me, and if I then don't keep clear of snags and sawyers, let me spring a leak and go to the bottom. It's natur that the big fish should eat the little ones. I've seen trout swallow a perch, and a cat would come along and swallow the trout, and perhaps, on the Mississippi, the alligators use up the cat, and so on to the end of the row. Well, I will walk tall into varmint and Indian; it's a way I've got, and it comes as natural as grinning to a hyena. I'm a regular tornado, tough as a hickory, and long-winded as a nor'-wester. I can strike a blow like a falling tree. and every lick makes a gap in the crowd that lets in an acre of sunshine. Whew, boys!" shouted Mike, twirling his rifle like a walking-stick around his head, at the ideas suggested in his mind. "Whew, boys! if the Choctaw divils in them ar woods thare would give us a brush, just as I feel now, I'd call them gentlemen. I must fight something, or I'll catch the dry rot—burnt brandy won't save me." Such were some of the expressions which Mike gave utterance to, and in which his companions heartily joined; but they never presumed to be quite equal to Mike, for his bodily prowess, as well as his rifle, were acknowledged to be unsurpassed. These displays of animal spirits generally ended in boxing and wrestling-matches, in which falls were received, and blows were struck without being noticed, that would have destroyed common men. Occasionally angry words and blows were exchanged, but, like the summer storm, the cloud that emitted the lightning purified the air; and when the commotion ceased, the combatants immediately made friends and became more attached to each other than before the cause that interrupted the good feelings occurred. Such were the conversation and amusements of the evening when the boat was moored under the bluffs we have alluded to. As night wore on, one by one of the hardy boatmen fell asleep, some in its confined interior, and others protected by a light covering in the open air. The moon arose in beautiful majesty; her silver light, behind the highlands, gave them a power and theatrical effect as it ascended; and as its silver rays grew perpendicular, they finally kissed gently the summit of the hills, and poured down their full light upon the boat, with almost noonday brilliancy. The silence with which the beautiful changes of darkness and light were produced made it mysterious. It seemed as if some creative power was at work, bringing form and life out of darkness. In the midst of the witchery of this quiet scene, there sounded forth the terrible rifle, and the more terrible war-whoop of the Indian. One of the flatboatmen, asleep on deck, gave a stifled groan, turned upon his face, and with a quivering motion, ceased to live. Not so with his companions— they in an instant, as men accustomed to danger and sudden attacks, sprang ready-armed to their feet; but before they could discover their

foes, seven sleek and horribly painted savages leaped from the hill into
the boat. The firing of the rifle was useless, and each man singled out a
foe and met him with the drawn knife.

The struggle was quick and fearful; and deadly blows were given amid
screams and imprecations that rent the air. Yet the voice of Mike Fink
could be heard in encouraging shouts above the clamour. "Give it to them,
boys!" he cried, "cut their hearts out! choke the dogs! Here's hell a-fire
and the river rising!" then clenching with the most powerful of the assailants, he rolled with him upon the deck of the boat. Powerful as Mike
was, the Indian seemed nearly a match for him. The two twisted and
writhed like serpents,—now one seeming to have the advantage, and then
the other.

In all this confusion there might occasionally be seen glancing in the
moonlight the blade of a knife; but at whom the thrusts were made, or
who wielded it, could not be discovered.

The general fight lasted less time than we have taken to describe it.
The white men gained the advantage; two of the Indians lay dead upon
the boat, and the living, escaping from their antagonists, leaped ashore,
and before the rifle could be brought to bear they were out of its reach.
While Mike was yet struggling with his antagonist, one of his companions
cut the boat loose from the shore, and, with powerful exertion, managed
to get its bows so far into the current, that it swung round and floated;
but before this was accomplished and before any one interfered with
Mike, he was on his feet, covered with blood, and blowing like a porpoise:
by the time he could get his breath, he commenced talking. "Ain't been
so busy in a long time," said he, turning over his victim with his foot;
"that fellow fou't beautiful; if he's a specimen of the Choctaws that live
in these parts, they are screamers; the infernal sarpents! the d—d pos-
sums!" Talking in this way, he with the others, took a general survey of
the killed and wounded. Mike himself was a good deal cut up with the
Indian's knife; but he called his wounds blackberry scratches. One of
Mike's associates was severely hurt; the rest escaped comparatively harmless. The sacrifice was made at the first fire; for beside the dead Indians,
there lay one of the boat's crew, cold and dead, his body perforated with
four different balls. That he was the chief object of attack seemed evident,
yet no one of his associates knew of his having a single fight with the
Indians. The soul of Mike was affected, and taking the hand of his
deceased friend between his own, he raised his bloody knife towards the
bright moon, and swore that he would desolate "the nation" that claimed
the Indians who made war upon them that night, and turned to his
stiffened victim, that, dead as it was, retained the expression of implacable
hatred and defiance; he gave it a smile of grim satisfaction, and then
joined in the general conversation which the occurrences of the night would
naturally suggest. The master of the "broad horn" was a business man,
and had often been down the Mississippi. This was the first attack he
had received, or knew to have been made from the shores inhabited by

the Choctaws, except by the white man, and he, among other things, suggested keeping the dead Indians until daylight, that they might have
an opportunity to examine their dress and features, and see with certainty
who were to blame for the occurrences of the night. The dead boatman
was removed with care to a respectful distance; and the living, except
the person at the sweep of the boat, were soon buried in profound slumber.

Not until after the rude breakfast was partaken of, and the funeral
rites of the dead boatman were solemnly performed, did Mike and his
companions disturb the corpses of the red men.

When both these things had been leisurely and gently got through with,
there was a different spirit among the men.

Mike was astir, and went about his business with alacrity. He stripped
the bloody blanket from the Indian he had killed, as if it enveloped
something disgusting, and required no respect. He examined carefully the
moccasins on the Indian's feet, pronouncing them at one time Chickasas,
at another time, the Shawnese. He stared at the livid face, but could not
recognise the style of paint that covered it.

That the Indians were not strictly national in their adornments, was
certain, for they were examined by practiced eyes, that could have told
the nation of the dead, if such had been the case, as readily as a sailor
could distinguish a ship by its flag. Mike was evidently puzzled; and as
he was about giving up his task as hopeless, the dead body he was examin-
ing, from some cause, turned on its side. Mike's eyes distended, as some
of his companions observed, "like a choked cat," and became riveted. He
drew himself up in a half serious, and half comic expression, and pointing
at the back of the dead Indian's head, there was exhibited a dead warrior
in his paint, destitute of his scalp-lock, the small stump which was only
left, being stiffened with *red paint*. Those who could read Indians' symbols learned a volume of deadly resolve in what they saw. The body of
Proud Joe was stiff and cold before them.

The last and best shot of Mike Fink cost a brave man his life. The
corpse so lately interred, was evidently taken in the moonlight by Proud
Joe and his party, as that of Mike's, and they had risked their lives, one
and all, that he might with certainty be sacrificed. Nearly a thousand
miles of swamp had been threaded, large and swift running rivers had
been crossed, hostile tribes passed through by Joe and his friends, that
they might revenge the fearful insult, of destroying *without the life*, the
sacred scalp-lock.

Trimming a Darky's Heel

IN THE early days of St. Louis, before the roar of commerce or manufac-
tures had drowned the free laugh and merry song of the jolly keel boat-

By Solitaire [John S. Robb]. From *The Saint Louis Weekly Reveille*, Vol. III
(January 25, 1847), No. 29, p. 1147.

men, those primitive navigators of the "Father of Waters" tied up their crafts beneath the bluff, which then, eighty feet in height, rose per-pendicular from the water's edge in front of the city. On top of the bluff then, as now, a number of *doggeries* [drinking places] held forth their temptations to the hardy navigator, and they were often the scene of the wildest kind of revelry.

At that time *Mike Fink,* the chief among keel boatmen, was trading to St. Louis, and he frequently *awoke* the inhabitants by his wild freaks and daredevil sprees. Mike was celebrated for the skill with which he used the *rifle*—then the constant companion of western men. It was his boast that he could "best shoot whar he'd a mind to with his *Betsy*," as he familiarly termed his "shooting iron," and his companions, for the pleasure of noting his skill, or exhibiting it to some stranger, would often put him to the severest kind of tests.

One day, while lying upon the deck of his boat below the St. Louis bluff, with two or three companions, the conversation turned upon Mike's last shot; and one of the party ventured the opinion that his skill was departing. This aroused the boatmen into a controversy, and from their conversation might be learned the manner of the shot which was the subject of dispute. It was thus: One of the party, at a distance of one hundred yards, had placed a tin cup between his knees, and Mike had, at that distance, bored the center of the cup.

"I'll swar I don't hold that cup agin for you, Mike," remarked the doubter, "for thur is the delicatest kind of a trimble comin' in your hand, and, some of these *yur* days, you'll miss the cup clear."

"Miss thunder!" shouted Mike; "why, you consarned corn-dodger mill, it war you that had the trimbles, and when I gin old Bets the wakin' tetch, you *squatted* es ef her bark war agoin' to bite you!"

"Oh, well," was the reply, "thar's mor'n one way of gettin' out of a skunk hole, and ef you kin pass the trimbles off on me, why, you kin *pass,* that's all; but I ain't goin' to trust you with a sight at my paddles agin at an hundred paces, that's sartin."

"Why, you scary varmint," answers Mike, bouncing to his feet and reaching for *Betsy,* which stood by the cabin door of the boat, "jest pint out a muskeeter, at a hundred yards, and I'll nip off his right hinder eend claw, at the second jint, afore he kin hum *Oh, don't!*"

"Hit a muskeeter, ha, ha!" was the tantalizing response of the others; "why, you couldn't hit the hinder part of that nigger's heel up thar on the bluff, 'thout damagin' the bone, and that ain't no shot to crow about."

The negro referred to was seated at the very edge of the bluff, astride of a flour barrel, and one foot hung over the edge. The distance was over a hundred yards, but Mike instantly raised his rifle, with the remark: "I'll jest trim that feller's heel so he kin wear a decent boot!" and off went *Betsy.*

The negro jumped from his seat, and uttered a yell of pain, as if, indeed, his whole heel had been trimmed off, and Mike stood a moment with his rifle listening to the negro's voice, as if endeavoring to define from the sound whether he was really seriously hurt. At last the boatman who had been doubting Mike's present skill remarked:

"You kin *leave,* now, Mike, fur that darky's master will be arter you with a sharp stick;" and then he further added as a taunt—"I knowed Betsy was feelin' for that nigger's bones jest by the way you held her!"

Mike now became a little wrathy, and appeared inclined to use *his* bones upon the tormentor, but some of the others advised him to hold on—that he would have a chance to exercise them upon the constable. In a short time an officer appeared with a warrant, but as soon as Mike looked at him he gave up the thought of either flight or resistance, and quietly remarked to his companions that the officer was a clever fellow, and "a small *hoss* in a fight."

"The only way you kin work him is to fool him," says Mike, "and he's a weazel in that bisness hisself!"

The warrant was produced by the officer and read to the offender, who signified his assent to the demand for his body, and told the representative of the law to lead the way. He did so, and when about to step off the boat he cast his eye back, supposing that Mike was following him, yet a little suspicious. The movement was a prudent one, for he discovered the tail of Mike's hunting shirt at the very moment the owner was retreating into the small cabin at the rear of the boat, which was immediately locked on the inside! All the boatmen, as if by previous concert, began to leave their craft, each bearing away upon his shoulder any loose implement lying about, with which an entrance into the cabin could be forced. The officer paused a moment, and then went to the cabin door, which he commenced persuading the offender to open, and save him the trouble of forcing it. He received no answer, but heard a horrible rustling within At length getting out of patience, he remarked aloud:

"Well, if you won't open the door I can burn you out!" and he commenced striking fire with a pocket tinder box. The door immediately flew open, and there stood a boatman in Mike's dress; but it *wasn't Mike!*

"You ain't arter me, are you, *hoss?*" inquired the boatman.

The officer, without reply, stepped inside of the small cabin and looked around. There appeared to be no place to hide a figure as large as Mike, and there was a fellow dressed just like him. The thought immediately came uppermost in the officer's mind, that the offender had changed coats outside, while his back was turned to go off the boat, and one of the parties that had walked off was Mike in disguise! He was about to step out when a moccasin-covered heel, sticking out of a hole in a large mattress, attracted his attention, and when he touched it the heel vanished. He put his hand in to feel, and Mike burst out in a hoarse laugh!

"Quit your ticklin'!" shouted he. "Consarn your cunnin' pictur', I'll *gin in* 'thout a struggle."

The other boatman now joined in the laugh, as he helped the officer to pull Mike out of his hiding place. He had changed his garments *inside* the cabin instead of outside. A crowd of the boatmen also gathered around, and they all adjourned to the bluff, where, after taking drinks, they started in a body for the magistrate's office, who, by the way, was one of the early French settlers.

"Ah, ha!" he exclaimed, as the party entered the door; "here is ze men of ze boat, raisin' ze *diable* once more time. I shall not know what to do wiz *him*, by gar. Vat is de mattair now?"

"Why, Squire," broke in Mike, "I've jest come up with the Colonel to collect a small bill offen you!"

"You shall collect ze bill from *me*?" inquired the Justice. "What for you do the city good to de amount of von bill? Ah, ha! You kick up your *heel* and raise de batter and de salt of de whole town wiz your noise so much as we nevair get some sleep in de night!"

All eagerly gathered around to hear what Mike would reply, for his having a bill against the Justice was news to the crowd.

"You jest hit the pint, Squire," said Mike, "when you said that that word *heel*! I want you to pay me fur trimmin' the heel of one of your town niggers! I've jest altered his breed, and arter this his posterity kin warr the neatest kind of a boot!"

The boatmen burst into a yell of laughter, and the magistrate into a corresponding state of wrath. He sputtered French and English with such rapidity that it was impossible to understand either.

"Leave ze court, you ras*kells* of ze boat!" shouted the Squire above the noise. "*Allez vous-en, vous* rogues, I shall nevair ave nosing to do wiz you. You ave treat ze court wiz *grand contempt*."

The boatmen, all but Mike, had retired to the outside of the door, where they were still laughing, when Mike again, with a sober and solemn phiz, remarked to the Squire:

"Well, old dad, ef you allays raise *h-ll* in this way fur a little laffin' that's done in your court, I'll be cussed ef I gin you any more of my cases!"

Another roar from the boatmen hailed this remark.

"Constable, clear ze court, in *une* instant, right avay! *Les sacre diables* of ze river, no know nosing about how to treat wiz de law. I shall ave nosing to do wiz de whole what you call pile of ze rogues!"

"I ain't agoin' to stand any more sich law as this," remarked Mike. "Consarn my pictur' ef I don't leave the town!"

"Go to ze *devil*!" shouted the magistrate.

"I won't," says Mike; "mabbe he's anuther French Jestis!"

Amid a torrent of words and laughter Mike retreated to his boat, where he paid the officer for his trouble, and sent a handful of silver to the darky to extract the pain from his shortened heel.

Death of Mike Fink

"THE Last of the Boatmen" has not become altogether a *mythic* personage. There be around us those who still remember him as one of flesh and blood, as well of proportions simply human, albeit he lacked not somewhat of the *heroic* in stature, as well as in being a "perfect terror" to people!

As regards Mike, it has not yet become that favourite question of doubt —"Did such a being really live?" Nor have we heard the skeptic inquiry —"Did such a being really die?" But his death in half a dozen different ways and places has been asserted, and this, we take it, is the first gathering of the *mythic* haze—that shadowy and indistinct enlargement of outline, which, deepening through long ages, invests distinguished mortality with the sublimer attributes of the hero and the demi-god. Had Mike lived in "early Greece," his flat-boat feats would, doubtless, in poetry, have rivalled those of Jason, in his ship; while in Scandinavian legends, he would have been a river-god, to a certainty! The Sea-Kings would have sacrificed to him every time they "crossed the bar," on their return; and as for Odin, himself, he would be duly advised, as far as any interference went, to "lay low and keep dark, or, *pre*-haps," &c.

The story of Mike Fink, including *a* death, has been beautifully told by the late Morgan Neville, of Cincinnati, a gentleman of the highest literary taste as well as of the most amiable and polished manners. "The Last of the Boatmen," as his sketch is entitled, is unexceptionable in style, and, we believe, in *fact,* with one exception, and that is, the statement as to the manner and place of Fink's death. He did *not die* on the Arkansas, but at Fort Henry, near the mouth of the Yellow Stone. Our informant is Mr. Chas. Keemle of this paper,[1] who held a command in the neighbourhood, at the time, and to whom every circumstance connected with the affair is most familiar. We give the story as it is told by himself.

In the year 1822, steamboats having left the "keels" and "broad-horns" entirely "out of sight," and Mike having, in consequence, fallen from his high estate—that of being "a little bit the almightiest man on the river, *any* how"—after a term of idleness, frolic and desperate rowdyism, along the different towns, he, at St. Louis, entered the service of the Mountain Fur Company, raised by our late fellow-citizen Gen. W. H. Ashley, as a trapper and hunter; and in that capacity was he employed by Major Henry, in command of the Fort at the mouth of Yellow Stone river, when the occurrence took place of which we write.

Mike, with many generous qualities, was always a reckless daredevil; but,

---

From *The Drama in Pokerville; The Bench and Bar of Jurytown, and Other Stories,* by "Everpoint" (J. M. Field, Esq., of the *St. Louis Reveille*), pp. 177-183. Philadelphia: Carey and Hart. 1847. Reprinted from the *St. Louis Reveille,* October 21, 1844.

[1] *St. Louis Reveille.*—J. M. F.

at this time, advancing in years and decayed in influence, above all become
a victim of whisky, he was morose and desperate in the extreme. There
was a government regulation which forbade the free use of alcohol at the
trading posts on the Missouri river, and this was a continual source of
quarrel between the men and the commandant, Major Henry,—on the
part of Fink, particularly. One of his freaks was to march with his rifle
into the fort, and demand a supply of spirits. Argument was fruitless,
force not to be thought of, and when, on being positively denied, Mike
drew up his rifle and sent a ball through the cask, deliberately walked up
and filled his can, while his particular "boys" followed his example, all
that could be done was to look upon the matter as one of his "queer ways,"
and that was the end of it.

This state of things continued for some time; Mike's temper and exac-
tions growing more unbearable every day, until, finally, a "split" took
place, not only between himself and the commandant, but many others
in the fort, and the unruly boatman swore he would not live among them.
Followed only by a youth named Carpenter, whom he had brought up,
and for whom he felt a rude but strong attachment, he prepared a sort
of cave in the river's bank, furnished it with a supply of whisky, and,
with his companion, *turned in* to pass the winter, which was then closing
upon them. In this place he buried himself, sometimes unseen for weeks,
his *protege* providing what else was *necessary* beyond the whisky. At
length attempts were used, on the part of those in the fort, to withdraw
Carpenter from Fink; foul insinuations were made as to the nature of
their connection; the youth was twitted with being a mere slave, &c., all
which (Fink heard of it in spite of his retirement) served to breed distrust
between the two, and though they did not separate, much of their cordiality
ceased.

The winter wore away in this sullen state of torpor; spring came with
its reviving influences, and to celebrate the season, a supply of alcohol was
procured, and a number of his acquaintances from the fort coming to
"rouse out" Mike, a desperate "frolic," of course, ensued.

There were river yarns, and boatmen songs, and "nigger break-downs,"
interspersed with wrestling-matches, jumping, laugh, and yell, the can
circulating freely, until Mike became somewhat mollified.

"I tell you what it is, boys," he cried, "the fort's a skunk-hole, and I
rather live with the *bars* than stay in it. Some on ye's bin trying to part
me and my boy, that I love like my own cub—but no matter. Maybe he's
*pi*soned against me; but, Carpenter (striking the youth heavily on the
shoulder), I took you by the hand when it had forgotten the touch of a
father's or a mother's—you know me to be a man, and you ain't a going
to turn out a dog!"

Whether it was that the youth fancied something insulting in the manner
of the appeal, or not, we can't say; but it was not responded to very
warmly, and a reproach followed from Mike. However, they drank together, and the frolic went on, until Mike, filling his can, walked off some

forty yards, placed it upon his head, and called to Carpenter to take his rifle.

This wild feat of shooting cans off each other's head was a favourite one with Mike—himself and "boy" generally winding up a hard frolic with this savage, but deeply-meaning proof of continued confidence;—as for risk, their eagle eyes and iron nerves defied the might of whisky. After their recent alienation, a doubly generous impulse, without doubt, had induced Fink to propose and subject himself to the test.

Carpenter had been drinking wildly, and with a boisterous laugh snatched up his rifle. All present had seen the parties "shoot," and this desperate aim, instead of alarming, was merely made a matter of wild jest.

"Your grog is spilt, for ever, Mike!"

"Kill the old varmint, young 'un!"

"What'll his skin bring in St. Louis?" &c., &c.

Amid a loud laugh, Carpenter raised his piece—even the jesters remarked that he was unsteady,—crack!—the can fell,—a loud shout,— but, instead of a smile of pleasure, a dark frown settled upon the face of Fink! He made no motion except to clutch his rifle as though he would have crushed it, and there he stood, gazing at the youth strangely! Various shades of passion crossed his features—surprise, rage, suspicion—but at length they composed themselves into a sad expression; the ball had grazed the top of his head, cutting the scalp, and the thought of treachery had set his heart on fire.

There was a loud call upon Mike to know what he was waiting for, in which Carpenter joined, pointing to the can upon his head and bidding him fire, if he knew how!

"Carpenter, my son," said the boatman, "I taught you to shoot differently from that *last* shot! You've *missed* once, but you won't again!"

He fired, and his ball, crashing through the forehead of the youth, laid him a corpse amid his, as suddenly hushed, companions!

Time wore on—many at the fort spoke darkly of the deed. Mike Fink had never been known to miss his aim—he had grown afraid of Carpenter —he had murdered him! While this feeling was gathering against him, the unhappy boatman lay in his cave, shunning both sympathy and sustenance. He spoke to none—when he did come forth, 'twas as a spectre, and only to haunt the grave of his "boy," or, if he did break silence, 'twas to burst into a paroxysm of rage against the enemies who had "turned his boy's heart from him!"

At the fort was a man by the name of Talbott, the gunsmith of the station: he was very loud and bitter in his denunciations of the "murderer," as he called Fink, which, finally, reaching the ears of the latter, filled him with the most violent passion, and he swore that he would take the life of his defamer. This threat was almost forgotten, when one day, Talbott, who was at work in his shop, saw Fink enter the fort, his first visit since the death of Carpenter. Fink approached; he was careworn, sick, and wasted; there was no anger in his bearing, but he carried his rifle, (had he ever gone without it?) and the gunsmith was not a coolly brave man; moreover, his life had been threatened.

"Fink," cried he, snatching up a pair of pistols from his bench, "don't approach me—if you do, you're a dead man!"

"Talbott," said the boatman, in a sad voice, "you needn't be afraid; you've done me wrong—I'm come to talk to you about—Carpenter—my boy!"

He continued to advance, and the gunsmith again called to him:

"Fink! I know you; if you come three steps nearer, I'll fire, by——!"

Mike carried his rifle across his arm, and made no hostile demonstration, except in gradually getting nearer—*if* hostile his aim was.

"Talbott, you've accused me of murdering—my boy—Carpenter—that I raised from a child—that I loved like a son—that I can't live without! I'm not mad with you *now,* but you must let me show you that I *couldn't* do it—that I'd rather died than done it—that you've wronged me——"

By this time he was within a few steps of the door, and Talbott's agitation became extreme. Both pistols were pointed at Fink's breast, in expectation of a spring from the latter.

"By the Almighty above us, Fink, I'll fire—I don't want to speak to you now—don't put your foot on that step—don't."

Fink did put his foot on the step, and the same moment fell heavily within it, receiving the contents of both barrels in his breast! His last and only words were,

"I didn't mean to kill my boy!"

Poor Mike! we are satisfied with our senior's conviction that you did *not* mean to kill him. Suspicion of treachery, doubtless, entered his mind, but cowardice and murder never dwelt there.

A few weeks after this event, Talbott himself perished in an attempt to cross the Missouri river in a skiff.

II. PSEUDO BAD MEN

I'm a two-gun man and a very bad man and won't do to monkey with.—COWBOY YELL

WITH the passing of the keelboat many of Mike Fink's tribe became raftsmen, joining the new crew of hardy adventurers that brought the forests down to the towns in the form of rafts, put together in "cribs" of logs or boards and then taken apart to be sold.

"The typical raftsman," writes Charles Edward Russell, in *A-Rafting on the Mississip'* (1928), "was reckless, dissolute, daring and all that, but he was more; he was humorous with a style of humor all his own and largely his own language in which to frame it; emotional at bottom, sophisticated on the surface; a singer, a dancer, an improviser of wild yarns, ready with fist, dagger, or pistol; something of a poet, curiously responsive to charitable appeals, something of a Lothario, something of a pirate, something of a blackguard, and in profanity equipped with resources incomparable for richness of invention and competence of authority."

Lumber rafting on the Upper Mississippi lasted roughly from 1840 to 1915; but the old-time raftsman began to disappear when the raft-boat, or steamboat used to tow or push rafts, came in, about 1865. The hardihood of the raftsman of the floating days tended to be measured by the strength of his whisky, which was so powerful that it would take the hair off a buffalo robe. Or, to cite another school of thought on the buffalo robe test, Mike Fink "drank so much whisky that he destroyed the coating of his stomach, and the doctor told him that before he could get well, he would need a new coat for it. Mike thought the thing over, and said, when he had a new coat for his stomach, he would have one that would stand the whisky; and he made up his mind that a buffalo robe with the hair on it was just the thing, and so he sat down, and swallowed it. He could drink any amount of whisky after that, and never so much as wink."[1]

But when a buffalo robe failed as a stomach lining, oqueejum did the trick. Something of the toughness of the raftsman and the humor of his invention may be gleaned from the following advice of one raftsman to another:

"Hey! Don't let that stuff drop like that on your boots!" I heard one raftsman say to another that was passing him a bottle. "I spilt some on my new shore shoes last week and it ate the uppers clean off down to the soles."

"Was them shoes tanned with oqueejum?" asked the other in a quietly interested way, as if he were seeking scientific knowledge.

"No, sir. That there leather was tanned with the best hemlock bark, and the shoes cost me $3 in Red Wing."

"Now, say, my friend"—gently remonstrative—"don't you know better than to buy leather tanned with hemlock? What you want is leather tanned with oqueejum and then whisky can't eat it. You see, whisky and hemlock, they get together on social terms, same's you and me, and then the whisky does its deadly work and swallers the leather. But whisky and oqueejum's enemies, and when they meet whisky gets licked every time. That's why I keep my stomach lined with it. Oqueejum's made from the bamjam tree which grows in India to a height of more than a thousand feet. Its wood is so hard they have to cut it with a cold chisel. It stands to reason that it's stronger than hemlock. Try some on your stomach and then your liquor won't get to your head like this."

The hardihood of the raftsman tended also to be measured by his boasting. In the famous raft scene in *Life on the Mississippi* (1874), which gives us our first glimpse of Huck Finn, Mark Twain has immortalized the "screamer." The "screamer" is the ring-tailed roarer grown maudlin, who boasts out of his weakness rather than his strength. He is the bogus bad man, who has already been glimpsed in the canebrake cockalorum and in the cock-of-the-walk pose of Mike Fink.

West of the Mississippi the scream of the backwoods boaster and bully passed into the howl of the pseudo or mock bad man, who, in his boasting

---

[1] *Underground, or Life Below the Surface,* by Thomas W. Knox (1873), pp. 680–684.

[2] *A-Rafting on the Mississip',* by Charles Edward Russell (1928), pp. 189–190.

chants and yells, proclaimed his intestinal fortitude with more and more weird anatomical details. In addition to the usual animal traits he claimed a mythical animal nurse and a more than usual endowment of teeth and other hard substance in his makeup. Crockett, too, it will be recalled, boasted of being "half chicken hawk and steel-trap" and of his wilderness birthplace—"born in a cane brake, cradled in a sap trough, and clouted with coon skins."

No one liked to play bad man more than the cowboy on a spree; and from his favorite interjection, "Whoopee!," originally a call to animals, "making whoopee" has become a general term for carousing. But if a would-be desperado announced that it was his time to howl, this was chiefly for the benefit of the uninitiated. For the rest knew that with the true bad man or killer the rule was: "Shoot first and talk afterward." [1]

On the frontier, however, "apparent rage" and "vigorous language" had their uses in bluffing or blustering one's way out of a tight place as well as in letting off steam. By such devices an Iowa squatter is reported to have got rid of a prospective settler from Illinois "who casually remonstrated against any one holding more than one claim and not even that 'unless he lived on it' ":

"My name, Sir, is Simeon Cragin. I own *fourteen* claims, and if any man jumps one of them I will shoot him down at once, Sir. I am a gentleman, Sir, and a scholar. I was educated in Bangor, have been in the United States army and served my country faithfully—am the discoverer of the Wopsey—can ride a grizzly bear, or whip any *human* that ever crossed the Mississippi; and if you dare jump one of my claims, die you must." [2]

The dramatized bad man yells not only lean heavily on one another but also become mixed with literary or semi-literary parodies and burlesques. Such, frankly, is "The Bad Man from the Brazos," beginning:

> I'm a blizzard from the Brazos on a tear, hear me hoot;
> I'm a lifter of the flowing locks of hair, hear me toot;
> I'm a rocker from the Rockies
> And of all the town the talk is,
> "He's a pirate from the Pampas on the shoot." [3]

Raftsman Talk

THE river's earliest commerce was in great barges—keelboats, broadhorns. They floated and sailed from the upper rivers to New Orleans, changed

[1] *Short Grass Country,* by Stanley Vestal (1941), pp. 26.

[2] "Justice in Early Iowa," by *George F. Robeson, The Palimpsest,* Vol. 5 (March, 1924), No. 3, p. 105.

[3] *Cowboy Songs and Other Frontier Ballads,* Revised and Enlarged, collected by John A. Lomax and Alan Lomax (1938), p. 138, where it is ascribed to *Texas Siftings.*

From *Life on the Mississippi,* by Mark Twain, pp. 41–49. Copyright, 1874 and 1875, by H. O. Houghton & Company; 1883, by Samuel L. Clemens. Boston: James R. Osgood & Company. 1883.

cargoes there, and were tediously warped and poled back by hand. A voyage down and back sometimes occupied nine months. In time this commerce increased until it gave employment to hordes of rough and hardy men; rude, uneducated, brave, suffering terrific hardships with sailor-like stoicism; heavy drinkers, coarse frolickers in moral sties like the Natchez-under-the-hill of that day, heavy fighters, reckless fellows, every-one, elephantinely jolly, foul-witted, profane, prodigal of their money, bankrupt at the end of the trip, fond of barbaric finery, prodigious brag-garts; yet, in the main, honest, trustworthy, faithful to promises and duty, and often picturesquely magnanimous.

By and by the steamboat intruded. Then, for fifteen or twenty years, these men continued to run their keelboats down-stream, and the steam-ers did all of the up-stream business, the keelboatmen selling their boats in New Orleans, and returning home as deck-passengers in the steamers.

But after awhile the steamboats so increased in number and in speed that they were able to absorb the entire commerce; and then keelboating died a permanent death. The keelboatman became a deck-hand, or a mate, or a pilot on the steamer; and when steamer-berths were not open to him, he took a berth on a Pittsburgh coal-flat, or on a pine raft constructed in the forests up toward the sources of the Mississippi.

In the heyday of the steamboating prosperity, the river from end to end was flaked with coal-fleets and timber-rafts, all managed by hand, and employing hosts of the rough characters whom I have been trying to describe. I remember the annual processions of mighty rafts that used to glide by Hannibal when I was a boy—an acre or so of white, sweet-smelling boards in each raft, a crew of two dozen men or more, three or four wigwams scattered about the raft's vast level space for storm-quarters —and I remember the rude ways and the tremendous talk of their big crews, the ex-keelboatmen and their admiringly patterning successors; for we used to swim out a quarter or a third of a mile and get on these rafts and have a ride.

By way of illustrating keelboat talk and manners, and that now de-parted and hardly remembered raft life, I will throw in, in this place, a chapter from a book which I have been working at, by fits and starts, during the past five or six years, and may possibly finish in the course of five or six more. The book is a story which details some passages in the life of an ignorant village boy, Huck Finn, son of the town drunkard of my time out West, there. He has run away from his persecuting father, and from a persecuting good widow who wishes to make a nice, truth-telling, re-spectable boy of him; and with him a slave of the widow's has also escaped. They have found a fragment of a lumber-raft (it is high water and dead summer-time), and are floating down the river by night, and hiding in, the willows by day—bound for Cairo, whence the negro will seek freedom in the heart of the free states. But, in a fog, they pass Cairo without knowing it. By and by they begin to suspect the truth, and Huck Finn is persuaded to end the dismal suspense by swimming down to a huge raft which they have seen in the distance ahead of them, creeping aboard under cover of the darkness, and gathering the needed information by eavesdropping:——

. . . There was thirteen men there—they was the watch on deck of course. And a mighty rough-looking lot, too. They had a jug, and tin cups, and they kept the jug moving. One man was singing—roaring, you may say; and it wasn't a nice song—for a parlor, anyway. He roared through his nose, and strung out the last words of every line very long. When he was done they all fetched a kind of Injun war-whoop, and then another was sung. It begun:

> "There was a woman in our towdn,
>   In our towdn did dwed'l [dwell],
> She loved her husband dear-i-lee,
>   But another man twyste as wed'l.
>
> "Singing too, riloo, riloo, riloo,
>   Ri-too, riloo, rilay - - - e,
> She loved her husband dear-i-lee,
>   But another man twyste as wed'l."

And so on—fourteen verses. It was kind of poor, and when he was going to start on the next verse one of them said it was the tune the old cow died on; and another one said: "Oh, give us a rest!" And another one told him to take a walk. They made fun of him till he got mad and jumped up and begun to cuss the crowd, and said he could lam any thief in the lot.

They was all about to make a break for him, but the biggest man there jumped up and says:

"Set whar you are, gentlemen. Leave him to me; he's my meat."

Then he jumped up in the air three times, and cracked his heels together every time. He flung off a buckskin coat that was all hung with fringes, and says, "You lay thar tell the chawin-up's done"; and flung his hat down, which was all over ribbons, and says, "You lay thar tell his sufferin's is over."

Then he jumped up in the air and cracked his heels together again, and shouted out:

"Whoo-oop! I'm the old original iron-jawed, brass-mounted, copper-bellied corpse-maker from the wilds of Arkansaw! Look at me! I'm the man they call Sudden Death and General Desolation! Sired by a hurricane, dam'd by an earthquake, half-brother to the cholera, nearly related to the smallpox on the mother's side. Look at me! I take nineteen alligators and a bar'l of whiskey for breakfast when I'm in robust health, and a bushel of rattlesnakes and a dead body when I'm ailing. I split the ever-lasting rocks with my glance, and I squench the thunder when I speak!

Whoo-oop! Stand back and give me room according to my strength! Blood's my natural drink, and the wails of the dying is music to my ear. Cast your eye on me, gentlemen! and lay low and hold your breath, for I'm 'bout to turn myself loose!"

All the time he was getting this off, he was shaking his head and looking fierce, and kind of swelling around in a little circle, tucking up his wristbands, and now and then straightening up and beating his breast with his fist, saying, "Look at me, gentlemen!" When he got through, he jumped up and cracked his heels together three times, and let off a roaring "Whoo-oop! I'm the bloodiest son of a wildcat that lives!"

Then the man that had started the row tilted his old slouch hat down over his right eye; then he bent stooping forward, with his back sagged and his south end sticking out far, and his fists a-shoving out and drawing in in front of him, and so went around in a little circle about three times, swelling himself up and breathing hard. Then he straightened, and jumped up and cracked his heels together three times before he lit again (that made them cheer), and he began to shout like this:

"Whoo-oop! bow your neck and spread, for the kingdom of sorrow's a-coming! Hold me down to the earth, for I feel my powers a-working; Whoo-oop! I'm a child of sin, *don't* let me get a start! Smoked glass, here, for all! Don't attempt to look at me with the naked eye, gentlemen! When I'm playful I use the meridians of longitude and parallels of latitude for a seine, and drag the Atlantic Ocean for whales! I scratch my head with the lightning and purr myself to sleep with the thunder! When I'm cold I bile the Gulf of Mexico and bathe in it; when I'm thirsty I reach up and suck a cloud dry like a sponge; when I'm hot I fan myself with an equinoctial storm; when I range the earth hungry, famine follows in my tracks! Whoo-oop! Bow your neck and spread! I put my hand on the sun's face and make it night in the earth; I bite a piece out of the moon and hurry the seasons; I shake myself and crumble the mountains! Contemplate me through leather—*don't* use the naked eye! I'm the man with a petrified heart and biler-iron bowels! The massacre of isolated communities is the pastime of my idle moments, the destruction of nationalities the serious business of my life! The boundless vastness of the great American desert is my inclosed property, and I bury my dead on my own premises!" He jumped up and cracked his heels together three times before he lit (they cheered him again), and as he come down he shouted out: "Whoo-oop! bow your neck and spread, for the pet Child of Calamity's a-coming!"

Then the other one went to swelling around and blowing again—the first one—the one they called Bob; next, the Child of Calamity chipped in again, bigger than ever; then they both got at it at the same time, swelling round and round each other and punching their fists most into each other's faces, and whooping and jawing like Injuns; then Bob called the Child names, and the Child called him names back again; next, Bob called him a heap rougher names, and the Child come back at him with the very worst kind of language; next, Bob knocked the Child's hat off, and the Child picked it up and kicked Bob's ribbony hat about six foot; Bob went and got it and said never mind, this warn't going to be the last of this thing, because he was a man that never forgot and never forgive, and so the Child better look out, for there was a time a-coming, just as sure as he was a living man, that he would have to answer to him with the best blood in his body. The Child said no man was willinger than he for that time to come, and he would give Bob fair warning, *now*, never to cross his path again, for he could never rest till he had waded in his blood, for such was his nature, though he was sparing him now on account of his family, if he had one.

Both of them was edging away in different directions, growling and shaking their heads and going on about what they was going to do; but a little black-whiskered chap skipped up and says:

"Come back here, you couple of chicken-livered cowards, and I'll thrash the two of ye!"

And he done it, too. He snatched them, he jerked them this way and that, he booted them around, he knocked them sprawling faster than they could get up. Why, it warn't two minutes till they begged like dogs—and how the other lot did yell and laugh and clap their hands all the way through, and shout, "Sail in, Corpse-Maker!" "Hi! at him again, Child of Calamity!" "Bully for you, little Davy!" Well, it was a perfect pow-wow for a while. Bob and the Child had red noses and black eyes when they got through. Little Davy made them own up that they was sneaks and cowards and not fit to eat with a dog or drink with a nigger; then Bob and the Child shook hands with each other, very solemn, and said they had always respected each other and was willing to let bygones be bygones. So then they washed their faces in the river; and just then there was a loud order to stand by for a crossing, and some of them went forward to man the sweeps there, and the rest went aft to handle the after sweeps.

Crockett's Brag

I'M THAT same David Crockett, fresh from the backwoods, half-horse, half-alligator, a little touched with the snapping-turtle; can wade the Mississippi, leap the Ohio, ride upon a streak of lightning, and slip without a scratch down a honey locust; can whip my weight in wild cats,—and if any gentleman pleases, for a ten dollar bill, he may throw in a panther,— hug a bear too close for comfort, and eat any man opposed to Jackson.

From *Sketches and Eccentricities of Col. David Crockett, of West Tennessee*, p. 164. New York: Printed and Published by J. & J. Harper. 1833.

Fink's Brag

I'M A Salt River roarer! I'm a ring-tailed squealer! I'm a reg'lar screamer from the ol' Massassip'! WHOOP! I'm the very infant that refused his milk before its eyes were open, and called out for a bottle of old Rye! I love the women an' I'm chockful o' fight! I'm half wild horse and half cock-eyed alligator and the rest o' me is crooked snags an' red-hot snappin' turkle. I can hit like fourth-proof lightnin' an' every lick I make in the woods lets in an acre o' sunshine. I can out-run, out-jump, out-shoot, out-brag, out-drink, an' out-fight, rough-an'-tumble, no holts barred, ary man on both sides the river from Pittsburgh to New Orleans an' back ag'in to St. Louiee. Come on, you flatters, you bargers, you milk-white mechanics, an' see how tough I am to chaw! I ain't had a fight for two days an' I'm spilein' for exercise. Cock-a-doodle-do!

Hurray for Me!

. . . "HURRAY for me, you scapegoats! I'm a land-screamer—I'm a water-dog—I'm a snapping-turkle—I can lick five times my own weight in wild-cats. I can use up Injens by the cord. I can swallow niggers whole, raw or cooked. I can out-run, out-dance, out-jump, out-dive, out-drink, out-holler, and out-lick, any white thing in the shape o' human that's ever put foot within two thousand miles o' the big Massassip. Whoop! holler, you varmints!—holler fur the Snapping Turkle! or I'll jump right straight down yer throats, quicker nor a streak o' greased lightening can down a nigger's! . . . I'm in fur a fight, I'll go my death on a fight, and a fight I must have, one that'll tar up the arth all round and look kankarifferous, or else I'll have to be salted down to save me from spiling, as sure nor Massassip alligators make fly traps o' thar infernal ugly jawrs."

Bully of Salt River

THE bully of Salt River war named Skippoweth Branch. He slept in his hat, chawed his vittles with his foreteeth, and could scream through his nose. He sunned himself in a thunder storm, went to meeting on two horses, never turned out for man or beast; and was sworn to lick every

From *Mike Fink, King of Mississippi Keelboatmen,* by Walter Blair and Franklin J. Meine, pp. 105–106. Copyright, 1933, by Henry Holt & Company, Inc. New York.

From *Mike Fink: A Legend of the Ohio,* by Emerson Bennett, pp. 24–25, 83. Cincinnati: Robinson & Jones. 1848.

From *Mince Pie for the Million.* Philadelphia and New York: Turner & Fisher. 1846.

thing he saw, except his own father and mother. He would walk ten miles, at any time of day or night, for a fight. He called himself the great oak that grows half its length underground, and turns up its roots unexpected. He sometimes took the name of floating iron and melted pewter, red hot cannon balls, and Big Snag of the Desert. He said he lived on the mountains and eat thunder, that he had a neckcloth at home made of double chain lightning, and that he could never come to his full height till the clouds were lifted a peace. He called himself a west wind full of prickles, a dose for old Kaintuck and a drawing plaster for the Allegheny mountains. The fact is he war too smart to live long, and screamed himself to death, one night, to show his spirrit. I knowed him when he war a boy, and seed him when he war a man, and went to his funeral when he war ded. He war the pride of the country, and could outscream seven cata-mounts tied together.

Billy Earthquake

As WE were passing by the court-house, a real "screamer from the Nob," about six feet four in height, commenced the following tirade:—"This is *me*, and no mistake! Billy Earthquake, Esq., commonly called Little Billy, all the way from No'th Fork of Muddy Run! I'm a small specimen, as you see, a remote circumstance, a mere yearling; but cuss me if I ain't of the true imported breed, and I can whip any man in this section of the country. Whoop! won't *nobody* come out and fight me? Come out, some of you, and die decently, for I'm spileing for a fight, I hain't had one for more than a week, and if you don't come out I'm flyblowed before sundown, to a certingty. So come up to taw!

"Maybe you don't know who Little Billy is? I'll tell you. I'm a poor man, it's a fact, and smell like a wet dog; but I can't be run over. I'm the identical individual that grinned a whole menagerie out of countenance, and made the ribbed nose baboon hang down his head and blush. W-h-o-o-p! I'm the chap that towed the Broad-horn up Salt River, where the snags were so thick that the fish couldn't swim without rubbing their scales off!—fact, and if any one denies it, just let 'em make their will! Cock-a-doodle-doo!

"Maybe you never heard of the time the horse kicked me, and put both his hips out of jint—if it ain't true, cut me up for catfish bait! W-h-o-o-p! I'm the very infant that refused its milk before its eyes were open, and called out for a bottle of old Rye! W-h-o-o-p! I'm that little Cupid!

From *An American Glossary*, Being an Attempt to Illustrate Certain Americanisms upon Historical Principles, by Richard H. Thornton, Vol. II, pp. 969–970. Philadelphia: J. B. Lippincott Company. 1912. Reprinted from a Florida newspaper, about the year 1840.

Talk about grinning the bark off a tree!—'tain't nothing; one squint of mine at a bull's heel would blister it. O, I'm one of your toughest sort,— live for ever, and then turn to a white oak post. I'm the ginewine article, a real double acting engine, and I can out-run, out-jump, out-swim, chaw more tobacco and spit less, and drink more whiskey and keep soberer than any man in these localities. If that don't make 'em fight (walking off in disgust) nothing will. I wish I may be kiln-dried and split up into wooden shoe-pegs, if I believe there's a chap among 'em that's got courage enough to collar a hen!"

Bad Man Yells

A CERTAIN class of chant-like yells emphasizing the badness of the man yelling them belongs to the lore of the bad man, I suppose, though oftener than not they originated in a spirit of mockery. The cowboy liked to "yip" them out when he was playing bad man—for the cowboy was truly "the playboy of the western world." Here is a yell that "hard customers" from the country around Harrisburg and Houston used to give fifty years ago. My father, who was a very quiet man, used to quote it to enforce his contempt for the "fly-up-the-creeks" from whom he learned it.

> Raised in a canebrake,
> Fed in a hog trough,
> Suckled by a she bear,
> The click of a six-shooter is music to my ear!
>   Wh-o-o-o-p-ee! [1]
>
> The further up the creek you go
> The worse they get,
> And I come from the head of it!
>   Wh-o-o-o-p-ee!

From "Ballads and Songs of the Frontier Folk," by J. Frank Dobie, *Texas and Southwestern Lore*, Publications of the Texas Folk-Lore Society, Number VI, edited by J. Frank Dobie, pp. 149–150. Copyright, 1927, by the Texas Folk-Lore Society. Austin.

[1] As an interjection "whoop," of which "whoopee" is a derivative, is at least as old as the fifteenth century. It is listed as a call to sheep in Mary Crawford's "English Interjections in the Fifteenth Century" (1913). When brought to the United States this call to animals found its chief home in the Southwest. Witness the familiar refrain of the cowboy song reported by John A. Lomax in 1910: "whoopee-ti-yi-yo, git along little dogies." When the World War broke out the Powder River cowboys carried the cry far and wide, making it known across the Atlantic as well as in the United States. From "whoopee" the interjection comes "whoopee" the noun, of recent American creation. Walter Winchell, the New York columnist, is probably the man responsible for floating the noun usage of the word. Mr. Winchell himself believes this and he is in a position to know. Then the adoption of the name for the well-known Ziegfeld show did the rest. With such publicity behind it, and launched during the jazz age, its popularity was assured.—J. D., *American Speech*, VI (June, 1931), No. 5, pp 394–395.

Another boast, adapted to a Texas river, was as follows:

> Born high up on the Guadalupe,
> Raised on a thorny prickly pear,
> Quarrelled witn alligators,
> And fought grizzly bears!

A. J. Sowell, who knew Texas frontier life as few men who have written of it knew it, says in his *Rangers and Pioneers of Texas* (San Antonio, 1884, page 330): "Occasionally in some Western village, you will hear a voice ring out on the night air in words something like these: 'Wild and woolly,' 'Hard to curry,' 'Raised a pet but gone wild,' 'Walked the Chisholm Trail backwards,' 'Fought Indians and killed buffalo,' 'Hide out, little ones,' and then you may expect a few shots from a revolver. It is a cowboy out on a little spree, but likely he will not hurt anyone, as some friend who is sober generally comes to him, relieves him of his pistol, and all is soon quiet again." Sowell adds that such yelling cowboys were exceptions.

Human Man-Eaters

PSEUDO "bad men" of the "I eat humans for breakfast" kind functioned in the presence of tenderfoots by fierce looks and snorts, by savage remarks, and sometimes by the recital of speeches ferocious in phrase and committed to memory. These men would "wild up" whenever they obtained an impressionable audience, and their braggadocio often was picturesque, even though made up at least in part from strings of stereotyped Western anecdotes. Old, harmless Jim ——, when in his cups, would fervently relate: "I'm the toughest, wildest killer in the West. When I'm hungry I bites off the noses of living grizzly bars. I live in a box canyon, where everybody is wild, and shoots so much they fills the ar plumb full of lead, so there ain't no ar to breathe. The further up the canyon you goes, the wilder the people gits, and I live at the very top end. Whoop!" If tenderfoots continued their presence, Jim would persist in this strain; and perhaps, because of him, a diary or two would receive the entry: "Saw to-day a real Western 'bad man.' He carried two large revolvers in holsters which hung, one just above each knee. This marks him as being what is called a 'two-gun man,' and a person who 'totes his weepens low.'" If only Westerners were auditors, Jim soon would quit his oratory, go to sleep, and snore himself to peaceability.

Bill ——, when alcoholically beset, would announce: "I live in Jack County, Texas. Thars whar the human man-eaters come from, and I'm

From *The Cowboy;* His Characteristics, His Equipment, and His Part in the Development of the West, by Philip Ashton Rollins, pp. 53–54. Copyright, 1922, by Charles Scribner's Sons. New York.

one on 'em. Every pusson they don't take no fancy to is drug out and scalped alive. My hum range is so plumb full of murder and sin that hell won't be no treat to me." He, too, presently would cease his clatter, and would slumber back to sobriety.

This Jim ——, this Bill ——, and the other men of their type had no wish to "try it out" with any "real Westerner," for it was a foregone conclusion as to which side in such a contest would "weaken," "back down," and "pull out."

The actual "bad man" was "short on conversation." He spoke infrequently, and when he opened his mouth what he said was to the point. He usually talked in quiet tones, for his nerves always were well in hand. His nerves had to be thus in order for him to do the jobs which he essayed.

The Boasting Drunk in Dodge

WHEN a group of cowboys reached Dodge City from Texas, they had not slept in a bed for months; nor had they shaved or enjoyed a hot bath or a haircut. Their clothing was dirty, often ragged. They had not seen a woman perhaps for half a year. The saloons of Dodge never shut their doors (on the opening day the proprietor threw away the keys). The red lights in back of the saloons beckoned. First the cowboys got rid of their extra hair, bought new outfits of clothing, and then they tanked up. They were ready to go. Some were quiet in their dissipation. Others talked— perhaps to keep up their courage—as does the "Boasting Drunk." Dodge was the toughest town known in 1883.

Raised on six-shooters till I get big enough to eat ground shotguns,
When I'm cool I warm the Gulf of Mexico and bathe therein,
When I'm hot there's an equinoxical breeze that fans me fevered brow,
The moans of widows and orphans is music to me melancholy soul.

Me the boy that chewed the wad the goat eat that butted the goat off the bridge,
Born in the Rocky Mountains, suckled by a grizzly bear,
Ninety-nine rows of jaw teeth and not a single hair.

From *Cowboy Songs and Other Frontier Ballads*, collected by John A. Lomax and Alan Lomax, pp. 135–136. Revised and Enlarged. Copyright, 1910, 1916, 1938, by The Macmillan Company; 1938, by John A. Lomax. New York.

Cf.:

> Raised in a canebrake, and suckled by a lion,
> Head like a bombshell and teeth made out of iron;
> Nine rows of jaw teeth and holes punched for more.
> I come from ourang-a-tang where the bullfrogs jump
> from north to south.
> —*Cowboy Songs and Other Frontier Ballads*, collected
> by John A. Lomax and Alan Lomax, p. 63.

Thirty-two inches 'tween the eyes and they feed me with a shovel,
Mount the wild ass and leap from crag to crag,
And roar like laughter in a tomb,
Jump from precipice to precipice and back to pice again.

Snatched him bald-headed and spit on the place where the hair come off;
Take a leg off him and beat him over the head with the bloody end of it,
Slap his head up to a peak and then knock the peak off,
Take his eye out and eat it for a grape.

Gimme one hundred yards start and I'll run plumb to Honolulu without even
    wettin' my feet,
Shoulder five hundred bushel of shot and wade through solid rocks up to my
    shoulder blades.
Any damn man don't believe it . . .

I'll lick him on a sheep hide and never tromp on the tail,
Knock a belch out of him that'll whiz like a nail,
Knock a belch out of him longer'n a rail,
Sharp enough to stick a pig with.

Other Cowboy Boasting Chants

I'm wild and woolly
And full of fleas;
Ain't never been curried
Below the knees.
I'm a wild she wolf
From Bitter Creek,
And it's my time
To h-o-w-l, whoop-i-e-e-ee.

Wasp nests and yaller jackets,
The higher you pitch, the sweeter my navy tastes.
Born on the Guadalupe,
Ten miles below Duck Pond,
Raised in the Rocky Mountains.
Hang one spur where the collar works
And the other where the crupper works.

Four rows of jaw teeth
And holes punched for more;
Steel ribs and iron backbone,
And tail put on with screws,
Double dew-clawed,
Knock-kneed and bandy-shanked,
Nine rows of teeth,
And holes punched for more.

From *American Ballads and Folk Songs*, collected and compiled by John A. Lomax
and Alan Lomax, pp. 382–383. Copyright, 1934, by The Macmillan Company. New
York.

Cowboy to Pitching Bronco

To be declaimed, not sung

Born on the Col-o-ra-do,

Sired by an al-li-ga-tor,

I'm a bold, bad man from Crip-ple Creek, Col-o-ra-do.

When I git back there'll be a tor-na-do!

Git high-er, git high-er,

The high-er you git's too low for me.

Want to git my po-ny back and throw my nig-gers through the crack.

I'm tell-in' you, flam-doo-zle-dum!

Born on the Colorado,
Sired by an alligator,
I'm a bold, bad man
    from Cripple Creek, Colorado.
When I git back
    there'll be a tornado!

Ibid., pp. 381–382.

A practice, once common in Texas, called for boasting talk from the probably scared cowboy as the wild horse, ridden for the first time, began his frantic pitching to dislodge his rider. Each line of the chant measures the period while the horse is in the air. The chant goes on indefinitely, other verses being added or the first being repeated, until the final exclamation when the horse suddenly stops to breathe.

The above rote and time values can but poorly, approximately, and arbitrarily reproduce the cowboy's *chant;* its freedom of motion, unusual disposition of accent, and rising and falling of the voice are never twice the same.—J. A. L. and A. L.

Git higher, git higher,
The higher you git's
    too low for me.
Want to git my pony back
    and throw my niggers through the crack.
I'm tellin' you,
    flamdoozledum!

Cowboy Yells

"HALF horse, half alligator, with a little touch of a snapping turtle, clumb a streak of lightning, and slid down a locust tree a hundred feet high, with a wild cat under each arm and never got a scratch. Whoopee-yip-ho!"

"I come to this country riding a lion, whipping him over the head with a .45 and picking my teeth with a .38 and wearing a .45 on each hip, using a cactus for a piller, whe-ee-e! I'm a two-gun man and a very bad man and won't do to monkey with. Whe-ee-o, I'm a bad man! Whoopee!"

"Raised in the backwoods, suckled by a polar bear, nine rows of jaw teeth, a double coat of hair, steel ribs, wire intestines, and a barbed wire tail, and I don't give a dang where I drag it. Whoopee-whee-a-ha!"

The Purple Blossom of Gingham Mountain

" ' "LET all the sons of men b'ar witness!" sings this gent, as he goes skatin' stiff-laig about in a ring like I relates, arms bent, an' back arched; "let all the sons of men b'ar witness; an' speshully let a cowerin' varmint, named Sam Enright, size me up an' shudder. I'm the maker of deserts an' the wall-eyed harbinger of desolation! I'm kin to rattlesnakes on my mother's side; I'm king of all the eagles an' full brother to the b'ars! I'm the bloo-eyed lynx of Whisky Crossin', an' I weighs four thousand pounds. I'm a he-steamboat; I've put a crimp in a cat-a-mount with nothin' but my livin' hands! I broke a full-grown allagator across my knee, tore him asunder an' showered his shrinkin' fragments over a full section of land! I hugged a cinnamon b'ar to death, an' made a grizzly plead for mercy! Who'll come gouge with me? Who'll come bite with me? Who'll come put his knuckles in my back? I'm Weasel-eye, the dead shot; I'm the blood-drinkin', skelp-t'arin', knife-plyin' demon of Sunflower Creek! The flash of my glance will deaden a whiteoak, an' my screech in anger will

As told by Walter R. Smith, St. Louis, Oklahoma. From "Tall Talk and Tall Tales of the Southwest," by B. A. Botkin, *The New Mexico Candle*, New Mexico Normal University, Las Vegas, New Mexico, June 28, 1933.

From "Old Man Enright's Love," in *Wolfville Days*, by Alfred Henry Lewis, pp. 273-274. Copyright, 1902, by Frederick A. Stokes Company. New York.

back the panther plumb off his natif heath! I'm a slayer an' a slaughterer, an' I cooks an' eats my dead! I can wade the Cumberland without wettin' myse'f, an' I drinks outen the spring without touchin' the ground! I'm a swinge-cat; but I warns you not to be misled by my looks! I'm a flyin' bison, an' deevastation rides upon my breath! Whoop! whoop! whoopee! I'm the Purple Blossom of Gingham Mountain, an' where is that son of thunder who'll try an' nip me in the bud! Whoop! whoopee! I'm yere to fight or drink with any sport; ary one or both! Whoopee! Where is the stately stag to stamp his hoof or rap his antlers to my proclamations! Where is that boundin' buck! Whoopee! whoop! whoop!" ' "

From College to Cowboy

I FOUND Cheyenne, Wyo., one of the wickedest places in the world when I visited it twelve years ago. It was a town of saloons, dance houses, and faro banks. Travelers for the Black Hills used to stop at Cheyenne and commit the last wicked act before burying themselves in the hills. Of course all this is changed now. While there, I wrote a letter to the New York *Sun* about "the wickedest town on earth." The humor of it amused the people and especially delighted McDonald, the manager of the leading dance house. He dramatized my letter, calling it "Eli among the Cowboys," and the play was enacted for many nights. I was the hero of the play, and was represented as a captured humorous lecturer. In the play three cowboys leveled their revolvers at the hero and compelled him to deliver a humorous lecture, or tell a funny joke, or die on the spot. It was funny to see a man, surrounded by desperadoes, and telling jokes to save his life. At the conclusion of a funny speech they would all dance around me with cocked revolvers, singing:

> *First Cowboy:*
> I'm the howler from the prairies of the West,
> If you want to die with terror, look at me.
> I'm chain-lightning; if I ain't, may I be blessed.
> I'm the snorter of the boundless perairie.
>
> *Chorus:*
> He's a killer and a hater;
> He's the great annihilator;
> He's a terror of the boundless perairie.

From "From College to Cowboy," in *Eli Perkins, Thirty Years of Wit, and Reminiscences of Witty, Wise and Eloquent Men,* by Melville D. Landon (Eli Perkins), pp. 295–296. Copyright, 1891, by Cassell Publishing Company. New York.

The song is also given by N. Howard Thorp ("Jack" Thorp) in *Songs of the Cowboys,* p. 9, where it is entitled "The Boozer" ("cut this out of a Colorado newspaper") and by John A. and Alan Lomax in *Cowboy Songs and Other Frontier Ballads,* pp. 137–138, as "The Desperado."

Second Cowboy:
I'm the snoozer from the upper trail;
I'm the reveler in murder and in gore;
I can bust more Pullman coaches on the rail
Than any one who's worked the job before.

Chorus:
    He's a snorter and a snoozer;
    He's the great trunk line abuser;
    He's the man who put the sleeper on the rail.

Third Cowboy:
I'm the double-jawed hyena from the East;
I'm the blazing bloody blizzard of the States;
I'm the celebrated slugger, I'm the beast;
I can snatch a man bald-headed while he waits.

Chorus:
    He's a double-jawed hyena;
    He's the villain of the scena;
    He can snatch a man bald-headed while he waits.

The Pike County Rip-Tail Roarer

"THE smartest fighters come from Pike. I kin whip my weight in wildcats, am a match for a dozen Indians to onst, and can tackle a lion without flinchin'."

"I'm from Pike County, Missouri, gentlemen. They call me the Rip-tail Roarer."

A Female Rip-Tail Roarer

MY FIRST sweetheart gave me this description of herself:

"You just ought to see me rigged out in my best. My bonnet is a hornet's nest, garnished with wolves' tails and eagles' feathers. My gown's made of a whole bear's hide, with the tail for a train. I can drink from the branch without a cup, shoot a wild goose flying, wade the Mississippi without getting wet, out scream a catamount, and jump over my own shadow. I've good, strong horse sense, and know a woodchuck from a skunk. I can dance down any fellow in Arkansas, and cut through the bushes like a pint of whisky among forty men. Your Sal."

From *Joe's Luck; or, A Boy's Adventures in California*, by Horatio Alger, Jr., pp. 141, 172. Copyright, 1887, by A. L. Burt. New York.

From *Harry Macarthy, the Arkansas Comedian; His Book of Original Songs, Ballads and Anecdotes*, as presented by the author in his well known Personation Concerts, p. 14. Indianapolis: State Sentinel Steam Printing Establishment. 1870.

Washoe

WE REACH Carson City about nine o'clock in the morning. It is the capital of the silver-producing territory of Nevada.

They shoot folks here somewhat, and the law is rather partial than otherwise to first-class murderers.

I visit the territorial prison, and the warder points out the prominent convicts to me, thus:

"This man's crime was horse-stealing. He is here for life.

"This man is in for murder. He is here for three years."

But shooting isn't as popular in Nevada as it once was. A few years since they used to have a dead man for breakfast [1] every morning. A reformed desperado told me that he supposed he had killed men enough to stock a graveyard. "A feeling of remorse," he said, "sometimes comes over me! But I'm an altered man now. I hain't killed a man for over two weeks! What'll yer poison yourself with?" he added, dealing a resonant blow on the bar.

There used to live near Carson City a notorious desperado, who never visited town without killing somebody. He would call for liquor at some drinking-house, and if anybody declined joining him he would at once commence shooting. But one day he shot a man too many. Going into St. Nicholas drinking-house, he asked the company present to join him in a North American drink. One individual was rash enough to refuse. With a look of sorrow rather than of anger, the desperado revealed his revolver, and said, "Good God! *Must* I kill a man every time I come to Carson?" and so saying he fired and killed the individual on the spot. But this was the last murder the bloodthirsty miscreant ever committed, for the aroused citizens pursued him with rifles and shot him down in his own door-yard.

III. KILLERS

He gained this recognition not because he was bad but rather because he was a man of swift and decisive action.
—CAPT. JOHN R. HUGHES

1. WILD BILL HICKOK

THE line of Western heroes is an unbroken one. As a boy in La Salle County, Illinois, James Butler Hickok, born the year after Crockett died, like him killed wolves for bounty, and idolized Kit Carson, who later

From *Artemus Ward: His Travels* (Part II: *Among the Mormons*), by Charles F. Browne, pp. 148–149. New York: Carleton, Publisher. 1866.

[1] "Dead man for breakfast"—a common phrase in California by which to designate a murdered man.—C. F. B.

praised him for his fearlessness. And when he was twenty, according to tradition, Wild Bill came to the aid of an eleven-year-old boy, named Will Cody, who was being rough-handled by his companions in Lew Simpson's wagon train. Wild Bill's prowess in knock-down and drag-out fighting and in marksmanship recall the feats of Mike Fink. On his first job as a towpath driver on the Illinois and Michigan Canal, he emerged as the victor of a fist fight that lasted over an hour, beginning on the towpath and ending in the water with his adversary nearly drowned. "I allers shoot well," he told George Ward Nichols, "but I come ter be perfeck in the mountains by shootin at a dime for a mark, at bets of half a dollar a shot." As a killer Wild Bill has been the subject of much controversy. Was he a gun fighter, who fought fair, or a gunman, who didn't? As a legend, he eclipses Bat Masterson, Wyatt Earp, and other marshalls who were also "bad men."

The killer arose out of the turbulent conditions of the frontier, where "the six-shooter was the law of the land," and a man shot to kill if self-preservation demanded that he kill or be killed. Since a split second, in which one got the drop on one's adversary, might mean the difference between these two alternatives, the mastery went to the man who combined agility of movement and steadiness of nerve, such as were required for drawing quickly and shooting straight, with coolness of head. " 'Whenever you get into a row,' said Wild Bill, 'be sure and not shoot too quick. Take time. I've known many a feller slip up for shootin' in a hurry.' "

The law of the six-shooter was based on an utter disregard for human life, which elevated murder to a cold-blooded science. " 'As ter killing men,' said Wild Bill, 'I never thought much about it. The most of the men I have killed it was one or t'other of us, and at sich times, you don't stop to think; and what's the use after it's all over?' " And as to how he got into fights: " 'D—d if I can tell . . . but you know a man must defend his honor.' " Again: " 'That I have killed men, I admit, but never unless in absolute self-defence, or in the performance of an official duty. I never, in my life, took any mean advantage of an enemy. Yet, understand,' he added, 'I never allow a man to get the drop on me.' " [1]

Thus, when confronted by a desperado with a gun in each hand, Bill stepped back, with upraised hand: " 'Don't shoot him—he's only in fun!' he called out. Mulvey turned, expecting to confront a deputy approaching from behind. In the instant that his attention was distracted Bill snatched out a revolver and dropped him with a bullet in the brain." [2]

Although no seasoned trouper like Buffalo Bill, with whom he appeared briefly in Ned Buntline's melodrama, *The Scouts of the Prairie*, in 1873, Wild Bill displayed considerable showmanship in living up to his early-acquired reputation as a "bad man to fool with." George Ward Nichols' account of his fabulous exploits was probably no more extravagant than Wild Bill's conception of himself. For throughout his varied career as stage-coach driver, Civil War sharpshooter and spy, Indian fighter, scout, guide, and peace officer, Wild Bill helped create his own legend by combining a certain amount of pose with a sense of his own mission. Thus do

[1] *Wild Bill Hickok*, The Prince of Pistoleers, by Frank J. Wilstach, p. 242.
[2] *Ibid.*, p. 162.

heroes both during and after their lifetime make it easier for the folklorist and harder for the historian.

Wild Bill's reputation as a bad man to fool with rested on his reputation as a gunfighter and this in turn on his use of all those tricks of gunplay which old-timers attribute to the pseudo bad man and the fancy shooter, such as carrying two guns, shooting from the hip, and "fanning" (firing a revolver by brushing back the hammer with the palm of the left hand). Whether this show of daredeviltry and flashiness were due to courage or the lack of it, Wild Bill made the most of it, while at the same time taking no chances. The result was such myths as the "McCanles massacre" and such stunts as simultaneously killing two assailants who had entered by opposite doors of a restaurant. He could do this not because he "had eyes in the back of his head, or some sixth sense," but because he "drew his pistols, both of them, with a movement almost quicker than the eye could perceive, and with one he killed the man in front of him, and at the same time with the other gun hand resting on the opposite shoulder he killed the man behind him, looking through the mirror" over the front door.[1]

His good looks and gallantry, plus his taste for fancy clothes, also gained for him the reputation of a lady-killer. Mrs. Cody was entranced at the actuality, as she had been terrified at the prospect, of meeting him.

I could have danced the Highland Fling, I believe, so happy was I to find mildness where I had been led to believe would be the most murderous of persons. Instinctively I looked for revolvers. There were none, not even the slightest bulge at the hips of the Prince Albert he wore. I was happier than ever. We danced. And I must confess that we danced and danced again until Will laughingly put a stop to it.[2]

There was no end of miracles. Many of his hair-raising exploits during the war involved his well-trained horse, Black Nell (reminiscent of the marvelous steeds of earlier heroes), whose "trick of dropping quick" saved his life time and again. With the warriors and tribal chieftains of other heroic ages this "prince of pistoleers" was linked not only by his saga of daring challenges, thrilling combats, and miraculous escapes but also by his tragic doom. In fact, the fairies presided at his death as well as at his birth. Even his remains, as evidenced at the time of their exhumation for reburial underwent the miracle of natural embalming.

2. Billy the Kid

The superman among killers was Billy the Kid, whose golden legend has grown out of all proportion to the few sordid facts of his short, lightning-swift career. Born as William H. Bonney in New York City in 1859, he was brought to Kansas at the age of three; at twelve killed his first man in Silver City, New Mexico, for insulting his mother; after a series of wanderings and crimes in Arizona, Mexico, Texas and New Mexico, joined the Murphy-Dolan faction in the Lincoln County war; made a

---

[1] *The Bad Man of the West*, by George D. Hendricks (1941), p. 96.

[2] *Memories of Buffalo Bill*, by his wife Louisa Frederici Cody, in collaboration with Courtney Riley Cooper (1919), p. 91.

sensational escape from his captors at Lincoln; and while visiting his sweetheart at Fort Sumner was shot in the dark by Sheriff Pat Garrett. This bare outline has been filled in by old-timers, journalists, and dime-novelists with some of the most lurid and fantastic traditions and fictions that the popular imagination has ever concocted. Both the hero-worshippers and the debunkers have had a field day with the apocrypha of the "Southwest's most famous desperado" and "best-loved hero in the state's history"—the "darling of the common people." The list of twenty-one killings in twenty-one years which was the Kid's boast has been repeatedly revised downward, conservative estimates ranging from twelve to three And the reputedly handsome, generous daredevil stands unmasked by his only authentic photograph, according to one unsympathetic critic, as "a nondescript, adenoidal, weasel-eyed, narrow-chested, stoop-shouldered, repulsive-looking creature with all the outward appearance of a cretin." [1]

His dual personality has made him something of an enigma, which has fascinated his biographers. According to Pat Garrett:

> The Kid had a lurking devil in him. It was a good-humored, jovial imp, or a cruel and blood-thirsty fiend, as circumstances prompted. Circumstances favored the worser angel, and the Kid fell.

The two sides of his nature met in a curious "nerveless imperturbability," which Walter Noble Burns analyzes as "a sub-zero vacuum—devoid of all human emotions."

> "A little while before we made a dash for our lives, the Kid rolled a cigarette. I watched him. It seemed just then as if he had about a minute and a half to live. But when he poured the tobacco from his pouch into the cigarette paper he did not spill a flake. His hand was as steady as steel. A blazing chunk of roof fell on the table beside him, barely missing his head. "Much obliged," he said; and he bent over and lighted his cigarette from the flame. Then he looked at me and grinned as if he thought that was a good joke. He didn't roll that cigarette because he was nervous but because he wanted a good smoke. You could tell by the way he inhaled the smoke and let it roll out of his mouth that he was getting real pleasure out of it. If you had seen Billy the Kid roll that cigarette and smoke it, señor, you would have known at once that he was a brave man." [2]

Like many another Western gun fighter—Wild Bill, Jesse James—Billy the Kid was killed without a chance to fight for his life. An extra touch of tragic irony is added to the Kid's fate by the fact that his slayer was, up to the time of his appointment as sheriff, a good friend. As his biographer Pat Garrett was a good friend after the Kid's death, too. And by his death the Kid did Garrett a good turn. Partly because of the fame of his victim and partly because of the special kind of courage that it took to carry out his assignment, Pat Garrett became a hero in his own right, as not the greatest (Wild Bill's title) but the "last great sheriff of the old frontier."

---

[1] *Belle Starr*, by Burton Rascoe (1941), pp. 9–10.
[2] *The Saga of Billy the Kid*, by Walter Noble Burns (1925), p. 145.

By writing his *Authentic Life of Billy the Kid,* Pat Garrett also tried to kill the monstrous lies that sprang up after Billy the Kid's death. But as late as 1926 the rumor persisted that the Kid was still alive, as reported in an El Paso paper for June 24:

Leland V. Gardiner . . . believes Billy the Kid, notorious outlaw of pioneer days, still lives, and has thought so for the past ten years, he said. He is not the El Pasoan, however, who communicated his belief to the New Mexico Historical Society. That informant said he had seen the Kid about ten years ago (in an eastern city).

"I am not certain, but believe I have seen the Kid," said Mr. Gardiner. "I am told that he is on an isolated ranch within 500 miles of El Paso. When strangers come to the ranch he disappears until they are gone. . . . He can't take chances on being detected." [1]

3. Jesse James and Others

Similar rumors have dogged the memory of Jesse James, and no less than seventeen persons, according to his granddaughter, have claimed to be the "original Jesse James." As Billy the Kid was the child of the cattle rustling wars, so Jesse James was the product of the bloody border warfare of Western Missouri and Eastern Kansas, beginning with the conflict over the Free Soil issue, passing into Civil War bushwhacking, and culminating in postbellum outlawry. As a boy on a Missouri farm, Jesse played at shooting or hanging Jim Lane or John Brown. In his youth, it will be recalled, Wild Bill Hickok was a member of Jim Lane's Red Legs and had his cabin burned down in retaliation by Missouri border ruffians; and Buffalo Bill's father, Isaac Cody, was likewise involved in the free-state cause. In 1863 what had been a game became for Jesse a life-and-death affair. While ploughing in a cornfield, he was seized and lashed with a rope by a squad of Federal militia, who nearly hanged his stepfather and subsequently arrested and jailed his mother and sister. Joining the guerrillas under "Bloody Bill" Anderson, he was outlawed at the close of the war. Whether or not they were "driven" to crime by "persecution," he and his brother Frank and their cousins, the four Younger boys, all ex-guerrillas, turned to robbing banks and trains for a livelihood.

This background in sectional conflict and civil strife perhaps helped to make Jesse James stand out in the popular imagination as a symbol of revolt and protest against the forces of tyranny and injustice. For most Americans he represents the Robin Hood tradition of the "good bad man," certain aspects of which are seen in Billy the Kid. In his bland, quixotic humor and impish wiliness, however, the Kid, like Wild Bill Hickok, has more in common with the tradition of the "cheerful rogue," which has given us "bad boys" and "bad good men" from Robin Hood and Tyl Eulenspiegel to Huckleberry Finn. Jesse James, on the other hand,

> robbed from the rich and he gave to the poor,
> He'd a hand and a heart and a brain.

---

[1] *A Vaquero of the Brush Country,* by J. Frank Dobie (1929), p. 174 n.

And he all but achieved martyrdom through death by treachery. These lines, reminiscent of the refrain of the ballad, were inscribed on his monument at his mother's request:

> Murdered by a Traitor and Coward Whose
> Name Is Not Worthy to Appear Here

The classic instance of Jesse James' chivalry is the episode in which he paid off the mortgage for a poor widow and then stole the money back from the mortgage owner. The same story is told of Sam Bass, the "Texas Robin Hood," who was also a victim of the treachery of one of his own men—the best example of the good boy gone wrong.

The last Robin Hood of the Southwest was Charley ("Pretty Boy") Floyd, of Sallisaw, Oklahoma, described as a "nice, soft-spoken boy, good to his mother," with a special grudge against bankers and sheriffs.

It was his custom . . . to inform the sheriffs ahead of time when he was about to rob a bank, and it was so well known that he would rather pot a sheriff any day than rob a bank that nowadays the sheriffs invariably locked themselves in and barred the doors or left town as the date approached. The list of sheriffs and deputies whom "Pretty Boy" had shot in the head—he never shot except at the head and there was only one record of his missing—was desperately long.[1]

Wild Bill

I. My First Meeting with Wild Bill

SEVERAL months after the ending of the civil war I visited the city of Springfield in Southwest Missouri. Springfield is not a burgh of extensive dimensions, yet it is the largest in that part of the State, and all roads lead to it—which is one reason why it was the *point d'appui,* as well as the base of operations for all military movements during the war.

On a warm summer day I sat watching from the shadow of a broad awning the coming and going of the strange, half-civilized people who, from all the country round, make this a place for barter and trade. Men and women dressed in queer costumes; men with coats and trowsers made of skin, but so thickly covered with dirt and grease as to have defied the identity of the animal when walking in the flesh. Others wore homespun gear, which oftentimes appeared to have seen lengthy service. Many of those people were mounted on horse-back or mule-back, while others urged forward the unwilling cattle attached to creaking, heavily-laden

---

[1] *Sweet Land,* by Lewis Gannett (1934), pp. 39–40.

From "Wild Bill" [by George Ward Nichols], *Harper's New Monthly Magazine,* Vol. XXXIV (February, 1867), No. CCI, pp. 273–285.

wagons, their drivers snapping their long whips with a report like that of a pistol-shot.

In front of the shops which lined both sides of the main business street, and about the public square, were groups of men lolling against posts, lying upon the wooden sidewalks, or sitting in chairs. These men were temporary or permanent denizens of the city, and were lazily occupied in doing nothing. The most marked characteristic of the inhabitants seemed to be an indisposition to move, and their highest ambition to let their hair and beards grow.

Here and there upon the street the appearance of the army blue betokened the presence of a returned Union soldier, and the jaunty, confident air with which they carried themselves was all the more striking in its contrast with the indolence which appeared to belong to the place. The only indication of action was the inevitable revolver which every body, excepting, perhaps, the women, wore about their persons. When people moved in this lazy city they did so slowly and without method. No one seemed in haste. A huge hog wallowed in luxurious ease in a nice bed of mud on the other side of the way, giving vent to gentle grunts of satisfaction. On the platform at my feet lay a large wolf-dog literally asleep with one eye open. He, too, seemed contented to let the world wag idly on.

The loose, lazy spirit of the occasion finally took possession of me, and I sat and gazed and smoked, and it is possible that I might have fallen into a Rip Van Winkle sleep to have been aroused ten years hence by the cry, "Passengers for the flying machine to New York, all aboard!" when I and the drowsing city were roused into life by the clatter and crash of the hoofs of a horse which dashed furiously across the square and down the street. The rider sat perfectly erect, yet following with a grace of motion, seen only in the horsemen of the plains, the rise and fall of the galloping steed. There was only a moment to observe this, for they halted suddenly, while the rider springing to the ground approached the party which the noise had gathered near me.

"This yere is Wild Bill, Colonel," said Captain Honesty, an army officer, addressing me. He continued:

"How are yer, Bill? This yere is Colonel N——. who wants ter know yer."

Let me at once describe the personal appearance of the famous Scout of the Plains, William Hitchcock, called "Wild Bill," who now advanced toward me, fixing his clear gray eyes on mine in a quick, interrogative way, as if to take "my measure."

The result seemed favorable, for he held forth a small, muscular hand in a frank, open manner. As I looked at him I thought his the handsomest *physique* I had ever seen. In its exquisite manly proportions it recalled the antique. It was a figure Ward would delight to model as a companion to his "Indian."

Bill stood six feet and an inch in his bright yellow moccasins. A deerskin shirt, or frock it might be called, hung jauntily over his shoulders, and revealed a chest whose breadth and depth were remarkable. These lungs had had growth in some twenty years of the free air of the Rocky Mountains. His small, round waist was girthed by a belt which held two of Colt's navy revolvers. His legs sloped gradually from the compact thigh to the feet, which were small, and turned inward as he walked. There was a singular grace and dignity of carriage about that figure which would have called your attention meet it where you would. The head which crowned it was now covered by a large sombrero, underneath which there shone out a quiet, manly face; so gentle is its expression as he greets you as utterly to belie the history of its owner, yet it is not a face to be trifled with. The lips thin and sensitive, the jaw not too square, the cheek bones slightly prominent, a mass of fine dark hair falls below the neck to the shoulders. The eyes, now that you are in friendly intercourse, are as gentle as a woman's. In truth, the woman nature seems prominent throughout, and you would not believe that you were looking into eyes that have pointed the way to death to hundreds of men. Yes, Wild Bill with his own hands has killed hundreds of men. Of that I have not a doubt. "He shoots to kill," as they say on the border.

In vain did I examine the scout's face for some evidence of murderous propensity. It was a gentle face, and singular only in the sharp angle of the eye, and without any physiognomical reason for the opinion, I have thought his wonderful accuracy of aim was indicated by this peculiarity. He told me, however, to use his own words:

"I allers shoot well; but I come ter be perfeck in the mountains by shootin at a dime for a mark, at bets of half a dollar a shot. And then until the war I never drank liquor nor smoked," he continued, with a melancholy expression; "war is demoralizing, it is."

Captain Honesty was right. I was very curious to see "Wild Bill, the Scout," who, a few days before my arrival in Springfield in a duel at noon-day in the public square, at fifty paces, had sent one of Colt's pistol-balls through the heart of a returned Confederate soldier.

Whenever I had met an officer or soldier who had served in the Southwest I heard of Wild Bill and his exploits, until these stories became so frequent and of such an extraordinary character as quite to outstrip personal knowledge of adventure by camp and field; and the hero of those strange tales took shape in my mind as did Jack the Giant Killer or Sinbad the Sailor in childhood days. As then, I now had the most implicit faith in the existence of the individual; but how one man could accomplish such prodigies of strength and feats of daring was a continued wonder.

II. THE DUEL WITH DAVE TUTT

Bill was born of Northern parents in the State of Illinois. He ran away from home when a boy, and wandered out upon the plains and into the mountains. For fifteen years he lived with the trappers, hunting and fishing. When the war broke out he returned to the States and entered the Union service. No man probably was ever better fitted for scouting than he. Joined to his tremendous strength he was an unequalled horseman; he was a perfect marksman; he had a keen sight, and a constitution which had no limit of endurance. He was cool to audacity, brave to rashness, always possessed of himself under the most critical circumstances; and, above all, was such a master in the knowledge of woodcraft that it might have been termed a science with him—a knowledge which, with the soldier, is priceless beyond description. Some of Bill's adventures during the war will be related hereafter.

The main features of the story of the duel was [sic] told me by Captain Honesty, who was unprejudiced, if it is possible to find an unbiased mind in a town of 3000 people after a fight has taken place. I will give the story in his words:

"They say Bill's wild. Now he isn't any sich thing. I've known him goin on ter ten year, and he's as civil a disposed person as you'il find he-e-arabouts. But he won't be put upon.

"I'll tell yer how it happened. But come inter the office; thar's a good many round hy'ar as sides with Tutt—the man that's shot. But I tell yer 'twas a far fight. Take some whisky? No! Well, I will, if yer'l excuse me.

"You see," continued the Captain, setting the empty glass on the table in an emphatic way, "Bill was up in his room a-playin seven-up, or four-hand, or some of them pesky games. Bill refused ter play with Tutt, who was a professional gambler. Yer see, Bill was a scout on our side durin the war, and Tutt was a reb scout. Bill had killed Dave Tutt's mate, and, atween one thing and another, there war an onusual hard feelin atwixt 'em.

"Ever sin Dave come back he had tried to pick a row with Bill; so Bill wouldn't play cards with him any more. But Dave stood over the man who was gambling with Bill and lent the feller money. Bill won about two hundred dollars, which made Tutt spiteful mad. Bime-by, he says to Bill:

" 'Bill, you've got plenty of money—pay me that forty dollars yer owe me in that horse trade.'

"And Bill paid him. Then he said:

" 'Yer owe me thirty-five dollars more; yer lost it playing with me t'other night.'

"Dave's style was right provoking; but Bill answered him perfectly gentlemanly:

" 'I think yer wrong, Dave. It's only twenty-five dollars. I have a memorandum of it in my pocket down stairs. Ef it's thirty-five dollars I'll give it yer.'

"Now Bill's watch was lying on the table. Dave took up the watch, put it in his pocket, and said: 'I'll keep this yere watch till yer pay me that thirty-five dollars.'

"This made Bill shooting mad; fur, don't yer see, Colonel, it was a-doubting his honor like, so he got up and looked Dave in the eyes, and said to him: 'I don't want ter make a row in this house. It's a decent house, and I don't want ter injure the keeper. You'd better put that watch back on the table.'

"But Dave grinned at Bill mighty ugly, and walked off with the watch, and kept it several days. All this time Dave's friends were spurring Bill on ter fight; there was no end ter the talk. They blackguarded him in an underhand sort of a way, and tried ter get up a scrimmage, and then they thought they could lay him out. Yer see Bill has enemies all about. He's settled the accounts of a heap of men who lived round here. This is about the only place in Missouri whar a reb can come back and live, and ter tell yer the truth, Colonel—" and the Captain, with an involuntary movement, hitched up his revolver-belt, as he said, with expressive significance, "they don't stay long round here!

"Well, as I was saying, these rebs don't like ter see a man walking round town who they knew in the reb army as one of their men, who they now know was on our side, all the time he was sending us information, sometimes from Pap Price's own head-quarters. But they couldn't provoke Bill inter a row, for he's afeard of hisself when he gits *awful* mad; and he allers left his shootin irons in his room when he went out. One day these cusses drew their pistols on aim and dared him to fight, and then they told him that Tutt was a-goin ter pack that watch across the squar next day at noon.

"I heard of this, for every body was talking about it on the street, and so I went after Bill, and found him in his room, cleaning and greasing and loading his revolvers.

" 'Now, Bill,' says I, 'you're goin ter git inter a fight.'

" 'Don't you bother yerself, Captain,' says he. 'It's not the first time I have been in a fight; and these d—d hounds have put on me long enough. You don't want me ter give up my honor, do yer?'

" 'No, Bill,' says I, 'yer must keep yer honor.'

"Next day, about noon, Bill went down to the squar. He had said that Dave Tutt shouldn't pack that watch across the squar unless dead men could walk.

"When Bill got onter the squar he found a crowd standin in the corner of the street by which he entered the squar, which is from the south, yer know. In this crowd he saw a lot of Tutt's friends; some were cousins of his'n, just back from the reb army; and they jeered him, and boasted that Dave was a-goin to pack that watch across the squar as he promised.

"Then Bill saw Tutt standin near the courthouse, which yer remember is on the west side, so that the crowd war behind Bill.

"Just then Tutt, who war alone, started from the courthouse and walked out into the squar, and Bill moved away from the crowd toward the west side of the squar. Bout fifteen paces brought them opposite to each other, and about fifty yards apart. Tutt then showed his pistol. Bill had kept a sharp eye on him, and before Tutt could pint it Bill had his'n out.

"At that moment you could have heard a pin drop in that squar. Both Tutt and Bill fired, but one discharge followed the other so quick that it's hard to say which went off first. Tutt was a famous shot, but he missed this time; the ball from his pistol went over Bill's head. The instant Bill fired, without waitin ter see ef he had hit Tutt, he wheeled on his heels and pointed his pistol at Tutt's friends, who had already drawn their weepons.

" 'Aren't yer satisfied, gentlemen?' cried Bill, as cool as an alligator. 'Put up your shootin-irons, or there'll be more dead men here.' And they put 'em up, and said it war a far fight.''

"What became of Tutt?" I asked of the Captain, who had stopped at this point of his story, and was very deliberately engaged in refilling his empty glass.

"Oh! Dave? He was as plucky a feller as ever drew trigger; but, Lord bless yer! it was no use. Bill never shoots twice at the same man, and his ball went through Dave's heart. He stood stock-still for a second or two, then raised his arm as if ter fire again, then he swayed a little, staggered three or four steps and then fell dead.

"Bill and his friends wanted ter have the thing done regular, so we went up ter the Justice, and Bill delivered himself up. A jury was drawn; Bill was tried and cleared the next day. It was proved that it was a case of self-defense. Don't yer see, Colonel?"

I answered that I was afraid that I did not see that point very clearly.

"Well, well!" he replied, with an air of compassion, "you haven't drunk any whisky, that's what's the matter with yer." And then, putting his hand on my shoulder with a half-mysterious, half-conscious look in his face, he muttered, in a whisper:

"The fact is, thar was an undercurrent of a woman in that fight!"

[The following conversation took place that afternoon at the hotel. —B. A. B.]

I had a curiosity, which was not an idle one, to hear what this man had to say about his duel with Tutt, and I asked him:

"Do you not regret killing Tutt? You surely do not like to kill men?"

"As ter killing men," he replied, "I never thought much about it. The most of the men I have killed it was one or t'other of us, and at sich times you don't stop to think; and what's the use after it's all over? As for Tutt, I had rather not have killed him, for I want ter settle down quiet here now. But thar's been hard feeling between us a long while. I wanted ter keep out of that fight; but he tried to degrade me, and I couldn't stand that, you know, for I am a fighting man, you know."

A cloud passed over the speaker's face for a moment as he continued:

"And there was a cause of quarrel between us which people round here don't know about. One of us had to die; and the secret died with him."

"Why did you not wait to see if your ball had hit him? Why did you turn round so quickly?"

The scout fixed his gray eyes on mine, striking his leg with his riding-whip, as he answered.

"I *knew* he was a dead man. I never miss a shot. I turned on the crowd because I was sure they would shoot me if they saw him fall."

"The people about here tell me you are a quiet, civil man. How is it you get into these fights?"

"D—d if I can tell," he replied, with a puzzled look which at once gave place to a proud, defiant expression as he continued—"but you know a man must defend his honor."

"Yes," I admitted, with some hesitation, remembering that I was not in Boston but on the border, and that the code of honor and mode of redress differ slightly in the one place from those of the other.

III. BLACK NELL

. . . A cry and murmur drew my attention to the outside of the house, when I saw Wild Bill riding up the street at a swift gallop. Arrived opposite to the hotel, he swung his right arm around with a circular motion. Black Nell instantly stopped and dropped to the ground as if a cannonball had knocked life out of her. Bill left her there, stretched upon the ground, and joined the group of observers on the porch.

"Black Nell hasn't forgot her old tricks," said one of them.

"No," answered the scout. "God bless her! she is wiser and truer than most men I know on. That mare will do any thing for me. Won't you, Nelly?"

The mare winked affirmatively the only eye we could see.

"Wise!" continued her master; "why, she knows more than a judge. I'll bet the drinks for the party that she'll walk up these steps and into the room and climb up on the billiard-table and lie down."

The bet was taken at once, not because any one doubted the capabilities of the mare, but there was excitement in the thing without exercise.

Bill whistled in a low tone. Nell instantly scrambled to her feet, walked toward him, put her nose affectionately under his arm, followed him into the room and to my extreme wonderment climbed upon the billiard-table, to the extreme astonishment of the table no doubt, for it groaned under the weight of the four-legged animal and several of those who were simply bifurcated, and whom Nell permitted to sit upon her. When she got down from the table, which was as graceful a performance as might be expected under the circumstances, Bill sprang upon her back, dashed through the high wide doorway, and at a single bound cleared the flight of steps and landed in the middle of the street. The scout then dismounted, snapped his riding-whip, and the noble beast bounded off down the street, rearing and plunging to her own intense satisfaction. A kindly-disposed individual, who must have been a stranger, supposing the mare was running away, tried to catch her, when she stopped, and as if she resented his impertinence, let fly her heels at him and then quietly trotted to her stable.

"Black Nell has carried me along through many a tight place," said the scout, as we walked toward my quarters. "She trains easier than any animal I ever saw. That trick of dropping quick which you saw has saved my life time and again. When I have been out scouting on the prarer or in the woods I have come across parties of rebels, and have dropped out of sight in the tall grass before they saw us. One day a gang of rebs who had been hunting for me, and thought they had my track, halted for half an hour within fifty yards of us. Nell laid as close as a rabbit, and didn't even whisk her tail to keep the flies off, until the rebs moved off, supposing they were on the wrong scent. The mare will come at my whistle and foller me about just like a dog. She won't mind any one else, nor allow them to mount her, and will kick a harness and wagon all ter pieces ef you try to hitch her in one. And she's right, Kernel," added Bill, with the enthusiasm of a true lover of a horse sparkling in his eyes. "A hoss is too noble a beast to be degraded by such toggery. Harness mules and oxen, but give a hoss a chance ter run."

IV. The McCanles Massacre

The scout's story of swimming the river ought, perhaps, to have satisfied my curiosity; but I was especially desirous to hear him relate the history of a sanguinary fight which he had with a party of ruffians in the early part of the war, when, singlehanded, he fought and killed ten men. I had heard the story as it came from an officer of the regular army who, an hour after the affair, saw Bill and the ten dead men—some killed with bullets, others hacked and slashed to death with a knife.

As I write out the details of this terrible tale from notes which I took as the words fell from the scout's lips, I am conscious of its extreme improbability; but while I listened to him I remembered the story in the Bible, where we are told that Samson "with the jawbone of an ass slew a thousand men," and as I looked upon this magnificent example of human strength and daring, he appeared to me to realize the powers of a Samson and Hercules combined, and I should not have been inclined to place any limit upon his achievements. Besides this, one who has lived for four years in the presence of such grand heroism and deeds of prowess as was seen during the war is in what might be called a "receptive" mood. Be the story true or not, in part, or in whole, I believed then every word Wild Bill uttered, and I believe it to-day.

"I don't like to talk about that M'Kandlas affair," said Bill, in answer to my question. "It gives me a queer shiver whenever I think of it, and sometimes I dream about it, and wake up in a cold sweat.

"You see this M'Kandlas was the Captain of a gang of desperadoes, horse-thieves, murderers, regular cut-throats, who were the terror of everybody on the border, and who kept us in the mountains in hot water whenever they were around. I knew them all in the mountains, where they pretended to be trapping, but they were there hiding from the hangman. M'Kandlas was the biggest scoundrel and bully of them all, and was allers a-braggin of what he could do. One day I beat him shootin at a mark, and then threw him at the back-holt. And I didn't drop him as soft as you would a baby, you may be sure. Well, he got savage mad about it, and swore he would have his revenge on me some time.

"This was just before the war broke out, and we were already takin sides in the mountains either for the South or the Union. M'Kandlas and his gang were border-ruffians in the Kansas row, and of course they went with the rebs. Bime-by he clar'd out, and I shouldn't have thought of the feller agin ef he hadn't crossed my path. It 'pears he didn't forget me.

"It was in '61, when I guided a detachment of cavalry who were comin in from Camp Floyd. We had nearly reached the Kansas line and were in South Nebraska, when one afternoon I went out of camp to go to the cabin of an old friend of mine, a Mrs. Waltman. I took only one of my revolvers with me, for although the war had broke out I didn't think it necessary to carry both my pistols, and, in all or'nary scrimmages, one is better than a dozen, ef you shoot straight. I saw some wild turkeys on the road as I was goin down, and popped one of 'em over, thinking he'd be just the thing for supper.

"Well, I rode up to Mrs. Waltman's, jumped off my horse, and went into the cabin, which is like most of the cabins on the prarer, with only one room, and that had two doors, one opening in front and t'other on a yard, like.

" 'How are you, Mrs. Waltman?' I said, feeling as jolly as you please.

"The minute she saw me she turned as white as a sheet and screamed: 'Is that you, Bill? Oh, my God! they will kill you! Run! run! They will kill you!'

" 'Who's a-goin to kill me?' said I. 'There's two can play at that game.'

" 'It's M'Kandlas and his gang. There's ten of them, and you've no chance. They've jes gone down the road to the corn-rack. They came up here only five minutes ago. M'Kandlas was draggin poor Parson Shipley on the ground with a lariat round his neck. The preacher was most dead with choking and the horses stamping on him. M'Kandlas knows yer bringin in that party of Yankee cavalry, and he swears he'll cut yer heart out. Run, Bill, run!—But it's too late; they're comin up the lane.'

"While she was a-talkin I remembered I had but one revolver, and a load gone out of that. On the table there was a horn of powder and some little bars of lead. I poured some powder into the empty chamber and rammed the lead after it by hammering the barrel on the table, and had just capped the pistol when I heard M'Kandlas shout:

" 'There's that d—d Yank Wild Bill's horse; he's here; and we'll skin him alive!'

"If I had thought of runnin before it war too late now, and the house was my best holt—a sort of fortress, like. I never thought I should leave that room alive."

The scout stopped in his story, rose from his seat, and strode back and forward in a state of great excitement.

"I tell you what it is, Kernel," he resumed, after a while, "I don't mind a scrimmage with these fellers round here. Shoot one or two of them and the rest run away. But all of M'Kandlas's gang were reckless, blood-thirsty devils, who would fight as long as they had strength to pull a trigger. I have been in tight places, but that's one of the few times I said my prayers.

" 'Surround the house and give him no quarter!' yelled M'Kandlas. When I heard that I felt as quiet and cool as if I was a-goin to church. I looked round the room and saw a Hawkins rifle hangin over the bed.

" Is that loaded?' said I to Mrs. Waltman.

" 'Yes,' the poor thing whispered. She was so frightened she couldn't speak out loud.

" 'Are you sure?' said I, as I jumped to the bed and caught it from its hooks. Although my eye did not leave the door, yet I could see she nodded 'Yes' again. I put the revolver on the bed, and just then M'Kandlas poked his head inside the doorway, but jumped back when he saw me with the rifle in my hand.

" 'Come in here, you cowardly dog!' I shouted. 'Come in here, and fight me!'

"M'Kandlas was no coward, if he was a bully. He jumped inside the room with his gun leveled to shoot; but he was not quick enough. My rifle-ball went through his heart. He fell back outside the house, where he was found afterward holding tight to his rifle, which had fallen over his head.

"His disappearance was followed by a yell from his gang, and then there was a dead silence. I put down the rifle and took the revolver, and I said to myself: 'Only six shots and nine men to kill. Save your powder, Bill, for the death-hug's a-comin!' I don't know why it was, Kernel," continued Bill, looking at me inquiringly, "but at that moment things seemed clear and sharp. I could think strong.

"There was a few seconds of that awful stillness, and then the ruffians came rushing in at both doors. How wild they looked with their red, drunken faces and inflamed eyes, shouting and cussing! But I never aimed more deliberately in my life.

"One—two—three—four; and four men fell dead.

"That didn't stop the rest. Two of them fired their bird-guns at me. And then I felt a sting run all over me. The room was full of smoke. Two got in close to me, their eyes glaring out of the clouds. One I knocked down with my fist. 'You are out of the way for a while,' I thought. The second I shot dead. The other three clutched me and crowded me onto the bed. I fought hard. I broke with my hand one man's arm. He had his fingers round my throat. Before I could get to my feet I was struck across the breast with the stock of a rifle, and I felt the blood rushing out of my nose and mouth. Then I got ugly, and I remember that I got hold of a knife, and then it was all cloudy like, and I was wild, and I struck savage blows, following the devils up from one side to the other of the room and into the corners, striking and slashing until I knew that every one was dead.

"All of a sudden it seemed as if my heart was on fire. I was bleeding every where. I rushed out to the well and drank from the bucket, and then tumbled down in a faint."

Breathless with the intense interest with which I had followed this strange story, all the more thrilling and weird when its hero, seeming to live over again the bloody events of that day, gave way to its terrible spirit with wild, savage gestures, I saw then—that my scrutiny of the morning had failed to discover—the tiger which lay concealed beneath that gentle exterior.

"You must have been hurt almost to death," I said.

"There were eleven buck-shot in me. I carry some of them now. I was cut in thirteen places. All of them bad enough to have let out the life of a man. But that blessed old Dr. Mills pulled me safe through it, after a bed siege of many a long week."

"That prayer of yours, Bill, may have been more potent for your safety than you think. You should thank God for your deliverance."

"To tell you the truth, Kernel," responded the scout with a certain solemnity in his grave face, "I don't talk about sich things ter the people round here, but I allers feel sort of thankful when I get out of a bad scrape."

"In all your wild, perilous adventures," I asked him, "have you ever been afraid? Do you know what the sensation is? I am sure you will not misunderstand the question, for I take it we soldiers comprehend justly that there is no higher courage than that which shows itself when the consciousness of danger is keen but where moral strength overcomes the weakness of the body."

"I think I know what you mean, Sir, and I'm not ashamed to say that I have been so frightened that it 'peared as if all the strength and blood had gone out of my body, and my face was as white as chalk. It was at the Wilme Creek fight. I had fired more than fifty cartridges, and I think fetched my man every time. I was on the skirmish line, and was working up closer to the rebs, when all of a sudden a battery opened fire right in front of me, and it sounded as if forty thousand guns were firing, and every shot and shell screeched within six inches of my head. It was the first time I was ever under artillery fire, and I was so frightened that I couldn't move for a minute or so, and when I did go back the boys asked me if I had seen a ghost. They may shoot bullets at me by the dozen, and it's rather exciting if I can shoot back, but I am always sort of nervous when the big guns go off."

"I would like to see you shoot."

"Would yer?" replied the scout, drawing his revolver; and approaching the window, he pointed to a letter O in a signboard which was fixed to the stone-wall of a building on the other side of the way.

"That sign is more than fifty yards away. I will put these six balls into the inside of the circle, which isn't bigger than a man's heart."

In an off-hand way, and without sighting the pistol with his eye, he discharged the six shots of his revolver. I afterward saw that all the bullets had entered the circle.

As Bill proceeded to reload his pistol, he said to me with a naïvete of manner which was meant to be assuring:

"Whenever you get into a row be sure and not shoot too quick. Take time. I've known many a feller slip up for shootin' in a hurry."

It would be easy to fill a volume with the adventures of that remarkable man. My object here has been to make a slight record of one who is one of the best—perhaps the very best—example of a class who more than any other encountered perils and privations in defense of our nationality.

One afternoon as General Smith and I mounted our horses to start upon our journey toward the East, Wild Bill came to shake hands goodby, and I said to him:

"If you have no objection I will write out for publication an account of a few of your adventures."

"Certainly you may," he replied. "I'm sort of public property. But, Kernel," he continued, leaning upon my saddle-bow, while there was a tremulous softness in his voice and a strange moisture in his averted eyes, "I have a mother back there in Illinois who is old and feeble. I haven't seen her this many a year, and haven't been a good son to her, yet I love her better than any thing in this life. It don't matter much what they say about me here. But I'm not a cut-throat and vagabond, and I'd like the old woman to know what'll make her proud. I'd like her to hear that her runaway boy has fought through the war for the Union like a true man."

(William Hitchcock—called *Wild Bill, the Scout of the Plains*—shall have his wish. I have told his story precisely as it was told to me, confirmed in all important points by many witnesses; and I have no doubt of its truth.—G.W.N.)

V. THE TRUTH ABOUT THE McCANLÉS AFFAIR

. . . That David C. McCanles's ardent Southern sympathies led him to appropriate horses for the Confederate cavalry seems irrefutable. It appears that he went to the Rock Creek Station of the Overland Mail and Pony Express Company to get either Wild Bill's horse or the company's stock, that he had previously threatened Wild Bill with personal violence for his attentions to Sarah Shull, and that his choleric temper made him a man apt to execute such threats. We come now to the events of July 12, 1861.

During the first days of July, Wellman left the Station. Tradition has it that he went to Nebraska City in the attempt to secure funds to pay

From *Wild Bill Hickok, The Prince of Pistoleers*, by Frank J. Wilstach, pp. [V], 71–75; [VI], 8–11, 269–270; [VII], 266–269, 270–275, 280–293. Copyright, 1926, by Doubleday, Page & Company. Garden City, New York.

McCanles for the property, but this is refuted by the testimony of the only living eye-witness of the shooting: Monroe McCanles, then a boy of twelve. He has kept his peace about the tragedy for more than sixty years, and the writer had difficulty in inducing him to discuss the affair, but at last he recounted the history of that fatal day as follows:

Wellman went, not to Nebraska City, but to Brownsville, and solely to get some supplies. Monroe McCanles accompanied him on his journey. They returned on the afternoon of July 12th, and soon after their arrival young McCanles met his father near the Station. With him were James Woods and James Gordon. These two walked toward the barn in which the horses were kept, while David McCanles and his son walked toward the house, in which were Wild Bill, Mr. and Mrs. Wellman, and Sarah Kelsey, a servant.

According to Monroe McCanles, while Wellman was away at Browns-ville Mrs. Wellman and his father had had a quarrel; but just what it was about no one ever knew. In his opinion this difficulty had more to do with the tragedy than anything else.

David C. McCanles, accompanied by his son Monroe, walked to the kitchen door and asked for Wellman. It is Monroe McCanles's recollection that Mrs. Wellman came to the door, and that his father asked if Wellman were in the house. Mrs. Wellman replied that he was, and McCanles asked that he come out. Mrs. Wellman then demanded to know what he wanted of her husband.

"I want to settle with him," McCanles replied to this.

Mrs. Wellman stated that her husband would not come out.

"Send him out or I'll come in and drag him out!" McCanles retorted.

Wild Bill now stepped to the door. McCanles looked him in the face and remarked, "Jim, we have been friends all the time, haven't we?"

"Yes," answered Wild Bill.

"Are we friends now?" McCanles went on.

"Yes," answered Wild Bill.

"Will you hand me a drink?"

Wild Bill turned and a moment later appeared with a dipper of water. McCanles drank, and as he handed the dipper back he started, having apparently seen something that threatened danger. An instant later the report of Wild Bill's rifle sounded and McCanles fell dead. Woods and Gordon ran up, and were also shot to death.

This version of the tragedy, as given by Monroe McCanles, the only living eye-witness, provides no reasonable motive for the killing of Mc-Canles, or of Woods and Gordon. It is inexplicable that either Mr. or Mrs. Wellman or Wild Bill should, after McCanles was shot, suddenly develop a frenzied desire to kill Woods and Gordon, with whom they had no apparent quarrel.

Monroe McCanles states that a week later there was a preliminary hearing at which all were acquitted. Asked for a statement of what happened at the trial, he replied:

"Jim Hickok, Horace Wellman, and Dock Brink made their defence before Justice Albert Towle that McCanles and his gang had come to take the stage stock, and that the battle was over the horses. They had the preponderance of evidence. I was the only witness, but was not called to testify."

VI. "THE PRINCE OF PISTOLEERS"

. . . Wild Bill and Charles Utter—known as Colorado Charlie—were once freighting supplies out of Wichita. Utter, somewhat of a wag, had riled a teamster to such a pitch that the angry man hurled a big stone at him, which would have killed him had it hit its mark. But, the story goes, as the missile left the teamster's hand Wild Bill's gun flashed. The bullet struck the stone, and turned it from its course. It was a masterly shot and won the applause of all.

No wonder!

And yet Bill made shots only a little less phenomenal. The late Joseph Wheelock, the actor, once told the writer that when he was a young man he had seen Wild Bill stand between telegraph poles and fire simultaneously with a revolver in each hand, hitting both poles. Another of Bill's feats was to cut a chicken's throat with a bullet from a distance of thirty paces, without breaking its neck or touching the head or body. He was also wont to amuse his friends by driving the cork into a bottle without breaking the bottle-neck. He was able to hit a dime at fifty paces nine times out of ten. These feats are all the more remarkable when it is taken into account that he fired from the hip without taking deliberate aim.

The old residents of Hays City teem with stories of Bill's pistolry. One day he was walking along the street when he observed a ripe apple hanging on a tree. Pulling two revolvers from their holsters, he shot with his left hand and nipped the stem. As the apple fell his right-hand revolver pierced it with a bullet. On another occasion he was riding in from the fort with General Custer. Bill pointed out a knot on a telegraph pole, remarking that he wanted to see how many bullets he could put in it as he rode by at a gallop. He fired all six chambers of his revolver, and every bullet hit the knot. This telegraph pole was pointed out for many years by the residents of Hays City as an example of Bill's remarkable marksmanship.

During the last years of his life, according to Ellis T. Peirce, Bill used two Colt's-.45 calibre cap-and-ball revolvers without triggers. He was a pulse shot. When he grasped the butt of his revolver his thumb would rest on the hammer, and the instant he had drawn the weapon clear of the holster its own weight would cock it. Bill had only to lift his thumb— and there was another death to record. The hammers were ground smooth so they would slip easily under the thumb when pressure was removed.

* * * * *

A story is told that, meeting the stagecoach a few miles out of Dead, wood, Bill dismounted and took a seat alongside the driver. For the amusement of the passengers, as the coach rolled along, he took eight shots at squirrels. He neglected, however, to recharge his pistols, little thinking that road-agents were about. A band of these worthies, five in all, had learned that the incoming coach contained a considerable amount of currency in the strong box consigned to the Wells Fargo express agent. Suddenly Bill and the driver discovered five horsemen ahead of them, each rider heavily armed and wearing a mask. The men dismounted, and one of them grabbed the bridle of the leaders, crying out, "Up with your hands, all of you!"

Bill's hands went up—blazing. With four rapid shots he dropped four of the outlaws. Necessity caused him to cease firing. The one man still on his feet, levelling a sawed-off shot-gun at him, ordered him to get down off the coach. Bill recognized the voice; it was "Mickey" Rose, an ex-Cheyenne barkeeper.

"So it is you, is it, Mickey?" Bill replied, and, rising from his seat, he hurled one of his empty pistols at Mickey with such accuracy that the heavy weapon struck the head of the desperado, and smashed his skull.

"Well, I saved the Vigilantes a little job that time, all right," Bill remarked, surveying the bodies of his victims.

Is it necessary to add that for this incident, which outshines even the stories of the "McCanles massacre," the writer has been able to unearth no supporting evidence. If it had really happened both Young and Peirce would have referred to it—which they did not.

VII. The Death of Wild Bill

Gold had been discovered in the Black Hills by Horatio Ross, one of Custer's scouts, in July, 1874. This find was reported to the War Department by General Custer, but as the Black Hills was included in the Sioux land, for which negotiations were then in progress, the report of the discovery was suppressed until June, 1875.

But the news leaked out and within six months of the discovery gold seekers were cradling for nuggets and dust in the streams of Black Hills gulches. As the Black Hills was on Sioux land, the Indians naturally resented the invasion. This, together with the Government's efforts to transfer them to a reservation, was the chief cause of the Sioux rebellion that resulted in the annihilation of General Custer and his entire command on the Little Big Horn.

Deadwood was an outlaw town in 1874. As the land belonged to the Indians the Government could not recognize it as a settlement. It was not so recognized until June, 1877. But when Wild Bill arrived there it was a free-and-easy place, everybody carrying a bag of gold nuggets as well as a brace of pistols. Doc Peirce was there at the time and in a letter to the writer dated October 18, 1925, he gives a minute description of the town and its people.

"Deadwood," he wrote, "had only one narrow street, filled with stumps.

boulders, lumber, and logs, with hundreds of men surging from saloon to saloon—so you had to get acquainted with a majority of them, and have a speaking acquaintance. Whenever a gunman came to the gulch the word was passed along as quickly as it would be at a ladies' sewing society.

"There was Johnny Bull, who killed Farmer Peals in Salt Lake; Billy Allen, gambler; Tom Hardwick, who with his party of prospectors had killed Indians across the Canadian line, so that it took all the persuasive powers of James G. Blaine to keep the Canadian Government from hanging them. The Indians had stolen the boys' horses; that was what saved them. They killed sixty Indians and came back over the line with their stock, but this country had to surrender them. Joel Collins, the Texas cattleman, was a gunman; but he was killed just after the Big Spring robbery on the Union Pacific Railroad in the fall of '77.

"There was Laughing Sam, another gunman; and Jim Levy, the top-notcher of them all, except Wild Bill. Jim was killed down in New Mexico by Milligan, whose claim Jim had jumped. Tom Mulqueen got his afterward at Cheyenne. C. C. Clifton, one of Quantrel's old band in Missouri, was another bad hombre. He cashed in down in the Indian Territory; Boone May—in fact, all three May brothers—were quick on the draw. Deadwood was then hog-wild; duels and gunfights in the streets, and often one had to duck or fall flat on the ground to escape a shower of lead."

Wild Bill and Charlie Utter, otherwise Colorado Charlie, made their way to Deadwood, via Cheyenne, leaving the latter town on April 12th.

* * * * *

Harry Young, the barkeeper of Carl Mann's saloon, has furnished a picturesque description of Wild Bill's arrival at Deadwood. We have already seen that Young had been befriended by Wild Bill when he was a resident of Hays City.

"About the middle of June," wrote Young, "there arrived in Deadwood my old friend Wild Bill. Accompanying him was Charlie Utter, commonly known as Colorado Charlie. They were mounted, and a more pictur-esque sight could not be imagined than Wild Bill on horseback. This character had never been north of Cheyenne before this. Many in Dead-wood knew him; many knew him only by reputation, particularly those who came from Montana. Among these Montana people were a good many men of note. I mean by that, gunmen, and the arrival of this character in town caused quite a commotion.

"They rode up to the saloon where I was working, both of them having known Carl Mann before. He being a great friend of Bill's they naturally called on him first. They dismounted and walked into the saloon, great crowds following them, until the room was packed. Mann cordially re-ceived them, asking them to make his saloon their headquarters, which they agreed to do. This meant money to Mann, as Bill would be a great drawing card. After the excitement of Bill's arrival had subsided a little Bill looked at me a few moments, then said:

" 'Kid, here you are again, like the bad penny, but I am awfully glad to see you.' And turning to Carl Mann, he remarked, 'I first met this kid in Hays City, Kansas, and wherever I go he seems to precede me, but he is a good boy and you can trust him. Take my word for that.'"

It has frequently been stated that Bill went to the hills merely as a gambler and with no idea of prospecting for gold. This is not true. In the Deadwood *Telegram* of November 13, 1922, the writer finds: "Wild Bill sought to accumulate gold by manipulating the picture cards rather than by digging in the earth for it."

Buel, however, makes the positive statement that "Bill established himself in Deadwood to watch for an opportunity to make a profitable strike. He had located several claims." This would not indicate that his sole interest in the Black Hills was the picture cards of Deadwood, although when not otherwise occupied it is pretty certain that he spent his spare time playing his favourite game, poker. There are two letters written by Wild Bill at the time to his wife. One of these, dated July 19, 1876, disproves the theory that he had no interest in those parts as a miner. Here follows the letter, now in the possession of Gil Robinson, whose wife was Wild Bill's daughter-in-law, Emma, who is mentioned in the letter:

My Own Darling Wife Agnes:

I have but a few moments left before this letter starts. I never was as well in my life, but you would laugh to see me now—just got in from prospecting. Will go away again tomorrow. Will write again in the morning, but God knows when the letter will start. My friend will take this to Cheyenne if he lives. I don't expect to hear from you, but it is all the same; I know my Agnes and only live to love her. Never mind, pet, we will have a home yet, then we will be so happy. I am almost sure I will do well here. The man is hurrying me. Goodbye, dear wife. Love to Emma.

J. B. Hickok

Had it not been for Bill's courage he might very well have met with a tragic fate even earlier than he did. There were a number of Montana gun fighters in Deadwood at the time of his arrival. Bill was envied by these men, for it appears that his reputation was much the same as that of a prize fighter who has sent all his opponents down to defeat. He was the champion. Gun fighters at that time aspired to kill any one of their number who had a superior record and thus lay claim to the championship. One night in the Montana saloon, six gun fighters, envious of Bill's prowess, were criticising him, and openly threatening that they would get rid of him. A friend of Bill's ove heard this talk and reported it to him. Bill immediately put his revolvers in order, and going straight to the Montana saloon, walked up to the crowd.

"I understand that you cheap, would-be gun fighters from Montana have been making remarks about me," he said. "I want you to understand unless they are stopped there will shortly be a number of cheap funerals in Deadwood. I have come to this town, not to court notoriety, but to live in peace, and do not propose to stand for your insults."

Whereupon Bill ordered the six men to stand against the wall and deliver up their guns. This they did in a sheepish manner. He then backed out of the saloon, and it was the last he heard of the Montana crowd aspiring to the championship.

*   *   *   *   *

. . . Wild Bill was now living in peace with everyone in Deadwood, as he had travelled far from his former conflicts with the bad men of Hays and Abilene. O. W. Coursey, the historian of the Black Hills, now a resident of Mitchell, South Dakota, has made a searching investigation of those wild times. He learned that Bill had a premonition when he entered Deadwood Gulch that his end was near. When the party reached the top of the upland divide (Break Neck Hill) and looked over into Deadwood Gulch for the first time, he said to Colorado Charlie Utter, "I have a hunch that I am in my last camp and will never leave this gulch alive."

"Quit dreaming," retorted Utter.

"No, I am not dreaming," replied Wild Bill. "Something tells me that my time is up, but where it is coming from I do not know, as I cannot think of one living enemy who would wish to kill me."

On the evening before he was killed he was standing up leaning against the jamb of the door to the building in which he was to be assassinated the next day, looking downcast.

"Bill, why are you looking so dumpy tonight?" Tom Dosier asked him.

"Tom, I have a presentiment that my time is up and that I am soon going to be killed," Bill replied.

"Oh, pooh, pooh!" said Tom. "Don't get to seeing things; you're all right."

A letter written by Wild Bill to his wife on that same evening lends reality to this legend:

AGNES DARLING:

If such should be we never meet again, while firing my last shot, I will gently breathe the name of my wife—Agnes—and with wishes even for my enemies I will make the plunge and try to swim to the other shore.

J. B. HICKOK.

On the following afternoon, Wednesday, August 2, 1876, he was engaged in a game of poker in a saloon owned by Carl Mann and Jerry Lewis.

There is some diversity of opinion as to the name of this place. O. W. Coursey says it was No. 6; Harry Young, the barkeeper, in his "Hard Knocks," says it was No. 66; while Brown and Willard, in "Black Hill Trails," give it as No. 10.

Those sitting at the table beside Wild Bill were Carl Mann, Charles Rich, and Captain Massey, the latter a former Missouri River pilot. As the game progressed the quartet were joking and laughing.

For the first time known, Wild Bill was sitting with his back to a door. While he was facing the front door, a rear door was standing open, Charlie Rich had taken Bill's seat next to the wall, just to plague him, and kept it, though several times Bill asked Charlie to exchange places, Rich said afterward that he was the cause of Bill's murder.

Jack McCall, the assassin, entered the saloon in a careless manner, not giving the least hint of his cowardly purpose. He walked up to the bar, at which Harry Young was officiating, and then sauntered around to a point a few yards behind Wild Bill. He then swiftly drew a .45-calibre Colt and fired. The bullet passed through Bill's head, issued beneath his right cheek bone and before it had spent its course, pierced Captain Massey's left arm. The time was 4:10 P. M.

In his letter to the writer Mr. Peirce gives several details that have not heretofore been revealed. Doc Peirce was the impromptu undertaker who took charge of the remains and looked after the details of the burial:

"Now, in regard to the position of Bill's body," writes Mr. Peirce, "when they unlocked the door for me to get his body, he was lying on his side, with his knees drawn up just as he slid off his stool. We had no chairs in those days—and his fingers were still crimped from holding his poker hand. Charlie Rich, who sat beside him, said he never saw a muscle move. Bill's hand read 'aces and eights'—two pair, and since that day aces and eights have been known as 'the dead man's hand' in the Western country. It seemed like fate, Bill's taking off. Of the murderer's big Colt's-.45 six-gun, every chamber loaded, the cartridge that killed Bill was the only one that would fire. What would have been McCall's chances if he had snapped one of the other cartridges when he sneaked up and held his gun to Bill's head? He would now be known as No. 37 on the file list of Mr. Hickok."

It has been stated that Bill occupied a cabin which stood in a little copse near the spot where the Burlington depot now stands in the city of Deadwood; but Doc Peirce states that Bill was living in a tent, a wagon cover stretched over a pole. Colorado Charlie Utter was his tent mate. It was to this tent that the body was taken by Doc Peirce to prepare it for burial.

In a former statement he said: "When Bill was shot through the head he bled out quickly and when he was laid out he looked like a wax figure. I have seen many dead men on the field of battle and in civil life, but Wild Bill was the prettiest corpse I have ever seen. His long moustache was attractive, even in death, and his long tapering fingers looked like marble."

The following funeral notice was printed and distributed among the miners of the district:

FUNERAL NOTICE

Died in Deadwood, Black Hills, August 2, 1876, from the effects of a pistol shot, J. B. Hickok (Wild Bill) formerly of Cheyenne, Wyoming. Funeral services will be held at Charlie Utter's camp on Thursday afternoon, August 3d, 1876, at three o'clock P. M.

All are respectfully invited to attend.

The body of Wild Bill was enclosed in a coffin made from rough boards. Mr. Peirce had deftly closed the wound in his cheek so that it was scarcely noticeable. Bill's countenance was one of perfect peace, while his long beautiful light brown hair lay parted evenly across his forehead and fell gracefully down to his broad shoulders. According to an eye witness, an expression of calm contentment crowned his features; the lips were slightly parted as if still smiling at the last joke that was passed around the table when the fatal shot was fired. Colorado Charlie had placed beside him in the coffin the Sharps rifle that Bill had carried for many years.

A grave had been dug at Ingleside, then a romantic spot on the mountain slope. A clergyman read the funeral service and on a large stump at the head of the grave was rudely carved the following inscription:

> A brave man, the victim of an assassin,
> J. B. Hickok (Wild Bill) age 39 years;
> murdered by Jack McCall, Aug. 2, 1876.

Captain Jack Crawford, the poet scout, and one of Wild Bill's most intimate friends, commemorated his burial in verse. This poem is dedicated to Colorado Charlie Utter:

BURIAL OF WILD BILL

Under the sod in the prairie land
    We have laid him down to rest,
With many a tear from the sad, rough throng,
    And the friends he loved the best;
And many a heartfelt sigh was heard
    As over the sward we trod,
And many an eye was filled with tears
    As we covered him with the sod.

Under the sod in the prairie land
    We have laid the good and true—
An honest heart and a noble scout
    Has bade us a last adieu.
No more his silvery voice will ring,
    His spirit has gone to God;
Around his faults let charity cling,
    While we cover him with the sod.

Under the sod in the land of gold
    We have laid the fearless Bill;
We called him Wild, yet a little child
    Could bend his iron will.
With generous heart he freely gave
    To the poorly clad, unshod—
Think of it, pards—of his noble traits—
    While you cover him with the sod.

Under the sod in Deadwood Gulch
You have laid his last remains;
No more his manly form will hail
The Red Man on the plains.
And, Charlie, may Heaven bless you!
You gave him a "bully good send";
Bill was a friend to you, pard,
And you were his last, best friend.

You buried him 'neath the old pine tree,
In that little world of ours,
His trusty rifle by his side—
His grave all strewn with flowers;
His manly form in sweet repose,
That lovely silken hair—
I tell you, pard, it was a sight,
That face so white and fair!

The pall-bearers were William Hillman, John Oyster, Charlie Rich, Jerry Lewis, Charles Young, and Tom Dosier.

In a letter written by Wild Bill's sister Lydia, in 1896, she gives a pathetic picture of the arrival of the news of her brother's death at Troy Grove, Illinois.

"I remember the day the paper came," she wrote, "with the news of Bill's murder. Mother had been a sufferer from inflammatory rheumatism for two years before that and had not taken a step for eighteen months. My sister was standing at the gate when a neighbor came by and brought the Chicago paper, giving an account of Bill's death. He handed it to my sister. She took it and saw the headlines, but did not read all of it. She folded it up and hurried into the house, hiding the paper in the kitchen behind the mirror on the shelf. Then composing herself she went in where Mother was sitting.

"'Mother,' she said, 'I am going over to the store a minute and will be right back.'

"She put on her bonnet and ran to the little store about two hundred yards away to tell one of my brothers. All came back to the house together. When they entered the sitting room, there sat Mother, the newspaper lying at her side, slowly rocking back and forth, while the blood from a hemorrhage of the lungs dyed the front part of her dress.

"'I saw you get the paper, Lydia,' she said, 'and when you did not bring it in, I went and got it.'

"She never fully recovered from the blow, and she died two years later, still mourning Bill's terrible death."

Within three years Deadwood had grown so rapidly that it was found necessary to remove the bodies in the old graveyard where Wild Bill lay. On August 3, 1879, Charlie Utter and Lewis Shoenfield, old friends of Bill's, arranged for the removal of the remains to Mount Moriah cemetery. Upon removing the coffin lid, it was found that few changes had taken place in the features. In short, Wild Bill lay after three years as if he had been merely asleep. The same smile lingered on his lips, as if the sleeper was in a pleasant dream.

An account of the exhumation of the remains was published in the Deadwood *Telegram* of November 13, 1922, in which it was stated that those who assisted the undertaker "were astounded to find that by some natural embalming process of the soil, accomplished by water which had percolated through the coffin, the body of Wild Bill had been so well embalmed as to preserve even the outlines of his features and the lines of the manifold pleatings of the dress shirt which he wore. This preservation of the body gave rise to the report that it had been petrified, but Mr. McClintock states that from his examination he would call it an embalming, rather than a petrification, by the deposition of minerals in the tissues of the body."

This lot and grave had been prepared by Colorado Charlie Utter, who had given the remains their second burial. A marble headstone was placed at the head of the grave inscribed as follows:

WILD BILL
J. B. HICKOK
KILLED BY THE ASSASSIN
JACK MC CALL
DEADWOOD CITY
BLACK HILLS
AUGUST 2, 1876
PARD, WE WILL MEET AGAIN IN THE HAPPY
HUNTING GROUNDS TO PART NO MORE.
GOODBYE
COLORADO CHARLIE.
C. H. UTTER.

So great had Wild Bill's fame become that in the ten succeeding years visitors to Mount Moriah cemetery had chipped off pieces of the headstone as souvenirs until little or nothing was left of it. Then a new headstone and full-length statue was arranged for, it was decided that in order to save the tomb from desecration by vandals it should be surrounded by a steel cage. This new monument and statue was erected in 1892. It was carved by James H. Riordan, a sculptor of New York, who was visiting in that locality.

Billy the Kid

I. THE PEOPLE REMEMBER THE KID

IF YOU would learn in what affectionate regard the people of New Mexico cherish the memory of Billy the Kid to-day, you have but to

From *The Saga of Billy the Kid*, by Walter Noble Burns, pp. 64–69. Copyright, 1925, by Doubleday, Page & Company. Garden City, New York.

journey in leisurely fashion through the Billy the Kid country. Every one will have a story to tell you of his courage, generosity, loyalty, light-heartedness, engaging boyishness. More than likely you yourself will fall under the spell of these kindly tales and, before you are aware, find yourself warming with romantic sympathy to the idealized picture of heroic and adventurous youth.

Sit, for instance, on one of the benches under the shade trees in the old square at Santa Fé where the wagon caravans used to end their long journey across the plains. Here the rich and poor of this ancient capital of the land of mañana and sunshine come every day to while away an hour and smoke and talk politics. Mention Billy the Kid to some leisurely burgher. Instantly his face will light up; he will cease his tirade against graft and corruption in high places and go off into interminable anecdotes. Yes, Billy the Kid lived here in Santa Fé when he was a boy. Many a time when he was an outlaw with a price on his head, he rode into town and danced all night at the dance hall over on Gallisteo Street. The house is still there; the pink adobe with the blue door and window shutters. Did the police attempt to arrest him? Not much. Those blue-coated fellows valued their hides. Why, that boy wasn't afraid of the devil. Say, once over at Anton Chico. . . .

Or drop into some little adobe home in Puerta de Luna. Or in Santa Rosa. Or on the Hondo. Or anywhere between the Ratons and Seven Rivers. Perhaps the Mexican housewife will serve you with frijoles and tortillas and coffee with goat's milk. If you are wise in the ways of Mexicans, you will tear off a fragment of tortilla and, cupping it between your fingers, use it as a spoon to eat your frijoles that are red with chili pepper and swimming in soup rich with fat bacon grease. But between mouthfuls of these beans of the gods—and you will be ready to swear they are that, else you are no connoisseur in beans—don't forget to make some casual reference to Billy the Kid. Then watch the face of your hostess. At mention of the magic name, she will smile softly and dream-light will come into her eyes.

"Billee the Keed? Ah, you have hear of heem? He was one gran' boy, señor. All Mexican pepul his friend. You nevair hear a Mexican say one word against Billee the Keed. Everybody love that boy. He was so kind-hearted, so generous, so brave. And so 'andsome. *Nombre de Dios!* Every leetle señorita was crazy about heem. They all try to catch that Billee the Keed for their sweetheart. Ah, many a pretty *muchacha* cry her eyes out when he is keel; and when she count her beads at Mass, she add a prayer for good measure for his soul to rest in peace. Poor Billee the Keed! He was good boy—*muy valiente, muy caballero.*"

Or ask Frank Coe about him. You will find him a white-haired old man now on his fruit ranch in Ruidoso Cañon. He fought in the Lincoln County war by the Kid's side and as he tells his story you may sit in a rocking chair under the cottonwoods while the Ruidoso River sings its pleasant tune just back of the rambling, one-story adobe ranch house.

"Billy the Kid," says Coe, "lived with me for a while soon after he came to Lincoln County in the fall of 1877. Just a little before he went to work for Tunstall on the Feliz. No, he didn't work for me. Just lived with me. Riding the chuck line. Didn't have anywhere else special to stay just then. He did a lot of hunting that winter. Billy was a great hunter, and the hills hereabouts were full of wild turkey, deer, and cinnamon bear. Billy could hit a bear's eye so far away I could hardly see the bear.

"He was only eighteen years old, as nice-looking a young fellow as you'd care to meet, and certainly mighty pleasant company. Many a night he and I have sat up before a pine-knot fire swapping yarns. Yes, he had killed quite a few men even then, but it didn't seem to weigh on him. None at all. Ghosts, I reckon, never bothered Billy. He was about as cheerful a little hombre as I ever ran across. Not the grim, sullen kind; but full of talk, and it seemed to me he was laughing half his time.

"You never saw such shooting as that lad could do. Not a dead shot. I've heard about these dead shots but I never happened to meet one. Billy was the best shot with a six-shooter I ever saw, but he missed sometimes. Jesse Evans, who fought on the Murphy side, used to brag that he was as good a shot as the Kid, but I never thought so, and I knew Jesse and have seen him shoot. Jesse, by the way, used to say, too, that he wasn't afraid of Billy the Kid. Which was just another one of his brags. He was scared to death of the Kid, and once when they met in Lincoln, Billy made him take water and made him like it. Billy used to do a whole lot of practice shooting around the ranch, and had the barn peppered full of holes. I have heard people say they have seen him empty his shooter at a hat tossed about twenty feet into the air and hit it six times before it struck the ground. I won't say he couldn't do it, but I never saw him do it. One of his favourite stunts was to shoot at snowbirds sitting on fence posts along the road as he rode by with his horse at a gallop. Sometimes he would kill half-a-dozen birds one after the other; and then he would miss a few. His average was about one in three. And I'd say that was mighty good shooting.

"Billy had had a little schooling, and he could read and write as well as anybody else around here. I never saw him reading any books, but he was a great hand to read newspapers whenever he could get hold of any. He absorbed a lot of education from his newspaper reading. He didn't talk like a backwoodsman. I don't suppose he knew much about the rules of grammar, but he didn't make the common, glaring mistakes of ignorant people. His speech was that of an intelligent and fairly well educated man. He had a clean mind; his conversation was never coarse or vulgar; and while most of the men with whom he associated swore like pirates, he rarely used an oath.

"He was a free-hearted, generous boy. He'd give a friend the shirt off his back. His money came easy when it came; but sometimes it didn't come. He was a gambler and, like all gamblers, his life was chicken one day and feathers the next, a pocketful of money to-day and broke to-morrow. Monte was his favourite game; he banked the game or bucked it, depending on his finances. He was as slick a dealer as ever threw a card, and as a player, he was shrewd, usually lucky, and bet 'em high— the limit on every turn. While he stayed with me, he broke a Mexican monte bank every little while down the cañon at San Patricio. If he happened to lose, he'd take it like a good gambler and, like as not, crack a joke and walk away whistling with his hands rammed in his empty pockets. Losing his money never made him mad. To tell the truth, I never saw Billy the Kid mad in my life, and I knew him several years.

"Think what you please, the Kid had a lot of principle. He was about as honest a fellow as I ever knew outside of some loose notions about rustling cattle. This was stealing, of course, but I don't believe it struck him exactly that way. It didn't seem to have any personal element in it. There were the cattle running loose on the plains without any owner in sight or sign of ownership, except the brands, seeming like part of the landscape. Billy, being in his fashion a sort of potentate ruling a large portion of the landscape with his six-shooter, felt, I suppose, like he had a sort of proprietary claim on those cattle, and it didn't seem to him like robbery—not exactly—to run them off and cash in on them at the nearest market. That's at least one way of figuring it out. But as for other lowdown kinds of theft like sticking up a lonely traveller on the highway, or burglarizing a house, or picking pockets, he was just as much above that sort of thing as you or me. I'd have trusted him with the last dollar I had in the world. One thing is certain, he never stole a cent in his life from a friend."

The history of Billy the Kid already has been clouded by legend. Less than fifty years after his death, it is not always easy to differentiate fact from myth. Historians have been afraid of him, as if this boy of six-shooter deadliness might fatally injure their reputations if they set themselves seriously to write of a career of such dime-novel luridness. As a consequence, history has neglected him. Fantastic details have been added as the tales have been told and retold. He is already in process of evolving into the hero of a Southwestern Niebelungenlied. Such a mass of stories has grown about him that it seems safe to predict that in spite of anything history can do to rescue the facts of his life, he is destined eventually to be transformed by popular legend into the Robin Hood of New Mexico —a heroic outlaw endowed with every noble quality fighting the battle of the common people against the tyranny of wealth and power.

Innumerable stories in which Billy the Kid figures as a semi-mythical hero are to be picked up throughout New Mexico. They are told at every camp fire on the range; they enliven the winter evenings in every Mexican home. There is doubtless a grain of truth in every one, but the troubadour touch is upon them all. You will not find them in books, and their chief interest perhaps lies in the fact that they are examples of oral legend kept alive in memory and passed on by the story-tellers of one generation to the story-teller of the next in Homeric succession. They are folklore in the making. As each narrative adds a bit of drama here and a picturesque detail there, one wonders what form these legends will assume as time goes by, and in what heroic proportions Billy the Kid will appear in fireside fairy tales a hundred years or so from now.

II. THE "WAR OF BILLY THE KID"

CHAPTER V

Lincoln County War

To the average dweller in that portion of the great West known as New Mexico, the Lincoln county war is as well known as was the internecine "war of the Roses" to the people of the time of York and Lancaster. Its causes and its results yet form the theme of conversation around the camp fire, on a winter's night, or a summer's evening, and it will be many years before the tale will have grown old and uninteresting. Were nothing else needed to make it live the mere fact that The Kid was a leading spirit in the deadly strife would suffice to give it a certain place in history. Much as small men are known as the husbands of Mrs. ——, the actress, or lecturer, will the Lincoln imbroglio be known as the war of "Billy the Kid."

According to Marion Turner, who was a prominent actor in the war, the trouble began with the determination of "Old John Chisum" and partner, Alex McSwain, to establish a monopoly of the stock-grazing business and make themselves in truth the cattle kings of the Pecos Valley. This valley is, next to that of the Rio Grande, the most important in the Territory, running as it does almost along its entire length from North to South, and is, with the exception of the Rio Hondo, the only one of any size in Lincoln county. To have entire command of such a range would be a fortune in itself. Chisum drove in 80,000 head of cattle. The herds of the smaller rancheros were swept away, as if by an avalanche, by this multitude of hoofs and horns; naturally enough those who lost their little all in this manner attempted to reclaim their animals. This was dangerous business and collisions between the herders were of daily occurrence. The smaller fry banded together under the leadership of Murphy, Dolan & Co., men who had important cattle interests and were anxious to defend them. Both sides enlisted all the strength and influence they could command and prepared for what bid fair to be a deadly conflict. Chisum and McSwain in a happy moment, hired The Kid, and his dare-devil ways, his deadly marksmanship, his perfect command of a horse, combined with what seemed to be an absolute delight in murder, soon caused him to be made the leader of his faction. The strife progressed with alternate success and

From *The Cowboy's Career, or The Dare Devil Deeds of "Billy, the Kid," The Noted New Mexican Desperado,* by "One of the Kids." Chicago: Belford, Clarke & Co. St. Louis: Belford & Clarke Publishing Co. 1881. (From a typewritten transcript loaned by Philip Edward Stevenson.)

defeat for each party. Early in 1879 Chisum arranged for the appointment of The Kid as deputy constable and clothed in this authority he was given a warrant for the arrest, on a trivial charge, of Billy Morton and Frank Baker, two herders employed by Tom Catron. This Catron, by the way, used to live in Lafayette county, Missouri, and was the partner of Hon. Stephen B. Elkins, himself a Missouri boy, later delegated to Congress from New Mexico and now one of the moneyed men of New York. The Kid saddled his horse, when told what was to be done, and, without a word to any of his comrades, silently rode off to the range in search of his prey, accompanied by one McCluskey. He found Morton and his companion in a camp near the eastern boundary of the county and showing him the warrant said:

"You are my prisoners. Come along."

"What do you want of me?" said Morton, in a threatening tone.

"Shut up, or I'll blow your brains out. You have been working against Chisum. That's enough."

"We'll see about this pretty soon, young man," said Baker. "It's a free country and no man arrests me without I know what it's for."

"Haven't I told your white-livered friend the reason. Hold your tongue or I'll stop it forever with a bullet."

At this point McCluskey interfered and remonstrated with the young desperado.

"You don't mean to kill a defenseless man do you?" he said.

"If I wish to, yes; and you, too."

With these words The Kid drew his revolver and before the astonished McCluskey could move his hand shot him in his tracks.

"You see how I treat men who fool with me, do you?" the murderer said, as he scornfully kicked the lifeless form at his feet. "Be careful what you do or I'll serve you as I have him."

Chaining the two men together by the wrists and carefully securing them to the saddle he placed them both upon McCluskey's horse and started back at a slow trot towards Chisum's ranch. The feelings of the prisoners can easily be imagined. Should they be taken into camp the vengeance of Chisum would be upon their heads. There was, at least, a chance of escape. If the handcuffs could only be loosened and the chain parted a successful break might be made. Those "ifs" must be gotten out of the way in the next twenty miles. The men worked cautiously and had almost freed themselves, when the watchful eye of The Kid espied their movements. Without saying a word he coolly drew his rifle to his shoulder and fired twice at them. As the distance was only ten feet and his aim sure the reports were followed by the simultaneous fall of both Morton and Baker, and in a moment their souls had flown to what we may hope was a greener range, where even the cow-boy has a place. Shot dead without hardly an excuse. Thus The Kid added two more to the list of those who had felt his deadly power. Thus far he had killed four men and the career of this pseudo James boy had hardly begun. Fearful in its beginning the reader must judge the righteousness of the end.

Riding into camp The Kid informed Chisum of what he had done and asked that two men be sent out to bury them.

"Where is McCluskey?" asked Chisum.

"None of your —— business," replied The Kid.

"It is my business and I will know. I am not afraid of you and you may as well understand it now as any time."

"Come, come, old feller," he said, changing his tone and manner, "I was just bantering you a little. Now to be honest about it I killed Mc."

"Killed him!"

"That's the racket."

"Why, what had he done?"

"Too infernally inquisitive. Didn't know his place, either. Thought he'd try to boss the job, but I settled him quick."

"He was my best man, next to you," said Chisum, after a pause, in which he eyed The Kid closely and rubbed his chin reflectively.

"Don't care if he was, he had to go."

"Do you know, Kid, that this affair will leak out and the officers will be down here to inquire into it and arrest you?"

"Chisum, you must think I'm a fool. I care no more for Brady and Hindman than I do for a dog. If they get the drop on me—all right, but The Kid won't be caught napping and don't you forget it."

"I'm afraid they'll bring the troops down on us!"

"Let them do it. If we can't whip any company of 'blue coats,' why then I'll change my name and herd sheep in the States," and with this assertion The Kid carelessly sauntered down to his tent and threw himself down to catch a few hours' sleep before morning should dawn.

CHAPTER VI

Numbers Five and Six

As hinted by Chisum, the news of the killing of Morton, McCluskey and Baker quickly reached the ears of the authorities of the county. Although a wild section, a triple murder could not be winked at, or a reign of lawlessness would ensue destructive of the already loose fabric of society and containing elements of disaster of great moment to the cattle men and their employes, as well as to the few farmers and store keepers of Lincoln county. When sheriff Brady first heard of The Kid's bloody deed from the lips of a special detective, who, in turn, learned the fact from one of Chisum's men—a friend of the murdered parties, and who had recently been discharged because of suspected intimacy with the opposing faction—he realized that in capturing the murderer he would have no easy task to perform. The matter was talked over carefully with his deputy, George Hindman, and it was resolved to at once proceed to Chisum's ranch and, if possible, effect the capture. No one else was taken into the secret, as it was feared that The Kid might be informed of the intended raid of the officers and prepare himself accordingly. The precaution was, however, an unnecessary one, since he was always ready to meet a personal enemy or an officer of the law, knowing himself to be practically an outcast, with the hand of almost every man against him.

The news came to Brady Wednesday. The murders were committed Monday. The officers left Thursday, bound for the home of The Kid. Each was heavily armed and rode horses of fine staying powers. The trip was a solemn one. They fully recognized the fact that the chances of coming back alive were hardly even. Indeed, before the start was made, they settled their business affairs and otherwise made ready for any emergency.

"I confess I don't like this," remarked Hindman to his superior as they galloped out of Lincoln.

"You are not afraid, are you?" responded Brady.

"No man ever saw George Hindman turn pale, even when looking down the barrel of a rifle in the hands of an enemy," he said, "but I can't shake off the feeling, somehow or other, that we won't come out of the fight alive."

"The Kid is a bad man, I know," replied Brady, after a moment's thought, "but if I take him off his guard he will be my prisoner and no blood will be spilled, either."

"Catch a cat sleeping. The Kid is surrounded by men who will defend him to the last. I tell you it's a bad job. We are in for it, though."

It will be seen that they did not walk into the trap blindly but with eyes open. It is all very well to praise the immortal six hundred who made the charge at Balaklava; one may become enthusiastic at the bravery of the men at Bunker Hill, or Vicksburg, but to the unprejudiced mind this act of Brady and Hindman had in it more elements of heroism than the others. The one faced death in behalf of an idea and surrounded by all the glory of conquest and insanity of battle; the other, in behalf of law and order, quietly took even chances of death or life without a murmur and alone.

A few words will tell the story. All day Thursday The Kid seemed possessed with the idea that something would happen. As he expressed himself to a comrade: "Either I or the man whom I meet will die to-day." At an early hour he cleaned his rifle carefully, loaded it with a heavy ball and an extra charge of powder, placed a new cap in position, looked to the proper equipment of his Derringers and was never for a moment off his guard. Between the hours of eleven and twelve his watchful eye discerned two horsemen slowly riding to the ranch from the west. At the instant he espied them they were fully five miles off. In forty minutes they would be at the ranch; in twenty they would be near enough to be recognized. As they came nearer, making a detour to the south, hoping to reach a grove and escape observation until almost at their destination, The Kid procured a spy glass and leveled it in the direction of the approaching horsemen.

"The officers!" was all he said.

Quietly walking to McSwain's adobe, which was located near the outside of the little hamlet, he placed himself in readiness. Five—ten—

fifteen—twenty minutes had elapsed. A sound was heard around the corner—the measured tramp of approaching feet. The Kid peered cautiously around the corner. The two officers. Then he discovered himself to them, at the same time raising his rifle to the shoulder, and pulling the trigger, with the barrel aimed at Brady's heart, there was a quick flash, followed by a loud report and a white cloud of smoke; then another flash and another report. The south wind quickly cleared the air, and stepping forward, with Derringer drawn The Kid saw Brady and Hindman at his feet, the one dead, the other breathing faintly and asking to be put out of his misery.

"You shall go as quick as I can send you," the cow-boy said. "Give Baker my love," and he placed the muzzle of his Derringer at Hindman's right temple and finished the bloody work.

By this time a crowd had gathered, but no one, if so inclined, dared to arrest The Kid. Instead, he ordered his comrades to join him in an hour, fully equipped with arms, ammunition and horses, saying that it would be too hot for them as soon as Baker's friends discovered the murder, and that escape must be made to the mountains where a defense could be more easily made. He accordingly gathered around him a band of outlaws and desperadoes and defied county, territory and United States authorities.

CHAPTER VII

The Crisis

The tacit defiance of law, the reign of terror and bloodshed inaugurated by The Kid were met in a determined manner by the proper authorities. June 15th, 1879, two days after the occurrence mentioned in the preceding chapter, Marion Turner, deputy sheriff of Lincoln county, had a warrant placed in his hands for the arrest of The Kid for the murder of Morton Baker, McCluskey, Brady and Hindman. Turner was not only a very brave but a very wise man. He knew that the man for whom he had a warrant was a desperate character, and therefore desperate measures were resorted to to effect his capture. Turner organized a posse of thirty-five men, consisting principally of ranchmen and cowboys of the anti-Chisum faction. In adopting this course Turner not only took advantage of the general horror which every man would feel at the cold-blooded murders, but also of the peculiar and intense hatred entertained against The Kid and his gang by those who conceived their rights had been trampled on by Chisum. The posse was not a very large one, but every man in the crowd was an expert handler of the rifle and could be depended on in an emergency. As emergencies were very liable to arise, this readiness and nerviness was a good and important factor of the problem.

On the seventeenth day of June, after being out two days, Turner and his posse came upon The Kid and his sixty-three men. The place where they met was in a narrow cañon at the mouth of a range of low foot hills

To the right was a thickly wooded expanse, to the left huge boulders, with here and there a straggling pine tree, while in front ran a small stream which had its source ten miles distant, to the north. The Kid's party had made their camp five miles up the stream, and had come down to the place where it left the hills in order to reconnoiter, when they were met by Turner's posse. The former divided, one division running back to protect their camp, and the other remaining to confront the posse, each side thus being evenly balanced. Turner halted nearly a hundred yards from where The Kid was standing, and arranging his forces in the best possible manner with each man's hand on his rifle, stepped out a few steps from the ranks and read his warrant. To the requisition a defiant answer was returned to the effect that they would never get him, dead or alive; whereupon Turner ordered his men to arrest him. They advanced at a double-quick, on horseback, but The Kid, wishing to avoid a fight until he could effect a junction with the remainder of his gang, as well as secure a better position, hastily retreated. Seeing his purpose the order was given to fire, but the aim of the posse was rendered uncertain by the motion of their horses and only two men were hit, one being seriously and the other fatally wounded. None of the Sheriff's party were touched by the return fusillade. The fight continued in this way for five miles, neither side scoring another fatal shot. A decided stand was made at the camp and Turner drew off for consultation. At the camp all was bustle and confusion. A rude embankment had been thrown up, behind which The Kid, his men, their horses and pack animals were waiting to receive the expected onslaught. The consultation between Turner and his men resulted in the employment of strategy. They retired a short distance and halted just on the edge of the wood. Ten of the party formed a line along its edge and the other twenty-five dashed into the wood with the intention of making a circuit and coming in upon the gang from the rear. This was easily accomplished, provided the ruse was successful, because The Kid's camp joined the woods on the right. The danger of the undertaking lay in the fact that if the plan was discovered the little party of ten would fall an easy prey to a foe outnumbering them six to one. The minutes that succeeded the departure of the twenty-five were anxious ones to those who remained. Every movement of the enemy was watched and a show of preparation for renewing the conflict was kept up. Five minutes had passed. The detour should have been made in that time. The Kid appeared at the head of his men and began to file out of the camp, confident of the superiority of numbers and his own charmed life. At this moment, and not a second too soon, a yell was heard from behind. Turner had flanked them. They turned, and another yell was heard. The ten who had guarded the operation of their comrades rushed up the stream. A deadly fire was poured in from two sides, and for a moment all was confusion and panic. At this juncture The Kid dashed forward, and calling upon his men to rally broke through the opposing force, killing one of them and slightly wounding two more. He was followed by Turner, the Nemesis. Volley after volley was fired. The flight was so rapid that neither the dead nor the wounded were cared for. On! On! in feverish haste. Crossing and recrossing the little stream, turning to fire and then savagely spurring their horses forward, they fairly flew. Of the sixty-five men whom The Kid led into the cañon only forty escaped alive, while Turner lost but five. The odds had changed, and they were not as favorable to the desperado. Across the plain, dodging hither and thither, now advancing, then retreating, the two forces went, each wreaking vengeance on the other, each paying old scores and getting even with bitter enemies. Strange as it may seem, this running fight lasted two days, with scarcely a stop for food or water. The forces by this time had become considerably reduced, numbering but twenty-five each. Lieut. Col. Dudley, of the famous 9th Cavalry (colored), learning that re-enforcements were being sent to The Kid, took two companies of his regiment and went to Turner's assistance. As luck would have it Dudley was first on the ground and The Kid and his gang at once retreated towards Lincoln which was but a few miles distant. They took shelter in McSwain's house, one of the most elegantly furnished dwellings in the Territory, in which only the most fashionable were wont to enter. The cavalry rushed up but were repulsed and fell back. Again the line was formed, this time on foot, and an advance was made. The fight raged furiously. It was a question of annihilation for one side or the other, and every man fought like a demon. Port holes were cut and rifle balls sent from them with unerring aim. The house became a fort and the garden surrounding it a battlefield. During the battle Mrs. McSwain encouraged the garrison by playing martial airs on her piano, and singing inspiring battle songs. The besieging posse soon got the range of the piano from its sound, and shot it to pieces with their heavy buffalo rifles, the wife of McSwain narrowly escaping. This siege was of three days' duration. On the third day of the fight Turner, being convinced that they could not be conquered by legitimate warfare, ordered the house to be fired by throwing bucketfuls of blazing coal oil on the roof and inside through the windows. This precipitated the crisis, and about dusk of the third day the desperadoes made a rush for their horses with the intention of thereby effecting an escape. A hand to hand combat ensued in which twelve of The Kid's men and two of Turner's posse were killed, McSwain being among the number. During the rush from the burning house, Tom O'Fallaher, a "pard" of The Kid's, young, and from San Antonio, Texas, noticed a friend fall. Although a storm of balls and buckshot rained around him he coolly stopped, picked up his comrade and was about to carry him out when he noticed that he was dead. Throwing the body down he drew a sword and fought his way out. This brave fellow was afterwards killed by deputy sheriff Garrett's posse, shortly after the capture of The Kid.

The leader of the gang, The Kid, seemed to bear a charmed existence. A hundred bullets were speeded towards him and not one reached the mark. He escaped without a scratch, and with barely a dozen men fled, hotly pursued but never caught. Immediately after this fearful flight he reorganized his followers, received accessions to his cause, and was again in condition to make the average New Mexican go to bed with a feeling of insecurity. The Kid in the meanwhile had added five names to his death-roll. It now numbered eleven.

III. Death of Billy the Kid

In March, 1881, a Deputy United States Marshal by the name of John W. Poe arrived in the booming mining camp of White Oaks. He had been sent to New Mexico by the Cattlemen's Association of the Texas Panhandle. Cattle King Charlie Goodnight, being the president of the association, had selected Mr. Poe as the proper man to put a stop to the stealing of Panhandle cattle by "Billy the Kid" and gang.

After the "Kid's" escape, Pat Garrett went to White Oaks and deputized John W. Poe to assist him in rounding up the "Kid."

From now on Mr. Poe made trips out in the mountains trying to locate the young outlaw. The "Kid's" best friends argued that he was "nobody's fool," and would not remain in the United States, when the Old Mexico border was so near. They didn't realize that little Cupid was shooting his tender young heart full of love-darts, straight from the heart of pretty little Miss Dulcinea del Toboso, of Fort Sumner.

Early in July, Pat Garrett received a letter from an acquaintance by the name of Brazil, in Fort Sumner, advising him that the "Kid" was hanging around there. Garrett at once wrote Brazil to meet him about dark on the night of July 13th at the mouth of the Taiban arroyo, below Fort Sumner.

Now the sheriff took his trusted deputy, John W. Poe, and rode to Roswell, on the Rio Pecos. There they were joined by one of Mr. Garrett's fearless cowboy deputies, "Kip" McKinnie, who had been raised near Uvalde, Texas.

Together the three law officers rode up the river towards Fort Sumner, a distance of eighty miles. They arrived at the mouth of Taiban arroyo an hour after dark on July 13th, but Brazil was not there to meet them. The night was spent sleeping on their saddle blankets.

The next morning Garrett sent Mr. Poe, who was a stranger in the country, and for that reason would not be suspicioned, into Fort Sumner, five miles north, to find out what he could on the sly, about the "Kid's" presence. From Fort Sumner he was to go to Sunny Side, six miles north, to interview a merchant by the name of Mr. Rudolph. Then when the moon was rising, to meet Garrett and McKinnie at La Punta de la Glorietta, about four miles north of Fort Sumner.

From *History of "Billy the Kid,"* by Chas. A. Siringo, pp. 124–133. The true life of the most daring young outlaw of the age. He was the leading spirit in the bloody Lincoln County, New Mexico, war. When a bullet from Sheriff Pat Garrett's pistol pierced his breast he was only twenty-one years of age, and had killed twenty-one men, not counting Indians. His six years of daring outlawry has never been equalled in the annals of criminal history. Copyright, 1920, by Chas. A. Siringo.

Failing to find out anything of importance about the "Kid," John W. Poe met his two companions at the appointed place, and they rode into Fort Sumner.

It was about eleven o'clock, and the moon was shining brightly, when the officers rode into an old orchard and concealed their horses. Now the three continued afoot to the home of Pete Maxwell, a wealthy stockman, who was a friend to both Garrett and the "Kid." He lived in a long, one-story adobe building, which had been the U. S. officers' quarters when the soldiers were stationed there. The house fronted south, and had a wide covered porch in front. The grassy front yard was surrounded by a picket fence.

As Pat Garrett had courted his wife and married her in this town, he knew every foot of the ground, even to Pete Maxwell's private bed room.

On reaching the picket gate, near the corner room, which Pete Maxwell always occupied, Garrett told his two deputies to wait there until after he had a talk with half-breed Pete Maxwell.

The night being hot, Pete Maxwell's door stood wide open, and Garrett walked in.

A short time previous, "Billy the Kid" had arrived from a sheep camp out in the hills. Back of the Maxwell home lived a Mexican servant, who was a warm friend to the "Kid." Here "Billy the Kid" always found late newspapers, placed there by loving hands, for his special benefit.

This old servant had gone to bed. The "Kid" lit a lamp, then pulled off his coat and boots. Now he glanced over the papers to see if his name was mentioned. Finding nothing of interest in the newspapers, he asked the old servant to get up and cook him some supper, as he was very hungry.

Getting up, the servant told him there was no meat in the house. The "Kid" remarked that he would go and get some from Pete Maxwell.

Now he picked up a butcher knife from the table to cut the meat with, and started, bare-footed and bare-headed.

The "Kid" passed within a few feet of the end of the porch where sat John W. Poe and Kip McKinnie. The latter had raised up, when his spur rattled, which attracted the "Kid's" attention. At the same moment Mr. Poe stood up in the small open gateway leading from the street to the end of the porch. They supposed the man coming towards them, only partly dressed, was a servant, or possibly Pete Maxwell.

The "Kid" had pulled his pistol, and so had John Poe, who by that time was almost within arm's reach of the "Kid."

With pistol pointing at Poe, at the same time asking in Spanish: "Quien es?" (Who is that?), he backed into Pete Maxwell's room. He had repeated the above question several times. On entering the room, "Billy the Kid" walked up to within a few feet of Pat Garrett, who was sitting on Maxwell's bed, and asked: "Who are they, Pete?"

Now discovering that a man sat on Pete's bed, the "Kid" with raised pistol pointing towards the bed, began backing across the room.

Pete Maxwell whispered to the sheriff. "That's him, Pat." By this time the "Kid" had backed to a streak of moonlight coming through the south window, asking: "Quien es?" (Who's that?)

Garrett raised his pistol and fired. Then cocked the pistol again and it went off accidentally, putting a hole in the ceiling, or wall.

Now the sheriff sprang out of the door onto the porch, where stood his two deputies with drawn pistols.

Soon after, Pete Maxwell ran out, and came very near getting a ball from Poe's pistol. Garrett struck the pistol upward, saying: "Don't shoot Maxwell!"

A lighted candle was secured from the mother of Pete Maxwell, who occupied a nearby room, and the dead body of "Billy the Kid" was found stretched out on his back with a bullet wound in his breast, just above the heart. At the right hand lay a Colt's-.41 calibre pistol, and at his left a butcher knife.

Now the native people began to collect,—many of them being warm friends of the "Kid's." Garrett allowed them to take the body across the street to a carpenter shop, where it was laid out on a bench. Then lighted candles were placed around the remains of what was once the bravest, and coolest young outlaw who ever trod the face of the earth.

The next day, this, once mother's darling, was buried by the side of his chum, Tom O'Phalliard, in the old military cemetery.

He was killed at midnight, July 14th, 1881, being just twenty-one years, seven months and twenty-one days of age, and had killed twenty-one men, not including Indians, which he said didn't count as human beings.

IV. SONG OF BILLY THE KID

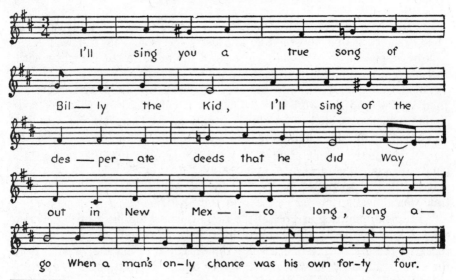

I'll sing you a true song of Bil—ly the Kid, I'll sing of the des—per—ate deeds that he did Way out in New Mex—i—co long, long a—go When a man's on—ly chance was his own for—ty four.

From *American Ballads and Folk Songs,* collected and compiled by John A. Lomax and Alan Lomax, pp. 137–138. Copyright, 1934, by The Macmillan Company. New York.

I'll sing you a true song of Billy the Kid,
I'll sing of the desperate deeds that he did
Way out in New Mexico long, long ago,
When a man's only chance was his own forty four.

When Billy the Kid was a very young lad,
In old Silver City he went to the bad;
Way out in the West with a gun in his hand
At the age of twelve years he first killed his man.

Fair Mexican maidens play guitars and sing
A song about Billy, their boy bandit king,
How ere his young manhood had reached its sad end
He'd a notch on his pistol for twenty-one men.

'Twas on the same night when poor Billy died
He said to his friends: "I am not satisfied;
There are twenty-one men I have put bullets through
And Sheriff Pat Garrett must make twenty-two."

Now, this is how Billy the Kid met his fate:
The bright moon was shining, the hour was late.
Shot down by Pat Garrett, who once was his friend,
The young outlaw's life had now come to its end.

There's many a man with a face fine and fair
Who starts out in life with a chance to be square,
But just like poor Billy he wanders astray
And loses his life in the very same way.

Jesse James

I. BALLAD OF JESSE JAMES

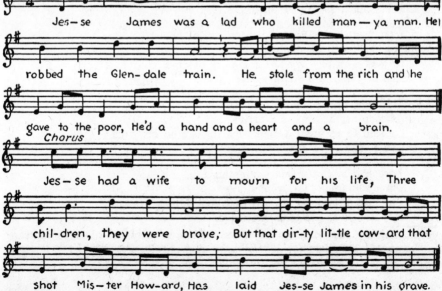

Jes—se   James was a lad   who   killed   man—ya man. He
robbed the Glen—dale train.   He stole from the rich and he
gave to the poor, He'd a   hand and a heart   and a   brain.

Chorus

Jes—se had a wife   to   mourn   for his life, Three
chil—dren, they were brave; But that dir—ty lit—tle cow—ard that
shot Mis—ter How—ard, Has   laid   Jes-se James in his grave.

Jesse James was a lad who killed many a man.
He robbed the Glendale train.
He stole from the rich and he gave to the poor,
He'd a hand and a heart and a brain.

Chorus:
  Jesse had a wife to mourn for his life,
  Three children, they were brave,
  But that dirty little coward that shot Mister Howard,
  Has laid Jesse James in his grave.

It was Robert Ford, that dirty little coward,
I wonder how he does feel,
For he ate of Jesse's bread and he slept in Jesse's bed,
Then he laid Jesse James in his grave.

Jesse was a man, a friend to the poor.
He'd never see a man suffer pain,
And with his brother Frank he robbed the Chicago bank,
And stopped the Glendale train.

It was on a Wednesday night, the moon was shining bright,
He stopped the Glendale train,
And the people all did say for many miles away,
It was robbed by Frank and Jesse James.

It was on a Saturday night, Jesse was at home,
Talking to his family brave,
Robert Ford came along like a thief in the night,
And laid Jesse James in his grave.

The people held their breath when they heard of Jesse's death,
And wondered how he ever came to die,
It was one of the gang called little Robert Ford,
That shot Jesse James on the sly.

Jesse went to his rest with hand on his breast,
The devil will be upon his knee,
He was born one day in the county of Shea
And he came of a solitary race.

This song was made by Billy Gashade,[1]
As soon as the news did arrive,
He said there was no man with the law in his hand
Could take Jesse James when alive.

Jesse had a wife to mourn for his life,
Three children, they were brave,
But that dirty little coward that shot Mister Howard,
Has laid Jesse James in his grave.

From *Singing Cowboy*, A Book of Western Songs, collected and edited by Margaret Larkin, pp. 158–159. Copyright, 1931, by Alfred A. Knopf, Inc. New York.
[1] An example of the ballad convention of "claim to authorship."

II. Jesse James and the Poor Widow

"One day," says Sam Allender, "Frank James told me that on a certain occasion he and his pals were traveling on horseback somewhere in northern Missouri. It being about noon, they were hungry. They pulled off the main road and found a lone woman in charge of a small farmhouse. They asked her if she could supply them with something to eat.

"At first the woman hesitated. The men displayed money and assured her they would be glad to pay for what they ate. She then proceeded to prepare such scant food as she had on hand. As she was making coffee and cooking eggs, the James crowd sat around the room. They noticed that she was weeping; tears were rolling down her cheeks, sobs were heaving her bosom.

" 'Jesse,' said Frank in telling me the story, 'was always tender-hearted—couldn't stand a woman's tears. He asked her why she was crying. She tried to smile it off, and said that seeing us men around the house reminded her of the happy time when her husband was living and had other men now and then helping him do the farm work; she was just thinking how sadly things had changed since his death, and that was what made her cry, so she said.

" 'Jesse kept on asking questions. The woman said she had several children at school, some miles down the road; there was a mortgage on her farm, she went on to say, for $1,400; it was overdue, and this was the last day of grace.

" ' "Aha!" said Jesse, "and so that's really what's making you cry—you're afraid you're going to lose your home. I see."

" 'Yes, that was it, she admitted. That very afternoon, said the weeping widow, the man who held the mortgage was coming out from town to demand his money. He was a hardhearted old miser, she stated, and she didn't have a dollar to apply on the debt. The man would be sure to foreclose and turn her and her helpless little ones out.

" ' "Huh!" said Jesse, "that so?" his eyes blinking fast and furiously. "Well, now ma'am, I don't know about that; I—well, now, I think maybe you won't lose your farm after all."

" 'The widow looked rather puzzled. She put the food on the table and all of us sat down and turned to. After we finished eating, Jesse produced a sack and counted out on the table $1,400.

" ' "Here, lady," said Jesse, "you take this money and pay off your mortgage."

" 'The lady was amazed. "I can't ever pay you back," she said, "and so I won't borrow it."

" ' "But it's no loan," said Jesse; 'it's a gift.'

From *The Rise and Fall of Jesse James*, by Robertus Love, pp. 289–292. Copyright 1926, by Robertus Love. New York: G. P. Putnam's Sons.

" 'The widow said she couldn't believe it was anything but a dream—things never happened that way—but Jesse assured her it was no dream; the money was good money and it was for her use. Jesse then sat down and wrote out a form of receipt, which he had the woman copy in her own handwriting. He put the original into his pocket, so that his handwriting wouldn't get into other hands. Jesse instructed the woman to pay the mortgage-holder the $1,400 and have him sign the receipt—in ink. He then handed her a handful of cash for her immediate needs.

" 'Jesse asked the grateful widow to describe the man who held the mortgage. She did so, telling the kind of rig he drove and about what hour she expected him, and the road by which he would come out from town. We then bade her good day and mounted our horses. The widow was still weeping, but weeping for joy.

" 'We rode some distance from the house and hid in the bushes beside the rocky road along which the mortgage man was to come in his buggy. Presently we saw him driving toward the widow's house, and pretty soon driving back, looking prosperous. He was humming "Old Dan Tucker was a fine old feller" as he came opposite. We stepped out into the road, held him up and recovered the $1,400.'

"I asked Frank James," said Sam Allender, "if they had any more difficulty in getting the money on that occasion than they had had on the occasion when they first acquired it; and he replied, with a laugh:

" 'Now, Sam, I'm not being sweated.' "

III. The Death of Jesse James

Between eight and nine o'clock yesterday morning Jesse James, the Missouri outlaw, before whom the deeds of Fra Diavolo, Dick Turpin and Schinderhannes dwindled into insignificance, was instantly killed by a boy twenty years old, named Robert Ford, at his temporary residence on the corner of Thirteenth and Lafayette streets, in this city.

In the light of all moral reasoning the shooting was unjustifiable; but the law is vindicated, and the $10,000 reward offered by the state for the body of the brigand will doubtless go to the man who had the courage to draw a revolver on the notorious outlaw even when his back was turned, as in this case.

· · ·

There is little doubt that the killing was the result of a premeditated plan formed by Robert and Charles Ford several months ago. Charles had been an accomplice of Jesse James since the 3d of last November, and entirely possessed his confidence. Robert Ford, his brother, joined Jesse

From the Kansas City *Journal*, April 4, 1882. Reprinted from the St. Joseph (Missouri) *Evening News*, April 3, 1882. Cited in *The Rise and Fall of Jesse James*, by Robertus Love, pp. 341–345. Copyright, 1926, by Robertus Love. New York: G. P. Putnam's Sons.

near Mrs. Samuel's (the mother of the James boys) last Friday a week ago, and accompanied Jesse and Charles to this city Sunday, March 23.

Jesse, his wife and two children, removed from Kansas City—where they had lived several months, until they feared their whereabouts would be suspected—to this city, arriving here Nov. 8, 1881, coming in a wagon and accompanied by Charles Ford. They rented a house on the corner of Lafayette and Twenty-first streets, where they stayed two months, when they secured the house No. 1381 on Lafayette street, formerly the property of Councilman Aylesbury, paying $14 a month for it, and giving the name of Thomas Howard.

The house is a one-story cottage, painted white, with green shutters, and is romantically situated on the brow of a lofty eminence east of the city, commanding a fine view of the principal portion of the city, river and railroads, and adapted by nature for the perilous and desperate calling of Jesse James. Just east of the house is a deep, gulchlike ravine, and beyond that a broad expanse of open country backed by a belt of timber. The house, except from the west side, can be seen for several miles. There is a large yard attached to the cottage, and a stable where Jesse had been keeping two horses, which were found there this morning.

Charles and Robert Ford have been occupying one of the rooms in the rear of the dwelling, and have secretly had an understanding to kill Jesse ever since last fall. Ever since the boys have been with Jesse they have watched for an opportunity to shoot him, but he was always so heavily armed that it was impossible to draw a weapon without James seeing it. They declared that they had no idea of taking him alive, considering the undertaking suicidal.

The opportunity they had long wished for came this morning. Breakfast was over. Charlie Ford and Jesse James had been in the stable currying the horses preparatory to their night ride. On returning to the room where Robert Ford was, Jesse said:

"It's an awfully hot day."

He pulled off his coat and vest and tossed them on the bed. Then he said:

"I guess I'll take off my pistols, for fear somebody will see them if I walk in the yard."

He unbuckled the belt in which he carried two .45-calibre revolvers, one a Smith & Wesson, and the other a Colt, and laid them on the bed with his coat and vest. He then picked up a dusting brush with the intention of dusting some pictures which hung on the wall. To do this he got on a chair. His back was now turned to the brothers, who silently stepped between Jesse and his revolvers.

At a motion from Charlie both drew their guns. Robert was the quicker of the two, and in one motion he had the long weapon to a level with his eye, and with the muzzle not more than four feet from the back of the outlaw's head.

Even in that motion, quick as thought, there was something which did not escape the acute ears of the hunted man. He made a motion as if to turn his head to ascertain the cause of that suspicious sound, but too late. A nervous pressure on the trigger, a quick flash, a sharp report, and the well-directed ball crashed through the outlaw's skull.

There was no outcry—just a swaying of the body and it fell heavily backward upon the carpet of the floor. The shot had been fatal, and all the bullets in the chambers of Charlie's revolver, still directed at Jesse's head, could not more effectually have decided the fate of the greatest bandit and freebooter that ever figured in the pages of a country's history.

The ball had entered the base of the skull and made its way out through the forehead, over the left eye. It had been fired out of a Colt's-.45, improved pattern, silver-mounted and pearl-handled pistol, presented by the dead man to his slayer only a few days ago.

Mrs. James was in the kitchen when the shooting was done, separated from the room in which the bloody tragedy occurred by the dining room. She heard the shot, and dropping her household duties ran into the front room. She saw her husband lying extended on his back, his slayers, each holding his revolver in his hand, making for the fence in the rear of the house. Robert had reached the enclosure and was in the act of scaling it when she stepped to the door and called to him:

"Robert, you have done this! Come back!"

Robert answered, "I swear to God I didn't!"

They then returned to where she stood. Mrs. James ran to the side of her husband and lifted up his head. Life was not yet extinct, and when she asked him if he was hurt, it seemed to her that he wanted to say something but could not. She tried to wash the blood away that was coursing over his face from the hole in his forehead, but it seemed to her that the blood would come faster than she could wipe it away, and in her hands Jesse James died.

Charlie Ford explained to Mrs. James that "a pistol had accidentally gone off." "Yes," said Mrs. James, "I guess it went off on purpose." Meanwhile Charlie had gone back in the house and brought out two hats, and the two boys left the house. They went to the telegraph office, sent a message to Sheriff Timberlake of Clay County, to Police Commissioner Craig of Kansas City, to Governor Crittenden and other officers, and then surrendered themselves to Marshal Craig [Enos Craig of St. Joseph].

When the Ford boys appeared at the police station they were told by an officer that Marshal Craig and a posse of officers had gone in the direction of the James residence, and they started after them and surrendered themselves. They accompanied the officers to the house and returned in custody of the police to the marshal's headquarters, where they were furnished with dinner, and about 3 p. m. were removed to the old circuit courtroom, where the inquest was held in the presence of an immense crowd.

Quantrell

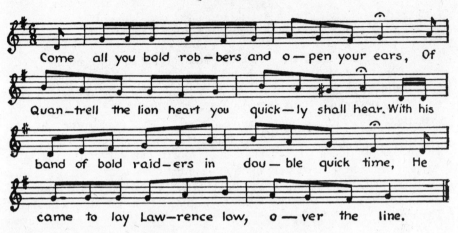

Come all you bold rob—bers and o—pen your ears, Of
Quan—trell the lion heart you quick—ly shall hear. With his
band of bold raid—ers in dou—ble quick time, He
came to lay Law—rence low, o—ver the line.

Come all you bold robbers and open your ears,
Of Quantrell the lion heart you quickly shall hear.
With his band of bold raiders in double quick time,
He came to lay Lawrence low, over the line.

Chorus:
　　All routing and shouting and giving the yell,
　　Like so many demons just raised up from hell,
　　The boys they were drunken with powder and wine,
　　And came to burn Lawrence just over the line.

They came to burn Lawrence, they came not to stay.
They rode in one morning at breaking of day,
With guns all a-waving and horses all foam,
And Quantrell a-riding his famous big roan.

They came to burn Lawrence, they came not to stay.
Jim Lane he was up at the break of the day;
He saw them a-coming and got in a fright,
Then crawled in a corn crib to get out of sight.

Oh, Quantrell's a fighter, a bold-hearted boy,
A brave man or woman he'd never annoy.
He'd take from the wealthy and give to the poor,
For brave men there's never a bolt to his door.

From *Frontier Ballads,* heard and gathered by Charles J. Finger, pp. 64–65. Copyright, 1927, by Doubleday, Page & Company. Garden City. New York.

Sam Bass

I. THE SAM BASS LEGEND

SOON after his death, relics of Sam Bass began to crop up in nearly every town of central and northern Texas. If all the "authentic" Bass guns could be gathered in one place, they would stock an arsenal. A contemporary newspaper supported the claim of Milt Tucker, of Georgetown, that Bass gave him his gun when captured. Other guns owned by two Rangers, Dick Ware and John L. Banister, were also said to have been surrendered by Bass when captured. A fourth gun for which the same claim was made was sold at auction in Austin soon afterwards. Sam's cartridge belt, with a few unused bullets, was given to the University of Texas Library. His compass went to Captain Dan W. Roberts, of the Texas Rangers, while Captain June Peak retained the bowie knife taken from the body of Arkansas Johnson at Salt Creek. Horns of steers said to have been killed by Bass were sold at fancy prices, and a carpenter at Snyder nailed to the top of his tool chest a horseshoe supposed to have been worn by the Denton mare.

G. W. Allen, a mule-team freighter and storekeeper in Old Round Rock, possessed a hat said to have been given him by Sam Bass. Another headpiece, described as "the identical hat which Sam Bass wore at the time of his capture," was displayed at the bar of the El Paso Hotel at Fourth and Main, Fort Worth, about three weeks after Sam was buried. The hat was a limp one with a low crown and a wide brim. The owner, C. A. Sparks, traveling agent for a St. Louis wholesale hat firm, said Bass gave him the hat; and he showed corroborative statements from citizens of Round Rock.

Near Belton, people pointed to live oaks in which Bass was said to have shot his initials while riding at full speed. In Round Rock, Henry Koppel and his successors showed visitors the bandits' bullet marks in the store, and the Sam Bass Cafe was opened across the street. Every cave within a wide area was said to have been a hiding place for the outlaw band. Boy Scouts from Denton have explored a cave at Pilot Knob, imagining they were in the brigands' rendezvous; and a wild recess in the hills of Palo Pinto County has become known as Sam Bass Hollow. Longhorn Cavern, about forty miles west of Georgetown, had been widely advertised as a former haunt of the famous outlaw, though it is doubtful if he ever was within thirty-five miles of the place.

Thickets, as well as caves, have been pointed out as the desperado's hiding places; Bass hideouts in Texas have become almost as numerous as George Washington beds in Virginia. On their way back to Denton

---

From *Sam Bass*, by Wayne Gard, pp. 239–247. Copyright, 1936, by Wayne Gard. Boston and New York: The Houghton Mifflin Company.

County from their fourth Texas train robbery at Mesquite, Sam and his
regulars were said to have hidden for a day or two in a bois d'arc thicket
just north of Dallas, on what later became the campus of Southern
Methodist University. A short distance west of this thicket, the story
goes, a Negro youngster named Bob was looking after a herd of hogs
when a stranger approached on a horse and asked what he was doing.

"Herdin' hogs, suh," the boy replied.

"Do you know who I am?" the rider asked.

"No, suh, ah sho don't, suh."

"I'm Sam Bass!"

This statement almost paralyzed the youngster, whose fear was not
lessened when Bass whipped out a gun, pointed it at Bob, then returned
it to the holster.

"Boy, I ought to kill you," he said. "But I won't. There are men following me. When they get here, you tell them I've gone toward the
Trinity River."

The bandit then rode off to the north, and Bob ran in the opposite
direction until out of breath. As he stopped to rest, a posse headed by
Sheriff Marion Moon rode up; and the frightened boy told them Bass
had ridden westward, toward the river.

Many of the legends that took root in cattle camps and hearthsides
magnified Sam's crimes as well as the size of his loot. Most of these
stories were as fictitious as that of the Texas verse writer who described
Bass as stealing a pig when the Indiana youth was only ten years old.
More plausible was the Denton County story that, at the outset of his
robbing career, Sam tried to hold up Henry Hill, of Little Elm. Hill, who
went by the name of Rawhide, was building a cotton gin and had gone to
Dallas to obtain money for wages and other expenses. Returning to Lewis-
ville by train, he hired a livery horse and started home. Sam and two
companions waylaid him and, after an exciting chase, shot his horse from
under him. At this, Hill grabbed his saddle-bags containing the money
and took refuge in a nearby farmhouse. The amateur robbers then gave
up the pursuit and rode away.

Although sheriffs and Rangers seldom sighted him, legendary encounters
with the elusive Sam were reported from many places. Once he stopped
a Negro near Cove Hollow and asked him to trade horses, but the well-
mounted darky refused.

"Do you know who I am?" asked the brigand. "I'm Sam Bass!"

At this news, the Negro tumbled off his horse and began to run for
his life. Sam called him back, however, and—after the saddles were
changed—handed him seventy-five dollars.

Until he ran short of money at the last, Bass always paid well for his
fresh mounts—usually with gold stolen from the Union Pacific express
at Big Springs.

Once he stopped a cattleman in the northern part of Dallas County
and asked for chewing tobacco. "You can buy more, but I can't," he

explained. The rancher handed over a plug; and Sam cut off a piece, returning the remainder with a half dollar.

Bass then offered fifty dollars for the man's horse, but he replied that he had paid only half that amount for the nag.

"That's all right; I'll take that mule of yours to make up the difference," said Sam.

A trade was made, and both men went off well satisfied.

Some of the stories have to do with banks Sam tried to rob or thought of robbing, but didn't. Although court testimony indicated that Bass sent Billy Scott to inspect the bank at Weatherford, legend has it that the desperado led his whole band there to look over the financial situation. They found Jim Couts, the trigger-fingered banker, seated on the curb in front of his place on the south side of the square. Sam already was acquainted with the rugged financier, and the setup didn't look promising. For some time, the bandit leader sat on a drygoods box and whittled while his men walked up and down in front of the bank. Later, they decided that before they could rob the bank they would have to kill Couts. As they didn't want to undertake that job, they mounted their horses and rode away.

The generosity of Sam with the twenty-dollar gold pieces he brought back from the big train robbery in Nebraska gave him fame as a Robin Hood even while he was living; and after his death the stories of his giving and spending were enlarged. Payments of twenty dollars for a dozen eggs or a pan of warm biscuits were reported from many directions. On one occasion, he was said to have stopped with his outlaw band at the farm home of a Denton County widow. Against the woman's wishes, the robbers stayed overnight; but Bass told his men that the widow was a lady and must be treated as such. The men behaved themselves and did no drinking; and when they left the next morning, Bass paid the widow fifty dollars.

Many stories were told at the expense of those who pursued the outlaw band. A cocky young Breckenridge lawyer was said to have led a heavily armed posse against Bass, whom he expected to capture by nightfall. But when the pursuers found the desperado, Sam refused to flee, and therefore the posse could not chase him. Rather than to approach too close to the notorious gunman, the men in the posse rode home and reported that Bass could not be found.

From Breckenridge came also the tale of a young detective who arrived with the announcement that he was going to kill Sam Bass. Walking along the road toward the supposed hideout of the brigands, he received a lift from a man in a buggy. He explained his mission to the driver, who asked if he would know Sam Bass if he saw him.

"No," answered the detective.

"Well, you're riding with him now," his companion calmly remarked.

The detective then began trembling and begging for his life and telling of his wife and children at home. He was released, and this was the last time he went out looking for Sam Bass.

However, another amateur detective in Breckenridge was said to have given a better account of himself. This young fellow, who roomed at the town's only hotel, began talking about capturing Bass when the outlaws were rumored to be camping in Stephens County. Not rating this self-appointed detective's courage as highly as they might, several young fellows of the town decided to play a trick on him by impersonating the train-robber band and giving the pursuer a big scare when he was decoyed in their direction. A young newspaper editor, Homer Davenport, agreed to lead the detective to a place in the country where the others would be hidden.

As the editor led the bandit-catcher up a hillside, shots were fired by the pranksters from behind rocks at the summit, and the two men started to run back. The editor fell on his rifle, as planned, and called out that he was killed. After running a little farther, the detective suddenly turned around and marched deliberately back to the supposed corpse, pistol in hand. Muttering, "I can't leave a man like that," he began firing at the men he took for brigands hiding behind the rocks—firing to kill. Not until the corpse rolled off to join the fleeing townsmen did he see through the trick. It was two days before Davenport mustered enough courage to resume his meals at the hotel.

The most persistent of all the Bass legends have been those of buried gold. A Denton saloonkeeper was said to have buried six hundred dollars' worth of Sam's double-eagles at a spot within the town; and thirty thousand dollars of his loot was reported buried in Montague County, northwest of Denton. A cave near McNeil, a few miles south of Round Rock, and another in Llano County were also said to have received some of his stolen treasure. For more than half a century, men armed with maps and spades—and sometimes with divining rods—have been looking for chests of gold they believed Sam buried.

One of the earliest stories of the outlaw's buried riches came from a young farmer, Henry Chapman, who lived near Springtown, in Parker County. In January, 1879, Chapman was riding a mule through the woods from Harrison's gin, at the pool on Clear Fork, to Squire Milliner's place near the mouth of Salt Creek. At a point near Skeen's Peak, his mule became scared, gave a hard lurch, and broke the saddle girth. While he was dismounted, mending the girth, Chapman discovered a pile of fresh dirt covered with pieces of brush. He supposed at first that some fellow had been enticed into the woods and murdered, but he was curious enough to remove the brush and loose earth.

Within a few minutes, as he related afterwards, he unearthed a walnut box big enough to hold a bushel and a half. The box was crammed with gold and silver coins, including many twenty-dollar gold pieces. His first impulse was to fill his pockets, but he remembered that he had a sack under his saddle. He quickly procured this sack and began to fill it with treasure from the walnut box.

As the coins were clinking into the sack, Chapman happened to look up and was terrified to see eight men advancing upon him with guns leveled at his head. As he was unarmed he hastily mounted his mule and galloped off. He never saw the gunmen again, but he was sure they were associates of Sam Bass, who had come back for treasure they had helped the outlaw bury in the previous summer.

From Austin to the Red River, caves were searched for gold the robber chieftain was supposed to have buried, but none was found. Before long, maps and diagrams began to appear. Several years after the turn of the century, N. B. Hamilton, a Round Rock liveryman, was in Mexico and obtained from an American there a map that showed just where the Bass treasure was buried. Hamilton brought the map back to Round Rock and let two of his friends, B. H. Allen and George Townsley, into the secret. The map indicated that the treasure was hidden in a hollow tree on the old Leander and Liberty Hill road, two miles northwest of Round Rock. Equipped with axes and lanterns, the men went to the scene late at night and chopped down the tree. The only metallic substance they found, however, was a single rusty nail. The next morning, people who passed along the road wondered why the tree-trunk had been chopped to bits and none of the wood carried away.

Two decades later, other men with other maps were observed digging for Sam's gold in the neighborhood of Cove Hollow, more than forty miles northwest of Denton. As late as January, 1928, feverish treasure-hunters carried the search into the city of Dallas. The searchers had seen an old penciled map that showed where Sam had buried two hundred thousand dollars' worth of gold bullion and other valuables. The hiding place was under a forked stump near a spring on the west side of Trinity River. The spot was located, and for several weeks nocturnal excavations were made on a section of the river bluff, owned by Marcus Plowman, two blocks north of the Oak Cliff end of the Houston Street viaduct.

II. THE SONG

THAT night the song of *Sam Bass* was sung. It generally is, where men are who know it. The old wanderer was the singer, and did his part with gusto, with the song halted frequently to enable the singer to give paren-thetical explanations. It was something like this:

"This is the song of Sam Bass. He was a true-blooded hero. He was a kindly natured fellow. I knew old Dad Egan, sheriff of Denton County, Sam's first boss. This is how the song goes:

From *Frontier Ballads,* heard and gathered by Charles J. Finger, pp. 65–71. Copy-right, 1927, by Doubleday, Page & Company. Garden City, New York.
The tune is from *Singing Cowboy,* by Margaret Larkin, pp. 162–163.

Sam Bass was born in Indiana, which was his native home.
Before he reached young manhood, the boy began to roam.
> *(In Lawrence County, he was born. Eighteen fifty-one if the grave stone don't lie, and July 21st.)*

He first came out to Texas a cowboy for to be
> *(Working for Dad Egan, like I said. Then he drifted down to San Antone and after a while out to Uvalde County.)*

He first came out to Texas, a cowboy for to be—
A better hearted fellow you scarce could hope to see.
> *(All them fellows is good hearted. That's their downfall. Their good heartedness is. But the dadgummed, jim-crow laws, they don't care about a man's good heartedness. Anyone knows that. See, where was I?)*

Sam bought him first some race stock and also the Denton mare.
He matched her in all races and took her to the fair.
He fairly coined money and spent it frank and free.
He drank the best of whiskey wherever he might be.
> *(Let me tell this. That mare was sure good. Sam he put right smart of money into her. Cleaned up a lot, too, he did, I'd say. A little sorrel she was. Dad Egan offered Sam to give up the mare or quit his job, but Sam, he loved her like a child. A man can love a mare or his dog more faithful than a woman.)*

He left where he was working one pretty summer day
A-headin' for the Black Hills with his cattle and his pay.
In Custer City sold the lot and then went on a spree,
His chums they was all cowboys rough and hard as they could be.
> *(Deadwood, it was—Deadwood, in the Dakotas. A wide-open town. Sam, his boss was Jo Collins who bought his cattle on time I've heard it said, but when he sold out, gambled and lost. So him and Sam they*

held up a stagecoach or two, though the song don't tell nothing of that.)

A-ridin' back to Texas they robbed the U. P. train,
For safety split in couples and started out again.
The sheriff took Jo Collins who had a sack of mail
And with his partner landed him inside the county jail.

(Big Springs, not Big Springs, Texas, but Big Springs in Nebraska it was. The express messenger said it was one of them dad-gummed time locks on the safe, so one of the men started to lay him out, but Sam, being kind hearted, wouldn't stand for that. So when they was about to quit, what did they come on but three boxes of gold, in twenty-dollar gold pieces, $60,000. To do the thing right, they went through the cars and took another $5,000 from the passengers. This Jo Collins, he had met up with a store clerk in Ogallala, and went back to buy things after the hold-up. Sam Leech, done give information and the posse caught up with Collins and Bill Heffridge in Kansas right where was some U.S. army men who lit out after the outlaws. They tried to stand off the soldiers, but the men fired and killed them both. So the song's wrong about the jail, but that's put in for poetry. You can't always have things like they are in poetry. Poetry hain't what you'd call truth There ain't room enough in the verses. About Sam. Him and Jack Davis they lit out for Texas. Jim Berry and Dad for Mexico City, Missouri. The song goes on about Sam.)

But Sam got back to Texas all right side up with care.
And in the town of Denton he did his money share.

(He was the boy to do that all right. I forgot to say that this here Jim Berry he got caught by a posse, shot in the knee and his leg bone was shattered. Old Dad he got away safe with his share. . . . I'll start up that again.)

But Sam got back to Texas all right side up with care,
And in the town of Denton he did his money share.
The lad he was so reckless, three robberies did he do,
The passenger and express car and U.S. mail car, too.

(What isn't in the song is that Sam and Bill met up with a crowd of cavalry men and camped with 'em, joking about the robberies and them soldiers never suspicioning anything. The Texas train robberies was on the T.P. at Eagle Ford and at Mesquite Junction.)

Now Sam he had four pardners, all bold and daring bad.
There was Richardson and Jackson, Jo Collins and Old Dad.
More daring bolder outlaws the rangers never knew,
They dodged the Texas rangers and beat them, too.

Sam had another pardner called Arkansaw for short,
But Thomas Floyd the ranger cut his career quite short.
This Floyd stood six feet in his socks and passed for mighty fly,
But them that knows will tell you he's a dead beat on the sly.

(That about Floyd the ranger is only put in for the poetry of it. I heard tell one of the best jokes on the rangers. Good enough to go in a book.

*There hain't nothing what a ranger won't tackle. Well, when Fort
Worth first started up there was some kind of trouble and pretty much
of a riot. So they wired down to headquarters for rangers to keep
order. What did they do but send this same Floyd. The mayor and
the people, all het up about the trouble, was down at the depot, when
this Floyd gets off. The mayor, he says, we sent for rangers. All right,
says Floyd, here I am. Well, hain't there no more than one of you,
asked the mayor. Why? asks Floyd. Is there more than one riot?
The joke comes in where he said that, this Floyd. He knew he could
handle a riot all right, single handed. Came natural to him. But the
mayor couldn't see it that way. That's where the joke comes in. One
ranger to one riot. It's shore funny. Anyway, him who killed Sam
was Dick Ware. Did it with a .45.)*

Jim Murphy was arrested and then let out on bail,
He jumped the train for Terrel after breaking Tyler jail.
But old Mayor Jones stood in with Jim and it was all a stall,
A put-up job to catch poor Sam, before the coming fall.
   *(About this Murphy. Sam he was suspicious of him and wanted to
   shoot Murphy. Murphy and Jackson they was cousins and there ought
   to be something about that in the song. But there hain't. Some poet
   ought to put it in. I tried but can't quite make it go right. This
   Murphy he agreed to doublecross Sam, agreed with General Jones, and
   Sam he got to hear of it. That's why he wanted to shoot him.)*

Sam met his fate at Round Rock, July the twenty-first.[1]
They dropped the boy with rifle balls and then they took his purse,
Poor Sam he is a dead lad, and six foot under clay.
And Jackson's in the mesquite aiming to get away.
   *(At Round Rock sure enough with Jackson holding the rangers back
   shooting with his right hand while he helped Sam get in the saddle.
   Jackson stuck by Sam to the end, with Sam shot through the kidneys.
   Three days Sam suffered and when he died he was buried at Round
   Rock. I seen the gravestone. Murphy, he committed suicide, drinking
   eye medicine, and there ought to be something about that in the song,
   but there hain't.)*

Jim, he had took Sam Bass's gold and didn't want to pay,
His only idea it was to give brave Sam away,
He sold out to Sam and Barnes and left their friends to mourn—
And Jim he'll get a scorching when Gabriel blows his horn.

Perhaps he's got to heaven, there's none of us can say,
My guess it is and surmise, he's gone the other way,
And if brave Sam should see him as in the place he rolls,
There'll be a lively mix-up down there among the coals.
   (I made up that last, to get the rights of it about Murphy going to hell.)

[1] 1878.

"There is a lot more verses," said the old man in ending, "a regular raft of 'em, a hundred or more, for this Sam Bass he had a horse," and then came a long tale of how Sam had been pursued by rangers from Denton to Fort Concho, the animal taking steep-banked creeks at a stride, carrying its rider down cañon sides where human foot could not find place, carrying on unfalteringly, and at last, when danger threatened, waking its sleeping master by shaking him. It was an adaptation of Swift Nick and Dick Turpin, with their boldest deeds given to the Indiana lad. And at the end,

"Sam Bass he looked to east and west, to sky and silver cloud
And took his every garment to make the horse a shroud,
He dropped a tear to think that he and his brave horse must part,
'Twas not the ride that killed her but 'twas a broken heart."

Stackalee

HE WAS BORN WITH A VEIL OVER HIS FACE

Gypsy told Stack's mother,
Told her like a friend,
Your double-jinted baby
Won't come to no good end.

AND the gypsy woman shore said a hatful, cause it all come out that very way. And how comes Stackalee's mother to call in the fawchin teller was cause he come kickin into this wide world double-jinted, and with a full set of teeth. But what scared her most was he had a veil over his face, and everybody knows that babies born with veils on their faces kin see ghosts and raise 41 kinds of hell.

SOLD HIS SOUL TO THE DEVIL

And so when Stackalee growed up he got to be an awful rascal and rounder wit lots of triflin women and he staid drunk all the time. One dark night as he come staggerin down the road the devil popped up real sudden, like a grinnin jumpin jack. He carried Stackalee into the grave yahd and bought his soul. And that's how come Stack could go round doin things no other livin man could do, such as:

Makin himself so little he could git into a bottle on a shelf and you could look at him settin there—yes suh! And fillin a small bottle full of water and settin it in a big glass jar where it would sink to the bottom

By Onah L. Spencer. From *Direction*, Vol. IV (Summer, 1941), No. 5, pp. 14–17. Copyright, 1941, by Direction, Inc.
Edna Ferber named a steamboat in *Showboat* after Stackalee. I am also told that policy players in American Black Bottoms highly prize luck charms bearing his name, that such charms, or (in Black Bottom vernacular) mojoes, sell from one dollar up.—O. L. S.

till he began to talk to it and make it rare up and drap back just how-soever he wanted it to. And by walkin barefoot on hot slag out of a pig iron furnace and never gittin burned and eatin all the hot fire you could hand him without burning his stummick and changin hisself into a mountain or varmint. Some old timers lowed they knowed him personal and that his favorite night time shape was a prowlin wolf. That's how it come they used to sing that old song about him:

> Stackalee didn't wear no shoe;
> Couldn't tell his track from horse or mule.

THE MAGIC HAT

You see, it happened like this: Stack was crazy about Stetson hats; specially them great big five gallon hats with dimples in the crown. And he had a whole row of em hangin on pegs and you could look at em along the wall of his rickety shanty on Market Street in St. Louis, where he lived with his woman, Stack o' Dollars, that I'm goin to tell you about later.

He had a dimpled and lemon colored yaller hat, and a black Sunday one with two white eyes to wear to funerals with his new brogans, and lots of other ones, all kinds and colors.

But his favorite was an oxblood magic hat that folks claim he made from the raw hide of a man-eatin panther that the devil had skinned alive. And like I told you, how come Stack to have it was because he had sold his soul to old Scratch. You see, Satan heard about Stack's weakness, so he met him that dark night and took him into the grave yahd where he coaxed him into tradin his soul, promisin him he could do all kinds of magic and devilish things long as he wore that oxblood Stetson and didn't let it get away from him. And that's the way the devil fixed it so when Stack did lose it he would lose his head, and kill a good citizen, and run right smack into his doom.

HIS GIRL FRIEND

Now Stackalee had a girl friend and her name was Stack o' Dollars. She blew into St. Louis off Cincinnati's old Bucktown on the Levee where she used to run gamblin games at a saloon there called the Silver Moon, long, long ago; and she always bet her whole stack of silver dollars.

> She walked into the Silver Moon
> Stacked her dollars, mountain high;
> Says they call me Stack o' Dollars
> Cause my limit is the sky.

She had two diamond teeth with gold fillin and when she opened her mouth with a sunburst smile, didn't they glitter! Proud of them sparklers, too, cause they shined like flashlights. Wouldn't pawn em, even to get old

Stackalee out on bond. And since they was fastened to her haid they was safe cause she was a fat mama with the meat shakin on her bones and she didn't need no man for a bouncer. She feared nothin and nobody. Her motto was: "Come clean, or come dirty and get cleaned." She could put a knot on a bully's haid so big that he wouldn't know whether the knot was on him or he was on the knot.

She had a full bosom, wore an eight-gallon Stetson, smoked cheroots, and was tougher than Big Mag of Chicago's old Cheyenne District. She ruled the levees with her big fist, and even old double-jinted Stackalee, big enough to go bear huntin with a willow switch, had to light out when they had them Saturday night fist fights, cause she would roll up her sleeves and begin smackin him around till their shanty shook like when Joshua fit the battle of Jericho and the walls come tumblin down. But she was good-hearted, though, when she was sober; and old long tall Stack who was a gambler with plenty of good-lookin browns claimed he like her cause she whupped him so good.

STACKALEE GOES WEST

Now like I told you, Stack was popular with the women folks cause he could whup the blues on a guitar, and beat out boogie woogie music piano bass and the like of that, but what they liked about him most was he was so stout he could squeeze the breath out of em almost. And his favorite one was a voodoo queen down in New Orleans French market.

Any way, the women got to braggin on him bein so stout that they reckoned he could even give old Jesse James a good tussle. So Stack, with his gun handle filled with notches, knowed there was a reward out for him for men he had washed away. He lowed he was lucky 'count of his magic Stetson to keep in hidin, but he figgered he had better light out while the goin was good. So he thought he would just look up old Jesse James and give him a trial.

> Stackalee went out West,
> Met Jesse James, and did his best.

Yes, sir, that fool even got mixed up with Jesse James. But Jesse was too much for him—turned old Stack every way but *loose*. And Lord knows what might not have happened to Stack if the devil hadn't come down the road in a cloud of dust that got in Jesse's eyes. Leastwise, it might have saved the city of San Francisco and it might have kept old Stack from gettin into all them other amazin things I'm goin to tell you about later. And leastwise the devil wouldn't have changed hisself to look like Billy Lyons and get poor innercent Billy killed.

STACKALEE CHANGES HIMSELF INTO A HORSE

Anyway, after the devil had saved him from Jesse James, Stack, knowin the law was hot after him, lit out again, headin west. And it was on the

way over the mountains that he run into two cullud deputies on the lookout
for him in order to collect the $5,000 reward offered for his arrest. So
Stack set down to swap a few words with 'em between two big mountains [1]
before they had caught on who he was. Then he told em he didn't aim
to hurt em, he just wanted to know what their names was. When they
told him, that sucker hauled out his forty-five and shot their initials in
their hats, changed hisself into a horse, and galloped away with a lot of
little baby red devils ridin on his back. And did them deputies run the
other direction! They knowed it was Satan's work and they thought
maybe Stack was the devil hisself.

> Tell you the truth!
> Think I'm lyin?
> Had to run sideways
> To keep from flyin.

So skeered they tore out through a graveyahd, knockin tombstones over
like ten pins in a bowlin alley. And so Stack he held his sides laughin,
and set down between them two big mountains and thought and thought,
and finally made up his mind to go on to Frisco, where he was later called
"the black Samson."

STACKALEE LAYS SAN FRANCISCO LOW

Now here comes the most amazin part of the story. Stack had been in
Frisco about a month, gettin leapin drunk, and just about runnin hisself
crazy. So one morning in April, 1906, after he had had a rocky night and
had a headache built for a hippopotamus he was out lookin for a sudden
jerk and an eye opener to cool the burnin thirst in his throat. Into the
first barroom he staggered. He didn't have penny one on him but he had
a fist full of tricks and his magic oxblood Stetson and he was sure he
could pull off some kind of conjuration to get his morning's juice.

But the bartender told him: "Listen here, cullud man! I ain't wettin
even the bottom of a glass with gin till you shows me the color of your
money."

Stack got all big at the nose and woofed: "All right, boss, you either
fixes me up with that gin, or I pulls down this bar!"

The bartender he just stood there grinnin and lookin sassy. So Stack
he laid a-holt of the bar with both hands and sweat as big as marbles
rolled down his face while he huffed and puffed and blew.

Stack knowed that he didn't know his own strength, so when he give
one last powerful jerk and down come the ceiling and whole building he
said: "Mah goodness, I sure didn't aim to get *so* rough! Damned if I
ain't gone and made a mess for sure!"

It happened so fast it almost skeered Stack hisself.

---

[1] Cf. "Po' Laz'us" in Part Six.

It Was the Watah Pipes

Outside was more wrecks than you could shake a stick at; buildings tumblin down all over town.

"Lordy! Sure didn't know mah own strength!" Stack said to a crowd of people in the street. They tried to tell him about an earthquake, but Stack didn't pay them no mind.

"It was the watah pipes," he said. "They was all fastened together all over town. When I give that last powerful jerk, I must have pulled out a faucet in the saloon and snatched down the whole town."

Then he lit out of there for St. Louis, where he run right smack into his doom.

How Old Scratch Tricked Stackalee

You see, Stack was gettin into so much devilment that he even worried the devil, and old Satan was gettin tired waitin for Stack's soul, so he figgered out a way to trick him.

Old Scratch knowed that if Stack was killed fightin another bad man like Jesse James maybe God wouldn't let his soul go to hell. So this is the way the devil fixed it. He schemed it out to make hisself look like Billy Lyons, an innercent family man. So when Stack killed an honest family man, the Lord would be mad at him and let Satan have him.

One cold, frosty Friday night when Stack was havin one of his lucky streaks in a big coon can game down at Jack o' Diamond's place in St. Louis, he was so busy pickin up his money that he hung his oxblood Stetson on the back of his cheer. That's when Old Scratch, keepin his eye peeled, changed hisself to look like Billy Lyons. Then he snatched the magic hat and tore out toward the White Elephant Barrel House where he knowed Billy was. When the devil got to the door he disappeared. Stack came runnin up and seen Billy standin by the door, lookin as innercent as you please, smokin, and watchin the can can dancers.

And there is where Stack shot him through and through. Billy pleaded for his life, on account of his wife and babies. But Stack, mad as blue blazes because he had lost the magic hat that kept the law from ketchin him, blazed away and blasted poor Billy down.

So the wagon come loaded with pistols and a big gatlin gun and hauled Stack off to jail. But the police didn't kill him like the devil, setting outside the window in the shape of a black cat, hoped they would.

Instead, they slapped Stack into jail where the judge sent him to Jefferson Pen for 75 years. He's already served 34 of em and got 41 more to serve there yet. The devil is waitin for him to die so he can snatch his soul just like this song tells you:

It was in the year of eight-een hun—dred

and six-ty—one In St. Lou-is on Mar—ket St. where

Stack-a-lee was born. Ev' ———— ry—bo—dys'

talk-in 'bout Stack-a—lee. It was

an one cold and frost——y night When

Stack-a-lee and Bil—ly Ly—ons had one aw—ful fight,

All a-bout an old Stet—son hat

Stack-a-lee got his gun Boy, he got it fast!

He shot poor Bil—ly through and through; the

bul-let broke a look-in glass Oh, oh, Lord,

Lord, Lord Stack-a-lee shot

Bil-ly once; his bod—y fell to the floor

He cried out, "Oh, please, Stack, please don't shoot me no more,"

Oh, oh, Lord, Lord, Lord "Have

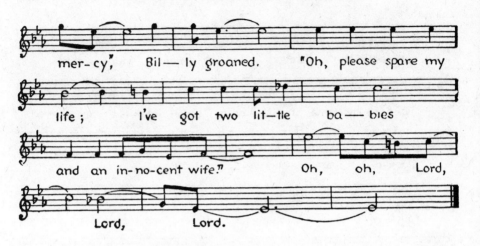

mer-cy," Bil—ly groaned.   "Oh, please spare my

life ; I've got two lit—tle ba——bies

and an in-no-cent wife."   Oh, oh, Lord,

Lord,   Lord.

It was in the year of eighteen hundred and sixty-one
In St. Louis on Market Street where Stackalee was born.
    Everybody's talkin 'bout Stackalee.[1]

It was on one cold and frosty night
When Stackalee and Billy Lyons had one awful fight,
    All about an old Stetson hat.

Stackalee got his gun. Boy, he got it fast!
He shot poor Billy through and through; the bullet broke a lookin glass.
    Oh, oh, Lord, Lord, Lord.

Stackalee shot Billy once; his body fell to the floor.
He cried out, "Oh, please, Stack, please don't shoot me no more."

The White Elephant Barrel House was wrecked that night;
Gutters full of beer and whisky; it was an awful sight.

Jewelry and rings of the purest solid gold
Scattered over the dance and gamblin hall.

---

[1] Refrain:
> Everybody's talkin 'bout Stackalee: (Use this one most.)
> That bad man Stackalee.
> Oh, tough man Stackalee.
> Oh, oh, Lord, Lord, Lord.
> All about an old Stetson hat.

For variation the following were often used:
> Oh, treacherous Stackalee.
> Oh, oh, what a shame.
> Oh, foolish Stackalee.
> Oh, scared Stackalee.
> Oh, scheming Stackalee.
> Oh, worried Stackalee.
> Oh, oh, what a lie.—O. L. S.

The can can dancers they rushed for the door
When Billy cried, "Oh, please, Stack, don't shoot me no more."

"Have mercy," Billy groaned. "Oh, please spare my life;
I've got two little babies and an innocent wife."

Stack says, "God bless your children, damn your wife!
You stole my magic Stetson; I'm gonna steal your life."

"But," says Billy, "I always treated you like a man.
'Tain't nothin to that old Stetson but the greasy band."

He shot poor Billy once, he shot him twice,
And the third time Billy pleaded, "Please go tell my wife."

Yes, Stackalee, the gambler, everybody knowed his name;
Made his livin hollerin high, low, jack and the game.

Meantime the sergeant strapped on his big forty-five,
Says, "Now we'll bring in this bad man, dead or alive."

And brass-buttoned policemen all dressed in blue
Came down the sidewalk marchin two by two.

Sent for the wagon and it hurried and come
Loaded with pistols and a big gatling gun.

At midnight on that stormy night there came an awful wail—
Billy Lyons and a graveyard ghost outside the city jail.

"Jailer, jailer," says Stack, "I can't sleep.
For around my bedside poor Billy Lyons still creeps.

"He comes in shape of a lion with a blue steel in his hand,
For he knows I'll stand and fight if he comes in shape of man."

Stackalee went to sleep that night by the city clock bell,
Dreaming the devil had come all the way up from hell.

Red devil was sayin, "You better hunt your hole;
I've hurried here from hell just to get your soul."

Stackalee told him, "Yes, maybe you're right,
But I'll give even you one hell of a fight."

When they got into the scuffle, I heard the devil shout,
"Come and get this bad man before he puts my fire out."

The next time I seed the devil he was scramblin up the wall,
Yellin, "Come an get this bad man fore he mops up with us all."[1]

---

[1] Cf. "The Farmer's Curst Wife" (Child, No. 278).

Then here come Stack's woman runnin, says, "Daddy, I love you true,
See what beer, whisky, and smokin hop has brought you to.

"But before I'll let you lay in there, I'll put my life in pawn."
She hurried and got Stackalee out on a five thousand dollar bond.

Stackalee said, "Ain't but one thing that grieves my mind.
When they take me away, babe, I leave you behind."

But the woman he really loved was a voodoo queen
From Creole French market, way down in New Orleans.

He laid down at home that night, took a good night's rest,
Arrived in court at nine o'clock to hear the coroner's inquest.

Crowds jammed the sidewalk, far as you could see,
Tryin to get a good look at tough Stackalee.

Over the cold, dead body Stackalee he did bend,
Then he turned and faced those twelve jury men.

The judge says, "Stackalee, I would spare your life,
But I know you're a bad man; I can see it in your red eyes."

The jury heard the witnesses, and they didn't say no more;
They crowded into the jury room, and the messenger closed the door.

The jury came to agreement, the clerk he wrote it down,
And everybody was whisperin, "He's penitentiary bound."

When the jury walked out, Stackalee didn't budge.
They wrapped the verdict and passed it to the judge.

Judge looked over his glasses, says, "Mr. Bad Man Stackalee,
The jury finds you guilty of murder in the first degree."

Now the trial's come to an end, how the folks gave cheers;
Bad Stackalee was sent down to Jefferson pen for seventy-five years

Now late at night you can hear him in his cell,
Arguin with the devil to keep from goin to hell.

And the other convicts whisper, "Whatcha know about that?
Gonna burn in hell forever over an old Stetson hat!"
Everybody's talkin 'bout Stackalee.

IV. FREE LANCES

Pioneers, or frontiersmen, are a class of men peculiar to our country, and seem to have been designed especially to meet the exigencies of the occasion.—JOHN C. DUVAL

1. ROY BEAN

THE thin and shifting line that separated law enforcement from law-breaking in the West permitted not only a peace officer like Wild Bill to become known as a "killer" but also a comic scalawag like Roy Bean to become known as the "Law West of the Pecos." A Kentuckian by birth, he counted the art of bluff as part of his backwoods heritage; and in his late fifties, after knocking about California, New Mexico, and Texas, playing for small stakes as adventurer and jack-of-all-trades—saloon-keeper, ranger, bull-whacker, blockade-runner, wood merchant—he gave up fortune-hunting and sought the limelight. In the lawless waste of the Trans-Pecos country he followed the construction of a new line on the Southern Pacific Railroad as camp saloon-keeper, first at Vinegarroon and then at Langtry, where in 1883 the tracks were joined and Bean moved in as a squatter on the railroad right of way. With some 8,000 workers on their hands, the railroad contractors learned the truth of the saying that "West of the Pecos there is no law" and called in the Texas Rangers to help counteract crime. On August 2, 1882, Roy Bean got himself appointed justice of the peace, on a hunch that it might be doubly profitable to preside over both the barroom and the bar of justice. From then until his death in 1903, he held court in the "Jersey Lily" saloon, named, like the town, for the English actress, whom Bean never met but who visited the place after his death.

The judge who specialized in finable cases and kept most of the fines was not uncommon in the West,[1] but Roy Bean was the most famous example of the type. In fact, even during his lifetime his legend reached such proportions that his brother Sam wrote of him:

You may have graduated at Yale or Harvard and carry a number of diplomas, but if you have not seen or heard of Judge Roy Bean of Texas you are groping in darkness and there yet remains a large space to be filled in your classical head.[2]

There was plenty of precedent for Roy Bean in the usual Western "Law" or sheriff, who was "judge, jury, and executioner" all in one, and in frontier vigilantism. In fact, he had had first-hand knowledge of the latter when he narrowly escaped from hanging for killing a rival in a love affair in California. And the many anecdotes of his shady business dealings before he became the "Law West of the Pecos" testify to the native shrewdness and bluster which enabled him to dispose of cases in his own way. At any

---

[1] Compare Justice of the Peace Jim Burnett of Charleston, Arizona, in *Tombstone*, by Walter Noble Burns.

[2] *Roy Bean, Law West of the Pecos*, by C. L. Sonnichsen (1943), p. 46.

rate, the red rope-burn that he wore about his permanently stiff neck, usually hidden by a bandana, was his only diploma, and his only law book was the *Revised Statutes of Texas* for 1876. But he inspired respect for the law with his two six-shooters and such bizarre punishments as the use of the bear-and-stake method for sobering up drunks, while the stories of his weird decisions and judgments entertained the newspaper public and have become classics of the Southwest bench and bar. In his comic rôle of fining-judge Roy Bean rivals the famous "hanging judge" of Fort Smith, Arkansas, Isaac C. Parker.

"Hear ye! Hear ye! This honorable court is now in session, and if anybody wants a snort before we start step up to the bar and name your poison."

"It is the judgment of this court that you are hereby tried and convicted of illegally and unlawfully committing certain grave offences against the peace and dignity of the State of Texas, particularly in my bailiwick, to wit: drunk and disorderly, and being Law West of the Pecos, I fine you two dollars; then get the hell out of here and never show yourself in this court again." [1]

2. BUFFALO BILL

In the same year that Roy Bean was appointed justice of the peace, another masterpiece of showmanship was being created. This was the Wild West, Rocky Mountain, and Prairie Exhibition, which opened at Omaha, Nebraska, on May 17, 1883, and its star, Buffalo Bill. Of all the types of showmen produced by the "histrionic West," none was more characteristic than the "professional Westerner," in long hair and fringed buckskins. For this rôle no one was more perfectly cast than William F. Cody, born on a farm in Scott County, Iowa, in 1846, who was endowed by nature and experience to be the epitome of all that was "high, wide, and handsome" in the Old West. Having lived all his life on the plains, in almost every capacity—"herder, hunter, pony express rider, stage driver, wagon master in the quartermaster's department, and scout of the army," to quote his press agent—and finding all Indian wars fought and himself out of a job in 1869, at the age of 26 Buffalo Bill discovered his true mission. As a buffalo hunter employed by the Kansas Pacific to supply meat to construction crews, he had won his name, killing 4,280 buffalo in one year. Always something of a show-off, he now took to performing stunts of horsemanship and marksmanship and fell in with the promotion schemes of James Gordon Bennett, editor of the New York *Herald*, who had employed him as a guide on a hunting trip, and Ned Buntline (E. Z. C. Judson), the author.

In February, 1872 Buffalo Bill came to New York at Bennett's expense for the opening of Fred G. Maeder's play, inspired by Buntline, *Buffalo Bill, the King of Bordermen*, taking a bow before the audience; and in December of the same year he made his first stage appearance in Chicago in Buntline's *The Scouts of the Prairie*. Ned Buntline, from who Buffalo Bill parted after his first theatrical success, was only the first of the four creators of Buffalo Bill. The second was Major John M. Burke, the

[1] *Law West of the Pecos*, The Story of Roy Bean, by Everett Lloyd (1936), pp. 74–75, 66–67.

world's greatest press agent, who publicized Buffalo Bill's duel with Yellow Hand in 1876 and was publicity man of his "Wild West," which Nat Salsbury, who was Number Three, suggested. The fourth was Prentiss Ingraham, author of over two hundred dime novels about Buffalo Bill. In this way, "Unlike those popular heroes who grow in folklore fortuitously, Buffalo Bill was the subject of the deliberate and infinitely skilful use of publicity." [1]

Although Buffalo Bill lived to see himself and the Wild West show outmoded, as he had once seen the passing of the Old West, the legend of the West, which was partly his creation as he in turn was its creature, still lives in Western pulp-paper magazines and movies and in the hearts of Americans.

3. BIG-FOOT WALLACE

Your true Western original was an unassuming fellow, free from sham heroics, who, though six feet two in his moccasin feet, and head and shoulders above the rest as fighter and story-teller, was yet "guileless and unsuspicious as a child, and whenever . . . in conflict with the shrewd, calculating man of business, . . . as helpless as a 'stranded whale.'" This is the stuff of which "provincial heroes" are made; and such was William A. ("Big-Foot"[2]) Wallace, born in Virginia, in 1816, and noted as a Texas scout and ranger. Like Buffalo Bill, he lived through the cycle of the West and saw the frontier pass; and although he would not have presumed to say with the former, "I stood between savagery and civilization most all my early days," in his later days, when he went back East for a visit, he was perfectly capable of seeing the humor of the "savagery" of civilization. *The Adventures of Big-Foot Wallace*, by John C. Duval, "first Texas man of letters," who served with Big-Foot in Jack Hays' company of Texas Rangers, is the result of a happy collaboration between a provincial hero and a provincial writer. "Always free and at home with himself," writes J. Frank Dobie,[3] "Big-Foot seems to have opened up to Duval with utmost gusto; and Duval took the bridle off him, slapped his rump with his reins and told him to hist his heels to heaven." Although the two are pretty well mixed, "Duval emerges an artist, and Big-Foot emerges robust, as natural as daylight, and as 'red-blooded' as a maverick yearling. . . . By virtue of Duval's narrative he remains the saltiest, rollickiest, most genial, most individualistic pioneer Indian fighter, Mexican layer-out, and lone-wolf dweller of the open range that Texas has ever had."

In the last portion of the book the lone-wolf character of Big-Foot is seen at its best by contrast with the settlements and with his "fish out of water" experience on the farm, proving that "You can take the boy out of the wilderness but you can't take the wilderness out of him" and that "innocence abroad" is still one of the best devices of satire.

---

[1] *The Making of Buffalo Bill*, A Study in Heroics, by Richard J. Walsh in collaboration with Milton S. Salsbury (1928), p. v.

[2] The town of Big Foot in Frio County, Texas, is named for him.

[3] "John C. Duval: First Texas Man of Letters," by J. Frank Dobie, *Southwest Review*, XXIV (April, 1939), No. 3, pp. 277–278.

Roy Bean, Law West of the Pecos

I. ROY BEAN

Cowboys, come and hear the story of Roy Bean in all his glory,
  "All the law west of the Pecos," read his sign;
We must let our ponies take us to a town on lower Pecos
  Where the High Bridge spans the cañon thin and fine.

He was born one day near Toyah, where he learned to be a lawyer,
  And a teacher and a barber and the Mayor.
He was cook and old-shoe mender, sometimes preacher and bartender,
  And it cost two bits to have him cut your hair.

He was right smart of a hustler, and considerable a rustler,
  And at mixing up an eggnog he was grand;
He was clever, he was merry, he could drink a Tom and Jerry,
  On occasion at a round-up took a hand.

Though the story isn't funny, there was once he had no money,
  Which was for him not very strange or rare;
So he went to help Pap Wyndid, but he got so absent-minded
  That he put his R.B brand on old Pap's steer.

As Pap was right smart angry, old Roy Bean went down to Langtry,
  Where he opened up an office and a store.
There he'd sell you drinks or buttons, or another rancher's muttons,
  'Though the latter made the other feller sore.

Once there came from Austin City a young dude reported witty,
  Out of Bean he sort of guessed he'd take a rise;
And he got unusual frisky as he up and called for whisky,
  Sayin', "Bean, now hurry up, goldurn your eyes."

Then a-down he threw ten dollars, which the same Roy quickly collars,
  Then the same Roy holds to nine and hands back one;
So the stranger gave a holler, as he saw that single dollar,
  And at that began the merriment and fun.

The dude he slammed the table just as hard as he was able,
  That the price of whisky was too high, he swore.
Said Roy Bean, "For all that fussin' and your most outrageous cussin'
  You are fined the other dollar by the law.

From *Frontier Ballads,* heard and gathered by Charles J. Finger, pp. 133–136. Copyright, 1927, by Doubleday, Page & Company. Garden City, New York.
The tune used was an adaptation of part of "Tramp, Tramp, Tramp, the Boys Are Marching" but without the chorus!—C. J. F.

"On this place I own a lease, sir, I'm the Justice of the Peace, sir.
    The law west of the Pecos all is here,
And you've acted very badly." Then the dude he went off sadly
    While down his lily cheek there rolled a tear.

One fine day they found a dead man who in life had been a redman,
    So it's doubtless he was nothing else than bad.
They called Bean to view the body, first he took a drink of toddy,
    Then he listed all the things the dead man had.

For a redman he was tony, for he had a pretty pony,
    And a dandy bit and saddle and a rope;
He'd a fine Navajo rug and a quart within his jug
    And a broncho that was dandy on the lope.

So the find it was quite rare-O, for he'd been a "cocinero," [1]
    And his pay day hadn't been so far away.
He'd a bran'-new fine white Stetson and a silver Smith and Wesson,
    While a purse of forty dollars jingled gay.

Said Roy Bean, "You'll learn a lesson, for you have a Smith and Wesson,
    And to carry implements of war is very wrong.
Forty dollars I will fine you, for we couldn't well confine you,
    As already you've been laying round too long."

So you boys have heard the story of Roy Bean in all his glory,
    He's the man who was the Justice and the Law;
He was handy with his hooks, he was orn'ry in his looks,
    And just now I ain't a-telling any more.

NOTE: The striking events related will carry this song to a successful end
    no matter how it be sung.——C. J. F.

II. NECKTIE JUSTICE

"Hear ye! Hear ye! This honorable court's now in session; and if any
galoot wants a snort afore we start, let him step up to the bar and name
his pizen. Oscar, serve the gentlemen." Thus did Judge Bean open court
to try one Carlos Robles, an opening typical of his original procedure.

"Carlos Robles," he said solemnly after witnesses and hangers-on had
downed their liquor, "it is the findin' of this court that you are charged
with a grave offense against the peace and dignity of the law West of the
Pecos and the State of Texas, to wit: cattle-rustlin'. Guilty or not guilty?"

Not being able to speak or comprehend English, Robles merely grunted.

"Court accepts yore plea of guilt. The jury will now deliberate; and if

From *Vinegarroon*, The Saga of Judge Roy Bean, "Law West of the Pecos," by
Ruel McDaniel, pp. 83–89. Copyright, 1936, by Ruel McDaniel. Kingsport, Tenn.:
Southern Publishers.
[1] A cook.

it brings a verdict short of hangin' it'll be declared in contempt. Gentlemen, is yore verdict ready?"

The twelve nondescript citizens cleared their throats in unison. "It is,
your honor," several spoke.

"Thank you, gentlemen. Stand up, Carlos Robles, and receive yore
sentence. You got anything to say why judgment shouldn't be passed on
you in this court?"

Of course Carlos had not, in view of the fact that he had only the
vaguest idea of what was transpiring.

"Carlos Robles," Judge Roy continued, his voice almost quaking with
the solemnity of the occasion, "you been tried by twelve true and good
men, not men of yore peers, but as high above you as heaven is of hell;
and they've said you're guilty of rustlin' cattle.

"Time will pass and seasons will come and go; Spring with its wavin'
green grass and heaps of sweet-smellin' flowers on every hill and in every
dale. Then will come sultry Summer, with her shimmerin' heat-waves
on the baked horizon; and Fall, with her yeller harvest-moon and the
hills growin' brown and golden under a sinkin' sun; and finally Winter,
with its bitin', whinin' wind, and all the land will be mantled with snow.
But you won't be here to see any of 'em, Carlos Robles; not by a dam'
sight, because it's the order of this court that you be took to the nearest
tree and hanged by the neck till you're dead, dead, dead, you olive-colored
son-of-a-billy-goat!" [1]

The Law West of the Pecos could be cruel in administering his brand
of justice; but he was cruel only when he deemed the accused and the
crime fully warranting such cruelty. He more frequently tempered justice
with his own peculiar brand of mercy, especially if there was any means
by which he could profit by that mercy.

One afternoon several ranchmen brought in a twenty-year old boy
accused of horse-stealing. They demanded that he be tried and dealt
with according to the enormity of the crime.

Judge Bean duly opened court. He appointed six men as jurors, the
actual number meaning nothing to him and depending entirely upon men
available. He would not appoint just any citizens to jury duty. They
must be good customers of the liquor bar at the other end of the shack
during intermissions, or their services as jurors no longer were desirable
or acceptable. Every transaction must be made to return the utmost in
profit, and non-drinking jurors were strictly dead timber.

"Hear ye! This honorable court is again in session. Anyone wishin'
a snort, have it now. This here prisoner is charged with the grave offense
of stealin' a horse and Oscar, where are the witnesses?" the Law West of
the Pecos opened. He appreciated his own sense of humor in varying his

---

[1] This rhetorical or mock-rhetorical address to a condemned prisoner has been attributed to other Western jurists, notably, Judge Parker ("The Hanging Judge") of
Fort Smith and Judge Benedict of Santa Fe, whose versions are given on pp. 147–150.

court openings to relieve the monotony; but he seldom varied to the extent of omitting the invitation to participate in a snort at the other bar.

"We caught him in the act of stealin' the animal," the ranchman testified. "He admitted his intentions."

"That right, young feller? You was stealin' the cayuse?"

The young prisoner dropped his head, unruly red hair tumbling down over his high forehead. "Yes, your honor," he mumbled.

"Gentlemen of the jury," His Honor instructed, "the accused pleads guilty to horse theft. You know as well as I do the penalty. I'm ready for yore verdict." And it was promptly forthcoming.

Gravely the judge passed sentence. "If there's any last word, or any-thing, I'll give you a few minutes," he told the pale Easterner, thus ex-tending an infrequent favor.

"I would like to write a note—to my mother back in Pennsylvania," the doomed prisoner mumbled with obvious emotion. "Thank you."

"Oscar, fetch the prisoner a piece of wrappin' paper and a pencil. I think we got a pencil back there behind that row of bottles." Bean gently handed the convicted thief these writing facilities, got up and tendered him the beer barrel and rickety table from which sentence had just been passed. Then he took a position directly behind the boy so that he could watch over his shoulder at what he wrote.

The victim wrote at length in apology for the grief and trouble he had caused his mother and earnestly sought her forgiveness. "In small part perhaps I can repay you for the money I have cost you in keeping me out of trouble. Enclosed is $400, which I've saved. I want you—."

Judge Bean started, cleared his throat, cut in at this point. "By gobs!" he exclaimed, "gentlemen, I got a feelin' there's been a miscarriage of justice, in this case. I hereby declare it re-opened. Face the bar, young man."

The prisoner removed himself from the beer keg and stood erect in front of the judicial bench, befuddled at this sudden turn.

"After all, that wasn't much of a cayuse the lad tried to steal; and he didn't actually steal him. So I rule it's a finable case. I hereby fine the accused three hundred dollars and get to hell outer this country afore I change my mind!"

The boy gladly enough paid three hundred of his four hundred dollars and assured the court that the next setting sun would find his brow well beyond El Rio Pecos.

Practically every cattleman and law-abiding citizen of the Bean bailiwick had an indefinite appointment as deputy constable to the Law West of the Pecos. Thus any citizen who apprehended any person in the act of com-mitting a crime or suspected any of crime had authority to bring him on forthwith for trial. Bean consistently encouraged such co-operation, for the more business they brought before the court, the greater the financial returns for the whole establishment. Naturally it was understood that such arresting constables did not in any manner participate in the fee accruing from such cases created by them. This doubtless was the only justice court in the State of Texas wherein only one official received all fees collected by the office.

Under authority as deputy constable, Reb Wise, Pecos rancher, brought in a cattle rustler on a hot August afternoon when business at the refreshment counter was exceptionally brisk. It was all both Roy and Oscar could do to handle the trade. Consequently Bean looked up with sour expression when Deputy Constable Wise approached the bar and informed the judge that a prisoner was awaiting attention at the bar of justice.

"What's he charged with, Reb?" Roy asked, opening another foaming bottle of Triple-X beer.

"Cattle-rustlin', yuhr honor," Reb replied.

"Whose cattle?"

"Mine."

"You positive he's guilty, Reb?"

"Positive? Say, Judge, I caught him with a runnin' iron on one of my finest calves!" the rancher replied with emphasis.

For the first time Roy glanced up at the scowling prisoner. He noticed blood dripping from his left ear. "Who plugged his ear?" he inquired.

"I did, yuhr honor, when he wouldn't stop."

"You ought'n shot at his head, Reb. You could 'a' killed him; and that would 'a' been bad, because he wouldn't have been saved for the punishment he deserves. You real shore he's guilty?"

"Didn't I say, Judge, I caught him runnin' a brand on my stuff?"

"All right then," the judge said. "What'll it be for you, feller?" to a newcomer at the bar, ". . . All right then. The court finds the accused guilty as charged; and as there ain't no worse punishment I know of right handy, I hereby sentence him to be hung. Reb, I'm busy's hell here. You and some of yore compadres take him out and tie his neck to some handy limb—some place where his cronies'll be positive to see him; and that's my rulin'. Court's adjourned and what'll it be for you down there, Slim?"

A VARIANT

"What is the prisoner charged with?" Roy Bean asked.

"Stealing horses."

"Whose horses?"

"Mine."

"You sure about it?"

"Caught him at it."

"Who nicked his ear?"

"I did when he didn't stop."

From "Roy Bean: Law West of the Pecos," by Myron W. Tracy, *Straight Texas*, Publications of the Texas Folk-Lore Society, Number XIII, edited by J. Frank Dobie and Mody C. Boatright, pp. 114–115. Copyright, 1937, by the Texas Folk-Lore Society. Austin.

"Poor shot, Jack, but if you had got him he would not have been properly finished as becoming a horse thief. It's my ruling that the prisoner is guilty. The rest is your business, Jack. You'd better buy him a drink before you string him up. Court is adjourned."

"The next prisoner I took before Judge Bean," said the sheriff, "was a man that everybody had for a long time known to be a rustler but that nobody had been able to pin the evidence down on.

" 'What is this galoot charged with?' asked the judge.

" 'Running stolen cattle across the Rio Grande down at Painted Cave.'

" 'Sure this is the man?'

" 'Caught him in the middle of the ford driving the cattle.'

" 'Then what did you bring him here fer when I am so busy? In a case like that always give the galoot what he deserves. Take him away and string him up.'

"Then turning to a line of men at the bar who had been listening, Roy Bean asked, 'Well, boys, what are you going to have?' "

III. Roy Bean, Coroner

The story that everybody knows about Roy Bean the coroner comes from another bridge accident which happened a little earlier than this.

It was a Sunday afternoon in February, 1892. A number of bridge carpenters from the Pecos project had come up to pass the day at the Jersey Lily, among them a quiet fellow named Pat O'Brien who didn't care much for the carousing and hell raising that was going on. Towards evening he decided to take a walk. There were no shady lanes or pasture paths in those parts so he started off down the railroad tracks, a smile on his face and a six-shooter in his hip pocket. Why he wanted the weapon is not clear. Maybe he was from the East. Easterners were more careful about this article of dress than native Texans.

When he got to the Myers Canyon bridge, three miles east of Langtry, a heavy wind was blowing as usual down the draw, and one gust was strong enough to take him off his feet and land him at the bottom where the

From *Roy Bean, Law West of the Pecos,* by C. L. Sonnichsen, pp. 126–128, 154, 119--123, 168–173. Copyright, 1943, by C. L. Sonnichsen. New York: The Macmillan Company.

The best known stories about Bean's decisions and judgments as a justice of peace were current during his lifetime. He was ready to confirm virtually all of them, but when I asked him about fining a dead man for carrying a six-shooter, he said that story was not true. It was probably occasioned by the way he disposed of a Mexican who had been killed in a shooting scrape at Painted Cave. His daughters told me and Billy Miller that they were with their father when he examined the dead man, finding ten dollars in his pocket and a six-shooter, four empty cartridges in it, still in his hand. Bean appropriated both the gun and the money, remarking to the girls at the same time that, "These greasers are poor shots. They waste a lot of good ammunition. Anyhow, there's no sense in this ten dollars' going to waste."—"Roy Bean: Law West of the Pecos," by Myron W. Tracy, *op. cit.,* p. 113.

sharp rocks ended his career. Section workers and track walkers were always very careful when they crossed this bridge, but the stranger never suspected his danger until it was too late.

That evening he was found and Roy was notified. He and Jim King (now Del Rio) went out in a buckboard, brought the body back, and laid it out on the table in the saloon. Nobody knew who the man was beyond his name, so they searched him for identification and in so doing found the six-shooter and forty dollars.

"Now," said Coroner Bean, "I've got to bury this poor devil and it's hard digging in these rocks. I hereby fine this defendant forty dollars for carrying concealed weapons."

Turning to Jim King he added, "Don't you think that's the way to handle it, Jimmy?" Jimmy thought so, and Roy had no idea that he had made a historic decision, but one man told another and pretty soon Texas was chuckling again at Roy Bean's way of conducting his business. The San Antonio *Express* got hold of the story of Roy's verdict in March and passed it on to the world.

"Gentlemen," said Roy to the jury and onlookers, "there is nothing to find out how that man came to his death. He fell from the bridge and that's all there is about it. But there is one thing that is not so plain, and that is what was he doing with that gun? Of course he is dead and can't explain, but that ain't the fault of the law; it's his own misfortune. Justice is justice, and law is law, and as he can't offer no satisfactory explanation of the matter I shall be obliged to fine him forty dollars for carrying on or about his person that pistol. Because a man chooses to put on a pair of wings is no reason why the great State of Texas should not have what is coming to her all the same."

IV. JUDGE ROY BEAN AGAIN

A man came to Roy once and says to him, Judge I have found a good place for a Hog Ranch down the River here and I want to go into the business. I think it will be a paying enterprise and as you have more money than I have, you can advance the necessary funds to set the scheme on foot. Very well, says Roy, I am always willing to go into anything that there is any money in. Enough said, the Hog Ranch was established, and it flourished for about two years, but Roy was not receiving any profits from the Ranch. Hitherto it had all been unlimited expenditure without results and Roy proposed to his partner to have a dissolution of partnership. But he objected and the Ranch had to wag along in the same old way. Roy wanted to bring suit against him, but there was no other court or authority except his own and what was he to do. Finally after a deep study an Idea struck him and he says now I have it, I will sue him before myself. He issued a citation for his partner who made his appearance in court. Roy made a speech in his own behalf and testified in the case while his partner viewed the proceedings with silent amazement

and had but little to say. The decision of the court in this case is briefly
this the Plaintiff who is the court itself will take one half the Hogs and
the other half the constable will sell at public auction to pay the damages
suffered by this Plaintiff and the cost of suit.

SAMUEL G. BEAN
Las Cruces

V. ROY BEAN AND THE CHINAMAN

It is time now to talk about Roy Bean's affair with the Chinaman.
The earliest and shortest version of the story appeared in the El Paso
Daily Times for June 2, 1884.

Here is the latest on Roy Bean:
Somebody killed a Chinaman and was brought up standing before the
irrepressible Roy, who looked through two or three dilapidated law books
from stem to stern, and finally turned the culprit loose remarking that
he'd be d—d if he could find any law against killing a Chinaman.

That is the core of what has become, after fifty years, one of the best
known anecdotes ever to come out of the Southwest. The time must have
been about the beginning of 1883 (the ends of track were joined in
January). From the west hundreds of Chinese laborers were building.
From the east came the Irish and other brawny sons of Europe. The
white laborers hated the Chinese for their willingness to work for low
wages, their saving ways, their squeaking gibberish, and their love of
peace. More killings than one occurred when the gangs from east and
west got close enough to rub elbows and cut throats, and there were many
narrow escapes. For example take the night in 1882 when the Irish, who
had built almost to the east side of the Pecos, got involved in a celebration,
and decided their lives would be wasted unless they crossed over to where
the Chinese were camped on the west bank and cut off a few pigtails.
They knew that a Chinaman did not like to fight and would not fight
under ordinary provocation, but would give a satisfactory performance
if his pigtail were cut off. So these drunk and joyful Irishmen organized
themselves and were all ready to start out when the foreman interfered
and averted a race riot by a very slim margin.

Even so, many Chinamen lost their lives by one means or another and
were buried where they fell. Later the bones of many of them were collected
and sent back to the west coast by Chinese friends who came in for the
purpose.

Usually the Americans concerned themselves very little about whether
a Chinaman lived or died, but somehow the historic case under discussion
was brought to Roy Bean for judgment and he turned the Irishman loose,
as most Americans in West Texas would have been glad of an excuse to
do. On account of the feeling between the Chinese and the other laborers

it would have been easy to start a race riot just then, and Roy knew it. Besides, as he once said, there were about two hundred of the toughest white men in the world around the saloon and they might have lynched him if he hadn't let the Irishman go free. His decision was merely his own peculiar way of preserving law and order, at the same time protecting the health of Judge Bean, but the ruling had the real gamy Western tang and stuck in men's minds. The story not merely lived; it grew. By 1899 it was getting into the newspaper exchanges this way:

At Langtry, Tex., says the San Francisco Wave, Squire Roy Bean, who administers justice and keeps the leading saloon, had to sit in judgment on a railroad clerk who had killed Ah Ling, a laundry man for, as he claimed, insulting him. The man was arrested and brought before magistrate Bean, who listened to the evidence, which was given by the accused himself, and then proceeded to turn the pages of the revised statutes: "This here book, which is a Texas law book," he announced, "says that hommyside is th' killin' of a human, male ur female. They is many kinds of hommyside—murder, manslaughter, plain hommyside, negl'gent hommyside, justifi'ble hommyside an' praiseworthy hommyside. They is three kinds of humans—white men, niggers, and Mexicans. It stan's to reason thet if a Chinym'n was human, killin' of him would come under th' head of praiseworthy hommyside. The pris'ner is discharged on condition that he pays f'r havin' th' Chinee buried."

In print and out of print the story went around, gathering details and variations. In the last ten years it has been reprinted a dozen times, and every fresh book about the old days in the Southwest tells it a new way. In 1934, F. H. Bushick put out this version in his book *Glamorous Days:*

Some cavalry soldier in passing through that way, it was thought, had lost his sabre. One of the bridge gang found it. When it was brought into camp nobody wanted the old corn cutter except this Irishman who took a shine to it because he had once been a soldier himself. He ground up the old blade and kept it as a handy weapon, he being a storekeeper of iron supplies, a responsible sort of job.

This Irishman was in the habit of now and then stealing a pie from the cook. The chink got to missing his pies and finally lay for the Irishman and caught him red handed. Armed with a big butcher knife, the Chink attacked the Irishman, who ran and got his old sabre and returned to the fray. He made just one pass at the chink with his sabre and cut off his head as clean as if the Lord High Executioner of China had done the job.

A ranger arrested the Irishman and took him before Judge Bean.

The most remarkable variation of all appeared in 1931 in Tom Rynning's book *Gun Notches.* Tom was an old cavalry man and peace officer who knew Roy, and this is the way he tells it:

Once Roy's son shot and killed a Chinaman because he charged too much for his laundry or something serious like that, and of course young Bean was tried before his old man. Naturally Roy wanted to give his boy as easy a deal as the law would allow, but he was a square-shooter and if his son turned out guilty of a misdemeanor or anything like that, it was a cinch he'd wrap it to him just like he was a stranger.

So the judge opened court with the usual formalities, throwing out a couple of drunks who wouldn't quit snoring during the proceedings, and started the justice mill to grinding. On account of his own kin being up for trial, and all the customers watching him more interested than usual, he went about things mighty careful and legal-like.

As a rule he give his decisions right out of his deep knowledge of the law, for he'd been a J. P. for a year or more then; but this time he figured he had to dig into the Unabridged Statutes of 1846, or somewheres round that date.

He hooked his spectacles onto his handsome big red nose and begun reading the law book out loud so's everybody could see he wasn't keeping any ace in the hole. And damned if he didn't read those Texas statutes from cover to cover, cussing every cowpuncher awake that went to sleep on him and refusing to let any of them go to the bar for a drink during that long spell of court.

When he'd waded plumb through the Texas law from murder to cow brands, in about two hours or so, those cowpunchers and rustlers had got a darned sight more legal knowledge screwed into their skulls than lots of the tin-horn lawyers of the state ever knew. In fact, they was a plumb nuisance after that, some of them spouting their information about Texas law by the hour every time they got drunked up and could get some unfortunate dogie to stand hitched long enough to pour it into him by the gallon.

"And there she is, gentlemen," says Roy Bean, when he'd got through. "That's the full unexpurgated law of the great State of Texas up to 1873, and it ain't noways likely there's been any fundamental changes run into since.

"The complete statutes of this here state from the Alamo on ahead, and there ain't a damned line in it nowheres that makes it illegal to kill a Chinaman. The defendant is discharged."

You can ask anybody over forty in West Texas, and many a man under forty, if he knows anything about Roy Bean, and you will get another edition of this same tale. It is already a part of American folklore.

The man who shot the Chinaman and started all this story-telling may still be alive. Uncle Bill Jones, who has kept a bar at Reserve, New Mexico, since 1886, says he is, and Uncle Bill was at Langtry when the trial happened. Bill doesn't think he should talk too much about the man, however. "I am not permitted to tell his name," he says. "The last time I heard of him he was tending bar. He is a pleasant sort of person and very agreeable."

Well, people do change!

VI. BEAN'S BEAR

It would be too bad if old Bruno couldn't have a chapter, considering how much Roy thought of him and how bad he felt when Bruno was—well, we might say murdered.

As far back as anybody can remember, Bruno was there—fat, fractious, and full grown. Other bears came and went, but it looked as if Bruno might go on indefinitely. Roy had a cage for him but never thought of asking him to stay in it. Most of the day he was attached to a corner post on the porch by a chain long enough to allow for a little circulation. The rest of the time he was fastened to a post midway between the tracks and the saloon.

He and Roy got along fine, for they had similar views on a good many of life's problems. They were both rugged souls who put up with no nonsense, and at the same time they liked to get friendly and relax with the right people. They were both acquisitive and anxious to pick up anything that came their way (the bear specialized in pullets). Both were also apt to be a bit of a shock to people who were unprepared for Beans or bears.

One day a tramp got off a freight train at Langtry and made a bee line for the well known charity of the Jersey Lily. Roy was ruminating on his porch and heard the hobo's plea.

"Go on around behind the saloon," he said, "and knock on the door. They'll give you something."

Joyfully the man skipped around the corner. Six seconds later he came tearing back in a mad scramble, eyes popping, face pale, coat missing.

"What in hell's going on here?" demanded Roy, startled out of his massive calm.

"There's a b-b-bear around there!" gibbered the frightened tramp.

A glance around the corner revealed the bear on his hind legs holding the tramp's coat and wondering what to do next. The man had run smack into him, and Bruno too was suffering from shock.

Naturally, being the Law West of the Pecos, Roy assumed the right of putting everybody else to work, and that went for Bruno. One of the bear's jobs was to assist the Judge in carrying out the mandates of the law.

It was in 1892 that a Mexican woman came to Roy for help (all the Mexicans regarded him with awe) when her husband went on a high-speed non-stop spree. Roy was sitting on his gallery with his son Sam, his constable Phil Forrest, and his friend M. W. Tracy (who tells the tale). The woman recited her sorrows with drama and pathos and Roy was much moved.

"Phil," he said, "you will find this woman's man down near Pedro's shack dead drunk. Bring him in here and look out for his knife. Sam, get that chain and lock in the back room."

In a little while Phil returned with the husband who was about as drunk and disorderly as a man might be. He could hardly hiccup an answer to the questions which were put to him. Finally Roy had him taken out and hitched by the chain to the post in front of the saloon. Then the bear was led over and padlocked to the same post, his chain being a little shorter than the one attached to the man.

Still too drunk to care about anything, the Mexican watched indifferently as the bear ambled up, drew back a paw, and slapped him into a somersault. Surprise and terror dawned upon the man's face as he rolled to the end of his chain to get out of the bear's reach. In the next half hour he sweated a week's supply of alcohol out of himself playing hide and seek with old Bruno, who was having a very happy time. When he was completely sobered up and ready to be brought before the seat of justice, Judge Bean handed down a decision. The woman was to have the family burro and household effects; the man was to have fifteen minutes to get out of town.

Roy told Tracy that the bear-and-stake method was frequently used for sobering up drunks.

That was one of Bruno's minor jobs, however. His real purpose in life was to help Roy Bean sell booze. Somehow or other he learned to like beer and became as conscientious a drinker as his master. All he asked was that somebody should loosen up the cork for him. He knew how to do everything else. He would catch a bottle that was thrown to him, get the cork out with his teeth, sit down contentedly, and tip her up. Of course people were always willing to buy a bottle of beer just to see the bear pour it down, and sometimes, along about train time, Roy would provide his pet with a free bottle so that passengers on the train would see, visit, and absorb.

Once the bear is supposed to have got drunk, broken loose, and run the Judge off into the brush, but that story is too good to be true. Bruno sometimes took offense at invasions of his personal liberty, but it was careless strangers who suffered for their rash acts. He did put a brakeman up on top of a box car one time, but he didn't mean any harm.

The brotherly relationship between Roy and his bear was really a beautiful thing, but like all beautiful things it had to end. Without realizing what he was doing Roy committed an act which made bare bones and bear skin out of Bruno.

The seed was sown when a whisky salesman for Hugo Schmelzer dropped in for a routine call. Some say his name was Sam Betters and some say his name was something else, but Sam Betters will do. Like all the other liquor salesmen he expected to be soaked when he visited the Jersey Lily, so he bought drinks for the crowd (including Bruno), saw half a dozen empties counted slyly in with the bottles he had really bought, and prepared to pay more than he really owed. Down deep in his pocket he fished for change and brought up nothing but a twenty-dollar bill— new, crisp, and noisy. It made Roy's eyes bulge and his mouth water.

He put it tenderly into his cash drawer, got a far-away look in his eyes, and seemed to forget the world around him.

The whisky salesman finally said, "Judge, don't I get any change out of that bill?"

"The only change you got coming around here is a change of heart," said the Judge, "and by God you need it."

About that time the train whistled and the drummer went out on the run, pausing only to shake his fist at the bear who was still consuming his free bottle of suds.

A few weeks later he got his chance for revenge. Dave McCormick, who still lives in San Antonio, happened on Roy Bean in the barroom of the Menger Hotel. They coasted over to the bar and bent an elbow.

About that time the whisky salesman came in and joined the party. They all bent elbows together.

"Where you been?" inquired Roy.

"El Paso," said the drummer.

"Did you stop in my town?"

"Sure did."

"Everything all right there?"

"Fine."

They bent elbows again.

"Oh, I forgot to tell you," said the salesman, "Bruno is dead."

"The hell you say!" Roy was deeply shocked.

"You remember you told me I could have the hide. Is your word good on that?"

"By God, you never heard of Roy Bean not making his word good, did you?"

"Well, will you sign a telegram to Sam and tell him to ship the hide to me?"

"Yes, by God!" boomed Roy. So a telegram was written out on the bar of the Menger Hotel to this effect:

> Sam Bean
> Langtry, Texas
> Skin Bruno and ship hide to Sam Betters at San Antonio.
> Roy Bean.

When the telegram arrived Sam was much puzzled. He knew of no reason for sacrificing one of the family in this way, but he was an obedient son. He put two charges of buckshot between the bear's ribs and did as he was told.

Next day Roy came home and the first thing he asked was, "What did Bruno die of?"

"Of buckshot," replied Sam. "Naturally."

"You mean you killed him?" asked Roy, stunned.

"Sure."

"Why in hell did you do that?"

"I couldn't skin him alive, could I?"

That was the only time Roy's friends ever saw him mad enough to kill anybody. Fortunately he didn't see the whisky drummer again till he had cooled off, so there was no bloodshed.

In 1896 when the big fight was run off at Langtry the bear was only a memory. A mangy mountain lion occupied the historic cage and snarled at the fight fans who looked at him.

Bears came and went around the Jersey Lily after that, but none of them could get a grip on Roy's affections. There were a couple of cubs with no personality or gumption. There was also one full-grown specimen who looked all right but soon showed signs of a nasty disposition. He clawed his chain, frightened children, and once broke the neck of a burro with a single blow of his paw. Everybody wondered what would happen if he ever got loose, and he very kindly satisfied this curiosity one day by breaking his chain and taking after his owner. The Judge dodged, ducked, and yelled for Mr. Trent, who seized his gun and solved the problem with buckshot.

After that Roy gave up trying to fill the vacant cage. Bruno had no successor.

VII. VARIANTS OF ROY BEAN'S SENTENCE

1. JUDGE PARKER'S SENTENCE

In the early cattle trail days, when Oklahoma was known as the Indian Territory, a certain Federal Judge, one Parker, was known for the severity of his decisions. In a cowcamp brawl of a passing trail herd, a Mexican cook shot and killed a cowboy in a dispute over a game of cards. Friends of the dead cowboy wanted to lynch the cook at once, but one of their number, the trail-herd boss, persuaded them to wait until he had seen Judge Parker about the matter. It is related that he and the Judge had several drinks together the next day in Fort Smith, Arkansas, and that the Judge readily agreed to pass sentence of death upon the Mexican according to the ideas of the trail herder. Plenty of oratory was asked for along with the sentence in order to make the proceedings entirely legal and proper. This is Judge Parker's sentence:

"José Manuel Miguel Xavier Gonzales, in a few months it will be spring, the snow of winter will flee away, the ice will vanish, and the air will become soft and balmy. In short, José Manuel Miguel Xavier Gonzales, the annual miracle of the year's awakening will come to pass, but you

From "Stop-Over at Abilene," by John A. Lomax, *Southwest Review,* Vol. XXV (July, 1940), No. 4, pp. 407–418.

A New Mexico Federal Judge, Franklin Pierce Benedict, also claims to be the hero of this story. For a more plausible account, see R. E. Twitchell's *Old Santa Fe,* pp. 348–350.—J. A. L.

won't be here. The rivulet will run its purling course to the sea, the timid desert flowers will put forth their tender shoots, the glorious valleys of this imperial domain will blossom as the rose, still you won't be here. From every tree-top some wildwood songster will carol his mating song, butterflies will sport in the sunshine, the busy bee will hum happily as it pursues its accustomed vocation, the gentle breezes will tease the tassels of the wild grasses, and all nature, José Manuel Miguel Xavier Gonzales, will be glad, but you won't be here to enjoy it; for I command the sheriff or some other officer or officers of this county to lead you out to some remote spot, swing you up by the neck to a nodding bough of some sturdy oak, and there let you hang till you are dead, dead, dead. And then, José Manuel Miguel Xavier Gonzales, I command further that such officer or officers retire quietly from your swinging, dangling corpse, that the vultures may descend from the heavens upon your filthy body and pick the putrid flesh therefrom till nothing remain but the bare, bleached bones of a cold-blooded, copper-colored, bloodthirsty, chili-eating, guilty, sheep-herding, Mexican son-of-a-bitch."

2. JUDGE BENEDICT'S SENTENCE

The most distinguished of the jurists who made Santa Fe his headquarters was . . . Kirby Benedict. He was appointed associate justice of the supreme court of New Mexico by Franklin Pierce in 1853. He was a native of the state of Connecticut, born in 1811. All of his adult life, up to the time of his appointment to the New Mexico judgeship, was spent in Illinois, where he was a distinguished member of the bar and a close friend of Stephen A. Douglas and Abraham Lincoln. He was a man of much more than ordinary ability. Literary pursuits had a charm for him, and this characteristic has a lasting memorial in some of his judicial opinions, which assume the form of essays and are to be found in Volume One of the reports of the supreme court of New Mexico.
. . . It was in Taos that he delivered the famous sentence of death, which will probably survive all of his more elaborate utterances or writings. It is so characteristic that it should be preserved, as repeated by a member of the bar present at the time it was given.[1]
José Maria Martín had been convicted of murder in the district court at Taos, the crime having been shown to be of a very aggravated nature and without provocation. The judge evidently concurred in the verdict as fully as if he had been a member of the jury. When the time for sentence was arrived the prisoner was brought before Judge Benedict, who addressed him as follows:

From *Old Santa Fe*, The Story of New Mexico's Ancient Capital, compiled, edited, and written with translations by Ralph Emerson Twitchell, pp. 349–350. Copyright, 1925, by R. E. Twitchell. Santa Fe: Santa Fe New Mexican Publishing Corporation.
[1] William Breeden, leader of the Bar, attorney general, 1872–1889.—R. E. T.

"José Maria Martín, stand up. José Maria Martín, you have been indicted, tried and convicted, by a jury of your countrymen, of the crime of murder, and the Court is now about to pass upon you the dread sentence of the law. As a usual thing, José Maria Martín, it is a painful duty for the Judge of a court of justice to pronounce upon a human being the sentence of death. There is something horrible about it, and the mind of the Court naturally revolts at the performance of such a duty. Happily, however, your case is relieved of all such unpleasant features and the Court takes positive pleasure in sentencing you to death!

"You are a young man, José Maria Martín; apparently of good physical condition and robust health. Ordinarily you might have looked forward to many years of life, and the Court has no doubt you have, and have expected to die at a green old age; but you are about to be cut off in consequence of your own act. José Maria Martín, it is now the springtime, in a little while the grass will be springing up green in these beautiful valleys, and, on these broad mesas and mountain sides, flowers will be blooming; birds will be singing their sweet carols, and nature will be putting on her most gorgeous and her most attractive robes, and life will be pleasant and men will want to stay; but none of this for you, José Maria Martín; the flowers will not bloom for you, José Maria Martín; the birds will not carol for you, José Maria Martín; when these things come to gladden the senses of men, you will be occupying a space about six feet by two beneath the sod, and the green grass and those beautiful flowers will be growing above your lowly head.

"The sentence of the Court is that you be taken from this place to the county jail; that you be kept there safely and securely confined, in the custody of the sheriff, until the day appointed for your execution. (Be very careful, Mr. Sheriff, that he have no opportunity to escape and that you have him at the appointed place at the appointed time); that you be so kept, José Maria Martín, until—(Mr. Clerk, on what day of the month does Friday about two weeks from this time come? 'March 22nd, your honor.') Very well, until Friday, the 22nd day of March, when you will be taken by the sheriff from your place of confinement to some safe and convenient spot within the county (that is in your discretion, Mr. Sheriff, you are only confined to the limits of this county), and that you there be hanged by the neck until you are dead, and the Court was about to add, José Maria Martín, 'May God have mercy on your soul,' but the Court will not assume the responsibility of asking an allwise Providence to do that which a jury of your peers has refused to do. The Lord couldn't have mercy on your soul.[1] However, if you affect any religious belief, or are connected with any religious organization, it might be well for you to send for your priest or your minister, and get from him,—well,—such

---

[1] Notwithstanding the statement of Judge Benedict that an allwise Providence could not do that which twelve of his peers had refused to do, the fact remains that José Maria Martín escaped and never paid the penalty of the law.—R. E. T.

consolation as you can, but the Court advises you to place no reliance upon
anything of that kind! Mr. Sheriff, remove the prisoner."

Buffalo Bill's "Wild West"

BUFFALO BILL'S "WILD WEST"
PRAIRIE EXHIBITION, AND ROCKY MOUNTAIN SHOW,
A DRAMATIC-EQUESTRIAN EXPOSITION
OF
LIFE ON THE PLAINS,
WITH ACCOMPANYING MONOLOGUE AND
INCIDENTAL MUSIC
THE WHOLE INVENTED AND ARRANGED BY
W. F. CODY
W. F. CODY AND N. SALSBURY, PROPRIETORS AND MANAGERS
WHO HEREBY CLAIM AS THEIR SPECIAL
PROPERTY THE VARIOUS EF-
FECTS INTRODUCED IN
THE PUBLIC PER-
FORMANCES
OF
BUFFALO BILL'S "WILD WEST"

MONOLOGUE

LADIES AND GENTLEMEN:

I desire to call your attention to an important fact. From time to time
it will be my pleasure to announce to you the different features of the
programme as they occur. In order that I may do so intelligently, I
respectfully request your silence and attention while I am speaking. Our
agents will pass among you with the biographical history of the life
of Hon. William F. Cody ("Buffalo Bill") and other celebrities who
will appear before you this afternoon. The Management desires to vouch
for the truth and accuracy of all the statements contained in this book,
and respectfully submitted to your attention, as helping you to understand and appreciate our entertainment. Before the entertainment begins,
however, I wish to impress upon your minds that what you are about to
witness is not a performance in the common sense of that term, but an
exhibition of skill, on the part of men who have acquired that quality
while gaining a livelihood. Many unthinking people suppose that the
different features of our exhibition are the result of what is technically

---

From copyright deposit typescript in the Library of Congress, dated June 1, 1885.
Entered according to Act of Congress, by W. F. Cody, at Washington, D. C., on the
22nd Day of December, 1883. All Rights Reserved.

called "rehearsals." Such, however, is not the fact, and anyone who witnesses our performance the second time will observe that men and animals alike are the creatures of circumstances, depending for their success upon their own skill, daring and sagacity. In the East, the few who excel are known to all. In the far West, the names we offer to you this afternoon are the synonyms of skill, courage and individual excellence. At the conclusion of the next overture our performance will commence with a grand processional parade of the "Wild West."

> Overture, grand processional parade of cowboys, Mexicans, and Indians, with incidental music.

I will introduce the different groups and individual celebrities as they pass before you in review.

> Enter a group of Pawnee Indians. Music. Enter Chief. Music. Enter a group of Mexican vaqueros. Music. Enter a group of Wichita Indians. Music. Enter Chief. Music. Enter a group of American Cowboys. Music. Enter King of Cowboys. Music. Enter Cowboy Sheriff of the Platte. Music. Enter a group of Sioux Indians. Music. Enter Chief. Music.

I next have the honor of introducing to your attention a man whose record as a servant of the government, whose skill and daring as a frontiersman, whose place in history as the chief of scouts of the United States Army, under such generals as Sherman, Sheridan, Hancock, Terry, Miles, Hazen, Royal, Merrit, Crook, Carr and others, and whose name as one of the avengers of the lamented Custer, and whose adherence throughout an eventful life to his chosen principle of "true to friend and foe," have made him well and popularly known throughout the world. You all know to whom I allude—the Honorable William F. Cody, "Buffalo Bill."

> Enter Cody. Bugle Call. Cody speaks.

Ladies and Gentlemen: Allow me to introduce the equestrian portion of the Wild West Exhibition.

> Turns to review.

Wild West, are you ready? Go!

> Exeunt omnes.

First on our programme, a —— mile race, between a cowboy, a Mexican, and an Indian, starting at ——. You will please notice that these horses carry the heaviest trapping, and that neither of the riders weigh less than 145 pounds.

Next on our programme, the Pony Express. The Pony Express was established long before the Union Pacific railroad was built across the continent, or even before the telegraph poles were set, and when Abraham Lincoln was elected President of the United States, it was important that the election returns from California should be brought across the mountains as quickly as possible. Mr. William Russell, the great government freighter, who at the time was in Washington, first proposed the Pony Express. He was told that it would take too long—17 or 18 days. The result was a wager of $200,000 that the time could be made in less than ten days, and it was, the actual time being nine days, seventeen hours, leaving seven hours to spare, and winning the wager of two hundred thousand dollars. Mr. Billy Johnson will illustrate the mode of riding the Pony Express, mounting, dismounting and changing the mail to fresh horses.

> Music. Enter express rider, changing horses in front of the grandstand, and exit.

Next on our programme, a one hundred yard race between an Indian on foot, and an Indian on an Indian pony, starting at a given point, running fifty yards, and returning to the starting point—virtually a race of a hundred yards.

> Race as described above. Music.

Next on our programme, an historical representation between Buffalo Bill and Yellow Hand, fought during the Sitting Bull war, on the 17th of July, 1876, at War Bonnet Creek, Dakota, shortly after the massacre of Custer. This fight was witnessed by General Carr's command and the Sioux army, and resulted in the death of Yellow Hand, and the first scalp taken in revenge of Custer's fate.

> Duel as described above. Cody, supported by cowboys, etc., Yellow Hand by Indians. Music.

I have the pleasure of introducing Mr. Seth Clover. Mr. Clover will give an exhibition of his skill, shooting with a Winchester repeating rifle, at composition balls thrown from the hand.

> Clover shoots as above.

Shooting two balls thrown in the air at the same time. You will notice that Mr. Clovis [sic] is obliged to replace the discharged cartridge before he can shoot at the second ball.

> Shoots as above.

Obscuring the sight by placing a card over the rifle.

> Shoots as above.

If any gentleman has a half-dollar he would like to have mutilated and take home as a pocket piece, if he will throw it in upon the track, where we can get it, Mr. Clover will try and oblige him.

> Shoots coin as above.

Shooting at a nickel.

> Shoots as above.

Shooting at a marble. You will notice that the mark is hardly larger than the bullet shot at it.

> Shoots as above.

Shooting a number of composition balls thrown in rapid succession.

> Shoots as above. Exit.

I have the pleasure of introducing Master Johnny Baker, of North Platte, Neb., known as the Cowboy Kid. Master Johnny is 16 years of age, and the holder of the boy's champion badge for rifle and revolver shooting, and stands ready to meet any opponent of his age. Master Baker will give an exhibition of his skill, holding his rifle in various positions.
Holding the rifle sideways.
Holding the rifle to the left shoulder.
Holding the rifle upside down, on the top of his head.
Standing with his back to the target, bending forward, and shooting between his knees.
Leaning backward, over a support, and shooting over his head.
Standing with his back to the target, and taking aim by the aid of a small mirror.
Shooting composition balls thrown in air.
Shoots each shot as above. Exit.

Miss Annie Oakley, the celebrated wing and rifle shot. Miss Oakley will give an exhibition of her skill, shooting with a shot gun at Ligowsky patent clay pigeons, holding the gun in various positions.
Shoots pigeons sprung from trap.
Shooting double, from two traps sprung at the same time.
Shoots as above.
Picking the gun from the ground after the trap is sprung.
Shoots as above.
Shooting double in the same manner.
Shoots as above.
Shooting three composition balls, thrown in the air in rapid succession, the first with the rifle held upside down upon the head, the second and the third with the shot gun.
Shoots as above. Exit.

Next on our programme, the cowboy's fun, or the riding of bucking ponies and mules, by Mr. ——, Mr. ——, and Mr. ——. There is an impression in the minds of many people that these horses are taught or trained to buck, or that they are compelled to do so by having foreign substances placed under their saddles. This, however, is not the fact. Bucking, the same as balking or running away, is a natural trait of the animal, confirmed by habit.
Riders announced, and mount in succession.
Watch Mr. Taylor pick up his hat.
Taylor rides past at full speed, leans out of his saddle and picks hat from the ground.
Watch Mr. Taylor pick up his handkerchief.
Taylor rides past at full speed, leans out of his saddle, and picks up handkerchief.

Hon. William F. Cody, champion all round shot of the world.

Enter Mr. Cody.

Mr. Cody will give an exhibition of his skill, shooting with shot gun, rifle and revolver at clay pigeons and composition balls, shooting first with a shot gun at clay pigeons, pulling the traps himself. (Shoots.) Shooting clay pigeons in the American style of holding the gun, the butt of the gun below his elbow. (Shoots.) Shooting clay pigeons in the English style of holding the gun, the butt of the gun below the arm-pit. Please notice the change of position. (Shoots.)

Shooting clay pigeons standing with his back to the trap, turning and breaking the pigeon while it is in the air. (Shoots.)

Shooting with his back to the trap, gun over his shoulder, turning and pulling the traps himself. (Shoots.)

Holding the gun with one hand. (Shoots.)

Holding the gun with one hand, pulling the trap with the other. (Shoots.)

Shooting clay pigeons double from two traps sprung at the same time. (Shoots.)

Shooting clay pigeons double, pulling the traps himself. (Shoots.)

Shooting twenty clay pigeons inside of one minute and thirty seconds. Any gentleman desiring to hold the time on this feat, will please take it, not from the pulling of the trap, but from the first crack of the gun. (Shoots.)

Mr. Cody will shoot next with a Winchester repeating rifle, at composition balls, thrown from the hand while he rides upon his horse. (Shoots.)

Missing with the first shot, hitting with the second. (Shoots.)

Missing twice, hitting the third time. (Shoots.)

Hitting three balls thrown in the air at the same time. (Shoots.)

Hitting a ball thrown from behind. (Shoots.)

Hitting a ball thrown to either side. (Shoots.)

Hitting a number of balls thrown in the air in rapid succession. (Shoots.)

Hitting a ball thrown in the air while he rides past it at full speed, a shot accomplished by no other marksman. (Shoots.)

Mr. Cody will next attempt the great double shot, hitting two balls thrown in the air at the same time. (Shoots.)

Mr. Cody will next attempt the great double shot! Hitting two balls thrown in the air at the same time, as he rides past at full speed. (Shoots.)

Hitting composition balls thrown in the air, while marksman and object thrower ride side by side at full speed, thus forming a picture of combined horsemanship and marksmanship never before presented to a public audience. (Shoots.)

Hitting composition balls thrown in air with an ordinary Colt's army revolver. (Shoots.)

Next on our programme, the Deadwood stage coach, formerly the property of Gilmore, Salsbury, & Co., and plying between Deadwood and Cheyenne. This coach has an immortal place in American history, having been baptized many times by fire and blood. The gentleman holding the reins, is Mr. John Higby, an old stage driver, and formerly the companion of Hank Monk, of whom you have all probably read. Seated beside him is Mr. John Hancock, known in the West, as the Wizard Hunter of the Platte Valley. Broncho Bill will act as out rider, a position he has occupied in earnest many times with credit. Upon the roof of the coach is seated Mr. Con Croner, the Cowboy Sheriff of the Platte, to whose intrepid administration of that office for several consecutive terms, covering a period of six years, Lincoln County, Neb., and its vicinity are indebted for the peace and quiet that now reigns. Mr. Croner's efforts having driven out the cattle thief and hoodlum element who formerly infested that section of the country, noticeably, the notorious Middleton gang. The coach will start upon its journey, be attacked from an ambush by a band of fierce and warlike Indians, who in their turn will be repulsed by a party of scouts and cowboys, under the command of Buffalo Bill. Will two or three ladies and gentlemen volunteer to ride as passengers.

> After passengers are seated in coach.

It is customary to deliver parting instructions to the driver before he starts on his perilous journey, something in the following fashion: Mr. Higby, I have intrusted you with valuable lives and property. Should you meet with Indians, or other dangers, *en route*, put on the whip, and if possible, save the lives of your passengers. If you are all ready, go!

> Coach is driven down track, meets Indians, turns, followed by Indians. Battle back to stand. Cody and cowboys come to rescue.
>
> Battle past stand. Cody, coach and cowboys return to stand. Exit [*sic*] omnes.

Next on our programme, a one-quarter mile race between Sioux boys and on barebacked Indian ponies from the Honorable William F. Cody's ranche [*sic*] at North Platte, Neb., starting at ——

> Race as above. Music.

I would next call your attention to an exciting race between Mexican thoroughbreds. These animals are bred with great care, and at considerable expense, their original cost being sixteen [hundred?] dollars per doz. All up! No jockeying! Go!

> Race as above. Music. "We Won't Come Home till Morning."

A portion of the Pawnee and Wichita tribes will illustrate their native sports and pastimes, giving first the war dance.

> War dance by Indians.

Next the grass dance.

> Grass dance by Indians.

Next, the scalp dance, in which the women of the tribe are allowed to participate.

> Scalp dance by Indians and squaws.

Keep your eyes on the burros!

> Burros return. Music. "Home Again!" or "We Never Speak as, Etc."

I have the pleasure of introducing "Mustang Jack," or as the Indians call him "Pet-se-ka-we-cha-cha," the great high jumper. Jack is the champion jumper among the cowboys of the West, and stands ready to jump with anybody in any manner or style for any amount of money. He will give you an exhibition of his skill, jumping over various animals, beginning with the small burro.

> Jack jumps over burro.

Jumping twenty-four feet in two jumps, and clearing the burro in the second jump.

> Jack jumps as above.

Jumping the Indian pony, Cha-sha-sha-na-po-geo, a feat which gave him his name of "Mustang Jack."

> Jumps as above.

Next, jumping the tall white horse, "Doc. Powell," sixteen and a half hands high. The best recorded standing high jump is one of five feet and three inches made by Mr. Johnson, of England. In order to clear this horse, Jack is obliged to make a jump of nearly six feet, thus beating the record daily.

> Jumps as above.

Next on our programme the roping, tying and riding of wild Texan steers by cowboys and Mexicans.

> Performance as above.

Next on our programme the riding of a wild elk, by Master Voter Hall, a Feejee Indian from Africa.

> Saddled elk ridden as above.

Next on our programme the attack upon a settler's cabin by a band of marauding Indians, and their repulse, by a party of scouts and cowboys, under the command of Buffalo Bill. After our entertainment you are invited to visit the Wild West camp. We thank you for your polite attention, and bid you all good afternoon.

> Battle as above. Review before the grand stand.
> Adieux and dismissal by Mr. Cody.

FINIS

The Adventures of Big-Foot Wallace

I. SKETCH OF WALLACE's LIFE

William A. Wallace was born in Lexington, Rockbridge County, Virginia, in the year 1816. He went to Texas in 1836, a few months after the battle of San Jacinto, for the purpose, he says, of taking pay out of the Mexicans for the murder of his brother and his cousin, Major Wallace, both of whom fell at "Fannin's Massacre." He says he believes accounts with them are now about square.

He landed first at Galveston, which consisted then of six groceries and an old stranded hulk of a steamboat, used as a hotel, and for a berth in which he paid at the rate of three dollars per day. From Galveston, Wallace went on to La Grange, then a frontier village, where he resided until the spring of 1839, when he moved to Austin, just before the seat of government was established at that place. He remained at Austin until the spring of 1840, when finding that the country was settling up around him too fast to suit his notions, he went over to San Antonio, where he resided until he entered the service.

He was at the battle of the Salado, in the fall of 1842, when General Woll came in and captured San Antonio. The fight began about 11 o'clock in the day, and lasted until night. General Woll had fourteen hundred men, and the Texans one hundred and ninety-seven, under Caldwell (commonly known as "Old Paint"). Between eighty and one hundred Mexicans were killed, while the Texans lost only one man (Jett). Forty men, however, from La Grange, under Captain Dawson, who were endeavoring to form a junction with them, were surrounded and captured by the Mexicans, who massacred them all as soon as they had surrendered their arms.

In the fall of 1842, he volunteered in the "Mier Expedition," an account of which appears in this volume. After his return from Mexico, he joined Colonel Jack Hays's Ranging Company, the first ever regularly enlisted in the service of the "old Republic," and was with it in many of those desperate encounters with the Comanches and other Indians, in which Hays, Walker, McCulloch, and Chevalier gained their reputations as successful Indian-fighters.

When the Mexican war broke out in 1846, Wallace joined Colonel Hays's regiment of mounted volunteers, and was with it at the storming of Monterey, where he says he took "full toll" out of the Mexicans for killing his brother and cousin at Goliad in 1836.

After the Mexican war ended, he had command of a Ranging Company for some time, and did good service in protecting the frontiers of the

From *The Adventures of Big-Foot Wallace, the Texas Ranger and Hunter*, by John C. Duval, pp. xiv–xv, 221–222, 229–254, 281–291. Copyright, 1870, by J. W. Burke & Co. Macon, Georgia.

State from the incursions of the savages. Subsequently he had charge of the mail from San Antonio to El Paso, and, though often waylaid and attacked by the Indians, he always brought it through in safety.

II. How Big-Foot Wallace Got His Name

It was while we were prisoners at the City of Mexico that I acquired the name of "Big-Foot," which has stuck to me like Texas mud ever since. It happened in this way: Some of the foreign residents of the city, observing that we were almost in a shoeless condition, made up by contribution among themselves a sufficient sum to purchase a pair of shoes for each of us. Every one was fitted with a suitable pair except myself; but I searched in vain every shop and "tienda" in the city for even a pair of No. 11's, though 12's fit me best, and finally I had no alternative left me but to buy the leather and have a pair put up on purpose for me by a "zapatero," or go barefooted. The Mexicans are generally a small people compared with the Americans, and their feet are still smaller in proportion; consequently they were much astonished at the size of mine, and from that time forward, and as long as I remained in the city, I was known among them as "Big-Foot."

I flatter myself, however, that my foot is not a very large one, taking into consideration the fact that I am just six feet two inches in height, and weigh upward of two hundred pounds net. But, even if it were otherwise, there is nothing dishonorable in the appellation, and I would rather be called "Big-Foot Wallace" than "Lying Wallace," or "Thieving Wallace." Such handles to my name would not be agreeable.

III. How He Started on His Journey

Wallace Hears from Virginia—Civilized Compared with Uncivilized Life—
He Determines to Take a Trip to "The Old States"—Lays in a "Civilized"
Wardrobe—An Old Friend Finds Him Disguised in His New Clothes—
Starts on His Journey.

Some years after the Mexican war, a stranger stopped at my "ranch" one night, and gave me a letter which he said the postmaster at San Antonio had requested him to deliver. I opened it, and found that it was from one of my relatives in Virginia, advising me to come on there at once, as my presence was necessary in the division of an estate, of which I was one of the heirs.

I had never been back to the "States" since I left Virginia in 1837, and made up my mind at once that I would go—not so much for the purpose of securing what property I might be entitled to, as to see how people managed to live in those old countries, without the excitement of an occasional Indian fight, or a "scrimmage" with the Mexicans, or even a "tussle" with a bear now and then to keep their blood in circulation. I thought to myself, it must be a mighty humdrum sort of a way of living, but I suppose custom enables one to get used to almost anything. The happiest people I ever saw on earth were the Keechies, who were at war with all the neighboring tribes, and ran a great risk of having their hair lifted, even when they went to the spring for a drink of water.

I don't say this to recommend a state of warfare, but only to prove that people can get used to almost everything but skinning. I once saw the Keechies skin some of their prisoners alive, and they didn't live twenty minutes afterward. Nothing can survive that operation long, except a snake.

But, to come back to my story: It was necessary, before I started on my trip, to replenish my wardrobe, as what I had on hand wasn't exactly suitable for civilized countries. Leather hunting-shirts and leggins are just the things for the prairies and chaparral; but I had a sort of idea they wouldn't be considered the "height of the fashion" by the people of the "Old States."

I had a splendid suit of buckskin given me by my old friend "Bah-pish-na-ba-hoo-tee" (which means "Little blue whistling thunder" in the Tonkawa language), made of the skins of the "big-horn," and rigged off with buffalo tags and little copper bells, that jingled musically as I walked along; and when I was dressed up in them, and had my coonskin cap on, with its tail hanging down behind, I do believe there wasn't a young woman in the settlement that could look at me with impunity. But even that, I concluded, wouldn't be exactly the thing for my travels; so the next day I got on my horse, and rode into San Antonio, to supply myself with such articles as I required.

A city friend, who was posted in the fashions, went around with me to the shops, and bought for me such things as he said I would want—a stove-pipe hat, and coat and pantaloons, and a pair of patent-leather boots that were as slick and shiny as a darky's face after a dinner of fat 'possum, and a pair of gloves that I never wore but once, for they "choked" my hands so that they made me short-winded. He bought me also a number of other little traps, combs, brushes, etc., and a two-story trunk to hold them all.

A day or two after I had made my purchases, I thought it advisable to rig myself out in my "toggery," so as to get a little used to their "hang" before I started on my journey. I squeezed myself into a pair of pants that fitted as tight as candle-moulds, and into a blue coat with metal buttons that was tighter still, and which split from stem to stern the first time I sneezed, and finally forced my feet into the shiny boots, without bursting either them or a blood-vessel, which was the greatest wonder of all.

When I had rigged myself out from head to foot, I felt as I suppose a man would feel who had a layer of "daubin" plastered over him, that had hardened in the sun. I couldn't bend my knees, nor crook my elbows; couldn't do anything except sit bolt upright in a chair, with my legs straight out before me. Even when I smiled at the ridiculous figure I cut, no matter how faintly or sweetly, I could hear a seam crack somewhere. If the shanty had caught fire just then, I would have been roasted to a certainty, before I could have made my retreat.

It so happened that while I was "trussed up" in that style, a fellow with whom I had a slight acquaintance came in to see me about buying a horse. I asked him to take a seat, which he did, all the time staring at me in a way that convinced me he didn't know me. At length he inquired if "Big-Foot" was at home. I laughed outright, at the expense of two buttons and a rent in my pants, and he then recognized me at once. "Why, 'Big-Foot'," he said, "what do you mean by disguising yourself in that way? Are you crazy, or are you going a-courting?"

"Neither," I replied. "I am tired of tending stock, and fighting Indians, and intend to play the gentleman awhile, and as a commencement of my new career, I have bought this suit of 'store clothes' on tick, which I am trying on to see how I feel in them. Though my education has been considerably neglected in these backwoods, just as soon as I can learn to play poker and cut-throat loo, swear like a trooper, and can run off with some man's wife, I have some hopes the fraternity will admit me as a member. It is true I haven't killed a man as yet in a duel, but I have 'got' 'severial' in fights with the enemies of my country, and perhaps they will consider that a fair offset. What do you think?"

My friend said he had no doubt I would do with a little training, and asked me when I proposed to make a start in my new line of business.

"I am off in the morning," said I. "I have just five hundred dollars in my pocket, and when I have got through with that and my 'inheritance,' I shall come back to my ranch here, put on my old buckskins, and run after stock and fight Indians for a livelihood the balance of my life."

My friend bid me good-by, and the next morning, leaving my "ranch" in the care of my old compadre, Jeff Bond, I went into San Antonio, and took the stage for Indianola. There I got on board a steamer that was just ready to start, and in two or three hours we were rolling and tossing on the Gulf.

*   *   *   *   *

IV. THE ST. CHARLES TAVERN

The St. Charles "Tavern"—How He Registered His Name—Wallace Is Afraid of a Fire—He Breakfasts at the St. Charles, and Gets Up an Excitement—The Bill of Fare—Fried Bullfrogs.

. . . I went to the St. Charles tavern, to hunt up quarters for the night, as I had been told it was the best in the city, and I was determined to have the best of everything going while I was on my travels. Some one had pointed the tavern out to me in the daytime, and as it was but a little way off, I soon came to it, and went up the broad steps in front, and then into a room where several men were putting their names down in a book.

I asked a fellow standing behind the railing at a desk, if the landlord was in, as I wanted to see him. He laughed a little, though I didn't see anything funny in the question, and told me the landlord was out just then, but that he would attend to any business I might have with him. I told him all I wanted was a room to sleep in, and as much "grub" as I could eat as long as I staid in New Orleans.

"Certainly," said he, "you can be accommodated. Will you please register your name?"

I took the pen and wrote down "Big-Foot Wallace" in the first column, "Buffalo-Bull Ranch, Texas," in the second, and "Old Virginny" in the third. Then the clerk, or whoever he was, struck something that sounded like a clock, and a fellow jumped up from the corner of the room, and came up to where we were.

"Show this gentleman to No. 395," and he handed the waiter a little piece of candle that didn't look to me nigh long enough to last us through three hundred and ninety-five rooms. But the whole tavern was lighted up with little brass knobs, that made every place as bright as day.

The waiter took me up one pair of stairs, and then up another and another, until I thought I was in a fair way to get to heaven at last, providing my breath didn't fail me. We then wound about through half a dozen lanes and alleys, until at last we came to No. 395. The waiter unlocked the door, lit my candle, and told me good night.

"Stop a minute, my friend," said I; "if this tavern should catch fire to-night, how am I to find my way back again to where we started from?"

"Oh," said he, "there's no danger of fire, for it is all built of rock; and besides, it's insured."

"Devil trust it," said I, "with that gas stuff burning all over it. If it can set fire to a brass knob, why can't it burn a rock, too? I'd rather trust myself in a dry prairie, with a stiff 'norther' blowing, and the grass waist high, and hostile Indians all around: my chances of being roasted alive wouldn't be half as good as they are up here in No. 395; and besides," said I, "I'm not insured!"

"Well," said he, "if the house catches fire, all you've got to do is to pull that string hanging down there with the tassel on the end of it, which rings a bell, and I'll come up and show you the road down."

"Look here, my friend," said I, "you can't satisfy me in that way. This is room 395, and I suppose there's at least 395 more of 'em, and when 790 bells are all ringing at the same time, how are you going to tell which one is mine? You might as well try to tell the bellowing of a particular buffalo-bull in a gang of ten thousand. No, sir; you stay up here with me, and when the row commences, if you are lucky enough to find your way down, I won't be far behind you."

"Well," said he, "when my watch is up, which will be in about half an hour, I'll come back."

" 'Nough said," I replied, "and I'll stand treat in the morning."

So I turned into bed, and in five minutes was fast asleep. I never knew whether the fellow came back or not, but I suppose he did, for he claimed the "treat" off me the first thing in the morning. I gave him a brand-new fifty-cent piece, and he said he'd like to take the job by the week at half the price: so I engaged him regularly at twenty-five cents a night, and considered it dirt-cheap at that.

I made an early start in the morning, for I knew I had a crooked way to travel and a dim trail to follow; and about 9 o'clock I found myself in the room where I had registered my name the night before, and feeling considerably snappish after my long tramp.

I inquired of one of the porters sitting there, how long it was till breakfast. He said any time I wanted it, and showed me the way into the breakfast-room. It was almost as large as a small prairie, and, instead of one long table, as we have in our taverns at home, there were at least forty or fifty little round ones scattered about all over it.

Being of rather a social disposition, although I have lived so much in the woods by myself, and seeing a tolerably jovial little party of ladies and gentlemen sitting around one of these tables, I walked up and took a seat with them. I saw in a minute I wasn't welcome, for the gentlemen looked as ill-natured as a sulky bull, and the ladies all tittered; but I pretended not to notice it, and called to one of the waiters who was running round, to bring me a pound or so of beefsteak and the "condiments."

At this, one of the men spoke up, and said "he presumed I was under a mistake, as that was a private table."

"Yes, sir," said I, "I am. I presumed you were gentlemen; and as to this being a private table, all I have to say is, it's the first one I ever saw in a 'public house.' However," I continued, "I've no wish to force my company where it isn't wanted," and I got up and took a seat at another table.

If a man had spoken to me at a tavern in Texas the way that chap did, I would have introduced him to "Old Butch" at once; but thinks I, maybe things are different here, and I bothered myself no more about it.

There was nothing to eat on the table where I had taken a seat but a plate of butter and a bowl of sugar; but in a minute or so a waiter stepped up and handed me a paper. I took it, folded it up, and laid it on the table.

"My friend," says I, "I'm 'remarkable' hungry just now, and I'll read that after I get something to eat, if you say there's anything special in it."

After a little while he says, "What'll you have for breakfast, sir?"

"Well," I answered, "anything that's fat and juicy. What have you got cooked?"

"If you'll read the 'bill of fare,' " says he, "you can see for yourself."

"Well! let's have it," said I.

"That's it you have just folded up and laid on the table there," he replied.

"Oh, yes," said I. "I understand now;" and I picked it up, and the first thing I saw on it was *"Café au lait,"* "and it's late enough too for it, heaven knows," said I; "for I am used to taking a quart cup every morning just at daybreak!"

"What else?" said the waiter, and I read on:

"*Pâte de fois gras*"—some sort of yerbs, thought I, and I never went high on greens, especially for breakfast. I found most of the names of the things on the "bill of fare" were French, or some other foreign lingo, and they were all Greek to me; but, to make the waiter believe I knew very well what they were, only I wasn't partial to their sort of "grub," I told him to bring me some "crapeau fricassee" and "gumbo filet," and I wish I may never take another "chaw" of tobacco if he did not bring me a plateful of fried bull-frogs' legs, and another full of their spawn, just the same sort of slimy, ropy stuff you see around the edges of shallow ponds. I might have known that everything French had frog in it in some shape or other, just as certain as "Chili pepper" is found in everything the Mexicans cook. However, I made out a tolerable breakfast on other things, but would have been much better satisfied if I could have had four or five pounds of roasted buffalo-meat and a *"marrow gut."*

V. The Quadroon Ball

Wallace Meets with an Adventure—Goes to a Quadroon Ball, and Teaches Them "the Stampede"—Wallace Takes a "White Lion," and Pays for It —Has His Fortune Told—What Followed.

After breakfast, I loaded my pipe and took a seat on the front porch, with my legs hoisted up on the iron railings, and while I was sitting there puffing away, as comfortable as an old sow in a mud-hole on a hot day, a young woman came along on the opposite side of the street, and stopped awhile to look at some pictures in a window. Presently she looked up and beckoned me to come to her! I couldn't believe my eyes at first, but she kept on motioning her hand to me until I knew there was no mistake about it.

I thought maybe she takes me for some acquaintance of hers, and I'll go down and let her know she is on the wrong trail, just to see how foolish she will look when she finds she has been making so familiar with a stranger. So I went down the steps and crossed over to where she was standing. When I got up close to her I noticed that her dress didn't look overly neat, and that her eyes were as red as if she had been on a burst for the last week. I made her a polite bow, however, and remarked that I supposed she was mistaken; but before I could finish my speech, which I had "cut and dried," like the politicians, she ran up to me and grabbed me by the hand.

"Oh, bosh!" said she, "not a bit of it: you are the hardest fellow to take a hint I ever saw. I've been beckoning to you for the last half hour. Come along, Johnny Green, I want to introduce you to some particular friends of mine."

"My name ain't Johnny Green," said I, trying to get my hand loose from her; but she held on to it like a vise.

"Oh! never mind that," said she; "come along with me, and we'll have a jolly time of it."

Thinks I, if you ain't a brazen piece I never saw one; for all the time she was talking she kept dragging me on, though there were half a dozen fellows on the stoop of the tavern, killing themselves laughing at us. This made me desperate, and I jerked my hand away by main force, though I hated to serve anything like a woman in such a rough way.

"Won't you go?" said she.

"No," said I, "not just now; I haven't time."

"Well," she answered, "if you won't go, I reckon you won't refuse to 'treat.' "

"Certainly not," said I. "What'll you take—a lemonade, or an ice-cream?"

"To the old boy," said she, "with your lemonades and ice-cream! I'll take a glass of brandy with a little schnapps in it."

"There," said I, and I threw her a slick quarter; "that'll buy you one;" and I turned on my heel and made tracks for the tavern as fast as I could.

Geminy! what a "cussin' " she gave me as I went! I thought I had heard the rangers on the frontiers of Texas make use of pretty hard language, but they couldn't hold a candle to that young woman. The farther I went the louder she "cussed," and I never got out of hearing of her until I found my way at last up to 395, where I bolted myself in, and never came out till dinner-time.

After supper, I fixed up a little, slicked down my hair with about a pint of bear's grease (some of my own killing), and went off to a "Quadroon Ball" in the French part of the city, for I was determined to see a little of everything going. Just as I entered the door of the house where the ball was given, a man stopped me and told me I would have to be searched before I could enter!

"What for?" said I; "anything been stolen about here?"

"No," said he; "but if you've got any weapons about you, you must give 'em up to me before you can go in, and I will be responsible for them."

"Well," said I, "the truth is, I am partially 'heeled,' " and I handed him out a pair of Derringers and "Old Butch."

"I don't care so much about the Derringers," said I, "but take good care of 'Old Butch,' for I have a sort of affection for him, on account of the many scrapes he has helped me out of, and the amount of hair I have lifted from the heads of Indians with it."

The doorkeeper looked at me and then at "Old Butch," as if he didn't know what to make of either of us exactly; but he took the weapons, and told me I could have 'em when I left; and said he, "If you have any money about you of account, you had better leave it with me; else you mayn't be able to put your hand on it when you want it."

"I've only a few Mexican dollars in my pocket," I answered, "and if anybody can get them, they are welcome to them."

"Very well," said he, "you can go in."

So I went up a pair of stairs, and into a long room filled with people, and lighted up as bright as a prairie on fire with gas-knobs. 'Most everybody had masks on, so you couldn't tell who they were, but that made no difference to me, for, of course, all there were strangers to me.

There were two or three sets on the floor dancing, besides a great many little squads scattered all about, laughing and talking, and making fun of themselves and everybody else. I sauntered about among 'em for some time, amusing myself with looking on as well as I could. I had begun to get rather tired of the concern, as I had no one to dance with, when a genteel-looking chap with a parrot-bill mask on, came up to me, and said "he presumed I was a stranger in the city."

I told him he had hit the nail on the head exactly.

"And how do you like our little fandango?" he asked.

"Oh! very well," said I; "but I see you haven't yet introduced the Texas national dance—the Stampede."

"No," said he; "have never heard of it before. Wouldn't you be kind enough to describe it to me, and I'll introduce it immediately; we are very much in want of something new just now."

"Of course," said I, "if you wish me. The 'Stampede' is danced in this way: The ladies range themselves on one side of the room, and the gentlemen on the other. Then one of the gentlemen neighs, and if a lady 'whinnies' in answer, they both step forward, and become partners for the dance. If the gentleman is very homely, and, after neighing three times, no lady should answer, he steps out of the 'ring,' and hopes for better luck next time.

"When the couples are all paired off in this way, the manager calls out, 'Gallopade all,' and all 'lope' around the room briskly three or four times. Then the gentlemen 'curvet' to their partners, and the ladies coquettishly back their ears and kick up at the gentlemen. Then the ladies canter up to the gentlemen, who rear and plunge for a while, then seize the ladies' hands, and pace gracefully off in couples around the room. First couple then wheel and go off at a two-forty lick, second couple ditto, and so on till the race becomes general, when the manager calls out 'Whoa!' and everybody comes to a sudden halt. The manager then calls out, 'Walk your partners'; 'pace your partners'; 'trot your partners'; and 'gallopade all' again, faster and faster, until the 'sprained' and 'wind-galled' and 'short stock' begin to 'cave in' when he calls out 'Boo!' and throws his hat in the 'ring.' A general 'stampede' follows; the gentlemen neigh, curvet, and pitch; the ladies whinny, prance, and kick, chairs and tables are knocked over, lights blown out, and everybody tumbles over everybody else, till the whole set is piled up in the middle of the room; and so the dance ends."

"By jingo," said my new friend, grabbing my hand, "it's glorious! It's the very thing for this latitude, and will create a sensation, you may depend. I'll introduce the 'Stampede' this very night."

"Very well," said I; "but you had better wait till it's time to go home, for, generally, things are smashed up so after the 'Stampede,' that it's hard to get the ball going again."

My new friend and myself soon got pretty thick with each other, and before I suspected what he was up to, he had pumped me dry of all the information I could give him about myself, where I was from, what was my name, where I was going to, etc.

After a while, he asked me if I ever indulged. I told him I was indulgent to a fault, providing the liquor wasn't certain death, like the most of it in Texas. (I once drank some in Castroville, that was so awful bad that it burnt a hole in my sleeve when I wiped my mouth afterward.) My friend, however, said they had pretty fair liquor there; and he took me to a little room off to one side, where refreshments of all sorts were ladled out to the crowd.

"What'll you take?" asked my new friend.

"Well, I don't care," said I; "I'm not particular, so it ain't stronger than fourth-proof brandy."

"'Spose," said he, "we try a 'white lion'?"

"Agreed," says I, off-hand like, just as if I knew perfectly well what he meant by a 'white lion,' though, of course, I hadn't the least idea what it was.

The bar-keeper took a tumbler, poured a little water in it, then put some sugar, and a good deal of brandy, then a little old Jamaica rum, and some pounded ice, and then clapping another tumbler to it, mouth downward, he shook 'em backward and forward till everything in them was well mixed up. He then slipped a slice of fresh pineapple into the tumbler and handed it to me. I put it to my lips, intending just to take a sip, to see how it would go; but it never left them till I had drained the last drop.

It was hard to beat, I tell you. I never tasted anything equal to it but once, and that was a drink of muddy water out of a Mexican gourd, after having been without any for five days and nights. I had already seen most of the "lions" of the city, but the "white lion" took the lead of them all. If I had joined the Temperance Society only the day before, I should have backslidden at once. There's no use at all of joining it, when you have to encounter one of these "lions" in the path every day. Father Mathew himself couldn't scare one of them out of the way!

Well, I was so much taken up with my "lion," I forgot my new friend for an instant, and when I turned to look for him he was gone. I started off to hunt him up, but the bar-keeper called to me and told me I had forgot something.

"What is it?" I asked.

"To pay for those 'lions,'" said he.

I handed out the change without a word. In Texas, when a man asks you to drink, it is expected that he will pay, of course; in the Old States, it seems the rule is reversed. But customs differ everywhere. I looked all around the room, but couldn't find my new friend anywhere, nor a buckskin "puss," filled with "six-shooter" bullets and percussion caps, that somebody had cut out of my coat-pocket. I didn't mind losing the bullets much, for I would freely have given them to the fellow that took 'em, if he had told me he needed 'em, but he had split my new coat about six inches on the side, and ruined it entirely. I suppose he thought he had got a purse full of California nuggets, from the weight of it; and I rather think he must have felt a little disappointed when he emptied it and found what it was filled with. I would have given a "slick quarter" just to have seen how he looked when the bullets and percussion caps rolled out.

But, he wasn't the first fellow, I thought to myself, by a long ways, that got only bullets from me when he expected something more agreeable. A good many others have carried off my lead with 'em, and some not very far, at that. I ain't in the habit, you know, of bragging in this way, but you see it was all owing to the "white lions" that somehow had got into my head, for by this time I had "repeated."

Well, I was beginning to get somewhat tired of the "fandango," and was just about to despatch another "white lion," with the full intention of exterminating the breed at once, when a young woman, dressed in a fanciful sort of costume, came up to me, and said "she presumed I was a stranger in the city."

"How in the world," thought I, "does everybody know I'm a stranger in the city? Perhaps it's my 'sombrero,' with its broad brim, and silver tassels hanging down behind;" and I remembered then I hadn't seen anybody else in the city with one on.

"Yes," said I, "Miss; I haven't been in the place long."

"I thought not," said she; "you look like you had lately been transported from your native soil; you haven't wilted a bit yet."

"I am afraid I will, though, now," said I, "since I have met with you;" for there was something about that young woman that was "monstrous" taking! She was built up from the ground, and she walked as springy as a "spike buck." Her foot wasn't longer than my thumb, and the prettiest sort of pigtail curls hung down all around her neck.

"Cross my hand," said she, holding out a little paw about the size of a possum's, with a flesh-colored glove on it, "and I'll tell you your fortune."

"My dear," said I—for by this time I wasn't afraid to say anything, the "lions" had made me so bold—"I don't care about having my fortune told; but I'll give you a two-and-a-half-dollar gold piece if you will take off that mask and let me have a peep at that pretty face of yours."

"Agreed," she answered, "but I must tell you your fortune first, anyhow, just to convince you that I understand my trade. Hold out your hand"; and I poked out a paw that will span the head of a flour-barrel "with ease and elegance." She took it in both of hers, and examined it closely for some time.

"You are from Texas," she said; and she followed a wrinkle on my hand with one of her little soft fingers till my blood tingled all the way up to my elbow. "That line runs straight back to that State."

"You are a witch, sure enough," said I.

"You are not married," said she, "but you will be before long, for that line" (following another with her finger that ran up to the bottom of my thumb) "reaches all the way to Cupid's dominions."

"Right again," said I; "I see you understand your 'trade,' sure enough."

"And this line," she went on, tracing another from the middle of my hand till it sprangled out toward the roots of my fingers, "shows you've roamed about a great deal in the prairies and backwoods of Texas. You have been a great hunter, and no doubt have taken the scalps from the heads of many an aborigine."

"No," said I, "we haven't any of those varmints in Texas; but I've lifted the hair from the head of many an Indian; and if I only had 'Old Butch' here, I'd show you the little instrument I did it with; but the fellow downstairs has got it. But how in the world did you find out all this? You are a witch to a certainty."

"Of course I am," she answered, "and therefore I can easily tell that you are now on your way to 'Old Virginny.' "

"That'll do," I said; "I see you know it all; and I won't let you read any more of the lines on my hand, for some of 'em, you see, run into places where I wouldn't like to be trailed up. Come, I'm as dry as a 'buffalo chip,' and wish you would ask me to take something."

"Why don't you ask me?" said she.

"Because," I answered, "it seems to be the custom here for the one that's invited to pay; and I don't want you to settle the bar bill."

"Oh, very well," she said, "suppose we do have something."

So we went up to the bar, and she asked me what I'd take.

"I'm after big game now," said I, "and we'll take a 'white lion.' "

She called for "a lemonade with the privilege," and the "privilege," I noticed (which was Cognac brandy) filled up the tumbler pretty well of itself. Well, we stood there laughing and talking, and sipping our liquor, until we got on the best of terms, and at length I ventured to take her hand in mine and give it a gentle squeeze; but I had drunk so many "white lions" I couldn't regulate the pressure exactly, and I squeezed harder than I intended.

The young woman gave a keen scream and jerked her hand away, and said I had crippled her for life. I begged a thousand pardons, laid the blame on the "lions" and "love at first sight," etc.; and finally got her in a good humor again. A woman will forgive a fellow anything, if he can only make her believe that it's all owing to her good looks or winning ways.

"And now," said I, "that we are friends again, I must have a peep at that pretty face of yours, as you promised," and I handed her the two-and-a-half-dollar gold piece.

"Well," says she, "it's about time to be going home, anyhow, and I suppose it will make no difference."

So she took off her mask, and—what do you think? If she wasn't a full-blooded "mulatto" I wish I may never lift the hair from another Indian! I was so astonished I couldn't say a word; and what I would have done I don't know, but just then I heard a terrible row going on, and looking round, I saw my first friend sitting on a table, and calling out the figures of the "Stampede." Nearly everybody in the room had joined in, and such neighing, curvetting, and prancing, and pitching, and kicking up, I never saw or heard on the prairies of Texas. At last the manager threw his hat among 'em and called out, "Stampede all," and the "rippit" commenced. The women screamed and made tracks down stairs, while the men kicked over the chairs and tables and pitched into each other right and left.

One fellow came along by where I was standing, and planted his boot-heel with all his might on the top of my toes! I gave him three or four pounds of my fist right in the middle of his forehead, and he tumbled over on the floor and didn't take any more stock in that "scrimmage." By this time the police came in and took a hand in the row, and things got livelier than ever. Two fellows grabbed me at once: I took an "under crop" out of the ear of one of 'em, and about half the hair off the head of the other. (It was well for him I didn't have "Old Butch" about me, or I should have got it all.) Pretty soon I saw a mahogany chair flying straight toward me, and I rather suppose, from the bump that was on my head the next morning, that it had finally stopped the chair. At any rate, that's the last thing I recollect about the "Quadroon Ball."

VI. His Opinion of Farming

Wallace Gives Jack Dobell His Opinion of Farming—Uncle Josh—The Jews a Sensible People—Wallace Makes His Arrangements for a Crop— He and "Keecheye" Try Ploughing—Both Disgusted—Queer Muskmelon —Ruined by the Drought—How Wallace Was Cheated Out of His "Roasting Ears"—Living on Watermelons and "Poor Doe"—Wallace's Future Prospects—Conclusion.

Some years ago, while on my way to the city of San Antonio, I lost my road, and after wandering about the prairies till nearly sunset, I concluded to strike camp, and make a fresh start in the morning. But, just as I had made up my mind to pass the night at "Sprawls," and put up as well as I could with such accommodations as are usually furnished by that extensive establishment, I thought I saw some faint symptoms of a "settlement" ahead of me. Spurring on my jaded horse, I at length came to a sort of hybrid between a log cabin and a half-faced camp, in front of which a man was seated on a fallen tree, busily engaged in rubbing up his rifle.

"Can you give me such directions, my friend," said I, "as will enable me to find my way back to the main road to San Antonio?"

The man looked up as he replied to my question, and to my astonishment I recognized my old friend and messmate, Big-Foot Wallace.

"Why, hello, Foot," said I, "have you forgotten your old 'compadre,' Jack Dobell?"

Big-Foot looked at me dubiously for a minute, then, springing up from the log, he seized me by the hand and gave it such a grip that my fingers stuck together for five minutes afterward.

"Get down, Dobell," said he, "and rest your face and hands. You must stay with me all night, and in the morning I'll pilot you out to the road myself. It's a fact, though," continued Big-Foot, looking ruefully around upon the apparently scant accommodations afforded by his "ranch," "it's a fact, though, I haven't got much to offer you. Crops have failed entirely, but there's pretty smart of good grass in that hollow yonder for your nag; and my partner, Jackson, was lucky enough to kill a fat buck to-day. So get down at once, for I have a heap to tell you about what has happened to me since we last met, and particularly about a scurvy trick my partner, Jim Jackson there" (pointing to a remarkably homely individual who was busily engaged near by in "peeling" the hide from the aforesaid buck), "played off upon me about a month ago."

Without further "palaver," I dismounted from my horse, and, under Big-Foot's guidance, proceeded to stake him out in a snug little valley, where the mesquite grass grew rank and luxuriantly.

"You needn't be afraid to stake him so far from camp—there's no Indians about here now," said Big-Foot, with a melancholy expression of countenance, as if he was heartily sick of "these piping times of peace," and longed to see once more the stirring scenes of bygones days. "I do believe there hasn't been an Indian in ten miles of this place for the last twelve months."

"Why, you don't tell me, Big-Foot," said I, "that you have been all that time without a single 'scrimmage' with the Mexicans or Indians?"

"Yes," said he, "with the exception of a little 'tussle' I had with the 'Tonks' about six months ago, on the Llaño, I haven't had a row of any sort since I 'drove my megs down' in this settlement. And no wonder, neither, for the people are 'piling in' here as thick as pig-tracks around a corn-crib door; and they have fenced up the prairies in such a way that the Indians won't venture in, for fear of being 'hemmed up.' If I only knew where all these people come from, I'd go there right off, for there can't be any one left behind, and a fellow wouldn't be 'scrouged' to death, as he is here now. Of all things in the world, I hate being 'fenced up'; I want plenty of elbow-room and plenty of 'outlet,' but here you can't travel half a dozen miles in any direction, without being headed off by somebody's fence."

On our return to the "ranch," we took a seat on the log which answered Big-Foot in place of a sofa, and he said to me, "Well, in the first place, I suppose you would like to know how I came to settle here, and take up with the business of farming.

"You see, after the Mexican war had ended, and that chap with the gold epaulets on his shoulders and the 'chicken fixings' on his coat-sleeves ɹad mustered us out of the service and paid us off, Jackson and I concluded, as we had saved up a smart pile of money between us, that we would try our hands at 'ranching.' Neither of us knew anything about it, but we thought it would be plain sailing enough, as things appeared to grow in this country pretty much of their own accord anyhow, without requiring a great deal of hard work, of which neither of us were 'overly' fond. So we bought two hundred acres of land here, from Uncle Josh (and by the same token, he made us pay a 'swingeing' price for it— twenty-five cents an acre, half cash down).

"You know Uncle Josh, don't you? There never was a better-hearted fellow in the world, and he has but one little failing: whenever he can get to where there's liquor, either the liquor gives out, or he gets 'Ingin drunk' certain—one or the other. I have often taken him out in the chaparral, and talked to him with tears in my eyes as big as glass marbles, about his carrying on so in that way; but all I can ever get out of him is, 'that it's all owing to the high price of putty,' which, he says, 'riz half a cent on the ton, just as he had sold out.'

"But, as I was telling you, after Jackson and I had bought this piece of land from 'Uncle Josh,' the first thing we did was to build this shanty, and fence in that 'truck-patch' you see yonder; and long before we got through with the job, I tell you I had taken a perfect disgust for farming. To sit here comfortably on this log, and look at that little shanty and the truck-patch alongside of it, you would think them a mere circumstance; and, in fact, they don't make a very imposing show in the way of improvements; but just you try your hand at riving a few hundred boards out of these knotty post-oaks, that split just as well crossways as lengthways, and if you don't lather 'a few,' and cuss a few more, then I'm mistaken. And, if that don't satisfy you, just pitch into that chaparral out yonder, where the thorns are as sharp and as crooked as cats' claws, and perhaps, by the time you are tattooed all over like a New-Zealander, and there's nothing left of your pants but the waistbands, and only the collar of your shirt, you will come to the same conclusion that I did, that farming ain't quite so pleasant a business as following an Indian trail on an easy-going horse, with a fair prospect of overtaking the women and children.

"In my opinion, the Jews are the most sensible people about 'farming,' after all. You'll find 'em everywhere making money at all sorts of trades and occupations: but whoever heard of a Jew that followed 'grubbing the ground' for a living? Even in the time of Moses, you know, they went 'scootin'' around the country for forty years, living on manna and grasshoppers, just for an excuse to keep from building shanties and hoeing corn. They are a shrewd, smart people, and I'd join 'em at once, only I'm opposed to their 'earmarks,' and don't like being circumscribed and hemmed up, as I told you. Besides, I don't want to give up old Ned,[1] of which I am remarkably fond. Take my advice, Dobell, and never do

---

[1] A Southern term for bacon.—J. C. D.

you try 'farming,' unless you have got half a dozen darkeys and a small 'trash gang' to clear away the 'roughness.'

"Well, as I was saying, after we had worked and 'fussed' around here more than a month, and got the shanty built and the ground fenced in, I went into town and bought a plough, shovels, spades, hoes, and all sorts of farming ammunition, so as to have everything ready when the planting season came round. I went to a drug-store and bought all kinds of seeds, done up in little brown paper parcels; for, thinks I, maybe farming is like shooting at ducks with mixed shot: if a No. 4 don't hit 'em in the body, perhaps a No. 7 will take 'em in the head. If parsnips don't do well, maybe beets will. I didn't forget muskmelons and watermelons (for I am powerfully fond of 'em, I am); and well it was I didn't, as I'll tell you before I'm done.

"The first thing I did, when I got back from town, was to hitch my saddle-horse, old 'Keecheye,' into the plough; and if ever I saw a shame-faced brute, he was one. He looked as if he thought he had got down to 'the lowest notch' at last. He was so cowed he went off as quiet as a lamb, and never cut up the first 'shine.' I had never tried ploughing before in my life, but I had seen other people at it, and I thought it was the easiest thing in the world; but I'm blamed if I have got the 'hang' of it rightly to this day. Sometimes the crazy thing would scoot along the top of the ground for a yard or so, and then, kerwhoop! it would come up against a grub, and jar the very nails off my fingers. Then again it would dive right down into the earth, as if it thought I was engaged in digging cellars by the job; and whenever I tried to bring it up, I was sure to overdo the thing, and away it would go again scooting along the top of the ground, until another grub would bring it up all standing. I pledge you my word, Dobell, after I had run the first furrow, and looked back at it, it made me dizzy, it was so monstrous crooked. However, we at last got through with the job; though, if you had seen the field after we had it done, you would have thought a gang of wild hogs had been rooting in it for the last month.

"Well, we planted the most of it in corn, and the rest we planted with the seeds I had bought at the drug-store. Among them was a paper labelled 'muskmelon seed,' (and I am remarkably fond of muskmelons, I am); so I planted them in the richest part of the patch, and tended them well till they began to grow finely. But, one day, as I was passing through the patch, I saw a young melon sprouting on one of the vines, and as it appeared to have a rather queer look, I stooped down to examine it closely, and may I never scalp another Indian if it wasn't a regular bottle-gourd! I turned in right away and dug all the vines up, for fear strangers might think I had a touch of nigger blood in me, for you know the old saying, 'A poor man for posterity, and a nigger for gourds.'

"Well, everything grew off splendidly for a spell, and the corn seemed to do just as well in the crooked furrows as if they had been straight; but after a while the drought set in, and the drier it got the more the corn turned 'yaller,' until at last it wilted right up. I tried my best to make it rain, but it was all no use. Sometimes, the frogs croaked powerfully in the 'slash' over yonder, but it never rained for all that; and at last the slash went dry, and the frogs would have died if they hadn't turned to highland toads. Sometimes the wind was due east, and my corns hurt me terribly, but still it didn't rain. Sometimes there was a great 'hello' around the moon, as big as a wagon-wheel, and I made sure we would have rain then; but we didn't, and never did until everything was as dry as this long yarn I am spinning now.

"But to cut it short, the crop turned out a perfect failure. And now I will tell you about the scurvy trick that Jackson there played off on me, not long ago. I wish my rifle may snap the next fair chance I get at an Indian, if I thought there was as much meanness in 'human natur.' You see, though it is true the crop had failed teetotally, there were about roasting-ears enough in the patch to make one pretty fair mess; and I told Jackson one morning that I would go out and kill a fat buck, and when I got back we would gather the crop, and have one good 'bait' out of it, anyhow. So I swabs out old Haco, as I call my rifle, and off I put, up one side of Doe Run and down the other, then over to York's Creek, and from there to Little Sandy, but not a single deer could I find. At last, however, when I had given up all hopes of killing a deer that day, and was making tracks for home, just after crossing Burnt Boot, I 'upped' as fine a buck as you ever saw. I peeled his hide off in short order, cut out the 'saddle,' and started for home at a double-quick, for by this time I was getting as hungry as a coyote wolf. When I got in about two hundred yards of the camp, I thought I smelt 'fried corn,' and mistrusted something was wrong immediately; and, sure enough, when I walked into the ranch, there sat that rascal Jackson 'shoveling' the last grain from the skillet down his throat.

"He had taken advantage of my absence to gather and eat up the whole crop we had been working four or five months to make! He hadn't left a nubbin as big as my thumb in the field, and consequently all my share of that crop was just one smell of fried corn; and I suppose I shouldn't have got that much if I hadn't happened to have the wind of Jackson as I came up.

"Well, from this time on, things got worse and worse. The potatoes took the dry rot—and who could blame 'em, as a drop of rain hadn't fallen in three months?—and everything else we had planted wilted right up, except the watermelons. They did finely, I suppose because they carry their own water along with 'em, and of course are independent of the weather. By this time, what with buying ploughs and hoes and other implements, etc., our money gave out entirely, and we were compelled to live on watermelons, with now and then a dish of 'poor doe,' which, as you know, isn't much stronger diet than the watermelons. I admit that watermelons are first rate in their way, but when a fellow has nothing but watermelons for breakfast, watermelons for dinner, and watermelons for supper, he fairly hates the sight of one after a while. I pledge my word, Dobell, that after I had lived for a week or so on 'em, I could hear the water 'jug' in me whenever I stumped my toe as I walked along! And then they are such unsatisfying and 'ill-convenient' diet! In fifteen minutes after eating a fellow that would weigh twenty pounds, I was just as hungry as ever.

"Once there came along some travelers here, who wanted dinner, and I tell you, Dobell, I have never felt so mean in my life since the time Polly Jenkins said, 'No, sir-ee, horse-fly, Bob,' to a little question I asked her, as I did when I took the travelers out to the 'patch,' and, giving them a butcher-knife apiece, told them to 'pitch in,' as their dinner was before them. However, I see Jackson has got the steaks ready for supper; so draw up a 'chunk,' Dobell, and take a 'bite.'

"No, Dobell," he continued, as he helped my tin platter to about a pound of juicy steak, "I'd rather be that old chunk you are sitting on, sailing forever round and round in a 'dead eddy,' than live here as I have done for the last six months."

"But, Big-Foot," said I, "if you are going to give up 'farming,' what will you go at? There won't be any more rangers wanted, you know, because the Government has settled all the Indians upon their 'reserves,' where they are learning them to farm and to eat fat beef in place of horse-meat."

"Yes," said Big-Foot, with a melancholy shake of the head, "all that is very true, I know, and I hear the Indians take to it kindly—least ways to the beef. However, Jackson tells me there's a couple of 'gals' moved into the settlement down below here, that are as rich as 'cow-yards,' and we have concluded to 'slick up' a little and hunt stock awhile in that neighborhood. I think I shall stand a pretty good chance to get one of them, seeing as how there are worse-looking chaps than I am; but as for Jackson there, he is so uncommonly ugly, that if a 'gal' was dying of some sort of sickness that could only be cured by marrying, I'm doubtful, if he was to offer himself, if she wouldn't rather 'kick the bucket,' and him, too. Look at them teeth of his, will you, how they stick out in front, just as if he had been made on purpose to 'eat pumpkins through a fence.' "

"But, Big-Foot," said I, "if you *should* accidentally fail in the 'gal speculation,' what will you do then?"

"That is what I call a 'poser,' " said he; "but there's one thing you may depend on: just as soon as I hear of a Comanche starving to death for want of a horse to eat, I'll try 'farming,' again, and not before. Jackson, bring out the bottle-gourd—there's a little 'wake robin' left in it yet, and I have talked till I am as dry as a 'buffalo-chip.' "

V. MIRACLE MEN

Whenever the sense of his own incapacity showed the need of some great artificer, some supernatural miracle-worker, man created gods in his own image.—MARIAN ROALFE COX

1. COMIC DEMIGODS

WHEN the heroes of history go, the demigods arrive. As the ring-tailed roarer is a comic version of the frontiersman who wrestles single-handed with the wilderness, so our tinkering demigods are the comic culture heroes of an industrial civilization who account for its wonders. Their miracles are also the pranks of trickster heroes, whose huge laughs provide much the same sort of comic relief as our comic strips. "All mythical heroes have been exaggerations," says Max Eastman, "but they have been serious ones. America came too late for that. . . . That is the natively American thing—not that her primitive humor is exaggerative, but that her primitive exaggerations were humorous." [1]

A typical American demigod is Pecos Bill, the culture hero of the cowboy, who is said to have "invented most of the things connected with the cow business." At the same time his affinity with the wild men of the West is attested by his title of the "king killer of the bad men." His toughness is of the kind that was the boast of the pseudo bad men: "He cut his teeth on a bowie knife, and his earliest playfellows were the bears and catamounts of East Texas." In the Davy Crockett tradition are his fights with two grizzly bears, which he hugged to death; with a rattlesnake, which he used as a lariat to spin at Gila monsters; and with a mountain lion, which soon hollered for mercy and let Bill ride him "a hundred feet at a jump . . . quirtin' him down the flank with the rattlesnake." He is the boasting cowboy par excellence; and his cyclone variant of the theme of the horse that couldn't be ridden and the cowboy that couldn't be thrown is only a little less poetic than Badger Clark's High-Chin Bob version. In the latter's poem of "The Glory Trail" (also recorded from tradition by John A. Lomax) Bob ropes a mountain lion; and since neither would or could let go, they continue together through eternity—a ghost rider on a ghost horse leading a ghost lion in a noose. Pecos Bill's death is a caricature of the death of a hero, caused, according to one version, by putting "fish-hooks and barbed wire in his toddy."

In a slightly different key is the "saga of inadvertence" of Bowleg Bill, whose fool stunts and outlandish exploits are more the result of happy accidents—"uncommon happen-quences"—than of design. His reckless playfulness links him with Pecos Bill, but this "gawdamnedest intelligent fool" outdoes the other in the "larger lunacy" of his antics. As a sea-going cowboy and an "inland furriner" he combines the freakishness of a hybrid with the innocence of the greenhorn, though in this case a green-horn who teaches the old hands some new tricks. Of the breed of pet

---

[1] *Enjoyment of Laughter* (1936), p. 168.

trout and rattlesnakes is Piccolo the whistling whale; and the bronco that could not be broken turns up again in Slickbritches the Hoss-Mackerel.

The American genius for invention has produced its hero in Paul Bunyan. Although he handles nature like a toy and accounts for the bigness of certain American geographical features, such as Puget Sound, he is primarily a work giant whose job is to invent logging. By reason of his having to start from scratch, there is something primordial about him; but unlike most Titans, he combines brain with brawn, and employs both for the good of mankind. He has gone a long way from the giant of nursery tales whose chief purpose was to scare little children and be slain by the hero.

Just as the "mightiest of loggers" appears in other settings and guises as Tony Beaver, Kemp Morgan, Finn MacCool, and Febold Feboldson, so his exploits are essentially prodigious lies of the Munchausen variety, which are much older than the heroes themselves. The "key stories" in the Bunyan cycle may be matched by hundreds of Old World parallels in Stith Thompson's *Motif-Index of Folk-Literature.*

Tales of the Paul Bunyan type originated as separate anecdotes or "gags" exchanged in competitive bragging or lying contests and involving "sells" and the pranking of greenhorns. "The best authorities," writes W. B. Laughead (and in this the experts all agree), "never recounted Paul Bunyan's exploits in narrative form. They made their statements more impressive by dropping them casually, in an offhand way, as if in reference to actual events of common knowledge." Such remarks often began with a phrase of reminiscence or reminder: "Time I was with Paul up in the Big Onion country ——"; "That happened the year I went up for Paul Bunyan"; "Did you ever hear of the —— that Paul Bunyan ——?"

James Stevens traces the mythical Paul Bunyan to a French-Canadian logger named Paul Bunyon, who won a reputation as a prodigious fighter in the Papineau Rebellion against the Queen in 1837, and later became famous as the boss of a logging camp—"he fight like hell, he work like hell, and he pack like hell."[1] But whatever his historical origins, if any, Paul Bunyan—the superman in a world of super-gadgets—has become an American symbol of bigness and a proverbial character on which to tack an extravagant anecdote. Although the tradition has spread to many other occupations—the oil fields, the wheat fields, and construction jobs, Paul Bunyan tales are told popularly, outside of the industry more than within it, and depend for their effect upon pure exaggeration rather than upon occupational coloring.

The first appearance of Paul Bunyan in print seems to have been an advertising man's idea. In 1914 the Red River Lumber Company issued a booklet of tales which has since gone through twelve editions, gradually incorporating more and more advertising matter along with the original stories. To-day Paul Bunyan is the company's trademark and "stands for the quality and service you have the right to expect from Paul Bunyan." The author and illustrator of these booklets, W. B. Laughead, who claims to have invented many of the names of characters and who is given credit for initiating the preservation of the Paul Bunyan stories, has never made

---

[1] *Paul Bunyan,* by James Stevens (1925), p. 1.

clear whether Paul Bunyan dreamed up the lumber business or *vice versa*.[1]
In 1914 also appeared Douglas Malloch's poem "The Round River Drive,"
published in *The American Lumberman*, to be followed in 1916 by the
first scholarly investigation of the legends by K. Bernice Stewart and
Homer A. Watt, in 1919 by the "first continuous narrative" of Ida
Virginia Turney, and in 1924 by Esther Shephard's volume. In the same
year James Stevens began to publish his dressed-up versions for readers
who do not like their folklore raw. How much of Paul Bunyan is folklore
and how much of it is literature is still an open question. But in the
absence of authentic oral versions, scholars give credence to the view that
he is, if not actually a hoax, at least the product of downward transmission.[2]

Paul Bunyan has been the inspiration of other demigods who are
probable inventions, such as Tony Beaver, the West Virginia lumberjack
hero of *Up Eel River* (1928), by Margaret Prescott Montague, and Febold
Feboldson, the plains hero. On the origins of the latter Paul R. Beath
writes:[3]

I first became aware of Febold Feboldson when stories of him were appearing
regularly in the Gothenburg, Nebraska, *Times*. As I recall this was in 1927 or
1928 while I was undergraduate at the University of Illinois. About this time
I read James Stevens' *Paul Bunyan* and immediately spotted the similarity. It
was during this period that I started contributing an occasional story to the
Times during my summer vacations which I spent in Nebraska. The stories
were mostly adaptations of those I had heard around town with elaborations and
embellishments to fit what I conceived to be Febold's character, i. e., an
indomitable Swedish pioneer who could surmount any difficulty.

I must add here that as a boy and young man I worked as night clerk in a
hotel in Gothenburg where I heard literally thousands of stories told by
travelling salesmen and other garrulous wayfarers. I suppose I received clues
to many of the stories I used from this ever flowing stream. At one time, after

---

[1] See his letter to Louise Pound in her article on "Nebraska Strong Men," *Southern
Folklore Quarterly*, Vol. VII (September, 1943), No. 3, pp. 133–143. For Paul Bunyan
bibliography see "Paul Bunyan Twenty-Five Years After," by Gladys J. Haney,
The Journal of American Folklore, Vol. LV (July-September, 1942), No. 217, pp. 155–
168.

[2] In a note on "Paul Bunyan—Myth or Hoax?", in *Minnesota History*, Vol. XXI
(March, 1940), No. 1, pp. 55–58, Carleton C. Ames places the burden of proof on
"those who are presenting Paul Bunyan as a native product of the imagination of
the shanty boy, and who are making him, in a sense, the patron saint of the old-
time logger." On the basis of the negative evidence that Paul Bunyan was unknown
to old-timers in Wisconsin and Minnesota and of certain anachronisms in Esther
Shephard's version, he reaches the "tentative conclusion" that "Paul Bunyan as the
legendary hero of the shanty boy, as true folklore, is spurious. He may have appeared
in the camps of a later day, possibly about the turn of the century, when the true
shanty boy had all but vanished. He may exist among the lumberjacks of the Pacific
Coast, where logging is a far different operation than the Minnesota and Wisconsin
jack ever knew, but he was a stranger to the loggers of the Middle West when logging
was at its height."

[3] Letter to Louise Pound, July 1, 1943, a copy of which, together with clippings
from the Gothenburg, Nebraska *Times*, and other Febold data, is on file at the Archive
of American Folk Song, Library of Congress, Washington, D. C.

I had read the Canterbury Tales in college, I contemplated a modern set based on this hotel experience.

. . . Don Holmes of the *Times* told me that the character had been created by Wayne T. Carroll, a local lumber dealer, who wrote a column under the name of Watt Tell in the now defunct Gothenburg *Independent*. This series, to the best of my knowledge, began about 1923. Later Carroll used Febold in advertising he wrote for his lumber company. Lumber magazines were the first to use Paul Bunyan and it seems obvious to me that Febold was patterned after Paul Bunyan. But Febold could never have been a lumber hero, because there are no trees on the Great Plains. So Febold became a hero wrestling with the adversities of the plains—tornadoes, drouths, extreme hot and cold, Indians, politicians, and disease.

Because I have published Febold the widest of any of his first champions— that is, Carroll, Holmes, and myself—I have been accused of creating him. I did not. Febold, a pioneer Swede, and all his nephews were in existence when I came upon the legend. Febold, the fabulous uncle, had already gone to his reward by retiring to California like a good middlewesterner. His exploits seemed always to be recounted by someone who knew him in the old days, usually his nephews, Bergstrom Stromberg, Herebold Farvardson, Hjalmar Hjalmarson, and Eldad Johnson. For some reason there was always a contemporary of Febold called Eldad Johnson's grandfather. The only historical basis for any of these characters is that Olof Bergstrom is Bergstrom Stromberg, . . . the immigration from Gothenburg, Sweden, to Nebraska of a band of Swedes [having been] led by Olof Bergstrom who founded both Stromberg (the reverse of his true name) and Gothenburg in the state of Nebraska. It is my opinion that Carroll had this man in mind, because tales of him were current when I was a boy. He had a most hectic career. He married a Swedish singer on one of his periodic returns to the old country; she later committed suicide. He worked for the Union Pacific selling railroad land to the incoming immigrants. He killed a man and was acquitted. He was said to have disappeared.

In 1928 these stories "caught on." Not only did Don write them, but contributions began coming in from the *Times* readers. From 1928 to 1933 at least one Febold story appeared in the *Times* without a break from week to week, a total of 260 stories.

Mr. Beath's account throws light on the making of legendary heroes. The early stages of the process are clearly reflected in the Febold stories, where the central conception of a heroic character has not yet attained full growth and tends to fall apart into the *disjecta membra* of tall stories.

2. Strong Men and Star Performers

Although American legendary heroes like Paul Bunyan and the other work giants are occupational heroes, they are industrial pioneers rather than industrialists. Thus Paul Bunyan represents the days before the timber beast became a timber mechanic and Old Stormalong, the days of wooden ships and iron men. Under the influence of the machine the hero undergoes a change. The work boss is supplanted by the ordinary worker, who distinguishes himself not so much for innovations as for doing a good job of whatever he is doing. He is a strong man or a star performer with tragic and social rather than comic significance. The tragedy usually results from his being overcome by a superior force—the machine. Thus John Henry dies in a contest with a steam drill and Casey Jones in a train wreck with one hand on the whistle cord and the other on the airbrake lever; while Joe Magarac offers himself up as a sacrifice to make better steel.

Originally a flesh-and-blood hero of the rock-tunnel gangs, the great steel-driver who died with his hammer in his hand while competing with a steam-drill at Big Bend Tunnel on the Chesapeake and Ohio Railroad in West Virginia in 1870, John Henry has become a legendary and mythical figure with various symbolic significances. In folk song tradition the "tiny epic of man's last stand against the machine" has produced a work song (the hammer song), a ballad, and a social song or blues, in which the central theme of the drilling contest has attracted to itself double meaning stanzas and conventional ballad lines and motifs. The few John Henry tales that have been recovered are of the Paul Bunyan type, elaborating the hero's size, strength, skill, and prowess with food, women, etc. As the tradition moved west, other kinds of labor were substituted for tunnel construction, until in Roark Bradford's version John Henry becomes the champion cotton picker, roustabout, and railroad man with more than a touch of the bad man and boaster or "big mouth."

"I'm f'm de Black River country," said John Henry, "and I kin roust what I kin git my hands on. But dat don't make me no rouster. I'm f'm de Black River country whar de sun don't never shine. My home ain't hyar, and I'm fixin' to git around."

". . . 'Scuse me for laughin', Cap'm," he said, "but dat tawk do sound funny. Dat winch might work like ten good men, but how about John Henry? I burned out all de men you got, and I kin burn dat steam winch out, too.

"So th'ow down another stage for me, so I kin git some action. I'll roll more cotton on de *Big Jim White* den you kin wid dat steam winch, 'cause I'm John Henry and I'm six foot tall and my strenk can't hit de bottom. Maybe de women fool me bad, and maybe, too, de gamblers. Maybe de happy dust cross me up and de preacher put me in de dozens. But rollin' cotton ain't nothin' but work, and can't nobody fool me. So stand back, you bullies, and gimme some room, and watch me roll dat cotton. I'll clean dat boat befo' de sun goes down or my name ain't John Henry."

The supreme symbol of industrial strength is Joe Magarac, who comments thus on his name and nature: "Sure! Magarac. Joe. Dat's me. All I do is eatit and workit same lak jackass donkey." He symbolizes not only the power of steel but the power of the men behind the steel, the human basis of our basic industry.

There is no glory comparable to poured iron or poured steel. The gushing out of fiery metal from a great wheel-like container seems like the beginning of Creation. This black container of molten iron is twenty feet high. A ladle advances on an overhead railway. It travels to the container of molten iron. It moves forward on its track and then laterally and then down. The black container swings around slowly on its axle as a man presses a lever.

Then follows the sudden magnificence of poured metal. Like giant fireworks, a thousand sparks fly from it, a river of white fire throwing off cascades of stars, a fiery shower on all sides. On a greasy platform above the ladle are the men who operate it. They look down with indifference into its seething deadly brightness.

My guide said: "A man fell into that once, and they buried him and all the tons of metal. Right here they held the burial service."

The story of the man who fell into the vat of molten metal and became part of it obsesses the men's minds. I have heard it told in different ways.

They tell you of a man made into iron rails, of another who went into the structure of great buildings.

This story is as old as time. There was a great bell once which was cast and re-cast and would not ring true until a human being was sacrificed to it.[1]

The Saga of Pecos Bill

It is highly probable that Paul Bunyan, whose exploits were told in a recent number of *The Century Magazine,* and Pecos Bill, mythical cow-boy hero of the Southwest, were blood brothers. At all events, they can meet on one common ground: they were both fathered by a liar.

Pecos Bill is not a new-comer in the Southwest. His mighty deeds have been sung for generations by the men of the range. In my boyhood days in west Texas I first heard of Bill, and in later years I have often listened to chapters of his history told around the chuck-wagon by gravely mendacious cow-boys.

The stranger in cattle-land usually hears of Bill if he shows an incautious curiosity about the cow business. Some old-timer is sure to remark mournfully:

"Ranchin' ain't what it was in the days Bill staked out New Mexico."

If the visitor walks into the trap and inquires further about Bill, he is sure to receive an assortment of misinformation that every cow-hand delights in unloading on the unwary.

Although Bill has been quoted in a number of Western stories, the real history of his wondrous deeds has never been printed. I have here collected a few of the tales about him which will doubtless be familiar to cow-men, but deserve to be passed on to a larger audience.

Bill invented most of the things connected with the cow business. He was a mighty man of valor, the king killer of the bad men, and it

---

[1] *Men and Steel,* by Mary Heaton Vorse (1920), p. 20.

By Edward O'Reilly. From *The Century Magazine,* Vol. 106 (October, 1923, No. 6), pp. 827–833. Copyright, 1923, by The Century Co.

was Bill who taught the broncho how to buck. It is a matter of record that he dug the Rio Grande one dry year when he grew tired of packin' water from the Gulf of Mexico.

According to the most veracious historians, Bill was born about the time Sam Houston discovered Texas. His mother was a sturdy pioneer woman who once killed forty-five Indians with a broom-handle, and weaned him on moonshine liquor when he was three days old. He cut his teeth on a bowie-knife, and his earliest playfellows were the bears and catamounts of east Texas.

When Bill was about a year old, another family moved into the country, and located about fifty miles down the river. His father decided the place was gettin' too crowded, and packed his family in a wagon and headed west.

One day after they crossed the Pecos River, Bill fell out of the wagon. As there were sixteen or seventeen other children in the family, his parents didn't miss him for four or five weeks, and then it was too late to try to find him.

That's how Bill came to grow up with the coyotes along the Pecos. He soon learned the coyote language, and used to hunt with them and sit on the hills and howl at night. Being so young when he got lost, he always thought he was a coyote. That's where he learned to kill deer by runnin' them to death.

One day when he was about ten years old a cow-boy came along just when Bill had matched a fight with two grizzly bears. Bill hugged the bears to death, tore off a hind leg, and was just settin' down to breakfast when this cow-boy loped up and asked him what he meant by runnin' around naked that way among the varmints.

"Why, because I am a varmint," Bill told him. "I'm a coyote."

The cow-boy argued with him that he was a human, but Bill wouldn't believe him.

"Ain't I got fleas?" he insisted. "And don't I howl around all night, like a respectable coyote should do?"

"That don't prove nothin'," the cow-boy answered. "All Texans have fleas, and most of them howl. Did you ever see a coyote that didn't have a tail? Well, you ain't got no tail; so that proves you ain't a varmint."

Bill looked, and, sure enough, he didn't have a tail.

"You sure got me out on a limb," says Bill. "I never noticed that before. It shows what higher education will do for a man. I believe you're right. Lead me to them humans, and I'll threw in with them."

Bill went to town with this cow-hand, and in due time he got to enjoyin' all the pleasant vices of mankind, and decided that he certainly was a human. He got to runnin' with the wild bunch, and sunk lower and lower, until finally he became a cow-boy.

It wasn't long until he was famous as a bad man. He invented the six-shooter and train-robbin' and most of the crimes popular in the old

days of the West. He didn't invent cow-stealin'. That was discovered
by King David in the Bible, but Bill improved on it.

There is no way of tellin' just how many men Bill did kill. Deep
down he had a tender heart, however, and never killed women or children,
or tourists out of season. He never scalped his victims; he was too
civilized for that. He used to skin them gently and tan their hides.

It wasn't long before Bill had killed all the bad men in west Texas,
massacred all the Indians, and eat all the buffalo. So he decided to
migrate to a new country where hard men still thrived and a man could
pass the time away.

He saddled up his horse and hit for the West. One day he met an old
trapper and told him what he was lookin' for.

"I want the hardest cow outfit in the world," he says. "Not one of
these ordinary cow-stealin', Mexican-shootin' bunches of amateurs, but a
real hard herd of hand-picked hellions that make murder a fine art and
take some proper pride in their slaughter."

"Stranger, you're headed in the right direction," answers the trapper.
"Keep right on down this draw for a couple of hundred miles, and you'll
find that very outfit. They're so hard they can kick fire out of a flint
rock with their bare toes."

Bill single-footed down that draw for about a hundred miles that
afternoon; then he met with an accident. His horse stubbed his toe on
a mountain and broke his leg, leavin' Bill afoot.

He slung his saddle over his shoulder and set off hikin' down that draw,
cussin' and a-swearin'. Profanity was a gift with Bill.

All at once a big ten-foot rattlesnake quiled up in his path, set his tail
to singin', and allowed he'd like to match a fight. Bill laid down his
saddle, and just to be fair about it, he gave the snake the first three
bites. Then he waded into that reptile and everlastingly frailed the pizen
out of him.

By and by that old rattler yelled for mercy, and admitted that when
it came to fightin', Bill started where he let off. So Bill picked up his
saddle and started on, carryin' the snake in his hand and spinnin' it in
short loops at the Gila monsters.

About fifty miles further on, a big old mountain-lion jumped off a cliff
and lit all spraddled out on Bill's neck. This was no ordinary lion. It
weighed more than three steers and a yearlin', and was the very same
lion the State of Nuevo León was named after down in old Mexico.

Kind of chucklin' to himself, Bill laid down his saddle and his snake and
went into action. In a minute the fur was flyin' down the cañon until
it darkened the sun. The way Bill knocked the animosity out of that
lion was a shame. In about three minutes that lion hollered:

"I'll give up, Bill. Can't you take a joke?"

Bill let him up, and then he cinched the saddle on him and went down
that cañon whoopin' and yellin', ridin' that lion a hundred feet at a
jump, and quirtin' him down the flank with the rattlesnake.

It wasn't long before he saw a chuck-wagon with a bunch of cow-boys squattin' around it. He rode up to that wagon, splittin' the air with his war-whoops, with that old lion a-screechin', and that snake singin' his rattles.

When he came to the fire he grabbed the old cougar by the ear, jerked him back on his haunches, stepped off him, hung his snake around his neck, and looked the outfit over. Them cow-boys sat there sayin' less than nothin'.

Bill was hungry, and seein' a boilerful of beans cookin' on the fire, he scooped up a few handfuls and swallowed them, washin' them down with a few gallons of boilin' coffee out of the pot. Wipin' his mouth on a handful of prickly-pear cactus, Bill turned to the cow-boys and asked:

"Who the hell is boss around here?"

A big fellow about eight feet tall, with seven pistols and nine bowie-knives in his belt, rose up and, takin' off his hat, said:

"Stranger, I was; but you be."

Bill had many adventures with this outfit. It was about this time he staked out New Mexico, and used Arizona for a calf-pasture. It was here that he found his noted horse Widow-Maker. He raised him from a colt on nitroglycerin and dynamite, and Bill was the only man that could throw a leg over him.

There wasn't anythin' that Bill couldn't ride, although I have heard of one occasion when he was thrown. He made a bet that he could ride an Oklahoma cyclone slick-heeled, without a saddle.

He met the cyclone, the worst that was ever known, up on the Kansas line. Bill eared that tornado down and climbed on its back. That cyclone did some pitchin' that is unbelievable, if it were not vouched for by many reliable witnesses.

Down across Texas it went sunfishin', back-flippin', side-windin', knockin' down mountains, blowin' the holes out of the ground, and tyin' rivers into knots. The Staked Plains used to be heavily timbered until that big wind swiped the trees off and left it a bare prairie.

Bill just sat up there, thumbin' that cyclone in the withers, floppin' it across the ears with his hat, and rollin' a cigarette with one hand He rode it through three States, but over in Arizona it got him.

When it saw it couldn't throw him, it rained out from under him This is proved by the fact that it washed out the Grand Cañon. Bill came down over in California. The spot where he lit is now known as Death Valley, a hole in the ground more than one hundred feet below sea-level, and the print of his hip-pockets can still be seen in the granite.

I have heard this story disputed in some of its details. Some historians claim that Bill wasn't thrown; that he slid down on a streak of lightnin' without knockin' the ashes off his cigarette. It is also claimed that the Grand Cañon was dug by Bill one week when he went prospectin'; but the best authorities insist on the first version. They argue that that streak of lightnin' story comes from the habit he always had of usin' one to light his cigarette.

Bill was a great roper. In fact, he invented ropin'. Old-timers who admit they knew him say that his rope was as long as the equator, although the more conservative say that it was at least two feet shorter on one end. He used to rope a herd of cattle at one throw.

This skill once saved the life of a friend. The friend had tried to ride Widow-Maker one day, and was thrown so high he came down on top of Pike's Peak. He was in the middle of a bad fix, because he couldn't get down, and seemed doomed to a lingerin' death on high.

Bill came to the rescue, and usin' only a short calf-loop, he roped his friend around the neck and jerked him down to safety in the valley, twenty thousand feet below. This man was always grateful, and became Bill's horse-wrangler at the time he staked out New Mexico.

In his idle moments in New Mexico Bill amused himself puttin' thorns on the trees and horns on the toads. It was on this ranch he dug the Rio Grande and invented the centipede and the tarantula as a joke on his friends.

When the cow business was dull, Pecos Bill occasionally embarked in other ventures; for instance, at one time he took a contract to supply the S. P. Railroad with wood. He hired a few hundred Mexicans to chop and haul the wood to the railroad line. As pay for the job, Bill gave each Mexican one fourth of the wood he hauled.

These Mexicans are funny people. After they received their share of the wood they didn't know what to do with it; so Bill took it off their hands and never charged them a cent.

On another occasion Bill took the job of buildin' the line fence that forms the boundary from El Paso across to the Pacific. He rounded up a herd of prairie-dogs and set them to dig holes, which by nature a prairie-dog likes to do.

Whenever one of them finished a nice hole and settled down to live in it, Bill evicted him and stuck a fence-post in the hole. Everybody admired his foresight except the prairie-dogs, and who cares what a prairie-dog thinks?

Old Bill was always a very truthful man. To prove this, the cow-boys repeat one of his stories, which Bill claimed happened to him. Nobody ever disputed him; that is, no one who is alive now.

He threw in with a bunch of Kiowa Indians one time on a little huntin'-trip. It was about the time the buffalo were getting scarce, and Bill was huntin' with his famous squatter-hound named Norther.

Norther would run down a buffalo and hold him by the ear until Bill came up and skinned him alive. Then he would turn it loose to grow a new hide. The scheme worked all right in the summer, but in the winter most of them caught colds and died.

The stories of Bill's love-affairs are especially numerous. One of them may be told. It is the sad tale of the fate of his bride, a winsome little maiden called Slue-Foot Sue. She was a famous rider herself, and Bill lost his heart when he saw her riding a catfish down the Rio Grande with only a surcingle. You must remember that the catfish in the Rio Grande are bigger than whales and twice as active.

Sue made a sad mistake, however, when she insisted on ridin' Widow-Maker on her weddin'-day. The old horse threw her so high she had to duck her head to let the moon go by. Unfortunately, she was wearin' her weddin'-gown, and in those days the women wore those big steel-spring bustles.

Well, when Sue lit, she naturally bounced, and every time she came down she bounced again. It was an awful sad sight to see Bill implorin' her to quit her bouncin' and not be so nervous; but Sue kept right on, up and down, weepin', and throwin' kisses to her distracted lover, and carryin' on as a bride naturally would do under those circumstances.

She bounced for three days and four nights, and Bill finally had to shoot her to keep her from starvin' to death. It was mighty tragic. Bill never got over it. Of course he married lots of women after that. In fact, it was one of his weaknesses; but none of them filled the place in his heart once held by Slue-Foot Sue, his bouncin' bride.

There is a great difference of opinion as to the manner of Bill's demise. Many claim that it was his drinkin' habits that killed him. You see, Bill got so that liquor didn't have any kick for him, and he fell into the habit of drinkin' strychnine and other forms of wolf pizen.

Even the wolf bait lost its effect, and he got to puttin' fish-hooks and barbed wire in his toddy. It was the barbed wire that finally killed him. It rusted his interior and gave him indigestion. He wasted away to a mere skeleton, weighin' not more than two tons; then up and died, and went to his infernal reward.

Many of the border bards who knew Pecos Bill at his best have a different account of his death.

They say that he met a man from Boston one day, wearing a mail-order cow-boy outfit, and askin' fool questions about the West; and poor old Bill laid down and laughed himself to death.

Old Stormalong, the Deep-Water Sailorman

"CERTAINLY, I 'member Old Stormalong," said the oldest skipper on Cape Cod. "I was a 'prentice fust on his ship and later on I was Second when he was bosun on the *Courser*, out o' Boston. *That* was a ship, a wooden ship with iron men on her decks, a ship that aint been eekaled by these hoity-toity steamboats. No, sir, an' never will. Donald McKay built that ship just because he found one sailorman who could handle her as

From *Here's Audacity! American Legendary Heroes*, by Frank Shay, pp. 17–31. Copyright, 1930, by Frank Shay. New York: The Macaulay Company.

she should be handled. But, you're aimin' to hear about a sailorman an not about ships.

"Only t'other day a young whippersnapper was a-telling me about Stormie sayin' as how he was fourteen fathoms tall. I've heared other tales about his height. I know! He was jes' four fathoms from the deck to the bridge of his nose.

"He was the first sailorman to have the letters 'A. B.' after his name. Those were jes' his 'nitials, put after his name on the ship's log just the same as always. Alfred Bulltop Stormalong was the name he gave his first skipper. The old man looked him over and says:

" 'A. B. S. Able-Bodied Sailor. By your size and strength they should measure the talents of all other seamen.'

"It makes me pretee mad when I see some of the hornswogglers of today with these letters after their names. They are only feeble imitators o' the greatest o' all deep-water sailormen.

"You landsmen know very little about real sailormen, that is, blue-water sailors. This chap Stormalong was not only a sailorman for all waters, he was a whaler too. I mind the time we was anchored in the middle of the North 'Lantic finishin' off a right whale. The lookout sights a school off to the east'ard and Stormie, the bosun, gives the order to h'ist the mudhook. All hands for'ard but not a h'ist. The hook 'ud give a bit and then it 'ud sink right back into the mud. Seemed to be hands clutchin' it and draggin' it out o' our hands. Once we got it clear o' the bottom and almost shipped it when we seed what was wrong. Nothin' short of an octopus was wropped all 'round that mudhook. He was holdin' the anchor with half of his tenacles and with the other half hangin' on to the seaweed on the bottom.

"The mate yelled 'vast heavin' ' and went back to tell the skipper. When the old man came for'ard to see for himself he was just in time to see Stormie go overboard with his sheath knife in his teeth. He went below the su'face and there began a terrific struggle. The water was churned and splashed about so that old hooker jes' rolled about like she was beam to the wind. All of us was sure our bosun had been tore 'part by the octopus. The struggle went on for about a quarter of an hour when Stormie's head came to the su'face. Some one called out to throw him a line but before one could be brought he had grabbed the anchor chain and came hand over hand to the deck. The strugglin' in the water kept on for a while but moved away from the ship.

" 'All right,' yelled Stormie, 'all hands lean on it and bring it home.'

"After the anchor was shipped I asked him what he had done to the octopus.

" 'Jes' tied his arms in knots. Double Carrick bends. It'll take him a month o' Sundays to untie them.'

"There was one peculiar thing about Stormalong that was due to his size. He was as loyal to his ship as any sailorman until he saw a bigger one. Then he'd get peevish an' sullen until he had signed aboard the bigger ship. His biggest complaint was that ships weren't built big enough for a full sized man.

"Well, the ship we were on at that time was *Lady of the Sea*, finest and fastest of the tea packets. Even that didn't satisfy him. He wanted a bigger ship or he'd go farmin'. Once he said to us as we sat 'round the forebitt:

"'When this hooker gets to port I'm goin' to put an oar over my shoulder and I'm goin' to start walkin' 'way from salt water. I'm goin' to keep right on walkin' until some hairlegger says to me, "What's that funny stick you have on your shoulder, matey?" an' right there I'm goin' to settle down and dig potaters.'

"'Yes,' said the Third-in-Command, skeptically, 'what potaters are you goin' to dig?'

"'Regular and proper spuds, fresh ones, not like the dead potaters you get on this hooker,' said the Sailor Who Was Tired of the Sea.

"'Got to plant them first,' said the Third. 'Then you got to hoe them, pick the bugs off'n them, spray them, hoe them some more. You got to irrigate them, too. Best irrigater for potatoes is the sweat off'n your brow. Just dig so hard and fast that the sweat rolls down along your nose and drops on the plant. Much harder'n holystoning the deck which, by the way, you'll begin on jus' as soon as you turn to in the mornin'.'

"'Nothin' can be as hard as holystoning a deck,' observed Stormie.

"'Compared with sailoring,' I cuts in, 'farmin' comes under the headin' of hard labor. The best part o' farmin', I'll admit, is that all the hard work comes in fine weather while with sailorin' it's jes' t'other way 'bout.'

"For the rest of that trip Stormalong was moody and preoccupied. He had been on the ship for over a year, a very long time for him, without seeing a bigger ship. When the ship hit Boston Stormie signed off. He came on deck with his duffel bag over his shoulder.

"'Where you goin'?' I asks him.

"'Farmin',' says he.

"Then he heaves the bag over the rail and follows it to the wharf. The crew of the *Lady of the Sea* just stood along the rail and gaped.

2

"Several years later when we were again lined against the wharf at Boston a big, tall man was seen coming down the wharf.

"'Stormie, or I'm a fool,' says I to myself.

"The big man came over the side and sure enough it was Alfred Bulltop Stormalong. There was a change immediately apparent. He was taller than ever but the flesh hung in dewlaps all over him and his eyes showed the marks of great suffering. Too, he looked hungrily at the sea. He breathed deep breaths of the salt air and in a few minutes seemed to regain some of his old spirit.

"'Stormie, where 'a' you been?' I asks him.

" 'Farmin',' says he.

" 'How'd you like it?' I goes on.

" 'Terrible,' says he. 'Nothin' but green grass an' trees an' hills an' hot work. Nary a breeze or the smell o' the sea. Never a storm to make a man pull out all the best that's in him. Nothin' but zephyrs an' a hot sun an' pushin' on a plow. All my muscles were made for pullin' an' on a farm there's nothin' to do but push. Sailorin's the best job after all.'

"He signed on for his old job of boatswain and after taking on water we got under way. We cruised about the Caribbean Sea taking on and discharging shipments for over six months. Then we made for Boston Harbor.

"Stormie was a loyal sailor until he saw a bigger ship and the *Lady of the Sea* was the biggest ship sailing the Atlantic. At least we thought she was but just before we got to Barnegat we came across what first appeared to be a mirage. She was just the biggest ship ever built and I heard the skipper say to the mate that she was Donald McKay's dream come to life. Her lines were perfect, her cloth pure white and hung on silver masts. She rolled lazily on a sea that made us bump about like a cork. I saw Stormie at the rail gazing in goggle-eyed admiration.

" 'Must take a million ordinary sailors to man her,' he gasped. 'Yes, sir! One million at the least. Well, I guess I'll be leavin' this packet.'

"The next mornin' we were without a bosun. The best explanation we could give was that during the night he had gone over the side and swum to the big ship. For a second time Stormalong had gone out of my life.

"After the *Lady of the Sea* discharged her cargo in Boston we got word that they were signing on a crew for a new ship, the *Courser*. I applied for a place as second mate and was signed on. We were told to report to a ship at the end of the wharf that was acting as a tender for the *Courser* which was too big to enter Boston Harbor.

"The next morning we boarded the tender and were taken out to the *Courser*. She was none other than the big ship we had seen from the *Lady of the Sea*, the ship that Stormie had gone over the side for. She looked like a ship that might have been built for a race of men of Stormalong's stature. The first thing that caught my eye as my feet hit the deck was a stableful of horses.

" 'Horse boat, huh!' I said.

" 'Horse boat nothin',' said the man in charge of the tender. 'Those horses are for the men on watch.'

"Believe it or not. That ship was so big that all officers and men on watch were mounted on horses. Manalive, her rigging was so immense that no living man could take her in at a single glance. Her masts penetrated the clouds and the top sections were on hinges so they could be bent over to let the sun and moon pass. Her sails were so big that the builders had to take all the able-bodied sailmakers out in the Sahara Desert to find room to sew them. Young men who were sent aloft usually came down as gray-beards. The skipper had to order all hands aloft six days before a storm. Every yard and every block and tackle had bunkhouses and cooks' galleys built into them to accommodate the men who worked aloft. She carried over six hundred men and some of the sailormen never saw all their shipmates. Once the Old Man, who gave his orders through a megaphone, ordered all hands forward. It took the after crew a week to get there and then over thirty were killed in the crush. Some of the men got lost because they had not taken the precaution to bring their compasses with them.

"The *Courser* was so big that she had to keep to the oceans, there was no harbor big enough for her to turn about in. Her wheel was so big it took thirty-two men working in unison to turn her and early in the cruise it was found that Stormalong was the only man aboard who could make her answer the wheel promptly. When we had to take on or discharge a cargo a whole fleet of ordinary ships used to come out and we would transship our load.

"But she was a great ship. There never was a storm great enough to cause her any real discomfort.

"There was one that caused us a bit of worry. One of those September gales that chivvy us in the North Atlantic. She was so big that the Skipper just let her ride out any storm, knowing that no matter how big a blow it was the *Courser* could weather it. Well, this was some storm, and we bobbed about like a regular sized vessel all over that ocean. Worst of it was that the clouds and fog made it so dark we couldn't make where we were at. This went on for over a fortnight when we awoke to see the sun bright and shining. The bosun put his mouth to his megaphone and shouted:

Rise and shine
For the Black Ball Line

and all hands turned to. There was Stormalong at the wheel holding her true to what he thought was her course. After the Captain and all the mates had 'taken the sun' and figured it out on paper they told us we were somewhere in the North Sea and headed south. That meant trouble. The *Courser* could never get through the English Channel and it meant that we'd pile up against the cliffs of Dover or on the French coast. You see, the North Sea wasn't big enough for us to turn around in. The skipper and the mates had a consultation and decided as they could not turn around to take a chance of easing through the Channel. The officers rode across the poop of that ship on their horses, yelling orders and squinting their eyes along the ship's sides. Stormie was at the wheel and the only man who could see everything at once. Just as they got to the point between Calais and the cliffs of Dover all sails were reefed and the skipper was ready to order the men to take to the boats. He looked back at Stormie and saw that the man at the wheel was calm and steady.

" 'Will she make it?' yelled the skipper through his megaphone.

" 'I think so!' answered the man at the wheel. 'May scrape a bit o' paint off'n our sides but she'll go through.'

"Then, squinting first along the port side an' then the starboard, he called to the man on the poop deck:

" 'Better send all hands over and soap the sides, put an extry heavy coat on the starboard.'

"The skipper got the whole crew plastering the sides with the best soap he had and the big ship eased through just as sweet as honey. But it's all due to the soap that we did get through. It was such a tight fit that the cliffs at Dover scraped every bit of soap off the starboard side. Ever since then the cliffs at that point have been pure white. That was from the *Courser's* soap and the action of the waves. Sometime when you are in the channel take a look at the waves. They are still a bit foamy from the soap.

"When the Old Man saw we had gotten through he called all hands forward to splice the main brace, which meant in nautical terms, to come and have a drink of grog.

"The *Courser* kept right on going but after a few hours we got into shallow water and we had to jettison all of our ballast. We threw so much overboard that you can still see the piles of dirt. The English call them the Channel Islands.

"In all the time I knew her the *Courser* had but one other storm that troubled her. Strange to relate but it was another September gale, one of those lads that generally does so much damage around Florida. The *Courser* was down among the Caribbees and the storm whipped her about pretty badly. The Skipper wasn't as much afraid of losing his ship as he was of hitting one of the islands and knocking it and the inhabitants into kingdom come. The ship just missed Haiti and headed west by south like a broncho with the bit in his teeth. Right down the Gulf she went until she came to Darien and without asking anybody's permission went right through the Isthmus. The *Courser* found herself out in the Pacific Ocean. The only eye-witnesses of the destruction outside the crew were a couple of army officers who had been sent down by the United States to make surveys for a canal. And right in front of their eyes a ship comes along and digs it for them. Naturally they took all the credit but the truth of it is Old Stormalong and the *Courser* dug that ditch."

The Oldest Skipper on Cape Cod paused in his narrative to yawn and give his cronies a chance.

"All I ever knowed about him," said another, "was that he took his whale soup in a Cape Cod dory, that his fav'rite meat was shark. He liked ostrich eggs for breakfast and then he would lie back on the deck and pick his teeth with an eighteen foot oar."

"Skippers came and skippers went," said the Oldest Skipper on Cape Cod, "but Stormie stuck to the *Courser* to the end. He died while we were discharging a cargo from the middle of the Gulf of Mexico."

"I heard how he was buried," said the Sailor Who Had Swallowed the Anchor. "They took him ashore and buried him right near the water so he could always have the salt spray over him."

Then he burst into song:

Stormie's gone, that good old man,

And all the rest joined in the chorus line:

To my way hay, storm along, John.
Stormie's gone, that good old man,
To my aye, aye, aye, Mister Stormalong!

They dug his grave with a silver spade,
To my way hay, storm along, John!
His shroud of finest silk was made,
To my aye, aye, aye, Mister Stormalong!

They lowered him with a silver chain,
To my way hay, storm along, John!
Their eyes all dim with more than rain,
To my aye, aye, aye, Mister Stormalong!

An able sailor, bold and true,
To my way hay, storm along, John!
A good old bosun to his crew,
To my aye, aye, aye, Mister Stormalong!

He's moored at last, and furled his sail,
To my way hay, storm along, John!
No danger now from wreck or gale,
To my aye, aye, aye, Mister Stormalong!

I wish I was old Stormie's son,
To my way hay, storm along, John!
I'd build me a ship of a thousand ton,
To my aye, aye, aye, Mister Stormalong!

I'd sail this wide world 'round and 'round,
To my way hay, storm along, John!
With plenty of money I would be found,
To my aye, aye, aye, Mister Stormalong!

I'd fill her with New England rum,
To my way hay, storm along, John!
All my shellbacks they would have some,
To my aye, aye, aye, Mister Stormalong!

Old Stormie's dead and gone to rest,
To my way hay, storm along, John!
Of all the sailors he was the best,
To my aye, aye, aye, Mister Stormalong!

The song ended and the old shellbacks looked wistfully across the harbor. Beyond the harbor entrance a steamship was making her smoky way to Minot's Light. The Sailor Who Had Swallowed the Anchor spat into the water and said:

"When I went to sea they had iron men and wooden ships; now they got iron ships and wooden men. I'd ruther be found dead than to be found on one o' them steamboats."

Bowleg Bill

I. THE CRIMPING OF BOWLEG BILL

SOME say 'Frisco, some say Provincetown. Nobody seems to know where Bowleg Bill first went down to the sea. But east or west, it was a long trail, for it began in Laramie County, Wyoming.

They called him "the sea-going cowboy," and though his adventures were keeping the Liars' Bench warm in every port from Cape Cod on "down to the east'ard," Bowleg never forgot his home acres. Through it all—whaling, fishing, the foreign trade—he remained at heart a ranch-hand; he longed again to feel out his saddle.

Once, when he came to Provincetown as third mate of the whaleship *Lily Queen*—"riding herd," as he called it, on a passel of fo'mast hands— three towns on Lower Cape Cod could hear him bellowing his favorite ditty across the waters of the bay, and there were echoes even on the far shore, in the very respectable towns of Brewster and Dennis. Unfortunately, my publishers tell me the words of this song do not lend themselves well to print. There were forty-eight stanzas, and from the lot I have picked one which I am allowed to include here if I change the last line. And I am including it because it shows how Bowleg Bill really felt about the sea, though he was at the height of his career. It goes:

> Oh, give me a bucket o' bull blood,
>   Give me the prai-rie grass!
> You kin take yore oceans
> And seafaring notions
>   And la, tra-la, tra-la.

Because he felt this way, Bowleg was never, technically, an able seaman. Those who spread his fame and were so generous with their own embroidery would readily admit that he "didn't know a thwart from a thunder-mug."

No, and he never bothered to learn. Throughout his career, he did

From *Bowleg Bill, The Sea-Going Cowboy,* or Ship Ahoy & Let 'Er Buck! by Jeremiah Digges, pp. 11–18, 21–28, 37–46. Copyright, 1938, by Josef Berger. New York: The Viking Press.

things in his own way, and ashore or afloat, it was the way of the ranch-hand, the mustanger, the bronc-peeler, from another world. On the Liars' Bench, he was always "the big furriner," and his "born-to trade" was touched on gingerly by the wharf-yarners, who described it as "launching crank horses on their maiden voyage across the flats of Wyoming," or, in other versions, "going harbor-pilot to them big schools of western cattle—them hermaphrodite-rig bulls that are growed for their meat."

But with such a background for their hero, the spell-weavers of dory and wharf-spile could cast off in waters worthy of their skill. They could sail close to the wind. They could soar above all demand for oath and affidavit and grandly omit the long assurances that everything was gospel-truth. If, in the pages that follow, heaven or any of its inhabitants is called upon as witness, it will be merely a matter of form; it is the language of the Liars' Bench; it is a concession of the proud and the lofty.

All that they have asked of Bowleg Bill—in Gloucester, in Boston, in Provincetown—was that he be true to himself. And the Liars' Bench has kept him so. A gawd-damned lubber he was when he went down to the sea. A gawd-damned lubber he remained through the height of his fame. And precisely because of this, the wonders he worked were the more engaging to those who heard them, the more gleefully seized on by those who would pass them along.

Wharf-yarns and spoondrift? Yes, else why should Bowleg Bill be picked as the man to perform the prodigious—Bowleg, who, to quote the Bench itself, "could not have told you the difference between a taffr'l and the skipper's left tit," Bowleg, who, by his own admission, could never learn to "sashay around on them poles and wires," Bowleg, who was ever unpleasantly surprised because he couldn't remember to spit to the looward? Why pick the supreme lubber to work wonders at sea?

Well, he who knows the New England fisherman of today will understand, and so would he who knew the New England whaleman of yesterday. Give them Paul Bunyan, if you will, on the Liars' Bench of any waterfront, but do not try to impress the boys with what a mighty man Paul was. Do not go into the dull statistics of felling a spruce six feet through in ten strokes of the ax—by virtue of great strength and great skill. No, if you would win these fellows over to Paul, let him fell his tree in one stroke—and with his eyes closed too—by virtue of a rotten spot in the trunk. Better still, let him lean on his ax while a bolt of lightning comes down at the proper moment and does the business for him.

It's not that they are lazy. God knows, the fisherman's work is as hard as any on earth, and a shade more hazardous. But through the ages, the man with the hook, the trawl, or the harpoon has insisted on "working shares," instead of for a fixed wage; and the hero who clicks with him must be endowed with something above strength, something beyond skill.

Thus, the entire story of Bowleg Bill becomes a saga of inadvertence. His career at sea began by accident, the mistake of a "crimp" operating in a waterfront "pulparee," or dive frequented by drifters from the deep water and by floaters from inland. The whaleships of that day had difficulty finding men who were willing to undergo the hardships of a voyage lasting from three to five years, and crimps were paid to bring hands aboard. The crimp would accost his prey in the pulparee, buy him a few drinks, and then slip him a dose of knockout drops. When the victim came to, he was lying on the deck of some outbound blubber-boiler, with a bucko mate standing over him, belaying pin in hand.

The Liars' Bench has never bothered, so far as I have been able to discover, with the question of Bowleg's presence in a pulparee. It was a long way from Wyoming, no matter which coast, and Bowleg had wandered in, for no matter which of the two major attractions a pulparee offered.

There he fell in with a crimp, who was naturally impressed with his height—eight foot four inches without them long-heeled boots!—drugged, and hoisted aboard the whaleship *Sawdust Sal*. The mate of the *Sawdust Sal* looked him over with great curiosity, paused to stare at his legs and marvel, at the way he "paid off on opposite tacks from the waist down," felt of the angora chaps he was wearing, and in bafflement finally remarked: "I've seen many a tough hide in my day, but I'll be damned if ever I seen a man that chafes so severe he needs rope-yarns on his drawers!" He kicked Bowleg's inert form over, slipped the gun out of "that inside-out leather pocket stuck on his belt," and left him there on the deck.

When Bowleg came to, it was morning and the *Sawdust Sal* was well out to sea on a cruise of three years or longer. He sat up and blinked. He looked out to starboard and saw deep water. He looked out to larboard and saw more deep water. He rose to his full height, saw deep water all around him, and exclaimed:

"Durned if I hain't flooded the range in my sleep!"

When the mate saw Bowleg on his feet, he came after him with a marline-spike. But Bowleg nodded and said sleepily:

"Mornin'. You hain't seen nawthing of a chestnut gelding tethered somewheres hereabouts, have you, stranger?"

"Git aloft there, ye swill-sotted son of a sarpint," the officer answered, "and take in the skys'l afore I start a little gelding of my own aboard this ship!"

That answer didn't mean a great deal to Bowleg, but the tone of it told him this was no exchange of good old Western pleasantries.

"Fly yore own balloons," he said. "I hain't got time for play, and my hoss never did like the wet too well."

The mate brought up his marline-spike, and Bowleg reached for his gun—which wasn't there. So he took hold of the spike and twisted it out of the fellow's hand.

"When a man asks after his own hoss," Bowleg lectured, "he's asking a civil question. Don't you know this thing is dangerous, with a sharp point to it?" and he tossed the marline-spike overboard.

The mate swung at Bowleg with his fist, and several other ship's officers ran to join in the fight. All accounts agree that it was a grand mêlée, there on the deck of the *Sawdust Sal*, with Bowleg's long arms bowling men down as quickly as they got to their feet, and with a lecture throughout from the giant bronco-buster, who kept asking them, didn't they know it wasn't civil to come at a man with "them tent-pegs and things" when he was merely asking after his hoss?

Finally Captain Slateface appeared on deck, with a pistol in his hand. Slateface, according to the Liars' Bench, was one of the most terrible, the bloodthirstiest bully captains ever to go a-whaling.

"You the foreman here?" Bowleg asked.

Slateface ignored him, and turned to the mate.

"Clap this mutinous son of a bitch in the run!"

But nobody stepped forward to carry out the order, and when the skipper looked back at Bowleg, he found a long six-shooter pointing his way. For the mate who had taken the gun from Bowleg's belt had never thought to look in his "long-heeled shoes." And with this gun, so the Liars' Bench avers, "you could have shot a fourteen-foot blue shark from dead astern and blowed his brains out!"

"Better put that little parlor-piece away, boss," Bowleg told the skipper. "Why, you might put somebody's eye out with that!" And when the Captain wavered, and could not make up his mind whether to give up or let fly, Bowleg warned the other men:

"All right, boys. If this place has a bar or something to give cover, better lay low behind it!"

Then—bang! The six-shooter roared out once, and when the smoke cleared, there stood the skipper "with his mustache clipped off clean at the second coil—port side." And—bang!—the six-shooter roared out twice, and when the smoke cleared, there stood the skipper, "with his mustache clipped off clean at the second coil—starboard side."

Well, the upshot of it was that Bowleg, after neatly bringing the skipper out of his whiskers and scaring him out of his wits, disarmed him and forced the crew to "hop up there and wheel this thing around for home— pronto!" And while the skipper sat by the after-hatch and growled through his short hairs about "mutiny" and "fur-legged lunatics," the whaleship *Sawdust Sal* was worked back into port.

And on these details of Bowleg Bill's first adventure at sea, the Liars' Bench is generally agreed. Several seaports have been named, several names have been given to the big cowpuncher. But these things do not matter, nor does it matter whether the stories of Bowleg Bill that follow were told on the Liars' Bench, of other men, in other ages. There was a way that all such stories had of popping up again and again in unexpected places, and in unexpected dress. There was a general overlapping, and I myself have heard parts of all these stories in still other stories; and the germ of no single one among them is new. The wharf-yarners do not invent. The truths they speak are the eternal verities; the words, spoondrift. . . .

II. SLICKBRITCHES THE HOSS-MACKEREL

The boys of the trap fleet are setting on the wharf as usual between trips, betting on the gulls as to which will be the next to decorate the spiles, when Bowleg Bill the sea-going cowboy shows up.

We have been hearing yarns for years of this wild Wyoming bronco-buster, and the uncommon happen-quences which are told of him since he took to seafaring, and now all of a sudden on our own waterfront here he is personal. But for all his rare seamanship, not even Bowleg Bill himself—personal as a spinster's dream—is going to take up much slack among the boys that goes out for swordfish or hoss-mackerel.

"Hoss-mackerel" is the name we give in Cape Cod waters to what off-Cape furriners calls "tuna." For a few days each summer they strike here and git caught in the weirs and float-traps which we set in the harbor for smaller fish. This summer the run of hoss-mackerel is heavy in the traps, and while the boys are talking of the elegant stocks it is rolling up for them, Bowleg Bill paces for'ard and aft on that wharf like a tomcat on one side of the fence which figures he is missing something on tother.

Finally the talk is more than he can put up with, and he walks over to Yank Daggett, who skippers the *Tossup,* and who is high-line fisher-man of the harbor fleet.

"This here hoss-mackerel," Bowleg inquires, "he's a sassy varmint, is he, stranger?"

Yank nods. "The strike is running uncommon heavy this season, with a long streak of hell in each of 'em."

"Mmm. Real cornfed he-man's work, is it, ridin' herd on 'em?"

"Well, you got to know how to gaff 'em in. Hoss-mackereling is no business for a green hand."

Bowleg Bill paces the wharf a couple more times, and comes back.

"What do you reckon the critters will weigh on the hoof?"

"Up to rising a thousand pounds. Most of 'em come a hundred to eight-nine hundred."

"Now, hain't that a shame!" says Bowleg. "Not enough to kick dust in yore eye! I was figgering I might admire to rope in a few, but where I come from, we don't bother with a rope on nawthing under a couple ton—that is, if it's extry good, smoke-snortin' bull with half a ton of devilment throwed in."

Yank bends a long grin between his ears.

"You jest throw back the small fry, eh?"

"Wa-al, them little fellers we pick up barehanded by the belly-slack, and toss 'em into the pens."

Yank nods. "Makes it handy, don't it? But with us, we got to watch out for the tail. A hoss-mackerel's tail ain't no slack hawser abaft, ending in a bunch of loose rope-yarns. When you git hoss-mackerel, you want to make sartin-sure you don't git slapped over the gunnels with his tail."

"Huh!" says Bowleg. "I have yet to meet up with the critter—two-legged or four, stranger—which I couldn't take keer of in that section. Where's yore foreman? I see I'll have to show you fellers how to haze yore herd, the way it's done back in old Wyoming!"

"I'm skipper here," Yank says, "but we ain't taking on no greenies while the run of hoss-mackerel keeps up."

"Mister," says Bowleg, "if you are a betting man, I'll jest hit the trail with you to them corral-things out yonder. And if I don't cut me out one of yore full-growed hoss-mackerel and bring him in bare-handed, without using none of them long-handled prod-sticks, I'll pay you twenty silver dollars and marry yore meanest of kin!"

Well, Yank figures this big cowboy has missed stays in the August heat, but he has heard so many yarns about him that finally he takes the bet. The boys at the wharf hurry upstreet to spread the news, and before dark the whole town is talking of the off-Cape lunatic who is going after hoss-mackerel barehanded. Big odds is offered against Bowleg, but these people knows fish, and there is no takers amongst 'em.

Next morning the whole harbor is cluttered up with dories, pungoes, and anything down to harness-casks, which the citizens can climb aboard to watch the *Tossup* draw the traps. As a fishing port, the town has took Bowleg's bet to heart as an insult, and he gets hootcalls aplenty on the way out. Even poor old Cap'n Dyer, who's been shorebound twenty years with the backsliding vertigo, is out there in one of the boats.

"Better go back inland, young feller!" he hollers. "Ye don't know what's waiting fer ye in that net!"

"Don't you fret over me, grandpaw!" Bowleg calls back. "That's a mighty shaky caboose yo're driving there. You get for cover pronto if I start a stampede!"

At the first trap, there is thrashing and white water, a commotion like a hurricane stoppered up under them net-buoys, and in the middle of it, the biggest hoss-mackerel Yank Daggett has ever seen. And the minute Yank does see him, he forgets all about Bowleg Bill, he forgets everything but that great blue-silver body and six foot of slapping, thrashing tail. And he stands ready with his gaff while the boys haul on the net.

Bowleg gets the measure of this big feller, and he climbs over, alongside Yank.

"That one over yonder!" he says. "Will he weigh up to our bet?"

"Will he weigh up to it! He's two thousand pounds if he's a Scotch ounce, you lubber!"

"All right, boys," Bowleg sings out, "give me a clear field!" And he pushes Yank and a couple of others aside and yells to the hoss-mackerel. "Come along, leetle dogie!"

"Hey, git aft, you blasted pig-farmer!" Yank hollers. "That fish is big money, and I ain't leaving it to no gawd-damned greeny to lose him!"

"Now, jest keep yore britches dry, boss," says Bowleg, "and lift that daggone spear out o' my road. I've picked my animal and I'm a-going after him for all creation and a barbwire fence! *Hy-up!* Come along, leetle dogie, come along!"

He reaches out, he gets hold of the fish in the small, and he heaves—though how in etarnity he figures to swing aboard two thousand pounds of game fish that way, only an inland furriner might know! The tail slips clear of his hands, and the hoss-mackerel slips clear of the backbone of the net.

"Look out!" Yank hollers. "He's clear! He's clear and away!"

"Oh, no. he hain't," Bowleg answers. Over the side he goes, boots and all, and before the fish has got under way, there is this shatterwitted cowpuncher, setting astride, whipping astern with his hat, and hollering like the yoho-bird of every dead sailor come home from hell!

"*Whoop-ee-ee! Hy-ee-ee—up!* Show some buck, now, you white-livered snubbin'-beetle, before I sell you off to a livery stable. Come on here, Slickbritches, *hy-up!*" And away goes that silver divil, and up he jumps, breaching clean out of the water like a porpoise. But when he comes down again, there is Bowleg Bill, still astraddle. still fanning his tail with the wide out-rigger hat.

Yank gives a groan. "There goes the biggest catch—and the gawddamnedest fool—that was ever set loose in these waters!"

But somebody aboard one of the craft hard by sets up a cheer: "Ride him. cowboy!" And other folks takes it up, till all over the harbor there is a wide sing-out of cheers for Bowleg Bill and the hoss-mackerel which he has named Slickbritches.

But the worst yells is from Bowleg himself, who is whooping like a wild Injun with the galloping chin-cough.

"*Yip, yip, yip-ee-ee!* Come on, you two-dollar fly-roost, hain't you going to throw no sand in their eyes?"

I don't know where he larned it, but somehow that cowboy has took a grip on the foretops'l fin, and no matter how bad Slickbritches broaches to, he can't shake him loose. They go scudding a wide circle of the harbor, with the big hoss-mackerel getting madder every minute. He dives to starboard, he lashes to larboard, he all but pitchpoles head-over. But somehow—and may the divil spit me over hell's hottest hearth if I can explain it!—Bowleg hangs on, with his knees bearing in close amidships, riding easy as grandmar in the Sunday-parlor rocker. Then Slickbritches makes one last big leap, like the flurry of an ironed whale—up in the air and clean over the bow of the *Tossup!*

"Buck away, you overgrowed sardine!" yells Bowleg. "I'll peel you if it takes to Kansas City!"

But after that last jump, it is plain that Slickbritches is losing wind.

He stops pitching, and jogs along easy among the harbor craft. And Bowleg, setting there and showing out of water from the knees up, starts stroking the fish abaft the gills, and talking to him, and—so help me Gawd!—little by little larning him to answer the helm! He hauls taut on that fin, and Slickbritches takes one tack; and he hauls again, and Slickbritches takes another tack; and when he has rode all the crank notions out of him, Bowleg veers about and heads in for the beach.

They make inshore till the hoss-mackerel is chafing his chin on the tideflats. Then—just when the whole town is fixing to send up a cheer for the landing of the biggest fish in history—this big beef-farmer gives a performance which none of us human folks will ever understand, and which I respectfully leave to some gawd-damned inlander to explain.

Instead of beaching that fish, he all of a sudden warps him around and jumps off!

Slickbritches heads for the open water, and Bowleg speeds him on his course, splashing after him and flogging him over the tail.

A crowd is gathered on the beach, and they are mad as a school of bees in a tar-barrel; for any man which lets a big fish get away has got some explaining to do before the law-abiding citizens of this town. When Bowleg wades out of the water, they all want to know why he done it, and is he gone clean whacky, and hadn't they better get him arrested and locked up as a dangerous character.

But Bowleg Bill just shakes his head at the crowd, and there is a sad, long-frayed look in his eyes, and he knuckles a tear off his cheek, and he says:

"That pore old windbroke waterbug! I tell you, folks, there ain't nawthing that'll break a cowhand's heart so quick as to find a critter—two-legged or four—with the rough all rode off at first mount!"

III. THE SKIPPER'S BULL BAZZOON [1]

The skipper is in his cabin, blowing brisk ditties on the bull bazzoon. OOMPA-DIDDLE-DIDDLE.

---

[1] . . . the story that Cap'n Sam told bore some resemblance to an old Cape Cod legend, or rather a whole group of legends, concerned with a "whistling whale," a musical giant whose talents were employed in various ways for the weal or woe of humankind.

According to one local version, a great whale was harpooned, the iron going in thwartships through his spouthole. That is a very effective but very dangerous place to harpoon a whale, I am told. At any rate, the whale got away. And ever after that, his breathing and spouting caused a great whistling sound which could be heard for miles.

Some say he learned to control it, and give the boys a tune; others, that he charmed other whales and treacherously turned decoy. And according to still another school, he had a pet hate on the chief of the Provincetown Volunteer Fire Department, who, in his younger days, had planted that very iron in his snoot. And so, he used to come into the harbor in the dead of night and reproduce the sound of the fire whistle so ably that the entire force would turn out three and four times a night.—J. D., pp. 153–154.

Me and Bowleg Bill is setting on the deck, the same as we have sot these hunderd and eighty long days at sea, with nary a heave of the long dart, nary a thimble of ile in the casks. Aye, we sets and we stews and we rots and we stinks, and Sparm Whale pokes his head out of the green water and gives us twenty barr'ls of the Injy Ocean in our faces with his compliments. And our skipper goes on a-blowing brisk ditties on the bull bazzoon.

"May the divil beach you on the hottest flats in hell!" I says to the whale.

"Shoo, you ornery gruller-hoss," Bowleg Bill says to the whale.

But he knows better, that whale. Him and all the whales in the Injy Ocean knows that Cap'n Epepharus Atkins of the *Duty Bound* has went clean whacky with a bull bazzoon, ever since he has picked it up in a New Bedford hand-me-along emporium. Aye, they knows the bazzoon is a bugle of Beelzebub, which will drive a man whacky blowing this everlasting oompa-diddle. And this particular bazzoon which our skipper has picked up is two yards long and big around as the spankerboom of the whaleship *Duty Bound*. And all the whales in the water knows that Epepharus Atkins will not show willing to lower so long as he can practice brisk ditties on that bazzoon.

OOMPA-DIDDLE-DIDDLE.

Like the groans and gripes of a bung-stoppered walrus, so help me! And this sparm whale is breaching under our lee quarter, till the lookout is nigh to gitting slapped out of the crow's nest.

"Thar she blows!" he hollers. "Blo-o-ow! Thar she blows and belches, thar she breaches and biles! My Gawd, thar she bilges the bottoms of my boots!"

OOMPA-DIDDLE-DIDDLE.

So long as he hears it, this whale knows he can blow like all the typhoons in the China Sea, for the skipper will never show willing to lower. And he twists his flukes up for'ard to the end of his nose, and he winks us an eye, and he gives to the whole of us a ancient and honorable invitation.

"Bowleg," I says, "I am discouraged. We ain't never going to git home again."

"Reckon not?" says Bowleg.

"Bowleg," I explains, "if the skipper don't show willing to lower, we don't git no whale. And if we don't git no whale, we don't try no blubber. And if we don't try no blubber, we don't bile no ile. And if we don't bile no ile, we don't stow no casks. And if we don't stow no casks—why, we jest cruise on and on! Bowleg"—and I breaks down under the whole of it—"we will jest cruise on and on till we have exhausticated the whole gawd-damned Injy Ocean!"

"Don't say!" says Bowleg. "Wa-al, durned if it don't look like a case for the possy!"

"And there is a girl back on Cape Cod, Bowleg, which I wish to see again," I goes on with a snag in my gullet. "We used to go out in the spring and pick mayflowers, her and me together," I goes on, with tears in my eyes. "Bowleg, I wish to go back to Cape Cod and pick mayflowers!"

Bowleg Bill lays a flipper on my shoulder, and I am crying like a baby, and the skipper is still in his cabin, blowing brisk ditties on the bull bazzoon. And Bowleg keeps saying it is a case for the possy—whatever the hell that is—and this gawd-damned whale keeps blowing barr'ls of the Injy Ocean in our faces, and I breaks down under the whole of it. And I turns to Bowleg.

"Bowleg Bill, you are a pore crimped sailor. By trade you are a cowhand, and your home acres is the cow country. But, Bowleg, you won't never navigate no cows again, you won't never climb aboard no horse, you will not see them long flats of Wyoming again to the end of your days!"

"*What?*" he bellers. "You aiming to say, pardner, *I can't ride the range no more?*"

"Never no more, Bowleg—till we have exhausticated the whole of the Injy Ocean."

He jumps to his feet. He walks to the rail. He looks this here sparm whale in the eye, and he says:

"You jest keep yore shirt on, stranger. I'm a-going downstairs for a leetle talk with the driver of this roundup wagon. But I'll take keer of you when I git back." And he crowds his eight-foot frame down through the coamings of the after-hatch.

OOMPA-DIDDLE-DIDDLE.

It goes on for a few more toots, and then I hears it taper off to one last belch. And then there is voices, coming from below in the skipper's cabin:

"So Seaman Salthorse is discouraged, is he?"

"Plumb discouraged, sir."

"Well, you jest tell Seaman Salthorse any time he gits so discouraged he would like to jump overboard, I have no anchors lodged whar they would hold him back. Now, git for'ard, ye long-eared lubber, and next time you break into my bazzooning I'll have you flogged a dozen lashes for every note I miss!"

OOMPA-DID—

"Jest a minute, boss. I hear this outfit's been hired to ride out yonder and stick a passel o' them floatin' pigs. And while I hain't never hankered for pig-stickin' work, here is one hombre that is about ready for the feel of his saddle. Now, I'll jest trouble you, boss, to hand me over that double-jointed flute."

Then I hears a ruckus breaking out, and the skipper hollers for the mate. And then more ruckus, and shouting and batterfanging about down below, but in a couple of minutes the noise abates, and up comes Bowleg Bill, with his big forty-five in one hand and—may Gawd sink my soul for a derelict!—the skipper's bazzoon in tother!

"Bowleg," I says, "where is the skipper?"

"He'll keep. Got him and that foreman of his hog-tied down there in the chuck-box."

"My Gawd, Bowleg, you have committed mutiny!"

"Hain't done no such of a thing," says he, setting down the bazzoon to roll a cigarette. "Yore boss has still got everything he was born with, pardner."

"Bowleg," I says, "I ain't no sea lawyer, but I knows a mutiny from a maypole dance. Now we can't never go back to the States!"

"Wa-al, now, out where I come from, Salthorse, when the feller that's driving the wagon falls asleep, a smart nag don't stop dead at the cross-roads." And he goes to the rail and looks out to sea. "Now, where is that daggone water-beetle?"

The sparm whale is standing by, and when Bowleg raises him again, he waves his hat and lets out a yell.

"*Hy-up!* Come on, you son of a squirt-gun, and let me tame you down with a good old tune from the country of the sage and the hardpan!" And with that, he starts a-blowing on the skipper's bull bazzoon. And if there is one thing worse in this miserable world than Cap'n Atkins's brisk ditties, it is the music which Bowleg Bill is making now.

OOMPA-DIDDLE-DIDDLE.

Like the mating season of a school of overdue sea elephants, and I am not the man to talk small of nature's wonders! But this sparm whale rises to Bowleg's music first off. In fact, he is clean spell-moored to it! He veers and he rolls, he scuds and he spins, he ups and he downs like a three-legged tailor with two left legs, and he launches into a hell-roaring hornpipe to the thunderbeats which Bowleg Bill sends rolling over the Injy Ocean.

OOMPA-DIDDLE-DIDDLE.

Closer and closer to the vessel comes the spell-betaken critter, and louder and louder Bowleg blows on the skipper's bull bazzoon. His face is gitting red, his eyes is nigh popped, I am afeard he is going to start a plank any time now, or pass his insides through that black foghorn of hell. But he jest keeps on a-blowing, and when the whale is come within a looward spit, this whacky cowboy climbs up on the bulwark and holds the bazzoon aloft.

"In the name of the Bar One Flying Bee, of old Wyoming," he hollers, "I christen you Piccolo Ike!" And with the heft of a spile-driver, he jams the bazzoon down into the spouthole of the whale. Then he takes the long steering oar out of the waist boat and brings it down—one, two, three —on that bazzoon, driving it in like a calker's stick, where all the ripping and snorting of hell's own hurricanes will never jar it clear.

Then—hey-diddle-diddle, away goes Piccolo Ike, a-trumpeting for Judgment Day! Every time he blows, he has got to blow through that bazzoon, and now it is gitting blowed like it was never blowed before. That whale is out of sight long before he is out of earshot, and while the *Duty Bound* is jogging along with a smart sou'wester at her heels, we can hear him running due no'theast, and far across the water—

OOMPA-DIDDLE-DIDDLE.

"Wa-al," says Bowleg Bill, "now that we got a bellwether turned out with the herd, reckon 'twon't do no harm to let the boss up out of the dugout." And he goes below and sets loose the skipper and the mate.

Cap'n Atkins is wild. When Bowleg tells him he can't give him back his bull bazzoon, he is wilder still. But this ain't nothing but sweet birdsong alongside of what he is next morning. We are idling over a flat sea, and he is pacing the quarterdeck, and growling to himself. And all of a sudden he hears, rolling over that blue water—

OOMPA-DIDDLE-DIDDLE.

Aye, then the skipper digs in and claws at his hair, and nigh jumps out of his boots. And the lookout calls down:

"Thar she—thar she whistles!"

"Where away?" the Cap'n bellers.

"Two points off the starboard bow. Sparm whale! Sparm whale with a steam calliope!"

All hands comes on deck, and there is Piccolo Ike, heading straight for the vessel, and a-blowing on the skipper's bull bazzoon, with all the whales in the Injy Ocean coming in his wake! They are follering him, and may the divil keel-haul me on hell's own bottom if it ain't because of the brisk ditties he is blowing on the skipper's bull bazzoon!

"Thar she whistles and toots!" the lookout yells. "Thar she warbles, thar she chirps! Thar—Gawd damn ye down below—thar she yodels lullabies!"

"Lower away!" the skipper orders. "Lower all boats! Lively there, ye blasted school o' mud turkles, lower and see that the whole of ye makes fast to the critter which is playing on my bazzoon!"

And so the whaleship *Duty Bound*—a hunderd and eighty-one long days at sea—lowers for whale at last! And when the boats come back, they has each of them killed three-four sparm whales, rolling fin out, and waiting to be cut in.

Cap'n Atkins is standing at the rail, and as the boats come back, one by one he asks them, where is the whale which has made off with his bazzoon. But we shakes our heads, every man amongst us, and the boatsteerers they look shy, and the mates they look ashamed. And from over the horizon, far out in the Injy Ocean, it comes again—

OOMPA-DIDDLE-DIDDLE.

Cap'n Atkins roars and rants, he stomps and he heaves at his hair. But there is whales to cut in, there is blubber to bile, and ile to stow in the hold of the *Duty Bound*. And all hands is at work, with every man a two-fathom grin spread under his jib.

Next day we picks up the whistling of Piccolo Ike again. And again Cap'n Atkins goes into a galloping frenzy, and orders all boats to lower. And whales is killed, and ile is biled, but no man amongst us has salvaged the bull bazzoon. And time and again, as the weeks go by we picks up Piccolo Ike by the brisk ditties which he is blowing, and the boatsteerers they look shy and the mates they look ashamed, and Cap'n Atkins roars and rants and bites out pieces of the cap rail. But we lowers, we makes fast, we gits whale. We cuts in, we biles blubber, we stows down. And all hands works with a two-fathom grin spread under their jibs. So I turns to Bowleg Bill, and I says:

"Bowleg, I am thinking of the girl back on Cape Cod, and I am thinking of the mayflowers which I will go a-picking. One things leads to another in this world, which is no place for a man to be discouraged."

And Bowleg Bill turns to me and says:

"Salthorse, it's a daggone elegant world! Reckon I'll be riding the range again in my time, and when I do, it'll be on some ornery gruller-hoss with jest enough daylight under him to clear the sagebrush!"

On this we shakes hands, and we looks out over that gawd-damned Injy Ocean, and I starts me a chantey!

> For it's Old Man Sparm
> With a iron in his back—

And Bowleg jines me in:

> Oh, it's Old Sulphurbottom
> With a iron in his middle—

And from far astern, we hears across that blue water—

> OOMPA-DIDDLE-DIDDLE.

Paul Bunyan

I. WHO MADE PAUL BUNYAN?

WHO made Paul Bunyan, who gave him birth as a myth, who joked him into life as the Master Lumberjack, who fashioned him forth as an apparition easing the hours of men amid axes and trees, saws and lumber? The people, the bookless people, they made Paul and had him alive long before he got into the books for those who read. He grew up in shanties, around the hot stoves of winter, among socks and mittens drying, in the smell of tobacco smoke and the roar of laughter mocking the outside weather. And some of Paul came overseas in wooden bunks below decks in sailing vessels. And some of Paul is old as the hills, young as the alphabet.

The Pacific Ocean froze over in the winter of the Blue Snow and Paul Bunyan had long teams of oxen hauling regular white snow over from China. This

From *The People, Yes,* by Carl Sandburg, pp. 97–99. Copyright, 1936, by Harcourt, Brace and Company, Inc. New York.

was the winter Paul gave a party to the Seven Axmen. Paul fixed a granite floor sunk two hundred feet deep for them to dance on. Still, it tipped and tilted as the dance went on. And because the Seven Axmen refused to take off their hob-nailed boots, the sparks from the nails of their dancing feet lit up the place so that Paul didn't light the kerosene lamps. No women being on the Big Onion river at that time the Seven Axmen had to dance with each other, the one left over in each set taking Paul as a partner. The commotion of the dancing that night brought on an earthquake and the Big Onion river moved over three counties to the east.

One year when it rained from St. Patrick's Day till the Fourth of July, Paul Bunyan got disgusted because his celebration of the Fourth was spoiled. He dived into Lake Superior and swam to where a solid pillar of water was coming down. He dived under this pillar, swam up into it and climbed with powerful swimming strokes, was gone about an hour, came splashing down, and as the rain stopped, he explained, "I turned the dam thing off." This is told in the Big North Woods and on the Great Lakes, with many particulars.

Two mosquitoes lighted on one of Paul Bunyan's oxen, killed it, ate it, cleaned the bones, and sat on a grub shanty picking their teeth as Paul came along. Paul sent to Australia for two special bumble bees to kill these mosquitoes. But the bees and the mosquitoes intermarried; their children had stingers on both ends. And things kept getting worse till Paul brought a big boatload of sorghum up from Louisiana and while all the bee-mosquitoes were eating at the sweet sorghum he floated them down to the Gulf of Mexico. They got so fat that it was easy to drown them all between New Orleans and Galveston.

Paul logged on the Little Gimlet in Oregon one winter. The cook stove at that camp covered an acre of ground. They fastened the side of a hog on each snowshoe and four men used to skate on the griddle while the cook flipped the pancakes. The eating table was three miles long; elevators carried the cakes to the ends of the table where boys on bicycles rode back and forth on a path down the center of the table dropping the cakes where called for.

Benny, the Little Blue Ox of Paul Bunyan, grew two feet every time Paul looked at him, when a youngster. The barn was gone one morning and they found it on Benny's back; he grew out of it in a night. One night he kept pawing and bellowing for more pancakes, till there were two hundred men at the cook shanty stove trying to keep him fed. About breakfast time Benny broke loose, tore down the cook shanty, ate all the pancakes piled up for the loggers' breakfast. And after that Benny made his mistake; he ate the red hot stove; and that finished him. This is only one of the hot stove stories told in the North Woods.

II. The Round River Drive

'Twas '64 or '65
We drove the great Round River Drive;
'Twas '65 or '64—
Yes, it was durin' of the war,
Or it was after or before.
Those were the days in Michigan,
The good old days, when any man
Could cut and skid and log and haul,
And there was pine enough for all.
Then all the logger had to do
Was find some timber that was new
Beside a stream—he knew it ran
To Huron or to Michigan,
That at the mouth a mill there was
To take the timber for the saws.
(In those old days the pioneer
He need not read his title clear
To mansions there or timber here.)
Paul Bunyan, (you have heard of Paul?
He was the king pin of 'em all,
The greatest logger in the land;
He had a punch in either hand
And licked more men and drove more miles
And got more drunk in more new styles
Than any other peavey prince
Before, or then, or ever since.)
Paul Bunyan bossed that famous crew:
A bunch of shoutin' bruisers, too—
Black Dan MacDonald, Tom McCann,
Dutch Jake, Red Murphy, Dirty Dan,
And other Dans from black to red,
With Curley Charlie, yellow-head,
And Patsy Ward, from off the Clam—
The kind of gang to break a jam,
To clean a bar or rassle rum,
Or give a twenty to a bum.

Paul Bunyan and his fightin' crew,
In '64 or '5 or '2,
They started out to find the pines
Without much thought of section lines.
So west by north they made their way
One hundred miles until one day
They found good timber, level land,
And roarin' water close at hand.

By Douglas Malloch. From *The American Lumberman,* Whole Number 2032, April 25, 1914, p. 33. Chicago, Ill.

They built a bunk and cook-house there;
They didn't know exactly where
It was and, more, they didn't care.
Before the Spring, I give my word,
Some mighty funny things occurred.

Now, near the camp there was a spring
That used to steam like everything.
One day a chap that brought supplies
Had on a load of mammoth size,
A load of peas. Just on the road
Beside the spring he ditched his load
And all those peas, the bloomin' mess,
Fell in the spring—a ton I guess.
He come to camp expectin' he
Would get from Bunyan the G. B.
But Joe the Cook, a French Canuck,
Said, "Paul, I teenk it is ze luck—
Them spring is hot; so, Paul, pardon,
And we will have ze grand bouillon!"

To prove the teamster not at fault,
He took some pepper, pork and salt,
A right proportion each of these,
And threw them in among the peas—
And got enough, and good soup, too,
To last the whole of winter through.
The rest of us were kind of glad
He spilt the peas, when soup we had—
Except the flunkeys; they were mad
Because each day they had to tramp
Three miles and tote the soup to camp.

Joe had a stove, some furnace, too,
The size for such a hungry crew.
Say what you will, it is the meat,
The pie and sinkers, choppers eat
That git results. It is the beans
And spuds that are the best machines
For fallin' norway, skiddin' pine,
And keepin' hemlock drives in line.
This stove of Joe's it was a rig
For cookin' grub that was so big
It took a solid cord of wood
To git a fire to goin' good.
The flunkeys cleaned three forties bare
Each week to keep a fire in there.
That stove's dimensions south to north,
From east to westward, and so forth,
I don't remember just exact,
And do not like to state a fact

Unless I know that fact is true,
For I would hate deceivin' you.
But I remember once that Joe
Put in a mammoth batch of dough;
And then he thought (at least he tried)
To take it out the other side.
But when he went to walk around
The stove (it was so far) he found
That long before the bend he turned
The bread not only baked but burned.

We had two coons for flunkeys, Sam
And Tom. Joe used to strap a ham
Upon each foot of each of them
When we had pancakes each A. M.
They'd skate around the stove lids for
An hour or so, or maybe more,
And grease 'em for him. But one day
Old Pink-Eye Martin (anyway
He couldn't see so very good),
Old Pink-Eye he misunderstood
Which was the bakin'-powder can
And in the dough eight fingers ran
Of powder, blastin'-powder black—
Those niggers never did come back.
They touched a cake, a flash, and poof!
Went Sam and Tommie through the roof.
We hunted for a month or so
But never found 'em—that, you know,
It was the year of the black snow.

We put one hundred million feet
On skids that winter. Hard to beat,
You say it was? It was some crew.
We took it off one forty, too.
A hundred million feet we skid—
That forty was a pyramid;
It runs up skyward to a peak—
To see the top would take a week.
The top of it, it seems to me,
Was far as twenty men could see.
But down below the stuff we slides,
For there was trees on all four sides.

And, by the way, a funny thing
Occurred along in early Spring.
One day we seen some deer tracks there,
As big as any of a bear.
Old Forty Jones (He's straw-boss on
The side where those there deer had gone)

He doesn't say a thing but he
Thinks out a scheme, and him and me
We set a key-log in a pile,
And watched that night for quite a while.
And when the deer come down to drink
We tripped the key-log in a wink.
We killed two hundred in the herd—
For Forty's scheme was sure a bird.
Enough of venison we got
To last all Winter, with one shot.

Paul Bunyan had the biggest steer
That ever was, in camp that year.
Nine horses he'd out-pull and skid—
He weighed five thousand pounds, he did.
The barn boss (handy man besides)
Made him a harness from the hides
Of all the deer (it took 'em all)
And Pink-Eye Martin used to haul
His stove wood in. Remember yet
How buckskin stretches when it's wet?
One day when he was haulin' wood,
(A dead log that was dry and good)
One cloudy day, it started in
To rainin' like the very sin.
Well, Pink-Eye pounded on the ox
And beat it over roads and rocks
To camp. He landed there all right
And turned around—no log in sight!
But down the road, around the bend,
Those tugs were stretchin' without end.
Well, Pink-Eye he goes in to eat.
The sun comes out with lots of heat.
It dries the buckskin that was damp
And hauls the log right into camp!

That was a pretty lucky crew
And yet we had some hard luck, too.
You've heard of Phalen, double-jawed?
He had two sets of teeth that sawed
Through almost anything. One night
He sure did use his molars right.
While walkin' in his sleep he hit
The filer's rack and, after it,
Then with the stone-trough he collides—
Which makes him sore, and mad besides.
Before he wakes, so mad he is,
He works those double teeth of his,
And long before he gits his wits
He chews that grindstone into bits.

But still we didn't miss it so;
For to the top we used to go
And from the forty's highest crown
We'd start the stones a-rollin' down.
We'd lay an ax on every one
And follow it upon the run;
And, when we reached the lowest ledge,
Each ax it had a razor edge.

So passed the Winter day by day,
Not always work not always play.
We fought a little, worked a lot,
And played whatever chance we got.

Jim Liverpool, for instance, bet
Across the river he could get
By jumpin', and he won it, too.
He got the laugh on half the crew:
For twice in air he stops and humps
And makes the river in three jumps.

We didn't have no booze around
For every fellow that we found
And sent to town for apple jack
Would drink it all up comin' back.

One day the bull-cook parin' spuds
He hears a sizzlin' in the suds
And finds the peelin's, strange to say,
Are all fermentin' where they lay.
Now Sour-face Murphy in the door
Was standin'. And the face he wore
Convinced the first assistant cook
That Murphy soured 'em with his look.
And when he had the parin's drained
A quart of Irish booze remained.
The bull-cook tells the tale to Paul
And Paul takes Murphy off the haul
And gives him, very willingly,
A job as camp distillery.

At last, a hundred million in,
'Twas time for drivin' to begin.
We broke our rollways in a rush
And started through the rain and slush
To drive the hundred million down
Until we reached some sawmill town.
We didn't know the river's name,
Nor where to someone's mill it came,
But figured that, without a doubt,
To some good town 'twould fetch us out

If we observed the usual plan
And drove the way the current ran.

Well, after we had driven for
At least two weeks, and maybe more,
We come upon a pyramid
That looked just like *our* forty did.

Some two weeks more and then we passed
A camp that looked just like the last.
Two weeks again another, too,
That looked like *our* camp, come in view.

Then Bunyan called us all ashore
And held a council-like of war.
He said, with all this lumbering,
Our logs would never fetch a thing.
The next day after, Silver Jim
He has the wits scared out of him;
For while he's breakin' of a jam
He comes upon remains of Sam,
The coon who made the great ascent
And through the cook-house ceilin' went
When Pink-Eye grabbed the fatal tin
And put the blastin' powder in.

And then we realized at last
That every camp that we had passed
Was *ours*. Yes, it was then we found
The river we was on was round.
And, though we'd driven many a mile,
We drove a circle all the while!
And that's the truth, as I'm alive,
About the great Round River Drive.

What's that? Did ever anyone
Come on that camp of '61,
Or '63, or '65,
The year we drove Round River Drive?
Yes, Harry Gustin, Pete and me
Tee Hanson and some two or three
Of good and truthful lumber men
Came on that famous camp again.
In west of Graylin' 50 miles,
Where all the face of Nature smiles,
We found the place in '84—
But it had changed some since the war.
The fire had run some Summer through
And spoiled the logs and timber, too.
The sun had dried the river clean
But still its bed was plainly seen.

And so we knew it was the place
For of the past we found a trace—
A peavey loggers know so well,
A peavey with a circle L,
Which, as you know, was Bunyan's mark.
The hour was late, 'twas gittin' dark;
We had to move. But there's no doubt
It was the camp I've told about.
We eastward went, a corner found,
And took another look around.
Round River so we learned that day,
On Section 37 lay.[1]

III. The Whistling River

It seems that some years before the winter of the Blue Snow (which every old logger remembers because of a heavy fall of bright blue snow which melted to ink, giving folks the idea of writing stories like these, so they tell) Ol' Paul was logging on what was then known as the Whistling River. It got its name from the fact that every morning, right on the dot, at nineteen minutes after five, and every night at ten minutes past six, it r'ared up to a height of two hundred and seventy-three feet and let loose a whistle that could be heard for a distance of six hundred and three miles in any direction.

Of course, if one man listening by himself can hear that far, it seems reasonable to suppose that two men listening together can hear it just twice as far. They tell me that even as far away as Alaska, most every camp had from two to four whistle-listeners (as many as were needed to hear the whistle without straining), who got two bits a listen and did nothing but listen for the right time, especially quitting time.

However, it seems that the river was famous for more than its whistling, for it was known as the orneriest river that ever ran between two banks. It seemed to take a fiendish delight in tying whole rafts of good saw logs into more plain and fancy knots than forty-three old sailors even knew the names of. It was an old "side winder" for fair. Even so, it is unlikely that Ol' Paul would ever have bothered with it, if it had left his beard alone.

It happened this way. It seems that Ol' Paul is sitting on a low hill one afternoon, combing his great curly beard with a pine tree, while he plans his winter operations. All of a sudden like, and without a word of warning, the river h'ists itself up on its hind legs and squirts about four thousand five hundred and nineteen gallons of river water straight in the center of Ol' Paul's whiskers.

---

[1] A township consists of thirty-six sections. Cf. the "nineteenth hole" of a golf course.

From *Ol' Paul, The Mighty Logger*, by Glen Rounds, pp. [III] 19–41; [IV], 42–51; [V], 117–133. Copyright, 1936, by Holiday House, Inc. New York.

Naturally Paul's considerably startled, but says nothing, figuring that if he pays it no mind, it'll go 'way and leave him be. But no sooner does he get settled back with his thinking and combing again, than the durn river squirts some more! This time, along with the water, it throws in for good measure a batch of mud turtles, thirteen large carp, a couple of drowned muskrat, and half a raft of last year's saw logs. By this time Ol' Paul is pretty mad, and he jumps up and lets loose a yell that causes a landslide out near Pike's Peak, and startles a barber in Missouri so he cuts half the hair off the minister's toupee, causing somewhat of a stir thereabouts. Paul stomps around waving his arms for a spell, and allows:

"By the Gee-Jumpin' John Henry and the Great Horn Spoon, I'll tame that river or bust a gallus tryin'."

He goes over to another hill and sits down to think out a way to tame a river, forgetting his winter operations entirely. He sits there for three days and forty-seven hours without moving, thinking at top speed all the while, and finally comes to the conclusion that the best thing to do is to take out the kinks. But he knows that taking the kinks out of a river as tricky as this one is apt to be quite a chore, so he keeps on sitting there while he figures out ways and means. Of course, he could dig a new channel and run the river through that, but that was never Paul's way. He liked to figure out new ways of doing things, even if they were harder.

Meanwhile he's gotten a mite hungry, so he hollers down to camp for Sourdough Sam to bring him up a little popcorn, of which he is very fond. So Sam hitches up a four-horse team while his helpers are popping the corn, and soon arrives at Paul's feet with a wagon load.

Paul eats popcorn and thinks. The faster he thinks the faster he eats, and the faster he eats the faster he thinks, until finally his hands are moving so fast that nothing shows but a blur, and they make a wind that is uprooting trees all around him. His chewing sounds like a couple hundred coffee grinders all going at once. In practically no time at all the ground for three miles and a quarter in every direction is covered to a depth of eighteen inches with popcorn scraps, and several thousand small birds and animals, seeing the ground all white and the air filled with what looks like snowflakes, conclude that a blizzard is upon them and immediately freeze to death, furnishing the men with pot pies for some days.

But to get back to Ol' Paul's problem. Just before the popcorn is all gone, he decides that the only practical solution is to hitch Babe, the Mighty Blue Ox, to the river and let him yank it straight.

Babe was so strong that he could pull mighty near anything that could be hitched to. His exact size, as I said before, is not known, for although it is said that he stood ninety-three hands high, it's not known whether that meant ordinary logger's hands, or hands the size of Paul's, which, of course, would be something else again.

However, they tell of an eagle that had been in the habit of roosting on the tip of Babe's right horn, suddenly deciding to fly to the other. Columbus Day, it was, when he started. He flew steadily, so they say, night and day, fair weather and foul, until his wing feathers were worn down to pinfeathers and a new set grew to replace them. In all, he seems to have worn out seventeen sets of feathers on the trip, and from reaching up to brush the sweat out of his eyes so much, had worn all the feathers off the top of his head, becoming completely bald, as are all of his descendants to this day. Finally the courageous bird won through, reaching the brass ball on the tip of the left horn on the seventeenth of March. He waved a wing weakly at the cheering lumberjacks and 'lowed as how he'd of made it sooner but for the head winds.

But the problem is how to hitch Babe to the river, as it's a well-known fact that an ordinary log chain and skid hook will not hold water. So after a light lunch of three sides of barbecued beef, half a wagon load of potatoes, carrots and a few other odds and ends, Ol' Paul goes down to the blacksmith shop and gets Ole, the Big Swede, to help him look through the big instruction book that came with the woods and tells how to do most everything under the sun. But though Paul reads the book through from front to back twice while Ole reads it from back to front, and they both read it once from bottom to top, they find nary a word about how to hook onto a river. However, they do find an old almanac stuck between the pages and get so busy reading up on the weather for the coming year, and a lot of fancy ailments of one kind and another that it's supper time before they know it, and the problem's still unsolved. So Paul decides that the only practical thing to do is to invent a rigging of some kind himself.

At any rate he has to do something, as every time he hears the river whistle, it makes him so mad he's fit to be tied, which interferes with his work more than something. No one can do their best under such conditions.

Being as how this was sort of a special problem, he thought it out in a special way. Paul was like that. As he always thought best when he walked, he had the men survey a circle about thirty miles in diameter to walk around. This was so that if he was quite a while thinking it out he wouldn't be finding himself way down in Australia when he'd finished.

When everything is ready, he sets his old fur cap tight on his head, clasps his hands behind him, and starts walking and thinking. He thinks and walks. The faster he walks the faster he thinks. He makes a complete circle every half hour. By morning he's worn a path that is knee-deep even on him, and he has to call the men to herd the stock away and keep them from falling in and getting crippled. Three days later he thinks it out, but he's worn himself down so deep that it takes a day and a half to get a ladder built that will reach down that far. When he does get out, he doesn't even wait for breakfast, but whistles for Babe and tears right out across the hills to the north.

The men have no idea what he intends to do, but they know from experience that it'll be good, so they cheer till their throats are so sore they have to stay around the mess hall drinking Paul's private barrel of cough syrup till supper time. And after that they go to bed and sleep very soundly.

Paul and the Ox travel plenty fast, covering twenty-four townships at a stride, and the wind from their passing raises a dust that doesn't even begin to settle for some months. There are those who claim that the present dust storms are nothing more or less than that same dust just beginning to get back to earth—but that's a matter of opinion. About noon, as they near the North Pole, they begin to see blizzard tracks, and in a short time are in the very heart of their summer feeding grounds. Taking a sack from his shoulder, Paul digs out materials for a box trap, which he sets near a well-traveled blizzard trail, and baits with fresh icicles from the top of the North Pole. Then he goes away to eat his lunch, but not until he's carefully brushed out his tracks—a trick he later taught the Indians.

After lunch he amuses himself for a while by throwing huge chunks of ice into the water for Babe to retrieve, but he soon has to whistle the great beast out, as every time he jumps into the water he causes such a splash that a tidal wave threatens Galveston, Texas, which at that time was inhabited by nobody in particular. Some of the ice he threw in is still floating around the ocean, causing plenty of excitement for the iceberg patrol.

About two o'clock he goes back to his blizzard trap and discovers that he has caught seven half-grown blizzards and one grizzled old nor'wester, which is raising considerable fuss and bids fair to trample the young ones before he can get them out. But he finally manages to get a pair of half-grown ones in his sack and turns the others loose.

About midnight he gets back to camp, and hollers at Ole, the Big Swede:

"Build me the biggest log chain that's ever been built, while I stake out these dadblasted blizzards! We're goin' to warp it to 'er proper, come mornin'."

Then he goes down to the foot of the river and pickets one of the blizzards to a tree on the bank, then crosses and ties the other directly opposite. Right away the river begins to freeze. In ten minutes the slush ice reaches nearly from bank to bank, and the blizzards are not yet really warmed to their work, either. Paul watches for a few minutes, and then goes back to camp to warm up, feeling mighty well satisfied with the way things are working out.

In the morning the river has a tough time r'aring up for what it maybe knows to be its last whistle, for its foot is frozen solid for more than seventeen miles. The blizzards have really done the business.

By the time breakfast is over, the great chain's ready and Babe all harnessed. Paul quick-like wraps one end of the chain seventy-two times around the foot of the river, and hitches Babe to the other. Warning the men to stand clear, he shouts at the Ox to pull. But though the great beast strains till his tongue hangs out, pulling the chain out into a solid bar some seven and a half miles long, and sinks knee-deep in the solid rock, the river stubbornly refuses to budge, hanging onto its kinks like a snake in a gopher hole. Seeing this, Ol' Paul grabs the chain and, letting loose a holler that blows the tarpaper off the shacks in the Nebraska sandhills, he and the Ox together give a mighty yank that jerks the river loose from end to end, and start hauling it out across the prairie so fast that it smokes.

After a time Paul comes back and sights along the river, which now is as straight as a gun barrel. But he doesn't have long to admire his work, for he soon finds he has another problem on his hands. You see, it's this way. A straight river is naturally much shorter than a crooked one, and now all the miles and miles of extra river that used to be in the kinks are running wild out on the prairie. This galls the farmers in those parts more than a little. So it looks like Paul had better figure something out, and mighty soon at that, for already he can see clouds of dust the prairie folks are raising as they come at top speed to claim damages.

After three minutes of extra deep thought he sends a crew to camp to bring his big cross-cut saw and a lot of baling wire. He saws the river into nine-mile lengths and the men roll it up like linoleum and tie it with the wire. Some say he used these later when he logged off the desert, rolling out as many lengths as he needed to float his logs. But that's another story.

But his troubles with the Whistling River were not all over. It seems that being straightened sort of took the gimp out of the river, and from that day on it refused to whistle even a bird call. And as Paul had gotten into the habit of depending on the whistle to wake up the men in the morning, things were a mite upset.

First he hired an official getter-upper who rode through the camp on a horse, and beat a triangle. But the camp was so big that it took three hours and seventy-odd minutes to make the trip. Naturally some of the men were called too early and some too late. It's hard to say what might have happened if Squeaky Swanson hadn't showed up about that time. His speaking voice was a thin squeak, but when he hollered he could be heard clear out to Kansas on a still day. So every morning he stood outside the cookshack and hollered the blankets off every bunk in camp. Naturally the men didn't stay in bed long after the blankets were off them, what with the cold wind and all, so Squeaky was a great success and for years did nothing but holler in the mornings.

IV. THE BEDCATS

Ol' Paul had quite a time with the Bedcats one winter, when he was using one of his old camps that had stood deserted for thirty years or more. It happened this way. As every one knows, most bunkhouses have a certain number of bedbugs. These don't annoy a real lumberjack to amount to anything, although you'll hear the greenhorns holler plenty when they first come into camp. But they either make friends with the little beasts or they don't last long. The story is that the loggers all had their pet bugs that followed them around camp and out in the woods like dogs, some even being trained, it is said, to steal blankets off adjoining bunks for their masters on especially cold nights. However, that is as it may be; I never saw it.

But it is a well-known fact that the intelligent little beasts always knew when camp was to be moved, and the night before would come out of wherever they were in the habit of staying and climb into the bedding rolls so as not to be left behind. Then when the new camp was set up, there they were, jumping up and down with excitement to greet the men when they came in from their first day's work.

One time, though, they got fooled. That was the time the Indian, Squatting Calf, comes running into camp just after breakfast with the news that gold has been discovered in the Black Hills. Right away all the men tear out over the hills without even waiting to pick up their blankets. Within three minutes the camp is as empty as an old maid's letter box on Valentine's Day. That night at sundown the little bugs are all lined up at the bunkhouse door waiting for the men to come home as usual. But they don't come.

Ol' Paul's in town at the time, and when he hears the news, he knows there's no use figuring on logging till the gold fever passes, so he goes on a timber cruising trip. He locates some fine timber down Kansas way, and when he finds his men ready to work, he starts a new camp there, as he has a ready market for his lumber in the new gold towns. And, what with one thing and another, it's about thirty years before he comes back to the old camp. But when he does, he finds trouble waiting for him.

He and the men get there about noon and start cleaning out the old buildings. They're a little surprised to find the bunks filled up with the bones of rabbits and other small animals, but suppose that owls or bobcats have been living there. By night the camp is ready, and after supper the men turn in early. Ol' Paul suddenly wakes up, hearing wild yells and snarls from the bunkhouse, and comes running out of his office to see the men clawing over one another in their underwear, trying to get out in the open. They swear that their bunks are full of wildcats which have been crawling all over them. Now Paul knows wildcats, and he's never heard of one that'll come within a hundred yards of a logger if it has its 'druthers. As he can find nothing in there when he looks, he figures that being as it's the day after payday, the men have probably eaten something that disagrees with them. But they won't go back in the bunkhouse, so he lets them sleep in the stables that night.

But the next night the same thing happens, so Paul decides to get his pistol and sleep in the bunkhouse himself. When a bunch of lumberjacks are scared to sleep in a place there must be something wrong somewhere. For a time things are quiet enough to suit anybody, and Paul finally decides that the men have been reading too many old mystery magazines, and dozes off. But he wakes up mighty soon. What feels like a couple of full-grown wildcats seem to have gotten tangled up in his beard, and his blanket is heaving around like he has a runaway cat show under it. The whole bunk is full of animals of some kind, hissing and snarling like all get out. It's none too comfortable there, but Ol' Paul doesn't lose his head. He grabs out in the dark and gets a couple of the beasts and stuffs them into a sack he's got handy. Of course as soon as he starts floundering around the things clear out, like any wild animal, and by the time the men come running with lanterns the place is quiet again.

They carefully open up the sack to see what they've caught. The animals inside are not bobcats. In fact nobody has ever seen anything like them. They are the size of bobcats, but they have several pairs of legs. They are covered with a heavy coat of reddish-brown fur, which is quite long on the back, but due to the shortness of their legs, is worn down to the length of plush on the bottom. Naturally Paul and the men are more than a little puzzled.

It is not until the Indians come into camp that they find out what it is they have caught. The Indians call them Bedcats, and from them Paul learns the story.

It seems that the little bugs, being left alone in camp, had to forage for themselves. At first many died, but the stronger ones survived and grew larger, soon attacking small mice and sparrows. As the years passed, they grew fur to keep them warm, and became more and more savage, each generation a little larger and wilder than the one before. Eventually they were bringing in gophers and small rabbits to feed their young. Later, it seems, they crossed with bobcats and the half-breeds were really fierce hunters. They took to running in packs like wolves, baying at the moon, and in a pitched fight a full-grown bobcat was no match for even an ordinary-sized Bedcat. The Indians set deadfalls for them, and made warm fur robes and mittens from the pelts. But with the return of the lumberjacks, some forgotten instinct seemed to urge them into the blankets in the bunks, which upset even the soundest sleepers.

Something had to be done. Ol' Paul buys the Indians a lot of number four wolf traps and offers a five-dollar bounty for the scalps, so they are soon trapped out. I haven't heard of any quite that big being seen since.

V. Johnny Inkslinger

Soon after Ol' Paul invented mass production in the logging business and got the system to working right, he found himself in a peck of trouble. It seems that the logging went so fast he couldn't begin to keep up with his office work.

At that time there were no figures as we know them now. So he has to do all his figuring in his head and keep all his records there too. It takes eight days and forty-seven hours to figure the payroll alone, and that's only the beginning. There are the commissary accounts, the logging records, hay and grain bills, and a thousand and one other things.

His fingers get blistered from counting on them, but he doesn't stop, and new blisters form and push the old ones back towards his wrists, and still he keeps on counting. Finally the tips of his fingers are blistered clear to his elbows. Luckily, they have time to get well by the time they reach the elbows, so go no farther. But strain as he may, he can never get more than half done.

In desperation he takes some time off and goes up to the North Pole, where he had left the Day-Stretcher he'd invented when he was logging off the Arctic. (Afterwards he'd sold it to the Eskimos, they being so pleased with the long nights it gave them.) Arriving there, he gives old chief Fancypants a broken jack-knife and a lead quarter to stretch a sackful of days he's brought with him. He only has them stretched to twice the usual length, being as how he's in quite a sweat to get back to camp, and doesn't want to wait.

As it turns out, this is just as well, for he finds that when he tries to use them he's worse off than before. Naturally, if he was getting behind with the figuring when he worked an ordinary day, it stands to reason that working twice as long a day, he'd get just twice as far behind. And that's exactly what happened, so after a few days he has to give the idea up.

However, he doesn't throw those extra long days out. But being very thrifty, he ships them to a second-hand dealer in the East who has been peddling them out ever since. Perhaps you yourself can remember days that seemed endless, especially of a Monday. If so, you may be sure that it was just one of those days. Almost every school and business has a supply of them.

But to get back to Paul's problem. He's in a stew, sure enough! It looks as though he'll have to invent mass production for figuring the same as he's done for logging. But seeing as how it takes a certain amount of time for even Paul to invent inventions, and him being so busy, he thinks he'll first look around camp and see if he can find someone who can help him.

Here he runs into trouble. He finds a top loader who can figure a little, but Shot Gunderson, the woods boss, insists that he can't be spared from the woods, seeing as how he hasn't any too many top loaders as it is. Then there's the fellow in the cookshack helping Hot Biscuit Slim, who's been heard to say he can both spell and cipher. But Sam lets it be known, in no uncertain terms, that dreadful things will probably find their way into the food if his helpers are interfered with. And not even Paul dares rile a camp cook.

So it looks like the only thing left is to try and teach Backward Bill Barber, the bull cook, to figure. You see, a fellow that's no good for anything else is given the job of carrying wood and water for the cooks, and looking after the bunkhouses. He's called the bull cook, for no good reason that I ever heard of. Naturally he can very easily be replaced, so Backward Bill gets the job. It's surprising how often people like Backward Bill get put into important jobs because they can be so easily replaced where they are.

For a while he seems to do all right. But soon Paul discovers that his figures never come out in anything but odd numbers, and finds that Bill has had a finger cut off at some time, which throws his counting into nines instead of tens. Being an odd number, nine is much harder to figure with than ten. So that finishes Backward Bill as a figurer.

Next Ol' Paul tries a crude system of bookkeeping by means of notches chopped in trees. On one tree he chops payroll notches, and on another commissary bills, and so on. For a time he keeps a crew of men busy chopping notches as he calls out the numbers. He gets so he can call out three numbers at once, and that's something not everyone can do. This system works fairly well for a time, although Paul hates to keep so many men out of the woods. But these men, not being real figurers, make many mistakes. A notch-chopper chopping payroll notches'll climb a timber record tree by mistake, or a commissary notch-chopper'll get onto a hay and grain tree, and soon the records get as badly mixed as before.

So again he's right back where he started from. He's losing sleep and weight from worrying, and even then he isn't really getting it all done, as he's so busy with other things. And he has so many notch-chopping crews out that he's kind of lost track of them and isn't at all sure that he's called them all in. He's haunted by the fear that maybe he's left a crew out in the woods somewhere to starve.

For a while he thinks seriously about going back to the great cave where he grew up, and spending the rest of his life whittling. I think this was the only time that any problem threatened to be more than Ol' Paul could solve. He kept getting thinner and thinner, and he didn't even have the heart to comb his great beard any more. It is said that the mess-hall was thrown into an uproar one morning at breakfast when two full-grown bobcats chased a snowshoe rabbit out of his whiskers. But that may or may not be true.

He gets in the habit of roaming the woods at night, with the faithful Ox at his heels, just worrying. One morning, finding himself in a part of the country that is strange to him, he decides to explore a little before going back to camp. (Although he doesn't know it, he is near Boston, which everyone knows is the seat of Learning, Culture, and Baked Beans. However, it is unlikely that he'd have cared even if he had known, as he's already learned practically everything there is to know. He's not interested in culture, and beans are no novelty to a logger.)

About ten-thirty he's sitting on a low hill, resting, when he's startled by a yell that uproots trees all around him. Up to that time he's supposed that he's the only man that can holler loud enough to knock down trees, so he's more than somewhat curious.

He stands up and steps over a couple of small mountains, and gets the surprise of his life. Sitting on a hill is a fellow almost as large as Paul himself. He has a high, smooth forehead, and instead of wearing a fur cap he's bareheaded, which even then was a sign of high learning. But the thing that takes Paul's eye is the collar. It is very high, stiff, and pure white, and looks very uncomfortable. (It is said that after he went to work for Paul he kept a crew of thirty-nine men busy every Sunday whitewashing it.)

The strange giant is busy scraping the limestone bluff on the other side of the river with a jack-knife the size of a fourhorse double-tree, scattering the pieces for miles around. When the rock is smooth enough to suit him, he takes an enormous pencil from behind his ear and starts writing down columns of queer marks with it. The pencil is over three feet in diameter and seventy-six feet long—the first one ever used.

Paul stands around, first on one foot and then on the other, waiting for him to look up so he can find out who he is and what he's doing. But it seems that the fellow has just invented concentration and is busy practicing it as he works. So of course he never bats an eye when Paul shuffles his feet, knocking down thirty-five acres of standing timber. Nor does he seem to hear when Paul says, "Reckon as how it's goin' to be a mighty dry summer if it don't rain soon." As I said before, he was concentrating, and concentrating is a mighty exacting operation when it's done right.

After a while, however, he finishes what he's doing and turns around to look at Paul. But he still says nothing, and Paul says the same thing, as the white collar has him impressed more than somewhat. So Paul gets out his can of Copenhagen and offers the stranger a chaw; then they both sit and squirt tobacco juice at ants for a bit until they raise the river almost to flood stage. After they discuss the chances of rain, Paul asks him what he's doing with the marks on the cliff. (He thinks maybe they're some kind of pictures.)

The fellow tells him he's Johnny Inkslinger and those are figures. But naturally Paul knows that figures are something that you think but can't see.

"Them is figures, and I'm sole owner and inventor of them," Johnny insists.

He shows Paul a little of how they work, even working out a couple of problems that Paul thinks up, and finally convinces him that they really work. Then Paul wants to know what he figures, and is completely flabbergasted when Johnny tells him that he just figures for the fun of it, as he has everything that needs figuring all figured.

Paul can't imagine a full-grown man sitting around all day figuring just for the fun of it, but Johnny tells him that he always liked it. As he grew older he got dissatisfied with just figuring in his head as everyone else did, so one day he sat down and instead of just sitting, he sat and thought about what he could do to make figuring more fun.

Finally he hit on the idea of inventing figures that could be seen as well as thought. He worked for many months, and the result was a system whereby he could not only figure anything, but see the figures at the same time. Moreover, figures figured this way could be written down in books and saved for future reference. (This is the system now used in all our schools.)

As you can well imagine, Ol' Paul is pretty excited by this time. Here is mass production in figures, the same as he has in logging. And the fellow seems to be a real artist, so probably could be hired for practically nothing. If he can get Johnny to work for him his worries will be over and he can get out in the woods again. So he puts on the expression a man wears when he holds a royal flush and wants to give the other fellow the impression he's bluffing on a pair of deuces, and asks Johnny how he'd like to have a job figuring for him.

Johnny reckons that would be mighty fine, but that he's a poor man and can't afford such luxuries. Finally Paul convinces him that he means it when he says that he'll furnish him with all the figuring he can do, besides giving him books to write them in, and pay him thirty dollars a month. He right away starts off for camp at a run, he's that anxious to begin work. He was the first bookkeeper in history, and his job with Ol' Paul lasted for many years, to the great advantage of both.

VII. Pipeline Days and Paul Bunyan

It was evening. The sun hung like a sandy ball above the rim of dull mesquite that surrounded the pipeline camp. For three weeks the line had been extending through a lifeless country of mesquite and dust. For three weeks the men had been broiling under the August sun with not even a wind to make the heat less deadening. Now they were sprawled on the grass in easy after-supper positions. Forming a half circle about the cook-shack, they rested uncomfortably and "razzed" the lone fat man who had not yet finished eating. "Fat" was always last—last to start work, last to stop eating, and certainly last to stop talking. "Fat" ate on, unconcerned with their tired humor. Gradually the men drifted into small groups and lay droning a preparation for the evening's talk.

"Git a scoop. That's what you need, Fat."

"Move the chuck wagon and he'll starve to death. He's too damn lazy to follow it."

"Hey, Fat, did you ever get all you wanted to eat?"

"They ought to grow square beans so he could get more of them on his knife."

"Talk about eating. Tell you what I saw once," said one who aspired to Fat's position as the camp's chief liar. "I saw a man eat a whole ham

By Acel Garland. From *Foller de Drinkin' Gou'd*, Publications of the Texas Folk-Lore Society, Number VII, edited by J. Frank Dobie, pp. 55–61. Copyright, 1928, by the Texas Folk–Lore Society. Austin.

once—well, not exactly a whole ham, we had eaten a meal on it—not exactly we, my brother-in-law Jim and his family. The man came to the house one morning and wanted something to eat. Sis was busy and didn't have no time to be fooling with him; so she just set the table and put this ham on it and then went on about her housework or whatever she was doing. Well, when she come back the man was gone and so was the ham—all except the bone and it had been gnawed so dry that even the dog wouldn't touch it. That's the God's truth. Jim swears it's the truth."

The men howled derisively, and Fat, who had been listening half attentively, arose from his stool and sauntered into the center of the group.

"Did you say something about eating?" he said. "Well, I had a funny thing happen to me the other day in Wichita Falls. I goes into one of them restaurants down by the railroad tracks to eat. When I come in I saw a couple of tough hombres setting at the counter and they looks me over kind of amused like. But I just goes on back and sets down a couple of seats from them. After a while the waiter comes out from behind and goes over to where they are setting and asks them what they want.

"They was sure tough-looking birds, and one of them speaks up and says, 'Gimme a T-bone steak a inch and a quarter thick. Just scorch it.' And he looks over at me kinda mean like.

"But I didn't pay him no mind but just set there. So the other one pulls his hat 'way down over his eye, and says, 'Gimme a hind quarter. Raw.' And then they both looks over at me.

"Well, when the waiter come over to where I am setting, I says to him, 'Gimme a sharp butcher knife and then just cripple a steer and run him through here. I'll cut off what I want!' "

"Speaking of steers," the Contender put in, "did you ever hear about the cattle line that Paul Bunyan laid from his ranch to Chicago?

"Well, Paul he got tired of paying such high freight to get his stock to market; so he just laid a pipeline all the way to the stockyards in Chicago and pumped them through it. Everything went all right except that the pipe was so big that the calves and half-grown yearlin's would get lost in the threads and starve to death before they could get to the outside. And one time the line sprung a leak and Paul lost thirty-five carloads of cattle before he could get it corked [caulked]. But he sure did do a good job of corking when he did get to it."

"How the devil did he cork a hole that big?" asked Fat after a minute or two of silence.

"Why with B. S., you big windbag, same as that that you have been spouting off."

Fat sat for a moment trying to think of a way to get "back at" the Contender. Then he started off on a new trail.

"You know so much about Paul Bunyan," he said. "Did you ever hear about that big steer that he had? He called her Babe and she just measured forty-two pick-handles lengths and the width of a size seven derby hat between the eyes. And strong! Why that steer could pull anything!

"I remember one time when we was drilling a well down Breckenridge way. Wasn't much of a hole, just sixteen inches. Well, we drilled and drilled and didn't ever strike nothing—except dust, and a God's plenty of that; so finally Paul he said we might as well give it up as a dry hole and let it go at that.

"But Paul was mad! He swore around for two or three days and smashed the derrick into kindling wood and was about to quit drilling when he saw a advertisement in the paper by some bird out on the plains that wanted to buy some post-holes. Ten thousand post-holes it was he wanted. Ten thousand holes three feet long.

"Well, Paul he hitched a chain around this duster hole and hooked up Babe and pulled fifteen thousand feet of it out of the ground. He got mad again because the hole broke off and left over half of it in the ground. But directly he said that they wasn't no use of a post-hole being sixteen inches across; so he just quartered the hole and then sawed it up into the right lengths.

"You know out on the plains they have a awful hard time digging post-holes, or any other kind of holes for that matter. The soil out there is only about a foot deep till you strike solid rock and they can't dig through this rock a-tall.

"Why, them guys used to come down into East Texas and buy all the old wells and dug-outs that they could get a-hold of and cut them up to use for post-holes. I used to know a feller down there that could dig and stack on cars more old wells than any man I ever saw before. He could stack twenty-nine of them on cars in a day and take two hours off for dinner.

"They finally moved so many wells from down there that they ruined the water; so they was a ordinance passed against it. But that didn't stop it. They bootlegged them out to the plains. I knew one guy that got rich bootlegging them. He had a patented jack that would lift a well or a dug-out right out of the ground.

"It don't do much good to build fences out on the plains, though. That there wind out there is awful. Soon as a man gets a good fence built, along comes the wind and blows it away, posts, post-holes, and all. Why, that wind even blows wells away and a guy told me that he seen it turn prairie dog holes wrong side out it blew so hard. But I never did believe it. Them guys are awful liars. One of them told me he had a horse throw him so high one time that he had to catch a-holt of a cloud to keep from falling and killing himself. It's cold out there too——"

"I'll say it is," a pipeliner broke in. "Like that guy that was up in Canada somewheres when it was fifty degrees below. He come up to another guy and said, 'God, man, wouldn't you hate to be in Amarillo today?'"

"Ja ever hear about them wells out in Colorado where the oil freezes when it comes out of the ground?" asked the Contender. "They can't pipe it away; so they just let it spout out on the ground and then shovel it into wagons with scoops and haul it off."

"That's like some of them wells that Paul Bunyan drilled in over at Smackover," said someone. "They was gushers and blew in so strong that they had to put roofs over the derricks to keep the oil from spouting a hole in the sky."

"I worked for Paul out in Arizona on the biggest well that I ever worked on," resumed the Contender. "It was a seventy-five inch hole, it was, and we had to make a derrick so tall that it had to be hinged in two places and folded up before the sun and stars could pass. Took a man fourteen days to climb to the top of it. It did. And Paul had to hire thirty derrick men so we could have a man on top all of the time. They was always fourteen men going up and fourteen men coming down, a man on top and a man off tower,[1] all the time. And they was dog houses built a day's climbing apart for the men to sleep in while they was going up and down.

"Why, when that well blew in, it took three days for the oil to reach the top of the derrick, and it rained oil for a week after we had got it capped.

"It was some well. We drilled it with one of Paul's patented rotary rigs. Never could have drilled so deep—it was sixty thousand feet—if Paul hadn't used flexible drill pipe. We just wound the drill stem up on the draw-works. Take a devil of a long time to come out of the hole if we had had to stack it.

"Well, when we was down sixty thousand and three feet, the well blew in. And when we had come out of the hole we seen that we had forgot to case it. Well, Paul he called out both towers and made up the casing on the ground—about ten miles of seventy-five-inch casing—and then he just picked it up and dropped it down into place."

"I worked for Paul on one of them deep wells once," said Fat. "It was out in Arkansas. Jimmy Blue was running the rig and we was drilling with standard tools. We got down thirty thousand feet and struck a rock formation that a bit wouldn't touch. And we was using a pretty good sized bit too, drilling a fifty-inch hole.

"Well, we worked on this formation for three weeks without doing any good and then we called up Paul. Paul he come out there and took charge of the rig himself and worked for three more weeks, day and night, without doing anything except ruin a lot of bits. And finally he got so mad that he jumped down on the derrick floor and pulled up the bit with

---

[1] The reader may take his choice of spellings: "tower" or "tour." The word is pronounced "tower," and means a shift of men. The drilling crews work in two towers of twelve hours each, from twelve o'clock to twelve. The tower that goes on at midnight is the "graveyard tower," the one that goes on at noon is the "gravy tower."—A. G.

his hands. Then he threw it down into the hole as hard as he could throw it. Well, we busted the rock that time. The bit just kept on going and when the line run out it pulled derrick, rig, and all into the hole after it.

"We got a gusher that time. But when Paul seen that the rig had pulled Jimmy into the hole with it he was just about to plug off the hole and abandon it. But in a few days we got a telegram from Jimmy in China saying that he had a 100,000 barrel gusher and was spudding in on another location."

"Did any of you guys work for Paul on that big line he laid?" asked the Contender. "Well, I worked for him on that 101-inch aluminum line that he laid from Pennsylvania to California. We laid it to pipe buttermilk out to his camp out there. Paul liked buttermilk so well himself that he had a twenty-four-inch petcock running wide open all the time to catch enough for him to drink."

"Yeh," said Fat, "I know all about that. I helped Paul drill the buttermilk well that furnished that line. We drilled down thirty-two thousand feet and then struck a formation of cornbread. We drilled for five hundred feet through the cornbread and then for twelve hundred feet through solid turnip greens—except that every few feet would be a layer of fried sow-belly. That's where the old song started: 'Cornbread, Buttermilk, and Good Old Turnip Greens.' "

"Fat, did you ever see Paul's wife?" asked a young boll-weevil who had started to work only a few days before. "She had a wooden leg and she was so homely that we used to scrape enough ugly off her face every day to mud off a well. The hardest six months' work I ever put in was painting that wooden leg of hers."

"When Paul worked on the highlines he had a wooden leg himself," added an ex-linesman. "It was ninety feet long and the men used to wear one out every three days climbing up to bum him for cigarettes."

"Paul discovered perpetual motion—of the jaw—when he got Fat to work for him," said the Contender.

"Huh," said Fat, "only perpetual motion Paul ever discovered was one time down in India. We was drilling a ninety-inch hole with standard tools. And when we got down twenty-seven thousand feet we struck the root of a rubber tree and the bit never did stop bouncing. Had to abandon the hole."

"I worked—" the Contender began.

"Yeh, and on another one of them wells we was drilling a eighty-inch offset. Had them big derricks all around us. And our camp was setting so far back in them derricks that we had to pipe the daylight in. We drilled down nearly fifty thousand feet and struck a flowing vein of alum water and the hole, rig, and everything drew up until we had to abandon it."

"Paul sure had drilling down to a fine point," said the Contender. "Why I worked for him on one hole where we was using rubber tools. We would just start the tools bouncing and then go to sleep until it was time to change the bit. And the men was so fast that the driller would just bounce the bit out of the hole and they would change it before it could fall back."

"Paul's camps wasn't nothing like this dump," said Fat. "I worked for him on a ninety-inch line once and we had so many men in the camp that it took fifteen adding machines running day and night to keep track of their time. Paul invented the first ditching machine while we was laying this line through Arkansas. He bought a drove of them razorback hogs and trained them to root in a straight line."

"You telling about that cattle line of Paul's a while back reminds me of the trees that used to grow down on the Brazos," said the "Old Man." "One time I was working through that country with a herd of cattle and come up to the river where I couldn't ford it. While I was setting on my horse looking at the water I heard a big crash up the river and when I went up to see what it was, it was a tree had fallen across the river. It was one of them big holler trees. So I just drove my herd across the river through the holler of it. But when I got to the other side and counted the herd I seen that they was nearly three hundred steers missing and I went back to look for them. They had wandered off into the limbs and got lost."

"That reminds me of the sand storms that they used to have down in East Texas," said the Contender. "One time they was a nigger riding along one of them sandy roads on a jackass and he stopped to go down to the creek and get a drink and tied his mule to a sapling by the side of the road. While he was gone it come one of them sand storms and when he come back he seen his ass hanging by the tie-rope about seventy feet up in a tree. The sand had blown away from under him and just left him hanging there."

"Say," said Fat, "did any of you guys ever see Paul Bunyan in a poker game. The cards he used were so big that it took a man five hours to walk around one of them. Paul used to play a lot of poker that time we was digging Lake Michigan to mix concrete in when he was building the Rocky Mountains. A little while after that we dug Lake Superior for a slush pit for one of them big wells we was drilling. Any of you birds want to play some poker?"

This, from Fat, was the signal for retiring. The sun was long past set and mosquitoes were buzzing in the darkened mesquite. Silently the men stalked off toward their tents—all except two or three who followed Fat to his tent for a session at poker.

Febold Feboldson

I. Real American Weather

SOMEBODY ought to do something about the weather. It's downright disgraceful that in most parts of the United States the climate is of foreign

By Paul R. Beath. From *Nebraska Folklore Pamphlets*, Number Five, pp. 2–3. Lincoln: Federal Writers' Project of the Works Progress Administration for the State of Nebraska. July 1, 1937.

origin. Florida and California brazenly boast of Mediterranean sunshine. Winter resorts in the Adirondacks are only imitations of those in Switzerland. Even the famous blizzard of 1888 came from Siberia. In fact, there's only one place where you can get real, genuine, American weather, and that's on the great plains between the Mississippi and the Rockies.

In the early days, I guess, it was even more American than it is now. At least that's what Bergstrom Stromberg says. He's way past ninety and has seen some big weather in his day. Besides, he's heard all about the climate of the early days directly from his uncle, the famous Febold Feboldson. Febold was the first white settler west of the Mississippi, not counting Spaniards and Frenchmen who don't count anyway.

Take 1848 for instance. That was the year the Petrified Snow covered the plains all summer and held up the '48ers in their gold rush to California with the result that they became '49ers. At that time Febold was operating an ox train between San Francisco and Kansas City, because the snow prevented him from doing anything else.

Since Febold was the only plainsman able to make the trip that year, the '48ers appealed to him for help. His secret was to load up with sand from Death Valley, California. The sands of the desert never grow cold, nor did Febold and his oxen. This sand he sold to the gold rushers at fifty dollars a bushel, and they were glad to get it.

Then the '49ers began to swarm over the snow-covered plains in their prairie schooners. But before they reached the Rockies the jolting of the wagons scattered the sand and covered up every bit of the Petrified Snow. And that's the reason, according to Bergstrom Stromberg, that the prairies are so all fired hot in the summer.

Febold cursed himself twenty times a day for twenty years for selling the '48ers that sand. Then he spent the next twenty years trying various schemes to moderate the climate. He finally gave up in disgust and moved to California. Thus he set an example which all good Middlewesterners have followed ever since.

Or take the popcorn ball. There's a genuine American product. Most people think that someone invented the popcorn ball, but it's actually a product of the American weather. It invented itself, so to speak, on Bergstrom Stromberg's ranch in the early days when Febold owned the place.

It was during that peculiar year known as the Year of the Striped Weather which came between the years of the Big Rain and the Great Heat. This year the weather was both hot and rainy. There was a mile strip of scorching sunshine and then a mile strip of rain. It so happened that on Febold's farm there were both kinds of weather. The sun shone on his cornfield until the corn began to pop, while the rain washed the syrup out of his sugar cane.

Now the cane field was on a hill and the cornfield was in a valley. The syrup flowed downhill into the popped corn and rolled it into great balls. Bergstrom says some of them were hundreds of feet high and looked like big tennis balls from a distance. You never see any of them now, because the grasshoppers ate them all up in one day, July 21, 1874.

But the Great Fog, I suppose, was the biggest piece of American weather that ever hit the great plains. It followed the year of the Great Heat which killed off the Dirtyleg Indians and Paul Bunyan's Blue Ox. Near the end of that remarkable year, according to Bergstrom Stromberg, it began to rain and kept it up for the proverbial forty days and forty nights.

"But nary a drop of water hit the ground," said Bergstrom.

"Then what became of it?" I asked.

"Why, it turned into steam, of course. That there rain had no more chance of hittin' the ground than you have of spittin' into a blast furnace."

This steam, as Bergstrom tells it, cooled enough to turn into fog. The whole country was fogbound. It was so thick that people had to go around in pairs, one to hold the fog apart while the other walked through it. The pioneer ranchers didn't need to water their stock. The cattle would simply drink the fog. It looked funny to see pigs with their noses up in the air rooting for fish and frogs. But the dirt farmers were as mad as the stockmen were happy. The sun couldn't shine through the fog and the seeds didn't know which way was up. So they grew downward.

Things were getting pretty serious. All the farmers had just about decided to go to California when Febold came to their rescue. He hit upon the idea of importing some English fog-cutters from London. But the English were so slow that Febold didn't get his fog-cutters until Thanksgiving, and then the fog had turned to slush. He finally got to work and cut up the fog and slush into long strips which he laid along the roads so as not to spoil the fields. In course of time the dust covered up the roads and today you can hardly tell where Febold buried the Great Fog.

But many a rural mail carrier has cursed Febold and his English fog-cutters. For every spring when it rains or thaws, that old fog comes seeping up and makes rivers of mud out of all the country roads.

II. Why Febold Went to California

Just why and when Febold went to California and whether he went for good or only for a visit no one perhaps will ever know. Bergstrom Stromberg thinks he's gone only for a visit. Eldad Johnson is probably of the same opinion, but in Bergstrom's presence he always takes the opposite view and gives vent to his exasperation with his native prairies and his own suppressed desire to go to California. All you need to start them off is to ask in a casual manner when Febold is coming back.

"He ain't never coming back," Eldad will snap at you in a voice anything but casual.

"How do you know he ain't?" Bergstrom will ask.

"Because any man as smart as Febold would know enough to stay away from this here man-killing, God-forsaken country. If you ain't burned up

Ibid., Number Eight, pp. 7–8. September 15, 1937.

by drouth and winds hot as hell or frozen out by blizzards and hail storms, you're eat up by grasshoppers, speculators, and politicians. Febold tried his damnedest to make this country fit for a white man to live in. But it can't be done and I don't blame him for going off to California with the rest of the sensible people."

"Whoa, there, ain't you just a little strong," Bergstrom will say. "Remember, Febold ain't no lily-livered cake-eater like you. These here plains is a tough country and it takes tough people to live here and Febold never backs out."

"Just the same he did go to California and he ain't back yet and never will be. Damned if I wouldn't go myself if I only had the time and money. I know Febold was a tough feller and liked a good big job, but he was smart, too, smart enough to know when he was licked."

"Licked, hell! He ain't begun to fight yet. All those tricks he used to pull in the early days ain't nothing to what's going to be done when he gets back. Say, do you really want to know just why Febold went to California?"

"Want to know! Cripes, I do know! And so does anybody else with a lick of sense. He went to get away from here and enjoy his old age without fighting this damned country for a living all the time. I heard he was a bartender at Tia Juana till he made a little money on the horses. Then he bought some steamships trading with China or somewhere. I think he had a fruit farm, too, and was in the movies for a while."

"Rot, you old fool! You ought to know Febold's too big a man to monkey with such things. Horse races, steamships, fruit farms, movies, bah! Do you think Febold would mess around with that stuff? Never! What he went to California for was to study."

"Study what?" Eldad always asks in a tone of utmost contempt.

"Irrigation and forestry," Bergstrom always replies. "Science, you know. Things is done different now. When Febold gets back he's going to put some water and trees on these here plains and no fooling."

"Can't be done," says Eldad.

"You just wait and see," says Bergstrom.

Thus Bergstrom and Eldad are wont to dispute the second coming of their famous Uncle far into the proverbial night, but just why and when Febold went to California and whether he went for good or only for a visit no one perhaps will ever know.

John Henry

I. JOHN HENRY, THE HERO

I [1]

ALL questions of authenticity of the John Henry tradition fade into insignificance before the incontrovertible fact that for his countless ad-

[1] From *John Henry: Tracking Down a Negro Legend,* by Guy B. Johnson, pp. 142–146. Copyright, 1929, by The University of North Carolina Press. Chapel Hill.

mirers John Henry is a reality. To them he will always be a hero, an idol, a symbol of the "natural" man.

It is often charged against the Negro that he glorifies his tough characters, his "bad men." But when one considers that the Negro has had little opportunity to develop outside the fields of labor and hell-raising, this tendency is not surprising. Bad men are nearly always interesting, and, incidentally, no one can sing of them any more heartily than the white man. But a working man fits into the drab scene of everyday life, and it is a miracle if he achieves any sort of notoriety by his hard labor. John Henry, then, is a hero indeed. With his hammer and his determination to prove his superiority over a machine, he made a name for himself in folk history. His superstrength, his grit, his endurance, and his martyrdom appeal to something fundamental in the heart of the common man. John Henry stands for something which the pick-and-shovel Negro idolizes— brute strength. He epitomizes the tragedy of man versus machine. In laying down his life for the sake of convincing himself and others that he could beat a machine, he did something which many a Negro would gladly do. The whole thing is a sort of alluring tragedy which appeals strongly to one's egotism.

So strong, indeed, has been the admiration, the envy, of other men for John Henry that some have tried to repeat his drama. I have no doubt but that some of these John Henry episodes said to have happened at so many places throughout the country (the Alabama episode, for instance) are based on real incidents in which would-be John Henry's did their best to put themselves beside the god of the hammer.

Mention John Henry to a group of Negro working men and the chances are that you start an admiration contest. The rare man who intimates that *he* could beat John Henry is laughed down by his fellows. "Why man," said a true John Henryite on such an occasion, "John Henry could take that hammer between his teeth and drive with his hands tied and beat you like all git-out." "Yes, Lawd," affirmed another, "that man had a stroke like a Alabama mule." "They tells me," said a third, "that he used to keep six men runnin' just to carry his drills back and forth from the man that sharpened 'em." And so on until no one could think of anything else to say about him.

F. P. Barker, an old Alabama steel driver who claimed to have known John Henry, said, "I could drive from both shoulders myself, and I was as far behind John Henry as the moon is behind the sun. The world has not yet produced a man to whip steel like John Henry."

A young woman in Georgia concluded an account of John Henry's life as follows:

When he died people came from all parts of the world to see this Famous man John Henry. His wife had it engraved on his tombstone.

his Epitah [*sic*]
"Here lies the steel driving man."

John Henry has a way of cropping up at unexpected times and places. I was standing on the street at Chapel Hill one night in a throng of people gathered to hear the Dempsey-Sharkey fight on the radio. When things looked bad for Dempsey, a Negro man who stood near me began to show his displeasure. "If they'd put old Jack Johnson in there," he said, "he'd lay that Sharkey man out." At the end of the round we discussed colored prize fighters. Suddenly he came out with, "I'll tell you another colored man would've made a real prize-fighter—that's John Henry. Yessir, anybody that could handle a thirty-pound hammer like that man could would make a sure-'nough fighter."

There is, on the whole, a surprisingly small amount of exaggeration in the stories about John Henry told by those who worship at his shrine. Occasionally you hear that John Henry used a thirty-pound hammer or that he wore out six shakers on the day of the famous contest or that his statue has been carved in solid rock at the portal of Big Bend Tunnel, but around John Henry there has not yet grown up a body of fantastic lore like that which surrounds certain other folk characters—Paul Bunyan, for example. The only really bizarre tale I have ever heard about John Henry is one which Professor Howard W. Odum obtained from a construction-camp Negro at Chapel Hill three years ago. I repeat it here just as it was published in *Negro Workday Songs*.

One day John Henry lef' rock quarry on way to camp an' had to go through woods an' fiel'. Well, he met big black bear an' didn't do nothin' but shoot 'im wid his bow an' arrer, an' arrer went clean through bear an' stuck in big tree on other side. So John Henry pulls arrer out of tree an' pull so hard he falls back 'gainst 'nother tree which is so full o' flitterjacks, an' first tree is full o' honey, an' in pullin' arrer out o' one he shaken down honey, an' in fallin' 'gainst other he shaken down flitterjacks. Well, John Henry set there an' et honey an' flitterjacks, an' after while when he went to get up to go, button pop off'n his pants an' kill a rabbit mo' 'n a hundred ya'ds on other side o' de tree. An' so up jumped brown baked pig wid sack o' biscuits on his back, an' John Henry et him too.

So John Henry gits up to go on through woods to camp for supper, 'cause he 'bout to be late an' he mighty hongry for his supper. John Henry sees lake down hill and thinks he'll get him a drink o' water, 'cause he's thirsty, too, after eatin' honey an' flitterjacks an' brown roast pig an' biscuits, still he's hongry yet. An' so he goes down to git drink water an' finds lake ain't nothin' but lake o' honey, an' out in middle dat lake ain't nothin' but tree full o' biscuits. An' so John Henry don't do nothin' but drink dat lake o' honey dry. An' he et the tree full o' biscuits, too. An' so 'bout that time it begin' to git dark, an' John Henry sees light on hill an' he think maybe he can git sumpin to eat, 'cause he's mighty hongry after big day drillin'. So he look 'roun' an' see light on hill an' runs up to house where light is an' ast people livin' dere, why'n hell dey don't give him sumpin to eat, 'cause he ain't had much. An' so he et dat, too.

Gee-hee, hee, dat nigger could eat! But dat ain't all, cap'n. Dat nigger could wuk mo' 'n he could eat. He's greates' steel driller ever live, regular giaunt, he was; could drill wid his hammer mo' 'n two steam drills, an' some say mo' 'n ten. Always beggin' boss to git 'im bigger hammer. John Henry was cut out fer big giaunt driller. One day when he was jes' few weeks ol' settin' on his mammy's knee he commence cryin' an' his mommer say, "John Henry, whut's matter, little son?" An' he up an' say right den an' dere dat nine-poun' hammer be death o' him. An' sho' 'nough he grow up right 'way into bigges' steel driller worl' ever see. Why dis I's tellin' you now wus jes' when he's young fellow; waits til' I tells you 'bout his drillin' in mountains an' in Pennsylvania. An' so one day he drill all way from Rome, Georgia, to D'catur, mo' 'n a hundred miles drillin' in one day, an' I ain't sure dat was his bes' day. No, I ain't sure dat was his bes' day.

But, boss, John Henry was a regular boy, not lak some o' dese giaunts you read 'bout not likin' wimmin an' nothin'. John Henry love to come to town same as any other nigger, only mo' so. Co'se he's mo' important an' all dat, an' co'se he had mo' wimmin 'an anybody else. Some say mo' 'n ten, but as to dat I don't know. I means, boss, mo' wimmin 'an ten men, 'cause, Lawd, I specs he had mo' 'n thousand wimmin. An' John Henry was a great co'tin man, too, cap'n. Always was dat way. Why, one day when he settin' by his pa' in san' out in front o' de house, jes' few weeks old, wimmin come along an' claim him fer deir man. An' dat's funny, too, but it sho' was dat way all his life. An' so when he come to die John Henry had mo' wimmin, all dressed in red an' blue an' all dem fine colors come to see him dead, if it las' thing dey do, an' was mighty sad sight, people all standin' 'roun', both cullud an' white.

II [1]

John Henry drove steel with a ten pound sheep-nose hammer with a regular size switch handle four feet long. This handle was made slim from where the hammer fitted on to a few inches back where it reduced to one half inch in thickness, the width being five eighths in this slim part. It was kept greased with tallow to keep it limber and flexible, so as not to jar the hands and arms.

He would stand from five and one half feet to six feet from his steel and strike with full length of his hammer. The handle was so limber that when it was held out straight the hammer would hang nearly half way down. He drove steel from his left shoulder and would make a stroke of more than nineteen and one half feet spending his power with all his might

---

[1] From *John Henry, A Folk-Lore Study* by Louis W. Chappell, pp. 22–23, 32–33. Jena: Frommannsche Verlag, Walter Biedermann. 1933.

making the hammer travel with the speed of lightning. He would throw his hammer over his shoulder and nearly the full length of the handle would be down his back with the hammer against his legs just below his knees. He would drive ten long hours with a never turning stroke.

. . . John Henry could stand on two powder cans and drive a drill straight up equally as fast as he could drive it straight down—with the same long sweep and rapidity of the hammer. He could stand on a powder can with two feet together, toes even and drive all day never missing a stroke. He was the steel driving champion of the country and his record has never been equalled.[1]

*   *   *   *   *

John Henry was the best driver on the C. & O. He was the only man that could drive steel with two hammers, one in each hand. People came from miles to see him use the two 20 lb. hammers he had to drive with.

It seems that two different contracting companies were meeting in what is called Big Bend Tunnel. One had a steam drill while the other used man power to drill with. When they met everyone claimed that the steam drill was the greatest of all inventions, but John Henry made the remark he could sink more steel than the steam drill could. The contest was arranged and the money put up. John Henry was to get $100.00 to beat the steam drill.

John Henry had his foreman to buy him 2 new 20 lb. hammers for the race. They were to drill 35 minutes. When the contest was over John Henry had drilled two holes 7 feet deep, which made him a total of 14 feet. The steam drill drilled one hole 9 feet which of course gave the prize to John.

When the race was over John Henry retired to his home and told his wife that he had a queer feeling in his head. She prepared his supper and immediately after eating he went to bed. The next morning when his wife awoke and told him it was time to get up she received no answer, and she immediately discovered that he had passed to the other world some time in the night. His body was examined by two Drs. from Baltimore and it was found his death was caused from a bursted blood vessel in his head.

The information I have given you came to me through my grandfather. He was present at Big Bend Tunnel when the contest was staged, at that time he was time keeper for the crew that John Henry was working with. I have often heard him say that his watch started and stopped the race. There was present all of the R. R. officials of the C. & O. The crowd that remained through the race at the mouth of the tunnel was estimated at 2500, a large crowd for pioneer days.

John Henry was born in Tenn. and at the time of his death he was 34 years old. He was a man weighing from 200 to 225 lbs. He was a full blooded negro, his father having come from Africa. He often said his

---

[1] Newton Redwine, *The Beattyville Enterprise*, Beattyville, Ky., Feb. 1, 1929

strength was brought from Africa. He was not any relation of John Hardy as far as I know. . . .[1]

II. JOHN HENRY

John Hen-ry was a li-'l ba-by, (uh-huh,) Sit-tin' on his ma——ma's knee, (oh, yeah,) Said: "De Big Bend Tun-nel on de C. and O. road Gon-na cause de death of me, (Lawd, Lawd,) gon-na cause de death of me."

I

John Henry was a li'l baby, uh-huh,[2]
Sittin' on his mama's knee, oh, yeah,
Said: "De Big Bend Tunnel on de C. & O. road
Gonna cause de death of me,
Lawd, Lawd, gonna cause de death of me."

---

[1] George Johnston, Lindside, W. Va.

Considerable verisimilitude hardly characterizes all these details. The presence of all the officials of the road, with a crowd of 2,500, at the drilling-contest had better be accepted as fictional embroidery. But the purpose of this study is not to emphasize the tissue of falsehood in popular reports. Big Bend Tunnel was built by a single contractor, as will be shown later, but the "two different contracting companies" may well represent two crews of workmen. The steel driver may have had "2 new 20 lb. hammers" and used only one at a time. Two doctors from Baltimore may have examined Henry's body, but that they came to the tunnel for that purpose seems impossible of belief. His John Henry suggests the frontier strong man, who does impossible things.—L. W. C.

From *American Ballads and Folk Songs*, collected and compiled by John A. Lomax and Alan Lomax, pp. 5–9. Copyright, 1934, by the Macmillan Company. New York.

[2] The syllables "uh-huh" and "oh, yeah" are to be repeated in each stanza.—J. A. L. and A. L.

John Henry, he had a woman,
Her name was Mary Magdalene,
She would go to de tunnel and sing for John,
Jes' to hear John Henry's hammer ring,
Lawd, Lawd, jes' to hear John Henry's hammer ring.

John Henry had a li'l woman,
Her name was Lucy Ann,
John Henry took sick an' had to go to bed,
Lucy Ann drove steel like a man,
Lawd, Lawd, Lucy Ann drove steel like a man.

Cap'n says to John Henry,
"Gonna bring me a steam drill 'round,
Gonna take dat steam drill out on de job,
Gonna whop dat steel on down,
Lawd, Lawd, gonna whop dat steel on down."

John Henry tol' his cap'n,
Lightnin' was in his eye:
"Cap'n, bet yo' las' red cent on me,
Fo' I'll beat it to de bottom or I'll die,
Lawd, Lawd, I'll beat it to de bottom or I'll die."

Sun shine hot an' burnin',
Wer'n't no breeze a-tall,
Sweat ran down like water down a hill,
Dat day John Henry let his hammer fall,
Lawd, Lawd, dat day John Henry let his hammer fall.

John Henry went to de tunnel,
An' dey put him in de lead to drive;
De rock so tall an' John Henry so small,
Dat he lied down his hammer an' he cried,
Lawd, Lawd, dat he lied down his hammer an' he cried.

John Henry started on de right hand,
De steam drill started on de lef'—
"Before I'd let dis steam drill beat me down,
I'd hammer my fool self to death,
Lawd, Lawd, I'd hammer my fool self to death."

White man tol' John Henry,
"Nigger, damn yo' soul,
You might beat dis steam an' drill of mine,
When de rocks in dis mountain turn to gol',
Lawd, Lawd, when de rocks in dis mountain turn to gol'."

John Henry said to his shaker,
"Nigger, why don' you sing?
I'm throwin' twelve poun's from my hips on down,
Jes' listen to de col' steel ring,
Lawd, Lawd, jes' listen to de col' steel ring."

Oh, de captain said to John Henry,
"I b'lieve this mountain's sinkin' in."
John Henry said to his captain, oh my!
"Ain' nothin' but my hammer suckin' win',
Lawd, Lawd, ain' nothin' but my hammer suckin' win'."

John Henry tol' his shaker,
"Shaker, you better pray,
For, if I miss dis six-foot steel.
Tomorrow'll be yo' buryin' day,
Lawd, Lawd, tomorrow'll be yo' buryin' day."

John Henry tol' his captain,
"Looka yonder what I see—
Yo' drill's done broke an' yo' hole's done choke,
An' you cain' drive steel like me,
Lawd, Lawd, an' you cain' drive steel like me."

De man dat invented de steam drill,
Thought he was mighty fine.
John Henry drove his fifteen feet,
An' de steam drill only made nine,
Lawd, Lawd, an' de steam drill only made nine.

De hammer dat John Henry swung
It weighed over nine pound;
He broke a rib in his lef'-han' side,
An' his intrels fell on de groun',
Lawd, Lawd, an' his intrels fell on de groun'.

John Henry was hammerin' on de mountain,
An' his hammer was strikin' fire,
He drove so hard till he broke his pore heart,
An' he lied down his hammer an' he died,
Lawd, Lawd, he lied down his hammer an' he died.

All de womens in de Wes',
When de heared of John Henry's death,
Stood in de rain, flagged de eas'-boun' train,
Goin' where John Henry fell dead,
Lawd, Lawd, goin' where John Henry fell dead.

John Henry's li'l mother,
She was all dressed in red,
She jumped in bed, covered up her head,
Said she didn' know her son was dead,
Lawd, Lawd, didn' know her son was dead.

John Henry had a pretty li'l woman,
An' de dress she wo' was blue,
An' de las' words she said to him:
"John Henry, I've been true to you,
Lawd, Lawd, John Henry, I've been true to you."

II

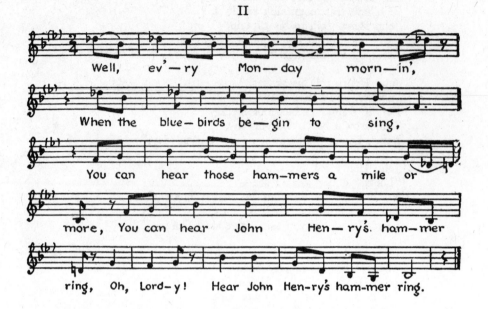

Well, ev'-ry Mon-day morn-in',
When the blue-birds be-gin to sing,
You can hear those ham-mers a mile or
more, You can hear John Hen-ry's. ham-mer
ring, Oh, Lord-y! Hear John Hen-ry's ham-mer ring.

Well, ev'ry Monday mornin',
When the bluebirds begin to sing,
You can hear those hammers a mile or more,
You can hear John Henry's hammer ring, Oh, Lordy!
Hear John Henry's hammer ring.

John Henry told his old lady,
"Will you fix my supper soon?
Got ninety miles o' track I've got to line,
Got to line it by the light of the moon, Oh, Lordy!
Line it by the light o' the moon."

John Henry had a little baby,
He could hold him in his hand;
Well, the last word I heard that po' child say,
"My daddy is a steel-drivin' man. Oh, Lordy!
Daddy is a steel-drivin' man."

John Henry told his old captain,
Said, "A man ain't nothin' but a man;
Before I let your steel gang down
I will die with the hammer in my hand, Oh, Lordy!
Die with the hammer in my hand."

From *Folk Music of the United States*, Album III, edited by Alan Lomax. Washington, D. C.: Archive of American Folk Song, Library of Congress. 1942. Sung by Arthur Bell, Gould, Arkansas, 1939. Recorded by John A. and Ruby T. Lomax. Transcribed by Ruth Crawford Seeger.

John Henry told his captain,
"Next time you go to town
Uh-jes' bring me back a ten-pound maul
For to beat your steel-drivin' down, Oh, Lordy!
Beat your steel-drivin' down."

John Henry had a old lady,
And her name was Polly Ann.
John Henry tuck sick and he had to go to bed;
Pauline drove steel like a man, Oh, Lordy!
'Line drove steel like a man.

John Henry had a old lady,
And the dress she wo' was red.
Well, she started up the track and she never looked back,
"Goin' where my man fell dead, Oh, Lordy!
Where my man fell dead."

Well, they taken John Henry to Washington,
And they buried him in the sand.
There is peoples from the East, there's peoples from the West
Come to see such a steel-drivin' man, Oh, Lordy!
See such a steel-drivin' man.

Well, some said-uh he's from England,
And some say he's from Spain;
But-uh J. say he's nothin' but a Lou's'ana man,
Just a leader of the steel-drivin' gang, Oh, Lordy!
Leader of the steel-drivin' gang.

III. The Birth of John Henry

Now John Henry was a man, but he's long dead.

The night John Henry was born the moon was copper-colored and the sky was black. The stars wouldn't shine and the rain fell hard. Forked lightning cleaved the air and the earth trembled like a leaf. The panthers squalled in the brake like a baby and the Mississippi River ran upstream a thousand miles. John Henry weighed forty-four pounds.

John Henry was born on the banks of the Black River, where all good rousterbouts come from. He came into the world with a cotton-hook for a right hand and a river song on his tongue:

"Looked up and down de river,
    Twice as far as I could see.
  Seed befo' I gits to be twenty-one,
    De Anchor Line gonter b'long to me, Lawd, Lawd,
    Anchor Line gonter b'long to me."

From *John Henry,* by Roark Bradford, pp. 1–4. Copyright, 1931, by Roark Bradford. New York: Harper & Brothers.

They didn't know what to make of John Henry when he was born. They looked at him and then went and looked at the river.

"He got a bass voice like a preacher," his mamma said.

"He got shoulders like a cotton-rollin' rousterbout," his papa said.

"He got blue gums like a conjure man," the nurse woman said.

"I might preach some," said John Henry, "but I ain't gonter be no preacher. I might roll cotton on de boats, but I ain't gonter be no cotton-rollin' rousterbout. I might got blue gums like a conjure man, but I ain't gonter git familiar wid de sperits. 'Cause my name is John Henry, and when fo'ks call me by my name, dey'll know I'm a natchal man."

"His name is John Henry," said his mamma. "Hit's a fack."

"And when you calls him by his name," said his papa, "he's a natchal man."

So about that time John Henry raised up and stretched. "Well," he said, "Ain't hit about supper-time?"

"Sho hit's about supper-time," said his mamma.

"And after," said his papa.

"And long after," said the nurse woman.

"Well," said John Henry, "did de dogs had they supper?"

"They did," said his mamma.

"All de dogs," said his papa.

"Long since," said the nurse woman.

"Well, den," said John Henry, "ain't I as good as de dogs?"

And when John Henry said that he got mad. He reared back in his bed and broke out the slats. He opened his mouth and yowled, and it put out the lamp. He cleaved his tongue and spat, and it put out the fire. "Don't make me mad!" said John Henry, and the thunder rumbled and rolled. "Don't let me git mad on de day I'm bawn, 'cause I'm skeered of my ownse'f when I gits mad."

And John Henry stood up in the middle of the floor and he told them what he wanted to eat. "Bring me four ham bones and a pot full of cabbages," he said. "Bring me a bait of turnip greens tree-top tall, and season hit down wid a side er middlin'. Bring me a pone er cold cawn bread and some hot potlicker to wash hit down. Bring me two hog jowls and a kittleful er whippowill peas. Bring me a skilletful er red-hot biscuits and a big jugful er cane molasses. 'Cause my name is John Henry, and I'll see you soon."

So John Henry walked out of the house and away from the Black River Country where all good rousterbouts are born.

Casey Jones

I. CASEY JONES, ENGINEER

I[1]

ON the last day of April [1928] occurs the 28th anniversary of the death of Casey Jones,—probably the most famous of a long line of locomotive engineer heroes who have died at their post of duty, one hand on the whistle and the other on the airbrake lever. Casey Jones' fame rests on a series of nondescript verses, which can hardly be called poetry. They were written by Wallace Saunders, a Negro engine wiper who had been a close friend of the famous engineer, and who sang them to a jigging melody all his own.

Mrs. Casey Jones still lives in Jackson, Tenn. She has two sons and a daughter. Charles Jones, her younger son, lives in Jackson; Lloyd, the older son, is with a Memphis auto agency; and her daughter, Mrs. George McKenzie, lives at Tuscaloosa, Ala.

Although 41 years have flitted by since Miss Janie Brady said "I do" and became the bride of John Luther (Casey) Jones, Mrs. Jones still keeps green the memory of that glad occasion. Today, still on the sunny side of 60, the plump blond woman with her cheery smile tells graphically the story of how her husband was killed, and how Wallace Saunders composed the original air and words that later swept the country for years as the epic ballad of the railroader.

"My husband's real name was John Luther Jones," she told her latest interviewer. "He was a lovable lad—6 feet 4½ inches in height, dark-haired and gray-eyed. Always he was in good humor and his Irish heart was as big as his body. All the railroaders were fond of Casey, and his wiper, Wallace Saunders, just worshipped the ground he walked on."

The interviewer asked Mrs. Jones how her husband got the nickname Casey.

"Oh, I supposed everyone knew that!" she replied. "He got it from the town of Cayce, Kentucky, near which he was born. The name of the town is locally pronounced in two syllables, exactly like 'Casey.'"

Mrs. Jones remembers Wallace Saunders very well, although she has not seen him for years.

"Wallace's admiration for Casey was little short of idolatry," she said. "He used to brag mightily about Mr. Jones even when Casey was only a freight engineer."

Casey Jones was known far and wide among railroad men, for his peculiar skill with a locomotive whistle.

"You see," said Mrs. Jones, "he established a sort of trade mark for

---

[1] From *Erie Railroad Magazine.* Vol. 24 (April, 1928), No. 2, pp. 13, 44.

himself by his inimitable method of blowing a whistle. It was a kind of long-drawn-out note that he created, beginning softly, then rising, then dying away almost to a whisper. People living along the Illinois Central right of way between Jackson and Water Valley would turn over in their beds late at night and say: 'There goes Casey Jones,' as he roared by."

After he had put in several years as freight and passenger engineer between Jackson and Water Valley, Casey was transferred early in 1900 to the Memphis-Canton (Miss.) run as throttle-puller of the Illinois Central's crack "Cannonball" train.

Casey and his fireman, Sim Webb, rolled into Memphis from Canton about 10 o'clock Sunday night, April 29. They went to the checking-in office and were preparing to go to their homes when Casey heard somebody call out: "Joe Lewis has just been taken with cramps and can't take his train out tonight."

"I'll double back and pull Lewis' old No. 638," Casey volunteered.

At 11 o'clock that rainy Sunday night Casey and Sim Webb clambered aboard the big engine and eased her out of the station and through the South Memphis yards.

> "All the switchmen knew by the engine's moans
> That the man at the throttle was Casey Jones."

Four o'clock of the 30th of April. The little town of Vaughn, Miss. A long, winding curve just above the town, and a long sidetrack beginning about where the curve ended.

"There's a freight train on the siding," Casey yelled across to Sim Webb.

Knowing the siding there was a long one, and having passed many other freights on it, Casey figured he would do the same this night.

But there were two separate sections of a very long train on the side-track this night. And the rear one was a little too long to get all its length off the main line onto the siding. The freight train crews figured on "sawing by"; that is as soon as the passenger train passed the front part of the first train, it would move forward and the rear freight would move up, thus clearing the main track.

But Casey's speed—about fifty miles an hour—was more than the freight crews bargained for.

But when old 638 was within a hundred feet of the end of the siding the horrified eyes of Casey Jones and Sim Webb beheld through the gloom the looming shape of several boxcars in motion, swinging across from the main line to the side-track. In a flash both knew there was no earthly way of preventing a smashup.

"Jump, Sim, and save yourself!" was Casey's last order to his fireman. As for himself, Casey threw his engine in reverse and applied the air-brakes—all any engineer could do, and rode roaring 638 into a holocaust of crashing wood that splintered like match boxes. Sim Webb jumped, fell into some bushes and was not injured.

When they took Casey's body from the wreckage (old 638 had plowed through the cars and caboose and turned over on her side a short distance beyond) they found one hand on the whistle cord, the other on the air-brake lever.

"I remember," Sim Webb told Casey's widow, "that as I jumped Casey held down the whistle in a long, piercing scream. I think he must have had in mind to warn the freight conductor in the caboose so he could jump."

Probably no individual, excepting a member of Casey's family, was more affected by the sad news than Wallace Saunders.

A few days later he was going about singing a song to a melody all his own. The air had a lilt that caught the fancy of every one who heard it. But Wallace, honest old soul, had no idea of doing more than singing it as a sort of tribute to his white friend's memory.

But one day a song writer passed through Jackson and heard the song and the details of Casey's tragic death. He went off and changed the words, but retained the lilting refrain and the name of Casey Jones. That was about 1902.

II [1]

There are many railroad men still living who knew and worked with Jones. The affection he aroused among all his acquaintances seems to have been an outstanding characteristic. He was 6 feet 4½ inches tall, dark-haired and gray-eyed. An excellent photograph of him, which has just come to light from the Memphis Press-Scimitar, is reproduced as a frontispiece in this issue.

His old friend R. E. Edrington, a fellow engineer on the Illinois Central writes: "The reputation which Casey enjoyed was richly earned by numerous feats of resourcefulness, skill and downright daring. He could perform feats with his famous 638 that no other engineer could equal with locomotives of the same class, or even with the same engine. Firing for him was a back-breaking and hair-raising job, but his mulatto fireman, Sim Webb, was equal to every demand, and held Casey in almost idolatrous regard, following him from one run to another through his entire career."

A. J. ("Fatty") Thomas, who often ran as conductor on trains pulled by Casey and the 638, writes: "I had often heard the song about Casey Jones, but on account of the phrases in it about the Southern Pacific and the Santa Fe, rounder, Frisco, and 'another papa on the Salt Lake Line,' I never figured that the song was intended for my Illinois Central Casey. For he was not a rounder but a car roller, and in my estimation the prince of them all. We had a number of fast men, and since then I have had hundreds of good engineers pull me on different western roads. But I never met the equal of Casey Jones in rustling to get over the road.

"The 'whistle's moan' in the song is right. Casey could just about play a tune on the whistle. He could make the cold chills run up your back with it, and grin all the time. Everybody along the line knew Casey Jones' whistle.

"I never saw him with his mouth closed—he always had a smile or a broad grin. The faster he could get his engine to roll, the happier he was. He would lean out of the cab window to watch his drivers, and when he got her going so fast that the side rods looked solid, he would look at you and grin all over, happy as a boy with his first pair of red boots. Yet he had a reputation as a safe engineer. With all his fast running I never knew of him piling them up, of any but a few derailments and never a rear-ender. He was either lucky, or else his judgment was as nearly perfect as human judgment can be."

Ed Pacey, another conductor who knew Casey Jones, writes: "In the early days of railroading there was a real glamor to the rails. Into this setting Casey, engineer of the Cannonball Express, fitted perfectly. He was a giant and came of a great railroad family. His nickname was derived from his native village, Cayce, Tenn., pronounced 'Casey.'

"Jones was famous for two things: he was a teetotaler in days when abstinence was rare, and he was the most daring of all engineers in the days when schedules were simply 'get her there and make the time, or come to the office and get your time.'"

Mr. Pacey lodges a protest against the popular song's line to the effect that Casey Jones' widow informed her orphan children that "you've got another papa on the Salt Lake line." Mr. Pacey chafes at the implied disrespect toward Mrs. Jones in that stanza. "There never was any other papa on the Salt Lake or any other line," he says. "Instead, the widow devoted her life to the hard struggle to maintain herself and educate her three children."

The common story of the wreck in which Jones was killed is that Casey had to meet two freight trains which were too long to clear the siding. For some reason, never clearly explained, Casey failed to stop and he piled them up when he struck the caboose and cars protruding out on the main line.

According to R. E. Edrington, however, the situation was even more complicated. "It was characteristic," he says, "of the desperate chances which were part of the period of railroading, when the engines were rapidly growing in size and the sidings, safety equipment and other appliances not keeping pace with them.

"There were not two but three trains. Two of these were north bound and had pulled into the siding. The third was racing, on short time, ahead of the Cannonball. As this train scurried down to the siding it dropped off a flagman but, after it had pulled down, this flagman rode in with the idea that the mother train would protest against the Cannonball.

"But the other train crew thought that he was still out and did not flag. So Casey came down, as fast as he could turn a wheel, with the result of one of the worst wrecks in the history of the road. . . ."

II. THE "CASEY JONES" SONG

Four years ago the Erie Railroad Magazine gathered up the real story of Casey's life and death, as told by his widow, who still lives in Jackson, Tenn. The article was reprinted in railroad magazines and newspapers all over the world and has brought a continuous stream of letters ever since. Scores of correspondents have sent in various versions of the Casey Jones song, not only in English but in French, German and even in the language of the native laborers on the South African railways.

Every branch of railroading has at least one version of the song. The hobo jungles and the I.W.W. song books contribute others. Still others come from the campfires and boarding cars of construction gangs, and several weird and often unprintable variations were composed by dough-boys in France during the world war.

Come all you rounders for I want you to hear
The story told of a brave engineer;
Casey Jones was the rounder's name
On a heavy six-eight wheeler he rode to fame.

Caller called Jones about half-past four,
Jones kissed his wife at the station door,
Climbed into the cab with the orders in his hand,
Says, "This is my trip to the promised land."

Through South Memphis yards on the fly,
He heard the fireman say, "You've got a white-eye,"
All the switchmen knew by the engine's moans,
That the man at the throttle was Casey Jones.

Erie Railroad Magazine, Vol. 28 (April, 1932), No. 2, p. 12. The present text (*ibid.*, Vol. 24, April, 1928, No. 2, p. 12), like the tune, is traditional, differing from the

It had been raining for more than a week,
The railroad track was like the bed of a creek.
They rated him down to a thirty mile gait,
Threw the south-bound mail about eight hours late.

Fireman says, "Casey, you're runnin' too fast,
You run the block signal the last station you passed."
Jones says, "Yes, I think we can make it though,
For she steams much better than ever I know."

Jones says, "Fireman, don't you fret,
Keep knockin' at the firedoor, don't give up yet;
I'm goin' to run her till she leaves the rail
Or make it on time with the south-bound mail."

Around the curve and a-down the dump
Two locomotives were a-bound to bump.
Fireman hollered, "Jones, it's just ahead,
We might jump and make it but we'll all be dead."

'Twas around this curve he saw a passenger train;
Something happened in Casey's brain;
Fireman jumped off, but Casey stayed on,
He's a good engineer but he's dead and gone—

Poor Casey was always all right,
He stuck to his post both day and night;
They loved to hear the whistle of old Number Three
As he came into Memphis on the old K.C.

Headaches and heartaches and all kinds of pain
Are not apart from a railroad train;
Tales that are earnest, noble and gran'
Belong to the life of a railroad man.

The Saga of Joe Magarac: Steelman

WHILE working in the steel mills along the Monongahela valley of Pennsylvania, I often heard one of the many Slavs who worked in the mills call one of his fellow-workers "*magarac*." Knowing that literally translated the word *magarac* meant jackass, but knowing also, from the tone of voice and the manner in which it was used, that it was seldom used derisively,

popular song version principally in the absence of the chorus. Copyright 1909 by Newton & Seibert. Copyright renewed. By permission of Shapiro, Bernstein & Co., Inc.

By Owen Francis. From *Scribner's Magazine*, Vol. XC (November, 1931), No. 5, pp. 505–511. Copyright, 1931, by Charles Scribner's Sons.

I questioned my Hunkie leverman as to its meaning as understood by the Hunkie workers. He gave me a vivid explanation. He said:

"Magarac! Dat is mans who is joost same lak jackass donkey. Dat is mans what joost lak eatit and workit, dats all."

Pointing a finger toward another of his race, a huge Hunkie by the name of Mike, who was walking from the open hearth, he yelled:

"Hay! Magarac!"

At once, Mike's thumbs went to his ears, and with palms outspread his hands waved back and forth while he brayed lustily in the best imitation of a donkey that he could give.

"See," my leverman said, "dere is *magarac*. Dat is Joe Magarac for sure."

Then they both laughed and spoke in their mother tongue, which I did not understand.

It was evident enough there was some definite reason for the use of the word, and obviously that reason was, to their way of thinking, very humorous.

By working for a considerable number of years with a Hunkie on my either side, by sitting many evenings in their homes, and, since turning my thoughts to writing, by spending a good deal of my time with them, I have been fortunate enough to hear considerably more about Mr. Joe Magarac.

I find that Joe Magarac is a man living only in the imagination of the Hunkie steel-mill worker. He is to the Hunkie what Paul Bunyan is to the woodsman and Old Stormalong is to the men of the sea. With his active imagination and his childlike delight in tales of greatness, the Hunkie has created stories with Joe Magarac as the hero that may in the future become folklore of our country. Conceived in the minds of Hunkie steel-mill workers, he belongs to the mills as do the furnaces and the rolling-mills. Although the stories of Joe Magarac are sagas, they have no tangible connection so far as I have been able to find, with the folklore of any of the countries which sent the Hunkie to these United States. It seems that the Hunkie, with the same adaptability that has made him into the best worker within our shores, has created a character and has woven about him a legend which admirably fits the environment in which he, the Hunkie, has been placed. Basically, the stories of Joe Magarac are as much a part of the American scene as steel itself.

I did not hear the story which I have set down here as accurately as I have been able, at one time. Some of it I heard in the mill; some of it while sitting on the hill above the mill on pleasant Sunday afternoons; the most of it while sitting in Agnes's kitchen with Hunkie friends at my side and well-filled tin cups of prune-jack before us.

The saga of Joe Magarac is more typical of the Hunkie than any tale or incident or description I might write. It shows his sense of humor, his ambitions, his love of his work, and, in general, shows what I know the Hunkie to be: a good-natured, peace- and home-loving worker.

One time long time ago mebbe one, two hundred years, dere was living by Hunkietown, Steve Mestrovich. Steve he workit by open-hearth and he have daughter Mary. Oh, my, Mary was pretty girls: she have big, blue eyes, hairs yellow lak hot steel, hands so little lak lady, and big strong teeths. She was prettier as Hunkie girls from any place and all fellows what workit for mill comit around and say for Steve:

"Mebbe pretty soon now be plenty good ting Mary gone catch hoosband."

Den Steve he always laughit and he say:

"Gone on home little mans. Mary no gone marry some one lak you who not catch much steam dis time. Mary gone marry only strongest mans what ever lived, ya betcha."

Mary say nothing. She joost sit around and hope dat pretty soon mans who be all right comit, for she was seventeen year old already and she no lak dat business of wait around. Steve get sick too from wait around and nobody comit. Steve say:

"What the hells kind business is dat. I catch best young girls as anybody: she pretty lak hell, she wanit mans, she wanit be good for mans and joost stay home and raise kids and no say nothing, dats all. And, by Gods, I catch two hundred dollar I give myself for wedding present and I no find mans for her. By Gods, I tink gone have party dis time and ask everybody comit and den we see who is best mans for Mary, ya damn right.

"So, Old Womans, next Sunday we gone have party. You makit plenty prune-jack and I gone to Pittsburgh and gone have two barrel beer sent out on truck."

Well, Steve's old lady she makit plenty prune-jack and all week she workit makit cake and Mary she help and she was glad lak anyting because Sunday gone be party and she tink mebbe she gone catch mans lak 'nother Hunkie girls who have mans who workit in mills. Steve tell everybody what gone be on Sunday and all dem young fellers start lift 'em up dolly bars in eighteen-inch mill, its big hunk steel what is heavy lak anyting, so dat dey strong for Sunday. Some people say dey betcha dat Pete Pussick be strongest mans for Pete lift 'em up dolly bars same lak it was toothpicks; other peoples tink maybe Eli Stanoski be better mans and he gone catch fine girls lak Mary for *frau*. But everybody wish it gone be him who is best mans and everybody dey lookit at Mary and dey feel strong lak anyting.

So pretty soon next Sunday be dere and Hunkie mans comit from Monesson, comit from Homestead, comit from Duquesne, comit from every place along Monongahela River and dey gone show everybody how strong dey be dis time. Steve have everything fix 'em up: in big field down by river bank he put two barrel beer what comit from brewery, he put table what he makit where Old Lady gone put prune-jack and cakes, and he have three dolly bar what he get from mill.

One dose dolly bar its joost little one what weigh three hundred fifty pound, 'nother dolly bars weigh five hundred pounds, and big ones she weigh more as 'nother two put together. On side of field Steve has fixed 'em up benches where womans can sit and nurse baby and see what gone happen and right by dere is platform lak have on Fourth July with red paper and flags and everyting. Mary she sit on platform where all young fellow can see good and see what dey gone get after dey lift 'em up dolly bars. Mary was dressed up lak dere was big funeral: she have on dress what mudder had made from wedding dress and it was pretty I tell you. It was all red and green, silk too, and on front was big bunch lace what *Groszmuter* in old country makit. On finger was ring with nice red stone what Steve buy from company store and on head was nice scarf. Oh, sure, when Mary go on platform everybody say she was prettier as Queen.

Steve was happy mans dat day, I tell you. He was dressed up with sleeves down and tie on his neck and he walkit 'round lak he was Boss everyting and he yell lak dis:

"Hi, yah, Pete. You tink you feelit all right to-day? By Gods, better you no be sick and have lots steam. It take plenty strong mans to lift 'em up dolly bars."

And den he say:

"Hi, yah, Eli. What matter you? Mebbe better you take 'nother drink prune-jack. You lookit little bit white in face lak you was 'fraid Pete nor Sam gone be stronger as you. By Gods, was I young mans same as you I lift 'em up whole damn three bars one time to catch fine girls lak Mary."

Den he laughit and pull mustache and walkit up and down same like nigger mans on pay day.

After everybody visit 'round little bit and everybody havit one, two, three drink all around, Steve get on platform and makit speech. He say:

"For coople year now everybody what is young mans and feelit pretty good dey comit for me and dey say: 'Pretty soon Mary gone lookit for mans. Me! I catch good job for blast furnace. Me, I be best mans what workit for mills, best mans what ever poke 'em out tap hole. Sure! I be strong lak anyting. Whats matter Mary no be *frau* for me?'"

Den Steve he stopit speech and he stickit out tongue lak he was not feelit so good for stomach and he say:

"By Gods, I hear so many mans talk lak dat dat it makit me sick. So I fix 'em up plan and now we gone see who be good mans for marry Mary, daughter of Steve Mestrovich, me, by Gods, what is best mans who was cinderman for open hearth any place. First, everybody gone lift 'em up small dolly bars. If anybody no lift 'em up dat little one den he joost go and play with little kids, dats all. Next, everybody gone to lift 'em up second dolly bars. Anybody no lift 'em up dat second dolly bars den dey go and sit with womans and stay out road of strong mans while strong mans gone show him something. Den, everybody gone lift 'em up last dolly bars. By Gods, dis dolly bar she be from bloomer mill and she is so heavy dis time dat I no can lift him myself. Somebody gone lift 'em up dat hunk steel den by Jezus, dats mans what gone marry Mary, ya damn right, ya betcha."

So all young fellows pull off shirt and get ready to lift dolly bars. First mans was Pete. Pete he walkit over by dolly bars and he lookit 'round for make sure everybody see and den he reach down and lift 'em up easy lak anyting. Everybody holler:

"Dats big mans, you Pete! Dats good fellow!"

Pete he no say nothing. He joost walkit away and he laughit lak he feel sure he gone be plenty strong dis time. Den Eli gone over by dolly bars and he lift 'em up easier as Pete and everybody yell some more. Two fellows what comit from Homestead try and lift 'em up and dey no can move dolly bars from ground. Den everybody laughit and say:

"Ho! Ho! Ho! What kinds mans you have dat place, Homestead? At home I got boy joost two year old and I tink mebbe I better send him over by your mill to help you out little bit. Better you go and play with kids little mans so dat you no monkey 'round with big mans and get hurt dis time."

Well, after dat dey lift 'em up second dolly bars and what you tink? Only three mans catch enough steam to do dat. Dat was Pete, dat was Eli, and dat was 'nother mans from Johnstown. Dis fellow from Johnstown was plenty big mans all right and he catch plenty steam to lift 'em up dolly bars. He do dat easy as anyting. Den all his friends dey yell hoorah for him and dey make face at Pete and Eli same lak dey was sure dat dis fellow was gone be strongest mans and take Mary Mestrovich back to Johnstown with him. People from dis place no lak dat business. Dey lak much better Pete nor Eli gone be strongest and den Mary Mestrovich stay dis place which have better mills as Johnstown anytime. Dat mills at Johnstown is joost little place what when do best she can no makit more as one, two hundred tons steel a day. So peoples get mad at dese peoples from Johnstown and dey gone makit bet dat Pete nor Eli gone be stronger as dis fellow. Pete say dat is good business and nobody gone worry nothing, he gone lift 'em up big dolly bars joost same lak he lift 'em up little ones. Den Pete he gone over take big, big drink prune-jack and he spit on hands. Den he reach down and grab hold dat big dolly bars. His arm crack lak paper bag, his eyes stick out from head lak apple, sweat run down face same lak he was workit in front furnace in July. By Jezus, dat dolly bars no movit one inch from ground. Den Eli try it and he was no good dis time. People from dis place groan lak somebody kick in stomach when dey see dat. Dey tink for sure now dey gone lose Mary Mestrovich, dey gone lose money, and den dey must listen when peoples from Johnstown say:

"Ho! Ho! Ho! Over by dis place mans is joost same lak old womans who talkit all time and no doit nothing. Comit over by Johnstown where mans so strong dat dey tear down mill and fix 'em up again every day joost for fun."

Den dis fellow from Johnstown takit two big, big drinks prune-jack, he twist mustache so she look lak King, and he wave hand for everybody. Den he fixit his feets so he no be shaky and bend down and grabit dat dolly bars. He give big pull, and den another big pull and he grunt all time lak pig at dinner time. He pullit so damn hard on dat dolly bars dat his hand come loose and he fallit down on ground.

Peoples from dis place feelit much better: she is not so easy as dis fellow tink. Johnstown fellow mad lak *frau* when hoosband get drunk and spend all money on pay days. He joomp up from ground and he cuss lak hell and he grabit dolly bars again. No good dis time neither.

"Ho! Ho! Ho!"

A laugh lak dat comit from somebody in crowd. Everybody lookit 'round to see who laughit lak dat; mans from Johnstown straighten back and he say:

"Who laughit for me? By Jezus Christ a Mighty, if dat fellow who laughit tink he be so strong mans whats matter he no comit here and pick 'em up dolly bars? Den after he do dat I gone broke his neck."

Den out from crowd walkit biggest mans whatever I see: he have back bigger as door, hands bigger as Pete nor Eli together, neck lak big bulls, and arm bigger as somebodys round waist. I betcha my life he was more as seven feets tall. Oh, he was prettiest mans whatever anybody ever see. Everybody lookit everybody and everybody say:

"Who is dat fellow anyhow?"

And everybody shake heads no dey never see before.

Dat fellow he walkit over to dolly bars and he was laughit so hard he have to holdit his belly so dat he can stand on feet. Dat fellow from Johnstown he takit pull at trousers, he spit on hands and he gone take slug at dat fellow. But dat mans he grabit fellow from Johnstown with one hands and with 'nother he pick 'em up dolly bars. Den he hold 'em out and shake until mans from Johnstown yell he was so 'fraid.

By Gods, everybody was white lak sheet. Dey never see before mans what was so strong lak dat. But dat fellow put dat fellow from Johnstown down so easy as little baby by mudder and he say:

"Nobody be 'fraid nothing. I no wanit hurt nobody, no wanit makit trooble. Joost havit little bit fun, dats all."

Steve Mestrovich walkit over and he say:

"What kind mans you are? Which place you comit from?"

And dat fellow answer:

"My name is Joe Magarac, what you tink of dat, eh?"

Everybody laughit for dat for *magarac* in Hunkie mean jackass donkey. Dey know dis fellow is fine fellow all right when he say his name is Joe Jackass. Den dis fellow say:

"Sure! Magarac, Joe. Dats me. All I do is eatit and workit same lak jackass donkey. Me, I be only steelmans in whole world, ya damn right. Lookit for me; I show you something."

He pull 'em off shirt and everybody lookit. By Gods, he no tell lie. He was steelmans all right: all over he was steel same lak is from open hearth, steel hands, steel body, steel everything. Everybody say:

"What the hells you tink of dat?"

Joe Magarac say:

"Dats all right, dats good business for me. Me, I was born inside ore mountain many year ago. To-day I comit down from mountain in ore train and was over in ore pile by blast furnace."

Den he laughit and twist dolly bars in two with hands.

Steve Mestrovich smile lak somebody givit him cold beer on hot day and he takit Mary by hand and leadit her over to Joe Magarac: dis time he gone catch best hoosband for Mary dat was in whole country. Joe Magarac takit long look at Mary and he say:

"Oh, boy, I never see such pretty girls as dat. You makit fine *frau* for anybodies. But dat is no business for me. What you tink, I catch time for sit around house with womans? No, by Gods, not me. I joost catch time for workit dats all. Be better all right if Mary have hoosband and I tink I see her get little bit dizzy in head when she lookit for Pete. Dats good, for after me dis Pete is best mans in country."

Joe Magarac close one eyes for Steve and Steve close one eyes for Joe Magarac and Mary was happy lak anyting for she lak dat Pete all right better as anybody. Fellow from Johnstown get black in face and he stomp 'round mad lak anyting, but he 'fraid say anyting for fellow who was made out of steel and who comit from ore mountain. So he go away.

Everyting was fixed 'em up all right den: Priest comit with altar boy and Pete and Mary kneel down and pretty soon dey was hoosband and *frau*. First one to dancit with bride was Joe Magarac. Den everybody get drunk, have big time and was happy as anyting.

So next day, Joe Magarac gone down to Mrs. Horkey, who catch boarding-house by mill gate and he say:

"Howdy do, Mrs. Horkey. My but you lookit nice dis morning and from kitchen comit smell of best breakfast whatever I smell anyplace. Dis place lookit all right for me. I gone work in mill dis place and I wanit good place for eat. I no wanit room, joost five big meals a day, dats all, for I workit night turn and day turn all at same time."

So Joe Magarac livit by Horkey's boarding-house and he catch job in mill. He workit on Noomber Seven furnace by open hearth and he workit all night and all day without finish and he no get tired nothing. He standit before Noomber Seven and he throw 'em in limestone, ore, scrap and everyting and den he go sit in furnace door with fires from furnace licking 'round chin. When steel melt 'em up, Joe Magarac put in hands and stir steel 'round while she was cookit and when furnace was ready for tap 'em out he crawl into furnace and scoop up big handfuls steel and dump 'em into ingot mould. After dat he run down to lower end and grab dat steel in hands and squeeze 'em out from fingers and he makit rails. Eight rails one time, four by each hand, he makit by Gods. Pretty soon he makit more steel as all other furnace together. Nobody ever see before such business lak dat, so boss of open hearth have big sign made and he put sign on mill fence where everybody see and dis sign say:

THE HOME OF JOE MAGARAC

Joe Magarac was workit every day and every night at mill and same lak before he was makit rails with hands. Pretty soon dat pile of rails in yard get bigger and bigger for Joe Magarac is workit so hard and after coople months yard was full, everyplace was rails. When Joe Magarac see dat he joost laughit and workit harder as ever. So one day roller-boss he comit up from down by finishing mills and he say to Joe Magarac who was workit by his furnace in open hearth. Roller-boss he say:

"Well, Joe Magarac, I guess we gone shut mill down early dis week. Dis time we catch plenty rails everyplace and we no catch many orders. So by Gods, we gone shut mill down Thursday night and we no start 'em up again until Monday morning. Mebbe you gone put slow heat in furnace: you tell stockman give you fifty-ton stock. You put 'em in stock and give furnace slow fire so dat she keepit warm and be ready for start 'em up on Monday."

Joe Magarac he act lak he gone say something and den he no say nothing and roller-boss tink everyting gone be all right dis time and he gone away.

When next Monday comit mans gone back to work for open hearth. Den dey see dat Joe Magarac is not workit on furnace dat morning. Everyplace dey lookit and dey no see Joe anyplace. 'Nother mans was workit on Noomber Seven and pretty soon when Noomber Seven was ready for tap 'em out melter-boss gone down to platform to see what kind steel dat slow heat makit. He was standit by ingot mould and pretty soon he hear voice what say:

"How she lookit dis time?"

Melter-boss lookit 'round and he no see nobody and den dat voice say again:

"It's me, Joe Magarac. I'm inside ladle."

Melter-boss turn around and he lookit inside ladle and he see Joe. Joe was sitting inside ladle with hot steel boiling up around neck. Melter-boss was scared lak anyting and he say:

"What the hells you do in dere, Joe Magarac? Better you gone crawl out dat ladle right 'way or I tink maybe for sure dat she gone melt you up."

Joe Magarac close one eyes for melter-boss and he say:

"Dats fine. Dats good business, dats joost what I wanit. By Gods, I be sick dis time of mill what shut down on Thursday and no start 'em up again untii Monday. What the hells I gone do all time mill is shut down anyway? I hear big boss say dat he was gone makit two, three good heats steel so dat he gone have best steel what we can makit for buildit new mill dis place. Dey gone tear down dis old mills and makit new ones what is gone be best mills in whole Monongahela valley, what gone be best mills in whole world. Den by Gods, I get plan: I gone joomp in furnace when steel is melted down and dey gone melt 'em up me, who was made from steel, to makit steel to makit dat mills. Now Mr. Boss you gone listen for me and I gone tell you someting. You gone take dis ladle steel what has me inside and you gone pour 'em out in ingot mould and den you gone roll 'em out and makit beam, channel, and maybe one, two piece angle and you gone take dat steel and makit new mills. You do lak I say for you and you gone see you gone have best mills for anyplace. Good-by."

Den Joe Magarac sit back down in ladle and hold his chin down in boiling steel until he was all melted up. Pretty soon dey pour him out in ingot mould.

Well, after dey roll 'em out dat heat and dey cut 'em up dey see dat dis time dey have best steel what was ever made. Oh, my, dat steel was smooth and straight and it no have seam or pipe nothing. Den melter-boss he gone 'round for everybody and he say:

"Now we gone have best mills for sure. You see dat steel? By Gods, nobody ever see steel lak dat before and dats joost because Joe Magarac he makit dat steel. Sure, he's inside and now we gone takit dat beam and dat channel and we gone build finest mills what ever was."

Dey do lak melter-boss say and dat is why all young boys want to go for mill, and dat is why when somebody call Hunkie *magarac* he only laughit and feel proud as anyting, and dat is why we catch the best mill for anyplace, ya damn right!

Songs of Popeye

I yam Popeye,
The Sailor Man.
    I yam what I yam
    'Cause tha's what I yam.
I yam Popeye,
The Sailor Man.

I yam Popeye,
The Sailor Man.
    Never more will I roam,
    Fer I feels right to home.
I yam Popeye,
The Sailor Man.

From *Popeye starring in Choose Your Weppins.* A Creation of E. C. Segar. Adaptation by Charles T. Clinton from the Max Fleischer Cartoon. A Paramount Picture. Copyright, 1935, 1936, by King Features Syndicate, Inc., New York. Akron, Ohio, and New York: The Saalfield Publishing Company.

I yam Popeye,
The Sailor Man.
  I yam jus' a little feller,
  But I hasn't any yeller.
I yam Popeye,
The Sailor Man.

I yam Popeye,
The Sailor Man.
  I have said I hates strife,
  But I'll fight fer me life.
I yam Popeye,
The Sailor Man.

I yam Popeye,
The Sailor Man.
  When spinach I eat
  I kin not be beat.
I yam Popeye,
The Sailor Man.

I yam Popeye,
The Sailor Man.
  I fights fer the right
  With all of me might.
I yam Popeye,
The Sailor Man.

I yam Popeye,
The Sailor Man.
  I yam strong as the breezes
  Wich blows down big treeses.
I yam Popeye,
The Sailor Man.

I yam Popeye,
The Sailor Man.
  I yam strong at the finitch
  'Cause I eats me spinitch.
I yam Popeye,
The Sailor Man.

VI. PATRON SAINTS

The hero is a man who has fought impressively for a cause of which we approve.—DUMAS MALONE.

ON THE purely patriotic level our heroes are apt to be too good to be true. Such is the case with that "typically good man," Washington, whose integrity is traditionally taught by means of what the Doubter in the

Sazerac Lying Club characterizes as the "doggonedest biggest lie as was ever told in this here Club." Yet in spite of more robust and even backwoodsy traits and episodes in young manhood, the juvenile Washington of Parson Weems' cherry-tree legend is of a piece with the "supercilious postage-stamp" likeness that the older Washington has become in the hearts of his countrymen.

As human being and folk hero, as American image and symbol, Lincoln is more satisfying. His "log cabin to White House" career fits the Horatio Alger pattern (which is essentially the fairy-tale pattern) of the poor boy who makes good; his genius as a folk story-teller helped in the making of his own legend; and he suffered the martyrdom which is the hero's apotheosis. He is also the perfect exemplar of the Freudian formula which sees in his homeliness the potentiality of our own impotence and of the American democratic creed of the self-made man. ("Any boy can become President.") Rather than too good to be true, Lincoln was great because he was not afraid to be common.

Although Americans as a rule have clung less tenaciously to the ideal of the good life than to that of the useful one, following Mr. Hoover's "American way" of "stimulating their ingenuity to solve their own problems," the doctrine of plain living and high thinking has produced spiritual heroes—saints and martyrs in whom self-abnegation is combined with service. That saints are not far from cranks is seen in the fanatic Johnny Appleseed, whose resemblance to Saint Francis is balanced by his likeness to a Yankee peddler, as the primitive Christian in him merged with the footloose type of hero. His "benevolent monomania" of "planting appleseeds in remote places" has overshadowed his less beneficent fixation of sowing the seed of dog-fennel, from a belief that it possessed valuable anti-malarial virtues. His inner meaning as a mystical pioneer cast in the unique rôle of a savior among wastrels is the intent of these lines written to be spoken in a pageant:

"My name is Johnny Appleseed. I lived in this part of the country a long time ago, when it had hardly been touched. I liked the Indians and I liked the white people and I liked the animals, and I didn't hurt any of them. I planted seeds and set out apple trees for the settlers and I took care of them. I told the people about God, and I tried to be a good man myself. I tried to be a good American, on this land we had found. Maybe I was, a little. Maybe I'm not dead yet." [1]

———

"I Cannot Tell a Lie"

NEVER did the wise Ulysses take more pains with his beloved Telemachus, than did Mr. Washington with George, to inspire him with an *early love*

---

[1] "The Return of Johnny Appleseed," by Charles Allen Smart, *Harper's Magazine,* Vol. 179 (August, 1939), pp. 233–234.

From *The Life of George Washington,* by Mason Locke Weems (fifth edition), 1806. Parson Weems, itinerant preacher and book peddler, published *The Life and Memorable Actions of George Washington* in 1800. The cherry-tree story was first included in the fifth of the more than seventy editions of the work.

of truth. "Truth, George," said he, "is the loveliest quality of youth. I would ride fifty miles, my son, to see the little boy whose heart is so *honest,* and his lips so *pure,* that we may depend on every word he says. O how lovely does such a child appear in the eyes of everybody! his parents doat on him. His relations glory in him. They are constantly praising him to their children, whom they beg to imitate him. They are often sending for him to visit them; and receive him, when he comes, with as much joy as if he were a little angel, come to set pretty examples to their children.

"But, Oh! how different, George, is the case with the boy who is given to lying, that nobody can believe a word he says! He is looked at with aversion wherever he goes, and parents dread to see him come among their children. Oh, George! my son! rather than see you come to this pass, dear as you are to my heart, gladly would I assist to nail you up in your little coffin, and follow you to your grave. Hard, indeed, would it be to me to give up my son, whose little feet are always so ready to run about with me, and whose fondly looking eyes, and sweet prattle make so large a part of my happiness. But still I would give him up, rather than see him a common liar."

"Pa," said George very seriously, "do I ever tell lies?"

"No, George, I *thank* God you do not, my son; and I rejoice in the hope you never will. At least, you shall never, from me, have cause to be guilty of so shameful a thing. Many parents, indeed, even compel their children to this vile practice, by barbarously beating them for every little fault: hence, on the next offence, the little terrified creature slips out a *lie!* just to escape the rod. But as to yourself George, you know I have *always* told you, and now tell you again, that, whenever by accident, you do anything wrong, which must often be the case, as you are but a poor little boy yet, without *experience* or *knowledge,* you must never tell a falsehood to conceal it; but come *bravely* up, my son, like a *little* man, and tell me of it: and, instead of beating you, George, I will but the more honour and love you for it, my dear."

This, you'll say, was sowing good seed!—Yes, it was: and the crop, thank God, was, as I believe it ever will be, where a man acts the true parent, that is, the *Guardian Angel,* by his child.

The following anecdote is a *case in point.* It is too valuable to be lost, and too true to be doubted; for it was communicated to me by the same excellent lady to whom I am indebted for the last.

"When George," said she, "was about six years old, he was made the wealthy master of a *hatchet!* of which, like most little boys, he was immoderately fond, and was constantly going about chopping every thing that came in his way. One day, in the garden, where he often amused himself hacking his mother's pea-sticks, he unluckily tried the edge of his hatchet on the body of a beautiful young English cherry-tree, which he barked so terribly, that I don't believe the tree ever got the better of it. The next morning the old gentleman, finding out what had befallen his tree, which, by the by, was a great favourite, came into the house; and with much warmth asked for the mischievous author, declaring at the same time, that he would not have taken five guineas for his tree. Nobody could tell him anything about it. Presently George and his hatchet made their appearance. *'George,'* said his father, 'do you know who killed that beautiful little cherry tree yonder in the garden?' This was a *tough question;* and George staggered under it for a moment; but quickly recovered himself: and looking at his father, with the sweet face of youth brightened with the inexpressible charm of all-conquering truth, he bravely cried out, 'I can't tell a lie, Pa; you know I can't tell a lie. I did cut it with my hatchet.'—'Run to my arms, you dearest boy,' cried his father in transports, 'run to my arms; glad am I, George, that you killed my tree; for you have paid me for it a thousand fold. Such an act of heroism in my son is more worth than a thousand trees, though blossomed with silver, and their fruits of purest gold.' "

It was in this way by interesting at once both his *heart* and *head,* that Mr. Washington conducted George with great ease and pleasure along the happy paths of virtue.

Honest Abe

I. The Young Store-Keeper

As A clerk he proved honest and efficient, and my readers will be interested in some illustrations of the former trait which I find in Dr. Holland's interesting volume.

One day a woman came into the store and purchased sundry articles. They footed up two dollars and six and a quarter cents, or the young clerk thought they did. We do not hear nowadays of six and a quarter cents, but this was a coin borrowed from the Spanish currency, and was well known in my own boyhood.

The bill was paid, and the woman was entirely satisfied. But the young store-keeper, not feeling quite sure as to the accuracy of his calculation, added up the items once more. To his dismay he found that the sum total should have been but two dollars.

"I've made her pay six and a quarter cents too much," said Abe, disturbed.

It was a trifle, and many clerks would have dismissed it as such. But Abe was too conscientious for that.

"The money must be paid back," he decided.

This would have been easy enough had the woman lived "just round the corner," but, as the young man knew, she lived between two and three miles away. This, however, did not alter the matter. It was night, but

---

From *Abraham Lincoln, The Backwoods Boy;* or How a Young Rail-Splitter Became President, by Horatio Alger, Jr., pp. 64–66. Copyright, 1883, by Horatio Alger, Jr. New York: John R. Anderson & Henry S. Allen.

he closed and locked the store, and walked to the residence of his customer.
Arrived there, he explained the matter, paid over the six and a quarter
cents, and returned satisfied. If I were a capitalist, I would be willing to
lend money to such a young man without security.

Here is another illustration of young Lincoln's strict honesty:

A woman entered the store and asked for half a pound of tea.

The young clerk weighed it out, and handed it to her in a parcel. This
was the last sale of the day.

The next morning, when commencing his duties, Abe discovered a four-
ounce weight on the scales. It flashed upon him at once that he had used
this in the sale of the night previous, and so, of course, given his customer
short weight. I am afraid that there are many country merchants who
would not have been much worried by this discovery. Not so the young
clerk in whom we are interested. He weighed out the balance of the half
pound, shut up store, and carried it to the defrauded customer. I think
my young readers will begin to see that the name so often given, in later
times, to President Lincoln, of "Honest Old Abe," was well deserved. A
man who begins by strict honesty in his youth is not likely to change as
he grows older, and mercantile honesty is some guarantee of political
honesty.

II. Spell "Defied!"

"Spell *defied!*"

This question was put to a class in spelling by the master.

The first pupil in the straggling line of backwoods boys and girls who
stood up in class, answered with some hesitation: "D-e-f-i-d-e, defied."

The master frowned.

"Next!" he called sharply.

The next improved upon the effort of the first speller, and in a confident tone answered:

"D-e-f-y-d-e."

"Wrong again! The next may try it," said the teacher.

"D-e-f-y-d!" said the third scholar.

"Worse and worse! You are entitled to a medal!" said Crawford, sar-
castically. "Next!"

"D-e-f-y-e-d!" was the next attempt.

"Really, you do me great credit," said the teacher, a frown gathering
on his brow. "You can't spell an easy word of two syllables. It is shameful. I'll keep the whole class in all the rest of the day, if necessary, till
the word is spelled correctly."

It now became the turn of a young girl named Roby, who was a
favorite with Abe. She was a pretty girl, but, nevertheless, the terrible
word puzzled her. In her perplexity she chanced to turn toward the seat
at the window occupied by her long-legged friend, Abe.

Ibid., pp. 34–35.

Abe was perhaps the best speller in school. A word like defied was easy enough to him, and he wanted to help the girl through.

As Miss Roby looked at him she saw a smile upon his face, as he significantly touched his *eye* with his finger. The girl took the hint, and spelled the word correctly.

"Right at last!" said Master Crawford, whose back was turned, and who had not seen Abe's dumb show. "It's lucky for you all that one of the class knew how to spell, or I would have kept my word, and kept you all in."

III. Working Out a Book

All the information we can obtain about this early time is interesting, for it was then that Abe was laying the foundation of his future eminence. His mind and character were slowly developing, and shaping themselves for the future.

From Mr. Lamon's Life I quote a paragraph which will throw light upon his habits and tastes at the age of seventeen:

"Abe loved to lie under a shade-tree, or up in the loft of the cabin, and read, cipher, and scribble. At night he sat by the chimney 'jamb,' and ciphered by the light of the fire, on the wooden fire-shovel. When the shovel was fairly covered, he would shave it off with Tom Lincoln's drawing-knife, and begin again. In the day-time he used boards for the same purpose, out of doors, and went through the shaving process ever-lastingly. His step-mother repeats often that 'he read every book he could lay his hands on.' She says, 'Abe read diligently. He read every book he could lay his hands on, and when he came across a passage that struck him, he would write it down on boards if he had no paper, and keep it there until he did get paper. Then he would rewrite it, look at it, repeat it. He had a copy-book, a kind of scrap-book, in which he put down all things, and thus preserved them.'"

I am tempted also to quote a reminiscence of John Hanks, who lived with the Lincolns from the time Abe was fourteen to the time he became eighteen years of age: "When Lincoln—Abe—and I returned to the house from work, he would go to the cupboard, snatch a piece of corn-bread, take down a book, sit down on a chair, cock his legs up as high as his head, and read. He and I worked barefooted, grubbed it, ploughed, mowed, and cradled together; ploughed corn, gathered it, and shucked corn. Abraham read constantly when he had opportunity."

It may well be supposed, however, that the books upon which Abe could lay hands were few in number. There were no libraries, either public or private, in the neighborhood, and he was obliged to read what he could get rather than those which he would have chosen, had he been able to select from a large collection. Still, it is a matter of interest to know what books he actually did read at this formative period. Some of

Ibid., pp. 38–42.

them certainly were worth reading, such as "Aesop's Fables," "Robinson Crusoe," "Pilgrim's Progress," a History of the United States, and Weems' "Life of Washington." The last book Abe borrowed from a neighbor, old Josiah Crawford (I follow the statement of Mr. Lamon, rather than of Dr. Holland, who says it was Master Crawford, his teacher). When not reading it, he laid it away in a part of the cabin where he thought it would be free from harm, but it so happened that just behind the shelf on which he placed it was a great crack between the logs of the wall. One night a storm came up suddenly, the rain beat in through the crevice, and soaked the borrowed book through and through. The book was almost utterly spoiled. Abe felt very uneasy, for a book was valuable in his eyes, as well as in the eyes of its owner.

He took the damaged volume and trudged over to Mr. Crawford's in some perplexity and mortification.

"Well, Abe, what brings you over so early?" said Mr. Crawford.

"I've got some bad news for you," answered Abe, with lengthened face.

"Bad news! What is it?"

"You know the book you lent me—the 'Life of Washington?'"

"Yes, yes."

"Well, the rain last night spoiled it," and Abe showed the book, wet to a pulp inside, at the same time explaining how it had been injured.

"It's too bad, I vum! You'd ought to pay for it, Abe. You must have been dreadful careless!"

"I'd pay for it if I had any money, Mr. Crawford."

"If you've got no money, you can work it out," said Crawford.

"I'll do whatever you think right."

So it was arranged that Abe should work three days for Crawford, "pulling fodder," the value of his labor being rated at twenty-five cents a day. As the book had cost seventy-five cents this would be regarded as satisfactory. So Abe worked his three days, and discharged the debt. Mr. Lamon is disposed to find fault with Crawford for exacting this penalty, but it appears to me only equitable, and I am glad to think that Abe was willing to act honorably in the matter.

Johnny Appleseed: A Pioneer Hero

THE "far West" is rapidly becoming only a traditional designation: railroads have destroyed the romance of frontier life, or have surrounded it with so many appliances of civilization that the pioneer character is rapidly becoming mythical. The men and women who obtain their groceries and dry-goods from New York by rail in a few hours have nothing in common with those who, fifty years ago, "packed" salt a

By W. D. Haley. From *Harper's New Monthly Magazine*, Vol. XLIII (November, 1871), No. CCLVIII, pp. 830–836.

hundred miles to make their musl. palatable, and could only exchange corn and wheat for molasses and calico by making long and perilous voyages in flat-boats down the Ohio and Mississippi rivers to New Orleans. Two generations of frontier lives have accumulated stores of narratives which, like the small but beautiful tributaries of great rivers, are forgotten in the broad sweep of the larger current of history. The march of Titans sometimes tramples out the memory of smaller but more useful lives, and sensational glare often eclipses more modest but purer lights. This has been the case in the popular demand for the dime novel dilutions of Fenimore Cooper's romances of border life, which have preserved the records of Indian rapine and atrocity as the only memorials of pioneer history. But the early days of Western settlement witnessed sublimer heroisms than those of human torture, and nobler victories than those of the tomahawk and scalping-knife.

Among the heroes of endurance that was voluntary, and of action that was creative and not sanguinary, there was one man whose name, seldom mentioned now save by some of the few surviving pioneers, deserves to be perpetuated.

The first reliable trace of our modest hero finds him in the Territory of Ohio, in 1801, with a horse-load of apple seeds, which he planted in various places on and about the borders of Licking Creek, the first orchard thus originated by him being on the farm of Isaac Stadden, in what is now known as Licking County, in the State of Ohio. During the five succeeding years, although he was undoubtedly following the same strange occupation, we have no authentic account of his movements until we reach a pleasant spring day in 1806, when a pioneer settler in Jefferson County, Ohio, noticed a peculiar craft, with a remarkable occupant and a curious cargo, slowly dropping down with the current of the Ohio River. It was "Johnny Appleseed," by which name Jonathan Chapman was afterward known in every log-cabin from the Ohio River to the Northern lakes, and westward to the prairies of what is now the State of Indiana. With two canoes lashed together he was transporting a load of apple seeds to the Western frontier, for the purpose of creating orchards on the farthest verge of white settlements. With his canoes he passed down the Ohio to Marietta, where he entered the Muskingum, ascending the stream of that river until he reached the mouth of the Walhonding, or White Woman Creek, and still onward, up the Mohican, into the Black Fork, to the head of navigation, in the region now known as Ashland and Richland counties, on the line of the Pittsburgh and Fort Wayne Railroad, in Ohio. A long and toilsome voyage it was, as a glance at the map will show, and must have occupied a great deal of time, as the lonely traveler stopped at every inviting spot to plant the seeds and make his infant nurseries. These are the first well-authenticated facts in the history of Jonathan Chapman, whose birth, there is good reason for believing, occurred in Boston, Massachusetts, in 1775. According to this, which was his own statement in one of his less reticent moods, he was, at the time of his appearance on Licking Creek, twenty-six years of age, and whether impelled in his eccentricities by some absolute misery of the heart which could only find relief in incessant motion, or governed by a benevolent monomania, his whole after-life was devoted to the work of planting apple seeds in remote places. The seeds he gathered from the cider-presses of Western Pennsylvania; but his canoe voyage in 1806 appears to have been the only occasion upon which he adopted that method of transporting them, as all his subsequent journeys were made on foot. Having planted his stock of seeds, he would return to Pennsylvania for a fresh supply, and, as sacks made of any less substantial fabric would not endure the hard usage of the long trip through forests dense with underbrush and briers, he provided himself with leathern bags. Securely packed, the seeds were conveyed, sometimes on the back of a horse, and not unfrequently on his own shoulders, either over a part of the old Indian trail that led from Fort Duquesne to Detroit, by way of Fort Sandusky, or over what is styled in the appendix to "Hutchins's History of Boguet's Expedition in 1764" the "second route through the wilderness of Ohio," which would require him to traverse a distance of one hundred and sixty-six miles in a west-northwest direction from Fort Duquesne in order to reach the Black Fork of the Mohican.

This region, although it is now densely populated, still possesses a romantic beauty that railroads and bustling towns can not obliterate— a country of forest-clad hills and green valleys, through which numerous bright streams flow on their way to the Ohio; but when Johnny Appleseed reached some lonely log-cabin he would find himself in a veritable wilderness. The old settlers say that the margins of the streams, near which the first settlements were generally made, were thickly covered with low, matted growth of small timber, while nearer to the water was a rank mass of long grass, interlaced with morning-glory and wild pea vines, among which funereal willows and clustering alders stood like sentinels on the outpost of civilization. The hills, that rise almost to the dignity of mountains, were crowned with forest trees, and in the coverts were innumerable bears, wolves, deer, and droves of wild hogs, that were as ferocious as any beast of prey. In the grass the massasauga and other venomous reptiles lurked in such numbers that a settler named Chandler has left the fact on record that during the first season of his residence, while mowing a little prairie which formed part of his land, he killed over two hundred black rattlesnakes in an area that would involve an average destruction of one of these reptiles for each rod of land. The frontiersman, who felt himself sufficiently protected by his rifle against wild beasts and hostile Indians, found it necessary to guard against the attacks of the insidious enemies in the grass by wrapping bandages of dried grass around his buckskin leggings and moccasins; but Johnny would shoulder his bag of apple seeds, and with bare feet penetrate to some remote spot that combined picturesqueness and fertility of soil, and there he would plant his seeds, place a slight inclosure around the place, and leave them to grow until the trees were large enough to be transplanted by the settlers, who, in the mean time, would have made their clearings in the vicinity. The sites chosen by him are, many of them, well known, and are such as an artist or a poet would select—open places on the loamy lands that border the creeks—rich, secluded spots, hemmed in by giant trees, picturesque now, but fifty years ago, with their wild surroundings and the primal silence, they must have been tenfold more so.

In personal appearance Chapman was a small, wiry man, full of restless activity; he had long dark hair, a scanty beard that was never shaved, and keen black eyes that sparkled with a peculiar brightness. His dress was of the oddest description. Generally, even in the coldest weather, he went barefooted, but sometimes, for his long journeys, he would make himself a rude pair of sandals; at other times he would wear any cast-off foot-covering he chanced to find—a boot on one foot and an old brogan or a moccasin on the other. It appears to have been a matter of conscience with him never to purchase shoes, although he was rarely without money enough to do so. On one occasion, in an unusually cold November, while he was traveling barefooted through mud and snow, a settler who happened to possess a pair of shoes that were too small for his own use forced their acceptance upon Johnny, declaring that it was sinful for a human being to travel with naked feet in such weather. A few days afterward the donor was in the village that has since become the thriving city of Mansfield, and met his beneficiary contentedly plodding along with his feet bare and half frozen. With some degree of anger he inquired for the cause of such foolish conduct, and received for reply that Johnny had overtaken a poor, barefooted family moving Westward, and as they appeared to be in much greater need of clothing than he was, he had given them the shoes. His dress was generally composed of cast-off clothing, that he had taken in payment for apple-trees; and as the pioneers were far less extravagant than their descendants in such matters, the homespun and buckskin garments that they discarded would not be very elegant or serviceable. In his later years, however, he seems to have thought that even this kind of second-hand raiment was too luxurious, as his principal garment was made of a coffee sack, in which he cut holes for his head and arms to pass through, and pronounced it "a very serviceable cloak, and as good clothing as any man need wear." In the matter of head-gear his taste was equally unique; his first experiment was with a tin vessel that served to cook his mush, but this was open to the objection that it did not protect his eyes from the beams of the sun; so he constructed a hat of pasteboard with an immense peak in front, and having thus secured an article that combined usefulness with economy, it became his permanent fashion.

Thus strangely clad, he was perpetually wandering through forests and morasses, and suddenly appearing in white settlements and Indian villages; but there must have been some rare force of gentle goodness dwelling in his looks and breathing in his words; for it is the testimony of all who knew him that, notwithstanding his ridiculous attire, he was always treated with the greatest respect by the rudest frontiersman, and, what is a better test, the boys of the settlements forbore to jeer at him. With grown-up people and boys he was usually reticent, but manifested great affection for little girls, always having pieces of ribbon and gay calico to give to his little favorites. Many a grandmother in Ohio and Indiana can remember the presents she received when a child from poor homeless Johnny Appleseed. When he consented to eat with any family he would never sit down to the table until he was assured that there was an ample supply for the children; and his sympathy for their youthful troubles and his kindness toward them made him friends among all the juveniles of the borders.

The Indians also treated Johnny with the greatest kindness. By these wild and sanguinary savages he was regarded as a "great medicine man," on account of his strange appearance, eccentric actions, and, especially, the fortitude with which he could endure pain, in proof of which he would often thrust pins and needles into his flesh. His nervous sensibilities really seem to have been less acute than those of ordinary people, for his method of treating the cuts and sores that were the consequences of his barefooted wanderings through briers and thorns was to sear the wound with a red-hot iron, and then cure the burn. During the war of 1812, when the frontier settlers were tortured and slaughtered by the savage allies of Great Britain, Johnny Appleseed continued his wanderings, and was never harmed by the roving bands of hostile Indians. On many occasions the impunity with which he ranged the country enabled him to give the settlers warning of approaching danger in time to allow them to take refuge in their block-houses before the savages could attack them. Our informant refers to one of these instances, when the news of Hull's surrender came like a thunder-bolt upon the frontier. Large bands of Indians and British were destroying everything before them and murdering defenseless women and children, and even the block-houses were not always a sufficient protection. At this time Johnny travelled day and night, warning the people of the approaching danger. He visited every cabin and delivered this message: "The Spirit of the Lord is upon me, and he hath anointed me to blow the trumpet in the wilderness, and sound an alarm in the forest; for, behold, the tribes of the heathen are round about your doors, and a devouring flame followeth after them." The aged man who narrated this incident said that he could feel even now the thrill that was caused by this prophetic announcement of the wild-looking herald of danger, who aroused the family on a bright moonlight midnight with his piercing voice. Refusing all offers of food and denying himself a moment's rest, he traversed the border day and night until he had warned every settler of the approaching peril.

His diet was as meagre as his clothing. He believed it to be a sin to kill any creature for food, and thought that all that was necessary for human sustenance was produced by the soil. He was also a strenuous opponent of the waste of food, and on one occasion, on approaching a log-cabin, he observed some fragments of bread floating upon the surface of a bucket of slops that was intended for the pigs. He immediately fished them out, and when the housewife expressed her astonishment, he told her that it was an abuse of the gifts of a merciful God to allow the smallest quantity of any thing that was designed to supply the wants of mankind to be diverted from its purpose.

In this instance, as in his whole life, the peculiar religious ideas of Johnny Appleseed were exemplified. He was a most earnest disciple of the faith taught by Emanuel Swedenborg, and himself claimed to have frequent conversations with angels and spirits; two of the latter, of the feminine gender, he asserted, had revealed to him that they were to be his wives in a future state if he abstained from a matrimonial alliance on earth. He entertained a profound reverence for the revelations of the Swedish seer, and always carried a few old volumes with him. These he was very anxious should be read by everyone, and he was probably not only the first colporteur in the wilderness of Ohio, but as he had no tract society to furnish him supplies, he certainly devised an original method of multiplying one book into a number. He divided his books into several pieces, leaving a portion at a log-cabin, and on a subsequent visit furnishing another fragment, and continuing this process as diligently as though the work had been published in serial numbers. By this plan he was enabled to furnish reading for several people at the same time, and out of one book; but it must have been a difficult undertaking for some nearly illiterate backwoodsman to endeavor to comprehend Swedenborg by a backward course of reading, when his first installment happened to be the last fraction of the volume. Johnny's faith in Swedenborg's works was so reverential as almost to be superstitious. He was once asked if, in traveling barefooted through forests abounding with venomous reptiles, he was not afraid of being bitten. With his peculiar smile, he drew his book from his bosom, and said, "This book is an infallible protection against all danger here and hereafter."

It was his custom, when he had been welcomed to some hospitable log-house after a weary day of journeying, to lie down on the puncheon floor, and, after inquiring if his auditors would hear "some news right fresh from heaven," produce his few tattered books, among which would be a New Testament, and read and expound until his uncultivated hearers would catch the spirit and glow of his enthusiasm, while they scarcely comprehended his language. A lady who knew him in his later years writes in the following terms of one of these domiciliary readings of poor, self-sacrificing Johnny Appleseed: "We can hear him read now, just as he did that summer day, when we were busy quilting up stairs, and he lay near the door, his voice rising denunciatory and thrilling—strong and loud as the roar of wind and waves, then soft and soothing as the balmy airs that quivered the morning-glory leaves about his gray beard. His was a strange eloquence at times, and he was undoubtedly a man of genius." What a scene is presented to our imagination! The interior of a primitive cabin, the wide, open fire-place, where a few sticks are burning beneath the iron pot in which the evening meal is cooking; around the fire-place the attentive group, composed of the sturdy pioneer and his wife and children, listening with a reverential awe to the "news right fresh from heaven"; and reclining on the floor, clad in rags, but with his gray hairs glorified by the beams of the setting sun that flood through the open door and the unchinked logs of the humble building, this poor wanderer, with the gift of genius and eloquence, who believes with the faith of apostles and martyrs that God has appointed him a mission in the wilderness to preach the Gospel of love, and plant apple seeds that shall produce orchards for the benefit of men and women and little children whom he has never seen. If there is a sublimer faith or a more genuine eloquence in richly decorated cathedrals and under brocade vestments, it would be worth a long journey to find it.

Next to his advocacy of his peculiar religious ideas, his enthusiasm for the cultivation of apple-trees in what he termed "the only proper way" —that is, from the seed—was the absorbing object of his life. Upon this, as upon religion, he was eloquent in his appeals. He would describe the growing and ripening fruit as such a rare and beautiful gift of the Almighty with words that became pictures, until his hearers could almost see its manifold forms of beauty present before them. To his eloquence on this subject, as well as to his actual labors in planting nurseries, the country over which he traveled for so many years is largely indebted for its numerous orchards. But he denounced as absolute wickedness all devices of pruning and grafting, and would speak of the act of cutting a tree as if it were a cruelty inflicted upon a sentient being.

Not only is he entitled to the fame of being the earliest colporteur on the frontiers, but in the work of protecting animals from abuse and suffering he preceded, while, in his smaller sphere, he equaled the zeal of the good Mr. Bergh. Whenever Johnny saw an animal abused, or heard of it, he would purchase it and give it to some more humane settler, on condition that it should be kindly treated and properly cared for. It frequently happened that the long journey into the wilderness would cause the new settlers to be encumbered with lame and broken-down horses, that were turned loose to die. In the autumn Johnny would make a diligent search for all such animals, and, gathering them up, he would bargain for their food and shelter until the next spring, when he would lead them away to some good pasture for the summer. If they recovered so as to be capable of working, he would never sell them, but would lend or give them away, stipulating for their good usage. His conception of the absolute sin of inflicting pain or death upon any creature was not limited to the higher forms of animal life, but every thing that had being was to him, in the fact of its life, endowed with so much of the Divine Essence that to wound or destroy it was to inflict an injury upon some atom of Divinity. No Brahmin could be more concerned for the preservation of insect life, and the only occasion on which he destroyed a venomous reptile was a source of long regret, to which he could never refer without manifesting sadness.

He had elected a suitable place for planting apple seeds on a small prairie, and in order to prepare the ground he was mowing the long grass, when he was bitten by a rattlesnake. In describing the event he sighed heavily, and said, "Poor fellow, he only just touched me, when I, in the heat of my ungodly passion, put the heel of my scythe in him, and went away. Some time afterward I went back, and there lay the poor fellow dead." Numerous anecdotes bearing upon his respect for every form of life are preserved, and form the staple of pioneer recollections. On one occasion, a cool autumnal night, when Johnny, who always camped out in preference to sleeping in a house, had built a fire near which he intended to pass the night, he noticed that the blaze attracted large numbers of mosquitoes, many of whom flew too near his fire and were burned. He immediately brought water and quenched the fire, accounting for his conduct afterward by saying, "God forbid that I should build a fire for my comfort which should be the means of destroying any of His creatures!" At another time he removed the fire he had built near a hollow log, and slept on the snow, because he found that the log contained a bear and her cubs, whom, he said, he did not wish to disturb. And this unwillingness to inflict pain or death was equally strong when he was a sufferer by it, as the following will show. Johnny had been assisting some settlers to make a road through the woods, and in the course of their work they accidentally destroyed a hornets' nest. One of the angry insects soon found a lodgment under Johnny's coffee-sack cloak, but although it stung him repeatedly he removed it with the greatest gentleness. The men who were present laughingly asked him why he did not kill it. To which he gravely replied that "It would not be right to kill the poor thing, for it did not intend to hurt me."

Theoretically he was as methodical in matters of business as any merchant. In addition to their picturesqueness, the locations of his nurseries were all fixed with a view to a probable demand for the trees by the time they had attained sufficient growth for transplanting. He would give them away to those who could not pay for them. Generally, however, he sold them for old clothing or a supply of corn meal; but he preferred to receive a note payable at some indefinite period. When this was accomplished he seemed to think that the transaction was completed in a business-like way; but if the giver of the note did not attend to its payment, the holder of it never troubled himself about its collection. His expenses for food and clothing were so very limited that, notwithstanding his freedom from the *auri sacra fames*, he was frequently in possession of more money than he cared to keep, and it was quickly disposed of for wintering infirm horses, or given to some poor family whom the ague had prostrated or the accidents of border life impoverished. In a single instance only he is known to have invested his surplus means in the purchase of land, having received a deed from Alexander Finley, of Mohican Township, Ashland County, Ohio, for a part of the southwest quarter of section twenty-six; but with his customary indifference to matters of value, Johnny failed to record the deed, and lost it. Only a few years ago the property was in litigation.

We must not leave the reader under the impression that this man's life, so full of hardship and perils, was a gloomy or unhappy one. There is an element of human pride in all martyrdom, which, if it does not soften the pains, stimulates the power of endurance. Johnny's life was made serenely happy by the conviction that he was living like the primitive Christians. Nor was he devoid of a keen humor, to which he occasionally gave vent, as the following will show. Toward the latter part of Johnny's career in Ohio an itinerant missionary found his way to the village of Mansfield, and preached to an open-air congregation. The discourse was tediously lengthy, and unnecessarily severe upon the sin of extravagance, which was beginning to manifest itself among the pioneers by an occasional indulgence in the carnal vanities of calico and "store tea." There was a good deal of the Pharisaic leaven in the preacher, who very frequently emphasized his discourse by the inquiry, "Where now is there a man who, like the primitive Christians, is traveling to heaven barefooted and clad in coarse raiment?" When this interrogation had been repeated beyond all reasonable endurance, Johnny rose from the log on which he was reclining, and advancing to the speaker, he placed one of his bare feet upon the stump which served for a pulpit, and pointing to his coffee-sack garment, he quietly said, "Here's your primitive Christian!" The well-clothed missionary hesitated and stammered and dismissed the congregation. His pet antithesis was destroyed by Johnny's personal appearance, which was far more primitive than the preacher cared to copy.

Some of the pioneers were disposed to think that Johnny's humor was the cause of an extensive practical joke; but it is generally conceded now that a widespread annoyance was really the result of his belief that the offensively odored weed known in the West as the dog-fennel, but more generally styled the May-weed, possessed valuable antimalarial virtues. He procured some seeds of the plant in Pennsylvania, and sowed them in the vicinity of every house in the region of his travels. The consequence was that successive flourishing crops of the weed spread over the whole country, and caused almost as much trouble as the disease it was intended to ward off; and to this day the dog-fennel, introduced by Johnny Appleseed, is one of the worst grievances of the Ohio farmers.

In 1838—thirty-seven years after his appearance on Licking Creek—Johnny noticed that civilization, wealth, and population were pressing into the wilderness of Ohio. Hitherto he had easily kept just in advance of the wave of settlement; but now towns and churches were making their appearance, and even, at long intervals, the stage-driver's horn broke the silence of the grand old forests, and he felt that his work was done in the region in which he had labored so long. He visited every house, and took a solemn farewell of all the families. The little girls who had been delighted with his gifts of fragments of calico and ribbons had become sober matrons, and the boys who had wondered at his ability to bear the pain caused by running needles into his flesh were heads of families. With parting words of admonition he left them, and turned his steps steadily toward the setting sun.

During the succeeding nine years he pursued his eccentric avocation on the western border of Ohio and in Indiana. In the summer of 1847, when his labors had literally borne fruit over a hundred thousand square miles of territory, at the close of a warm day, after traveling twenty miles, he entered the house of a settler in Allen County, Indiana, and was, as usual, warmly welcomed. He declined to eat with the family, but accepted some bread and milk, which he partook of sitting on the door-step and gazing on the setting sun. Later in the evening he delivered his "news right fresh from heaven" by reading the Beatitudes. Declining other accommodation, he slept, as usual, on the floor, and in the early morning he was found with his features all aglow with a supernal light, and his body so near death that his tongue refused its office. The physician, who was hastily summoned, pronounced him dying, but added that he had never seen a man in so placid a state at the approach of death. At seventy-two years of age, forty-six of which had been devoted to his self-imposed mission, he ripened into death as naturally and beautifully as the seeds of his own planting had grown into fibre and bud and blossom and the matured fruit.

Thus died one of the memorable men of pioneer times, who never inflicted pain or knew an enemy—a man of strange habits, in whom there dwelt a comprehensive love that reached with one hand downward to the lowest forms of life, and with the other upward to the very throne of God. A laboring, self-denying benefactor of his race, homeless, solitary, and ragged, he trod the thorny earth with bare and bleeding feet, intent only upon making the wilderness fruitful. Now "no man knoweth of his sepulchre"; but his deeds will live in the fragrance of the apple blossoms he loved so well, and the story of his life, however crudely narrated, will be a perpetual proof that true heroism, pure benevolence, noble virtues, and deeds that deserve immortality may be found under meanest apparel, and far from gilded halls and towering spires.

PART TWO

BOOSTERS AND KNOCKERS

*Everything is upon a great scale upon this conti-
nent. The rivers are immense, the climate violent in
heat and cold, the prospects magnificent, the thunder and lightning tremendous. The disorders incident to the country make every constitution tremble. Our own blunders here, our misconduct, our
losses, our disgraces, our ruin, are on a great scale.*
—LORD CARLISLE TO GEORGE SELWYN (1778)

I. TALL TALK

I can outspeak any man.—DAVY CROCKETT

We pride ourselves in the backwoods upon being original, and perpendicular, like the blow of a hammer.—TIMOTHY FLINT

1. MAKING A NOISE IN LANGUAGE

THE language of the ring-tailed roarer—and without his language he was like Samson without his hair—was tall talk. Tall talk may be defined as the art of making a noise in language. As such, it is characterized by grandiloquence, boasting, and exaggeration. At its best it is a kind of poetry. At its worst it is bombast and buncombe. For the most part, however, it is comic in effect or intention, insofar as exaggeration is a source of humor or as tall talk has been associated with the local-color sketches, yarns, and tall tales of the old Southwest. "Froth and specks" of the "fermentation processes" of language (as that tall-talking poet, Whitman, described slang), tall talk is the slang of the frontier movement, when windy bragging and laughing at bragging were at their height.

Tall talk is not only "frontier" in spirit; it is also national and regional. Since "broad exaggeration" has been identified with American humor and through it with the character of the people and the physical features of the country, tall talk has come to be considered a part of our national heritage, along with tall tales and tall heroes. During the growth of nationalism and the "new nation" after the War of 1812, "rankness and protestantism in speech" accompanied the release of political and industrial energies in this country. Robert Kempt, the British compiler of *The American Joe Miller*, wrote in 1865 of his American cousins: "Their ordinary speech is hyperbole, or tall talk. They never go out shooting unless with the long bow."

Regional characteristics are clearly stamped upon tall talk. In the United States what has been called the "dividing line of loquacity" runs East and West as well as North and South. It corresponds roughly to the Mason and Dixon Line and the Mississippi or Missouri River. The tradition of good talk and talkativeness has been at home South by West. Here country frolics and public gatherings—parties, picnics, barbecues, camp and political meetings, muster and court days—have invited talk—folk talk, man talk, back talk—and encouraged yarn-swapping and stump-speech eloquence. Such backwoods eloquence is "expansive eloquence," in contrast to the "reluctant" Yankee cracker-box philosopher brand.

It must not be thought, however, that tall talk was illiterate. In its "bundle of crooked and stupendous" words and phrases it possessed many of the features of a "literary dialect."

"Gentle reader," admonishes the anonymous author of *Sketches and Eccentricities of Col. David Crockett, of West Tennessee,* in a prefatory

272

statement belied by "A Vote for Crockett," "I can promise you, in no part of this volume, the wild rhodomontades of 'Bushfield'; nor can I regale you with the still more delicate repast of a constant repetition of the terms *'bodyaciously,' 'tetotaciously,' 'obflisticated,'* &c. Though I have had much intercourse with the West, I have never met with a man who used such terms unless they were alluded to, as merely occupying a space in some printed work. They have, however, thus been made to enter, as a component part, into the character of every backwoodsman. . . ."

Like most literary dialects, tall talk was spread on thick by its practitioners. The picturesque, grotesque tropes and expletives attributed to backwoodsmen and boatmen in fiction, for all their allusions to everyday objects and activities of the time and place, constitute a species of literary folklore. Basic to this "strong language" is, of course, what John Russell Bartlett (in his *Dictionary of Americanisms,* 1848) refers to as the fondness of Americans, especially in the South and West, for "intensive and extravagant epithets"—awful, powerful, monstrous, dreadful, mighty, almighty, all-fired. Tall talk was "strong language" constantly striving to outdo itself. Thus Bartlett defines *teetotaciously* as "A strange Western term, meaning a little more than teetotally, if such a thing be possible." By means of strained blends and coinages, coupled with far-fetched comparisons and extravagant conceits—as shaggy and rambunctious as the backwoodsmen who were supposed to utter them—tall talk went the whole hog.

2. "An Entire Zoölogical Institute"

Tall talk also had its mythology, in which animal allusions figure prominently. These point to a hunting and trapping existence and to love of sports of "turf and field," such as produced the hunting and sporting yarns that filled William T. Porter's virile journal of oral and anecdotal humor, *The Spirit of the Times* (1831–1861). Like the woods, the Crockett almanacs were full of bear, catamount, beaver, panther, moose, wolf, raccoon, possum, turkey, etc. Of the word *screamer* ("a bouncing fellow or girl"), Bartlett notes: "This, like the word roarer, is one of the many terms transferred from animals to men by the hunters of the West." It is not too fantastic to see in this transfer of names as in nicknames, a totemic transfer of traits, reflected in the application to humans of such terms as hoss (old hoss), colt (a pretty severe colt), coon (a right smart coon, a gone coon), varmint, critter.

Strong Language

I. Fanciful, Facetious, and Factitious Intensifying Words
(From the Specimens in Part One)

absquatulate, v. (cf. *abscond* and *squat*), to depart, run away
anngelliferous, a. angelic
bodaciously, bodyaciously, adv. (cf. *bold* and *audacious*; or, possibly "an absurd exaggeration of bodily") wholly, completely (Southern dialect: "bodaciously tired," "bodaciously ruint")

boliterated, p. p. see exfluncted

exfluncted, exfluncticated, exflunctificated, explunctified, explunctificated, **p. p.**
  (cf. *flunkt, flunked,* overcome, outdone) exhausted, crushed, demolished,
  beaten thoroughly

obflisticated, obflusticated, obfusticated, p. p. obfuscated, bewildered, confused,
  put out of the way

ramsquaddled, rumsquaddled, p. p. see *exfluncted*

ring-tailed roarer or *squealer,* n. a stentorian braggart (Thornton)

ripstaver, n. a first-rate person or thing (Thornton); a dashing fellow (Bartlett)

screamer, n. a bouncing fellow or girl (Bartlett)

slantindicular, adv. in a slanting direction

tarnal, tarnacious, a. eternal, a Yankee form of swearing (Thornton)

tetotal, teetotal, a. total

tetotaciously, teetotaciously, adv. totally

wolfish, wolfy, a. savage

II. FIGURATIVE EXPRESSIONS

I [1]

Shut pan, and sing dumb, or I'll throw you into the drink.

Hold your tongue, you beauty, or you shall smell brimstone through
a nail hole.

I wish I may run on a sawyer if I didn't.

I'll be choked with a saw-log if I do.

See if I don't row you up Salt River before you are many days older.

I wouldn't risk a huckleberry to a persimmon that we don't every soul
get treed and sink to the bottom like gone suckers.

Drive him like a flash of lightning through a gooseberry-bush.

A mighty grist of rain.

I'll be shot.

Prayed like a horse.

He had turned the edge of a razor in attempting to cut through a fog.

I'll wool lightning out of you if you interrupt me.

He'll find I'm from the forks of Roaring River, and a bit of a screamer.

I told him I knew him as well as a squirrel knows a hickory-nut from
an acorn.

I told him stories that were enough to set the Mississippi afire.

You do take the rag off the bush.

Poking his nose everywhere like a dog smelling out a trail.

You don't know a B from a Buffalo's foot.

II [2]

Hang me up for bar-meat, ef I don't push off without them.

Bile me fur a sea-horse, ef I wouldn't rather crawl into a nest o' wildcats, heels foremost, than be cotched alone with you in the night-time.

---

[1] From *Westward Ho!* by James K. Paulding (1832).
[2] From *Mike Fink: A Legend of the Ohio,* by Emerson Bennett (1848).

Quicker nor a alligator can chew a puppy.
Choked to death like a catfish on a sandbank.
Dumb as a dead nigger in a mud-hole.
Harder nor climbin' a peeled saplin', heels uppard.
Travel like a nigger in a thunder-storm.

Animal Comparisons

I'm a hoss what never war rode.[1]
I can walk like an ox, run like a fox, swim like an eel . . . make love like a mad bull.[2]
I'm shaggy as a bear, wolfish about the head, active as a cougar, and can grin like a hyena, until the bark will curl off a gum log. There's a sprinkling of all sorts in me, from the lion down to the skunk; and before the war is over, you will pronounce me an entire zoological institute, or I miss a figure in my calculation.[3]
A man that comes to settle in these parts must be wide awake, and rip and tear away like a horse in a canebrake.
A man must begin with the eggshell on him, as the partridge learns to run, and get up before daylight many a year in and year out, before he can get to be worth much—I mean in the way of living in these parts.[4]
Ar'n't I the leaping trout of the waters? [5]
One said, "I am a man; I am a horse; I am a team. I can whip any man *in all Kentucky*, by G-d."
The other replied, "I am an alligator; half man, half horse; can whip any *on the Mississippi*, by G-d."
The first one again, "I am a man; have the best horse, best dog, best gun, and handsomest wife in all Kentucky, by G-d."
The other, "I am a Mississippi snapping turtle: have bear's claws, alligator's teeth, and the devil's tail; can whip *any man*, by G-d." [6]

---

[1] From "Fight with a Puke," in *Mince Pie for the Million*.
[2] See "Speech of Colonel Crockett in Congress."
[3] From *Col. Crockett's Exploits and Adventures in Texas*, Written by Himself (1836), p. 129.
[4] From Paulding's *Westward Ho!*
[5] From Bird's *Nick of the Woods*.
[6] From *Travels on an Inland Voyage*, by Christian Schulz, Jr., Volume II, pp. 145–146. New York: Printed by Isaac Riley. 1810.

II. THE SKY'S THE LIMIT

A Kentuckian was once asked what he considered the boundaries of the United States. "The boundaries of our country, sir?" he replied. "Why sir, on the north we are bounded by the Aurora Borealis, on the east we are bounded by the rising sun, on the south we are bounded by the procession of the Equinoxes, and on the west by the Day of Judgment."

—THE AMERICAN JOE MILLER

1. THE EAGLE SCREAMS

IN A wild country, it was good business for "wild men" to go about scaring people with strange noises and by "making terrible faces playfully." But as the hunter was displaced by the second and third orders of "back settlers," the squatter and the homesteader, the roarers and screamers were not only out-hollered but out-licked by a new type of boaster and tall talker. This was the boomer and booster, drunk not with his own powers but with the bigness of the country and the illusion of inexhaustible resources and opportunities.

Here history repeated itself. As the backwoodsman's antics and war-cries were partly in imitation of the Indian,[1] so the advocates of Western expansion and settlement borrowed from the backwoodsman the elbow-room motif. This had been given expression for all time by Daniel Boone when in 1799, at the age of 65, he was asked why he was leaving Kentucky for frontier Missouri: "Too many people! Too crowded! Too crowded! I want more elbow room!" The frontier also had a saying: "When you see the smoke of your neighbor's chimney, it's time to move."

"The backwoodsman," says the Crockett Almanac for 1838, "is a singular being, always moving westward like a buffalo before the tide of civilization. He does not want a neighbor nearer than ten miles; and when he cannot cut down a tree that will fall within ten rods of his log house, he thinks it is time to sell out his betterment and be off."

But to the expansionists and the promoters of free land and the West, elbow-room meant room for improvements, for free enterprise, and so for more neighbors—in terms of nothing less than a continent and manifest destiny.

With the movement for territorial expansion and free land, the country entered upon one of the greatest advertising campaigns in history—the booming of the West. This was a campaign in which statesmen and orators joined with land and railroad companies, farmers' organizations, departments of agriculture, bureaus of immigration, boards of trade, and chambers of commerce. The theme of countless speeches, immigrant handbooks, emigrants' and railroad guides, state and regional guidebooks and gazetteers, state year books, rural almanacs, real estate directories, and government reports was "The sky's the limit," "Watch us grow," "We don't have to prove it—we admit it."

---

[1] Cf. "The Histrionic West," by Stanley Vestal, *Space*, Vol. I (June, 1934), No. 2, pp. 13–16.

In style this propaganda rivalled the "expansive eloquence" of the ring-tailed roarer and the stump-speaker. Its flamboyant ballyhoo proved that, more than the protective coloration of the homespun hero playing the tough guy and the smart aleck, tall talk is the highfalutin style of all provincial Americans whose motto is "Braggin' saves advertisin'."

In the vanguard of Western expansion was another screamer, the American eagle. This "favorite fowl of orators" was derived from the American emblem in the Great Seal and in coinage—not, according to Franklin, the most appropriate emblem of America. But the bird suffers not so much from the "bad moral character"—"generally poor, and often very lousy" and a "rank coward"—ascribed to it by Franklin, as from sheer triteness.

From the apex of the Allegheny to the summit of Mount Hood, the bird of America has so often been made to take flight, that his shadow may be said to have worn a trail across the basin of the Mississippi. . . .[1]

The scream of the expansionist eagle is heard in the swelling peroration of Samuel C. Pomeroy's impassioned plea for the Homestead Bill, whose passage climaxed the ten-years' debate in Congress on the free land question. Both the "patriotic epidemic" and the spread-eagle oratory of expansionism are taken off in the mock-speech on the Oregon question by the comedian, Yankee Hill, whose peroration is in the tall-talking tradition of "Change the Name of Arkansas? Hell, No!"

2. THE WONDER STATE

In his speech on the land policy of the United States, cited above, the Hon. Richard Yates expressed the hope that "we will not be governed by the narrow considerations of a sectional jealousy. . . . A railroad in Illinois, like a light-house on the seacoast, is the common property of the nation. . . . We have one country; our interests are one, our history is one; our destiny is the same—a glorious destiny of free and sovereign States to unexampled power and renown." But it was the destiny and the prerogative of free and sovereign states to claim, each in its own way, "unexampled power and renown."

State nicknames, which have become part of the folklore of American places, crystallized these local aspirations or pretensions to uniqueness and excellence: the Boomer's Paradise (Oklahoma), the Garden of the West (Illinois, Kansas), the Land of Heart's Desire, or the Land of Sunshine (New Mexico), the Land of Plenty (New Mexico, South Dakota), the Wonder State (Arkansas).[2]

As an instance of the willingness with which state governments took the lead in "telling the world of our wonderful possibilities," one may point to the concurrent resolution of the Arkansas Senate approving the nickname, "The Wonder State"—virtually an argument in favor of changing the name of Arkansas. The objection to the earlier nickname of "The Bear State" is typical of the desire of the self-conscious West to

[1] Mr. Cathcart, of Indiana, in the House of Representatives, February 6, 1846. Cited by Thornton, in *An American Glossary* (1912), Vol. II, p. 985.

[2] Cf. the similar nicknames of cities: The City Beautiful, the City of Magic, the City of Opportunities. the City of Prosperity, the Crown City, the Queen City.

live down its frontier past, commemorated in such uncomplimentary terms as the Puke State (Missouri) and the Grasshopper State (Kansas).

The prince of state greeters and boosters was Robert Love Taylor (1850–1912), the "Fiddling Governor" of Tennessee and the apostle of "Love, Laughter, and Sunshine," who devoted his sky-painting talents as orator, editor, and writer chiefly to booming the South. His "village apocalypse quality" and "inventive, epic earnestness" have been praised by another village improver, Vachel Lindsay, in his poem, "Preface to Bob Taylor's Birthday." For all his Pollyanna optimism and mush-and-syrup sentiment, Taylor had something of the folk touch in his art of improvisation and a backwoodsy homeliness in his native figures and allusions. Above all, he had a big heart, which went out to all things big, such as Uncle Sam, Dixie, and Tennessee, or any state that exerted or felt the influence of the sunny South. Here is tall talk in the plug hat, swallow-tailed coat, and striped trousers of a "glad-handed" Uncle Sam.

The advertising pages of *Bob Taylor's Magazine,* a monthly addressed to "all Parts of the Prosperous South," were filled with the "come-on" invitations of Southwest railroad and land companies and "commercial clubs," for whose promotion Taylor set the pace in his editorials and essays and, in October, 1906, gave the cue with the following query:

Have you a Board of Trade, or a Chamber of Commerce, or a Boosters' Club? . . . A Southern Town now without a live Board of Trade might as well disincorporate and go back into the woods.

One of the most elaborate of these advertisements rivalled Taylor's lush pen in depicting the farm lands of the Nueces River Valley as a paradise on earth worthy of Theodore Roosevelt's characterization of Texas as the "garden spot of the land."

3. GOD'S COUNTRY

Besides manifest destiny, free land, and state pride, the West had another string to its bow—the long bow which it drew in order to live down its wild and woolly reputation and to attract settlers. This was the myth of a land flowing with milk and honey—part of the American dream of a promised land of plenty, opportunity, and "beginning," which had first attracted settlers from the Old World to the New and was now transferred to the fabulous, far-off West. To make its ardors outweigh its endurances, orators, promoters, and guidebook writers painted this unknown country in the rosy hues of fairyland.

The land of "nature's bounty" was "God's country," defined as "a special part of the United States or the country as a whole, viewed nostalgically as almost a paradise."[1] "God's country" was sometimes the

---

[1] *A Dictionary of American English on Historical Principles,* edited by Sir William A. Craigie and James R. Hulbert, Vol. II (1940), p. 646.

The idea of a country "under God's care" or "that God remembers" is encountered frequently in the West, especially in the language of boosters: "Colorado is a land whereon the Creator has stamped his eternal monogram" (the Colorado Association); "Out in Arizona where God is all the time" (the Hon. David Kincheloe, of Kentucky, in the *Congressional Record*). See "Rocky Mountain Metaphysics," by Thomas Hornsby Ferril, *Folk-Say, A Regional Miscellany: 1930,* edited by B. A. Botkin, pp. 305-316.

country one was going to—perhaps always going to and never reaching, like the pot of gold at the end of the rainbow; and it was sometimes the place that one was going back to. Or perhaps it was only in the heart—not a place but a state of mind. To Boone in retrospect it was real enough —the Kentucky he had left behind him. " 'I have traveled,' he said in his old age, 'over many new countries in the great Mississippi Valley; I have critically examined their soils; their mineral wealth; their healthful climates; their manufacturing situations; and the commercial advantages given them by nature. I have discovered where these endowments were given most bountifully in many localities, singly and in groups, *but I have never found but one Kentucky—a spot of earth where nature seems to have concentrated all her bounties.*' " [1] For many a pioneer settler, however, who, while in quest of God's country, often had to ask: "Is this God's Country or not?" and "Had God forsaken us?" there was only this consolation left at the end of the search:

We learned that God's Country isnt in the country. It is in the mind. As we looked back we knew that all the time we was hunting for God's country we had it. We worked hard. We was loyal. Honest. We was happy. For 48 years we lived together in God's Country.

The potency of this phrase was part of the "pioneer myth." This assumed that land, which should be as free as the air and the sunshine, was a symbol of the inalienable rights of man; that all land was good land and all settlers were good farmers; that in its "green pastures" one should not want; that the land had certain imperishable values of its own from which one could derive, not only sustenance and profit, but also strength and courage; and that the pioneer, "inured to self-reliance" through hardship and discouragement, was a soldier of civilization and of God.

4. "WITHAL THERE IS AN EFFECT OF CLIMATE"

In a land of violent extremes and abrupt contrasts of weather and climate, the quest for health and happiness put a premium on optimum environment. Land advertisements boasted of such advantages as dry, bracing air; three hundred (or more) days of sunshine a year; and—negatively—no killing frosts, hail, blizzards, hot winds, heat waves, tornadoes, cyclones, whirlwinds, hurricanes, earthquakes, and similar afflictions. "Why Shovel Snow and Shiver?" was one rhetorical question. "No chills, no negroes, no saloons, no mosquitoes," went a sweeping statement from Arkansas.

The guidebooks were equally reassuring.

It is complained that the "wind blows." As it blows elsewhere, so it blows in Colorado—occasionally. Sometimes these winds are momentarily disagreeable, but they serve nature as one of her sanitary measures and their effect is refreshing and beneficial. [2]

---

[1] "Kentucky," *The Southern Guide*, Vol. I (January, 1878), No. 1, p. 59.
[2] *The Resources and Attractions of Colorado for the Home Seeker, Capitalist and Tourist* (Union Pacific Railway, Omaha, 1888), pp. 61–62.

Withal there is an effect of climate, and something of freedom caught from the outdoorness of life. Sunshine and green salads all the year will promote cheerfulness. Where there are no bitter winds, no sleet or hail, no blizzards to kill flocks and herds, no "cold snaps" to freeze poultry on the perch or water-pipes in the kitchen, it is not at all surprising that people laugh and are affected by the great world of sun and summer in which they dwell.[1]

Emigrant and Western songs fell in line with the chauvinism, utopianism, and arcadianism of the guidebooks, reflected in many a state song and poem of the "sweet singer" or boosting variety and many a popular song of nostalgia for this, that, or the other "wonder state."[2]

The boast of a climate "so healthy that people rarely die, except from accident or old age," as in the Nueces River Valley land advertisement, was a common one.[3] One of the best of the stories on this theme is related by Barnum, as he heard it from a sleight-of-hand artist named Henry Hawley.

Related to the stories of life-prolonging air are the stories of air that restores life.

In East Texas it is the wind that revives corpses.

Truth of it is, Dad was dead, but when that coffin bust open and that strong healthy plains wind hit him it just filled his lungs full of good revivin air, and Dad nor no one else could stay dead.[4]

In Florida it is the sunshine, as on the occasion when the corpse of a gangster had been imported from Chicago so that a funeral could be staged by the local dealer in cemetery lots.

The coffin was taken to the graveside and the lid was opened to give the bystanders a glimpse of the beautiful way the corpse had been laid out, a masterpiece of the undertaker's art. As the Florida sunshine hit the body, there was an immediate stir. The gangster arose with a yell, feeling for his gun. The bystanders had to kill him again before they could go on with the funeral.[5]

Variations on the theme are found in the stories of a dying person being revived by the air expelled from a bicycle or automobile tire, which had been pumped up in California or Arizona, or of an incurable victim of tuberculosis being healed by a single ray of Florida sunshine.[6]

---

[1] *California for the Settler*, by Andrew Jackson Wells (Southern Pacific Company, San Francisco, 1915), p. 62.

[2] See *The Facts of Life in Popular Song* (1934), by Sigmund Spaeth.

[3] "I saw a cowboy in California once who was a hundred if he was a day. It's astonishing how old these greasers get to be. I have traveled a great deal in Mexico, and it don't occur to me just now where I ever saw a graveyard. There's the Tomb-stone district in Arizona, and I know there isn't a tombstone in it. The people just dry up and blow away, and maybe you think it don't blow down there some-times." . . . *Ten Wise Men and Some More*, by William Lightfoot Visscher (1909), p. 89.

[4] See "The Wind," by Frank Neff and William Henry, Part Four.

[5] Told by B. A. Trussell, of Miami, Florida, in *Tall Stories*, by Lowell Thomas (1931), pp. 236–237.

[6] *Tall Stories*, by Lowell Thomas (1931), pp. 232–235.

Rival claims of salubrious climate are accompanied by mutual recrimination in which state rivalry is keen. Thus Florida papers cast aspersions on California as a "terrible place, going rapidly to the bad with frost, storms, earthquakes, and other calamities. California and other resort places reciprocate."[1] To the older feud between Florida and California has more recently been added the competition between California and the Rio Grande Valley.

But we have the healthiest climate in California. It is so healthy we had to shoot a man in order to start a graveyard.

That's no comparison with our Valley climate for health. One of our citizens went out to California, took sick and died there. They shipped his remains back to the Valley, the friends of the deceased were gathered around the corpse. When they opened the casket he raised up, greeted his friends and walked off.[2]

Tacked on to Hawley's yarn is the tale of the "monstrous large gun," which "required one pound of powder and four pounds of shot to load it properly" and with which Hawley shot off four-and-a-half bushels of wild pigeons' feet and legs (without killing a single bird) when the flock rose off the ground just a half second ahead of his shot. The great number of pigeons and the large field of buckwheat which it was feared they would destroy reflect the abundance of crops and game associated with the marvels of climate and soil. Here brags about rich land and big crops shade off into yarns of varying degrees of exaggeration. The boosters' club gives way to the liars' club—with an occasional knock for the famine that often followed the feast or the bust that followed the boom.

In 1851 the Commissioner of Patents reported an "address delivered by A. Williams, Esq., at a meeting in San Francisco, for presenting the premium of a silver goblet, offered by Mr. C. A. Shelton for the best varieties of vegetables and grains." Among other prize products are an onion weighing 21 pounds, a turnip "which equalled exactly in size the top of a flour barrel," another weighing 100 pounds, a cabbage measuring 13 feet, six inches around, a beet weighing 63 pounds, and carrots three feet in length, weighing 40 pounds, not to mention a single potato, "larger than the size of an ordinary hat," of which twelve persons partook at a dinner in Stockton, "leaving at least the half untouched." Then the speaker added ironically:

And we have some still larger and taller specimens of other things nearer home, here in our own city, to which many who hear me will bear witness from experience, and which come to maturity *"monthly in advance"*—rents, the tallest kind of rents, put up higher than the pines, and sometimes harder to get around than red-wood![3]

---

[1] *North America,* by J. Russell Smith and M. Ogden Phillips (1942), p. 349.

[2] *Thomas W. Jackson with all the "Funny Ones,"* by Thomas W. Jackson (1938), p. 79.

[3] *Report of the Commissioner of Patents for the Year 1851,* Part II, Agriculture (1852), pp. 3–7.

5. Laughing It Off

Praise of the wonders and glories of the new country was offset by a healthy skepticism which viewed with alarm instead of pointing with pride. Hardship and failure gave rise to inverse exaggeration and defensive boasting—of the kind that proceeds from having too little rather than too much.

A common symbol of disillusionment was the returning emigrant or prospector admonishing the westward traveler to turn back. In the frontispiece of "Major Wilkey's" *Narrative*,[1] the fashionable young man in the smart chaise behind the spirited horse, proclaims: "I am going to Illinois!" whereas from the lips of the broken-down owner of a "broken down waggon!—a ·broken winded horse!—a broken hearted wife!—a broken legged dog! and, what is still more to be lamented, the irreparable broken constitutions of my three Fever and Ague sons, Jonathan, Jerry, and Joe!"—the reply emanates: "I have been!" A modern parallel is furnished by *The Grapes of Wrath*, in which the Joads, on their way to "where it's rich an' green," and they can get work and a "piece a growin' land with water," are laughed at by a ragged man who inquires:

"You folks all goin' to California, I bet." "I tol' you that," said Pa. "You didn' guess nothin'." The ragged man said slowly, "Me—I'm comin' back. I been there. . . . I'm goin' back to starve. I ruther starve all over at oncet." [2]

Disappointed victims of gold fever, who had been advised "not to be too sanguine of success," turned back with mottoes properly amended to express their disgust. "Busted, by thunder!" set the pattern in slogans for all settlers who did not have the "grit, grace, and gumption" necessary to tough it out in a tough country.

Disillusionment in turn was seasoned with stoical humor of the type known as "laughing it off," or smiling in the face of adversity. Grasshopper plagues were commemorated in the wagon inscription, "Hoppers et all but the wagonsheet," in the saying that the grasshoppers had eaten everything except the mortgage, and in the story of the grasshopper who ate the farmer's team of mules and then pitched the horseshoes for the wagon. In Nebraska one could stand by the side of a field and hear the grasshoppers threatening. "On the potato vines they would eat downward, and when they came to a potato bug would calmly kick it and go on their devastating way." [3]

On the Great Plains, it has been said, "If you ain't burned up by drought and winds hot as hell or frozen out by blizzards and hail storms, you're

---

[1] Although the author of this anonymous satire on land frauds maintains that "never could there be experienced just such another confounded take-in," Major Wilkey's misfortunes in "Edensburgh" may have furnished suggestions to Dickens (even to the name of the place) for the somewhat similar experiences of Martin Chuzzlewit in the city of "Eden," published four years later.

[2] *The Grapes of Wrath*, by John Steinbeck (1939), p. 257.

[3] *Pioneer Life in Nebraska*, Pamphlet One, *We Settled the Plains*, Series One, compiled by Workers of the WPA Writers' Program of the Work Projects Administration in the State of Nebraska (Oct. 1941), p. 3.

eat up by grasshoppers, speculators, and politicians." [1]—and, it might have been added, centipedes, snakes, bedbugs, fleas, and other pests that infested the primitive shelters of pioneer settlers. This is the plaint of Western "hard times" songs like "The Lane County Bachelor," which prove that only a thin line separates stoicism from revolt.

—And Nothing but the Continent

"MR. SPEAKER: When I take my eyes and throw them over the vast expanse of this expansive country: when I see how the yeast of freedom has caused it to rise in the scale of civilization and extension on every side; when I see it growing, swelling, roaring, like a spring-freshet—when I see all *this*, I cannot resist the idea, Sir, that the day will come when this great nation, like a young schoolboy, will burst its straps, and become entirely too big for its boots!

"Sir, we want *elbow-room*—the continent—the *whole* continent—and nothing *but* the continent! And we will *have* it! Then shall Uncle Sam, placing his hat upon the Canadas, rest his right arm on the Oregon and California coast, his left on the eastern sea-board, and whittle away the British power, while reposing his leg, like a freeman, upon Cape Horn! Sir, the day *will*—the day *must* come!"

Manifest Destiny

MR. CHAIRMAN, the population of the Valley of the Mississippi already constitutes more than one third of the entire population of the Union. And, sir, the time is not distant when the seat of empire, the stronghold of numerical power, will be west of the Alleghanies. The handwriting is on the wall. It is *manifest destiny*, sir. It is written on the signs of the times in clear, fresh and unmistakable lines. . . .

. . . The same flag that flashes its stars to the sun on the banks of the Hudson and Potomac is hailed by millions of rejoicing freemen on the banks of the Mississippi and the Columbia.

. . . Within the last five years three new States have been added to the Union, and there is the territory at the head of the Missouri and the Arkansas, the Territories of Nebraska, New Mexico, Utah, and Oregon—

---

[1] "Legends of Febold Feboldson," by Paul R. Beath, in *Nebraska Folklore Pamphlets*, Number Eight, p. 7. Lincoln: Federal Writers' Project in Nebraska. September 15, 1937.

". . . 'specimen of eloquence' from an authentic speech made by General Buncombe, in the House of Representatives, in the days of 'Fifty-four Forty or Fight,'" *Knickerbocker Magazine*, XLVI (August, 1855), No. 2, p. 212. New York: Samuel Hueston.

From "Speech of Hon. Richard Yates, of Illinois, on the Land Policy of the United States, and in Defense of the West," delivered in the House of Representatives, April 23, 1852.

and the vision of an ocean-bound Republic is now a reality. Sir, what a mighty theater for American enterprise! What a mighty course for the race of democratic liberty! . . .

It is already our boast as a nation, sir, that we enjoy more of liberty, a more universal diffusion of knowledge, and a more exalted national character than any nation on the globe. But the striking feature of the American character is its enterprise—an enterprise that knows no obstacles, counts no cost, fears no dangers, triumphs over all obstacles. . . .

The Proudest Bird upon the Mountain

. . . OUR country is yet but in the infancy of its being, not yet three centuries old. And our settlements are but specks dotted round upon the edge of the map of the continent. The great heart of America, with treasures as precious as the lifestrings, is as yet unexplored, and almost unknown.

This bill, enacted into a law, shall give civilization and life throughout the silent gorges and gentle sleeping valleys, far away into the deep recesses of the continent. Where it leads the way, there shall go in triumph the American standard, the old flag of the Union. And when once thus planted, it shall never again be trailed in the dust. The proudest bird upon the mountain is upon the American ensign, and not one feather shall fall from her plumage here. She is American in design, and an emblem of wildness and freedom. I say, again, she has not perched herself upon American standards to die here. Our great Western valleys were never scooped out for her burial place. Nor were the everlasting untrodden mountains piled for her monument. Niagara shall not pour her endless waters for her requiem; nor shall our ten thousand rivers weep to the ocean in eternal tears. No, sir; no. Unnumbered voices shall come up from the river, plain and mountain, echoing the songs of our triumphant deliverance, while lights from a thousand hilltops will betoken the rising of the sun of freedom, that shall grow brighter and brighter until a perfect day.

Speech on the Oregon Question

. . . YET the time is not far off, when the locomotive will be steaming its way to the Rocky Mountains, with a mighty big train of cars running after

From "Speech of Hon. S. C. Pomeroy, of Kansas, on the Homestead Bill," delivered in the Senate of the United States, May 5, 1862.

From "Speech on the Oregon Question," by Yankee Hill, in *Life and Recollections of Yankee Hill: together with Anecdotes and Incidents of His Travels,* edited by W. K. Northall, pp. 101–104. New York: Published for Mrs. Cordelia Hill, by W. F. Burgess. 1850.

In 1846, Mr. Hill paid a visit to Washington City. He was there during the excite-

it. Yes, the whistle of the engine will echo through the South-west Pass,
and sharply hint to the free people of that great territory the approach of
hundreds and thousands tew, who are to be their neighbors. No, sir, the
time is not far distant, when our commerce with China will equal that
of all the world; when the Pacific Ocean will be crossed with as much ease
as the Frog pond on Boston Common. Yes, Mr. Speaker, as my eloquent
friend from the Hoosier State remarks, "Men of blood, and friends of
General Washington, and that old hoss, General Jackson, I want your
attention. *Lightnin'* has burst upon us; and Jupiter has poured out the ile
of his wrath. Thunder has broke loose and slipped its cable, and is now
rattling down the mighty Valley of the Mississippi, accompanied by the
music of the alligator's hornpipe. Citizens and fellers; on the bloody
ground on which our fathers catawampously poured out their claret free
as ile, to enrich the soil over which we now honor and watch with hyena
eyes, let the catamount of the inner varmint loose and prepare the engines
of vengeance, for the long looked-for day has come. The crocodile of the
Mississippi has gone into his hole, and the sun that lit King David and his
host across the Atlantic Ocean, looks down upon the scene, and drops a
tear to its memory." I am with you, and while the stars of Uncle Sam, and
the stripes of his country, triumph and float in the breeze, whar, whar
is the craven, low-lived, chicken-bred, toad-hoppin', red-mouthed mother's
son of ye who will not raise the beacon-light of triumph, snouse the
citadel of the aggressor, and press onward to liberty and glory? Wha-ah!
Hurrah! where's the inimy?

The Wonder State

WHEREAS, it is an admitted fact that the State of Arkansas excels all
others in natural resources, its store of mineral wealth being practically

---

ment which prevailed upon the Oregon question. It would have been impossible,
perhaps, for a man of much less excitable temperament than Mr. Hill, to have been
in Washington at that time, and have escaped the patriotic epidemic which then prevailed to such an alarming extent. His patriotism became rampant, and he opened
the flood-gates of his eloquence, and poured forth such a powerful stream, that all who
opposed his views were nigh swept from the face of the earth. The speech which he
made in Washington, night after night, to immense audiences, will be found carefully reported below. Daniel Webster might possibly have made a more solid speech,
Clay a more eloquent one, John Quincy Adams, one more fruitful of sage experience;
but neither of them, I will venture to say, could have made one quite like it. But let
the reader judge for himself.—W. K. N.

*Acts of Arkansas, 1923: General Acts and Joint and Concurrent Resolutions and
Memorials and Proposed Constitutional Amendments of the Forty-fourth General
Assembly of the State of Arkansas, Passed at the Session at the Capitol, in the City
of Little Rock, Arkansas, Commencing on the 8th Day of January, 1923, and Ending
on the 18th Day of March, 1923,* by authority (Democrat Printing and Lithographing
Company, Little Rock, Arkansas, 1923), pp. 803–804. Cited in *American Nicknames;
Their Origin and Significance,* by George Earlie Shankle, p. 19. Copyright, 1937, by
George Earlie Shankle. New York: The H. W. Wilson Company.

inexhaustible, its vast forests supplying pine and hardwoods in quantities sufficient to place the state in the forefront, and its agricultural and horticultural prowess recognized not only in the United States, but in foreign countries as well, and

Whereas, the publicity campaign of the Arkansas Advancement Association has so indelibly stamped upon the mind of the world that Arkansas is "The Wonder State," and

Whereas, this title is so befitting, while the old one, "The Bear State" is a misnomer, and leads to a false impression, while "The Wonder State" is accurate and is deserving of special recognition:

Now, Therefore,

Be It Resolved by the Senate of the State of Arkansas, the House of Representatives Concurring:

That we accept the name, "The Wonder State," given us by this Patriotic association which has done much to acquaint the world with Arkansas and its wealth of resource, and we hereby specially proclaim that hereafter Arkansas shall be known and styled "The Wonder State."

Uncle Sam

THE most striking and picturesque in all history is the picture of a lean and sinewy old man, with long hair and chin whiskers, and wearing an old-fashioned plug hat. His pantaloons are in stripes of red and white, and his blue swallow-tail coat is bespangled with stars. He is the personification of the United States, and we call him Uncle Sam.

He is the composite of the wild-cat and the cooing dove, the lion and the lamb, and "summer evening's latest sigh that shuts the rose." He is the embodiment of all that is most terrible. The world stands appalled at his wonderful power, and bows in admiration to his matchless magnanimity.

He is the tallest figure on this mundane sphere, and when he steps across the continent and sits down on Pike's Peak, and snorts in his handkerchief of red, white, and blue, the earth quakes and the monarchs tremble on their thrones. From the peaceful walks of life he can mobilize a mighty army in sixty days, and in ninety days he can destroy a powerful navy and demolish an empire. He is boss of the Western Hemisphere, Sheriff of Cuba, Justice of the Peace of Porto Rico, and guardian *ad litem* of the Philippine Islands. He is as brave as Caesar and as meek as Moses.

He is as fierce as a tiger, and as cool as a cucumber. He wears the tail feathers of the eagle of France in his hat, and the scalp of Mexico in his

Extract from "Speech of Governor Taylor, on Presenting a Flag to the Fourth Tennessee Volunteers, November, 1897, at Knoxville." From *Echoes, Centennial and other Notable Speeches, Lectures, and Stories,* by Governor Robt. L. Taylor, pp. 78–79. Copyright, 1899, by S. B. Williamson & Co. Nashville, Tennessee.

belt. He laughs at the roar of the Russian bear, and is always ready for a schooner of German beer.

All that is left of Spain is her "Honah," since her combat with Uncle Sam. No longer the lion of England roars at our door, but the twain now stand together for liberty and humanity.

In the Land of Dixie

I LOVE to live in the land of Dixie, under the soft Southern skies, where summer pours out her flood of sunshine and showers, and the generous earth smiles with plenty. I love to live on Southern soil, where the cotton-fields wave their white banners of peace, and the wheat-fields wave back their banners of gold from the hills and valleys which were once drenched with the blood of heroes. I love to live where the mocking-birds flutter and sing in the shadowy coves, and bright waters ripple in eternal melody, by the graves where our heroes are buried. I love to breathe the Southern air, that comes filtered through jungles of roses, whispering the story of Southern deeds of bravery. I love to drink from Southern springs and Southern babbling brooks, which once cooled the lips of Lee and Jackson and Forrest and Gordon, and the worn and weary columns of brave men, who wore the gray. I love to live among Southern men and women, where every heart is as warm as the Southern sunshine, and every home is a temple of love and liberty.

I love to listen to the sweet old Southern melodies, which touch the soul and melt the heart and awaken to life ten thousand precious memories of the happy long ago, when the old-time darkeys used to laugh and sing, and when the old-time black "mammy" soothed the children to slumber with her lullabies. But, oh, the music that thrills me most is the melody that died away on the lips of many a Confederate soldier as he sank into the sleep that knows no waking—

"I'm glad I am in Dixie."

We Will Show You

CANEY, Queen City of the B. I. T. In the Choctaw Nation, the Garden Spot of Indian Territory, Surrounded by a Healthful and Productive

---

Extract from "Address of Welcome by Governor Taylor to the Ex-Confederates, at Ex-Confederate Reunion, on Confederate Day, at Tennessee Centennial, June 24, 1897." From *Echoes, Centennial and other Notable Speeches, Lectures, and Stories*, by Governor Robt. L. Taylor, pp. 26-27. Copyright, 1899, by S. B. Williamson & Co. Nashville, Tennessee.

From *Bob Taylor's Magazine*, October and December, 1906. Copyright, 1906, by the Taylor Publishing Company. Nashville, Tennessee.

Country, Inhabited by a High Class of Prosperous and Contented People. . . . Come and Grow and Prosper With Us.

Pryor Creek, Indian Territory. . . . A good moral town and sociable people. Plenty of room for pushing, progressive people.

Watch Eufaula Grow. The Best Town and the Best Country in Oklahoma. We don't have to prove it—we admit it.

The Gulf Coast Country of Texas is the World's Garden Spot and the St. Louis, Brownsville, and Mexico Railway traverses it from end to end. Opportunities There are Golden Now!

Great, Grand, Glorious Texas. Its Stupendous Resources can hardly be exaggerated. A Mild Climate, Fertile Soil, Thrifty Healthy People. 90 per cent of the prospectors from other States become permanent settlers. I. & G. N., "The Texas Railroad."

Nueces River Valley Paradise

. . . LOCATED on that middle plain between East Texas, where it rains too much, and the arid section of West Texas, where it does not rain enough; . . .

Where the constant sea breeze makes cool summers and warm winters without snow or hard freezes;

Where there are no blizzards, nor tornadoes, nor earthquakes, nor cyclones;

Where the flowers bloom ten months in the year;

Where the greatest variety of products can be grown;

Where the farmers and gardeners, whose seasons never end, eat home grown June vegetables in January, and bask in midwinter's balmy air and glorious sunshine;

Where the land yield is enormous, and the prices always remunerative;

Where something can be planted and harvested every month in the year;

Where the climate is so mild that the Northern farmer here saves practically all his fuel bills and three-fourths the cost of clothing his family in the North;

Where the country is advancing and property values rapidly increasing;

Where all stock, without any feed, fatten, winter and summer, on the native grasses and brush which equal any feed pen;

Where the same land yields the substantials of the temperate and the luxuries of the tropic zones;

Where the farmer does not have to work hard six months in the year

---

From an advertisement of C. F. Simmons, San Antonio, Texas, "How to Secure a River Farm and Home in Town for $120," in *Bob Taylor's Magazine*, November, 1906. Copyright, 1906, by the Taylor Publishing Company. Nashville, Tennessee.

to raise feed to keep his stock from dying during winter, as they do in the North and Northwest;

Where the winter does not consume what the summer produces, and there are markets for all produced;

Where two full crops of the same kind, three vegetable crops, or four mixed crops, can be raised from the same land in one year;

Where vegetation is so rapid that in two years the home is surrounded by trees and shrubs which would require five years to develop in a colder climate;

Where there are no aristocrats and people do not have to work hard to have plenty and go in the best society;

Where ten acres, judiciously planted in fruits, will soon make one independent, all varieties being wonderfully successful and profitable;

Where the natives work less and have more to show for what they do than in any country on earth;

Where houses, barns and fences can be built for less than half the cost in the North;

Where the average temperature is about 60 degrees, varying from 50 in winter, to 90 in summer, which is rendered cool by constant sea breezes;

Where the average rainfall for the past five years is over 39 inches, and well distributed, as shown by the government's report, which is more than some of the older States have;

Where sun-strokes and heat-prostrations are unknown;

Where the residents have charming homes surrounded by trees and flowers of a semi-tropical climate;

Where sufferers with Asthma, Bronchitis, Catarrh, Hay-Fever and Throat troubles find relief;

Where one can work out of doors in shirt sleeves, without inconvenience, 29 out of every 30 days the year around;

Where, surrounded by fruits and vegetables, which ripen every month in the year, the living is better and less expensive than in the North;

Where the water is pure, soft and plentiful;

Where the laws protect both the investor and the settler;

Where the people are so law abiding that usually only two days of District Court every six months are required to dispose of all the Civil and Criminal business;

Where the taxes are so low that the amount is never missed;

Where Public and Private schools and Churches of all denominations are plentiful;

Where peace, plenty and good will prevail to such an extent that the people sleep with their doors and windows open the year around, without danger of molestation;

Where it is so healthy that people rarely die, except from accident or old age; . . .

He Shall Not Want

. . . For my own part, I believe it should not be the policy of the Government to derive a revenue from a sale of the land, any more than from a sale of the air or the sunshine. These natural elements and auxiliaries of human life are God's great gifts to man, and the Government may as well bottle up the one as deed away the other. The great command was, when our earth came fresh, green, and beautiful from a divine hand, to take it, to people and subdue it. . . .

. . . I am, sir, for opening these lands for the landless of every nation under heaven. . . .

. . . With one hundred and sixty acres of God's free earth under a man in his own right, and genial skies above him, he shall not want. For "seed time and harvest, summer and winter, day and night" shall not fail him till the heavens be no more.

I need not disguise the fact that while this system of small farms of a quarter section of land each will greatly promote the wealth, strength, and glory of the Republic, thus conducing to human happiness, near and remote, now and for all ages, still as a consequence and by virtue of the same law, it will secure the entire public domain to human freedom forever! The pioneer struggling amidst many discouragements upon the frontier prairies of the West, comes nearer obeying the divine injunction to "gain his bread by the sweat of his brow," than any other man. The men who have, from their circumstances and education, been inured to self-reliance, can safely volunteer as soldiers of civilization in its onward progress across this continent, from the great valleys of the Mississippi and Missouri to the shores of the Pacific. The man who is able to put all he owns on earth into one canvas covered wagon, wife, children, household goods, all and move with slow pace into what has been called the "wilderness of the West," far out upon the frontier, beyond all law and civilization, and there plant himself down upon a homestead for life, is doing a work for himself, his family, for civilization, his country, and his God, that can never be fully known, or its influence told, until the final disclosure.

Going to God's Country

WE WERE going to God's Country. Eighteen hunderd and 90. With a husle and busle to get things ready. With five litel childern and the oldest

From "Speech of Hon. S. C. Pomeroy, of Kansas, on the Homestead Bill," delivered in the Senate of the United States, May 5, 1862.

From *Going to God's Country*, by Martha L. Smith, with an introduction by Dr. Clara E. Krefting. Copyright, 1941, by the Christopher Publishing House. Boston.

only 10 years old. And geting food and clothing for a long journey. We could do that job very well for we did not realise what we were geting into. We had some cousens that had gone 2 years before to the Indian Territory way down on what was called the Fleet Wood Farms in the Chicksaw Nation. Its part of Oklahoma now. And that was where we were going. (P. 11.)

It was prety hard to part with some of our things. We didn't have much but we had worked hard for everything we had. You had to work hard in that rocky country in Missouri. I was glad to be leaving it. We were going to God's Country. (Pp. 12–13.)

TOUGHF MISSOURI

Old Missouri was after all a pretty toughf place. I hated to leave it though for it was all I knew. But we were going to God's Country. We were going to a new land and get rich. Then we could have a real home of our own. But we didn't know what was ahead of us. (P. 41.)

WE ALL DRIVE IN

We were all tired from the long wearysome trip. And it seemed that every river we crossed was up. Our first was Sock, the next bad river was the Arkansaw and the next was the Cimarron. And then the North Canadian and the South Canadian and hundreds of others it seemed. We went through part of Missouri, Kansas, Osage Nation, Pawnee Nation, Old Oklahoma proper, Chicksaw Nation and then we landed on the Fleet Wood Farms. It was on the Red River just across from Texas. So there we were at our cousens. And was we ever so hapy. We all drove in his lot with the seven coverd wagons. And so tired from thirty three days drive. But at last we were in God's Country. (Pp. 56–57.)

WE SLEEP WITH CENTIPEADS

The dug out was so full of centipeads that we had to sleep with a bucher knife under our pillows so we could have something to protect our selfs.

Sleeping with the bucher knives under our pillows at night to kill the centipeads in our half dug out was exsiting. The dug out was made of logs with mud in between so when we would put the lights out at night the centipeads would go runing in the cracks. Then we would whak them to pieces. Some nights we would kill as many as twenty. Next morning first thing was to move the beds and sweep the dead ones out. But that was pioneering in God's Country. (Pp. 59–60.)

WE COUNT BLESSINGS

We thought that it was indeed God's Country. We had worked hard for eleven years in Missouri and left there with eight hunderd dolars and our teams and wagons. And after we paid for picking and gining and all expenses we had eight hunderd and twenty dolars left. And besides we had our corn and our garden truck.

And our garden was the best garden that we ever had. It seemed like every seed came up. And how the garden did grow. We had onions, tomatose, cabages, peas, beans, potatose, pepers, letuce, parsnips, musk melons, water melons and every thing in that line. People came from all around to see that garden. So when fall came we went to Henrietta for groceries. But this time it was for barels. I made one barel of catchup and a barel of soar crout.

But many things hapend while we were living on the small lease. Many hardships along with the pioneering. But we tried to overlook all for everything was so difernt and new to us with heaps of exsitement. And besides we were in God's Country. (Pp. 70–71.)

SOWING WHEAT

We picked coton most all fall but when October came it was geting time for wheat sowing. Then there was a wheat drill to buy and that was eighty five more dolars of the coton money gone. So that was that. It seemed like we never looked ahead untell we had to have some implements to work with. Then it was another long trip to the rail road. But that was done with good grace. We were in God's Country.

But at least we had a drill to sow the wheat. Back in Missouri we would sow by hand. You would put about a peck of wheat in a sack and swing it across your shoulder. Then you would take out a hand full and sling it around. You could just sow about ten feet at once. You would have to walk around the field till you got it all done. Then harrow the ground to cover the wheat. The harrow was made by tying some brush together with a chain and fastening the brush to a double tree. Then two singel trees were fastened to the double tree and horses fastened to them. That was the way it was done for a good many years. But in God's Country we had a drill to sow the wheat. (Pp. 83–84.)

A PRARIE FIRE

In 1892 the prarie grass was most as high as our coverd wagons. One day by some means a fire got started. We never knew how but any way it was exsiting. You could see the blaze leap. It looked like it was fifty feet in the air. We had burned a very small patch around our house. Perhaps one half an acer. We had just built us a shed for our teams and a chicken house for a cow corell. Our horses were all tied in the shed and the fire was coming so fast that we could not tell whether we would have time to get them out or what to do. It looked like our horses and our milk cows and our famly too would go up in the flames. We did manage to get the teams and harness out of the shed and close to the house. But the fire was geting very close. Just about half mile away I should judge.

We were so frightent. The litel childern crying and screaming and the horses snorting and I was praying and working too. We had a well that we had dug just in front of the house. We had to draw the water by hand with a bucket and I was drawing water so as we might try to save our house and childern. The fire was geting prety close and we could see jack rabits, prarie dogs, prarie chickens, cyotes, all kinds of birds and antilopes, runing in front of the fire. While we were watching the animels and birds I had every available thing full of water that I had drawn from the well. We could hear the fire roaring and see the flames leaping. We were all covered with the burning grass. We put the six litel childern all in the house and fastened the door and the one window.

While we were standing in front of the hut watching the fire I just hapend to turn my head to get some of the burned grass out of my eyes and I thought that I could see some moving objects coming from the north. I wiped my eyes again and looked. Then I said to my husband, "Look, there is something coming from the north." He wiped his eyes and looked. It looked like a herd of stampeded catle. And if it was that, we were goners for they were coming toward us. We watched for a moment but it was smokey and so much burned grass flying in the air, for the fire was coming from the south west and was blowing very hard, we couldn't see. All that we could do was to stand there and wait.

There we were, we thought, between two fires. We could plainly see the fire coming from the south west and my husband said if it was a stampeded herd of catle that we were in for something. I ask him if we hadnt beter go in the house with the childern and he said that I might but that he would watch. But I never did go in, for just about that time I wiped my eyes again and I could see that it wasnt catle. But we couldn't make out just what it was. It looked like men the best we could see through all that smoke. We just stood and looked and I told my husband perhaps it was Indians on the war path. He said it might be but he did not think so. But I do believe he thought it was Indians for he turned white. So white that I could see he was scerd. And so was I. The fire coming one way and the Indians or stampeded catle the other.

We just stood there most petrified for a few seconds and then I could see that it was men. But what kind of men. Cow boys or Indians? But all at once one man whiped ahead of the rest and then I felt like it was cow boys. And shure enoughf he just came chargen up. I felt some relief but I was shakin so I could hardly stand on my feet and so was my husband. The six litel childern in the house got over being scerd and were just playing. When we opened the door they looked so surprised to see so many cow boys. They never said a word but just looked so amased.

Cow Boys Save the Day

Then the boys said that Roof Benton had sent them for he could see the fire and thought we might be in danger and some of his catle might too. All the water I had drawd out of the well was used for when the cow boys got there they got off their horses, droped their briedl reins, went to the shed, gathered up all the old feed sacks and two of them picked up the water and walked out to the edge of the high grass. Then they all wet the feed sacks and began to set the grass a fire but they did not tell us what they were going to do. We soon found out. They were back firing.

BACK FIRING WORKS

They burned all along past the shed and then let it burn quite a ways. But they would whip it out with the wet sacks. So when the fire got to the burned grass it would stop. They had a very hard time of it because the wind was so strong and they were burning against the wind.

They worked most all that night and when they began it was about three oclock in the afternoon. About six oclock my husband said that we would give them something to eat. I tryed to get them something nice to eat but it was a hard job for most every thing we had in the house was black with burned grass. But anyway I made some buisquit and some coffe. They ate and drank the coffe but they told my husband that they would stay untell we was out of danger. Later we made some more coffe and some more buisquit and by that time I had goten some of the burnt grass washed off of the things so we could cook some food.

When my husband took the food to them the second time they told him for us to go to bed and rest for we had gone through some exsperence. And they was right too for we had. I washed the litel folks the best that I could and put them to bed. Of course they thought it funny to have the burnt black grass all over them and their rag dolls.

Finly we did try to sleep but I did not sleep very much and was up early next morning. I wanted to see how things looked. It all looked black. The cow boys were gone and the fire was all out. But every thing did look so queer. We looked around, fed the litel folks and went to work to clean our house. Every thing was so black we had to wash all our beding and every thing that we had. And wash the house outside and inside. We worked all day. Then the childerns heads and my own head was to wash. It was a long time before I could get the black off of things.

IS THIS GOD'S COUNTRY OR NOT?

In just a few days we noticed the buzards sailing over where the fire had burned. So we hitched a team to the wagon and piled the childern in and drove over the prarie. Was we surprised to see the dead rabits, snakes and all kinds of birds. And when the wind blew from the south west we could smell some thing that smelled like burned hair.

Well it wasnt very long untell it came a big rain and that helpt to wash the black off things and prety soon the grass came up so green and every thing did look so beautifull and before long it was coverd with catle.

After several days of hard work I got every one cleaned up and the house cleaned too. While I was doing that, H. H. went to the rail road and brought some fence posts and the hired man back with him. The hired man had gone to visit some one. He said that he was sorry that he had missed all the fun. I told him that it wasnt much fun but that he could have the fun of seting the fence posts back where the fire had burned them out. They went to work but it took several days. We finly got every thing in shape again. But I never looked over the praire that way but what I could imagin that I could see smoke. It took me a long time to forget it. In fact I never did and it makes my flesh creep today when I think about that terable fire and smoke. I said to myself, "Is this God's Country or not?" I didn't talk about it to my husband but just kept saying, "go on for every thing will be O. K." But some times I all most gave up. Then something kept saying. "It must be God's Country. Go on." (Pp. 90–96.)

Rock Botem

As time went on every thing went to rock botem. Wheat, corn, coton, hogs, catle and every thing.

One of the men that was in the drunken spree was wanting to go back to Texas. He had raised quite a lot of corn and fed a bunch of hogs and they were very nice. But he could not sell them on the market for there wasnt any market. So he came to our place and wanted us to buy them. We told him that we could not handle them for the weather was too warm to butcher. He just stayed and stayed and talked and cussed the country and finly he said that if we would buy them that we could have them for a dolar a head. We didn't know what to do but we finly said that we would take them if he would bring them over. He said that he had his wagon in the shop for he was geting ready to leave the damned country. "Well," I told him, "This is God's Country." "But," he said, "It's a hell of a country." He was one of those good Methodists, but he did get drunk and got in jail. Foster was his name. Any way we felt sory for him, so we told him that we would take the hogs and we would come that evening when it got cool to get them.

We got a top on the wagon and went to get the hogs. They were nice young hogs and very fat. He put his dog in the pen to help catch them. One of the hogs got too hot and keeled over so H. H. just cut his throat. One of the hogs dead out of the whole batch wasn't so bad. We got the rest loaded and put the dead one on top of the planks that we had to keep the hogs from jumping out. We gave Foster eight dolars and went home.

We heated some water and cleaned the dead one and put the others in the pen. We worked most all night before we got our work done, and the next day I worked all day frying the meat down in big stone jars. It was lovly meat too. The Texas man was ready to go back to Texas. We never did see him again but hope he got back to his good old Texas.

Things just was on the bed rock but we staid and fought it out and came out all right in the end. But it was a toughf go. We raised thirty five bales of coton that year and sold three bales early and had the rest jined and hauled home. We piled it in the yard untell the next spring and then we sold it for three and a half cents a pound. It did not ever pay for the picking. But we were in God's Country. Or so they said. (Pp. 101–102.)

A SAND STORM

The very day that the school was out we had the worst sand storm. It came up about two o'clock in the afternoon. It was so bad that we could not see fifty yards. We went in the house and closed all the doors and windows. But that did not make any diference. The house was just made of boxing lumber. And the sand came through the cracks. Every thing was coverd. We just had to sit and take it. We could not cook nor do any thing but try to keep from choking to death. There was two hired men at that time and my brother and nine of our own famly so there we all sat and the sand poring in. No super. We could not cook nor even get out to milk our cows. It lasted eighteen hours. We had to just sit.

Besids the sand blowing it was an electric storm. Every thing was so full of electricity that we could not tuch any thing. If you tuched any thing the fire would fly like you had struck a match. The sun was shining but the air was full of electricity. Abe Gunn, a hired man, came in from the field, threw his lines on the fence and the electricity flew down the fence. The childern would get drinks of water so they could slide the tin cup over the stove to see the sparks fly. And the electricity killed streaks of wheat and oats. Some places in the fields for fifty feet looked like the fire had run over it and that was dead. It never did grow any more and there was streaks all over the whole country. We estimated about one fifth of our crop was killed. We sure wondered if that was God's Country.

Well the next morning, first thing was to dig out the sand from the house. We moved every thing outside, swept out the best we could and then we tried to cook some breakfast. But every thing was so grity we could hardly eat. Most all our groceries were ruined. So was every ones else for the sand storm was all over the country where the land was plowed. The house was cleaned the best we could, the cows milked, and breakfast over. Every one went to work.

Was we ever blue and home sick. But our cousen, Joe Parker, came over to cheer us up. He said that it was the worst storm that he ever saw. I laughft and said that I thought so, for it was God's Country. He did not like it. He said that he was sory for me for I had worked so hard and had been such a good sport about every thing but he thought every thing would be allright.

Then in a few days we had a good rain. Things began to look pretty good. We felt beter. But we did not have a very good crop. Wheat was short and corn not very good, coton pretty fair. But the price of coton was down. It looked like we were going back from where we started from in 91. One thing, we had our big lease for four more crops so we tried to console our selfs and look ahead for beter times. (Pp. 112–114.)

HAD GOD FORSAKEN US?

It was July 1895. I comenced to wonder if God had forsaken this country. Crops was bad. And most all our money gone. And all those teams to feed. The corn all burned. Five hunderd acers of wheat and not one grain cut. It was all too short. Just a very few oats cut. The coton was about a foot high, then the jack rabits cleaned it up. We had about fifty acers of cotton but it did not last long when the jack rabits took to it. And it looked like the grass was going to dry up too. No gardens. No feed for our hogs. No feed for the childern. But our credit was good so we still bought goods.

The Post Office was still going. Not much pay for we just got what we canceled. That wasnt very much for every body was too poor to buy stamps. Then we had a big rain that pepped things up. We would make some hay and have some feed and the grass would green up so our cows could give some milk.

We plowed some ground and went to town and bought a bushul of black eyed peas and planted them. We planted a new garden of most every thing. Our neighbors laughft at us. But when fall came they did not laughf. So did H. H. laughf when I told him that I was going to plant a garden. I said, "Why not for we are in God's Country." So he didn't say any more.

He helped me plant the garden and we had a nice garden and lots of black eyed peas. I sold some of them peas.

Every body in the neighborhood, what did not leave the country, went to plowing. Turning under their wheat land and the wheat that did not make any thing. A lot of people left. Some left in the night and took all their belongings and some things that did not belong to them. They had bought plows and other impliments and my husband had gone on their notes. So that left us to pay for their things. And nothing to pay with.

We went to Ryan and told the merchants what had hapened. So they said, "Well H. H. you go and put in your crop. We will cary you over and let you have money to buy your seed." They bought a car load of seed wheat and a car load of oats for seed and the merchants let every body have seed. But most of them had to give a morgage on their teams and impliments. They said that they would trust us. I felt like we were favord. And we was too. (Pp. 123–124.)

Perhaps the Cheyenne Arapaho Was God's Country

We were still working on, but all the time wishing that we could really have a home. We were not afraid of work but it seemed that just when you thought you had something it would burn up or it would rain so much that everything would be ruined. The childern were growing up and we knew that we must get a home.

So we went up to the town of Geary. We looked around and saw some nice places for sail. We made a deal for one claim and that would be one hunderd and sixty acers. And another claim was to be relinquished. The man relinquished and H. H. filed on the eighty acers.

We paid the man three hunderd dolars for his claim. I had the money in gold. We had sold part of our catle for twenty dolars a head and I had made a litel sack and fasened it to my under skirt band. When I gave him the three hunderd dolars in gold the mans eyes got as big as a hen egg. He was so sceard that he jumped on his horse and started to El Reno. We told him that it was thirty miles and the bank would be closed. But he said that if he couldnt get to the bank he would hide out untell morning. If people knew that he had that much money he would be robed before morning.

We put up the money for the other farm in the bank at El Reno. We had to write to Washington and prove up on it, so that took quite a while. We got what is called a paton from the goverment. That hunderd and sixty acers cost us about seven hunderd dolars and the other eighty, three hunderd.

It was a beautiful land in the valey on the south side of the North Canadian River. We had about made up our minds that the Chicksaw Nation wasnt God's Country. But we had hopes of finding it in this new territory. So we started back home. Or what we caled home. It was our seven year home and five of that was lived out.

We thought we would stay one more year and then sell our box houses. We had kept building one most every year as the family would grow till we had five litel box houses, the store and Post Office combined, the litel black smith shop and the chicken houses. Those we could move if we wished to. All we had to leave was the four wire fence.

We had sold all of our milch cows to get money to buy the two farms. So I told my husband that something would have to be done. I couldn't go out and round up one like I did in the ninetys. He laughft and said, "Wasnt them good old days." I told him that he might think so but I didn't. Then he joked me and said that when I was a young girl that I had debated the question that "Persuit is beter than posession." "Yes," I told him and that I still believed that persuit was the beter. That I was still in persuit of the home we had talked about. That I did not believe that I could have fought the snakes, centipeeds, cyotes, and all the rest of the varments and live like we did if I all ready had a home.

And I was still thinking that persuit was beter than posession. He laughft and said, "You are a queer woman but one that will stay with it." But anyway we knew that we had to do something about some milch cows. (Pp. 146–148.)

Looking Ahead

This new God's Country was much farther north and we would camp out while we were building. One thing was that we had a lumber yard in Geary, the place where we were going, and it wouldn't be so far to hall lumber. Our new place was just four miles from Geary. We had been going so much farther four miles would seem just like play.

We sold our building to Charley Willis, the man that had worked for us for four years. He bought all of our improvements and was going to run the farm.

When it came time for us to move I felt like I wanted to stay for we had had lots of exsitement and lots of fun, lots of hardships too and lots of hard work. But it was all over now. We did like pioneering very much for you would get something out of it.

We had not found God's Country but we were sure we would find it in our new home in the Cheyenne Country. So again we were on our way. We were going to God's Country. (Pp. 155–156.)

The Wind and Plaster

We were going to build a two story house but every one said that was too high. So we just built one story and a half. We wanted to plaster, "No," the people said, "The wind will shake the plaster all off." So we just sealed and papered. But that was all a mistake. The people did not know what they were talking about for we have built two story houses and plastered too. But later. So I think it does not pay to take every ones advice. Just do like you want to. But anyway we built. And it was the show house of the whole country. You could see it for miles. At last we were in God's Country. (Pp. 159–160.)

We Sell Again

We stayed about four years and then one day a man came to our place looking for a home. Ours being the best improved and the best looking farm, he wanted to know what we would take for the place. "Well," I said, "I wont sell for I am tired of moving." Then H. H. said that he would sell if he could get his price and that was sixty five hundred. The man said that he would take it if we would wait for part of the money. We said that we guessed we could. So we sold. (Pp. 163–164.)

ANOTHER HOUSE, ANOTHER BABY

Then it was to look out for some place to live. We had to give posession in May so we moved in a small house again and looked for another place. On August the twenty fourth, 1901, while we were still living in the litel house, we had another baby. We called her Daisy Lincoln.

H. H. was still looking for a beter place to live. There was much talk of the Caddo Country coming in for setlement. That was a good place to setle if you got the right farms. Some places were bad. So H. H. went to El Reno to regester. When you regestered you would get the numbers in a sealed envelope. Then you would have to go and locate your land. He regestered but he never drew. (Pp. 164–165.)

A BIG PLACE

We finly bought a lovly place just south of our old place. . . . It was a new place and a beautiful place. But again it was too small so we had to build on a big kitchen twenty feet long and eighteen feet wide. And a big back porch. It was a lovly place with all kinds of fruits and berys. Apricots, all kind of buded fruit, and all kind of ornimentel trees. So we could work very haply with such a lovly home. And we thought that we would be there for life. We were sure that we had landed in God's Country. Or almost sure. (Pp. 165–166.)

ANOTHER BABY

In 1904 there was another baby girl, Lily, on hand. This was our twelfth child. She was born in November so work was slacked up for some time. (P. 170.)

WE BUY SOME TEXAS LAND

We heard of good land that was selling around Vernon, Texas, so we desided that we would go to Texas and see. We thought that we were in God's Country now and might take a chance on something. We went to Geary and took the train to Texas. Of course we were met by a lot of real estate men. They drove us all over the country. . . . But anyway we bought seven hunderd and forty acers. We just paid five hunderd dolars down. . . . We had paid ten dolars per acer. And that was quite a lot of money. We let a man have the place to sow wheat but it did not make very much. So then did some of the Geary people laugh and say that we were crazy. We didn't say very much for we began to think that maby we had made a mistake.

Pay day came around and we had to pay five hunderd dolars and the interest so that was over one thousand dolars gone. And no crop. We didn't say much to our neighbors about it. Some of them felt sory and some of them were tickled. It didn't weary me for I knew that we had been in so many tight places before and had all ways come out all right and I felt that we would this time. And we did.

That fall we got a telegram from the same man that we bought from saying that we could get fifteen dolars per acer. So we talked it over and sent him a telegram saying, "Twenty dolars an acer and no less." The next day here came a telegram saying, "Sold. Deeds will folow." Was we ever hapy.

But since then that land was worth lots of money for there was big produsing oil wells all over the seven hunderd acers. So you see one never knows what to do. But we made good for we cleard four thousand dolars. We thought that was prety good and we bought another farm close to us with what we made. We thought that was the easiest money we had ever made. And only one thousand dolars invested for eight months. And then we wonderd if maybe Texas wasnt God's Country. (Pp. 170–172.)

We Sell Again

It was not long untell a man from Kentucky came to our place and wanted to know how much we wanted for our home place. I said that I wanted to quit moving but he kept hanging around so H. H. told him that he would take ten thousand dolars. He said, "Sold." I had to have a big cry for we had bought a lot of new furnature and we also had the other farm. But I didn't say any thing. I wonderd where we were going to go this time.

The next thing was to sell the other place just across the road. That did not take long. We just put up a sign, "For Sail," and in a few days a man from Kansas came by looking for a farm. We sold our farm that we had bought with the money we had made from the Texas deal. We paid four thousand and sold it for forty five hunderd. (Pp. 172–173.)

Hunting Again

So now we were all set for another search for God's Country. For another wild goose chase. And this time it was Oregon. My father was there and I had a sister there too and they had been writing what a wonderful country it was. They wrote that "Oregon is really God's Country." We had been in search of God's Country ever since we left Missouri so we decided we would taken another chance. We decided that it was—on to Oregon. (P. 173.)

A Trek across Country

That was nineteen and eight. And there were seven childern and H. H. and myself. Two of the boys were in college, one was about twelve, three litel girls and the baby boy, Harley. He was born in nineteen and seven, the money panic year and the year Oklahoma became a State.

It was a husel around to get off but this time we were going on the train and not in the coverd wagons. I thought it would be much beter. And of course it was. We were only five days on the train. But believe me it was some job even then with all those litel folks. It was a big trek across the country. Easy though. For it was made by train.

We landed in Salem Oregon about the midle of June. It was so difernt but it was a lovly country. Somehow I did not like it. But we thought that we would try it.

We had to have some place to live and we could not find anything to rent that was fit to live in so we began to look for something to buy. (Pp. 174–175.)

ANOTHER HOME

The real estate men hauled us all over the country. In spring wagons. Some with tops and some without. And the dust was about three inches deep on all the roads but anyway we did get to see lots of country. And it was very beautifull with all the groves of tall fir trees and the Royal Ann cherys. Salem was noted for its cherys.

We soon found a big two story house that belonged to a widow and two girls. They wanted to sell and buy a smaller house. We bought it. And it was more furnature to buy and it took quite a lot of money. (Pp. 175–176.)

WE LOOK BACK TOWARD OKLAHOMA

It was geting fall now and we began to think of going back to our old stomping ground. We did not like it in Oregon. It was a very good place but just wasnt what we thought it would be.

I was geting discouraged hunting for God's Country. I knew there must be such a place. But where? We decided that maybe Oklahoma wasn't so bad. Any way we decided to go back. (P. 179.)

WE FIND GOD'S COUNTRY

We found just about every kind of person in every part of the country we lived. We worked, made friends, helped out where we could and usually found that others were willing to help us when we had our troubles. We were comencing to wonder if there was a certain place that was God's Country. Or if God's Country was everywhere? Or if God wasnt in the country—then in what?

H. H. and I did a lot of thinking and a litel talking. We had been living out on the farm in Woodward County for three years when H. H. had a stroke of paralysis. We moved back to Enid so we could be near good doctors. He lived for two years. Then my beloved died. We had spent

48 years together hunting for God's Country. Before he died we learned something. Something teribly important.

We learned that God's Country isnt in the country. It is in the mind. As we looked back we knew that all the time we was hunting for God's Country we had it. We worked hard. We was loyal. Honest. We was happy. For 48 years we lived together in God's Country. (Pp. 185–186.)

Beautiful and Healthful Iowa

I [1]

IOWA is noted for the glory and beauty of its autumns. That gorgeous season denominated "Indian Summer" cannot be described, and in Iowa it is peculiarly charming. Day after day, for weeks, the sun is veiled in a hazy splendor, while the forests are tinged with the most gorgeous hues, imparting to all nature something of the enchantments of fairyland. Almost imperceptibly, these golden days merge into winter, which holds its stern reign without the disagreeable changes experienced in other climes, until spring ushers in another season of life and beauty. And so the seasons pass, year after year, in our beautiful and healthful Iowa.

II [2]

Our climate is one of the most delightful in nature. Our spring usually commences in March, and by the middle of April the prairies are green with mild, beautiful weather. In May, all the face of nature is covered with flowers and the foliage of the prairies bends before the breeze like the waves of an enchanted lake, whilst the whole atmosphere is scented with the breath of flowers. At all seasons of the year, a gentle breeze is fanning the prairies, and a day is never so sultry but that a cooling breath comes to moderate the melting temperature.

The Kinkaiders

Air: "Maryland, My Maryland."

1 You ask what place I like the best,
   The sand hills, O the old sand hills;
   The place Kinkaiders make their home,
   And prairie chickens freely roam.

---

[1] From *Iowa: The Home for Immigrants*, prepared by Secretary A. R. Fulton of the Iowa Board of Immigration, in 1870. Cited in *The Palimpsest*. XVIII (July 1937), pp. 226–242.

[2] From *The Iowa Handbook for 1857*, by Nathan H. Parker. Boston: J. P. Jewett and Company.

From *The American Songbag*, by Carl Sandburg, pp. 278–279. Copyright, 1927, by Harcourt, Brace and Company, Inc. New York.

Chorus:

> In all Nebraska's wide domain
> 'Tis the place we long to see again;
> The sand hills are the very best,
> She is the queen of all the rest.

2   The corn we raise is our delight,
   The melons, too, are out of sight.[1]
   Potatoes grown are extra fine
   And can't be beat in any clime.

3   The peaceful cows in pastures dream
   And furnish us with golden cream,
   So I shall keep my Kinkaid home
   And never far away shall roam.

Chorus:

> Then let us all with hearts sincere
> Thank him for what has brought us here,
> And for the homestead law he made,
> This noble Moses P. Kinkaid.[2]

A Home on the Range

> Oh, give me a home where the buffalo roam,
> Where the deer and the antelope play;
> Where seldom is heard a discouraging word
> And the skies are not cloudy all day.

Chorus:

> Home, home on the range,
> Where the deer and the antelope play;
> Where seldom is heard a discouraging word
> And the skies are not cloudy all day.

---

[1] The phrase "out of sight" in the late 1880's was slang indicating excellence or superfine quality.—C. S.

[2] Moses P. Kinkaid, Congressman from the Sixth District, 1903–1919, introduced a bill for 640-acre homesteads and was hailed as a benefactor of the sandhill region.—C. S.

From *Cowboy Songs and Other Frontier Ballads*, collected by John A. Lomax and Alan Lomax, Revised and Enlarged, pp. 424–426. Copyright, 1910, 1916, 1938, by The Macmillan Company. Copyright, 1938, by John A. Lomax.

Oscar J. Fox, San Antonio, Texas, published an arrangement of this song after it had remained unnoticed for many years in *Cowboy Songs*. For a time "Home on the Range" was the most popular song on the air. A suit for a half-million dollars was brought on copyright—probably the largest sum ever asked for one song. A Negro saloon keeper in San Antonio gave me the music to "Home on the Range" as herein reprinted. The words are also identical with the version of *Cowboy Songs*, 1910. They were assembled from several sources and have since often been pirated.—J. A. L. and A. L.

Where the air is so pure, the zephyrs so free,
The breezes so balmy and light,
That I would not exchange my home on the range
For all the cities so bright.

The red man was pressed from this part of the West,
He's likely no more to return
To the banks of Red River where seldom if ever
Their flickering campfires burn.

How often at night when the heavens are bright
With the light of the glittering stars,
Have I stood here amazed and asked as I gazed
If their glory exceeds that of ours.

Oh, I love these wild flowers in this dear land of ours;
The curlew I love to hear scream;
And I love the white rocks and the antelope flocks
That graze on the mountain-tops green.

Oh, give me a land where the bright diamond sand
Flows leisurely down the stream;
Where the graceful white swan goes gliding along
Like a maid in a heavenly dream.

Then I would not exchange my home on the range,
Where the deer and the antelope play;
Where seldom is heard a discouraging word
And the skies are not cloudy all day.

Hawley's Yarn

. . . EMBOLDENED by his success, Hawley proceeded to relate that there
was, in that same section, an area of twenty miles where the air was so
pure that people never died, unless by accident.

"Never died!" exclaimed several of his hearers in astonishment.

"No, gentlemen, it was quite possible. The rare purity of the atmosphere prevented it. When persons got too old to be useful, they would
sometimes be blown away, and, once outside of the charmed circle, they
were lost."

"Is that really possible?" asked one of his hearers, in some doubt.

"A fact, upon my honor," rejoined old Hawley. "Indeed, some years
ago several philanthropic gentlemen erected a museum at that place, where
persons who became too old for usefulness were put into sacks, labelled,
registered at the office, and hung up. If at any subsequent period their

---

From *Struggles and Triumphs: or The Life of P. T. Barnum*, Written by Himself,
edited with an introduction, by George S. Bryan, Volume I, pp. 168–169. Copyright,
1927, by Alfred A. Knopf, Inc. New York and London.

Cf. Barnum's account of Hawley: "We reached Montgomery, Ala., February 28th,
1837. Here we met a legerdemain performer by the name of Henry Hawley. He was
about forty-five years of age, but being prematurely gray, he had the appearance of
a venerable gentleman of seventy. He purchased one half of my exhibition. . . .

"After the performances in country places, Hawley usually sat in the village bar-
room, and a knot of astonished and credulous persons would gather about him. They
were also attracted by the marvellous stories in which he indulged. His gray head,
grave countenance, and serious manner, carried conviction in the more probable narratives—the barely possible were swallowed, though with occasional signs of choking
—but when he enlarged in his Munchausen vein, some of his auditors would forget his
venerable presence, and cry out, 'That's a lie, by thunder!' Hawley would laugh
heartily and reply, 'It is as true as anything I have yet told you.'

"He had a singularly lively imagination, and his inventive faculty regarded neither
rhyme nor reason. Had he lived in the times of the Arabian Nights' Entertainments, he
would have been celebrated, as I think a few specimens of his bar-room stories will
show." *Op. cit.*, pp. 163, 165.

friends wished to converse with them, for a fee of fifty cents the old friend would be taken down, placed in a kettle of tepid water, and would soon be enabled to hold a conversation of half an hour, when he would be taken out, wiped off, and hung up again."

"That *seems* incredible!" remarked one of the listeners.

"Of course it does," replied Hawley. "It is nevertheless true. Why, gentlemen," he continued, "on one occasion I went to the museum, and asked if they had a subject there named Samuel Hawley. I had an uncle by that name who went to the Rocky Mountains thirty years before, and we had not heard from him in a long time. The clerk, having examined the register, replied that Samuel Hawley was in Sack No. 367, and had been there nineteen years. I paid the fee and called for an interview. The contents of that particular sack were placed in the warm water, and in a short time I proceeded to inform my old uncle who I was. He seemed pleased to see me, although I was a child when he left our part of the country. He inquired about my father and other friends. His voice was very weak, and after a conversation of twenty minutes, he said his breath was failing him, and if I had nothing more to say he would like to be hung up again. I remarked that I believed he formerly owned a large gun, and asked him where it was. He informed me that it was lying on the cross-beam in my father's garret, and that I was welcome to it. I thanked him, and bidding him good-bye, the keeper of the museum took him in hand, and soon placed him in his proper locality. If any of you should ever go that way, gentlemen, I hope you will call on my uncle and present him my compliments. Remember his number is 367."

The First California Booster Story

THE wear and tear of this covered-wagon life on the plains discourages many, although (who can doubt it?) we are journeying to a land unexcelled in all the world—even if there isn't a single nugget of gold within its boundary lines! This is illustrated by the yarn of a man who had lived in California, until he had reached the interesting age of 250 years. In most countries a man that old would be pretty feeble and decrepit, but not in California—Oh no! In fact such were the exhilarating, life-giving, and youth-preserving qualities of that climate that our hero at 250 was in the perfect enjoyment of his health and every faculty of mind and body. But he had become tired of life. The perpetual responsibility of managing a large fortune made him long for a new state of existence, unencumbered with this world's cares, passions, and strifes. Yet, notwithstanding his desire—for which he daily and hourly prayed to his

From *Forty-Niners, the Chronicle of the California Trail,* by Archer Butler Hulbert, pp. 20–21. Copyright, 1931, by Archer Butler Hulbert. Boston: Little, Brown & Company.

maker—health and vigor typical of residents of California clung persistently to him. He could not shake them off. At times he contemplated
suicide; but the holy padres (to whom he confessed his thoughts) ad-
monished him that that was damnation; being a devout Christian, he
would not disobey their injunction. A lay friend, however, no doubt the
heir to his estate, with whom he daily consulted on this subject, at last
advised him to a course which, he thought, would produce the desired
result. It was to make his will and then travel into a foreign country.
This suggestion was pleasing to our California patriarch in search of
death, and he immediately adopted it. He visited a foreign land; and
very soon, in accordance with his plan and his wishes, he fell sick and died.
In his last will and testament, however, he required his heir and executor,
upon pain of disinheritance, to transport his remains to his own beloved
country and there entomb them. This requisition was faithfully complied
with. His body was interred with much be-candled pomp and ceremony
in his own California, and prayers were duly rehearsed in all the churches
for the rest of his soul. He was happy, it was supposed, in Heaven, where,
for a long series of years, he had prayed to be; and his heir was happy
that he was there. But who can safely mock Providence? Being brought
back and interred in Californian soil, with the health-breathing, youth-
preserving, Californian zephyrs rustling over his grave, the energies of life
were immediately restored to his inanimate corpse! Herculean strength
was imparted to his frame and, bursting the prison-walls of death, he
appeared before his chapfallen heir reinvested with all the vigor and
beauty of early manhood! He submitted to his fate with Christian resignation and determined bravely to live his appointed time.[1]

The Abundant and Luxuriant
Produce of the West

. . . "PURE air—sweet water—*healthy climate*—(mark that, fellow
traveler)—fertile and easy cultivation of the prairies—extensive and self-
sown wheat fields!"—and, what was wonderful indeed, always free and
accessible to innumerable droves of well-fatted wild Hogs! ripe for the
slaughter, and so exceedingly kind and accommodating to Maine emigrants, as to approach their barn-yards once a week (not to be *fed*, but lo)

---

[1] This tale, although oft repeated by Forty-Niners, was originally published by E.
Bryant in 1848. Is it not the first California "booster" story?—A. B. H.

From *Western Emigration, Narrative of a Tour to, & One Year's Residence in
"Edensburgh,"* (Illinois), by Major Walter Wilkey, An Honest Yoeman of Mooseboro',
State of Maine . . . , pp. 6–7. New York: G. Claiborne, and Others, Publishers, 1839.
Reprinted by William Abbatt, 1914, being Extra No. 28 of *The Magazine of History
with Notes and Queries.*

to be *butchered!* Indeed, there was nothing of that country's produce which the "Squire" did not most extravagantly boast, the Fever and Ague excepted, about which he was as mum as a toad-fish! although the whole country so abounded therewith, that had seven-eighths been *barrelled* and *exported* to other parts of the world, there would have remained enough in all conscience, to have set half New England into the *shivers!*

The Elephant

I [1]

AMONG thousands of returning emigrants we passed one jovial party with a huge charcoal sketch of an elephant upon their wagon cover labeled: "What we saw at Pike's Peak."

II [2]

. . . Here we begin to meet people who are turning back, discouraged. They had seen enough of "the Elephant." No one seems able to explain that expression—which is the commonest heard along the California Trail. "I suppose," said Meek, "that it comes from circus talk, like if you went to the circus folks'll ask: 'Well, did you see the Elephant?'—meaning in general, Did you go where you set out for? Did you see what you went to see? Did you see the thing you started on through to the end?" As applied to our case it means undergoing the hardships and privations of the California trip, and getting there. You hear the phrase used variously of these quitters that are heading back for Independence as: "They've seen too much of the Elephant," or "The Elephant's tracks got too close." In rare instances the continent is referred to as "the Elephant," and the continental divide ahead of us (South Pass) as the top of the Elephant's back.[3]

---

[1] From *Beyond the Mississippi: From the Great River to the Great Ocean;* Life and Adventure on the Prairies, Mountains, and Pacific Coast, by Albert D. Richardson, p. 202. Entered according to Act of Congress, in the year 1867, by Albert D. Richardson, in the Clerk's Office of the District Court of the Southern District of New York. Hartford, Conn. American Publishing Company.

[2] From *Forty-Niners, The Chronicle of the California Trail,* by Archer Butler Hulbert, p. 41. Copyright, 1931, by Archer Butler Hulbert. Boston: Little, Brown & Company.

[3] E. P. Hatheway, Ms. *Letters.*—A. B. H.

Busted

I

"Pike's Peak or Bust" [1]

AMONG the most significant mottoes we have seen upon any of the wagons going out to the mines, was upon that of an Illinoisan, about three weeks ago, inscribed in flowing letters of red chalk, though not in the most approved style of art—"Pike's Peak or bust." The indefatigable and energetic sucker, returned the other day upon a gaunt and starving mule, that looked as if he had climbed the Peak. He was asked why he didn't go through, "Wal," he said, "he'd got clean on beyond Kearny, and—he busted, so he just rubbed out 'Pike's Peak or bust,' and turned back."

II

Wagon Inscriptions—Emphatic [2]

We have been somewhat amused in noticing the inscriptions and devices on the wagon covers of the Pike's Peak emigrants. One went through a day or two since, with a large elephant painted over the whole cover. Another had a rude attempt at a pike, with a pyramid to represent the Peak. But the most unequivocal inscription yet, we noticed on the wagon cover of a returned emigrant on Saturday. It reads: "Oh Yes! Pike's Peak in H—l and D—n nation!" We think the man owning that wagon must be of the opinion that he has been badly humbugged, and he thus emphatically expressed himself.

Disgusted

THE legend "Pike's Peak or Bust" began to appear on wagon covers. Others had "Ho for the gold fields of Kansas" painted on them. Still

---

From *Colorado Gold Rush,* Contemporary Letters and Reports 1858–1859, edited by LeRoy R. Hafen, p. 319. The Southwest Historical Series, edited by LeRoy R. Hafen, X. Copyright, 1941, by the Arthur H. Clark Company. Glendale, California.

[1] *Nebraska City News,* May 28, 1859. This item, showing the first use of the famous expression, was first given me by Dr. R. P. Bieber of Washington University, St. Louis. It was later found among the Willard items.—L. R. H.

[2] *Jefferson Inquirer,* May 28, 1859; copied from the *St. Joseph Journal.*— L. R. H.

From *Three Frontiers; Memories, and a Portrait of Henry Littleton Pitzer, as Recorded by his Son, Robert Claiborne Pitzer,* pp. 78, 79, 83–84. Copyright, 1938, by Robert Claiborne Pitzer. Muscatine, Iowa: The Prairie Press.

others, the names of places from which they hailed, or the owners' names, or sometimes even a verse of Scripture. I noticed that the men who meant business mostly had no time for signs, and that the more romantic a man was the more he painted his wagon cover.

. . . It wasn't long before we began to see the word "Busted" scrawled under the "Pike's Peak or Bust" legend. Then the rush got as thick coming as going. . . .

. . . D. C. Oakes came east to get a saw mill outfit, and was almost lynched going back again when a group of busted boomers who had read his book discovered his identity. . . .

. . . Again we came across that legend, "Pike's Peak or Bust," this time with "Busted, by Thunder." It was said that some of our returning pilgrims were so passionately exercised that they dug Major Oakes' grave every time they camped.

Timid but Wise

IN TIMES of adversity the faint-hearted forsake the country. Even after a few weeks of drouth many timid ones desert their farms, some remain away only a year, and others give them up entirely or sell them for a small amount to some sharp speculator. . .

Consternation seizes the settlers in these districts when the real condition dawns upon them, and they begin at once to fix up a "prairie schooner" preparatory to going East to make a protracted visit among their relations. . . .

. . . One covered wagon had written on it: "In God we trusted, in Kansas we busted." It was in all probability the same fellow who, returning next year, wrote: "We fled Kansas' sun and dust, and in Missouri's mud stuck fast." One man who had left Kansas several times, while returning the last time silenced any who might question or ridicule by posting these words: "Wise men change their minds; fools, never."

I Got Busted

MANY carried slogans painted on the sides of wagon covers. The most popular was "Oklahoma or Bust." Frequently on the opposite side were the words, "In God We Trust."

The old saying was "Oklahoma or Bust," but when I got to Oklahoma I got busted.

From *A Kansas Farm, or The Promised Land*, by Fannie McCormick, pp. 76–79. Copyright, 1891, by Fannie McCormick. New York: John B. Alden, Publisher.

From *The Last Run, Kay County, Oklahoma, 1893*, Stories Assembled by the Ponca City Chapter of the Daughters of the American Revolution, pp. 120, 201. Ponca City: The Courier Printing Company, 1939.

A Grasshopper Was Seen

WHEN the hoppers were thickest the air was full of them and the ground literally covered with them. Mr. Hoisington, then editor of the *Register*, greatly amused the people by placing this unique sentence at the head of a leading news column: "A grasshopper was seen on the court-house steps." This patient man brushed the pests out of his eyes, and off his nose, but with true Kansas grit and editorial dignity absolutely ignored their presence so far as any further remarks were concerned in that copy of the paper.

Hell on Earth

"YOU see them heat waves out there on the prairie? Them's the fires of hell, licking round your feet, burning your feet, burning your faces red as raw meat, drying up your crops, drawing the water out of your wells! You see them thunderheads, shining like mansions in the sky but squirting fire and shaking the ground under your feet? God is mad, mad as hell!"

"Oklahoma Rain"

IT WAS reported that dust had been found in the vault at the bank, that a banana crate used as a wastepaper basket by the local editor was full and running over with dust. One man claimed that gravel had come through his windowpane and wakened him during the night. Another, finding his car stalled by the grit in the engine, opened the door and shot ground squirrels overhead which were tunneling upward for air! A local paper reported finding gold nuggets in the street which had been blown from the mines in New Mexico. The county farm agent advised his clients that it would be unnecessary to rotate crops in the future, since the wind was rotating soils. One of the natives proposed a test for wind velocity: "Fasten one end of a logchain to the top of a fence-post. If

From *A Kansas Farm, or The Promised Land*, by Fannie McCormick, pp. 75–76. Copyright, 1891, by Fannie McCormick. New York: John B. Alden, Publisher.

From "Sandhill Sundays," by Mari Sandoz, in *Folk-Say, A Regional Miscellany: 1931*, edited by B. A. Botkin, p. 291. Copyright, 1931, by B. A. Botkin. Norman: University of Oklahoma Press.

From *Short Grass Country*, by Stanley Vestal, pp. 205–206, 208. *American Folkways*, edited by Erskine Caldwell. Copyright, 1941, by Stanley Vestal. New York: Duell, Sloan & Pearce.

the wind does not blow the chain straight out from the post, the breeze is moderate. You have a calm day."

Allergy in its various forms became so common that, it was said, even the snakes had learned to sneeze; in the night you could tell when a duster was coming by the sneezing of the rattlesnakes on the prairie. Everyone jestingly referred to a dust storm as an "Oklahoma rain." A man caught some huge bullfrogs, so he said, and put them in his watertank to multiply; but, he said, the poor things all drowned immediately. It hadn't rained for so long that they had never had a chance to learn to swim.

A housewife claimed that she scoured her pans by holding them up to a keyhole. The sand coming through in a stream polished them better than she could by the usual method. One old lady, on hearing a man compare the climate to that of hell, put her chin up and declared that if the good Lord sent *her* to hell, he'd have to give her a constitution to stand it.

They laughed about the Black Snow which covered their fields. One farmer said he was going to leave Texas and move to Kansas to pay taxes—"There's where my farm is now."

Another said he could not keep up with his farm, which had taken a trip north. "But next week she'll be back," he said. "I can plow then."

One leather-faced dry farmer said, "I hope it'll rain before the kids grow up. They ain't never seen none." . . .

Those who left the Plains generally did so unwillingly, and, in the midst of their disaster, with a joke on their lips: "Well, the wind blew the dirt away. But we haven't lost everything. We still got the mortgage!"

Dakota Land

Air: After "Beulah Land."

We've reached the land of desert sweet,
Where nothing grows for man to eat.
The wind it blows with feverish heat
Across the plains so hard to beat.

Chorus:

O Dakota land, sweet Dakota land,
As on thy fiery soil I stand,
I look across the plains
And wonder why it never rains,
Till Gabriel blows his trumpet sound
And says the rain's just gone around.

From *The American Songbag*, by Carl Sandburg, p. 280. Copyright, 1927, by Harcourt, Brace & Company. New York. As "Nebraska Land" this is sung to "Maryland, My Maryland" or "Sweet Genevieve."

We've reached the land of hills and stones
Where all is strewn with buffalo bones.
O buffalo bones, bleached buffalo bones,
I seem to hear your sighs and moans.

We have no wheat, we have no oats,
We have no corn to feed our shoats;
Our chickens are so very poor
They beg for crumbs outside the door.

Our horses are of bronco race;
Starvation stares them in the face.
We do not live, we only stay;
We are too poor to get away.

The Lane County Bachelor

My name is Frank Bolar, 'nole bachelor I am,
I'm keepin' ole bach on an elegant plan.
You'll find me out West in the County of Lane
Starving to death on a government claim;
My house it is built of the national soil,
The walls are erected according to Hoyle,
The roof has no pitch but is level and plain
And I always get wet when it happens to rain.

Chorus:

But hurrah for Lane County, the land of the free,
The home of the grasshopper, bedbug, and flea,
I'll sing loud her praises and boast of her fame
While starving to death on my government claim.

Ibid., pp. 120–122. Tune: "The Irish Washerwoman." From *Folk–Dance Music*, selected and compiled by Elizabeth Burchenal and C. Ward Crampton (n.d.), p. 22.

My clothes they are ragged, my language is rough,
My head is case-hardened, both solid and tough;
The dough it is scattered all over the room
And the floor would get scared at the sight of a broom;
My dishes are dirty and some in the bed
Covered with sorghum and government bread;
But I have a good time, and live at my ease
On common sop-sorghum, old bacon and grease.

Chorus:

But hurrah for Lane County, the land of the West,
Where the farmers and laborers are always at rest,
Where you've nothing to do but sweetly remain,
And starve like a man on your government claim.

How happy am I when I crawl into bed,
And a rattlesnake rattles his tail at my head,
And the gay little centipede, void of all fear
Crawls over my pillow and into my ear,
And the nice little bedbug so cheerful and bright,
Keeps me a-scratching full half of the night,
And the gay little flea with toes sharp as a tack
Plays "Why don't you catch me?" all over my back.

Chorus:

But hurrah for Lane County, where blizzards arise,
Where the winds never cease and the flea never dies,
Where the sun is so hot if in it you remain
'Twill burn you quite black on your government claim.

How happy am I on my government claim,
Where I've nothing to lose and nothing to gain,
Nothing to eat and nothing to wear,
Nothing from nothing is honest and square.
But here I am stuck, and here I must stay,
My money's all gone and I can't get away;
There's nothing will make a man hard and profane
Like starving to death on a government claim.

Chorus:

Then come to Lane County, there's room for you all,
Where the winds never cease and the rains never fall,
Come join in the chorus and boast of her fame,
While starving to death on your government claim.

Now don't get discouraged, ye poor hungry men,
We're all here as free as a pig in a pen;
Just stick to your homestead and battle your fleas,
And pray to your Maker to send you a breeze.
Now a word to claim-holders who are bound for to stay:
You may chew your hard-tack till you're toothless and gray
But as for me, I'll no longer remain
And starve like a dog on my government claim.

Chorus:

Farewell to Lane County, farewell to the West,
I'll travel back East to the girl I love best;
I'll stop in Missouri and get me a wife,
And live on corn dodgers the rest of my life.

The State of Arkansas

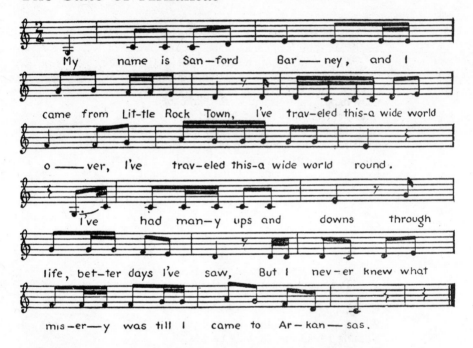

My name is Sanford Barney, and I came from Little Rock Town,
I've traveled this-a wide world over, I've traveled this-a wide world round.
I've had many ups and downs through life, better days I've saw,
But I never knew what misery was till I came to Arkansas.

'Twas in the year of '82 in the merry month of June,
I landed at Hot Springs one sultry afternoon.
There came a walking skeleton, then gave to me his paw,
Invited me to his hotel, 'twas the best in Arkansas.

I followed my conductor unto his dwelling place.
It was starvation and poverty pictured on his face.
His bread it was corn dodgers, and beef I could not chaw.
He charged me fifty cents a meal in the state of Arkansas.

From *Folk Music of the United States*, Album VII, edited by B. A. Botkin. Washington, D. C.: Archive of American Folk Song, Library of Congress. 1943. Sung by I. F. Greer, Thomasville, N. C. Recorded by Fletcher Collins. Transcribed by Charles Seeger.

I started back next morning to catch the early train.
He said, "Young man, you better work for me. I have some land to **drain.**
I'll give you fifty cents a day, your washing and all chaw.
You'll feel quite like a different man when you leave old Arkansas."

I worked for the gentleman three weeks, Jess Harold was his name.
Six feet seven inches in his stocking length, and slim as any crane.
His hair hung down like ringlets beside his slackened jaw.
He was a photygraft of all the gents that 'uz raised in Arkansas.

His bread it was corn dodgers as hard as any rock.
It made my teeth begin to loosen, my knees begin to knock.
I got so thin on sage and sassafras tea I could hide behind a straw.
I'm sure I was quite like a different man when I left old Arkansas.

I started back to Texas a quarter after five;
Nothing was left but skin and bones, half dead and half alive.
I got me a bottle of whisky, my misery for to thaw;
Got drunk as old Abraham Linkern when I left old Arkansas.

Farewell, farewell, Jess Harold, and likewise darling wife,
I know she never will forget me in the last days of her life.
She put her little hand in mine and tried to bite my jaw,
And said, "Mr. Barnes, remember me when you leave old Arkansas."

Farewell, farewell, swamp angels, to canebrake in the chills.
Fare thee well to sage and sassafras tea and corn-dodger pills.
If ever I see that land again, I'll give to you my paw,
It will be through a telescope from here to Arkansas.

III. LOCAL CRACKS AND SLAMS

Crack . . . Slang. *A gibing retort; a quip.*
Slam . . . Colloq. *A violent criticism.*
—WEBSTER'S COLLEGIATE DICTIONARY, Fifth Edition (1936)

From time immemorial . . . pointing sarcasm or humor at localities has been recognized as an element in human nature and its literature.—SAMUEL S. COX

1. NAMES AND NICKNAMES

IN ALL times and places popular tradition embraces terms, phrases, sayings, allusions, rhymes, songs, and jokes that poke fun at a particular locality or group.[1] In America geographical and cultural diversity intensifies rather than modifies the spirit of clannishness, provincialism, and

---

[1] For the proverbial aspects of local witticisms—the French *blason populaire* and the German *ortsneckereien*—see *The Proverb*, by Archer Taylor (1931), pp. 97–105.

rivalry which motivates local gibes. Minority and sectional conflicts and the mobility of the population are contributing factors. The restlessness of travel and internal migration makes local differences stand out in sharp relief and heightens the power of observation and the sense of the incongruous. Corresponding to "local color" in fiction, the humor of local characters and customs is an integral part of our folklore.

From another point of view, local taunts and insults are inspired by reaction against the excessive optimism and confidence of boasting and boosting. This boosting in reverse has already been noted in mock brags and orations, inverse brags, and "laughing it off." Mockery and skepticism also break out in open scoffs and jeers, pricking the inflated self-opinion of places. Exaggeration is the weapon as well as the object of attack.

The thrusts and shots of deflating sarcasm are also related to the national habit of "knocking" or faultfinding. The fact that knocking is as much at home in America as boosting may be attributed to the see-saw of American life, with its ups and downs of feasts and famines, booms and busts—"always up in the clouds or down in the dumps." More than the opposite of boosting, however, knocking is the spirit of social criticism and protest at work on the inequalities and contradictions of "individual competitive aggressiveness." When accompanied by wit and humor, knocking is relieved of rancor and in the guise of panning or razzing becomes not only good fun but an effective form of debunking.

In the matter of name-calling nicknames go even further and call a spade a shovel. Slang names of the states and their inhabitants popular during the last century were mostly uncomplimentary. One of the harshest of these is Puke, for a Missourian. "Early Californians christened as 'Pukes' the immigrants from Missouri, declaring that they had been vomited forth from that prolific State."[1] Collections of these sportive and slighting sobriquets illustrate not only local pride and prejudice but also the fondness for "intensive and extravagant epithets" noted by Bartlett and the "perennial rankness and protestantism" in speech which Whitman identified with slang.

A simple form of local witticism is nomenclature. Out of a realistic sense of humor and the apt phrase, frontier communities assumed disreputable, hard-sounding names, with a rough-and-ready appropriateness

---

[1] *Beyond the Mississippi: From the Great River to the Great Ocean,* Life and Adventure on the Prairies, Mountains, and Pacific Coast. . . . 1857–1867, by Albert D. Richardson (1867), p. 132.

"Puke" has also been interpreted as a corruption of "Pike," from Pike County, Missouri. The Pike County dialect—a generalized Southwestern speech (largely "low colloquial") made popular by the writings of John Hay and Bret Harte—is identified with the "poor white" character described by Bayard Taylor: "A pike in the California dialect is a native of Missouri, Arkansas, Northern Texas, or Southern Illinois. The first emigrants that came over the plains were men from Pike County, Missouri; but the phrase, 'Pike County Man,' . . . was soon abbreviated into 'A Pike.' He is the Anglo-Saxon relapsed into semi-barbarism. He is long, lathy, and sallow; he expectorates vehemently; he takes naturally to whisky; he has 'the shakes' his life long at home, though he generally manages to get rid of them in California; he has little respect for the rights of others; he distrusts man in 'store clothes,' but venerates the memory of Andrew Jackson."

For a full-length portrait of "squatter types," see *Mark Twain's America,* by Bernard DeVoto (1932), pp. 54–62.

and facetious raciness. Bret Harte has capitalized and popularized such places as Roaring Camp, Poker Flat, Red Gulch, One Horse Gulch, Rough and Ready.

In these hardy, improvised names, born out of the moment's humor—good or bad—, the American expressed the same irreverence and impudence as in the "barbaric yawp" of tall talk and boasting. "The appetite of the people of These States," wrote Whitman in *An American Primer*, "is for unhemmed latitude, coarseness, directness, live epithets, expletives, words of opprobrium, resistance. . . . Words of Names of Places are strong, copious, unruly, in the repertoire for American pens and tongues."

Such names, far from being confined to the West, had been anticipated in the East, where they have entered into mountain speech and thence into mountain fiction. John Fox, Jr.'s readers are familiar with the grotesque or whimsical sound and the native salt and savor of Hell fer Sartain, Cutshin, Frying Pan, Kingdom Come, Troublesome, Lonesome.

2. Poor Country

A common butt of ridicule is "poor country," whose lack of fertility and productiveness has given rise to almost as many jests as rich land has to brags.[1] In the East, especially the Southeast, "poor country" is apt to be exhausted or impoverished land, eroded and inefficiently farmed.

The typical "poor country" of the West is dry country. In the geography books of the last century the Great American Desert extended as far east as the Mississippi Valley, but as more and more of the land was put under cultivation or grazing, the desert was pushed farther and farther west. Recently, as a result of overgrazing and plowing under of the grassland, the desert—this time man-made—has moved east again, in what, since the dust storms of May, 1933, has become known as the Dust Bowl.

At their best, however, the Great Plains are semi-arid or sub-humid. The formula has thus been stated by Walter Prescott Webb: "east of the Mississippi civilization stood on three legs—land, water, and timber: west of the Mississippi not one but two of these legs were withdrawn—water and timber—and civilization was left on one leg—land."[2]

In this land where "You can see farther and see less than anywhere else on earth" and "Between Amarillo and the North Pole there is nothing to stop the wind but a barbed wire fence," many a jest and saying speak of too much wind and too little water.

Although applicable to and diffused over the entire Plains area, "dry country" jests become attached to individual states. Thus the genial "hymn of hate" describing the "hell" of the arid Southwest is known variously as "Hell in Texas," "The Birth of New Mexico," and "Arizona."[3] Similarly, "Dakota Land," "Kansas Land," and "Nebraska Land" (cited above) are essentially the same song about another "land of little rain." In

---

[1] See Part Four.

[2] *The Great Plains* (1931), p. 9.

[3] For a discussion of the cycle, see "Hell in Texas," by George E. Hastings, *Southwestern Lore* (Publications of the Texas Folk-Lore Society, Number IX, 1931), edited by J. Frank Dobie, pp. 175–182. For a Texas-Mexican legend on a similar theme, see "The Devil on the Border," by Jovita Gonzáles, Publications of the Texas Folk-Lore Society, Number VIII, 1930, pp. 106–109.

other cases a song, in spite of many parallels, is more or less definitely associated with a single state. This is true of "In Kansas," whose prototype is "Over There" and which is akin to songs like "The Cows Fly High" and "The Eagles They Fly High."

In the hill country of New England and the South a related type of local jest has grown up around the humors of hillside cultivation.[1]

3. "—WHO WOULD SOONER BE FUNNY THAN ACCURATE"

According to the author of *The Truth about Arkansas* (1895), "Probably about no other State are there so many misconceptions and so many inaccurate ideas as about Arkansas. . . . For this we may credit the class of writers who would sooner be funny than accurate. The chronicler of the wanderings of that noted personage, 'The Arkansas Traveler,' for example, may be said to have cost the State millions of dollars. . . . In spite of all that the State has suffered at the hands of traducers and thoughtless writers, it is undergoing a wonderful development." [2]

As a form of criticism or propaganda, local satire may be a power for good as well as for evil. Beyond its uses for mere entertainment, in the hands of journalists and politicians the humorous treatment of localities has had a serious purpose. Its range of possibilities is indicated by two widely differing examples—the *Salome Sun* and *Duluth!* In the former the local sage and wit assumes the mask of naïveté and the rustic, drawling accents of the "cracker-box philosopher." In the latter a leading Congressional humorist summons all the resources of polished wit, learning, and eloquence in an elaborate burlesque as felicitous as it is devastating. Both have their springs in the native humor of local allusion and popular jest.

In what is perhaps the most humorous speech ever delivered in Congress —*Duluth!*, by J. Proctor Knott, of Kentucky—, which proved to be a boomerang, the author unwittingly turned out to be a booster in the guise of a knocker. The reason was his curiously mistaken notion (based on ignorance of Minnesota geography and history) that Duluth rather than its rival Superior would profit from the proposed St. Croix & Bayfield Railroad grant. Turning the full force of his ridicule on Duluth, he caused the defeat of the bill—which was precisely what Duluth wanted. As an unexpected result of the speech, however, Duluth was flooded with inquiries concerning the location and price of lots; a grateful real estate dealer sent Knott some handsome photographs of the city and an invitation to accept its hospitality (which he did in 1890); the speech was reprinted by local boosters; and in 1895 the village of Proctorknott (now a part of Duluth) was named for him. Thus not only the speech itself, which is mined out of the lore of boosting and knocking, but the ironic sequel, which was a good joke on Knott, constitutes an amusing chapter in the history of American humor and "floating literature." [3]

---

[1] Cf. "Brown's Descent, or, The Willy-Nilly Slide," by Robert Frost.

[2] *The Truth about Arkansas*, by William H. Edmonds (1895), pp. 6, 15.
For an exhaustive investigation of the "comic notoriety" of Arkansas, see *Tall Tales of Arkansaw*, by James R. Masterson (1943).

[3] Cf. *Uncle Dudley's Odd Hours;* Being the Vagaries of a Country Editor; Also, as an Appendix, J. Proctor Knott's Famous Speech on Duluth, by M. C. Russell (Duluth, 1882), pp. 283–284; *Why We Laugh*, by Samuel S. Cox (1876), Chapter XII

Proceeding on the theory that "every knock's a boost," Dick Wick Hall (1877–1926), of Salome (rhymes with "home"), Arizona (population, 100), put the town and himself on the map by playing the role of Salome's "best friend and severest critic." Homesteading, ranching, and mining had given him an intimate knowledge of the region. As postmaster, garage owner, and editor and publisher of a one-man, single-sheet mimeographed newspaper, the Salome *Sun* (issued monthly beginning in January, 1921), he combined civic responsibility and business with literature. His puns, whoppers, and wisecracks, often in rhymed prose, are in the "Bingville Bugle" tradition of the comic country newspaper. His frog who had never learned to swim is straight out of American folklore. And his small town stuff—overtly good fun and covertly agitation for improved roads—sums up a whole phase of American life and humor, best described by the sign on his "Laughing Gas" filling station: "Smile—You Don't Have to Stay Here but We Do." [1]

The classic of American humorous folklore is *The Arkansas Traveler* (1840). Local in origin and allusion, it belongs to the older and larger tradition of the saucy, riddling dialog, or cross questions and crooked answers, between a traveler and a crotchety innkeeper.[2] The wit and humor of the dialog are largely elementary—a mixture of puns, paradoxes, insults, involving misunderstanding, the matching of wits, the naïveté of the rustic, the discomfiture of the stranger, and the solecisms of dialect. In style it is characterized by the humor of understatement, more typically identified with Yankee laconic wit or "reluctant eloquence," as opposed to the "expansive eloquence" of the backwoods.[3] Here the grudging response of the Squatter is associated with the stubborn cantankerousness of the native, due in part to suspicion and dislike of strangers (which in the Crockett almanacs inspired pugilistic encounters, including those of the purely verbal order) and in part to the low standard of living of the "unfit of the frontier," with its shiftless wantlessness and attendant ills of malaria, hookworm, and pellagra. Certainly the piece, for all its broadness, is far from a caricature; and the spoofing of the well-groomed Traveler on his milk-white horse (as pictured in the famous painting of the same name by Edward Payson Washbourne, 1858) derives an added social interest and significance from its realism as well as an extra satirical fillip from the outwitting of the socially superior by the socially inferior.

The Arkansas Traveler has other backwoods connotations. In the love of music that unites the Traveler and the Squatter when the former supplies the "Turn of the Tune" (also pictured by Washbourne in the

---

[1] For discussions of Hall, see *Arizona, A State Guide*, compiled by Workers of the Writers' Program of the Work Projects Administration in the State of Arizona (1940) and *Desert Country*, by Edwin Corle (1941).

[2] Cf. "Whimsical Dialogue between an Irish Innkeeper and an Englishman," *Wit and Wisdom; or The World's Jest-Book* . . . (London: Thomas Allman . . . , 1853), pp. 28–29; "A Musical Tennessee Landlord," by "Dresbach," *Spirit of the Times*, XVI (February 13, 1847), p. 603.

[3] See "The Inquisitive Yankee Descendants in Arkansas," by Walter Blair, *American Speech*, XIV (February, 1939), 11–22, where Blair points out that whereas in the East the native is usually the questioner and the traveler the questioned, the rôles have been reversed in the West, *The Arkansas Traveler* being a case in point. Cf. " 'Old Sense' of Arkansas," Part Three.

companion painting of that name) is reflected the popularity of the fiddle as a socializing agent, following the frontier. Again, the character of the Squatter may be a reflection of the dislike and contempt which the yeomanry has felt for the "poor white," as signified in such derogatory nicknames as poor white trash, no 'count, po' buckra, peckerwood, mean whites, low downers, sand-hillers, pineywoods tackies, hill-billies, dirt-eaters, clay-eaters.[1] Something, too, of the conservative's distrust of the pioneer and "coonskin" democracy enters into the treatment of back-woods hospitality, which is here taken off as somewhat less spontaneous and generous than usually represented in backwoods sketches and travel accounts.

The dialog is not only a piece of folk humor; it is also a popular entertainment. Essentially a folk drama, it is known to have been acted out by wagoners in at least one tavern bar-room, at Salem, Ohio,[2] and has inspired a play, *Kit, the Arkansas Traveler,* besides being used in plays like Paul Green's *Saturday Night,* for folklore color. As a recitation, with or without music, it has circulated in songbooks and jokebooks, to many of which it has given its name.[3] The tune itself (first printed in 1847) [4] rivals *Turkey in the Straw (Zip Coon)* as the liveliest and most popular of American fiddle tunes.

Apart from its local color interest, *The Arkansas Traveler* remains one of the most American of folklore themes, in both its symbolism—that of the backwoods, defined as a "state of society where rusticity reigns supreme"—and its form—that of a question-and-answer "frame" dialog which has attracted to itself a number of typically rural jokes.

No less vigorous, if more scurrilous, is that other Arkansas classic, *Change the Name of Arkansas? Hell, No!,* a mythical speech which takes off the fulminating rhetoric of backwoods legislators. Though the un-printable version smacks more of the smoking car than of the halls of state, it represents the less seemly side of tall talk, which in another version

---

[1] Cf. *The Southern Poor-White from Lubberland to Tobacco Road,* by Shields McIlwaine (1939).

[2] See *The Arkansas Traveler,* by Thomas Wilson (1900).

[3] *The Arkansas Traveller's Songster, Containing the Celebrated Story of the Arkansas Traveller, with the Music for Violin or Piano, and Also an Extensive and Choice Collection of New and Popular Comic and Sentimental Songs* (New York: Dick & Fitzgerald, copyright 1863), which reprints, on pages 5–9, the Blodgett & Bradford version (Buffalo, *ca.* 1850) ascribed to Mose Case. Of the several newspapers of this name (see F. W. Allsopp's *History of the Arkansas Press,* 1922), the most famous is that founded and edited by the Arkansas humorist, Opie Read. The first weekly issue (June 6, 1882) reprinted Faulkner's *Arkansas Traveler,* together with the tune and the two Washbourne paintings.

[4] *The Arkansas Traveller and Rackinsac Waltz,* arranged by William Cumming (Louisville: Peters & Webster; Cincinnati: Peters & Field, copyright, 1847).

The authorship of the tune has been assigned variously to Sandford C. Faulkner of Little Rock, Joseph Tosso of Cincinnati, and Mose Case of Buffalo, who, together with Edward P. Washbourne, claim the authorship of the dialog. For an account of these disputed and unsettled claims see James R. Masterson, *Tall Tales of Arkansaw* (1943), pp. 220–232; and for the several versions, *ibid.,* pp. 186–219; also Catherine Marshall Vineyard, "The Arkansas Traveler," *Backwoods to Border,* edited by Mody C. Boatright and Donald Day, Texas Folk-Lore Society Publications No. XVIII (1943), pp. 11–60.

has been cleaned up with the aid of passages lifted from the raftsman talk in Mark Twain's *Life on the Mississippi*.

In the role of inquiring traveler American humorists have developed a type of humorous travelog, which has been made popular by jokebooks and has served as a vehicle for monologists and lecturers. Its origin may be traced, on the one hand, to serious and imaginary travel literature and, on the other, to the humorous travel or local color sketch of the almanac variety. It has developed mainly in two directions: the comic account of "'scapes and scrapes" (represented in this book by *The Adventures of Big-Foot Wallace*) and the satiric commentary on local manners. Various "literary comedians"—William Tappan Thompson ("Major Jones"), Bill Nye, Artemus Ward, and Mark Twain—have worked this vein of local humor in one form or another.

On the popular or quasi-folk level it is almost pure vaudeville—rapid-fire, sure-fire stuff, interspersing wisecracks with gags and puns. Thomas W. Jackson's *On a Slow Train through Arkansaw* (1903)[1] has had many imitators, including a dozen or so jokebooks on the same pattern by Jackson himself. On a more sophisticated level it has produced the "hick-baiting" and "Babbitt-baiting" "Americana" of the *American Mercury* type. The inquiring traveler, with his gibes at local fads, freaks, and follies, is one of the many incarnations of the "cracker-box philosopher," providing material for a comic social history of the U.S.A.

Mining Localities Peculiar to California

Jim Crow Cañon	Puke Ravine	Blue-Belly Ravine
Happy Valley	Shanghai Hill	Gas Hill
Ground Hog's Glory	Mad Cañon	Dead Man's Bar
Red Dog	Plug-Head Gulch	Wild Goose Flat
Hell's Delight	Shirt-tail Cañon	Sluice Fork
Jackass Gulch	Guano Hill	Ladies' Valley
Devil's Basin	Slap Jack Bar	Brandy Flat
Bogus Thunder	Skunk Gulch	Shinbone Peak
Ladies' Cañon	Rattlesnake Bar	Graveyard Cañon
Dead Wood	Quack Hill	Gridiron Bar
Last Chance	Snow Point	Seven-up Ravine
Miller's Defeat	Wild Cat Bar	Gospel Gulch
Gouge Eye	Paradise	Hen-Roost Camp
Greenhorn Cañon	Nary Red	Loafer's Retreat
Loafer Hill	Dead Mule Cañon	Chicken-Thief Flat

[1] For a discussion of "slow train" humor, see James R. Masterson, *op. cit.*, pp. 269–280.

From *Put's Golden Songster*, Containing the Largest and Most Popular Collection of California Songs Ever Published, by the Author of "Put's Original California Songster," pp. 63–64. Entered according to Act of Congress, in the year 1858, by John A. Stone, in the Clerk's Office of the District Court of the United States for the Northern District of California. San Francisco: D. E. Appleton & Co.

Lousy Ravine	Rough and Ready	Yankee Doodle
Humpback Slide	Hog's Diggings	Gold Hill
Hungry Camp	Rat Trap Slide	Stud-Horse Cañon
Lazy Man's Cañon	Ragtown	Horsetown
Swellhead Diggings	Brandy Gulch	Pancake Ravine
Coon Hollow	Pike Hill	Bob Ridley Flat
Murderer's Bar	Sugar-Loaf Hill	Petticoat Slide
Whiskey Bar	Liberty Hill	Centipede Hollow
Pepper-Box Flat	Port Wine	One Eye
Poor Man's Creek	Poker Flat	Chucklehead Diggings
Poverty Hill	Love-Letter Camp	Nutcake Camp
Nigger Hill	Mud Springs	Push-Coach Hill
Humbug Cañon	Logtown	Mount Zion
Greasers' Camp	Cayote Hill	Seven-by-nine Valley
Seventy-Six	Skinflint	Puppytown
Bloomer Hill	Git-up-and-git	Barefoot Diggings
Christian Flat	Poodletown	Paint-Pot Hill
Piety Hill	American Hollow	
Grizzly Flat	Gopher Flat	

"Hasty and Grotesque"

. . . AMONG the far-west newspapers, have been, or are, *The Fairplay* (Colorado) *Flume, The Solid Muldoon,* of Ouray, *The Tombstone Epitaph,* of Nevada, *The Jimplecute,* of Texas, and *The Bazoo,* of Missouri. Shirttail Bend, Whiskey Flat, Puppytown, Wild Yankee Ranch, Squaw Flat, Rawhide Ranch, Loafer's Ravine, Squitch Gulch, Toenail Lake, are a few of the names of places in Butte County, Cal.

Perhaps indeed no place or term gives more luxuriant illustrations of the fermentation processes I have mention'd, and their froth and specks, than our Mississippi and Pacific coast regions, at the present day. Hasty and grotesque as are some of the names, others are of an appropriateness and originality unsurpassable. . . . Hog-eye, Lick-skillet, Rake-pocket, and Steal-easy are the names of some Texas towns. . . .

"Slops and Parings of Names"

. . . IN SHORT, Texas is one great, windy lunatic; or if you please, a bundle of crooked and stupendous phrases, tied together with a thong of rawhide.

From "Slang in America," by Walt Whitman, *The North American Review,* CXLI (November, 1885), No. 348, p. 435. Copyright, 1885, by Allen Thorndike Rice. New York.

From "South-Western Slang," by Socrates Hyacinth, *The Overland Monthly,* Devoted to the Development of the Country, Vol. III (August, 1869), No. 2, p. 125. Entered . . . 1869, by John H. Carmany. San Francisco: A. Roman & Company.

But it is in geography that this gift gives forth its most amazing manifestations. We all have heard some of our exquisite American names, such as Last Chance, Sorrel Horse, Righteous Ridge, Scratch Gravel, Pinchtown, Marrow Bones, etc.; but now read these from Texas: Lick Skillet, Buck Snort, Nip and Tuck, Jimtown, Rake Pocket, Hog Eye, Fair Play, Seven League, Steal Easy, Possum Trot, Flat Heel, Frog Level, Short Pone, Gourd Neck, Shake Rag, Poverty Slant, Black Ankle, Jim Ned.

Not Lovely but Honest

THE classic tradition belongs in any educational program, but let it not lay hands on those rural schools named Greasy Neck, Mud Dig, Mud, Way Back, Big Lump, and Allseeing Eye! Steal Easy Mountain, Tallow Face Mountain, Yearling Head, Hog Skin, Sodville, Peg Leg Crossing, Smuggler's Gap, Sixshooter Draw, and the creeks of Sparerib, Toewash, Troublesome, Wall Eye, Squabble, Skinout, and Gunsight, so named either because an Indian shot the front sight off a gun with which a teamster was drawing a bead on him or because in the vicinity a hill and a gap line up like the sights of a gun—these may not be lovely names, but they are honest.

How Louse Creek Was Named

"AIN'T you ever heard how Louse Creek got its name?" inquires Rawhide Rawlins. "Well, I ain't no historian, but I happen to savvy this incident. The feller that christens it ain't like a lot of old-timers that consider it an honor to have streams an' towns named after 'em. His first name's Pete, and he still lives in the Judith, but I ain't goin' no further exceptin' to say he's a large, dark-complected feller, he's mighty friendly with Pat O'Hara, and his hangout is the town of Geyser.

"When I knowed him first he's a cowpuncher. From looks you'd say he didn't have nothin' under his hat but hair, but what he knows about cows is a gift. Right now he's got a nice little bunch rangin' in the foothills. There's a lot of talk about the way he gets his start—you can believe it or not, suit yourself—but I think it's his winnin' way among cows. He could come damn near talkin' a cow out of her calf. Some say they've seen calves follerin' his saddle hoss across the prairie. One old

From "Stories in Texas Place Names," by J. Frank Dobie, *Straight Texas*, Publications of the Texas Folk-Lore Society, Number XIII, 1937, edited by J. Frank Dobie and Mody C. Boatright, pp. 47–48. Austin: The Steck Company, Publishers.

From *Trails Plowed Under*, by Charles M. Russell, p. 77. Copyright. 1927, by Doubleday, Page & Company. Garden City, New York.

cowman says he's seen that, alright, but lookin' through glasses, there's a rope between the calf and Pete's saddle horn.

"But goin' back to the namin' of Louse Creek, it's one spring roundup, back in the early '80s. We're out on circle, an' me an' Pete's ridin' together. Mine's a center-fire saddle, and I drop back to straighten the blanket an' set it. I ain't but a few minutes behind him, but the next I see of Pete is on the bank of this creek, which didn't have no name then. He's off his hoss an' has stripped his shirt off. With one boulder on the ground an' another about the same size in his hand, he's poundin' the seams of the shirt. He's so busy he don't hear me when I ride up, and he's cussin' and swearin' to himself. I hear him mutter, 'I'm damned if this don't get some of the big ones!'

"Well, from this day on, this stream is known as Louse Creek."

"Bizarre and Original Place Names" of Appalachia

THE qualities of the raw backwoodsman are printed from untouched negatives in the names he has left upon the map. His literalness shows in Black Rock, Standing Stone, Sharp Top, Twenty Mile, Naked Place, The Pocket, Tumbling Creek, and in the endless designations taken from trees, plants, minerals, or animals noted on the spot. Incidents of his lonely life are signalized in Dusk Camp Run, Mad Sheep Mountain, Dog Slaughter Creek, Drowning Creek, Burnt Cabin Branch, Broken Leg, Raw Dough, Burnt Pone, Sandy Mush, and a hundred others. His contentious spirit blazes forth in Fighting Creek, Shooting Creek, Gouge-eye, Vengeance, Four Killer, and Disputanta.

* * * * *

A sardonic humor, sometimes smudged with "that touch of grossness in our English race," characterizes many of the backwoods place-names. In the mountains of Old Virginia we have Dry Tripe settlement and Jerk 'em Tight. In West Virginia are Take in Creek, Get In Run, Seldom Seen Hollow, Odd, Buster Knob, Shabby Room, and Stretch Yer Neck. North Carolina has its Shoo Bird Mountain, Big Bugaboo Creek, Weary Hut, Frog Level, Shake a Rag, and the Chunky Gal. In eastern Tennessee are No Time settlement and No Business Knob, with creeks known as Big Soak, Suee, Go Forth, and How Come You. Georgia has produced Scataway, Too Nigh, Long Nose, Dug Down, Silly Cook, Turkey Trot, Broke Jug Creek, and Tear Breeches Ridge.

* * * * *

. . . Rip Shin Thicket, Dog-hobble Ridge, the Rough Arm, Bear-wallow, Woolly Ridge, Roaring Fork, Huggins's Hell, the Devil's Race-

From *Our Southern Highlanders*, by Horace Kephart, pp. 301, 302, 304. Copyright. 1913, by Outing Publishing Company, and 1922, by The Macmillan Company.

path, his Den, his Courthouse, and other playgrounds of Old Nick—they, too, were well and fitly named.

"Circuitous Styles of Expression"

. . . THE propensity to approach a meaning not directly and squarely, but by circuitous styles of expression, seems indeed a born quality of the common people everywhere, evidenced by nick-names, and the inveterate determination of the masses to bestow subtitles, sometimes ridiculous, sometimes very apt. . . . Among the rank and file, both armies, it was very general to speak of the different States they came from by their slang names. Those from Maine were called Foxes; New Hampshire, Granite Boys; Massachusetts, Bay Staters; Vermont, Green Mountain Boys; Rhode Island, Gun Flints; Connecticut, Wooden Nutmegs; New York, Knickerbockers; New Jersey, Clam Catchers; Pennsylvania Logher Heads; Delaware, Muskrats; Maryland, Claw Thumpers; Virginia, Beagles; North Carolina, Tar Boilers; South Carolina, Weasels; Georgia, Buzzards; Louisiana, Creoles; Alabama, Lizzards; Kentucky, Corn Crackers; Ohio, Buckeyes; Michigan, Wolverines; Indiana, Hoosiers; Illinois, Suckers; Missouri, Pukes; Mississippi, Tad Poles; Florida, Fly up the Creeks; Wisconsin, Badgers; Iowa, Hawkeyes; Oregon, Hard Cases. . . .

Illinois As It Was

A SMART sprinkling of the inhabitants of Illinois are from New England, a heap from Kentucky, and the balance are John Bulls, Paddies, Pukes, Wolverines, Snags, Hoosiers, Griddle-greasers, Buckeyes, Corn-crackers, Pot-soppers, Hard Heads, Hawk Eyes, Rackensacks, Linsey-Woolseys, Greenhorns, Whigs, Conservatives, Canada Patriots, Loafers, Masons, Anti-Masons, Mormons, and some few from the Jarseys. The Loafers are perfectly peaceable; the Mormons and politicians wrathy, and fond of hunting, cock-fighting, and getting into trouble in order to get out again.

From "Slang in America," by Walt Whitman, *The North American Review*, Vol. CXLI (November, 1885), No. 348, p. 433. Copyright, 1885, by Allen Thorndike Rice. New York.

From "Olympia Pioneer," in the *Bangor Mercury* of 1845. Cited by Thornton, in *An American Glossary* (1912), Vol. II, p. 974.

Hoosier

I [1]

HOOSIER. A nickname given at the West to a native of Indiana.

A correspondent of the Providence Journal, writing from Indiana, gives the following account of the origin of this term: "Throughout all the early Western settlements were men who rejoiced in their physical strength, and on numerous occasions, at log-rollings and house-raisings, demonstrated this to their entire satisfaction. They were styled by their fellow citizens, 'hushers,' from their primary capacity to still their opponents. It was a common term for a bully throughout the West. The boatmen of Indiana were formerly as rude and as primitive a set as could well belong to a civilized country, and they were often in the habit of displaying their pugilistic accomplishments upon the Levee at New Orleans. Upon a certain occasion there, one of these rustic professors of the 'noble art' very adroitly and successfully practised the 'fancy' upon several individuals at one time. Being himself not a native of this Western world, in the exuberance of his exultation he sprang up, exclaiming, in foreign accent, 'I'm a hoosier, I'm a hoosier.' Some of the New Orleans papers reported the case, and afterwards transferred the corruption of the epithet 'husher' (hoosier) to all the boatmen from Indiana, and from thence to all her citizens.

There was a long-haired hoosier from Indiana, a couple of smart-looking suckers from Illinois, a keen-eyed, leather-belted badger from Wisconsin; and who could refuse to drink with such a company?—Hoffman, Winter in the West, p. 210.

The hoosier has all the attributes peculiar to the backwoodsmen of the West. . . . One of them visited the city [New Orleans] last week. As he jumped from his flat-boat on to the Levee, he was heard to remark that he "didn't see the reason of folks livin' in a heap this way, where they grew no corn and had no bars to kill."—Pickings from the Picayune.

II [2]

"The citizens of this State, known as Hoosiers, who gave the State its name, are proverbially inquisitive. They are said to have got their nickname, because they could not pass a house without pulling the latchstring and crying out, Who's here?" (W. Ferguson, America by River and Rail, p. 338.) Another version derives the name from the word husher, denoting a man of superior strength and skill, who could hush or overcome every adversary, and hence an equivalent for the modern "bully."

[1] From Dictionary of Americanisms by John Russell Bartlett, pp. 180–181. New York: Bartlett and Welford, 1848.

[2] From Americanisms; The English of the New World, by M. Schele de Vere, p. 659. Copyright, 1871, by Charles Scribner & Co. New York.

Sucker

Sucker. A nickname applied throughout the West to a native of Illinois. The origin of this term is as follows:

The Western prairies are, in many places, full of the holes made by the "crawfish," (a fresh water shell-fish similar in form to the lobster) which descends to the water beneath. In early times, when travellers wended their way over these immense plains, they very prudently provided themselves with a long hollow weed, and when thirsty, thrust it into these natural artesians, and thus easily supplied their longings. The crawfish-well generally contains pure water, and the manner in which the traveller drew forth the refreshing element gave him the name of *"Sucker."—Let. from Illinois, in Providence Journal.*

A correspondent of the New York Tribune, writing from Illinois, says:

We say to all friends of association, come West; to the land of *suckers* and liberal opinions.

The Poorest Ground You Ever Seen

"Yeah," says Larkins White, "dat was some pretty rich ground, but whut is de poorest ground you ever seen?"

Arthur Hopkins spoke right up and said:

"Ah seen some land so poor dat it took nine partridges to holler 'Bob White.' "

"Dat was rich land, boy," declared Larkins. "Ah seen land so poor dat de people come together and 'cided dat it was too poor to raise anything on, so they give it to de church, so de congregation built de church and called a pastor and held de meetin'. But de land was so poor they had to wire up to Jacksonville for ten sacks of commercial-nal [1] before dey could raise a tune on dat land."

From *Dictionary of Americanisms,* by John Russell Bartlett, p. 343. New York: Bartlett and Welford, 1848.

From *Mules and Men,* by Zora Neale Hurston, p. 151. Copyright, 1935, by Zora Neale Hurston. Philadelphia and London: J. B. Lippincott Company.

---

[1] Commercial fertilizer.—Z. N. H.

A Poor Country

I [1]

PLEASE goodness! but that's a poor country down yander; it makes the tears come into the kildear's eyes when they fly over the old fields. Dod drot me, if you can even get a drink of cider!! They a'n't got no apples but little runts of things, about as big as your thumb, and so sour, that when a pig sticks his tooth into 'em, he lays back his jaw, and hollers, you might hear him a mile; but it's "eat, pig, or die"—for it's all he's got. And then again, they're great for huntin of foxes; and if you were to see their hounds! lean, lank, labber-sided pups, that are so poor they have to prop up agin a post-and-rail fence, 'fore they can raise a bark at my tin-cart. It's the poorest place was ever made.

II [2]

The dogs, in a certain county in Maryland, are so poor, that they have to lean against the fence to bark. The kildees are so poor, that they have to let down the draw-bars to enable them to go into a field; and the pigs are so poor, that to prevent them from upsetting as they run down hill, they are compelled to suspend a lump of lead to their tails to balance them.

III [3]

An eastern editor, in alluding to a rival town, says, that it takes several of their pigs to pull up a blade of grass; that they are so poor, the fore-most seizes the spear in his mouth, the balance having taken each other by the tail, when they give a pull, a strong pull, and a pull altogether, and if it breaks, the whole tumble to the ground for want of sufficient strength to support themselves. It must take three or four such pigs to make a shadow.

Hill-Country Wonders

WEST VIRGINIA is a hill-country State, and this has produced a type of farm surprising to newcomers within its borders. Planted fields seem to

---

[1] From *An Account of Col. Crockett's Tour to the North and Down East . . .* Written by Himself, p. 90. Philadelphia: E. L. Carey and A. Hart. 1835.

[2] From "Vive la Bagatelle!" in *The Southern Literary Messenger,* Vol. VI (June, 1840), No. 6, p. 416.

[3] From *Yankee Notions; or The American Joe Miller,* by Sam Slick, Junr., p. 47. London: Ball, Arnold, & Co.; Edinburgh: Fraser and Crawford; Glasgow: John Robertson. 1839.

From *Hill-Country Wonders,* by C. S. Barnett, in *American Stuff; An Anthology of Prose & Verse by Members of the Federal Writers' Project, with Sixteen Prints by the Federal Art Project,* pp. 53–54. Copyright, 1937, by the Guild's Committee for Federal Writers' Publications, Inc. New York: The Viking Press.

hang precariously on steep hillsides. The visitor is apt to be told by a native, quite earnestly, that the corn is sown by standing on one hillside with a gun and firing it into the opposite hillside. Pumpkins and squash, as soon as they begin to grow, have to be tethered to the cornstalks to hold them till harvest time. Cultivation on these slopes is so difficult that the native son at times will say with a perfectly straight face that he has to roughlock his harrow to get it down off the hill.

In the steep grazing country, it is told without even the suggestion of a smile that a breed of cattle has been developed with legs shorter on one side so they can graze around the hill without discomfort. The only herd of goats in the district had to be equipped with telephone linemen's climbers before they could get to pasture.

One man with an apple orchard on a steep hill just behind his house is said to have nothing to do when he harvests his crop except to open the gate to the orchard, shake the trees, and the apples roll right into his cellar.

A farmer with a cornfield on top of a high hill is reported to shuck out his corn and toss it down a natural chute of rock, so that when it gets to the bottom, all he has to do is to separate the corncobs from the shelled corn, put the corn in the bin for the winter, and stack up the corncobs in a little outhouse in case the mail-order catalogue should be used up.

There is also some extremely hardscrabble country in West Virginia. A visitor in Webster Springs, having had supper at the hotel, went out for a smoke and a little walk. Zip! A cat ran past. He watched it in surprise. Zip! Zip! Two more cats ran by in the same direction. Within about fifteen minutes he saw twenty-seven cats, all running in the same direction. "Where are all those cats going?" he asked a native. "Aw, don't pay no attention to that," the man replied. "They do it every day. It's seventeen miles down to the junction and that's the only place around here where they can find any dirt."

There is one place in the State where the country is so rough that the people have no teeth. The reason for this is said to be that level land is so scarce that cabin chimneys always open out close under the slope of the hills, and when beans are cooked in the fireplace, gravel from the hills runs down into the chimney and mixes with the beans, and the people wear out their teeth chewing on them. In this area folks always watch up the chimney to see the cows come home.

Some of the valleys are very narrow. The razorback hog is thought to have got his start in these narrow valleys: if he got too fat, he just naturally stuck between the walls of the valleys and had to get thin again before he could amble along. And there are valleys so narrow that the dogs wag their tails up and down. In fact, some valleys are so narrow that it is said you have to lie down and look up to see out; but one is so extremely narrow that the moonshine has to be wheeled out on a wheelbarrow early every morning, and the daylight wheeled in.

Dry Country

. . . OF COURSE it gets dry out there, they say, so dry sometimes that the cattle starve down and climb through the holes in the chicken wire, and hide among the chickens, and that's annoying . . . and they say that you're a tenderfoot until you can taste the difference between Texas, Oklahoma, Colorado, Kansas, and the Dakotas.

A drop of water hit a man, and they had to throw two buckets of dirt in his face to bring him to. . . . We keep track of the wind by hanging a log chain on a post. If it stands out straight, that's a breeze, but when it gets to whipping around, and links snap off, look out; it's likely to be windy by sundown.

What They Say on the Plains

I

"DOES the wind blow this way here all the time?" asked the ranch visitor in the West.

"No Mister," answered the cowboy; "it'll maybe blow this way for a week or ten days, and then it'll take a change and blow like hell for a while."

*   *   *   *   *

"This," said the newcomer to the Plains, "would be a fine country if we just had water."

"Yes," answered the man whose wagon tongue pointed east, "so would hell."

"In this country," said the cowboy, "we climb for water and dig for wood."[1]

"No woman should live in this country who cannot climb a windmill or shoot a gun."

"On the plains," said another, "the wind draws the water and the cows cut the wood."

From *Behold Our Land,* by Russell Lord, pp. 2, 211. Copyright, 1938, by Russell Lord. Boston: Houghton, Mifflin Company.

From *The Great Plains,* by Walter Prescott Webb, pp. 22, 320. Copyright, 1931, by Walter Prescott Webb. Boston: Ginn and Company.

[1] That is, climb the windmill tower to turn the wheel by hand, and dig mesquite roots.—W. P. W.

Cf. J. Frank Dobie, *The Flavor of Texas* (1936), p. 15: "Texas is where 'a man has to dig (mesquite roots) for wood and climb (go up gravely canyons) for water.' "

II [1]

Where you can go farther and see less,
Where there are more creeks and less water,
Where there are more cows and less milk,
Where there is more climate and less rain,
Where there is more horizon and fewer trees,
Than any other place in the Union.

From One Extreme to Another

A GAUNT westerner, fed up on dry farming in the arid Southwest, decided
to migrate to a place of eternal rain. Upon being asked why, he drawled:

"I'm tard uv sweatin' dust, that's WHY. Out here the only rains are
dust storms. Buzzards hev to wear goggles an' fly back'ards to keep from
chokin' to death, an' grasshoppers carry haversacks to keep from starvin'.
The only fish to be ketched in dry lakes are dried herring an' blind robin,
an' my mouth is allers so DRY, the only way I kin whistle to my dog is
by ringin' a bell."

A traveller from the wet delta region of Arkansas, attracted by the reports
of a land where rain was a novelty, decided to go to the Southwest for
relief. When asked why, he replied:

"This dang Delty's too wet for ME. Why, here the onliest time the
sun ever shines is when it rains. Even the pores uv ma hide air sproutin'
WATER CRESS. But I could stand ma ole houn' dawg havin' crawdads
'stid uv fleas; fer water bugs to take the place uv flies; fer the chickens to
grow web footed an' their aigs to hatch out turtles. Why I just laffed at the
bullfrogs croakin' on the haid uv ma bed; at the pollywogs in the drinkin'
water; an' I even stood it without too much cussin' when all the young'uns
tookd down with water rash an' the ole woman got water-on-the-knee. But,
when I started ketchin' CATFISH in the settin' room MOUSE TRAP,
I figgered 'twuz time to MOVE!"

---

[1] Opening stanza of a poem written by Leona Mae Austin, a fourteen-year-old
high-school girl, who had lived in Childress, Texas. From *Cowboy Songs and Other
Frontier Ballads*, collected by John A. Lomax and Alan Lomax, pp. 413–414. Revised
and Enlarged. Copyright, 1910, 1916, 1938, by The Macmillan Company; 1938, by
John A. Lomax.

Cf. J. Frank Dobie, *The Flavor of Texas*, p. 15: "Texas has more rivers and less
water, more climate and less rain, more earth and less dirt, more cows and less milk,
more preachers and less religion, more hot days and more cold nights, etc.—than
any other place on earth."

From *Tall Tales*, Compiled by Jim Blakley, p. 12. Copyright, 1936, by Eldridge
Entertainment House, Inc. Franklin, Ohio, and Denver, Colorado.

Hell in Texas

Oh, the Dev-il in Hell they say he was chained, And
there for a thous——and years he re—mained; He
nei—ther com—plained nor did he groan, But de-
cid—ed he'd start up a hell of his own, Where
he could tor—ment the souls of men With—out
be—ing shut in a pris——on pen, So he
asked the Lord if He had an—y sand Left
o—ver from mak—ing this great land.

Oh, the Devil in Hell they say he was chained,
And there for a thousand years he remained;
He neither complained nor did he groan,
But decided he'd start up a hell of his own,
Where he could torment the souls of men
Without being shut in a prison pen,
So he asked the Lord if He had any sand
Left over from making this great land.

From "Hell in Texas," by George E. Hastings, *Southwestern Lore*, Publications of the Texas Folk-Lore Society, Number IX, edited by J. Frank Dobie, pp. 178–180. Copyright, 1931, by the Texas Folk-Lore Society. Dallas: The Southwest Press.

The song is attributed by John A. Lomax to John R. Steele of the United States Signal Corps, "stationed at Brownsville in early frontier days."

The Lord He said, "Yes, I have plenty on hand,
But it's away down south on the Rio Grande,
And, to tell you the truth, the stuff is so poor
I doubt if 'twill do for hell any more."
The Devil went down and looked over the truck,
And he said if it came as a gift he was stuck,
For when he'd examined it carefully and well
He decided the place was too dry for a hell.

But the Lord just to get the stuff off His hands
He promised the Devil He'd water the land,
For He had some old water that was of no use,
A regular bog hole that stunk like the deuce.
So the grant it was made and the deed it was given;
The Lord He returned to His place up in heaven.
The Devil soon saw he had everything needed
To make up a hell and so he proceeded.

He scattered tarantulas over the roads,
Put thorns on the cactus and horns on the toads,
He sprinkled the sands with millions of ants
So the man that sits down must wear soles on his pants.
He lengthened the horns of the Texas steer,
And added an inch to the jack rabbit's ear;
He put water puppies [1] in all the lakes,
And under the rocks he put rattlesnakes.

He hung thorns and brambles on all of the trees,
He mixed up the dust with jiggers and fleas;
The rattlesnake bites you, the scorpion stings,
The mosquito delights you by buzzing his wings.
The heat in the summer's a hundred and ten,
Too hot for the Devil and too hot for men;
And all who remained in that climate soon bore
Cuts, bites, stings, and scratches, and blisters galore.

He quickened the buck of the bronco steed,
And poisoned the feet of the centipede;
The wild boar roams in the black chaparral;
It's a hell of a place that we've got for a hell.
He planted red pepper beside of the brooks;
The Mexicans use them in all that they cook.
Just dine with a Greaser and then you will shout,
"I've hell on the inside as well as the out!"

---

[1] The word that went here was a corrupt form of *ajalote*—Texas–Mexican for that
wondrous and hideous form of aquatic salamander, so common in the tanks and
troughs of West Texas, known as water-dog or water-puppy.—G. H.

In Kansas

Oh, they chaw tobacco thin
   In Kansas.
They chaw tobacco thin
   In Kansas.
They chaw tobacco thin
And they spit it on their chin
And they lap it up agin
   In Kansas.

Oh, they churn the butter well
   In Kansas.
They churn the butter well
   In Kansas.
They churn the butter well
And the buttermilk they sell
And they get as lean as hell
   In Kansas.

Oh, the potatoes they grow small
   In Kansas.
Potatoes they grow small
   In Kansas.
Oh, potatoes they grow small
And they dig 'em in the fall
And they eat 'em hides and all
   In Kansas.

Oh, they say that drink's a sin
   In Kansas.
They say that drink's a sin
   In Kansas.
They say that drink's a sin
So they guzzle all they kin,
And they throw it up agin
   In Kansas.

Come all who want to roam
   To Kansas.
Come all who want to roam
   To Kansas.
Come all who want to roam
And seek yourself a home
And be happy with your doom
   In Kansas.

From *Nebraska Folklore* (Book Three), Written and Compiled by Workers of the Writers' Program, Work Projects Administration in the State of Nebraska, pp. 11–12. Copyright, 1941, by the State Superintendent of Public Instruction. Lincoln: Woodruff Printing Company. For one tune see *Ballads and Songs Collected by the Missouri Folk-Lore Society*, by H. M. Belden (1940), p. 429.

Salome—"Where She Danced"

I

MANY tourists and easterners ask about the past, present and future history of Salome—so here is it. Salome is the principal stopping point on the Santa Fe Railroad and the International Auto & Air Route, between Phoenix and Los Angeles—which means that when you are not in the auto you ought to be in the air—and Salome put the air in Arizona.

The train stops here twice each day—when it goes from Phoenix and when it comes back from Los Angeles. Some folks have wondered why it comes back from Los Angeles but the engineer's wife has the asthma and lives in Phoenix—so he comes back. The train stops here because Salome has the only good water for a long ways—and the engine has to have water. The train goes through here becuz it can't get through the Granite Wash Mountains without going right through Salome—otherwise some of the natives might not know what a train looks like.

Some sweet day someone with a trained and talcum powdered tongue and an unlimited vocabulary of alluring and entrancing adjectives will attempt to describe the wonders and beauties of Salome. Meantime, it is a good place to live, if you like it—and a good place to die, if you don't.

Salome is not as large as Los Angeles, but larger than Phoenix used to be—and a much better town than either of them to live in—if you like them small and quiet—not dead, but sleeping.

Twenty years ago there was no one here but me—and now there's folks a living as far as you can see. On some nights when the Tourists are thick and the section men all in town and a good game going at Blarney Castle, as many as 75 or 90 people have been counted here—which is a big increase from nothing in twenty years.

It is a characteristic of the country, however, as one cow man who now has over a thousand head of cattle is said to have come here riding a blind mule and driving one red steer. It really would be fine cattle country if we had more grass & water.

Almost everything grows well here. Squint Eye Johnson built a barn last year and on account of the high price of lumber cut four big cotton-wood posts and set them in the ground for the corners, nailing boards

From *Salome Sun*, Vol. 1, Nos. 2 and 4, February and April, 1921. Dick Wick Hall, Editor and Miner. Salome, Arizona.

on to complete the barn. It rained soon after and the corner posts started to grow—and it kept Squint Eye busy all summer nailing on more boards at the bottom to keep the cows from getting out—and now he has a two story barn and uses the top story for a hen house. Squint Eye says one more wet year and he will have to buy an aeroplane to feed his chickens.

Melons don't do very well here becuz the vines grow so fast they wear the melons out dragging them around the ground—and in dry years we sometimes have to plant onions in between the rows of potatoes and then scratch the onions to make the potatoes eyes water enough to irrigate the rest of the garden—and the kids sure do hate to scratch the onions on moonlight nights.

Salome has the purest water and the clearest air in the whole world—including Texas. Don't mix Salome with Yuma, where the bad soldier lived, and when he died—well, he sent for his blankets and overcoat. Yes, it was through the streets of Yuma that the coyote chased the jack rabbit—and they were both walking—and it wasn't more than three figures in the shade at midnight either. Just warm.

II

Stop when you get to Salome—where she danced and fill your tires with that soft Salome air—it rides easier and is used to dodging bumps—use our laughing gas—a free smile with every quart—we laugh becuz we like to live here—we have to and you don't—you just keep on riding by and buy asking which road and dodging bumps and chucks coming and going—we wonder where—and why becuz we've been here a long time—a l-o-n-g time trying to save something for a rainy day—Rockefeller and Henery Ford used to get all the money before we started.

But we haven't saved anything—and it hasn't rained—there's frogs here seven years old that haven't learned to swim yet—so why should we worry about rainy days? We thank you—and if you have to come this way again why—stop and say hello! Maybe Salome will dance again or the frog might learn to swim by that time. Adios!

My Frog

PLEASE help buy a Bath Tub for Our Frog. He will be Seven Years Old next month and he hasn't learned to swim yet. If it does not rain soon we are afraid he will turn into a long horned toad.

From *Salome Sun*, Vol. 1, Nos. 2, 3, and 4, Vol. 2, No. 1, Vol. 3, No. 1, Vol. 5, No. 1, and Vol. 7, No. 11, February, March, April, and October, 1921, January, 1922, April, 1923, and November, 1924. Dick Wick Hall, Editor and Miner. Salome, Arizona.

Our Frog went out to play, one day, in youthful froglike folly; he let the sun shine on his back and the sand was hot, By Golly! But he hasn't learned to swim yet. He was asleep the last time it rained and when he woke up the water was all gone. Better luck next time.

> Our poor Old Frog is getting gray
> Waiting for a Rainy Day;
> If it don't hurry up and rain,
> I fear he'll have a window pane.

Put the Frog out, Bill, I think it's going to rain.

Our Frog says: "Arizona is dry—my tears are dusty when I cry; my chances here look pretty slim—7 years old and I can't swim. I'm a dry land Frog away from Home—but watch me when I get to Salome."

Wanted AT ONCE—A Bushel of Lightning Bugs or a Dozen Lightning Bug Eggs. Major Jo Hardie of Santa Monica has just told us about a Frog he once owned down in South Carolina that used to eat Lightning Bugs until his Belly would stick out like a Toy Balloon—and the Light from the Bugs shining through His Bay Window—the Frog's I mean—was strong enough to read by. I've got the Biggest Frog in Captivity and if I can just get the Lightning Bugs I will soon have an Electric Light Plant at Salome—"Where She Danced." I'll fill Him full of Lightning Bugs and then feed him about 10 lbs. of Buckshot so he can't jump around and sit him out in front of the Laughing Gas Station at Night so Tourists can find their way Home. Patents being applied for now.

My Frog says Arizona sure is Dry When a Frog has to Carry a Big Canteen and Water His back to keep it Green and Prime Himself when he wants to Cry and His Belly gets Burned with the Alkali and Life on the Desert ain't No Joke to a Frog out here Alone and Broke and Seven Years Old, can't Swim a Stroke—so He's just trying to Learn to Smoke.

Hot & Yumaresque

IT is the hot and Yumaresque season again, when lazy folks can lie around and sweat without working or exercising. That is the main reason why some folks like to live in Arizona, or any place where the wind blows from down around Yuma. June is here, school is over and it is getting quite comfortably warm. The women folks are all either gone or getting ready to go to the California beaches again, not on account of the heat,

From *Salome Sun*, Vol. 4, No. 2, June, 1922. Dick Wick Hall, Editor and Miner, Salome, Arizona.

oh no, but just so the children can learn to swim, there being no water here and so much of it around the beaches—although not many of the Arizona men find it.

Every child really ought to learn to swim, especially if they live on the desert, where they are so apt to get drowned in some of those dry lakes, mirages and cloudbursts. Any Arizona woman can tell you that—and prove it, if you are married to her. So the women take the children down to the beaches in the summer—to teach them how to swim and we men generally have to drop all our work, no matter how important it is, and go along to see that none of them get drowned. A married man's first duty is to his family and after all the trouble it is to raise a family out here in this dry country we can't afford to take any chances on losing them in the water.

Last summer, after we had gotten located down at the beach in a "seaside villa" about five feet wide and 27 feet long, at $25 a foot a month, where I had to stick my leg out of the window to get my pants on and the next "villa" neighbor's dog bit it the second morning there, my wife remembered that she had forgotten to put any water in the piano and was going to send to one of the neighbors to put some in when I happened to think of 2 bottles of old Gordon Gin I had left in the box couch—so I had to come back to Arizona to water the piano and un-gin the box couch, not wishing to bother any of the neighbors; not that they are not good neighbors, but I know them too well to risk 2 bottles of good Gordon Gin in a box couch. In Arizona, you know, you have to water the pianos in the summer time or they get hoarse—and so do I when I think of Gordon Gin.

It was night when I got here and the wind was blowing from down towards Yuma and the house was hot and stuffy when I unlocked it and lit a match to find a lamp or candle long enough to un-gin the box couch before getting out in the open air to sleep. I knew the piano could wait until morning for water but the gin couldn't. I thought of a pair of pink candles my wife always kept on top of the piano, for ornament and to look at, so I lit another match and turned to light the candles. I had to laugh. What I saw would have made a preacher laugh, or even a sour old maid. When we left the candles were standing up stiff and straight, just waiting for a match and ready to burn. Not now though. Both of them were hanging over the edge of the candlesticks, sick, limp and weary looking, with their heads hanging towards the floor in disgust. I managed to light one after turning it bottomside up and went out in the kitchen to get some water—after un-ginning the box couch—and there on the floor I found a big yellow mess in front of the cupboard. No, nothing had been in there but my wife had left a pair of yellow rubber gloves on the cupboard shelf and the heat had melted the fingers all off and they had fallen on the floor. Yes, it really does get a little warm here—when the sun shines and the wind blows from down around Yuma.

I am saving the candles and what is left of the gloves, just to show and prove that I am an honest man and Arizona truth is greater than any fiction. I was showing them to a lady from Massachusetts the other day and she said: "For the Land's Sakes A-live! How DO you stand it here?" "We don't," I answered, "we get like the gloves and candles; that's why the women all go to the coast in the hot and Yumaresque season."

The Old Indian Trail

(Dedicated to the Tourists by the Salome Service Station)

SIXTY years ago the Indians chased an old prospector from the Colorado River to where Phoenix now is—he hit some of the high places and dodged around through the brush something like a spring chicken after a grass-hopper—like a cricket on a hot stove—or the lady on the back seat. This old prospector made the trail you are now hitting—the natural and shortest route to the coast—the scenic highway—scenery high and in the way—but don't blame the old prospector—he was in a hurry—he knew the Indians were following him but he never expected you to—and he didn't know the Yuma County Democratic Boards of Supervisors were going to relocate his trail and call it a county road—a Yuma County Arizona Road—just because they are Democrats and this isn't a road. They come up here every two years full of Democratic promises—after our votes and every year after our taxes to help build roads through the sand down around Yuma—our county seat which is so far from here it costs $17 to send a postal card to find out who is sheriff again—this year they are so busy saving the rest of the world and trying to make it safer for Democrats that they forget all about us up here on the old Indian Trail—which is just the same as it was sixty odd years ago—only worse—as 137556 tourists can and do swear to and swear at and then swear some go to it—keep right on swearing and maybe some day Henry Ford himself will come bump chuckin along this way and shake a few $$$$$$$ out of his system and help remove some of the scenery and cuss words and corkscrews out of the old Indian Trail so that Lizzie can go 100 yards without getting curvature of the spine shimmying through the cactus and jumping greasewood like a jack rabbit—trying to find the tracks the old prospector left here sixty odd years ago—never mind Henry—you can dodge the bumps like he dodged the Indians and have a hell of a time—he did—and maybe if you hurry you can beat his record from the Colorado River to Phoenix—no one ever has yet—but with a Republican Administration everything is going to move faster now—step on her bill—let's go.

From *Salome Sun*, Vol. 1, No. 4, April, 1921. Dick Wick Hall, Editor and Miner. Salome, Arizona.

Duluth!

. . . YEARS ago, when I first heard that there was somewhere in the vast *terra incognita,* somewhere in the bleak regions of the great North-west, a stream of water known to the nomadic inhabitants of the neighborhood as the river St. Croix, I became satisfied that the construction of a railroad from that raging torrent to some point in the civilized world was essential to the happiness and prosperity of the American people, if not absolutely indispensable to the perpetuity of republican institutions on this continent. [Great laughter.] I felt instinctively that the boundless resources of that prolific region of sand and pine-shrubbery would never be fully developed without a railroad constructed and equipped at the expense of the Government, and perhaps not then. [Laughter.] I had an abiding presentiment that, some day or other, the people of this whole country, irrespective of party affiliations, regardless of sectional prejudices, and "without distinction of race, color, or previous condition of servitude," would rise in their majesty and demand an outlet for the enormous agricultural productions of those vast and fertile pine-barrens, drained in the rainy season by the surging waters of the turbid St. Croix. [Great laughter.]

*   *   *   *   *

From *Duluth!* Speech of Hon. J. Proctor Knott, of Kentucky, delivered in the House of Representatives, on the St. Croix and Superior Land Grant, January 27, 1871.

Cf. Cox's comment on the "humors" of the speech and its circumstances:

"Until the Duluth speech was made, the House had little thought of the rich plenitude of humor in store for them. The surprise was enhanced because Mr. Knott spoke rarely. He was not an active, rather a lazy, member—ostensibly so. . . . They took the alligator for a log, till they sat on him. Grudgingly was the floor yielded to him on the Duluth debate. He was offered only ten minutes; whereupon he remarked that his facilities for getting time were so poor that, if he were standing on the brink of perdition, and the sands were crumbling under his feet, he could not in that body get time enough to say the Lord's Prayer. The St. Croix and Bayfield Bill asked for some of the public domain. Mr. Knott disavowed any more interest in the bill than in an orange-grove on the bleakest summit of Greenland's icy mountains. . . .

". . . A close student of men and books, once attorney-general of Missouri, familiar with frontier and prairie life, he had the rare perception to observe the queerness and oddity of things, and the rarer gift so to mix his colors and limn his figures that all should recognize beneath the heightened colors the graphic genuineness and design of his art. But the special humor of this Duluth speech lies in its magnifying, with a roaring rush of absurdity, the exaggerations of a Western Eden, in which utter nakedness and fragrant luxuriance alternate, and between whose aisles of greenery the sly devil of selfishness sat squat at the ear of Congress, tempting it to taste the forbidden fruit of subsidy. . . . Like the allegory or the parable, there is moral hidden beneath this elaborate imagery. It is this moral which exalts the American mind to the sublimity of its own peculiar fun, and relieves the leviathanic lawlessness of exaggeration of its strain upon the faculties. No speech that I can recall produced at once so signal an effect." (*Op. cit.,* pp. 215–216, 221.)

Now, sir, who, after listening to this emphatic and unequivocal testimony of these intelligent, competent, and able-bodied witnesses [laughter;] who that is not as incredulous as St. Thomas himself, will doubt for a moment that the Goshen of America is to be found in the sandy valleys and upon the pine-clad hills of the St. Croix? [Laughter.] Who will have the hardihood to rise in his seat on this floor and assert that, excepting the pine bushes, the entire region would not produce vegetation enough in ten years to fatten a grasshopper? [Great laughter.] Where is the patriot who is willing that his country shall incur the peril of remaining another day without the amplest railroad connection with such an inexhaustible mine of agricultural wealth? [Laughter.]

Duluth! The word fell upon my ear with peculiar and indescribable charm, like the gentle murmur of a low fountain stealing forth in the midst of roses, or the soft, sweet accents of an angel's whisper in the bright, joyous dream of sleeping innocence. Duluth! 'Twas the name for which my soul had panted for years, as the hart panteth for the water-brooks. [Renewed laughter.] But where was Duluth? Never in all my limited reading had my vision been gladdened by seeing the celestial word in print. [Laughter.] And I felt a profounder humiliation in my ignorance that its dulcet syllables had never before ravished my delighted ear. [Roars of laughter.] I was certain the draughtsman of this bill had never heard of it, or it would have been designated as one of the termini of this road. I asked my friends about it, but they knew nothing of it. I rushed to the library and examined all the maps I could find. [Laughter.] I discovered in one of them a delicate, hair-like line, diverging from the Mississippi near a place marked Prescott, which I supposed was intended to represent the river St. Croix, but I could nowhere find Duluth.

Nevertheless, I was confident it existed somewhere, and that its discovery would constitute the crowning glory of the present century, if not of all modern times. [Laughter.] I knew it was bound to exist, in the very nature of things; that the symmetry and perfection of our planetary system would be incomplete without it [renewed laughter]; that the elements of material nature would long since have resolved themselves back into original chaos if there had been such a hiatus in creation as would have resulted from leaving out Duluth. [Roars of laughter.] In fact, sir, I was overwhelmed with the conviction that Duluth not only existed somewhere, but that, wherever it was, it was a great and glorious place. I was convinced that the greatest calamity that ever befell the benighted nations of the ancient world was in their having passed away without a knowledge of the actual existence of Duluth; that their fabled Atlantis, never seen save by the hallowed vision of inspired poesy, was, in fact, but another name for Duluth; that the golden orchard of the Hesperides was but a poetical synonym for the beer-gardens in the vicinity of Duluth. [Great laughter.] I was certain that Herodotus had died a miserable death because in all his travels and with all his geographical research he had never heard of Duluth. [Laughter.] I knew that if the immortal spirit of Homer could look down from another heaven than that created by his own celestial genius upon the long lines of pilgrims from every nation of the earth to the gushing fountain of poesy opened by the touch of his magic wand, if he could be permitted to behold the vast assemblage of grand and glorious productions of the lyric art called into being by his own inspired strains, he would weep tears of bitter anguish that, instead of lavishing all the stores of his mighty genius upon the fall of Illion, it had not been his more blessed lot to crystallize in deathless song the rising glories of Duluth. [Great and continued laughter.] Yet, sir, had it not been for this map, kindly furnished me by the Legislature of Minnesota, I might have gone down to my obscure and humble grave in an agony of despair because I could nowhere find Duluth. [Renewed laughter.] Had such been my melancholy fate, I have no doubt that with the last feeble pulsation of my breaking heart, with the last faint exhalation of my fleeting breath, I should have whispered, "Where is Duluth?" [Roars of laughter.]

But, thanks to the beneficence of that band of ministering angels who have their bright abodes in the far-off capital of Minnesota, just as the agony of my anxiety was about to culminate in the frenzy of despair, this blessed map was placed in my hands; and as I unfolded it a resplendent scene of ineffable glory opened before me, such as I imagine burst upon the enraptured vision of the wandering peri through the opening gates of paradise. [Renewed laughter.] There, there for the first time, my enchanted eye rested upon the ravishing word "Duluth."

* * * * *

If gentlemen will examine it, they will find Duluth not only in the centre of the map, but represented in the centre of a series of concentric circles one hundred miles apart, and some of them as much as four thousand miles in diameter, embracing alike in their tremendous sweep the fragrant savannas of the sunlit South and the eternal solitudes of snow that mantle the ice-bound North. [Laughter.] How these circles were produced is perhaps one of those primordial mysteries that the most skilful paleologist will never be able to explain. [Renewed laughter.] But the fact is, sir, Duluth is pre-eminently a central place, for I am told by gentlemen who have been so reckless of their own personal safety as to venture away into those awful regions where Duluth is supposed to be, that it is so exactly in the centre of the visible universe that the sky comes down at precisely the same distance all around it. [Roars of laughter.]

I find by reference to this map that Duluth is situated somewhere near the western end of Lake Superior, but as there is no dot or other mark indicating its exact location I am unable to say whether it is actually confined to any particular spot, or whether "it is just lying around there loose." [Renewed laughter.] I really cannot tell whether it is one of those ethereal creations of intellectual frostwork, more intangible than the rose-tinted clouds of a summer sunset; one of those airy exhalations of the speculator's brain, which I am told are ever flitting in the form of towns and cities along those lines of railroad, built with Government subsidies, luring the unwary settler as the mirage of the desert lures the famishing traveler on, and ever on, until it fades away in the darkening horizon, or whether it is a real, *bona fide,* substantial city, all "staked off," with the lots marked with their owners' names, like that proud commercial metropolis recently discovered on the desirable shores of San Domingo. [Laughter.] But, however that may be, I am satisfied Duluth is there, or thereabout, for I see it stated here on this map that it is exactly thirty-nine hundred and ninety miles from Liverpool [laughter]; though I have no doubt, for the sake of convenience, it will be moved back ten miles, so as to make the distance an even four thousand. [Renewed laughter.]

Then, sir, there is the climate of Duluth, unquestionably the most salubrious and delightful to be found anywhere on the Lord's earth. Now, I have always been under the impression, as I presume other gentlemen have, that in the region around Lake Superior it was cold enough for at least nine months in the year to freeze the smoke-stack off a locomotive. [Great laughter.] But I see it represented on this map that Duluth is situated exactly half way between the latitudes of Paris and Venice, so that gentlemen who have inhaled the exhilarating airs of the one or basked in the golden sunlight of the other may see at a glance that Duluth must be a place of untold delights [laughter], a terrestrial paradise, fanned by the balmy zephyrs of an eternal spring, clothed in the gorgeous sheen of ever-blooming flowers, and vocal with the silvery melody of nature's choicest songsters. [Laughter.] In fact, sir, since I have seen this map I have no doubt that Byron was vainly endeavoring to convey some faint conception of the delicious charms of Duluth when his poetic soul gushed forth in the rippling strains of that beautiful rhapsody—

> "Know ye the land of the cedar and vine,
> Where the flowers ever blossom, the beams ever shine;
> Where the light wings of Zephyr, oppressed with perfume,
> Wax faint o'er the gardens of Gul in her bloom;
> Where the citron and olive are fairest of fruit,
> And the voice of the nightingale never is mute;
> Where the tints of the earth and the hues of the sky,
> In color though varied, in beauty may vie?"

[Laughter.]

As to the commercial resources of Duluth, sir, they are simply illimitable and inexhaustible, as is shown by this map. I see it stated here that there is a vast scope of territory, embracing an area of over two million square miles, rich in every element of material wealth and commercial prosperity, all tributary to Duluth. Look at it, sir [pointing to the map]. Here are inexhaustible mines of gold, immeasurable veins of silver, impenetrable depths of boundless forest, vast coal-measures, wide, extended plains of richest pasturage, all, all embraced in this vast territory, which must, in the very nature of things, empty the untold treasures of its commerce into the lap of Duluth. [Laughter.]

Look at it, sir [pointing to the map], do not you see from these broad, brown lines drawn around this immense territory that the enterprising inhabitants of Duluth intend some day to inclose it all in one vast corral, so that its commerce will be bound to go there whether it would or not? [Great laughter.] And here, sir [still pointing to the map], I find within a convenient distance the Piegan Indians, which, of all the many accessories to the glory of Duluth, I consider by far the most inestimable. For, sir, I have been told that when the small-pox breaks out among the women and children of that famous tribe, as it sometimes does, they afford the finest subjects in the world for the strategical experiments of any enterprising military hero who desires to improve himself in the noble art of war [laughter]; especially for any valiant lieutenant general whose

> "Trenchant blade, Toledo trusty,
> For want of fighting has grown rusty,
> And eats into itself for lack
> Of somebody to hew and hack."

[Great laughter.]

The Arkansas Traveler

A LOST and bewildered Arkansas Traveler approaches the cabin of a Squatter, about forty years ago, in search of lodgings, and the following dialogue ensues:

From *The Arkansas Traveler*, B. S. Alford, Photographer, Little Rock, Arkansas. Entered according to Act of Congress, in the Year 1876, by B. S. ALFORD, LITTLE ROCK, ARK., in the Office of the Librarian of Congress, Washington, D. C.

COL. SANDY FAULKNER, the original "Arkansaw Traveler," was born in Georgetown, Scott county, Kentucky, March 3, 1803. He came to Arkansas in 1829, and settled in Chicot county on the Mississippi river, as a cotton planter. In 1839, Col. Faulkner, (with his father, the late Nicholas Faulkner, a Virginian by birth,) took up his residence in Little Rock where he died August 4, 1874, at the age of seventy-one years.

It is well known throughout the Northwest that Col. Faulkner was the original personator of the "Arkansaw Traveler"; it was his pride to be known as such. The story, it is said, was founded on a little incident which occurred in the campaign of 1840, when he made the tour of the state in company with the Hon. A. H. Sevier, Gov. Fulton, Chester Ashley and Gov. Yell. One day in the Boston mountains, the party approached a squatter's for information of the route, and Col. "Sandy" was made spokesman of the company, and it was upon his witty responses the tune and story were founded. On return to Little Rock, a grand banquet was given in the famous "bar room" which used to stand near the Anthony house, and Col. "Sandy" was called upon to play the tune and tell the story. Afterward it grew into popularity. When he subsequently went to New Orleans, the fame of the "Arkansas Traveler" had gone ahead of him, and at a banquet, amid clinking glasses and brilliant toasts, he was handed a violin by the then governor of Louisiana, and requested to favor them with the favorite Arkansas tune. At the old St. Charles hotel a special room was devoted to his use, bearing in gilt letters over the door, Arkansas Traveler.—B. S. A.

According to James R. Masterson, in *Tall Tales of Arkansaw* (1943), p. 359, the

DIALOGUE

Traveler.—Halloo, stranger.

Squatter.—Hello yourself.

T.—Can I get to stay all night with you?

S.—No, sir, you can't git to—

T.—Have you any spirits here?

S.—Lots uv 'em; Sal seen one last night by that ar ole hollar gum, and it nearly skeered her to death.

T.—You mistake my meaning; have you any liquor?

S.—Had some yesterday, but Ole Bose he got in and lapped all uv it out'n the pot.

T.—You don't understand; I don't mean pot liquor. I'm wet and cold and want some whisky. Have you got any?

S.—Oh, yes—I drunk the last this mornin.

T.—I'm hungary; havn't had a thing since morning; can't you give me something to eat?

S.—Hain't a durned thing in the house. Not a mouffull uv meat, nor a dust uv meal here.

T.—Well, can't you give my horse something?

S.—Got nothin' to feed him on.

T.—How far is it to the next house?

S.—Stranger! I don't know, I've never been thar.

T.—Well, do you know who lives here?

S.—Yes sir!

T.—As I'm so bold, then, what might your name be?

S.—It might be Dick, and it might be Tom; but it lacks right smart uv it.

T.—Sir! will you tell me where this road goes to?

S.—It's never gone any whar since I've lived here; it's always thar when I git up in the mornin'.

T.—Well, how far is it to where it forks?

S.—It don't fork at all; but it splits up like the devil.

T.—As I'm not likely to get to any other house to night, can't you let me sleep in yours; and I'll tie my horse to a tree, and do without anything to eat or drink?

Alford version, "in all except a few phrases, is identical with that dated between 1858 and 1860 [now unavailable]. Colonel Faulkner's connection with the earlier version we do not know. He may have given Washbourne a manuscript; he may have dictated to him; or Washbourne may have written down the dialogue from memory after hearing it recited (whether by Faulkner or by someone else). We do know that Colonel Faulkner was popularly regarded as the composer of the dialogue, and hence we can hardly doubt that he would have obtained a copy of the early printed version, even if Washbourne had published without his permission. In this copy he doubtless made marginal changes, or he may have embodied the changes in a separate manuscript, prepared with the printed copy before him. From one source or the other, we may presume, the version of 1876 was published."

S.—My house leaks. Thar's only one dry spot in it, and me and Sal sleeps on it. And that thar tree is the ole woman's persimmon; you can't tie to it, 'caze she don't want 'em shuk off. She 'lows to make beer out'n um.

T.—Why don't you finish covering your house and stop the leaks?

S.—It's been rainin' all day.

T.—Well, why don't you do it in dry weather?

S.—It don't leak then.

T.—As there seems to be nothing alive about your place but children, how do you do here anyhow?

S.—Putty well, I thank you, how do you do yourself?

T.—I mean what do you do for a living here?

S.—Keep tavern and sell whisky.

T.—Well, I told you I wanted some whisky.

S.—Stranger, I bought a bar'l more'n a week ago. You see, me and Sal went shars. After we got it here, we only had a bit betweenst us, and Sal she didn't want to use hern fust, nor me mine. You see I had a spiggin in one eend, and she in tother. So she takes a drink out'n my eend, and pays me the bit for it; then I'd take un out'n hern, and give her the bit. Well, we's getting long fust-rate, till Dick, durned skulking skunk, he born a hole on the bottom to suck at, and the next time I went to buy a drink, they wont none thar.

T.—I'm sorry your whisky's all gone; but, my friend, why don't you play the balance of that tune?

S.—It's got no balance to it.

T.—I mean you don't play the whole of it.

S.—Stranger, can you play the fiddul?

T.—Yes, a little, sometimes.

S.—You don't look like a fiddlur, but ef you think you can play any more onto that thar tune, you kin just try it.

(The traveler takes the fiddle and plays the whole of it.)

THE TURN OF THE TUNE.

S.—Stranger, tuck a half a duzen cheers and sot down. Sal, stir yourself round like a six-horse team in a mud hold. Go round in the hollar whar I killed that buck this mornin', cut off some of the best pieces, and fotch it and cook it for me and this gentleman, d'rectly. Raise up the board under the head of the bed, and get the ole black jug I hid from Dick, and gin us some whisky; I know thar's some left yit. Til, drive ole Bose out'n the bread-tray, then climb up in the loft, and git the rag that's got the sugar tied in it. Dick, carry the gentleman's hoss round under the shead, give him some fodder and corn; much as he kin eat.

Til.—Dad, they ain't knives enuff for to sot the table.

S.—Whar's big butch, little butch, ole case, cob-handle, granny's knife, and the one I handled yesterday! That's nuff to sot any gentleman's table, outer you've lost um. Durn me, stranger, ef you can't stay as long as you please, and I'll give you plenty to eat and to drink. Will you have coffey for supper?

T.—Yes, sir.

S.—I'll be hanged if you do, tho', we don't have nothin' that way here, but Grub Hyson,[1] and I reckon it's mighty good with sweetnin'. Play away, stranger, you kin sleep on the dry spot to-night.

T.—(After about two hours' fiddling.) My friend, can't you tell me about the road I'm to travel to-morrow?

S.—To-morrow! Stranger, you won't git out'n these diggins for six weeks. But when it gits so you kin start, you see that big sloo over thar? Well, you have to git crost that, then you take the road up the bank, and in about a mile you'll come to a two-acre-and-a-half corn-patch. The corn's mityly in the weeds, but you needn't mind that: jist ride on. About a mile and a half or two miles from thar, you'll cum to the damdest swamp you ever struck in all your travels; it's boggy enouff to mire a saddle-blanket. Thar's a fust rate road about six feet under thar.

T.—How am I to get at it?

S.—You can't git at it nary time, till the weather stiffens down sum. Well, about a mile beyant, you come to a place whar thar's no roads. You kin take the right hand ef you want to; you'll foller it a mile or so, and you'll find its run out; you'll then have to come back and try the left; when you git about two miles on that, you may know you're wrong, fur they ain't any road thar. You'll then think you're mity lucky ef you kin find the way back to my house, whar you kin cum and play on thata'r tune as long as you please.

---

[1] Sassafras tea.

"Change the Name of Arkansas? Hell, No!"

I [1]

MR. SPEAKER, You blue-bellied rascal! I have for the last thirty minutes been trying to get your attention, and each time I have caught your eye, you have wormed, twisted and squirmed like a dog with a flea in his hide, damn you!

Gentlemen, you may tear down the honored pictures from the halls of the United States Senate, desecrate the grave of George Washington, haul down the Stars and Stripes, curse the Goddess of Liberty, and knock down the tomb of U. S. Grant, but your crime would in no wise compare in enormity with what you propose to do when you would change the name of Arkansas! Change the name of Arkansas—hell-fire, no!

Compare the lily of the valley to the gorgeous sunrise; the discordant croak of the bull-frog to the melodious tones of a nightingale; the classic strains of Mozart to the bray of a Mexican mule; the puny arm of a Peruvian prince to the muscles of a Roman gladiator—but never change the name of Arkansas. Hell, no!

II [2]

The member arose, shook his head, looked fierce, rolled up his sleeves, pounded the table, and saying, "Hear me, gentlemen," waded in:

Mr. Speaker: The man who would CHANGE THE NAME OF ARKANSAS is the original iron-jawed, brass-mounted, copper-bellied corpse-maker from the wilds of the Ozarks! Sired by a hurricane, dammed by an earthquake, half-brother to the cholera, nearly related to the small-pox on his mother's side, he is the man they call Sudden Death and General

---

From *Folklore of Romantic Arkansas*, by Fred W. Allsopp, Volume II, pp. 87–90. Copyright, 1931, by the Grolier Society.

[1] There is a tradition that away back yonder—about the time when the Arkansaw Traveler story came into being—it was proposed to change the name of Arkansas by legislative enactment. Some say the question was actually introduced at a session of the Legislature, and that a member delivered a fiery speech on the subject. "Change the name of Arkansas? Hell, No!" he is supposed to have declared. The writer has been requested many times for a copy of that speech. Investigation fails to reveal any official record of such a deliverance, but it seems certain that there was some discussion of the matter, in or out of the halls of state, and the speech may have been delivered sub rosa at a committee meeting, or, more likely, in a bar-room. It has frequently been referred to at banquets and on other convivial occasions, always being described as a wickedly lurid gem. As often rehearsed by George Williams, a member of the Arkansas Legislature from Pulaski County, some 25 years ago, it went something like this, barring its unprintable profanity and obscenity.—F. W. A.

[2] Here is another version of what is supposed to have been the speech, delivered by Cassius M. Johnson, as printed in a pamphlet at Cleveland, Ohio. Printed by J. H. Philips, Cleveland, Ohio, no date.—F. W. A.

Desolation! Look at him! He takes nineteen alligators and a barrel of whiskey for breakfast, when he is in robust health; and a bushel of rattlesnakes and a dead body when he is ailing. He splits the everlasting rocks with his glance, and quenches the thunder when he speaks!

Change the name of Arkansas! Hell, no! stand back and give him room according to his strength. Blood's his natural drink! and the wails of the dying is music to his ears! Cast your eyes on the gentleman, and lay low and hold your breath, for he's 'bout to turn himself loose! He's the bloodiest son of a wild-cat that lives, who would change the name of Arkansas! Hold him down to earth, for he is a child of sin! Don't attempt to look at him with your naked eye, gentlemen; use smoked glass. The man who would change the name of Arkansaw, by gosh, would use the meridians of longitude and the parallels of latitude for a seine, and drag the Atlantic ocean for whales! He would scratch himself awake with the lightning, and purr himself asleep with the thunder! When he's cold, he would "bile" the Gulf of Mexico and bathe in it! When he's hot, he would fan himself with an equinoctial storm! When he's thirsty, he would reach up and suck a cloud dry like a sponge! When he's hungry, famine follows in his wake! You may put your hand on the sun's face, and make it night on the earth; bite a piece out of the moon, and hurry the seasons; shake yourself and rumble the mountains; but, sir, you will never change the name of Arkansaw!

The man who would change the name of Arkansaw, would massacre isolated communities as a pastime. He would destroy nationalities as a serious business! He would use the boundless vastness of the Great American Desert for his private grave-yard! He would attempt to extract sunshine from cucumbers! Hide the stars in a nail-keg, put the sky to soak in a gourd, hang the Arkansas River on a clothesline; unbuckle the belly-band of Time, and turn the sun and moon out to pasture; but you will never change the name of Arkansaw! The world will again pause and wonder at the audacity of the lop-eared, lantern-jawed, half-breed, half-born, whiskey-soaked hyena who has proposed to change the name of Arkansaw! He's just starting to climb the political banister, and wants to knock the hay-seed out of his hair, pull the splinters out of his feet, and push on and up to the governorship. *But change the name of Arkansaw, hell, no!*

From El Paso to San Antonio

After hanging around El Paso for a few days I bought a ticket over the Sunset Line to Alpine, Texas.

From *Bill Jones of Paradise Valley,* His Life and Adventures for Over Forty Years in The Great Southwest. He was a Pioneer in the Days of the Buffalo, The Wild Indian, The Oklahoma Boomer, The Cowboy and The Outlaw, by John J. Callison, pp. 281–289. Copyright, 1914, by J. J. Callison. Kingfisher, Oklahoma.

From El Paso to Alpine is one of the most desolate pieces of country I ever saw. There is absolutely nothing. The railroad has water cars standing at every siding for the Mexicans that work on the railroad. If anyone else wants a car of water it costs him from twenty to fifty dollars a car. The railroad over the mountains is so crooked that you can't tell in what direction you are going, or whether you are going straight up or down.

As I was riding along, looking out of the car window, I saw a lot of crows, or ravens, flying west. Everyone of them had a tin can or a little sack hung to its neck by a string. At one place where we stopped to let a train pass I saw a lot of ants going west. They were rigged up like a lot of Indians moving camp. At another place where we made a short stop I noticed a freight train standing on the side track. Lots of the passengers got out to rest themselves while we were looking at that freight train. We discovered that nearly every truck had a few tramps or hoboes on it. All were going west. We also saw several coyotes on the trucks going west. Each tramp had something to eat along with him. Someone threw a stale loaf of bread out of the car window. Then the coyotes and a bunch of hoboes had a fight over it. When the train started I looked out of the window and saw them still fighting over that piece of bread.

I asked an old Texan who happened to be in the car what made the crows and ravens carry the can and the little sacks? He said the country between San Antonio and El Paso was so poor that they had to carry along something to eat and drink. He also said that the ants had to do the same thing, and that was the reason why the coyotes rode the freight train.

I asked him why they were all going west. He said the crows, ravens, ants, and coyotes in New Mexico had more sense than to come to Texas. He said that as soon as they get their eyes opened they all left Texas. He said there were so many suckers coming to Texas from the North that an honest, hard-working, respectable ant or coyote could not make a living in Texas any more. He said that down in east Texas, in the pine woods, where he lived, they had quit trying to raise anything except goats and frogs. He said "Befo' de wah" they could raise a few Arkansaw hogs, until some man brought in a lot of goats and they ate up all the pine cones, as well as all the young trees and shrubs. Then a lot of men from Chicago, the location of which place might be in Oshkosh for all he knew, came to Ft. Worth and built a big slaughter house, the smell from which had killed all the fish in the Trinity River. Then Bill Bailey, Governor of Texas, and one of the owners of the Standard Oil Company, went to Washington and got Uncle Sam to let him have six million dollars to dig the Trinity River deep enough to allow a few sharks to come up the river as far as Dallas. He said that most all the sharks in Texas lived in the Gulf Coast country, with headquarters at Houston, and if they could get the snags pulled out of the river as far as Dallas the sharks could meet all the suckers from the North at Dallas. He said there were a big lot of men at Havana, Illinois, who do nothing else but hatch out thousands of fish every year, mostly of the sucker variety, who come to Texas to buy big farms, and that all the suckers do not come from Chicago, either. He said they come from every place except Kansas. The darn Kansas suckers have gotten too smart to swallow anything except a lot of barb wire whiskey. He said the only way you could catch a Kansas sucker was to put the cork on the hook. There was no use putting the cork on the line and the bait on the hook; you had to change things a little to get them to bite. He said there were so many Kansas people in the Texas Panhandle that the ticks were all coming farther south. He had a brother at Waco who wrote and told him that the ticks and boll weevils were so bad in the Brazos River Valley that the people could hardly live there any longer. He said the boll weevils would eat up the cotton in the summer and fall, and then in the winter they would all move to town and get in the hotels and boarding houses, so thick that a Dutchman from Chicago only lived a short time after staying at a hotel a few weeks. They just acted like an Iowa hog with the cholera; went to bed feeling fine and woke up the next morning dead as a mackerel. He said it was different with a tick. All you had to do to get rid of the ticks was to take a bath in crude coal oil once or twice a week. Or you could take a bath in that new tick remedy, called Car Sul, and the ticks would quit you and go on the hunt of another tenderfoot from the North.

About dark I got to Alpine. When I got off the train I thought everybody who lived in that town was at the depot to meet me. That is the way it looked to Willie. I had to shake hands with almost a dozen before I could get away to find a hotel.

I met one of the most crooked real estate agents in Alpine I ever saw in my life. He was so crooked that he could not sleep in a fence corner. He was so crooked that you could not tell by his tracks which way he was going. He had a barrel of snakes beat a country block. You could not tell by his city plot whether you were trying to buy a lot in Alpine or in a prairie dog town four miles out. He dug a well that was so crooked that the water ran out at both ends. He had to have his shoes made to order at the blacksmith shop in order to get a fit. He was the same old scout who found the way through Arkansaw for the most crooked railroad in the United States. He was the same man that discovered the hogs in Arkansaw that have hoofs like a mule. His writing was as crooked as the streets in El Paso. He said that in San Antonio, where he used to live, the streets are so crooked that he could not tell in what part of the town he lived, so the policeman had to take him home. He was so crooked that he had to put his hat on with a monkey wrench. He was so crooked that he could not go through a round house.

Liberty still survives. You can locate in Alpine if you wish to, but life is too short to stay there over a week. When I was in Alpine there was a water famine. but as far as I could see everybody had plenty to drink.

I noticed that the real estate agent always kept his fore finger close to a live trigger.

While I was in Alpine I noticed that the steam roller gang and the city street cleaning department were always working around the free lunch counter.

A guest at the Alpine Hotel broke his jawbone eating a spring chicken.

After a few days spent in the magic city I went to San Antonio. It is a fine farming country from Alpine to San Antonio—if you look at it with your eyes shut. But if you happen to open your eyes and look out of the car window it's not so good. I would advise you to travel through Texas by night, or keep your eyes shut, especially after you have been reading all the good things the real estate agents, hotel keepers and immigration agents have said about the State. Then you will not be disappointed.

San Antonio is said to be the glory spot of Texas, and from what I saw of it I think it is—not. I think Huntsville has San Antonio beat seven to one. Huntsville is where Sam Houston used to live. I think he is there yet. Most of the people in San Antonio, when I was there, were wearing soldiers' uniforms. I noticed a great many Northern people there. They all had coughs, "lungers" they call them in Texas. Most all of the hotels, boarding houses and rooming houses are full of "lungers." In reading over the Furnished Room for Rent advertisements I noticed that nearly all of them said "No sick." I asked a man what that meant, and he told me that those were the places that do not want to be bothered with sick people. I picked out a house that I thought would suit me, and as the advertisement said "No sick," I went to hunt it. When I rang the door bell a woman came to the door. I told her I wanted a room. She said she had one that would just suit me, and the price would be seven dollars a week. I asked her if that was not a little high for a room four by six on the first floor coming down. She said that was cheap, and that they always made a Dutchman from up North pay a double price. That was the only way they had to get pay for the "Niggers" the North took away from them.

I asked her how I would get my clothes off when I went into that room, and where I would set my suitcase. She said the last man who occupied the room took off his clothes in the alley and climbed up the fire escape when he went to bed. She said he left his suitcase out in the back yard close to the alley. I asked her if there were any sick people in the house. "Lord no," she responded, "I would not have any sick people in my house." To make a long story short, I rented the room. I asked her if she would give any of the money back if I only stayed a few days.

"No, you bet your life I won't. I will have to charge you extra if you do not stay a full week."

The first night I stayed there the boll weevils nearly ate me up. You see, a Texas hotel or rooming house never has such things as bed bugs or fleas in them. A state law of Texas says that the bed sheets shall be nine feet long. That keeps out every kind of a bug except the boll weevil.

After a boll weevil eats up the cotton crop, the cactus and the mesquite brush they take to the hotels and boarding houses for the winter.

A boll weevil will not bother a native Texas woman. That's why the Texas women use snuff—to keep away the boll weevil. A coyote won't eat a dead Mexican because the Mexican eats chili.

Some time in the night a man in the adjoining room commenced to cough. From the way he coughed, and the length of time he was at it, I thought he must have jarred the foundation of the house. Of course, there was no "lungers" in that house. After he quit, I had just gotten to sleep again when a woman in the other room adjoining mine began coughing, and I thought she would jar the windows out. Of course, there was no "lungers" in that house. When she quit, another one across the hall commenced, and I looked next morning to see if the roof was still there. "No sick" in that house. Then it dawned upon me why the land⋅ lady wanted to charge me extra if I did not stay a week.

Next morning she wanted to know what ailed me that I had come to San Antonio. I told her there was nothing particular the matter with me. She said she would have to know, as the health officers required her to make a report of all suspicious characters stopping at her house. This was done so the doctors and undertakers would know about what amount of business they could count on from each house in the town. I told her I had a very severe headache all the time; I was partly deaf; had a cataract in one eye; had a bad case of catarrh in my head; one of my arms was nearly shot off in the fight at Casas Grandes; I was suffering with mountain fever I had contracted in coming over the mountains from El Paso to Alpine. I said I was suffering with appendicitis; that I had rheumatism in my hips and knew that I had a very weak back; and I had to stay in bed about half the time on account of the gout I had caught in Kansas City; that I had eczema, doby itch and a few ticks that had gotten on me at Lipscomb. Then she wanted to know if I had been scalped by the Mexicans, as there was no hair on my head; also if I had a cork leg, as I limped when walking. She wanted to know if I had ever had smallpox and how long I had been doctoring for the asthma. She wanted to know how many times I had been in a bughouse; if I was a moderate or hard drinker; how many times I had been married and if my last wife was living; how long it had been since I was divorced, and how much of a reward was offered for me in the United States, Canada, Mexico or Arkansaw. She wanted to know if I was a republican, and if I expected to run for an office of any kind. She said that the last republican that ran for office in San Antonio got across the Rio Grande before daylight. She wanted to know if I really had a glass eye.

I tried to break in several times, but she cut in so fast that I saw there was no use. I just backed out of the door, ran around to the alley, reached over the fence, grabbed my old suitcase and lit out and hid in a box car for fear she would have me arrested for slipping off without paying extra. If I had stayed half a week the doctors would have gotten me, and if I had stayed the week out the undertakers would have gotten me, and that was the reason she wanted extra if I did not stay a week. They aim to get all you have in some way.

To be on the safe side, I just stayed in that old box car till I got to Houston. When I got up town I bought a "San Antonio Express" to see what they had to say about me. The only thing I could find that covered my case was a two-column piece about Teddy Roosevelt, "The Rough Rider," coming to San Antonio in disguise, meeting a lot of the boys and having a big time. It said that he got so bad that to keep from getting arrested he had gone down to the river and drowned himself; or at least he had made a complete get-away, like he did at San Juan Hill.

PART THREE

JESTERS

Amerikans luv caustic things; they would prefer turpentine to colone water, if they had to drink either. So with the relish of humour; they must hav it on the half-shell with cayenne. An Englishman wants his fun smothered deep in mint sauce, and he iz willing tew wait till next day before he tastes it. If yu tickle or convince an Amerikan yu have got tew do it quick. An Amerikan luvs to laff, but he don't luv to make a bizziness ov it; he works, eats, and hawhaws on a canter. I guess the English hav more wit, and the Amerikans mor3 humour. We havn't had time yet to bile down our humour and get the wit out ov it.

— Josh Billings

I. PRANKS AND TRICKS

*Of course all boys are not full of tricks, but the best of them are.
That is, those who are readiest to play innocent jokes, and who
are continually looking for chances to make Rome howl, are the
most apt to turn out to be first-class business men.*
> —George W. Peck

1. From Gibes to Sells

THE lore of "sells" (which, as Peck indicates, are only a step removed
from sales) centers in the Yankee peddler. As the "American Auto-
lycus," the Yankee has been the peddler not only of wares but also of wit
and wisdom—"Yankee notions" in the intellectual sense—to the nation. In
fact, as cracker-box philosopher, he has become a national type, from Seba
Smith to Will Rogers, much as Cousin Jonathan has become Brother
Jonathan or Uncle Sam.

During the last century the feud between the backwoodsman and the
Yankee peddler, who sold the other things he didn't want, assumed
the proportions of a comic contest of wits. As a butt of ridicule and the
victim of counterplots, the Yankee was penalized for his superior sagacity.
"You might as well try to hold a greased eel as a live Yankee." For Yankee
trickiness or slickness the name Sam Slick has become proverbial. The
original clockmaker of that name (who has had many namesakes) was
the creation of a Nova Scotia judge, T. C. Haliburton, and was in reality
half Yankee or down-easter and half ring-tailed roarer, by a curious blend
of rival traits.[1] Perhaps a truer embodiment of the Yankee spirit of sharp-
ness of wit and trade was P. T. Barnum, of whom one of his friends said:
"If he was shipwrecked and thrown on a desert island, he would try to sell
maps of the island to the inhabitants."[2]

Back of the similar libels of sheepherders are the feuds between cowmen
and sheepmen and, within the ranks of the latter, between herders and
shearers, old hands and new, and bosses and men. Comic feuds develop
in other occupations, with give and take of "hot ones," as between the
Texas and Mormon cowpunchers in "Shipping Out," where the joke about
the sheepherder who could only bleat is told in a goat variant.

2. Practical Jokes

In popular tradition the spirit of mischief and roguery has been em-
bodied in trickster heroes of varying degrees of innocence and malice—
Robin Goodfellow, Tyl Eulenspiegel, Reynard the Fox, and Brer Rabbit.
It has also inspired the countless pranks and tricks that are part of the

---

[1] See *Thomas Chandler Haliburton*, by V. L. O. Chittick (1924).
[2] *Here We Are Again*, by Robert Edmund Sherwood (1926), p. 191.

folkways and folk humor of everyday life, from the wild-goose chases and ridiculous deceptions of April Fool's Day [1] to what Governor Bob Taylor calls the "eternal war between the barefooted boy and the whole civilized world."

The apotheosis of the "bad boy" in American humor is Peck's Bad Boy.[2] George W. Peck saw no contradiction between the vagaries of the Bad Boy—"wide awake, full of vinegar"—and success in life, and in fact admitted the possibility of a correlation between toughness and smartness. The charm of the Bad Boy, as distinguished from such plaguy brats as the Katzenjammer Kids, lies not so much in pure deviltry as in ingenuity and gumption, the horse sense in his horseplay taking the form of sly, shrewd digs at grown-up frauds and shenanigans.

A modern, sophisticated, feminine counterpart of Peck's Bad Boy is Little Audrey (as she is generally known), whose rôle is that of a spectator at life's little tragedies rather than a perpetrator of mischief. The catastrophes, however, are in the nature of ironic tricks or pranks of fate; and Little Audrey has a trick of her own, that of just laughing and laughing, followed by an I-knew-it-all-the-time observation involving a pun or a surprise.

In backwoods, frontier, and small-town America practical jokes (ranging from the low comedy of badger fights and snipe hunts to pure orneriness) are similarly both a pastime and a means of getting along by hook or by crook. Together with fighting, drunkenness, blackguarding, boasting, and savage sports, horseplay and fool stunts afford relief from monotony, loneliness, and strain; an outlet for surplus energy and animal spirits; and an opportunity for exhibitionism. Western humorists have used the practical joke as a form of democratic attack on pretense and affectation. To realists and satirists village japes and monkeyshines are an expression of the sadistic or moronic in American life.[3]

The practicalness of a "practical joke" is said to consist in the fact that something is done rather than said. Such a joke differs from a mere gibe in that the butt of the joke is also its victim. Functionally, a practical joke is intended to take advantage of ignorance, in the person of the newcomer or the green hand, and as such is related, on the one hand, to the dislike of strangers, and, on the other, to the exploitation of the weak. From the point of view of the victim, practical jokes exemplify the gullibility of human nature.

Even verbal jests may partake of the nature of a practical joke when a whopper or a riddle ends with a "sell," which pulls the leg of the victim or leaves him holding the sack.

"There I was out in that prairie, not a tree or a bush in a thousand miles, and a bald-faced bull took after me. I run about fifty feet and climbed up a tall tree."

---

[1] In addition to such April Fool stunts as tying a string to a pocketbook left lying on the sidewalk and jerking it away from the victim who tries to pick it up, there are such time-honored gags as telephoning the zoo to ask for Mr. Wolf or Mr. Fox.

[2] According to G. W. Orians, *Peck's Bad Boy* was inspired by Thomas Bailey Aldrich's *The Story of a Bad Boy*. It will be observed, however, that Tom Bailey was a "good bad boy."

[3] See the stories of Ring Lardner, George Milburn, and Erskine Caldwell.

"Why. you —— liar, you said there was no trees or bushes in a thousand miles."

"There had to be one—just had to be one." [1]

Or the narrator gets himself cornered by hostile Indians or wild animals in order to elicit a query as to what happened to him and to permit the solemn announcement: "Why—then them damn redskins killed me," or "They got me."

Riddles often conceal a surprise which is akin to a sell. Lincoln liked to ask: " 'If three pigeons sit on a fence and you shoot and kill one of them, how many will be left?' . . . The answer was, 'Two, of course.' To which Lincoln responded, 'No, there won't, for the other two will fly away.' " [2]

Here, too, belong children's riddling tricks and catches, such as "Just like me," "I'm a gold lock," "Adam and Eve and Pinchme," [3] and arithmetical jokes like Barnum's.

In almost every occupation, part of the education or initiation of the new hand consists in sending him on fool's errands, usually in search of a mythical or impossible object, such as a left-handed monkey wrench, a bottle stretcher, a four-foot yard stick. or a sky-hook, or in otherwise exposing his ignorance ridiculously and perhaps painfully.

The youngest fellow on the works always had to take the "rawhiding," but I soon learned to hold my own. I was hired to work on "macaroni" farms, sent to buy "striped paint," but was not as bad as the fellow who looked all day in a mud puddle for a frog, because they needed it on the railroad. [4]

Greenhorns and tenderfeet are pranked by falsifying narratives and dialogs (often acted out in a little byplay) as well as by practical jokes. These recitals usually involve animals surrounded by mystery and terror, such as inhabit Paul Bunyan's woods. Yarns of "fearsome critters" have the double purpose of taking in the newcomer and entertaining the old-timers, and so belong to the kingdom of lies as well as of pranks. Sometimes the hazing narratives take the form of circular stories, or "long-winded tales that ingeniously held the listener's interest, but eventually disclosed that they had no point, making this disclosure sometimes by reverting to the starting-place and reiterating word for word." [5] In national parks and on Western ranches the hazing of "dudes" and tenderfeet has produced many classics among sells.

Besides "breaking in" new hands, practical jokes also serve the purpose of getting even with enemies or getting rid of intruders. Where the element of revenge is present, as in "Casting Anchor," the idea is to give "trick for

---

[1] *A Song of the Pipeline*, by Daniel M. Garrison, *Folk-Say, A Regional Miscellany: 1930*, edited by B. A. Botkin, p. 110. See "Mirages," Part Four.

[2] *Abraham Lincoln, The Prairie Years*, by Carl Sandburg (1926), Vol. II, p. 81.

[3] See "Tricks and Catches," Part Six.

[4] "Range Lore," by W. W. Adney, San Angelo, Texas. Manuscripts of Federal Writers' Project for the Works Progress Administration in the State of Texas.

[5] *The Cowboy*, by Philip Ashton Rollins (1922), p. 184. For an example of a conversational sell "in the way of a string of plausibly worded sentences that didn't mean anything under the sun," see "First Interview with Artemus Ward," in *Mark Twain's Sketches New and Old*, pp. 283-286.

trick." Where the presence of the victim is unwelcome, the aim is to frighten him away. In any case, as in love or war, all is what Davy Crockett calls "fairation" when one is dealing with a rival.

3. A Pretty Cute Little Stunt

The ruses of trade and swindling are more practical than practical jokes in that they are a means to an end—the end being gain—rather than an end in themselves. At the same time, many swindling dodges, such as selling a greenhorn gold bricks, the Brooklyn Bridge, Grant's Tomb, or the Woolworth Building, are hoaxes. The hoax differs from the ordinary prank in that it is played for greater stakes and before a larger audience. As a "deliberately concocted untruth, made to masquerade as truth," [1] the hoax differs also from true superstition or myth as deliberate falsification differs from erroneous observation or false inference. Yet in their fictitious build-up, hoaxes involve mythical elements and are "folklore in the making." In between the more elaborate hoaxes, like Barnum's Mermaid, which belong to history and journalism rather than to folklore, and the myth-making stunts involving freaks and monsters, such as sea serpents, petrified men, and "fearsome critters" of the hodag type, are the hoaxing, cheating tricks akin to practical jokes—the pretty cute little stunts by which one outsmarts a customer in a trade, whether it be selling or swapping.

Yankee Headwork

MOTHER always said I was the smartest baby that she ever see. I don't speak of this by way of bragging, but as I am writing a history to go before the world, I'm bound to be impartial. She says before I was a week old I showed that I was real grit, and could kick and scream two hours upon the stretch, and not seem to be the least bit tired that ever was. But I don't remember anything about this. The first I remember, I found myself one cold November day, when I was about six years old, bareheaded and barefoot, sliding on the ice. It had been a snapping cold night, and all the boys in the neighborhood, and most all the gals turned out and had a fine frolic that day, sliding and running on the pond. Most of the larger boys had shoes, but we little fellers that wan't big enough to wear shoes had to tuff it out as well as we could. I carried a great pine chip in my hand, and when my feet got so cold I couldn't stand it no longer, I'd put the chip down and stand on that a little while and warm 'em, and then at it to sliding again.

We used to have a school in Downingville about three months in the Winter season and two months in the Summer, and I went to the Winter

---

[1] *Hoaxes,* by Curtis D. MacDougall (1940), p. vi. Among the folkloric hoaxes treated by MacDougall are mythical monsters (the hodag), historical myths (Parson Weems' cherry tree myth), tall stories, and legendary heroes (Johnny Appleseed).

From *My Thirty Years Out of The Senate,* by Major Jack Downing (Seba Smith), pp. 25-26, 28-29. New York: Oaksmith & Company. 1859.

school three Winters, from the time I was twelve till I was fifteen. And
I was called about the best scholar of my age that there was in school.
But to be impartial, I must confess the praise didn't always belong to me,
for I used sometimes to work headwork a little in order to get the name
of being a smart scholar. One instance of it was in reading. I got along
in reading so well, that the master said I read better than some of the
boys that were considerable older than I, and that had been to school
a dozen Winters. But the way I managed it was this. There was cousin
Obediah was the best reader there was in school, and as clever a boy as
one in a thousand, only his father hadn't got no orchard. So I used to
carry a great apple to school in my pocket every day and give to him
to get him to set behind me when I was reading, where he could peak into
my book, and when I come to a hard word, have him whisper it to me,
and then I read it out loud. Well, one day I was reading along so, pretty
glib, and at last I come to a pesky great long crooked word, that I
couldn't make head nor tail to it. So I waited for Obediah. But it proved
to be a match for Obediah. He peaked, and squinted, and choked, and I
was catching my breath and waiting for him to speak; and at last he
found he could do nothing with it, and says he "skip it." The moment
I heard the sound I bawled out, *skip it*. "What's that?" said the master,
looking at me as queer as though he had catched a weazel asleep. I stopt
and looked at the word again, and poked my tongue out, and waited for
Obediah. Well, Obediah give me a hunch, and whispered again, "skip it."
Then I bawled out again, *skip it*. At that the master and about one-half
the scholars yaw-hawed right out. I couldn't stand that; and I dropt
the book and streaked it out of school, and pulled foot for home as fast
as I could go, and I never showed my head in school again from that day
to this. But for all that, I made out to pick up a pretty good education.
I got so I could read and spell like a fox, and could cypher as far as the
rule of three. And when I got to be about twenty years old, I was strongly
talked of one Winter for schoolmaster. But as a good many of the same
boys and gals would go to me, that were in the school when I read
"skip it," I didn't dare to venture it for fear there would be a sort of a
snickering among 'em whenever any of them come to a hard word.

A Yankee Pedlar

YES! I have laughed this morning, and that heartily, but I fear I shall
scarce be able to amuse you at second-hand with what depends altogether
on certain *un-writable* turns of countenance and manner. The hero of the
occasion was an old pedlar, who came jogging along in his hearse-shaped

From *The Americans at Home;* or, Byeways, Backwoods, and Prairies, edited by
the Author of "Sam Slick" (T. C. Haliburton), Vol. II, pp. 212–215. London:
Hurst and Blackett, Publishers. 1854.

cart, soon after breakfast, and before this dripping humour beset the weather. He stopped his cart on seeing several men at work, and it was not long before the laughter of the men, who usually pursue their business in solemn silence, drew my attention. The aspect of the pedlar secured it, for he was a personification of Momus. His face was very red, and of a most grotesque turn, and his nutcracker nose and chin were like nobody but Punch. His grey eyes twinkled through a pair of mock spectacles made of a strip of tin twisted into the requisite form and placed far down his nose, so that he was obliged to throw his head back in order to look through them. When I went to the window, he was enumerating the contents of his covered cart with a bewildering rapidity, but as soon as he observed me, he stopped short, pulled off the remains of an old straw hat, and made a very low bow in the style of Sir Pertinax, who thought the world was to be won by "booing."

"My dear beautiful lady," said he, "could I sell you anything this morning? I sell things for nothing, and I've got most everything you ever heard tell on. Here's fashionable calicoes,"—holding up a piece of bright scarlet,—"splendid French work collars and capes,"—and here he displayed some hideous things, the flowers on which were distinctly traceable from where I stood,—"elegant milk pans, and Harrison skimmers, and *ne plus ultry* dippers! patent pills, cure anything you like—ague bitters— Shaker yarbs—essences, winter green, peppermint, lobely—tapes, pins, needles, hooks and eyes—broaches and brasslets—smelling bottles—castor ile—corn-plaster—mustard—garding seeds—silver spoons—pocket combs —tea pots—green tea—saleratus—tracts, songbooks—thimbles—babies' whistles—copybooks, slates, playin' cards—puddin' sticks—butter-prints —baskets—wooden bowls—"

"Any wooden nutmegs, daddy?" said one of the men.

"No, but as I come past I see your father a turnin' some out o' that piece o' lignum vitae you got him last week," said the pedlar quietly; then turning again to the window—"Can I suit you today, ma'am? I've all sorts o' notions—powder and shot, (but I s'pose you do all your shootin' at home), but may be your old man goes a gunnin'—I shan't offer you lucifers, for ladies with sich eyes never buys matches,—but you can't ask me for any thing I haven't got, I guess."

While I was considering my wants, one of the men must try a fall with this professed wit.

"Any goose-yokes, mister?" said he.

"I'm afraid I've sold the last, sir; there is so many wanted in this section of the country. But I'll take your measure, and fetch you a supply next time I come along." This of course produced a laugh.

"Well! I want a pair o' boots, any how," said the prostrate hero, rallying, to show that he was not discomforted. "These here old ones o' mine lets in gravel, but won't let it out again. If you've got any to fit me, I'll look at 'em." And thus saying he stretched out a leg of curious wire-drawn appearance. "Any to fit, old boss?"

"Fit you like a whistle, sir," said the pedlar, fumbling among his wares, and at length drawing forth a pair of *candle moulds,* much to the amusement of the bystanders.

The rain which had begun to fall now cut short our conference. I bought a few trifles, and the pedlar received his pay with a bow which was almost a salaam. Mounting his blue hearse, he drove off in triumph, not minding the rain, from which he was completely sheltered by a screen of boughs fitted in the sides of his wagon, and meeting over his head,—a protection against sun and rain which I much admired.

"Sheepmen" in Montana

TALKING about sheepmen reminds me of Joe, the big bronco-buster, and his *mot.* I was doing the town with Joe, and he was carefully educating me in all the Western mysteries. He told me about "day-wranglers" and "night-hawks" and "war-bags" and "round-ups"; showed me how to tie a "bull-noose" and a "sheep-shank" and a "Mexican hackamore"; put me onto the twist-of-the-wrist and the quick arm-thrust that puts half-hitches 'round a steer's legs; showed me how a cowboy makes dance music with a broom and a mouth-harp—and many other wonderful feats, none of which I can myself perform.

I wanted to feel the mettle of the big typical fellow, and so I said playfully: "Say, Joe, come to confession—you're a sheepman, now, aren't you?"

He clanked down a glass of long-range liquid and glared down at me with a monitory forefinger pointing straight between my eyes: "Now, you look here, Shorty," he drawled; "you're a friend of mine, and whatever you say *goes,* as long as I ain't all caved in! But you cut that out, and don't you say that out loud again, or you and me'll be having to scrap the whole outfit!"

He resumed his glass. I told him, still playfully, that a lot of mighty good poetry had been written about sheep and sheepmen and crooks and lambs and things like that, and that I considered my question complimentary.

"You're talkin' about sheepmen in the old country, Shorty," he drawled. "There ain't any cattle ranges there, you know. Do you know the difference between a sheepman in Scotland, say, and in Montana?"

I did not.

"Well," he proceeded, "over in Scotland, when a feller sees a sheepman coming down the road with his sheep, he says: 'Behold the gentle shepherd with his fleecy flock!' That's poetry. Now, in Montana, that same feller says, when he sees the same feller coming over a ridge with the same sheep:

From *The River and I,* by John G. Neihardt, pp. 88–92. Copyright, 1910, by John G. Neihardt. New York and London: G. P. Putnam's Sons.

Look at that crazy blankety-blank with his woolies!' 'That's fact. You mind what I say, or you'll get spurred."

A Sheep Herder from Yale

REED & CASHION and other sheepmen come down here into Happy Valley every spring to lamb and shear—the sheep, I mean, not Reed & Cashion or the sheepmen; also to eat up all of Mrs. Peck's cow feed and help out some of the poor people around Wenden, the side track 5 miles up the line from Salome, the Mining Metropolis.

Algernon McGoogle—"Hotfoot Mac" they called him at Yale, on account of his sprinting ability—also came out here this spring, on account of his health, having exercised too much in his BVD's while training to beat the 100 yard record, and taken a bad cold, which settled on his lungs, so the doctors ordered Arizona and outdoor life for Mac. Mac had lived all his life in the city and Happy Valley, Arizona was a new experience to him.

Mac landed in Happy Valley soon after the sheep—and he has been after them most of the time since, he says. Reed was short of herders and Mac was short of cash, and Scotch by descent, so Mac was soon hired to herd a band of about 2,000 ba ba's. It is customary to herd the sheep around the desert among the greasewood and sage brush during the day, bringing them back to the corrals at night on account of the coyotes.

Mac was started out the first morning with his band and instructed to wander along slowly towards a little butte several miles away, letting the sheep feed as they went along, and to start back towards camp so as to get in before dark. "Try and get them back here by five o'clock," Reed called to him as he left, "and don't let any of the lambs get away from the band," he added jokingly, as there were no lambs in the band and the ewes were not due to lamb for several weeks yet.

The sheep and Mac soon disappeared in the brush and nothing more was thought of them until supper time came and no sign of Mac or the sheep. Reed commenced to worry, about the sheep, and about seven o'clock was about to start out looking for them when Mac at last came driving them up through the brush into the corral and, after shutting them in, came up to the chuck tent, streaked with dust and perspiration and, from all appearances, tired out. Before Reed could say anything, Mac burst out:

"Boss," he said, "I'm through. They thought back east that I was a foot racer, but I'm not. Almost any sheep herder that can herd that band for a week and not lose those lambs can beat all the world's records. I didn't lose any today and I ran every one of those damn lambs back into the band every time they tried to get away, but one day is enough for me.

From *Salome Sun*, Vol. 3, No. 2, February, 1922. Dick Wick Hall, Editor and Miner. Salome, Arizona.

I'm all in, but they are all there. Go and count them up and then give me my time. I'm done."

Reed, knowing that there were no lambs in the band and that none of the ewes could have lambed yet, went down to the corral to investigate and, off, in one corner, huddled up by themselves, he counted 47 jackrabbits and 16 cottontails.

"A Sheepman Ain't Got No Friends"

"A SHEEP shearer is a sheep herder with his brains knocked out." Something tells me that this definition, current in the sheep country, originated with a sheep herder rather than a sheep shearer. Certainly I never heard a shearer quote it or subscribe to it, but, as a herder, I could much more easily believe it than I could the reverse saying, which is also sometimes heard.

Another libel is to the effect that the omnipresent bleating of the sheep combined with the total absence of human speech so works on the herder's very limited intelligence that he soon forgets human speech entirely and adopts instead the language of his charges. In proof of this there is told the story of the traveling man who took a seat in a crowded train beside an old sheep herder, and by way of breaking the conversational ice asked him where he was from. "Montanaa-aa-aa-aa," replied the herder with the general intonation of a ewe calling her long-lost lamb. "Where are you going?" was the next question. "Baa-aa-aack," bleated the herder, and the traveling man, hastily pulling down his trousers to cover his wool socks, sought a seat in another car.

Then there was the herder who fell foul of the law, and since it was an open and shut case his lawyer advised him that his only chance lay in feigning a touch of herder's complaint and answering every question with a plaintive blat. Like a wise client the herder followed his lawyer's instructions, and was forthwith discharged as incompetent, irresponsible, and a total intellectual loss. Outside in the corridor his lawyer congratulated him on beating the case and then said, "Now how about my fee?" "Baa-aa-aa," answered the herder.

"A sheepman ain't got no friends" is the customary complaint of the flock owner. To this the classic retort is, "A sheepman don't want no friends." In other words, the farther away a sheepman's neighbors are, the more grass he has for his stock. Besides, it is often easier to be on good terms with someone at a distance whose interests do not in any way conflict with yours than it is with your neighbor whose lands may join

From *Sheep*, by Archer B. Gilfillan, pp. 130, 152–153, 159–160, 161–162. Copyright, 1928, 1929, by Archer B. Gilfillan. Boston: Little, Brown & Company.

yours for miles. If distance alone is enough to make friends, we all ought to be friendly in this part of the country where the population is less than two to the square mile and where, in spite of the one crop that never fails, there are fewer people than there were ten years ago. The ranch on which I work, one of average size, comprises about nineteen square miles, which would seem to give plenty of elbow room. Size, however, is only relative. Several years ago the boss was talking with the representative of a sheep company out in Montana. This man said that they had been dried out the previous year and had run short of range, and so had had to lease six additional townships. A township is thirty-six square miles.

Sometimes a herder's difficulties are the fault of the sheepman. A new herder beginning work on a certain ranch asked his boss where the lines were. "Oh!" said the sheepman, making large and expansive gestures, "herd anywhere you like. It's all my range." The trustful herder set out with the sheep, but every time he crossed a boundary line someone popped up, and if he wasn't the owner, then the land belonged to his brother or his aunt or his grandmother, and he had been especially commissioned to keep any and all sheep off it. That night the new herder tendered his resignation, to take effect at once.

Sometimes the shoe is on the other foot. A certain sheepman, hiring a herder with a reputation for quarrelsomeness, warned him before he went out to the wagon to begin work, "You can get into all the fights you want to, and you can get out of them yourself."

Shipping Out

THEY were a great bunch of rough-joshers, these cowboys; and the butts of many a joke were Bishop and Kinch, the Mormons. Or at least the boys claimed they were Mormons—Jack Mormons, anyway. Mormons when they were at home, and something else out on the range. They were always feeling of Bob's red head, upon which they professed to find "bishop's horns," sure sign he was going to be a bishop of the Church and have at least four wives.

"Aw," he would say, "you boys are jealous." And come back with some joke of his own, with many allusions to Bugscuffle, Texas. This was a legendary town, to which they referred all big liars; and from there they would proceed to Ticklegrass Canyon, another liar's paradise.

"Oh, he's from Bugscuffle," they would say; and the man whose veracity had been questioned would answer back:

From *Texas Cowboys*, by Dane Coolidge, pp. 145–151. Copyright, 1937, by Dane Coolidge. New York: E. P. Dutton & Co., Inc.

"No, suh! I come from that big, black canyon, away over on the other side."

"Oh, you mean Ticklegrass Canyon. I was through there once, and the grass had drifted in until it was a hundred feet deep. Never did git all them stickers out of my clothes—but what was *you* doing there?"

"That's just what the sheriff wanted to know, when he finally caught up with me. He was riding the best hawse in the country, barring one, and he made it from where we started in eighteen hours and twenty-two minutes. I made it in eighteen flat."

There were a thousand other jokes about men who had beat the sheriff to the line, and many more sly remarks about how come they had stolen that horse.

"I was walking along one day when I see a nice new rope in the road, and I says to myself:

" 'I'd better pick that up and take it along or some son-of-a-goat might *steal* it.'

"Well, suh, believe it or not, when I got back home there was a hawse on the other end of it. Now I knowed them ornery neighbors of mine wouldn't believe that that was an accident, so I stepped up on the hawse and come out to New Mexico."

But sooner or later they would get back to the Mormons, until Bishop Greenhouse pulled a good one that finally shut them up. It went off something like this.

"Mighty funny about these Tee-hannos," he observed. "They say, back in Texas, when a man gits where he can count fifty they set him to teaching school—and when he can count a hundred he gits onto himself and leaves the cussed country. Ordinary folks kin only count to twenty—ten fingers and ten toes, like an Injun. It's sure a fine country to come away from."

He glanced over at Kinch Talley who nodded, not being much on talk, and Buck Buchanan took up the cudgels for Texas.

"They tell me, Bob," he said, "that them Mormons down on the river can't talk no more—jest git along by signs and a kind of sheep-blat they have."

"Nope," answered Greenhouse, "they is such people, but don't live along the Heely. Them fellers you're thinking of is in the goat business. They don't say *baaa* like a sheep; they go *maaa* like a goat. I've heeard tell of them, too. It seems they don't wear no pants—nothing but shirts—and when they have a dance the gals have to tie a red rag on their big toe, so they can tell 'em apart. They live on them goat ranches, back in Western Texas."

He paused and looked about triumphantly, but only Kinch Talley laughed.

"I was driving a bunch of strays through that Mormon country," explained Buck Buchanan. "That's where I got the idee. That's a great country, ain't it Bishop? Lots of houses, too. I remember I stopped one time at a street crossing, and there was houses on all four corners. They was a lot of kids playing around, and I asked one of them whose houses they were, and he says:

" 'My father's.'

" 'How come your father has so many?' I says. 'Does he rent 'em?'

" 'No sir,' the kid says, 'he lives in 'em. Don't you know him? He's the bishop!' "

There was a roar of laughter at this unkind jest, but Bishop had become accustomed to it.

"Aw, you're jest jealous," he grunted, and let them holler awhile, until he finally got back the lead.

"That's one thing you'll never find around a Mormon town," he said, "you'll never find no Texicans. Of course a Mormon has to work, and that bars most of them at the start. But I don't know, seems like the first settlers took a prejudice agin' 'em. I remember my old man telling how it come that way. Course they must be mistaken, but the Mormons think a Texan ain't got no sense.

"The Mormons was the first people to settle along the Heely, and my grandpaw was one of the leaders. He killed a lot of Injuns, believe me! But one day, when he was gitting kind of old and feeble-like, he got a notion into his head that he wanted a squirrel-skin, and so he called in my father and said:

" 'Son, you take your rifle and ride up on the peaks and git me a gray tree-squirrel; and be careful not to shoot him in the head, because I want the brains to tan the skin with.'

"So my father he went up in the pines and hunted around; but the only gray squirrel he could find was sticking his head over a limb, and rather than not git nothing he shot him anyhow. Well, he brought it back and said to the old man:

" 'I'm mighty sorry, Dad. The squirrels was awful scarce and, rather than not git any, I had to shoot this one through the head.'

" 'Oh, that's all right,' the old man says. 'You got a nice skin, anyway, and I reckon we can fix it somehow. I tell you what you do! They's a bunch of Texans camped down on the lower water—you go down and kill one of them, and mebby we can use *his* brains.' "

Greenhouse paused and looked around with squinched-up, twinkling eyes; and at last Buck Buchanan broke the silence.

"Well," he demanded roughly, "what's the joke?"

"Well, sir," ran on the Bishop, "you wouldn't hardly believe it, but my old man told me he had to kill six of them Texicans to git brains enough to tan that squirrel-skin! That's why they won't take 'em into the Church!"

There was a near-riot after that; but the Texans, like Bishop, were accustomed to taking hot ones, and they were giving off at the head mightily when we took the long trail for the Gila River and Bylas, where we were due to ship the beef-herd.

His Pa Plays Jokes

A man shouldn't get mad at a joke—The magic bouquet—The grocery man
takes a turn—His Pa tries the bouquet at church—One for the old maid—
A fight ensues—The bad boy threatens the grocery man—-A compromise

"SAY, do you think a little practical joke does any hurt?" asked the bad
boy of the grocery man, as he came in with his Sunday suit on, and a
bouquet in his buttonhole, and pried off a couple of figs from a new box
that had been just opened.

"No sir," said the grocery man, as he licked off the syrup that dripped
from a quart measure, from which he had been filling a jug. "I hold that
a man who gets mad at a practical joke, that is, one that does not injure
him, is a fool, and he ought to be shunned by all decent people. That's
a nice bouquet you have in your coat. What is it, pansies? Let me smell
of it," and the grocery man bent over in front of the boy to take a whiff
at the bouquet. As he did so a stream of water shot out of the innocent
looking bouquet and struck him full in the face, and run down over his
shirt, and the grocery man yelled murder, and fell over a barrel of axe
helves and scythe snaths, and then groped around for a towel to wipe his
face.

"You condemn skunk," said the grocery man to the boy, as he took
up an axe helve and started for him, "what kind of a golblasted squirt gun
have you got there. I will maul you, by thunder," and he rolled up his
shirt sleeves.

"There, keep your temper. I took a test vote of you on the subject of
practical jokes, before the machine began to play upon the conflagration
that was raging on your whiskey nose, and you said that a man who
would get mad at a joke was a fool, and now I know it. Here let me show
it to you. There is a rubber hose runs from the bouquet, inside my coat to
my pants pocket, and there is a bulb of rubber, that holds about half
a pint, and when a feller smells of the posey, I squeeze the bulb, and you
see the result. It's fun, where you don't squirt it on a person that gets
mad."

The grocery man said he would give the boy half a pound of figs if he
would lend the bouquet to him for half an hour, to play it on a customer,
and the boy fixed it on the grocery man, and turned the nozzle so it
would squirt right back into the grocery man's face. He tried it on the
first customer that came in, and got it right in his own face, and then
the bulb in his pants pocket got to leaking, and the rest of the water ran
down the grocery man's trousers' leg, and he gave it up in disgust, and
handed it back to the boy.

"How was it your Pa had to be carried home from the sociable in a

From *Peck's Bad Boy and His Pa*, by George W. Peck, first and only complete
edition, pp. 210-215. Chicago: W. B. Conkey Co. 1893.

hack the other night?" asked the grocery man, as he stood close to the stove so his pants leg would dry. "He has not got to drinking again, has he?"

"O, no," said the boy, as he filled the bulb with vinegar, to practice on his chum. "It was this bouquet that got Pa into the trouble. You see I got Pa to smell of it, and I just filled him chuck full of water. He got mad and called me all kinds of names, and said I was no good on earth, and I would fetch up in state's prison, and then he wanted to borrow it to wear to the sociable. He said he would have more fun than you could shake a stick at, and I asked him if he didn't think he would fetch up in state's prison, and he said it was different with a man. He said when a man played a joke there was a certain dignity about it that was lacking in a boy. So I lent it to him, and we all went to the sociable in the basement of the church. I never see Pa more kitteny than he was that night. He filled the bulb with ice water, and the first one he got to smell of his button-hole bouquet was an old maid who thinks Pa is a heathen, but she likes to be made something of by anybody that wears pants, and when Pa sidled up to her and began talking about what a great work the christian wimmen of the land were doing in educating the heathen, she felt real good, and then she noticed Pa's posey in his button-hole and she touched it, and then she reached over her beak to smell of it. Pa he squeezed the bulb, and about half a teacupful of water struck her right in the nose, and some went into her strangle place, and O, my, didn't she yell. The sisters gathered around her and they said her face was all covered with perspiration and the paint was coming off, and they took her in the kitchen, and she told them Pa had slapped her with a dish of ice cream, and the wimmin told the minister and the deacons, and they went to Pa for an explanation, and Pa told them it was not so, and the minister got interested and got near Pa, and Pa let the water go at him, and hit him in the eye, and then a deacon got a dose, and Pa laughed; and then the minister who used to go to college, and be a hazer, and box, he got mad and squared off and hit Pa three times right by the eye, and one of the deacons kicked Pa, and Pa got mad and said he could clean out the whole shebang, and began to pull off his coat, when they bundled him out doors, and Ma got mad to see Pa abused, and she left the sociable, and I had to stay and eat ice cream and things for the whole family. Pa says that settles it with him. He says they haven't got any more christian charity in that church than they have in a tannery. His eyes are just getting over being black from the sparring lessons, and now he has got to go through oysters and beefsteak cure again. He says it is all owing to me."

"Well, what has all this got to do with your putting up signs in front of my store, 'Rotten Eggs,' and 'Frowy Butter a specialty,'" said the grocery man as he took the boy by the ear and pulled him around. "You have got an idea you are smart, and I want you to keep away from here. The next time I catch you in here I shall call the police and have you pulled. Now git!"

The boy pulled his ear back on the side of his head where it belonged, took out a cigarette and lit it, and after puffing smoke in the face of the grocery cat that was sleeping on the cover to the sugar barrel he said:

"If I was a provision pirate that never sold anything but what was spoiled so it couldn't be sold in a first-class store, who cheated in weights and measures, who bought only wormy figs and decayed cod-fish, who got his butter from a fat rendering establishment, his cider from a vinegar factory, and his sugar from a glucose factory, I would not insult the son of one of the finest families. Why, sir, I could go out on the corner, and when I saw customers coming here, I could tell a story that would turn their stomachs, and send them to the grocery on the next corner. Suppose I should tell them that the cat sleeps in the dried apple barrel, that the mice made nests in the prune box, and rats run riot through the raisins, and that you never wash your hands except on Decoration day and Christmas, that you wipe your nose on your shirt sleeves, and that you have the itch, do you think your business would be improved? Suppose I should tell customers that you buy sour kraut of a wooden-shoed Polacker, who makes it of pieces of cabbage that he gets by gathering swill, and sells that stuff to respectable people, could you pay your rent? If I should tell them that you put lozengers in the collection plate at church, and charge the minister forty cents a pound for oleomargarine, you would have to close up. Old man, I am onto you, and now you apologize for pulling my ear."

The grocery man turned pale during the recital, and finally said the bad boy was one of the best little fellows in this town, and the boy went out and hung up a sign in front: Girl wanted to cook.

The Adventures of Little Audrey

LITTLE AUDREY is a folk-lore character about whom thousands of nonsensical short tales—during the past five or six years—have been told. Sometimes Little Audrey parades as Little Emma or Little Gertrude, but she usually is recognizable by a catch phrase—"she just laughed and laughed." The amusing incident is typically a catastrophe. Little Audrey sees the humor in any situation.

A nice thing about Little Audrey is her integrity. She is no hypocrite; she does what she wants to do, says what she wants to say, and makes no bones about it. Little Audrey will never have inhibitions. Further, she is a very modern girl. She is having new adventures constantly, as indicated by the puns on floating power automobiles and the carioca dance steps. To her, irony predominates over sentiment. She has few illusions.

Little Audrey is nation-wide in distribution. In Texas she is well-known,

By Cornelia Chambers. From *Straight Texas*, Publications of the Texas Folk-Lore Society, Number XIII, 1937, edited by J. Frank Dobie and Mody C. Boatright, pp. 106–110. Copyright, 1937, by the Texas Folk-Lore Society. Austin.

particularly in universities and high schools. Approximately one out of ten students is a Little Audrey fan with a number of her adventures tucked away in his mind. The following are some of the stories known and collected by the author.

Little Audrey and her papa were out riding one day in their new streamlined car. Papa was proud of the car, and he was giving it the gas; he wanted to see how much it would make. All of a sudden the road turned, but papa did not; he went straight on and into the lake. Little Audrey saw what was going to happen, and she just laughed and laughed. She knew all of the time that their car had floating power.

Once upon a time all the children in Little Audrey's neighborhood were taking lessons. It was the proper thing to do; if you did not take lessons, you simply were not in the social swim. So Little Audrey cried and cried, 'cause she was not taking lessons.

After a while her mama said, "Little Audrey, if you will just stop that bawling, I'll let you take lessons." That made Little Audrey awful happy; so she sat down to think about what kind of lessons she would take. Well, after a long time she decided to take parachute lessons. So Little Audrey practiced and practiced, and after a while it was time to give her recital; you know if you take lessons you just have to give recitals.

Well, people came from far and near to see Little Audrey parachute jump. She went way up high in the airplane and got ready to jump. She looked down and saw all those people watching her, and then she jumped out. On her way down she just laughed and laughed, 'cause she knew she was going to fool those people; she didn't have on her parachute.

Once upon a time Little Audrey got lost on a desert island. Along came a big bunch of black cannibals and kidnapped her. They tied her up to a tree and started their pot to boiling. Little Audrey knew they were going to make stew out of her; so she looked around at those lean, hungry cannibals and counted them. There were nineteen. Little Audrey just laughed and laughed, 'cause she knew she was not big enough to make enough stew to go around.

One day Little Audrey and her mother went for a walk in the forest where some lumbermen were felling trees. Just as they came along, the men cut down a big oak, and it fell right on mother! Little Audrey just laughed and laughed, 'cause she knew all the time that Mother couldn't carioca.

That night Little Audrey and her mama and papa and her little brunette sister were sitting at the dinner table. Papa said, "Little Audrey, pass the cream, please." So Little Audrey passed the cream to her papa, and he poured some into his coffee. Then he put the pitcher down, and Little Audrey noticed that right on the tip end of the spout there was a little drop of cream all ready to fall. Little Audrey just laughed and laughed, 'cause she knew all the time that the little cream pitcher couldn't go *sniff, sniff*.

One day Little Audrey was standing on the corner just a-crying and a-crying, when along comes a cop, who said, "Little Audrey, why are you crying?" And Little Audrey said, "Oh, I've lost my papa!" The cop said, "Why, Little Audrey, I wouldn't cry about that. There's your papa right across the street leaning against that bank building." Little Audrey was overjoyed; without even looking at the traffic she started across the street. Along came a big two-ton truck that ran over Little Audrey and killed her dead. The cop just laughed and laughed. He knew all the time that that was not Little Audrey's papa leaning against the bank building.

One time Little Audrey and her little brother were inspecting a ship. They went over it from top to bottom, and then little brother decided he wanted to go way up high to the crow's nest. Little Audrey told him he better not go, but he was awful hard-headed; so up he went. When he got up there he waved to Little Audrey, lost his balance, and came tumbling down. Little Audrey looked at the remains and just laughed and laughed, 'cause she knew all the time that her brother just could not stand hard ships.

One time Little Audrey took her grandpa out walking. Little Audrey got awful hot; so she said, "Grandpa, let's go down to the old swimming hole and take a swim." But grandpa didn't much want to, 'cause he was blind. But Little Audrey begged and begged, and finally grandpa agreed to go. So they went down to the old swimming hole and put on their bathing suits. There was a big tree, growing out over the water, that the kids used as a diving board. Little Audrey told her grandpa to climb up the tree and dive off. But he didn't want to; so Little Audrey had to make him. When he jumped off, Little Audrey just laughed and laughed. She knew all the time that the swimming hole had dried up.

Little Audrey's brother was a jailbird. One time when he was up for three years he broke out of jail. The sheriff looked and looked for him, but he couldn't find him anywhere. After about a month the sheriff decided to put the bloodhounds on the trail. And that made Little Audrey just laugh and laugh, 'cause she knew all the time that her brother was anemic.

One day Little Audrey and her mother were driving along when all of a sudden the car door flew open and Little Audrey's mother fell out. Little Audrey just laughed and laughed, 'cause she knew all the time that her mother had on her light fall suit.

The nurse was going to take Little Audrey out for a walk; but the nurse was absent-minded, and she forgot until she was outside to take Little Audrey with her. So she called up to the cook and said, "Cook, throw Little Audrey out the window, and I'll catch her on the second bounce." The cook threw Little Audrey out the window and then she just laughed and laughed. She knew all the time that Little Audrey was not a rubber ball.

One day Little Audrey's mama went to town, and while she was gone Little Audrey decided to bake a cake, 'cause she wanted to show her mama how smart she was. She got down the recipe book and mixed the cake according to directions. She sifted the flour, creamed the butter and sugar, beat the eggs, and stirred the ingredients together. Then she was ready to cook the cake; so she looked at the recipe book and it said: "Now set in the oven for thirty minutes." So Little Audrey crawled into the oven and closed the door.

By and by Little Audrey's mama came home. She looked everywhere for Little Audrey, but she couldn't find her. All of a sudden she smelled something burning. She opened the oven door, and there was Little Audrey, burned to a crisp. Her mother just laughed and laughed. She didn't know that Little Audrey could read.

The next day Little Audrey and her grandma were standing on their front porch watching the men pave their street. There was a cement mixer, a steam roller, and all kinds of things to watch. All of a sudden grandma saw a quarter out there right in the middle of the street. She dashed right out to get it, but just as she picked it up along came that old steam roller and rolled her out flatter than a sheet of theme paper. Little Audrey just laughed and laughed, 'cause she knew all the time it was only a dime.

One day Little Audrey was playing with matches. Mama said, "Ummm, you better not do that." But Little Audrey was awful hard-headed; she kept right on playing with matches, and after a while she set the house on fire, and it burned right down to the ground. Mama and Little Audrey were looking at the ashes, and mama said, "Uh huh, I told you so! Now, young lady, just wait until your papa comes home. You certainly will catch it!" Little Audrey just laughed and laughed. She knew all the time that papa had come home an hour early and had gone to bed to take a nap.

The next night Little Audrey and her date were sitting on the sofa when all of a sudden the lights went out. "Oh," said Little Audrey's boy friend, "it sure is dark in here. I can't even see my hand in front of me." Little Audrey just laughed and laughed, 'cause she knew all the time that his hand wasn't in front of him.

Arithmetical Jokes

ONE night, after the performances were over, a dozen or more jovial fellows, with Old Turner and myself, were enjoying ourselves in the sitting room of the hotel, over a few bottles of wine and a box of prime Havanas. Stories were told, songs sung, etc. Finally one man proposed several difficult and funny arithmetical questions, which were soon solved by the company.

From *Struggles and Triumphs: or The Life of P. T. Barnum*, Written by Himself edited, with an introduction, by George S. Bryan, Volume I, pp. 145–147. Copyright 1927, by Alfred A. Knopf, Inc. New York & London.

Hoping to catch Turner with a trick, I got behind him, and winking to the rest of the company, and pointing at him, I gravely proposed the following question:

"Suppose," said I, "a man is thirty years of age and he has a child one year of age, he is *thirty times* older than his child. When the child is thirty years old, the father, being sixty, is only *twice* as old as his child. When the child is sixty the father is ninety, and therefore only *one third* older than the child. When the child is ninety the father is one hundred and twenty, and therefore only *one fourth* older than the child. Thus you see, gentlemen, the child is gradually but *surely gaining* on the parent, and as he must certainly continue to come nearer and nearer, in time he must overtake him. The question therefore is, suppose it was possible for them to live long enough, how old would the father be when the child overtook him and became of the same age?"

All the company, except Turner, saw the joke, and perceiving that I intended it for him, they gravely commenced figuring. Presently one of them remarked that it would take too long to figure it out then, though it was plain that such an event would occur if the parties lived long enough.

"I think," I replied, "it is 999 years, but I have almost forgotten, as it is some years since I figured it out."

Turner was much interested in the question. Said he, "I never heard that before, and I would not have believed it; but it is plain that it is so, for the son is gradually gaining on the father, and although I don't know much about arithmetic, one thing is certain, if you give a slow horse five miles or fifty miles the start, and a faster horse is put behind him, I am sure *he must catch the slow one in time if they run far enough!*"

As he appeared to be now convinced beyond doubt, an old gentleman gravely remarked that he knew nothing about figures, but that the idea of a son becoming as old as his father while both were living was nonsense; and he would bet a dozen of champagne that the thing was impossible. Turner, who was a betting man, especially when he felt sure of winning, remarked that it appeared odd, but for reasons just stated it *must* be true, and he therefore took the bet. When the wager was fairly concluded, and judges appointed, the company all burst into laughter, and after much talk, Turner became convinced that although relatively the boy would gain on his father, there must always be thirty years' difference between them. Turner paid the champagne, which cost him $25, and it was several months before I could convince him there was any fun in the joke.

The Cowboy and the Riveter

WE WERE on the riveting gang driving by hand; we picked up a Western guy to buck rivets for me.

As told by a structural steel worker to Marion Charles Hatch. Manuscripts of the Federal Writers' Project of the Works Progress Administration in New York City.

A fellow by the name of Big Bill Hearn says to him, "Slim, can you buck?" "Oh," he says, "I was never knocked off a rivet in my life." So 1, like a good friend of him, asked how old is he. He says he was 28 years old.

Bill says to him, "Got any friends in the undertakin' business?" He says, "No and I don't need any."

"Well," he says, "get on the rivet." We stuck a rivet in, O. K. "He held that up fine and dandy." Bill says, "By gosh, you're good." "Ah," he says, "you can hit it as hard as you like."

By the time it was finished, he had a cold rivet stuck in red lead. It's nice and red and he put it in the hole. The Westerner gets on the rivet. Bill Hearn hits the rivet and the Westerner goes out like a light. The dolly bar goes in the hole and the Westerner after the dolly bar. He fell out twenty feet.

The cold rivet is so hard it knocks the man off immediately. He must have turned three times over before he landed. When he landed he said, "Jesus Christ that son of a bitch can hit." I slid down the column but Bill stayed up there. Bill says, "Ask him if he got any friends in the undertakin' business." We shook him up, revived him and he sat up but he refused to get up. He was sitting on his poo poo. I said to him, "Got any friends in the undertakin' business?"

"No," he says. "But I've got a friend that's a cemetery caretaker." He says, "I'll never buck a rivet in the east while I stay here. You Irish are too tough for a cowboy." He bought us a drink and he says he learned something for two drinks of whiskey that he would have paid a fortune to know before, so he parted.

I believe he's still going. He'll never come back. He never did find out that was a cold rivet.

The Slide-Rock Bolter

(Macrostoma saxiperrumptus)

IN THE mountains of Colorado, where in summer the woods are becoming infested with tourists, much uneasiness has been caused by the presence of the slide-rock bolter. This frightful animal lives only in the steepest mountain country where the slopes are greater than 45 degrees. It has an immense head, with small eyes, and a mouth somewhat on the order of a sculpin, running back beyond its ears. The tail consists of a divided flipper, with enormous grab-hooks, which it fastens over the crest of the mountain or ridge, often remaining there motionless for days at a time, watching the gulch for tourists or any other hapless creature that may

From *Fearsome Creatures of the Lumberwoods,* With a Few Desert and Mountain Beasts, by William T. Cox, p. 21. Copyright, 1910, by William T. Cox. Washington, D. C.: Press of Judd & Detweiler, Inc.

enter it. At the right moment, after sighting a tourist, it will lift its tail, thus loosening its hold on the mountain, and with its small eyes riveted on the poor unfortunate, and drooling thin skid grease from the corners of its mouth, which greatly accelerates its speed, the bolter comes down like a toboggan, scooping in its victim as it goes, its own impetus carrying it up the next slope, where it again slaps its tail over the ridge and waits. Whole parties of tourists are reported to have been gulped at one swoop by the slide-rock bolter, and guides are becoming cautious about taking parties far back into the hills. The animal is a menace not only to tourists but to the woods as well. Many a draw through spruce-covered slopes has been laid low, the trees being knocked out by the roots or mowed off as by a scythe where the bolter has crashed down through from the peaks above.

A forest ranger, whose district includes the rough country between Ophir Peaks and the Lizzard Head, conceived the bold idea of decoying a slide-rock bolter to its own destruction. A dummy tourist was rigged up with plaid Norfolk jacket, knee breeches, and a guide book to Colorado. It was then filled full of giant powder and fulminate caps and posted in a conspicuous place, where, sure enough, the next day it attracted the attention of a bolter which had been hanging for days on the slope of Lizzard Head. The resulting explosion flattened half the buildings in Rico, which were never rebuilt, and the surrounding hills fattened flocks of buzzards the rest of the summer.

A Most Original Wager

I

THE CAPE COD SAILOR AND THE GANNINIPPER

A CAPE COD sailor laid a wager, that he would lie down naked in the salt meadow a quarter of an hour, and submit to the utmost fury of the moschetoes for that term without once wincing. Accordingly the wager was staked; he lay down in one of the calm hot evenings of August, on the side of a marsh where the moschetoes were flying about by millions. Thirteen minutes and a half he lay in this situation, without shrinking, and put the whole host of the winged little fiends at defiance. One of the company, fearing at last that the fellow would win the wager, stept aside, and put the small end of a walking stick into the fire, with which he returned, and slily applied it to the man's naked back; he could hold out no longer, but shrunk from the touch with some violence, taking it for the bite of a large fly. "You have lost the wager," said one of the company. "I have lost it surely," said he, "but if it had not been for that d—d

From *Jack's Kit; or, Saturday Night in the Forecastle*, by An Old Salt, p. 156. New York: Bunce & Brother.

ganninipper I should have won it!" [A ganninipper is a large green fly, abounding in pine woods, of a very keen sting, peculiarly painful and venomous.]

II

ON THE BIG BLUE

One of the funniest ruptures in friendship that we have heard of occurred on the pretty, but mosquito-ridden, Big Blue. Some of the boys belonging to one outfit sought temporary relief in the river while the mosquitoes hovered over them, whetting their daggers all the time. During the bath a most original wager was made betwixt two young fellows. One bet that he could remain exposed without his clothes longer than the other. It was agreed that both could smoke cigars. So, after each got a light, they sat down on the river bank, close to each other, wincing as stings were inflicted on a tender quarter, and smoking with a fiercer energy in proportion as the pain became more excessive. Both held out manfully for minutes, when one, in the very act of giving up the contest, accidentally touched the rear of his adversary with the end of his cigar, causing the latter to jump into the river in agony, swearing that "the great-grandfather of the whole flock had stabbed him." When a healthy blister developed where only a mere sting should have appeared, the murder was "out" and war to the death was declared.

How to Make Rattlesnake Soup

JACK's escapade with the lariat had suggested the need for mildly chastening him, and now the subject of reptiles suggested the method. It was a method which demanded the presence of enough ingenious raconteurs to maintain a seemingly serious discussion of an absurd topic. Happily, in addition to Pieface, Hyena Bob, Saunders, and Pete, the camp contained Bigfoot, the cowboy who had caught the runaway horse, Dirty Shirt, the cowboy who had brought the snake, and also Dishwater and Fatbelly, punchers who had halted on their way from Glendive for the pleasurable purpose of wasting time. All of these visitors were adepts at the prospective game.

Pieface led off: "Does your ma make her rattlesnake soup good an' rich?"

At first Jack thought the question a bit of nonsense, but was immedi-

From *Forty-Niners, The Chronicle of the California Trail,* by Archer Butler Hulbert, pp. 49–50. Copyright, 1931, by Archer Butler Hulbert. Boston: Little, Brown & Company.

From *Gone Haywire,* Two Tenderfoots on the Montana Cattle Range in 1886, by Philip Ashton Rollins, pp. 31–36. Copyright, 1939, by Charles Scribner's Sons. New York.

ately deluded when Fatbelly added: "I sure like that kind o' soup better'n any other." Dirty Shirt chimed in: "Mean to say you's never ate it? Shucks! All Western folks hankers fer it; but they can't often get it acause it's hard to make jus' right."

Jack's final doubt of the horrific dish was ended when Bigfoot volunteered: "Cuttle, your ol' woman here, contrives it nicer'n anybody in this region; but she ain't got time to make none now, for it's an awful complicated job."

Jack was fully snared. "Saunders," he begged, "won't you tell me how you do it?"

Cuttle began the dialogue.

"First off, you get yourself a couple o' tin pails; one big an' t'other smaller, so's you won't get 'em mixed. Them pails mus' jus' nacherally be sort o' rusty on th' inside, else th' soup won't turn out good. Fatbelly, you askin' what size pails I finds best suitin'? Well, lemme think. Oh! generally, 'less it's fer a barbecue or a perlitical rally, a gallon pail fer th' big un an' an empty termater can'll do fer th' little un.

"What's that, Pieface? You mean 'bout th' rust? Oh, yea! Pertainin' to that rust, be sure th' tin ain't ate all th' way through, otherwise th' best part o' th' soup'll leak out; an' too, th' rust puts iron int' your blood an' tonics up your system. No, Dishwater, th' pails don't have to be round. Any shape'll do, acause, jus' as I was 'bout to tell young Hilton here, you don't coil the snakes int' th' pails, you puts 'em in in pieces."

After a few moments of colloquy, all of which was intended for Jack's misguidance, Cuttle once more took up the thread. "Hilt, you savvy now all 'bout th' pails, but acourse you's also got to get some sugar an' salt an' pepper an', ef you likes high seasonin', some mustard an' a big patch o' young leaves from sagebrush.

"What's that, Pete an' Pieface? One o' you at a time. Pete's inquirin' 'bout th' pepper, whether red or black. Bein' Mexican, he prob'ly puts 'is money on th' red; but I usually mixes 'em, 'bout one-third, two-thirds. An' Pieface's suggestin' rabbit-brush. No, Pie, ain't so tasty as sagebrush—sort o' flat. There's some folks thinks addin' a touch o' prickly pear tones it up. Thank you, Bigfoot, for mentionin' th' black-strap merlasses—I'd clean disremembered it—use jus' a few spoonfuls o' it, 'long with a few drops o' vinegar. No, Hyena, I never uses cinnamon nor nutmeg."

Several additional ingredients were mentioned and properly discussed; then, fearing lest further intricacies in the recipe might make Jack suspicious, Cuttle embarked on the second stage of the recital.

"Now, Jack, you's learned all th' necessary fixin's an' flavorin's, an' snakes is th' next thing. Some folks insists on assorted sizes, but I don't necessarily hold with them. Why, o' course, Fatbelly, ef it's all little snakes, it lacks body, an' all big snakes tends to make it tough. Folks mostly disagrees whether th' snakes should be skun or left with th' skins on. For me myself, I absosurely likes th' skins kept on.

"What's that, Dishwater, 'bout th' next step? Oh, yea! Wall, you lays th' snakes out flat, cuts off th' heads right behin' th' ears, puts all them heads int' th' little pail, pours in water 'nough to jus' cover 'em, an' sets that keerfully to one side. Then you takes off th' rattles an' lays 'em nigh th' little pail so's you can easy find 'em when you need 'em for th' decoratin'. An' now, with a sharp knife you slices th' snakes crosswise into pieces three inches long. Th' knife's got to be sharp so's not to make no rough gashes in th' flesh. No, Dirty Shirt, it's contrary to reason to slice 'em lengthwise—'ll make the soup stringy."

This was followed by a short debate as to what region produced the most desirable reptiles. In the course of it, plausible anecdotes were detailed of alleged soups which had made a cook famous in Texas and wrecked another man's reputation in Oregon.

Jack's attention was still holding fast and Cuttle resumed his falsifying.

"You takes th' big pail, covers th' bottom inside with th' sagebrush leaves, an' starts to stack up th' pieces o' snake into it; th' first layer lengthwise, th' next crosswise or antigodlinlike an' so on till all th' snakes is in. Then you reaches fer your flavorin's. That's all."

Cuttle had stopped talking and was stuffing tobacco into his mouth. Jack exclaimed: "Tell me honest what happens next?" His plea invited the denouement which all the Westerners had gleefully been anticipating. After a geyserlike expectoration and a moment's pretense of deep thought, Cuttle solemnly announced:

"I said that's all, an' 'tis. Th' only other thing you does is put on your hat an', in a respectful an' dignified way, ride off an' quit th' stinkin' mess."

Young Hilton's discomfiture at the outburst of joyous howls was possibly the greater because Bill was so noisy. To lessen Jack's chagrin, Pieface promptly challenged: "Steady there, Bill King; don't josh your cousin too hard, remember th' circular story you swallowed three years ago." Bill remembered, and he secretly approved Pieface's defense of Jack. He meekly recalled how he himself had breathlessly listened to a long-winded description of an imaginary thief chase—a description of the type which Westerners styled a circular story because its final words were the same as the opening ones. He also remembered that he had been inveigled into a so-called snipe hunt in which, having been equipped with a bag ostensibly for snaring birds, he was left outdoors all night while his tormentors deserted him and furtively returned to bed.

Bill was now familiar with three of the principal methods by which ranchmen gently plagued their pilgrim guests—the snipe hunt, the circular story, the recipe for snake soup—and in a few weeks he was to meet a fourth, the wouser.

Attacked by a Wouser

He was so sleepy when he crawled into bed that he failed to notice that all cartridges had been extracted from the cylinder of his pistol and the belt of his chaparejos. Also he failed to notice that the earliest outgoing night herder carried a shovel, an ax, and a bottle of tomato catsup. And there was no reason for him to know that Pete, when herding the remuda into its grazing area, had found a recently dead cow.

Some two hours before dawn his heavy sleep was broken by a sudden commotion in the camp. Though only half awake, he realized that Cuttle was violently dashing water onto the charred remnants of the campfire and that Abilene in a loud stage whisper was pleading: "Don't dare to leave a single spark else 'e might see it. Gosh! wasn't 'e awful lookin'!"

Still more disturbing was Cuttle's apparently terror-stricken query—also in a loud stage whisper—"Did 'e ruin Kansas Ed arter Terril tried to save 'em?"

Bill, now thoroughly awake and not a little scared, rose in bed; but before he could say a word, Pieface rushed out from the darkness, pushed him down and urged: "Don't speak, too dangerous!"

Suddenly there came a long-drawn booming sound followed by a piercing scream.

At Cuttle's cry of "Boys, he's headin' back, we's got ter fight 'im!" Bill tried to ask: "What is it?" but his mouth was sealed by Pieface's hand. Jerked to his feet by Pieface on one side and Hyena on the other, he was hustled out of camp. Whatever qualms he may have had in deserting Jack and Red were dissipated by Hyena's hissing: "Th' kids is safe, 'e won't touch 'em; an' fer Heaven's sake don't make a sound, too all-fired resky." When he protested: "The cartridges in my belt are gone," he was told: "Can't help it, can't stop, don't talk, too dangerous."

Floundering through the sagebrush—the cowboys were purposely taking Bill through it rather than around it—they came to an open spot where, by the dim aid of matches, Bill glimpsed a ground that was deeply scarified and bushes with branches that were sharply broken and heavily matted with red fluid. The night herder had been industrious. Bill tried again to ask "What is it?" but once more his mouth was stopped and he was hustled onward. "Shut up! don't talk, too dangerous!"

At the next open spot, matches were used for a scant two seconds and

---

Ibid., pp. 248–251.

A mythical animal known to cowboy raconteurs as the "wouser" sometimes was descanted upon. The wouser was accorded any physical appearance and predatory habits which the course of the earlier conversation had seemed to warrant. He usually, however, was permitted to have hydrophobia, and was made a subspecies of either the bear or the mountain-lion.—*The Cowboy*, by Philip Ashton Rollins (1922), pp. 184–185.

revealed the dead cow lying on its side. Bill was not given a chance to inquire the meaning of Pieface's puzzling utterance: "Queer 'e didn't rip its head off, mos'ly does."

Pieface and Hyena were now out of breath, and their escort duties were assumed by Terril and Kansas Ed who were waiting according to pre-arrangement, and who plausibly explained their presence by asserting: "Got 'way from 'im at last an', Gosh, he's savage!"

At last Bill was able to phrase his question, "What is it, man-killing horse or mad wolf?" but the only answer was another of the long-drawn booming sounds, succeeded by a shriek.

He was further bewildered when Terril, having lit still another match, pointed to an old wagon track and a maze of hoofprints and exclaimed: "Look there, Ed, that's where 'is tail got tangled with 'is foot. Let's run!"

While Bill was floundering on a detour with his new chaperons, Pieface had time to use the ax; thus, when Bill returned and reinspected the dead cow, it had been decapitated. At sight of the mangled body Hyena, pre-tending thankfulness, averred: "We's safe now an' can go back to camp; th' dragon's gone off somewheres plum' full of blood, an'll bust wide open in egsactly nineteen minutes."

A short walk brought them back to camp to find the fire blazing and the coffee boiling. Jack sat up in bed with a taunt: "Bill, did you catch the wouser?" A cousinly riding boot was thrown at his head, and Pieface warned: "Jack, if you rasps Bill any further 'an 'e has been, you'll be eatin' snake soup for breakfast."

The only other comment was made to Pete when he appeared. "You sure can pull appallin' noises from a conch shell."

Needless to say, the actual breakfast was delayed till long after the sun had risen—incidentally allowing Pieface to ascertain the brand on the decapitated cow for the purpose of reporting to its owner.

A Snipe Hunt

ONE of our most popular forms of amusement was playing practical jokes on each other, and some of them were of a pretty rough character. I re-member one joke we played on Rector, a jolly and useful member of the troop, albeit so deaf one had to yell at him to make him hear. The boys called him "Reck." He was fond of natural history, and was never so delighted as when he captured a curious insect, or shot a rare bird, or killed a fine specimen of a snake. One day, one of the boys asked Reck if he'd ever gone "sniping."

"Shooting snipe?" said Reck. "Lots of times."

From *A Texas Ranger*, by N. A. Jennings, foreword by J. Frank Dobie, pp. 185–189. Copyright, 1930, by Southwest Press. Dallas, Texas.

"No, no," said the Ranger, "not shooting them; catching them in a bag. I thought nearly everyone knew about 'sniping.'"

"Never heard of it," said Reck. "How can anyone catch snipe in a bag?"

"Oh, it's simple enough when you know how," explained the other. "A party of half a dozen or more men start out about sundown and go to some marshy place, near a river, where the snipe are apt to be at night. They take a bag—an old gunny-sack is best—and some candles with them. They select a likely spot and, when it is quite dark, one of the party holds the mouth of the bag open and places a lighted candle in front of it, on the ground. The others go off and make a big circle, which they gradually narrow as they approach the one who is holding the bag. They beat the chaparral and make all the noise they can as they get near to him, and they frighten all the snipe and start them running toward him, too. The snipe are attracted by the light from the candle and, as they get close to it, are blinded by its rays. They run straight into the mouth of the open sack. It's great sport, and I know a place, about three miles from here, where the snipe are as thick as hops. Let's get up a party to go after them to-night."

Reck was delighted with the idea and a party of nine snipe-hunters was quickly made up. Strangely enough, all of the men except Reck had often been on sniping expeditions and knew all about them. I was in the secret and formed one of the party.

We started soon after sundown and went up the river, led by the Ranger who proposed the sport. He took us, by winding, roundabout paths, to a swampy piece of ground where we sank to our ankles at every step. The place was swarming with mosquitoes. When we reached what we agreed was a favorable spot, we stopped and had an animated discussion as to who should hold the sack. We all wanted to hold it apparently, because it was so much more fun to bag the snipe than to go tramping around in the brush, beating up the birds. Finally someone said that it took more skill to beat up the snipe than it did to hold the sack and, as Reck was green at the work, perhaps it would be better to let him have the coveted part. The rest agreed to this as a fair solution of the question and two candles were lighted and stuck in the marshy ground, while Reck squatted down and held the mouth of the sack open behind them. It took both his hands to hold the sack properly, and when we left him the mosquitoes were singing in high glee about his head.

And so we came away from him. To beat up the snipe? Oh, no; to get by the nearest way out of that mosquito-infested marsh and back to camp. We reached there shortly, and the boys howled with wicked delight as we drew graphic pictures of poor Reck holding on with both hands to that sack, while every mosquito in the swamp within sight of the candles made a bee line for the spot.

Reck came into camp about midnight. He got lost in hunting it and came near having to pass the night in the brush. He brought the sack with him and went straight to where the man who had invited him to go "sniping" lay asleep. He woke him up and all near him with a wild warwhoop.

"Hello, Reck!" exclaimed the practical joker, as he sat up; "did you get any snipe?"

"You bet your boots I did!" cried Reck, as he suddenly shook the contents of his sack all over the joker. "Look at all those fine fellows."

The man gave a yell and scrambled to his feet. Reck had shaken about two quarts of big black ants all over him, and he knew from experience that ants in Texas bite like fiends. Reck had stumbled over an ant-hill in wandering back to camp and gathered a lot of them into his sack, so as to get even with the sniping party. He did it very effectually, for the ants spread in all directions and made things decidedly uncomfortable for us the rest of the night. That was the last "sniping" party we ever had in the Rangers, but it was far from being the last practical joke played. . . .

Tying a Cow's Tail to His Boot Strap

I WENT to another place to stay all night; and, as they had a lot of cows to milk, the whole family went along. The old man was milking a cow that was bad about switching her tail; first, into the milk bucket, then in the old man's face. I asked him if he had ever tried tying her tail to his boot strap. I told him that was the way the Dutch do, and he thought it was a good idea. He tied the cow's tail to his boot strap and went on milking. It worked all right for awhile. But suddenly she got scared at something and started off in a hurry, jerking the old man off his stool. That spilled the bucket of milk all over him, and she dragged him around the lot a few times through the mud. All the time he kept yelling: "Head her off and don't let her get into the brush." The cow stopped once, long enough to let the old man get up on his feet, but away she went again. Part of the time he had his hands on her hips, and part of the time he had her by the tail, and all the time he was running. Sometimes he could use both feet. It put me in mind of a lot of boys playing leap frog. All the time the old man and the cow were playing circus, the rest of the family were laughing to beat the band. When the boot strap gave way, the old man was on the ground out of breath, covered with mud and slime, and mad. Yes, he was all swelled up. After he got over it, he said he did not care to try any more Dutch tricks, especially if a Yankee school teacher was mixed up in it.

From *Bill Jones of Paradise Valley,* His Life and Adventures For Over Forty Years in The Great Southwest. He was a Pioneer in the Days of the Buffalo, The Wild Indian, The Oklahoma Boomer, The Cowboy and The Outlaw, by John J. Callison, pp. 39–40. Copyright, 1914, by J. J. Callison. Kingfisher, Oklahoma.

Swallowing an Oyster Alive

A STORY OF ILLINOIS—BY A MISSOURIAN [1]

AT A late hour, the other night, the door of an oyster house in our city was thrust open, and in stalked a hero from the Sucker state. He was quite six feet high, spare, somewhat stooped, with a hungry, anxious countenance, and his hands pushed clear down to the bottom of his breeches pockets. His outer covering was hard to define, but after surveying it minutely, we came to the conclusion that his suit had been made in his boyhood, of a dingy yellow linsey-woolsey, and that, having sprouted up with astonishing rapidity, he had been forced to piece it out with all colours, in order to keep pace with his body. In spite of his exertions, however, he had fallen in arrears about a foot of the necessary length, and consequently, stuck that far through his inexpressibles. His crop of hair was surmounted by the funniest little seal-skin cap imaginable. After taking a position, he indulged in a long stare at the man opening the *bivalves,* and slowly ejaculated—"Isters?"

"Yes, sir," responded the attentive operator,—"and fine ones they are, too."

"Well, I've heard of isters afore," says he, "but this is the fust time I've seed 'm, and *pre-haps* I'll know what *thar* made of afore I git out of town."

Having expressed this desperate intention, he cautiously approached the plate and scrutinized the uncased shell-fish with a gravity and interest which would have done honour to the most illustrious searcher into the hidden mysteries of nature. At length he began to soliloquize on the difficulty of getting them out, and how queer they looked when out.

"I never seed any thin' hold on so—takes an amazin' site of screwin,

---

From *The Big Bear of Arkansas, and Other Sketches,* Illustrative of Characters and Incidents in the South and South-West, edited by William T. Porter, pp. 80–86. Entered, according to Act of Congress, in the year 1845, by Carey & Hart, in the Clerk's Office of the District Court of the United States, of the Eastern District of Pennsylvania. Philadelphia.

---

[1] We should hate to bet *"Straws"* that J. M. Field, the principal editor of the St. Louis "Reveille," was not the writer of the following story. Unlike his late brother "Poor Mat"—better known as "Phazma"—who recently died at sea, our friend "Joe" is full of fun and frolic, and ready to "go at any thing in the ring—from pitch-and-toss to manslaughter!" When he became an editor by profession, the stage sustained a material loss. He was indeed one of "the best actors in the world, either for tragedy, comedy, history, pastoral, pastoral-comical, historical-pastoral, tragical-historical, tragical-comical-historical-pastoral, scene undividable, or poem unlimited." For several years he has been a contributor to the periodical press; but quite recently he has embarked in the enterprise of a new daily journal at St. Louis, which appears to have succeeded almost beyond his hopes. The annexed sketch is "a taste of the quality" of the "Reveille" and himself.—W. T. P.

hoss, to get 'em out, and aint they slick and slip'ry when they does come? Smooth as an eel! I've a good mind to give that feller lodgin', jist to realize the effects, as uncle Jess used to say about speckalation."

"Well, sir," was the reply, "down with two bits, and you can have a dozen."

"Two bits!" exclaimed the Sucker, "now come, that's stickin' it on rite strong, hoss, for *isters.* A dozen on 'em aint nothin' to a chicken, and there's no gettin' more'n a picayune a piece for *them.* I've only realized forty-five picayunes on my first ventur' to St. Louis. I'll tell you what, I'll gin you two chickens for a dozen, if you'll conclude to deal."

A wag, who was standing by indulging in a dozen, winked to the attendant to shell out, and the offer was accepted.

"Now mind," repeated the Sucker, "all fair—two chickens for a dozen —you're a witness, mister," turning at the same time to the wag; "none of your tricks, for I've heard that your city fellers are mity slip'ry coons."

The bargain being fairly understood, our Sucker squared himself for the onset; deliberately put off his seal-skin, tucked up his sleeves, and, fork in hand, awaited the appearance of No. 1. It came—he saw—and quickly it was bolted! A moment's dreadful pause ensued. The wag dropped his knife and fork with a look of mingled amazement and horror —something akin to Shakespeare's Hamlet on seeing his daddy's ghost— while he burst into the exclamation—

"Swallowed alive, as I'm a Christian!"

Our Sucker hero had opened his mouth with pleasure a moment before, but now it *stood* open. Fear—a horrid dread of he didn't know what— a consciousness that all wasn't right, and ignorant of the extent of the wrong—the uncertainty of the moment was terrible. Urged to desperation, he faltered out—

"What on earth's the row?"

"Did you swallow it alive?" inquired the wag.

"I swallowed it jest as he gin it to me!" shouted the Sucker.

"You're a dead man!" exclaimed his anxious friend, "the creature is alive, and will eat right through you," added he, in a most hopeless tone.

"Get a pizen pump and pump it out!" screamed the Sucker, in a frenzy, his eyes fairly starting from their sockets. "O gracious!—what 'ill I do?— It's got holds of my innards already, and I'm dead as a chicken!—do somethin' for me, do—don't let the infernal sea-toad eat me afore your eyes."

"Why don't you put some of this on it?" inquired the wag, pointing to a bottle of strong pepper-sauce.

The hint was enough—the Sucker, upon the instant, seized the bottle, and desperately wrenching out the cork, swallowed half the contents at a draught. He fairly squealed from its effects, and gasped and blowed, and pitched, and twisted, as if it were coursing through him with electric effect, while at the same time his eyes ran a stream of tears. At length becoming a little composed, his waggish adviser approached, almost bursting with suppressed laughter, and inquired,—

"How are you now old fellow—did you kill it?"

"Well, I did, hoss'—ugh, ugh o-o-o my inards. If that *ister* critter's dyin' agonies didn't stir a 'ruption in me equal to a small arthquake, then 'taint no use sayin' it—it squirmed like a sarpent, when that killin' stuff touched it; hu' "—and here with a countenance made up of suppressed agony and present determination, he paused to give force to his words, and slowly and deliberately remarked, "If you git two chickens from me for that live animal, I'm d—d!" and seizing his seal-skin he vanished.

The shout of laughter, and the contortions of the company at this finale, would have made a spectator believe that they had all been *swallowing oysters alive.*

Casting Anchor

I've met with a darned many odd sort o' fish, in my travels, but them are salt water critters, called sailors, be the all strangest sarpents that frequent Terra Firma; they are tarnacious cute when they're on board o' their great big boats an play all sorts o' tricks upon poor travellers, as one o' 'em did me once, by stickin my feet fast to the floor o' the boat with tar, an given me a puke by a drink o' salt water, an all that 'ere kind o' nonsense; but I caught this same walken tar kettle on shore one day, an the way I gin him trick for trick, was about what I call fairation. You see, the tarnal crittur come up to Uncle Paradise's one day, for to hire a horse o' him, so I jist slipped up a little, an telled the old chap to leave it all to me, an I'd fix it off about square, an so I reckon I did, for I gin him the all-starten skittyiest critter in all New England, so etarnal shy, that she used to rear up an run at the sound o' her own snort. Well, I got him fixed a top o' her, but the tarnal critter still thinkin o' the boat, would take one o' them ere great double fish-hook lookin things, called ankers, along with him, and fasten about the mare's neck; well, up he got, lookin for all the world like a tree frog on a fence rail; the first thing, he poked his heels into her flank, an the way she did rear an whinner and squirm about, was enough to skeer a jockey; at last off she started like a barn swallow, while he hung on to the mane like a wild cat to the bark of a tree, till finally the feller got the wind so fur jolted out o' him, that he couldn't hardly hang on to her any longer, and hollered out, "Avast, you lubber!" but the crittur was determined to run him under a tree, an brush him off, an the sarpent throwed out his great fish hook, around the trunk of a tough hickory; this of course, brought her to a sudden and almost awful halt, an the way she pitched the salt sea sarpent over her head made him never want to sail on horse back agin.

From *Mince Pie for the Million*. Philadelphia and New York: Turner & Fisher. 1846

The Pedlar's Fright

JIST befour the frost cum, one fall, a long-legged cream-faced Yankee Pedlar brot his plunder into the forrest, for to tice our gals out of their munny. He put up for a time with a feller called Flunkey Bill, who lived in a log cabin on the edge of Skunk's Paradise. This Pedlar war most abominable onscrupulus in his dealings, and knowed no more about handling a rifle than a goose knoes about rib stockings; but he borrowed a rifle one arternoon, and went out into the woods to kill some varmints. He didn't cum back that nite, and Flunkey sot up for him and kept a pine knot burning haff the nite. And the way he didn't cum home all the nixt day war a caution. So Bill didn't know but what something had happent to the pesky critter, and he razed the nabors to go and hunt arter him. I war won of the number, and sumtimes I forgot that it war a human we war arter, and placed my hand on the lok of my rifle, whenever I heered a noise, as if I war goin to take a blizzard at a painter. It war the first time I went a hunting arter a two-legged varmint. I shood a thort he had run away a purppus, only he left his plunder behind, and I knowed very well he wouldn't do that if he didn't expect to cum back. We went a day's jurny into the forrest, and kepp a lookout on every hand; but we seed nothing of the pedlar. So when it begun to grow dark, we kindled a fire, and sot down and took out the whiskey. As soon as the fire begun to burn well, we heered a sort of groaning noise, and as the fire war made under the branches of a big tree, we looked up, and, my eyes, reeder! thar we seed a pare of long legs dangling down in the smoke, and they twisted and writhed like frying an eel alive! So we begun to skatter the fire, and Flunkey Bill bawled out, "There's the Pedlar's legs—I shood kno them from a thousand." True enuff, it war the Pedlar, and we helped him dowr. from the tree. When he got down he looked around him haff fritened to death, till he seed Flunkey Bill, and then he knowed he war safe. The coward varmint told us he had been up in that tree nite and day, ever sense he left the cabin. He had seed a big snapping turtle that had come out of a pond close by, and he thort it war a alligator. So he had clum up into the tree, and if we hadn't a cum, he would have staid up thar till he rotted. The pesky cretur wanted to kno, if he war safe arter he cum down. Ses I, "You are along with Davy Crockett, who is part snapping turtle himself, and a piece of the alligator; so if you are afeered of them varmints you had better git up in the tree agin." Arter we got home, the gals got hold of the story, and the pedlar cleered out pritty quick, for they used to shuv a turtle in his face whenever he wanted to sell 'em ennything.

Ibid.

Concerning Bald-Headed Whizzers

TYPICAL adjunct to life in the hell-roarin' days of the Argonauts when camps reeked gold and the humors of men were raw as new-plowed prairie land, was that effervescent phenomenon known as the Whizzer.

The Whizzer was the high ace in the deck of life as it was dealt over gravel bar and auriferous stream bank. Individuals and towns reaped fame by it. A successful Whizzer not only crowned its originator and perpetrator with glory, but shed an enviable light upon the entire community that witnessed—or suffered—its execution. Whizzers of superlative merit have been embalmed in the memories of very old men who still sun themselves in the ghost towns of gold and who can be led, with much chuckling, to recount them. In a few rare volumes of reminiscences long out of print you'll find samples of this long extinct genus pinned like gorgeous butterflies to the pages.

A noteworthy swindle, a practical joke, a brilliant hoax: these were the magic components of which the Whizzer was made. They were of two classes, the plain and the bald-headed. A bald-headed Whizzer was one so adroitly built upon a human foible or frailty, so carefully exploited by its author as to bring a whole community into the arena of mocking laughter. The distinction between the two varieties was comparative; the gage, you might say, of genius.

One of the earliest Whizzers of the gold diggin's to gain immortality was that one perpetrated by a genius whose name comes down as Pike Sellers—undoubtedly one of the Wild Missouri hellions generically lumped as "Pikes," in the vocabulary of the mines. This Pike had an imagination and a devilishly sly humor which would qualify him to-day for one of our highly specialized lines of salesmanship.

It was in the spring of '50 when word of the incredible richness of Downie's Flat, away up near the headwaters of Yuba's north fork, swept downstream and set a crowd of wild-eyed boomers hurrying thither. Original discoverers of Downie's Flat were digging a pound of gold a day to the man out of crevices under the rim rock with the point of a butcher knife. Major Downie himself had sifted downstream to Bullard's Bar with $3000 in nuggets, result of three days' work! So rumor exploded.

When the first of the rush commenced to lower themselves hand over hand down the precipitous wall of the gorge to Downie's camp on the forks of white water they were not very cordially received by the ten or a dozen original discoverers who'd spent a hard winter there. It was, in fact, quite true that Downie and his associates had been hitting raw gold out of the bank with butcher knives and iron spoons over several months; and they did not welcome a division of riches.

From *The Hell-Roarin' Forty-Niners*, by Robert Welles Ritchie, pp. 233–237, Copyright, 1928, by J. H. Sears & Co., Incorporated. New York.

Then it was that Pike Sellers had his inspiration.

He was working away at the soft dirt of the stream bank one day when he saw one of the boomers, pack on back, crawling precariously down trail. Pike, unseen himself, scrambled up out of the stream bed and commenced furiously prying with his long knife at the bark slabs on a jack-pine. Just as the stranger came up one of the rough shags of bark became loosened. Pike pushed two fingers behind it and withdrew a fat gold nugget.

Eyes of the stranger popped. Pike tackled another bark slab without so much as a glance over shoulder at the fascinated onlooker. By a simple trick of legerdemain that hunk yielded a second alluring gold pebble.

"My Gawd!"—from the tenderfoot. "I hearn ye was diggin' the yaller stuff outa cracks in the rocks, but I didn't know she grew on trees."

"Gits lodged thar when th' tree's pushing up through th' зoil," indifferently from Pike. "Most of th' nuggets is up higher, but too dam'd much trouble to shin up th' trees. Me, I'm jist satisfied to peck round nigh th' ground."

Under the believing eyes of the newcomer Pike found a couple more nuggets. Then the former whipped out his bowie-knife and started to work on a near-by jack-pine.

"Hold on thar!" commandingly from the Sellers person. "Yo're on my claim. Rule in this camp ev'ry fella's entitled to ten gold bearin' pines; that thar one belongs to me."

The boomer wanted to know in an excited whine where he could stake himself to a tree. Reluctantly Pike Sellers abandoned his work to stride through the forest to where a jack-pine of smaller growth reared.

"Like I said, she's richest nigh th' top. Ye can climb this one 'thout a ladder iffen yo're so minded." Pike showed a commendable interest in seeing the newcomer make his first strike of jack-pine gold. The latter dropped his pack and, bowie in teeth, commenced to shin up the rough trunk.

"Higher up's better," bawled Pike when his protege had come to the first limbs. "Nothin' but flake gold low down mostly."

Up went the avid tenderfoot, before his eyes the vision of a man prying nuggets from beneath tree bark. Pike let him risk his neck until the luckless light-wit was fifty or sixty feet from the ground.

"That's a likely 'nough place to begin on. Only be mighty keerful not to drop any nuggets. I kain't be held responsible fer losses like that."

The searcher after tree gold began to attack the bark with his bowie knife. Pike Sellers sifted back to the stream bed to bring an audience for the farce comedy he had staged. Thereafter "jack-pine gold" became a synonym through all the Northern Mines.

Pike Sellers reaped enduring fame as the father of a Whizzer.

A Voice from Shiloh

ANSWERING questions in rapid succession at the close of a New York banquet, Mark Twain said:

"In writing, it is usually stronger and more dramatic to have a man speak for himself than to have someone else relate a thing about him."

Billy Boynton, whom I had introduced to Mark Twain a few moments before, interrupted, "Suppose a man dies. Is it stronger to have the man himself say that he has died?"

Mark Twain smiled affably. "Sometimes," he answered. "Take the case of Major Patterson, down in Missouri, when a squatter had moved in on some of the extensive lands he laid claim to. Deciding to use the frightening method to get the squatter off, the major donned a mask one dark night, mounted an enormous black horse, rode to the squatter's door, called him out, and asked for a bucket of water. The major had also availed himself of a contrivance used by the Ku Klux Klan, a large leather bag on his chest and stomach, buttoned securely under his coat.

"When the squatter had brought the water the major raised the three-gallon bucket, slowly poured its contents into the bag through an opening at his throat, turned to the astonished squatter and said, 'Ah-h-h—— That's the first drink of water I've had since I was killed at the battle of Shiloh!'

"The squatter disappeared from that part of the country," concluded Mark Twain. "And I think you will agree that when the major spoke for himself, the effect was stronger than otherwise."

Yankee Notions

I

"WHAT is the price of razor-strops?" inquired my grandfather of a peddler, whose wagon, loaded with Yankee notions, stood in front of our store.

From *Mark Twain and I*, by Opie Read, p. 3. Copyright, 1940, by the Reilly & Lee Co. Chicago.

From *Struggles and Triumphs: or, The Life of P. T. Barnum*, Written by Himself, edited, with an introduction, by George S. Bryan, Vol. I, pp. 19–20, 48–50. Copyright, 1927, by Alfred A. Knopf, Inc. New York and London.

In nearly every New England village, at the time of which I write, there could be found from six to twenty social, jolly, story-telling, joke-playing wags and wits, regular originals, who would get together at the tavern or store, and spend their evenings and stormy afternoons in relating anecdotes, describing their various adventures, playing off practical jokes upon each other, and engaging in every project out of which a little fun could be extracted by village wits whose ideas were usually sharpened at brief intervals by a "treat," otherwise known as a glass of Santa Cruz rum, old Holland gin, or Jamaica spirits.

Bethel was not an exception to this state of things. In fact no place of its size could

"A dollar each for Pomeroy's strops," responded the itinerant merchant.

"A dollar apiece!" exclaimed my grandfather. "They'll be sold for half the money before the year is out."

"If one of Pomeroy's strops is sold for fifty cents within a year, I'll make you a present of one," replied the peddler.

"I'll purchase one on those conditions. Now, Ben, I call you to witness the contract," said my grandfather, addressing himself to Esquire Hoyt.

"All right," responded Ben.

"Yes," said the peddler, "I'll do as I say, and there's no backout to me."

My grandfather took the strop, and put it in his side coatpocket. Presently drawing it out, and turning to Esquire Hoyt, he said, "Ben, I don't much like this strop now I have bought it. How much will you give for it?"

"Well, I guess, seeing it's you, I'll give fifty cents," drawled the Squire, with a wicked twinkle in his eye, which said that the strop and the peddler were both incontinently sold.

"You can take it. I guess I'll get along with my old one a spell longer," said my grandfather, giving the peddler a knowing look.

The strop changed hands, and the peddler exclaimed, "I acknowledge, gentlemen. What's to pay?"

"Treat the company, and confess you are taken in, or else give me a strop," replied my grandfather.

"I never will confess nor treat," said the peddler, "but I'll give you a strop for your wit"; and suiting the action to the word, he handed a second strop to his customer. A hearty laugh ensued, in which the peddler joined.

"Some pretty sharp fellows here in Bethel," said a bystander, addressing the peddler.

"Tolerable, but nothing to brag of," replied the peddler. "I have made seventy-five cents by the operation."

"How is that?" was the inquiry.

"I have received a dollar for two strops which cost me only twelve and a half cents each," replied the peddler; "but having heard of the cute tricks of the Bethel chaps, I thought I would look out for them and fix my prices accordingly. I generally sell these strops at twenty-five cents each,

---

boast more original geniuses in the way of joking and story-telling than my native village. As before stated, my grandfather, Phineas Taylor, was one of the sort. His near neighbor, Benjamin Hoyt, or "Esquire" Hoyt, as he was called, on account of being a justice of the peace, was one of the most inveterate story-tellers I ever knew. He could relate an anecdote with better effect than any man I have ever seen. He would generally profess to know all the parties in the story which he related, and however comic it might be, he would preserve the most rigid seriousness of countenance until its *dénouement*, when he would break forth into a hearty haw! haw! which of itself would throw his hearers into convulsions of laughter.

Luckily or unluckily, our store was the resort of all these wits, and many is the day and evening that I have hung with delight upon their stories, and many the night that I have kept the store open until eleven o'clock, in order to listen to the last anecdotes of the two jokers who had remained long after their companions had gone to rest.—P. T. B., *op. cit.*, pp. 12–13.

but, gentlemen, if you want any more at fifty cents apiece, I shall be happy to supply your whole village."

Our neighbors laughed out of the other side of their mouths, but no more strops were purchased.

II

Dr. Carrington, Esquire James Clarke, and other well-known jokers of Danbury, were the authors of many anecdotes which I heard in my younger days. The doctor kept a country store. A small farmer coming to trade with him one day, asked him if he took cheese in exchange for goods. "Certainly," was the reply. The farmer brought in a large bag and emptied out eleven very small cheeses. "Only eleven!" said the doctor counting them. "I can't do any thing with them."

"Why not?" asked the farmer.

"There is not a full set—there should be twelve," responded the doctor.

"A full set of what?" inquired the farmer.

"Button molds, of course," was the reply.

Fortunately the farmer was of a humorous turn and took the joke in good part.

"Tin peddlers," as they were called, were abundant in those days. They travelled through the country in covered wagons, filled with tin ware and small Yankee notions of almost every description, including jewelry, dry goods, pins, needles, etc., etc. They were a sharp set of men, always ready for a trade whether cash or barter, and as they generally were destitute of moral principle, whoever dealt with them was pretty sure to be cheated. Dr. Carrington had frequently traded with them, and had just as frequently been shaved. He at last declared he would never again have any business transaction with that kind of people.

One day a peddler drove up to the doctor's store, and jumping from his wagon went in and told him he wished to barter some goods with him.

The doctor declined trading, quietly remarking that he had been shaved enough by tin peddlers, and would have nothing more to do with them.

"It is very hard to proscribe an entire class because some of its members happen to be dishonest," said the wary peddler, "and I insist on your giving me a trial. I am travelling all through the country, and can get rid of any of your unsaleable goods. So, to give you a fair chance, I will sell you any thing I have in my wagon at my lowest wholesale price, and will take in exchange any thing you please to pay me from your store at the retail price."

"Your offer seems a fair one," said the doctor," and I will look over your goods."

He proceeded to the wagon, and seeing nothing that he wanted except a lot of whetstones, of which the peddler had a large quantity, he inquired the price.

"My wholesale price of whetstones is $3 per dozen," replied the peddler.

"Well, I will take a gross of them," said the doctor.

The twelve dozen whetstones were brought in, counted out, and carefully placed upon a shelf behind the counter.

"Now," said the peddler, "you owe me $36, for which I am to take such goods as you please at the retail price. Come, doctor, what are you going to pay me in?"

"In whetstones at fifty cents each, which will take just six dozen," replied the doctor gravely, at the same time commencing to count back one half of his purchase.

The peddler looked astonished for a moment, and then bursting into what is termed "a horse laugh," he exclaimed, "Took in, by hokey! Here, doctor, take this dollar for your trouble (handing him the money); give me back my truck, and I'll acknowledge for ever that you are too sharp for a tin peddler!"

The doctor accepted the proposed compromise, and was never troubled by that peddler again.

Preëmption Dodges

DURING this fall many residents were preëmpting their claims. The law contemplates a homestead of one hundred and sixty acres at a nominal price for each actual settler and no one else; but land is plenty and everybody preëmpts. A young merchant, lawyer, or speculator, rides into the interior, to the unoccupied public lands, pays some settler five dollars to show him the vacant 'claims,' and selects one upon which he places four little poles around a hollow square upon the ground, as children commence a cobhouse. Then he files a notice in the land-office that he has laid the foundation of a house upon this claim and begun a settlement for actual residence. He does not see the land again until ready to 'prove up,' which he may do after thirty days. Then he revisits his claim, possibly erects a house of rough slabs, costing from ten to twenty dollars, eats one meal and sleeps for a single night under its roof. More frequently, however, his improvements consist solely of a foundation of four logs.

Hundreds of men whose families are still in the East find witnesses to testify that their wives and children are residing upon the land. I have known men to preëmpt who had never been within twenty miles of their claims, facile witnesses swearing with the utmost indifference that they were residing upon them.

The preëmptors must state under oath that they have made no agreement direct or indirect for selling any part of the land. But in numberless instances these statements are falsehoods, connived at by the officers.

From *Beyond the Mississippi: From the Great River to the Great Ocean; Life and Adventure on the Prairies, Mountains, and Pacific Coast . . . 1857–1867*, by Albert D. Richardson, pp. 137–138; 140–141. Entered, . . . 1867, by Albert D. Richardson. Hartford: American Publishing Company.

In most land-offices a man cannot preëmpt unless he has a house at least twelve feet square. I have known a witness to swear that the house in question was 'twelve by fourteen,' when actually the only building upon the claim was one whittled out with a penknife, twelve *inches* by fourteen.

Some offices require that the house must have a glass window. While traveling in the interior, I stopped at a little slab cabin, where I noticed a window-sash without lights hanging upon a nail. As I had seen similar frames in other cabins, I asked the owner what it was for.

"To preëmpt with," was the reply.

"How?"

"Why, don't you understand? To enable my witness to swear that there is *a window in my house!*"

Sometimes the same cabin is moved from claim to claim, until half a dozen different persons have preëmpted with it. In Nebraska a little frame house, like a country daguerrean car, was built for this purpose *on wheels*, and drawn by oxen. It enabled the preëmptor to swear that he had a bona fide residence upon his claim. It was let at five dollars a day, and scores of claims were proved up and preëmpted with it. The discovery of any such malpractice and perjury would invalidate the title. But I never knew of an instance where the preëmptor was deprived of his land after once receiving his title.

No woman can preëmpt unless she is a widow or the "head of a family." But sometimes an ambitious maiden who wishes to secure one hundred and sixty acres of land, *borrows* a child, signs papers of adoption, swears that she is the head of a family, and preëmpts her claim; then annuls the papers and returns her temporary offspring to its parents with an appropriate gift.

Cheating a Greenhorn

THEN old Packsaddle Jack got to telling about Senator Dorsey, of Star Route fame, selling a little herd of cattle he had in northern New Mexico. He said the Senator had got hold of some eye-glass Englishmen, and, representing to them that he had a large herd of cattle, finally made a sale at $25 a head all around. The Englishmen however, insisted on count-

From *A Vaquero of the Brush Country*, by J. Frank Dobie, pp. 165–166. Copyright, 1929, by the Southwest Press. Dallas.

The average old time range man would not have known a "folk-tale," by name, from Adam's off ox; just the same the open range was "lousy" with folk-tales, and one of them was about the way a cowman sold cattle to a greenhorn and in delivering them had the buyer count the same animals over and over. This tale has been told many times in connection with many cowmen and many greenhorns—generally some unnamed Englishman; but perhaps the best of all versions of the yarn fastens the trick on Senator Dorsey. It is to be found in a small, rollicky, and long out-of-print book called *Cowboy Life on a Sidetrack*, by Frank Benton. It seems appropriate here to quote the story as Frank Benton, a thoroughgoing waddie, spun it.—J. F. D.

ing the herd and wouldn't take the Senator's books for them. Dorsey agreed to this; he then went to his foreman, Jack Hill.

"Jack," he said, "I want you to find me a small mountain around which a herd of cattle can be circled several times in one day. This mountain must have a kind of natural stand where men can get a good count on cattle stringing by but where they can't possibly get a view of what is going on outside. Sabe?"

Jack selected a little round mountain with a canyon on one side of it. Here on the bank of the canyon he stationed the Englishmen and their bookkeepers and Senator Dorsey. The Senator had only about 1,000 cattle, and these Jack and the cowboys separated into two bunches out in the hills. Keeping the two herds about a mile apart, they now drove the first herd into the canyon. . . . It was hardly out of sight before the second bunch came stringing along. Meantime cowboys galloped the first herd around back of the mountain and had them coming down the canyon past the Englishmen again for a second count. And they were hardly out of sight before the second division was around the mountain and coming along to be tallied again. Thus the good work went on all morning, the Senator and the Englishmen having only a few minutes to snatch a bite and tap fresh bottles.

At noon Dorsey's foreman told the English party that his men were yet holding an enormous herd back in the hills from which they were cutting off these small bunches of 500 and bringing them along to be tallied. But about three o'clock in the afternoon the cattle began to get thirsty and footsore. Every critter had already traveled thirty miles that day, and lots of them began to drop out and lie down. In one of the herds was an old yellow steer. He was bobtailed, lophorned, and had a game leg. When for the fifteenth time he limped by the crowd that was counting, milord screwed his eyeglass a little tighter on his eye and says:

"There is more bloody, blarsted, lophorned, bobtailed, yellow crippled brutes than anything else, it seems."

Milord's dogrobber speaks up and says, "But, me lord, there's no hanimal like 'im hin the other 'erd."

The Senator overheard this interesting conversation, and, taking the foreman aside, told him when they got that herd on the other side of the mountain again to cut out the old yellow reprobate and not let him come by again. So Jack cut him out and ran him off a ways. But old yellow had got trained to going around that mountain, and the herd wasn't any more than tallied again till here come old Buck, as the cowboys called him, limping down the canyon, the Englishmen staring at him with open mouths and Senator Dorsey looking at old Jack Hill in a reproachful, grieved kind of way. The cowboys ran old Buck off still farther next time, but half an hour afterwards he appeared over a little rise and slowly limped by again.

The Senator now announced that there was only one herd more to count and signalled to Jack to ride around and stop the cowboys. . . .

But as the party broke up and started for the ranch, old Buck came by again, looking like he was in a trance. That night the cowboys said the Senator was groaning in his sleep in a frightful way, and when one of them woke him up and asked if he was sick, he told them, while big drops of cold sweat dropped off his face, that he'd had a terrible nightmare. He said that he thought he was yoked up with a yellow, bobtailed, lophorned, lame steer and was being dragged by the animal through a canyon and around a mountain, day after day, in a hot, broiling sun, while crowds of witless Englishmen and jibbering cowboys were looking on. He insisted on saddling up and going back through the moonlight to the mountain to see if old Buck was still there. A cowboy went with him and after they had got to the canyon and waited a while they heard something coming. Sure enough, directly in the bright moonlight they saw old Buck painfully limping along, stopping now and then to rest.

A week later a cowboy reported finding old Buck dead on his well-worn trail. No one ever rides that way on moonlight nights now, for the cowboys have a tradition that during each full moon old Buck's ghost still limps down the canyon.

The Sky Foogle

THERE was a printer named Dan Shriner who lived in Chillicothe in the early nineties. His chief claim to fame was for his invention of the "sky foogle." The "sky foogle," according to Shriner, was a ferocious animal that had never before been seen or captured. Shriner hired a hall, charged the eager crowd admission for a glimpse of the "terror." When the good Chillicotheans were assembled, there was a fearful rattling of chains, some horrible cries off stage and Shriner, torn and dishevelled, burst upon the scene crying, "Run for your lives, the terrible 'sky foogle' has escaped." The audience ran. They forgot to ask for their money back on the way out. Nobody ever knew what became of Shriner, or, for that matter, of the "sky foogle."

Young Melvin

AFTER his pappy passed on Young Melvin decided he wanted to travel. He'd always lived back at the forks of the creek and he hadn't ever at no time been farther from there than the crossroads.

From *Chillicothe and Ross County*, compiled and written by Federal Writers' Project of Ohio, Works Progress Administration, pp. 29–30. Copyright, 1938, by the Ross County Northwest Territory Committee.

By James R. Aswell. From *God Bless the Devil! Liars' Bench Tales*, by James R. Aswell, Julia Willhoit, Jennette Edwards, E. E. Miller, and Lena E. Lipscomb, of the Tennessee Writers' Project, pp. 3–10. Copyright, 1940, by the University of North Carolina Press. Chapel Hill.

So Young Melvin put out the fire and hid the ax and skillet and called up his hound named Bulger and he was on his way. He went over the hill and a good piece further and he come to the crossroads. He went straight to Old Man Bill Blowdy's house there. He knocked on the door.

Old Man Bill Blowdy come to the door and stuck his nose out the crack. "Who's there?" says he, not daring to come out for fear it was somebody he'd beat in some deal.

"It's me," says Young Melvin. "Just me and my hound dog Bulger."

Old Man Bill Blowdy opened the door then and gave Young Melvin a sly look. "Come in and rest and eat a bite," he says, faint-like.

He was a great big fat red man that was always grinning and easy talking, like butter wouldn't melt in his mouth. And he was just about the slickest, double-dealingest old cooter in the country or anywhere else at all. Nobody could beat him in a deal—never had, anyway—or when it come to a law-suit. Always lawing somebody, Old Man Bill Blowdy was.

"Why don't you come in, Young Melvin?" he says.

"Because I'm on my way, Mister Old Man Bill Blowdy. I'm a-going to town for sure. It's forty miles and across two counties but I aim to see that town. That's why I come to see you."

Old Man Bill Blowdy started shutting the door. "Now, now, Young Melvin," he says. "I'm hard up for money right now. I couldn't loan my sweet mother, now in heaven praise be, so much as a penny."

"I don't want no money," says Young Melvin. "I ain't the borrowing kind."

So Old Man Bill Blowdy poked his head out again. "What can I do for you then?"

"Well, it's like this. You're my twenty-third cousin, my only kin in this world. I got a favor for you to do for me."

Old Man Bill Blowdy started sliding that door shut. "No, no favors. I make it a rule to do no favors and don't expect none from nobody."

"It's a favor I'm aiming to pay for," says Young Melvin.

"Oh," says Old Man Bill Blowdy, opening the door once more, "that's different now. Come right in, Young Melvin."

"No sir, no need to come in, for I'd just be coming out again. What I want you to do is keep my fox hound Bulger while I'm off on my travels. I'll pay his keep, I'll pay what's right when I come back to get him."

Old Man Bill Blowdy grinned all over his face. He thought he saw a way to make himself something extry or get him a fox hound one. Everybody knew Young Melvin was simple. Honest as the day's long but simple.

"Why yes," says Old Man Bill Blowdy. "Why yes, I'll keep Bulger for you, Young Melvin, and glad to."

So Young Melvin gave his hound dog over and bid Old Man Bill Blowdy farewell. "I'll be back next week or month or sometime. I don't know how long it'll be, for it's forty miles and across two counties to town."

Well, one day the week or month or anyhow sometime after that, here come Young Melvin down the pikeroad to the crossroads, limping and dusty and easy in mind. He went straight to Old Man Bill Blowdy's house and knocked his knuckles on the door.

Old Man Bill Blowdy stuck his nose out the crack and says, "Who's there?"

"It's me, it's Young Melvin."

"How are you, Young Melvin?"

"Fair to piddling. I walked to town and saw all the sights and then walked back here again. Forty miles and across two counties. Don't never want to roam no more. I'm satisfied now."

Old Man Bill Blowdy started shutting the door. "Glad to hear it, Young Melvin. Next time you come down to the crossroads, drop in and say hello. Any time, just any time, Young Melvin."

"Hold there! Wait a minute!" says Young Melvin.

"I'm busy," says the old man.

But Young Melvin got his foot in the door. "How about Bulger, Old Man Bill Blowdy? How about him?"

Old Man Bill Blowdy kept trying to shut the door and Young Melvin kept shoving his foot in.

"See here!" says Young Melvin. "I mean my fox hound."

"Oh him? Why, I declare to my soul I'd almost forgot that hound dog, Young Melvin. I sure almost had."

"Where is he at?" says Young Melvin, still trying to keep the old man from closing the door.

"I'll tell you," says Old Man Bill Blowdy, still trying to shut it, "I feel mighty bad about it, Young Melvin, but your Bulger is no more."

"How come? What do you mean?"

"Why, he's perished and gone, Young Melvin. The first night after you left I sort of locked him up in that little busted-down house over in the Old Ground. Well sir, Young Melvin, those last renters of mine that lived there was powerful dirty folks. They left the place just lousy with chinch bugs. Them bugs was mortal hungry by this time. So they just eat that Bulger of yours alive. Eat all but the poor thing's bones by morning—and the bones was pretty well gnawed.

"It was my fault in one way. I ought to known better than put your dog in there, Young Melvin. But I done it. So I won't charge you a penny for his keep the night I had him. I aim to do the fair thing."

Well, Old Man Bill Blowdy stuck his sly eye to the crack of the door to see how Young Melvin was taking it. He knew the boy was simple. He figured he had him. Because Old Man Bill Blowdy had Bulger hid out and he aimed to swap him for something to a man he knew in the next county.

So Young Melvin stood there looking like the good Lord had shaken him off His Christian limb. Tears come in his eyes and he sleeved his nose. "That dog was folks to me," he says. "Them chinch bugs don't know what they done to me."

He pulled his foot out of the door and he backed down the steps. He started towards home.

Old Man Bill Blowdy eased out on the porch to watch him go.

About that time Young Melvin turned around. "Mister Old Man Bill Blowdy," he says, "my place is way over the hill and a good piece further. I'm beat out and tired. Wonder if you'd loan me your mule to ride on? I'll bring it back tomorrow."

The old man knew Young Melvin was honest as the livelong day. Besides, he was so tickled with how he'd got him a good hound to swap and it not costing anything that he just called across the way to the crossroads store and got a witness to the loan and let Young Melvin take the mule. It was a fine mule, too, with the three hind ribs showing, the best sort of sign in a mule—shows he's a hard worker.

Next morning Young Melvin never showed up and Old Man Bill Blowdy got worried. He got worrieder still in the middle of the day when no sign of Young Melvin did he see.

But along about afternoon he saw Young Melvin come walking over the hill and down towards the crossroads. He run out on his porch and yelled, "Hey, Young Melvin, where's my mule?"

Young Melvin kept walking. He just shook his head. "I feel mighty bad about that mule, Mister Old Man Bill Blowdy," he called. "I sure do."

"Hey! Wait there!"

But Young Melvin went on, heading for the store at the crossroads.

So Old Man Bill Blowdy was so mad he didn't wait to get his shoes. He just jumped off the porch and run across to Square Rogers, that good old man's house up the road a ways.

"Square," he says, "I want you to handle Young Melvin. He stole my mule."

The Square waked up his deputy and the deputy went down and brought in Young Melvin. Everybody at the crossroads come tagging along behind.

Square said, "Son, they tell me you stole a mule."

"No sir, Square Rogers, I never done it," says Young Melvin.

Old Man Bill Blowdy stomped his bare feet and shook his fists. "He's a bald-faced liar!"

"Curb yourself down, Old Man Bill Blowdy," says the Square, "and let the boy tell his side. Go ahead, Young Melvin."

So Young Melvin told his side, told how he borrowed the mule and started for home. "Well," he says, "you know I live over the hill and a good piece further. I rode that mule to the top of the hill. I was minding my own business and not giving nobody any trouble. Then all on a sudden I see a turkey buzzard dropping down out of the sky. Here it come, dropping fast and crowing like a game rooster.

"First thing I knew that old buzzard just grabbed Old Man Bill Blowdy's mule by the tail and started heaving and the mule's hind legs lifted off the ground and I went flying over his head and hit a rock head-on. I failed in my senses a minute. When I could see straight I saw that buzzard sailing away with the mule, most a mile high and getting littler all the time.

"And that's how it happened. I sure am sorry, but there ain't much you can do with a thing like that, Square."

"Hold on there!" says Square Rogers, that good old man. "I've seen many a turkey buzzard in my time, Young Melvin, but never a one that could crow."

"Well," says Young Melvin, "it surprised me some too. But in a county where chinch bugs can eat up a full-grown fox hound in one night, why I just reckon a turkey buzzard has a right to crow and fly off with a mule if he wants to."

So it all come out and Square Rogers, that good old man, made Old Man Bill Blowdy fork up Bulger and then Young Melvin gave back the mule.

Old Man Bill Blowdy was mocked down to nothing. He just grieved and pined away and it wasn't no more than ten years before he taken sick and wasted away and died.

The Glorious Whitewasher

SATURDAY morning was come, and all the summer world was bright and fresh, and brimming with life. There was a song in every heart; and if the heart was young the music issued at the lips. There was cheer in every face and a spring in every step. The locust trees were in bloom and the fragrance of the blossoms filled the air. Cardiff Hill, beyond the village and above it, was green with vegetation, and it lay just far enough away to seem a Delectable Land, dreamy, reposeful, and inviting.

Tom appeared on the sidewalk with a bucket of whitewash and a long-handled brush. He surveyed the fence, and all gladness left him and a deep melancholy settled down upon his spirit. Thirty yards of board fence nine feet high. Life to him seemed hollow, and existence but a burden. Sighing he dipped his brush and passed it along the topmost plank; repeated the operation; did it again; compared the insignificant whitewashed streak with the far-reaching continent of unwhitewashed fence, and sat down on a

From *The Adventures of Tom Sawyer,* by Mark Twain, pp. 12–19. Copyright, 1875, 1899, and 1903, by Samuel L. Clemens, 1917, by Clara Gabrilowitsch, 1917, 1920, by Mark Twain Company. New York: Harper & Brothers.

At mention of Mark Twain's name the average Man of the Street is likely to say: "Why yes, of course; he wrote that piece about Tom Sawyer whitewashing the fence. I read it as a boy, and never forgot it."

Later, he will recall other, perhaps more important, achievements; but he will begin with Tom and his fence.

There is a reason for this: the famous "whitewashing" episode is to-day something more than mere literature. It has entered the realm of folk-lore—taken its place in that corner of Story Land, where the old tales remain always fresh, and never lose their fashion, because they are immortal.—Albert Bigelow Paine, *Tom Sawyer, Whitewasher* (1933), pp. v–vi.

tree-box discouraged. Jim came skipping out at the gate with a tin pail, and singing "Buffalo Gals." Bringing water from the town pump had always been hateful work in Tom's eyes, before, but now it did not strike him so. He remembered that there was company at the pump. White, mulatto, and Negro boys and girls were always there waiting their turns, resting, trading playthings, quarreling, fighting, skylarking. And he remembered that although the pump was only a hundred and fifty yards off, Jim never got back with a bucket of water under an hour—and even then somebody generally had to go after him. Tom said:

"Say, Jim, I'll fetch the water if you'll whitewash some."

Jim shook his head and said:

"Can't, Mars Tom. Ole missis, she tole me I got to go an' git dis water an' not stop foolin' roun' wid anybody. She say she spec' Mars Tom gwine to ax me to whitewash, an' so she tole me go 'long an' 'tend to my own business—she 'lowed *she'd* 'tend to de whitewashin'."

"Oh, never you mind what she said, Jim. That's the way she always talks. Gimme the bucket—I won't be gone only a minute. *She* won't ever know."

"Oh, I dasn't, Mars Tom. Ole missis she'd take an' tar de head off'n me. 'Deed she would."

"*She!* She never licks anybody—whacks 'em over the head with her thimble—and who cares for that, I'd like to know. She talks awful, but talk don't hurt—anyways it don't if she don't cry. Jim, I'll give you a marvel. I'll give you a white alley!"

Jim began to waver.

"White alley, Jim! And it's a bully taw."

"My! Dat's a mighty gay marvel, *I* tell you! But Mars Tom, I's powerful 'fraid ole missis—"

"And besides, if you will I'll show you my sore toe."

Jim was only human—this attraction was too much for him. He put down his pail, took the white alley, and bent over the toe with absorbing interest while the bandage was being unwound. In another moment he was flying down the street with his pail and a tingling rear, Tom was whitewashing with vigor, and Aunt Polly was retiring from the field with a slipper in her hand and triumph in her eye.

But Tom's energy did not last. He began to think of the fun he had planned for this day, and his sorrows multiplied. Soon the free boys would come tripping along on all sorts of delicious expeditions, and they would make a world of fun of him for having to work—the very thought of it burnt him like fire. He got out his worldly wealth and examined it—bits of toys, marbles, and trash; enough to buy an exchange of *work*, maybe, but not half enough to buy so much as half an hour of pure freedom. So he returned his straitened means to his pocket, and gave up the idea of trying to buy the boys. At this dark and hopeless moment an inspiration burst upon him! Nothing less than a great, magnificent inspiration.

He took up his brush and went tranquilly to work. Ben Rogers hove in sight presently—the very boy, of all boys, whose ridicule he had been dreading. Ben's gait was the hop-skip-and-jump—proof enough that his heart was light and his anticipations high. He was eating an apple, and giving a long, melodious whoop, at intervals, followed by a deep-toned ding-dong-dong, ding-dong-dong, for he was personating a steamboat. As he drew near, he slackened speed, took the middle of the street, leaned far over to starboard and rounded to ponderously and with laborious pomp and circumstance—for he was personating the *Big Missouri,* and considered himself to be drawing nine feet of water. He was boat and captain and engine-bells combined, so he had to imagine himself standing on his own hurricane-deck giving the orders and executing them:

"Stop her, sir! Ting-a-ling-ling!" The headway ran almost out and he drew up slowly toward the sidewalk.

"Ship up to back! Ting-a-ling-ling!" His arms straightened and stiffened down his sides.

"Set her back on the stabboard! Ting-a-ling-ling! Chow! ch-chow-wow! Chow!" His right hand, meantime, describing stately circles—for it was representing a forty-foot wheel.

"Let her go back on the labboard! Ting-a-ling-ling! Chow-ch-chow-chow!" The left hand began to describe circles.

"Stop the stabboard! Ting-a-ling-ling! Stop the labboard! Come ahead on the stabboard! Stop her! Let your outside turn over slow! Ting-a-ling-ling! Chow-ow-ow! Get out that head-line! *Lively* now! Come—out with your spring-line—what're you about there! Take a turn round that stump with the bight of it! Stand by that stage, now—let her go! Done with the engines, sir! Ting-a-ling-ling! *Sh't! sh't! sh't!*" (trying the gauge-cocks).

Tom went on whitewashing—paid no attention to the steamboat. Ben stared a moment and then said:

"Hi-*yi!* *You're* up a stump, ain't you!"

No answer. Tom surveyed his last touch with the eye of an artist, then he gave his brush another gentle sweep and surveyed the result, as before. Ben ranged up alongside of him. Tom's mouth watered for the apple, but he stuck to his work. Ben said.

"Hello, old chap, you got to work, hey?"

Tom wheeled suddenly and said:

"Why, it's you, Ben! I warn't noticing."

"Say—*I'm* going in a-swimming, *I* am. Don't you wish you could? But of course you'd druther *work*—wouldn't you? Course you would!" Tom contemplated the boy a bit, and said:

"What do you call work?"

"Why, ain't *that* work?"

Tom resumed his whitewashing, and answered carelessly:

"Well, maybe it is, and maybe it ain't. All I know, is, it suits Tom Sawyer."

"Oh come, now, you don't mean to let on that you *like* it?"

The brush continued to move.

"Like it? Well, I don't see why I oughtn't to like it. Does a boy get a chance to whitewash a fence every day?"

That put the thing in a new light. Ben stopped nibbling his apple. Tom swept his brush daintily back and forth—stepped back to note the effect—added a touch here and there—criticized the effect again—Ben watching every move and getting more and more interested, more and more absorbed. Presently he said:

"Say, Tom, let *me* whitewash a little."

Tom considered, was about to consent; but he altered his mind:

"No—no—I reckon it wouldn't hardly do, Ben. You see, Aunt Polly's awful particular about this fence—right here on the street, you know— but if it was the back fence I wouldn't mind and *she* wouldn't. Yes, she's awful particular about this fence; it's got to be done very careful; I reckon there ain't one boy in a thousand, maybe two thousand, that can do it the way it's got to be done."

"No—is that so? Oh come, now—lemme just try. Only just a little— I'd let *you*, if you was me, Tom."

"Ben, I'd like to, honest injun; but Aunt Polly—well, Jim wanted to do it, but she wouldn't let him; Sid wanted to do it, and she wouldn't let Sid. Now don't you see how I'm fixed? If you was to tackle this fence and anything was to happen to it—"

"Oh, shucks, I'll be just as careful. Now lemme try. Say—I'll give you the core of my apple."

"Well, here— No, Ben, now don't. I'm afeard—"

"I'll give you *all* of it!"

Tom gave up the brush with reluctance in his face, but alacrity in his heart. And while the late steamer *Big Missouri* worked and sweated in the sun, the retired artist sat on a barrel in the shade close by, dangled his legs, munched his apple, and planned the slaughter of more innocents. There was no lack of material; boys happened along every little while; they came to jeer, but remained to whitewash. By the time Ben was fagged out, Tom had traded the next chance to Billy Fisher for a kite, in good repair; and when *he* played out, Johnny Miller bought in for a dead rat and a string to swing it with—and so on, and so on, hour after hour. And when the middle of the afternoon came, from being a poor poverty-stricken boy in the morning, Tom was literally rolling in wealth. He had besides the things before mentioned, twelve marbles, part of a jews'-harp, a piece of blue bottle-glass to look through, a spool cannon, a key that wouldn't unlock anything, a fragment of chalk, a glass stopper of a decanter, a tin soldier, a couple of tadpoles, six firecrackers, a kitten with only one eye, a brass door-knob, a dog-collar—but no dog—the handle of a knife, four pieces of orange-peel, and a dilapidated old window-sash.

He had had a nice, good, idle time all the while—plenty of company— and the fence had three coats of whitewash on it! If he hadn't run out of whitewash, he would have bankrupted every boy in the village.

Tom said to himself that it was not such a hollow world, after all. He had discovered a great law of human action, without knowing it—namely, that in order to make a man or boy covet a thing, it is only necessary to make the thing difficult to attain. If he had been a great and wise philosopher, like the writer of this book, he would now have comprehended that Work consists of whatever a body is *obliged* to do, and that Play consists of whatever a body is not obliged to do. And this would help him to understand why constructing artificial flowers or performing on a treadmill is work, while rolling tenpins or climbing Mont Blanc is only amusement. There are wealthy gentlemen in England who drive four-horse passenger-coaches twenty or thirty miles on a daily line, in the summer, because the privilege costs them considerable money; but if they were offered wages for the service, that would turn it into work and then they would resign.

The boy mused awhile over the substantial change which had taken place in his worldly circumstances, and then wended toward headquarters to report.

II. HUMOROUS ANECDOTES AND JESTS

It was common in the bar-rooms, the gatherings in the "country store," and finally at public meetings in the mouths of "stump orators." Arguments were clinched, and political principles illustrated by a "funny story." It invaded even the camp meeting and the pulpit. It at last received the currency of the public press. But wherever met it was so individual and characteristic, that it was at once known and appreciated abroad as "an American story."—BRET HARTE

1. VARIETIES OF THE AMERICAN ANECDOTE

THE anecdote may be defined as a story with a point or a point with a story, depending upon where the emphasis falls. Unlike the fable or parable, the anecdote is not allegorical and is generally based on an actual occurrence. Because the point of an anecdote is wise or witty rather than moral, it is close to the aphorism; and in its use to enliven or illustrate conversation and oratory, it resembles the allusion and the figure of speech. All these values are embodied in Lincoln's remark—an anecdote in epitome —on the lawyer's paper: "It's like the lazy preacher that used to write long sermons, and the explanation was, he got to writin' and was too lazy to stop."

Typically, the anecdote is associated with character and custom, being commonly used to illustrate a trait of an individual or a community. Thus we are familiar with anecdotes (etymologically, "unpublished" stories) of famous persons and of places. In the broad sense, however, the anecdote is any traditional narrative of a single incident and of a realistic and usually humorous character, which is intended to be believed. Although all anecdotes are not humorous, all jests involving a narrative situation, with some development and elaboration, may be classed as anecdotes.

The evolution of an anecdote from a mere joke is illustrated by two versions of "Ain't Lost." In its simplest form the gag is a comeback, as given by Carl Sandburg in *The People, Yes:* "Which way to the post-office, boy?" "I don't know." "You don't know much, do you?" "No, but I ain't lost."

In general, three types of anecdotes may be distinguished: the anecdote based on a witty remark, or *jeu d'esprit,* such as "Ain't Lost," involving repartee, quibbles, and quiddities; the anecdote of character; and the social or cultural anecdote, which involves a comment on a way of living. In the United States, all three types are given local coloring and significance in what may be called the local anecdote.

It is perhaps in the local anecdote of character (e.g., "The Grist Mill") that one may best see the American anecdote on its way to becoming a short story, in line with Bret Harte's theory that the American anecdote was the "parent of the American 'short story.'"

2. PRACTICAL STORY-TELLERS

On the one hand, story-telling is a pastime or a form of social inter-course, associated with leisure, gregariousness, and travel. On the other hand, it may have a practical application, enforcing a point and enlivening a discourse with a parable or example. Because wit and humor add an extra seasoning to the sauce of narrative, the humorous anecdote has always been effective for the purposes of homiletic or forensic illustration, as demonstrated by the popularity of collections of stories and jokes for speakers. Thus the medieval Latin collections of *exempla,* or illustrative stories for use in sermons, which drew upon the storehouses of classical legend, fable, and merry tales, served as a link between the folk literatures of ancient and modern times and as a forerunner of the jest-book.

In America the practical value of the humorous anecdote lies not so much in teaching a lesson as in making a point. Hence the wide use of the practical story in business and politics. The master of the story with a point was Lincoln, unique among story-tellers and presidents in his ability "to tell his stories, and by them to illustrate matters of great pith."

Lincoln touches the art of the humorous American anecdote at almost every point. In young manhood he discovered the secret that the Yankee peddler had learned before him and that traveling salesmen, storekeepers, lawyers, and politicians have always known—how to mix business and sociability by making a good story break down resistance, build up good will, clinch or bolster an argument, or simply pass the time of day. Whether his business was floating a flatboat or raft down the river, logging, clerking in a store, practising law, representing his district in the state legislature or Congress, or directing the destiny of his country in a great Civil War, he knew that the apt saying or anecdote, expressive of a principle or truth, constituted one of his greatest assets.[1]

From the prize story-teller of his community and its spokesman at all

---

[1] The backwoods Lincoln has often been compared to Davy Crockett as a stump-speech story-teller. With Crockett, however, as has been pointed out above, the funny story was, like the treat, chiefly a vote–getting expedient.

the neighborhood gatherings, he rose to be story-teller to the nation and the voice of the people. He is our only folk hero who is also a folk artist. Akin to Aesop and Poor Richard, he differs from our other great folk story-teller, Mark Twain, in that he was not a professional humorist, and from other "funny men" in Congress—Hardin, Corwin, Knott, and Cox— in that with him the anecdote rather than repartee or satire was the weapon. Drawing his homely incidents, allusions, figures, aphorisms, and idioms from backwoods experience, he differs from all the ordinary raconteurs who have used funny stories to garnish oratory or tickle an audience. At the same time, steeped in the lore of humor, he learned many of his tricks from the cracker-box philosophers and jesters before him, including Joe Miller. He raised the wisecrack to the level of scripture.

The practical anecdote also has its religious uses, as parables, to illustrate sermons, to point the meaning of true religion, or perhaps to satirize a rival sect.

3. RURAL JESTS

Both Lincoln and Crockett, in common with many of our popular humorists and comedians, had hayseed in their hair. Near the end of the last century the vogue of rural humor coincided with the vogue of rural and provincial drama, fiction, and poetry of the *Old Homestead, David Harum,* and James Whitcomb Riley stamp. The appeal of rural character and illiteracy in American literature is based on various motives and related to various movements in American life. The frontier, the democratic tradi- tion of the common man, local color, and naturism, with their cults of the soil, the "homely pathetic," and the "native," have conspired to make the dry wit and the slow drawl of the countryman the most effective and characteristic expression of American independence, ingenuity, and irrever- ence. In rural humor, with its blend of Yankee shrewdness, backwoods eccentricity, and Western breeziness, the central trait is the contrast between apparent simplicity and underlying wit and wisdom or between pretended knowledge and actual ignorance, coupled in either case with gumption and nerve. The spectacle of rustic follies and blunders affords entertainment not only to the city-dweller, who is something of a hick- baiter, but also to the countryman ruminating on the odds and ends of his daily life. The best of rural jests are local anecdotes of character and custom. On the "make-it-yourself-or-do-without" level of culture, more- over, story-telling is one of the chief leisure-time activities and an integral part of fun-making.

4. NEGRO JESTS

The laughter of the Negro, like that of other minorities, is a solace and a source of courage; but it is on the attack rather than merely on the defensive, emphasizing the Brer Rabbit resourcefulness of a highly adaptive and infinitely patient folk. Negro jests strike a note of defiance rather than of protest, as is the case with Negro blues and folk rhymes. As High John de Conquer (the folk name for the marsh St. John's wort, whose root wards off evil, in the form of disease, hants, witches, nightmares, and the like), the "John" of slavery anecdotes is a symbol of the Negro's brier-patch-bred ability to land on his feet in the briers and "skip out des ez lively ez a cricket in de embers." Old John gets out of tight places and turns the joke on Old Massa, by dint of what Zora Neale Hurston calls "hitting a straight lick with a crooked stick." "Now, High John de Conquer, Old Massa couldn't get the best of *him*. That Old John was a case!" High John de Conquer's laughter is a secret laughter, with a subtle power like that of the root of the same name—the power to help Negroes "overcome things they feel that they could not beat otherwise."[1]

5. Fools and Bunglers

On the credit side, the countryman is as commonsensical as he is unlearned; on the debit side, he is apt to be as nonsensical as he is simple. The humor of rustic ignorance and gullibility, with the stupid person being taken in by the clever one, is part of the larger humor of mistakes and misunderstandings. From ancient times men have laughed at "that droll stupidity which is the characteristic of noodles or simpletons" and which, as in the following drolleries, takes the form of Irish bulls, Gaulardisms, pedantry, making easy things hard, absentmindedness, imagining troubles, and literal following of directions.[2]

6. Gags and Wisecracks

From the perennial humor of wit and nitwit emerge stock themes, such as the absent-minded man, Scotch and "so tight" jokes, the ugliest man, the meanest man, as well as certain vogues, such as slow train and Ford jokes and, among sayings, "knock knocks" and "You tell 'em" English. The ephemeral humor of gags and wisecracks—the temporal counterpart of local anecdotes and sayings—provides a laboratory for the study of the patterns, variations, and diffusion of popular material. The idiom is largely urban and sophisticated, since the principal means of transmission is by press, stage, film, and radio, but the mold is the folk mold of popular fantasy patterned by repetition.

Almost every form of wit and rhetorical device is employed in the wisecrack or "jocular smart remark": puns, malapropisms, boners, and other varieties of word play and humorous mistakes (She was so dumb she thought a subordinate clause was one of Santa's offspring; He is a big needle and thread man from So-and-So; She is not my best girl—just necks best; Lettuce is a proposition); Wellerisms (As the pencil sharpener said, "Now to get down to the point"); Irish bulls and paradoxes (I couldn't commit suicide if my life depended on it; She would be cute if it wasn't for her face); extravagant impossibilities (Yours till elephants roost on rose bushes); nonsense (More fun than I've had since the day the cow catcher had a calf); exaggeration (She was so thin that she could fall through a flute and never strike a note); the fabulous or the tall tale (It was so cold the cows gave ice cream); *reductio ad absurdum* (If steam-

---

[1] "High John de Conquer," by Zora Neale Hurston, *The American Mercury*, Vol. LVII (October, 1943), No. 238, pp. 450–458.

[2] For a classification of "fool" motifs, see *Motif-Index of Folk-Literature*, by Stith Thompson, under "J. The Wise and the Foolish."

ships sold for a nickel, I couldn't buy the echo of a whistle); *non sequitur* (Let's you and him fight until I get tired).

The use of the formula is basic to the wisecrack: so dumb, so tight, you tell 'em, they call, she was only, you don't have to, you may be. Certain formulae are identified with disparaging or insulting wisecracks, or "slams" (They call her a toe dancer because she dances on other people's toes; You don't have to hang from a tree to be a nut; You may be bread in old Kentucky but you're just a crumb around here).

The habit of wisecracking is related to the American trait of "laughing it off" and to the love of mottoes and slogans. Many trade slogans are nothing but wisecracks: We wash everything but the baby; You can whip our cream but you can't beat our milk; You furnish the girl, we furnish the rest; Look at your hat, everyone else does; Why kill your wife? Let us do the dirty work; You wreck 'em, we fix 'em.

The value of this floating linguistic material for both the poet and the social historian is evinced by the successful use of talk, jokes, and lingo made by Carl Sandburg in both *Abraham Lincoln, the Prairie Years* and *The People, Yes.*

Ain't Lost

A FINE city man had a brand-new buggy and a prize-winning pair of trotters that he wished to try out. He drove along the country roads, speeding a little here and walking a little there, studying the good points and admiring the beauty of his new rig. He was so delighted with the prospect that he failed to notice the road. Later on he realized that he was lost, but he hoped by driving on to find his way, or at least to meet someone who could tell him how to get back to the city.

But it was a long lonesome road. For a long time he followed the windings, hoping every hilltop would bring him within sight of some dwelling. When it was almost dark he saw in front of him a cotton patch and a good-sized country boy chopping away in the rows. He reined his tired team near the fence and called out, "Hello, boy."

"Hello yourself," the boy replied, still wielding his hoe.

"Where does this road go to?"

"Hain't never seed it go nowhars. Hit allus stays right whar hit is," said the boy, still digging away.

"How far is it to the next town?"

"Don't know; never measured it," replied the boy.

Thoroughly disgusted, the man said with some heat, "You don't know anything. You are certainly the biggest fool I ever saw."

From "Anecdotes from the Brazos Bottoms," by A. W. Eddins, *Straight Texas*, Publications of the Texas Folk-Lore Society, Number XIII, 1937, edited by J. Frank Dobie and Mody C. Boatright, p. 94. Copyright, 1937, by the Texas Folk-Lore Society. Austin.

The boy looked a long time in the man's eyes; then he said with contempt, "I knows I don't know nothing. I knows I'se a fool. But I ain't lost."

The Grist Mill

THERE is no land on earth which has produced such quaint and curious characters as the great mountainous regions of the South, and yet no country has produced nobler or brainier men.

When I was a barefooted boy my grandfather's old grist mill was the Mecca of the mountaineers. They gathered there on rainy days to talk politics and religion, and to drink "mountain" dew and fight. Adam Wheezer was a tall, spindle-shanked old settler, as dark as an Indian, and he wore a broad, hungry grin that always grew broader at the sight of a fat sheep. The most prominent trait of Adam's character, next to his love of mutton, was his bravery. He stood in the mill one day with his empty sack under his arm, as usual, when Bert Lynch, the bully of the mountains, with an eye like a game rooster's, walked up to him and said: "Adam, you've bin a-slanderin' of me, an' I'm a-gwine to give you a thrashin'." He seized Adam by the throat and backed him under the meal spout. Adam opened his mouth to squall and it spouted meal like a whale. He made a surge for breath and liberty, and tossed Bert away like a feather. Then he shot out of the mill door like a rocket, leaving his old battered plug hat and one prong of his coat-tail in the hands of the enemy. He ran through the creek and knocked it dry as he went. He made a bee-line for my grandfather's house, a quarter of a mile away, on the hill. He burst into the sitting-room, covered with meal and panting like a bellowsed horse, frightening my grandmother almost into hysterics. The old lady screamed and shouted: "What in the world is the matter, Adam?" Adam replied: "That thar durned Bert Lynch is down yander a-tryin' to raise a fuss with me."

But every dog has his day. Brother Billy Patterson preached from the door of the mill on the following Sunday. It was his first sermon in that "neck of the woods" and he began his ministrations with a powerful discourse, hurling his anathemas against Satan and sin and every kind of wickedness. He denounced whisky. He branded the bully as a brute and a moral coward, and personated Bert, having witnessed his battle with Adam. This was too much for the champion. He resolved to "thrash" Brother Patterson, and in a few days they met at the mill. Bert squared himself and said: "Parson, you had your turn last Sunday; it's mine to-day. Pull off that broadcloth an' take your medicine. I'm a-gwine to suck the marrow out'n them ole bones o' yourn." The pious preacher

From "Visions and Dreams," in *Echoes, Centennial and other Notable Speeches, Lectures, and Stories,* by Governor Robt. L. Taylor, pp. 175–177. Copyright, 1899, by S. B. Williamson & Co. Nashville, Tennessee.

pled for peace, but without avail. At last he said: "Then, if nothing but a fight will satisfy you, will you allow me to kneel down and say my prayers before we fight?" "Oh, yes, that's all right, Parson," said Bert, "but cut yer prayer short, for I'm a-gwine to give you a good sound thrashin'."

The preacher knelt and thus began to pray: "O Lord, thou knowest that when I killed Bill Cummins, and John Brown, and Jerry Smith, and Levi Bottles, that I did it in self defense. Thou knowest, O Lord, that when I cut the heart out of young Sliger, and strewed the ground with the brains of Paddy Miles, that it was forced upon me, and that I did it in great agony of soul. And now, O Lord, I am about to be forced to put in his coffin, this poor, miserable wretch, who has attacked me here to-day. O Lord, have mercy upon his soul, and take care of his helpless widow and orphans when he is gone!"

And he arose, whetting his knife on his shoe-sole, singing:

> "Hark, from the tomb a doleful sound,
> Mine ears attend the cry."

But when he looked around, Bert was gone. There was nothing in sight but a little cloud of dust far up the road, following in the wake of the vanishing champion.

Two Pioneer Folk Tales

I. YALLER BREAD

THE "yaller bread" incident preluded an "infare" dinner that was being prepared for a newly wedded couple. The table was set but the company was not due to arrive for an hour or so when the ladies of the house found their hospitality required by an unexpected guest. He was a man living some miles "up the creek" who had obligingly stopped on his way home from the mill below to deliver a supply of freshly ground cornmeal. He was a person of considerable ignorance and of little consequence, and his

From "Pioneer Folk Tales," by Mary Jourdan Atkinson and J. Frank Dobie, *Foller De Drinkin' Gou'd*, Publications of the Texas Folk-Lore Society, Number VII, edited by J. Frank Dobie, pp. 69–70, 71. Copyright, 1928, by The Texas Folk-Lore Society. Austin.

One class of these early day folk narratives—a class now rapidly disappearing as a result of luxuries—was designed to teach the children manners—a purpose that has inspired children's stories from time immemorial. Besides educating their offspring in the ways of general courtesy, the pioneer parents, particularly of the better class of settlers, felt it necessary to inform them concerning the elegancies of civilization that had been left behind. Naturally the burden of this instruction was borne by the mother. The settlements became "alive" with stories ridiculing the backwoodsman and enforcing the rules of etiquette.—M. J. A. and J. F. D.

presence was not desired at the wedding dinner; nevertheless, custom demanded that he leave the house with his appetite satisfied and his feelings uninjured. It was decided to say nothing of the impending sociable, and the hostess graciously suggested that he sit down and eat immediately so that he should not be delayed on his long ride home. The man sat down at his ease and began eating. In fact, he made so free with the good things on the table that he was obliged to let his belt out notch by notch until finally he got up and took it off. He hung it on the back of his chair and forgot to put it on again when the meal was over. But that omission was not the worst of his backwoods violations of good manners.

As he ate on, he seemed to relish in particular a huge plate of sliced pound cake. He kept spreading the pieces thick with butter and making away with them, while he ate chicken, beef, venison, and other solid food, until the hostess, alarmed at the rate at which her cherished and rare cake was disappearing, pressed him to take some biscuits. With white flour at a premium, biscuits, as well as cake, were a delicacy, a luxury; cornbread was the staple breadstuff. Surely, thought the hostess, the biscuits will divert him from the pound cake.

But the backwoodsman, apparently with perfect sincerity, waved them away. "No thank you, ma'am," he said. "You just save them there biscuits. This here yaller bread is good enough for me."

II. The Woven Rug

A boy was sent by his parents to the home of some new and well-to-do neighbors. He had been used to deer skins and bull hides for carpets, and when he was invited into the elegantly furnished parlor of his hosts, he was very much intimidated. By sidling around the edge of the floor, he managed to get to a chair without walking on a rug that covered most of the floor space. When he left a few moments later he got out of the room by the same circuitous route.

"Well, son, how did you like our new neighbors?" his mother inquired when he got back home.

"Oh," the boy replied, "the lady seemed to be mighty nice, but she is terrible car'less like. Why, she had a fine piece of cloth spread right out in the middle of the floor, and danged if she didn't put her foot right down on it. But I knowed better than to do anything like that and so managed to hop around and keep from steppin' on it."

Catching a Corn Thief

"Did you hear about Owl Skinner getting a corn thief by the hand in a steel trap? Well, old Owl's a mart'n. He kept his crib locked all the

From *Beyond Dark Hills*, A Personal Story, by Jesse Stuart, pp. 88–89. Copyright, 1938. by E. P. Dutton & Co., Inc. New York.

time. And he said he kept saying: 'Boys, you're feeding a little too heavy on that corn. Now you must go lighter or we won't have enough to last us all winter.' But he said the boys said: 'Pap, we ain't feeding corn that way. We don't feed the cattle anything but roughness. And the mules are going down on what we are feeding them. They're weak on pulling a little drag of wood into the yard.' Then Owl goes out to the crib and finds a hole worn slick as a ground-hog hole. He gets him a heavy-jawed steel trap and sets it right at that hole. He puts a little corn silk over it so the jaws won't show. He fastens it to a crib log with a trace chain and locks the chain. The next morning when he goes out there stands old Pete Woodrow with his sack at his feet. Owl didn't say a word. He went right on and done up his feeding. Then he comes around and says: 'Now let this be a lesson to you, Pete, you won't forget.' He goes in the crib and unlocks the trace chain and lets Pete's hand out of the trap. 'Come on and get you some breakfast now, Pete.' He makes Pete go in, wash the blood off his hand and eat breakfast with him. Pete looks from shameful eyes ever since then. But don't you know Owl Skinner said: 'Now, Pete, I am the law here in this case. What I want you to do is go out there and fill up that sack out of my best corn and take it home with you this time.' It hurt Pete to take the corn but he went and done it. Owl Skinner ain't lost any more corn since."

Weather Prophets

It has been said that George B. Erath, the famous German pioneer and Indian fighter, was the author of the expression: "Nobody prophesies about Texas weather except newcomers and damn fools."

For many years this has been a favorite gag in Texas social life. It was one of the sells in the old saloon days, and the unfortunate tenderfoot who fell for it always had to set up the drinks to the crowd.

One dull, slow evening when things were at an absolute standstill in the saloon, a fresh young guy with a derby hat and store-bought clothes breezed into the place, walked up to the bar, and ordered a drink. The usual crowd of loafers looked on disapprovingly but said nothing. Leisurely finishing his drink and wiping his mouth with a bright silk handkerchief, the newcomer said, "Well, I believe it's going to rain."

The golden opportunity had arrived; the whole crowd was alert and watchful. Then the old nester, the leader in all the local wars of wits, said very fatherly, "My friend, did you know that there were only two kinds of people who prophesy about Texas weather?"

From "Anecdotes from the Brazos Bottoms," by A. W. Eddins, *Straight Texas*, Publications of the Texas Folk-Lore Society, Number XIII, 1937, edited by J. Frank Dobie and Mody C. Boatright, pp. 88–89. Copyright, 1937, by the Texas Folk-Lore Society. Austin.

"Two kinds of people who prophesy on Texas weather?" mused the stranger. "That's very queer. Who are they?"

Then the old nester, with all the contempt and sarcasm in his power, sneered, "Newcomers and damn fools."

The crowd rose with a mighty shout and gathered around the newcomer shouting, "Haw, haw, haw." "He got you that time." "You are it." "He got you good." "Set um up. Set um up." "You owe the drinks to the house." "Come on, set um up."

The young fellow stood smiling at all their hurrah. He was not the least troubled about their demands for the drinks. When the hubbub had died down and they were all properly up against the bar, he said very calmly and slowly, "You say there are only two kinds of people who prophesy about Texas weather—newcomers and damn fools. You are right. Those are the only two kinds in Texas."

All Face

ON A cold dreary day an Indian and a white man were making a journey together. The Indian had on no clothing except a blanket, while the white man was bundled up in all the clothes he possessed. The white man continued to complain about the cold and to wonder why the Indian was not freezing. He said to the Indian, "I don't understand it. With all my clothes I am about to freeze, and you, with only a thin blanket, do not seem to be cold at all."

"Is your face cold?" asked the Indian.

"No, my face is not cold, but I'm just about to freeze everywhere else."

"Me all face," said the Indian.

Predestination for the Indian

IN THE early days of the Republic of Texas when the Indians were especially bad, an old Primitive Baptist preacher was preparing for a long trip across the Indian country. He was especially careful in cleaning and loading the long rifle that was to accompany him. A friend, seeing his preparation and knowing his belief in predestination, said to him, "Uncle Billie, why are you so careful about your gun? If you meet the Indians and you are predestined to die at that time, why you will die anyway; so why worry about the gun? 'What is to be will be anyway,' you know."

"Yes, I know all about that," said Uncle Billie, "but it might be the Indian's time."

Ibid., p. 90.

Ibid., p. 98.

Contradictory Dream Revelations

IT IS said of this same minister that a notorious character of the community thought he would be able to take advantage of him because of his belief in mystic visions. So one morning he drove his wagon up to Uncle Billie's crib and said to him, "The Lord told me in a dream last night to come to your crib and get a load of corn."

Uncle Billie reached up over the door and took down his long rifle and said, "Yes, but the Lord must have changed His mind, for He told me this morning not to let you have it."

G. P. C.

THE church was in an uproar. The congregation was badly divided on the question of whether or not they should grant a certain young brother, whose reputation for piety was none too good, a license to preach.

A few of the older conservative members were a little doubtful about the sudden call to the ministry, and wanted to put him off until they could be a little surer about the reality of the call. Many of the younger brethren were very enthusiastic about the wonderful conversion and vocation of the applicant. They thought a real miracle had happened, and they were anxious to see him licensed and put to work in the Lord's vineyard. They recounted with great seriousness how, according to the young man's own testimony, the Lord had appeared to him in a vision and had shown him the three letters "G. P. C." flaming in the sky, and how a still small voice had said, "Follow these." There could be no doubt about the interpretation. G. P. C. meant "Go Preach Christ." And the young man should be sent on his way.

But the old deacon was on his feet, replying, "Brethren, I do not deny the vision. I am sure that the Lord has spoken to this young man. But knowing this young man as I do, and appreciating to some degree the great wisdom of the Lord, I am sure that you all misinterpret what this vision meant. 'G. P. C.' in this case can only mean, 'Go Pick Cotton.'"

The Laughing President

RESPECTABLE friends, who cared about reputations as gentlemen and scholars, took it as a little queer, a little like "a country Jake," beneath

Ibid., p. 98.

Ibid., pp. 99–100.

From *Abraham Lincoln, The Prairie Years*, by Carl Sandburg, Vol. II, pp. 295–301, 312–313. Copyright, 1926, by Harcourt, Brace & Company, Inc. New York.

dignity, that Lincoln should carry with him the book "Joe Miller's Jests," generally called Joe Miller's joke book. English puns, Irish bulls, Greek repartee, folk tales of Jews and Egyptians, brisk anecdotes, filled the book —more than a thousand, each with a serial number. No. 997 told of "the celebrated organist Abbe Vogler, once imitating a thunderstorm so well that for miles round all the milk turned sour." The Irishman was told of, who had been living in Scotland and was asked how he liked the country, replying, "I was sick all the time I was there, and if I had lived there till this time, I'd been dead a year ago." Lord Russell on the scaffold ready to have his head cut off, handed his watch to a bishop, with the remark, "Take this—it shows time; I am going into eternity and no longer need it." Another lord, owing many debts, was asked how he could sleep at night, and answered: "I sleep very well, but I wonder how my creditors can." A wounded officer on a bloody battlefield was howling with pain when another wounded officer near by called to him: "What do you make such a noise for? Do you think nobody is killed but yourself?"

Such was some of the foolery in the book that Lincoln occasionally took out of his carpetbag and read aloud to other lawyers. Some had the pith and poignancy of the grave-digger in the play of Hamlet, one joke reading: "An Irishman going to be hanged, begged that the rope might be tied under his arms instead of round his neck; for, said Pat, I am so remarkably ticklish in the throat, that if tied there, I will certainly kill myself with laughing." Or again Joke No. 506, reading: "Lieutenant Connolly, an Irishman in the service of the United States, during the American war, chanced to take three Hessian prisoners himself, without any assistance; being asked by the commander-in-chief how he had taken them—'I surrounded them,' was the answer."

There were tales of the people. A traveler in Egypt said to a worker on the land: "I suppose you are quite happy now; the country looks like a garden and every village has its minaret." "God is great," replied the worker. "Our master gives with one hand and takes with two." Another traveler, reporting that he and his servant had made fifty wild Arabs run, said there was nothing surprising about it. "We ran and they ran after us." And again and again little tales of the people, the people. Into the street before Dean Swift's deanery came "a great rabble," waiting "to see the eclipse." And Dean Swift had the big bell rung, and a crier bawling: "O Yes, O Yes, all manner of persons here concerned take notice the eclipse be put off till tomorrow this time! so God save the King and his Reverence the dean." And the rabble went away, all but one Irishman who said he would stay because "the dean might change his mind and have the eclipse that day after all."

Thus Joe Miller's jests. They were a nourishing company to Lincoln. Once in a while he told a story that seemed to have been made over from Joe Miller and placed in Indiana. In his lighter moods his humors matched with the Rabelais definition, "a certain jollity of mind, pickled in the scorn of fortune."

He told of the long-legged boy "sparking" a farmer's daughter when the hostile father came in with a shotgun; the boy jumped through a window, and running across the cabbage patch scared up a rabbit; in about two leaps the boy caught up with the rabbit, kicked it high in the air, and grunted, "Git out of the road and let somebody run that knows how." He told of a Kentucky horse sale where a small boy was riding a fine horse to show off points, when a man whispered to the boy, "Look here, boy, hain't that horse got the splints?" and the boy answered: "Mister, I don't know what the splints is, but if it's good for him, he has got it; if it ain't good for him, he ain't got it."

Riding to Lewiston an old acquaintance, a weather-beaten farmer, spoke of going to law with his next neighbor. "Been a neighbor of yours for long?" "Nigh onto fifteen year." "Part of the time you get along all right, don't you?" "I reckon we do." "Well, see this horse of mine? I sometimes get out of patience with him. But I know his faults; he does fairly well as horses go; it might take me a long time to get used to some other horse's faults: for all horses have faults."

The instant dignity became bogus his eye caught it. He enjoyed such anecdotes as the one of a Brown County, Indiana, man who killed a neighbor's dog, and the proof of guilt was clear. The defendant's attorney cleared his throat and began a speech, "May it please the court, we are proud to live in a land where justice is administered to the king on the throne and the beggar on his dunghill." The squire then interrupted, "You may go ahead with your speech, but the case *are* decided."

Little folk tales and snatches of odd wisdom known to common people of the ancient kingdoms of the Persians and the Arabians, came to be known among the common people of the farming districts in Illinois, hitched up somehow to Abe Lincoln. When a story or saying had a certain color or smack, it would often be tagged as coming from Lincoln. He had said to a book agent, "For those who like that kind of a book, that's the kind of a book they'll like." He was the man walking along a dusty road when a stranger, driving a buggy came along. And he asked the stranger, "Will you be so good as to take my overcoat to town for me?" And the man in the buggy said he would. "But how will you get your overcoat back again?" "Oh, that's easy! I'm going to stay right inside of it." And of course, said some jokers, it was Abe Lincoln who first told a hotel waiter, "Say, if this is coffee, then please bring me some tea, but if this is tea, please bring me some coffee." And on Abe Lincoln was laid the remark, after tasting ice cream, "Say, waiter, I don't want to slander this hotel, but this here pudding's froze."

He had come out of a slushy snow into a courtroom to try a case and sat down to dry his feet at the stove. The words of the lawyer arguing against him came to his ears. All of a sudden he was out in the middle of the courtroom, one shoe off, calling: "Now, judge, that isn't fair. I'm not going to have this jury all fuddled up."

Did he not say when he met a man somewhat matching his own height,

"Well, you're up some"—had they not seen how the clay of the earth clung to him? Before posing for a photographer, he stepped into a barber shop, saying, "I better get my hair slicked up." Then, sitting before the camera, he ran his fingers through his hair, caught himself, and said, "Guess I've made a bird's nest of it again." It was he who agreed to make a horse trade, sight unseen, with a judge. First came the judge the next morning with a broken-down bone-rack of a horse; then came Lincoln carrying a wooden sawhorse on his shoulders, saying, "Well, judge, this is the first time I ever got the worst of it in a horse trade."

A walking, stalking library of stories he was. Some of them could have had musical accompaniments from barn-dance fiddles. The prize story tellers of one neighborhood and another had met him and they had competed. "That reminds me." "That's like the feller down at Goose Holler." And occasionally was one with a shine of many cross-lights in it. Lincoln told of a balloonist going up in New Orleans, sailing for hours, and dropping his parachute over a cotton field. The gang of Negroes picking cotton saw a man coming down from the sky in blue silk, in silver spangles, wearing golden slippers. They ran—all but one old timer who had the rheumatism and couldn't get away. He waited till the balloonist hit the ground and walked toward him. Then he mumbled: "Howdy, Massa Jesus. How's yo' Pa?"

Lincoln had stood with two umbrellas at an imaginary rat hole, impersonating Sam'l, the Quaker boy whose father wanted to stop the boy's using swear words. The two umbrellas were blacksmith tongs. Sam'l's father had said, "Now, Sam'l, thee will sit here until thee has a rat. If I hear thee swear, thee will sit here till thee has another." And Sam'l had sat there for hours, snipping the tongs a few times, but no rat caught. At last one came out from the rat hole, the whiskers peeping up, then the black nose, and the eyes blinking. And the two umbrella tongs snapped together in a flash. And Sam'l yelled, "By God, I have thee at last!" And Lincoln with a shaking, swaying frame let out a squeal aud stood holding an imaginary wriggling rat between the two umbrellas. He had told this in Illinois towns during the debates with Douglas. And Robert R. Hitt, the phonographic reporter, said he forgot himself and politics and business and nearly believed there was a live squeaking rat caught between the two umbrellas. For a roomful of men in a hotel, Lincoln would perform this drama of Sam'l, Sam'l's father, and the rat, acting subtly the rôles of the earnest father, the obstreperous boy, and the furtive rat.

He picked up comedy, as he met it, and passed it on to others. In Cumberland County, one Dr. Hamburgher, a Democrat, forced his way to the front to reply to Lincoln's speech. As Hamburgher worked into a frothy and threatening speech, a little man with a limp came over to Lincoln and said: "Don't mind *him*. I know *him;* I live here; I'll take care of *him*. Watch me." And he took the platform, and replying brought from Hamburgher the cry, "That's a lie." To which the little man with the limp called out with high defiance, "Never mind, I'll take that from *you*—yes, I'll take anything from you, except your pills." At the mention of pills, the doctor snorted, "You scoundrel, you know I've quit practicing medicine." And the little man dropped down on the knee of his best leg, raised his hands toward the sky in thankfulness, and shouted, "Then, thank God! The country is safe."

Plato, the Kane County lawyer, had told him a story about a man who had beaten a dog to death and was in such a rage that he would go out of the house and again beat the dog to death. When Plato came one day to Lincoln's office in Springfield, Lincoln's greeting was, "Well, Plato, have you got that dog killed yet?"

A family in Indiana, according to Lincoln, picked dandelion tops or other leaves and boiled "greens" for dinner in the spring and early summer. Once after a mess of greens the whole family went out of commission. After that when they had greens a big helping would first be forked out for Zerah, a half-wit boy, as the family said: "Try it on Zerah. If he stands it, it won't hurt the rest of us." And a man had a horse that would balk and settle down on all four legs like a bird dog. He traded off the horse as good for hunting birds. As the horse crossed a creek he settled down in the middle of it like a bird dog and the man who had owned him called to the new rider: "Ride him! Ride him! He's as good for fish as he is for birds."

People looked at Lincoln, searching his face, thinking about his words and ways, ready to believe he was a Great Man. Then he would spill over with a joke or tell of some new horse-play of wit or humor in the next county. The barriers tumbled. He was again a strange friend, a neighbor, a friendly stranger, no far-off Great Man at all. "His face," Moncure D. Conway noted, "had a battered and bronzed look, without being hard." He fitted the measurements, "three parts sublime to one grotesque."

A crowd was bubbling with mirth in an Ohio town as a short friend stood alongside Lincoln to introduce him. Lincoln, pointing at himself, said, "This is the long of it," and putting an arm on the friend's shoulder, "and this is the short of it."

Joe Fifer, an eighteen-year-old corn husker, heard Lincoln at Bloomington after Swett made the opening address. "When Lincoln was starting to speak," Fifer noticed, "some men near me said Lincoln was no great shakes as a public speaker and Swett would make a better showing against Douglas. But when Lincoln got to going they listened; they stood still without moving out of their foot tracks. Lincoln looked out on a wall of faces still as if they had been made of stone."

The Springfield doctor, William Jayne, trying to fathom why Lincoln had carried the crowds with him usually in debating with Douglas, said: "Everybody thinks he is honest and believes what he says. If he was really a great man, or if people regarded him as a great man, he could not do half so much."

He was the man who had started a little circle of people to giggling one morning in Judge Davis's courtroom, and the judge sputtered out: "I am not going to stand this any longer, Mr. Lincoln. You're always disturbing this court with your tomfoolery." The fine was $5.00, for disorderly conduct. Lincoln sat with his hand over his mouth trying to keep his face straight. Later the judge called Lawrence Weldon to him and Weldon whispered into his ear what it was that Lincoln had told. Then the judge giggled. Getting his face straight, he announced, "The clerk may remit Mr. Lincoln's fine." The joke had to do with "taking up a subscription to buy Jim Wheeler a new pair of pants."

He could speak of So-and-So as "a quiet, orderly, faithful man." And he could hand a bottle to a baldheaded man he wished to get rid of, with the remarks: "Try this stuff for your hair. Keep it up. They say it will grow hair on a pumpkin. Come back in ten months and tell me how it works." When it was intimated to him that he was consulting too much with Judge Davis, he told of a New Hampshire judge who said: "The only time the chief judge ever consulted was at the close of a long day's session, when he turned and whispered, 'Don't your back ache?'" He liked to tell of the strict judge of whom it was said: "He would hang a man for blowing his nose in the street, but he would quash the indictment if it failed to specify which hand he blew it with."

When he presented Coles County relatives with a sad-faced photograph of himself, he said, "This is not a very good-looking picture, but it's the best that could be produced from the poor subject."

* * * * *

The left corner of Lincoln's mouth had the lines of a laughing man. Beyond a struggle in which he was loser he could see another struggle, and write in a letter, "There will be another blow-up and we shall have fun again." But the right corner of his mouth had a droop; he could say, "I laugh because if I didn't I would weep."

Sometimes a poetry of fine wisdom in short words came from his tongue as carelessly as raindrops on high corn. Milt Hay, whose law office was on the same floor as Lincoln's, told Joe Fifer and others about a goat Lincoln met on the street one morning going to the office.

"Boys had been deviling the goat to make for people and butt them off their feet," said Hay, "and this morning Lincoln with his hands folded behind him, and his chin sunk in his bosom, comes along the street. And the goat makes for him. Well, Lincoln could be pretty quick when he wanted to be. And he stooped over and his two hands got hold of the two horns of the goat."

Then Lincoln dropped down, put his face close to the goat's face and slowly drawled: "Now—there—isn't—any—good—reason—why—you—should—want—to—harm—me; and—there—isn't—any—good—reason—why—I—should—want—to—harm—you. The—world—is—big—enough—for—both—of—us—to—live—in. If—you—behave—yourself—as—you—ought—to,—and—if—I—behave—myself—like—I—ought—to,—we'll—get—along—without—a—cross—word—or—action—and—we'll—live—in—peace—and—harmony—like—good—neighbors."

Then Lincoln lifted at the two horns, dropped the goat over a high fence, and walked up the street.

An Old Time Sermon

IN THE early days of Kentucky there lived a celebrated Methodist preacher by the name of Prater. He was a very corpulent man, weighing over three hundred pounds, and always rode to his appointments on a mule. When seated in the saddle his person protruded over both ends and spread out on the mule each way.

In those days it was quite common for services to be held in the houses of the earnest and working members. Among these was Granny Short, a good old sister of Madison county. An appointment was made at her house for Brother Prater to preach and the neighbors had promptly gathered and anxiously awaited his coming. At length he rode up, dismounted from his faithful mule, threw the bridle over a fence post, and started up to the house, shaking hands with first one and then another. Finally, all entered the house and the good old brother, standing before a little table, commenced his sermon.

"My brethren and sistrin, I was delayed a little today because I arose with a severe backache which is still annoying me. Consequently, I cannot say what sort of a sermon I shall preach, though I once married a couple when I had the backache, and I never married a couple that succeeded better than them. I shall preach to you from a text somewhar between the lids of the Bible, the chapter and verse of which I am not able to name. It runs as follows: 'Like a crane or a swaller, so did I chatter. Oh, Lord, undertake Thou for me.'

"Now, my beloved, you will see that there are two birds mentioned in this chapter—vizard: a crane and a swaller. It is necessary to a proper understanding that we should look carefully into the habits of these fowls."

By this time the old man had commenced warming up, his voice gradually increasing in volume.

"A crane, my brethren, is a tall bird, with long legs and a long bill, and will reach down into the water and snatch a fish that another bird would never think of—ah! And a swaller, my brethren, is a little pestiferous bird that congregates in great numbers in the chimneys and chatter, chatter, and flutter, flutter, causing the sut to fall and black all it teches, to the great annoyance of the good wimmen—ah! These swallers are jest like the Campbellites—they will gather around a hole of water and chatter, chatter, and flutter, flutter, while they are baptizin' one another, and the very next day they will not know the hole they were baptized in—ah!

From *Stories and Speeches of William O. Bradley*, with Biographical Sketch by M. H. Thatcher, pp. 56–57. Copyright, 1916, by Transylvania Printing Co. Lexington, Kentucky.

A Powerful Sermon on a Peculiar Text

REVEREND PETER TURNIPSEED—no one ever knew how he received his name—was a famous Negro preacher in Kentucky several decades ago. He was a tall, ungainly man, black as Egyptian darkness, with hands as large as canvas hams, feet like baby coffins, and a voice like a fog horn. One beautiful summer day, he preached under the spreading limbs of an old elm tree to a large concourse of his people.

"My brudders and sistahs," said he, "I am gwine fur to preach to you one uv my most famousest sarmints.

"You will fine my tex sum whar betwixt the leds of the Bibel, zact pint not now recumembered. Hit reads as follus:—'Wharsumebber de hen scraitch dar she fine de bug; also cept she pick him up an eat him.'

"Now, my bruddahs and sistahs, you will desarve dar am two figgers uv speech in dis tex. De fust am de hen; de secon am de bug. Dar is no use in my 'splainin to you whut a hen is, fur dar is not a niggah under de sound ob mi voice who is not well 'quainted wid dat bird and does not know its 'culiarties, bof nite and day, spechuly in de nite.

"As to de bug, my bruddahs, you all know what he is, and how many ob dem crawl on de groun. Dar is de June bug dat de chilluns tie by de laig an maks um fly. Dar am de lady bug, wich is so called, 'cause she war a spotted coat and puts on ars. But I will not bodder you to tel all abowt de bugs 'cept to say dat uv all de bombile bugs in de worl de wust am de humbug.

"You will desarve from my tex dat de hen am doin' sumtin; az uzal she am a scratchin' and not only am she a scratchin', but she am scratchin' in de groun—ah! An not only am she a scratchin' in de groun—ah! but she am a scratchin' for a bug—ah! An, my sistahs, she am sho to fine that bug 'cept she pic him up an eat him—ah! In case ef she pic him up an eat him he is a goner and she cain't fine him—ah! Dar-foah, ef de hen reely wants to fine de bug she mus be keerful not to pic 'im up an eat 'im, because ef she does she puts it outen her powah to fine him—ah!

"Dis tex, my bruddahs, haz a powful meenin. It teachers dat it am de duty of ebbery man an wummin to scraitch in de groun fur a libbin—ah! And as sho as God made littel apples, ef da ack de hog an eat things soon as da cum acrost um—ah! da will nebber fine nuthin—ah! De same may be sed ob deligion; ef yo want it, you must scraitch, an keep on scraitchin' till you fine it—ah! But ef you swallers down ebberyting you come acrost, you'll ruen yore digeschum an nebber fine enny thing—ah!

"In clushen, my beloved! Let me sa yoo mus scraitch in de mornin, scraitch in de middel ub de da, scraitch as de sun am gwine doun, and scraitch ob an endurin' ob de nite—an keap on scraitchin' an scraitchin' till yoo fine deligeon—ah! And when yu fine it yu will hab ebberyting dat is

Ibid., pp. 64–65.

wuth ennyting in dis wurl an de nex—ah! An now while de congregation
sing dat good old hymn—'Work fur de nite am cummin,' de invitashun iz
lovinly throwed out fur awl dat want to scraitch fur deligeon to cum forrard
an scraitch, an scraitch while dey has de prars of de congration—ah."

The Hard-Shell Baptist

THERE will be an old Hard-shell clock resurrected, with throat whiskers,
and wearing a shad-bellied coat and flap breeches. And when he is wound
up a little, and a little oil is squirted into his old wheels, he will swing out
into space on the wings of the gospel with: "My dear beloved brethren—
ah: I was a-ridin' along this mornin' a-tryin' to study up somethin' to
preach to this dying congregation—ah; and as I rid up by the old mill
pond—ah, lo and behold! there was an old snag a sticking up out of the
middle of the pond—ah, and an old mud turtle had clim up out uv the
water and was a-settin' up on the old snag a-sunnin' uv himself—ah; and
lo! and behold—ah! when I rid up a leetle nearer to him—ah, he jumped
off of the snag, 'ker chugg' into the water, thereby proving emersion—ah!"

The Baptist Ox

DE BIBLE tell how all de creeters what Marse Norah gwine 'low ter come
inter de Ark en be saved, is 'bleedzed t' be babtized.

Dey be a river—I done fergits what dey names hit, but hit sho 'nuff
be dar—dey a river right in front er Marse Norah's do'. En dey all, when
dey gits t' de river, kin choose how dey's gwine be babtized.

Wellum, de las' er de creeturs what comes up is de oxen. En de Mef'dis'
oxen, he be des' a-blowin' his ole bazzoo, en 'lowin' he gwine lead de way
en be at de haid er de percession, en be de fust un t' git inter de Ark.
Yassum, he do, he say he gwinter.

He des' comes struttin' 'long till he git right t' de water's aidge; den
he stop en kneel down en bow his haid, en say, "Moo-moo-moo!" whilst
he takes up a li'l soop o' water, narrer es he kin. Den he gits up en 'gins
lookin roun' fer ter see effen he kin fin' a shaller place t' wade 'cross.

Whilst he be lookin' up en down de bank, huntin' a shaller place fer
crossin', 'long comes ole Presbyteern oxen, walkin' des' so, en holden' his
haid so high, hit look like he hab de stiff neck. He didn' even down see dey
was a river, till he hear de Mef'dis' oxen a-askin' whar be de shalleres'
place in de water.

From "The Paradise of Fools," in *Echoes, Centennial and other Notable Speeches,
Lectures, and Stories,* by Governor Robt. L. Taylor, p. 159. Copyright, 1899, by S. B.
Williamson & Co. Nashville, Tennessee.

From *The Journal of American Folk-Lore,* Vol. XXXIV (October-December, 1921),
No. CXXXIV, pp. 397-398. Copyright, 1921, by the American Folk-Lore Society.
As told by a Negro in South Carolina to Mrs W. C. Burt, Asheville, N. C.

Wellum, when de Presbyteern oxen see dat river, he des' fetch de mos' polite bow you mos'ly ever see, en he ax de river, "Howdy?"—distant like. He 'low he ain' gwineter babtize hisse'f 'long wid de yuddern. Den he 'gins lookin' 'roun' fer t' see effen dey ain' er foot-log 'cross dat river, whar he kin walk over on.

Now Marse Norah see him thinkin' 'bout hit, en he calls out, "You is 'bleedzed ter fust be babtized, den you kin hoof it 'cross on de log effen you wanter."

De Presbyteern oxen, he 'low dat he ain' 'bleedzed ter do nothin' lessen he choose ter, 'caze hit done been 'p'inted dat he gwineter git inter dat Ark an' be saved.

Marse Norah, he make answer, he did, "Fust en last, dat's de law, I's been tellin' you. You kin *take hit er leave hit.*"

Now de Presbyteern oxen des' sorter wall he eyes 'roun', en he see de clouds was lookin' mighty black. En he 'low t' his-se'f—he did—dat 'cordin' ter de bes' er his jedgment, dey mought be a harrycane somers 'mongst dat pile er clouds, fixin' fer t' bus' loose presen'ly an' come splungin' 'long an t'ar up de whole yearth. So he des' bow he haid, slow en gran', en he take er li'l soop o' water, en he 'low he too perlite ter make a auger wid Marse Norah. Now he take sich a li'l soop o' water, dat Marse Norah ain' so mighty sure he done drink a solemn drap, but all de samer he say he gwineter take his word fer it. So he p'ints out de whar'bouts o' de foot-log.

De las' one dat come 'long, was de great big ole Babtis' oxen, en by dat time hit was drizzin' rain a li'l, an' de thunder was a-rum'lin'. He des' comes on de run; en by de way he was a-puffin' en a-snortin', you'd a thought he'd 'a' been plum' tuckered out. But I be boun'! when he gits ter dat river, he don' stop ter ax no odds er nobody. He des' 'gins a-bellerin', en he give a runnin' jump en lan's spang in de deepes' place he kin see in dat river—des' div right in haid fust—en when he comes up, he's on de yudder shore. En he shakes his haid, en switches his tail, en goes a-tearin' up de bank right inter de front do' o' de Ark, he did.

Baptist Chitlins, Methodist Chitlins

THIS man had a tub on his head and with a musical voice was singing:—

> "Here's yer chitlins, fresh an' sweet,
> Who'll jine de Union?
> Young hog's chitlins hard to beat,
> Who'll jine de Union?

From *My Southern Home; or, The South and its People,* by Wm. Wells Brown M.D., pp. 172–175. Copyright, 1880, by Annie G. Brown. Boston: A. G. Brown & Co., Publishers.

> Methodist chitlins, jest been biled,
>   Who'll jine de Union?
> Right fresh chitlins, dey ain't spiled,
>   Who'll jine de Union?
> Baptist chitlins by de pound,
>   Who'll jine de Union?
> As nice chitlins as ever was found,
>   Who'll jine de Union?

"Here's yer chitlins, out of good fat hog; jess as sweet chitlins as ever yer see. Dees chitlins will make yer mouf water jess to look at 'em. Come an' see 'em."

At this juncture the man took the tub from his head, sat it down, to answer a woman who had challenged his right to call them "Baptist chitlins."

"Duz you mean to say dat dem is Baptiss chitlins?"

"Yes, mum, I means to say dat dey is real Baptist chitlins, an' nuffin' else."

"Did dey come out of a Baptiss hog?" inquired the woman.

"Yes, mum, dem chitlins come out of a Baptist hog."

"How duz you make dat out?"

"Well, yer see, dat hog was raised by Mr. Roberson, a hard-shell Baptist, de corn dat de hog was fatted on was also raised by Baptists, he was killed and dressed by Geemes Boone, an' you all know dat he's as big a Baptist as ever lived."

"Well," said the woman, as if perfectly satisfied, "lem-me have two poun's."

By the time the man had finished his explanation, and weighed out her lot, he was completely surrounded with women and men, nearly all of whom had their dishes to get the choice morsel in.

"Now," said a rather solid-looking man. "Now, I want some of de Meth-diss chitlins dat you's bin talking 'bout."

"Here dey is, ser."

"What," asked the purchaser, "you take 'em all out of de same tub?"

"Yes," quickly replied the vender.

"Can you tell 'em by lookin' at 'em?" inquired the chubby man.

"Yes, ser."

"How duz you tell 'em?"

"Well, ser, de Baptist chitlins has bin more in de water, you see, an' dey's a little whiter."

"But, how duz I know dat dey is Meth-diss?"

"Well, ser, dat hog was raised by Uncle Jake Bemis, one of de most shoutin' Methodist in de Zion connection. Well, you see, ser, de hog pen was right close to de house, an' dat hog was so knowin' dat when Uncle Jake went to prayers, ef dat hog was squealin' he'd stop. Why, ser, you could hardly get a grunt out of dat hog till Uncle Jake was dun his prayer. Now, ser, ef dat don't make him a Methodist hog, what will?"

"Weigh me out four pounds, ser."

"Here's your fresh chitlins, Baptist chitlins, Methodist chitlins, all good an' sweet."

And in an hour's time the peddler, with his empty tub upon his head, was making his way out of the street, singing,—

> "Methodist chitlins, Baptist chitlins,
> Who'll jine de Union?"

Methodist Grasshopper and Baptist Possum

DE METHODISS, my bruddren, is like de grasshopper—hoppin', all de time hoppin'—hop into heaven, hop out, hop into heaven, hop out. But, my bruddren, de Baptiss, when he get to heaven, *he's dar!* De Baptiss is like de 'possum. Hunter get after him, he climb de tree; he shake de limb, one foot gone; he shake de limb, anudder foot gone; but tink you, my bruddren, *'possum fall?* You know, my bruddren—you cotch too many—you know *'possum hang on by de tail,* and de berry debbil can't shake him off!

"De Reason Niggers Is Working So Hard"

DIS is de way *dat* was.

God let down two bundles 'bout five miles down de road. So de white man and de nigger raced to see who would git there first. Well, de nigger out-run de white man and grabbed de biggest bundle. He was so skeered de white man would git it away from him he fell on top of de bundle and hollered back: "Oh, Ah got here first and dis biggest bundle is mine." De white man says: "All right, Ah'll take yo' leavings," and picked up de li'l tee-ninchy bundle layin' in de road. When de nigger opened up his bundle he found a pick and shovel and a hoe and a plow and chop-axe and then de white man opened up his bundle and found a writin'-pen and ink. So ever since then de nigger been out in de hot sun, usin' his tools and de white man been sittin' up figgerin', ought's a ought, figger's a figger; all for de white man, none for de nigger.

From *In the Brush; or Old-Time Social, Political, and Religious Life in the Southwest,* by Rev. Hamilton W. Pierson, pp. 267–268. Copyright, 1881, by D. Appleton and Co. New York.

From the sermon of a colored Baptist preacher at a county-seat village on the Ohio River, in Kentucky, who waged a "war of extermination" against Methodism "on account of what he esteemed the heretical doctrines and bad influence of Methodism."

From *Mules and Men,* by Zora Neale Hurston, p. 102. Copyright, 1935, by Zora Neale Hurston. Philadelphia and London: J. B. Lippincott Company.

Why the Sister in Black Works Hardest

KNOW how it happened? After God got thru makin' de world and de varmints and de folks, he made up a great big bundle and let it down in de middle of de road. It laid dere for thousands of years, then Ole Missus said to Ole Massa: "Go pick up dat box, Ah want to see whut's in it." Ole Massa look at de box and it look so heavy dat he says to de nigger, "Go fetch me dat big ole box out dere in de road." De nigger been stumblin' over de box a long time so he tell his wife:

" 'Oman, go git dat box." So de nigger 'oman she runned to git de box. She says:

"Ah always lak to open up a big box 'cause there's nearly always something good in great big boxes." So she run and grabbed a-hold of de box and opened it up and it was full of hard work.

Dat's de reason de sister in black works harder than anybody else in de world. De white man tells de nigger to work and he takes and tells his wife.

All Folks Was Born Black

ALL folks was born black, an' dem what's turnt white, dey jest had more sense. Angel o' de Lord come down an' told de ontire bunch to meet on de fo'th Friday at de dark o' de moon an' wash deyselves in Jordan. He oxplained to 'em dat dey'd all turn white an' straighten de kinks outen deir hair. Angel kept preachin' an' preachin', but dem fool niggers didn't pay him no mind. Angel can't teach a nigger nothin'. When de fo'th Friday come a mighty little sprinklin' of 'em went down to de river an' commenced to scrub. Water was mighty low. 'Twarn't like Old Missip'— 'scusin' de Lord's river—'twarn't no more'n a creek. You jest oughter seed dat crowd o' niggers settin' on de fence snickerin' at dem what went in washin'. Snickerin' an' throwin' slams. More niggers dan you ever see in Vicksburg on circus day.

Dem what went in de river kept scrubbin' and washin', special deir hair to git de kinks out. Old Aunt Grinny Granny—great-grandmammy of all dem niggers—she sot on a log all day long, eatin' cheese and crackers and lowratin' dem what was washin'. When fust dark come, she jumped up and clapped her hands: " 'Fore Gawd, dem niggers *is* gittin' white!" Grinny Granny jerked off her head handkercher an' went tumblin' down

Ibid., pp. 101–102.

Recorded by Harris Dickson, Vicksburg, Mississippi. From "Phrases of the People," *American Stuff*, An Anthology of Prose & Verse by Members of the Federal Writers' Project, pp. 150–151. Copyright, 1937, by The Guilds' Committee for Federal Writers' Publications, Inc. The Viking Press. New York.

de bank to wash her hair, an' all dem fool niggers followed her. But de water was all used up, jest a tiny drap in de bottom, no more'n enough to moisten de palms o' deir hands and de soles o' deir feet. So dat's why a nigger is white in dem places.

Sleepy Head, Kinky Head

"EF'N de nigger hadn't ben so sleepy-headed, he'd er ben wite, an' his hyar'd er ben straight des like yourn. Yer see, atter de Lord make 'im, den he lont him up 'gins de fence-corner in de sun fur ter dry; an' no sooner wuz de Lord's back turnt, an' de sun 'gun ter come out kin'er hot, dan de nigger he 'gun ter nod, an' er little mo'n he wuz fas' ter sleep. Well, wen de Lord sont atter 'im fur ter finish uv 'im up, de angel couldn't fin' 'im, caze he didn't know de zack spot whar de Lord sot 'im; an' so he hollered an' called, an' de nigger he wuz 'sleep, an' he nuber hyeard 'im; so de angel tuck de wite man, an' cyard him 'long, an' de Lord polished uv 'im off. Well, by'mby de nigger he waked up; but, dar now! he wuz bu'nt black, an' his hyar wuz all swuv'llt up right kinky.

"De Lord, seein' he wuz spilte, he didn't 'low fur ter finish 'im, an' wuz des 'bout'n ter thow 'im way, wen de wite man axt fur 'im; so de Lord he finished 'im up des like he wuz, wid his skin black an' his hyar kunkt up, an' he gun 'im ter de wite man, an' I see he's got 'im plum tell yit."

Essence of Rural Humor

THE scene is Kennicott's store at Blue Eye, a situation but slightly commercial. The group includes Dave Beatty, Forgy Dell, Marcus Feitz, Henstep Creaseley, Tola Summerlin, Homer Bullteeter, Homer's hired boy Bill Skeats, and the storekeeper. These occupy poultry crates and such. They whittle matches into infinitesimal slivers. They draw strange diagrams on the dusty porch floor and whistle tunes that take after nothing in particular. They indulge in slight sounds, slow gyrations, slight parleyings, patterings of feet, uproarious yawnings, and stretchings in the form of capital Xs and Ys.

Their relish for the wisecrack inevitably forthcoming is enhanced a dozenfold by such interludes of speculative waiting. The first spiel is by Bill Skeats, since hired boys are among the most cherished perpetrators of store-porch mirth.

From *Diddie, Dumps, and Tot; or Plantation Child-Life,* by Louise Clarke Pyrnelle, pp. 206–207. Copyright, 1882, by Harper & Brothers, and 1910, by Mary C. Motley. New York and London.

From *Backwoods America,* by Charles Morrow Wilson, pp. 15–26. Copyright, 1934, by the University of North Carolina Press. Chapel Hill.

Bill Skeats, then, sitting in sunny oblivion on the lowest estate of the store-porch steps, opens in dialect at his boss:

"Homer, how's hit do for me to ride your hoss home?"

The employer quivers slightly.

"It wouldn't do so good, I've got to ride him myse'f." Then with a soft ripple of merriment: "Mought be you could walk alongside me though."

"No, I reckon I'd better jest be pattin' down the road now by myself. If I was to walk aside you, I'd have to open and shet ever' gate and fence-gap between here and thar."

There is freely given laughter. The afternoon flow of jocundity has started. Homer faces unsteadily towards his lolling hired help.

"By the way, how come you ain't workin' today?"

The youth deliberately readjusts his battered felt hat and leers.

"W'y, I was workin' but I got hurt. You see I was plowin' corn in that fur squirrel patch and drekly I come to the field—I fell off—and wrenched my knee."

Backbrush humor hangs upon pegs that are unashamedly obvious: the old gentleman who can't get any satisfaction out of reading the dictionary because it changes the subject too often; the itinerant parson who agrees that a spring wagon and a span of mules are fool proof, but not necessarily damn-fool proof; the upbrush politician who craves a postmastership within easy walking distance of a distillery; the clodhopper who overwhelms the school-teacher's suggestion that the burning of Mart Miller's barn must have been the work of an incendiary with, "Incendiary, hell! Somebody sot it."

The humor carries an amiable plenitude, too, of anecdotes of stupidity.

The sheriff of a brush county in Southwestern Missouri was forming a posse to recapture a depraved culprit who had broken jail while the defender of justice was away investigating. A store-porch commentator reported that the fugitive had spent half the afternoon strolling about the village; that he had last been seen taking out westward down the old wire road. Then the observing countryman added that he had seen the sheriff pass by the escaped prisoner not an hour before. The upholder of sovereign justice admitted it.

"Oh, yes, yes! I seed him all right—passed him on the town branch bridge a while after dinner time—passed him and spoke howdy to him. But I didn't know the low hound reprobate was out of jail."

The store-porcher relishes so simple an episode as that of the rural lad and his first banana. The youth from Alpena was taking his first train ride, and when the newsman came through acclaiming "chawklets—bernanners!" the mountain lad invested readily in the latter. On the next round the caller stopped to ask after the qualities of his wares.

"Well, Mister, I can't say so bodaciously much for it. In the first place it was mainly all cob; and when I'd throwed that away, what little they was left was bitter and sort of 'ornery to eat."

Sometimes the gentleman of the store-porch is tickled almost beyond endurance by ignorance of rural ways, by unfamiliarity with the dictates of soil and season which he himself knows so well. The newcomer who figures to get rich off a few slanting acres of stump ground; who would bear down on his plow handles, tie up fodder with string, buckle the throat-latch of a bridle before he set the bit, undertake to keep the birds from his cherries or the squirrels from his corn—such a yahoo provides material for slow perceptive smiles based upon first-hand understanding of the ways and wiles of wooded hill and brushy dale.

The conversation on the store-porch drifted around to the chinch bugs, which had descended upon the tasseling corn in leeching multitudes. The drummer from Saint Looie wanted to know what a chinch bug looked like.

"You say it's no bigger than a seed tick?"

Nods and salivary assent.

"Why, I wouldn't have my crops wiped out by a little thing like that."

The sitters nudged one another and one soberly asked what the commercial ambassador might figure to do about it.

"Do about it? Why, I'd get me a good two-handed brush and frail 'em off my place."

The store-porch humorist is not, of course, above a pun. An old codger from Red Star was telling of his family.

"Yes, suh, they come three boys, then a girl, then another boy. So I named 'em Matthew, Mark, Luke, Ann, John."

And he knows the value of hyperbole. One time I asked an old countryman why he preferred cushaws (large hooked squashes) to pumpkins. He spat.

"Well suh, if I was to grow punkins on them slopin' fields, they'd likely break loose from the vines and roll down and kill somebody. But cushaws —they hook theirselves to corn stalks and ketch on."

Nor is the store humorist immune to the potency of slap-stick. There is no good reason why he should be. Mimicry can also put him into the high rhapsodies of mirth. And the countryside idiot is a dependable source of laughter.

The rural commoner likewise is amused at the plight of the singing master who started to cross Brush Creek by means of a log bridge, and went to where the log bridge wasn't. There moonlight and a black shadow had fallen across the way, so the singing master, mistaking the shadow for the bridge, decided that he would just hunker down and 'coon across it. So he knelt, putting his elbows forward and painstakingly plunged head first into a stream of ice-cold water.

Backwoods fondness for burlesque mingles mirthfully with the liking for the humor of ignorance. For that very reason countrymen enjoy country jokes and relish the opportunity for embellishment and parody.

"You know, over at Post Oak Hill where we come from, that there's the reel brush. Pap Eason he's about the only feller down that there creek bend as knows how to read and write. So about seven or eight of us chipped in and taken the Springfield newspaper, figgerin' as how Pap could read it to us.

"Well, we done hit, and one day we was settin' around listenin' and Pap was readin' about where the paper said as how ever'body ought to plant a lot of corn and plow hit a lot because some mighty bad droughts was comin'. Mart Miller set and puzzled awhile and then he says:

" 'Pap, what's a drought?'

"Pap chawed his terbaccer a minute and stroked his chin-whiskers and then says:

"Well, I couldn't be jest shore, but if I ain't mighty mistaken, a drought is one of them new-fangled varmints that's a cross betwixt a coon and a wildcat. Anyhow they shore is hell on corn.' "

Another tale of the same timbre tells of a rural countryside in the throes of a summertime political campaign. Squire Techstone was running for circuit clerk against a slicked-up county seat lawyer. The two were orating at an August picnic. The legal member was offering belligerent argument.

"That man is as ignorant of the law as he is of the responsibilities of office. I would even defy my opponent to define so simple a legal term as *habeas corpus*."

Squire Techstone lifted off his battered felt hat and cogitated.

"Well, unless I'm mighty fur wrong that term means a red Jersey heifer fresh with a first calf."

There are rural epics of the sort that came about when Newt Finnen's wife prevailed upon Newt to take all their children to the protracted meeting.

"Newt said he couldn't rightfully bear to set and listen to preachin's, but one time his wife got come over with holiness and she hawg-an'-pantered him till he had to take her an' the young 'uns to meetin'. Newt set out on the back porch till the preachin' was all over, then he commenced gettin' oneasy about was the young 'uns still there. He figgered he'd better round 'em up. So he strolled inside and brushed back the black bristles from his forehead and says,

" 'Emmy, Dan'l, Sady, Jude, Prosey, Tom, Virgil, Dessie, Newtie, Violeeny, you-all here?'

"They says, 'Yes, Pa, we're here.'

"So then Newt lined 'em up and struck out for home."

There are times when the edge of satire may become a bit cutting. A countryside revival meeting had reached the stage of spiritual orgies. The parson preached, the congregation rolled and grovelled and kicked up straw. Then came the hour for testifying.

Brother Amos, the countryside cripple, squatted upon a convenient corner bench. He was a paralytic, an invalid hopelessly cramped and drawn, with gangling and unruly limbs. During the course of the testifying the parson called upon the crippled one to rise and tell what the Lord had done for him.

Brother Amos roused jerkily, raised his chin a bare inch from his chest in painful deliberation and struggled to manipulate his lagging limbs. There was a silence of expectation and awaited revelation. Then the lame one shrilled:

"You was askin' what the Lord done for me. Well, I'll tell you. He jest blamed near ruint me."

The run of store-porch humor is withal a gentle humor, a garnishment for extensive leisure, cornmeal mush, sun and rain, dew and moonlight, and backwoods stillness. It rarely carries bitterness. It may be brusque but it is seldom vengeful. It is rarely ulterior. A man does not use it to sell his hen's eggs, or to acquire a soft job, or to swarm with the village social bees. The peasant laughs because he sees no reason why he shouldn't.

As an example of the kindliness of the humor, there is a recitation dealing with a lad from Gulch Hollow, who on first coming to Eureka, was lured by the tempting yellowness of the store-window lemons. The youth had never seen lemons before and he figured to sample them. So he bought a dime's worth and proceeded to try out the purchase. A first attempt to bite through the tough rind revealed an appalling mistake. But in the sight of a half-dozen onlookers the lad from Gulch Hollow did not once hesitate. He ate the first lemon whole; then the second and third. Nobody laughed. There was not even the suggestion of a smile. The rural youth addressed a sober audience.

"Yessir, fer a considerable spell I've been honin' to get my fill of these here tropical fruits because I shorely do pleasure in the flavor of 'em and now I aim to revel in it."

Then with puckering lips he retreated toward the village pump, his departure unmarred by laughter, his sensitive spirit unchafed.

And one time the folks were having a moonlight supper up at the Brush Ford schoolhouse. Uncle Zeb Hatfield, who hadn't been out to any manner of funmaking in a month of moons, was a bit unsteady about his etiquette, and in consequence chanced to pour buttermilk into his coffee instead of cream. An observing farm wife moved to fetch him another cup. But Uncle Zeb would be the subject of no such bother. He blew at the murky fluid and assured the company that taking buttermilk in coffee was to him an invariable habit. Steady faces accepted that declaration. There was not even an adolescent snigger.

Backwoods humor has its subtle side, too. The commoner from Low Gap is capable of a cerebral chuckle now and then, fully as capable of it as his brethren of the town.

He enjoys his Aunt Lulu Pettigrew's complaint of pains in her abominable muscles, or that most of her family have died of nobility, or that with one of them New Fords her son Wid can climb any manner of mountain in neutral. He relishes such picturesque generalities as those of Judge Patton of Kentucky, who once offered these instructions to his jury:

"Gentlemen, whenever you see a big overgrown buck a-settin' at the mouth of some holler or the fork of some road, with a big slouch hat on, a blue collar, a celluloid rose in his coat lapel and a banjo strung across his chist, fine that man, gentlemen. Fine him! Because if he ain't done somethin' already, he blame soon will."

He enjoys hearing the Tannehill child assure a younger brother that if he will only stop hollerin' he can watch the old gentleman fall off the hay wagon.

He enjoys the strategy of the thrifty old lady of didactic leanings who in remonstrating with some little boys for their stealing a pocketful of pears, assured them that if they would only be forward and honest about it and bring along something in which to carry the fruit home, she would be glad to give them the pears. Five minutes later she was faced by the pack of youngsters who brought an old-style clothes basket capable of holding at least four bushels.

There is an ephemeral freshness to backwoods humor due in part to its nearness to earth; in part to the ways of its perpetrators—their slowness of speech and droll maneuverings of expression; their posture and inflections which cannot be adequately reproduced even in the most accommodating of type.

The great majority of upcountry jests are neither scrupulously original nor sparklingly clever. Often enough a rustic gem will shine for generations. And this fact is easier to understand when one understands that in Elizabethan America one generation is very much like another.

What's the Matter?

A GENTLEMAN was once travelling through Alabama when water was not the most abundant article, when he discovered a specimen of a one-mule cart—such as some of the good citizens of North Carolina use for purposes of emigration, when they are necessitated to seek a new location, in consequence of the supply of material for the manufacture of tar failing in the old homestead. Every appearance indicated a camp for the night, though the only person moving was a "right smart chunk of a boy," who was evidently in trouble. The inside of the cart gave a constant strain of baby music, and a succession of groans, indicating deep distress. This, and the grief of the boy, aroused the kind sympathy of the traveller, and he rode up and inquired if anything was the matter.

"Is anything the matter?" replied the boy—"I should think there was. Do you see that old feller lying there, drunk as thunder?—that's dad. Do you hear them groanings?—that's the old woman; got the ague like blazes! Brother John he's gone off in the woods to play poker for the

From *The Americans at Home; or, Byeways, Backwoods, and Prairies*, edited by The Author of "Sam Slick" [T. C. Haliburton], Vol. II, pp. 237–239. London: Hurst and Blackett, Publishers. 1854.

mule, with an *entire* stranger. Sister Sal has gone scooting through the bushes with a half-bred Ingen, and—if *I* know what *they* are up to; and do you hear that baby? don't he go it with a looseness!—well he does that—and he is in a bad fix at that, and it is a mile to water, and there isn't the first drop of licker in the jug; and ain't that matter enough? Won't you light, stranger?—Dad'll get sober, and Sal will be back arter a bit. Darn'd if this ain't moving, though. *Is anything the matter?*—shouldn't think there was much, no how. Give us a chaw of terbacker, will ye, stranger?"

"Old Sense" of Arkansas

THE way the natives sometimes talk here is amusing. The following dialogue lately occurred here on the Devil's Fork of the Little Red (River). Old Sense met Dan Looney; they were strangers to each other. Says "Old Sense,"

"Good morning, sir; are you well?"

"If you call a man 'well' that has run twenty miles, I am *that*.

"Did you see any bear?"

"If you call a big black thing about the size of *Pete Whetstone's* black mar, a hoss, 'a bar,' I did."

"Had you a gun?"

"Now you hit me."

"Did you draw blood?"

"Do you call my double, double handsfull of brains, blood?"

"Had you a dog?"

"Is *Old Bose* a dog?"

"Did you skin him?"

"Well, if you call a man in his shirt sleeves, with a knife seventeen inches in the blade, among ribs and meat, *skinning*, I was *thar*!"

"Was he fat?"

"Do you call cutting eighteen inches on the ribs, *fat*?"

"Did you pack him in?"

"If you call four pony loads *packing*, why I packed *some*!"

"Light loads, I reckon."

"If *four hundred pounds* to a pony is a light load, they were light."

"Did you eat any of it?"

"Do you call drinking a *quart of bar's ile*, eating?"

"You must have meat."

By "N" of that Ilk [C. F. M. Noland]. From *The Big Bear of Arkansas, and Other Sketches*, Illustrative of Characters and Incidents in the South and South-West, edited by William T. Porter, pp. 143–145. Entered, according to Act of Congress, in the year 1845, by Carey & Hart, in the Clerk's Office of the District Court of the United States, of the Eastern District of Pennsylvania. Philadelphia.

"If you call *two thousand seven hundred pounds* of clean meat, without a bone, safe inside of a smoke-house, *meat*, we have got *some*."

"They must be fat at your house?"

"Do you call a *candle* fat?"

Here Old Sense brought a perfect squeal, and swore he had found the very man he had been looking for.

P. S. They had closed a quarter race up to the last accounts.

Two Plantation Tales

I. According to How the Drop Falls

"Is I gwine tell you a tale right now?" said Uncle Remus, in response to a question by the little boy. "Well, I ain't right certain en sho' 'bout dat. It's 'cordin ter how de drap falls."

"Pshaw!" exclaimed the youngster, "I've heard you say that before. I don't know what you mean when you say it's according to how the drop falls."

"Ah-yi!" retorted Uncle Remus triumphantly, "den I'm a punkin ahead er yo' 'simmon, is I?"

"It's according to how the drop falls," rejoined the little boy, laughing.

"De way dat sayin' come 'bout," said Uncle Remus, "may be funny, but 't ain't no tale. It des happen so. One time dey wuz a 'oman call on a neighbor 'oman des' fo' dinner-time. I dunner whedder de neighbor 'oman like dis mighty well, but she 'uz monst'us perlite all de same.

"She 'low, 'Come right in, en take off yo' things an make yo'se'f at home. You'll hatter skuzen my han's, kaze I'm makin' up dough. Fling yo' bonnet on de bed dar, en take a seat en be seated.'

"Well, de tudder 'oman, she sot dar en talk, en watch de neighbor 'oman mix dough fer de bread, en dey run'd on des like wimmin folks does. It seem like de neighbor 'oman got a bad col', en her eyes run water twel some un it crope down ter de een er her nose en hang dar. De tudder 'oman, she watch it, whiles dey er talkin'. De neighbor 'oman she work up de dough, en work it up, en talk. Sometimes she'd hol' her head fum over de tray en talk, en den ag'in she'd hol' it right spang over de dough, en shake 'er head en talk.

"Bimeby she 'low, 'Won't you stay ter dinner? I'll have dis bread done in two shakes uv a sheep's tail.'

"De tudder 'oman say, 'I can't tell you, ma'am; it's 'cordin' ter how de drap falls.'

From *Uncle Remus and His Friends, Old Plantation Stories, Songs, and Ballads with Sketches of Negro Character,* by Joel Chandler Harris, pp. 147–153. Copyright, 1892, by Joel Chandler Harris. Boston and New York· Houghton, Mifflin and Company.

"De tudder 'oman say, 'Dey ain't a cloud in de sky, so 't ain't gwine ter rain. You des ez well stay.'

"De tudder 'oman 'low, 'I done tole you de trufe; hit's 'cordin' ter how de drap falls.'

"So, atter dat, when folks wan't right certain en sho' 'bout what dey gwine do, dey'd up en say 't wuz 'cordin' ter how de drap fall."

"Well, how did it fall, Uncle Remus—in the bread-tray, or on the table, or on the floor?" the little boy inquired.

"Lawsy, honey!" responded the old man, "ef I 'uz er tell you, I'd hatter dream it, en dreamin' ain't gwine do you er me any mo' good dan it done de nigger man what had de possum."

"I never heard of that," said the little boy.

"Oh, yes you is!" Uncle Remus asserted with some emphasis. "You been hearin' 'bout it off'n on sence you 'uz knee-high ter a duck, en you ain't much mo'n dat right now. No, suh! You des got de idee in yo' min' dat when I set down fer ter tell you sump'n hit's bleedz ter be a tale, en when yuther folks tells it 't ain't nothin' but talk. I ain't got no secret 'bout dish yer nigger man what had de possum, but I tell you right now, 'tain't no tale. Too many folks done been fool wid it.

II. THE MAN WHO HAD THE POSSUM

"Well, den, one time dey wuz a nigger man, en dish yer nigger man had a big fat possum en a half er peck er sweet 'taters. He tuck de possum en de taters home, en he lay um down,—de possum on one side de fireplace en de taters on tudder side. Den he get some wood and chips en make 'im a fier, en den he fotch out de skillet. He put de possum in dar, he did, en he put de taters in de ashes close by fer ter keep 'im comp'ny. Den he raked out some hot embers en sot de skillet on um, en he put on de skillet led, en piled some embers 'pon topper dat.

"He sot dar, he did, en wait fer de possum fer ter git done, en whiles he wuz a-waitin' he struck up a song. Maybe you done hear it 'fo' now, but dat ain't make no diffunce ter me, kaze when I git started dis away, I'm like de bull yearlin' gwine down de lane; dem what gits in de way gwine ter git run'd over—dey mos' sholy is!"

Uncle Remus leaned back in his chair, closed his eyes, and began to pat his foot. Then, after a little pause, he sang this fragment of a song:

> "Virginny cut, chaw terbacker,
> Nigger dance ter merlatter;
> Hoe de corn, dig er tater,
> Plant terbacker, 't is no matter.

> "Mix de meal, fry de batter,
> Nigger dance ter merlatter;
> Warm de cake in er platter,
> Fry um in de cooney fat.

"Grab er tater out de ash,
Nigger dance ter merlatter;
Possum meat dar in der platter,
Shoo! he make de nigger fatter."

Uncle Remus's voice was full of melody, and he sang the song to a rollicking tune. The little boy was so much pleased that he asked the old man to sing it again.

"Bless yo' soul, honey. If I git in a fa'r way er singin', de niggers 'll all quit der work en crowd 'roun' here en jine in wid me, en we'll have a reg'lar ole-timey camp-meetin' gwine on here 'fo' you know it. I ain't got no time fer dat.

"Now, den, dish yer nigger man, what I been tellin' you 'bout, he got his taters in de ashes en his possum in de skillet, en he sot dar en sing de song, en watch um all cook. Atter so long a time dey got done, en he pull de taters out'n de embers, en push de skillet 'way fum de fier. He 'low ter hisse'f, he did, dat col' possum is better'n hot possum, dough bofe un um is good nuff fer anybody. So he say he'll des let it set dar en cool, en soak in de gravy. Den he say he b'lieve he'll do some noddin', kaze den he'll dream he eatin' de possum, en den he'll wake up en eat 'im sho nuff, en have de 'joyment er eatin' 'im two times.

"Well, suh, dat des de way he done. He sot back in his cheer, de nigger man did, en he nodded en nodded, en he work his mouf des like he eatin' possum, en he grunt in his sleep like he feelin' good. But whiles he settin' dar sleepin', a nudder nigger man smell de possum, en he crope up ter de door en peep in. He seed how de lan' lay en he slipped off his shoes en stole in. He lif' up de led er de skillet, en dar wuz de possum. He look on de side er de h'ath, en dar wuz de taters. Now, den, when dat de case, what gwine ter happen? Possum, en tater, en hongry nigger! Well, suh, de fust news you know, de possum wuz all bones, de taters wuz all peelin's, en de nigger wuz mo' dan a nigger. He fix de bones in one little pile, en he fix de peelin's in anudder little pile, en den he tuck some er de possum gravy en rub it on de tudder nigger's mouf en han's, en den he went on 'bout his business.

" 'T wan't so mighty long atter dat 'fo' de noddin' nigger wake up. He open his eyes, he did, en stretch hisse'f, en look at de skillet en laugh.

"He 'low, 'You er dar, is you? Well, I'll tell you howdy now, en ter-reckly I'll tell you good-by!'

"He tuck de led off'n de skillet, en dey ain't no possum dar. He look 'roun' fer de taters, en dey ain't no taters dar. Dey ain't nothin' dar but a pile er bones en a pile er tater-peelin's. De nigger sot down in his cheer en went ter studyin'. He look at his han's, en he see possum grease on um. He lick out his tongue, en he tas'e possum gravy on his mouf. He shuck his head en study. He look at his han's: 'Possum been dar!' He lick his mouf: 'Possum been dar, too!' He rub his stomach: 'But I be bless ef any possum been here!' "

Way Down in Georgia

ONCE upon a time, 'way down in Georgia, it wuz Sunday mawnin', an' de sun wuz hot. De folks in de big house didn' wake up, an' de crows, down in de cawn fiel', wuz a-pullin' up all de cawn. De ol' rooster see de crows a-pullin' up all de cawn an' he lifted up his voice an' say, "De crows a-pullin' up all de cawn! De crows a-pullin' up all de cawn! De crows a-pullin' up all de cawn!" [Imitation of a cock crowing.] An' de crows dey keep on sayin', "Cawn! Cawn! Cawn!" [Imitation of cawing]

An' de sun keep a-gittin' hotter an' hotter, an' de folks in de big house didn' wake up, an' de crows keep on a-pullin' up de cawn. De ol' rooster he git more an' more excited an' lift up his voice a little higher an' say, "De crows a-pullin' up all de cawn! De crows a-pullin' up all de cawn! De crows a-pullin' up all de cawn!" An' de crows, way down in de fiel', keep on sayin', "Cawn! Cawn! Cawn!"

An' de sun keep a-gittin' hotter an' hotter, an' de folks in de big house didn' wake up, an' de crows keep on pullin' up de cawn. De ol' rooster he git more an' more excited an' lift his voice 'way up an' say, "De crows a-pullin' up all de cawn! De crows a-pullin' up all de cawn! De crows a-pullin' up all de cawn!" An' de crows, 'way down in de fiel', dey keep on a-sayin', "Cawn! Cawn! Cawn!"

By-m-by, de ol' turkey gobbler, a-settin' on de fence, he git excited, too. He flopped his wings er time er two, flew down inter de yahd, an' called as loud as he could, "Put! put! put! put! W'at de heck yer goin' ter do 'bout it? W'at de heck yer goin' ter do 'bout it? W'at de heck yer goin' ter do' bout it?"

De Pot-Song

TEXAS nigger didn't have to stay on one planteration all de time lessen he want to. Lord, no! Too many big woods to run aroun' in. Sometimes de soup git moughty thin and de rations moughty measly on some planterations. Den a nigger git up an' leave. He hide in de woods fo' a spell, den he slip aroun' to de kitchen of anudder planteration just 'bout supper time.

From *Negro Tales from West Virginia*, by John Harrington Cox, *The Journal of American Folklore*, Vol. XLVII (October-December, 1934), No. CLXXXVI, pp. 356–357. New York.

Learned by the Editor from Mr. Richard Wyche, Washington, D. C., 1919.—J. H. C.

From "De Pot-Song," by Palmer A. Throop, *Foller de Drinkin' Gou'd*, Publications of the Texas Folk-Lore Society, Number VII, edited by J. Frank Dobie, p. 139. Copyright, 1928, by The Texas Folk-Lore Society. Austin.

My grandmother's cook, a former slave, at Anderson, in Grimes County, once told me this tale when I was a little boy, watching the oatmeal bubble on the stove. —P. A. T.

He stick he haid in de do' an' listen to de pot-song. Ef'n de pot-song sing "Z-z-z-z-z-z," nigger says, "Leave dis trash alone; I done heared dat water-song too long already." Den he take to de woods agin tell de nex' night. 'Long 'bout supper time, he stick he haid in anudder do' an' listen to de pot-song. Ef'n de pot sing, "Flippity-flop, flippity-flop," nigger say, "Dat chune sho' got a sight of water in hit." So he up'n take to de woods agin tell de nex' night. 'Long 'bout supper time, he stick he haid in anudder do' an' listen to de pot-song. Ef'n de pot sing slow and puffin', "Ker-plop , . . ker-plop . . . ker-plop," nigger say, "Lord! Dar's *my* chune; dat pot-song say, 'Thick an' plenty, thick an' plenty.' "

The Talking Mule

OLE feller one time had uh mule. His name wuz Bill. Every mornin' de man go tuh ketch 'im he say, "Come round, Bill!"

So one mornin' he slept late, so he decided while he wuz drinkin' some coffee he'd send his son tuh ketch Ole Bill.

Told 'im say, "Go down dere, boy, and bring me dat mule up here."

Boy, he sich a fast Aleck, he grabbed de bridle and went on down tuh de lot tuh ketch Ole Bill.

He say, "Come round, Bill!"

De mule looked round at 'im. He told de mule, "Tain't no use you rollin' yo' eyes at *me*. Pa want yuh dis mawnin'. Come on round and stick yo' head in dis bridle."

Mule kept on lookin' at 'im and said, "Every mornin' it's 'Come round, Bill! Come round, Bill!' Don't hardly git no night rest befo' it's 'Come round, Bill!' "

De boy throwed down dat bridle and flew back tuh de house and told his Pa, "Dat mule is talkin'."

"Ah g'wan, boy, tellin' yo' lies! G'wan ketch dat mule."

"Naw suh, Pa, dat mule's done gone tuh talkin'. You hatta ketch dat mule yo' ownself. Ah ain't gwine."

Ole man looked at ole lady and say, "See whut uh lie dat boy is tellin'?"

So he gits out and goes on down after de mule hisself. When he got down dere he hollered, "Come round, Bill!"

Ole mule looked round and says, "Every mornin' it's come round, Bill!"

De old man had uh little fice dog useter foller 'im everywhere he go, so he lit out wid de lil fice right behind 'im. So he told de ole lady, "De boy ain't told much of uh lie. Dat mule *is* talkin'. Ah never heered uh mule talk befo'."

Lil fice say, "Me neither."

De ole man got skeered agin. Right through de woods he went wid de

From *Mules and Men*, by Zora Neale Hurston, pp. 217–218. Copyright, 1935, by Zora Neale Hurston. Philadelphia and London: J. B. Lippincott Company.

fice right behind 'im. He nearly run hisself tuh death. He stopped and commenced blowin' and says, "Ah'm so tired Ah don't know whut tuh do."

Lil dog run and set down in front of 'im and went to hasslin' [1] and says, "Me too."

Dat man is runnin' yet.

The Ventriloquist

TAD: Is you hear de tale 'bout de white man an' de nigger an' de mule?

VOICE: I hear a heap er tales 'bout white folks an' niggers an' mules. Wuh you have in mind?

TAD: One time dere was a white man an' he runned a big farm, an' he notice one er he mule was gitten mighty poor, so he got to watchin'. He s'picion dat de nigger wuh was workin' de mule was stealin' he feed. Dis white man was one er dem people wha' kin pitch dey voice any wey dey wants. He could throw he voice into a cow or dog or any kind er animal an' have 'em talkin'—make 'em carry on reg'lar compersation.

VOICE: I has heared dem kind er people.

TAD: Well, he git to de crack er de stable an' he seed de nigger wid a bag reach in de mule' trough an' take out some corn an' put it in de bag. When de nigger do dat, de white man pitched he voice right into de mule' mout' an' make de mule say:

"Nigger, don't take my little bit er feed."

When he say dat, de nigger walk off an' look at de mule for awhile an' de mule ain' say nothin' more. Den he walk back an' dip in de trough again an' start takin' de mule' corn, an' de white folks make de mule say again:

"Nigger, please don't take my feed."

An' again de nigger walk off an' look at de mule.

VOICE: Ain' no mule ever would er spoke but one time to me.

TAD: Dis here nigger ain' have good sense, an' he went back de third time an' dive into dat corn. An' dis time de mule turn he head an' look at him, an' de white folks th'owed he voice into de mule' mout' one more time an' make de mule say:

"Nigger, ain' I axe you please for God' sake quit takin' my feed. You mighty nigh done perish me to de'te."

When he say dat, de nigger drap he bag an' bu's' out er dat stable, an' de next mornin' he went to he boss an' say:

"Boss, I guh quit."

An' he boss say:

"John, I ain' want you to quit me. I satisfy wid you."

[1] Panting.—Z. N. P.

From *Nigger to Nigger*, by E. C. L. Adams, pp. 136–138. Copyright, 1928, by Charles Scribner's Sons.

An' de nigger say:

"Well, Boss, I ain' zackly satisfy. You mought as well gee me my time, kaze I done quit."

Scip: Dere ain' no nigger ever would er been zackly satisfy atter he heared a mule talkin'.

Voice: It was quittin' time.

Tad: Dat ain' all. De white folks paid de nigger he wages an' de nigger walk off a piece down de road an' turn 'round an' walk back to de white folks an' say:

"Boss, I done quit. Dere ain' no nuse for nobody to say nothin' to me. I done quit an' I is guine, but 'fore I goes I got one thing to say to you."

An' de white folks look at him jes as kind an' say:

"Wha' it is, John?"

An' de nigger say:

"Boss, I done quit sho' 'nough, but 'fore I goes I wants to tell you one thing. Anything dat mule say to you is a damn lie."

An' den he leff.

Scip: I knowed in de first place dat de white folks done loss a nigger.

Ole Massa and John
Who Wanted to Go to Heaven

You know befo' surrender Ole Massa had a nigger name John and John always prayed every night befo' he went to bed and his prayer was for God to come git him and take him to Heaven right away. He didn't even want to take time to die. He wanted de Lawd to come git him just like he was —boot, sock and all. He'd git down on his knees and say: "O Lawd, it's once more and again yo' humble servant is knee-bent and body-bowed— my heart beneath my knees and my knees in some lonesome valley, crying for mercy while mercy kin be found. O Lawd, Ah'm astin' you in de humblest way I know how to be *so* pleased as to come in yo' fiery chariot and take me to yo' Heben and its immortal glory. Come Lawd, you know Ah have such a hard time. Ole Massa works me *so* hard, and don't gimme no time to rest. So come, Lawd, wid peace in one hand and pardon in de other and take me away from this sin-sorrowing world. Ah'm tired and Ah want to go home."

So one night Ole Massa passed by John's shack and heard him beggin' de Lawd to come git him in his fiery chariot and take him away; so he made up his mind to find out if John meant dat thing. So he goes on up to de big house and got hisself a bed sheet and come on back. He throwed de sheet over his head and knocked on de door.

From *Mules and Men*, by Zora Neale Hurston, pp. 96–99. Copyright, 1935, by Zora Neale Hurston. Philadelphia and London: J. B. Lippincott Company.

John quit prayin' and ast: "Who dat?"

Ole Massa say: "It's me, John, de Lawd, done come wid my fiery chariot to take you away from this sin-sick world."

Right under de bed John had business. He told his wife: "Tell Him Ah ain't here, Liza."

At first Liza didn't say nothin' at all, but de Lawd kept right on callin' John: "Come on, John, and go to Heben wid me where you won't have to plough no mo' furrows and hoe no mo' corn. Come on, John."

Liza says: "John ain't here, Lawd, you hafta come back another time."

Lawd says: "Well, then Liza, you'll do."

Liza whispers and says: "John, come out from underneath dat bed and g'wan wid de Lawd. You been beggin' him to come git you. Now g'wan wid him."

John back under de bed not sayin' a mumblin' word. De Lawd out on de doorstep kept on callin'.

Liza says: "John, Ah thought you was so anxious to get to Heben. Come out and go on wid God."

John says: "Don't you hear him say 'You'll do'? Why don't you go wid him?"

"Ah ain't a goin' nowhere. Youse de one been whoopin' and hollerin' for him to come git you and if you don't come out from under dat bed Ah'm gointer tell God youse here."

Ole Massa makin' out he's God, says: "Come on, Liza, you'll do."

Liza says: "O, Lawd, John is right here underneath de bed."

"Come on John, and go to Heben wid me and its immortal glory."

John crept out from under de bed and went to de door and cracked it and when he seen all dat white standin' on de doorsteps he jumped back. He says: "O, Lawd, Ah can't go to Heben wid you in yo' fiery chariot in dese ole dirty britches; gimme time to put on my Sunday pants."

"All right, John, put on yo' Sunday pants."

John fooled around just as long as he could, changing them pants, but when he went back to de door, de big white glory was still standin' there. So he says agin: "O, Lawd, de Good Book says in Heben no filth is found and I got on dis dirty sweaty shirt. Ah can't go wid you in dis old nasty shirt. Gimme time to put on my Sunday shirt!"

"All right, John, go put on yo' Sunday shirt."

John took and fumbled around a long time changing his shirt, and den he went back to de door, but Ole Massa was still on de doorstep. John didn't had nothin' else to change so he opened de door a little piece and says:

"O, Lawd, Ah'm ready to go to Heben wid you in yo' fiery chariot, but de radiance of yo' countenance is so bright, Ah can't come out by you. Stand back jus' a li'l way please."

Ole Massa stepped back a li'l bit.

John looked out agin and says: "O, Lawd, you know dat po' humble me is less than de dust beneath yo' shoe soles. And de radiance of yo' countenance is so bright Ah can't come out by you. Please, please, Lawd, in yo' tender mercy, stand back a li'l bit further."

Ole Massa stepped back a li'l bit mo'.

John looked out agin and he says: "O, Lawd, Heben is so high and wese so low; youse so great and Ah'm so weak and yo' strength is too much for us poor sufferin' sinners. So once mo' and agin yo' humber servant is knee-bent and body-bowed askin' you one mo' favor befo' Ah step into yo' fiery chariot to go to Heben wid you and wash in yo' glory—be so pleased in yo' tender mercy as to stand back jus' a li'l bit further."

Ole Massa stepped back a step or two mo' and out dat door John come like a streak of lightning. All across de punkin patch, thru de cotton over de pasture—John wid Ole Massa right behind him. By de time dey hit de cornfield John was way ahead of Ole Massa.

Back in de shack one of de children was cryin' and she ast Liza: "Mama, you reckon God's gointer ketch papa and carry him to Heben wid him?"

"Shet yo' mouf, talkin' foolishness!" Liza clashed at de chile. "You know de Lawd can't outrun yo' pappy—specially when he's barefooted at dat."

"God an' de Devil in de Cemetery"

Two mens dat didn't know how tuh count good had been haulin' up cawn and they stopped at de cemetery wid de last load 'cause it wuz gittin' kinda dark. They thought they'd git thru instead uh goin' 'way tuh one of 'em's barn. When they wuz goin' in de gate two ear uh cawn dropped off de waggin, but they didn't stop tuh bother wid 'em, just then. They wuz in uh big hurry tuh git home. They wuz justa 'vidin' it up. "You take dis'un and Ah'll take dat'un, you take dat'un and Ah'll take dis'un."

An ole nigger heard 'em while he wuz passin' de cemetery an' run home tuh tell ole Massa 'bout it.

"Massa, de Lawd and de devil is down in de cemetery 'vidin' up souls. Ah heard 'em. One say, 'You take that 'un an' Ah'll take dis'un.' "

Ole Massa wuz sick in de easy chear, he couldn't git about by hisself, but he said, "Jack, Ah don't know whut dis foolishness is, but Ah know you lyin'."

"Naw Ah ain't neither, Ah swear it's so."

"Can't be, Jack, youse crazy."

"Naw Ah ain't neither; if you don't believe me, come see for yo'self."

"Guess Ah better go see whut you talkin' 'bout; if you fool me, Ah'm gointer have a hundred lashes put on yo' back in de mawnin' suh."

They went on down tuh de cemetery wid Jack pushin' Massa in his rollin' chear, an' it wuz sho dark down dere too. So they couldn't see de two ears uh cawn layin' in de gate.

Ibid., pp. 117–119.

Sho nuff Ole Massa heard 'em sayin', "Ah'll take dis'un," and de other say, "An' Ah'll take dis'un." Ole Massa got skeered hisself but he wuzn't lettin' on, an' Jack whispered tuh 'im, "Unh hunh, didn't Ah tell you de Lawd an' de devil wuz down here 'vidin' up souls?"

They waited awhile there in de gate listenin' den they heard 'em say, "Now, we'll go git dem two at de gate."

Jack says, "Ah knows de Lawd gwine take you, and Ah ain't gwine let de devil get me—Ah'm gwine home." An' he did an' lef' Ole Massa settin' dere at de cemetery gate in his rollin' chear, but when he got home, Ole Massa had done beat 'im home and wuz settin' by de fire smokin' uh seegar.

The Fortune Teller

IN SLAVERY time dere was a colored man what was named John. He went along wid Ole Massa everywhere he went. He used to make out he could tell fortunes. One day him and his Ole Massa was goin' along and John said, "Ole Massa, Ah kin tell fortunes." Ole Massa made out he didn't pay him no attention. But when they got to de next man's plantation Ole Massa told de landlord, "I have a nigger dat kin tell fortunes." So de other man said, "Dat nigger can't tell no fortunes. I bet my plantation and all my niggers against yours dat he can't tell no fortunes."

Ole Massa says: "I'll take yo' bet. I bet everything in de world I got on John 'cause he don't lie. If he say he can tell fortunes, he can tell 'em. Bet you my plantation and all my niggers against yours and throw in de wood lot extry."

So they called Notary Public and signed up de bet. Ole Massa straddled his horse and John got on his mule and they went on home.

John was in de misery all that night for he knowed he was gointer be de cause of Ole Massa losin' all he had.

Every mornin' John useter be up and have Ole Massa's saddle horse curried and saddled at de door when Ole Massa woke up. But *this* mornin' Ole Massa had to git John out of de bed.

John useter always ride side by side with Massa, but on de way over to de plantation where de bet was on, he rode way behind.

So de man on de plantation had went out and caught a coon and had a big old iron wash-pot turned down over it.

There was many persons there to hear John tell what was under de wash-pot.

Ole Massa brought John out and tole him, say: "John, if you tell what's under dat wash-pot Ah'll make you independent, rich. If you don't, Ah'm goin' to kill you because you'll make me lose my plantation and every thing I got."

Ibid., pp. 111–112.

John walked 'round and 'round dat pot but he couldn't git de least inklin' of what was underneath it. Drops of sweat as big as yo' fist was rollin' off of John. At last he give up and said: "Well, you got de ole coon at last."

When John said that, Ole Massa jumped in de air and cracked his heels twice befo' he hit de ground. De man that was bettin' against Ole Massa fell to his knees wid de cold sweat pourin' off him. Ole Massa said: "John, you done won another plantation fo' me. That's a coon under that pot sho 'nuff."

So he give John a new suit of clothes and a saddle horse. And John quit tellin' fortunes after that.

Massa and the Bear

ONE day Ole Massa sent for John and tole him, says: "John, somebody is stealin' my corn out de field. Every mornin' when I go out I see where they done carried off some mo' of my roastin' ears. I want you to set in de corn patch tonight and ketch whoever it is."

So John said all right and he went and hid in de field.

Pretty soon he heard somethin' breakin' corn. So John sneaked up behind him wid a short stick in his hand and hollered: "Now, break another ear of Ole Massa's corn and see what *Ah'll* do to you."

John thought it was a man all dis time, but it was a bear wid his arms full of roastin' ears. He throwed down de corn and grabbed John. And him and dat bear!

John, after while got loose and got de bear by the tail wid de bear tryin' to git to him all de time. So they run around in a circle all night long. John was so tired. But he couldn't let go of de bear's tail, do de bear would grab him in de back.

After a stretch they quit runnin' and walked. John swingin' on to de bear's tail and de bear's nose 'bout to touch him in de back.

Daybreak, Ole Massa come out to see 'bout John and he seen John and de bear walkin' 'round in de ring. So he run up and says: "Lemme take holt of 'im, John, whilst you run git help!"

John says: "All right, Massa. Now you run in quick and grab 'im just so."

Ole Massa run and grabbed holt of de bear's tail and said: "Now, John you make haste to git somebody to help us."

John staggered off and set down on de grass and went to fanning hisself wid his hat.

Ole Massa was havin' plenty trouble wid dat bear and he looked over and seen John settin' on de grass and he hollered:

Ibid., pp. 100–101.

"John, you better g'wan git help or else I'm gwinter turn dis bear aloose!'"

John says: "Turn 'im loose, then. Dat's whut Ah tried to do all night long but Ah couldn't."

The Bear Fight

DEACON JONES an' he gal live in a section of de country wey dere been a heap er bears. An' one night he been guine to an experience meetin', an' dere been two roads, an' he gal say:

"Papa, le's we don't go through de woods road, kaze I seen a bear dere today."

An' de deacon say:

"I ain' care notin' 'bout no bear. I a Christian an' loves God an' God loves me, an' I puts my trust in Him. I loves God. God is good. I'm guine through dem woods."

An' de gal say:

"Papa, le's we don't make no mistakes. Le's we go 'round."

An' de deacon say:

"I'm guine through dem woods. I trust God. I puts my faith in God. God is good an' will pertec' me."

An' de gal say:

"I ain' trustin' all dat. I'm guine 'round."

An' de deacon say:

"Well, I'm guine through de woods. God is my pertecter."

An' he went through de woods, an' de gal went 'round.

An' when de deacon git half way through de woods, a bear jumped on him an' he had a terrible time fightin' wid dat bear. De bear tored mighty nigh all he clothes off, an' bit him up an' mighty nigh ruint him. But when he git loose, he made he way to de experience meetin'. An' when he git dere, dem niggers been tellin' 'bout dey experience wid God an' Jesus an de devil an' wid angels an' a passel er lies.

An' den dey spied Deacon Jones in de back er de congregation, an' dey call on him for his experience an' he say he ain' got nothin' to say. An' all dem brother an' all dem sister keep on hollerin' for him. An' atter while de deacon git up an' say:

"My brothers an' sisters, all I kin say is: God is good. God is good. I loves God. I sho' loves Him, an' I puts my faith in Him. God is good an' He'll help you in a lot er little things, but, my brothers an' sisters, good as God is, He ain' worth a damn in a bear fight."

From *Nigger to Nigger*, by E. C. L. Adams, pp. 223–224. Copyright, 1928, by Charles Scribner's Sons. New York.

End of the World

WHEN I wus a boy livin in de country, some Seven Day Adventis preachers comes intuh de community, an holes a tracted-meetin fur bout two-weeks in a big tent, an era, da preaches dat de worl hit gwina comes tuh a en, on Wednesday atter de close uv de meetin, Sunday night!

Hit look lack evy-body in dat hole county quits work, an comes tuh dat meetin whar da preaches three times a day, ten-clock in de mornin, three in de evenin an seven at night. Da proves fum de Bible dat de world hit gwina comes tuh a en real soon. I member des ez well ez ef twus yistidy, one uv de proofs wus dat de trees wus dyin in de tops. Da urges pun yuh tuh fess yuh sins tuh each uther, an gits ready fur Gabrel tuh blows fur de en. Kose we had big trees den, but yuh aint got um now, an when we looks out sho-nuff, some uv de big trees wus dead in de tops!

A man name John Hunnycut whut lives in de county went purty often tuh de meetin, an git so he bleven um, an jine de church an de mornin de worl wus comin tuh a en, he go out, clime pun a straw-stack tuh waits tell time be no-mo, an bein bout "half-full a licker" he draps off tuh sleep. Some boys comes along, an seein im up-dar, cludes tuh has some fun, so da sets de straw-stack afire on three sides, and when de flames gins tuh shoot-up, all roun im, he jump up an say: "In Hell jest as I expected!"

In a little town uv de community wus a man an his wife name Jerry Horner an Miss Horner. Da went tuh evy meetin so da bleves in um, an jines dat chuch too, an purty soon bleven de doctrin, da makes ready fur de las day.

On de las night, fo de time fur de worl tuh comes tuh a en, Mr. an Miss Horner cludes tuh fess tuh each uther da pass sins. Miss Horner she wants Mr. Horner tuh fess-up fuss, but he sist on her fessin fuss, so she do dat. Miss Horner she say dat she doan wants tuh has tuh tell her sins, but lows hit mus be done an she say:

"When I was a young woman about eighteen years old, I met a young man name Giles Buford, an he commenced coming to see me. After he had been coming to see me for about six months, he commenced to make love to me, and began to squeeze my hand. Somehow I liked that, and he soon got to squeezing my arms then my body, and then to kissing me. I went wild about him, and that went on for a year, but he got killed." (Mr. Horner, he say: "My! My!")

"About a year after Buford was killed I met a man named Will Hughes, and it warnt long till he was doing what Buford did, and I went wild about him, too, (Mr. Horner say: "Just think of that!") but he died, and then the old wooden-legged shoemaker down the street, commenced to pay attention

From *Humorous Short Stories*, by Uncle Eaph (Jacob Thompson Johnson), pp. 20–23. Copyright, 1928, by Jacob T. Johnson. Atlanta, Ga.: Jacob T. Johnson Publishing Co

to me, but that was before he lost his leg, in a saw-mill accident, and he did about what the others had done. (Mr. Horner say: "The Devil, an Tom Walker!") but when he lost his leg he was laid-up a long time."

"After that I met and married you, but while I have appeared happy, I never have been, and the old shoemaker still makes love to me." (De ole-man, wid head bowed down, an press tween his hans, groans loud, an say: "Oh, my God! Blow Gabrel, I'm ready!!")

"Man Above"

MAN was jealous of his wife, an' he come in one day an' ask her who had been there. An' she said, "No one." But he said, "Yes, there have, an' I'm goin' to beat you." She said, "Well, you can, but there's a man above knows all things." An' the man above said, "Yes, an' there's a man under the bed knows as much as I do."

The Lazy Man

'BOUT a man who was goin' to be married. He was so po', he had to go 'roun' to de citizen an' ask help. Dey all assis' him in clothin' an' in weddin'. Done all dey could for him. Promise dem if he live, he ketch up again an' he give all return. Dey give enough so he could live a while widout goin' to work. Dey get so hard on him, dey 'peal back to his wife. Said, "Oh, I remember my promise!" She ask him, "What was your promise?" Said, "I promise all of my people that help me when I was goin' to get married, I live quite a while on dat. Times gettin' hard for me. I got to go to work. I believe dat is my trouble."—"I believe it is," she says. "Now, dis is de en' of de week. I have to go to work Monday. Wake me up on Monday mornin'." She did. When she call upon him, said, "I kyan' work Monday, Monday is Sunday broder. Wake me Tuesday mornin'." Tuesday mornin' when she call upon him, he said "Kyan't work Tuesday, Tuesday is Monday broder. Wake me Wednesday mornin'." She call upon him Wednesday mornin'. "Kyan't work Wednesday, Wednesday is de middle of de week," he says. Says, "Well, de week goin' fast. De rations goin' fas'. Wake me Thursday mornin'." She call upon him. "Kyan't work Thursday, Thursday is day o' fas'."—"Two more days. Got to work, cause de neighbors is tired of us. Have somet'in

From "Tales from Guilford County, North Carolina," by Elsie Clews Parsons, *The Journal of American Folk-Lore*, Vol. XXX (April-June, 1917), No. CXVI, p. 186. Copyright, 1917, by the American Folk-Lore Society.

Informant, Bill Cruse. About 68. Born and bred in Forsyth County.—E. C. P.

From *Folk-Lore of the Sea Islands, South Carolina*, by Elsie Clews Parsons, Memoirs of the American Folk-Lore Society, Volume XVL, pp. 56–57. Copyright, 1923, by the American Folk-Lore Society. Cambridge, Mass., and New York.

Informant, Toby Byas, of John Tripp Plantation, St. Helena.—E. C. P.

to eat Sunday. Said, "Kyan't work Friday, Friday is hangman day. Everybody go see a man hang. Call me Saturday mornin'." She call upon him Saturday mornin'. "Kyan't work Saturday, Saturday is jus' de same as Sunday. Wake me up Monday. Have somet'in to eat nex' week." Kep' on wid dat. Nex' week met a man wid some money. While he roamin' out, get him to talk. He killed de man, took away his money. Nex' Friday he was hang. Everybody wen' to see *him* hang.

"All of These Are Mine"

WELL, the startin' of it is, a farmer was courtin' a girl and after he decided to marry her, they married and started home. So when he passed a nice farm he said to the girl: "You see dat nice farm over yonder?" She said, "Yes." He said: "Well, all of these are mine." (Strokes his whiskers.)

Well, they traveled on further and they saw a herd of cattle and he said, "See dat nice herd of cattle?" She said, "Yes." "Well, all of these are mine." He smoothed his whiskers again.

So he traveled on a piece further and come to a big plantation with a big nice house on it, and he said: "All of these are mine."

So he traveled on further. He said, "See dat nice bunch of sheep?" She said, "Yes." "Well, all of these are mine."

Traveled on further. Come across a nice bunch of hogs and he said: "See dat nice bunch of hogs?" "Yes." "Well, all of these are mine."

So the last go 'round he got home and drove up to a dirty li'l shack and told her to get out and come in.

She says, "You got all those nice houses and want me to come in there? I couldn't afford to come here. *Why you told me a story.* I'm going back home."

He says, "Why no, I didn't tell you a story. Everytime I showed you those things I said 'all of these were mine' and Ah wuz talkin' 'bout my whiskers." So the girl jumped out of the wagon and out for home she went.

Goat fell down and skint his chin
Great God A'mighty how de goat did grin.

The Two Hogs

LAS week Jedge Patrick, whut live fo mile in de country, come tuh town an load-up wid corn licker, an on de way back home, his hoss shy an thow im in a mud-hole, wid a big fat hog.

From *Mules and Men*, by Zora Neale Hurston, p. 214. Copyright, 1935, by Zora Neale Hurston. Philadelphia and London: J. B. Lippincott Company.

From *Humorous Short Stories*, by Uncle Eaph (Jacob Thompson Johnson), pp. 5–6. Copyright, 1928, by Jacob T. Johnson. Atlanta, Ga.: Jacob T. Johnson Publishing Co.

When de Jedge lan in de mud-hole, de sho-nuff hog he say, "Huh!"
but de Jedge, he say nuthin—kose da bofe hogs at dat time. Few hours
later, de Jedge he sober-up, an turn ovah, an seein de sho-nuff hog, he say:
"Good morning brother!" De sho-nuff hog he say back: "Huh! Huh!"
De Jedge he den rise-up his head an say: "You drunk too?" De sho-nuff
hog say: "Huh! Huh!"

By an by, de Jedge sober up some-mo, an he say: "Bright morning for
two hogs to be in the same mud-hole." De sho-nuff hog say: "Huh! Huh!"
De Jedge he den git kinda-huffy at de sociation uv de sho-nuff hog, an
he say: "I recognize brother, that we are both common hogs, in the same
mud-hole to-day, (de sho-nuff hog say: "huh! huh!), but tomorrow you
will be the same darned-old-hog, and I will be Judge Patrick of the
Supreme Court." De sho-nuff hog say: "Huh!"

Story of a Cow

Soon atter de negroes wus sot-free by Mr. Lincoln, two uv-um, by name
uv Mose Smiff an Rastus Jones, cludes tuh buys a cow tuhgether, ez da
lives on jinen places, an da goes ovah tuh a neighbor, an buys a cow fur
$20.00 an each uv-um tuh pays $10.00 fur his haff.

Comin on back home, Mose say tuh Rastus: "Rastus, whut haff uv de
cow you wants?" Rastus he say back: "I wants de front-en uv de cow."
Mose say: "All right, I takes de hine-en fur mine." Few days later da
goes ovah, pays fur de cow, an brings her back an turns her in Rastus'
clover-patch, whar she main sevel days.

One mornin, Mose wife wake up an say: "Mose, aint you an Rastus
Jones bought a cow tuther day?" He say: "Yes." She say: "Aint you
done paid fur haff de cow?" He say: "Yes." She say: "Whut haff uv de
cow longs tuh you?" He says: "De hine-en uv de cow." She say: "Well
era, ef de hine-en longs tuh you, how comes, yuh aint nuver looks atter
yo-en, an melks de cow?" He say: "I hadnt thought uv dat." She say:
"Now, you git-up an gits a bucket, an go ovah an melks dat cow, don't
I gwina bus yo head wide-open wid a boad, nigger!"

Mose gits up an gits a bucket, an goes-ovah an says: "Rastus, aint
me-en-you bought a cow tuther day?" He say: "Yes." Mose say: "Aint
I done pay fur haff de cow, an tuck de hine-en?" He say: "Yes." Mose
say: "Well era, I wants tuh melk my-en." Rastus say: "I been melkin
de cow." Mose say: "De front en longs tuh you, an you tuh feeds de
cow, an I tuh melks de cow!"

Ibid., pp. 35–36.

He Got the Possum

FOUR of us went to Possom-hunting—Bill and John and Pete and I—all four of us niggers, and we didn't catch but one; one possom, and we knew somebody would be without sweet potatoes and possom. So Bill said:

"I tell you what, we will all lay down and go to sleep, and the one that dreams the biggest dream will get the possom."

"All right," said we, and all laid down.

Bill dreamt that he was rich.

"Well, he got the possum."

"No, you forget, John was there, and he dreamt he was a millionaire."

"Oh, he got the possom."

"No, you forget, Pete was there; he dreamt he owned the whole round world."

"Well, that gives the possom to Pete."

"No, you forget that I was there yet."

"What did you dream?"

"I didn't go to sleep. I staid awake and got the possom myself. It is not the man that sleeps that gets the gravy, it's the man that stays awake."

The Three Dreams

Two Irishmen and a Hebrew one day
    Went out for recreation.
They took enough provisions along
    To spend a week's vacation.
One night they got lost in the woods;
    The night was dark and lonely.
At last the food they had gave out,
    Except a piece of baloney.

From *The Arkansaw Cracker Jack*, compiled by Taylor Beard, p. 17. Entered according to Act of Congress, in the year 1905, by the Rhodes & McClure Publishing Company, in the office of the Librarian of Congress, Washington, D. C. Chicago, Ill.

From *The Journal of American Folk-Lore*, Vol. XXXIV (July-September, 1921), No. CXXXIII, pp. 327–328.
The following verses (to the tune of "Pop goes the Weasel") were communicated to me through the mediation of Mr. Max Deutch by Mr. Frank Wolff. They were composed by the latter in conjunction with an employee of the St. Louis Post-Office. He is unable to identify any part as his contribution, and knows the tale merely as a floating anecdote. The theme will be recognized at once as that of the "Three Dreams, or the Dream-Bread Story," which has been discussed at length by Paull F. Baum in this Journal (30 [1917]: 378 ff.). The substitution of "heaven" for "hell" as the destination of the second dreamer is a minor innovation not restricted to this version. This is one more testimony of the immortality of the three-dreams motif; and it has, I am told, even descended to the vaudeville repertory.—Archer Taylor.

As one of them took up a knife,
  I said, "It's no use of carving,
For if we share this piece of baloney,
  It won't keep us from starving."
So I suggested we all go to sleep,
  And so did Maloney.
And the one that had the best of dreams
  Wins the piece of baloney.
The following morn we all got up,
  It was quarter after seven.
One of them said: "I had a dream,
  I died and went to heaven;
St. Peter met me at the gate,
  Riding on a pony.
I guess that dream couldn't be beat,
  So that wins the piece of baloney."
The other one said: "I too had a dream;
  I died and went to heaven;
St. Peter met me at the gate,
  Stuck out his hand, and said, 'Hello, Maloney!'
I guess that dream couldn't be beat,
  So that wins the piece of baloney."
The Hebrew said: "It's true, my friend,
  That you were sleeping.
The reason why I know it is
  'Cause I was peeping.
I saw you both go up in heaven;
  And, believe me, I was lonely;
I thought you'd never come back again,
  So I got up and ate the baloney."

The Goat That Flagged a Train

AH KNOW my ole man had a goat and one Sunday mornin' he got mama
to wash his shirt so't would be clean for him to wear to church. It was
a pretty red silk shirt and my ole man was crazy about it.

So my ole lady washed it and hung it out to dry so she could iron it
befo' church time. Our goat spied pa's shirt hangin' on de line and et it
up tiddy umpty.

My ole man was so mad wid dat goat 'bout his shirt till he grabbed him
and tied him on de railroad track so de train could run over him and kill
him.

But dat old goat was smart. When he seen dat train bearin' down on
him, he coughed up dat red shirt and waved de train down.

From *Mules and Men,* by Zora Neale Hurston, p. 148. Copyright, 1935, by Zora
Neale Hurston. Philadelphia and London: J. B. Lippincott Company.

Deer-Hunting Story

You know Ole Massa took a nigger deer huntin' and posted him in his place and told him, says: "Now you wait right here and keep yo' gun reformed and ready. Ah'm goin' 'round de hill and skeer up de deer and head him dis way. When he come past, you shoot."

De nigger says: "Yessuh, Ah sho' will, Massa."

He set there and waited wid de gun all cocked and after a while de deer come tearin' past him. He didn't make a move to shoot de deer so he went on 'bout his business. After while de white man come on 'round de hill and ast de nigger: "Did you kill de deer?"

De nigger says: "Ah ain't seen no deer pass here yet."

Massa says: "Yes, you did. You couldn't help but see him. He come right dis way."

Nigger says: "Well Ah sho' ain't seen none. All Ah seen was a white man come along here wid a pack of chairs on his head and Ah tipped my hat to him and waited for de deer."

Racing the Train

Once there was two Archman who had never seen a train. They decided they wanted to see one. They went out in the road an' lay down till the train came along. Train came along an' frightened them. An' they run along the railroad, follerin' the train. One of them left the railroad-track an' ran into the woods. The other remained on the railroad-track, an' called to him runnin' in the woods if he couldn't outrun the train on that pretty road how could he runnin' in the woods?

The Damaged Locomotive

'Bout a man who got drunk an' lay on de side de railroad. He lays his han' across de steel. He was asleep an' forgot about de train comin' dat

Ibid., pp. 102–103.

From "Tales from Guilford County, North Carolina," by Elsie Clews Parsons, *The Journal of American Folk-Lore*, Vol. XXX (April-June, 1917), No. CXVI, p. 186. Copyright, 1917, by the American Folk-Lore Society.

Informant Bill Cruse. About 68. Born and bred in Forsyth County. This story can hardly be accounted a folk-tale—as yet. I include it, however, as an illustration of the type of narrative which appears to be taking the place of the more familiar tale in North Carolina. Anecdotes about Irishmen have a distinct vogue. Indeed, the Archman has become as much of a stock character as Rabbit or Hant.—E. C. P.

From "Folk-Tales Collected at Miami, Fla.," by Elsie Clews Parsons, *The Journal of American Folk-Lore*, Vol. XXX (April-June, 1917), No. CXVI, p. 224. Copyright, 1917, by the American Folk-Lore Society.

way. De train come along, cut off his arm. His pardner said to him, "What do you want me to do? Mus' I go an' get a doctor?" He said, "No, go an' get my lawyer."—"What fer?" He said, "I have run over de locomotive an' knock off one of de drivers. De reason why I want a lawyer, I want to enter suit between myself an' de locomotive. I think I have damaged de locomotive. I want to pay de damage." Got de lawyer. "De locomotive sued you?" asked de lawyer. "I broke de driver."—"De State attorney wants to know from me what is de driver." He said, "Dat t'ing dat you tu'n over."—"Did you ketch de driver in you han'?"—"I did, si'."—"What did you do to de driver?"—"I car'ed it home with me, si'."—"What did you do when you got home?"—"I put it in my trunk, si'."—"What did you do with the arm you said de driver cut off?"—"I put it in de trunk wi' de driver."—"How much did it cost you to injur' dat locomotive?"—"It jus' cos' me my arm, si', dat's all."

The Boy and the Colt

DE COLT was at de river drinkin' water. De boy hid hisself way in de bushes. De boy said to hisself, "What a good time I'm goin' to have terday shovin' dat colt inter de river!" De boy didn't know at dat time dat while de colt was drinkin' water, he had one eye upon de boy. De boy makes a lunge at de colt. De colt see de boy comin' to him. De colt step aside an' t'row hisself into de river. After much scramblin' an' scufflin', de boy got out de river. De boy said to hisself, "It is a good thing dat I laugh befo' I lunge at de colt, because dere was no time to laugh in de river."

The Son Who Went to College

A MAN and his wife had a boy and they thought so much of him that they sent him off to college. At de end of seven years, he schooled out and come home and de old man and his ma was real proud to have de only boy 'round there dat was book-learnt.

So de next mornin' after he come home, de ma was milkin' de cows and had one young cow dat had never been to de pail befo' and she used to kick every time anybody milked her.

She was actin' extry bad dat mornin' so de woman called her husband and ast him to come help her wid de cow. So he went out and tried to hold her,

Ibid., p. 225.

From *Mules and Men*, by Zora Neale Hurston, pp. 163–164. Copyright, 1935, by Zora Neale Hurston. Philadelphia and London: J. B. Lippincott Company.

but she kept on rearin' and pitchin' and kickin' over de milk pail, so he said to his wife: "We don't need to strain wid dis cow. We got a son inside that's been to school for seben years and done learnt everything. He'll know jus' what to do wid a kickin' cow. Ah'll go call him."

So he called de boy and told him.

De boy come on out to de cow-lot and looked everything over. Den he said, "Mama cow-kickin' is all a matter of scientific principle. You see before a cow can kick she has to hump herself up in the back. So all we need to do is to take the hump out the cow's back."

His paw said, "Son, Ah don't see how you gointer do dat. But 'course you been off to college and you know a heap mo' than me and yo' ma ever will know. Go 'head and take de hump outa de heifer. We'd be mighty much obliged."

De son put on his gold eyeglasses and studied de cow from head to foot. Then he said, "All we need to keep this animal from humping is a weight on her back."

"What kinda weight do she need, son?"

"Oh, any kind of a weight, jus' so it's heavy enough, papa," de son told him. "It's all in mathematics."

"Where we gointer git any weight lak dat, son?"

"Why don't you get up there, papa? You're just about the weight we need."

"Son, you been off to school a long time, and maybe you done forgot how hard it is for anybody to sit on a cow, and Ah'm gittin' old, you know."

"But, papa, I can fix that part, too. I'll tie your feet together under her belly so she can't throw you. You just get on up there."

"All right, son, if you say so, Ah'll git straddle of dis cow. You know more'n Ah do, Ah reckon."

So they tied de cow up short to a tree and de ole man got on by de hardest,[1] and de boy passed a rope under her belly and tied his papa on. De old lady tried to milk de cow but she was buckin' and rearin' so till de ole man felt he couldn't stand it no mo'. So he hollered to de boy, "Cut de rope, son, cut de rope! Ah want to git down."

Instead of de boy cuttin' loose his papa's feet he cut de rope dat had de cow tied to de tree and she lit out 'cross de wood wid de ole man's feet tied under de cow. Wasn't no way for him to git off.

De cow went bustin' on down de back-road wid de ole man till they met a sister he knowed. She was surprised to see de man on de cow, so she ast: "My lawd, Brother So-and-so, where you goin'?"

He tole her, "Only God and dis cow knows."

---

[1] With great difficulty.—Z. N. H.

The Twist-Mouth Family

THERE was once a father and a mother and several children, and all but one of them had their mouths twisted out of shape. The one whose mouth was not twisted was a son named John.

When John got to be a young man he was sent to college, and on the day he came home for his first vacation the family sat up late in the evening to hear him tell of all he had learned. But finally they prepared to go to bed, and the mother said, "Father, will you blow out the light?"

"Yes, I will," was his reply.

"Well, I wish you would," said she.

"Well, I will," he said.

So he blew, but his mouth was twisted, and he blew this way (the narrator shows how he did it—blowing upward), and he couldn't blow out the light.

Then he said, "Mother, will you blow out the light?"

"Yes, I will," was her reply.

"Well, I wish you would," said he.

"Well, I will," she said.

So she blew, but her mouth was twisted, and she blew this way (blowing downward) and she couldn't blow out the light.

Then she spoke to her daughter and said, "Mary, will you blow out the light?"

"Yes, I will," was Mary's reply.

"Well, I wish you would," said her mother.

"Well, I will," Mary said.

So Mary blew, but her mouth was twisted, and she blew this way (blowing out of the right corner of the mouth), and she couldn't blow out the light.

Then Mary spoke to one of her brothers and said, "Dick, will you blow out the light?"

"Yes, I will," was Dick's reply.

"Well, I wish you would," said Mary.

"Well, I will," Dick said.

So Dick blew, but his mouth was twisted, and he blew this way (blowing out of the left corner of the mouth), and he couldn't blow out the light.

Then Dick said, "John, will you blow out the light?"

"Yes, I will," was John's reply.

"Well, I wish you would," said Dick.

"Well, I will," John said.

By Clifton Johnson, Hadley, Mass. From *The Journal of American Folk-Lore*, Vol. XVIII (October-December, 1905), No. LXXI, pp. 322–323. Copyright, 1905, by the American Folk-Lore Society. Boston and New York: Houghton, Mifflin & Company.
The story hails from Plymouth, Mass.—C. J.

So John blew, and his mouth was straight, and he blew this way (blowing straight), and he blew out the light.

The light was out and they were all glad that John had succeeded, and the father said, "What a blessed thing it is to have larnin'!"

Salting the Pudding

I NEVER will forget one time Old Lady Simpson was going to have a wood-sawing and thought she'd show off some by having puddin for the crowd. Course, she was bound to have a candy pulling and a goober popping same as usual. The puddin was extry.

Well, that day everything was a-hustle and a-bustle over at Simpson's and here it comes on night and no puddin cooked. The old lady she'd done made her brags all around and she just had to have that puddin. All the gals—they was five of them Simpson gals—was as busy as a bee in a tar barrel, washing and ironing, primping and cleaning up the house like they was looking for a preacher during big meeting. So the old lady she tore out to the kitchen and started chunking things together to make that puddin.

Now, she was give out to be the best puddin maker in the whole settlement. But she was so mixed up that evening she plumb forgot to salt the puddin. Now your *reel* good puddin don't take but just a *tee-nincy* pinch of salt, but if it ain't got that, it just ain't puddin.

Old Lady Simpson got the fire going just right in the stove and slammed the puddin in there. Then she rushed around a-dusting the cheers and the organ in the setting room.

About that time it hit her about the salt. Her hands was that filthy-dirty she knowed she couldn't salt the puddin without washing them. So she just went ahead a-dusting and a-scrubbing around, figgering she'd have one of the gals tend to it for her.

"Sue," she says, "will you go salt the puddin? I done got my hands dirty."

"Can't, Maw. I'm greasing my shoes."

"Sairy, how about you?"

"Maw, you know I'm a-trying to git this dress done."

"Berthy, can you salt the puddin?"

"No'm."

"Jenny, go salt the puddin."

"Let Lil do it, Maw. I'm starching and arning to beat the bobtail."

"All right. Lil, you run salt the puddin now, Honey."

"Shan't. I'm a-looking high and low for my hair ribbon. I ain't going do nothing else till I find it."

By Luther Clark and James R. Aswell. Manuscripts of the Federal Writers' Project of the Works Progress Administration for the State of Alabama.

So the old lady she throwed her dust rag across a cheerback and went and washed her hands and salted the puddin.

Just along about the time the old lady got back to her dusting, Lil got to thinking how she had ought to mind her Maw. So she sort of eased into the kitchen there and salted the puddin.

Well, she hadn't no more than got back to s'arching for her hair ribbon when Jenny got to feeling oneasy about being so sassy. So here she come and salted that puddin.

Well, so help me, she hadn't scarcely set back down on the back piazzer and picked up the slipper she was greasing when here come Sairy and salted that puddin.

Berthy always was the lady of the family. She didn't do nothing much none of the time. She was propped in her room a-reading a novelty when all this come off. But if they was one thing that gal liked better than reading a novelty it was eating puddin. She got to thinking about that puddin and got into a twidget. By and by she got up and she tiptoed to the kitchen. She got there right after Sairy left.

Well, that puddin sure baked pretty and when Old Lady Simpson come a-mincing out with it that night you could just hear everybody sort of bend back and smack their lips.

The preacher had come over to sort of look over the goings on, so naturally he got the first helping. His face just got to shining and he said something about puddin was the best eating going. Then he took a whopping big jawful.

When he bit down to kind of let the flavor soak in, his face looked like somebody had covered up the sun with a blanket.

"Upthem!" he said, and he grabbed for the water gourd.

Well, everybody just set there with their mouths full of teeth and their eyes bugged out. Old Lady Simpson sort of caught on that something was wrong, so she up and takes a taste herself. Then she knowed.

"Which one of you gals put salt in this puddin?"

"I done it, Maw!" all five of them says together.

"And I done it, too!" the old lady says. "It sure looks like too many cooks sp'iled the puddin."

And nobody couldn't deny it.

Borrowing Trouble

A FOLK-TALE common and often quoted by country people belonging to the States of New York and Ohio, in ridicule of those who unnecessarily "borrow trouble," is as follows:—

Once there was a girl. One day her mother came into the kitchen and

From "Borrowing Trouble," by Fanny D. Bergen, *The Journal of American Folk-Lore*, Vol. XI (January-March, 1898), No. XL, pp. 55–59. Copyright, 1898, by the American Folk-Lore Society.

found the girl sitting crying with all her heart. The mother said, "Why, what is the matter?" The girl replied, "Oh, I was thinking. And I thought how some day perhaps I might be married and how I might have a baby, and then I thought how one day when it would be asleep in its cradle the oven lid would fall on it and kill it," and she began to cry again.

A variant from Greenfield, Mass., which can be traced back fifty years, runs thus:—

A girl sat on a river bank crying. On being asked the cause of her grief, she replied, "Oh, I was thinking if I had a darter and my darter had a darter and she should fall into the warter, how dreadful it would be." [1]

Three More Fools

ONCE upon a time there was a woman with three girls. Her older girl was engage to get married to a boy. So one day he come to the house to see this girl. Her mother sent one of the girls to the spring. She stay so long 'til her mother say, "Go to the spring and see what are sister doing." So when she got to the spring, she ask the girl what was she staying so long? "I am studying up a name for sister to name the baby when she marry."— "Well, that is a good idea. I guess I had better study too." So she sit down to help study. So they stay so long 'til her mother went down there to see what they were doing. She ask them what they were doing. They told her they was studying a name for sister to name the baby when she

---

[1] Both of these folk-jests are probably fragmentary survivals of a popular European folk-tale. In Mr. Joseph Jacobs's volume of "English Fairy Tales," the tale of "The Three Sillies" is a well-sustained story, having exactly the same *motif* as that which gives point to both of the very brief stories that I have found in the United States. In the English folk-tale the girl goes to the cellar to draw beer, and falls to crying after indulging in fancies similar to those of the girl in our American stories. There is a Scotch variant of the tale. Grimm's "Clever Elsie" is very similar to the English version of this old folk-tale. There is also more than one Russian variant. In "Bastianelo," No. 93, in Crane's "Italian Popular Tales," a bride goes down cellar to draw wine, and muses in the same manner. It is interesting to note little details that relate to the various environments where the tale takes root and becomes a part of the local folk-lore. In Germany and England, it is while drawing beer that the maiden falls into soliloquy. In Italy it is wine, the national beverage, that runs away while the girl goes on with her idle dreaming. In New York and Ohio, where the great brick ovens were so often built into the wall beside the kitchen chimney, it is the oven lid that will fall and kill the sleeping child. The Western Massachusetts variant, told in the midst of the great meadows over which meander their rivers, describes the girl as sitting on a river bank while she worries over the drowning of her future grandchild. These stories are told in the United States as true, and the incidents are generally supposed to have happened long ago in the same neighborhood.—F. D. B.

From "Folk-Lore from Aiken, S. C.," by Elsie Clews Parsons, *The Journal of American Folk-Lore*, Vol. 34 (January-March, 1921), No. 131, pp. 18–19. Copyright, 1921, by the American Folk-Lore Society.

Written by Emma Lee Quarles. For bibliography see MAFLS 13:128 (note 3).

marry. "Well, that is a good idea; I guess I had better study too." So she sit down to study too. They stay so long 'til the last girl went what had the company. "What are you all doing?"—"Sat down study up a name for sister to name the baby when she marry."—"Well, that is a good idea; I guess I had better study." So they sat down to study. So the boy went down there. He ask them what they was doing there? Say they was studying a name "for you and sister to name the baby when you are married." He told them that if he find three more fool like them, he would come back and marry the girl. So he went, an' he saw a lady scrubbing floor. She was trying to get the sun to come in to dry the floor with a wheelbarrow. The boy said, "What are you doing?"—"I am trying to get the sun in to dry my floor."—"Why do [?] you ask the door and let the sun shine in and dry it?"—"Well, that is a good idea." So he went, an' saw a man with a oxen. He say, "Try to get the oxen to climb up there [1] to eat the moss." He was just beating the oxen, trying to make him get up there to eat the moss. The boy say, "What are you doing?"—"I am trying to make the oxen eat the moss."—"Why don't you take a hoe and rake it down?" —"Well, that is a good idea." So the boy went until he came to a tree. He saw a man with a new pair of overalls. He was trying to jump in them, had them hanging up in the tree. He say, "Why don't you put a sheet on the ground and stand on the sheet an' put them on?" So he say he hadn' thought about that. So he went on back an' married the girl.

"Little Moron"

I

THE little moron was nailing shingles on the house. Somebody noticed that he was throwing about half the nails away, and asked him why. "Because," said the little moron, "the heads are on the wrong ends." "Well, you dope," said the other, "those are for the other side of the house."

The little moron got up in the middle of the night to answer the tele-

---

[1] On the roof.

From "'Little Moron' Stories," by Ernest W. Baughman, *Hoosier Folklore Bulletin*, edited by Herbert Halpert, Vol. II (June, 1943), No. 1, pp. 17–18.

These stories were heard by my sister, Ruth Baughman, from students on the campus of Ball State Teachers College, Muncie, Indiana, during the past year. Since then I have heard them in many localities. Such jokes seem to circulate orally among city people, office workers and college people in particular. Most of these stories would probably be classified by Professor Stith Thompson in his Motif-Index under *Absurd Misunderstandings*. Some of the people I have heard seem to make a specialty of telling stories of this type which depend on gestures for their effectiveness. I have not included any of this type.—E. W. B.

Cf. *Little Moron*, by Abbott ("Heck") Hoecker and Clydene ("Ilda") Oliver (1943).

phone. "Is this one one one one?" says the voice. "No, this is eleven eleven." "You're sure it isn't one one one one?" "No, this is eleven eleven." "Well, wrong number. Sorry to have got you up in the middle of the night." "That's all right, mister. I had to get up to answer the telephone anyway."

Two little morons went hunting. The first one shot at a duck, and when it fell at his feet he felt bad that the little duck had died when he shot it. The other said, "Oh, don't feel so bad. The fall would have killed it anyway."

Little moron was painting the house when another one came up and said, "Got a good hold on that brush?" "Yep." "Well, if you are sure you got a good hold on that brush I'll borrow your ladder for a second." "O.K. but don't keep it long. The handle of this paint brush is kind of slippery."

Little moron's wife sent him down town after a bucket of ice. He came back with a pail of water. "I got this for half price because it was melted."

Little moron took two slices of bread and went down and sat on the street corner waiting for the traffic jam. A big truck came along and gave him a jar.

Why did the little moron go to the lumber yard?—To look for his draft board.

Then there was the little moron who broke his leg when he threw his cigarette butt down the manhole and tried to step on it.

And the one who took his nose apart to see what made it run.

Little moron tried to light his cigarette. He struck the first match on the seat of his pants, but it wouldn't light. He tried another. It wouldn't light. The third one finally lit. He lit his cigarette, carefully blew the match out and put it in his vest pocket. "What for did you put that match in your vest pocket." "That's a good match. I'll use it again."

Two little morons were in jail. They were trying to find a way out. "I know. I'll shine the flash light up to that window, you crawl up the beam and open that window." The other little moron objected. "Nothing doing. I'd get halfway up the beam and you'd turn the light off."

II

WHY did the little moron lock his papa in the icebox? Because he wanted cold pop.

Do you know why the little moron took some hay to bed with him? Because he wanted to feed his nightmare.

Can you tell me why the little moron took his clock to bed with him? Because it was fast.

From "The Demise of the Little Moron," by Rudolph Umland, *Esquire*, The Magazine for Men, Vol. XX (September, 1943), No. 3, pp. 32–33, 154–155. Copyright, 1943, by Esquire, Inc.

What did the little moron do when he was told he was dying? He moved into the living room.

*   *   *   *   *

A little moron went to a show. The usher asked him, "Would you like to sit down front?" The little moron answered, "I'm sorry, sir, but I don't bend that way."

And did you hear about the little moron who stayed up all night to study for his blood test? And the little moron who took some sugar and cream with him to the movie because he heard there was going to be a serial? And the little moron who saved burnt-out light bulbs to use during blackouts? And the little moron who took some pepper out with him because he heard it was hot stuff? And the little moron who ate some dynamite so his hair would grow out with bangs? And the little moron who put a chair in the coffin for rigor mortis to set in? And the little moron who slept on the chandelier because he was a light sleeper? And the little moron who went to a football game because he thought a quarterback was a refund? And the little moron who took off his knee cap to see if there was any beer in the joint? And the little moron who sat up all night on his wedding night gazing out of the window because his mother had told him it would be the most wonderful night he ever saw?

There were two little morons who were waiting for a streetcar. One asked the other if he thought the car had already gone. "Yes, it must have gone," the other exclaimed. "There's it's tracks!"

Did you hear about the little moron who cut his arms off? He wanted to wear a sleeveless sweater.

Did you hear about the little moron bride who sat down and cried bitterly when her husband went out to shoot craps? She didn't know how to cook them.

Did you hear about the little moron who went strolling along the beach and saw a nude woman come out of the water? He said, "Boy wouldn't she look good in a bathing suit!"

Have you heard about the little moron who was so bashful that he had to go into another room to change his mind?

There was the one about the two little morons who were walking along a railroad track and spied a human arm beside the rails. "That looks like Joe's arm," exclaimed the first little moron. "It is Joe's arm," said the other. They walked a little farther and saw a human leg lying beside the rails. "That looks like Joe's leg," exclaimed the first little moron. "It is Joe's leg," said the other. A short way farther they saw a head lying beside the rails. "That looks like Joe's head," exclaimed the first little moron. "It is Joe's head," said the other little moron, and he stooped, picked the head up by the ears, shook it, and cried, "Joe, Joe, are you hurt?"

Then there was the one about a group of little morons who were building a house. One of the little morons went to the boss and asked if they should start building the house from the top down or from the bottom up.

"Why, start from the bottom and build up, of course!" replied the boss. The little moron turned and yelled to his fellow workers: "Tear 'er down, boys! Gotta start all over!"

The little moron told his friend, "I only weighed three pounds when I was born." "Did you live?" asked the friend. "Did I live! Say, you oughta see me now!"

Absence of Mind

I

A MAN, thinking he was at home, one evening lately, lay down on the common, and put his boots outside the gate to be blacked in the morning. Another person, after getting home one rainy night, put his umbrella in the bed, and leaned up in the corner himself.

II

We have just heard of a truly distressing instance of absence of mind, of which, we understand, our venerable friend, and contemporary, Mr. Bot Smith, was the victim. The other evening he proceeded bed-ward, as usual, and, in a fit of absence of mind, put the candle into the bed, *and blew himself out!*

III

The last "modern instance" recorded in the Yankee papers, is that of a Vermont waggoner going to market, who lifted his horse into the waggon, and tacked himself to the traces. The veracious chronicler adds, the waggoner did not discover his error until he endeavored to neigh!

T'other day a man in Baltimore, intending to wind up his watch, through a sudden attack of absence of mind, wound up himself. . . .

The *Nashville Observer* informs us of the following case of absence of mind, which took place in the person of an old lady, who, after stirring the fire with her knitting needle, proceeded to knit with the poker, and did not discover her error till she commenced scratching her head with it.

A woman in Ohio put her baby into the washing-tub, and its dirty frock and petticoat into the cradle, and set her little boy to rock it. She did not discover her mistake until the baby cried out when she pinned its left leg to the line, as she hung it out in the yard to dry.

We learn from the *Nashville Banner*, that a land-agent down there, by name Hiram S. Botts, having to ride out in great haste one day last week,

From *Yankee Notions; or The American Joe Miller*, by Sam Slick, Junr., pp. 20, 28, 33, 39. London: Ball, Arnold & Co. Edinburgh: Fraser and Crawford. Glasgow: John Robertson. 1889.

actually clapped the saddle upon his own back instead of his mare's, and never found out the mistake till he was quite fatigued with vainly trying to get upon himself.

IV

A highly respectable inhabitant of the city of New York lately died under very remarkable circumstances. He was subject to fits of extreme absence of mind from childhood, and one night, upon retiring to bed, having carefully tucked his pantaloons under the bed-clothes, he threw himself over the back of a chair, and expired from the severe cold he experienced during the night. The editor of the *New York Morning Herald,* who relates this extraordinary fact, assures his readers, as a guarantee of its truth, that he received his information from the individual in question!

Big Talk

I. COLOR [1]

THEN Gold spoke up and said, "Now, lemme tell one. Ah know one about a man as black as Gene."

"Whut you always crackin' me for?" Gene wanted to know. "Ah ain't a bit blacker than you."

"Oh, yes you is, Gene. Youse a whole heap blacker than Ah is."

"Aw, go head on, Gold. Youse blacker than me. You jus' look my color cause youse fat. If you wasn't no fatter than me you'd be so black till lightnin' bugs would follow you at twelve o'clock in de day, thinkin' it's midnight."

"Dat's a lie, youse blacker than Ah ever dared to be. Youse lam' black. Youse so black till they have to throw a sheet over yo' head so de sun kin rise every mornin'. Ah know yo' ma cried when she seen *you.*"

"Well, anyhow, Gold, youse blacker than me. If Ah was as fat as you Ah'd be a yaller man."

"Youse a liar. Youse as yaller as you ever gointer git. When a person is poor he look bright and de fatter you git de darker you look."

"Is dat yo' excuse for being so black, Gold?"

II. AN UGLY MAN [2]

"Hey, Jim, where the swamp boss? He ain't got here yet."

"He's ill—sick in the bed Ah hope, but Ah bet he'll git here yet."

"Aw, he ain't sick. Ah bet you a fat man he ain't," Joe said.

"How come?" somebody asked him and Joe answered:

[1] From *Mules and Men,* by Zora Neale Hurston, p. 47. Copyright, 1935, by Zora Neale Hurston. Philadelphia and London: J. B. Lippincott Company.

[2] *Ibid.,* p. 94.

"Man, he's too ugly. If a spell of sickness ever tried to slip up on him, he'd skeer it into a three weeks' spasm."

Blue Baby [1] stuck in his oar and said: "He ain't so ugly. Ye all jus' ain't seen no real ugly man. Ah seen a man so ugly till he could get behind a jimpson weed and hatch monkeys."

Everybody laughed and moved closer together. Then Officer Richardson said: "Ah seen a man so ugly till they had to spread a sheet over his head at night so sleep could slip up on him."

They laughed some more, then Clifford Ulmer said:

"Ah'm goin' to talk with my mouth wide open. Those men y'all been talkin' 'bout wasn't ugly at all. Those was pretty men. Ah knowed one so ugly till you could throw him in the Mississippi river and skim ugly for six months."

"Give Cliff de little dog," Jim Allen said. "He done tole the biggest lie."

"He ain't lyin'," Joe Martin tole them. "Ah knowed dat same man. He didn't die—he jus' uglied away."

III. A MEAN MAN [2]

ALLEN asked: "Ain't dat a mean man? No work in the swamp and still he won't let us knock off."

"He's mean all right, but Ah done seen meaner men than him," said Handy Pitts.

"Where?"

"Oh, up in Middle Georgy. They had a straw boss and he was so mean dat when the boiler burst and blowed some of the men up in the air, he docked 'em for de time they was off de job."

Tush Hawg up and said: "Over on de East Coast Ah used to have a road boss and he was so mean and times was so hard till he laid off de hands of his watch."

Wiley said: "He's almost as bad as Joe Brown. Ah used to work in his mine and he was so mean till he wouldn't give God an honest prayer without snatching back 'Amen.'"

So Tight

1

YOU'VE probably heard about the Scotchman who lived in an efficiency flat because it was CLOSE, and how he refused to wear rubber heels be-

---

[1] "Blue Baby" was so black he looked blue.—Z. N. H.

[2] *Ibid.*, pp. 95–96.

From *Tall Tales*, compiled by Jim Blakely, pp. 32, 43, 54. Copyright, 1936, by Eldridge Entertainment House, Inc. Franklin, Ohio, and Denver, Colorado.

cause he was afraid they would GIVE, but how about the one who fed his little boy JUMPING BEANS to keep from buying him a POGO STICK?

2

It is said there was a Scotchman who married the tattooed woman from a side show so his children could see moving pictures FREE.

3

A Scotchman in order to teach his small son thrifty habits gave him a penny each day and saw to it that he deposited them in a white pig-bank. As soon as the boy had five pennies thus saved, the father removed the coins and gave the lad a nickel in exchange and had him place it in a larger blue china bank. And when five nickels had been accumulated again the father took the smaller coins and gave him a quarter for them which the boy was taught to place in a large red receptacle. BUT—the LARGE RED RECEPTACLE was a quarter-in-the-slot gas meter.

Eli Perkins on Mean Men

I WAS talking with Senator Blaine in Saratoga one day about mean men when Sam Cox stepped up and said he knew a very mean man—the meanest man on earth.

"How mean is that?" I asked.

"Why, Eli," he said, "he is so mean that he keeps a five-cent piece with a string tied to it to give to beggars; and when their backs are turned he jerks it out of their pockets!

"Why, this man is so confounded mean," continued Mr. Cox, "that he gave his children ten cents apiece every night for going to bed without their supper, but during the night, when they were asleep, he went upstairs, took the money out of their clothes, and then whipped them in the morning for losing it."

"Does he do anything else?"

"Yes, the other day I dined with him, and I noticed the poor little servant girl whistled all the way upstairs with the dessert; and when I asked the mean old scamp what made her whistle so happily, he said: 'I keep her whistling so she can't eat the raisins out of the cake.'"

I was down in Uncle Hank Allen's grocery today, telling about Sam Cox's mean man, when Oliver Wilcoxen remarked:

"That was a pretty mean man, but I could tell you about meaner men

From *Library of Wit and Humor* by *Mark Twain and Others, with the Philosophy of Wit and Humor,* by Melville D. Landon, A. M. (Eli Perkins), pp. 203–205. Copyright, 1883, by L. W. Yaggy and, 1898, by Star Publishing Co. Chicago: Thompson and Thomas.

than that right in this town. Now there is old Backus Long. You remember about the sausage skins?"

"No, what was it?" asked several voices at once.

"Well, I don't speak of this as a case of meanness, but I put it forward as an instance of careful thrift when I say that when I ran the butcher's shop Backus Long always used to send back his sausage skins and have them refilled."

"That was simply business shrewdness," said John Whitney. "Now I always do those kind of things myself. For instance, it is always my custom to stop the clock nights."

"What for?" asked Stanley Westfall.

"I do it to keep it from wearing out the cogs."

"I call that rather close," said Deacon Monson. "I call that mean, but we've got a man over in Lebanon who beats that. Old Calkins over there is so mean that he skims his milk o' top, and then, when no one is looking, he turns it over and skims it on the bottom."

Uncle Hank now uncrossed his legs, took a quid of fine cut, and remarked:

"Gentlemen, you don't appear to be aware of the many mean things done every day in this community. I tell you there is an all-killin' sight of meanness in this town."

"Who's meaner than old Calkins?" asked Calvin Morse.

"Why, the meanest man in this town, and none of you seems to have heard of him," said Uncle Hank. "I say the meanest man in this town, if my memory does not fail me, is old Deacon Crawford, and—"

"What was the meanest thing he ever did?" asked a dozen voices.

"Well, gentlemen, you may call me a liar, but it's the solemn truth. One day Deakin Crawford found a stray bung hole over around Stanley Westfall's cooper shop, and—"

"What did he do with a stray bung hole?" asked Jonas White.

"Why, gentlemen, you may call it a lie, but if he didn't take it up to Morse's cooper shop, and, handing it out, ask Gardner Morse to please give him a barrel to fit that ere bung hole. He did, by gosh!"

Yankee Exaggeration

"WAS Aaron Burr a mean man?" I asked a Yankee deacon up at Hartford.

"Mean? I should say he was. Aaron Burr mean? Why, I could take the little end of nothing, whittled down to a point, punch out the pith of a hair, and put in forty thousand such souls as his, shake them up, and they'd rattle!"

Ibid., p. 198.

Slow Train

I[1]

SOME trains in northern Idaho are as slow as the one out of Salmon City. Between Lewiston and Kamiah it's so slow that farmers who load hay at Kamiah discover that the cars are empty by the time they reach Lewiston, because cows along the way have eaten it. One time a salesman was so indignant that he swore to high heaven he could get out and walk and arrive more quickly. The conductor gazed at him for a moment and sighed. "So could I," he said, "but the company won't let me."

Among intolerably slow trains in Idaho is the branch to the Twin Falls area. Once an impatient passenger wanted to know of the conductor why the train had stopped. "There's a cow on the track," he said. "We have to chase her off." When, a little later, the train stopped again, the passenger roared: "Now what's wrong?" "Oh," said the conductor serenely, "We just caught up with the cow."

II[2]

Talk about your slow trains through Arkansaw and your snail specials over the Rockies, but I struck a train in Indiana that was sure enough slow. I got on it to go up the state about seventy-five miles. The thing ran so slow that I went to the conductor and said, "Look here, if you don't ginger the gait of this thing up a little, I'll get out and walk." He flared up and said, "Who's the boss of this train?" I said, "I suppose you are." He said, "Then dry up." I said, "Whose dead body have you on board?" He said, "Nobody's; why?" I said, "Because you're running so slow I thought maybe you were bossing a funeral procession." That made him still madder, and we hooked up. We jumped out on the right-o'-way, and the train running at full speed, and had a fight, and I knocked the breath out of him and ran down to a pond and got my hat full of water and poured it in his face and brought him to, and we both caught the hind end of the train as it came by—and it wasn't a long train either.

But the walloping I gave the conductor didn't make the thing go any faster. A fellow standing on the side of the track held up a knife and hollered, "Got a frog-sticker yer want to swap?" I lit out and looked his knife over, swapped with him and skinned him too bad to talk about, and

<hr>

[1] From *Idaho Lore,* prepared by the Federal Writers' Project of the Work Projects Administration, Vardis Fisher, State Director, American Guide Series, pp. 119–120, 132. Copyright, 1939, by George H. Curtis, Secretary of State for the State of Idaho. Caldwell, Idaho: The Caxton Printers, Ltd.

[2] From *I Blew in from Arkansaw,* A Trip of Fun through Hoosierdom, by Geo. D. Beason, pp. 48–49. Copyright, 1908, by Geo. D. Beason. Chicago: Geo. D. Beason, Publisher.

caught the hind end of the train again as it came by. I went to the conductor next day and apologized for banging him up. He said, "Oh, that's all right. The only thing I regret is, I lost my cap back where we had the fight." I said, "I'll go back and get it." He said, "Don't put yourself to any trouble." I said, "It won't be any trouble." I went back and got his cap and caught up with the train at the next station.

I was on the slow outfit so long that I wore out one of the cushion seats, and had train sores. You may think I'm overdrawing it, but I'm not, when I tell you that a fellow took down with typhoid fever on the thing just after I got on, and when I got off at the end of my journey, he was sound and well, and he had a long siege of it, too.

Origin of Names

A young Oil Citizen calls his sweetheart Revenge, because she is sweet.—*Oil City Derrick*.

And the young married man in South Hill calls his mother-in-law Delay, because she is dangerous.—*Burlington Hawkeye*.

And a South End man calls his wife Fact, because she is a stubborn thing.—*Boston Globe*.

And a fourth wife of a district attorney calls him Necessity, because he knows no law.—*New Orleans Times*.

And a Cincinnati man names his coachman Procrastination, because he stole his watch.—*Breakfast Table*.

And we called a beautiful schoolma'am that we used to go to Experience, because she was a dear teacher.—*Eli Perkins*.

And a Yonkers man names his wife Frailty, because Shakespeare says: "Frailty, thy name is woman."—*Yonkers Gazette*.

Eli Perkins calls his wife Honesty, because he says it is the best policy. —*N. Y. Herald*.

Umpire Bait, and Jollys for Pitchers and Batters

That base isn't made for a shelter, get into the open.

My kindergarten was the Polo Ground bleachers.

From *Library of Wit and Humor by Mark Twain and Others, with the Philosophy of Wit and Humor*, by Melville D. Landon, A. M. (Eli Perkins), p. 98. Copyright, 1883, by L. W. Yaggy and, 1898, by Star Publishing Co. Chicago: Thompson and Thomas.

From *Choice Slang*, by High Jinks Junior [Harold Poe Swartwood], pp. 74–75. Copyright, 1915, by The Coronodo Company.

The first spiral staircase was built after the design of my fast curve.

Every time I swing the bat they have to give the ball a hydraulic treat-ment to coax it back into shape.

He couldn't hit a bunch of bananas with a bass fiddle.

Every time that Umps starts talking his tongue gets twisted around his eye tooth and he can't see what he's saying.

Data boy smoke, hit him on the head, you can't hurt him there.

Long fly to the pitcher, that's his noise.

Like a gate the way he swings.

Let him hit, let him hit, I got it.

He hasn't any more on that ball than September Morn wears.

Shut the gate, Nanny is wandering.

He hasn't got a thing today, but a grin and a belt buckle.

On the hill with nothing but a glove and a prayer.

You're not so rotten, kid, in about forty years you'll be a ball player.

This fellow is made to order for you, get up there and sting one.

Let's pick him to pieces, piece by piece, and see what makes him tick.

Take him out, get the hook, the hook.

He never touched me, Umps, I'll leave it to you.

If rags were ribbon, you'd be silk.

Look out, you fellows on the bench, this bloat at bat is liable to spike you.

Come on, Smoke, old boy, give him the spitter.

That ball was so low it would have to reach up to touch bottom.

Put on your chains, Umps, you're skidding.

Cancel that rave, Umps.

A cozy corner in the nuttery for yours.

Back to the oven, you aren't done yet.

Is this a union of some kind? Does everybody strike?

Come on fellows, keep working. We gotta beat ten men, but one of them is blind.

Slang and Near Slang of Some Length

BACK to the oven, you're not done yet—Repartee. Conveys the impression of a lack of intelligence. Implies that the person's intelligence is in a "half baked" condition.

Come down from the walls—Be natural. Get down to facts. "Get off your high horse."

Come wipe your feet on our welcome mat—An invitation to make a visit.

Daggers at eighty paces—A mock challenge to a duel.

Do you follow me or do I go alone?—Do you understand what I am saying?

Ibid., pp. 64–67.

If you took a glass of water, the fumes would go to your brains—Repartee.

If you took laughing gas, you would cry—Repartee.

It was old when St. Louis was a blue print—It is old, old as the hills.

Jump on the bread wagon and loaf with the rest of the bundles—An invitation to become more idle and do things easier.

Put grease in your pan, your fish is burning—An intimation that what you are saying is incorrect.

Put in a quarter, your gas is low—You are getting out of breath or ideas.

Put on your chains, you're skidding—You are getting away from the idea or off the track.

Ring off, your wires are crossed—You are talking nonsense.

Ring the bell, conductor, I'm on, I'm on—I get your meaning.

Sit down, you're rocking the boat—You're causing a disturbance.

Six men will walk slow with you—You will be on your way to your funeral.

Sneeze, your brains are dusty—Your brain is not in good working order.

Snow again, I don't get your drift—I don't get your meaning. I don't understand you.

You are so low you have to reach up to touch bottom—Means your lowness almost surpasses description or imagination.

You've got more stalls than a stable—You abound in subterfuges and excuses.

I Should Worry——

LIKE a ball and get bounced.
Like a button and get the hook.
Like a chandelier and get lit up every night.
Like dice and get shaken.
Like an elephant and carry my trunk
Like a fresh clam and get the lemon.
Like a fireman and lose my hose.
Like glue and stick around.
Like a hat and order a colored band.
Like a lump of butter and get strong.
Like the ocean and get fresh like the lakes.
Like a patrol wagon and do in a pinch.
Like a peanut and get roasted.
Like a peninsula and stretch out to see.
Like a pin cushion and get all stuck up.
Like a piano stool and go for a spin.

Ibid., pp. 105–106.

Like a plumber and get all around the joints.
Like a railroad track and get some new ties.
Like a raisin and go on a bun.
Like a rolling pin and gather the dough.
Like a smokestack and get all puffed up.
Like a tree and get trimmed.
Like a washboard and get full of wrinkles.
Like a window washer and feel a pain.

"You Tell 'Em" English

You tell 'em, mail carrier,
You're a man of letters!

You tell 'em,
My tongue's in my shoe!

You tell 'em, powder puff,
My lips stick.

You tell 'em, parcel post,
I can't express it.

You tell 'em, pony,
I'm a little horse.

You tell 'em, corsets,
You've been around women longer than I have.

You tell 'em, salad,
I'm dressing.

You tell 'em, Sahara,
You've got the sand.

You tell 'em, pieface,
You've got the crust.

You say it, goldfish,
You've been around the globe.

You tell 'em, victrola,
You've got the record.

From *Stuff That Travels*, by William G. Bradshaw, pp. 37, 51. Copyright, 1921, by William G. Bradshaw. Saratoga Springs, New York.

you tell 'em, coffee,
You've got the grounds.

You tell 'em, little stream,
You've been through the mill.

You tell 'em, toothache,
You've got the nerve.

She Was Only a Daughter

SHE was only a professor's daughter, but she learned her lesson.
She was only a fireman's daughter, but she sure did go to blazes.
She was only the tailor's daughter, but she pressed well.
She was only a photographer's daughter, but she delivered the goods.
She was only an electrician's daughter, but she had good connections.
She was only a blacksmith's daughter, but she knew how to forge ahead.
She was only a milkman's daughter, but she was the cream of the crop.
She was only a convict's daughter, but she knew all the bars.
She was only the parson's daughter, but she had her following.
She was only an acrobat's daughter, but she never turned over.
She was only a convict's daughter, but she knew when to faint.
She was only a florist's daughter, but she potted all the pansies.
She was only a dairyman's daughter, but what a calf.
She was only a woodcutter's daughter, but she hadn't been axed.
She was only a barber's daughter, but what a mug she had.
She was only a surgeon's daughter, but oh what a cut-up.

Knock Knock, Who's There?

CHESTER. Chester who? Chester song at twilight.
  Cecil. Cecil who? Cecil have music wherever she goes.
  Hoffman. Hoffman who? I'll hoffman I'll puff an' I'll blow yer house in.
  Gretta. Gretta who? Gretta long little doggie—gretta long.
  Gwen. Gwen who? Gwen an' out the winda. Gwen an' out the winda.
  Shixa. Shixa who? Shixa one—half dozen of another.

From *Laughter for the Millions*, The Drollest Wit, The Funniest Gags, The Gayest Laughs, The Merriest Humor, The Greatest Hilarity, edited by Louis Shomer, p. 117. Copyright, 1938, by Louis Shomer. New York: Louellen Publishing Co.

From *Knock Knock*, Featuring Enoch Knox, by Bob Dunn. Copyright, 1936, by Whitman Publishing Co. Racine, Wisconsin. Published by Dell Publishing Company, Inc. New York.

Argo. Argo who? Argo chase yerself.

Hiram. Hiram who? Hiram I doin' hey hey.

Morris. Morris who? Morris Saturday—next day's Sunday.

Marcella. Marcella who? Marcella's fulla water.

Major. Major who? Major answer the door didn't I?

Thermos. Thermos who? Thermos be some one wait-ting who feels the way I do.

Arthur. Arthur who? Arthur any more at home like you?

Agatha. Agatha who? Agatha feeling you're foolin'.

Mortimer. Mortimer who? Mortimer pitied than scorned.

Akron. Akron who? Akron give you anything but love baby.

Alby. Alby who? Alby glad when you're dead you rascal you.

Hassan. Hassan who? Hassan a body here seen Kelly?

Irving. Irving who? Irving a good time wisha were here.

Upton. Upton who? Just upton and downtown.

Dick. Dick who? Dick 'em up—I'm tongue-tied.

Bob. Bob who? Bob ba black sheep hevya eny wool?

Cigarette. Cigarette who? Cigarette life if ya don't weaken.

Domino. Domino who? Domino thing if ya ain't got that swing.

Fletcher. Fletcher who? Fletcher self go—relax an' fletcher self go.

Wendy. Wendy who? Wendy moon comes over the mountain.

Sonia. Sonia who? Sonia shanty in ol' shanty town.

Igloo. Igloo who? Igloo through here—the music goes down an' round.

Caesar. Caesar who? Caesar jolly good fellow, caesar jolly good fellow.

Ennui. Ennui who? I'm a dreamer, ennui all?

Thistle. Thistle who? Thistle be a lesson to me.

Tex. Tex who? Tex us to pull a good one, don't it?

Pettygil. Pettygil who? Pettygil is like a melody.

Edsall. Edsall who? Edsall there is—there is no more.

Small Town Stuff

A MAN appears on the streets with more than a day's growth on stubble on his face. "Say, John, yah gonna have to pay dog tax pretty soon!"

A desperate man has cranked his flivver for thirty minutes and the motor has not coughed once. "What'll yah take fer it; spot cash?"

An ugly man or a handsome man, or a fairly respectable-looking man is having his picture made. "Mr. Photographer, yah gonna bust yah machine taking a picture o' Frank Goza."

Some brave soul, for vanity's sake, begins the culture of a mustache. "Say, guy, yah eyebrow has slipped," or "Why didn't yah swallow all o' the horse, Jim?"

From *Small Town Humor*, by Robert Peery, Little Blue Book No. 1397, edited by E. Haldeman-Julius, pp. 7–8. Copyright, 1929, by Haldeman-Julius Company, Girard, Kansas.

A man loses his house by fire. "Sam, did yah have time to git the furniture out befo' yah sot her afire?"

John Purdy and his wife stand at the depot waiting for the train. "Yah goin' on a pleasure trip, John?" "Nope, the wife's goin' along."

A shining straw hat appears upon the head of a native. "Say, feller, the cows are gonna take after yah!"

The circus comes to town. "Goin' to the circus?" "Sure, mike!" "Goin' in?" "Naw, I reckon not."

A man trudges home with a chicken swinging from his hand. "All right, Sim! Much oblige; I'll be up fer supper."

Phrases of the People

Put yo' brains in a jaybird's head an' he'd fly backwards.

Jump down your throat an' gallup your insides out.

Yessuh, my little boy he's tol'able honest for his age.

Dat road got littler an' littler til it jest run up a tree.

Been ponderin' so hard I ain't had time to think.

Got de hookworm hustle.

Mouth's so wide ef 'twarn't for his ears de top of his head would be an island.

Steppin' high like a rooster in deep mud.

When dat preacher leaves my house I steps out in de backyard an' counts my chickens.

*   *   *   *   *

I give him thunder an' lightning stewed down to a fine pizen.

Dat white cussed me from de birth o' Saul an' Silas to de death o' de devil, an' called me ev'ything 'cept a child o' God.

Cunnel, dat nigger sprinkled dis here peedee root an' love powders over me, an' dat's what fust injuced me to commit love.

So lazy yo' vittles don't taste good.

Water's so low dat de garfishes is gittin' freckle-faced.

Got tuk down drunk.

A fool's tongue is long enough to cut his throat.

Money thinks I'm dead.

You ain't got enough sense to deliver a chaw of tobacco in a spittoon.

The bosom of his trousers.

*   *   *   *   *

Make your face look like a dime's wuth o' dog meat.

Jaybird jabber. [Gabble of women.]

From "Phrases of the People," recorded by Harris Dickson, Vicksburg, Mississippi, in *American Stuff*, An Anthology of Prose & Verse by Members of the Federal Writers' Project, pp. 149–152. Copyright, 1937, by The Guilds' Committee for Federal Writers' Publications, Inc. The Viking Press. New York.

Ef you wants to see how much folks is goin' to miss you, jest stick yo' finger in de pond den pull it out an' look at de hole.

Cavortin' like a fat pony in high oats.

Make a straight coattail. [Scared man running.]

Grinnin' like a baked 'possum.

Lean hound for a long race and a poor man for chillun.

So hongry my belly think's my throat's cut.

Cluttered with trouble.

Dat nigger ain't skeered o' work; he'll lie down beside de biggest kind o' job an' go to sleep.

*   *   *   *   *

Enjoyin' poor health.

Swamp's so dry dere's four million bullfrogs ain't never learned how to swim.

Dat ooman's nine years older'n God.

A mighty miration. [Make a to-do.]

De devil gits up when de sun goes down, an' comes to plow his field.

Life is short an' full o' blisters.

Wish I was at home sick in bed.

"How is you today?" "Po'ly, thank God!"

Heap o' stir an' no biskits.

Busy as a bumblebee in a bucket of tar.

Don't remember yo' name, but I knows yo' favor.

Why don't you put sugar in yo' shoes to coax yo' breeches down?

Rather tell a lie on credit dan de truth for cash.

Yo' head's a-blossomin' fer de grave.

Overspoke myself.

Got d' runnin' off at de mouth.

Honest farmer puts straight wood on de outside his load.

On dat day seven women shall take hold of one man.

Dey 'scused me wrongful. [False charge of crime.]

A dunghill gentleman.

Beat him into doll rags.

It's agin nature and can't be did.

Afterclaps can go to the devil.

In a turkey dream.

Handful o' the dockyments. [Playing cards.]

Wake, snakes, day's a-breakin'.

Busted to flinderjigs.

See him deep in hell as a pigeon can fly in a week.

Rich as mud.

A dog will cry if you beat him with a bone.

Tread in my footsteps ef you can spraddle far enough.

Full of wrath and cabbage.

Manhood distended his hide.

Whip you from the point of a dagger to the anchor of a ship.

The Proverbs of a People

I[1]

A code arrives; language; lingo; slang;
behold the proverbs of a people, a nation:
Give 'em the works. Fix it, there's always
a way. Be hard boiled. The good die young.

Be a square shooter. Be good; if you can't
be good be careful. When they put you in
that six foot bungalow, that wooden kimono,
you're through and that's that.

Sell 'em, sell 'em. Make 'em like it. What
if we gyp 'em? It'll be good for 'em. Get their
names on the dotted line and give 'em the haha.

The higher they go the farther they drop.
The fewer the sooner. Tell 'em. Tell 'em.
Make 'em listen. They got to listen when
they know who you are. Don't let 'em know
what you got on your hip. Hit 'em where
they ain't. It's good for whatever ails
you and if nothing ails you it's good for
that. Where was you raised—in a barn?

They're a lot of muckers, tin horns; show
those slobs where they get off at. Tell 'em
you're going to open a keg of nails. Beat 'em
to a fare-thee-well. Hand 'em the razz-berries.
Clean 'em and then give 'em car-fare home.
Maybe all you'll get from 'em you can put in
your ear, anyhow.

They got a fat nerve to try to tie a can
on you. Send 'em to the cleaners. Put the
kibosh on 'em so they'll never come back.
You don't seem to know four out of five
have pyorrhea in Peoria.

Your head ain't screwed on wrong, I trust.
Use your noodle, your nut, your think tank,
your skypiece. God meant for you to use it.
If they offer to let you in on the ground
floor take the elevator.

---

[1] From *Good Morning, America,* by Carl Sandburg, pp. 15–18. Copyright, 1928, by Carl Sandburg. New York: Harcourt, Brace & Company.

Put up a sign: Don't worry; it won't last;
nothing does. Put up a sign: In God we
trust, all others pay cash. Put up a sign:
Be brief, we have our living to make. Put
up a sign: Keep off the grass.

Aye, behold the proverbs of a people:
The big word is Service.
Service—first, last and always.
Business is business.
What you don't know won't hurt you.
Courtesy pays.
Fair enough.
The voice with a smile.
Say it with flowers.
Let one hand wash the other.
The customer is always right.
Who's your boy friend?
Who's your girl friend?
O very well.
God reigns and the government at Washington lives.
Let it go at that.
There are lies, damn lies and statistics.
Figures don't lie but liars can figure.
There's more truth than poetry in that.
You don't know the half of it, dearie.
It's the roving bee that gathers the honey.[1]
A big man is a big man whether he's a president or a prizefighter.[2]
Name your poison.
Take a little interest.
Look the part.
It pays to look well.
Be yourself.
Speak softly and carry a big stick.[3]
War is hell.
Honesty is the best policy.
It's all in the way you look at it.
Get the money—honestly if you can.
It's hell to be poor.
Well, money isn't everything.
Well, life is what you make it.
Speed and curves—what more do you want?
I'd rather fly than eat.[4]
There must be pioneers and some of them get killed.[5]

---

[1] On hearing from his father "A rolling stone gathers no moss," John L. Sullivan won one of his important early fights and telegraphed this reply.—C. S.

[2] John L. Sullivan's greeting spoken to President Theodore Roosevelt in the White House.—C. S.

[3] A Spanish proverb first Americanized by Theodore Roosevelt.—C. S.

[4] & [5] Charles A. Lindbergh.—C. S.

The grass is longer in the backyard.[1]
Give me enough Swedes and snuff and I'll build a railroad to hell.[2]
How much did he leave? All of it.[3]
Can you unscramble eggs? [4]
Early to bed and early to rise and you never meet any prominent people.[5]
Let's go. Watch our smoke. Excuse our dust.
Keep your shirt on.

II

Come on, superstition, and get my goat.[6]
I got mascots.
The stars of my birthday favor me.
The numbers from one to ten are with me.
I was born under a lucky star and nothing can stop me.
The moon was a waxing moon and not a waning moon when I was born.
Every card in the deck and both of the seven-eleven bones are with me.
So you hear them tell it and they mean if it works it's good and if it don't it
     costs nothing.
How to win love, how to win games, the spells and conjurations are named for
     fever, burns, convulsions, snakebite, milksick, balking horses, rheumatism,
     warts.
"Tie the heart of a bat with a red silk string to your right arm and you will win
     every game at which you play."
If your right foot itches you will soon start on a journey, if it's your left foot
     you will go where you are not wanted.
If you sing before breakfast you will cry before night, if you sneeze before
     breakfast you will see your true love before Saturday night.
Lightning in the north means rain, lightning in the south means dry weather.
Frost three months after the first katydid is heard. Three white frosts and then
     a rain.

For toothache the faith doctor wrote the words "galla gaffa gassa" on the wall.
     With a nail he pointed at each letter of the words, asking if the toothache
     was better. At the letter where the tooth was feeling easier he drove the
     nail in and the tooth stopped aching. Galla gaffa gassa. Gassa galla gaffa.

Goofer dust comes from the goofer tree.
Sprinkle it in the shoes of the woman you love and
     she can never get away from you.
          Galla gaffa gassa.

---

[1] Based on a Republican campaign story in 1892 alleging that a man on all fours
eating grass on the White House lawn told President Grover Cleveland, "I'm hungry"
and was advised, "The grass is longer in the backyard."—C. S.

[2] A saying that took rise from James J. (Jim) Hill.—C. S.

[3] A folk tale in Chicago chronicles two ditch diggers on the morning after Marshall
Field I died, leaving an estate of $150,000,000, as having this dialogue.—C. S.

[4] J. Pierpont Morgan's query as to court decrees dissolving an inevitable industrial
combination.—C. S.

[5] George Ade.—C. S.

[6] From *The People, Yes,* by Carl Sandburg. Copyright, 1936, by Harcourt, Brace
& Co. This and succeeding lines are from pp. 123–124.

Even a lousy cur has his lucky days.
Sweep dirt out of the door after night and
    you sweep yourself out of a home.
Shake the tablecloth out of doors after sunset
    and you will never marry.
The first to drive a hearse is the next to die.
Kill cats, dogs or frogs and you die in rags.
Point at a shooting star or even speak of it **and**
    you lose your next wish.

Better born lucky than rich.
Marry in May, repent always.
May is the month to marry bad wives.

The son of the white hen brings luck.
So does a horse with four white feet.

He planted gravel and up came potatoes.
When a bitch litters pigs that is luck.
The lucky fellow gets eggs from his rooster
    and his hen eggs have two yolks.
Luck for the few, death for the many.

aw nuts aw go peddle yer papers [1]
where did ja cop dat monkeyface
    jeez ja see dat skirt
    did ja glom dat moll
who was tellin you we wuz brudders
how come ya get on dis side deh street
go home and tell yer mudder she wants yuh
chase yer shadder aroun deh corner
yuh come to me wid a lot uh arkymalarky
    a bing in de bean fer you yeah
how come ya get on dis side deh street
go home and get yer umbreller washed
    den get yer face lifted
dis corner is mine—see—dis corner is mine
gwan ja tink ya gonna get dis f'm me fer nuttin
    nobody gets nuttin fer nuttin
    gwan monkeyface peddle yer papers
ya can't kiss yerself in here   dis is all fixed

What have you above the ears? [2]
Or are you dead from the neck up?
If you don't look out for yourself nobody else will.
What counts most is what you got under your own hat.
    Your best friend is yourself.
Every man for himself and the devil take the hindmost.

---

[1] *Ibid.*, pp. 130–131.
[2] *Ibid.*, p. 163.

I'm the only one of my friends I can count on.
    I'm not in business for my health.
    I'm a lone wolf; I work by myself.
    I'm for me, myself and company.
Who said you could work this side of the street?

The rich own the land and the poor own the water.[1]
The rich get richer and the poor get children.
The rich have baby napkins, and the poor have diapers.
The big houses have small families and the small
    houses big families.
Why did Death take the poor man's cow and the rich
    man's child?

The mazuma, the jack, the shekels, the kale,[2]
    The velvet, the you-know-what,
    The what-it-takes, a roll, a wad,
    Bring it home, boy.
    Bring home the bacon.
    Start on a shoestring if you have to.
    Then get your first million.
The second million is always easier than the first.
And if you get more of them round iron men than you can use
    you can always throw them at the birds: it's been done.
Now take some men, everything they touch turns into money:
    they know how the land lays: they can smell where the
    dollars grow.
Money withers if you don't know how to nurse it along: money
    flies away if you don't know where to put it.
The first question is, Where do we raise the money, where is the
    cash coming from?
A little horse sense helps: an idea and horse sense take you far:
    if you got a scheme ask yourself, Will it work?
And let me put one bug in your ear: inside information helps:
    how many fortunes came from a tip, from being on the
    ground first, from hearing a piece of news, from fast riding,
    early buying, quick selling, or plain dumb luck?
Yes, get Lady Luck with you and you're made: some fortunes
    were tumbled into and the tumblers at first said, Who would
    have believed it? and later, I knew just how to do it.
Yes, Lady Luck counts: before you're born pick the right papa
    and mama and the news-reel boys will be on the premises
    early for a shot of you with your big toe in your mouth.

The cauliflower is a cabbage with a college education.[3]
All she needs for housekeeping is a can opener.
    They'll fly high if you give them wings.
Put all your eggs in one basket and watch that basket.
Everybody talks about the weather and nobody does anything about it

---

[1] *Ibid.*, p. 164.
[2] *Ibid.*, pp. 165–166.
[3] *Ibid.*, pp. 62–61.

The auk flies backward so as to see where it's been.

Handle with care women and glass.

Women and linen look best by candlelight.

One hair of a woman draws more than a team of horses.

Blessed are they who expect nothing for they shall not be disappointed.

You can send a boy to college but you can't make him think.

The time to sell is when you have a customer.

Sell the buffalo hide after you have killed the buffalo.

The more you fill a barrel the more it weighs unless you fill it with holes.

A pound of iron or a pound of feathers weighs the same.

Those in fear they may cast pearls before swine are often lacking in pearls.

May you live to eat the hen that scratches over your grave.

He seems to think he's the frog's tonsils but he looks to me like a plugged nickel.

If you don't like the coat bring back the vest and I'll give you a pair of pants.

The coat and the pants do the work but the vest gets the gravy.

"You are singing an invitation to summer," said the teacher, "you are not defying
it to come."

Where you been so long? [1]
What good wind blew you in?
Snow again, kid, I didn't get your drift.
Everything now is either swell or lousy.
"It won't be long now," was answered,
"The worst is yet to come."

Why repeat? I heard you the first time. [2]
You can lead a horse to water, if you've
got the horse.
The rooster and the horse agreed not to
step on each other's feet.
The caterpillar is a worm in a raccoon coat
going for a college education.
The cockroach is always wrong when it
argues with the chicken.
If I hadn't done it Monday somebody else
would have done it Tuesday.
Money is like manure—good only when
spread around.
You're such a first-class liar I'll take a
chance with you.
A short horse is soon curried.
A still pig drinks the swill.
Small potatoes and few in a hill.
A fat man on a bony horse: "I feed
myself—others feed the horse."
No peace on earth with the women, no life
anywhere without them.
Some men dress quick, others take as much
time as a woman.

[1] *Ibid.*, p. 65.

[2] *Ibid.*, pp. 83–84.

"You're a liar." "Surely not if you say so."
He tried to walk on both sides of the street
    at once.
He tried to tear the middle of the street in
    two.
"When is a man intoxicated?" "When he
    tries to kiss the bartender good-night."
"He says he'll kick me the next time we
    meet. What'll I do?" "Sit down."
He's as handy as that bird they call the
    elephant.
Now that's settled and out of the way what
    are you going to do next?
"From here on," said the driver at an
    imaginary line near the foothills of the
    Ozarks, "the hills don't get any higher
    but the hollers get deeper and deeper."
So slick he was his feet slipped out from
    under him.
The ground flew up and hit him in the face.
Trade it for a dog, drown the dog, and
    you'll be rid of both of them.
There'll be many a dry eye at his funeral.
"Which way to the post-office, boy?" "I
    don't know." "You don't know much,
    do you?" "No, but I ain't lost."

In the farm house passing another crock of apples,[1]
On the street car riding to the roller coasters,
At picnics, clam-bakes, or the factory workbench
They have riddles, good and bad conundrums:
    Which goes through the plank first, the bullet or the hole?
    Where does the music go when the fiddle is put in the box?
    Where does your lap go when you stand up? The same place your fist
        goes when you open your hand.
    What are the two smallest things mentioned in the Bible? The widow's
        mite and the wicked flee.
    Who are the shortest people mentioned in the Bible? Bildad the Shuhite,
        Knee-high-miah, and the man who had nothing but from whom even
        that which he had was taken away.
    What was the last thing Paul Revere said to his horse on the famous ride?
        "Whoa!"
    "Did you hear about the empty barrel of flour?" "No." "Nothing in it."
    What is there more of in the world than anything else? Ends.

    They have Irish bulls timeworn and mossgrown:
You are to be hanged and I hope it will prove a warning to you.
I took so much medicine I was sick a long time after I got well.
I can never get these boots on till I have worn them for a while.
One of us must kill the other—let it be me. We were boys together—at least
    I was.

---

[1] *Ibid.*, pp. 95–96.

If all the world were blind what a melancholy sight it would be.
This will last forever and afterward be sold for old iron.
They would cut us into mince-meat and throw our bleeding heads on the table
    to stare us in the face.
On the dim and faroff shore of the future we can see the footprint of an unseen
    hand.
We pursue the shadow, the bubble bursts, and leaves in our hands only ashes.

> "Ah there tootsie wootsie," has its day
> till the good old summertime has gone
> with the kit and caboodle of its day
> into the second-hand bins, the rummage sales,
> and another whim emerges in, "Okay toots!"

The people, yes, the customers,
In short-order lunch rooms they read signs:
    If the ice-box gets on fire ring the towel.
    Don't tip the waiters—it upsets them.
    Eat here—why go somewhere else to be cheated?
    Your face is good but it won't go in the cash register.
"There ain't no strong coffee, there's only weak people," said one heavy on
    the java.

The people is a child at school writing howlers,
writing answers half wrong and half right:
    The government of England is a limited mockery.
    Gravitation is that which if there were none we would all fly away.
    There were no Christians among the early Gauls; they were mostly lawyers.

You can't come back to a home unless it was a [1]
    home you went away from.
Between hay and grass neither one nor the other.
Can't you be useful as well as ornamental?
Why don't you go roll a peanut around the corner?
    When did they let you out?
The mules went to ask horns and came back without ears.
When you get hold of a good thing freeze onto it.
    Nothing to do and all day to do it in.
So dumb he spent his last dollar buying a pocketbook to put it in.
    A little more sandpaper and this will be smooth.
Write on one side of the paper and both sides of the subject.
Swear to it on a stack of Bibles and they wouldn't believe you.
    Be not a baker if your head be of butter.
Yesterday? It's a nickel thrown on a Salvation Army drum.
How could I let go when it was all I could do to hold on?
Thousands drink themselves to death before one dies of thirst.
    He didn't have much till he married a hunk of tin.
    There's always a nut on every family tree.
    The mosquitoes organized and drove me out of bed.
We'll fight till hell freezes over and then write on the ice, "Come on, you
    bastards."

---

[1] *Ibid.*, 111–113.

The yes-man spent his vacation yelling, "No! no! I tell you No!"

A man having nothing to feed his cow sang to her of the fresh green grass to come; this is the tune the old cow died on.

The man feeding a hatful of doughnuts to a horse explained to the curious, "I want to see how many he'll eat before he asks for a cup of coffee."

"I fired the man," said the new section boss, "not because I had anything agin him but because I had the authority."

"Don't I argue? Don't I sputify?" the backwoods preacher inquired of the complaining committee whose chairman responded, "Yes, you do argue and you do sputify but you don't tell wherein!"

The late riser is asked, "Are you up for all day?"

Shut the door—do you want to hear all outdoors?

He won't go to a wedding unless he's the bride nor a funeral unless he's the corpse.

"May you have the sevenyear itch," was answered, "I hope your wife eats crackers in bed."

He was always a hell of a big fellow in Washington when he was in Rhode Island and a hell of a big fellow in Rhode Island when he was in Washington.

You say you are going to Warsaw (or Boston) because you want me to think you are going to Lemberg (or Buffalo) but I know you are going to Warsaw (or Boston).

He got on a horse and rode off in all directions at once.

Did they let you out or did you let yourself out?

"Why!" said a Republican Governor of Illinois, "Why the Democrats can't run the government! It's all us Republicans can do."

This will last a thousand years and after that to the end of the world.

When a member died the newspaper men of the Whitechapel Club of Chicago gave the toast:

"Hurrah for the next who goes!"

In Vermont a shut-mouthed husband finally broke forth to his wife, "When I think of how much you have meant to me all these years, it is almost more than I can do sometimes to keep from telling you so."

> "Is it far to the next town?" [2]
> asked the Arkansas traveller
> who was given the comfort:
> "It seems farther than it is
> but you'll find it ain't."

> Six feet six was Davy Tipton
> and he had the proportions
> as kingpin Mississippi River pilot
> nearly filling the pilothouse
> as he took the wheel with a laugh:
> "Big rivers ought to have big men."

---

[1] *Ibid.*, p. 9.

"A long, tall man won't always make a good fireman," said the Santa Fe[1] engineer to a couple of other rails deadheading back. "Out of a dozen wants to be firemen you can pick 'em. Take one of these weakly fellers he'll do his best but he's all gone time you get nine miles. Take a short, stout feller, low down so he can get at his coal, and he'll beat one of those tall fellers has to stoop. But if a tall feller's got long arms he can do wonders. I knowed one engineer used to say he had a fireman he never saw him throw a shovel of coal on the fire—his arms was so long he just reached and laid the coal on!"

He can turn around on a dime.
He has an automobile thirst and a wheelbarrow income.
I don't know where I'm going but I'm on my way.
I'll knock you so high in the air you'll starve coming down.
A bonanza is a hole in the ground owned by a champion liar.
All you get from him you can put in your eye.
He tried to get a bird in the hand and two in the bush but what he got was a horse of another color.
If the government tried to pay me for what I don't know there wouldn't be enough money in all the mints to pay me.
You can't tell him anything because he thinks he knows more now than he gets paid for.
It's a slow burg—I spent a couple of weeks there one day.
He bit off more than he could chew.
Don't take a mouthful bigger than your mouth.
Let's take it apart to see how it ticks.
If we had a little ham we could have some ham and eggs if we had some eggs.
He always takes off his hat when he mentions his own name.
What's the matter with him? The big I, always the big I.
"Why didn't you zigzag your car and miss him?" "He was zigzagging himself and outguessed me."
"Are you guilty or not guilty?" "What else have you?"
"Are you guilty or not guilty?" "I stands mute."

"I never borrowed your umbrella," said a[2] borrower, "and if I did I brought it back."
He was quiet as a wooden-legged man on a tin roof and busy as a one-armed paper-hanger with the hives.
When a couple of fried eggs were offered the new hired man he said, "I don't dirty my plate for less than six."

Ugly? Sleep stays away from him till he covers his[3] face.
Poor? He can't raise money enough to buy lumber for a backhouse.
Big Feet? Buying shoes he don't ask for a number, he says, "Lemme see the biggest you got."

---

[1] *Ibid.*, pp. 59–60.
[2] *Ibid.*, p. 64.
[3] *Ibid.*, p. 119.

The name of a stub line under the Lone Star banner is The Houston Eastern [1] and Western Texas railroad.

On the passenger and freight cars is the monogram, the initials H. E. W. T.

And nearly everybody in the territory traversed and the adjacent right of way calls it "Hell Either Way you Take It."

The Never Did and Couldn't railway is the N. D. & C., Newburgh, Duchess and Connecticut.

The Delay Linger and Wait is the D. L. & W., the Delaware, Lackawanna and Western.

Come Boys and Quit Railroading ran the slogan of the 1888 engineer's strike on the C. B. & Q. RR., the Chicago Burlington & Quincy Rail Road.

No matter how thick or how thin you slice it it's still baloney. [2]

I would if I could and I could if I would but if I couldn't how could I, could you?

I never made a mistake in grammar but once in my life and as soon as I done it I seen it.

He was a good shoveler but I don't know as I would say he was a fancy shoveler.

"You're always talking about liberty, do you want liberty?" "I don't *know* as I do and I don't know *as* I do."

"The train is running easier now." "Yes, we're off the track now."

The chorus goes, "They take him by the hand, and they lead him to the land, and the farmer is the man who feeds them all."

"I hear a burglar in the house." "Wait, if he finds anything worth stealing we'll take it away from him."

"Did you say the sky is the limit?" "Yes, we won't go any higher than the sky."

"That dwarf ain't worth ten cents to see—he's five feet high if he's a foot." "Exactly, my good sir, he's the tallest dwarf in the world."

> The big fish eat the little fish, [3]
> the little fish eat shrimps
> and the shrimps eat mud.
> You don't know enough to come in when it rains.
> You don't know beans when the bag is open.
> You don't know enough to pound sand in a rat hole.
> All I know is what I hear.
> All I know is what I read in the papers.
> All I know you can put in a thimble.
> All I know I keep forgetting.
>
> We have to eat, don't we?
> You can't eat promises, can you?
> You can't eat the Constitution, can you?

---

[1] *Ibid.*, p. 149.
[2] *Ibid.*, p. 160.
[3] *Ibid.*, p. 234.

PART FOUR

LIARS

An authentic liar knows what he is lying about, knows that his listeners—unless they are tenderfeet, greenhorns—know also, and hence makes no pretense of fooling either himself or them. At his best he is as grave as a historian of the Roman Empire; yet what he is after is neither credulity nor the establishment of truth. He does not take himself too seriously, but he does regard himself as an artist and yearns for recognition of his art. He may lie with satiric intent; he may lie merely to make the time pass pleasantly; he may lie in order to take the wind out of some egotistic fellow of his own tribe or to take in some greener; again, without any purpose at all and directed only by his ebullient and companion-loving nature, he may "stretch the blanket" merely because, like the redoubtable Tom Ochiltree, he had "rather lie on credit than tell truth for cash." His generous nature revolts at the monotony of everyday facts and overflows with desire to make his company joyful

—J. FRANK DOBIE

I YARNS AND TALL TALES

*To string incongruities and absurdities together in a wandering
and sometimes purposeless way, and seem innocently unaware
that they are absurdities, is the basis of the American art, if my
position is correct. Another feature is the slurring of the point.
A third is the dropping of a studied remark apparently without
knowing it, as if one were thinking aloud. The fourth and last
is the pause.—*MARK TWAIN

1. THE ART OF CASUAL NARRATIVE: THE YARN

A YARN is a long, rambling, extravagant tale, with that quality of deliberate casualness and improvisation which stamps the "humorous
story," in Mark Twain's view, as the distinctive development of story-
telling in America.

The humorous story may be spun out to great length, and may wander around
as much as it pleases, and arrive nowhere in particular; but the comic and witty
stories must be brief and end with a point.

In Mark Twain's distinction between the comic or witty story and the
humorous story is implied the difference between the anecdote and the
yarn—a difference in form, style, and structure, based on a difference in
purpose. Since the purpose of the anecdote as a wise or witty story is
to make or illustrate a point, its business is to get to the point as quickly
as possible (but not too quickly) and to make it clear and unmistakable.
To that end the anecdote is bright and snappy, as brisk in movement as
it is sharp in point. Since the purpose of the yarn is to create an effect
of the odd, grotesque, or whimsical and to accumulate a certain kind
of detail in order to produce that effect, the yarn takes its time, building
up a good case for itself and delaying the ending or let-down, which is
frequently an anti-climax.

The difference is essentially one of timing. The anecdote is closer to
the short story, and the yarn to the sketch or tale in tempo. Whereas the
former moves directly toward its goal, with, as the short-story text-books
put it, the greatest economy of means that is consistent with the utmost
emphasis, the latter is leisurely, even to the point of being long-winded,
and profuse to the point of diffuseness. The prolixity of the yarn is an
oral quality, reflecting the relaxed mood of men who sit around and swap
stories. While the anecdote suggests the give-and-take of conversational
repartee, the yarn tends toward the monolog and garrulousness, with all
the repetitions and digressions of monopolizing talk. In print the yarn
becomes a mock-oral tale, imitating the slow drawl and sprawling ease of
spoken, spontaneous narrative.

The enormous popularity of the mock-oral yarn which was the vehicle of backwoods and frontier humorists in the thirties is due as much to the naturalness and informality of the medium as to the genuineness of its humor. The humble art of humble life, the yarn presupposes leisure and loquacity. It was something both the teller and the listener could sink their teeth into. Though it may have lost its appeal for a generation used to a snappier lore, it still has the freshness that marked the discovery made by its first literary practitioners—the discovery that "something old in talking might look new in writing." [1]

As in the case of "The Celebrated Jumping Frog of Calaveras County," the same story may be told as an anecdote or as a yarn. Based on a bit of mining-camp lore of the gold rush days, Mark Twain's version is a perfect example of the method of oral, vernacular humorous story-telling discussed in "How to Tell a Story" and exemplified by the description of Simon Wheeler's narrative manner. The dead seriousness of the narrator, which stands in marked contrast to the tomfoolery of the characters, is in the tradition of the deadpan, monotone performance of the folk story-teller and the folk singer. The piece sets a high standard for the insinuating mimicry of such garrulous recitals as "The Saga of Little Ab Yancey," with its quizzical, drawling innocence, and "Thar She Blows," with its cumulative dudgeon.

2. STRETCHING FACTS: THE TALL TALE

A special, and to some the most distinctive, type of yarn is the tall tale. "Exuberant combinations of fact with outrageous fiction," in Walter Blair's definition, tall tales originate when the delicate balance between truth and untruth is turned in favor of the latter. "Some of the incidents I know to be true," writes the narrator of "The Wind," "—just enough truth in them to make good story material and to incite the imagination to try to improve on actual happenings."

This improving on actual happenings rather than outright lying is the distinguishing feature of the tall tale, which carries it beyond the mere incongruity or absurdity of the yarn and saves it from the whole-cloth invention of the ordinary whopper. The tall tale has a twofold relation to fact. On the one hand, as in the tall tales which were the chief stock-in-trade of Southern and Western humorists of the 1830's and 1840's, the eccentric or outlandish traits of backwoods and frontier life are singled out for realistic portrayal, the object being to create a "cumulative effect of the grotesque, romantic, or humorous." On the other hand, as in the later development of the genre, the prevailing interest is in the freaks of nature and in establishing a circumstantial basis for subhuman or super-human marvels. In either case, the incongruity proceeds partly from the contrast between fact and fancy and is enhanced by enclosing the story in a realistic framework and employing the traditional device of the frame-tale, or group of stories within a story. This tendency of tall tales to grow and move in cycles also leads to their attraction about a central figure or hero of the Paul Bunyan variety.

Old-timers' reminiscences seem to make the best tall tales, all things considered, because the tricks of memory and distance come to the aid of

[1] *Humor of the Old Deep South*, by Arthur Palmer Hudson (1936), pp. 16–17.

the imagination in improving on actual happenings, while the exaggerations themselves are mellowed by time and immunized against criticism by the venerability that belongs to the narrator's years. Personal reminiscences gain further credence from the fact that they are the first-hand accounts of eye-witnesses or participants, backed up by the expressed or implied guarantee of "I saw or heard (if not actually did) these things myself." Sometimes the narrator employs the device of quoting an informant, named or unnamed, "long since dead" or lost track of, or of drawing upon travels (his own or some one else's) to report the wonders of distant places beyond checking up on. Credibility is also established by liberal use of local color and circumstantial detail. As the narrator of "The Rawhide Railroad" avers, "the wealth of detail and circumstantial accuracy leaves no doubt of the truth of the story as a whole."

In spite of the pretense of verisimilitude, which smacks of a hoax, the tall tale deals frankly with marvels, with the remarkable or prodigious, as the epithet signifies. As J. Frank Dobie points out, the tall-tale teller does not expect to be believed, except by the uninitiated. His task is essentially that of the poet; namely, to heighten fact and deal in illusions by creating a mood and an atmosphere favorable to the "willing suspension of disbelief that constitutes poetic faith." In "The Wind," for example, to the usual embellishments of garrulous elaboration and digression, the narrator adds the poetry of odd comparisons and conceits, akin to the hyperbole of tall talk. In these tales the wind itself, "pesky" and "cavortin'," takes on some of the attributes of poetic personification, playing pranks and performing miracles like any mythical hero. In "The Rawhide Railroad," the poetry takes the form of gorgeous nonsense, involving burlesque of stories of Indians and other Western romances.

The use of freaks of nature for tall tale material is associated not only with the experience of old-timers and travelers in their capacity as historians of the primitive type of a Herodotus or as naturalists of the credulous order of a Pliny but also with the American habit of boosting (as in stories of healthful climate and fertile soil) or boasting (as in brags of hunting and fishing) and with the pioneer trait of "laughing it off," or making light of misfortunes. Next to rural brags and gags, the most fertile source of tall tales is industry and remarkable inventions, as in "The Rawhide Railroad"—an expression of the mechanical genius of Americans which has flowered in folklore ranging from Yankee contraptions like the bone-picking machine to the large-scale contrivances of Paul Bunyan. The bone-picking machine is of the same breed as the automatic feeder in Chaplin's *Modern Times*.

"I've got a new machine," said a Yankee pedlar, "for picking bones out of fish. Now, I tell you, it's a leetle bit the darndest thing you ever did see. All you have to do is to set it on a table and turn a crank, and the fish flies right down your throat and the bones right under the grate. Well, there was a country greenhorn got hold of it the other day, and he turned the crank the wrong way; and, I tell you, the way the bones flew down his throat was awful. Why, it stuck that fellow so full of bones, that he could not get his shirt off for a whole week!" [1]

---

[1] *The Complete Works of Charles F. Browne, better known as "Artemus Ward."* (London: John Camden Hotten), pp. 316–317.

3. Tall Tales of Occupations

In a sense a railroad yarn such as "The Rawhide Railroad," together with most yarns of occupational groups—cowboys, miners, lumberjacks, farmers—may be considered occupational—the sense, namely, of involving experiences encountered in the course of making a living. A true occupational tale, however, is told by as well as about workers and gives the feel of the job—something of how the work is done and how the workers feel about it. Although frequently incorporating sayings, jokes, and anecdotes that go the rounds, occupational tall tales are traditional tales which fall midway between the more esoteric or technical lore of the group and popular jokes and stories. They are to be distinguished also from the stories of practical jokes in which new hands are sent in search of impossible objects and from the legendary cycles of the Paul Bunyan type, into which these occupational tall tales may grow.

Like the best tall tales, occupational tall tales have a strong realistic and sociological coloring, even to a note of social criticism and protest. Although boastful, in the ring-tailed roarer tradition, they temper their brags with humorous complaints of hard work and bad conditions and with satire at the expense of bosses and fellow-workers. The spirit of an ironic Joe Hill hovers over a fable like "Crumbs," which has passed beyond the stage of glorification of the timber beast to the militant stage of Wobbly unrest.

At the same time occupational tall tales tell us much of the inside story of craftsmanship and industry and what happens when machine labor displaces hand labor and when one kind of tool is outmoded by another. Technological changes and differences give rise to feuds and contests, involving deeds of prodigious strength or skill. Rivalries take such subtle forms as the feud between cable-tool drillers and rotary workers in the oil fields or such obvious forms as the feud between old and new hands. Resentment against the machine and nostalgia for the good old days also creep in as normal reactions of displaced hand workers.

The language of the tales is colored by occupations, both in the use of technical terms and trade slang and in the sprinkling of tall talk of men who work with their hands. In spite of the fact that freaks of machinery have replaced freaks of nature as subjects of these tall tales, there is a distinct hangover of the frontier-hero tradition of strong men and tough customers—hell-raisers or star performers. "I'm a man as is work-brickle," says the Demon Bricksetter from Williamson County. "I'm a man as can't say quit. When I lay a-holt, I'm like a turtle and I don't let loose till it thunders. I'm from Williamson County, and maybe you've heerd of the men they raise down there where the screech owls roost with the chickens."

The Celebrated Jumping Frog
of Calaveras County

IN COMPLIANCE with the request of a friend of mine, who wrote me from the East, I called on good-natured, garrulous old Simon Wheeler, and inquired after my friend's friend, Leonidas W. Smiley, as requested to do, and I hereunto append the result. I have a lurking suspicion that *Leonidas W.* Smiley is a myth; that my friend never knew such a personage; and that he only conjectured that, if I asked old Wheeler about him, it would remind him of his infamous *Jim* Smiley, and he would go to work and bore me nearly to death with some infernal reminiscence of him as long and as tedious as it should be useless to me. If that was the design, it certainly succeeded.

I found Simon Wheeler dozing comfortably by the barroom stove of the old, dilapidated tavern in the ancient mining camp of Angel's, and I noticed that he was fat and bald-headed, and had an expression of winning gentleness and simplicity upon his tranquil countenance. He roused up, and gave me good-day. I told him a friend of mine had commissioned me to make some inquiries about a cherished companion of his boyhood named *Leonidas W.* Smiley—*Rev. Leonidas W.* Smiley—a young minister of the Gospel, who he had heard was at one time a resident of Angel's Camp. I added that, if Mr. Wheeler could tell me anything about this Rev. Leonidas W. Smiley, I would feel under many obligations to him.

Simon Wheeler backed me into a corner and blockaded me there with his chair, and then sat me down and reeled off the monotonous narrative which follows this paragraph. He never smiled, he never frowned, he never changed his voice from the gentle-flowing key to which he tuned the initial sentence, he never betrayed the slightest suspicion of enthusiasm; but all through the interminable narrative there ran a vein of impressive earnestness and sincerity, which showed me plainly that, so far from his imagining that there was anything ridiculous or funny about his story, he regarded it as a really important matter, and admired its two heroes as men of transcendent genius in *finesse*. To me, the spectacle of a man drifting serenely along through such a queer yarn without ever smiling, was exquisitely absurd. As I said before, I asked him to tell me what he knew of Rev. Leonidas W. Smiley, and he replied as follows. I let him go on in his own way, and never interrupted him once.

There was a feller here once by the name of *Jim* Smiley, in the winter of '49—or may be it was the spring of '50—I don't recollect exactly, somehow, though what makes me think it was one or the other is because I remember the big flume wasn't finished when he first came to the camp;

From *The Celebrated Jumping Frog of Calaveras County, and Other Sketches*, by Mark Twain, edited by John Paul, pp. 7–19. New York: C. H. Webb, Publisher. 1867.

but any way, he was the curiosest man about always betting on anything that turned up you ever see, if he could get anybody to bet on the other side; and if he couldn't, he'd change sides. Any way that suited the other man would suit him—any way just so's he got a bet, *he* was satisfied. But still he was lucky, uncommon lucky; he most always come out winner. He was always ready and laying for a chance; there couldn't be no solit'ry thing mentioned but that feller'd offer to bet on it, and take any side you please, as I was just telling you. If there was a horse-race, you'd find him flush, or you'd find him busted at the end of it; if there was a dog-fight, he'd bet on it; if there was a cat-fight, he'd bet on it; if there was a chicken-fight, he'd bet on it; why, if there was two birds setting on a fence, he would bet you which one would fly first; or if there was a camp-meeting, he would be there reg'lar to bet on Parson Walker, which he judged to be the best exhorter about here, and so he was too, and a good man. If he even seen a straddle-bug start to go anywheres, he would bet you how long it would take him to get wherever he was going to, and if you took him up, he would foller that straddle-bug to Mexico but what he would find out where he was bound for and how long he was on the road. Lots of the boys here has seen that Smiley, and can tell you about him. Why, it never made no difference to *him*—he would bet on *any* thing—the dangdest feller. Parson Walker's wife laid very sick once, for a good while, and it seemed as if they warn't going to save her; but one morning he come in, and Smiley asked how she was, and he said she was considerable better—thank the Lord for his inf'nit mercy—and coming on so smart that with the blessing of Prov'dence she'd get well yet; and Smiley, before he thought, says, "Well, I'll risk two-and-a-half she don't anyway."

Thish-yer Smiley had a mare—the boys called her the fifteen-minute nag, but that was only in fun, you know, because of course she was faster than that—and he used to win money on that horse, for all she was so slow and always had the asthma, or the distemper, or the consumption, or something of that kind. They used to give her two or three hundred yards' start, and then pass her under way; but always at the fag-end of the race she'd get excited and desperate-like, and come cavorting and straddling up, and scattering her legs around limber, sometimes in the air, and sometimes out to one side amongst the fences, and kicking up m-o-r-e dust and raising m-o-r-e racket with her coughing and sneezing and blowing her nose—and always fetch up at the stand just about a neck ahead, as near as you could cipher it down.

And he had a little small bull-pup, that to look at him you'd think he wa'n't worth a cent but to set around and look ornery and lay for a chance to steal something. But as soon as money was up on him he was a different dog; his under-jaw'd begin to stick out like the fo'castle of a steamboat, and his teeth would uncover and shine savage like the furnaces. And a dog might tackle him and bully-rag him, and bite him, and throw him over his shoulder two or three times and Andrew Jackson—which was the name of the pup—Andrew Jackson would never let on but what *he* was satisfied, and hadn't expected nothing else—and the bets being doubled and doubled on the other side all the time, till the money was all up; and then all of a sudden he would grab that other dog jest by the j'int of his hind leg and freeze to it—not chaw, you understand, but only jest grip and hang on till they throwed up the sponge, if it was a year. Smiley always come out winner on that pup, till he harnessed a dog once that didn't have no hind legs, because they'd been sawed off by a circular saw, and when the thing had gone along far enough, and the money was all up, and he come to make a snatch for his pet holt, he saw in a minute how he'd been imposed on, and how the other dog had him in the door, so to speak, and he 'peared surprised, and then he looked sorter discouraged-like, and didn't try no more to win the fight, and so he got shucked out bad. He give Smiley a look, as much as to say his heart was broke, and it was *his* fault, for putting up a dog that hadn't no hind legs for him to take holt of, which was his main dependence in a fight, and then he limped off a piece and laid down and died. It was a good pup, was that Andrew Jackson, and would have made a name for hisself if he'd lived, for the stuff was in him and he had genius—I know it, because he hadn't had no opportunities to speak of, and it don't stand to reason that a dog could make such a fight as he could under them circumstances if he hadn't had no talent. It always makes me feel sorry when I think of that last fight of his'n, and the way it turned out.

Well, thish-yer Smiley had rat-tarriers, and chicken cocks, and tom-cats and all them kind of things, till you couldn't rest, and you couldn't fetch nothing for him to bet on but he'd match you. He ketched a frog one day, and took him home, and said he calk'lated to edercate him; and so he never done nothing for three months but set in his back yard and learn that frog to jump. And you bet you he *did* learn him, too. He'd give him a little punch behind, and the next minute you'd see that frog whirling in the air like a doughnut—see him turn one summerset, or maybe a couple, if he got a good start, and come down flat-footed and all right, like a cat. He got him up so in the matter of ketching flies, and kept him in practice so constant, that he'd nail a fly every time as far as he could see him. Smiley said all a frog wanted was education, and he could do 'most anything—and I believe him. Why, I've seen him set Dan'l Webster down here on this floor—Dan'l Webster was the name of the frog—and sing out, "Flies, Dan'l, flies!" and quicker'n you could wink he'd spring straight up and snake a fly off'n the counter there, and flop down on the floor ag'in as solid as a gob of mud, and fall to scratching the side of his head with his hind foot as indifferent as if he hadn't no idea he'd been doin' any more'n any frog might do. You never see a frog so modest and straightfor'ard as he was, for all he was so gifted. And when it come to fair and square jumping on a dead level, he could get over more ground at one straddle than any animal of his breed you ever see. Jumping on a dead level was his strong suit, you understand; and when it come to that, Smiley would ante up money on him as long as he had a red. Smiley was monstrous proud of his frog, and well he might be, for fellers that had traveled and been everywheres, all said he laid over any frog that ever *they* see.

Well, Smiley kept the beast in a little lattice box, and he used to fetch him down town sometimes and lay for a bet. One day a feller—a stranger in the camp, he was—come across him with his box, and says:

"What might it be that you've got in the box?"

And Smiley says, sorter indifferent-like, "It might be a parrot, or it might be a canary, maybe, but it ain't—it's only just a frog."

And the feller took it, and looked at it careful, and turned it round this way and that, and says, "H'm—so 'tis. Well, what's *he* good for?"

"Well," Smiley says, easy and careless, "he's good enough for *one* thing, I should judge—he can outjump any frog in Calaveras county."

The feller took the box again, and took another long, particular look, and give it back to Smiley, and says, very deliberate, "Well," he says, "I don't see no p'ints about that frog that's any better'n any other frog."

"Maybe you don't," Smiley says. "Maybe you understand frogs and maybe you don't understand 'em; maybe you've had experience, and maybe you ain't only a amature, as it were. Anyways, I've got *my* opinion and I'll risk forty dollars that he can outjump any frog in Calaveras county."

And the feller studied a minute, and then says, kinder sad like, "Well, I'm only a stranger here, and I ain't got no frog; but if I had a frog, I'd bet you."

And then Smiley says, "That's all right—that's all right—if you'll hold my box a minute, I'll go and get you a frog." And so the feller took the box, and put up his forty dollars along with Smiley's and set down to wait.

So he set there a good while thinking and thinking to hisself, and then he got the frog out and prized his mouth open and took a teaspoon and filled him full of quail shot—filled him pretty near up to his chin—and set him on the floor. Smiley he went to the swamp and slopped around in the mud for a long time, and finally he ketched a frog, and fetched him in, and give him to this feller, and says:

"Now, if you're ready, set him alongside of Dan'l's, with his fore-paws just even with Dan'l's, and I'll give the word." Then he says, "One—two—three—jump!" and him and the feller touched up the frogs from behind, and the new frog hopped off, but Dan'l give a heave, and hysted up his shoulders—so—like a Frenchman, but it wa'n't no use—he couldn't budge; he was planted as solid as an anvil, and he couldn't no more stir than if he was anchored out. Smiley was a good deal surprised, and he was disgusted too, but he didn't have no idea what the matter was, of course.

The feller took the money and started away; and when he was going out at the door, he sorter jerked his thumb over his shoulders—this way—at

Dan'l, and says again, very deliberate, "Well, *I* don't see no p'ints about that frog that's any better'n any other frog."

Smiley he stood scratching his head and looking down at Dan'l a long time, and at last he says, "I do wonder what in the nation that frog throw'd off for—I wonder if there ain't something the matter with him— he 'pears to look mighty baggy, somehow." And he ketched Dan'l by the nap of the neck, and lifted him up, and says, "Why, blame my cats, if he don't weigh five pound!" and turned him upside down and he belched out a double handful of shot. And then he see how it was, and he was the maddest man—he set the frog down and took out after that feller, but he never ketched him. And—

[Here Simon Wheeler heard his name called from the front yard, and got up to see what was wanted.] And turning to me as he moved away, he said: "Just set where you are, stranger and rest easy—I an't going to be gone a second."

But, by your leave, I did not think that a continuation of the history of the enterprising vagabond *Jim* Smiley would be likely to afford me much information concerning the Rev. *Leonidas W.* Smiley, and so I started away.

At the door I met the sociable Wheeler returning, and he button-holed me and re-commenced:

"Well, thish-yer Smiley had a yaller one-eyed cow that didn't have no tail, only jest a short stump like a bannanner, and—"

"Oh! hang Smiley and his afflicted cow!" I muttered, good-naturedly, and bidding the old gentleman good-day, I departed.

The Jumping Frog

(The Earliest Known Printed Version: From the Sonora *Herald* of June 11, 1853)

A TOAD story.—A long stupid-looking fellow used to frequent a gambling saloon, some time since, and was in the habit of promenading up and down, but never speaking. The boys began to play with him, at last, and in down east drawl he gave them Rolands for their Olivers till they left him alone. At night he spread out his blankets on an empty monte table and lived like a gambler, except that he talked to no one nor gambled a cent. He became, at length, an acknowledged character, slunk in and out, and the boys tittered as they saw him pass. One day he came in with an important air, and said:

"I have got a toad that'll leap further than any toad you can scare up."

They soon surrounded him, and roared and laughed.

From *The Origin of The Celebrated Jumping Frog of Calaveras County*, by Oscar Lewis, pp. 31-32. Copyright, 1931, by The Book Club of California. San Francisco.

"Yes," says he, "I'll bet money on it. Barkeeper, give me a cigar box to hold my toad in."

The fun was great, and the oddity was the talk of all hands. A gambler, in the evening, happened to come across a big frog, fetched him to the gaming house and offered to jump him against the Yankee's toad.

"Well," says Yank, "I'll bet liquors on it." A chalk line was made and the toad put down. They struck the boards behind the toad and he leaped six feet, then the frog leaped seven. Yank paid the liquors; but, next morning, he says aloud:

"My toad waren't beat. No man's toad can leap with my toad. I have two ounces and two double eagles, and all of them I bet on my toad." The boys bet with him again, and his toad leaped six feet, but the frog leaped only two feet.

"The best two out of three," said the gamblers.

"Very well," says Yank. But still the frog could not go over two feet. Yank pocketed the bets.

"My frog is darn heavy this morning," says the gambler.

"I reckoned it would be, stranger," says the Yankee, "for I rolled a pound of shot into him last night."

How to Tell a Story

The Humorous Story an American Development.—Its Difference from Comic and Witty Stories.

I DO not claim that I can tell a story as it ought to be told. I only claim to know how a story ought to be told, for I have been almost daily in the company of the most expert story-tellers for many years.

There are several kinds of stories, but only one difficult kind—the humorous. I will talk mainly about that one. The humorous story is American, the comic story is English, the witty story is French. The humorous story depends for its effect upon the *manner* of the telling; the comic story and the witty story upon the *matter*.

The humorous story may be spun out to great length, and may wander around as much as it pleases, and arrive nowhere in particular; but the comic and witty stories must be brief and end with a point. The humorous story bubbles gently along, the others burst.

The humorous story is strictly a work of art—high and delicate art—and only an artist can tell it; but no art is necessary in telling the comic and the witty story; anybody can do it. The art of telling a humorous

From *How to Tell a Story and Other Essays,* by Mark Twain (Samuel L. Clemens), pp. 7–15. Copyright, 1897, 1898, 1899, by Harper & Brothers; 1892, by C. L. Webster & Co.; 1898, by The Century Co.; 1898, by The Cosmopolitan; 1899, by Samuel E. Moffett; 1900, by American Publishing Company. Autograph Edition, The Writings of Mark Twain, Vol. XXII. Hartford, Conn. The American Publishing Company.

story—understand, I mean by word of mouth, not print—was created in America, and has remained at home.

The humorous story is told gravely; the teller does his best to conceal the fact that he even dimly suspects that there is anything funny about it; but the teller of the comic story tells you beforehand that it is one of the funniest things he has ever heard, then tells it with eager delight, and is the first person to laugh when he gets through. And sometimes, if he has had good success, he is so glad and happy that he will repeat the "nub" of it and glance around from face to face, collecting applause, and then repeat it again. It is a pathetic thing to see.

Very often, of course, the rambling and disjointed humorous story finishes with a nub, point, snapper, or whatever you like to call it. Then the listener must be alert, for in many cases the teller will divert attention from that nub by dropping it in a carefully casual and indifferent way, with the pretence that he does not know it is a nub.

Artemus Ward used that trick a good deal; then when the belated audience presently caught the joke he would look up with innocent surprise, as if wondering what they had found to laugh at. Dan Setchell used it before him. Nye and Riley and others use it to-day.

But the teller of the comic story does not slur the nub; he shouts it at you—every time. And when he prints it, in England, France, Germany, and Italy, he italicizes it, puts some whooping exclamation-points after it, and sometimes explains it in a parenthesis. All of which is very depressing, and makes one want to renounce joking and lead a better life.

Let me set down an instance of the comic method, using an anecdote which has been popular all over the world for twelve or fifteen hundred years. The teller tells it in this way:

The Wounded Soldier

In the course of a certain battle a soldier whose leg had been shot off appealed to another soldier who was hurrying by to carry him to the rear, informing him at the same time of the loss which he had sustained; whereupon the generous son of Mars, shouldering the unfortunate, proceeded to carry out his desire. The bullets and cannon-balls were flying in all directions, and presently one of the latter took the wounded man's head off—without, however, his deliverer being aware of it. In no long time he was hailed by an officer, who said:

"Where are you going with that carcass?"

"To the rear, sir—he's lost his leg!"

"His leg, forsooth?" responded the astonished officer; "you mean his head, you booby."

Whereupon the soldier dispossessed himself of his burden, and stood looking down upon it in great perplexity. At length he said:

"It is true, sir, just as you have said." Then after a pause he added. *"But he TOLD me* IT WAS HIS LEG!!!!!"

Here the narrator bursts into explosion after explosion of thunderous horse-laughter, repeating that nub from time to time through his gaspings and shriekings and suffocatings.

It takes only a minute and a half to tell that in its comic-story form; and it isn't worth the telling, after all. Put into the humorous-story form it takes ten minutes, and is about the funniest thing I have ever listened to—as James Whitcomb Riley tells it.

He tells it in the character of a dull-witted old farmer who has just heard it for the first time, thinks it is unspeakably funny, and is trying to repeat it to a neighbor. But he can't remember it; so he gets all mixed up and wanders helplessly round and round, putting in tedious details that don't belong in the tale and only retard it; taking them out conscientiously and putting in others that are just as useless; making minor mistakes now and then and stopping to correct them and explain how he came to make them; remembering things which he forgot to put in in their proper place and going back to put them in there; stopping his narrative a good while in order to try to recall the name of the soldier that was hurt, and finally remembering that the soldier's name was not mentioned, and remarking placidly that the name is of no real importance, anyway—better, of course, if one knew it, but not essential, after all—and so on, and so on, and so on.

The teller is innocent and happy and pleased with himself, and has to stop every little while to hold himself in and keep from laughing outright; and does hold in, but his body quakes in a jelly-like way with interior chuckles; and at the end of the ten minutes the audience have laughed until they are exhausted, and the tears are running down their faces.

The simplicity and innocence and sincerity and unconsciousness of the old farmer are perfectly simulated, and the result is a performance which is thoroughly charming and delicious. This is art—and fine and beautiful, and only a master can compass it; but a machine could tell the other story.

To string incongruities and absurdities together in a wandering and sometimes purposeless way, and seem innocently unaware that they are absurdities, is the basis of the American art, if my position is correct. Another feature is the slurring of the point. A third is the dropping of a studied remark apparently without knowing it, as if one were thinking aloud. The fourth and last is the pause.

Artemus Ward dealt in numbers three and four a good deal. He would begin to tell with great animation something which he seemed to think was wonderful; then lose confidence, and after an apparently absent-minded pause add an incongruous remark in a soliloquizing way; and that was the remark intended to explode the mine—and it did.

For instance, he would say eagerly, excitedly, "I once knew a man in New Zealand who hadn't a tooth in his head"—here his animation would die out; a silent, reflective pause would follow, then he would say dreamily, and as if to himself, "and yet that man could beat a drum better than any man I ever saw."

The pause is an exceedingly important feature in any kind of story, and a frequently recurring feature, too. It is a dainty thing, and delicate, and also uncertain and treacherous; for it must be exactly the right length—no more and no less—or it fails of its purpose and makes trouble. If the pause is too short the impressive point is passed, and the audience have had time to divine that a surprise is intended—and then you can't surprise them, of course.

On the platform I used to tell a Negro ghost story that had a pause in front of the snapper on the end, and that pause was the most important thing in the whole story. If I got it the right length precisely, I could spring the finishing ejaculation with effect enough to make some impressible girl deliver a startled little yelp and jump out of her seat—and that was what I was after. This story was called "The Golden Arm," and was told in this fashion. You can practise with it yourself—and mind you look out for the pause and get it right.

THE GOLDEN ARM

Once 'pon a time dey wuz a monsus mean man, en he live 'way out in de prairie all 'lone by hisself, 'cep'n he had a wife. En bimeby she died, en he tuck en toted her way out dah in de prairie en buried her. Well, she had a golden arm—all solid gold, fum de shoulder down. He wuz pow'ful mean—pow'ful; en dat night he couldn't sleep, caze he want dat golden arm so bad.

When it come midnight he couldn't stan' it no mo'; so he git up, he did, en tuck his lantern en shoved out thoo de storm en dug her up en got de golden arm; en he bent his head down 'gin de win', en plowed en plowed en plowed thoo de snow. Den all of a sudden he stop (make a considerable pause here, and look startled, and take a listening attitude) en say: "My *lan'*, what's dat!"

En he listen—en listen—en de win' say (set your teeth together and imitate the wailing and wheezing singsong of the wind), "Bzzz-z—zzz"— en den, way back yonder whah de grave is, he hear a *voice!*—he hear a voice all mix' up in de win'—can't hardly tell 'em 'part—"Bzzz-zzz— W-h-o—g-o-t—m-y—g-o-l-d-e-n *arm?*—zzz—zzz—W-h-o g-o-t m-y g-o-l-d-e-n *arm?*" (You must begin to shiver violently now.)

En he begin to shiver en shake, en say, "Oh, my! *Oh,* my lan'!" en de win' blow de lantern out, en de snow en sleet blow in his face en mos' choke him, en he start a-plowin' knee-deep towards home mos' dead, he so sk'yerd—en pooty soon he hear de voice agin, en (pause) it 'us comin' *after* him! "Bzzz—zzz—zzz—W-h-o—g-o-t—m-y—g-o-l-d-e-n—*arm?*"

When he git to de pasture he hear it agin—closter now, en *a-comin'!*— a-comin' back dah in de dark en de storm—(repeat the wind and the voice). When he git to de house he rush up-stairs en jump in de bed and kiver up, head and years, en lay dah shiverin' en shakin'—en ōen way out dah he hear it *agin!*—en *a-comin'!* En bimeby he hear (pause—awed, listening attitude)—pat—pat—pat—*hit's a-comin' up-stairs!* Den he hear de latch, en he know it's in de room!

Den pooty soon he know it's *a-stannin' by de bed!* (Pause.) Den—he know it's *a-bendin' down over him*—en he cain't skasely git his breath! Den—den—he seem to feel someth'n *c-o-l-d,* right down 'most agin his head! (Pause.)

Den de voice say, *right at his year*—"W-h-o—g-o-t—m-y g-o-l-d-e-n *arm?* (You must wail it out very plaintively and accusingly; then you stare steadily and impressively into the face of the farthest-gone auditor— a girl, preferably—and let that awe-inspiring pause begin to build itself in the deep hush. When it has reached exactly the right length, jump suddenly at that girl and yell, *"You've* got it!"

If you've got the *pause* right, she'll fetch a dear little yelp and spring right out of her shoes. But you *must* get the pause right; and you will find it the most troublesome and aggravating and uncertain thing you ever undertook.)

The Saga of Little Ab Yancey

WINDY BILL HATFIELD was the best talker in the entire Holler when he got started, and it wasn't very hard to get him started, either. One day I asked Windy if he had ever known any real honest-to-God bad men in the Ozark country. "Wal now, lemme see," he drawled. "Them James brothers—Jesse slept in our house a many a time—was bad 'nough in some ways, an' th' Younger boys warn't exactly whut you might call sody-squirts, neither. Some o' th' Dalton gang come through hyar oncet in a while, too, an' so did Cherokee Bill an' Henry Starr an' that Doolin feller whut kilt all them folks over t' Southwest City."

But these men, as I pointed out, were merely hard-working bank-robbers, while I wanted to hear about genuine desperadoes, light-hearted gunfighters such as Billy the Kid. Windy had never heard of the Kid, but he got my meaning all right, and immediately bethought himself of one Abner Yancey, who had terrorized these wilds in the eighties. "Yes sir," he said, "I reckon Leetle Ab was 'bout th' fightin'est feller whut ever showed up in th' Holler. He'd fight a circle-saw, an' turn it hisse'f! He drinked a right smart o' licker, an' played cyards for money, an' run atter th' womenfolks, an' kilt three-four fellers whut crowded him too fur. But me an' him allus got 'long fine—they warn't no rale meanness in him.

By Vance Randolph. From *Folk-Say IV, The Land Is Ours,* edited by B. A. Botkin, pp. 235–238. Copyright, 1932, by B. A. Botkin. Norman: The University of Oklahoma Press.

"Hit puts me in mind o' whut Lew Merriwether said, th' time they was a-tryin' Ab for killin' a feller over t' Durgenville. Th' prosecutin' attorney was a newcomer, an' he heerd how Lew an' Ab had fit two-three years back, so he got Lew up on th' stand t' testify whut a bad character Ab was. Atter th' jury heerd all 'bout th' fraction th' lawyer he says: 'Now, Mister Merriwether, you think Ab Yancey is a mighty dangerous man, don't ye?' Lew he studied a-while an' then he says: 'Naw, I wouldn't go so fur as t' say that.' Th' 'torney he hollers out: 'Whut? This hyar defendant shot you twicet an' battered your head all up an' run you plumb home an' set your house afire—an' you figger he ain't dangerous?' Lew he jest grinned kinder foolish-like an' says: 'Wal sir, I wouldn't want t' call nobody out'n their name,' says he. Th' pore lawyer was turrible sot back. 'Lord Gawd, Mister Merriwether,' says he, 'whut kind of a man *is* this hyar Yancey, then?' Lew he scratched his head a minute an' then he says: 'Wal Jedge, I reckon Ab is jest a feller whut it won't do t' monkey with, nohow!'

"Ab was a right comical leetle cuss, too—allus a-doin' somethin' t' make folks laugh. I 'member th' time him an' Batty Ross was 'rested for fightin', an' ol' Squire Perkins he fined 'em five dollars apiece. Batty was a turrible big feller, an' he'd ketched Ab drunk an' beat him purty nigh t' death, but Ab he spoke right up in court jest th' same. 'Hell fire, Jedge,' says he, 'hit ain't right t' fine that pore leetle scallywag—ever'body knows he couldn't do no fightin'. Hit was *me* whut done th' fightin', Jedge, an' I shore aim t' pay th' hull damage myse'f!'—an' with that he slapped out a ten-spot on th' counter. Batty he jest stood thar plumb flabbergasted, an' even ol' Squire Perkins had t' chuckle a leetle.

"He was purty cagey in his young days, an' had a name for tom-cattin' round atter th' married women. Hit shore did git him into a heap o' trouble, too, but seems like he allus wiggled out'n it some way. One time Ab had snuck in t' visit one o' th' neighbor women—I ain't a-callin' no names, mind ye—an' while he was in thar they heerd somebody open th' gate. Th' heifer she says, 'Oh Gawd, that's my ol' man, shore!' an' Ab he says, 'Wal, whut'd I better do?' She was that skeered she couldn't say nothin', but Ab he run quick an' hid in th' scaldin'-bar'l. Purty soon hyar come a feller in, but it warn't her husband nohow. Hit was Big Jim Applegate, an' he run up t' th' woman an' begin a-huggin' an' a-kissin' an' a-lallygaggin' an' all like that. Ab he jest set thar still as a mouse. He couldn't see nothin', but he shore heerd a plenty. Purty soon th' gate slammed ag'in, an' this time it *was* her ol' man shore 'nough. Big Jim he put on his hat an' coat mighty quick, an' when th' feller walked in he says, 'Howdy, neighbor! I jest come over t' borry your scaldin'-bar'l— we-uns is aimin' t' butcher t'morrer.' Th' feller didn't like the looks o' things none too good, but he jest says, 'Wal Jim, thar it is, over thar in th' corner.'

"When Big Jim picked th' dang thing up he tuck note it was all-fired heavy, but he figgered this hyar warn't no time t' argufy 'bout th' heft of a scaldin'-bar'l, nohow. So he jest hustled off down th' road with it, an' he never did stop till he was plumb out o' sight. 'My Gawd,' says he, when he finally got whar he could set her down an' rest hisse'f a minute, 'I shore did git out o' that mess mighty slick!' 'Bout that time Leetle Ab he pushed th' led off'n th' bar'l an' crope out. 'You shore did, Jim,' says he, 'an' I didn't do so *turrible* bad myse'f!' ' "

It seemed to me that this tale was reminiscent of something I had read in Boccaccio, or some other old writer. I intimated as much to Windy Bill, too, but on learning that Boccaccio had lived in Europe several hundred years ago he scouted my theory in no measured terms. "Ab Yancey," he said impressively, "was borned an' raised right up thar on Greasy Creek. He never went nowhar outside th' county, an' he shore didn't have no truck with no furriners. How could this hyar Bo-whut-do-ye-call-him feller of knowed whut Ab done hyar in Poot Holler? Hit's plumb redic'lous, Doc—sometimes I think you ain't jest right in your head!"

No satisfactory reply to this sort of logic occurred to me at the moment, so I dropped the matter of origins rather precipitately, and pressed Bill for more information about Yancey's exploits. Most of them were commonplace enough—Ab's fights and frolics and sprees and adulteries had not differed very much from those of any other mountain bravo. When I asked for the particulars of his death Bill said shortly that he died from drinking too much popskull whisky, but admitted later on that it was no ordinary case of alcoholic poisoning.

"Wal, ye see, Ab got t' drinkin' in th' tavern an' I don't mind tellin' you he drinked jest a leetle more'n he'd orter. Atter while he got t' talkin' kinder wild, a-makin' out like he figgered on killin' somebody afore sun-up. So finally me an' Bob Nowlin jest jumped onto him all of a suddent an' tuck his gun away, an' then we put him t' bed on a pile o' gunnysacks. . . . When he come t' hisse'f next mornin' Ab begun t' holler whar was his gun at? An' then he says how come me all skun up like this, an' my clothes all tore? Frank Pease he was a-tendin' bar that mornin', an' he seen how Ab didn't remember nothin' whut happened last night. So he says, 'Wal Ab, we all drinked a leetle too much, an' you got t' fightin' with a couple o' furriners from th' Injun Territory, an' they jest knocked you plumb senseless,' says he. Frank he didn't mean no harm—he was jest tryin' t' fix it so's Ab wouldn't hold nothin' ag'in me an' Bob Nowlin. So then he give Ab his gun back from under th' counter, an' Ab he jest clicked th' loadin'-gate an' stuck it in his britches same as allus. Hit was one o' these hyar ol' single-action thumb-busters, an' he allus carried it thataway with th' gate stuck out for a hook onto his belt, so's it wouldn't slip down his pants-leg. . . . Ab warn't a-feelin' peart 'nough t' eat no breakfast but he tuck three-four good snorts o' licker an' went a-rampin' off down th' road. An' that's th' last time I ever seen Ab Yancey till they fetched th' corpse back home in th' wagon.

"But th' way I heerd it next mornin', Ab jest walked on down by th' creek, an' purty soon he perked up a leetle—he was a-whistlin' when he passed Ol' Man Joslyn's place, anyhow. He met up with two strangers down by th' ford, an' they howdied him civil as anybody. But Ab he figgered it was maybe these hyar fellers whut got th' best of him last night. 'Whar-bouts do you-uns live at?' he ast 'em, an' when they says they been a-workin' over in th' Nation he out with his six-shooter. 'Wade out in th' creek, Gawd damn ye!' he hollers t' th' biggest 'un. 'Git down on your knees, an' drink water like a cow!' an' th' feller done it. But t'other 'un he jest stood thar, an' when Ab started in a-cussin' *him* he jest pulled out his pistol an' shot Ab right squar' in th' belly! Ab snapped his thumb-buster four times, an' he'd of kilt both of 'em shore, only his gun warn't loaded. Me an' Bob Nowlin had done tuck th' hulls out'n it that night, an' pore Ab was so fuddled he never noticed 'em bein' gone, an' Frank Pease he never thought t' tell him.

"Some o' Ab's kinfolks was mighty high ag'in them fellers from th' Nation, but I never could make out t' blame 'em much myse'f. Whut'd you do, if you was a-walkin' 'long 'tendin' t' your own business, an' some feller tuck t' pullin' out guns an' a-carryin' on like whut Ab done? Ol' Joe Yancey allus helt it ag'in Frank Pease—said he hadn't orter of give Ab no empty gun thataway—an' Ab's woman she 'lowed me an' Bob Nowlin didn't have no business a-takin' th' ca'tridges out like we done. . . . But I allus figgered it was drinkin' bad whisky whut kilt Ab Yancey. Hit stands t' reason, if Ab hadn't of got drunk we wouldn't never of snatched his gun off'n him thataway, or tuck th' hulls out'n it. An' if he'd kept sober he'd of knowed whut happened, an' Frank wouldn't never told him that big windy 'bout fellers from th' Nation, neither. An' more'n that, if his head had been a-workin' he'd of loaded his gun an' kilt both them fellers easy, an' ever'thing would of been all right. . . . We-uns give him a high-tone buryin' as was ever saw in these parts, an' he's got th' biggest grave-rock in th' hull dang country. Hit ain't no more'n right, neither, 'cause Ab was one o' th' best-liked fellers ever lived in th' Holler."

Thar She Blows!

IT WAS the good ship Mozambique, Cap'n Symes commandin', his name bein' the same as mine but no kin, thank God. We wuz four months an' twenty days out o' New Bedford an' not a drop o' ile in the tanks. I'm standin' my watch when the man aloft calls out, "Thar she blows!"

"Where away?" sez I.

"Four points off the starboard quarter," sez he.

An' I goes aft.

"Cap'n Symes," I sez, "thar she blows."

"Where away?" sez he.

"Four points off the starboard quarter," sez I. "Shall we lower away?"

As told by Edmund Fuller.

Cap'n Symes sez, "It's blowin' right too pert. 'Tain't fitten fer to lower. Go for'ard an' stan' yer watch!"

An' I goes for'ard. Purty soon the man aloft calls out, "Thar she blows and spouts!"

An' I goes aft. An' I sez, "Cap'n Symes, thar she blows and spouts. Shall we lower away?"

Cap'n Symes sez, "I tole ye once and I tell ye twice. By the left hind leg o' the Lamb o' God, it's blowin' right too pert, an' 'tain't fitten fer to lower. Go for'ard an' stan' yer watch."

An' I goes for'ard. Purty soon the man aloft calls out, "Thar she blows an' spouts, an' breaches an' bellows!"

An' I goes aft. "Cap'n Symes," I sez, "thar she blows an' spouts, an' breaches an' bellows. Shall we lower away?"

Cap'n Symes sez, "I tole ye once and I tole ye twice and I tell ye three times. By the twenty-three legs of the Twelve Apostles, it's blowin' right too pert an' 'tain't fitten fer to lower. Go for'ard an' stan' yer watch."

An' I goes for'ard. Purty soon the man aloft calls out, "Thar she blows, an' spouts, an' breaches an' bellows, an' a sparm at that!"

An' I goes aft. "Cap'n Symes," I sez, "thar she blows an' spouts, an' breaches an' bellows, an' a sparm at that. Shall we lower away?"

Cap'n Symes sez, "By the forty-eight fat-cheeked Cherubim that flutter 'round the thrice-sanctified throne of the thrice-sanctified Christ, it's blowin' right too pert, an' 'tain't fitten fer to lower. But if yew want to lower, lower away an' be damned!"

Well, we chased that whale through the first watch an' 'long about eight bells we come alongside and I sez to the men in the boat, "Shall I let 'er have the long dart?" An' they sez, "Sock it to 'er." An' I socked it to 'er an' it tuk! Well sir, when we cut that whale up we took out eighty-six bar'ls o' the finest sparm ile an' forty-eight pounds o' ambergris. That night I'm down in the fo'c'sle when Cap'n Symes comes down the lee gangway an' he sez to me, "Mr. Symes," he sez, "you're the best man out o' New Bedford with the long dart. Down in my cabin there's a box o' fine Hay-vana seegars and a case o' Jee-maica rum. They're yours for the rest o' the v'ige."

"Cap'n Symes, sir," I sez, "I don't want none o' yer fine Hay-vana seegars an' I don't want none o' yer Jee-maica rum. All I want out o' yew, Cap'n Symes sir, is a little Christian civility—an' goddamned little o' that."

A Texas Norther

IT WAS on this journey that I first experienced a Texas "norther." It came upon us early one afternoon. Will Ross and I were riding about a mile

From *A Texas Ranger*, by N. A. Jennings, foreword by J. Frank Dobie, pp. 17–21. Copyright, 1930, by Southwest Press. Dallas, Texas.

ahead of the wagon. We were coatless, and our shirts were open at the throats, for the heat was stifling. Suddenly, without the slightest warning, an icy wind swept across the prairie from the north. It chilled us, through and through, in a few seconds.

"Hello! a norther's coming," said Will Ross. "We'd better go back and get our coats."

We turned back to the wagon, but when we attempted to ride in the teeth of that terribly cold wind, we suffered so that we gave up the attempt. We dismounted and stood in the lee of our horses until the wagon came lumbering up. Then we bundled into our coats and overcoats and rode on to a creek, a mile or so ahead. There, under the shelter of one of the banks, we built a great fire and went into camp, to remain until the "norther" should blow itself out. This, Ross knew from experience would be in two days.

A "norther" invariably blows from the north for twenty-four hours, Then it comes back, almost as cold, from the south for twenty-four hours more. The third day there is no wind, but the cold continues, gradually abating until, on the fourth day, the temperature is what it was before the "norther" came. I have been in New Hampshire when the thermometer marked forty degrees below zero; I have passed a night, lost in a snowstorm, in the Rocky Mountains in Colorado; but never have I suffered so from the cold as I have in a "Texas norther." One's blood gets thin in a warm climate, and it is not so easy to resist cold as in Northern latitudes. Not infrequently thousands of cattle will die, frozen to death, in a Texas "norther." During the winter months the "northers" sweep over Texas about once in every two or three weeks.

Lawrence Christopher Criss, an old Texas guide and buffalo-hunter, is responsible for the following tale of a "norther." Criss vouched for the absolute truth of it, and even offered to take me to the spot where it happened and show me the ashes of the camp-fire to prove it.

"It was along in the winter of '69 that I was out huntin' buffalo with a little hunch-back we called Twisted Charley," said Criss, telling me the yarn one night, sitting by a camp-fire near El Paso, Texas. "We were up in the Panhandle, and dead oodles of buffalo grazed around us. We had run across a herd in the afternoon, and killed nineteen between us. Twisted Charley and I were skinnin' them, and were takin' off the hides of four or five when the worst norther I ever remembered struck us.

"We piled all the wood we could find on the fire, but we couldn't begin to keep warm, and when night come on it got colder, and colder, and colder, till the coffee, boilin' in the coffee-pot on the fire, had a skim of ice on it that we had to break before we could pour the coffee out.

"Well, a bright idea struck me, and I took one of the green buffalo-hides and wrapped myself up in it, and in a minute I was as warm and comfortable as a man could wish to be anywhere. You know there's nothin' warmer than a buffalo-hide, and this one was extra thick. Charley saw what I had done, and he went and got a hide, too, and wrapped himself up in it. We were not long in fallin' asleep after that, and I was peacefully dreamin' about skinnin' Jacarilla Apache buck Injuns to make moccasins out of, when, all of a sudden, I was woke up by the most awful howlin' I ever heard.

"I was sure the Injuns were down on us, and I jumped up and grabbed my rifle in a hurry. Then I saw it was Twisted Charley who was doing the yellin'. I went over to where he lay, wrapped up in the green buffalo-hide, and I gave him a kick to wake him up, for I thought, of course, he had a nightmare.

"'Help me out, help me out!' he yelled.

"'What's the matter with you?' I asked.

"'Don't you see I'm froze up in this hide and can't get out?' he howled.

"I took hold of the hide and tried to unroll it, but it was froze 'round him as hard as boiler-iron. He was warm enough, for he had wrapped himself in it with the hairy side next to him, but he wanted to get out bad.

"'I can't unwrap that hide any way,' I said, after I'd made a trial at it.

"'Cut it open,' said Twisted Charley.

"I took my skinning-knife and tried to cut it, but the hide was so hard it turned the knife-edge.

"'I'll have to give it up,' I said, at last.

"'What?' yelled Charley. 'Man, I can't stay in this hide forever.'

"'You won't have to,' I says; 'this norther'll blow itself out in three days, and then you'll thaw out naturally.'

"'Thaw me out at the fire,' said Charley.

"That seemed reasonable, and I rolled him over by the fire and began toastin' first one side and then the other. I thought I'd never get him out; but after awhile, when the hide was actually roasted, I managed to unroll it enough for him to get out. He sat up by the fire the rest of the night, swearin'. He was a beautiful swearer, and the air moderated a whole lot while he was sittin' there inventin' new oaths and lettin' 'em out."

Mirages

ONE evening in the early fall of 1891, while on a round-up in the West Pasture, we got through supper early and had an hour or two to sit around the fire before we crawled into our "hot-rolls." One of the first northers of the season had blown up the day before, and the air was so crisp that evening that the fire felt good. The boys kept adding cow chips, and the coals glowed red but never blazed much. Some of the punchers sprawled full length on the ground, some leaned back against their saddles, and some sat on their heels and smoked cigarettes.

From *Rollie Burns or An Account of the Ranching Industry on the South Plains*, by W. C. Holden, pp. 171–176. Copyright, 1932, by W. C. Holden. Dallas, Texas: The Southwest Press.

We got to talking about mirages. To cow-punchers who knew nothing of scientific explanations, there was something mysterious about mirages. All the boys who had been on the Plains very long had seen freakish things happen. I had observed cattle which looked twenty-five feet tall, grazing near a mirage, and a man riding a horse that appeared forty feet tall. All kinds of peculiar things have happened in a mirage. Men have traveled miles towards a most realistic lake only to find it was not there. At a time when there were no houses, fences or trees within forty miles, one frequently saw such things only a few miles away. Newcomers on the Plains, unaccustomed to the peculiarities of mirages, sometimes thought of them as good or bad omens.

I told the boys about a mirage I saw during the spring of 1890. Estacado was twenty-two miles from the I O A headquarters and over a considerable ridge. The region immediately around Estacado was much more rolling than land commonly is in the vicinity of Crosby County. Approaching from the south, one could not see the town until he was in four or five miles of the place. One clear, frosty morning I stepped out into the back yard and saw Estacado elevated just above the horizon. Every house was visible. I could have counted the panes of glass in the west and south sides of the courthouse. I could see horses tied to the hitching posts in front of the stores and blacksmith shop, and people walking about the place. It seemed to me that, with the aid of field glasses, I would have been able to recognize the faces of the individuals.

In the late fall of 1890 I witnessed another illusion equally strange. Our rounding-up outfit was camped about eight miles from the Yellow House Canyon, practically due south of Buffalo Springs. The morning was chilly, still and frosty. When I got up between daylight and sunrise, the cook called to me, "Boss, I thought we camped several miles from the Canyon last night."

"We did."

"Look, we are right on the edge of it this morning."

I looked, and I never beheld a more perfect mirage. It was so realistic it would have fooled an old-timer. There was the bottom of the Canyon just below us, water running along the creek, a few hackberry trees along the edges of the water course, and cattle grazing along the sides of the Canyon. I saw familiar landmarks in the creek, trees and rocks. It seemed that I could have thrown a rock into the center of the Canyon. If I had not known that we were eight miles from the rim of the Canyon and over a slight rise, I would have sworn we were on the very edge.

"Last spring," said T Bar Dick, "while I was 'reping' for our outfit over on the Syndicate range, I heard an old punch tell about a mirage he had seen about fourteen years before when he was a buffalo hunter. His camp was beside a lake in one of the wide, shallow basins on the Plains. He got lost from camp and rode several days looking for it. There was plenty of water in the lakes and buffaloes everywhere; so he was in no danger in that respect, but he had to get back to camp eventually. Each morning he would get his bearings the best he could when the sun came up, and ride

all day eyeing the horizon in every direction for the lost camp. One
morning after riding a couple of hours, ne looked back and saw an
unusual mirage behind him. There were buffaloes, wild horses, antelopes,
and wolves moving about without touching the earth. The reality of the
scene impressed him so much he stopped to study it awhile. Directly he
recognized his camp beside the lake. There were his wagon, piles of
buffalo hides, and his horses grazing not far away. He knew enough
about mirages to know that this was a reflected image of his camp. He
took his bearing and headed back toward the mirage. The illusion soon
vanished, but he kept the direction. He rode hard all day, and just
before sun-down he topped a ridge, and there was his camp. That morning
when he saw the mirage he must have been thirty or forty miles away."

None of us who had been on the Plains for a season or more doubted the
story. "Shorty" Anderson had been stretched by the fire listening with
rapt attention. Shorty always had a mischievous twinkle in his eye, and
when he was up to something the twinkle became downright devilish.

"Speaking of buffaloes," he said, "I was out on the Plains once before
any cowmen had ever ventured on top of the Caprock. I don't suppose
there was a tree, or a post, or a man in fifty miles. I rode up on a ridge
once and saw a big buffalo bull grazing near a lake. He didn't see me,
and I rode back quickly and circled around to get on the wind side. I had
only my Colt .45, and my horse was afraid of buffaloes. I thought my
only chance was to leave my horse over the ridge and stalk the bull on
foot. I figured that if everything worked just right I stood a chance to
get within pistol range. I got up within thirty yards before the big brute
sighted me. He looked at me a moment and couldn't decide whether to
run at me or from me. In either case, I decided I had better let him
have it. I banged away at him, and didn't hit where I aimed. The first
shot caused him to turn towards me. I let him have five more shots, but
you can't kill a buffalo with a .45 unless you hit him right behind his
shoulder blade. If he had been in doubt about what to do beforehand,
he didn't have any doubts after I put six lumps of lead under his hide.
He gave a wild bellow and took after me. My horse was a mile away, and
somehow I didn't get started in that direction. The bull gained on me for
a little bit; he was snorting and blowing and it seemed like I could feel
his breath. But after the first hundred yards I began to hold my own."

Shorty stopped suddenly as if that was the end of the story, but "Red"
Wheeler couldn't leave him in that predicament.

"What did you do next?" asked Red.

"I climbed a tree."

"But you said there was not a tree in fifty miles."

"Well, you see, it was this way. It happened that one of those mirages
like the boss has been telling about was right in front of me. There was
a big hackberry tree growing by a water hole. Well, I climbed that
mirage tree."

The boys bellowed, swayed, and slapped their knees. Most of them concluded that the joke was on Red, but one or two took a sheepish side

glance at me. I was never any hand at repartee, and was for letting it pass. But there was a young puncher there from Estacado. He was about five feet, eight inches tall, slender, wiry, hot-tempered and could ride any horse in the country. He was easy to get along with until you nettled him, and then it was too bad. The biggest, toughest roughneck in the outfit would have thought twice before getting this stripling riled up. He had an Irish wit and a deep booming voice like all United States senators aspire to have. The boys were mighty leery about pulling anything on him. His name was Winford Hunt. When the haw-hawing died down, Winford came to my and Red's rescue.

"Now, Shorty, don't you reckon that buffalo bull that was chasing you was just a mirage buffalo?"

Then it was Shorty's turn for the back-slapping.

The Wind

I

WELL—yes, the wind does get up and blow out here in West Texas sometimes. Most generally it comes from wherever it happens to be, but

---

By Frank Neff and William Henry. From *Folk-Say, A Regional Miscellany: 1930*, edited by B. A. Botkin, pp. 48–60. Copyright, 1930, by B. A. Botkin. Norman: University of Oklahoma Press.

Frank Neff, who worked up the Wind stories, was born in Pennsylvania. When a small boy he had read a number of nickel novels of the type of *Bloody-Hand the Avenger, Dead-Shot Dick, The Terror of the Gulch, Three-Finger Jake*, etc., which fired him with the ambition to go west and make the "redskins bite the dust." He arrived in the Panhandle of Oklahoma in time to see the victims of the Hay Meadows Massacre in 1889, all of whom were white men, killed by other white men from Kansas in a county seat fight.

He was short, thick-set, light complexioned; had steel-gray eyes, a mustache that would have been the envy of the Kaiser; and feared neither God, man, nor devil. He was barely five feet tall but weighed close to one-hundred seventy pounds, and was as clever with boxing gloves as any man in his section of the Panhandle. He was a crack shot with rifle and pistol, able to shoot the heads off the mountain quail running from him at full speed, or to split a card or a coin at fifty steps. He had a good education and served more than one term as county superintendent.

His height was reduced several inches by his having fallen into a well which with the help of his brother he was digging in a region where the nearest water was ninety feet straight down. His brother drew him up astride a galvanized bucket that was raised and lowered by a windlass. When the bucket was near the top the rope broke, dropping Frank about sixty feet and breaking both legs halfway between the knee and the thigh. When I knew him, he had recovered, but there was a heavy band of very thick cartilage around each leg, covering the break.

He was witty, cheerful, a great lover of sport—anything from a badger fight to riding an unbroken nineteen-year-old mule at a Fourth of July celebration. He was a mine of useful information as well as an excellent spinner of fanciful and amusing yarns. Some of the incidents I know to be true—just enough truth in them to make good story material and to incite the imagination to try to improve on actual happenings.—W. H.

the real good hard winds out here come from the north or from the south unless, as happens every once in a while, it gets to goin whirligig fashion, and when that happens you might say that things do move.

But that reminds me of the time I was workin with a watermelon seedin crew here about twenty year ago last summer. Or have I ever told you this story before? Well, you see, we had begun seedin melons along right just after sun-up, and there was just a nice gentle little breeze a-blowin, almost seemed like the answer to a maiden's prayer. But along about noon the sun commenced glarin down on us hotter and hotter and pretty soon we begin to see little whirligigs of wind scuddin around here, there, and yonder over the purairie pickin up little patches of dry grass and whippin up sand sky-high until it begun to look like the whole damn purairie was all afire. Of course, what looked like smoke rings was only sand, but it was real enough to make a tenderfoot start a backfire and get a fireguard ready.

I'm tellin you, 'i gosh, I never did see so many of them little twisters all a-goin at one and the same time as I did that day, and then all at once the funniest thing happened.

It seems as though the wind had just been pickin up speed and about this time it decided to set in for some real straight blowin. Well, 'bout one o'clock, when the sun had switched over to the west side of things, here she come from the west like a ball out of hell. Not a cloud any-wheres but just a good old west wind eastbound tryin to get acrost Texas immediately if not sooner. Talk about speed now. There was a couple of greyhounds chasin a rabbit in the next field and they just about had him caught when he raised his ears and the wind caught him and blew him clear out of sight 'fore the hounds ever missed him.

I never was exactly sure till that day why there won't nothin grow on these here purairies except buffalo grass. But I realize now that any other kind that was to try to grow would be blowed plumb away 'fore it'd even have time to turn green or take root. And nothin else'd have the nerve to crawl right out from under the sand and keep right on a-growin regard-less of whether it rained last week or last year.

Well—to get back to this here particular wind, which I just don't rightly understand. Here we was seedin watermelons at one o'clock in the after-noon and the wind just blowin hell's bells out of the west. By two o'clock the wind had got so much harder that everything was a-leanin east and we had to put the seeds eight inches in the ground to keep them from blowin out. Well—the wind kept gettin harder and harder until at three o'clock the sun was *actually standin still*. 'I gosh, mister, I hope to tell you it was. Yes, sir, I believe that there old Bible story 'bout Joshuer makin the sun and moon both stand still now. The only reason the moon didn't stand still that day was because it hadn't come up in time to meet this here wind.

Well—we just kept right on a-seedin watermelons and a-watchin that there damn sun a-standin still, and it stood there and stood there until we finally all agreed that it was at least three hours late goin down. And you never saw a sicklier-lookin thing anywhere than that poor old sun. The damn thing kept a-tryin to go down and tryin but it just was stuck up there and couldn't budge. It even stayed around till the stars come out and began to look around sorta surprised-like.

Then the wind finally begun to let up and the dog star come up and chased the sun away off over a hill, and then it got too dark to seed any more melons so we quit and went on home to supper. But I never yet seen just a plain straight old wind like that one was.

II

Wind? Wind? Did you ever see the wind blow? Stranger, I don't reckon you've lived in these here parts very long, have you? Let me tell you some of the things I've seen the wind do, right around in this particular community.

Man! I've seen the wind blow—by note and also by ear, you might say.

Just now I remember me of the time when it hadn't rained in these here regions for all of one summer—and a good part of the next one. The landscape had got so dry that there was rabbit tracks and gopher trails and coyote runs marked out in every direction like a college surveyor was a-tryin to set grade stakes for a new paper railroad that was to run from the North Pole to Nowhere—if only enough suckers could be induced to put their money into its watered stock so as it could loosen up a bit and get to runnin.

Well sir—'i gosh, this time that I'm a-thinkin about nobody but a tenderfoot would even dream that it would ever rain again. And as I was a-walkin along one side of my homestead and a-wonderin if there was enough buffalo grass to carry the stock through another winter, I looked away off to'ds the west, and as sure as shootin there was a little cloud a-peepin up over the west state line, and it just wasn't a mite bigger than a man's hand.

I just heaved another sigh and give up hopin for rain right then. But I want to tell you what happened. As I was a-moseyin along to'ds the shack the wind begins to blow. No, you ain't got it right—it did not come from the little cloud I'd just seen hidin on the rim of the world. No, sir, that wind was a-comin from the contrariwise direction, and man! how it did blow! But just before I got to the shack I looked back, a kinda helpless look to see what'd happen to the little cloud when that wind hit her.

You wouldn't expect anything but that the poor little cloud would be blown helter-skelter every which way from hell to breakfast. But it had just kinda rose up, and that heavy wind had missed her, and the little cloud was a-gettin bigger and was a-sailin along and was a-gettin bigger and bigger and a-comin nearer and nearer. But it still wasn't anything to think twice about.

And mister, right there was where I made my big mistake. And it come.

anigh ruinin all the rest of my life, and it did make a considerable dent in my future fortunes.

The contrary wind blowed stronger and stronger, and the little cloud puffed up and got blacker and blacker and bigger and then some; and she just come sailin on into our country. By that time the ground wind, seein it couldn't make no headway buckin the oncomin cloud—'i gosh, if it didn't turn right around and blow along with the cloud too. And by this time that little old cloud was as big as all out-o-doors and a-gettin blacker every minute.

Fust off henhouses and hog sheds seemed like they just give one look to'ds the black cloud rushin onto them, and then scairt-like they looked like they just flapped up into the sky, and off they all went. There was a regular whirlpool of boards and shingles gyratin round and round and up and off cross country.

It didn't seem like it lasted more'n a minute—and then there was some of the curiousest sights. One shingle had hit a tree, and the little end of it had hit the tree fust, and it was still a perfectly good shingle but stuck into the tree until no one could pull it out any way. Two boards had come together, crisscross, and one was driv' just exactly halfway through the other, and they was left a-sittin up on the ground like a letter X. My windmill wheel was blown away a slat at a time, and more'n a mile away I found them slats a-stickin in the ground in the shape of the letter S, and the top ends were all feathered out like some one had started to make toothpicks and didn't get done with the job. Where the storm crossed my field and the stalks of last year's crop was standin, it just took and wrapped every one of them stalks right down near the ground and round and round. Every one of my hens was blowed a mile or more out onto the purairie, and when I went out to look for them they had not a feather of any kind left on them, but the wind had done blowed them feathers so hard that they had hit my hogs, and one side of each hog was stickin full of chicken feathers, and they didn't seem hurt a bit.

The last look I had at the sky, before I took to my cave, was to see my settin hens' nests and my home brew go up together. And the sheriff found some good eggnog all blown into jugs and corked up regular way over into the next county, and there was talk of turnin me in to the revenooers.

Yes sir—the wind sure did blow out here that day.

III

A-speakin about wind. Now since you've mentioned *seein* the wind blow reminds me of some of the times the wind has blew out here on the west plains country. Many a time I've started to town with the wind at my back, and have met the same wind comin back to meet me 'fore I'd got more than halfway there. And it always come back with a bang, lookin like it was a-tryin to push all the real estate over into the next county

Sure enough, mister, I've actually come home to find that my farm was all piled up along the section line on the south side of my place; and when I left home it had been a-layin as purty and as peaceful as any man could wish.

More'n once in the fall I've seen the wind come a-hustlin them tumbleweeds along at a mile a minute gait; and it looked like there was no end to the tumblin, twistin, rollin things, bigger'n a washtub, and a-pilin up as high as the roof of the shed or the barn or wherever they happened to lodge. When two or three of us would get together on these windy days, we'd bet on which tumbleweed would outrun the rest to a certain point. It's a right interestin sport, and Old Lady Luck and Old Man Chance has to give you all the breaks to make you winner.

'Nother time I seen smoke a-risin way off to'ds the Oklahoma line. A-course, that meant only one thing—some camper had left the fire get away from him, and the purairie was afire! It wasn't no time at all till all the wild things that was footloose begun driftin by, not aimin to go anywhere in particular, only just so it was away from the fire that was a-gainin headway and comin on now at a great rate.

One of them purairie fires is sure one grand sight if you ain't got nothin at stake and you're plumb sure that your fireguard can't be jumped. There's clouds of smoke and pillars of flame and whirlpools of flame and smoke a-risin and a-twistin and a-bowin and a-sashayin alaman left and do-se-do, and all the time travelin acrost the country at a speed that would make you dizzy. I've timed these fires more'n once and found them makin a mile a minute—and with not more'n a forty-mile wind behind them.

Time I'm thinkin of we hadn't got our fireguards plowed yet, and all we could do was to hitch up and start a furrow, team at a lope and one of us aholt of the plow-handles, while some one else run behind a-startin the back-fires. And then I've seen the wind set the heat over acrost a hundred-foot fireguard which was already plowed and burned off slick and clean, and then the race was all on again.

This same time everything was swept by the fire. Next day we found smokin bodies of birds and rabbits and now and then a coyote that the fire had outrun.

It sure was a grand and a terrible sight to see the whirlin wind start at one end of the line of fire, and by blowin the burnin tumbleweeds, and cow-chips rollin on edge, and little and big whirlpools of fire dancin along the advancin line, set the fire half or quarter of a mile ahead by the time you could bat your eye twicet.

And more'n once that spring that I'm thinkin about—'i gosh, if I didn't find when I got to town that the danged wind had blew up the streets.

Yes s-i-r—it did for a fact.

IV

Did you ever hear me tell about Old Dad Thornberg and the funny trick the wind played on him? Dad was one of them fellers who never could support himself, and so he up and gets married so as to have a wife to help in the support. Dad and Mom Thornberg had reared a good-size family, and Mom a-doin all the work, with Dad helpin some. They had run a hotel and had managed to scrape along till the children was all growed up and gone out to hustle their own livin's.

It's a pity for Mom that it couldn't have happened sooner, but soon after the last youngster left the old home roof Dad just naturally give up the ghost. Mom kept him around for several days a-waitin so the children could all get home for the funeral. Finally the day come when they was to take Dad out to the old buryin ground and inter the last of his mortal remains.

After all the singin and the preacher had had his say and had done the best he could by Dad, they all started off for the buryin ground. It looked most of the way like it was a-goin to be a success, and that sure enough Old Dad was a-goin to be put where the moth and rust wouldn't corrupt nor the thieves break through and steal—when as they was a-crossin a little ravine one of the wheels dropped into a chuck hole and the coffin slid out onto the ground so hard that it bust right open.

A-course, every one was horrified and looked away, and each one was a-waitin to see if some one else wouldn't do something 'fore he would have to make a move. The minutes dragged by, and no one stirred until they heard Dad holler. Yes sir. And when they all looked around there come Dad, dressed up for the only time in his life, and for the first time since his death, comin straight to'ds them and lookin as surprised as time.

Course Dad wanted to know where in time they was a-goin with him, him not havin noticed the coffin which had dropped into the ditch. So they had to explain that they thought that he was dead and was on the way to find a doctor or something.

Truth of it is, Dad was dead, but when that coffin bust open and that strong healthy plains wind hit him it just filled his lungs full of good revivin air, and Dad nor no one else could stay dead.

A few years later Dad had another narrow escape. The wind started in kinda playful-like, and Dad was a-lookin after something out in the barnyard and a-potterin around doin his daily dozen a-lookin for the eggs and some other little tricks Mom had sent him for—when he noticed there was a little stronger breeze a-blowin than commonly. He did not think about it any too much, just then. It'd been hot and dry a long time, and no one thought there was any chance for a storm of any kind 'fore time to do the spring plowin next year.

So he just went on a-tendin to his little chores and enjoyin thinkin what a fine meal Mom would be a-gettin him pretty soon. In the meantime the wind was a-gettin stronger and stronger, and if any one had took one look off acrost the purairie he could have seen that the " 'fraid hole" was the place for him, and he'd been gone for it like time runnin for the bank when your note's comin due.

Finally the wind come full force, twistin and turnin and blowin up and down over and over. Dad was right in the path it finally took, and 'fore he even had time to yell it had picked him up and had smacked him flat against the side of the barn. And there poor old Dad was, spread out flatter'n a sheet of paper, and no way to get down.

The wind stopped blowin as quick as it had started, and Mom, who had seen it begin and had ducked into the 'fraid hole, come out and saw fust off what it'd done to Dad. She couldn't think of nothin better than to get a hoe and start to scrape Dad down off the barn. She got him all down finally and started sorrowfully for the house with Dad loaded into a wheelbarrow. Well sir—I'll be everlastingly a liar if that wind didn't spring up again and blew so strong against her that it blew Dad clean out of the wheelbarrow and back into the natural shape. Yes sir, it did, 'i gosh.

Did you ask me, "Didn't Dad ever die?" Not yet. There he is right over there. He's more'n a hundred years old right this minute, and he'll tell you this tale just like I have—if'n you give him a little time to remember what happened.

V

Well now—that there story of yourn is real interestin, and I suppose if a measly little twister'd come along and untwist the top off my house I'd be real excited about it like you say you was. But sure enough, man, you didn't see the wind blow anything like it did when I fust come here— not any at all.

Let me tell you about an incident or two. Maybe that'll put you in mind of how the wind used to blow when these here purairies was young and there was nothin but lone wolfs and Injuns to cavort and howl here-abouts.

See that old dugout over there 'bout two mile? Well just now I'm thinkin of some tricks I seen the wind do right over at that old dugout. Course it was a new house then, and one of them everlastin cheerful galoots from somewheres east of Abilene was a-tryin to make a go of it with one cow and some chickens and a woman and some little yaller-haired children.

Every other year he'd just about make a crop, and could purty near support his wife and all until time come for him to try it again. Then dry weather'd set in or a hail would drive in or a purairie fire'd sweep down, and then the poor cuss'd have to have aid from the county or from his wife's folks or any place aid could be got from.

Time I'm a-thinkin about he had a durn good prospect for makin more than enough to carry him through. Broom corn and maize was a-lookin the best it ever had in the middle of August, and the ground had enough moisture to make a crop without any more rain at all.

It begun gettin hot, and day after day it kept a-gettin hotter and drier on top of the ground. We didn't worry any about that as the soil is sandy and crops can stand drouth for a long time and not to say hurt them any. But this time it was different, and after a few days of bright hot sun the weather woke up and decided to do something about things.

Day I'm a-thinkin about the sun come up clear as a whistle but hot as the hinges of tarnation and all. By ten o'clock the cattle had all drifted down the draw and was a-lookin for the shady side of a hill or some place to get away from the heat and flies.

'Bout two in the afternoon I seen the little whirlwinds begin to twist up and go a-tumblin off over the plains, and they kept gettin bigger and bigger. I was right busy and didn't pay the weather any more heed until 'bout five o'clock, and at that I didn't think anything serious was a-brewin. Sure, I noticed a little cloud 'bout as big as a man's hand kinda loafin along the edge of the purairie, but there didn't seem anything unusual about that. But I wish I'd give it more thought, for then we'd-a been better prepared for what come to pass quicker'n I can in reason tell about it.

'Twasn't long till I heard a low rumblin sound way off like, and it kept a-gettin louder and seemed to be comin nearer. And finally it got so loud that I stuck my head out of the door to see what's in the wind anyhow. What I see was enough for me, but it wasn't all I was a-goin to see that day. No siree!

Here was that little old black cloud a-sky-hootin crost the plain like it had to go elsewhere and in less than no-time. It was a-turnin and a-twistin, but it looked so little and waspy that it has always been a wonder to me the things that pesky wind cloud did that day.

It struck right at the corner of my fence, and I'm tellin you it come right down my fence line a-rollin up the posts and the bobwire plumb along one side of my place. And then it struck out to'ds my house, but changed again and went for a shed where as luck would have it I kept my machinery. It blew this shed away and piled up all the machinery in one big contwisted heap that it took me days and days to unscramble. It missed my house by inches, but the funnel-shape tail did get in a swipe at the chimley and turned it half around and blew my prancin pony wind-pointer plumb away.

The next house in line was this here tenderfoot's dugout that was half hole in the ground and half pine boards and 'dobe sod. There wasn't much of it a-stickin up for the wind to tug at, but you won't believe me when I say that that tarnal wind took another twist around that house, dived straight down into the doorway and on into the house, and it sure tore up jack down there. Pots and kettles and pans and tubs and the boxes they was a-usin for chairs come up out of that dugout like they was a-floatin on water 'stead of just being lifted out and up and away by the wind.

The only thing left standin in the whole place was a sugar barrel that they'd been keepin their flour in, and the wind had scooped the flour out of that slick and clean as a whistle.

The next place it struck was 'bout two miles off—a neighbor of Old Dad Thornberg's, and one of these shiftless cusses that cain't think of nothin but goin huntin or a-fishin. It was thirty mile or more to the Beaver, but this onry cuss would dig for fishbait every day, just to aggravate his wife, it looked as if. He'd had more'n his usual run of luck this day and had a good-sized can 'bout full of worms. Well sir—what-a you think that wind done with that can of worms?

It didn't do a thing but empty the can and blow it smack through a windowpane like it had been shot out of a gun. And it blowed them worms right up against the side of his grindstone, and more'n an hour after we found them, heads hanging out on one side of the grindstone and tails hangin out on the other side, and every worm alive and a-wrigglin.

No sir, no, I ain't seen the wind blow like that all my life—not yet anyway. I'm only seventy-nine now, and I'm feelin real peart. Well—so long. Sorry you can't stay and have a snack with me and let me tell you more about these health-bringin, cavortin purairie winds.

The Rawhide Railroad

FOREWORD

THIS is a story of a remarkable steam railroad actually constructed and successfully operated in the beautiful Walla Walla Valley many years ago, on which rawhide, overlaying wooden beams, was used in place of iron or steel rails. This unique road, later modernized, is now operated as part of a large railway. It is doubtful, however, if through the roll of years, the changing managements of the big line have preserved either record or recollection of the once famous rawhide railroad, which was the germ of the present transportation system.

More than a quarter century ago, while in railroad service, it was my good fortune to come in contact with an old Irish section foreman, long since dead, who had been actually employed on the singular railroad. The outlines of the narrative were extracted from him disjointedly and at different times, but the wealth of detail and circumstantial accuracy leaves no doubt of the truth of the story as a whole.

After the catastrophe, which closes the last chapter, the railroad was operated successfully for many years with iron plates fastened on top of the wooden rails.

From *The Rawhide Railroad*, by George Estes, pp. 10, 38–42, 46–48, 49–54. Copyright, 1916, by George Estes. Canby, Oregon: Publishing House of the Clackamas County News.

One Thousand Plug Hats

The question of bringing the locomotives and equipment up the Columbia was one of great moment not unmixed with danger. The red robbers of Wish-ram, if they permitted the locomotives to pass around the rapids at all, would exact enormous tribute, or there would be a great battle which would gradually extend to the neighboring tribes and the result might be the complete annihilation of the whites, who in the whole northwest were at that time greatly outnumbered by the Indians.

When the barges containing the two locomotives, one hundred pairs of car wheels and the thousand plug hats arrived at the rapids of Wish-ram the wisdom of Doc Baker shone out anew. The resplendent breeches of Seekolicks, though with luster now slightly impaired by coatings of salmon scales, still continued to attract the admiring glances of Wish-ram maidens, to the intense disgust of all the other bucks who from necessity were without breeches. This general feeling was, one might say, openly and nakedly displayed without attempt at concealment. Doc Baker had studied this situation from the first and now decided to profit by working with, instead of against, human passions and desires. He called a council of the head villains of Wish-ram and with the astuteness of an oriental peddler in the ancient city of Bagdad, displayed for the first time to the astonished gaze of the assembled robbers the wonders of a dress silk hat, and with consummate cunning bargained at the price of one stove-pipe for each of the doughty warriors of Wish-ram, not only for free passage of the locomotives, but for the combined power of a thousand naked but plug-hatted villians to drag the locomotives around the rapids.

What boots it now that Seekolicks' breeches displayed the glories of a sunset (apologies to the Pacific Monthly)? For influence with an Indian maiden a shiny plug hat will do more than a thousand dollars in stock of the Standard Oil Company, and Seekolicks' breeches fell behind in the mad race of changing fashions along the river.

At last the locomotives and one hundred pairs of car wheels reached Wallula, where Bill Green had built an incline running down to the water in order to bring them up to the roadway.

This he did without difficulty by hitching his great team of forty oxen to each locomotive in turn. It is safe to say that this team of oxen could pull as much as either locomotive, though not so rapidly, perhaps.

When the locomotives were at last on the main line the names "Loco Ladd" and "Loco Blue Mountain" were painted on their cab panels. Thus Doc Baker honored the two greatest objects, to him, in the world. The road was ready for service, the cars having been previously constructed entirely of wood and the car wheels brought from New York had been placed under them.

The chief engineer had conducted all these operations from the saddle of his mule. He galloped back from the leading yoke of the forty-ox team, to where Doc Baker stood near the locomotives, now on the main line, and solemnly announced to his chief that the road was ready for business. Then turning to the train dispatcher, also mounted on a long-legged mule with two big horse pistols hanging low on his hips, the chief engineer formally turned over the completed railroad from the Construction to the Operating Department in these terse terms: "Their your'n. Get to hell out o' here with 'em."

COWCATCHERS

But the most intensely practical side of the train dispatcher was perhaps best illustrated in his conception of the locomotive pilots sometimes called "cowcatchers." When the locomotives first arrived at Wallula the train dispatcher, taking Pat Prunty the source of all railroad wisdom, along with him, proceeded to look them over. He inquired of Prunty the purpose of the "V" shaped combination of slats on the front ends of the locomotives. Prunty explained that these were called "cowcatchers" and were to clear the track of cattle. The train dispatcher remarked that the bunch of corset staves might be serviceable for catching cows in the City of New York, but in the great west cows were harder to catch and more dangerous when caught. His authority in reality being as absolute as the country operator thinks the authority of the average dispatcher is today, he ordered the pilots ripped off the two locomotives and low platforms built in their stead. On each of these platforms he stationed one of his best hunting dogs which he quickly trained, when cattle on the tracks were approached, to leap to the ground and drive them away. The dogs at once grasped the responsibility of their important railroad positions and thirty minutes before departure of each train from their respective terminals at Walla Walla and Wallula, without the service of the caller, they took their positions on their locomotive platforms and, like the great figure heads on the ship prows of the conquering Vikings, they piloted the trains across the Walla Walla Valley faithful to their duties as "cowcatchers" in fact as well as in name.

The Rawhide Railroad, though operating in a cattle country, under the wise direction of Bill Green and Josh Moore paid fewer claims for cattle killed according to its size than any other railroad in the world.

Nor did the two "cowcatchers," "Ponto" and "Thor" ever "bark" on account of their overtime being short on payday. They were watchful of other things besides six o'clock and the pay car.

DESTRUCTION OF THE RAILROAD

Soon it was found that the gnawing movements of the tread and flanges of the locomotive drivers quickly wore off the tops and edges of the wooden rails making it necessary constantly to renew them.

The pioneer of the Pacific coast has one favorite "metal" on which he relies to surmount all difficulties—the renowned rawhide. He who understands it can accomplish wonders with it. But its antics are strange to those from eastern lands, unfamiliar with its peculiar properties.

The pioneers delight to tell of the tenderfoot who did not know how rawhide would stretch when wet and contract when dry. He hitched up his team with rawhide harness in a rain storm, and attached a drag chain to a log, intending to pull it to his cabin for fuel. Driving the team to the cabin, he looked back and saw that the log had not moved, the rain causing the rawhide harness to stretch all the way to the house. Disgusted, he unharnessed the horses and threw the harness over a stump. The sun came out, and contracting the harness, pulled the log up to the house.

Possessed of enormous quantities of this durable material, Doc Baker directed that the wooden rails be "plated" with rawhide from Walla Walla to Wallula. It hardened in the summer sun and made the roadway practically indestructible.

In the rainy season the rawhide became soft and the road could not be operated, but there was no occasion to operate it in the winter time, for the reason that there was no traffic, and when the snow melted in the spring, the sun blazing out over the valley quickly put the rawhide railroad in good condition and ready for train service.

Finally there came a winter of terrible severity on the Pacific coast which was long spoken of as the "hard winter."

In the empire of Walla Walla it did untold damage. The snow fell very deep throughout the land. With the first rains and snows the rawhide railroad ceased operation for the winter, according to its usual custom, as the rawhide had become soft as mush.

Provisions became scarce. Great hardships and suffering were experienced. Cattle raisers were obliged to begin feeding their stock earlier than usual and soon the feed ran short. In desperation they turned the cattle out on the range, which was covered with deep snow. Blizzards swept over the prairie lands and many of the cattle froze to death standing erect, a gruesome sight.

The deer in the Blue Mountains were starved and frozen and the wolves from the fastnesses of the distant Rockies on the east and from icebound Canada on the north swept over the country, devouring the carcasses of the frozen deer and after these were all gone, forced on by famishing hunger, and growing bolder as the winter became more and more severe, they crept out over the great valley of Walla Walla in search of food.

Driven at last in desperation, to sustain their lives, the red-throated, ravening monsters, running in great packs, crowded on and on to the very edge of the village of Walla Walla, searching for carcasses of frozen cattle which they pawed out of the snow and quickly devoured.

The beleaguered village now felt that it was only a question of days, perhaps hours, if the storm did not break, when they would have to fight the oncoming horde of famished fiends to preserve their very lives. And everyone was prepared for the final conflict.

One night, late in midwinter, the blizzard was roaring and howling across the prairie and snow was falling in long slanting sheets, when a tremendous disturbance was made at the door of Doc Baker's home.

Grabbing up a loaded pistol, the doctor ran to the door, fearing the last stand against the wolves was at hand. Opening the door cautiously, he saw outside the two faithful Indians, Sapolil and Seekolicks, seeking admission. They hurled their shivering bodies through the doorway and began in a mixture of English and Chinook, a wild effort to communicate some disastrous intelligence to their friend, Doc Baker.

Their excitement was so great that the only word the doctor could catch in the first rush of their attempt to talk, was "wolves."

Without waiting for more, the doctor called to all the men of the household to arm themselves quickly and prepare for a fight against the coming onslaught of the wolves. Then turning to his sideboard he poured a good big drink of strong whiskey for each of the Indians, now trembling with cold and excitement. This disposed of, he pushed them down by the roaring fire-place and forced them to deliver their message slowly and in a manner that could be understood.

In broken English, interwoven with Chinook, Sapolil finally succeeded in disclosing the terrible information, which ran as follows:

"Railroad—him gonum hell. Damn wolves digum out—eatum all up— Wallula to Walla Walla."

Crumbs

PAUL BUNYAN was all right in his time, but he didn't have the big shots of today to deal with—and he never was able to get rid of the crumbs. It was the Wobblies—and you got to give 'em credit for it—that really done something about the crumbs. That was one of their big fights.

In Bunyan's day the camps was crummy, the bunks was crummy, and the men were so used to being crummy that they wouldn't of knowed what to do without 'em. After the Wobs began to have some say-so on the jobs they begun to holler for clean bedding, and that sort of put the skids under the crumbs—a lot of 'em anyway.

A crumb is what you'd call a louse. They was called "cooties" by the soldiers during the war, but they're the same thing; we always called 'em crumbs. Anyhow, as I was going to say, one time when one of the big shots come out to look things over, he stuck his head in one of the bunk-house doors. Before he could duck back again he heard a bunch of voices yelling at him, "Hello, Brother." It kinda puzzled him. After a while,

---

By Wayne Walden. Manuscripts of the Federal Writers' Project of the Works Progress Administration in New York City.

when he seen that the crumbs were coming to meet him, and was actually calling him their brother, the boss got mad. He figured that that was an insult to his dignity, you see.

"What do you mean by calling me your brother?" he says to them. "Well, we are, ain't we?" they says. "We don't need no interpreter," they says, "we may be a little different looking on the outside, but we got the same souls, ain't we?" they says to him. "We get our living from the same source, don't we?" they says. "It's the blood of the guys you got working for you," they says. "You bleed 'em by day, and we bleed 'em by night," they says, "that makes you and us blood-brothers," they says to the boss.

"Yeah?" says the boss, "well, as you weaken 'em and rob 'em of some of their energy, I'm going to kill you," the boss says to the crumbs.

"All right," says the crumbs, "hop to it; but you'll lose the best ally you got, or ever had."

"How so?" says the boss.

"Well," says the crumbs, "ain't it our gouging into the hides of your slaves that keeps 'em so busy scratching they can't do any thinking? And as long as they can't think," they says, "your slaves won't bother to organize," they says. "They won't demand any improvements," they says. . . .

And, well, by that time, I was kinda tired of listening to their damned propaganda.

Big Frank

TIME was when a man had no trouble at all following the wheat harvest from Texas to the Dakotas and making a few dollars. That was when all wheat was cut with a binder, shocked, stacked sometimes, and then threshed. Farmers needed many hands during the harvesting season. Now combine machines that cut and thresh the grain in one operation are becoming more common every year. Farmers need fewer and fewer hands. One of the migratory hands that used to come up through this part of Nebraska was Frank McDarmit—Big Frank, we called him. He was a bundle-slinger if ever there was one.

The first time I had dealings with Big Frank, he took a hundred dollars from me easy as nothing. I had just finished cutting fifty acres of wheat that I wanted shocked right away. I was afraid a rainy spell of weather might come along and spoil some of the grain. That was the finest field of

By Rudolph Umland. From the Manuscripts of the Federal Writers' Project of the Works Progress Administration for the State of Nebraska.

The material for "Big Frank" was drawn from "tall ones spun in the shade of the racks" by threshers with whom I worked in southeastern Nebraska.—R. U.

wheat I ever raised; the bundles lay scattered three-deep over every inch of stubble. I hired Big Frank in the morning and told him I'd go to town and fetch some other shockers to help him.

Big Frank looked over the field, spat some tobacco juice, and said, "I don't need any help. I can shock that field myself and be finished by sundown."

"You're crazy," I said.

"Maybe I am," he said, "but I can still shock that field myself and be inished by sundown."

"Man, you can't."

"I can."

I looked at him and wondered what institution he'd escaped from.

"I'll bet you fifty dollars I can," he said.

"I'll bet a hundred you can't."

Big Frank spat on his hands, pulled on his gloves, and went to work. I never saw a bundle-slinger move so fast before. In less than an hour, I knew I was going to lose that bet.

Big Frank could shock wheat faster than any two binders could kick out the bundles. He could set up a shock thirty feet away by just tossing the bundles where they belonged. Sometimes he'd pick up eight or ten bundles at once, set them down, and have as pretty a shock as you ever saw. No matter how hard a windstorm blew, Big Frank's shocks kept standing. He could hurl a bundle into the ground so deep that nobody could pull it up. He frequently did this out of pure orneriness to make the threshers cuss when they were gathering the bundles.

He was a one, that Big Frank! He never hired out as a shocker by the day. He always demanded pay by the acre. He wouldn't work in a field where there were other shockers; they got in his way. Why, damn it, he wouldn't even start shocking in a field where the grain wasn't all cut; he'd catch up with the binder in no time and then have to wait.

When Big Frank blew into a community, other hands moved on. They knew there wouldn't be much work left for them. All the farmers wanted to hire Big Frank. He was such a handy man to have around. The women-folk liked him too; that's why there are so many youngsters named Frank in this part of the country. Big Frank had only one bad fault. Summer after summer he made the ensilage spoil in silos. It took the farmers several years before they discovered that Big Frank was to blame for this. Old Sam Bates, my neighbor, rose early one morning and found Big Frank sound asleep at the foot of his silo with a straw in his mouth that had some brown juice on it. Old Sam shook him and shook him but he couldn't get him wakened. Then he sniffed the straw. Corn juice! Big Frank had been boring small holes in the bottom of the silo and sucking out the juice from the ensilage. When he finally woke from his stupor, he was as shamefaced as a schoolboy caught in a bad act. But the next night he did the same thing. He couldn't be broke of the habit. Old Sam Bates was mad at first, then he became curious. After tasting the juice himself, he didn't blame Big Frank any more. In fact he slept at the foot of silos himself. That was during prohibition and fermented corn juice tasted mighty good. All the silos in the neighborhood soon had little holes bored in them.

The first years Big Frank came here, he used to move north as soon as the wheat was all in shock. Then one year he stayed to help thresh. It was a sight to see him load a rack. He heaved entire shocks into the rack and in only a few minutes had bundles piled so high that you had to crane your neck to see the top of the load. Sam Bates and I ran the rig. Old Sam kept the engine running at full speed while I squirted oil in all the cracks and crannies of the separator so the contraption wouldn't take fire. It took only two throws for Big Frank to have his rack unloaded but the separator would still be choking and sputtering and spitting out straw and chaff from that load when Big Frank would be returning with his next. The other bundle-haulers quit as soon as they found that Big Frank didn't need any help. He could haul bundles a mile and keep engine and separator going at full speed all the while himself. He was a bundle-slinger, that fellow!

Sam Bates, Big Frank and I made up a three-man threshing outfit. We went from farm to farm and threshed all the wheat in the county that summer. Our little separator kept twenty wagons busy hauling away the threshed grain to granaries and elevators. The next year we bought a larger separator and kept thirty wagons busy. We threshed out seven Nebraska counties that year and two in South Dakota. Big Frank became better and better all the time. He pitched bundles so fast that our separator couldn't keep up with him. Old Sam and I got our heads together and agreed that something had to be done. We'd have to get a still larger separator. The next year we bought the largest separator on the market. It was a beauty! You probably won't believe me when I tell you, but we kept fifty wagons busy that year hauling away the threshed grain. We threshed out nineteen Nebraska counties and fifteen more in the Dakotas. Big Frank had to work hard to keep up with the separator but he always remained in good humor. As long as there was a silo somewhere near, Big Frank was contented. He would curl up beside it at night, suck corn juice, and get a good sleep. We never threshed in a county that didn't have at least half-a-dozen silos.

Big Frank was a playful fellow. The second year that we had our big separator he managed to find time between loads to play "toss" with the grain-haulers. This was a sport he really enjoyed; you could hear his booming laughter three miles away. He'd pick out the heaviest hauler—usually a fat Bohemian or German weighing over two hundred pounds—take him by the scruff of the neck and throw him to the top of the strawstack. When the stack was fifty feet high, it was something to see that hauler come rolling down, kicking up the straw, his legs and arms flying. He-he-ho! Big Frank would roar. Once Big Frank miscalculated the distance and threw a hauler directly under the blower. Before Sam

Bates could stop the engine the poor fellow had been covered up with so much straw that it took two days to dig him out.

Big Frank got so he wanted more and more time to play "toss." One day he pitched bundles so fast into the separator that he choked it up. That hurt me. I don't know anything that hurts a separator-man's pride more than to have someone do that very thing. Of course I had to clean out the separator and, while I was doing that, Big Frank played "toss." After that, whenever Big Frank felt the urge to play come over him, he'd choke up the separator. Sam Bates and I got our heads together and agreed that something had to be done again.

The next year we bought another separator and engine and operated two rigs side by side. Big Frank drove his rack between the separators and pitched bundles first into the feeder of one, then into the feeder of the other. He had his hands really full now trying to keep up with two separators. No time for monkeyshines! Man alive, but that fellow pitched bundles! Ninety wagons were kept busy hauling away the threshed grain. In only a few weeks we had forty-two counties in Nebraska threshed out. Then we moved north into South Dakota. We threshed out the eastern half of the state and moved west. The wheat became poorer and poorer. Finally we struck a county that had suffered from drouth for several years.

"We'd better not waste our time here," I said. "Let's move north where the wheat's better."

But Big Frank felt sorry for the drouth-stricken farmers. "Let's thresh them out," he said, "and not charge them anything."

Big Frank was tender-hearted all right. He had to work a lot harder here because the wheat shocks were so far apart. At night he had to tramp forty miles sometimes to find a silo. He complained that the juice didn't taste good either. One morning he failed to come home. We searched for him two days and found him lying beside a rickety silo on an abandoned farm. When he got up we hardly recognized him. He had a wild look in his eyes and froth on his lips. He turned and ran as we approached. After running awhile, he doubled up like a ball and rolled faster than anything we had ever seen before.

"He rolls just like a tumbleweed," one of the farmers said.

"What do you fill your silos with hereabouts?" Sam Bates asked.

"Well, since the drouth, we've been filling them with tumbleweeds, locoweeds and prickly pear. We hain't raised no corn for three years."

"Good Lord!" Sam Bates said.

We never saw Big Frank again. The last report we had of him said he was rolling across the prairies of Saskatchewan, Canada.

The Sissy from the Hardscrabble County Rock Quarries

THE men that work in the rock quarries of Hardscrabble County are so tough they crack great big rocks just by spitting on them. The farther you go west in the county the tougher the men get, and the rock quarries are right on the western boundary line. When they set off a blast, those bullies are right out there with ten-year-old white oaks in their hands batting those big boulders around, or else they're playing catch without any gloves.

When they get constipated in the rock quarry camp they never use anything but blasting powder, and they whip their children with barb wire until the kids get to be ten years old and then they thresh their parents.

Strangers almost never travel into the rock quarry country, because no man, woman, beast or child that dared to try it ever returned to tell about it no more than any soul ever fetched back a report from hell.

When the quarrymen leave their camp, everybody but invalids, little children, and cripples take to the hills till danger's past. It's lucky that they usually come in a drove, and you can see their dust for miles away and hear their fearsome blackguarding and whooping for a good hour and a half before they strike the city limits.

Gentlemen, it's no lie nor fairy tale when I tell you that those Hard-scrabble County quarrymen are enough to plague a saint. They use them in the farm villages to scare little children and make them behave, but the grownups are even scareder than the young ones.

One day a lone wolf got right into town before anybody knew he was on the way. He came riding two snapping, snarling panthers, straddling them with a foot on each, and he was lashing them into a lather with a whip made of three six-foot rattlesnakes knotted together.

This fellow was a sight to behold, and everybody knew in a minute that he was a quarryman. He stood a good eight feet without tiptoeing, and not enough fat on him to grease a one-egg skillet. That man was muscled like a draft mule, and he moved around like a bolt of lightning on its holiday.

First thing off he went to the shoe store and bought him a pair of brogans. Then he got a nickel's worth of stout roofing nails from the hardware store and asked for the loan of a hammer. He drove these roofing nails right through the soles and heels of the shoes and put the shoes back on his feet. He wore a size fifteen, broad last.

"That's the way I like it," he said. "It gives you a good grip and all you got to do when your foot itches is to wiggle it around a little.

"I want to get prettied up a little," the quarryman said, and went into

By Jack Conroy. From "Chicago Industrial Folklore." Manuscripts of the Federal Writers' Project of the Works Progress Administration for the State of Illinois.

the barber shop. The barber took the edge off his shears when he tried to cut his hair.

"Ain't you got no tinsmiths in this town?" asked the quarryman. "Get a pair of tinsnips, extra large. And fetch a blowtorch from the plumber's. I ain't had a decent shave for a month of Sundays."

He dropped in the Blue Moon Saloon then and asked for a good stiff drink, talking as polite as chips. The bartender planked down a bottle of his strongest brand of fortyrod. Some of it sloshed over and ate a spot of varnish off the bar the size of a five-dollar bill. The quarryman lost his temper then, and snorted and fumed fit to kill.

"None of that bellywash for me! I'd as soon have a pinky, sticky ice cream sody with a cherry on it."

"What sort of a charge do you crave, stranger?" asked the bartender, his false choppers almost shaking out of his mouth.

"Gimme a prussic acid cocktail with a little sulphuric for a chaser," ordered the quarryman, "and see that you don't go diluting it with no carbolic, neither. What are you, anyway? One of them temperance cranks? You must think I'm a plumb teetotaler!"

The bartender dashed out the back way and hotfooted it to the drug store and got the stuff for the drinks. The quarryman got in a little better humor then, and began passing the time away by spitting on the floor and burning holes right through to the ground underneath.

"Not bad!" he said. "A little weak. Only trouble with this tipple is that it's hell on underwear. Every time you break wind it burns a hole in them."

"I guess you aim to get back to the quarries before nightfall, don't you, stranger?" said the bartender, hoping to God it was so.

"No, no!" answered the quarryman, shaking his head kind of sad. "I don't reckon I'll ever go back."

He grabbed a can of tomatoes off the shelf behind the bar and gulped it down without chewing it open.

"Don't it lay heavy on your stomach, stranger?" asked the bartender, terribly put out that the quarryman wasn't leaving that night.

"Not long," answered the quarryman. "I soon digest the can from around the tomatoes. It's easy. A doorknob is harder, but I can do it easy as pie when I set my head to it."

"You aim to make your home in our little Magic City?" asked the bartender, still hoping he had heard wrong.

"Hell's fire and damnation no, man!" said the quarryman, so riled he bit a foot long chunk out of the mahogany bar and spat it right in the bartender's face. "I wouldn't live here for love nor money. I wouldn't be caught dead here."

"Well, then," said the bartender, getting a little bolder, "why did you leave the quarries?"

"Aw, I didn't *want* to," answered the quarryman. "I had to."

"You had to? Why? Get in a fight or some kind of trouble there?"

"A fight? Are you plumb stark, staring looney, man? Whoever heard of a man getting into trouble over fighting in the Hardscrabble County rock quarries?"

"Why did you have to leave then?"

"Well," said the quarryman, looking like a sheepkilling dog. "They chased me out because they said I was a sissy."

The Demon Bricksetter from Williamson County

A MAN that sets brick in a pavement only needs to have a weak mind, a strong back, and a great big hand with long fingers that will stretch and won't strain easy. It ain't no job for a violin player, you can bet your sweet life. You've got to kneel down on your prayerbones, or stoop over up and down like a little clown on a peanut roaster if your poor old backbone can stand it, and set the bricks three rows at a time. For every other row you set down a half brick to break the joints. Right ahead of you there's a crew smoothin' out the sand bed with a drag, hollerin' "Yo, drag!" all day long and humptediddyin' to keep ahead of the setters. The bricks are piled alongside the street, and a crew of men keep trottin' up to the setters with a pair of tongs holdin' four or five bricks. They ain't overly careful the way they drop the bricks, and if a setter ain't watchful he's liable to have his finger dressed in mournin'.[1] And whilst you're watchin' your fingers, they're apt as not to dump a load on your feet.

Behind the bricksetters there's a tar kettle, with the tar bubblin' hot. They draw it out of a spigot into coal scuttles, and then spread it as thin as possible, like molasses on a slice of bread, over the bricks. Two or three fellows push it into the cracks with long, stiff brushes. Their shoe soles get to be a foot thick from the tar stickin' on 'em. They're like flies on Tanglefoot, and long about the time that evening sun goes down and it's mighty hard to pick 'em up and lay 'em down anyhow, they're hardly able to walk about, let alone do their work.

The bricksetters, though, have the hardest job. There's a sand hard as diamonds that sticks to the bricks closer'n a brother and eats through a rawhide mitt damned nigh as quick as hell could scorch a feather. If you kneel down to save your poor old back, the little grains of sand eat into your prayerbones same as a rat would gnaw a hunk of cheese.

The Wild Man from Williamson County blew into town ridin' a panther broke to saddle and usin' a rattlesnake sportin' seventeen rattles and a

---

Ibid.

The demon bricksetter's place of residence varies with localities. For example, on a Missouri job he was represented as hailing from Harrison, Arkansas.—J. C.

[1] That is, the nails bruised until they turn black or purple.—J. C.

button for a whip. First thing he done he dropped in a bar and called for a nitric acid cocktail with a lysol chaser. When he spat, he melted the copper spittoon till it ran along the floor like a crick when the snows melt in the spring. He throwed two-bits on the bar, and it went plumb through slick as a bullet. His muscles looked like they had been blowed up with a bicycle pump and was about to bust out with a big "pouf." When that man walked, I tell you he shook the earth for miles about and the windows cracked and dishes fell off the shelves. He was that much of a man, and that's the God's truth.

When the Wild Man asked for a job on the paving gang, the boss was glad enough to give it to him. It was sizzlin' hot in July and you could fry a steak to a cinder anywhere on the sidewalk or on a cake of ice, as far as that goes. Three or four of the setters had keeled over and was pantin' in the shade with their tongues hangin' out a foot, like dogs that had been chasin' a spry rabbit for days and days and days.

"I'm a man as is work-brickle," said the Wild Man. "I'm a man as can't say quit. When I lay a-holt, I'm like a turtle, and I don't let loose till it thunders. I'm from Williamson County, and maybe you've heer'd of the men they raise down there where the screech owls roost with the chickens. I'm a rambunctious, ruttin' rookaroo with fourteen tits and holes bored for more."

"Brother," said the foreman, "if it's labor your heart craves for, you got it right here on the premises. Just lay your lily whites on some of them brick, slap 'em down on that there sand, and show me you know how to back up your mouth. The wind blows where I come from, too, but it takes that old willy and some backbone to git by here."

Well, sir, when that Wild Man started in, he jumped up ten feet in the air and cracked his heels together three times before he ever touched the ground, crowin' like a Dominecker rooster on a frosty mornin'. He wouldn't take the buckskin mitts, and the first brick he nailed a-holt of was mashed into a red powder. The sparks flew like Fourth of July. After that he was more careful. The way he dropped them bricks sounded like a terrible, awful hailstorm on a tar roof. The carriers done their best to slow him down, because these pavin' jobs they don't last none too long, nohow. They slammed bricks on his heels and they bounced 'em off his fingers, but he never paid 'em the least teensy bit of mind. Fourteen men was huffin' and puffin' on the sand drag, clippin' along fifteen miles an hour, and then he had to wait for 'em lots of times. While he was waitin' he packed two hundred bricks under each arm back and forth across the street just to keep limbered up. Or sometimes he lay on the flat of his back and juggled ten brick at once with his feet.

Pretty soon he was the only setter left; all the rest was packin' brick to him and fallin' all over one another's feet. They went so fast they'd meet theirselves comin' back. You couldn't get enough men on that street, I tell you, to keep that Wild Man satisfied. He was the doin'est man that ever hit this burg, and that ain't no lie nor whore's dream.

It was time to give up when he taken off his shoes and started in to
layin' 'em with his toes.

What do they feed 'em in Williamson County, for God's sakes?

Well, nothin' but punkins and crick water, they tell me. It's sure a
wonder to nature.

We had aimed to have us a job all winter, but soon that old wind got
to whistlin': "What have you done with your summer's wages?" The
job was finished in three days, and would have been in one if they could
have kept brick and sand on hand.

I tell you, good peoples, if you want to work on ary paving gang,
be sure to ask and inquire if they's a man from Williamson County on
the job or if one has been seen in them parts lately. If there is, or if
he has, don't never bother to start.

What do they raise them on down there in Williamson County, for
God's sakes? Is it wildcat's milk or wild boar's meat that puts that old
willy and double-jointed backbone in 'em?

Well, I can't say as to that, stranger. I heer'd they touch nothin'
but turnip greens and weak well water down there, but it sure is a
curiosity to nature how they get that way. If ary man can tell me,
I'll fetch him one of the finest pretties you ever clapped eyes on.

The Boomer Fireman's Fast Sooner Hound

A BOOMER fireman is never long for any one road. Last year he may
have worked for the Frisco, and this year he's heaving black diamonds
for the Katy or the Wabash. He travels light and travels far and doesn't
let any grass grow under his feet when they get to itching for the greener
pastures on the next road or the next division or maybe to hell and gone
on the other side of the mountains. He doesn't need furniture and he
doesn't need many clothes, and God knows he doesn't need a family or a
dog.

When the Boomer pulled into the roadmaster's office looking for a job,
there was that sooner hound of his loping after him. That hound would
sooner run than eat and he'd sooner eat than fight or do something useful
like catching a rabbit. Not that a rabbit would have any chance if the
sooner really wanted to nail him, but that crazy hound dog didn't like
to do anything but run and he was the fastest thing on four legs.

"I might use you," said the roadmaster. "Can you get a boarding place
for the dog?"

"Oh, he goes along with me," said the Boomer. "I raised him from
a pup just like a mother or father and he ain't never spent a night or a
day or even an hour far away from me. He'd cry like his poor heart would

Ibid.

break and raise such a ruckus nobody couldn't sleep, eat or hear themselves think for miles about."

"Well, I don't see how that would work out," said the roadmaster. "It's against the rules of the road to allow a passenger in the cab, man or beast, or in the caboose and I aim to put you on a freight run so you can't ship him by express. Besides, he'd get the idea you wasn't nowhere about and pester folks out of their wits with his yipping and yowling. You look like a man that could keep a boiler popping off on an uphill grade, but I just don't see how we could work it if the hound won't listen to reason while you're on your runs."

"Why, he ain't no trouble," said the Boomer. "He just runs alongside, and when I'm on a freight run he chases around a little in the fields to pass the time away."

> "That may be so, I do not know;
> It sounds so awful queer.
> I don't dispute your word at all,
> But don't spread that bull in here,"

sang the roadmaster.

"He'll do it without half trying," said the Boomer. "It's a little bit tiresome on him having to travel at such a slow gait, but that sooner would do anything to stay close by me, he loves me that much."

"Go spread that on the grass to make it green," said the roadmaster.

"I'll lay my first paycheck against a fin [1] that he'll be fresh as a daisy and his tongue behind his teeth when we pull into the junction. He'll run around the station a hundred times or so to limber up."

"It's a bet," said the roadmaster.

On the first run the sooner moved in what was a slow walk for him. He kept looking up into the cab where the Boomer was shoveling in the coal.

"He looks worried," said the Boomer. "He thinks the hog law [2] is going to catch us, we're making such bad time."

The roadmaster was so sore at losing the bet that he transferred the Boomer to a local passenger run and doubled the stakes. The sooner speeded up to a slow trot, but he had to kill a lot of time, at that, not to get too far ahead of the engine.

Then the roadmaster got mad enough to bite off a drawbar. People got to watching the sooner trotting alongside the train and began thinking it must be a mighty slow road. Passengers might just as well walk; they'd get there just as fast. And if you shipped a yearling calf to market, it'd be a bologna bull before it reached the stockyards. Of course, the trains were keeping up their schedules the same as usual, but that's the way it looked to people who saw a no-good mangy sooner hound beating all the

---

[1] Five dollar bill.—J. C.
[2] Rule forbidding excessive over time.—J. C.

trains without his tongue hanging out an inch or letting out the least little pant.

It was giving the road a black eye, all right. The roadmaster would have fired the Boomer and told him to hit the grit with his sooner and never come back again, but he was stubborn from the word go and hated worse than anything to own up he was licked.

"I'll fix that sooner," said the roadmaster. "I'll slap the Boomer into the cab of the Cannon Ball, and if anything on four legs can keep up with the fastest thing on wheels I'd admire to see it. That sooner'll be left so far behind it'll take nine dollars to send him a post card."

The word got around that the sooner was going to try to keep up with the Cannon Ball. Farmers left off plowing, hitched up, and drove to the right of way to see the sight. It was like a circus day or the county fair. The schools all dismissed the pupils, and not a factory could keep enough men to make a wheel turn.

The roadmaster got right in the cab so that the Boomer couldn't soldier on the job to let the sooner keep up. A clear track for a hundred miles was ordered for the Cannon Ball, and all the switches were spiked down till after that streak of lightning had passed. It took three men to see the Cannon Ball on that run: one to say, "There she comes," one to say, "There she is," and another to say, "There she goes." You couldn't see a thing for steam, cinders and smoke, and the rails sang like a violin for a half hour after she'd passed into the next county.

Every valve was popping off and the wheels three feet in the air above the roadbed. The Boomer was so sure the sooner would keep up that he didn't stint the elbow grease; he wore the hinges off the fire door and fifteen pounds of him melted and ran right down into his shoes. He had his shovel whetted to a nub.

The roadmaster stuck his head out of the cab window, and—whosh!— off went his hat and almost his head. The suction like to have jerked his arms from their sockets as he nailed a-hold of the window seat.

It was all he could do to see, and gravel pinged against his goggles like hailstones, but he let out a whoop of joy.

"THE SOONER! THE SOONER!" he yelled. "He's gone! He's gone for true! Ain't *nowhere* in sight!"

"I can't understand that," hollered the Boomer. "He ain't *never* laid down on me yet. It just ain't like him to lay down on me. Leave me take a peek."

He dropped his shovel and poked out his head. Then he whooped even louder than the roadmaster had.

"He's true blue as they come!" the Boomer yelled. "Got the interests of the company at heart, too. He's still with us."

"Where do you get that stuff?" asked the roadmaster. "I don't see him nowhere. I can't see hide nor hair of him."

"We're going so fast half the journal boxes are on fire and melting the axles like hot butter," said the Boomer. "The sooner's running up and down the train hoisting a leg above the boxes. He's doing his level best to put out some of the fires. That dog is true blue as they come and he's the fastest thing on four legs, but he's only using three of them now."

Greedy-Gut Gus, the Car Toad

THERE'S nobody better at hogging and cheating than a piece-working car toad when he's cut from a selfish pattern. He'd steal the pennies off his poor old dead grandmother's eyes or acorns from a blind sow if it'd put a deemer [1] extra on his time slip at whistling time. He sashays around the livelong day like a blind dog in a meatshop, hollering for lumber jacks and bolt house boys. And if he leaves his box car for one minute, some creeper may come sneaking up and cabbage [2] onto castings or nails or bolts or siding or flooring or sills or drawbars or coupling springs he needs for his own job.

Car toads have lungs like glassblowers. They come by that bellowing like a bull natural; they shake the slats over their cradles with their bass voices before their navel cords are clipped loose. It's worth traveling miles and paying a pretty price to see and hear those leather-lunged rascals standing by their cars and yelling from one end of the yards to the other:

> "Lumber jack! Double track!
> Oughta been here and half way back!"

"That lumber jack wasn't hardly out of his didies when he started out after my roofing, but he'll have a beard long enough to play Sandy Claus with before he gets back."

"You have to drive a stake in the ground to see whether he's moving at all or not."

"Every time he takes one step forward he slips back two. I wish to God he'd turn around and start this way so's he'd get there hindside before."

"He's too slow to catch a cold. He's slower 'n molasses in January."

Boys, I'm here to say and state that that piece-working merry-go-round will make a man slap his own dear baby brother square in the mouth and pick his pockets or steal his sugartitty when he ain't looking. It's a dog eat dog and the devil take the hindmost. A man had better get him a tin bill and pick horse apples with the chickens. He'd better let somebody punch out his eyes and get him some blue glasses and a cup and a sign "Please Help the Blind" and sit on a corner the rest of his natural days.

"Come on, Sleepin' Jesus! Come and see me! Come and see me! I miss you so and it's been, oh, so long since we said goodbye."

Ibid.
[1] Dime.—J. C.
[2] Seize, or take possession of.—J. C.

That's the way a piece-working car toad has to holler at the lumber hustlers all day long if he wants to keep sow tits and hominy on the table and the seat in his pants.

Greedy-Gut Gus was born a twin, but he soon rooted the other one away till it died of starvation before it had a chance to cut a tooth. The old man got tired of Gus eating him out of house and home, so he put him out in a pen with the hogs. Gentlemen, ladies, and little children, I'm here to swear on oath that it wasn't a month until Gus was fat as a butterball, but every pig that had the misfortune to be in that pen with him was so gaunt he had to lean twice to make a shadow.

If there ever was a born piece-working car toad, it was Gus. He could holler louder and sneak more than any other man in the yards. It got so the other car toads had to chain down everything loose about their cars when they left at night. They didn't dare go away for lunch, because by the time they came back Gus would have packed off everything but the rails the car had stood on.

Gus learned how to skimp his work, too. This can be done by putting a whole side on a car with only one nail holding all the boards or by not tightening nuts on drawbar bolts or leaving the nuts off altogether. You can leave an old journal brass in the journal box and put fresh dope around it and get paid for putting in a new one. Of course, it may run a hot box and throw the truck off the rails and play glory hallelujah with a whole train and send the crew to kingdom come, but Gus never bothered his head about that. Just so he was smart enough to make the inspectors believe he was doing the work right.

A man can't do wrong and get by for always. A dog never run so fast that his tail didn't follow close behind. There came a time when Greedy Gus was in too much of a hurry to go after a good jack and in too much of a hurry to put tripods under the car after he had jacked it up with a condemned jack that always slipped its cogs when the weight on it was too much. The jack slipped, the car came down—boom!, and splat! went Gus. It was the end of Greedy-Gut Gus's piece-working on this earth.

When the devil saw Greedy-Gut Gus coming in with his tool box, he said: "You're just the man I need to keep my Central of Hell Railroad rolling stock in tiptop shape. I'll make you king of all the car toads in hell. No piece-work here, though. You may not like that, being born and raised to it, and you won't get retired on a pension, either. You're signed up for me from now on."

Well, friends, it went all right for a few million years. Gus was supposed to keep in good shape all the coal cars on the line running from the coal mines to the fiery furnaces that run three shifts a day to keep the temperature at frying heat.

Then Gus's old piece-working habits got the best of him, and he started to skimping and robbing Peter to pay Paul. He'd take castings and wheels off one car and put them on another. He did his nailing and bolting so slipshod that the cars got to falling to pieces all along the right of way and the shovelers were leaning on their shovels and the fires smouldering low. The first cool breeze in seventeen hundred and eighty-nine trillion centuries sprang up in the southeast corner of the northeast section of hell and started blowing pretty strong on the graying cinders. It worried the devil half crazy. You can't have a first-class hell without plenty of heat.

Greedy-Gut Gus got his time. He isn't going to be a car toad for all eternity after all. The devil just couldn't put up with a man that has been spoiled by the piece-work system. Pretty soon a car toad who had been a day worker turned in his checks on the Baltimore and Ohio, and he was too wicked a man for any place but down below. He's a man that always took his time, being a day worker, and, taking his time, he does a good job of it. He'll hold the job from now on and the fires will roar and burn while Gus shovels in that coal forevermore.

"Snake" Magee and the Rotary Boiler

I HEAR it spread around in some fields that the reason a rotary rig uses four boilers while cable tools only use one is because a rotary got so much more work to do, all of which is a fundamental lie. It taken four boilers for a rotary, because none of them is any good, as to which no man in the country is in better shape to testify than I am.

I only work with one rotary boiler in my time. It was not a rotary rig otherwise—just good old cable-tools—and I would not have working with it if I known what it was. The first intimation I got that anything was

---

By Jim Thompson. From Manuscripts of the Federal Writers' Project of the Works Progress Administration for the State of Oklahoma.

Drillers from West Virginia are commonly called "snakes." The best cable-tool men in the world came from this State where, it is said, the drilling formations were so hard that no one but a snake could get through them.

The average boiler is set to pop off at one hundred pounds. Any pressure above that is dangerous and is released through the safety valve.

In exceedingly soft structure it might be possible to drill two hundred feet a day with cable-tools, but one hundred feet would be a pretty good day's work, and both tool dresser and driller would have plenty to do.

The feud between cable-tool men and rotary workers was at one time very real. Many cable-tool men, whose fathers and grandfathers had spent their lives in the trade, preferred learning some other work rather than have anything to do with the despised rotary. The rotary machine now is, of course, almost the only kind used, while cable tools, once so predominant that they were called standard, have almost disappeared.

The ignorance of the laws of elementary science as depicted in this story is a libel which cable-tool men humorously assumed. Actually, a group better schooled in practical engineering would be hard to find. I accompanied one cable-tool driller to an abandoned well where a drilling bit had been lost at the bottom of a 1,600 foot hole. He ran his fishing tools into the hole once, brought them out and made some seemingly casual adjustment. On the second run the tools closed tightly over the top of the bit and lifted it up through 1,000 feet of salt water and silt to the derrick floor.

I have heard this story, with variations, from a number of cable-tool men in West Texas and Oklahoma.—J. T.

wrong was with the safety valve. You taken a good cable-tool boiler and hang a six-inch bit on the safety valve, and you got a head a steam that pulls a mile of hole right up on top of the ground and pulls the derrick right down where the hole used to be. But this rotary boiler—I didn't know that was what it was—didn't react properly. I hang a six-inch bit on the safety, and she goes to jumping up and down, like a walking-beam on soft structure. And I hang a Stillson wrench, a sledge hammer, and a short piece of fifteen-inch pipe on the safety, and the results was alarming. The pressure gauge only showed three hundred and eighty pounds to the square inch, but them boiler plates begin to wiggle and squirm like mustard plasters on a itchy back, and the whole thing begin to jiggle like a little boy when the teacher can't see his hand.

We only making about fourteen hundred feet of hole a day, so my tool dresser been staying in town until I need him. But I work with tricky boilers before and need no help. I do not even need to put the fire out. It was a secret of mine, but I will tell it to you in case you should need to fix a boiler when the fire is going.

Take and jump into the slush-pit where the mud is fresh and damp. Then, before the mud getting hard, think of something that throws you into a cold sweat. The cold cause your body to contract, and the first thing you know there is a wall of perspiration between your body and the mud. This keeps the mud pliable and easy to work in, like a big glove, and the sweat keeps you from scorching, when you step into the fire-box.

How do you keep from breathing the flame? Well, I will tell you another secret. Most people taken breath from the outside and breathe in; when you are working in the fire, you taken a breath from the inside and breathe out. You can do this, when you know how, because the body is ninety-nine per cent water, and water is nothing but h-two-o. Besides, water purifies itself every fifteen feet and all you got to do is keep moving and you always got a fresh supply of air.

I leave the rig to run itself because we are not making more than nineteen hundred feet of hole a day, and there is really not nah-thing to do. Then, I take a Stillson, a ball-peen hammer, a acetyline torch, and a new set of flues and go out and climb into the fire-box.

Right away, I says to myself, "Magee," I says, "this boiler is uncommonly frail. I would almost suspect it of being a rotary boiler. We have only four hundred and thirty-six pounds of steam and the heat indicator only shown eleven hundred and ninety-nine degrees Fahrenheit, but there is every evidence of inferior materials. Something must be done with expediency."

I see there is no use putting new flues in the old can, because the plates have begin to melt and will not hold a flue, so I think rapidly. If I have had my sky-hooks there, I would have flipped the boiler over so the pressure is against the bottom instead of the top, but I loan them out that very morning. I finally see the boiler will have to be reversed, so that the outside of the plates, which is cool, will be turned in. This is just like turning a coat wrongside out, and I have done it many times. But just as I am pulling the smokestack down through the fire-box this rotary boiler explodes.

When I wake up I think I am in jail, like I have sometimes seen pictures of men of, because there is bars all around me. But then there is nahthing beneath my feet or over my head and I am sailing through the air at a terrific speed, and I remember what happen. "Magee," I says, "these are the grates that are wrapped around you, and you are in the air because the boiler blown up." I worry somewhat because I am a law-abiding citizen and do not have a license to fly, but then I begin to see that I am slightly hurt. The mud protecting me some, but I have six broken ribs, a fractured back, concussion of the brain, a ruptured appendix, a busted nose, both arms and legs broken in from three to twelve places, and a slight headache.

"Magee," I says, "you have excellent grounds for a damage suit against the rotary manufacturing company. When you are through collecting there will be no more rotaries and wells will be drilt with cable-tools as God originally intended."

I do not think anything very long, of course, because I am traveling somewhat faster than light which is forty-four thousand foot pounds per second, and before I know it I am back in town sixteen miles away and dropping down in front of our boarding house.

I holler for my tool-dresser, Haywire Haynes, who is still sleeping, to come out, and he does so swiftly.

"Are you hurt, Magee?" he asks.

"Only slightly," I says. "I doubt if I will be incapacitated for more than thirty or forty years. But I am going to sue the rotary manufacturing company for every cent they are worth. When I am through there will not be a rotary left on the face of the earth."

He shaken his head. "You can't do that, Magee. You been blown back here so fast you arrived before you got started. You can't sue for being injured because you ain't been to work yet this morning."

I thought a moment and seen he was right. "If that's the case," I says, "I may as well get well, right now."

Hank, the Free Wheeler

HANK LORD was a man that wanted everything on wheels and moving about long before he owned an automobile factory. When he was still in his didies, he yelped till his poor old dad had to rollerskate the floor with him instead of walking to and fro like it's always proper for dads to do.

By Nelson Algren. From "Chicago Industrial Folklore." Manuscripts of the Federal Writers' Project of the Works Progress Administration for the State of Illinois.

He fetched his lunch to the little red school house in a little red wagon and tried to make the cows learn to ride a bicycle so's they'd make better time from the pasture when he called them up for milking. He traveled that fast he wore goggles around the barnyard before anybody ever heard of an automobile, and was called Speedrow in five states and twenty counties when the Indianapolis racing track was still a hayfield, a frogpuddle, and a couple of turnip patches. He was speed on wheels; he knew good and well that wheels make the world go round and get the job done and done right and for keeps while you would be scratching your head and thinking of it any other way.

When he started his automobile factory, a man could have roamed it from front to back and from ceiling to floor without seeing more than a few trucks and barrows and such like on wheels. In them days a bunch of men got around in a ring and pretty soon here come one with a part of the frame and laid it down on the floor and another one soon follows suit until they got enough to start out on. Then they started reaming and trueing and whamming and bamming and sledging and boring and bolting until it looked like a thing that might take a snifter of gasoline and go skedaddling down the pike to a faretheewell.

I tell you, boys, when you put in a wheel here and a roller there and a belt in the other place, it ain't long till you got to be hell on wheels and no brakes, and it was goodbye crapping a smoke or drinking a rest. If you had to hold up two fingers like a kid being excused in school, you'd meet yourself coming back or they'd know the reason why. You had to pick 'em up and lay 'em down right there at your post and make believe you liked it or ask them to pull your card. You would just walk outside talking to yourself if you couldn't stand the gaff.

Hank decided that iron was too high and lasted too long so he got to scouring the back alleys for every tin can he could lay his hands on and made flivvers out of them. As long as they held together long enough to get off the belt and outside the gates he never worried his mind but hollered: "More tin! More wheels! Roll 'em, boys, roll 'em!"

I told 'em what would come to pass, and it will yet. It will yet as sure as God made little apples. Two men will run the whole shooting-match. Number one will just politely dump a load of cans on a great big steel block, and—bing! flash! bing! bang! squeak! just like that, down'll come a million-ton die and when it raises they'll be a new black flivver ready to be driven away by number two or maybe even a radio, for chrissakes. Maybe one man would do the whole job and mow the old man's lawn when he's got nothing to do but just fool around and keep busy.

This will come to pass, good peoples, as sure as you're born, and plenty of men already without a hair on their heads or a tooth in it will live to see that day. It's been inching along ever since Hank found his first wheel and put it on a wagon and when he found out that anything round will roll and speed up work and take the beans and bacon right out of a man's jaws because he ain't needed no more.

It got so you couldn't throw a pork-and-beans can in the alley that it wasn't picked up and hustled right along to Hank's factory. The little children on street corners and in vacant lots began to sing:

> "There was an old man, he had a wooden leg,
> He had no auto nor no auto could he beg.
> He got two spools and an old tin can;
> He made him a flivver and the darned thing ran!"

A man's got wheels same as a factory, and no matter how much you pour the old oil to them, they wear out. You can get your two-thousand-dollar-an-ounce oil and it'll keep them bearings rolling a little longer than 3-in-1 or two-bit cylinder oil, but there's nothing lasts forever, not even the bearings of a man like Hank Lord.

Hank's bearings began to wear out. Old age sprinkles the worst kind of emery dust in a man's bearings, and even if you take some of them out and put in a diamond-studded one, it's going to feel that wear and tear and get lopsided and go to jumping and gum up the works.

There was ten thousand doctors with half a million shots in the arm shaking their heads mournful around Hank's five-hundred-room house when he turned in his checks to the tool crib. Fifty thousand nurses couldn't do a thing but cry a little and say: "He was a good man for the shape he was in. It's a shame he's gone."

They sent his coffin down the assembly line, and its gold plate and diamonds shone so that it hurt a man's eyes to look at it, leave alone lay a hand on it. Everybody had on his white gloves and a white suit and the coffin went slow out of respect for the dead. A man had plenty of time to put in the bolts and screws and tighten the handles.

Hank might have been dead, but there's too far you can go with the dead. Six pallbearers all drawing a six-dollar-day minimum started pacing respectfully to the hearse with the coffin. It was too much, boys, even for the dead, even for a man that's earned his last long rest away from the wheels and the belts and the conveyers and the tin that rusts so easy when the enamel cracks off it as enamel will in spite of you.

The pallbearers almost dropped the coffin when Hank reared up and smashed the glass and yelled:

"WHAT THE HELL IS THIS? YOU CALL THIS EFFICIENCY? PUT THIS THING ON WHEELS! LAY FIVE OF THESE BIRDS OFF, AND CUT THE OTHER ONE'S WAGES 'CAUSE THE WORK IS EASY AND THE HOURS AIN'T LONG AND THE PACE IS SLOW!"

Sven, the Hundred Proof Irishman

OLD Gallagher polished his bald head. "It's too bad," he says to himself. "Every son of the Old Sod I hire turns out to be a booze-histing floater. And what work they do ain't much good. But I can't help liking the lads from the land of me dear old Mother."

Old Gallagher scratched and sighed.

"What I ought to do is hire me a Swede," he says. "They turn out good work and they're steady. But I don't like the daggone lunkheads! They just naturally rub me the wrong way. Still, it's a cinch I got to get somebody. I need another blower bad."

Next morning a floater came in the plant.

"What kin ye blow?" says old Gallagher.

"Anything you want, from pints to five gallons," says the floater.

"What's your name?" says the old man.

"Shaemas O'Toole," says the floater. "Burprrrp!"

"O.K.," says the old man, "get on out to the five-gallon tank before your breath makes me drunk."

Shaemas staggered on back in the plant. Next morning he drew his day's pay to pay board and never showed up again.

The old man roared.

"Out drunk again, the bottle-busting boozer! He never had got good and sober, even. Two five-gallon jugs he made. Two! Two for eleven bucks!"

In a few days in came number two floater. The old man looked at him hard.

"What kin ye blow?" says he.

"Anyshing from pintsh to five gallonsh," says number two.

"Good, ain't you?" says the old man. "How about window glass?"

"Shure, all winnow glash you want," says number two.

"I bet," says the old man. "What's your name?"

"Patrick Michael Shulliwan," says number two.

"All right. Get on back and make one gallons if you can walk that far. Say, ye ain't drunk, are ye?"

"Never toush drop shtuff," says Sullivan, reeling out.

He lasted a week and drew full pay. Fifty-five dollars.

"Never see him again," says the old man.

He didn't.

So a few days later Sven Murphy came in. Old Gallagher glared at him fierce.

"What kin ye blow best, boy?"

"Anything from pints to five gallons," says Sven. "Or window glass if you want it."

By Edward Miller. From the Manuscripts of the Federal Writers' Project of the Works Progress Administration for the State of Tennessee.

The old man let out a roar.

"Anything, huh? I bet! How much do ye weigh, boy?"

"Ninety-one pounds and six ounces," says Sven, "with my shoes on."

"Been drinking, ain't you?" says the old man.

"Sure," says Sven, "I just had breakfast."

The old man hit the ceiling.

"Git out!" he howls. "Another dog hair! I just been stung by two in a row and not another one will I hire! No dog hair! No floater! No booze-hister! Git out!"

"I ain't no dog hair at all," says Sven, never batting an eyebrow. "I ain't no floater. My name is Sven Murphy and I just got to this country from Ireland. I ain't no booze-hister. I just drink for my health. Just a few quarts a day to keep my nerves steady. On Saturday maybe a few gallons more so I can sort of feel it."

"From Ireland, huh?" says the old man, very nice now. "Sven Murphy, ye say? What kind of a name is that? Are ye Irish or not?"

"My father was Irish, my mother was Swedish," says Sven.

"Swede huh?" Old Gallagher frowned. "But your father was Irish? Go on back and make pint bottles, boy. I'm afraid ye couldn't handle fifteen pounds of glass and you only weighing ninety. Fifteen ounces is nearer your size."

"Ninety-one pounds and six ounces with my shoes on," says Sven, starting back to the tanks. "But I'll make pint bottles if you say so. Thank you kindly."

The old man took an interest in Sven. That evening when Sven was leaving he stopped him.

"How did they go today, boy?" he says.

"Just so-so," says Sven. "Not so good. But I'll do better tomorrow."

"How many pints did ye make today?"

"Three hundred dozen," says Sven. "But I'll do better tomorrow."

The old man swallowed three times. Then he went back to the tanks. The foreman was there.

"Flaherty," says the old man, "how many pints did the new man make today?"

"Three hundred dozen," says Flaherty. "And he knocked off twice to go out for a drink. The glass-blowingest fool I ever seen."

"Praise the saints!" says old Gallagher. "Maybe he's the man I've been needing. An Irishman that works like a Swede! Put him on quarts tomorrow."

Next evening he stopped Sven again.

"Well, how many quarts did ye make, me boy?"

"Not many," says Sven. "Two hundred and sixty dozen. But I'll do better tomorrow."

"Put him on gallon jugs tomorrow," old Gallagher says to the foreman. "He's a glass-blowing fool, all right. Now if he just sticks with me."

Next day Sven made a hundred dozen gallons.

"But I'll do better tomorrow," he says.

"Make five-gallon jugs tomorrow," says the old man.

Next day he went out to watch Sven work.

Sven stood by the five-gallon tank. The gathering boy gathered fifteen pounds of glass on the end of a pipe and gave it to Sven.

Sven took the pipe and blew. He swung it right. He swung it left. He clamped it into the mould and blew.

Sven broke the pipe loose and gave it back to the gathering boy.

The finisher put a rim on the jug.

The gathering boy handed Sven his pipe. Sven swung it right. He swung it left. He clamped it into the mould and blew.

Another five-gallon jug.

Old Gallagher's mouth hung open.

"Boy, ye're a glass-blowing fool!" he says. "How do ye do it so easy?"

"My wind is good and my nerves are steady," says Sven. He grabbed the pipe and swung it right. "But I'm not going so good today." He swung it left. "I'll do better tomorrow." He clamped it into the mould and blew.

The old man roared. "Ye're a glass-blowing fool!" he says. "Make window glass tomorrow. I want to see that."

Next day the whole crew stood around to see Sven Murphy blow window glass.

The gathering boy handed Sven his pipe. Ninety pounds of glass on the end. Sven swung it as easy as a mother swings her baby. Ninety pounds of glass on one end and ninety pounds of man on the other. He swung it right and left in the trench. He drew such a breath you could feel the draft and blew like Hell's own bellows.

Then he swung it up and they caught it and broke it off the pipe. A six-foot cylinder of glass, two feet through and shining like silver. They carted it off to split it and melt it down flat in the oven.

Sven grabbed his pipe and swung it.

"Praise the saints!" says old Gallagher. "Boy, ye're a glass-blowing fool! No Irish, no Swede nor no human could blow glass like you can. Ye must be a son of the devil!"

"I'll do better next week," says Sven, breaking the pipe loose again.

That was the end of the week.

Monday morning old Gallagher went to the plant feeling fine. All his troubles were over. He was humming: "Sure, I love the dear silver that shines de da dum; and de dum da, de dum—"

He opened the door to his office.

Sounded like the roof fell in. Old Gallagher swallowed his upper plate.

Sounded like a riot back in the plant. Glass breaking and people yelling at the tops of their voices.

Old Gallagher was fat but he moved fast. He took the other end of the plant in no time.

He busted in the door to the tank and storage room. The place was a wreck. The floor was covered with broken jugs, bottles and window glass. Men were lying around in the mess, some bleeding from cuts, some with big lumps on their heads. Gallagher was just in time to see Sven Murphy smash a five-gallon jug to the floor and Flaherty bend a blower's pipe over young Murphy's head. Murphy went down in a heap.

"Flaherty! Flaherty!" says the old man, running up. "Name of the saints! What's the matter?"

Flaherty was panting and blowing.

"This crazy fool," he says. "When we got here this morning he was here busting all the glassware he had made. Every last piece he had made last week. He just then busted the last jug. We tried to stop him but he couldn't be stopped. He laid out every man in the plant but me and went right on with his busting."

Sven Murphy stirred a little. Old Gallagher bent over and shook him.

"Murphy!" he says. "Murphy! It's old Tom Gallagher, boy. Name of the saints, what's the matter? Have ye gone plumb looney, boy?"

Sven opened his mouth a little.

"Alla men," he mumbles, "alla lil green men."

"What men, boy?" says old Gallagher, propping him up in his arms. "What men are ye speaking of?"

"Alla lil green men," says Sven, "inna bottlesh I made lash week. Got to worrying 'bout 'em Shaturday night. Been in here all lash night bushting bottlesh to let 'em out."

Slappy Hooper, World's Biggest, Fastest, and Bestest Sign Painter

SLAPPY HOOPER wasn't big because he was six foot nine and wide between the eyes, no more than he weighed three hundred pounds without his cap on or his bucket in one hand and his brush in the other. It was just that there wasn't no job any too big for Slappy, and he never wanted a helper to mess around with.

Even when he was painting a high stack, he didn't want any rube staggering and stumbling around the lines to his bosun's chair. He knew too well that lots of times a helper can be more trouble than he's worth. He'll yawn and gape around or send up the wrong color or the wrong

By Jack Conroy. From "Chicago Industrial Folklore." Manuscripts of the Federal Writers' Project of the Works Progress Administration for the State of Illinois.

I have no idea how general the legend of Slappy Hooper is among sign painters, since I have not encountered so very many of these craftsmen. There were quite a number of the incidents telling the results of Slappy's realism on billboards, and I have chosen only two representative ones.

The attitude of the craftsman toward the helper is characteristic of most occupations.—J. C.

brush, or he'll throw rocks at birds, or he'll make goo-goo eyes at dames passing by. Like as not, he'll foul the lines or pull the wrong one and send you butt over appetite to kingdom come.

At any rate, a helper keeps a man uneasy, and when a man's uneasy he ain't doing his best work. They ought to make it a penitentiary act for a helper "gapering, mopering, and attempting to gawk." Slappy said his life was too short to take a helper to raise up. He could let himself up and down as fast as a monkey could skin up a cocoanut tree or a cat lick its hind leg with its leg up and its tongue out. Anything Slappy wanted on the ground he could lasso with his special long and tough rawhide lariat and pull it up to where he was working.

Slappy done some big jobs in his day, and he done them right and fast. He says if there ever was a crime against nature it's this way they got here of late of blowing paint on with a spray gun like you was slaying cockroaches or bedbugs or pacifying a cow to keep the flies off her until she can get milked. Slappy liked to splash it on with a good old eight-inch brush, and he never was known to leave a brush lap or a hair on the surface when the job was finished. Slapping it on up and down or slapping it on crossways or anti-goggling [1] you couldn't tell the difference. It was all of a solid sheet.

With all these new inventions like smoke-writing from airplanes and painting signs from a pounce [2] (even pictures they do that way), it's hard to appreciate an old-timer like Slappy.

He used to get jobs of lettering advertising on the sky, and it didn't fade away in a minute like smoke that pours out of a plane and gets torn to pieces by the wind before you can hardly spell out what it says. It was all pretty and fancy colors, too; any shade a man's heart could wish for, and it'd stay right there for days if the weather was fair. Of course, birds would fly through it, and when it'd rain the colors would all run together and when the clouds rolled by, there'd be what folks got to calling a rainbow. It really was nothing but Slappy Hooper's sky-writing all jumbled together. It seems that no man, woman, child or beast, alive or dead, was ever able to invent waterproof sky paint. If it could have been done, Slappy would have done it.

His biggest job was for the Union Pacific Railroad, and stretched from one end of the line to the other. The only way you could read it all was to get on a through train and look out of the window and up at the sky all the time. Everybody got stiff necks, of course, so Slappy had the bright idea of getting Sloan's Liniment to pay him for a big sign right at the end of the Union Pacific sign.

Nobody ever did understand how Slappy managed to do the sky paint-

---

[1] Slantwise, or crooked.—J. C.

[2] Perforated outline or stencil for painters unable to do freehand work efficiently. Derived from the bag of chalk, or pounce, used to pat the stencil onto the billboard or sign. Sometimes the outline is transferred by blowing powdered chalk against the pounce.—J. C.

ing. He'd have been a chump to tell anybody. He always used to say when people asked him: "That's for me to know and you to find out," or, "If I told you that, you'd know as much as I do."

The only thing people was sure of was that he used sky hooks to hold up the scaffold. He used a long scaffold instead of the bosun's chair he used when he was painting smokestacks or church steeples. When he started in to fasten his skyhooks, he'd rent a thousand acre field and rope it off with barbed wire charged with electricity. He never let a living soul inside, but you could hear booming sounds like war times and some folks figured he was firing his skyhooks out of a cannon and that they fastened on a cloud or some place too high for mortal eyes to see or mortal minds to know about. Anyways, after a while—if you took a spy glass— you could see Slappy's long scaffold raising up, up, up in the air and Slappy about as big as a spider squatting on it.

But that played out, somehow. It wasn't that people didn't like his skypainting any more, but the airplanes got to buzzing around as thick as flies around a molasses barrel and they was always fouling or cutting Slappy's lines, and he was always afraid one would run smack into him and dump over his scaffold and spill his paint if nothing worse. Besides, he said, if advertisers was dumb enough to let a farting airplane take the place of an artist, the more he'd fool them, and it wasn't no skin off his behind. He could always wangle three squares a day and a pad at night by putting signs on windows for shopkeepers if he had to. If I can stay off public works,[1] I'll be satisfied, he thought to himself.

So Slappy said to hell with the *big* jobs. I'll just start painting smaller signs, but I'll make them so *real* and true to life that I can still be the fastest and bestest sign painter in the world, if I ain't the biggest any more. It's pure foolishness for a man to try to match himself against an airplane at making *big* signs.

He knew he could do it with one hand tied behind and both eyes punched out. Some sign painters couldn't dot the letter "i" without a pounce to go by. It was enough to make a dog laugh to see some poor scissorsbills wrastling around with a pounce, covered all over with chalk wet by sweat until they looked like a plaster of Paris statue.

Then, like as not, they'd get a pounce too small for the wall or billboard they was working on. When it was all on there was a lot of blank space left over. The boss'd yell: "Well, well, Bright Eyes! Guess the only thing to do is fetch a letter stretcher!" If the pounce happened to be too big, it was every bit as bad. "A fine job, Michael Angelo," the boss'd holler, "except you'll have to mix the paint with alum so's it'll shrink enough that we can squeeze it in with a crowbar."

One of Slappy's first jobs after he took to billboard painting was a

---

[1] It is the pride of many independent craftsmen and boomers that they have never been chained to a job on "public works," i.e., in a large factory where a time clock is punched and the routine is deadening. To the freelancing artisans, going on "public works" is a fate worse than death.—J. C.

picture of a loaf of bread for a bakery. It would make you hungry just to look at it. That was the trouble. The birds begin to flying on it to peck at it, and either they'd break their bills and starve to death because they didn't have anything left to peck with, or they'd just sit there perched on the top of the billboard trying to figure out what was the matter until they'd just keel over. Some of them'd break their necks when they dashed against the loaf, and others'd try to light on it and slip and break their necks on the ground. Either way, it was death on birds. The humane societies complained so much and so hard that Slappy had to paint the loaf out, and just leave the lettering.

He didn't like this a bit, though, because, as he often said, any monkey who can stand on his hind legs and hold anything in his fingers can make letters. The loaf of bread business sort of gave Slappy a black eye. People was afraid to hire him.

Finally the Jimdandy Hot Blast Stove and Range Company hired him to do a sign for their newest model, showing a fire going good inside, the jacket cherry red, and heat pouring off in ever which direction. In some ways it was the best job Slappy ever done. The dandelions and weeds popped right out of the ground on the little plot between the billboard and the sidewalk, and in middle January of the coldest winter ever recorded by the Weather Bureau.

It was when the bums started making the place a hangout that the citizens and storekeepers of the neighborhood put in a kick. The hoboes drove a nail into the billboard so they could hang kettles and cans against the side of the heater and boiled their shave or boilup [1] water. They pestered everybody in the neighborhood for meat and vegetables to make mulligan stews. They found it more comfortable on the ground than in any flophouse in the city, so they slept there, too. They ganged up on the sidewalk so that you couldn't push through, even to deliver the United States mails. Mothers was afraid to send their little children to school or to the grocery store.

The company decided to hire a special watchman to shoo hoboes away, but this was a terrible expense. Not only that, but the watchman would get drowsy from the warmth, and no sooner did he let out a snore than the bums would come creeping back like old home week. Finally, the Company got the idea of having Slappy make the stove a lot hotter to drive the bums clean away.

So he did. He changed the stove from a cherry red to a white hot, and made the heat waves a lot thicker.

This drove the bums across the street, but it also blistered the paint off all the automobiles parked at the curb. Then one day the frame building across the way began to smoke and then to blaze. The insurance company told the Jimdandy Hot Blast Stove and Range Company to jerk that billboard down and be quick about it, or they'd go to law.

---

[1] Boiling of clothing to kill body lice.—J. C.

Slappy says now he feels like locking up his keister [1] and throwing away the key. They don't want big sign painting and they don't want true-to-life sign painting, and he has to do one or the other or both or nothing at all.

The Type Louse

TIMES have changed since the old days when a good typesetter could walk in any shop in the country, hang up his coat, and get to work. Green hands, such as a new devil, would always be asked to look at the type louse at the bottom of a type case, and they always had some water or even ink in the bottom of the case. When the greenhorn leaned over, he'd get his face full, all right.

I never did actually believe there was such a thing as a type louse until quite recently, any more than I did in Santa Claus, though I'd talked about them a lot, joshing around with greenhorns, and all that.

But now I know different. I'm fired in my old days after taking all the trouble to learn to use the lino, too. Back in the old days we used to hear tales about a steam typesetter they were inventing. It was like some of the mechanical men they have nowadays, the kind that can answer questions and do all sorts of things by an electric ray or something of the kind. This steam typesetter never did pan out, but it scared a lot of us, just like the men are being scared and put out of their jobs by labor-saving machinery the last twenty years.

I always maintained that the linotype like anything else that takes away the work of a man's hands is the work of the devil. God gave a man hands that can pick up type better than any machine that was ever invented. You just look at a handset job and then at a lino set job if you want to know what I mean. There's as much difference as night from day.

We had our hardships in the old days. I've worked in shops where it was that dark you could hardly see your hand before you, leave alone set the smaller fonts of type. There would be dust and trash and mice dirt in the type cases and nobody would ever think of sweeping up the place. Most of the smaller shops never had enough leads, quads or spaces, so we'd be told to "plug the Dutchman" when we complained. That meant you simply had to make out with pasteboard, toothpick slivers, tin or anything else to be found.

When you were working piecework, so much per thousand ems, all this

---

[1] Satchel, resembling a rigid suitcase, in which itinerant sign painters keep their work materials and often their clothing as well.—J. C.

Ibid.

The type louse story has been compiled from conversations with a number of printers but principally from information given by Harold Gunn and Floyd Nims.—J. C.

cut right in on the pay envelope. Whether you set solid or leaded, you had to work fast to make anything.

Green men, too, were taken advantage of. All the fat takes [1] were off the copy hook before you could get at them, and when you went to the copy hook for a take and didn't watch out whatever quads you might have by you would disappear, nobody knew where. I used to take a pocketful of leads and quads with me when I went to the toilet or to hook for a take.

In some of the shops we had to punctuate the matter ourselves. It was just written out in a continuous stream, and the typesetter had to use his own judgment. The rule I learned as an apprentice was: "Set up as long as you can hold your breath without getting blue in the face, then put in a comma. When you gape, put in a semi-colon, and when you want to sneeze, that's the time to make a paragraph."

I started to tell you how the type louse got me; how I found out there really is such a creature and he's capable of causing a man all sorts of troubles.

I am working for a firm that specializes in church magazines and the like, all religious stuff, and uncommonly dull. A typesetter can get a good education because he has to comprehend at least something of the stuff he's putting into type. That's the way I first read Shakespeare, setting up a one-volume edition of his plays. I still know a lot of the best lines by heart.

I don't blame the type louse for one of the mistakes in my copy, but it had got spread around the shop that I was an agnostic and my job was none too safe anyhow.

This boner was in the Church magazine *Good Tidings*. It was about a B.Y.P.U. convention, and it gets past the proofreaders and everything with this sentence: "After the meeting, we brayed and sang together." Of course, "brayed" should have been "prayed," but I had a devil of a time convincing them that I hadn't made it that way on purpose. The proofreaders were all God-fearing folks and they were equally to blame, in a way, so the firm gave me another chance.

But I couldn't get out of the Foreign Missionary job so slick. We'd printed ten thousand copies of the booklet reporting on the year's activities, and I set it up. The boss comes back shaking a copy and swearing like no boss in a religious press should swear.

"Look at that!" he says, and showed me a sentence in the preface:

"Your president is pained to report that the work of the Society during the past year has not been blessed, by God."

The whole thing had to be reset at the expense of the company, of course. The proofreader got the gate, and so did I, though I'm an innocent man. I've done some investigating, and I can put my finger right on the cause.

It's the type louse.

---

[1] Copy quickly and easily set in short lines, such as poetry or short conversations. —J. C.

I can prove it, if they'll let me. Just back of where I worked there was a stack of old typecases, and the top one reached a height of about a foot above my shoulder. I'd been bothered by dust and dirt falling down from these cases, but I didn't pay much attention to it since the floor vibrates quite a bit from the heavy presses.

Everybody had been telling me that the type louse eats nothing but metal, and sometimes he holes away in old typecases for years. Just like a bedbug, he can live a long time just on the expectation of getting a good meal. He lives mostly in the ffl and ffi compartments, because they're about the least used. The type louse is smart as a wharf rat when it comes to hiding away, and he's so tiny you have to have a magnifying glass to see him at all. I didn't exactly believe the stories about the type louse, but I could have sworn that when I went to lunch I had just left the line this way:

"year has not been blessed"

without any comma at all.

So I thought to myself: "Supposing a type louse had somehow got a bellyful of lime metal and had been using the top of that typecase for a promenade. He might have lost his balance and fell kerplunk on that comma key. He'd be heavy enough to depress the key. I might have overlooked the comma matrix altogether and just set 'by God' after coming back from lunch."

So I get me a magnifying glass and I take a squint on the ffl and ffi compartment in top typecase, and, sure enough, there are a number of queer-looking insects lazing around like they were too gorged to walk.

When I see one of them coming out of the hell box where there's a lot of dross lino metal, I know that I was right. I guess a diet of kerns and about fifty-year old 10 pt. italic foundry type like he had been having in the top case had got too tiresome for him. The smell of that fresh-cast metal just got the best of his native caution and he, and probably several of his brethren, had been making the trip up and down. One of them was too full, lost his balance and fell on the comma key. His bellyful of lead did the trick, and caused two people to lose their jobs, one of them me—as innocent as an unborn babe. But try to tell the boss that; that's the trouble.

The High Divers

You ask me why I'm all bunged up this way, going on crutches, both arms busted and what may still be a fractured skull. The doctor ain't

Ibid.

From Charlie DeMelo, a superannuated circus clown and strong man who frequents the near North Side theatrical district. He has two performing Chihuahua hounds, and occasionally gets a booking in taverns for his clown and dog act. He also does a strong arm act, lifts tables with his teeth, etc., though he is well past fifty. His "professional name" is "Sum Sum, the Hollywood Klown. Klassy, Klever Komedy with a Kick."—J. C.

sure about that yet. I'll live, I guess, but I don't know what for. I can't never be a high diver any more. I'll go to selling razor blades, like as not, and there's plenty doing that already.

Eddie La Breen is to blame for it all. High diving was an easy and high-paying profession before he tried to root me and every other performer out of it. I would go traveling in the summer with a carnival company, and my high dive would be a free feature attraction. The local merchants would kick in for signs to put on my ladder and advertise their goods. Sometimes I'd make a little spiel from the top of the ladder just before I dived off into the tank.

Eddie La Breen called himself "The Human Seal." He bragged that he could dive higher into shallower water than any man alive. I was pretty good myself, being billed as Billie the Dolphin, spectacular and death-defying high diver extraordinary.

I'm doing all right with Miller's Great Exposition Shows, using a twenty-five foot ladder and diving into a ten-foot tank. Big crowds of people would come from miles around to see me, and not a soul ever seemed dissatisfied until we happen to be playing Omaha on a lot over ten blocks away from where Eddie La Breen is playing with Barker's World's Fair Shows.

Just when I come up out of the tank and start to take a bow one night I hear somebody say: "That ain't *nothing*. You ought to see Eddie La Breen over on Farnum Street diving twice as high into water half as deep."

I found out it's so. Eddie has been diving into five feet of water from a fifty-foot ladder, and Mr. Miller threatens to let me go if I can't do as well.

It sure looked high when I got up there and I could feel my nose scraping on the bottom of the tank just as I made the upturn. But I'm no slouch at the high dive myself, and Eddie La Breen ain't going to outdo me if I can help it.

I added the fire act to my dive, too, and most of the time I could hardly see where to dive. For the fire act you have a little bit of gasoline pouring into the tank. It stays right on top of the water and when you fire it it makes a fearful sight, splashing fire in every direction when you hit the water.

Eddie sends me word that I might as well give up. "I'm going to dive next from a thousand feet into a tank of solid concrete," he says, "and I'll do it while playing the ukulele, eating raw liver, and keeping perfect time. Why, when I was a kid of ten or so I could dive off a silo onto the dew in the grass, bellybuster, and never even grunt when I lit."

He didn't do quite that, but he did enough. He raised his ladder to a hundred feet, and kept only two and a half feet of water in the tank.

I practised and practised and got a few bruises, but I cut that depth to two feet and I raised my ladder to a hundred and fifty feet.

By this time Eddie sent word he was good mad, and he's going to call himself the Minnow. "You know how a minnow just skitters along on top of a pond," he says. "Well, that's the way I'll light on that tank. From two hundred feet I'll dive into six inches of water and just skim off without hardly making a bubble."

If ever a man practised hard to make a shallow dive, that was me. I did that minnow dive in four inches of water from a height of 250 feet, lit right on my feet after barely touching the water, and didn't even muss my hair.

When Eddie makes it from 300 feet into three inches, I'm a little put out but I don't give up. I tell Miller to get me a good heavy bath mat and soak it good all day. First time I hit that bath mat it sort of knocked me dizzy. You know how it is when you have the breath knocked out of you and all you can do is croak like a frog. But I got better and better at it until I hardly puffed at all.

I beat Eddie La Breen fair and square, but he wasn't man enough to admit it or take it like a man. He showed that he was rotten to the core and treacherous from the word go.

We were playing Sheboygan, Wisconsin, and I had no idea that Eddie was anywhere within miles. I had heard that Barker had told him to pack his keister and get out when I bested him.

When I hit that bath mat that night I thought my time had come. That was six months ago, and look at me now. Still on crutches, and lucky if I ever get off of them.

Well, sir, I don't know anybody but Eddie who wanted to have done me that dirt. They had soaked my heavy bath mat in water, all day, the same as usual, but they must have let it get out of their sight some time or other, because some one had wrung it out practically dry.

That's the way I had it done to me. I heard somebody say later that a man answering to the description of Eddie La Breen had been seen lurking around the show grounds that evening.

And if he didn't do it, who did?

II. FROM THE LIARS' BENCH

These men weren't vicious liars. It was love of romance, lack of reading matter, and the wish to be entertainin' that makes 'em stretch facts and invent yarns.—CHARLES M. RUSSELL

1. "EXAGGERATIVE INVENTION": THE LYING TALE

As a product of the untrammeled imagination, lying tales, whoppers, big windies, or big lies are a further specialization of the yarn and tall tale in the direction of the fabulous and mythical. Outside the realm of both probability and possibility, the world of lies is the world of supermen who perform miracles midway between nonsense and magic and who inhabit a land of giant vegetables and delightfully preposterous canny or composite creatures. Although more nearly akin to fairyland, this otherworld bears a faint resemblance and direct relation to the earthly paradise of Western guidebooks and land advertisements, out of whose boasts of marvels of climate and soil many whoppers have sprung.

In a land of vast distances and vast natural resources, where topographical features and human enterprises alike are on a grand scale, the line between fact and fantasy is hard to draw. Especially is this true in the "enchanted" Southwest, amidst flat, shining expanses of plain and desert, where the atmosphere, light, and distance play queer tricks with one's vision and imagination, making for mirage and legend.

The rabbits have somehow gotten the body of the hare and the ears of the ass; the frogs, the body of the toad, the horns of the stag-beetle, and the tail of the lizard; the trees fall up-hill, and the lightning comes out of the ground.[1]

Equally intense and dramatic is the history of the Southwest, with its kaleidoscope of land-openings, migrations, and industrial developments, centering in the kingdoms of cattle and oil, cotton and citrous fruit. Landscape and history thus combine to keep one in a state of restless excitement and stimulation, in which it is easy to confuse illusion with reality, and a highly sharpened dramatic sense causes travelers and old-timers to feed their own and others' love of marvels, relating not what they have seen but what they think they have seen and what their listeners want to hear.

A similar enchantment is bred by the mountains and valleys of the South and the West. Among the concealments and surprises of winding creek trails, mysterious woods, and misty hollows, the marvelous hunters and fishermen of Appalachia and Ozarkia keep alive the name or tradition and the fictions of Davy Crockett and Baron Munchausen. Amidst the less intimate and more frigid wonders of the Rockies and the coastal range, where "streams run uphill and Nature appears to lie some herself," scouts, trappers, hunters, and explorers like Jim Bridger, Jim Beckwourth, Joe Meek, and Black Harris acquired a reputation as spectacular wind-jammers.[2]

2. COMPETITIVE LYING: THE LIARS' CLUB

Since whoppers are based on extravagant claims, artistic lying, like artistic boasting, thrives on competition. And once the element of competition or contest is introduced, the artistic lie gives rise to the burlesque lie, as the artistic boast gives rise to the burlesque boast. The whopper then becomes a monstrous take-off, a lie to end all lies.

As a convenient device for lying contests, the tradition of the Liars' Bench has sprung up in rural America. Generally, this is a purely figurative

---

[1] "South-western Slang," by Socrates Hyacinth, *The Overland Monthly*, Vol. III (August, 1869), p. 125.

[2] "An eastern visitor once wrote in a bread-and-butter letter to a Roundup newspaper editor: 'Out there every prairie dog hole is a gold mine; every hill a mountain; every creek a river; and everybody you meet is a liar.' "—*Montana, A State Guide Book* (1939), p. 258.

expression for a mythical gathering of story-tellers in any setting, from courthouse steps or square, country store, barber shop, or bar-room to campfire or bunkhouse. In some cases, however, the bench is an actual one rather than a mere symbol.[1] Thus in Indiana:

In Nashville, county seat of Brown County, the bench stands beneath the locust trees on the courthouse lawn. It is an old wooden seat with iron legs, and a single arm, and has occupied the same position winter and summer for a number of years. Its seating capacity is limited to six. Here the Brown County story-tellers swap yarns.

There is an unwritten law that when this bench is full and other tale-tellers come to join those seated there, the one at the foot—the end without the arm—is pushed off to make room for the new recruits. Efforts are sometimes made to dislodge the man at the head, but the iron arm blocks this move and as a result one of the middle men is pushed out when the grand shove begins. It is to this comfortable loafing place that Nashville women come whenever they cannot find their husbands nearer home.

Gentryville has always had its loafing place since the days when the Gentry boys, Baldwin the blacksmith, Abe Lincoln, and Dennis Hanks used to congregate around Jones' store. But it was not until 1894 that a definite place was established where a man might go and be sure of an audience any time of day. A large heavy bridge plank was wedged between two locust trees near the entrance to one of the crossroad stores. The plank was thick and long, and with a brace in the center gave enough room for a number of men and boys who kept the bench full throughout the day and far into the night. As fast as one would leave some other would take his place.[2]

In response to the same urge for competitive lying and an audience, Liars' Clubs have also arisen, ranging from such hoaxes as the Sazerac Lying Club to regular organizations like the Tall Story Club of Lowell Thomas, the Burlington, Wisconsin, Liars' Club ("Originators and Promoters of the National Liars' Contest"), and the Goofy Liars' Club of Decatur, Illinois ("Organizers and Promoters of International Liars' Contest"). The Sazerac Lying Club was the creation of Fred H. Hart, born of a dearth of "local" copy to fill the columns of the *Reese River Reveille*, an Austin, Nevada, daily, of which he became editor in 1873.[3] The Tall Story Club grew out of a flood of fan-mail mosquito stories following a *Literary Digest* radio news commentary in which Lowell Thomas had cited the fact that the Arctic tundras rather than the tropics breed the biggest and worst mosquitoes.[4] The Burlington Liars' Club, like the Sazerac Lying Club, grew out of a newspaper hoax:

---

[1] The "deacon's seat" was the lumberjack's name for the place on the "liars' bench" occupied successively by the bunkhouse story-tellers at the evening session of yarning. See *The Hodag, and Other Tales of the Logging Camps,* by Lake Shore Kearney (Wausau, Wisconsin, 1928).

[2] *Hoosier Tall Stories* (Federal Writers' Project in Indiana, 1937), pp. 1–2.

[3] The *Sazerac Lying Club,* a Nevada Book, by Fred. W. Hart (Henry Keller & Co., San Francisco, 1878).

[4] *Tall Stories,* the Rise and Triumph of the Great American Whopper, by Lowell Thomas (1931).

Back in 1929 a Burlington newspaper reporter wrote a story to the effect that these "old timers" got together each New Year's day at the police station, and lied for the championship of the city. He told a brother reporter of his plan, and the story was "sprung" just before New Year's.

They considered the story a good local joke, and after it had appeared in their respective newspapers, forgot about it. However, city editors, with an eye for interesting features, "put it on the wire," and the following December the Associated Press and other news agencies began phoning Burlington to find out if the city's annual contest would be repeated. By this time one of the reporters had left Burlington, but the other one, feeling it would be a shame to miss an opportunity to hornswoggle the public, concocted a story and sent it on its way. Letters began to trickle in from the four corners of the country commenting on the "contest." They furnished the inspiration for a real contest instead of a phoney one, national in scope, and the Burlington Liars' Club was formed to carry it on.[1]

The themes of whoppers are the perennial ones of weather, climate, soil, pests, monsters, hunting, fishing, marksmanship, in any extreme or excess that constitutes an asset or a liability, or both. On the asset side, stories of fertile land are perhaps the most common. From nearly all states comes a chorus of brags of giant vegetables—turnip, pumpkin, beet, potato, cucumber, corn—harking back to old world stories of the great cabbage and the pot that matched it, with disaster following in the trail of phenomenally large or rapid growth. On the liability side, stories of grasshoppers and potato bugs vie with those of mosquitoes as most destructive of crops or most annoying to mankind. Side by side with traditional whoppers are the individual inventions of professional humorists and literary men. Through all this lavish, contagious, and expansive mendacity runs a strain of elaborate hoaxing and jesting that belongs to the humor of exaggeration and deception but more often borders on pure nonsense or fantasy.

Nonsense and fantasy reach their height in the freakish behavior of animals and the lore of mythical monsters. Harking back to the "unnatural natural history" and bestiaries of ancient and medieval times, the most fearsome of these fabulous creatures are those that haunt the big woods, from Maine to Vancouver Island, where, as part of the lore of the lumberjack, they have been attracted into the Paul Bunyan cycle.

Black Harris and the Putrified Forest

THEY were a trapping party from the north fork of Platte, on their way to wintering-ground in the more southern valley of the Arkansas; some, indeed, meditating a more extended trip, even to the distant settlements of New Mexico, the paradise of mountaineers. The elder of the company

---

[1] *The 25 Best Lies of 1933* (Burlington, Wisconsin, 1934), p. 1.

From *Life in the Far West*, by George Frederic Ruxton, pp. 14–18. New York: Harper & Brothers, 1849.

was a tall, gaunt man, with a face browned by twenty years' exposure to the extreme climate of the mountains; his long black hair, as yet scarcely tinged with gray, hanging almost to his shoulders, but his cheeks and chin clean shaven, after the fashion of the mountain-men. His dress was the usual hunting-frock of buckskin, with long fringes down the seams, with pantaloons similarly ornamented, and moccasins of Indian make. Whilst his companions puffed their pipes in silence, he narrated a few of his former experiences of western life; and whilst the buffalo "hump-ribs" and "tender-loin" are singing away in the pot, preparing for the hunters' supper, we will note down the yarn as it spins from his lips, giving it in the language spoken in the "far west":—

" 'Twas about 'calf-time,' maybe a little later, and not a hundred year ago, by a long chalk, that the biggest kind of rendezvous was held 'to' Independence, a mighty handsome little location away up on Old Missoura. A pretty smart lot of boys was camp'd thar, about a quarter from the town, and the way the whisky flowed that time was 'some' now, I can tell you. . . .

"Surely Black Harris [1] was thar; and the darndest liar was Black Harris —for lies tumbled out of his mouth like boudins out of a bufler's stomach. He was the child as saw the putrified forest in the Black Hills. Black Harris come in from Laramie; he'd been trapping three year an' more on Platte and the 'other side'; and, when he got into Liberty, he fixed him- self right off like a Saint Louiy dandy. Well, he sat to dinner one day in the tavern, and a lady says to him:—

" 'Well, Mister Harris, I hear you're a great travler.'

" 'Travler, marm,' says Black Harris, 'this niggur's no travler; I ar' a trapper, marm, a mountain-man, wagh!'

" 'Well, Mister Harris, trappers are great travlers, and you goes over a sight of ground in your perishinations, I'll be bound to say.'

" 'A sight, marm, this coon's gone over, if that's the way your 'stick floats.' [2] I've trapped beaver on Platte and Arkansas, and away up on Missoura and Yaller Stone; I've trapped on Columbia, on Lewis Fork, and Green River; I've trapped, marm, on Grand River and the Heely (Gila). I've fout the 'Blackfoot' (and d—d bad Injuns they ar); I've

---

[1] Among the few famous raconteurs of the genuine tall tale type of frontier ad- venture story to whom the Northwest has some right to lay claim is one Moses ("Black" or "Major") Harris, who guided the Gilliam and Ford emigrants into Oregon in 1844, and is said to have conducted Marcus Whitman on his first journey into the same country. Harris also rendered valuable service in helping to discover a feasible trail across the Cascade mountains. In 1847 he trapped and fur-traded east to Missouri, in which section of the union he had originally begun his wanderings, and died there. It had been his intention to return west, to either Oregon or California. According to another account of his death he was shot for his traps and tobacco while on a hunting expedition in the Rockies.—V. L. O. Chittick, *The Frontier*, Vol XII (January, 1932), Number 2, p. 173.

[2] Meaning—if that's what you mean. The "stick" is tied to the beaver trap by a string; and, floating on the water, points out its position, should a beaver have carried it away.—G. F. R.

raised the hair [1] of more *than one* Apach, and made a Rapaho 'come'
afore now; I've trapped in heav'n, in airth, and h—; and scalp my old
head, marm, but I've seen a putrified forest.'

" 'La, Mister Harris, a what?'

" 'A putrified forest, marm, as sure as my rifle's got hind-sights, and
she shoots center. I was out on the Black Hills, Bill Sublette knows the
time—the year it rained fire—and every body knows when that was.
If thar wasn't cold doins about that time, this child wouldn't say so.
The snow was about fifty foot deep, and the bufler lay dead on the
ground like bees after a beein'; not whar we was tho', for *thar* was no
bufler, and no meat, and me and my band had been livin' on our moccasins
(leastwise the parflesh [2]) for six weeks; and poor doins that feedin' is,
marm, as you'll never know. One day we crossed a 'cañon' and over a
'divide,' and got into a peraira, whar was green grass, and green trees, and
green leaves on the trees, and birds singing in the green leaves, and this
in Febrary, wagh! Our animals was like to die when they see the green
grass, and we all sung out, 'hurraw for summer doins.'

" 'Hyar goes for meat,' says I, and I jest ups old Ginger at one of them
singing birds, and down come the crittur elegant; its darned head spinning
away from the body, but never stops singing, and when I takes up the
meat, I finds it stone, wagh! 'Hyar's damp powder and no fire to dry it,'
I says, quite skeared.

" 'Fire be dogged,' says old Rube. 'Hyar's a hos as 'll make fire come';
and with that he takes his ax and lets drive at a cotton wood. Schr-u-k
—goes the ax agin the tree, and out comes a bit of the blade as big as
my hand. We looks at the animals, and thar they stood shaking over
the grass, which I'm dog-gone if it wasn't stone, too. Young Sublette
comes up, and he'd been clerking down to the fort on Platte, so he
know'd something. He looks and looks, and scrapes the trees with his
butcher knife, and snaps the grass like pipe stems, and breaks the leaves
a-snappin' like Californy shells.

" 'What's all this, boy?' I asks.

" 'Putrefactions,' says he, looking smart, 'putrefactions, or I'm a niggur.'

" 'La, Mister Harris,' says the lady, 'putrefactions! why, did the leaves,
and the trees, and the grass smell badly?'

" 'Smell badly, marm!' says Black Harris, 'would a skunk stink if he
was froze to stone? No, marm, this child didn't know what putrefaction
was, and young Sublette's varsion wouldn't "shine" no how, so I chips
a piece out of a tree and puts it in my trap-sack, and carries it in safe to
Laramie. Well, old Captain Stewart (a clever man was that, though he
was an Englishman), he comes along next spring, and a Dutch doctor
chap was along too. I shows him the piece I chipped out of the tree,
and he called it a putrefaction too; and so, marm, if that wasn't a putrefied

---

[1] Scalped.—G. F. R.
[2] Soles made of buffalo hide.—G. F. R.

peraira, what was it? For this hos doesn't know, and *he* knows "fat cow"
from "poor bull," anyhow.' . . ."

Mushmouth Charlie's Lecture
on the Petrified Forest

AWAY out yonder in Arizony where it ain't rained since Noah and it's
so dry you have to prime yourself to spit thar's a wonderful forest whar
the trees is a-growin' jest the same as they did centuries and centuries ago,
but a-a-ll pewtrified, ladies and gentlemen, a-a-ll pewtrified. And the roots
of them thar trees is a-growin' way down in the ground—a-spreadin' out
and a-takin' holt on the dirt jest the same as they did centuries and
centuries ago—but a-a-ll pewtrified, ladies and gentlemen, a-a-ll pewtrified;
and the branches of them thar trees is a-growin' full of twigs and leaves
and birds' nests jest the same as they did centuries and centuries ago.
And flyin' around in them thar branches and through the pewtrified air
is a number of pine hens, sandhill cranes, white-necked ravens, and
yellow-headed blackbirds, all a-singin' their beautiful songs just as they
did centuries and centuries ago but a-a-ll pewtrified, ladies and gentlemen,
a-a-ll pewtrified.

Now when I give a lecture on Arizony up to Boston last week and told
this interestin' scientific fact, some unbelievin' miscreant sings out, "What
about the law of gravitation?" and I sings right back at him, "Seems to
me anybody with the sense of a coyote'd know that way out there in
Arizony this here now law of gravitation hain't worked for centuries and
centuries but is like everythin' else aout there—a-a-ll pewtrified, ladies
and gentlemen, completely pewtrified.

The Wild Texan Tells Some Big Stories

FROM Richmond I went on to Lexington, where my relatives lived. They
were all glad to see me, and did all they could to make my time pass
pleasantly while I was with them; though I could see very plainly that
they all looked upon me as a sort of half-civilized savage that never could

From *The Hurricane's Children*, Tales from Your Neck o' the Woods, by Carl
Carmer, p. 58. Copyright, 1937, by Carl Carmer. Farrar & Rinehart, Inc. New York.
Toronto.

From *The Adventures of Big-Foot Wallace, the Texas Ranger and Hunter*, by John
C. Duval, 274–281. Entered, according to Act of Congress, in the year 1870, by J. W.
Burke & Co., in the Clerk's Office of the District Court of the United States for the
Southern District of Georgia. Philadelphia: Claxton, Remsen & Haffelfinger. Macon,
Ga.: J. W. Burke & Co.

be entirely tamed; and perhaps they were right. I had lived too long the free and independent life of a ranger, to be contented a great while with the steady habits and humdrum existence of the people of the "Old States." I longed for the excitement of the chase, an Indian foray, a buffalo-hunt, or a bear-fight. However, everything for a time was new and strange to me, and I enjoyed myself as much as I could have expected.

A few weeks after my arrival I went to a "fandango" that was given for my especial benefit. There was a great crowd there, and everybody was anxious to see the "Wild Texan," as they called me. I was the "lion" of the evening, particularly with the young ladies, who never tired of asking me questions about Mexico, Texas, the Indians, prairies, etc. I at first answered truly all the questions they asked me; but when I found they evidently doubted some of the stories I told them which were facts, I branched out and gave them some "whoppers," which they swallowed down without "gagging." For instance, one young woman wanted to know how many wild horses I had ever seen in a drove. I told her perhaps thirty or forty thousand.

"Oh! now! Mr. Wallace," said she, "don't try to make game of me in that way. Forty thousand horses in one drove! well, I declare you are a second 'Munchausen'!"

"Well, then," said I, "maybe you won't believe me when I tell you there is a sort of spider in Texas as big as a peck measure, the bite of which can only be cured by music."

"Oh, yes," she answered, "I believe that's all so, for I have read about them in a book."

Among other "whoppers," I told her there was "varmint" in Texas, called the "Santa Fé," that was still worse than the tarantula, for the best brass band in the country couldn't cure their sting; that the creature had a hundred legs and a sting on every one of them, besides two large stings in its forked tail, and fangs as big as a rattlesnake's. When they sting you with their legs alone, you might possibly live an hour; when with all their stings, perhaps fifteen or twenty minutes; but when they sting and bite you at the same time, you first turn blue, then yellow, and then a beautiful bottle-green, when your hair all fell out and your finger nails dropped off, and you were as dead as a door-nail in five minutes, spite of all the doctors in America.

"Oh! my! Mr. Wallace," said she, "how have you managed to live so long in that horrible country?"

"Why, you see," said I, "with my tarantula boots made of alligator-skin, and my centipede hunting-shirt made of tanned rattlesnakes' hides, I have escaped pretty well; but these don't protect you against the stinging scorpions, 'cow-killers,' and scaly-back chinches, that crawl about at night when you are asleep! The only way to keep them at a distance is to 'chaw' tobacco and drink whisky, and that is the reason the Temperance Society never flourished much in Texas."

"Oh!" said she, "what a horrible country that must be, where people have to be stung to death, or 'chaw' tobacco and drink whisky! I don't know which is the worst."

"Well," said I, "the people out there don't seem to mind it much; they get used to it after a while; in fact, they seem rather to like it, for they chaw tobacco and drink whisky even in the winter-time, when the 'cow-killers' and stinging-lizards are all frozen up!"

I had been introduced to one young woman by the name of Matilda, who was as pretty as a pink! Her teeth were as white as an alligator's, and her eyes were as bright as two mesquite coals, and her mouth looked like a little gash cut in a juicy peach. She was a "deadener," I tell you, and a regular "knee-weakener," in the bargain; and I wanted to have a little talk with her the worst in the world; but somehow I felt a little afraid to venture. After a little while, however, she came up to me of her own accord, and began to ask me a great many questions about Texas and the Indians, wild horses, and the prairies, etc. Among other things, she asked me if young women were in great demand in Texas.

"I should think they were," said I. "The day the first young woman came into our settlement there were fourteen Spanish horses badly foundered on sedge-grass, by the young men who flocked in to see her, from forty miles around; and the next morning she had seventeen offers of marriage before breakfast! The young woman was a little confused by so many applications at once, and before she could make up her mind which one to take, one of the 'rancheros' watched his chance, and the first time she walked out he caught her up behind him on his horse, rode off full speed to San Patricio, drew his six-shooter on the padre, and forced him to marry them on the spot. This saved the young woman all further trouble on the subject, and they are now living happily together on one of the finest cattle ranches in the County of Karnes."

"Oh! I declare," said Miss Matilda, "that is delightful! How romantic to be run off with in that way by a handsome young 'ranchero.' I think, Mr. Wallace, I shall have to go to Texas."

"You might do worse," said I; "and besides, you would stand a chance of being run away with by some great Comanche or Tonkawa chief; with a bow and quiver on his back and eagle's feathers on his head, and nothing else to speak of in the way of clothes."

Miss Matilda didn't seem to hear that last part of my speech, for she jumped up and clapped her little hands: "Oh," said she, "wouldn't that be fine? To gallop over the flowery prairies, free as the wind, from morning till night, and listen to the feathered songsters pouring forth their untaught melodies from every grove and shady dell! Oh, it would be splendid, Mr. Wallace!"

"Yes," said I, "it would. One of the handsomest young women in our settlement was carried off, three or four years ago, by 'He-che-puck-sa-sa,' the 'Bellowing Bull,' and when I went on a visit to his tribe, not long ago, she was the favorite wife and head squaw of the wigwam, and had brass rings enough on her arms and legs to have made a pair of 'dog-irons,' if they had been melted up, besides one in her nose as big as the palm of my hand."

"Why! how many wives did the Mormon have?" asked Miss Matilda, looking a little down in the mouth.

"Oh! I can't say exactly," I answered; "I only saw six; but he had another wigwam at the village below. But," said I, "Miss Matilda, after riding over the flowery prairies all day, and listening to the coyotes howling in every grove and dell, where will you *put up* at night; and how will you manage to get along without hot rolls for breakfast, and baked custard for dinner?"

"Oh," said she, "I don't care for them; I can do very well without them; all I want is a nice cup of coffee in the morning, and a biscuit or a slice of toast, and a little fresh butter, or a few fresh-laid eggs; and for dinner a few vegetables and wild fruits, and now and then a nice beefsteak or a saddle of venison roasted before the fire!"

"Yes," says I, "that's all reasonable enough, and you could get them, I suppose, at any time; but you see, the Indians don't cook their meat."

"The cannibals!" exclaimed Miss Matilda; "they certainly don't eat it raw, do they?"

"Yes," said I, "as a general thing; only sometimes, when a fellow feels a little squeamish, he fastens a beef or mule steak under his saddle, and after riding and jolting on it all day, he finds it nicely 'done' when he stops at night; and it's a very convenient way of cooking, too, especially when a fellow is in a hurry (which the Indians always are, for they are always after somebody, or else somebody is after them); and besides, they say it is the best thing in the world for a sore-back horse!"

"Oh! dear," said Miss Matilda, "I don't believe I'll go to Texas, after all; for if I do, I must put up with a 'ranchero'—they don't eat their meat raw, do they?"

"No," said I, "except when they are out on the plains, and can't find buffalo-chips enough to cook it with."

"Oh! tell me, Mr. Wallace," said she, "did you ever see a 'mirage' on the plains?"

"A mirage?" said I, rather taken aback, for I hadn't the least idea what she meant, unless it was a drove of mustangs or a herd of buffalo; "why, certainly, I have seen a thousand of 'em."

"I didn't think they were so common," said she.

"Oh, yes," I answered; "the last one I saw was just back of Santa Fé, and it stampeded when we got in about a quarter of a mile of it; and such a dust as was kicked up you never saw, for there hadn't been a drop of rain in six months."

"Well, I declare!" said Miss Matilda; "I always heard that the mirage would disappear as you approached it, but I never heard of one kicking up a dust before."

"No," said I; "they don't in other countries, where the ground is kept wet by constant rain; but in Texas, you see, it is different."

Just then a dapper-looking young fellow came up and asked Miss Matilda if he might have the pleasure of dancing with her that set, and she walked off with him. I took a dislike to that young fellow at once, and felt for "Old Butch," without knowing what I was about! The fact is, I rather fancied this young woman, and I determined, the next time I met up with her, to give her a better account of Texas, and leave out all the centipedes and "raw meat."

Well, sir! I staid with my kinsfolk in Old Virginny till I began to pine for the prairies and woods once more. They were as kind to me as they could be, but feather beds, tight rooms, and three meals a day were too much for me, and, like old General Taylor, when he was taken from "camps" to the "White House," I fell away daily, and "went off my feed" entirely; and, like him, I suppose I should have gone up the spout, if I had staid much longer. I helped matters a little by taking a camp-hunt of a couple of weeks in the Blue Ridge Mountains, where I killed the last bear, I suppose, that was ever seen in that part of Old Virginny, for when his carcass was hauled in, people came from twenty miles around to have a look at it. But I never got entirely to rights again till I returned to Texas and got into an Indian "scrimmage," and lifted the hair off of one or two of them with the aid of "Old Butch." That night, for the first time, my appetite came back to me, and I ate six pounds of buffalo-hump, a side of ribs, and a roasted marrow-gut, and ever since I have been "as well as could be expected."

Some Liars of the Old West

SPEAKIN' of liars, the Old West could put in its claim for more of 'em than any other land under the sun. The mountains and plains seemed to stimulate man's imagination. A man in the States might have been a liar in a small way, but when he comes west he soon takes lessons from the prairies, where ranges a hundred miles away seem within touchin' distance, streams run uphill and Nature appears to lie some herself.

These men weren't vicious liars. It was love of romance, lack of reading matter, and the wish to be entertainin' that makes 'em stretch facts and invent yarns. Jack McGowan, a well-known old-timer now livin' in Great Falls, tells of a man known as Lyin' Jack, who was famous from Mexico to the Arctic.

McGowan says one of Jack's favorite tales is of an elk he once killed that measured 15-feet spread between the antlers. He used to tell that he kept these horns in the loft of his cabin.

"One time I hadn't seen Jack for years," said McGowan, "when he shows up in Benton. The crowd's all glad to see Jack, an' after a round or two of drinks, asks him to tell them a yarn.

From *Trails Plowed Under*, by Charles M. Russell, pp. 191–194. Copyright, 1927, by Doubleday, Page & Company. Garden City, New York.

" 'No, boys,' says Jack, 'I'm through. For years I've been tellin' these lies—told 'em so often I got to believin' 'em myself. That story of mine about the elk with the 15-foot horns is what cured me. I told about that elk so often that I knowed the place I killed it. One night I lit a candle and crawled up in the loft to view the horns—an' I'm damned if they was there.' "

Once up in Yogo, Bill Cameron pointed out Old Man Babcock an' another old-timer, Patrick, sayin', "There's three of the biggest liars in the world."

"Who's the third?" inquired a bystander.

"Patrick's one, an' old Bab's the other two," says Cameron.

This Babcock one night is telling about getting jumped by 50 hostile Sioux, a war party, that's giving him a close run. The bullets an' arrows are tearin' the dirt all around, when he hits the mouth of a deep canyon. He thinks he's safe, but after ridin' up it a way, discovers it's a box gulch, with walls straight up from 600 to 1,000 feet. His only get-away's where he come in, an' the Indians are already whippin' their ponies into it.

Right here old Bab rares back in his chair, closes his eyes, an' starts fondlin' his whiskers. This seems to be the end of the story, when one of the listeners asks:

"What happened then?"

Old Bab, with his eyes still closed, takin' a fresh chew, whispered: "They killed me, b' God!"

The upper Missouri River steamboats, they used to say, would run on a light dew, an' certainly they used to get by where there was mighty little water. X. Beidler an' his friend, Major Reed, are traveling by boat to Fort Benton. One night they drink more than they should. X. is awakened in the morning by the cries of Reed. On entering his stateroom, X. finds Reed begging for water, as he's dying of thirst.

X. steps to the bedside, and takin' his friend's hand, says: "I'm sorry, Major, I can't do anything for you. That damned pilot got drunk, too, last night, and we're eight miles up a dry coulee!"

"Some say rattlers ain't pizen," said Buckskin Williams, an old freighter, "but I know different. I'm pullin' out of Milk River one day with 14, when I notice my line hoss swing out an' every hoss on the near side crowds the chain. My near wheel hoss, that I'm ridin', rares up an' straddles the tongue. It's then I see what the trouble is—a big rattler has struck, misses my hoss an' hits the tongue. The tongue starts to swell up. I have to chop it off to save the wagon, an' I'm damn quick doin' it, too!"

"Cap" Nelse, a well-known old-timer around Benton in the early days, tells of coming south from Edmonton with a string of half-breed carts. They were traveling through big herds of buffalo. It was spring and there were many calves. They had no trouble with the full-grown buffalo, Cap said, but were forced to stop often to take the calves from between the spokes of the cart-wheels!

A traveling man in White Sulphur Springs makes a bet of drinks for the town with Coates, a saloon keeper, that Coates can't find a man that will hold up his hand and take his oath that he has seen 100,000 buffalo at one sight. When the bet's decided, it's agreed to ring the triangle at the hotel, which will call the town to their drinks.

Many old-timers said they had seen that many buffalo, but refused to swear to it, and it looked like Coates would lose his bet until Milt Crowthers showed up. When a smile of confidence spread over Coates' face as he introduces Crowthers to the drummer.

"Mr. Crowthers," said the traveling man, "how many antelope have you seen at one time?"

Crowthers straightens up and looks wise, like he's turning back over the pages of the past. "Two hundred thousand," says he.

"How many elk?" asks the traveling man.

"Somethin' over a million," replies Crowthers.

"Mr. Crowthers, how many buffalo will you hold up your hand and swear you have seen at one sight?"

Crowthers holds up his hand. "As near as I can figure," says he, "about three million billion."

This is where Coates starts for the triangle, but the traveling man halts him, saying, "Where were you when you saw these buffalo, Mr. Crowthers?"

"I was a boy travelin' with a wagon train," replies Crowthers. "We was south of the Platte when we was forced to corral our wagons to keep our stock from bein' stampeded by buffalo. For five days an' nights 50 men kep' their guns hot killin' buffalo to keep 'em off the wagons. The sixth day the herd spread, givin' us time to yoke up an' cross the Platte, an' it's a damn good thing we did."

"Why?" asks the traveling man.

"Well," says Crowthers, "we no more than hit the high country north of the Platte, than lookin' back, here comes the main herd!"

Stories Told around the Camp Fire

BUFFALO BILL, Pawnee Bill, and Three Dollar Bill were out scouting in Colorado, on the hunt of a war party of Cheyenne and Arapahoe Indians

From *Bill Jones of Paradise Valley, Oklahoma*. His Life and Adventures for Over Forty Years in The Great Southwest. He was a Pioneer in the Days of the Buffalo, The Wild Indian, The Oklahoma Boomer, The Cowboy and The Outlaw, by John J. Callison, pp. 115–118, 119–123. Copyright, 1914, by J. J. Callison. Kingfisher, Oklahoma.

that were said to have captured a Mormon emigrant who was going from St. Joseph, Mo., to Salt Lake City. All at once the three Bills stopped and sniffed the air to see if they could locate their camp.

"There it is," said Buffalo Bill, "just in the edge of that clump of timber, and it is just ten miles to their camp."

"Yes," said Pawnee Bill, "and they are in the center of the clump. That makes them ten miles and a half from here."

"No," said Three Dollar Bill. "They are on the farther side of the clump, and that makes them eleven miles away, and there are three hundred of the braves. Do you think we had better wait until night before we attempt to rescue the Mormons?"

"Yes," said Buffalo Bill. "We will wait until just before the moon comes up. Then we will slip in and rescue them, and by the time we can get those emigrants together the moon will be up, so we can be off about ten."

That night the three Bills slipped into the Indian camp and had no trouble in locating the Mormons. Buffalo Bill put the seventeen women on his pony and started for Ft. Hays, Kansas. Pawnee Bill gathered up the fifty-one kids, put them on his pony and started after Buffalo Bill. Three Dollar Bill was to trail along behind and keep a lookout for the Indians, in case they should attempt to recapture them. That old Mormon was so tickled over his capture that he just stayed in the Indian camp, and was captured three years later by some cowboys and hanged for stealing horses.

The three Bills had gone about five miles when they discovered that the Indians were on their trail. Buffalo Bill and Pawnee Bill whipped up the ponies into a good fast dog trot, and Three Dollar Bill dropped behind to stand the Indians off. As quick as the Indians got within gunshot, Three Dollar Bill began to shoot. His shots were so accurate and deadly that you could have jumped from one dead Indian to another for four miles.

"What became of that Mormon's wives, Texas Jack?"

"They all married soldier boys at Ft. Hays and lived happily ever afterwards as company laundresses."

"Next man on the program," said Big Jim. "Say, 'Old-Man-Afraid-of-His-Squaws,' tell us when and where you were killed and scalped by the Indians."

"Well, boys," commenced the man with the jaw-breaking name, "you know that I was not killed, I only thought so, but I was scalped all right, as you can see for yourselves."

"It's funny," said one of the boys, "that we have worked together for a long time and never knew you was scalped by the Indians."

"In 1877 we were hunting buffalo out on the Staked Plains, when we were rounded up by the Apaches, and the fight started.

"I went to a little creek after a bucket of water, when the Indians cut me off from camp, and I was shot and scalped before the other boys could get to me. I was carried to camp and the boys turned in and fixed me up the best they could. They killed our dog, cut off some of his hide and fit it to my head, bandaged it up, and in six weeks I was all right, as you can see by looking at my hair."

Deacon White will now lead in singing the doxology:

"And now we are across the Brazos,
    And homeward we are bound;
No more in that cursed country
    Will ever we be found;
We will go home to our wives and sweethearts
    Tell others not to go
To that God-forsaken cactus country
    Way out in Mexico.

"We lived on sage brush, buffalo hump,
    And a lot of sour dough bread;
Strong coffee and alkali water to drink,
    And a bull hide for a bed;
The way the mosquitoes and graybacks worked
    On us was not so slow,
God grant there's no worse place on earth
    Than among the buffalo."

* * * * *

"Say, kid, you promised to tell us about the Mormons. You told us you were born and raised in Utah, now let us have one from you. It's your turn."

"Bet your life I'm a Mormon and I am proud of it, too," remarked the young man called the "Salt Lake Kid."

"Before I start to tell you about the Mormons, I want to say that I am going to tell you the truth and nothing but the truth, so help me Brigham Young, just as I saw it.

"My people were all Mormons, and lucky or unlucky for me, I am the oldest of my father's kids, and my mother is the first wife. A man in Utah is limited as to the number of wives he may have. Twenty-five is the highest number any man can have, and the number gets less, according to who you are. But in addition to his legal wives, he can have all the proxies he wants or needs in his business.

"My father had fifteen wives and fifteen proxies. If one of your wives dies you are supposed to marry one of the proxies; then you can get a few more young women as second wives or proxies if you want to, and we always want to.

"We lived on a big farm, and in addition to the farm, we had a big ranch where we raised lots of horses, cattle and sheep. As I was the oldest boy I was started out as a kid herder. I was promoted to a sheep herder at ten, and was a full-fledged cowboy at fifteen."

"What's a kid herder? And did you raise goats, too?" "Goats, nothing," said the kid. "You know that we call children kids out there."

"How many brothers and sisters did you have, anyway?" I wanted to know.

"Say, Bill, you know that when I went to work with you fellows fifty was all I could count, and I had a lot more brothers and sisters than I could count."

"When you would take them out to herd, how would you know how many to bring in at night?" "When I would start out I would take a stick and cut a notch in it, like a gun man does when he kills another man. Say, boys, it's some fun to herd a bunch of kids ranging in age from a yearling to a ten-year-old. Did any of you boys ever have a job herding a bunch of dogies?"

"What's a dogie?" one of the tenderfeet wanted to know.

"I started to tell about the Mormons," said the kid.

"Go ahead and tell the boys about a dogie," said Whiskers. "Well, a dogie is a tenderfoot, and it don't make any difference whether he walks on two legs or four. I will tell you about the four-legged kind," said the kid. "When father went to Utah there was very little stock of any kind there, so he would go back to the States and buy a train load of calves from the farmers, ship them home and turn them loose on the range. Now, a calf raised on a farm don't savey the range any better than a boy raised in a city. For down-right misery, and for a nerve-wrecking job, a bunch of dogies is the limit. Take my word for it, boys, if you are ever caught out in a howling wilderness, with a bunch of dogies or a bunch of Mormon kids, the bug house is not far away for you. Sheep herding is a picnic in comparison, for the reason that the sheep will stick together.

"I remember having two thousand sheep out, the summer I was sixteen years old, and we drifted to the railroad, when along comes a freight train making about eight miles an hour. The old bell wether that was the leader took a notion to cross the track ahead of the train and every blamed one of them sheep started to follow him. Well, so help me Brigham Young, if that wasn't the worst mixup I ever saw. The air was full of flying sheep, and sheep were jammed into that engine and cars wherever a sheep could stick his head. When the train came to a stop, sheep were still crossing the track, under the cars, and it took the train crew two hours to get the dead sheep out of the engine so they could go on.

"After I got the bunch rounded up and got them to grazing again I went back to see the wreck of sheep. A section boss and his gang were cleaning the road and counting the dead sheep."

"Say, kid, you started out to tell us about the Mormons."

"Well, herding a bunch of Mormon kids has its drawbacks, like herding dogies and sheep, only it's more like dogies or worse.

"In the summer season, when the wild strawberries were ripe, I would have to take the bunch out on the prairies to let them fill up on the wild strawberries, and that was when the trouble started. Every blamed one

of them kids had a notion in his head that the best strawberries were at
least half a mile away from where he was at, and the kids would all start
in a different direction at the same time. Then I would have to put in
some hard running to gather them together and get them home by sundown.

"Say, kids, did any of youse ever have the job of driving the calf wagon
up the trail?" the kid wanted to know. "One day I had all the kids out
in the prairie, when one of these sudden rain storms came up so quick
that I had no time to get them home. All I could do was to round them
up like a bunch of calves, and, of course, they all began to squall at the
same time; it beats a wagon load of calves or even a drove of coyotes.
Honest to Brigham it does."

The Razorback

COARSELY and variously colored, long-snouted, long-tailed, long-bodied,
long-legged, long-tusked, even long in his squeal, the razorback of Texas
and the South became the theme for a whole cycle of folk jokes and
yarns. Modern pipeliners swear that their mythological hero, Paul Bunyan,
laid his famous line through Arkansas by driving ahead of him a herd
of razorbacks that rooted the ditch for the pipe. The story goes, too, that
in early days an Eastern tenderfoot who had recently arrived in South
Texas became very much interested in the native hogs. After learning how
the settlers had to scour the country for hours sometimes before catching
one of their hogs and then had to carry its dirty carcass for miles before
getting home to butcher it, he exclaimed:

"All this must take an awful lot of trouble and time!"

"Yes," replied a settler, "it does take time, but, hell, what's time to
a hog—and besides we have lots of fun."

The Tennessee version of the story—as told by the fertile anecdoter,
L. L. Click of Austin—goes better. A mountaineer was holding a razorback
shoat in his arms and lifting him up so that he could "graze" on ripe
persimmons still hanging on the tree. A stranger came along.

"You may get that hog fat after a while," he said to the mountaineer,
"but it's going to take a mighty long time."

"Huh," replied the mountaineer, "what's time to a derned hawg?"

There was a time when Texans and citizens of other Southern states
were not a bit ashamed of their respective varieties of razorbacks. One
time, so one story goes, a real estate agent was showing a stranger some
land in the Trinity River bottoms. The stranger saw what he took to be
highwater marks far up on the trunks of the various trees and he called
attention to these evidences of overflow.

"Oh, no, no," the agent corrected the prospective buyer, "them's not

From *A Vaquero of the Brush Country*, by J. Frank Dobie, pp. 35–38. Copyright,
1929, by the Southwest Press. Dallas.

highwater marks at all. That's jest where our hawgs rubbed their backs. Let me tell you, man, this land grows the tallest hawgs in America."

A. L. Steele, of Lovington, New Mexico, who was born in Grimes County, Texas, 1841, tells another anecdote of the patriotic zeal with which some frontiersmen supported the razorback.

"Right after the close of the Civil War," says Mr. Steele, "I was in Natchez, Mississippi, with a herd of steers, from Navarro County. After we got them sold, Wash Little, who was with me, began to tank up on red-eye and to brag on Texas hogs. A Mississippian began glorifying the Mississippi variety, and in order to prevent a possible killing I had to take Wash across the river and stay all night in Vidalia."

Arkansas had zealous—and logical—advocates also, as a story recorded by Dallas T. Herndon in his *Centennial History of Arkansas* will illustrate. "Some swine breeders from other states brought their best specimens of fine stock—Chester White, Poland China, etc.—to a county fair in Arkansas. The local farmers exhibited their hogs, which still retained many of the points of the true razorback, and, to the surprise of the owners of the thoroughbreds, the native hogs won every prize. After the awards had been made, one of the importers approached one of the judges and said:

" 'We are not offended with your action in giving the prizes to your neighbors, but we feel confident that our hogs are superior in many respects to those you have favored, and just for information I would like to ask upon what points you judges based your decision.'

" 'Well, stranger,' replied the judge, 'there's no doubt that your hogs could be fattened easier and made to weigh more, but the trouble is they can't run fast enough.'

" 'Can't run fast enough?' exclaimed the swine breeder. 'This is the first time I ever heard of speed being a good qualification in a hog. Why should a hog be able to run fast?'

" 'The niggers, sir, the niggers,' replied the judge. 'Your hogs would be all right for meat, but the niggers could steal them too easily. With our hogs they would have more trouble in catching them. Do you get the point?'

"The exhibitor evidently got the point, as the conversation ended and he took his fine hogs back home, having learned a lesson in swine breeding that he had previously overlooked."

Razorbacks

"LITTLE pig, big pig, root, hog, or die," was a trite saying current some years ago in the daily press. It was used to express the certainty that

By H. B. Parks. From *Southwestern Lore*, edited by J. Frank Dobie, Publications of the Texas Folk-Lore Society. Number IX, 1931, pp. 15–26. Copyright, 1931, by the Texas Folk-Lore Society. Austin.

human life depended on personal exertion. This saying, almost meaningless now, has a direct and continuous lineage back to the dawn of history. This sonorous sentence, almost as meaningless as the famous "Eni, meni, mini, mo," comes directly from a salutation to a hog totem. It is easy to see why in the warm lands, which were the cradles of the infant races, the hog, with its sagacity, its quickness to learn, and its attachment for man, should have furnished the theme for a totemic demigod; indeed, it is highly probable that this totem has yet many followers.

In the Egyptian pantheon, the hog appears in several forms but plays no important part. As a rule it is just the homely family sow with her mess of fat babies, and it is the deity of fecundity, of happiness, and of wealth. In India, on the other hand, the hog is somebody. Its earliest record in myth is on a par with the razorback stories of today. In the oldest version of the religion of Brahma it is recorded that when Brahma wished to create the world he took the form of a hog, waded out into the sea of Nothingness, and rooted up mud which when dry became India. This same idea was expressed several years ago at a meeting of the National Live Stock Association at Chicago, when a farmer in boasting of his state and its hogs said, "If all the hogs in the state of Iowa were made into one big hog, it could root out the Panama Canal in a single day."

The hog belongs not only to the Eastern and classic mythologies but also to those of the North. When Freyr, the Apollo of the Norse Gods, wished to go to battle, although he possessed the swiftest of all horses, Bloodyhoof, he would mount a sandy-haired boar which could outrun any horse and at the same time protect itself with its tushes. This story has a counterpart current in Northern Mississippi. A farm demonstration agent was anxious to improve the stock of hogs raised in his county. He imported a nine-months-old pig that weighed 300 pounds and brought in a three-year-old razorback that weighed ninety pounds. Then, calling the farmers together, he showed the two animals, pointing out the advantages of good stock and good feeding. When he thought the proper impression had been made, he called on the leading farmer of the county to express his opinion. "Well," said the farmer, "the fat boy is a dandy and all that, but the slim hog is the hog for this county. You see, a hog to be worth anything has just got to be able to outrun the niggers and scallywags."

In every country where free range still exists the razorback is common, and tales relative to his behavior hold an important place in the lore of the folk. The collection of tales that follows comes from East Texas. While these tales exist in many forms and are very old, yet the East Texas versions have a certain individuality.[1]

The setting for the story-telling is a farmyard in a clearing in Houston County. Against the pines stands a story-and-a-half log house with a

---

[1] For something of a historical treatment of the razorbacks and also for various additional folk yarns about the animal, read Chapter IV, "The Razorbacks," in *A Vaquero of the Brush Country*, by J. Frank Dobie, Dallas, Texas, 1929.—H. B. P.

gallery in front. The house is almost a century old and shows its age. The proper amount of discarded house and farm implements decorates the yard. The time is early winter, and twilight has brought the dwellers in from labor. The patriarch, Old Jim Baker, sits in a rocker on the gallery. In the yard some sons and grandsons are doing the chores.

One by one the group on the gallery increased as the male Bakers finished their day's work and assembled for supper. In the side yard Miss Sue, as the old maid sister, aunt, and grandaunt was called, was taking in the wash.

"Hi, you, you needn't expect any supper till I get this wash sprinkled and rolled; so make yourselves comfortable," came from around the corner, and with varying expression of face and some underbreath comments, the Bakers picked the least splintery planks on the gallery as resting places, awaiting Miss Sue's call to supper.

"Hi, Jim," somebody said, and out of the growing darkness came what appeared to be another Baker.

"What's the hurry? Stay, eat and gas awhile."

"Don't care if I do," came from Jim, as he lumped down heavily on an empty board.

"Where ya been?" asked Old Man Baker.

"Down to Ev Libbie's helping kill horgs."

"What you so glum about?"

"Well," answered Jim, "I'm dead tired, and somehow it makes me sorter sick when things don't go right, whether they're mine or not, and poor old Ev has the worst luck."

"What's wrong with Ev now? You say you been helping kill horgs for two days and you're dead tired and are pitying old Ev. Why, last spring he had the pertest passel of pigs I ever laid eyes on. What's wrong? Somebody steal 'em? Got cholery, or can't he find them?"

"Well, yes and no. You see Ev had those dandy little pigs fat as butter and as tame as cats. When summer came, he turned 'em out on the south fork of the crick to grow up on mast, and in July he sent me to look 'em up. Well, they had grown into big rangy shoats, and then the drouth came on and the mast ended and them pigs took to eating pine sprouts. Every time Ev saw 'em they were longer and rangier than ever. Yesterday morning he sent me and Bob out to drive 'em up to the pen and when I found 'em I couldn't believe my eyes. They were the longest, skinniest razorbacks I ever laid eyes on. We killed 'em yesterday and hung 'em up to cool last night and today we cut 'em up and made sausage and tried out the lard."

"Where's the catch?" came from the elder Baker.

"They ain't none. It's just Ev's poor luck. You see, them razorbacks looked rich in fat, but they'd been runnin' in the pine woods, and when we tried out that fat, them pigs averaged a pound of lard and two gallons of turpentine apiece and turpentine's got no selling price. It does beat all what poor luck some folks have."

"Huh!" snorted Dad Baker.

"Send him to the head of the class!" came from the darkness, and every-body laughed.

"Well, Bud"—this came from the only non-Baker in the group, a son-in-law—"Old Ev is just behind the times. He ought to wake up and get out of the dumps. You remember, Dad (this addressed to old man Baker), the year I worked for Dave McCullum down by Grovetown. Dave was right up to the spot. Went everywhere, read everything, and nothing got past him. He'd take an old machine and tinker it up in no time and sell it for twice what he paid. Was always a-buying sick or crippled animals and a-doctoring them and a-making money, but that year he almost found his match."

"Hay, what'd he do with it, light it?"

"Don't get ahead of yourself. It's your turn next. That summer he bought a dozen runty pigs, well along to'rd razorbacks, and 'lowed he'd make 200 pounders out of 'em agin' frost. I went way down in the thicket after 'em and they was thin and scairt. Had to put a lid on the wagon box to keep 'em from jumping out. The whole lot wouldn't weigh 500 pounds. I unloaded 'em in the barn lot. You see, the barn and lot is on top a hill over a little creek. It ain't much of a hill but when it goes down, it goes all at once and then you are in Dave's bottom land where the spring is. Right beside the barn was a little draw and acrost it on the next ridge was Dave's goober patch fenced in, hog tight and bull high.

"The next morning Dave says to me, 'Take Ben and Georgie (his two boys) and the dogs, and take those pigs over and put 'em in the goober patch.' So we did and closed up the gap tight. Just after noon Mrs. Dave came a-hollering that the pigs were in the garden patch, and sure enough they were all there, and the way they ate when we put 'em in the barn lot, they hadn't got many goobers. Next morning we put 'em in again and by noon half of 'em were out and by night all were back at the barn begging for corn.

"'Dag gum,' says Dave, 'I don't believe those pigs like goobers, but what gets me is how they get out.'

"By Saturday night, the pigs had finished a week of getting out and Dave says, 'Dag gum, I'm clear beat out. I've watched those pigs a whole week and I don't know how they get out. I'll give you a dollar if you'll find out.'

"So Sunday I put the pigs in the patch early and picked a nice shady place. Thinks I, now I'll sit here and see how they get out and make a dollar easy. I sat there and watched the pigs. They didn't seem to have much luck rooting up goobers. The ground was too hard for 'em. They would root and root but just couldn't turn up the goobers. I was a-sitting there a-watching the pigs and a-thinking what I'd do with that dollar, and the first thing I knowed I waked up and it was way past noon and when I looked there wasn't a pig in that patch. I'll be beat if those pigs didn't get to the house ahead of me—and the hurrahing I got! Dave says it's no use, that he'll have to take a day off and find out himself.

"Monday morning Dave put the pigs in the goobers and sent me to the bottom field to cut out some 'simmon sprouts. Along about two by the sun I got hot and tired and went to the edge of the field at the foot of the hill and sat there in the shade a-resting, when all at once something came smashing through the branches of the tree and down cawhollop on the ground in front of me and there lay one of the razorbacks. Huh! I thinks, hole under that fence and that pig fell out. So I sat there to watch. The pig went a-limping off and in a few minutes way down at the end of the field I saw another pig come a-sailing down. Then I beat it for the house.

" 'Dave,' I hollers, 'them pigs fall out of that pen.'

" 'No,' says he.

" 'Shure as shootin',' says I.

"So we went out to the patch and only four pigs were a-rooting in the goobers. We went round on the bluff side but there was no hole to fall out of. Well, we was just a-standing there guessing when, zip, a pig flew past us 'bout head high and went over the fence into the bushes.

" 'Dag gum,' says Dave.

" 'Huh!' says I, and we climbed up on the rail fence and sat there and watched those pigs. One close to us had a hole rooted right up against a goober hill but couldn't bust out the goobers. He pushed and pushed, but the dirt didn't move, and he backed outa the hole and looked at it thoughtful like, and backed off a rod or so and took a run at it and drove his snoot under that goober hill. Out it come, and how that pig gulped the goobers! Then he rooted at another hill and took another run, and this time he didn't get his nose far enough down and it stuck in the hard top soil, and, it's the Gospel truth, his hind end flew up and away he went a-sailing over the fence.

" 'Dag gum,' says Dave, 'I fix that.' And we went back to the house.

"Dave was thoughtful all evening. The next morning he says, 'I'll take the razorbacks out this morning.'

"Well, I didn't hear about a hog or see one for two or three weeks; so one Sunday morning I strolls over to the goober patch and there was all the pigs a-fattening nicely, all a-rooting and turning up the soil like mad. You see, those pigs were just too light behind to root in hard dirt and Dave had tied a chunk of cast iron to each one of their tails."

"Hay, you, don't you know the first liar hasn't got a ghost of a chance," "Give him the medal," "Throw him out," all came as the approval of the Bakers.

"Say, boy, those pigs of Dave McCullum's may be all right, but both them and Dave had better take lessons. They don't know nothing. You know three year ago when I stayed up to Grandpa Johnson's? Well, he had a little long razorback he called Sheffield because he was like English steel. Take it and make you like it. But he paid the penalty. He sure did. Grandpa had put in a new clearing on the east road and fenced it with an eight-rail, stake-and-rider fence.

" 'Bout the time roastenears were ripe that pig got to getting into that patch of corn and a-smashing it something terrible. Grandpa walks round that fence four or five times before he found how that razorback got in, and then it was so funny that Grandpa comes home to dinner and all through the meal he was a-chuckling to himself. Finally he told us that the razorback had a private tunnel into the corn patch, and he took us all out there to see it. Sure enough, in one low place there had been a little gully under the fence, and when the field was cleared a holler log was used to fill the gully and the fence was built right acrost it. The little razorback had found by going through the holler log he could git into the field. Now, Grandpa just set a-laughing and laughing.

" 'What's funny?' I asked.

" 'Nothing now, but wait and see. You boys pull down about three lengths of that fence and I show you a Yankee trick.'

"Well, we did.

" 'Now,' says Grandpa, 'get that holler log out of that gully,' and we did.

" 'Now, lay it in the line of the fence so both ends is out,' and we did.

" 'Now, put the fence back like it always was,' and we did.

" 'Now, pile stumps till you fill up the gully under the fence,' and we did.

" 'Now, come over here behind these bushes and you'll see a sight worth seeing, or I'm no Johnson,' and we did.

"Well, in about a half hour that razorback came a-easing up to where the end of the log had been and couldn't find it. Then he rooted around and around, and by the by he spies the open end of the log. He looks all around and takes a header into the log and pops out in the pasture at the other end. He looked all around mighty queer; then he roots a bit, and pop into the log he goes again. This time he came out and looked queerer than ever, and before you could say 'Scat' he went through the log again. Grandpa was a-laying on the ground just a-rolling with laughter but we dar'n't make a noise because we'd miss the fun if we scared that pig. Well, the pig got to running through that log and 'round to the other end of the log time and again; the more he ran the faster he went till all you could see was a sandy-like streak and all to once he rolled over and lay still.

" 'Well, I declare to goodness, he wrung his own neck,' says Grandpa."

"You're no amatoor," put in somebody. "Best liar of the Bakers," added another.

"Huh! you boys ain't heard nothin' yet." Old man Baker came to life with a snap. He had pretended to be asleep while all this story-telling was going on. "Right after the War between the States your Grandpa lived in Palestine and hauled freight from the landing down on the Trinity River to outside towns. He and Nick Busby was pardners in a livery stable and stage coach line. Pa did the freighting and Busby drove the coach and I was just a sizer boy and worked 'round, curried horses, fed, and was general help. Old Nick took a shine to me, and when he made the long trip to Jacksonville, he took me along for company.

"One day we carried an English woman who was going from St. Louis to Houston. Everywhere we stopped she'd say, 'Boots, go get me a drink of water,' and she never thanked me or anything. But when we got to the landing on the river, she told me to carry her things on board the *Leon*. That was the steamboat, and when I set them down in her room, she gave me an English coin.

"Now, at this time there were a lot of Yankee sharpers coming to Texas to buy cheap land. You see, the War took all the men and all the niggers and all the money, and there was nothing left to farm with and no one to farm. So land was cheap. One day we was a-waiting at Jacksonville for time to start with the coach, when Amos Whitecombe came up to Busby, and, leading him behind the coach, says, 'Nick, I've got a Yank who wants to buy river bottom land and I want you to talk river bottom land all the way from here to the Landing and call his attention to that land of mine that used to belong to the Bowdens. If he buys, you get 20 per cent. I can't go and need to make the sale.'

" 'Bring him on,' and Mr. Nick got up on the stage and looked very important. I, not knowing what to do, just stood there. Here come Whitecombe and a tall slim Yank who was introduced as Mr. Caldwell of Cincinnati. He got in and I put in the trunk and the carpet bag and away we went. The passenger was solemn as a preacher at a baptizing, but when we hit the Neches bottom he asked Nick to stop. He wanted to see the trees. We stopped, and then he was more social, and, say, he liked trees and plants and river bottoms.

"Nick said, 'You get up here in front so you can see. The boy will ride inside.'

" 'No, let the boy stay. No boy wants to be inside,' and he got back in and off we went again.

" 'Well,' says Nick, 'Neches is a nice river but it's nothing to the Trinity. Just wait till we see that and you'll see trees.'

"When we reached the hill that is over the Trinity bottom, Nick stopped and pointed over the bottom and says, 'There's Trinity bottom, fifteen miles wide and a hundred miles long. The finest hardwood forest in the world.'

"The Yank didn't say much. He just looked. As we got down the hill and started across the bottom, Mr. Nick pointed out the pecans, the gums, the oaks, and made talk a-plenty. The man didn't say much, just 'um hu' and 'unt o.' When he was about a mile out from the hill, he says all of a sudden, 'What are those muddy places on all those trees.'

" 'Why,' says Nick, 'that's just where old man Brown's hogs been scratching the mud off their sides.'

" 'Huh!' says the Yank. 'Some hogs! Those marks are at least three feet off the ground.'

" 'Well,' says Nick, 'you haven't seen anything yet,' and went on a-talking about rich bottom land and what it would raise.

"In near the six-mile slough, all at once the Yank hollers out. 'What about those muddy streaks on those trees? They must be at least seven feet high.'

" 'Why, sure they are,' replies Mr. Nick. 'This is Lon Benson's range, and he's got them improved Georgia porkers. On this fine range with all this rich mast of acorns, pecans, and crawdads, and such, 'tain't nothing uncommon to find hogs that high.' Nick went right on talking about what that land would be worth when it would be cleared and how the logs would pay for the clearing.

"By that time we'd hit the river road, and the stranger wasn't interested in the river. He kept looking at the trees. When we were at the East Bend, he says, 'Now, tell me what made those muddy streaks on those trees,' and he points to the line the last high water left, some thirteen feet or more up the trees.

" 'Didn't I tell you, you hadn't saw nothing yet?' said Mr. Nick. 'Why, we're in Jake Long's range now, and he keeps the regular genuwine Texas razorbacks that can shake the acorns and pecans off the trees, can jump the river, and produce more bacon than any other kind of hogs. If you buy this land and put it into corn, you'll need that kind of hogs, because the ears will be so big no ordinary hog can handle 'em.'

"That settled it, and the Yank says, 'You tell Mr. Whitecombe to draw up the deeds and I'll be back in a week,' and he gave Mr. Nick a bunch of papers. 'This is the collateral.' I have always remembered that word.

"We got to the Landing and the *Leon* was there almost busting to get away. A mate was a-cussing a nigger and the captain was a-showing a lady aboard and then just as we were all ready to say goodby, that Yankee looked queer and said, 'Mr. Busby, you are quite a land salesman.'

"Mr. Nick was tickled and says, 'You do me proud, Mr. Caldwell. I can do a good job at almost anything.'

" 'Well,' says the Yankee, 'you did a good job of explaining about those mud marks on those trees. You see, I'm a sawmill man and I know high water marks when I see them, and this whole trip was made to see if there was sufficient water in the Trinity to raft lumber, and as for your razorbacks, you're certainly some liar.'

"With that he jumped on the boat, or I think Mr. Nick would have killed him, he was so mad."

"Hey, all of you out there, wash and come to supper."

Shortly the rattle of knives and forks spoke most eloquently of the appetites of the Bakers and of the culinary efforts of Miss Sue. As the meal neared its end, she cleared her throat, saying, "You men did the razorbacks proud, but you did not tell the best one of them all. Years ago before I joined the Baker tribe I lived over to Henry Woodword's at Cherokee Springs. Henry had a lot of hogs he was fattening that fall, and every day he snapped out a load of corn and drove into the woods pasture. Here he'd break the ears over the edge of the wagon box so that the hogs could get at the grain. This made considerable noise, and the hogs soon learned it meant corn. That fall there was little cold weather, and the corn ran out before killing time. Henry noticed the hogs were falling off very rapidly and one day in going through the pasture saw the whole bunch of hogs running like mad toward an old dead pine. Before they reached it, they suddenly turned and made for another pine across the hill. After watching them for half an hour, Henry realized that the hogs were following a woodpecker around. They thought the woodpecker's hammering was Henry a-breaking ears of corn."

Out in western Iowa the story of razorbacks with weights tied to their tails has a counterpart that cannot be omitted.

One afternoon in mid-summer a good many years ago a mechanic working in Council Bluffs for the McCormick Harvester Company set out to repair a binder for a farmer living up the Missouri River. He boarded a combination freight and passenger train, and it was not long before restlessness on account of slow progress drove him to the caboose. Here he entered into conversation with the conductor and was invited to ride in the cupola. As the train crept along he could see the rich bottom lands green with alfalfa and yellow with wheat. The mechanic was an observant fellow, and he noticed in many of the alfalfa fields circular bare spots, all of about the same size. He asked the conductor for an explanation, but the conductor could not explain. At last he reached his destination, and soon had the binder repaired.

Night was near; there was no train back until next morning; so the farmer was the host. After supper while the harvesters were sitting around waiting for bedtime and talking, the mechanic brought up again the observation that had aroused his curiosity.

"Mr. Bronson," he said, "while I was riding up here on the train, I noticed in many of the alfalfa fields circular bare spots, probably six to eight feet across. What are they? Can it be some disease?"

Someone gave a kind of a cross between a laugh and a cough. Mr. Bronson replied, "You are a stranger in this part of Iowa, I know from your remarks. We live where the Old Missouri has left us the blackest, richest soil in the world and also the stickiest.

"About those round bare spots in the alfalfa, this is how they happen to be. We raise hogs out here, the finest and best in the whole corn belt. Those alfalfa patches you noticed were hog pastures. Now, you see most of these have water holes for the hogs to wallow in. Well, Mr. Pig wallows in the mud and it sticks to him, and then he goes out to eat alfalfa. The mud commences to dry and that hurts; so he goes to a fence post and scratches off the mud till he is reasonably clean, but he can't scratch the mud off his tail; so a lump is left in the curlicue at the end. Well, that pig goes through this performance three or four times a day, and each time the lump on his tail gets larger and heavier. Finally comes a day when he tries to pull his tail load out and he can't. He gets scared and gives a mighty jump and pulls the lump out into the alfalfa until it sticks in the hay and then he is tied, tied by his own tail. He must eat, and so he eats round and round till the circle is cleaned as far as he can wiggle and twist.

"About this time the farmer misses the pig and knows just what to do. He takes a sledge hammer and goes down to the alfalfa patch and there is the pig anchored by the tail. He hits the ball of hard black soil; it shivers like glass and the pig makes tracks for the slop trough. Now, go back to Council Bluffs and tell the boys that one."

King Solomon's Power-Pump

CRAWDADS is the leggiest things in cr'ation, yit they kin claw theirselves into a hole slicker than a minute, and kin mine thar for water deep as coal-diggers.

Well, summer afore the Big Snow hit it were the Gret Drougth: hottest, dry-uppedest, dog-dayest time in the world! Couldn't only loll your tongue out and laze around. Hit were a sight!

Green leaves curled up yaller on the timber. Crow-birds settin' in a gang thar, gappin' their beaks. God couldn't squeeze a song outen a mipkin lesser than a squawk. Ole Greasy Creek were drippin' a puny dreen like a sorghum barrel. The trails was dried up to salt.

Well, my ole sow, Chinkapin, she'd jist farrered a new litter o' piggies, and her dugs was gone dry. So she 'lowed, I reckin, she'd go prospectin' for liquor to raise the gang.

Anyways she squandered off, and arter a spell, as usual, I went huntin' of her. Fer me and Chinky us nacherly was chum-fellers, which hit were what allers grumbled my ole woman.

Well, I won't bescribe ye now the len'th and days o' my hunt in that all-fired drougth. I'll cut to the finish.

I were crawlin' up the dry bed o' Gabe's Branch, and I come to the head of a holler where there used to onct was a waterfall had fell high down off over a bench-rock. But nary a drap now!

And I were gazin' up thar, lickin' the thirst of mimory, till slow thar I waked like in a dream. And thar in my dream hit come over the bench-rock, drip-fallin', the wee purtiest leetle water-stream, and run off down the branch-bed.

"Dad fetch me!" says I in my dream, "hit's gittin' moughtier and biggerer."

And right hit were so; for soon hit were roarin' down like a mill-dam shower. And up over beyand the bench-rock I heerd thar the quarest suck-chuggerin' noise, like hit were a gret stranglin'.

"Sol, air ye dreamin' fer shore?" says I.

From *Tall Tales of the Kentucky Mountains*, by Percy MacKaye, pp. 59–63. Copyright, 1924, by the Century Company; 1926, by Percy MacKaye. New York: George H. Doran Company.

"Dadburn me ef I be!" says Solomon.

And I climbs up over that bench-rock, and thar, on a leetle hollock be-yand, I sees my ole sow Chinkapin, ring-arounded by her gang o' shoats, and her nose-snout glued in a ground-hole.

Doin'? What were she doin' of?

That's what I run thar to look.

Chilluns, hit were a crawfish hole, that's what! And thar she was pumpin' water with her snout from the bottom of hit—*chug-chug! chucky-chuck!*—seventeen gallons a second, and the little shoats splashin' in the aidge of the tide. I up and kicked her in the snout and jest saved her babies bein' drownded. And thar I measured the hole by drappin' a rock in. Hit were forty-nine foot deep with a plumb string.

The ole she-pump up and run fer home, squealin' a river-brook from her snout behint her. But I tuck arter her with the shoat-gang. To home she were moughty shy and shame-bashed, ole Chinkapin. She tried for to hide her snout under the cabin timber. Reckon she thought I'd onscrew hits gum-nozzle and pack hit to the fair, to bog first prize in water-weetchery. But I warn't huntin' blue ribbons.

I jist called my ole woman, and we catched a bushel o' crawdabs and planted 'em in our gyarden-patch holler. And afore night I had sicked the ole pumper-deevil at ary crawdab's hole in the patch and set her a-pumpin' thar with her snout end.

Well, sirs, next day I hired my neebors and builded a splash-dam. And all that summer and fall I sold 'em water for two bits a barrel, and run nine corn-grindin' mills in the creek-bed o' Greasy. Folks do say that water-flux was cause o' the Big Snow come next winter.

Day and night in the Mount'ins, miles round, ye could hear ole Chinkapin suck-chuggerin' thar. And that season she doubled her record litterin' new piggies, which I raised 'em to bacon and kep' the hull country from starvin' that year.

Yea, my rounders! When hit come for hog-flesh and water-power, that time o' the Gret Droughth they shore did call me King Solomon.

Uncle Davy Lane

I MUST not forget, in these random sketches, my old friend and neighbor, Uncle Davy Lane. Some men make an early and decided impression upon you—features, actions, habits, all the entire man, real and artificial. "Uncle Davy" was that kind of man.

I will mention a few things that make me remember him. His looks were peculiar. He was tall, dark, and rough-skinned; lymphatic, dull,

---

From *Fisher's River (North Carolina) Scenes and Characters,* by "Skitt" [H. E. Taliaferro], pp. 50–58, 63–74, 79–93. New York: Harper & Bros. 1859.

For additional material on and by "Skitt," cf. *Carolina Humor,* Sketches by Harden E. Taliaferro . . . , Foreword by David K. Jackson (1938).

and don't-care-looking in his whole physiognomy. He had lazy looks and movements. Nothing could move him out of a slow, horse-mill gait but snakes, of which "creeturs he was monstrous 'fraid." The reader shall soon have abundant evidence of the truth of this admission in his numerous and rapid flights from "sarpunts."

Uncle Davy was a gunsmith, and, as an evidence of the fact, he carried about with him the last gun he ever made. His gun, a rifle, was characteristic of its maker and owner—rough and unfinished outside, but good within. It was put in an old worm-eaten half-stock which he had picked up somewhere, and the barrel had never been dressed nor ground outside. He would visit a neighbor early in the morning, sit down with his rifle across his knees, in "too great a hurry" to set it aside, would stay all day, would lay it by only at meals, which he seldom refused, but "never was a-hongry."

He had a great fund of long-winded stories and incidents, mostly manufactured by himself—some few he had "hearn"—and would bore you or edify you, as it might turn out, from sun to sun, interspersing them now and then with a dull, guttural, lazy laugh.

He became quite a proverb in the line of big story-telling. True, he had many obstinate competitors, but he distanced them all farther than he did the numerous snakes that "run arter him." He had given his ambitious competitors fair warning thus:

"Ef any on 'um beats me, I'll sell out my deadnin' and hustle off to other deadnin's."

In sheer justice to Uncle Davy, however, and with pleasure I record the fact, that he reformed his life, became a Christian, I hope, as well as a Baptist, and died a penitent man.

As stated, he was never known to get out of a snail's gallop only when in contact with snakes; and the reader shall now have, in Uncle Davy's own style, an account of his flight from a coachwhip snake.

I. The Chase

"I had a hog claim over beyant Moor's Fork, and I concluded I'd take old Bucksmasher (his rifle), and go inter the big huckleberry patch, on Round Hill, in sarch for 'um. Off I trolloped, and toddled about for some time, but couldn't find head nur tail uv 'um. But while I was moseyin' about, I cum right chug upon one uv the biggest, longest, outdaciousest coachwhip snakes I uver laid my peepers on. He rared right straight up, like a May-pole, licked out his tarnacious tongue, and good as said, 'Here's at you, sir. What bizness have you on my grit?' Now I'd hearn folks say ef you'd look a vinimus animil right plump in the eyes he wouldn't hurt you. Now I tried it good, just like I were trying to look through a millstone. But, bless you, honey! he had no more respect fur a man's face and eyes than he had fur a huckleberry, sure's gun's iron. So I seed clearly that I'd have to try my trotters.

"I dashed down old Bucksmasher, and jumped 'bout ten steps the fust leap, and on I went wusser nur an old buck fur 'bout a quarter, and turned my noggin round to look fur the critter. Jehu Nimshi! thar he were right dab at my heels, head up, tongue out, and red as a nail-rod, and his eyes like two balls uv fire, red as chain lightnin'. I 'creased my verlocity, jumped logs twenty foot high, clarin' thick bushes, and bush-heaps, deep gullies, and branches. Again I looked back, thinkin' I had sartinly left it a long gap behind. And what do you think? By jingo! he'd hardly begun to run—jist gittin' his hand in. So I jist put flatly down again faster than uver. 'T wasn't long afore I run out'n my shot-bag, I went so fast, then out'n my shirt, then out'n my britches—luther britches at that—then away went my drawers. Thus I run clean out'n all my linnen a half a mile afore I got home; and, thinks I, surely the tarnul sarpunt are distanced now.

"But what do you think now? Nebuchadnezzar! thar he were, fresh as a mounting buck jist scared up. I soon seen that wouldn't do, so I jumped about thirty-five foot, screamed like a wildcat, and 'creased my verlocity at a monstrous rate. Jist then I begun to feel my skin split, and, thinks I, it's no use to run out'n my skin, like I have out'n my linnen, as huming skin are scarce, so I tuck in a leetle.

"But by this time I'd run clean beyant my house, right smack through my yard, scaring Molly and the childering, dogs, cats, chickens—uvrything —half to death. But, you see, I got shet uv my inimy, the sarpunt, fur it had respect fur my house, ef it hadn't fur my face and eyes in the woods. I puffed, and blowed, and sweated 'bout half an hour afore I had wind to tell Molly and the childering what were the matter.

"Poor old Bucksmasher staid several days in the woods afore I could have the pluck to go arter him."

When Uncle Davy told one snake story, he must needs exhaust his stock, big and little. After breathing a little from telling his coachwhip story, which always excited him, he would introduce and tell the story of his adventure with

II. THE HORN-SNAKE

"Fur some time arter I were chased by that sassy coachwhip, I were desput 'fraid uv snakes. My har would stand on eend, stiff as hog's bristles, at the noise uv uvry lizzard that ran through the leaves, and my flesh would jerk like a dead beef's.

"But at last I ventured to go into the face uv the Round Peak one day a-huntin'. I were skinnin' my eyes fur old bucks, with my head up, not thinkin' about sarpunts, when, by Zucks! I cum right plum upon one uv the curiousest snakes I uver seen in all my borned days.

"Fur a spell I were spellbound in three foot uv it. There it lay on the side uv a steep presserpis, at full length, ten foot long, its tail strait out, right up the presserpis, head big as a sasser, right toards me, eyes red as forked lightnin', lickin' out his forked tongue, and I could no more move

than the Ball Rock on Fisher's Peak. But when I seen the stinger in his
tail, six inches long and sharp as a needle, stickin' out like a cock's spur,
I thought I'd a drapped in my tracks. I'd ruther a had uvry coachwhip on
Round Hill arter me en full chase than to a bin in that drefful siteation.

"Thar I stood, petterfied with relarm—couldn't budge a peg—couldn't
even take old Bucksmasher off uv my shoulder to shoot the infarnul
thing. Nyther uv us moved nor bolted 'ur eyes fur fifteen minits.

"At last, as good luck would have it, a rabbit run close by, and the
snake turned its eyes to look what it were, and that broke the charm,
and I jumped forty foot down the mounting, and dashed behind a big
white oak five foot in diamatur. The snake he cotched the eend uv his tail
in his mouth, he did, and come rollin' down the mounting arter me jist
like a hoop, and jist as I landed behind the tree he struck t'other side
with his stinger, and stuv it up, clean to his tail, smack in the tree. He were
fast.

"Of all the hissin' and blowin' that uver you hearn sense you seen daylight, it tuck the lead. Ef there'd a bin forty-nine forges all a-blowin'
at once, it couldn't a beat it. He rared and charged, lapped round the
tree, spread his mouf and grinned at me orful, puked and spit quarts an'
quarts of green pisen at me, an' made the ar stink with his nasty breath.

"I seen thar were no time to lose; I cotched up old Bucksmasher from
whar I'd dashed him down, and tried to shoot the tarnil thing; but he kep'
sich a movin' about and sich a splutteration that I couldn't git a bead at
his head, for I know'd it warn't wuth while to shoot him any whar else. So
I kep' my distunce tell he wore hisself out, then I put a ball right between
his eyes, and he gin up the ghost.

"Soon as he were dead I happened to look up inter the tree, and what
do you think? Why, sir, it were dead as a herrin'; all the leaves was
wilted like a fire had gone through its branches.

"I left the old feller with his stinger in the tree, thinkin' it were the best
place fur him, and moseyed home, 'tarmined not to go out again soon.

"Now folks may talk as they please 'bout there bein' no sich things as
horn-snakes, but what I've seen I've seen, and what I've jist norated is true
as the third uv Mathy.

"I mout add that I passed that tree three weeks arterwards, and the
leaves and the whole tree was dead as a door-nail."

*   *   *   *   *

I shall not record a tithe of the hunting stories of my Western Hercules,
for they would make a ponderous volume. Only a few samples of the
many shall be given; and I here take occasion to express the sincere hope
that my countrymen will never return to such a state of barbarism as to
deify our Fisher's River hero, as the ancients did Hercules, and make for
him a mythology out of these imperfect records; for I now testify to all
coming generations that Uncle Davy Lane was but a mortal man, and has
been gathered to his fathers for several years. But excuse this digression:
my plea is, The importance of the subject demanded it.

I will give but a *few* of my hero's stories, and will begin, without being choice, with

III. The Fast-Running Buck

"Now I'd smashed up so many master old bucks 'bout Fisher's Gap, Blaze Spur, Flour Gap, clean round to Ward's Gap,[1] I 'cluded they mout be gittin' scass, and I'd let 'um rest a spell, and try my luck in other woods; so I toddled off to the Sugar-Loaf.[2]

"Now I know'd it were the time uv year fur old bucks to be hard'nin' thar horns, so I tuck the sunny side uv the Sugar Loaf. I kep' my eyes skinned all the way up, but nuver seen any thing tell I got nairly to the top, when up jumped one uv the poxtakedest biggest old bucks you uver seen. He dashed round the mounting faster nur a shootin' star ur lightnin'. But, howsomever, I blazed away at him, but he were goin' so fast round the Loaf, and the bullet goin' strait forrud, I missed him. Ev'ry day fur a week I went to that spot, allers jumped him up in ten steps uv the same place, would fire away, but allers missed him as jist norated.

"I felt that my credit as a marksman, and uv old Bucksmasher, was gittin' mighty under repair. I didn't like to be outgineraled in any sich a way by any sich a critter. I could smash bucks anywhar and any time, but that sassy rascal, I couldn't tech a har on him. He were a perfect dar-devil. One whole night I didn't sleep a wink—didn't bolt my eyes—fixin' up my plan. Next mornin' I went right smack inter my blacksmith shop, tuck my hammer, and bent old Bucksmasher jist to suit the mounting, so that when the pesky old buck started round the mounting the bullet mout take the twist with him, and thus have a far shake in the race.

"I loadened up, and moseyed off to try the 'speriment. I 'ruv at the spot, and up he jumped, hoisted his tail like a kite, kicked up his heels in a banterin' manner, fur he'd outdone me so often he'd got raal sassy. I lammed away at him, and away he went round the mounting, and the bullet arter him—so good a man, and so good a boy. I stood chock still. Presently round they come like a streak uv sunshine, both buck and bullit, bullit singin' out, 'Whar is it? whar is it?' 'Go it, my fellers,' says I, and away they went round the Loaf like a Blue Ridge storm. Afore you could crack yer finger they was around again, bucklety-whet. Jist as they got agin me, bullit throwed him.

"I throwed down old Bucksmasher, out with my butcher-knife, jerked off my shot-bag and hung it on the horn uv one uv the purtiest things you uver seen. I thort I'd look at it better when I stuck my buck. I knifed him monstrous quick, and turned round to look at the curious thing I'd hung my shot-bag on, and it were gone most out'n sight. I soon seen it

---

[1] Different crossing-places of the Blue Ridge.—H. E. T.

[2] A lofty peak of the Blue Ridge, running up in a beautiful conical form, resembling a sugar-loaf.—H. E. T.

were the moon passin' along, and I'd hung my shot-bag on the corner uv it. I hated mightily to lose it, fur it had all my ammernition in it, and too 'bout a pound uv Thompson's powder.[1]

But I shouldered my old buck, moseyed home, skinned and weighed him, and he weighed 150 pounds clean weight. I slep' sound that night, fur I'd gained the victory. I went next day to look fur the moon, and to git my shot-bag, pervided it hadn't spilt it off in moseyin' so fast. Sure 'nuff, it came moseyin' along next day, jist at the same time o' day, with my shot-bag on its horn. I snatched it off, and told it to mosey on 'bout its business.

"Now thar's some things I'll describe the best I can, and I'm a tolluble hand at it, though I say it; but I nuver will tell a human critter how that moon looked. But I'll say this much: all that talk of 'stronimy and 'lossify 'bout the moon are nonsense; *that's what I know.* They can't fool this old 'coon, fur what I know I know—what I've seen I've seen."

After a lazy laugh, in which he cared not whether you engaged or not— at leas' his looks would so indicate—Uncle Davy would straighten himself, fetch a long breath, charge his mouth with a fresh chew of tobacco, and would proceed to tell of his

IV. RIDE IN THE PEACH-TREE

"Now when I got my shot-bag off uv the moon, I lost no time, which I'd lost a great deal arter that old buck, as jist norated. I moseyed home in a hurry, straightened old Bucksmasher, and piked off to Skull Camp,[2] to smash up a few old bucks on that grit. Soon as I landed I seen 'bout a dozen old bucks and one old doe. I planted myself, fur they was comin' right smack to'ads me, and I waited tell they got in shootin' range, as it were. I knowed ef I smashed Mrs. Doe fust I'd be right apt to smash all the Mr. Bucks. That's the way with all creation—the males allers a-traipsin' arter the females.

"So I lammed away at her, fotched her to the yeth, and the bucks scampered off. Agin I got loadened up they come back to the doe, smellin' round, and I blazed away again, and tripped up the heels uv one uv 'um. They'd run off a little ways uvry time, but again I'd load up thar'd allers be one ready to be smashed, and I jist kep' smashin' away tell there were but one left, and he were a whopper.

"I felt in my shot-bag, and, pox take the luck! there warn't a bullit in it—nothin' but a peach-stone. I crammed it down, thort I'd salute him with that, and blazed away, aimin' to hit him right behind the wethers,

---

[1] A favorite powder with hunters in that section, made by a man named John Thompson. I have no doubt of its being the best powder in the world.—H. E. T.

[2] A spur of the Blue Ridge, at the foot of which one or two human skeletons were found at the first settling of the country, where there were signs of an old hunters' camp; hence the name of the mountain.—H. E. T.

and, by golly! ef he didn't slap down his tail and outrun creation, and give it two in the game. I run up, out with my butcher-knife, stuck uvry one on 'um afore you could cry 'cavy. And sich a pile on 'um, all lyin' cross and pile, you nuver seen in yer borned days.

"I moseyed home in a turkey-trot, got Jim and Sanders and the little waggin, went arter 'um, and, I tell you, we had nice livin' fur a fortnight. Some o' the old bucks would a cut four inches clare fat on the rump. Molly didn't hev to use any hog fat nur fry no bacon with 'um. We sopped both sides uv ur bread, and greased ur mouths from ear to ear. It made the childering as sassy as it does a sea-board feller when he gits his belly full uv herrin'. Thar was skins plenty to make me and all the boys britches, and to buy ammernition to keep old Bucksmasher a-talkin' fur a long time, fur he's a mighty gabby old critter to varmunts uv uvry kind, well as to old bucks, he is.

"Arter makin' a desput smash among old bucks uvry whar else fur three very long years, I thort I'd try my luck in Skull Camp agin. I took plenty uv ammernition with me this time—didn't care about shootin' peach-stones any more out'n old Bucksmasher—and piked off full tilt.

"Soon as I got on good hunting yeth, I seen right by the side uv a clift uv rocks (I were on the upper side uv the clift) a fine young peach-tree, full uv master plum peaches. I were monstrous hongry and dry, and thanked my stars fur the good luck. I sot down old Bucksmasher, stepped from the top uv the clift inter the peach-tree—nuver looked down to see whar it were growin'—jerked out old Butch, and went to eatin' riproarin' fashion.

"I hadn't gulluped down more'n fifty master peaches afore, by golly! the tree started off, with me in it, faster nur you uver seen a scared wolf run. When it had run a mile ur so, I looked down to see what it mout mean. And what do you think? True as preachin', the peach-tree was growin' out'n an old buck, right behind his shoulders.

"I thort my time had come, for on he moseyed over logs, rocks, clifts, and all sorts o' things, and me up in the tree. He went so fast, he did, that he split the wind, and made it roar in my head like a harricane. I tried to pray, but soon found I had no breath to spar in that way fur he went so orful fast that my wind was sometimes clean gone. He run in that fashion fur fifteen mile, gin out, stopped to rest, when I got out'n my fast-runnin' stage mighty soon, and glad o' the chance.

"I left him pantin' away like he were mighty short o' wind, returned thanks fur once, tuck my foot in my hand, and walked all the way back to old Bucksmasher. I seen more old bucks on my way than I uver seen in the same length uv time in all my borned days. They knowed jist as well as I did that I had nothin' to smash 'um with. Thar they was a-kickin' up thar heels and snortin' at me fur fifteen long miles—miles measured with a 'coon-skin, and the tail throwed in fur good measure, fur sure. It were a mighty trial, but I grinned and endured it. I piked on and landed at the place whar I started in my peach-tree stage, found old Bucksmasher, shouldered him, and moseyed fur home, with my feathers cut, fur I'd made a water haul that time, fur sure and sartin."

"To—be—shore, Mr. Lane?" said old Mr. Wilmoth, a good, credulous old man; "ef I didn't know you to be a man of truth, I couldn't believe you. How do you think that peach-tree come up in the back of that deer?"

"Bless you, man! it was from the peach-stone I shot in his back, as jist norated—nothin' plainer."

V. The Pigeon-Roost

"Now, do ye see, a man will git tired out on one kind o' meat, I don't care a drot what it is ('ceptin' Johnson Snow, who nuver gits tired o' hog's gullicks and turnup greens). So I got tireder of them thar turkeys, which thar was so many, than I uver did uv old buck meat. I hearn uv a mighty pigeon-roost down in the Little Mountings,[1] so I 'tarmined to make a smash uv some uv 'um, to hev a variety uv all sorts o' meat. I had got to turnin' up my nose whenuver Molly sot turkey on the table, which I hated to do, fur she's a mighty kind critter.

"So I jist fixed up old Tower,[2] and filled my shot-bag chug full uv drap-shot, mounted old Nip,[3] and moseyed off fur the pigeon-roost. I 'ruv thar 'bout two hours by the sun, and frum that blessed hour till chock dark the heavens was dark with 'um comin' inter the roost. It is unconceivable to tell the number on 'um, which it were so great. Bein' a man that has a character fur truth, I won't say how many there was. Thar was a mighty heap uv saplins fur 'um to roost in, which they would allers light on the biggest trees fust, then pitch down on the little uns ter roost.

"Now jist at dark I thort I'd commence smashin' 'um; so I hitched old Nip to the limb uv a tree with a monstrous strong bridle—a good hitchin' place, I thort. I commenced blazin' away at the pigeons like thunder and lightnin'; which they'd light on big trees thick as bees, bend the trees to the yeth like they'd been lead. Uvry pop I'd spill about a pint uv drap-shot at 'um, throwed at 'um by Thompson's powder, which made a drefful smash among 'um. By hokey! I shot so fast, and so long, and so often, I het old Tower so hot that I shot six inches off uv the muzzle uv the old slut. I seen it were no use to shoot the old critter clean away, which I mout have some use fur agin; so I jist quit burnin' powder and flingin' shot arter I'd killed 'bout a thousand on 'um, fur sure.

"Arter I'd picked up as many on 'um as my wallets would hold, I looked for old Nip right smack whar I'd hitched him, but he were, like King Saul's asses, nowhar to be found. I looked a consid'able spell next to the yeth, but, bless you, honey! I mout as well a sarched fur a needle

---

[1] A range of mountains by that name, an offshoot from the Blue Ridge, in the "Hollows of the Yadkin."—H. E. T.

[2] The name of his musket.—H. E. T.

[3] The name of his horse.—H. E. T.

in a haystack. At last I looked up inter a tree 'bout forty foot high, and thar he were swingin' to a limb, danglin' 'bout 'tween the heavens and the yeth like a rabbit on a snare-pole. I could hardly keep from burstin' open laughin' at the odd fix the old critter were in. The way he whickered were a fact, when I spoke to him—wusser nur ef I'd a had a stack uv fodder fur him ur a corn-crib to put him in."

"How come him up thar, Uncle Davy?" said Bill Holder, a great quiz.

"Why, I hitched him to the limb uv a big tree bent to the yeth with pigeons, you numskull, and when they riz the tree went up, and old Nip with it, fur sure."

"But how did you get him down?" said Bill, again.

"That's nuther here nor thar; I got him down, and that's 'nuff fur sich pukes as you ter know. Soon as I got him down I piked fur home with my pigeons, and we made uvry pan and pot stink with 'um fur one whet, and they made us all as sassy as a Tar River feller when he gits his belly ful uv fresh herrin'."

VI. BIG PEACH-EATING

"These is the oncommonest biggest plum peaches I uver seen sense my peepers looked on daylight," said Uncle Frost Snow, in the presence of Uncle Davy Lane, while a party were making a desperate havoc of some very fine peaches. "They is 'most as good as I use' to eat in ole Albermarle, Fudginny. While I lived thar I eat a bushel on jist sich peaches at one eatin'." This was said to draw out a story from our hero. Uncle Frost was good at that.

"Pshaw! fidgittyfudge!" said Uncle Davy; "that's nothin' to a bait I once tuck in ole Pitsulvany, Virginny. I and Uncle John Lane went into his orchard one day, and thar was two grate big plum peach-trees so full that the limbs lay on the ground all round.

" 'Dave,' said Uncle John, 'do ye see them big peaches thar? I can beat you eatin' 'um so fur that you won't know yerself.'

" 'Not so fast, Uncle John,' says I.

" 'I'll bet you ten buckskins,' says he.

" 'Done, by Jeeminny!' says I.

" 'Take yer choice uv the trees,' says he.

" 'Here's at you! this one,' says I.

"And at it we went, like Sampson killin' the Philistines, with our butcher-knives, commencin' at 'bout twelve ur clock, and moseyed into 'um till 'most night.

" 'How do ye come on, Dave?' said Uncle John.

" 'Fust-rate,' says I—'jist gittin' my hand in. How do you navigate, Uncle John?' says I.

" 'I gin up,' says he. 'My craw's full,' says he.

"I looked up, and, Jehu Nimshi! ef we hadn't eat till all the limbs on his tree had riz from the yeth two foot, and mine had riz three foot

The peach-stones lay in two piles, and they looked fur all the world like two Injun mounds—mine a nation sight the biggest."

"Haw! haw! haw!" laughed Uncle Frost; "that takes the rag off the bush."

VII. SOME APPLE-EATING

"I'm danged," said Dick Snow, "ef I can't beat any man in this crowd eatin' apples."

"How many can you eat, yearlin'?" said Uncle Davy. "I'm a snorter in that line, sartin."

"Don't know adzackly; a half a bushel, I s'pose," said Dick.

"Bah! that's nothin'. No more'n a bar to an elephant. That same Uncle John Lane which I won the buckskins from, eatin' peaches, not satisfied with one lickin', tuck me into his apple orchard, and 'Dave,' says he, 'do you see yon two big leathercoat apple-trees?'

" 'Yes,' says I; 'and what of that?'

" 'You see,' says he, 'they're mighty full, with thar limbs lyin' on the yeth?' says he.

" 'Yes,' says I; 'and what does all that signify? Don't be beatin' the bush so long. Come out! Be a man, and tell me what you're arter,' says I.

" 'I want to win them thar buckskins back agin,' says Uncle John.

" 'Can't do it,' says I.

" 'Which tree will you take?' says he.

" 'This bully un,' says I.

" 'Bad choice,' says he; 'but I'll beat you the easier,' says he.

"So we moseyed into 'um yearly in the mornin', and 'bout twelve o'clock he called fur the calf-rope. I'd beat him all holler. Uncle John were swelled out like a hoss with the colic, while I looked as trim as a grayhound. We looked, and the limbs uv my tree had riz from the yeth full four foot and his'n three foot. Thar was apple-peelin's and cores enough under them thar trees to a fed five dozen hogs, sartin."

"I'm danged," said Dick Snow, "ef that don't take the huckleberry off uf my 'simmon."

VIII. THE TAPE-WORM

Patent medicines go every where; so do the almanacs of the inventors of such medicines. Soon after Dr. Jayne commenced publishing his almanacs, one of them got into the Fisher's River region. It was quite a wonder. It was as great a show as the elephant. Some one showed Uncle Davy the picture of the tape-worm, and read the account of it. He was determined not to be outdone, and held forth as follows:

"Fiddlesticks and Irish 'taters! For to think that a man of larnin', like Dr. Jaynes, should prent sich a little flea-bitten story as that! He sartinly nuver seen any *crape*-wurrums."

"*Tape-worms*, Uncle Davy," said one.

"Nuver mind, and save your breath," said he, very emphatically; "I know what I'm explanigatin' about. I say Dr. Jaynes were mighty pushed fur a wurrum story to prent sich a little baby story as that you have jist norated frum his book. If he'd a called on me, I'd a g'in him one what was wuth prentin'."

"Let's have it, Uncle Davy," said several voices.

"I'm a great mind not to tell it here by the side uv this poor little thing uv Dr. Jayneses. It makes me rantankerous mad to hear sich little stuff, it does. But here's at you, as you look like you'd die ef you don't hear it.

"Where I cum from, in ole Pitsulvany, Virginny, thar lived a strange-lookin' critter by the name uv Sallie Pettigrew. I sha'n't try to describe her, for it is onpossible. She were a sight, sure. She looked more like a bar'l on stilts than anything I can think on. She could eat as much meat sometimes as five dogs, and soon arter eatin' it could drink as much water as a thirsty yoke uv oxen, sartin'. You needn't be winkin' and blinkin' thar; truth, uvry word uv it. She was monstrous fond uv fish, which it was onpossible almost to git anuff fur her to make a meal on. And then arter eatin' the fish, she would drink galluns upon galluns uv water. The people got mighty tired uv her eatin' and drinkin' so much, and thort suthin must be the matter. They bought a whole bar'l uv salt herrin's; they cooked 'um, and she gulluped down the last one uv 'um. They tied her fast, so that she couldn't git to water. She hollered and bawled fur water, and seemed like gwine inter fits. They brought a bowl uv water, and placed it close to her mouth, not close enough fur her to drink, though. They helt it thar fur some time; at last they seed suthin' poke its head out'n her mouth, tryin' to drink. One uv 'um run and got the shoe-pinchers and nabbed it by the head, and commenced drawin' it out. He drawed and drawed, wusser nur a man drawin' jaw teeth, till it looked like he would nuver git done drawin' the critter out. At last he got done; and sich a pile! and sich a tape-wurrum! The poor 'oman fainted away, and we like to a nuver a fotched her to. But when she did cum to, Jehu Nimshi! you mout a hearn her a shoutin' two miles and a half. We detarmined to measure the critter. We tuck it up, and tuck it out'n doors, druv a nail through its head at the corner uv the house, then stretched it clean round the house where we started from, which the house was thirty foot long and eighteen foot wide, makin' the wurrum ninety foot long. I tell you, boys, Dr. Jayneses tape-wurrum were nothin' to it."

"Deng it! we'll gin it up," said Dick Snow.

"You mout as well," said Uncle Davy, "fur it were a whaler."

I promised the reader one more hunting story from Uncle Davy. I will now give it, as it seems to have been the cause of his reformation, and with it I close the sketches of our hunting hero. Here it is:

IX. The Buck-Horned Snake

"I piked out one day," said Uncle Davy, "in sarch uv old bucks, but they was monstrous scace, and I couldn't find none. I got 'most home, and thort I hated to return havin' smashed nothin'—didn't like to be laughed at. Jist then an old sucklin' doe got right smack in my way. I leveled old Bucksmasher, and down she fell. I tuck her home, and, meat being ruther scace, we eat her up monstrous quick.

"I furgut to mention that it was on Sunday I smashed that old doe. My feelings sorter hurt me fur killin' her on Sunday, and frum her young fawn too, poor critter! So in two ur three days arter, I thort I'd go out and git the fawn. I made me a blate,[1] went out to the laurel and ivy thicket whar I'd killed the doe, blated, and the fawn answered me, fur it thought it was its mammy, poor thing! I kep' blatin' away, and uvry time I'd blate it would answer me, but it cum to me mighty slow, sartin. I got onpatient, and moseyed a little to'ads it, and got on a log where I could see a leetle, which the laurel and ivy was monstrous thick. I blated agin, which it answered close by. I blated agin, and then I streeched up my neck liken a scared turkey, lookin' 'mong the laurel and ivy, and what do you think I seen?"

"I can not imagine," said Taliaferro, to whom he was relating this adventure.

"Well, I'll tell you. Thar lay the biggest, oncommonest black snake the Lord uver made, sartin—which he has made a many a one—full fifteen foot long, with a pair of rantankerous big buck's horns, big as antelope's horns. It fixed its tarnacious eyes on me, but afore it could get its spell on me I jumped off uv that log, and run so fast that I nuver hev nur nuver will tell any man—which it is onpossible to tell any man—how fast I did pike fur home. But sartin it is that the runnin' from the coachwhip on Round Hill were no more to it than the runnin' uv a snail to a streak uv lightnin'."

"What do you think it was?" inquired Taliaferro.

"I jist think it were suthin' sent thar to warn me 'bout huntin' on Sundays. It blated jist like a fawn, and I thort it were the fawn I were arter; but Jehu Nimshi! it were no more a fawn than I am a fawn, sartin. But as sure as old Bucksmasher is made uv iron, and is the best gun in the world, I've nuver hunted on Sunday sense."

---

[1] Hunters split a stick, put a leaf into it, and by blowing it can imitate the bleating of deer so as to deceive them. They call it a "blate."—H. E. T.

Larkin Snow, the Miller, and His Fast-Running Dog

FOX-HUNTING was a favorite sport with many; indeed, all loved it, but only a few kept hounds and gave chase to mischievous Reynard. Foxes were quite plenty, and renowned for deeds of daring. The women hated hounds most cordially, yet they would endure them for the sake of their fowls. If their fowls were destroyed, they could neither make soup nor their rich pot-pies, both of which were much admired. Wylie Franklin was a great favorite with chicken-raisers, for if a hen-roost was invaded a *hint* to him was all that was needed, and the marauder was soon taken. The compositions of Mozart, Handel, and Haydn were no music to these fox-hunters compared with the voice of hounds in the chase. Sometimes there would be a great rally of fox-hunters at some point to have a united chase, to see who had the fastest and the toughest hound. This must be kept in view in reading the story of Larkin's fast-running dog.

"You see," said Larkin, "a passel uv fellers cum frum 'bout Rockford, Jonesville, and the Holler to have a fox-hunt, and kep' a-boastin' uv thar fast dogs. I told 'um my little dog Flyin'-jib could beat all thar dogs, and give 'um two in the game. I called him up and showed him to 'um, and you mout a hearn 'um laugh a mile, measured with a 'coonskin and the tail throwed in. I told 'um they'd laugh t'other side o' thar mouths afore it were done. They hooted me.

"We went out with 'bout fifty hounds, and, as good luck would hev it, we started a rale old Virginny red fox, 'bout three hours afore day, on the west side uv Skull Camp Mountin'. He struck right off for the Saddle Mountin', then whirled round over Scott's Knob, then to Cedar Ridge, up it, and over Fisher's Peak, round back uv the Blue Ridge, then crossed over and down it at Blaze Spur, then down to and over Round Peak, then down Ring's Creek to Shipp's Muster-ground, and on agin to'ads Skull Camp. Not fur from Shipp's Muster-ground they passed me, and Flyin'-jib were 'bout half a mile ahead on 'um all, goin' fast as the report of a rifle gun. Passin' through a meader whar thar were a mowin' scythe with the blade standin' up, Flyin'-jib run chug agin it with sich force that it split him wide open frum the eend uv his nose to the tip uv his tail. Thar he lay, and nuver whimpered, tryin' to run right on. I streaked it to him, snatched up both sides uv him, slapped 'um together, but were in sich a hurry that I put two feet down and two up. But away he went arter the fox, scootin' jist in that fix. You see, when he got tired runnin' on two feet on one side, he'd whirl over, quick as lightnin', on t'other two, and it seemed ruther to hev increased his verlocity. He cotch the fox on the east side uv Skull Camp, a mile ahead uv the whole kit uv 'um.

"Now when the fellers cum up, and seen all thar dogs lyin' on the

---

Ibid., pp. 149–151.

ground pantin' fur life, and Flyin'-jib jist gittin' his hand in, they was mighty low down in the mouth, I warrant you. All the conserlation they had was seein' my dog in sich a curious fix. But I jist kervorted, and told 'um that were the way fur a dog to run fast and long, fust one side up, then t'other—it rested him."

They Have Yarns

They have yarns
Of a skyscraper so tall they had to put hinges
On the two top stories so to let the moon go by,
Of one corn crop in Missouri when the roots
Went so deep and drew off so much water
The Mississippi riverbed that year was dry,
Of pancakes so thin they had only one side,
Of "a fog so thick we shingled the barn and six feet out on the fog,"
Of Pecos Pete straddling a cyclone in Texas and riding it to the west coast where "it rained out under him,"
Of the man who drove a swarm of bees across the Rocky Mountains and the Desert "and didn't lose a bee,"
Of a mountain railroad curve where the engineer in his cab can touch the caboose and spit in the conductor's eye,
Of the boy who climbed a cornstalk growing so fast he would have starved to death if they hadn't shot biscuits up to him,
Of the old man's whiskers: "When the wind was with him his whiskers arrived a day before he did,"
Of the hen laying a square egg and cackling "Ouch!" and of hens laying eggs with the dates printed on them,
Of the ship captain's shadow: it froze to the deck one cold winter night,
Of mutineers on that same ship put to chipping rust with rubber hammers,
Of the sheep counter who was fast and accurate: "I just count their feet and divide by four,"
Of the man so tall he must climb a ladder to shave himself,
Of the runt so teeny-weeny it takes two men and a boy to see him,
Of mosquitoes: one can kill a dog, two of them a man,
Of a cyclone that sucked cookstoves out of the kitchen, up the chimney flue, and on to the next town,
Of the same cyclone picking up wagon-tracks in Nebraska and dropping them over in the Dakotas,
Of the hook-and-eye snake unlocking itself into forty pieces, each piece two inches long, then in nine seconds flat snapping itself together again,
Of the watch swallowed by the cow—when they butchered her a year later the watch was running and had the correct time,
Of horned snakes, hoop snakes that roll themselves where they want to go, and rattlesnakes carrying bells instead of rattles on their tails,

Of the herd of cattle in California getting lost in a giant redwood tree that
    had hollowed out,

Of the man who killed a snake by putting its tail in its mouth so it swallowed
    itself,

Of railroad trains whizzing along so fast they reach the station before the
    whistle,

Of pigs so thin the farmer had to tie knots in their tails to keep them from
    crawling through the cracks in their pens,

Of Paul Bunyan's big blue ox, Babe, measuring between the eyes forty-two
    ax-handles and a plug of Star tobacco exactly,

Of John Henry's hammer and the curve of its swing and his singing of it as
    "a rainbow round my shoulder."

            "Do tell!"
            "I want to know!"
            "You don't say so!"
            "For the land's sake!"
            "Gosh all fish-hooks!"
            "Tell me some more.
           I don't believe a word you say
           but I love to listen
           to your sweet harmonica
           to your chin-music.
           Your fish stories hang together
           when they're just a pack of lies:
           you ought to have a leather medal:
           you ought to have a statue
           carved of butter: you deserve
           a large bouquet of turnips."

    "Yessir," the traveler drawled,
"Away out there in the petrified forest
 everything goes on the same as usual.
The petrified birds sit in their petrified nests
and hatch their petrified young from petrified eggs."

A high pressure salesman jumped off the Brooklyn Bridge and was saved by
    a policeman. But it didn't take him long to sell the idea to the policeman.
    So together they jumped off the bridge.

One of the oil men in heaven started a rumor of a gusher down in hell. All the
    other oil men left in a hurry for hell. As he gets to thinking about the
    rumor he had started he says to himself there might be something in it
    after all. So he leaves for hell in a hurry.

"The number 42 will win this raffle, that's my number." And when he won
    they asked him whether he guessed the number or had a system. He said he
    had a system, "I took up the old family album and there on page 7 was my
    grandfather and grandmother both on page 7. I said to myself this is easy
    for 7 times 7 is the number that will win and 7 times 7 is 42."

Once a shipwrecked sailor caught hold of a stateroom door and floated for hours till friendly hands from out of the darkness threw him a rope. And he called across the night, "What country is this?" and hearing voices answer, "New Jersey," he took a fresh hold on the floating stateroom door and called back half-wearily, "I guess I'll float a little farther."

An Ohio man bundled up the tin roof of a summer kitchen and sent it to a motor car maker with a complaint of his car not giving service. In three weeks a new car arrived for him and a letter: "We regret delay in shipment but your car was received in a very bad order."

A Dakota cousin of this Ohio man sent six years of tin can accumulations to the same works, asking them to overhaul his car. Two weeks later came a rebuilt car, five old tin cans, and a letter: "We are also forwarding you five parts not necessary in our new model."

Thus fantasies heard at filling stations in the midwest. Another relates to a Missouri mule who took aim with his heels at an automobile rattling by. The car turned a somersault, lit next a fence, ran right along through a cornfield till it came to a gate, moved onto the road and went on its way as though nothing had happened. The mule heehawed with desolation, "What's the use?"

Another tells of a farmer and his family stalled on a railroad crossing, how they jumped out in time to see a limited express knock it into flinders, the farmer calling, "Well, I always did say that car was no shucks in a real pinch."

When the Masonic Temple in Chicago was the tallest building in the United States west of New York, two men who would cheat the eyes out of you if you gave 'em a chance, took an Iowa farmer to the top of the building and asked him, "How is this for high?" They told him that for $25 they would go down in the basement and turn the building around on its turntable for him while he stood on the roof and saw how this seventh wonder of the world worked. He handed them $25. They went. He waited. They never came back.

This is told in Chicago as a folk tale, the same as the legend of Mrs. O'Leary's cow kicking over the barn lamp that started the Chicago fire, when the Georgia visitor, Robert Toombs, telegraphed an Atlanta crony, "Chicago is on fire, the whole city burning down, God be praised!"

Nor is the prize sleeper Rip Van Winkle and his scolding wife forgotten, nor the headless horseman scooting through Sleepy Hollow

Nor the sunken treasure-ships in coves and harbors, the hideouts of gold and silver sought by Coronado, nor the Flying Dutchman rounding the Cape doomed to nevermore pound his ear nor ever again take a snooze for himself

Nor the sailor's caretaker Mother Carey seeing to it that every seafaring man in the afterworld has a seabird to bring him news of ships and women, an albatross for the admiral, a gull for the deckhand

Nor the sailor with a sweetheart in every port of the world, nor the ships that set out with flying colors and all the promises you could ask, the ships never heard of again,

Nor Jim Liverpool, the riverman who could jump across any river and back without ouching land he was that quick on his feet,

Nor Mike Fink along the Ohio and the Mississippi, half wild horse and half cock-eyed alligator, the rest of him snags and snapping turtle. "I can out-run, out-jump, out-shoot, out-brag, out-drink, and out-fight, rough and tumble, no holts barred, any man on both sides of the river from Pittsburgh to New Orleans and back again to St. Louis. My trigger finger itches and I want to go redhot. War, famine and bloodshed puts flesh on my bones, and hardship's my daily bread."

Nor the man so lean he threw no shadow: six rattlesnakes struck at him at one time and every one missed him.

A Trip Down East

STRANGER—I expect you are about the tallest kind of a coon there is in these diggings. Your little Buffalonian walks straight into things, like a squash vine into a potato patch.

I come down the other day in the steamboat Cleaveland. She's pretty fixin, Golly! ain't she a smasher? Once coming down, a streak of lightning followed three miles and better. The Captain seeing it was gaining on us a little, so he told the man to starboard the helm and let it go by. It did go like a horse, and we were so near it that the passengers smelt brimstone. Then the Captain felt a little cheap, at first, about letting it beat him, and said the steam wasn't up; but I told him he did perfectly right to turn out, as there were so many women on board, and then there was so much iron, that it drew the lightning and helped it along, so it warn't fair play. You should have heard the thunder that came along just after it. Perhaps you don't know where I came from. Give us your fist now and I'll tell you all about it. When I'm at home I stops in Chuckahokee digging in the state of Indiana. We raised a mighty crop of wheat this year, I reckon upon nigh four thousand bushels, and a sprinklin of corn, oats, potatoes and garden sass. You could hear the earth groan all round our settlement, the crops were so heavy, and that's what gives rise to the stories about the earthquakes. It was near enough to make a young earthquake to hear the corn grow as it did, and as to the potatoes, I'll be skinned alive, if ever I saw any thing like it. Why, any one of them warm nights, you just go out into a little patch of fifty acres, close to the house, and hold your ear down, you could hear the young potatoes quarrelling, and the old ones grumbling at them because they didn't lay along and stop crowding. I calculate you didn't raise such crops in these parts. Why one day one of our squash vines chased a drove of hogs better than half a mile, and they ran and squealed as if the old boy was after them. One little pig stubbed his toe and fell down and never was heard of afterwards. We got in pretty much all the crops, and I told the old man I would take a trip down east and see the old folks, grandfather and mother, aunts,

From *Mince Pie for the Million.* Philadelphia and New York: Turner & Fisher. 1846.

and cousins, a pretty considerable heap of them I calculate down to old Vermont. So I packed up my plunder and started.

"According to Nature"

"Such timber, and such bottom land, why you can't preserve any thing natural you plant in it unless you pick it young, things thar will grow out of shape so quick. I once planted in those diggins a few potatoes and beets: they took a fine start, and after that an ox team couldn't have kept them from growing. About that time I went off to old Kentuck on bisiness, and did not hear from them things in three months, when I accidentally stumbled on a fellow who had stopped at my place, with an idea of buying me out. 'How did you like things?' said I. 'Pretty well,' said he; 'the cabin is convenient, and the timber land is good; but that bottom land ain't worth the first red cent.' 'Why?' said I. ' 'Cause it's full of cedar stumps and Indian mounds,' said he, *and it can't be cleared.'* 'Lord,' said I, 'them ar "cedar stumps" is beets, and them ar "Indian mounds" ar tater hills.' As I expected, the crop was overgrown and useless: the sile is too rich, *and planting in Arkansaw is dangerous.* I had a good-sized sow killed in that same bottom land. The old thief stole an ear of corn, and took it down where she slept at night to eat. Well, she left a grain or two on the ground, and lay down on them: before morning the corn shot up, and the percussion killed her dead. I don't plant any more: natur intended Arkansaw for a hunting ground, and I go according to natur."

American Soil—Its Natural Richness

I took a handful of guano, that elixir of vegetation, and sowed a few cucumber seeds in it. Well, sir, I was considerable tired when I had done it, and so I just took a stretch for it under a great pine-tree, and took a nap. Stranger! as true as I am talking to you this here blessed minute, when I woke up, I was bound as tight as a sheep going to market on a butcher's cart, and tied fast to a tree. I thought I should never get out of that scrape; the cucumber vines had so grown and twisted round, and wound me and my legs while I was asleep! Fortunately, one arm was free; so I

From "The Big Bear of Arkansas," by T. B. Thorpe. Originally published in *The Spirit of the Times,* 1841; reprinted in *The Big Bear of Arkansas and Other Sketches, Illustrative of Characters and Incidents in the South and South-West,* edited by William T. Porter, Philadelphia, 1845, and *The Hive of the Bee Hunter,* by T. B. Thorpe. New York. 1854.

From *The American Joe Miller;* A Collection of Yankee Wit and Humor, compiled by Robert Kempt, pp. 149–150. London: Adams and Francis. 1865.

got out my jack knife, opened it with my teeth, and cut myself out, and off for Victoria again, hot foot. When I came into the town, says our captain to me, "Peabody, what in natur is that ere great yaller thing that's a sticking out of your pocket?" "Nothin'," sais I, looking as mazed as a puppy nine days old, when he first opens his eyes, and takes his first stare. Well, I put in my hand to feel, and I pulled out a great big ripe cucumber, a foot long, that had ripened and gone to seed there. ——*Sam Slick.*

"Nothing to What I Have Seen"

EARLY in the forenoon Dr. Binninger, Tom Fenton, Jim Hart, the retired miner, and Fraser, the Canadian, came up and began inspecting the crops.

"Oh, this is very well; very well, indeed, for Jersey," said Dr. Binninger, at last, as they sat on the fence by the cornfield, after their labors, smoking; "but nothing to what I have seen. In Gastley County, Missouri, I once saw the corn growing to such an unprecedented height, and the stalks so exceptionally vigorous, that nearly every farmer stacked up, for winter firewood, great heaps of cornstalks, cut up into cord-wood length by power saws run by the threshing engines. One man, Barney Gregory, took advantage of the season to win a fortune by preparing cornstalks for use as telegraph poles. . . ."

"What is one man's meat is another man's poison," said Fenton. "Fine growing weather, similar to that which made Gregory's fortune in Missouri, has come near ruining those of the Western Nebraska farmers who raised pumpkins. Just as, by all ordinary rules, the crop should have been ready to house, a mysterious rot began to destroy the great green globes glowing to yellow in the sun. An examination by the chemists of the State Agricultural College, showed that the trouble was due to the too rapid growth of the vines, which dragged the pumpkins about after them, all over the fields, until the pumpkins' lower cuticle, being worn out by the abrasion, they succumbed easily to rot in the bruised portion. Should another such year come, the farmers will avoid a like catastrophe by providing each pumpkin with a straw-lined nest, or a little truck with casters.

"A good illustration of nature's bounty happened some time ago in Doniphan County, Kansas," continued Fenton. "A seven-year-old daughter of James Steele was sent, in the middle of the forenoon, to carry a jug of switchel to the men, who were at work near the middle of one of those vast Kansas cornfields. The corn was about up to little Annie's shoulders as she started, but as she went along it rose and rose before her eyes, shooting out of the soil under the magic influence of the sun and the abundant moisture. Almost crazed with fear, she hastened on, but before she could

From *The Book of Lies,* by John Langdon Heaton, pp. 143–146. Copyright, 1896, by John Langdon Heaton. New York: The Morse Company.

reach the men, the stalks were waving above her head. The men were threatened in a like manner, but by mounting a little fellow on a big man's shoulders, to act as a lookout, they managed to get out, when they promptly borrowed a dog, to follow little Annie's trail. It was not until late in the afternoon that they reached her, where she lay, having cried herself to sleep, with the tear-stains streaking her plump cheeks."

"The soil of some of the Southern California counties is so rich as to become an actual detriment to the farmer," observed Eckels. "In San Bernardino County, a farmer, named Jones, has been forced entirely to abandon the culture of corn, because the stalks, under the influence of the genial sun, mild air, and mellow soil, shoot up into the air so fast that they draw their roots after them; when, of course, the plant dies as a rule. Cases have been known, however, where cornstalks thus uprooted, and lifted into the air, have survived for some time upon the climate alone."

"Why," said Dr. Binninger, "we used to have the same trouble in Kentucky, but it was solved long ago by burying a heavy stone under each cornstalk, and wiring the stalk down to it. I have known the price of stone to treble in one season in consequence of the purely agricultural demand."

Rich Land, Poor Land

"Yeah," said Sack Daddy, "you sho is tellin' de truth 'bout dat big old mosquito, 'cause my old man bought dat same piece of land and raised a crop of pumpkins on it and lemme tell y'all right now—mosquito dust is de finest fertilizer in de world. Dat land was so rich and we raised pumpkins so big dat we et five miles up in one of 'em and five miles down and ten miles acrost one and we ain't never found out how far it went. But my old man was buildin' a scaffold inside so we could cut de pumpkin meat without so much trouble, when he dropped his hammer. He tole me, he says, 'Son, Ah done dropped my hammer. Go git it for me.' Well, Ah went down in de pumpkin and begin to hunt dat hammer. Ah was foolin' 'round in there all day when I met a man and he ast me what Ah was lookin' for. Ah tole him my ole man had done dropped his hammer and sent me to find it for him. De man tole me Ah might as well give it up for a lost cause, he had been lookin' for a double mule-team and a wagon that had got lost in there for three weeks and he hadn't found no trace of 'em yet. So Ah stepped on a pin, de pin bent and dat's de way de story went."

"Dat was rich land but my ole man had some rich land too," put in Will House. "My old man planted cucumbers and he went along droppin'

From *Mules and Men*, by Zora Neale Hurston, pp. 135–136. Copyright, 1935, by Zora Neale Hurston. Philadelphia and London: J. B. Lippincott Company.

de seeds and befo' he could git out de way he'd have ripe cucumbers in his pockets. What is the richest land you ever seen?"

"Well," replied Joe Wiley, "my ole man had some land dat was so rich dat our mule died and we buried him down in our bottom-land and de next mornin' he had done sprouted li'l jackasses."

"Aw, dat land wasn't so rich," objected Ulmer. "My old man had some land and it was so rich dat he drove a stob[1] in de ground at de end of a corn-row for a landmark and next morning there was ten ears of corn on de corn stalk and four ears growin' on de stob."

"Dat lan' y'all talkin' 'bout might do, if you give it plenty commercial-nal[2] but my old man wouldn't farm no po' land like dat," said Joe Wiley. "Now, one year we was kinda late puttin' in our crops. Everybody else had corn a foot high when papa said, 'Well, chillun, Ah reckon we better plant some corn.' So I was droppin' and my brother was hillin' up behind me. We had done planted 'bout a dozen rows when Ah looked back and seen de corn comin' up. Ah didn't want it to grow too fast 'cause it would make all fodder and no roastin' ears so Ah hollered to my brother to sit down on some of it to stunt de growth. So he did, and de next day he dropped me back a note—says: 'passed thru Heben yesterday at twelve o'clock sellin' roastin' ears to de angels.' "

The Pumpkin

Tol' Jack to get de fastes' horse in de lot. He got up on de horse to go out on de plantation to drop de pum'kin-seed. He made a hole wi' de stick, dropped de seed. Horse ran as fas' as he could. Vine ran faster. You clim' up on top of that leaf an' holler.[3] Dat pum'kin-vine had pum'kins on it. My marster had two hawgs. Dey went away. De hawg-feeder name Jack. "Jack, we got to look for dem hawgs. Won't do to let 'em run away. Go to house, ask mistress for half a shoulder of meat, an' cook me some bread." De hawgs had eat a hole in dat pum'kin, an'

---

[1] Stake.—Z. N. H.
[2] Commercial fertilizer.—Z. N. H.

From "Tales from Guilford County, North Carolina," by Elsie Clews Parsons, *The Journal of American Folk-Lore,* Vol. XXX (April-June, 1917), No. CXVI, pp. 190–191. Copyright, 1917, by the American Folk-Lore Society.

Informant, Carter Young. About 70. Father of Lulu, Nancy, and Katherine Young. Born in Guilford County; but he has lived in Alabama, Georgia, Mississippi. This tale and the following present a type whose pattern or ornament is maximum exaggeration. These two tales are instances of the same type I have found well marked in Bahama and in Cape Verde Islands tales. This type of expression appears to make a peculiar appeal to certain narrators, who indulge in it whenever the tale affords opportunity. These narrators are comparatively few.—E. C. P.

[3] Lulu Young told me about a stalk of corn that "kep'" on growing. There was a squirrel up on the ear of corn. The man climb on up. It kep' growing. He had to take an' make a ladder to come back on to de groun' on."—E. C. P.

staid in dere until nex' plantin'-time. From dat pum'kin-vine they build a hotel in Richmon'. Made pretties' doors an' winders you ever saw.

The Turnip

ONE day there was a man in this country. An' he called to de man to stay all night. His name was John. He 'plied to him, "What's your occupation?" Says, "Turnip-grower." Says he cultivated an acre of land. He put it knee-deep manure. He sowed de seed. Didn't but one come up. It growed so big that they put a fence aroun' it. It raised de fence.[1] Says, "What's your occupation?" He said, "Pottery." He was three weeks amouldin' a big pot. It wore out three-power hammer before it struck the ground. He 'plied to him, "What you better do in that big pot?" He said, "Jus' to cook that turnip in." [2]

Paul's Oklahoma Farm

WHEN Paul farmed, he had a variety of corn he produced himself. One morning the corn plant broke out of the ground. It was about six feet high. One of the neighbors tied his team to it and stopped to talk. Pretty soon the sun came out and the corn began to grow and took the team, wagon, and all right up into the air with it. Paul called for one of the ax men from his timber land. The corn grew so fast the ax man couldn't hit twice in the same place. He called for one of his telephone linemen to climb up and untie the horses. The corn was growing so fast he couldn't come down. Paul finally coiled one of his railroad lines around the stalk and let it pinch itself to death. When it fell one ear stuck in the ground and made Paul's famous corn liquor well. He dug out the cob and left the well all bricked up with corn which fermented and furnished him with the liquor. They got to looking for the farmer and his team. They found him in another ear making a crop. This all happened the year after they

---

Ibid., p. 191. Informant, Bill Cruse. About 68. Born and bred in Forsyth County. —E. C. P.

[1] *Variant:* A band of soldiers come along. Come up a storm, an' they shelter under one leaf of the turnup.—E. C. P.

[2] *Variant:* They made a barrel to cook the turnup in,—a mile long an' half a mile wide.—E. C. P.

As told by Kara Fullerton, at the University of Oklahoma, Norman, Oklahoma. From "Tall Talk and Tall Tales of the Southwest," by B. A. Botkin, *The New Mexico Candle.* New Mexico Normal University, Las Vegas, New Mexico, June 28, 1935.

made Paul quit growing watermelons because one broke a dam and killed several people. Those watermelons were so big they had to tunnel through them.

Paul had such a fertile farm that when he left the walnut staff he always carried sticking in the cornfield and lost it he later found a bushel of walnuts and ten ears of corn all growing from the same stalk. The next year he left it sticking in the ground and sprinkled some broken glass around and got a bedroom suite out of it.

Idaho Potatoes

IN THE Snake River Valley lives an old-timer who is known as Old Jim. Old Jim comes to town now and then and boasts of the fertility of his land, but complains that he is unable to market the stuff. He grew pumpkins, but they were so large he could not get them on to a wagon, and then ventured into potatoes. When, two years ago, a CCC camp was established nearby, Old Jim was approached by a man who wanted to buy a hundred pounds of spuds. "Only a hundred pounds?" he asked, scratching his pate. "No, I can't do it. I wouldn't cut a spud in two for no one."

A Preacher's Pack

I. A BIG TURNIP

MANY years ago there lived a preacher in Garrard county, whose name will not be given lest the feeling of his numerous descendants might be wounded. He was a man of great intellectual force and lived a blameless life, except for the wonderful stories he told, all of which he appeared to believe to be true.

He said that he once cleaned up a quarter of an acre of ground, fenced it in and sowed it in turnips. Some time after he noticed that the turnips near the center were forced out of the ground, and thus continued outward until there was but one turnip top visible, and that was in the center of the patch. After careful investigation he found that this turnip

From *Idaho Lore*, prepared by the Federal Writers' Project of the Work Projects Administration, Vardis Fisher, State Director, American Guide Series, p. 139. Copyright, 1939, by George H. Curtis, Secretary of State for the State of Idaho. Caldwell, Idaho: The Caxton Printers, Ltd.

From *Stories and Speeches of William O. Bradley*, with Biographical Sketch by M. H. Thatcher, pp. 131–133. Copyright, 1916, by Transylvania Printing Company. Lexington, Kentucky.

had grown until it covered the entire field, forcing the others out. About this time he lost a valuable heifer, and after looking everywhere on the place, he found that she had eaten her way into the turnip. Said he:

"I knew I would have to procure an enormous kettle in which to cook that turnip; so I went to the Red River Iron Works, in Bath county, and ordered it made. Three hundred men worked on it night and day for three weeks, and on Saturday night of the last week, when it was completed, the head workman carelessly dropped his hammer and just as we reached the spot on Monday morning early, we heard the hammer strike the bottom."

II. A Great Hunter

In the adjoining county of Madison, there is a hill of considerable size called "Round Hill." The name is very appropriate, for the base of the hill forms a perfect circle. The preacher located one of his most remarkable experiences at that place. He was really a very successful hunter, but from his accounts it will be seen that he was a remarkable hunter, as well. Talking to an admiring group of friends, he remarked:

"I once went to Round Hill a-hunting. In those days there was a forest around it. When I neared the hill a buck started up and took out around the hill. I followed for some time, but could not get a shot; so I bent my gun-barrel across my knee to correspond with the curve of the hill and fired, when the bullet followed the buck and killed him. I went on to where the buck had fallen and straightened the barrel. Near at hand, I saw some honey running out of a tree, where the ball had entered, and I drove a peg in the tree until I could return, which I did, in a few days, and me and my friends took home five pounds of splendid honey. But this, aside. I cut off the hind quarters from the buck, slung them across my shoulders, and started home. I had on a very large and loose pair of pants which turned out to my advantage, for when I reached the creek the water was up and I had to wade. When I got on the other side of the creek I took fifteen pounds of jumpin' perch out of my pants, and you may easily understand how we lived on the deer, honey and fish, for some time."

III. Capturing a Young Eagle

"Many years ago," said he, "when I was a young man I had business in the State of Maine. It was during the winter and was exceedingly cold. I located an eagle's nest at the top of a crag and determined to capture one of the young eagles. To do this, I was compelled to climb an icicle for about fifty feet to reach the place. Just as I got the young bird the two old eagles appeared on the scene; and, to escape their beaks and claws, I slid down the icicle so fast that I set the seat of my pants on fire, and from that day to the present I have always been prejudiced against eagles."

IV. The Roar of a Lion

"When I was a small boy," remarked the old man, "I attended the first circus and menagerie that ever came into the county. Some man punched the lion, which was an enormous beast, and he uttered a terrible roar—a roar that fairly shook the earth. When I undertook to run away I could not move. Looking down to see what was the cause, I found that I had sunk into the ground up to my knees. I had great difficulty in releasing myself, so much so, that I have never attended such a place from that day to this."

V. The Squirrels and the Corn

Another story that he told was:

"I once had a hundred-acre river bottom farm as fine as a crow ever flew over. One year I raised an enormous crop of corn. After the corn had ripened, I noticed on the side adjoining the river that a large quantity had disappeared. So I concluded to watch and see who was stealing my corn. I concealed myself the following morning, early, in a small thicket that bordered the river. I had not been there long before I saw a number of objects start from the opposite bank. For a time I could not discern what they were, but as they came closer, I discovered they were squirrels —about a hundred of them—each seated on a shingle and propelling it with his tail. When they reached the bank they left their shingles in a little cove and went out in the field. Presently, each one returned with an ear of corn, and, mounting his shingle, propelled himself to the opposite side of the river. The next day, in company with a dozen expert woodchoppers, we cut down every hollow tree on the side where the squirrels landed, and found four hundred barrels of corn, besides killing many of the squirrels; indeed, we lived on squirrels for several weeks."

VI. Some Hewer

He also related the following:

"Many years ago I was in New Orleans, and saw in the papers that a 'hewing match' was to take place near the city; the best hewer to receive a premium of twenty-five dollars in gold. I concluded to compete for it; so, I sharpened my broad-ax until I could have easily shaved with it, and was there bright and early. There were many expert axmen present, and I waited until all of them were through, when, fastening the ax handle in my belt, I climbed a cypress tree two hundred feet high, and then went down it head foremost, cutting off the limbs and hewing it to a perfect eight square until I reached the ground. Of course the crowd was greatly astonished and when the twenty-five dollars was paid to me there was much hand-shaking and congratulations."

Differences betwixt Clear-Water Rivers and Muddy-Water Ones

. . . THE man they called Ed said the muddy Mississippi water was wholesomer to drink than the clear water of the Ohio; he said if you let a pint of this yaller Mississippi water settle, you would have about a half to three-quarters of an inch of mud in the bottom, according to the stage of the river, and then it warn't no better than Ohio water—what you wanted to do was to keep it stirred up—and when the river was low, keep mud on hand to put in and thicken the water up the way it ought to be.

The Child of Calamity said that was so; he said there was nutritiousness in the mud, and a man that drunk Mississippi water could grow corn in his stomach if he wanted to. He says:

"You look at the graveyards; that tells the tale. Trees won't grow worth shucks in a Cincinnati graveyard, but in a Sent Louis graveyard they grow upwards of eight hundred foot high. It's all on account of the water the people drunk before they laid up. A Cincinnati corpse don't richen a soil any."

And they talked about how Ohio water didn't like to mix with Mississippi water. Ed said if you take the Mississippi on a rise when the Ohio is low, you'll find a wide band of clear water all the way down the east side of the Mississippi for a hundred mile or more, and the minute you get out a quarter of a mile from shore and pass the line, it is all thick and yaller the rest of the way across. Then they talked about how to keep tobacco from getting moldy, and from that they went into ghosts and told about a lot that other folks had seen. . . .

"Dat Ain't No Lie"

I. "DAT WASN'T HOT"

. . . "IT SHO is gittin' hot. Ah'll be glad when we git to de lake so Ah kin find myself some shade."

"Man, youse two miles from dat lake yet, and otherwise it ain't hot today," said Joe Wiley. "He ain't seen it hot, is he, Will House?"

"Naw, Joe, when me and you was hoboing down in Texas it was so hot till we saw old stumps and logs crawlin' off in de shade."

From *Life on the Mississippi*, by Mark Twain, p. 50. Copyright, 1874 and 1875, by H. O. Houghton & Company; 1883, by Samuel L. Clemens. Boston: James R. Osgood & Company. 1883.

From *Mules and Men*, by Zora Neale Hurston, pp. 132–137, 149–151. Copyright, 1935, by Zora Neale Hurston. Philadelphia and London: J. B. Lippincott Company.

Eugene Oliver said, "Aw dat wasn't hot. Ah seen it so hot till two cakes of ice left the ice house and went down the street and fainted."

Arthur Hopkins put in: "Ah knowed two men who went to Tampa all dressed up in new blue serge suits, and it was so hot dat when de train pulled into Tampa two blue suits got off de train. De men had done melted out of 'em."

Will House said, "Dat wasn't hot. Dat was chilly weather. Me and Joe Wiley went fishin' and it was so hot dat before we got to de water, we met de fish, coming swimming up de road in dust."

"Dat's a fact, too," added Joe Wiley. "Ah remember dat day well. It was so hot dat Ah struck a match to light my pipe and set de lake afire. Burnt half of it, den took de water dat was left and put out de fire."

Joe Willard said, "Hush! Don't Ah hear a noise?"

Eugene and Cliffert shouted together, "Yeah—went down to de river—

Heard a mighty racket
Nothing but de bull frog
Pullin' off his jacket!"

II. Giant Insects

"Dat ain't what Ah hea'd," said Joe.

"Well, whut did you hear?"

"Ah see a chigger over in de fence corner wid a splinter in his foot and a seed tick is pickin' it out wid a fence rail and de chigger is hollerin', 'Lawd, have mercy.'"

"Dat brings me to de boll-weevil," said Larkins White. "A boll-weevil flew onto de steerin' wheel of a white man's car and says, 'Mister, lemme drive yo' car.'

"De white man says, 'You can't drive no car.'

"Boll-weevil says: 'Oh yeah, Ah kin. Ah drove in five thousand cars last year and Ah'm going to drive in ten thousand dis year.'

"A man told a tale on de boll-weevil agin. Says he heard a terrible racket and noise down in de field, went down to see whut it was and whut you reckon? It was Ole Man Boll-Weevil whippin' li' Willie Boll-Weevil 'cause he couldn't carry two rows at a time."

Will House said, "Ah know a lie on a black gnat. Me and my buddy Joe Wiley was ramshackin' Georgy over when we come to a loggin' camp. So bein' out of work we ast for a job. So de man puts us on and give us some oxes to drive. Ah had a six-yoke team and Joe was drivin' a twelve-yoke team. As we was comin' thru de woods we heard somethin' hummin' and we didn't know what it was. So we got hungry and went in a place to eat and when we come out a gnat had done et up de six-yoke team and de twelve-yoke team, and was sittin' up on de wagon pickin' his teeth wid a ox-horn and cryin' for somethin' to eat."

"Yeah," put in Joe Wiley, "we seen a man tie his cow and calf out

to pasture and a mosquito come along and et up de cow and was ringin'
de bell for de calf."

"Dat wasn't no full-grown mosquito at dat," said Eugene Oliver. "Ah
was travellin' in Texas and laid down and went to sleep. De skeeters bit
me so hard till Ah seen a ole iron wash-pot, so Ah crawled under it and
turned it down over me good so de skeeters couldn't git to me. But you
know dem skeeters bored right thru dat iron pot. So I up wid a hatchet
and bradded their bills into de pot. So they flew on off 'cross Galveston bay
wid de wash-pot on their bills."

"Look," said Black Baby, "on de Indian River we went to bed and
heard de mosquitoes singin' like bull alligators. So we got under four
blankets. Shucks! dat wasn't nothin'. Dem mosquitoes just screwed off
dem short bills, reached back in they hip-pocket and took out they long
bills and screwed 'em on and come right on through dem blankets and
got us."

"Is dat de biggest mosquito you all ever seen? Shucks! dey was li'l
baby mosquitoes! One day my ole man took some men and went out
into de woods to cut some fence posts. And a big rain come up so they
went up under a great big ole tree. It was so big it would take six men
to meet around it. De other men set down on de roots but my ole man
stood up and leaned against de tree. Well, sir, a big old skeeter come up
on de other side of dat tree and bored right thru it and got blood out of
my ole man's back. Dat made him so mad till he up wid his ax and
bradded dat mosquito's bill into dat tree. By dat time de rain stopped and
they all went home.

"Next day when they come out, dat mosquito had done cleaned up ten
acres dying. And two or three weeks after dat my ole man got enough
bones from dat skeeter to fence in dat ten acres."

Gallinipper and Mosquito

GALLINUP an' de musquiter. Oncet I was travellin' 'long de road. An'
I was in quite of a haste. An' it was a very thick pon'; an' I heard in that
pon' a cur'ous noise, but the noise was very serious. An' I stop an' listen.
An' I heard a man sing, "O Lawd! O Lawd!" Say, "Have mercy!" An'
I say, "I wonder what is dat!" An' de noise continue goin'. An' I say,
"I will go an' see what is dat." An' when I get dere where de noise was,
dere was a gallinipper pullin' a rail out of musquiter rib. An' I leave him,
but I don' know what become of dat musquiter. I t'ink he mus' be died.

From *Folk-Lore of the Sea Islands, South Carolina*, by Elsie Clews Parsons, Memoirs
of the American Folk-Lore Society, Volume XVI, p. 135. Copyright, 1923, by the
American Folk-Lore Society. Cambridge, Mass., and New York.
Informant. Henry Bryan, of Defuskie.—E. C. P.

Tough Yarns

A Mr. H. furnished some minor details of fact concerning this region
which I would have hesitated to believe, if I had not known him to be
a steamboat mate. He was a passenger of ours, a resident of Arkansas City,
and bound to Vicksburg to join his boat, a little Sunflower packet. He was
an austere man, and had the reputation of being singularly unworldly, for
a river-man. Among other things, he said that Arkansas had been injured
and kept back by generations of exaggerations concerning the mosquitoes
there. One may smile, said he, and turn the matter off as being a small
thing; but when you come to look at the effects produced, in the way of
discouragement of immigration and diminished values of property, it was
quite the opposite of a small thing, or thing in any wise to be coughed
down or sneered at. These mosquitoes had been persistently represented
as being formidable and lawless; whereas "the truth is, they are feeble,
insignificant in size, diffident to a fault, sensitive"—and so on, and so on;
you would have supposed he was talking about his family. But if he was
soft on the Arkansas mosquitoes, he was hard enough on the mosquitoes of
Lake Providence to make up for it—"those Lake Providence colossi," as
he finely called them. He said that two of them could whip a dog, and
that four of them could hold a man down; and except help come, they
would kill him—"butcher him," as he expressed it. Referred in a sort
of casual way—and yet significant way, to "the fact that the life policy
in its simplest form is unknown in Lake Providence—they take out a
mosquito policy besides." He told many remarkable things about those
lawless insects. Among others, said he had seen them try to *vote*. Noticing
that this statement seemed to be a good deal of a strain on us, he modified
it a little; said he might have been mistaken as to that particular, but
knew he had seen them around the polls "canvassing."

There was another passenger—friend of H.'s—who backed up the harsh
evidence against those mosquitoes, and detailed some stirring adventures
which he had had with them. The stories were pretty sizable, merely
pretty sizable; yet Mr. H. was continually interrupting with a cold,
inexorable "Wait—knock off twenty-five per cent of that; now go on";
or, "Wait—you are getting that too strong; cut it down, cut it down—
you get a leetle too much costumery onto your statements: always dress
a fact in tights, never in an ulster"; or, "Pardon, once more; if you are
going to load anything more onto that statement, you want to get a couple
of lighters and tow the rest, because it's drawing all the water there is
in the river already; stick to facts—just stick to the cold facts; what these
gentlemen want for a book is the frozen truth—ain't that so, gentlemen?"

From *Life on the Mississippi*, by Mark Twain, pp. 372–374. Copyright, 1874 and
1875, by H. O. Houghton & Company; 1883, by Samuel L. Clemens. Boston: James
R. Osgood & Company. 1883.

He explained privately that it was necessary to watch this man all the time, and keep him within bounds; it would not do to neglect this precaution, as he, Mr. H., "knew to his sorrow." Said he, "I will not deceive you; he told me such a monstrous lie once that it swelled my left ear up, and spread it so that I was actually not able to see out around it; it remained so for months, and people came miles to see me fan myself with it."

Remarkable Tenacity of Life

A FEW evenings since, in the "private crib" of one of our exchanges, there was a learned dissertation, subject, "Bed-bugs, and their Remarkable Tenacity of Life." One asserted of his own knowledge that they could be boiled, and then come to life. Some had soaked them for hours in turpentine without any fatal consequences. Old Hanks, who had been listening as an outsider, here gave in his experience in corroboration of the facts. Says he, "Some years ago I took a bed-bug to an iron-foundry, and dropping it into a ladle where the melted iron was, had it run into a skillet. Well, my old woman used that skillet pretty constant for the last six years, and here the other day it broke all to smash; and what do you think, gentlemen, that 'ere insect just walked out of his hole, where he'd been layin' like a frog in a rock, and made tracks for his old roost upstairs! But," added he, by way of parenthesis, "he looked mighty pale."

Grasshoppers

THERE are lots of people who remember the summer, fall, and winter of 1874; hot winds, grasshoppers and government aid. First, came the hot winds. They were like a furnace, and would blister the hands and face like fire. We had to get into the house and shut the windows and doors to keep cool. A few days later came the grasshoppers, and they were a hungry bunch of tramps. They got everything that was green, and ate a good many things that were not green. They ate up forty rods of stone fence in thirty-seven and a half minutes by the watch. They destroyed more stone fences that fall than all the boys, dogs, and rabbits put together. The green-headed horseflies were pretty bad that fall, and they made it hot for the stock. We had a pet cow, and in order to keep

From *The American Joe Miller*, A Collection of Yankee Wit and Humor, compiled by Robert Kempt, pp. 8–9. London: Adams and Francis. 1865.

From *Bill Jones of Paradise Valley, Oklahoma*, His Life and Adventures for Over Forty Years in The Great Southwest. He Was a Pioneer in the Days of the Buffalo, The Wild Indian, The Oklahoma Boomer, The Cowboy and The Outlaw, by John J. Callison, pp. 25–26. Copyright, 1914. by J. J. Callison. Kingfisher, Oklahoma.

the flies from eating her, we covered her with some green paint that we had left over, after painting the house. The hoppers came along, ate up the cow, paint and all.

The hoppers would hold up the children on their way to school and take their lunches away from them. After the grasshoppers had eaten everything, we turned in and ate the grasshoppers. One old fellow said he used to live with the digger Indians in Idaho, and they considered a grasshopper equal to or better than oysters, crawdads, clams, chili, or chop suey. So we all learned to eat grasshoppers, and I can say from experience that they were fine; but I do not want to live long enough to eat them three times a day again. After that we had grasshoppers for about six weeks and had them cooked and served in every way that could be thought of.

Famous Wind Storms

(Remarks Made at the Hatchet Club)

"TALKING about hard blows out west," said Mr. Lewis, of the *Detroit Free Press*, at a meeting of the "Hatchet Club," "talking about heavy winds, why I saw a man out in Michigan sitting quietly on his doorstep eating a piece of pie. Suddenly, before he could get into the house, the wind struck him. The gale first blew the house down, and then seized the man, carried him through the air a hundred yards or so, and landed him in a peach-tree. Soon afterward a friendly board from his own house came floating by. This he seized and placed over his head to protect himself from the raging blast, and—finished his pie." *(Sensation.)*

"That was a windy day for Michigan, I presume," said Mr. Wm. Nye, of Laramie, "but that would not compare with one of our Laramie zephyrs. Why, gentlemen, out in Laramie, during one of our ordinary gales, I've seen boulders big as pumpkins flying through the air. Once, when the wind was blowing grave-stones around, and ripping water-pipes out of the ground, an old Chinaman with spectacles on his nose was observed in the eastern part of the town seated on a knoll, calmly flying his kite—an iron shutter with a log-chain for a tail." *(Hear, Hear!)*

"That was quite windy," said a Boston man, who had just returned from Nevada. "We had some wind out there. One day as I was passing a hotel in Virginia City, the cap blew from one of the chimneys. It was a circular piece of sheetiron, painted black, slightly convex, and the four supports were like legs. The wind carried it down street, and it went straddling along like a living thing."

From *Library of Wit and Humor* by Mark Twain and Others, with the Philosophy of Wit and Humor, by Melville D. Landon, A. M. (Eli Perkins), pp. 214–216. Copyright, 1883, by L. W. Yaggy and, 1898, by Star Publishing Co. Chicago: Thompson and Thomas.

"Well, what was it?" asked a member.

"Why, it turned out to be a bed bug from the hotel, and, by George! I never saw anything like it," then he added, "outside of Boston." *(Sensation.)*

"You have seen some strong winds, gentlemen," observed Eli Perkins, "but I have seen some frisky zephyrs myself, and, as tonight is the 22d of February, the birthday of the patron saint of the 'Hatchet Club,' I will tell you about them.

"Once, out in Kansas, they told me the wind blew a cook-stove eighty miles, and came back the next day and got the griddles. *(Wonder and applause.)*

"A reporter of the Kansas City paper was standing out in the street looking at the stove as it floated away, when the wind caught him in the mouth, and turned him completely wrong side out. *(Sensation.)*

"In Topeka," continued Mr. Perkins, "post holes were ripped out of the ground and carried twenty miles *(hear, hear)*, and careless citizens who ventured out were blown right up against brick walls and flattened out as thin as wafers *(Sensation, and a voice, 'that's too thin')*. Yes, thousands of citizens," continued Eli, "were thus frescoed onto the dead walls of Topeka. The next day after the wind subsided, Deacon Thompson went around with a spade and peeled off a wagon load of citizens, and—"

"What did he do with them?" gasped the members of the Club.

"Why, gentlemen, if I remember rightly, he shipped them to Texas and sold them for circus posters and liver pads."

"Arise and sing!"

In Colorado

TENDERFOOT: How did you get started in this cattle ranch?

OLD TIMER: Well, you see, first I put all my wages as a top rider in an oil well, but it didn't have no oil in it. Then a cyclone came along and blew it inside out and left it sticking a thousand feet up into the air. So I cut it down, sawed it into two-feet sections. and shipped it east for postholes.

TENDERFOOT: Wind blow much out here?

OLD TIMER: We had a little breeze last week that blew the cook's stove clear to Kansas, and yesterday it came back for the lids.

TENDERFOOT: Why don't you raise chickens on this ranch too?

OLD TIMER: Well, we did have some hens round here but we ran out of buckshot.

TENDERFOOT: Buckshot? How's that?

From a letter by Chauncey Thomas, of Colorado. "Tall Talk and Tall Tales of the Southwest," by B. A. Botkin, *The New Mexico Candle*, New Mexico Normal University, Las Vegas, New Mexico, June 28, 1933.

OLD TIMER: Well, you see if we don't feed them lots of buckshot the wind blows them all away.

TENDERFOOT: What's the matter with those chickens? Moulting?

OLD TIMER: Naw, wind blew their feathers off.

Hail and Farewell

"HAIL?" said an old-timer scornfully after listening to a dozen stories. "Why, it don't hail no more. It usta, by the chumblechooks! I remember one time I was out in my old whitetop when I see a wall of hail comun that reached plumb from the sky to the earth. I whacked them-there old plow nags on their shin bones and we headed for home. We went like old sixty, with that storm right at the rear wheels; and when I got home and dashed into the machine shed, I couldn't get my breath for nigh half a hour. Then I looked around me and was I rum-guzzled to see that the rear end of the old buggy was loaded with hail as big as hen's eggs. All the way home I had kept just half a buggy length ahead of the storm."

The Sway-Back Horse

THE chickens were digging at their oil sacks and the colts were racing along the pasture fence, tails erect like banners. A very sway-backed old gelding had hung his head over the fence and was asking dumbly to be let into the barn.

"Ol' cuss!" said Mike O'Day. "He knows it's gonna rain pitchforks an' he wants in the barn, though he won't be gittin' no grain of a Sunday when he ain't workin'."

The old man and the old horse had the same air of weariness and lost energy. The driving sand had taken the shine from the horse's coat, and the sun had faded the man's eyes and his overalls to a gray blue.

Mike walked over to the gate and scratched the old horse under the chin. "Me an' you's gittin' along, ain't we?" he said. "Ain't 'lopin' around the pasture fence with our tails in the air."

"Mister O'Day," said the Gunn boy shrilly, "whut makes that horse's back bent like it's bent?"

"Well," Mike said, "you see it was like this. One day when we was

From *Idaho Lore*, prepared by the Federal Writers' Project of the Work Projects Administration, Vardis Fisher, State Director, American Guide Series, p. 119. Copyright, 1939, by George H. Curtis, Secretary of State for the State of Idaho. Caldwell, Idaho: The Caxton Printers, Ltd.

From *The Codder*, by William Cunningham, *Folk-Say IV: The Land Is Ours*, edited by B. A. Botkin, pp. 210–211. Copyright, 1932, by B. A. Botkin. Norman: University of Oklahoma Press.

livin' up in Kansas this critter got out into the green corn an' filled hisself up with roastin' ears, which he allays was a fool about roastin' ears. An when he was so blamed full that he was about to bust he come up to the water trough to git hisself a drink. It was a hot day an' he was thirsty, an' he allays was careless about the way he *stood*."

Mike paused for his audience to get the full significance of this fact.

"The way he stood, with his hind feet too far from his front feet. You know, a critter has to be careful to keep his hind feet a certain distance behind his front feet, an' likewise to keep his front feet the same distance in front of his hind feet. If he don't he'll stretch hisself.

"Well, this ol' cuss come up to the trough full of green roastin' ears an' he started to drinkin'. An' he musta drunk a tubful, an' all the time his hind feet was too far behind, an' his front feet too far in front.

"Well, I seen him jist as he was finishin', an' I seen how he was standin', an' I yells at him, but it was too late. All that weight in his belly had bent him like that, an' he won't never straighten out."

Shriveled, pasty-faced, toothless old Walt Harper had just enough wit to share in the codding. "Couldn't ya lay 'im on 'is back, Mike, an' git a pole er somepin' an' bend 'im back?" he asked. "Couldn't ya straighten 'im out, like? Kinda git 'im on 'is back an' bend 'im like he otta be?" He was overcome by mirth at his own joke. Baring his gums to the heavens, he leaned far back and filled his lungs with the dusty air. Then he doubled up, emitting a series of gasps and whoops, slapped one knee after the other and marched about in a circle, apparently at the point of choking to death.

The senior Gunn grinned. His boy was being codded, but it was part of the Western code that the young and tender should be taught the great verities by generous untruths. The dull red glow that filled the spaces between the boy's freckles showed that he was learning. The boy was bright, no doubt of that, like his mother, who could read and write.

Mike's expression did not change. "No," he said, "I seen that tried with a sway-back horse oncet when I was a boy on the ranch. They got the critter straight all right, but after that his back was so limber that it'd bend in any direction. Finally one day he tried to kick another horse, an' you know, he kicked hisself plumb in two, he was that weak in the back. I never seen a critter look so surprised, when his hind end come off. We felt awful sorry for him, because he'd been a good horse in his day, an' allays pushed in the collar. We shot 'is front end, an' buried him in the same hole."

At that instant a whirlwind was born in the barnyard. A fog of blinding, stinging sand rose up and the three men and the boy ducked their heads and clasped hands over their hats.

When it was gone, they sputtered and rubbed their eyes and brushed their sleeves. "Damn!" said Mike. "That shore come of a sudden. You know, I seen a whirlwind come up like that oncet in Kansas when a bunch of us was standin' on the porch of the general store. An' you know, Ike

Marlow who was runnin' the store had hung a sack of meal up on the porch fer advertisin', an' that blamed whirlwind blew the sack off an' left the meal hangin' there."

Mike opened the gate and let the old horse waddle past him into the barn.

The whirlwind was now sweeping through a field of tall, blue-green wheat, billowing and tangling the stocks, and plucking one here and there and lifting it hundreds of feet into the air.

Pulling Teeth

OUR Doctor in Demijohnville was an old man and had seen hard times in his day, especially in pulling teeth. He says that when the country was new and thinly settled, teeth came out much harder than they do in these days. A nail and hammer were indispensable in reforming out a grinder, and sometimes they would not start then; but the worst case that he knew, was a long-sided fellow by the name of Barney, who sent for him on Sunday. On applying the hammer and nail to Barney's tooth, it was found impossible to loosen it by the ordinary means, he cut away the gum around it, and fastened on a stout line made of cat gut. Then having tied Barney's heels to a ring bolt in the barn floor, he called on the inmates of the house to assist him in pulling. Barney's wife took hold of the Doctor's coat tail, and the rest ranged themselves in a regular line; but they could not start the tooth, although they pulled so hard that the patient could scarcely keep on his feet. Several foot passengers were called on to assist; and now they gave "a long pull, and a strong pull, and a pull altogether"; but the tooth remained firm, although they could hear poor Barney's neck snap, so violent was the strain; but twelve o'clock arrived, and the good people begun to bundle home from meeting. As they went by, they were called upon to hitch on, until the line of pulling men and women extended over the hill, and several lads at the tail, were even compelled to stand in the swamp. These benevolent individuals then begun to pull—in a moment Barney was hauled off his feet, and hung horizontally in the air like a man on the rack. He cried, "stop"; but it was too late, for the whole line of operators suddenly fell backward, and tumbled over each other; when it was supposed the tooth had come out; but, on looking, it was discovered that Barney's head had come off, near the shoulders. The Doctor examined the tooth, and found that the roots went down through the whole length of his body, and were clinched on the bottom of his foot.

From *The Crockett Almanac, 1841*, p. 19. Entered According to the Act of Congress, in the year 1840, by Turner & Fisher, in the Clerk's Office of the District Court of the United States, in and for the Eastern District of Pennsylvania. Boston: Published by J. Fisher.

Just Set

IN THE old days, we didn't have no automobiles and paved roads and all sich fancy likes. We didn't even have no trails and bridges. One time I 'member my wife was sick and I had to go Orofino for to bring a doctor. But when I got to the river I couldn't figger out how to cross. I decided to jump but when I was about three-fourths across I seen I wouldn't make it so I come back to think some more. Then I had to put my mind to it. There was a big tree on the edge of the river, so I hooked my lasso on a limb and got back and run for it, using the lasso to give me a swing across. That was good thinkun, but not everybody woulda 'membered the lasso would bring him right back agin if he wasn't durned keerful. Me, I cut the lasso when I was half way across. I tell you, I don't know what some of them-there modern squirts woulda done in a case like that. Just set on the bank, I guess.

John Hance, Darby, and the Grand Cañon

"I WAS ridin' on the rim just below here, one day, when Darby come round an uprooted pine and stepped right up on top of a she-grizzly as big as a buffalo—and you ought to seen him pull his freight! Stop him? Why, man, the Day o' Judgment wouldn't have stopped that hoss! I tried to haul him to one side into my wood-trail; but he just naturally *helled* straight for the rim, and before I could fall off, there we was way out in the sky, pretty near half-way across the cañon! I give him the rowels and the quirt, sort o' hoping he could reach the other bank; but it wasn't in him; and we went down like a rock—down and down and d-o-w-n —plumb to the bottom. Pore old Darby! I never *will* get another hoss like him!"

"But how about you, John? Why weren't you killed, too?"

"Huh! Too smart! You see Darby fell about sixty-five hundred feet; but just before he lit, I jumped off—so *I* only fell about twenty feet!"

From *Idaho Lore*, prepared by the Federal Writers' Project of the Work Projects Administration, Vardis Fisher, State Director, American Guide Series, p. 135. Copyright, 1939, by George H. Curtis, Secretary of State for the State of Idaho. Caldwell, Idaho: The Caxton Printers, Ltd.

From *Mesa, Cañon and Pueblo*, by Charles F. Lummis, p. 43. Copyright, 1925, by The Century Co. New York and London.

Tall Jumping

"I, too, am a jumper, I came from a family of jumpers. I have a brother who jumped ten thousand dollars in debt, but he couldn't jump out again; and I had another brother who jumped from a church steeple into a wagon-load of hay. When he got half-way down, I yelled, 'Look out, Jimmy, there's glass in the hay.' "

"Terrible—and what did he do?"

"What did he do? He turned right around and jumped back again."

"You Jus' Ain't Seen No Real Guns"

"DAT's put me in de mind of a gun my ole man had," said Gene Oliver "He shot a man wid it one time and de bullet worked him twice befo' it kilt him and three times after. If you hold it high, it would sweep de sky; if you hold it level, it'd kill de devil."

"Oh Gene, stop yo' lyin'! You don't stop lyin' and gone to flyin'."

"Dat ain't no lie, dat's a fact. One night I fired it myself," said Pitts.

"It's a wonder you didn't shoot it off dat time when de quarters boss was hot behind you."

"Let dat ride! Ah didn't want to kill dat ole cracker. But one night Ah heard somethin' stumblin' 'round our woodpile, so Ah grabbed de gun, stepped to de back door and fired it at de woodpile, and went on back to bed. All night long Ah heard somethin' goin' 'round and 'round de house hummin' like a nest of hornets. When daybreak came Ah found out what it was. What you reckon? It was dat bullet. De night was so dark it was runnin' 'round de house waitin' for daylight so it could find out which was the way to go!"

"Dat was a mighty gun yo' pa had," agreed Larkins, "but Ah had a gun dat would lay dat one in de shade. It could shoot so far till Ah had to put salt down de barrel so de game Ah kilt wid it would keep till Ah got to it."

"Larkins—" Jim Allen started to protest.

"Mr. Allen, dat ain't no lie. Dat's a fack. Dat gun was so bad dat all Ah need to do was walk out in de woods wid it to skeer all de varmints. Ah went huntin' one day and saw three thousand ducks in a pond. Jus' as Ah levelled dis gun to fire, de weather turned cold and de water in de lake froze solid and them ducks flew off wid de lake froze to their feets."

From *Here We Are Again*, Recollections of an Old Circus Clown, by Robert Edmund Sherwood, p. 73. Copyright, 1926, by the Bobbs-Merrill Company. Indianapolis.

From *Mules and Men*, by Zora Neale Hurston, pp. 149–150. Copyright, 1935, by Zora Neale Hurston. Philadelphia and London: J. B. Lippincott Company.

"Larkins, s'posin' you was to die right now, where would you land?—
fus' as straight to hell as a martin to his gourd. Whew! you sho kin lie.
You'd pass slap thru hell proper. Jus' a bouncin' and a jumpin' and
go clear to Ginny Gall,[1] and dat's four miles south of West Hell; you
better stop yo' lyin', man."

"Dat ain't no lie, man. You jus' ain't seen no real guns and no good
shootin'."

"Good Shootin' "

A MAN had a wife and a whole passle of young 'uns, and they didn't
have nothin' to eat.

He told his ole lady, "Well, Ah got a load of ammunition in my gun,
so Ah'm gointer go out in de woods and see what Ah kin bring back for
us to eat."

His wife said: "That's right, go see can't you kill us something—if
'tain't nothin' but a squirrel."

He went on huntin' wid his gun. It was one of dese muzzle-loads.
He knowed he didn't have but one load of ammunition so he was very
careful not to stumble and let his gun go off by accident.

He had done walked more'n three miles from home and he ain't saw
anything to shoot at. He got worried. Then all of a sudden he spied
some wild turkeys settin' up in a tree on a limb. He started to shoot at
'em, when he looked over in de pond and seen a passle of wild ducks;
and down at de edge of de pond he saw a great big deer. He heard some
noise behind him and he looked 'round and seen some partiges.

He wanted all of 'em and he didn't know how he could get 'em. So
he stood and he thought and he thought. Then he decided what to do.

He took aim, but he didn't shoot at de turkeys. He shot de limb de
turkeys was setting on and de ball split dat limb and let all dem turkeys'
feets dropped right down thru de crack and de split limb shet up on 'em
and helt 'em right dere. De ball went on over and fell into de pond and
kilt all dem ducks. De gun had too heavy a charge in her, so it bust and de
barrel flew over and kilt dat deer. De stock kicked de man in de breast
and he fell backwards and smothered all dem partiges.

Well, he drug his deer up under de tree and get his ducks out de pond
and piled them up wid de turkeys and so forth. He seen he couldn't tote
all dat game so he went on home to get his mule and wagon.

Soon as he come in de gate his wife said:

"Where is de game you was gointer bring back? You musta lost yo'
gun, you ain't got it."

---

[1] A mythical place.

Ibid., pp. 151–153.

He told his wife, "Ah wears de longest pants in dis house. You leave me tend to my business and you mind yours. Jus' you put on de pot and be ready. Plenty rations is comin'.''

He took his team on back in de woods wid him and loaded up de wagon. He wouldn't git up on de wagon hisself because he figgered his mule had enough to pull without him.

Just as he got his game all loaded on de wagon, it commenced to rain but he walked on beside of the mule pattin' him and tellin' him to "come up," till they got home.

When he got home his wife says: "De pot is boilin'. Where is de game you tole me about?"

He looked back and seen his wagon wasn't behind de mule where it ought to have been. Far as he could see—nothin' but them leather traces, but no wagon.

Then he knowed de rain had done made dem traces stretch, and de wagon hadn't moved from where he loaded it.

So he told his wife, "De game will be here. Don't you worry." So he just took de mule out and stabled him and wrapped dem traces 'round de gate post and went on in de house.

De next day it was dry and de sun was hot and it shrunk up dem traces, and about twelve o'clock they brought dat wagon home, "Cluck-cluck, cluck-cluck," right on up to de gate.

Shooting Match

I LEARNED that an old-fashioned shooting match was to be pulled off out at a country store, and I wended my way thither. I was told that two of the biggest liars of that section would be there, and I would hear something worth while.

When I arrived the contestants were lined up ready to go to shooting. Most of them were long, lean, hungry-looking specimens with guns to match. It was agreed that each contestant could use his own fowling-piece, and fire three shots for the prize, which was a caddy of chewing tobacco. I stood and watched them shoot and saw the winner, an eagle-eyed fellow from back in the brush where the timber grows tall, receive the prize. He opened up the tobacco and told all present to help themselves.

The crowd took seats on dry goods boxes around the front of the store, went for the tobacco, spit red and started the ball to rolling. The lying was what I went to hear, and I heard it. A dry-talking fellow told about a marksman he knew once who could shave a squirrel's nose at

From *I Blew in from Arkansaw*, A Trip of Fun through Hoosierdom, by Geo. D. Beason, pp. 50–53. Copyright, 1908, by Geo. D. Beason. Chicago: Geo. D. Beason, Publisher.

the top of the tallest tree on the Wabash. Bill Sikes, one of the notorious liars present, said, "That's nothing."

"What's nothing?"

"Why, that squirrel nose shaving. I knew a marksman by the name of Buck Mabre who could sure enough shoot. Did any of you ever hear of him?"

All present shook their heads.

"Well, Mabre was the slickest fellow with a gun I ever saw. He could shoot a cigar out of your mouth, burst marbles, cut a rooster's comb off, shoot through a gimlet hole, hit a knitting needle every crack ten steps, spat a target in the same place fifty times hand running, kill quail on the wing with a rifle, and—"

"And what?"

"Why, Buck Mabre could actually shoot so fast and so true that he could shoot away twenty-five cartridges and you would think he had shot but once, and when you looked to see where he hit, you would find but one hole."

Rube Allen, the other notorious liar present, said, "That's shooting, but I knew a fellow by the name of Bob Neely who could lift your man clear out of his boots. Did any of you know him?"

Nobody present had ever heard of him.

"Bob was a clipper. He made his living by his superior marksmanship. You could see him shoot, and if you had any money about your clothes, you would offer to give him the last cent you had. You couldn't help it. He mesmerized you with his fine shooting."

"How did he do it?"

"By the way he made his bullets whiz. He would put up a series of India rubber targets off about fifty yards, and by shooting at them and making his bullets bounce back at different angles and whiz, he could play any tune he ever heard. I've stood and heard him play Yankee Doodle, Dixie, Turkey in the Straw, and many other tunes. He had a red bullet he shot. He would shoot and the red ball would hit a target and bounce right back into his rifle barrel, and he was so quick that he could slap in a fresh charge of powder before the ball bounced back every time. The ball passed to and fro so rapidly that it looked like a red clothes line."

"But where did the mesmerizing come in?"

"Well, just before he closed a performance he would make his bullets whiz in such a way that he said it went like the Siren's singing, and his audience would become so charmed, or mesmerized, that it would do just anything he said. He would take up a collection and those present would try to chip in every cent they had. He wouldn't accept a contribution of more than a dollar."

This broke up the crowd and Rube lingered behind and said to the storekeeper, "I do admire a man who will tell the truth under any and all circumstances, but I hate a liar."

Salvanus Cobb, Jr., on Long Range Shooting

NAT. WILLEY did not like to give up beat when it came to yarns of shooting; for Nat., in his youth and early manhood, had been somewhat noted as a sportsman, both with the gun and the fishing-rod. Born and reared in the shadows of the White Mountains; nearly related to the unfortunate family whose monument in the "Willy Notch" is the work of thousands of sympathizers—he had lived in the time when game was plenty, both in wood and water.

On a certain autumnal evening Nat. sat in the spacious barroom of the Conway House, where a goodly company were gathered around a great open fire of blazing logs, when the conversation turned upon rifle shooting as compared with the shot-gun; and those who advocated the rifle based their claims for superiority partly on its longer range. And this led to stories of long ranges; and the distances to which one or two of those present had fired a rifle ball, with killing effect, was wonderful. Nat. had listened, but had said nothing of his own prowess. One man, from Virginia, told several marvellous stories, one of which was to the effect that his father, who had been one of the pioneers into Kentucky, had once owned a rifle with which he had killed a deer at the distance of two miles!

"I know it seems almost incredible," he said, in conclusion; "but the ground was measured by a practiced surveyor, and that was the sworn result."

A brief silence followed this, which was broken by Charley Head, who said to Old Nat.:

"Look here, Uncle Nat., how about that rifle that General Sam. Knox gave to you? If I don't forget, that could shoot some."

"You mean the one that I had to fire salted balls from, eh?"

"Yes. Tell us about it."

"Pshaw! It don't matter. Let the old piece rest in its glory."

And the old resident would have sat back out of the way, but the story-tellers had become suddenly interested.

"Let us hear about it," pleaded the gentleman whose father had been a compatriot with Daniel Boone. "Did I understand you that you salted your bullets?"

"Always," said Nat., seriously and emphatically.

"And wherefore, pray?"

"Because," answered the old mountaineer, with simple honesty in look and tone, "that rifle killed at such a distance that, otherwise, especially in warm weather, game would *spoil with age before I could reach it.*"

From *Library of Wit and Humor by Mark Twain and Others, with the Philosophy of Wit and Humor*, by Melville D. Landon, A.M. (Eli Perkins), pp. 181–182. Copyright, 1883, by L. W. Yaggy and, 1898, by Star Publishing Co. Chicago: Thompson and Thomas.

Cougar Tamers

YUP, we usta have quite a bit of trouble with cougars and we wuz pretty keerful to have a gun with us when we ambled out. One time though, I plumb forgot my gun and I had a narrow squeak with one of them-there varmints. 'Twas over to that place I usta have in the valley. I goes out after supper to bring the cows home and I was right dog-eared busy when I happened to look up. There was a cougar comun down the hill after me, and me without a gun. I had to think right smart about it. When the varmint got up to me with wide open mouth I just reached in and grabbed his tail and turned him wrong side out quickern a flash. Of course, he was headed in the wrong direction then, and so doggone surprised that he went lickety-split right back up the hill and out of sight.

Big as an Idaho Potato

YES, I'n tell you about wolves. My partner and me, we went up in the Sawtooths and got two elk and was headun home when we looked around and seen eleven wolves after us. We cut a elk loose and they et that. In another mile we give them the other elk and they et that. Then we left our horses and run for it, and they came up and et the horses. I said to my partner that I would rest and shoot a wolf and then run while he was restun and then he could shoot one. So we did. I shot one and the wolves pounced on it while I was runnin; and then my partner, he shot one. Well, we kept that up till we had shot ten of them. Then my partner yelled, "God a-mighty, Jim, look!" I looked behind me and there right on our tails was the biggest wolf anybody ever laid eyes on. He was as big as a house. And then I remembered he'd have to be that big, seeing as how he'd et two elk, two horses, and ten wolves.

They Make Excellent Pets

WHEN I was just a wee lad I wanted to be a cowboy and it was then that I found out what a swell friend a rattlesnake could be. I was riding

From *Idaho Lore,* prepared by the Federal Writers' Project of the Work Projects Administration, Vardis Fisher, State Director, American Guide Series, p. 121. Copyright, 1939, by George H. Curtis, Secretary of State for the State of Idaho. Caldwell, Idaho: The Caxton Printers, Ltd.

Ibid., p. 126.

Ibid., p. 116.
By Mrs. Jennie E. Schmelzel. Coeur d'Alene.

through a pass one day when I saw a rattler pinned under a stone: dismounting, I made ready to kill him, but changed my mind. Didn't seem fair. So I pushed the rock off and went home. As I went along I kept hearing funny noises behind me and looked back and saw it was that silly snake. It came right to my cabin and I opened some canned milk; and that snake drank it all, and you could just see the gratitude in his eyes. He stayed around and got so friendly he slept under my bed.

One night I was sleeping soundly when a bang awakened me. I could hear someone panting and struggling, so I grabbed my gun and said, "Hands up! If you move it wouldn't surprise me if I shot something!" A loud voice yelled, "For God's sake, take this damned thing off of me!" I lit a candle. There, sprawled on the floor, was a guy who had sneaked in to steal my gold dust. But my rattler had wrapped himself around the man's leg and the leg of the table—and had his tail through the keyhole, rattling for the sheriff!

A Bear for Work

PAUL PEAVY was in town from his logging camp buying supplies when Ted Chelde asked: "What in darnation you feedun so much honey to lumberjacks for? Ain't that pretty fancy feed for them?"

"This honey ain't for them. It's an investment."

"How come?" propounded Ted.

"Well, I make lumberjacks leave their coats in camp and in freezun weather I get more out of them. But it ain't enough. So I got the idea to make my silvertip cub work too. He's crazy about honey and will climb a rainbow to get it. So I strap a pair of broadaxes on his feet, and give him a sniff at a can and then shin up a tree with it. Up comes Annabel, the axes scoring the tree on two sides. Then I lower the can and down he goes, and raise it and up he shins, just hewing the tree as smooth as a whistle. Then to make railroad ties all I gotta do is chop it over and whack it up into lengths."

A Family Pet

ACME SULPHIDE came in from his prospect on Caribou creek, bringing a big cougar to Larry Frazee's taxidermist shop. "Want him skun out and made into a rug?" asked Larry.

"No sir. Stuff him as is. I wouldn't think of walkun on Petronius."

"Why not? Just a cougar, ain't he?"

Ibid., p. 124.

Ibid., p. 117.

"Not by your tin horn. He's an institution, that's what he is. When he was just a kitten I ketched him by the mine shaft. Him and Pluto, they was great friends until Petronius growed up. Then one evening when I comes back, my Pluto was gone and Petronius wouldn't eat his supper. I was plumb mad, but I figgered Pluto was gettun old and wasn't so much account nohow. Then, by gum, I missed Mary, the goat. When I missed the last of the chickens and Petronius showed up with feathers in his whiskers, I made up my mind to shoot him. But I got to thinkun how that goat could butt, and the hens wasn't layun anyhow. So I let it go. But I shoulda bumped him then.

"Lydie, she's my old woman—or she was. Partner of my joys and sorrows for forty years. One evening when I gets back she was gone. No sign of her anywhere exceptun one shoe. And Petronius didn't want no supper agin. That got me mad, danged if it didn't, and I went for my gun to blast the varmint. Then I got to thinkun. Lydie wasn't much for looks and besides, she was about to leave me. She was all for hittun the trail, so I puts my gun up."

"Then what happened?"

"Well, last night he jumped me on the trail and took a big hunk right out of me. That was too danged much. So mount him up pretty. He repersents my whole family."

A Pet Trout

. . . It is a likely story enough, as such things go, but there are points about it here and there which seem to require confirmation. I am told that it is a story well known and often repeated in Nova Scotia, but even that cannot be accepted as evidence of its entire truth. Being a fish-story it would seem to require something more. This is the tale as Charlie told it.

"Once there was a half-breed Indian," he said, "who had a pet trout named Tommy, which he kept in a barrel. But the trout got pretty big and had to have the water changed a good deal to keep him alive. The Indian was too lazy to do that, and he thought he would teach the trout to live out of water. So he did. He commenced by taking Tommy out of the barrel for a few minutes at a time, pretty often, and then he took

---

From *Angling in America*, by Charles Eliot Goodspeed, pp. 315–316. Copyright, 1939, by Charles E. Goodspeed. Boston: Houghton Mifflin Company.

. . . a story which may be familiar to many anglers as it is a favorite yarn of the guides. Albert Bigelow Paine, who prints it in *The Tent Dwellers*, credits it to his own guide, but in its dress, at least, the work of a more accomplished literary artist is indicated. . . . This pet-trout story has attained heights of fame loftier than those of printed page. Altered to meet the requirements of the screen it has been appropriated by Hollywood. In a recent movie season Wild Bill Hickok (impersonated by Gary Cooper), figuring in the film *The Plainsman*, re-enacts the occurrence of this moving tale at the steamboat landing in St. Louis; the date, conjecturally, coinciding with the close of the Civil War—C. E. G.

him out oftener and kept him out longer, and by and by Tommy got so he could stay out a good while if he was in the wet grass. Then the Indian found he could leave him in the wet grass all night, and pretty soon that trout could live in the shade whether the grass was wet or not. By that time he had got pretty tame, too, and he used to follow the Indian around a good deal, and when the Indian would go out to dig worms for him, Tommy would go along and pick up the worms for himself. The Indian thought everything of that fish, and when Tommy got so he didn't need water at all, but could go anywhere—down the dusty road and stay all day out in the hot sun—you never saw the Indian without his trout. Show people wanted to buy Tommy, but the Indian said he wouldn't sell a fish like that for any money. You'd see him coming to town with Tommy following along in the road behind, just like a dog, only of course it traveled a good deal like a snake, and most as fast.

"Well, it was pretty sad the way that Indian lost his trout, and it was curious, too. He started for town one day with Tommy coming along behind, as usual. There was a bridge in the road and when the Indian came to it he saw there was a plank off, but he went on over it without thinking. By and by he looked around for Tommy and Tommy wasn't there. He went back a ways and called, but he couldn't see anything of his pet. Then he came to the bridge and saw the hole, and he thought right away that maybe his trout had got in there. So he went to the hole and looked down, and sure enough, there was Tommy, floating on the water, bottom-side up. He'd tumbled through that hole into the brook and drowned."

The Fence That Moved

ONE night in camp two boys, Ira and Tom, got in rather late. Some of the boys already in camp after having retired to the bunkhouse asked the late comers what they had been doing that day.

Tom sez: "You tell 'em, Iry, 'cause I'm too tired."

Iry sez: "Well, it ain't much to tell, ceptin' that we saved the boss lots of time and money today. He set us out to fence in a section pasture. When we got over there, there wasn't enough fence posts and in going up a draw I smelt a terrible smell and asked Tom what it might be. He said he didn't think, he knowed already what it was. It was a snake den, and the snakes were crawlin' out to get the sunshine. I sed to him, 'There ain't much sunshine, for it's cold today.'"

"Well," sez he, "mebbe they come out yesterday to warm themselves when it was good and warm and stayed out too late last night and got froze to death."

From *Cowboy Lore*, by Jules Verne Allen, pp. 29–31. Copyright, 1933, by the Naylor Printing Company. San Antonio, Texas.

"Shore enough, when we got up to this snake den there was somewhere between five and ten thousand rattlesnakes all the way from six to fourteen feet long, lying stretched out and froze stiff. I sez to Tom, 'Right here's where we get our fence posts,' so we just throwed a rope around a bundle of 'em and drag 'em to where we was goin' to fence the 'trap' and I'd hold the pointed end of the snake with the rattles on it into the ground, and while Tom'd sit on his horse he'd hammer on the blunt end, that is the end his head's on, with a six pound sledge hammer, and drove him in the ground. We got through by about eleven o'clock, and thinkin' we was through so quick that the boss wouldn't care if we laid down and took a nap. Which we did, an' in the meantime the sun come shinin' out and the boss thought he'd ride over to see how we was gettin' along and caught us sleepin'. I told him he needn't to git mad because we had saved him a lot of time and money but I wouldn't tell him just how we done it. I told him to come and go with me and I would show him. Well, sir, I'll be dadgoned if he didn't show his appreciation by tellin' me an' Tom to come on down to the bunkhouse and go to sleep, bein' as how we was in such need of sleep and come to the office in the morning and get our money."

One of the boys sed: "Why, Iry, why did he want to fire you, you savin' him all that money expense of cutting fence posts like you did?"

Iry sed: "Oh hell, when that sun commenced to shinin' them damned snakes thawed out and carried off two miles of good barbed wire."

Paul Bunyan on the Water Pipeline

I. Paul Bunyan's Greyhounds

DIJEVER hear the story about Paul Bunyan's greyhoun's? Well—me'n another man was caretakers on Paul's ranch fer a long time. We lived

From "Paul Bunyan on the Water Pipeline," as told by Wayne Martin to B. A. Botkin, *Folk-Say, A Regional Miscellany,* edited by B. A. Botkin, pp. 55–58, 59–60, 61. Copyright, 1929, by B. A. Botkin. Publications of the Oklahoma Folk-Lore Society, No. 1. Norman: University of Oklahoma Press.

"These stories were picked up while the narrator was employed on a city water pipeline at Big Spring, Texas, from October to December, 1928. . . .

"The stories were swapped at work and at dinner (which was eaten on the job), about five miles outside of town 'on the hill.' . . .

". . . 'I decided that these Paul Bunyan stories were figments of the imagination and, while I hadn't had any experience in telling these things, why, I wasn't going to be outdone. So I picked up whatever I could find, put it together, and told it to them. That story there (Number III) is the first tall story I can remember in my life. As I remember it, it was one my Dad read to me—I was about eight or nine, I guess—and later, when I got to the omnivorous age of reading, why, I read it myself more than once. It's either in *Smiles Yoked with Sighs*—a collection of poems—or it's one of Riley's. . . .' Number V is based on two stories by A. W. Somerville in the *Saturday Evening Post:* the whistle episode from 'Comin' down the Railroad,' Septem-

in seprit houses about twenty miles apart. It ust' get mighty cold where we was, an when it did these damn dawgs ust' come around t' the house an bark. When they come we ust' build up a big hot fire, pack up all our stuff, open the door, whistle t' the dawgs, an go off fer a two weeks' visit. Then by the time we come back the dawgs 'd be in the house an we c'd shut the door.

The dawgs ust' start in the door an around the stove, then they'd keep walkin until they was all inside an then lay down with their tail-end first an then keep on layin down till they was all laid down.

One dawg ust' always have trouble gettin out again, so I spent about two days with im an learned im t' come in back'ards and then go out straight, 'nstead uh comin in straight an goin out back'ards. Well—one day Paul's other caretaker died, an he had t' hire a new one. Nobody remembered t' tell im about these greyhoun's, an that was what killed im in the end.

One day it uz cold as hell, about three hund'ed 'n eighty b'low, I think, an this new man looked outa the winduh an saw one uh these here greyhoun's settin out in the snow 'n sleet, jis shiverin 'n shakin like a bygod, so he thought: "Well—goddam, here I've got a nice warm fahr in here an that poor devil's cold as hell. I'll jis open the door an let im in a while." So he walks over an opens the door and whistles at the dawg. Well—that dawg started comin in an he jis kep a-comin.

There was a helluva blizzard outside, an this poor caretaker standin there holdin the door open caught cold. Well—this cold turned int' pneumonia, an fer weeks he was between life 'n death an finally died an was buried b'fore 'at damn dawg got in the house.

II. BARBED WIRE

Dijever hear about Paul Bunyan's shootin match with me? Well— one day ol Paul 'n me got in an argument about which one was the best shot. So we rigged us up a contest t' see which was the best. We picked out a stretch uh road that hadda four stran barb-wahr fence along both sides uv it, an the deal was t' ride a hoss at full gallop down the road, see, an see which one c'd shoot the mos barbs off uh this fence on both sides uh the road with a single shot .22 rifle fer one mile.

So—we rigged us up a hoss an put a long light-weight bar across 'is back with a magnet tied t' each end so's it ud drag on the ground right under the fence an catch the barbs when they fell.

ber 15, 1928, and the President's daughter's marriage from 'Highball!', September 22, 1928 (the rail-setting being the narrator's own addition). . . . Of Number VI he says: 'This isn't exactly a Paul Bunyan story. . . . I had a half-wit friend that told it to me. You might give him credit for the "Barbed Wire" story, too. . . . That "Barbed Wire" outfit was his own invention. He used to ride up and down the road and shoot at barbed wire fences with his B. B. gun. I don't know that he ever shot any off, though.' "

Well—Paul rode the first mile an shot off all the barbs, an then I rode the next mile an shot off all but two.

Then after we had did that we taken a ol muzzle-loadin musket, see, an put a layer uh powder in the bottom, and then we taken an melted some solder so's it ud drip in it, an dropped in some barbs, an put in another pinch er two uh powder, an we jis kep on mixin em up this way until we had the barrel full, then ol Paul rode back along at road an shot all uh them barbs back on the fence again.

(Chorus of *Yeah's?* with rising inflection.)

An—by God, if ya don't bulieve me, I'll take ya back there an show ya the fence.

III. Popcorn

Dijever hear about me 'n Paul 'n our popcorn farm? Well—one time me 'n Paul planted a four-thousand acre tract uh popcorn. There'd been a pretty good d'mand fer popcorn the season b'fore, so we thought we'd see if we c'd make a little money on it. Well—it jis happened that this particular year ever'body planted popcorn, so there wasn' no d'mand fer it. We went on ahead an harvested it an put it in ten big barns.

Not s' long after we stored it a hot wind come blowin up from Mexico, an the thing was so bloomin hot it set fahr t' these barns an popped all the popcorn. Well—this popcorn jis popped 'n popped, an popped all over that part uh the country. The' was a herd uh cattle some six er eight miles from there, an when they looked up an saw all this popcorn flyin around in the air an comin down they d'cided it was snow an froze t' death.

The owner uh this herd raised a big fuss, an Paul 'n me had t' pay him about $80,000 damages. But then that wasn' all lost 'cause Paul 'n me jis boxed up the whole herd, packed em in popcorn t' keep em cold, an shipped em t' Chicago an sold em t' a packin house fer $60,000.

IV. The Macaroni Farm

Dijever hear about Paul Bunyan's macaroni farm? Well—one time me 'n Paul d'cided t' raise some macaroni with spaghetti on the side. Well— the macaroni farm went along pretty good fer a few years. Then we had three or four crop failures in a row, an durin these failures the d'mand got away ahead uh the supply. So after seven er eight years uh this crop failure, why, we had a bumper crop, an it jis happened this bumper crop give us a corner on the macaroni market. Well—the d'mand was still great, and we had a good supply. The only thing was we jis couldn' hire enough men t' bore the holes.

(Voice: An what about the spaghetti?)

Why, we got that outa the cores uh the macaroni.

V. PAUL BUNYAN, RAILROADER

One time me 'n Paul was workin fer—I think it uz the B. 'n O. We had a run from Washington, D. C., t' Baltimore. One day the President's daughter got all hooked up t' run off 'n get married. So she come down t' see me 'n Paul about takin out a special run train from Washington t' Baltimore t' meet er sweetheart. So the next day me 'n Paul hauled out the biggest locomotive in the shop, hooked er up with three cars, slapped on a train crew, loaded on the President's daughter 'n some newspaper boys, an away we went.

We started off at 9 o'clock an had t' be there by 9:20. Me 'n Paul ust' run a double shift in the cab. I'd fahr till I got tired an then he'd fahr till I got rested. Well—I petered out in jis a little while, so Paul was fahrin 'n I was drivin. Well—we went shootin around a bend an up a hill when I seen a place up on the track ahead where the section hands had took out a ol rail an brought up a new one without puttin it in. This wasn' but about three hund'ed yards away. So I seen right away sumpthin ud have t' be did er we'd have a wreck. So I yanked on the air brakes, but they didn' hold. So then I started whistlin fer brakes from the train crew, but I didn' get em. Ya see, we was goin s' fast that when I blew the whistle they'd catch up with the sound of it and go on by b'fore they c'd hear it.

So I yelled at Paul t' tell im what the trouble was, an we d'cided t' put it in reverse. So we put it in reverse an went back up the hill an caught up with the sound uh the whistle, an the crew heard it and put on the brakes an stopped us. Then me 'n Paul run down, threw this ol rail out t' the side, spiked in the new one, got back in the cab, an went on t' Baltimore. An then we made it with two minutes t' spare.

VI. FALL RIVER

One night Fall River was froze up tight, an I was walkin on the ice from the ranch t' town, which was about thirty-three er four miles away. I was walkin along smokin my pipe with my teeth in my mouth an I stepped in a hole an fell in. Now when I come up from the bottom I missed the hole, an as I couldn' see no use standin where I was, I started downstream from one air hole between the water an the ice t' another until I c'd see the lights uh the town about eight er ten miles away. Well, after a while I found a air hole a little bigger 'n the rest, an I stopped fer a long breath. I looked up through the ice an saw Paul walkin up the river bank. So I whistled at im, an he come over an broke the ice fer me and helped me out.

When I got out the air was s' cold that me 'n my clothes froze up tight. But the heat from my pipe saved my face. So me 'n Paul went over b'hin a bush an he struck a match an I thawed out by it, an I took em off an Paul struck another an I dried em. Then we walked on t' town. Then I got tired uh smokin my pipe an knocked out the fire.

Tall Tales of the Mines

I worked in the Enterprise mine when it was only a drift many years ago. The vein didn't have much surface on to it and when I throwed a fall, the damn toppin' caved in on me—sand, slate, coal 'n' all. I shook it off all right, but when I cleared me eyes I found meself face to face with a buck which had pretty two-pointed antlers. "I guess we're into it, butty," says I to meself, "and so let's make the best of things." Well, sir, the buck he gave a snort and started to run off. I caught him by the tail and lifted meself on to his back. Then I took hold of his antlers. Bucky ran from one breast to another and then into the gangway, and from the gangway he hopped out of the mine to the surface, and with one leap he bounded up to the top of the mountain. From there he looked down to the cave-in and turned his head as if to ask me if I wanted to get down into the mine again. With one leap he was inside the mine again with me holding on to his antlers. Once again he leaped from breast to breast, into the gangway and up to the top of the mountain and down into the mine again. He repeated this a third time after which, wantin' to put an end to the nonsense, I slashed his throat with me big toenail and he bled to death.

*   *   *   *   *

Two miners made a bet over their beer to see who knew of a deeper shaft.

"I went into a colliery engine house onc't," said one, "and found the h'isting engineer asleep at the lever. Seein' as the engine was at top speed I quick woke him up. The engineer looked at his watch with half an eye open and yawned, 'I got three hours' sleep yet; she won't land on my shift.'"

"Ugh," grunted the other. "That ain't much of a shaft. I went to a mine for a job onc't. It was Wednesday, as I recall. I asked the topman where I could find the boss and he told me the boss had just stepped on the cage at the bottom and if I came back Saturday night I could catch him as he landed."

Yarns of the Sea

I. THE FLYING SPOUSE

ALL 'eddicated seafarin' men' have heard of the ship built from designs of a Cornishman, the frigate that scraped off Dover Cliff, trying to wedge

From *Minstrels of the Mine Patch*, Songs and Stories of the Anthracite Industry, by George Korson, pp. 72–73. Copyright, 1938, by the University of Pennsylvania Press. Philadelphia.

From *The Narrow Land*, by Elizabeth Reynard, pp. 247–251, 255–259. Copyright, 1934, by Elizabeth Reynard. Boston: Houghton Mifflin Company.

through the Channel. Young sailors went into the shrouds of her and came down with long white beards on them; and one of her discarded jackstays, sunk into the London mud, made 'Piccalilly Circus.'

The New Peninsula built such a ship under direction of Asey Shiverick. She was so tall that sailors took their wives when they went up to furl the toproyals. Later they sent down their grandsons to report that orders had been filled.

The Dover Cliff was a thornberry scratch compared with what befell Cape Cod when the *Flying Spouse,* as she was christened, tried to turn around in the Bay. She could not make it, could not come 'nigh to it,' so Asey sawed off her flying jib boom at the cap. That took three years. Still she could not make it, so he sawed off her Dolphin striker and her whisker boom. That took five years. Still she could not make it, so he sawed off her jib boom and her bowsprit. Hard sawing and Sunday-work, that took him ten years. Then he put her helm down hard and swung her till her nose knocked, whacking Billingsgate Island, plunging it under water. After that, Asey thought: how about taking her out stern first? So he cleared her neatly, but by that time the good meadows of Billingsgate, all owned by ministers, had disappeared in the Bay. The pirates up by Wellfleet had buried their gold on Billingsgate Island, and they lost a 'deal of treasure.'

Asey's ship was rigged with sheets so heavy that no gang could haul them. A team of mules was put aboard, and with this and that, so many mules were required to work ship that no room was left in the hold for cargo. She was nothing but a fancyman's dream. Yet Asey was so proud of her that he bet Captain Obed Paine of Eastham that the *Flying Spouse* could sail to Ireland, there and back in six days and rest upon the seventh. Obed took Asey up, and went along to see fair play. The mules hauled anchor on a Monday.

For all her size the *Flying Spouse* was no faster than the wind blows, so Obed was sure that Asey could never get her to Ireland and return in a matter of six days. What he forgot when he made his reckonings, was that her bow, when her stern was three days out, would be wedged tight into Queenstown Harbour and likely to get stuck there.

'You're a right smart sailorman, Asey,' said Obed, when the ship reached Ireland, Wednesday night, 'but how're y' goint' pull 'er out an' swing 'er aroun', Asey?'

Captain Shiverick grinned. 'God save King George!' he yelled, jumping on the fore deck. 'God save England! Horray for Parlyment!'

The Irish were that mad they pushed the prow of the *Flying Spouse* so hard out of Queenstown Harbour that she shot backward across the Atlantic into the Clay Pounds. Broke them up with a blow from her counter, scarred them, cracked them; all in strips they are, grooved by her stern timbers.

Saturday night at six o'clock Obed shook hands with Asey, and he handed over his Old Woman's recipe for quahaug fritters, due-money

on the bet. Asey ate fritters on Sunday morning—bad ballast amidships
—and that night he gave orders to scuttle the *Flying Spouse*.

II. The Lyars' Bench

Old Hutta Dyer, 'Prince of Yarners,' stretched out his legs, thrust his
cob through his whiskers and made himself comfortable on the Lyars'
Bench that overlooked the sea. There he sat through the long summer
'noonings,' his gray eyes somnolent, his expression mild, mournful; but let
a cat so much as spread its tail or a ship lift her maintruck over the
horizon, and Hut Dyer saw that cat, shivered and 'smelt trouble'; saw
that sail and by some process outside of human deduction 'reco'nised ship.'
His constitution needed a 'deal o' rest.' This he obtained, as he fished
the Backside, by half-hitching his line around his big toe. When he felt
a nibble he waked a 'leetle,' hauled line and brought up a bluefish.

Once a squidhound bass hit the hook and ran to sea with the line in
his stomach and Hut Dyer in tow. That was a ride. Hut moved fast,
almost as fast as the squidhound bass. Soon Hut's toe began to hurt
him, so he folded himself together, got a handhold on the line and began
hauling in. By and by he and the bass met face to face. They were
a long way from home, so Hut talked fast and friendly, and promised
to let bygones be bygones if the bass would tow him to shore. The
squidhound was no shark, only a 'leetle' playful. He towed Hut to the
beach again, and Hut held nothing against him; for he baked him and
ate him, just like a bluefish, with pickle and Dennis salt.

Hut Dyer was as kind as that to almost any animal. Shearjashub and
Bathsheba, his oxen (named after the Bourne family because they were
all slow and stubborn), had bog-water dispositions, neither of them
cheerful; and when the two swayed together, swinging their heads, slow
and mournful, and Hut up aloft swinging his head to be 'soci'ble,' the
sight would make a Nantucket whaleman weep. Only three things ever
make a Nantucketer woeful. One is when a Cape man brings home the
ambergris; one is when an Island girl marries a 'cod-faced peninsula-man';
the third is when the Nantucketer meets Hut Dyer swaying his head in
rhythm with his oxen, all three of them rolling along like a three-ply junk
on the China Sea. The Nantucket whaleman seeing a sight like that lays
down his head on the tattoo of his mother and weeps like a broken comber.

Hut Dyer never discouraged Shear and Sheba, his oxen. One day he
hitched them with traces made of new rawhide and drove them into the
back lot to gather winter wood. When he started for home, the load was
so heavy that it stuck while the traces stretched. Longer and longer they
grew as the oxen plodded ahead. Hut never mentioned the matter to
Shear and Sheba lest they feel disheartened, and the beasts-o-burden
ambled peacefully into Hut's barn. By that time the traces were thin
as ribbons and the load was still up in the back lot. Old Hut told the
oxen not to worry, just to wait for the Lord; and that night Hut left the

barn door open. The weather turned cold; the traces shrank; and when he went out in the morning, there was his load of wood come down from the back lot in the night and standing inside his barn.

Hut Dyer owned a handsome weathervane but was too kind-hearted to oil it; afraid he might fall off the roof, injure himself and be an expense on the town. He made a slingshot out of green rawhide and a forked ash bough. When the vane needed a 'leetle' reminder that the wind was shifting, Hut took a pebble and slingshot the vane till it pointed in the way that the wind blew. This, Hut found out by wetting his finger. Sometimes it took him two hours or more, knocking that vane with pebbles, but he never 'give up' till it pointed dead true, 'the airy-most vane in Truro.'

III. 'One fer the Arkyologists'

'One fer the Arkyologists,' said Captain John Flanders of Sippican as he told the yarn of the last Cape whaler. You cannot find any more Cape whalers. Neither can you find Sippican.

'Durin the blockade before the War (1812) the brig *Nautilus* come home from a viage. I don't know nothin bout the trip nor how she dodged the men-o-war that was standin off-and-on, but I heered the story from my grandther and I know that the brig was full of ile. Prime sparm, right through, and nary a drop scorched in the tryin-out. But business was shot to pieces, so the owners jest laid the brig up. Longside their dock she lay, and they run out chains to the wooden bollards, sent down her upper masts, unslung the spars and stowed everythin away in the riggin-loft. In time, the bollards chafed; so they set stone posts down in the fillin of the pier which was dirt and stone, built like most Cape piers, with only the chafin-spiles of wood.

'The war was fought and won. Then some whalers, fitted out, were sent to sea again. But the owners of the *Nautilus* had died and the wrangle over their leavins kep the brig tied up for years. When the tangle fin'lly got straight, the only livin heirs was two-three fellers that had gone out West and couldn't be located nohow. So the court appointed a feller to keep tract of the prop'ty and make expenses if he could. A kind of a white-livered feller he was, from inshore. He didn't even know that a whaler was layin alongside.

'When a vessel idles fer a long time, she begins to go back. Bein mostly of a veg'table nater, she goes veget'ble agen; fer no kind of veg'tation ever loses all the life that's in it, no matter what. So the seagrass grew fathoms long on the old brig's bottom; and the deck seams opened up; and dust blew in and, fust thing you knew, grass sprouted from the seams and stood up a couple of feet high on deck and on top of the deck-houses. More dust and sand blew in, betwixt the brig and the dock; and fin'lly all the space filled in until it was solid earth. The dock grew over with grass too, till the morin chains were buried deep in sward. All this took gen'rations. unnerstand. and by that time the brig was so covered with green growin things that nobody would have guessed that she was a whaler. Nobody was left to remember her when she was in commission.

'Now the masts, made out of Norway pine, standin in the mixture of bilge-water and ile began to sprout. What with all the changes they had seen and the sort of stuff they was soakin in, they grew a soft, smooth bark, and limbs put out nearly the whole ship's length. Aside from bein unusual straight, they looked like any tree.

'I dunno how long she laid there, but the whalin business died away cept for a few craft sailin from New Bedford, and those that went into the Arctic from West Coast ports. Out in Pennsylvanie some fellers struck min'ral ile and the story got afloat that ile might be found any-wheres, if the soil and bottom was right. A lot of smart-alecks went around with hand-drills lookin fer deposits in every beach hummock and sheep pasture; so nobody paid any attention when a feller showed up at Sippican and begun to bore around the old whale-dock. Nobody watched him as he sunk little holes, and fin'lly he walked out onto the cur'ous little point of land with the two straight trees in the middle of it. He begun to bore there. When he hauled up that drill from bout fifteen-sixteen feet down, looked at it and smelt it, he let out a yell you could hear on Nan-tucket. "Ile!" he yelled, "Ile, by Judas!" He had drilled right into the old cargo and didn't know the diff'ence between whale ile and ker'sene.

'Waal, he located and secured his claim, set up a watchman, and ordered ile riggin. It come, all manner of heavy gear that was stacked up on the wharf. Some parts was late showin up so the feller couldn't set up his riggin fer a space. A good thing, too, fer here's what happened!

' 'Twas September, ruther late, and we got the Line Gale. It breezed out of the nothe-east and kep risin til a hurricaine was blowin. The sea made up higher than ary man has ever seen it round this place; and bime-by there rolled up a reg'ler tidal wave that come rolling in, past the island, gittin higher and higher, curlin, featherin, risin, so high that it shut off the wind from the folks that watched it from the shore. It hit the old whale dock, and went clean over it.

'A little mite of life was left in the old brig yet. When she felt that comber, she riz, and she riz until her old chains parted. And when that sea run back agen, she went along with it, the most cur'ous lookin craft that ever sailed the ocean.

'Jest like a little floatin island, she was all covered with grass and nettles, with two straight trees amidships, full of green leaves and loaded down with ripe, yellow apricots. I fergot to menshun that apricots is what the masts fin'lly bore on em. So she went pitchin and rollin across-bay, shakin showers of leaves out of the branches, and heavin them apricots to port and starboard.

'If a man could have got an anchor over and saved her, she would have been worth a fortune to the Arkyologists. But all hands were too upsot. Besides, the sea was so bad that they couldn't have done it nohow.

'Slowly she drifted out with the swell, sagged back and forth in the wind, and fin'lly come down with a thump on the ledge, where she jest fell apart like a rotten punkin. Tussocks of sward, broken timbers, ile casks floated in all directions. Folks picked em up.'

IV. THE SAUCER-BACK HALIBUT

Whiskery as a 'porkypine,' tanned to the colour of an old leather boot, Jereboam Thacher of Provincetown, longshore fisherman, looked old enough to have fished in the flood. One leg, missing from the knee-joint, was pieced out with the loom of an oar.

'How did I lose my leg?' asked he. 'It's a tale that would turn your hair gray. I don't often tell about it, for folks won't believe me. Haint nobody left these days that kin remember what the fishin was like when I was a young feller. But I'm tellin you life was different when a man could walk alongshore with a pitchfork and load up an oxcart with squiteague, and when the cod schooled right in to the rocks and laid there for days. In them times the lobsters used to crawl in on the marshes and bed down for the winter as soon as the weather cooled up, and men dug em out by the bushel along in Januwary—Febuwary.

' 'Twas a halibut took my leg off, although the critter didn't mean no harm. Used to be a lot of em around inshore in them days, big fellers, shaped like a sole or a flounder, broad, with both eyes on one side of their heads; spotted light and dark brown on the back and dead white underneath. Only place they git em now is well offshore, but in them days they used to run right in to the beach. And they run from twenty-five pound weight up to, waal, no man ever knew how big the biggest one was. They get em now that run to three-four hundred pound.

'There was bigger ones than that when I was young.

'A halibut is a bottom fish, but there's times when they come up. They'll skitter acrost-water, jump out clean, and then there's times when they'll lay almost awash, with their sides and fins curled up like a saucer. Jest lay there. What for? The Lord only knows.

'Waal, this day, I had run off-shore into the bay, haulin lobsterpots, doin a little hand-linin and managin to git a hundred er two pounds of lobsters and bout as many fish. I was runnin right along under sail in my smack-boat, makin good time before a light southerly that was blowin, and glad of it, too, because the fog was makin. I must have been three mile from land when all to oncst I fetched up solid. Pretty nigh capsized. Figgered 'twas a piece of driftin wreck, and I went forrad to shove clear and look for damage, but it waant a wreck at all. It looked like bottom, but no bottom that I ever seen before. Besides, there was forty foot of water there.

'I got clear, put her on the other tack and stood off, wonderin about it. I run on for mebbe twenty minutes, then tacked inshore and bingo! I was aground agen! Bout six times I hit before I fin'lly tuk in that there was somethin between me and home. What it was I couldn't tell, but it was there. And then, jest as I was pushin off the last time, I noticed a flurry some fathoms ahead of me, and I see somethin big break water, a oval brown thing that opened and shet. It was a head, but, Godfreys, what a head! I could see two eyes, twice the length of a whaleboat oar apart. Lookin around they was.

'Bimeby I reelized what the eyes belonged to. A halibut! Layin awash. And I had been sailin acrost his saucer-back for nigh on an hour!

'Things didn't look too good to me, but I waant real worried. How to git clear, that was the question. Fin'lly I figgered that I'd run on to his fin agen, climb out, stand on it, and hang onto my boat, which might be lightened enough to ride over. I trimmed aft my sheet and headed for where I knew his side laid. I miscalkerlated some, and hit it before expected, hit it hardish, too. Then I passed the slack of my halliards round me, and jumped over the bow. Something hit my knee, and I never felt sech pain before. I crawled over the gunnel, more dead than alive, saw that my leg was bleedin bad, and wound a line tight around it. Then I took an oar, and dizzy with pain, I tried to shove the boat over. As she moved ahead, and went clear, I saw what had done the damage:

'I had struck that fish solid and started up a couple of scales. There they laid, four foot acrost, standin half on edge, sharp as a meat-axe, hard as flint. I had stumbled onto the edge of one, and later, when some of the bunch picked me up, they found that my leg was so nigh cut off that they had to finish the job.'

V. Jack Taffril and Tom Staysil

Back in the Seventeen Hundreds lived two ancient sailormen, Jack Taffril who sailed on the *Mary Ann*, Tom Staysil who sailed on the *Nancy*. Whenever they made the home port, the old salts met in Sandwich Tavern, and after a round or two of rum they swapped the 'logs' of their voyages. Whatever the waves or the whales or the mate had done to Jack Taffril, the waves and the whales and the 'murderish mate' had done Tom Staysil one better.

Once Jack came home from sea and told how porpoises followed ship till a sailor spilled a pail of red paint over the side. All the porpoises ate that paint. All of them turned red.

But that same voyage Tom Staysil, given a bottle of rum by the mate and suspicioning that it was poison, poured the firewater over the taffrail. A shark alongside opened his mouth and received a dose of grog. Was that shark happy? Was that shark faithful? It followed the *Nancy* around the Horn, and west to the Island of Tahiti.

Now at Tahiti sailors go ashore 'to git their eddication,' and when Tom no longer appeared, leaning over the ship's rail to pour out a share of his rum, the Faithful Shark 'took to worritin'.' Likewise the shark grew thirsty, so he slowly cruised around the shoreline looking for his old friend, Tom. By and by he found him, sitting on a sea-cliff singing tunes to a Yoo-hoo Lady decked out in floral ornaments and playing on a twang-stringer. The shark stuck his snout over the cliff, opened his mouth, and bared his teeth like a long white row of tombstones.

Tom picked the twang-stringer off the Yoo-hoo and cast it down the shark's throat, where it sunk athwartships and stuck in the gullet. Every time the shark swallowed, his palate swept across the cords of that Yoo-hoo love-fiddle. Thereafter the Faithful Shark made music wherever he went.

On the next voyage, Jack Taffril was capsized from a stove-in boat. He landed on a whale's back and held to the driven harpoon. With perilous speed he rode the whale, above seas and below seas, till the great mammal bled, weakened, drifted. No. 2 boat rescued Jack.

That was the year in which Tom Staysil took an oar in a whaleboat out to strike a Killer! The plunging brute came under the keel and smashed the boat to driftwood. Tom, still clinging to an oar, was taken between gaping jaws; swallowed by the whale. Once inside, Tom struck his flint, looked around and thought about Jonah. He tickled the ribs of the Killer for a time but the whale would not cough up. Then Tom drew out his knife and thrust it in the Killer's heart. Two hours later, while the pious seaman was reading his pocket Bible by whale-oil taper, the mammal sighed, floated on the ocean, and Tom climbed aloft.

He peered out through a picket-fence of white whale's teeth. A full gale beat the waves skyward. Icebergs clung to the Killer's whiskers. Glaciers floated on the sea. Tom went below where the weather was warmer, cut a hole in the stern of the whale, stuck his oar through; then he sculled and he sculled, till he sculled that Killer to Fairhaven.

A year later Jack Taffril was captured by the cannibals. Stripped, trussed, ready for the kettle, he decided to die like a Christian. He raised his voice in a psalm:

> 'And I shall be like to ye tree
> Implanted by ye rivers,
> That in my season yield my fruits
> Unlike ye leaf that withers.'

Jack sang valiantly. The cannibals rejoiced. They appeased their hunger with missionary-men, and the chief kept Jack beside him to sing during council-meetings. Jack married a cannibal lady and lived like a king till the captain of the *Mary Ann,* needing an able seaman, paid for him with ransom.

Tom Staysil likewise was captured, off the African coast. The head cook felt him all over, then decided not to boil him. They called him Very Tough Meat.

Very Tough Meat became a slave and was driven by a lash to work all day for the chief's nine wives. Living inland from the coast, he despaired of ever seeing Sandwich again, but decided to die like a hero. So, to restore his dolorous spirits, he lifted his voice in song. All nine wives came out of the mud hut, and listened to him gravely. Then they summoned the chief. The chief summoned the council; the council summoned the tribe. Soon the whole village stood listening to Tom Staysil's song.

Before he had finished, the chief placed a firm hand on his shoulder. Holding a whip in the other hand, he directed the singer to the coast. As Very Tough Meat departed, the Africans gave him a rousing cheer. And not only did the great chief lead him to the waterfront, he even insisted on signalling a vessel and placing Tom aboard. So careful was he of Tom's voice that if the appreciative seaman so much as opened his mouth, the chief struck it with a thong.

At this point in the Tavern Log, Jack and Tom sang the psalms that saved them from slavery or death in a boiling kettle. But mine host of the tavern dealt with them as the chief had dealt with Tom. He led them firmly out of the taproom, starting them toward Fairhaven. Hand in hand, singing sweet songs, they journeyed down the Highroad.

Birds and Beasts

"WHAT sort of a bird is the milamo?" asked Lanky. "What is he like?"

"Oh," replied Hank, "he's like a milamo. They ain't nothin' else jest like him."

"Is he large or small?" asked Lanky.

"He's rather large," said Hank, "though not as big as an ostrich I reckon, though somewhat bigger than a crane, which he somewhat resembles in general make-up and conformation.

"In the fall when the rains comes and fills up the lakes, like they are now, the critters comes in, or used to, and feeds around the edges of the water. They've got long legs like stilts for wadin' in the water, a long neck, and a long beak that they uses to bore into the soft ground for the earthworms, which is their principal food and diet.

"I ain't talkin' about the little puny earthworms like school boys use to fish with. Naw, sir, a milamo bird would be ashamed of his self if he et one of them kind. He digs down into the ground and ketches the big fellers, shore-nuff he-man worms that looks like inner-tubes. I've seen holes you could hide a hoss's leg in where them critters 'ad been escavatin' for grub. More than one good cow hoss has had to be shot from steppin' in holes that these birds has made, not to say nothin' of the good cow-hands that has had their necks broke.

"But as I was sayin' about the milamo bird, he jest has a way of knowin' where the big worms lives, and when he comes to a place where he knows one of them big fellers is all curled up takin' a nap down under the ground, he sticks his bill into the soil and begins to bore and bore,

---

From *Tall Tales from Texas*, by Mody C. Boatright, pp. 29–39. Copyright, 1934, by the Southwest Press. Dallas, Texas.

walkin' around and around. Purty soon his bill goes out of sight, then his head, then his neck, clean up to his shoulders. That's the way you can slip up on one of 'em. If you can ketch him in jest that stage, maybe you can git sight of him.

"Well, he bores around a while in the hole he has dug; then all at once he sets back like a hoss when there's a big steer on the other end of the rope; and you know then he's got a-holt of one of them big worms. The more he pulls, the more the worm stretches. If he lets up the least bit, the worm jerks his head and neck back into the hole. I seen one once a-bobbin' up and down like that for two hours and fifteen minutes before he finally got his worm.

"Well, he pulls and tussles and yanks and jerks, and finally the worm jest can't stand it no longer and has to let go. He shoots out jest like a nigger-shooter when you turn it loose, and like as not he hits the milamo in the eye. But he's a good-natured bird and don't git ringy about it. Jest why he does it, I don't know; maybe he's so glad to git the worm out, or maybe he sees the joke's on him, after all; anyhow, when the worm comes out and hits him in the eye, he jest naturally gits tickled and rears back on his hind legs and laughs through his beak so you can hear him a mile or more."

"I see," said Lanky. "A strange bird."

"But mighty shy," replied Hank, "mighty shy."

"Yeah, they're shy critters all right," agreed Joe, "but they ain't near as shy as the whiffle-pooffle. Why, them things is so bashful they don't feel comfortable unless they're hid in the bottom of a bottomless lake."

"Are they a fish?" asked Lanky.

"Not exactly a fish," explained Joe, "a sort of cross, I reckon, between an eel and a gila monster."

"Are there any around here?" asked Lanky.

"Well, maybe," replied Joe; "maybe a few. Still I doubt it. You see right around here the lakes go dry sometimes in the dry season, and the whiffle-pooffle wants water, and plenty of it, *mucha agua*. Still there may be a few. Out in the Roswell country, they used to be numerous. Also in Toyah Creek and Leon waterholes. I expect, though, they're gittin' scerce out in them parts now. All game is gittin' scerce. Still, them critters is mighty hard to ketch, and it's jest a few that knows how to do it. Mighty few in fact."

"Do people fish for them, then?" asked Lanky.

"Some does," replied Joe, "but it ain't no use to fish for 'em with a regular fishing outfit. I've seen them rich dudes from the East come out with their fine tackle, rods and reels and all that fool finery, and fish and fish for 'em all day long and never git a nibble. Still they can be caught."

"How does one catch them?" asked Lanky.

"So far as I know it was Pecos Bill that discovered the method. During Pecos Bill's time there was a lot of people that didn't believe there was any sech animal as the whiffle-pooffle livin' in the bottom of the lakes.

Bill said he knowed there was, and he'd show 'em. So he studied and studied, and finally he found a way to capture the critters. First he gits together a rowboat, a long post-hole auger, and a can of oil. Then he hunts up the funniest story-teller he can find and takes him along and sets out.

"He rows out on the lake to where the water's deep; then he takes the post-hole auger and bores a hole clean down to the bottom so as the whiffle-pooffle can come up to the top. Then he has the story-teller tell the funniest stories he can think of—all about Pat and Mike and an Englishman and a Scotchman, and all that.

"Purty soon the whiffle-pooffle gits interested and pricks up his ears. Then Bill tells the story-teller to git funnier. Then purty soon the whiffle-pooffle is so amused that he comes up through the hole and sticks out his head. Bill tells the man to keep on gittin' funnier and funnier till the whiffle-pooffle comes clean out on top of the water. Then Bill begins to ply the oars, very gentle-like at first. The whiffle-pooffle is so interested and amused that he jest naturally can't help but foller the story-teller, who all the time is gittin' funnier and funnier. Bill rows faster and faster, all the time makin' straight for the bank.

"Jest before he gits there, when he is rowin' as fast as he can, he pours the oil out on the water and cuts sharply to the left. By that time the whiffle-pooffle has got up so much speed on the slick water that he can't stop, and he jest naturally slides right out on the bank. Then Pecos Bill lands on him. If you ever git one of the critters on the land, he's jest as helpless as a year-old baby. But they're mighty bashful, mighty bashful."

"In that particular, they ain't a-tall like the club-tailed glyptodont," said Red, "which is a very ferocious and vicious beast. I'll tell you, Lanky, when you're ridin' around in the canyons and meet one of them fellers, you'd better not git into any disputes with him about your highway rights. Jist give him the whole road and don't argue with him. And be careful you don't hang around under the rim-rock when them critters is around."

"I take it they are animals," said Lanky.

"Yeah, I guess they belong to the kingdom of beasts," replied Red. "Some people call 'em whang-doodles, but they ain't real whang-doodles, bein' much bigger and more ferocious. They're purty scerce now, but when we work the canyon tomorrow, I can show you places where they have been. Yes, sir, I can show you the very spot where one of them fellers took off one of the very best friends I ever had in this world."

"A sort of mountain lion, I suppose," said Lanky.

"Son, one of them babies would make a mountain lion look like a kitten. Besides, they don't belong to the feline species nohow, bein' more like a kangaroo in build, and about sixteen hands high when on all-fours, though most of the time they hop along on their hind legs and tail and keep their forepaws ready to biff anything that gits in their way.

And if one of them critters hits you—well, you're lucky if they find anything to bury.

"However, that ain't their main method of combat; that ain't the way one of 'em took off my dear friend—Jack Snodgrass was his name. The glyptodont has got a big flat tail made out of stuff like cow's horn, except there ain't no bone in it. This tail bein' springy is a great aid and help in more ways than one. He can jump along with it and clear the brush, and he can land on it when he wants to jump off of a cliff, and he don't feel no bad effects from the jar.

"Well, I started to tell you how one of them beasts took off my dear friend Jack Snodgrass. Jack used to work on this outfit, and one fall he was workin' the canyon, jist like we'll be tomorrow, and Jack gits a glimpse of the glyptodont. Jack was always a curious lad; so he tarried around to see what the critter was about. Jack was on the other side of a canyon, anyway, and he 'lowed he'd have plenty of time to make his stampede if the critter showed any signs of combat. So Jack jist looks across to see what's goin' on.

"Directly the glyptodont gits wind of him and looks at him right straight for a minute or two. But Jack still ain't worried none, havin' the canyon between him and the ferocious beast. He jist stands there and watches him to see what he is about. Purty soon he notices that the glyptodont is spadin' around on the ground with his tail. Presently he scoops up a big boulder, jist like you'd lift it with a shovel. He carries this on his tail, bein' careful not to let it fall off, and backs up and eases it off on the top of a bigger boulder. Jack begins to try to figure out a way to capture the brute; he 'lows if he ever could git him broke, he'd be a mighty handy animal to have around the place about tankin' time.

"Well, the glyptodont walks over to the other side of the rock he's set up and squats on his hind legs; then he draws up his front legs and begins to whirl around and around on his hind legs, jist like a spool of barbed wire on a crowbar when you're stringin' fence. After he spins around a while, he lets down his tail, which hits the rock he's set up, which comes through the air like a cannon-ball. That was the last thing pore Jack ever knowed. We buried him, pore feller, next day—that is, all of him we could find. When we're over there tomorrow, I'll show you the place where he got kilt, as well as a lot of other places where them critters has catapulted rocks up and down the canyons jist to keep in practice and for the fun of seein' 'em roll. Yeah, them club-tailed glyptodonts is ferocious animals."

"They're vicious brutes," agreed Joe, "but they ain't got much on the gwinter."

"I never heard of a gwinter," said Lanky.

"Well," replied Joe, "did you ever hear of a godaphro?"

"No."

"Did you ever hear of a side-swiper?"

"No."

"Did you ever hear of a mountain-stem-winder?"

"No, I never heard of them, either."

"Well, they're really all one and the same thing, but the real true and correct name is gwinter."

"And what sort of a beast is he?" asked Lanky.

"Well, he's a grass-eatin' quadruped," said Joe, "something like a cross between a buffalo and a mountain-goat, only he's a lot more ferocious. The peculiar thing about the gwinter is his legs. Instead of havin' four legs of equal length like a critter ought to have, or two short legs in front and two long ones behind, like the glyptodont, these brutes have two long legs on the downhill side and two short legs on the uphill side. This is mighty convenient for 'em, since they don't live on level ground nohow. Some of 'em has their right legs long, and some of 'em has their right legs short, dependin' on which way they graze around the mountains. The Chisos and the Davis and the Guadalupe mountains used to be full of 'em. Up there, them critters was thicker than the buffalo or the antelope on the plains, but they're gittin' mighty scerce now. Still, they took off many a cow-hand in the early days, and sometimes yet a tenderfoot gits in the way of one of 'em and don't come back home to the chuck wagon at night.

"If one of them critters ever starts toward you, Lanky, don't for anything let him know you're scered. If you try to run, he'll git you shore. Jest stand there and look him right in the eye like you was glad to see him. He'll be comin' right toward you with his head down like a bat shot out of a cannon. Still, don't move, and if you're in the saddle, hold your hoss. Jest let that gwinter alone till he gits in two steps of you, then take a couple of steps down the hill. He can't run the other way, and you'll be safe. Ten to one he'll be so mad about it he'll try to foller you, anyway, and when he gits his short legs down hill, he's a goner. Jest stand by and watch him roll down the mountain and break his fool neck. That's one reason why they're so scerce, the cowboys learned that trick. Another reason is that they fought among themselves too much. You see, them that has their long legs on the right used to meet them that has their long legs on the left as they grazed around the mountains. And when two of 'em met like that, they always tangled up. Finally they fought till the weaker side all got kilt, so now there's only one kind on each mountain. On some mountains it's the right-leggers, and on some mountains it's the left-leggers."

"If somebody would capture one alive," said Lanky, "he could sell him to a circus for five thousand dollars."

"That's been tried, son; that's been tried," replied Joe. "However, your figger's too small. Once when I was punchin' cattle in the Chisos, Barnum and Bailey sent a feller all the way down from New York City with fifty thousand dollars to pay any man that would cage him a gwinter. For a long time he couldn't git nobody to try it, till finally he come to our outfit.

" 'I won't endanger the lives of my men in any sech manner and fashion,' says the boss. 'However,' he says, turnin' to us, 'if any of you men want to try it on your own hook, you can. They ain't much work to do right now, and I'll let you off for a few days.'

"Well, we gits our best mounts and ropes, and looks after our cinches, and sets out. We scouts around a while, and shore nuff we hears one snort right near the foot of Egg-shell Mountain. We lets out our wildest yells and fires off our six-shooters, and somehow, by luck I guess, we gits the critter buffaloed, and he goes tearin' around the mountain and us after him. Each time he goes around the mountain he gits a little higher. We sees our hosses is goin' to give out if we don't figger out some way to spell 'em. We 'lows that since we got the critter on the run, two of us will be enough to go around the mountain, and the others stays put. Then on the next round, two more goes, and so on and so forth. Each time we gits a bit nearer the top. Finally, we all joins in, in order to be there when he gits to the top and can't go no further. And purty soon there he is at the top."

"How did he escape?" asked Lanky.

"Why, the brute jest turned right through his self, jest clean wrong side out like a sock, and run the other way."

"And that was the last you saw of him?"

"Oh, we used to see him occasionally, as we knowed by his long legs bein' on the other side; but when winter come, he caught cold and died. And that's what you'll do, Lanky, if you set there by the coals and shiver. You'd better git a little shut-eye before you stand guard."

Paul Bunyan Natural History

INHABITING the big pine woods, the swamps, lakes and streams in the vicinity of Paul Bunyan's old-time logging camps were a considerable number of very wild animals. These differed considerably or greatly from the common bear, deer, wildcats and wolves of the timber lands. Most of them are now extinct or but rarely seen. Some were quite harmless, but most of them were of a very vicious or poisonous nature. Most were active only during the winter months, during the summer they hid in thickets or windfalls, hibernated in caves or hollow trees, or migrated to the North Pole. Tall tales of encounters with some of these mythical wild animals were often told in the lumber camp bunkhouses at night to create mirth or to impress and frighten the greenhorns. The information here collected concerning these Bunyan beasts, birds, reptiles and fish was obtained from

Paul Bunyan Natural History. Describing the Wild Animals, Birds, Reptiles and Fish of the Big Woods about Paul Bunyan's Old Time Logging Camps, Habitat and Habits of the Flitterick, Gumberoo, Hangdown, Hidebehind, Hodag, Luferlang, Rumptifusel, Sliver Cat, Shagamaw, Goofus Bird, Hoop Snake, Whirligig Fish and Others, by Charles Edward Brown. Madison, Wisconsin: C. E. Brown. 1935.

various reliable, as well as unreliable and doubtful sources. The descriptions of these are arranged in alphabetical order for convenience of ready identification.

I. ANIMALS

AXEHANDLE HOUND. Like a dachshund in general appearance, with a hatchet-shaped head, a short handle-shaped body and short, stumpy legs. It prowled about the lumber camps at night looking for axe or peavy handles, this being the only kind of food it was known to touch. Whole cords of axe handles were eaten by these troublesome wild hounds.

ARGOPELTER. This hoary beast lived in the hollow trunks of trees. From this point of vantage it dropped or threw chunks or splinters of wood on its victims. It but seldom missed its aim and a considerable number of lumberjacks were annually maimed by its gunnery. No complete description of it has ever been obtained and its life history is unknown.

CAMP CHIPMUNK. Originally small animals, they ate the tons of prune stones discarded from Paul Bunyan's camp cook shanty and grew so big and fierce that they killed all of the bears and catamounts in the neighborhood. Later Paul and his men shot them for tigers.

FLITTERICKS. The variety of flying squirrels which frequented the vicinity of the lumber camps were very dangerous because of the great rapidity of their flight. It was impossible to dodge them. One struck an ox between the eyes with such force as to kill the animal.

GUMBEROO. It lived in burned-over forests and was therefore easily avoided. It was very ferocious. It was "larger than a bear and had a round, leathery body that nothing could pierce. Bullets bounded off its tough hide. Often they struck the hunter on the rebound and killed him. The only thing that could kill a gumberoo was fire. Often at night the lumberjacks were awakened by loud explosions. These were caused by gumberoos blowing up in flames." A foolhardy photographer once took a picture of one but this also finally blew up.

GYASCUTUS. Also called the Stone-eating Gyascutus. This sordid beast has been described as "about the size of a white-tailed deer. Has ears like a rabbit and teeth like a mountain lion. It has telescopic legs which enables it to easily graze on hills. It has a long tail which it wraps around rocks when its legs fail to telescope together. It feeds on rocks and lichens, the rocks enabling it to digest the tough and leathery lichens. It is never seen except after a case of snake-bite."

HANGDOWN. Its Latin name is unknown. This utterly foolish animal lives in big woods "where it hangs down from the limbs of trees, either with its fore or hind paws, either head down or head on, either way making no difference to its digestion. It climbs along the bottom of a limb after the manner of a sloth. Its skin brings a high price. It is more easily hunted at night when a tub must be placed over it. It is then killed with an axe."

HIDEBEHIND. A very dangerous animal which undoubtedly accounted for many missing lumberjacks. It was always hiding behind something, generally a tree trunk. Whichever way a man turned it was always behind him. From this position it sprang upon its human prey, dragged or carried the body to its lair and there feasted on it in solid comfort. Because of its elusive habits no satisfactory description of it has ever been obtained.

HODAG. The Black Hodag (Bovinus spiritualis) was discovered by E. S. "Gene" Shepard, a former well-known timber cruiser of Rhinelander, Wisconsin. Its haunts were in the dense swamps of that region. According to its discoverer, this fearful beast fed on mud turtles, water snakes and muskrats, but it did not disdain human flesh. Mr. Shepard found a cave where one of these hodags lived. With the aid of a few lumberjacks he blocked the entrance with large rocks. Through a small hole left in the barricade he inserted a long pole on the end of which he fastened a sponge soaked in chloroform. The hodag, thus rendered unconscious, was then securely tied and taken to Rhinelander, where a stout cage had been prepared for it. It was exhibited at the Oneida County fair. An admission fee was charged and a quite large sum of money earned. Later Mr. Shepard captured a female hodag with her thirteen eggs. All of these hatched. He taught the young hodags a series of tricks, hoping to exhibit the animals for profit.

This ferocious beast had horns on its head, large bulging eyes, terrible horns and claws. A line of large sharp spikes ran down the ridge of its back and long tail. Colored photographs of it can be obtained at Rhinelander. The hodag never laid down. It slept leaning against the trunks of trees. It could only be captured by cutting deeply into the trunks of its favorite trees. It was a rare animal of limited distribution.

LUFERLANG. A curious animal with a dark blue stripe running down the length of its back. Its brushy tail was in the middle of the back. Its legs were triple-jointed and it could run equally fast in any direction. It attacked its prey without provocation and its bite was certain death. "It bites but once a year, so if one met one that had already bitten someone, one was perfectly safe."

ROPERITE. A very active animal as large as a pony. It had a rope-like beak with which it roped the swiftest rabbits. Sometimes it got a tenderfoot logger. It generally traveled in small herds. Probably now extinct.

RUMPTIFUSEL. A very ferocious animal of large size and great strength. When at rest it wraps its thin body about the trunk of a tree, a clever stratagem for securing its prey. A lumberjack mistakes it for a fur robe, approaches it and is thereafter missing.

SIDEHILL DODGER. It lived on the sides of hills only. It had two short legs on the up-hill side. It burrowed in hillsides, having a number of such burrows and was always dodging in and out of these. It was harmless but its very strange antics frightened many a lumberjack into fits.

SLIVER CAT. This fierce denizen of the pineries was a huge cat with tasseled ears. Its fiery red eyes were in vertical instead of horizontal eye-slits. It had a very long tail with a ball-shaped knob at its end. The lower side of this knob was bare and hard, on its upper side were sharp spikes. The big cat would sit on a limb waiting for a victim. When one passed beneath it would knock him down with the hard side and then pick him up with the spikes. Paul Bunyan's crews suffered continual losses from the depredations of these big cats.

TEAKETTLER. A small animal which obtains its name from the noise which it made, resembling that of a boiling teakettle. Clouds of vapor issued from its nostrils. It walked backward from choice. But few woodsmen have ever seen one.

TOTE-ROAD SHAGAMAW. An animal enigma. Its hind legs have the hoofs of a moose and its fore legs the claws of a bear, making it very hard to track. When it tires of using one set of legs it travels on the other set. It prowls along the tote roads devouring any coats or other articles of lumberjacks' clothing which it finds hung on trees or logs. It is fierce in appearance but is shy and harmless.

TRIPODERO. It had tripod legs. "Its beak is like the muzzle of a gun with a sight on the end. Going through the brush it raises and lowers itself to look for game. Upon seeing a bird or small animal it tilts itself to the rear, sights along its beak and lets fly a pellet of clay. A quantity of squids of this material it carries in its cheeks. It never misses a shot." This is more particularly an animal of the vicinity of the civil engineering and railroad construction than of the logging camps.

II. BIRDS

GOOFUS BIRD. One of the peculiar birds nesting near Paul Bunyan's old time camp on the Big Onion River. It was the opposite of most other birds—it always flew backwards instead of forwards. This curious habit an old lumberjack explained: "It doesn't give a darn where it's going, it only wants to know where it's been." It also built its nest upside down.

GILLYGALOO. This hillside plover nested on the slopes of Bunyan's famous Pyramid Forty. Living in such a locality it laid square eggs so that they could not roll down the steep incline. The lumberjacks hardboiled these eggs and used them as dice.

PINNACLE GROUSE. This bird had only one wing. This enabled it to fly in only one direction about the top of a conical hill. The color of its plumage changed with the seasons and with the condition of the observer.

PHILLYLOO BIRD. It had a long beak like a stork and long legs. It had no feathers to spare. It flew upside down the better to keep warm and to avoid rheumatism in its long limbs. It laid Grade D eggs.

MOSKITTOS. The naturalist in Paul Bunyan's camp classified these as birds. When Paul was logging in the Chippewa River region the mosquitos were particularly troublesome. They were so big that they could straddle the stream and pick the passing lumberjacks off the log drive. Sometimes a logging crew would find one in this position, quickly tie his legs to convenient trees and use him for a bridge across the river. Paul imported from Texas a drove of fighting bumblebees to combat the mosquitos. They fought for a while, then made peace and intermarried. The result of this crossing made the situation worse than ever before for the loggers. The offspring had stingers at both ends.

III. Snakes

Hoop Snake. A very poisonous reptile. It could put its tail in its mouth and roll with lightning-like rapidity after its prey. The only way to avoid it was to quickly jump through its hoop as it approached. This so confused the large serpent that it rolled by and could not get back. Its sting was in its tail. A hoop snake once stung a peavy handle. This swelled to such great size that Paul Bunyan cut one thousand cords of wood out of it.

Snow Snake. These reptiles came over from Siberia by frozen Bering Strait during the very cold year of the two winters. Being pure white in color they were always more plentiful during the winter time. They were very poisonous and savage. Tanglefoot oil was the only remedy for their bite.

IV. Fish

Cougar Fish. This savage fish, armed with sharp claws, lived in the Big Onion River. It was the cause of the disappearance and death of many river drivers, whom it clawed off the logs and beneath the water. Paul Bunyan offered a big reward for their capture and extermination, but the fish heard of it and stayed away. None were taken.

Giddy Fish. They were small and very elastic, like India rubber. They were caught through holes in the ice during the winter. The method pursued was to hit one on the head with a paddle. This fish would bounce up and down. Taking the cue from him the other fish would bounce also. Presently all would bounce themselves out of the water onto the ice. There they were easily gathered up.

Goofang. This curious fish always swam backward instead of forward. This was to keep the water out of its eyes. It was described as "about the size of a sunfish, only larger."

Log Gar. These big fish had a snout so well armed with large saw teeth that they could saw right through a log to get at a juicy lumberjack. Once in the water they made mince meat of him.

Upland Trout. These very adroit fish built their nests in trees and were very difficult to take. They flew well but never entered the water. They were fine pan fish. Tenderfeet were sent out into the woods to catch them.

Whirligig Fish. Related to the Giddy Fish. They always swam in circles. They were taken in the winter months through holes in the ice, like their relatives. The loggers smeared the edges of the holes with ham or bacon rind. Smelling this the fish would swim around the rims of the holes, faster and faster, until they whirled themselves out on the ice. Thousands were thus taken.

V. Bugs

Chiefly bed bugs and greybacks. The men soon got used to them and tolerated them. Wood ticks were in the brush but were out of date and inactive in the winter time.

Fearsome Critters

I. The Cactus Cat

(Cactifelinus inebrius)

How many people have heard of the cactus cat? Thousands of people spend their winters in the great Southwest—the land of desert and mountain, of fruitful valleys, of flat-topped mesas, of Pueblos, Navajos, and Apaches, of sunshine, and the ruins of ancient Cliff-dwellers. It is doubtful, however, if one in a hundred of these people ever heard of a cactus cat, to say nothing of seeing one sporting about among the cholla and palo verde. Only the old-timers know of the beast and its queer habits.

The cactus cat, as its name signifies, lives in the great cactus districts, and is particularly abundant between Prescott and Tucson. It has been reported, also, from the valley of the lower Yaqui, in Old Mexico, and the cholla-covered hills of Yucatan. The cactus cat has thorny hair, the thorns being especially long and rigid on its ears. Its tail is branched and upon the forearms above its front feet are sharp, knifelike blades of bone. With these blades it slashes the base of giant cactus trees, causing the sap to exude. This is done systematically, many trees being slashed in the course of several nights as the cat makes a big circuit. By the time it is back to the place of beginning the sap of the first cactus has fermented into a kind of mescal, sweet and very intoxicating. This is greedily lapped up by the thirsty beast, which soon becomes fiddling drunk, and goes waltzing off in the moonlight, rasping its bony forearms across each other and screaming with delight.

II. The Squonk

(Lacrimacorpus dissolvens)

The range of the squonk is very limited. Few people outside of Pennsylvania have ever heard of the quaint beast, which is said to be fairly

From *Fearsome Creatures of the Lumberwoods, With a Few Desert and Mountain Beasts,* by William T. Cox, pp. 27, 31, 37, 43, 45. Copyright, 1911, by William T. Cox. Washington, D. C.: Press of Judd & Detweiler, Inc., 1910.

common in the hemlock forests of that State. The squonk is of a very retiring disposition, generally traveling about at twilight and dusk. Because of its misfitting skin, which is covered with warts and moles, it is always unhappy; in fact it is said, by people who are best able to judge, to be the most morbid of beasts. Hunters who are good at tracking are able to follow a squonk by its tear-stained trail, for the animal weeps constantly. When cornered and escape seems impossible, or when surprised and frightened, it may even dissolve itself in tears. Squonk hunters are most successful on frosty moonlight nights, when tears are shed slowly and the animal dislikes moving about; it may then be heard weeping under the boughs of dark hemlock trees. Mr. J. P. Wentling, formerly of Pennsylvania, but now at St. Anthony Park, Minnesota, had a disappointing experience with a squonk near Mont Alto. He made a clever capture by mimicking the squonk and inducing it to hop into a sack, in which he was carrying it home, when suddenly the burden lightened and the weeping ceased. Wentling unslung the sack and looked in. There was nothing but tears and bubbles.

III. THE SPLINTER CAT

(Felynx arbordiffisus)

A widely distributed and frightfully destructive animal is the splinter cat. It is found from the Great Lakes to the Gulf, and eastward to the Atlantic Ocean, but in the Rocky Mountains has been reported from only a few localities. Apparently the splinter cat inhabits that part of the country in which wild bees and raccoons abound. These are its natural food, and the animal puts in every dark and stormy night shattering trees in search of coons or honey. It doesn't use any judgment in selecting coon trees or bee trees, but just smashes one tree after another until a hollow one containing food is found. The method used by this animal in its destructive work is simple but effective. It climbs one tree, and from the uppermost branches bounds down and across toward the tree it wishes to destroy. Striking squarely with its hard face, the splinter cat passes right on, leaving the tree broken and shattered as though struck by lightning or snapped off by the wind. Appalling destruction has been wrought by this animal in the Gulf States, where its work in the shape of a wrecked forest is often ascribed to windstorms.

IV. THE BILLDAD

(Saltipiscator falcorostratus)

If you have ever paddled around Boundary Pond, in northwest Maine, at night you have probably heard from out the black depths of a cove a spat like a paddle striking the water. It may have been a paddle, but the chances are ten to one that it was a billdad fishing. This animal occurs

only on this one pond, in Hurricane Township. It is about the size of
a beaver, but has long, kangaroo-like hind legs, short front legs, webbed
feet, and a heavy, hawk-like bill. Its mode of fishing is to crouch on a
grassy point overlooking the water, and when a trout rises for a bug,
to leap with amazing swiftness just past the fish, bringing its heavy, flat
tail down with a resounding smack over him. This stuns the fish, which is
immediately picked up and eaten by the billdad. It has been reported
that sixty yards is an average jump for an adult male.

Up to three years ago the opinion was current among lumber jacks that
the billdad was fine eating, but since the beasts are exceedingly shy
and hard to catch no one was able to remember having tasted the meat.
That fall one was killed on Boundary Pond and brought into the Great
Northern Paper Company's camp on Hurricane Lake, where the cook
made a most savory slumgullion of it. The first (and only) man to taste
it was Bill Murphy, a tote-road swamper from Ambegegis. After the first
mouthful his body stiffened, his eyes glazed, and his hands clutched the
table edge. With a wild yell he rushed out of the cook-house, down to the
lake, and leaped clear out fifty yards, coming down in a sitting posture—
exactly like a billdad catching a fish. Of course, he sank like a stone. Since
then not a lumber jack in Maine will touch billdad meat, not even with
a pike pole.

V. The Tripodero

(*Collapsofemuris geocatapeltes*)

The chaparral and foothill forests of California contain many queer
freaks of one kind and another. One of the strangest and least known is
the tripodero, an animal with two contractile or telescopic legs and a tail
like a kangaroo's. This peculiarity in structure enables the animal to
elevate itself at will, so that it may tower above the chaparral, or, if it
chooses, to pull in its legs and present a compact form for crowding
through the brush. The tripodero's body is not large but is solidly built,
and its head is nearly all snout, the value of which is seen in the method
by which food is obtained. As the animal travels through the brush-covered
country it elongates its legs from time to time, thus shoving itself up above
the brush for purposes of observation. If it sights game within a range
of ten rods it takes aim with its snout and tilts itself until the right elevation is obtained, then with astounding force blows a sundried quid of
clay, knocking its victim senseless. (A supply of these quids is always
carried in the left jaw.) The tripodero then contracts its legs and bores
its way through the brush to its victim, where it stays until the last bone
is cracked and eaten.

PART FIVE

FOLK TALES AND LEGENDS

'Twas so much of a tale spun out to pass daylight.
—Robert L. Morris

Item. To my beloved grandnephew and namesake, Matthew, I do bequeath and give (in addition to the lands devised and the stocks, bonds and moneys willed to him, as hereinabove specified) the two mahogany bookcases numbered 11 and 13, and the contents thereof, being volumes of fairy and folk tales of all nations, and dictionaries and other treatises upon demonology, witchcraft, mythology, magic and kindred subjects, to be his, his heirs, and his assigns, forever.
—Eugene Field

I. ANIMAL TALES

Animals talk to each other, of course. There can be no question about that; but I suppose there are very few people who can understand them.—MARK TWAIN

NEXT to hero tales and tall tales, animal tales are perhaps the most congenial to American folk story-tellers and their audiences. Animal tales proper, as distinct from mere tales about animals, are those in which animal characters talk and act like human beings. Originating in the primitive's sense of kinship with animals, animal tales have lent themselves to the purposes of allegory, satire, and children's "bedtime" stories. The fact that the best-known of our animal tales, the Uncle Remus stories, survive on the nursery level is another illustration of the "downward process" of tradition (also seen in games), by which children retain what was once the property of adults.

Historically, the social rôle of the Negro slave as story-teller to his master's children accounts for the large proportion of African survivals in Negro animal tales as compared with the predominance of white traits in other parts of his lore. At the same time, a good many of the plantation stereotypes linger in the nostalgic versions of Negro folk stories and story-tellers by Joel Chandler Harris, Louise Clarke Pyrnelle, and Virginia Frazer Boyle.

Although Harris discounted the literary value of the "old darkey's poor little stories" and the art of his own retelling, his renditions of "fantasies as uncouth as the original man ever conceived of" are perhaps more properly literature than folklore. More scientific, if what Harris would term more "painful" in their dialect, are the Gullah versions of Mrs. A. M. H. Christensen, Ambrose E. Gonzales, and Charles C. Jones, Jr. But whether quaint or stark, Negro animal tales project the "compensatory dreams of the subject races and serf-populations, expressed both in folk-tale and folk-ballad, [which] delight in the victory of the weak over the strong and in the triumph of brains over brute strength."[1] The way in which the Negro, more peculiarly than any other minority group, has made this symbolism his own and a vehicle for his philosophy, constitutes one of his most important contributions to folk literature and wisdom.

---

[1] *Rumors and Hoaxes; Classic Tales of Fraud and Deception,* collected and arranged with an introduction by Peter Haworth (1928), p. xviii.

The Wonderful Tar-Baby Story

I. How Mr. Fox Caught Mr. Rabbit

"Didn't the fox *never* catch the rabbit, Uncle Remus?" asked the little boy next evening.

"He come mighty nigh it, honey, sho's you born—Brer Fox did. One day atter Brer Rabbit fool 'im wid dat calamus root, Brer Fox went ter wuk en got 'im some tar, en mix it wid some turkentime, en fix up a contrapshun wat he call a Tar-Baby, en he tuck dish yer Tar-Baby en he sot 'er in de big road, en den he lay off in de bushes fer to see wat de news wuz gwineter be. En he didn't hatter wait long, nudder, kaze bimeby here come Brer Rabbit pacin' down de road—lippity-clippity, clippity-lippity—dez ez sassy ez a jay-bird. Brer Fox, he lay low. Brer Rabbit come prancin' 'long twel he spy de Tar-Baby, en den he fotch up on his behime legs like he wuz 'stonished. De Tar-Baby, she sot dar, she did, en Brer Fox, he lay low.

" 'Mawnin'!' sez Brer Rabbit, sezee—'nice wedder dis mawnin',' sezee.

"Tar-Baby ain't sayin' nothin', en Brer Fox, he lay low.

" 'How duz yo' sym'tums seem ter segashuate?' sez Brer Rabbit, sezee.

"Brer Fox, he wink his eye slow, en lay low, en de Tar-Baby, she ain't sayin' nothin'.

" 'How you come on, den? Is you deaf?' sez Brer Rabbit, sezee. 'Kaze if you is, I kin holler louder,' sezee.

"Tar-Baby stay still, en Brer Fox, he lay low.

" 'Youer stuck up, dat's w'at you is,' says Brer Rabbit, sezee, 'en I'm gwineter kyore you, dat's w'at I'm a gwineter do,' sezee.

"Brer Fox, he sorter chuckle in his stummuck, he did, but Tar-Baby ain't sayin' nothin'.

" 'I'm gwineter larn you howter talk ter 'spectubble fokes ef hit's de las' ac,' sez Brer Rabbit, sezee. 'Ef you don't take off dat hat en tell me howdy, I'm gwineter bus' you wide open,' sezee.

"Tar-Baby stay still, en Brer Fox, he lay low.

"Brer Rabbit keep on axin' 'im, en de Tar-Baby, she keep on sayin' nothin', twel present'y Brer Rabbit draw back wid his fis', he did, en blip he tuck 'er side er de head. Right dar's whar he broke his merlasses jug. His fis' stuck, en he can't pull loose. De tar hilt 'im. But Tar-Baby, she stay still, en Brer Fox, he lay low.

" 'Ef you don't lemme loose, I'll knock you agin,' sez Brer Rabbit, sezee, en wid dat he fotch 'er a wipe wid de udder han', en dat stuck. Tar-Baby, she ain't sayin' nothin', en Brer Fox, he lay low.

" 'Tu'n me loose, fo' I kick de natal stuffin' outen you,' sez Brer Rabbit, sezee, but de Tar-Baby, she ain't sayin' nothin'. She des hilt on, en den Brer Rabbit lose de use er his feet in de same way. Brer Fox, he lay low. Den Brer Rabbit squall out dat ef de Tar-Baby don't tu'n 'im loose he butt 'er cranksided. En den he butted, en his head got stuck. Den Brer Fox, he sa'ntered fort', lookin' des ez innercent ez one er yo' mammy's mockin'-birds.

" 'Howdy, Brer Rabbit,' sez Brer Fox, sezee. 'You look sorter stuck up dis mawnin',' sezee, en den he rolled on de groun', en laughed twel he couldn't laugh no mo'. 'I speck you'll take dinner wid me dis time, Brer Rabbit. I done laid in some calamus root, en I ain't gwineter take no skuse,' sez Brer Fox, sezee."

Here Uncle Remus paused, and drew a two-pound yam out of the ashes.

"Did the fox eat the rabbit?" asked the little boy to whom the story had been told.

"Dat's all de fur de tale goes," replied the old man. "He mout, en den agin he moutent. Some say Jedge B'ar come 'long en loosed 'im—some say he didn't. I hear Miss Sally callin'. You better run 'long."

II. How Mr. Rabbit Was too Sharp for Mr. Fox

"Uncle Remus," said the little boy one evening, when he had found the old man with little or nothing to do, "did the fox kill and eat the rabbit when he caught him with the Tar-Baby?"

"Law, honey, ain't I tell you 'bout dat?" replied the old darkey, chuckling slyly. "I 'clar ter grashus I ought er tole you dat, but old man Nod wuz ridin' on my eyelids twel a leetle mo'n I'd a disremember'd my own name, en den on to dat here come yo' mammy hollerin' atter you.

"W'at I tell you w'en I fus' begin? I tole you Brer Rabbit wuz a monstus soon creetur; leas'ways d'at's w'at I laid out fer ter tell you. Well, den, honey, don't you go en make no udder calkalashuns, kaze in dem days Brer Rabbit en his fambly wuz at de head er de gang w'en enny racket wuz on han', en dar dey stayed. 'Fo' you begins fer ter wipe yo' eyes 'bout Brer Rabbit, you wait en see whar'bouts Brer Rabbit gwineter fetch up at. But dat's needer yer ner dar.

"W'en Brer Fox fine Brer Rabbit mixt up wid de Tar-Baby, he feel mighty good, en he roll on de groun' en laff. Bimeby he up'n say, sezee:

" 'Well, I speck I got you dis time, Brer Rabbit,' sezee; 'maybe I ain't, but I speck I is. You been runnin' roun' here sassin' atter me a mighty long time, but I speck you done come ter de een' er de row. You bin cuttin' up yo' capers en bouncin' 'roun' in dis neighborhood ontwel you come ter b'leeve yo'se'f de boss er de whole gang. En den youer allers some'rs whar you got no bizness,' sez Brer Fox, sezee. 'Who ax you fer ter come en strike up a 'quaintance wid dish yer Tar-Baby? En who stuck you up dar whar you iz? Nobody in de roun' worril. You des tuck en jam yo'se'f on dat Tar-Baby widout waitin' fer enny invite,' sez Brer Fox, sezee, 'en dar you is, en dar you'll stay twel I fixes up a bresh-pile and fires her up, kaze I'm gwineter bobbycue you dis day, sho,' sez Brer Fox, sezee.

"Den Brer Rabbit talk mighty 'umble.

" 'I don't keer w'at you do wid me, Brer Fox,' sezee, 'so you don't fling me in dat brier-patch. Roas' me, Brer Fox,' sezee, 'but don't fling me in dat brier-patch,' sezee.

" 'Hit's so much trouble fer ter kindle a fier,' sez Brer Fox, sezee, 'dat I speck I'll hatter hang you,' sezee.

" 'Hang me des ez high ez you please, Brer Fox,' sez Brer Rabbit, sezee, 'but do fer de Lord's sake don't fling me in that brier-patch,' sezee.

" 'I ain't got no string,' sez Brer Fox, sezee, 'en now I speck I'll hatter drown you,' sezee.

" 'Drown me des ez deep ez you please, Brer Fox,' sez Brer Rabbit, sezee, 'but do don't fling me in dat brier-patch,' sezee.

" 'Dey ain't no water nigh,' sez Brer Fox, sezee, 'en now I speck I'll hatter skin you,' sezee.

" 'Skin me, Brer Fox,' sez Brer Rabbit, sezee, 'snatch out my eyeballs, t'ar out my years by de roots, en cut off my legs,' sezee, 'but do please, Brer Fox, don't fling me in dat brier-patch,' sezee.

"Co'se Brer Fox wanter hurt Brer Rabbit bad ez he kin, so he cotch 'im by de behime legs en slung 'im right in de middle er de brier-patch. Dar wuz a considerbul flutter whar Brer Rabbit struck de bushes, en Brer Fox sorter hang 'roun' fer ter see w'at wuz gwineter happen. Bimeby he hear somebody call 'im, en way up de hill he see Brer Rabbit settin' cross-legged on a chinkapin log koamin' de pitch outen his har wid a chip. Den Brer Fox know dat he bin swop off mighty bad. Brer Rabbit wuz bleedzed fer ter fling back some er his sass, en he holler out:

" 'Bred en bawn in a brier-patch, Brer Fox—bred en bawn in a brier-patch!' en wid dat he skip out des ez lively ez a cricket in de embers."

The Tar Baby [Water-Well Version]

ONCE upon a time there was a water famine, and the runs went dry and the creeks went dry and the rivers went dry, and there wasn't any water to be found anywhere, so all the animals in the forest met together to see

From *Negro Tales from West Virginia*, by John Harrington Cox, *The Journal of American Folklore*, Vol. XLVII (October-December, 1934), No. CLXXXVI, pp. 344–347.

"The Rabbit That Wouldn't Help Dig A Well." Contributed by Miss Dora Lee Newman to a book, *Marion County in the Making*, Fairmont, Marion County, West Virginia, 1918. Privately printed. Learned from her father, who, in turn, learned it when a child from "our Old Sukey and black Canada. . . ."—J. H. C.

what could be done about it. The lion and the bear and the wolf and the fox and the giraffe and the monkey and elephant, and even the rabbit, —everybody who lived in the forest was there, and they all tried to think of some plan by which they could get water. At last they decided to dig a well, and everybody said he would help,—all except the rabbit, who always was a lazy little bugger, and he said he wouldn't dig. So the animals all said, "Very well, Mr. Rabbit, if you won't help dig this well, you shan't have one drop of water to drink." But the rabbit just laughed and said, as smart as you please, "Never mind, you dig the well and I'll get a drink all right."

Now the animals all worked very hard, all except the rabbit, and soon they had the well so deep that they struck water and they all got a drink and went away to their homes in the forest. But the very next morning what should they find but the rabbit's footprints in the mud at the mouth of the well, and they knew he had come in the night and stolen some water. So they all began to think how they could keep that lazy little rabbit from getting a drink, and they all talked and talked and talked, and after a while they decided that someone must watch the well, but no one seemed to want to stay up to do it. Finally, the bear said, "I'll watch the well the first night. You just go to bed, and I'll show old Mr. Rabbit that he won't get any water while I'm around."

So all the animals went away and left him, and the bear sat down by the well. By and by the rabbit came out of the thicket on the hillside and there he saw the old bear guarding the well. At first he didn't know what to do. Then he sat down and began to sing:

> "Cha ra ra, will you, will you, can you?
> Cha ra ra, will you, will you, can you?"

Presently the old bear lifted up his head and looked around. "Where's all that pretty music coming from?" he said. The rabbit kept on singing:

> "Cha ra ra, will you, will you, can you?
> Cha ra ra, will you, will you, can you?"

This time the bear got up on his hind feet. The rabbit kept on singing:

> "Cha ra ra, will you, will you, can you?
> Cha ra ra, will you, will you, can you?"

Then the bear began to dance, and after a while he danced so far away that the rabbit wasn't afraid of him any longer, and so he climbed down into the well and got a drink and ran away into the thicket.

Now when the animals came the next morning and found the rabbit's footprints in the mud, they made all kinds of fun of old Mr. Bear. They said, "Mr. Bear, you are a fine person to watch a well. Why, even Mr. Rabbit can outwit you." But the bear said, "The rabbit had nothing to do with it. I was sitting here wide-awake, when suddenly the most beautiful music came right down out of the sky. At least I think it came down out of the sky, for when I went to look for it, I could not find it, and it must have been while I was gone that Mr. Rabbit stole the water." "Anyway," said the other animals, "we can't trust you any more. Mr. Monkey, you had better watch the well tonight, and mind you, you'd better be pretty careful or old Mr. Rabbit will fool you." "I'd like to see him do it," said the monkey. "Just let him try." So the animals set the monkey to watch the well.

Presently it grew dark, and all the stars came out; and then the rabbit slipped out of the thicket and peeped over in the direction of the well. There he saw the monkey. Then he sat down on the hillside and began to sing:

> "Cha ra ra, will you, will you, can you?
> Cha ra ra, will you, will you, can you?"

Then the monkey peered down into the well. "It isn't the water," said he. The rabbit kept on singing:

> "Cha ra ra, will you, will you, can you?
> Cha ra ra, will you, will you, can you?"

This time the monkey looked into the sky. "It isn't the stars," said he The rabbit kept on singing.

This time the monkey looked toward the forest. "It must be the leaves," said he. "Anyway, it's too good music to let go to waste." So he began to dance, and after a while he danced so far away that the rabbit wasn't afraid, so he climbed down into the well and got a drink and ran off into the thicket.

Well, the next morning, when all the animals came down and found the footprints again, you should have heard them talk to that monkey. They said, "Mr. Monkey, you are no better than Mr. Bear; neither of you is of any account. You can't catch a rabbit." And the monkey said, "It wasn't old Mr. Rabbit's fault at all that I left the well. He had nothing to do with it. All at once the most beautiful music that you ever heard came out of the woods, and I went to see who was making it." But the animals only laughed at him. Then they tried to get someone else to watch the well that night. No one would do it. So they thought and thought and thought about what to do next. Finally the fox spoke up. "I'll tell you what let's do," said he. "Let's make a tar man and set him to watch the well." "Let's do," said all the other animals together. So they worked the whole day long building a tar man and set him to watch the well.

That night the rabbit crept out of the thicket, and there he saw the tar man. So he sat down on the hillside and began to sing:

> "Cha ra ra, will you, will you, can you?
> Cha ra ra, will you, will you, can you?"

But the man never heard. The rabbit kept on singing:

> "Cha ra ra, will you, will you, can you?
> Cha ra ra, will you, will you, can you?"

But the tar man never heard a word. The rabbit came a little closer:

> "Cha ra ra, will you, will you, can you?
> Cha ra ra, will you, will you, can you?"

The tar man never spoke. The rabbit came a little closer yet:

> "Cha ra ra, will you, will you, can you?
> Cha ra ra, will you, will you, can you?"

The tar man never spoke a word.

The rabbit came up close to the tar man. "Look here," he said, "you get out of my way and let me down into that well." The tar man never moved. "If you don't get out of my way, I'll hit you with my fist," said the rabbit. The tar man never moved a finger. Then the rabbit raised his fist and struck the tar man as hard as he could, and his right fist stuck tight in the tar. "Now you let go of my fist or I'll hit you with my other fist," said the rabbit. The tar man never budged. Then the rabbit struck him with his left fist, and his left fist stuck tight in the tar. "Now you let go of my fists or I'll kick you with my foot," said the rabbit. The tar man never budged an inch. Then the rabbit kicked him with his right foot, and his right foot stuck tight in the tar. "Now you let go of my foot or I'll kick you with my other foot," said the rabbit. The tar man never stirred. Then the rabbit kicked him with his left foot, and his left foot stuck tight in the tar. "Now you let me go or I'll butt you with my head," said the rabbit. And he butted him with his head, and there he was; and there the other animals found him the next morning.

Well, you should have heard those animals laugh. "Oh, ho, Mr. Rabbit," they said. "Now we'll see whether you steal any more of our water or not. We're going to lay you across a log and cut your head off." "Oh, please do," said the rabbit. "I've always wanted to have my head cut off. I'd rather die that way than any other way I know." "Then we won't do it," said the other animals. "We are not going to kill you any way you like. We are going to shoot you." "That's better," said the rabbit. "If I had just stopped to think, I'd have asked you to do that in the first place. Please shoot me." "No, we'll not shoot you," said the other animals; and then they had to think and think for a long time.

"I'll tell you what we'll do," said the bear. "We'll put you into a cupboard and let you eat and eat and eat until you are as fat as butter, and then we'll throw you up into the air and let you come down and burst." "Oh, please don't!" said the rabbit. "I never wanted to die that way. Just do anything else, but please don't burst me." "Then that's exactly what we'll do," said all the other animals together.

So they put the rabbit into the cupboard and they fed him pie and cake and sugar, everything that was good; and by and by he got just as fat as butter. And then they took him out on the hillside and the lion took a paw, and the fox took a paw, and the bear took a paw, and the monkey took a paw; and then they swung him back and forth, and back and forth, saying: "One for the money, two for the show, three to make ready, and four to go." And up they tossed him into the air, and he came down and lit on his feet and said:

> "Yip, my name's Molly Cotton-tail;
> Catch me if you can."

And off he ran into the thicket.

Sheer Crops

BR'ER BEAR en Br'er Rabbit dey wuz farmers. Br'er Bear he has acres en acres uf good bottom land, en Br'er Rabbit has des' er small sandy-land farm. Br'er Bear wuz allus er "raisin' Cain" wid his neighbors, but Br'er Rabbit was er most engenerally raisin' chillun.

Arter while Br'er Rabbit's boys 'gun to git grown, en Br'er Rabbit 'lows he's gwine to have to git more land if he makes buckle en tongue meet.

So he goes ober to Br'er Bear's house, he did, en he say, sez he, "Morning, Br'er Bear. I craves ter rent yer bottom field nex' ye'r."

Br'er Bear he hum en he haw, en den he sez, "I don't spec I kin 'commodate yer, Br'er Rabbit, but I moughten consider hit, bein's hit is you."

"How does you rent yer land, Br'er Bear?"

"I kin onliest rent by der sheers."

"What is yer sheer, Br'er Bear?"

"Well," said Br'er Bear, "I takes der top of de crop fer my sheer, en you takes de rest fer yo' sheer."

Br'er Rabbit thinks erbout it rale hard, en he sez, "All right, Br'er Bear, I took it; we goes ter plowin' ober dare nex' week."

Den Br'er Bear goes back in der house des' er-laughin'. He sho is tickled ez to how he hez done put one by ole Br'er Rabbit dat time.

Well, 'long in May Br'er Rabbit done sont his oldest son to tell Br'er Bear to come down to de field to see erbout dat are sheer crop. Br'er Bear he comes er-pacin' down to de field en Br'er Rabbit wuz er-leanin' on de fence.

From "Brazos Bottom Philosophy," by A. W. Eddins, *Southwestern Lore*, Publications of the Texas Folk-Lore Society, Number IX, 1931, edited by J. Frank Dobie, pp. 153–156. Copyright, 1931, by the Texas Folk-Lore Society. Dallas: The Southwest Press.

"Mo'nin', Br'er Bear. See what er fine crop we hez got. You is to hab de tops fer yer sheer. Whare is you gwine to put 'em? I wants ter git 'em off so I kin dig my 'taters."

Br'er Bear wuz sho hot. But he done made dat trade wid Br'er Rabbit, en he had to stick to hit. So he went off all huffed up, en didn't even tell Br'er Rabbit what to do wid de vines. But Br'er Rabbit perceeded to dig his 'taters.

'Long in de fall Br'er Rabbit 'lows he's gwine to see Br'er Bear ergin en try to rent der bottom field. So he goes down to Br'er Bear's house en after passin' de time of day en other pleasant sociabilities, he sez, sez he, "Br'er Bear, how erbout rentin' der bottom field nex' year? Is yer gwine ter rent hit to me ergin?"

Br'er Bear say, he did, "You cheat me out uf my eyes las' year, Br'er Rabbit. I don't think I kin let yer hab it dis ye'r."

Den Br'er Rabbit scratch his head er long time, en he say, "Oh, now, Br'er Bear, you know I ain't cheated yer. Yer just cheat yerself. Yer made de trade yerself en I done tuck yer at yer word. Yer sed yer wanted der tops fer yer sheer, en I gib um ter you, didn't I? Now you des' think hit all ober ergin en see if you can't make er new deal fer yerself."

Den Br'er Bear said, "Well, I rents to you only on dese perditions: dat yer hab all de tops fer yer sheer en I hab all de rest fer my sheer."

Br'er Rabbit he twis' en he turn en he sez, "All right, Br'er Bear, I'se got ter hab more land fer my boys. I'll tuck hit. We go to plowin' in dare right away."

Den Br'er Bear he amble back into de house. He wuz shore he'd made er good trade dat time.

Way 'long in nex' June Br'er Rabbit done sont his boy down to Br'er Bear's house ergin, to tell him to come down ter de field ter see erbout his rent. When he got dare, Br'er Rabbit say, he did:

"Mo'nin', Br'er Bear. See what er fine crap we hez got? I specks hit will make forty bushels to der acre. I'se gwine ter put my oats on der market. What duz yer want me ter do wid yer straw?"

Br'er Bear sho wuz mad, but hit wa'n't no use. He done saw whar Br'er Rabbit had 'im. So he lies low en 'lows to hisself how he's gwine to git eben wid Br'er Rabbit yit. So he smile en say, "Oh, der crop is all right, Br'er Rabbit. Jes' stack my straw enywheres eround dare. Dat's all right."

Den Br'er Bear smile en he say, "What erbout nex' year, Br'er Rabbit? Is you cravin' ter rent dis field ergin?"

"I ain't er doin' nothin' else but wantin' ter rent hit, Br'er Bear," said Br'er Rabbit.

"All right, all right, you kin rent her ergin. But dis time I'se gwine ter hab der tops fer my sheer, en I'se gwine ter hab de bottoms fer my sheer too."

Br'er Rabbit wuz stumped. He didn't know what ter do nex'. But he finally managed to ask, "Br'er Bear, ef yer gits der tops en der bottoms fer yer share, what will I git fer my sheer?"

Den old Br'er Bear laff en say, "Well, you would git de middles."

Br'er Rabbit he worry en he fret, he plead en he argy, but hit does no good.

Br'er Bear sez, "Take hit er leave hit," en jes' stands pat.

Br'er Rabbit took hit.

Way 'long nex' summer ole Br'er Bear 'cided he would go down to der bottom field en see erbout dat dare sheer crop he had wid Br'er Rabbit. While he wuz er-passin' through de woods on his way, he sez to himself, he did:

"De fust year I rents to de ole Rabbit, I makes de tops my sheer, en ole Rabbit planted 'taters; so I gits nothin' but vines. Den I rents ergin, en der Rabbit is to hab de tops, en I de bottoms, en ole Rabbit plants oats; so I gits nothin' but straw. But I sho is got dat ole Rabbit dis time. I gits both de tops en de bottoms, en de ole Rabbit gits only de middles. I'se bound ter git 'im dis time."

Jes' den de old Bear come ter de field. He stopped. He look at hit. He shet up his fist. He cuss en he say, "Dat derned little scoundrel! He done went en planted dat fiel' in corn."

Old Mr. Rabbit, He's a Good Fisherman

"BRER Rabbit en Brer Fox wuz like some chilluns w'at I knows un," said Uncle Remus, regarding the little boy, who had come to hear another story, with an affectation of great solemnity. "Bofe un um wuz allers atter wunner nudder, a prankin' en a pester'n 'roun', but Brer Rabbit did had some peace, kaze Brer Fox done got skittish 'bout puttin' de clamps on Brer Rabbit.

"One day, w'en Brer Rabbit, en Brer Fox, en Brer Coon, en Brer B'ar, en a whole lot un um wuz clearin' up a new groun' fer ter plant a roas'n'year patch, de sun 'gun ter git sorter hot, en Brer Rabbit he got tired; but he didn't let on, kaze he 'feared de balance un um'd call 'im lazy, en he keep on totin' off trash en pilin' up bresh, twel bimeby he holler out dat he gotter brier in his han', en den he take'n slip off, en hunt fer cool place fer ter res'. Atter w'ile he come 'crosst a well wid a bucket hangin' in it.

"'Dat look cool,' sez Brer Rabbit, sezee, 'en cool I speck she is. I'll des 'bout git in dar en take a nap,' en wid dat in he jump, he did, en he ain't no sooner fix hisse'f dan de bucket 'gun ter go down."

"Wasn't the Rabbit scared, Uncle Remus?" asked the little boy.

"Honey, dey ain't been no wusser skeer'd beas' sence de worril begin dan dish yer same Brer Rabbit. He fa'rly had a ager. He know whar he cum fum, but he dunner whar he gwine. Dreckly he feel de bucket hit de water, en dar she sot, but Brer Rabbit he keep mighty still, kaze he dunner w'at minnit gwineter be de nex'. He des lay dar en shuck en shiver.

"Brer Fox allers got one eye on Brer Rabbit, en w'en he slip off fum de new groun', Brer Fox he sneak atter 'im. He knew Brer Rabbit wuz atter some projick er nudder, en he tuck'n crope off, he did, en watch 'im. Brer Fox see Brer Rabbit come to de well en stop, en den he see 'im jump in de bucket, en den, lo en beholes, he see 'im go down outer sight. Brer Fox wuz de mos' 'stonish Fox dat you ever laid eyes on. He sot off dar in de bushes en study en study, but he don't make no head ner tails ter dis kinder bizness. Den he say ter hisse'f, sezee:

"'Well, ef dis don't bang my times,' sezee, 'den Joe's dead en Sal's a widder. Right down dar in dat well Brer Rabbit keep his money hid, en ef 'tain't dat den he done gone en 'skiver'd a gole-mine, en ef 'tain't dat, den I'm a gwineter see w'at's in dar,' sezee.

"Brer Fox crope up little nigher, he did, en lissen, but he don't year no fuss, en he keep on gittin' nigher, en yit he don't year nuthin'. Bimeby he git up close en peep down, but he don't see nuthin' en he don't year nuthin'. All dis time Brer Rabbit mighty nigh skeer'd outen his skin, en he fear'd fer ter move kaze de bucket might keel over en spill him out in de water. W'ile he sayin' his pra'rs over like a train er kyars runnin'. ole Brer Fox holler out:

"'Heyo, Brer Rabbit! Who you wizzitin' down dar?' sezee.

"'Who? Me? Oh, I'm des a fishin', Brer Fox,' sez Brer Rabbit, sezee. 'I des say ter myse'f dat I'd sorter sprize you all wid a mess er fishes fer dinner, en so here I is, en dar's de fishes. I'm a fishin' fer suckers, Brer Fox,' sez Brer Rabbit, sezee.

"'Is dey many un um down dar, Brer Rabbit?' sez Brer Fox, sezee.

"'Lots un um, Brer Fox; scoze en scoze un um. De water is natally live wid um. Come down en he'p me haul um in, Brer Fox,' sez Brer Rabbit, sezee.

"'How I gwineter git down, Brer Rabbit?'

"'Jump inter de bucket, Brer Fox. Hit'll fetch you down all safe en soun'.'

"Brer Rabbit talk so happy en talk so sweet dat Brer Fox he jump in de bucket, he did, en, ez he went down, co'se his weight pull Brer Rabbit up. W'en dey pass one nudder on de half-way groun', Brer Rabbit he sing out:

> "'Good-by, Brer Fox, take keer yo' cloze,
> Fer dis is de way de worril goes;
> Some goes up en some goes down,
> You'll git ter de bottom all safe en soun'.' [1]

---

[1] As a Northern friend suggests that this story may be somewhat obscure, it may be as well to state that the well is supposed to be supplied with a rope over a wheel, er pulley, with a bucket at each end.—J. C. H.

"W'en Brer Rabbit got out, he gallop off den tole de fokes w'at de well b'long ter dat Brer Fox wuz down in dar muddyin' up de drinkin' water, en den he gallop back ter de well, en holler down ter Brer Fox:

> " 'Yer come a man wid a great big gun—
> W'en he haul you up, you jump en run.' "

"What then, Uncle Remus?" asked the little boy, as the old man paused.

"In des 'bout half n'our, honey, bofe un um wuz back in de new groun' wukkin des like dey never heer'd er no well, ceppin' dat eve'y now'n den Brer Rabbit'd bust out in er laff, en ole Brer Fox, he'd git a spell er de dry grins."

How Sandy Got His Meat—A Negro Tale from the Brazos Bottoms

BRER RABBIT an Brer Coon wuz fishermuns. Brer Rabbit fished fur fish an Brer Coon fished fur f-r-o-g-s.

Arter while de frogs all got so wile Brer Coon couldent ketch em, an he hadn't hab no meat to his house an de chilluns wuz hongry and de ole oman beat em ober de haid wid de broom.

Brer Coon felt mighty bad an he went off down de rode wid he haid down wundering what he gwine do. Des den ole Brer Rabbit wuz er skippin down de rode an he seed Brer Coon wuz worried an throwed up his years an say-ed:

"Mornin, Brer Coon."

"Mornin, Brer Rabbit."

"How is yer copperrosity segashuatin, Brer Coon?"

"Porely, Brer Rabbit, porely. De frogs haz all got so wile I caint ketch em an I aint got no meat to my house an de ole oman is mad an de chilluns hongry. Brer Rabbit, I'se got to hab help. Sumthin' haz got to be dun."

Old Brer Rabbit looked away crost de ruver long time; den he scratch his year wid his hind foot, an say:

"I'll tole ye whut we do, Brer Coon. We'll git eber one of dem frogs. You go down on de san bar an lie down an play des lack you wuz d-a-i-d. Don't yer mobe. Be jes as still, jest lack you wuz d-a-i-d."

Ole Brer Coon mosied on down to de ruver. De frogs hear-ed em er comin an de ole big frog say-ed:

"Yer better look er roun. Yer better look er roun. Yer better look er roun."

By A. W. Eddins. From *Publications of the Folk-Lore Society of Texas, No. I,* edited by Stith Thompson, pp. 47–49. Copyright, 1916, by the Folk-Lore Society of Texas. Austin.

Nother ole frog say-ed:

"Knee deep, knee deep, knee deep."

An "ker-chug" all de frogs went in de water.

But Ole Brer Coon lide down on de san an stretched out jest lack he wuz d-a-i-d. De flies got all ober em, but he never moobe. De sun shine hot, but he never moobe; he lie still jest lack he wuz d-a-i-d.

Drectly Ole Brer Rabbit cum er runnin tru de woods an out on de san bar an put his years up high an hollered out:

"Hay, de Ole Coon is d-a-i-d."

De ole big frog out in de ruver say-ed:

"I don't bleve it, I don't bleve it, I don't bleve it."

An all de littul frogs roun de edge say-ed:

"I don't bleve it, I don't bleve it, I don't bleve it."

But de ole coon play jes lack he's d-a-i-d an all de frogs cum up out of de ruver an set er roun whare de ole coon lay.

Jes den Brer Rabbit wink his eye an say-ed:

"I'll tell you what I'de do, Brer Frogs. I'de berry Ole Sandy, berry em so deep he never could scratch out."

Den all de frogs gun to dig out de san, dig out de san from under de ole coon. When dey had dug er great deep hole wid de ole coon in de middle of it, de frogs all got tired an de ole frog say-ed:

"Deep er nough,—deep er nough,—deep er nough."

An all de littul frogs say-ed:

"Deep er nough,—deep er nough,—deep er nough."

Ole Brer Rabbit was er takin er littul nap in der sun, an he woke up an say-ed:

"Kin you jump out?"

De ole big frog look up to de top of de hole an say-ed:

"Yes I kin. Yes I kin. Yes I kin."

An de littul frogs say-ed:

"Yes I kin. Yes I kin. Yes I kin."

Ole Brer Rabbit tole em:

"Dig it deeper."

Den all de frogs went to wuk an dug er great deep hole way down inside de san wid Ole Brer Coon right in de middle jest lack he wuz d-a-i-d. De frogs wuz er gittin putty tired an de ole big frog sung out loud:—

"Deep er nough. Deep er nough. Deep er nough."

An all de littul frogs sung out too:—

"Deep er nough. Deep er nough. Deep er nough."

An Ole Brer Rabbit woke up er gin an exed em:—

"Kin yer jump out?"

"I bleve I kin. I bleve I kin. I bleve I kin."

Ole Brer Rabbit look down in de hole agin an say-ed:—

"Dig dat hole deeper."

Den all de frogs gin to wuk throwin out san, throwin out san, clear till most sun down and dey had er great deep hole way, way down in de san, wid de ole coon layin right in de middle. De frogs wuz plum clean tired out and de ole big frog say-ed:—

"Deep er nough. Deep er nough. Deep er nough."

An all de littul frogs say-ed:—

"Deep er nough. Deep er nough. Deep er nough."

Ole Brer Rabbit peeped down in de hole agin an say:—

"Kin yer jump out?"

An de ole frog say:—

"No I cain't. No I cain't. No I cain't."

An all de littul frogs say:—

"No I cain't. No I cain't. No I cain't."

Den Ole Brer Rabbit jump up right quick an holler out:—

"RISE UP SANDY AN GIT YOUR MEAT."

An Brer Coon had meat fer sepper dat nite.

The Give-Away (Mock Funeral)

ONCET Ber Wolf an' Ber Rabbit had a confusion [trouble] over somet'in'. Ber Wolf an' Ber Tiyger was fixin' a plan to ketch Ber Rabbit. Ber Tiyger tol' Ber Wolf he mus' go in his house an' lay down, an' do like he was dead. Ber Tiyger he went out, an' tol' Ber Rabbit he mus' come to see Ber Wolf 'cause Ber Wolf wus dead. An' after Ber Rabbit went to Ber Wolf house, de firs' t'in' he said was, "Dead people raise up some time." Ber Wolf raise up. Said, "I never seed a person what was dead could raise up." An' he ran all de way home.

Who Stole Buh Kinlaw's Goat?

> Once upon a time de cat drink wine,
> De monkey chaw tobacco on de street-car line.

DEH been a man name Buh Kinlaw. Buh Rabbit t'ief Buh Kinlaw goat, an' Buh Kinlaw gwine hab court fuh fin' who t'ief um. So Buh Rabbit see Buh Wolf an' say, "Buh Wolf, deh's t'irty dollahs on a song, t'irty

From *Folk-Lore of the Sea Islands, South Carolina,* by Elsie Clews Parsons, Memoirs of the American Folk-Lore Society, Volume XVI, p. 143. Copyright, 1923, by the American Folk-Lore Society. Cambridge, Mass., and New York.

Informant, Viola Jones, pupil of Penn School, St. Helena, of Paris Island. For bibliography see JAFL 30: 179 (note 2); also South Carolina (Christensen, 22, 70–72).—E. C. P.

From *Folk Culture on St. Helena Island, South Carolina,* by Guy B. Johnson, p. 140. Copyright, 1930, by the University of North Carolina Press. Chapel Hill.

Cf. Parsons, p. 145.—G. B. J.

dollahs on a song. Big time on court day. You bass me on de song **an** we make a heap o' money. Now, w'en I sing,

[Chanted]   Buh Wolf t'ief Buh Kinlaw goat,

you sing,

Yes, indeed, indeed I did."

So Buh Wolf agree, an' dey try out de song till dey can sing um good.

W'en de court day come Buh Rabbit an' Buh Wolf come in to town. W'en dey come close to de court place, Buh Rabbit, say, "All right Buh Wolf, time to staa't singin' "; an' 'e begin:

"Buh Wolf t'ief Buh Kinlaw goat,"

an' Buh Wolf come in strong on

"Yes, indeed, indeed I did."

So de jedge yeddy um an' say, "So dat's de man wuh stole Buh Kinlaw goat." An 'e gib Buh Wolf t'irty days 'stead o' t'irty dollahs.

Playing Godfather: Tub of Butter

BUH RABBIT an' Buh Wolf been frien'. Day hab tub o' buttah fuh eat w'en wintah come. Dey wukkin' een de fiel' w'en Buh Rabbit say, "Buh Wolf, me yeddy my sistah duh cali me. I gwine see w'at 'e want." So 'e went off. Attah w'ile 'e come back. Buh Wolf say, "W'at yo' sistah want?" "Oh, my sistah hab a fine baby an' 'e want me fuh name um." "Well, w'at you name um?" "I name um Buh Start-um."

Dey wuk a lee' wile, den Buh Rabbit say, "Lissen to dat! My sistah duh call me ag'in. I wish 'e leave me 'lone." Buh Wolf say, "Man, you bettah go see w'at 'e want." So Buh Rabbit go off again. Fin'ly 'e come back, say, "Buh Wolf, my sistah done hab 'nuddah baby an' want me to name um." "Well, w'at you name um?" "Oh, I name um Buh Half-um."

Dey wuk a lee' w'ile mo' den Buh Rabbit say, "Lissen, Buh Wolf, my sistah duh call me again. I t'ink I not go dis time." Buh Wolf say, "Oh, man, I t'ink you bettah go." "All right, I be back in a lee' w'ile." Fin'ly Buh Rabbit come back, say, "Law, Buh Wolf, my sistah done hab 'nuddah chile." "W'at you name um dis time?" "Oh, I name um Buh Done-um." Dat mean 'e done eat all de buttah.

Ibid., pp. 138–140.

From a student in Penn School. See Parsons, pp. 5–8. Sometimes the names of the children are varied, as, for example, Begin-um, Buh Quartah-um, T'ree-fourt' Gone-um, Mos' Done-um, etc.—G. B. J.

Dey wuk on till Buh Wolf say, "Buh Rabbit, le's go see 'bout dat tub o' buttah." So dey go fuh git buttah an' de buttah all gone. Buh Wolf say, "Buh Rabbit, you been uh eat de buttah, enty?" "No, 'fo' Gawd, Buh Wolf, I yent eat um." Buh Wolf say, "I t'ink we fin' out who eat um. We gwine een de sun an' lay down, an' de one de sun melt de buttah out ob, 'e de one wuh eat um." Buh Rabbit agree, so dey go een de hot sun an' lay down. Buh Wolf go to sleep. De buttah melt out o' Buh Rabbit, an' 'e take an' smear um on Buh Wolf. Den 'e wake up Buh Wolf an' say, "Look, Buh Wolf, de buttah melt out on you. Dat prove you eat um." Buh Wolf say, "Yeah, Buh Rabbit, I guess you been right. I eat um fo' trute."

Brer Dog and Brer Rabbit

I

How Brer Dog Lost His Beautiful Voice

Joe Wiley said, " 'Tain't nothin' cute as a rabbit. When they come cuter than him, they got to have 'cute indigestion." He cleared his throat and continued:

Dat's de reason de dog is mad wid de rabbit now—'cause he fooled de dog.

You know they useter call on de same girl. De rabbit useter g'wan up to de house and cross his legs on de porch and court de girl. Brer Dog, he'd come in de gate wid his banjo under his arm.

"Good evenin', Miss Saphronie."

"My compliments, Brer Dog, come have a chair on de pe-azza."

"No thank you ma'am, Miss Saphronie. B'lieve Ah'll set out here under de Chinaberry tree."

So he'd set out dere and pick de banjo and sing all 'bout:

> If Miss Fronie was a gal of mine
> She wouldn't do nothin' but starch and iron.

So de girl wouldn't pay no mind to Brer Rabbit at all. She'd be listenin' to Brer Dog sing. Every time he'd stop she'd holler out dere to him, "Won't you favor us wid another piece, Brer Dog? Ah sho do love singin' especially when they got a good voice and picks de banjo at de same time."

Brer Rabbit saw he wasn't makin' no time wid Miss Saphronie so he waylaid Brer Dog down in de piney woods one day and says:

"Brer Dog, you sho is got a mellow voice. You can sing. Wisht Ah could sing like dat, den maybe Miss Fronie would pay me some mind."

From *Mules and Men*, by Zora Neale Hurston, pp. 145–148. Copyright, 1935, by Zora Neale Hurston. Philadelphia and London: J. B. Lippincott Company.

"Gawan, Brer Rabbit, you makin' great 'miration at nothin'. Ah can whoop a little, but Ah really do wish Ah could sing enough to suit Miss Fronie."

"Well, dat's de very point Ah'm comin' out on. Ah know a way to make yo' voice sweeter."

"How? Brer Rabbit, how?"

"Ah knows a way."

"Hurry up and tell me, Brer Rabbit. Don't keep me waitin' like dis. Make haste."

"Ah got to see inside yo' throat first. Lemme see dat and Ah can tell you exactly what to do so you can sing more better."

Brer Dog stretched his mouth wide open and the rabbit peered way down inside. Brer Dog had his mouth latched back to de last notch and his eyes shut. So Brer Rabbit pulled out his razor and split Brer Dog's tongue and tore out across de mountain wid de dog right in behind him. Him and him! Brer Rabbit had done ruint Brer Dog's voice, but he ain't had time to stop at Miss Fronie's nor nowhere else 'cause dat dog is so mad he won't give him time.

"Yeah," said Cliff.

II

What the Rabbit Learned

De dog is sho hot after him. Run dem doggone rabbits so that they sent word to de dogs dat they want peace. So they had a convention. De rabbit took de floor and said they was tired of runnin', and dodgin' all de time, and they asted de dogs to please leave rabbits alone and run somethin' else. So de dogs put it to a vote and 'greed to leave off runnin' rabbits.

So after de big meetin' Brer Dog invites de rabbit over to his house to have dinner wid him.

He started on thru de woods wid Brer Dog but every now and then he'd stop and scratch his ear and listen. He stop right in his tracks. Dog say:

"Aw, come on Brer Rabbit, you too suscautious. Come on."

Kept dat up till they come to de branch just 'fore they got to Brer Dog's house. Just as Brer Rabbit started to step out on de foot-log, he heard some dogs barkin' way down de creek. He heard de old hound say, "How o-l-d is he?" and the young dogs answer him: "Twenty-one or two, twenty-one or two!" So Brer Rabbit say, "Excuse me, but Ah don't reckon Ah better go home wid you today, Brer Dog."

"Ah, come on, Brer Rabbit, you always gitten scared for nothin'. Come on."

"Ah hear dogs barkin', Brer Dog."

"Naw, you don't, Brer Rabbit."

"Yes, Ah do. Ah know, dat's dogs barkin'."

"S'posin' it is, it don't make no difference. Ain't we done held a convention and passed a law dogs run no mo' rabbits? Don't pay no 'tention to every li'l bit of barkin' you hear."

Rabbit scratch his ear and say,

"Yeah, but all de dogs ain't been to no convention, and anyhow some of dese fool dogs ain't got no better sense than to run all over dat law and break it up. De rabbits didn't go to school much and he didn't learn but three letter, and that's trust no mistake. Run every time de bush shake."

So he raced on home without breakin' another breath wid de dog.

"Dat's right," cut in Larkins White. "De Rabbits run from everything. They held a meetin' and decided. They say, 'Le's all go drown ourselves 'cause ain't nothin' skeered of us.' So it was agreed.

"They all started to de water in a body fast as time could wheel and roll. When they was crossin' de marsh jus' befo' they got to de sea, a frog hollered, 'Quit it, quit it!' So they say, 'Somethin' is 'fraid of us, so we won't drown ourselves.' So they all turnt 'round and went home."

Ole Sis Goose

OLE sis goose wus er sailin' on de lake, and ole brer fox wus hid in de weeds. By um by ole sis goose swum up close to der bank and ole brer fox lept out and cotched her.

"O yes, ole sis goose, I'se get yer now, you'se been er sailin' on mer lake er long time, en I'se got yer now. I'se gwine to break yer neck en pick yer bones."

"Hole on der', brer fox, hole on, I'se got jes as much right to swim in der lake as you has ter lie in der weeds. Hit's des as much my lake as hit is yours, and we is gwine to take dis matter to der cotehouse and see if you has any right to break my neck and pick my bones."

And so dey went to cote, and when dey got dere, de sheriff, he wus er fox, en de iudge, he wus er fox, and der tourneys, dey wus foxes, en all de jurrymen, dey was foxes, too.

And dey tried ole sis goose, en dey 'victed her and dey 'scuted her, and dey picked her bones.

Now my chilluns, listen to me, when all de folks in de cotehouse is foxes, and you is jes er common goose, der ain't gwine to be much jestice for you pore nigger.

From "Brazos Bottom Philosophy," by A. W. Eddins, *Publications of the Texas Folk-Lore Society*, No. II, 1923, edited by J. Frank Dobie, pp. 50–51. Copyright, 1923, by the Texas Folk-Lore Society. Austin.

"Buh Alligettuh en' Buh Deer"

ONE time, w'en nutt'n cep' de bu'd en' de annimel en' de Injun bin yuh, buh deer en' buh alligettuh ain' bin fr'en', en' buh alligettuh blan does kill buh deer en' nyam'um w'enebbuh 'e git uh chance, en' buh deer does 'f'aid fuh swim 'cross ribbuh, en' w'enebbuh 'e go down to de ribbuh' aige fuh drink, 'e does cock 'e yez en' squint 'e yeye fuh buh alligettuh befo' 'e pit 'e mout' down fuh drink; but, bimeby, yuh come de buckruh, en' bimeby 'gen, de buckruh fetch de nigguh, en' bimeby 'e fetch houn' dog, en' den de Injun gone, en' de buckruh biggin fuh hunt buh deer wid dem English houn', en' de dog' so swif' en' dem blan push buh deer so close, de only chance 'e hab fuh git'way is fuh tek de watuh 'spite uh buh alligettuh, so, w'edduh de ribbuh dey close uh fudduh, buh deer mek fuhr'um w'enebbuh de dog jump'um.

Now, de fus' time de buckruh run buh deer wid houn', buh deer ain' 'quaintun' wid'um, en' 'e leddown een 'e bed een one mukkle t'icket on de aige uh de broom grass fiel' duh tek 'e res', 'tell de dog mos' git up tuhr'um, den 'e fin' him ain' able fuh hide, en' 'e buss' out de mukkle en' lean fuh de ribbuh fuh who las' de longes'! Yuh come de ole buck, yuh come de English houn'! Buh deer 'f'aid. 'E jump. 'E run. 'E git dey fus'. Jis ez 'e ketch de bluff fuh jump off een de ribbuh, buh alligettuh' two eye' rise out de watuh duh wait fuhr'um! De alligettuh hongry. Bittle berry sca'ceful. 'E belly pinch'um. Buh deer fat. 'E fat fuh sowl. Buh deer dey een one hebby trouble. Alligettuh dey befor'um, beagle' dey behin'um, en' den toung duh roll t'ru de swamp en' dem comin' *fas'*. Wuh buh deer gwi' do? 'E yeye dey 'pun de alligettuh, 'e yez dey 'pun de beagle'. 'E mek uh sudd'n twis jis befo' de dog' sight'um, en' bu'n de win' down de ribbuh bank 'bout seb'n acre f'um de bluff and tek de watuh 'cross weh buh alligettuh nebbuh shum.

Yuh come de beagle' uh bilin' fuh de bluff. Dem come so fas' 'pun buh deer track dem nebbuh stop, en' two't'ree gone obuh de bank en' drap een de watuh close buh alligettuh' snout. Buh alligettuh reason wid 'eself. "Wuh dis t'ing? I nebbuh see shishuh annimel befo', but, duh bittle!" en' 'e graff one de beagle' en' pull'um onduhneet' de water. Todduh dog' swim out en' tek dem foot een dem han' en' gone home.

Buh deer git'way dis time. 'E gone! W'en 'e ready fuh tu'n back 'cross de ribbuh, 'e walk easy to de bank duh skin 'e yeye fuh buh alligettuh, en' bimeby 'e shum 'tretch out 'pun one mud bank een de sunhot. 'E belly full'uh beagle. 'E sattify. 'E duh sleep. Buh deer sneak close to de ribbuh fuh tek a chance fuh git 'cross, but befo' him kin wet 'e foot, buh alligettuh shum, en' e' slip off de bank fuh meet'um. Yuh de debble now! How buh

From *The Black Border*, Gullah Stories of the Carolina Coast (With a Glossary), by Ambrose E. Gonzales, pp. 216–218. Copyright, 1922, by The State Company Columbia, S. C.: The State Company.

deer kin git 'cross to 'e fambly? Him biggin fuh study, but befo' him
kin crack 'e teet' fuh talk, buh alligettuh op'n de cumposhashun.

"Budduh," 'e tell buh deer, "dat t'ing wuh I done eat, wunnuh call'um
beagle, berry good bittle. Me lub um berry well. 'E easy fuh ketch, en'
'e ent gots no hawn fuh 'cratch me t'roat. Me *done* fuh lub'um!"

"Ef you lub'um, mekso wunnuh don' ketch'um, en' lef' me my fambly
'lone?" buh deer ax'um. Buh alligettuh mek ansuh: "Me cyan' ketch
de dog 'cep'n' wunnuh fetch'um t'ru de ribbuh, so leh we mek 'greement
fuh las' long ez de ribbuh run. Wunnuh tek de ribbuh, me tek de beagle'.
Me fuh you, en' you fuh me, en' all two fuh one'nurruh."

Dat w'ymekso ebbuh sence de' 'greement mek, w'enebbuh dog run'um,
buh deer tek de ribbuh en' buh alligettuh lem'lone, en' w'en de beagle'
come 'e ketch'um, but ef buh deer ebbuh come duh ribbuh bidout dog dey
att'um, him haffuh tek 'e chance.

Buh Hawss en' Buh Mule (A Fable)

Buh Hawss' tail long sukkuh willuh switch,
Buh Mule' own stan' lukkuh t'istle.

ONE time Buh Hawss en' Buh Mule tu'n out duh pastuh duh Sunday.
Dem alltwo blonx to high buckruh. Buh Hawss binnuh dribe een buggy,
en' Buh Mule binnuh wu'k duh plow. Dem alltwo glad fuh git out en'
dem alltwo kick up dem foot en' play 'bout de fiel'. Buh Hawss cantuh.
'E bow 'e neck sukkuh gobbluh duh strut, en' 'e tail heng sukkuh willuh
switch. Buh Mule trot. 'E 'tretch 'e neck out 'traight sukkuh Muscoby
duck duh fly. 'E step high en' e' tail stan' up sukkuh t'istle. Buh Mule
tail oagly, fuh true, but da' duh all de tail wuh 'e got en' 'e berry well
sattify 'long um. Buh Hawss biggin fuh brag. "Look 'puntop oonuh tail,"
'e say. "Mekso oonuh ent hab tail lukkuh my'own?" 'e ax'um. "Oonuh
yent kin switch fly 'long'um 'cause 'e shabe. Shishuh no'count tail ent
wut'," 'e tell'um. "Me duh buckruh, you duh nigguh!" Buh Mule biggin
fuh shame. 'E yent sattify 'long 'e tail no mo'. Buh Mule cyan' switch
fly, fuh true, but 'e skin tough, en' fly don' bodduh'um, but Buh Hawss
git'um so agguhnize' een 'e min' e' fuhgit fuh tell'um suh 'e yent hab
cajun fuh switch fly 'long 'e tail, en' 'e heng 'e head en' 'e tail alltwo, en'
'e lef' Buh Hawss en' 'e gone off todduh side de fiel' en' 'e study. Bimeby,
'e look obuh de pastuh, en' todduh side de fench 'e see one las'yeah
cawnfiel' weh de nigguh lef' 'nuf sheep buhr duh stan' 'long de cawnstalk.
Buh Mule biggin fuh laugh. 'E op'n 'e mout'. 'E blow 'e hawn. "Aw-e-
Aw-e-Aw-e!" Buh Hawss cantuh. 'E come close. 'E ax'um 'smattuh
mek 'e duh laugh. Buh Mule say 'e laugh 'cause Buh Hawss ent smaa't
'nuf fuh jump de fench en' run'um uh race t'ru de cawnfiel'. Buh hawss

tek'um up. 'E jump de fench. 'E behin' foot ketch de top rail en' knock'um off. Buh Mule tumble t'ru. Yuh dem come! Buh Hawss cantuh, Buh Mule trot, up en' down de fiel' t'ru de sheep buhr. Buh Mule tail shabe 'tell 'e slick. 'E switch'um roun' en' roun' 'mong de buhr but none nebbuh stick. Bimeby, Buh Hawss' tail biggin fuh hebby. 'E ketch full'uh buhr. Dem tanglety een 'e tail 'tell 'e stan' sukkuh timbuh cyaa't rope. 'E duh drag. Eb'ry time 'e switch'um roun' 'e hanch, de buhr sting'um. 'E say to 'eself, "wuh dis t'ing? Me fuh lick me own self! Me fuh hab spuhr een me own tail! De debble! Me dey een trubble, fuh true!" 'E talk trute. 'E tail lick'um en' spuhr'um alltwo one time.

Buh Mule pass'um. 'E look 'puntop Buh Hawss' tail, en', 'e yent shame no mo'. "Tengk Gawd," 'e say, "fuh shabe tail. Low tree stan' high win'!"

Buh Tukrey Buzzud and de Rain

BUH TUKREY BUZZARD, him yent hab no sense no how. You watch um.

Wen de rain duh po down, eh set on de fench an eh squinch up isself. Eh draw in eh neck, an eh try fur hide eh head, an eh look dat pittyful you rale sorry for um. Eh duh half cry, an eh say to isself: "Nummine, wen dis rain ober me guine buil house right off. Me yent guine leh dis rain lick me dis way no mo."

Wen de rain done gone, an de win blow, an de sun shine, wuh Buh Tukrey Buzzud do? Eh set on de top er de dead pine tree way de sun kin wam um, an eh tretch out eh wing, an eh tun roun an roun so de win kin dry eh fedder, an eh laugh to isself, an eh say: "Dis rain done ober. Eh yent guine rain no mo. No use fur me fuh buil house now." Caless man dis like Buh Tukrey Buzzud.

The Hawk and the Buzzard

You know de hawk and de buzzard was settin' up in a pine tree one day, so de hawk says: "How you get yo' livin', Brer Buzzard?"

"Oh Ah'm makin' out pretty good, Brer Hawk. Ah waits on de salvation of de Lawd."

Hawk says, "Humph, Ah don't wait on de mercy of nobody. Ah takes mine."

"Ah bet, Ah'll live to pick yo' bones, Brer Hawk."

"Aw naw, you won't, Brer Buzzard. Watch me git my livin'."

From *Negro Myths from the Georgia Coast, Told in the Vernacular,* by Charles C. Jones, Jr., p. 4. Copyright, 1888, by Charles C. Jones, Jr. Boston and New York: Houghton, Mifflin & Company.

From *Mules and Men* by Zora Neale Hurston, pp. 153–154. Copyright, 1935, by Zora Neale Hurston. Philadelphia and London: J. B. Lippincott Company.

He seen a sparrer sittin' on a dead limb of a tree and he sailed off and dived down at dat sparrer. De end of de limb was stickin' out and he run his breast right up on de sharp point and hung dere. De sparrer flew on off.

After while he got so weak he knowed he was gointer die. So de buzzard flew past just so—flyin' slow you know, and said, "Un hunh, Brer Hawk, Ah told you Ah was gointer live to pick yo' bones. Ah waits on de salvation of de Lawd."

And dat's de way it is wid some of you young colts.

The Knee-High Man

DE KNEE-HIGH man lived by de swamp. He wuz alwez a-wantin' to be big 'stead of little. He sez to hisself: "I is gwinter ax de biggest thing in dis neighborhood how I kin git sizable." So he goes to see Mr. Horse. He ax him: "Mr. Horse, I come to git you to tell me how to git big like you is."

Mr. Horse, he say: "You eat a whole lot of corn and den you run round and round and round, till you ben about twenty miles and atter a while you big as me."

So de knee-high man, he done all Mr. Horse tole him. An' de corn make his stomach hurt, and runnin' make his legs hurt and de trying make his mind hurt. And he gits littler and littler. Den de knee-high man he set in his house and study how come Mr. Horse ain't help him none. And he say to hisself: "I is gwinter go see Brer Bull."

So he go to see Brer Bull and he say: "Brer Bull, I come to ax you to tell me how to git big like you is."

And Brer Bull, he say: "You eat a whole lot o' grass and den you bellow and bellow and fust thing you know you gits big like I is."

And de knee-high man he done all Brer Bull tole him. And de grass make his stomach hurt, and de bellowing make his neck hurt and de thinking make his mind hurt. And he git littler and littler. Den de knee-high man he set in his house and he study how come Brer Bull ain't done him no good. Atter wile, he hear ole Mr. Hoot Owl way in de swamp preachin' dat de bad peoples is sure gwinter have de bad luck.

Den de knee-high man he say to hisself: "I gwinter ax Mr. Hoot Owl how I kin git to be sizable," and he go to see Mr. Hoot Owl.

And Mr. Hoot Owl say: "What for you want to be big?" and de knee-high man say: "I wants to be big so when I gits a fight, I ken whup."

And Mr. Hoot Owl say: "Anybody ever try to kick a scrap wid you?"

De knee-high man he say naw. And Mr. Hoot Owl say: "Well den, you

From *Stars Fell on Alabama*, by Carl Carmer, pp. 177-178. Copyright, 1934, by Carl Carmer. New York: Farrar & Rinehart, Inc.

ain't got no cause to fight, and you ain't got no cause to be mo' sizable 'an you is."

De knee-high man says: "But I wants to be big so I kin see a fur ways." Mr. Hoot Owl, he say: "Can't you climb a tree and see a fur ways when you is clim' to de top?"

De knee-high man, he say: "Yes." Den Mr. Hoot Owl say: "You ain't got no cause to be bigger in de body, but you sho' is got cause to be bigger in de BRAIN."

Compair Lapin and Mr. Turkey

EVERY evening when Compair Lapin returned from his work he passed through a yard where there was a large turkey sleeping on its perch, and like all other turkeys that one also had its head under its wing to sleep.

Every evening Compair Lapin stopped to look at the turkey, and he asked himself what it had done with its head. Finally, one evening, he was so curious that he stopped underneath the perch, and said: "Good evening, Mr. Turkey."

"Good evening," said the turkey, without raising its head.

"Do you have a head, Mr. Turkey?"

"Yes, I have a head."

"Where is it?"

"My head is here."

Compair Lapin looked in vain, but he could not see Mr. Turkey's head. As he saw that the turkey did not want to talk to him or show him where was its head, he went to his house and said to his sister: "Do you know that to go to sleep turkeys take off their heads? Well, I believe I shall do the same thing, because it is less trouble to sleep without a head, and one can speak without a head, for the turkey spoke to me."

Before his sister had the time to tell him anything, he took an axe and cut off his head. His sister tried in every way possible to stick it on again, but could not do so, as her brother had killed himself.

From *Louisiana Folk-Tales*, in French Dialect and English Translation, collected and edited by Alcée Fortier, Memoirs of the American Folk-Lore Society, Volume II, p. 25. Copyright, 1895, by the American Folk-Lore Society. Boston and New York: Houghton, Mifflin & Company.

In this story Compair Lapin is not as cunning as usual, and we can hardly believe that he acted as foolishly as Compair Bouki would have done. The tale is genuine Negro folklore. as is evidenced by the exact knowledge of the habit of turkeys sleeping on their perches.

Informant, Julia, 7 Prvtania Street, New Orleans.—A. F.

Compair Bouki and the Monkeys

COMPAIR BOUKI put fire under his kettle, and when the water was very hot he began to beat his drum and to cry out:

> Sam-bombel! Sam-bombel tam!
> Sam-bombel! Sam-bombel dam!

The monkeys heard and said: "What? Bouki has something good to eat, let us go," and they ran up to Bouki and sang: "Molési cherguinet, chourvan! Chéguillé, chourvan!" Compair Bouki then said to the monkeys: "I shall enter into the kettle, and when I say 'I am cooked,' you must take me out." He jumped into the kettle, and the monkeys pulled him out as soon as he said "I am cooked."

The monkeys, in their turn, jumped into the kettle, and cried out, immediately on touching the water, "We are cooked." Bouki, however, took his big blanket, and covering the kettle, said: "If you were cooked you could not say so." One little monkey alone escaped, and Bouki ate all the others. Some time after this Compair Bouki was hungry again, and he called the monkeys:

> Sam-bombel! Sam-bombel tam!
> Sam-bombel! Sam-bombel dam!

When the monkeys came, he jumped into the kettle again and said: "I am cooked, I am cooked." The monkeys, however, which had been warned by the little monkey which had escaped the first time, did not pull Bouki out, but said: "If you were cooked you could not say so."

II. NURSERY TALES

"You des got de idee in yo' min' dat when I set down fer ter tell you sump'n hit's bleedz ter be a tale. . . ."—JOEL CHANDLER HARRIS

STORY-TELLING for children has kept alive not only folk tales but also the art of oral narration. For young and old alike the fairy tale is the most appealing of folk tale types. This is the story of the trials and ulti-

---

Ibid., pp. 25, 27.

The monkey, in our Louisiana stories is often a dupe. He is, however, more cunning than Bouki, whose stratagems always fail in the end. Here we have words supposed to indicate the language of the monkeys, and of Bouki, and it is interesting to see a negro imitate an animal in his stories. In Ouolof *Bouki* means the hyena, and is always a dupe. . . . Informant, an old Negro at *la Vacherie*, St. James Parish. —A. F.

mate success of an imaginary hero or heroine, involving elements of the supernatural or the marvelous. The nature of the fairy tale, as compared with other folk-tale types, is that it is told not to be believed but to be enjoyed and admired or wondered at. For, unlike the lying tale, which deceives, the fairy tale or wonder tale may inculcate a certain imaginative wisdom and even instruction. It is imaginatively true in the way that dreams are true—a projection of subconscious desires and a survival of primitive patterns of experience and faith. The appeal of the fairy tale lies not only in the ingeniousness of the incidents but also in its beauty of form and style. Here stock motifs, episodes, and plots play an important part. The effectiveness of repetition and especially cumulative iteration as a device of oral narration is demonstrated by its wide use in both fairy tales and ballads. Above all, the atmosphere of the fairy tale, as of the ballad, weaves a spell of far away and long ago and diffuses a light that never was on land or sea.

The most effective American folk tales employ homely vernacular or dialect and other oral devices. Certain tales, like "Tailypo" (which may be traced to the "Teeny-Tiny" of English fairy tales), depend almost entirely upon the voice for their effect. Mark Twain gave this technique an amusing twist in his platform recital of a variant of "The Golden Arm." This is the tale in which the husband has stolen the coppers from the eyelids of his dead wife and is haunted by her ghost, which repeatedly appears wailing, "Who's got my money? I want my money." After working up his audience to an excruciating pitch, Mark Twain remained silent for a couple of seconds and, slowly advancing, with appropriate gestures, suddenly stamped and yelled "Boo!" [1]

The Talking Eggs

THERE was once a lady who had two daughters; they were called Rose and Blanche. Rose was bad, and Blanche was good; but the mother liked Rose better, although she was bad, because she was her very picture. She would compel Blanche to do all the work, while Rose was seated in her rocking-chair. One day she sent Blanche to the well to get some water in a bucket. When Blanche arrived at the well, she saw an old woman, who said to her: "Pray, my little one, give me some water; I am very thirsty." "Yes, aunt," said Blanche, "here is some water"; and Blanche rinsed her bucket, and gave her good fresh water to drink. "Thank you, my child, you are a good girl; God will bless you."

A few days after, the mother was so bad to Blanche that she ran away

---

[1] "Mark Twain's Ghost Story," by E. P. Pabody, *Minnesota History*, Vol. 18 (March, 1937), No. 1, pp. . 8–35.

From *Louisiana Folk-Tales*, in French Dialect and English translation, collected and edited by Alcée Fortier, Memoirs of the American Folk-Lore Society, Volume II, pp 117–119. Copyright, 1895, by the American Folk-Lore Society. Boston and New York: Houghton, Mifflin & Company.

into the woods. She cried, and knew not where to go, because she was afraid to return home. She saw the same old woman, who was walking in front of her. "Ah! my child, why are you crying? What hurts you?" "Ah, aunt, mamma has beaten me, and I am afraid to return to the cabin." "Well, my child, come with me; I will give you supper and a bed; but you must promise me not to laugh at anything which you will see." She took Blanche's hand, and they began to walk in the wood. As they advanced, the bushes of thorns opened before them, and closed behind their backs. A little further on, Blanche saw two axes, which were fighting; she found that very strange, but she said nothing. They walked further, and behold! it was two arms which were fighting; a little further, two legs; at last, she saw two heads which were fighting, and which said: "Blanche, good morning, my child; God will help you." At last they arrived at the cabin of the old woman, who said to Blanche: "Make some fire, my child, to cook the supper"; and she sat down near the fireplace, and took off her head. She placed it on her knees, and began to louse herself. Blanche found that very strange; she was afraid, but she said nothing. The old woman put back her head in its place and gave Blanche a large bone to put on the fire for their supper. Blanche put the bone in the pot. Lo! in a moment the pot was full of good meat.

She gave Blanche a grain of rice to pound with the pestle, and thereupon the mortar became full of rice. After they had taken their supper, the old woman said to Blanche: "Pray, my child, scratch my back." Blanche scratched her back, but her hand was all cut, because the old woman's back was covered with broken glass. When she saw that Blanche's hand was bleeding, she only blew on it, and the hand was cured.

When Blanche got up the next morning, the old woman said to her: "You must go home now, but as you are a good girl I want to make you a present of the talking eggs. Go to the chicken-house; all the eggs which say 'Take me,' you must take them; all those which will say 'Do not take me,' you must not take. When you will be on the road, throw the eggs behind your back to break them."

As Blanche walked, she broke the eggs. Many pretty things came out of those eggs. It was now diamonds, now gold, a beautiful carriage, beautiful dresses. When she arrived at her mother's, she had so many fine things that the house was full of them. Therefore her mother was very glad to see her. The next day, she said to Rose: "You must go to the woods to look for this same old woman; you must have fine dresses like Blanche."

Rose went to the woods, and she met the old woman, who told her to come to her cabin; but when she saw the axes, the arms, the legs, the heads, fighting, and the old woman taking off her head to louse herself, she began to laugh and to ridicule everything she saw. Therefore the old woman said: "Ah! my child, you are not a good girl; God will punish you."

The next day she said to Rose: "I don't want to send you back with nothing; go to the chicken-house, and take the eggs which say 'Take me.'"

Rose went to the chicken-house. All the eggs began to say: "Take me,"

"Don't take me"; "Take me," "Don't take me." Rose was so bad that she said: "Ah, yes, you say 'Don't take me,' but you are precisely those I want." She took all the eggs which said "Don't take me," and she went away with them.

As she walked, she broke the eggs, and there came out a quantity of snakes, toads, frogs, which began to run after her. There were even a quantity of whips, which whipped her. Rose ran and shrieked. She arrived at her mother's so tired that she was not able to speak. When her mother saw all the beasts and the whips which were chasing her, she was so angry that she sent her away like a dog, and told her to go live in the woods.

The Singing Bones

ONCE upon a time there lived a man and a woman who had twenty-five children. They were very poor; the man was good, the woman was bad. Every day when the husband returned from his work the wife served his dinner, but always meat without bones.

"How is it that this meat has no bones?"

"Because bones are heavy, and meat is cheaper without bones. They give more for the money."

The husband ate, and said nothing.

"How is it you don't eat meat?"

"You forget that I have no teeth. How do you expect me to eat meat without teeth?"

"That is true," said the husband, and he said nothing more, because he was afraid to grieve his wife, who was as wicked as she was ugly.

When one has twenty-five children one cannot think of them all the time, and one does not see if one or two are missing. One day, after his dinner, the husband asked for his children. When they were by him he counted them, and found only fifteen. He asked his wife where were the ten others. She answered that they were at their grandmother's, and every day she would send one more for them to get a change of air. That was true, every day there was one that was missing.

One day the husband was at the threshold of his house, in front of a large stone which was there. He was thinking of his children, and he wanted to go and get them at their grandmother's, when he heard voices that were saying:

Ibid., p. 61.

This is a variant of a story found everywhere. Informant, old Negress, 77 Esplanade Avenue, New Orleans.—A. F.

Cf. the tell-tale harp made of the drowned sister's bones and hair in Old World versions of the ballad of "The Twa Sisters."

Our mother killed us,
Our father ate us.
We are not in a coffin,
We are not in the cemetery.

At first he did not understand what that meant, but he raised the stone, and saw a great quantity of bones, which began to sing again. He then understood that it was the bones of his children, whom his wife had killed, and whom he had eaten. Then he was so angry that he killed his wife; buried his children's bones in the cemetery, and stayed alone at his house. From that time he never ate meat, because he believed it would always be his children that he would eat.

Tailypo

ONCE upon a time, way down in de big woods ob Tennessee, dey lived a man all by hisself. His house didn't hab but one room in it, an' dat room was his pahlor, his settin' room, his bedroom, his dinin' room, an' his kitchen, too. In one end ob de room was a great, big, open fiahplace, an' dat's wha' de man cooked an' et his suppah. An' one night atter he had cooked an' et his suppah, dey crep' in troo de cracks ob de logs de curiestes creetur dat you ebber did see, an' it had a *great, big, long tail.*

Jis' as soon as dat man see dat varmint, he reached fur his hatchet, an' wid one lick, he cut dat thing's tail off. De creetur crep' out troo de cracks ob de logs an' run away, an' de man, fool like, he took an' cooked dat tail, he did, an' et it. Den he went ter bed, an' atter a while, he went ter sleep.

He hadn't been 'sleep berry long, till he waked up, an' heerd sumpin' climbin' up de side ob his cabin. It sounded jis' like a cat, an' he could heer it *scratch, scratch, scratch,* an' by-an'-by, he heerd it say, *"Tailypo, tailypo; all I want's my tailypo."*

Now dis yeer man had t'ree dogs: one wuz called Uno, an' one wuz called Ino, an' de udder one wuz called Cumptico-Calico. An' when he heerd dat thing he called his dawgs, *huh! huh! huh!* an' dem dawgs cum bilin' out from under de floo', an' dey chased dat thing way down in de big woods. An' de man went back ter bed an' went ter sleep.

Well, way long in de middle ob de night, he waked up an' he heerd sumpin' right above his cabin doo', tryin' ter git in. He listened, an' he could heer it *scratch, scratch, scratch,* an' den he heerd it say, *"Tailypo,*

From *Negro Tales from West Virginia,* by John Harrington Cox, *The Journal of American Folk-Lore,* Vol. XLVII (October-December, 1934), No. CLXXXVI, pp. 341-342. New York.

Learned by the Editor from Mr. Richard Wyche, Honorary President of The Story-Tellers' League, Washington, D. C. Printed by his permission. A quite different version of this story is printed in Harris, *Uncle Remus Returns,* pp. 52-78.—J. H. C.

tailypo; all I want's my tailypo." An' he sot up in bed and called his dawgs, huh! huh! huh! an' dem dawgs cum bustin' round de corner ob de house an' dey cotched up wid dat thing at de gate an' dey jis' tore de whole fence down, tryin' ter git at it. An' dat time, dey chased it way down in de big swamp. An' de man went back ter bed agin an' went ter sleep.

Way long toward mornin' he waked up, an he heerd sumpin' down in de big swamp. He listened, an' he heerd it say, "You know, I know; all I want's my tailypo." An' dat man sot up in bed an' called his dawgs, huh! huh! huh! an' you know dat time dem dawgs didn' cum. Dat thing had carried 'em way off down in de big swamp an' killed 'em, or los' 'em. An' de man went back ter bed an' went ter sleep agin.

Well, jis' befo' daylight, he waked up an' he heerd sumpin' in his room, an' it sounded like a cat, climbin' up de civers at de foot ob his bed. He listened an' he could heer it scratch, scratch, scratch, an' he looked ober de foot ob his bed an' he saw two little pinted ears, an' in a minute, he saw two big, roun', fiery eyes lookin' at him. He wanted to call his dawgs, but he too skeered ter holler. Dat thing kep' creepin' up until by-an'-by it wuz right on top ob dat man, an' den it said in a low voice, "Tailypo, tailypo; all I want's my tailypo." An' all at once dat man got his voice an' he said, "I hain't got yo' tailypo." And dat thing said, "Yes you has," an' it jumped on dat man an' scratched him all to pieces. An' sum folks say he got his tailypo.

Now dey ain't nothin' lef' ob dat man's cabin way down in de big woods ob Tennessee, 'ceptin' the chimbley, an' folks w'at lib in de big valley say dat when de moon shines bright an' de win' blows down de valley you can heer sumpin' say, "Tailypo . . . ," an' den, die away in de distance.

The Singing Geese

A MAN went out one day to shoot something for dinner, and as he was going along, he heard a sound in the air above him and looking up saw a great flock of geese, and they were all singing.

"La-lee-lu, come quilla, come quilla, bung, bung, bung, quilla bung."
He up with his gun and shot one of the geese and it sang as it fell,
"La-lee-lu, come quilla, come quilla, bung, bung, bung, quilla bung."
He took it home and told his wife to cook it for dinner and each feather, as she picked it, flew out of the window. She put the goose in the stove, but all the time it was cooking, she could hear in muffled tones from the stove,
"La-lee-lu, come quilla, come quilla, bung, bung, bung, quilla bung."

From Folk-Lore from Maryland, collected by Annie Weston Whitney and Caroline Canfield Bullock, Memoirs of the American Folk-Lore Society, Volume XVIII, 1925, p. 179. New York.

When the goose was cooked, she set it on the table, but as her husband picked up his knife and fork to carve it, it sang,

"La-lee-lu, come quilla, come quilla, bung, bung, bung, quilla bung."

When he was about to stick the fork in the goose, there came a tremendous noise, and a whole flock of geese flew through the window singing,

"La-lee-lu, come quilla, come quilla, bung, bung, bung, quilla bung."

And each one stuck a feather in the goose. Then they picked it up off the dish and all flew out of the window singing,

"La-lee-lu, come quilla, come quilla, bung, bung, bung, quilla bung."

The Gunny Wolf

A MAN and his little daughter lived alone in a forest and there were wolves in the forest. So the man built a fence round the house and told his little daughter she must on no account go outside the gate while he was away. One morning when he had gone away the little girl was hunting for flowers and thought it would do no harm just to peep through the gate. She did so and saw a little flower so near that she stepped outside to pick it. Then she saw another a little farther off and went for that. Then she saw another and went for that and so she kept getting farther and farther away from home. As she picked the flowers she sang a little song. Suddenly she heard a noise and looked up and saw a great gunny wolf and he said,

"Sing that sweeten, gooden song again."

(This is said in a low, gruff voice.)

She sang, "Tray bla-tray bla-cum qua, kimo."

Pit-a-pat, pit-a-pat, pit-a-pat, pit-a-pat.

(This is said softly to represent the child's steps.)

She goes back. Presently she hears, pit-a-pat, pit-a-pat, pit-a-pat,

(coarse deep voice)

coming behind her and there was the wolf, an' 'e says:

"You move?" (Gruff voice.)

"O no my dear, what 'casion I move?" (In childish voice.)

"Sing that sweeten, gooden song again."

She sang, "Tray-bla, tray-bla, cum qua, kimo."

Wolf he gone.

Pit-a-pat, pit-a-pat, pit-a-pat.

She goes back some more. Presently she hears,

Pit-a-pat, pit-a-pat, pit-a-pat,

coming behind her, and there was the wolf, an' 'e says,

"You move."

"O no my dear, what 'casion I move?"

Ibid., pp. 178–179.

"Sing that sweeten, gooden song again."
She sang, "Tray-bla, tray-bla, tray-bla, cum qua, kimo."
Wolf, he gone.
Pit-a-pit, pit-a-pat, pit-a-pat coming behind her and there was the wolf, an' 'e say,
"You move."
"O no my dear, what 'casion I move?"
"Sing that sweeten, gooden song again."
She sang, "Tray bla-tray bla-cum qua, kimo."
Wolf he gone.
Pit-a-pat, pit-a-pat, pit-a-pat.
She goes back some more and this time when she hears pit-a-pat, pit-a-pat, pit-a-pat coming behind her, she slips inside the gate and shuts it and wolf, he can't get her.

Wiley and the Hairy Man

WILEY's pappy was a bad man and no-count. He stole watermelons in the dark of the moon, slept while the weeds grew higher than the cotton, robbed a corpse laid out for burying, and, worse than that, killed three martins and never even chunked at a crow. So everybody thought that when Wiley's pappy died he'd never cross Jordan because the Hairy Man would be there waiting for him. That must have been the way it happened, because they never found him after he fell off the ferry boat at Holly's where the river is quicker than anywhere else. They looked for him a long way down river and in the still pools between the sand-banks, but they never found pappy. And they heard a big man laughing across the river, and everybody said, "That's the Hairy Man." So they stopped looking.

"Wiley," his mammy told him, "the Hairy Man's done got yo' pappy and he's go' get you 'f you don't look out."

"Yas'm," he said, "I'll look out. I'll take my hound-dogs ev'rywhere I go. The Hairy Man can't stand no hound-dog."

Wiley knew that because his mammy had told him. She knew because she was from the swamps by the Tombigbee and knew conjure. They don't know conjure on the Alabama like they do on the Tombigbee.

One day Wiley took his axe and went down in the swamp to cut some poles for a hen-roost and his hounds went with him. But they took out after a shoat and ran it so far off Wiley couldn't even hear them yelp.

"Well," he said, "I hope the Hairy Man ain't nowhere round here now."

He picked up his axe to start cutting poles, but he looked up and there came the Hairy Man through the trees grinning. He was sure ugly

By Donnell Van de Voort. From the Manuscripts of the Federal Writers' Project of the Works Progress Administration for the State of Alabama.

and his grin didn't help much. He was hairy all over. His eyes burned like fire and spit drooled all over his big teeth.

"Don't look at me like that," said Wiley, but the Hairy Man kept coming and grinning, so Wiley threw down his axe and climbed up a big bay tree. He saw the Hairy Man didn't have feet like a man but like a cow, and Wiley never had seen a cow up a bay tree.

"What for you done climb up there?" the Hairy Man asked Wiley when he got to the bottom of the tree.

Wiley climbed nearly to the top of the tree and looked down. Then he climbed plumb to the top.

"How come you climbin' trees?" the Hairy Man said.

"My mammy done tole me to stay 'way from you. What you got in that big croaker-sack?"

"I ain't got nothing yet."

"Gwan 'way from here," said Wiley, hoping the tree would grow some more.

"Ha," said the Hairy Man and picked up Wiley's axe. He swung it stout and the chips flew. Wiley grabbed the tree close, rubbed his belly on it and hollered, "Fly, chips, fly, back in yo' same old place."

The chips flew and the Hairy Man cussed and damned. Then he swung the axe and Wiley knew he'd have to holler fast. They went to it tooth and toe-nail then, Wiley hollering and the Hairy Man chopping. He hollered till he was hoarse and he saw the Hairy Man was gaining on him.

"I'll come down part t'way," he said, " 'f you'll make this bay tree twicet as big around."

"I ain't studyin' you," said the Hairy Man, swinging the axe.

"I bet you cain't," said Wiley.

"I ain't go' try," said the Hairy Man.

Then they went to it again, Wiley hollering and the Hairy Man chopping. Wiley had about yelled himself out when he heard his hound-dogs yelping way off.

"Hyeaaah, dog. Hyeaaah," he hollered. "Fly, chips, fly, back in yo' same old place."

"You ain't got no dogs. I sent that shoat to draw 'em off."

"Hyeaaah, dog," hollered Wiley, and they both heard the hound-dogs yelping and coming jam-up. The Hairy Man looked worried.

"Come on down," he said, "and I'll teach you conjure."

"I can learn all the conjure I wants from my mammy."

The Hairy Man cussed some more, but he threw the axe down and balled the jack off through the swamp.

When Wiley got home he told his mammy that the Hairy Man had most got him, but his dogs ran him off.

"Did he have his sack?"

"Yas'm."

"Nex' time he come after you, don't you climb no bay tree."

"I ain't," said Wiley. "They ain't big enough around."

"Don't climb no kind o' tree. Jes stay on the ground and say, 'Hello, Hairy Man.' You hear me, Wiley?"

"No'm."

"He ain't go' hurt you, chile. You can put the Hairy Man in the dirt when I tell you how to do him."

"I puts him in the dirt and he puts me in that croaker-sack. I ain't puttin' no Hairy Man in the dirt."

"You jes do like I say. You say, 'Hello, Hairy Man.' He says, 'Hello, Wiley.' You say, 'Hairy Man, I done heard you 'bout the best conjureman 'round here.' 'I reckon I am.' You say, 'I bet you cain't turn yo'self into no gee-raff.' You keep tellin' him he cain't and he will. Then you say, 'I bet you cain't turn yo'self into no alligator.' And he will. Then you say, 'Anybody can turn theyself into somep'n big as a man, but I bet you cain't turn yo'self into no 'possum.' Then he will, and you grab him and throw him in the sack."

"It don't sound jes right somehow," said Wiley, "but I will." So he tied up his dogs so they wouldn't scare away the Hairy Man, and went down to the swamp again. He hadn't been there long when he looked up and there came the Hairy Man grinning through the trees, hairy all over and his big teeth showing more than ever. He knew Wiley came off without his hound-dogs. Wiley nearly climbed a tree when he saw the croaker-sack, but he didn't.

"Hello, Hairy Man," he said.

"Hello, Wiley." He took the sack off his shoulder and started opening it up.

"Hairy Man, I done heard you 'bout the best conjure man round here."

"I reckon I is."

"I bet you cain't turn yo'self into no gee-raff."

"Shux, that ain't no trouble," said the Hairy Man.

"I bet you cain't do it."

So the Hairy Man twisted round and turned himself into a gee-raff.

"I bet you cain't turn yo'self into no alligator," said Wiley.

The gee-raff twisted around and turned into an alligator, all the time watching Wiley to see he didn't try to run.

"Anybody can turn theyself into somep'n big as a man," said Wiley, "but I bet you cain't turn yo-self into no 'possum."

The alligator twisted around and turned into a 'possum, and Wiley grabbed it and threw it in the sack.

Wiley tied the sack up as tight as he could and then he threw it in the river. He went home through the swamp and he looked up and there came the Hairy Man grinning through the trees.

"I turn myself into the wind and blew out. Wiley, I'm go' set right here till you get hongry and fall out of that bay tree. You want me to learn you some more conjure."

Wiley studied a while. He studied about the Hairy Man and he studied about his hound-dogs tied up most a mile away.

"Well," he said, "you done some pretty smart tricks. But I bet you cain't make things disappear and go where nobody knows."

"Huh, that's what I'm good at. Look at that old bird-nest on the limb. Now look. It's done gone."

"How I know it was there in the fus' place? I bet you cain't make somep'n I know is there disappear."

"Ha ha," said the Hairy Man. "Look at yo' shirt."

Wiley looked down and his shirt was gone, but he didn't care, because that was just what he wanted the Hairy Man to do.

"That was jes a plain old shirt," he said. "But this rope I got tied round my breeches been conjured. I bet you cain't make it disappear."

"Huh, I can make all the rope in this county disappear."

"Ha ha ha," said Wiley.

The Hairy Man looked mad and threw his chest way out. He opened his mouth wide and hollered loud.

"From now on all the rope in this county has done disappeared."

Wiley reared back holding his breeches with one hand and a tree-limb with the other.

"Hyeaaah, dog," he hollered loud enough to be heard more than a mile off.

When Wiley and his dogs got back home his mammy asked him did he put the Hairy Man in the sack.

"Yes'm, but he done turned himself into the wind and blew right through that old croaker-sack."

"That is bad," said his mammy. "But you done fool him twicet. 'F you fool him again he'll leave you alone. He'll be mighty hard to fool the third time."

"We gotta study up a way to fool him, mammy."

"I'll study up a way tereckly," she said, and sat down by the fire and held her chin between her hands and studied real hard. But Wiley wasn't studying anything except how to keep the Hairy Man away. He took his hound-dogs out and tied one at the back door and one at the front door. Then he crossed a broom and an axe-handle over the window and built a fire in the fire-place. Feeling a lot safer, he sat down and helped his mammy study. After a little while his mammy said, "Wiley, you go down to the pen and get that little suckin' pig away from that old sow."

Wiley went down and snatched the sucking pig through the rails and left the sow grunting and heaving in the pen. He took the pig back to his mammy and she put it in his bed.

"Now, Wiley," she said, "you go on up to the loft and hide."

So he did. Before long he heard the wind howling and the trees shaking, and then his dogs started growling. He looked out through a knot-hole in the planks and saw the dog at the front door looking down toward the swamps, with his hair standing up and his lips drawn back in a snarl. Then an animal as big as a mule with horns on its head ran out of the swamp past the house. The dog jerked and jumped, but he couldn't get loose. Then an animal bigger than a great big dog with a long nose and big teeth ran out of the swamp and growled at the cabin. This time the dog broke loose and took after the big animal, who ran back down into the swamp. Wiley looked out another chink at the back end of the loft just in time to see his other dog jerk loose and take out after an animal, which might have been a 'possum, but wasn't.

"Law-dee," said Wiley. "The Hairy Man is coming here sho'."

He didn't have long to wait, because soon enough he heard something with feet like a cow scrambling around on the roof. He knew it was the Hairy Man, because he heard him damn and swear when he touched the hot chimney. The Hairy Man jumped off the roof when he found out there was a fire in the fire-place and came up and knocked on the front door as big as you please.

"Mammy," he hollered, "I done come after yo' baby."

"You ain't go' get him," mammy hollered back.

"Give him here or I'll bite you. I'm blue-gummed and I'll pizen you sho'."

"I'm right blue-gummed myself," mammy sang out.

"Give him here or I'll set yo' house on fire with lightnin'."

"I got plenty of sweet-milk to put it out with."

"Give him here or I'll dry up yo' spring, make yo' cow go dry and send a million boll-weevils out of the ground to eat up yo' cotton."

"Hairy Man, you wouldn't do all that. That's mighty mean."

"I'm a mighty mean man. I ain't never seen a man as mean as I am."

" 'F I give you my baby will you go on way from here and leave every-thing else alone."

"I swear that's jes what I'll do," said the Hairy Man, so mammy opened the door and let him in.

"He's over there in that bed," she said.

The Hairy Man came in grinning like he was meaner than he said. He walked over to the bed and snatched the covers back.

"Hey," he hollered, "there ain't nothin' in this bed but a old suckin' pig."

"I ain't said what kind of a baby I was givin' you, and that suckin' pig sho' belonged to me 'fo' I gave it to you."

The Hairy Man raged and yelled. He stomped all over the house gnashing his teeth. Then he grabbed up the pig and tore out through the swamp, knocking down trees right and left. The next morning the swamp had a wide path like a cyclone had cut through it, with trees torn loose at the roots and lying on the ground. When the Hairy Man was gone Wiley came down from the loft.

"Is he done gone, mammy?"

"Yes, chile. That old Hairy Man cain't ever hurt you again. We done fool him three times."

Wiley went over to the safe and got out his pappy's jug of shinny that had been lying there since the old man fell in the river

"Mammy," he said, "I'm goin' to get hog-drunk and chicken-wild."

"You ain't the only one, chile. Ain't it nice yo' pappy was so no-count he had to keep shinny in the house?"

Little Eight John

ONCE an long ago dey was a little black boy name of Eight John. He was a nice lookin little boy but he didn't act like he look. He mean little boy an he wouldn't mind a word de grown folks told him. Naw, not a livin word. So if his lovin mammy told him not to do a thing, he go straight an do hit. Yes, spite of all de world.

"Don't step on no toad-frawgs," his lovin mammy told him, "aw you bring de bad lucks on yo family. Yes you will."

Little Eight John he say, "No'm, I won't step on no toad-frawgs. No ma'am!"

But jest as sho as anything, soon as he got out of sight of his lovin mammy, dat Little Eight John find him a toad-frawg an squirsh hit. Sometime he squirsh a heap of toad-frawgs.

An the cow wouldn't give no milk but bloody milk an de baby would have de bad ol colics.

But Little Eight John he jes duck his haid an laugh.

"Don't set in no chair backwards," his lovin mammy told Eight John. "It bring de weary troubles to yo family."

And so Little Eight John he set backwards in every chair.

Den his lovin mammy's cawn bread burn an de milk wouldn't churn.

Little ol Eight John jes laugh an laugh an laugh cause he know why hit was.

"Don't climb no trees on Sunday," his lovin mammy told him, "aw hit will be bad luck."

So dat Little Eight John, dat bad little boy, he sneak up trees on Sunday.

Den his pappy's taters wouldn't grow an de mule wouldn't go.

Little Eight John he know howcome.

"Don't count yo teeth," his lovin mammy she tell Little Eight John, "aw dey come a bad sickness in yo family."

But dat Little Eight John he go right ahaid an count his teeth. He count his uppers an he count his lowers. He count em on weekdays an Sundays.

Den his mammy she whoop an de baby git de croup. All on count of dat Little Eight John, dat badness of a little ol boy.

By James R. Aswell. From *God Bless the Devil! Liars' Bench Tales,* by James R. Aswell, Julia Willhoit, Jennette Edwards, E. E. Miller, and Lena E. Lipscomb, of the Tennessee Writers' Project, pp. 172–175. Copyright, 1940, by the University of North Carolina Press. Chapel Hill.

"Don't sleep wid yo haid at de foot of the baid aw yo family git de weary money blues," his lovin mammy told him.

So he do hit and do hit sho, dat cross-goin little ol Eight John boy.

An de family hit went broke wid no money in de poke. Little Eight John he jes giggle.

"Don't have no Sunday moans, faw fear Ol Raw Haid Bloody Bones," his lovin mammy told him.

So he had de Sunday moans an he had de Sunday groans, an he moan an he groan an he moan.

An Ol Raw Haid Bloody Bones he come after dat little bad boy an change him to a little ol grease spot on de kitchen table an his lovin mammy wash hit off de next mawnin.

An dat was de end of Little Eight John.

An dat whut always happen to never-mindin little boys.

III. WITCH TALES

Where folks believe in witches, witches air;
But when they don't believe, there are none there.

STORIES of witches survive long after people have ceased to believe in witchcraft or take it seriously. The cult itself, allied to the black art, may linger in remnants of spells and charms or counter-charms, as in conjure or hoodoo, becoming mixed with beliefs in hants and spirits generally. But present-day witch tales, like ghost and devil tales, are told either to thrill or to amuse.

On the eerie and blood-chilling side is the favorite motif of the witch prevented from reëntering her skin. This is based on the "slip-skin" belief that a skinless person is invisible and that witches slip off their skin after midnight in order to perform their nefarious deeds unseen. In "De Witch-'ooman an' de Spinnin'-Wheel" this motif is combined with that of the witch-wife. The shape-shifting witch-woman may be discovered by a mutilated hand or foot or other part of the body, according to the notion that wounds inflicted on the animal shape persist in the human form.

On the prankish side, witches are tricksters who make a nuisance of themselves in all the ways known to playfully malevolent spirits. Their pranks range from milk-stealing to riding a person in his sleep. In one of the best of American legends of the supernatural, "The Bell Witch of Tennessee and Mississippi," the hag or disembodied spirit is both revenant and hobgoblin, combining the destructive persecution of the vampire with the obstreperous annoyance of the poltergeist or noisy ghost.

De Witch-'ooman an' de Spinnin'-Wheel

THE WITCH PREVENTED FROM REËNTERING HER SKIN: A TALE FROM LOUISIANA.

ONE time dey wuz a man whar rid up at night ter a cabin in de eedge o' de swamp. He wuz dat hongry an' ti'd dat he say ter hissef: "Ef I kin git a hunk o' co'n-pone and a slice o' bakin', I doan kur what I pays!" On dat here come a yaller-'ooman spankin' out'n de cabin. She wuz spry on her foot ez a catbird, an' her eyes wuz sof' an' shiny. She ax de man fer ter light an' come in de cabin, an' git some supper. An' Lawd! how he mouf do water when he cotch a glimpst er de skillet on de coals! He luk it so well dat he stay; an' he sot eroun' in dat cabin ontwel he git so fat dat de grease fa'r run out'n he jaws when he look up at de sun. De yaller-'ooman she spen' her time cookin' fer him, an' waitin' on him wi' so much oberly, dat at las' de man, he up an' marry dat yaller-'ooman.

At fus' dey git erlong tollable well, but a'ter erwhile he gin ter notice dat sump'n curus 'bout dat yaller-'ooman. She ain' never in de cabin when he wake up in de night time! So, he mek up his min' fer ter spy on her. He lay down one night on de fo' pos' bed in de cornder, 'ten luk he sleep. De yaller-'ooman watch him out'n de een o' her eye, an' when she hear him gin a sno' (caze *cose* he 'ten luk he sno') she jump up an' pat a juba in de middle o' de flo'. Den she reach down a big gridi'on fum de wall, an' rake out some coals, an' haul de big spinnin'-wheel close ter de ha'th. Den, she sot herself down on dat gridi'on, an' soon ez it wuz red-hot she 'gin ter spin her skin off'n her body on de spinnin'-wheel. "Tu'n an' spin, come off skin, tu'n an' spin, come off skin." An' fo' de Lawd, de skin come off'n dat witch-'ooman's body, berginning at de top o' her head, ez slick es de shush come off de ear o' corn. An' when it wuz fa'r off, dan she wuz a gret big yaller cat. Den, she tuk her skin an' chuck it onder de bed. "Lay dar, skin," she say, "wi' dat fool nigger sno'in' in de bed, ontwel I come back. I gwine ter ha' some fum, I is."

Wi' dat she jump out'n de winder an' lope off. Soon ez she wuz gone de man, he jump out'n de bed an' tuk out skin an' fill it plum full o' salt an' pepper, un' th'ow it back onder de bed. Den he crope out an' watch thro' de key-hole ontwel de witch-'ooman come home. She laugh whilse she wuz rakin' out de skin fum onder de bed, an' shakin' herse'f inter it. But when she feel de salt an' pepper, she laugh on de yether side her mouf. She moan an' groan so you kin hear her a mile! But she ain' able ter git out'n dat skin, an' de man watch her thoo de key-hole twel she fall down an' die on de flo'.

By Mrs. M. E. M. Davis, New Orleans, La. From *The Journal of American Folk-Lore*, Vol. XVIII (July-September, 1905), No. LXX, pp. 251-252. Copyright, 1905, by the American Folk-Lore Society. Boston and New York: Houghton, Mifflin & Company.

Aunt Sally Hillock's Witch Story

UNCLE PHIL was a great deer hunter, and he had two favorite short-eared hounds, old Salty and young Jerry. One day in the fall of the year they had been hunting with rare luck in the Little Valley which lies between the two ridges of the Bald Eagle Mountains north of Nippenose Valley, and when night came on he went into his cabin on the side of the mountain, grallocked and hung up three stags, built a big fire, ate supper and lay down in his bunk by the wall, his dogs resting on the ground close beside him. In a short time a handsome heath hen entered the shack—there was no door on the hinges—and sat down on the hearth with one side of her to the fire. She was not long in that position when she began to swell. After a while she rose and turned the side under her to the fire, and if she swelled before, she now swelled seven times bigger. At last she became an old woman, in a brownish grey cloak, and her toppy was a tall, pointed hat with a broad brim, which almost concealed her peaked brown face. She walked over to the bunk and stood before Uncle Phil, who had been wide awake all the time. As soon as the hounds noted her nearness to their master they assumed an angry attitude and sprang at her fiercely. "Tell your dogs to lie down," demanded the old woman. "I cannot make them mind," answered Uncle Phil. She pulled a white hair from her head and gave it to the hunter, who noticed that after he took it in his hand it became jet black. "Tie them up with that," she said.

He pretended to be fastening them with her hair, but he put one of the hairs from his beard, which was equally black, on them instead. As soon as the hag thought the dogs were tied she reached into the bunk and laid hold of Uncle Phil. The dogs sprang again to seize her. "Tighten my hair," she now said. "Slacken *my* hair," replied the hunter. At last the dogs broke loose and caught hold of the old cotton-head. She loosened her hold on Uncle Phil, and bolted for the open door, the dogs close at her heels. The hounds followed her until they drove her over the side of the bench which sloped down just in front of the cabin. It was very steep and rocky, and when they reached the creek which flowed in the bottom of the valley, the fight was resumed in earnest and lasted a good long time. But at length the battle came to an end. The dogs returned to their master, much bedraggled and torn, while the old woman staggered down

From *Two Pennsylvania Mountain Legends*, collected by Henry W. Shoemaker, pp. 13–15, Publications of The Pennsylvania Folk-Lore Society, Volume I, Number 4. Published by The Reading Eagle Press, Reading, Pa. 1928.

Aunt Sally Hillock says that her old Uncle Jake could not understand at first why his Uncle Phil had deserted from Colonel Loudon's riflemen and derricked himself in Cable's Woods. One cold wintry night, at Old Christmas time, in 1827, when only his mother, Peter Pentz and himself were sitting in front of the great open fire—it was only a few months before the old scalp-hunter died—she told the story, interpolated by Pentz, who knew most of the details of the strange occurrence.—H. W. S.

the hollow toward the head of Kearns' Run, saying, "If the young hound's tush had been in the old hound's mouth, or the old hound's wit in the young hound's head, I would never have escaped them."

Next day Uncle Phil went home, and when he arrived at his log-cabin on the river bluff he met his wife, Aunt Minerva, going in a hurry to a neighbor lady's house, whose daughter, dark Cathlin Drago, was in great pain, and to all appearance, at the point of death. He prevailed on Aunty to first return home and give him a snack, as he was hungry; then they both went together to the double log house of the sick girl, which was the most pretentious dwelling in the whole of the Fair Play Men's Country. When the girl, who was very beautiful and had been greatly beloved by Uncle Phil, though he feared to declare himself to such quality—she was the late Col. Michael Q. Drago's only child—saw him coming with his wife, she ordered the Indian servants in the house to shut and bar the doors. They did as she told them, while she lay on her face, watching through the window lights. But as soon as Uncle Phil and Aunt Minerva came near enough and saw the unfriendly conduct, they curled and picked up a pur-line and drove in one of the doors. When they entered they went straight to the bed where the beautiful black-haired girl lay on her face, her faultlessly lovely features pinched in dreadful agony.

Stung with curiosity, Uncle Phil threw the kivers back as far as the girl's knees. A terrible sight was now revealed to them. The girl's buttocks were torn off and her hips and thighs horribly lacerated by the hounds' fangs. Uncle Phil understood the cause, and bent over to whisper something in dark Cathlin's ear, for he knew that it was she who was with him the previous night at his shanty in the shape of an old woman and had been attacked by his hounds when they chased her from his bunk. Aunt Minerva, who had been jealous of this lovely girl for a long time, had her fears verified by her husband's concern, and quickly drew her dirk and stabbed the girl in the small of the back, and she died the death of a hechs.

Uncle Phil was raving mad and left that night in his canoe to 'list under Colonel Loudon at Fort Augusta. But in the army he could not shake off the memory that he was the cause of dark Cathlin's death, especially since he knew that after all she had returned his love and had visited him at his hunting shanty in the Little Valley in the form of a hechs.

Andres Hironimus, his messmate, had the Black Book, or Hechsenhammer, so he lifted it one night and struck out for the mountains. He arrived at the Little Valley with the book and tried to raise dark Cathlin's spook by pow-wowing. But she would not return, so he went to his home, thinking that he would have better luck among scenes where she had been last in life, or at her grave. But he could not bring her ghost and he hated his wife more than ever for having murdered her as a hechs. He was quarreling every day with Aunt Minerva and was in constant fear of arrest for deserting from his regiment, and even his father, who was an Ensign in the Rangers, sent word from the front that unless he reported

for duty at once he would come home on leave and shoot him down like
a penny dog.

One dark night, after pow-wowing for several hours without success
over dark Cathlin Drago's grave in Spook Hollow, a neighbor saw Uncle
Phil walking up the hill in the direction of Cable's Woods with a stout
rope tied around his waist. Climbing the tallest oak—it is still standing—
he fastened the rope around his neck and to the stoutest branch, and
leaped off. That night there was a terrible storm, such as usually follows
a suicide, but after it was over they found Uncle Phil's body with a smile
on his dead face.

Witches and Witch-Masters

So LONG as the loafers in Bib Tarkey's blacksmith shop discussed crops
and politics I paid them scant attention, but when the talk turned to
witchcraft I pricked up my ears at once. The old-timers spoke tolerantly
of modern disbelief. "Wal," said old Lem Whatley, "I reckon maybe thar
ain't many witches a-runnin' loose nowadays, but in my day an' time th'
woods was full of 'em. My pappy follered gunsmithin' mostly, but he was
a witch-master too, an' he shore kilt a many un when we lived up thar
on Flat Crick.

"I mind th' time somebody witched our hawgs, so's when I went out
t' slop 'em they never come t' th' trough—jest lent back on their tails an'
squole. An' th' cow never give no milk, neither, for seven days a-runnin'.
Pap he figured it mought be ol' Gram French, whut laid up in a rock-
house t'other side o' th' Narrers.

"Funny thing about Gram was, she allus had plenty o' cream an' butter
in th' spring-house, but nobody ever seen her do no milkin'. Wal, Pap he
snuck over an' bushed up back o' her place, an' peeked in th' winder ever'
chanst he got. Finally he seen Gram hang a ol' dirty dishrag on th' potrack
an' start in a-squeezin' milk out'n it—she squoze out four big gourdfuls
whilst he set thar a-watchin' her, with his eyes a-buggin' out like a
tromped-on toadfrog. An' now he knowed how come ol' Muley never give
down no milk for seven days a-runnin'.

"When Pap got home he looked mi-ighty solemn. Th' first thing he done
was t' git down his ol' silver-mounted witch-rifle, an' th' next thing he
done was t' melt up th' dollar an' mold hisse'f a silver bullet. Next mornin'
he tuck him a burnt stick an' drawed a pitcher o' ol' Gram French on a
peeled sycamore. Hit didn't look much like Gram, but he written her name
on it good an' big, so's not t' resk no boggle. Soon's he got th' hull thing

---

By Vance Randolph. From *Folk-Say, A Regional Miscellany: 1931*, edited by B. A.
Botkin, pp. 86–93. Copyright, 1931, by B. A. Botkin. Norman: University of Oklahoma Press.

drawed an' wrote t' suit him, back he come an' picked up th' ol' witch-killer.

"I was jest a teen-age boy then, an' I got kinder skeerylike, but Pap he'd kilt a lot o' witches in his time, an' he jest stood thar stiddy as a rock. *Bang,* says th' ol' witch-rifle, an' when we run up t' th' pitcher we seen whar th' silver bullet plunked her right squar' in th' middle. We-uns begun t' feel a heap better then, I tell you! An' thet same day, mind you, ol' Gram French fell off'n th' bluff an' kilt herse'f—busted plumb wide open like a rotten apple! Ol' Muley give down lashin's o' milk thet night, too, an' we never had no more trouble with our hawgs, neither."

The blacksmith had stopped his work to listen to old man Whatley's tale, and appeared to be particularly impressed by its happy conclusion. "Witches," he said with feeling, "is for them ol' fellers whut knows how t' handle 'em, like your paw, Lem. Hit's plumb resky for a common ord'nary evr' day feller t' fool with 'em. One o' them Pea Ridge witch-hunters come dang near killin' me one time. . . . Hit was th' year o' th' big freshet, an' th' Bradford boys had lost most ever'thing. They warn't very bright, nohow, an' 'pears like they was loonier'n usual thet fall.

"When their ol' cow died hit jest about wiped out th' Bradford family. It was holler-horn kilt her, I reckon, but Poly Bradford he figgered she was witched. So he went an' got him a silver spoon somers an' loaded up a ol' scatter-gun they had. Then he ambled out in th' flat-woods an' raked up a big circle o' leaves an' bresh—musta been purty nigh sixty foot acrost, I reckon. 'Long 'bout midnight he set them 'ar bresh afire, an' then he hid out in back of a big cedar stump t' wait for th' witch.

"Wal sir, it jest happened I was a-comin' home 'crost th' flats thet night—I'd been over a-settin' up t' th' Widder Lane's biggest gal Iny— an' I seen this hyar big fire-ring. I'd orter o' knowed better, but my head was all gaumed up with sparkin', an' I never oncet thought o' witches. Anyhow, I rid right into thet 'ar ring, an' th' next thing I knowed hyar come Poly a-prancin' out, 'ith th' ol' gun a-p'intin' fa'r an' squar' at my stummick! 'Bib Tarkey!' he hollers out, 'who'd ever a' thunk *you* was a witch! Wal, anyhow, I got ye now, an' I got a silver bullet in this hyar gun, an' I'm obleeged for t' kill ye!'

"My Gawd, boys, I thought I was a goner shore, an' th' bar'l o' thet ol' musket looked big as a stovepipe. I lent backwards jest as Poly made his fire, an' th' bullet ploughed a big lane right through my whiskers. Th' horse jumped an' throwed me, too, an' hyar was thet fool Poly right on top o' me, a-swingin' at my head with th' butt o' his gun.

"I dodged him ag'in, though, an' finally I got my thumb in his eye an' wrassled him down. I was purty dang mad by this time, an' I jest churned his head up an' down, an' beat him dang nigh t' death. 'Go on an' kill me, Bib,' says he, 'you've done kilt th' critters, an' me an' Lizzie'll starve t' death this Winter anyhow'—an' with thet he begun t' beller like a calf. 'I ain't no witch, you pore ignor'nt, misbegotten eediot,' I says, 'I been over t' Widder Lane's an' I rid into this hyar witch-ring unthoughted-like, 'fore I rightly knowed whar I was at.' Poly he kept on a-grumblin', but he was plumb docile now, so I let him up, an' wiped th' blood off'n his face. 'An' th' next time your danged ol' cow gits witched,' I says, 'you go tell ol' Pap Whatley, an' let him tend to it. You jest leave witches t' th' witch-masters,' says I, 'an' don't you never do no more cunjurin' roun' hyar of a night. Hit's too dang resky-like for th' neighbors.'"

With this Tarkey returned to his blacksmithing, but Charley Howard was moved to rehearse the exploits of his cousin Tom, who had wrestled mightily with the powers of darkness in the Eighties. "Hit all happened way back yander afore me an' my wife was married, an' th' first I heerd of it was one day Tom he come over an' told us how their cow was a-comin' home jest plumb stripped, an' Gran'paw Langley was a-follerin' th' critter round all day t' see who was a-milkin' her. Wal sir, he snuck an' he watched, an' finally he seen two big ol' swamp-rabbits a-suckin' her! Sich a thing was never saw nor heerd tell of afore, I reckon, but Gran'paw he up with th' ol' shotgun an' made his fire jest as them two rabbits was a-hoppin' off together. Th' ol' gun was loaded heavy with turkey-shot, an' they warn't more'n thirty foot off, but danged if he didn't clean miss 'em! Right then an' thar th' ol' man seen how things was, an' he come a-runnin' up t' th' house a-hollerin', 'Witches! Witches!' with his eyes a-buggin' out bigger'n duck-aigs.

"Wal sir, Tom he shucked right out an' dug up th' corner post whar th' money was vaulted, an' they melted up a dollar. Gran'paw he run th' bullets hisse'f, a-shakin' like a white-oak leaf in a Christmas wind, an' Mary she loaded up th' ol' rifle-gun afore th' ball was cold scarcely. Tom got a soon start in th' mornin', an' we was all a-settin' on th' stake-an'-rider when he kilt th' ol' she-rabbit—th' buck run off afore he could git th' gun charged. . . . An' then 'bout four o'clock come th' news thet somebody had went an' kilt ol' Miz' Ricketts over in Hell Holler—shot her plumb through th' heart. Doc he never did find th' bullet, but ever'body knowed how it was, all right."

The subject must certainly be exhausted now, I thought, but another hillman, a stranger to me, had something to contribute to the symposium. "Speakin' o' witches," he said, after helping himself to a big drink of corn from the fruit-jar provided by Whatley, "puts me in mind of a 'sperience Buck Peters had one time when we was berry-pickin' down on Bug Scuffle. Buck was th' loud-talkin'est, drinkin'est, fightin'est feller ever come t' them parts. He'd fight a circle-saw an' turn it hisse'f, an' he warn't skeered o' nothin' in this world or th' next 'un, neither. Thar was a ol' tore-down shanty in back o' Lum Hobart's grocery whar witches had been a-usin' round, an' one day some o' th' boys bannered Buck t' sleep in thar all night. Buck he says if they git him a jug o' right good drinkin' likker he'll sleep anywhar, an' if any witches come round *him* a-lookin' for trouble they'll shore git a lavish of it. Wal, Lum says he'd furnish th' jug hisse'f, pervidin' Buck was still alive come mornin', an' they set thar a-drinkin' an' a-jowerin' an' a-spewin' ambeer over each an' ever', till finally Buck he loaded up with whiskey an' went into th' ol' shanty an' shet th' door. I tuck notice he packed in a-plenty o' candles, too—reckon he warn't a-hankerin' t' fight no witches in th' dark.

"Buck he set thar a long time, a-studyin' 'bout witches an' hants an' th' like o' thet, when all of a suddint up jumps th' Gawd-awfullest big she-cat ever saw in Arkansas, a-yowlin' an' spittin' like a Injun with his tail-feathers afire! Buck he was feelin' kinder mean an' narvish-like anyhow, so he drawed his ol' horse-pistol an' pulls back th' rooster. Lucky for him he done it, too, for jest a ha'r later th' varmint jumped right squar' at him. Th' ol' gun roared like a Christmas anvil, an' one o' th' cat's hind feet was blowed plumb off. Somers a woman hollers out, 'Oh my Gawd!' an' Buck allus swore he seen a woman's bare foot, all shot up an' bloody, a-wigglin' round on th' table. But jest then th' candle went out. Buck he went out too, right through th' winder, an' never stopped a-runnin' till he got plumb home. I never did blame him none, myse'f. Gawda'-mighty! Sich doin's as thet 'ar 'd skeer anybody! . . . Purty soon hyar come a feller name Burdick a-ridin' in for t' git Doc Holton—says his ol' woman has done shot her foot off accidental-like. She up an' bled t' death, though, spite of all Doc could do. They do say she died a-yowlin' an' a-spittin' like a cat. . . ."

At the end of the stranger's story I tore myself away, and repaired to the log residence of Uncle Bill Hatfield and his wife, who provided me with bed and board. After supper I broached the general subject of witchcraft and demonology to Uncle Bill, remarking that I myself gave no credence to such idle superstitions as appeared to obtain in this benighted region.

"I ain't superstitious, neither," said Uncle Bill mildly, "but a lot o' things whut some folks *call* superstitions is jest as true as Gawd's own gospel. An' as for witches, it ain't no manner o' use t' tell me thar ain't none, 'cause I know better. Why, I've been rode by 'em myse'f, many th' time!

"I war jest a-dozin' off one night, in th' ol' cabin way back in up on Leetle Piney, when in come th' purtiest gal I ever seen, with a bran'-new bridle in her hand. She fetched a whoop an' jumped plumb astraddle o' my back, an' th' first thing I knowed she had thet 'ar bridle onto me, with th' big cold bit a-cuttin' into my gooms! An' th' *next* thing I knowed she turned me into a flea-bit gray pony, an' we was a-tearin' down th' road hell-bent for 'lection, with th' spurs a-sockin' into my hams at ever' jump.

"Up hills an' down hollers an' 'crost branches an' through berry-patches we went, till we met up with some furriners a-packin' big sacks full o' money—bankrobbers, I reckon they was, or somethin'. Th' witch-woman she lit down then, an' holp them fellers, an' danged if they didn't pile all them big pokes on my back! Hit was all gold money, 'peared like, an' it shore was heavy. Purty soon we come t' a big cave in under a clift, an' she tied me up t' a white oak-saplin', whilst they all tuck th' money inside for t'hide it, I reckon. Atter while th' furriners come out, a-talkin' an' a-laughin' 'mongst theirse'fs, an' purty soon she come out too, an' rid me back home ag'in.

"Wal, th' next night she come an' rid me some more, an' we met up with th' same fellers, an' they drug in another turrible big load o' money. . . . An' th' next night th' same an' more of it, an' the next night, too— hit seemed like thar warn't no end t' th' money we-uns toted into thet 'ar cave-noie. Ever' mornin' I'd wake up plumb tuckered out an' brier-scratched; my head was full o' cockleburrs constant, an' my mouth a-tastin' like a cat had done littered in it.

"I never said nothin' t' th' ol' woman 'bout this hyar witch-ridin' an' all, but I shore done a heap o' studyin' over it. I spent a lot o' time a lookin' for thet 'ar cave, too, but I couldn't make out t' find it noways, so one mornin' I hobbled off down t' ol' Pap Jennin's shanty an' told him th' hull story. Pap he was a witch-master from who laid th' chunk, an' I knowed in reason he'd tell me whut I better do. Th' ol' man he jest pondered awhile, a-shakin' of his head kinder juberous, an' then he says: 'Wal, Bill, I reckon you-all better mark thet 'ar cave so we kin find it easy. When you git it marked I'll jest lay for this hyar witch-woman an' kill her with a silver bullet. Then we-uns 'll git th' gold-money, o' course.'

"The next night, when she hitched me outside th' cave, I jest drapped as many drappin's as I could, an' started in for t' chaw me a good big blaze on th' white-oak saplin', like Pap told me. I chawed an' I chawed. All of a suddint come a hell of a noise an' a big flash o' light, an' then I heerd a lot o' hollerin'—my ol' woman was a-doin' th' hollerin'. . . . Quick as a wink I seen I was home ag'in, an' it seemed like"—and here Uncle Bill stole a furtive glance at his wife, who sat stolidly smoking by the fireplace—"hit seemed like I'd went an' benastied th' bed-blankets bad, an' dang near bit th' ol' woman's laig off!"

The unexpected conclusion of the story "sot me back right smart," and the whole shanty shook with Bill's uproarious laughter. Uncle Bill is one of the very few old-time Ozarkers whom I have heard speak lightly of these matters. They sometimes assert their unbelief, but they don't joke about it. . . . Aunt Lavina told me later that deep down in his heart Bill still believes in witchcraft, but refuses to admit it to any but his most intimate friends nowadays. And so it is with others of his generation.

The Bell Witch of Tennessee and Mississippi

A FOLK LEGEND

BACK in the days before the War there lived somewhere in old North Carolina a man by the name of John Bell. Bell was a planter and was well-

By Arthur Palmer Hudson and Pete Kyle McCarter. From *The Journal of American Folk-Lore*, Vol. XLVII (January-March, 1934), No. CLXXXIII, pp. 45–63.
The legend of the Bell Witch recounts the misfortunes of a family named Bell

tixed. He had a good-sized plantation and a dozen niggers of field-hand age, and mules and cows and hogs a-plenty. His family was made up of his wife, a daughter thirteen or fourteen years old they say was mighty pretty, and two or three young-uns that don't figure much in this story. Until he hired him an overseer, Bell got along fine.

The overseer was a Simon Legree sort of fellow, always at sixes and sevens with other folks, and especially with the niggers. He didn't even mind jawing with his boss. They say Mr. Bell was half a mind to fire the scoundrel and hire another one. But he tended to his business. He had a way with the women-folks. Some say he had an eye open for Mary, the daughter. And Mrs. Bell stood up for him. So he stayed on for a good while, and the longer he stayed the uppiter he got. Whenever he and Bell had a row—and their rows got bigger and bitterer—the overseer went out and blacksnaked three or four niggers, for they were the only critters in the shape of man that he could abuse without a come-back. He was the worst kind of a bully, and a man of high temper, in fact, a regular overseer of the kind you hear about in Yankee stories.

---

who moved from North Carolina to the midlands of Tennessee in the early 1800's and then, in one branch, to northern Mississippi, about forty years later. It is well known to oral tradition in the designated sections of the two latter states. The Tennessee versions of it have been made the subject of at least two obscurely published books. In 1894, at Clarksville, Tennessee, appeared M. V. Ingram's *An Authenticated History of the Famous Bell Witch. The Wonder of the 19th Century, and Unexplained Phenomenon of the Christian Era. The Mysterious Talking Goblin that Terrorized the West End of Robertson County, Tennessee, Tormenting John Bell to his Death. The Story of Betsy Bell, Her Lover and the Haunting Sphinx.* This book professes "to record events of historical fact, sustained by a powerful array of incontrovertible evidence. . . . The author only assumes to compile data, formally presenting the history of this greatest of all mysteries, just as the matter is furnished to hand, written by Williams Bell, a member of the family some fifty-six years ago, together with corroborative testimony by men and women of irreproachable character and unquestioned veracity." Ingram's book is now rare and hard to get. Drawing on much the same sources and telling much the same story is Harriett Parks Miller's *The Bell Witch of Middle Tennessee* (Clarksville, 1930). This pamphlet and letters from residents of Middle Tennessee attest the independent oral survival of the legend in that region. As late as 1910 it was still told, "under the most appropriate surroundings—country parties, hayrides, and fireside gatherings."

In northern Mississippi, where descendants of the original family concerned still live, the legend survives in somewhat fragmentary but independent, orally traditional form. Of the considerable number of people who told it, or parts of it, to us, a few said that they had seen "the book" (Ingram's) a long time ago, and most of the others had heard of the book; but we were unable to find a copy in Mississippi.

Our following version of the legend has been recovered exclusively from oral tradition in Mississippi, and was put together before we ever saw a printed version. Most of our sources know the main outlines but remember especially some particular episodes or motives. A few tell the whole substantially as we reproduce it. But there is great diversity in the details and motives. We have taken the main outline on which all agree and have sketched in, as consistently as possible, the minutiae from numerous Mississippi sources. The dialect used, the few simple figures of speech, and the folk locutions are genuine and are true to the speech of our informants.— A. P. H. and P. K. M.

Mr. Bell had a tall temper too, and the men did not spend a lot of time patting each other on the back and bragging about each other's good points. A stand-up fight was bound to come off.

It did. Some say it was about the way the overseer had beat up one of the niggers. Some say it was about something Mr. Bell heard and saw from behind a cotton-house one day when Mary rode through the field where the overseer was working a gang of niggers. Bell went away blowing smoke from his pistol barrel, and mumbling something about white trash. The overseer didn't go away at all.

Of course Bell was brought into court, but he plead self-defense, and the jury let him off. He went home, hired him another overseer, and allowed that everything was settled. But the truth was that everything was now plumb unsettled.

That year and the next and the next the crops on the Bell place were an out-and-out failure: bumblebee cotton and scraggly tobacco and nubbin corn. His mules died of colic or some strange disease like it. His cows and hogs got sick of something the horse-doctor couldn't cure. He had to sell his niggers one by one, all except an old woman. Finally he went broke. He got what he could for his land—lock, stock, and barrel—and moved with his family to Tennessee. They say that where he settled down the town of Bell, Tennessee, was named for him. Anyway, he bought him a house and a patch of land near the home of old Andy Jackson, who had knocked off from being President and was living in a big house called the Hermitage.

Not long after the move to Tennessee, strange things began to happen in the Bell home. The children got into the habit of tumbling, or being tumbled, out of bed at least once a week, and of waking up every morning with every stitch of the bed-clothes snatched off and their hair all tangled and mussed up. Now for young-uns to tumble out of bed and to wake up in the morning with their heads uncombed is a mighty strange thing, and the Bells realized it. The children couldn't explain this carrying-on, for they were always asleep till they hit the floor; and it was a peculiar fact that they were never tumbled out while awake.

The old nigger woman told them it was the ha'nt of the overseer Mr. Bell had killed that was pestering the children. She was as superstitious as any other nigger, and she said she had always felt jubous about what the ha'nt of a man like the overseer would do. But she had spunk, and one day she allowed she would find out whether she was right by spending the night under the young-uns' bed. In the middle of the night Mr. and Mrs. Bell were fetched out of their bed by a squall like a pant'er's. When they lit a lamp and ran into the room, they found the old nigger woman sprawled in the middle of the floor, dripping cold sweat like an ash-hopper, her face gray-blue as sugar-cane peeling, and her eyes like saucers in a dish-pan. She was stiff-jointed and tongue-tied. When they got her sitting up and her tongue loosened, she screeched: "Hit's him! Hit's him! Fo' Gawd, hit's him! Hit peenched me all over, stuck pins in me, snatched de keenks outen ma haiuh, an' whup me, Lawd Gawd, how hit whup me, whup me limber and whup me stiff, whup me jes' lack *him*. Ain't gwine back dauh no mo', ain't gwine back dauh no mo'."

The Bells were so scared they told some of the neighbors. Old Andy Jackson heard about it and decided to ride over. He didn't take any stock in ha'nts, and as he rode through the gate he spoke his mind out loud about tarnation fools that believed nigger tales about them. He hadn't got the words out of his mouth before something whaled him over the head and skipped his hat twenty or thirty yards back down the road. Old Andy didn't say any more. He motioned his nigger boy to hand him his hat, and he went away from there.

It seems like the Witch could get hungry like folks, and was satisfied with folks' grub. But it had to be the best. One day the old nigger woman came tearing into the front room where Mrs. Bell was quilting and said the Witch was back in the kitchen drinking up all the sweet milk.

Mrs. Bell was scared and said the old woman was lying.

"Come see fo' yo'se'f, missus. Come see fo' yo'se'f. Ah was back dauh a-mixin' up de biscuit, an' Ah retched ovah to git a cup o' miu'k, an' fo' Gawd, de cup was in de middle o' de auh, an' de miu'k was a-runnin' rat outen hit—an' hit wa'n't gwine nowheah, missus—hit wa'n't gwine nowheah. Jes' run outen de cup, an' den Ah couldn' see hit no mo'."

"You're just seeing things," said Mrs. Bell.

"Jes' whut Ah ain' doin'—ain' seein' de miu'k. Go on back in de kitchen efen you don' believe hit. Go on back dauh an' look fo' yo'se'f. . . . No, ma'am, Ah hain' gwine back in dat place. No, ma'am, dat ha'nt kin guzzle an' bile up all de miu'k de cows evah give 'fo' Ah raise mah finger to stop hit."

Mrs. Bell went back into the kitchen and looked. There was a cup there that had had milk in it, and the milk was gone, sure as shootin'. She was now as scared as the old nigger woman, and sent right away for her husband to come out of the field.

They couldn't figure out how a ghost could drink milk, or what becomes of the milk if he does. Does the milk dry up into the ghost of itself? If not, where does it go when the ghost swallows it? Ghosts can't be seen. At least, this one couldn't. They could see through where it was. If they could see through it, why couldn't they see the milk as plain when it was inside the ghost as when it was outside? The old nigger woman said the milk was running out of the cup, but it "wa'n't gwine nowheah." An old Holy Roller preacher from down in Tallahatchie bottom who rode over to talk about it argued that if the old woman's tale was so milk must be of a higher class than folks. When it turns into the soul of itself, it leaves nothing behind; but folks leave behind a corpse that must be covered up with dirt right away. Folks argued about it on front galleries in the summer time and around the fire in winter—but they didn't argue about it on the Bells' front gallery or by the Bells' fire. And the preachers preached about it at camp meetings.

But the Witch didn't let up on the Bells' grub. No one ever saw it; but lots of times some member of the family would see something to eat dive out of the cupboard or pop out of the safe. The Witch's favorite was cream, and he got to skimming it from every pan in the spring-house. The Bells were never able to get any butter from the churning.

Mr. Bell might have stood for having his young-uns' rest disturbed and his old nigger woman all tore up this way, but he couldn't stand for letting the ghost eat him out of house and home. So he called the family together and allowed he would move again—this time to Mississippi, where land was rich and cheap. Mrs. Bell raised up.

"Pa," said she, "it seems like to me we have been gettin' along tolerable well here. I don't see any use moving away. What would be to keep the Witch from following us down there?"

"Nothing in the world," spoke up a hide-bottomed chair from a corner of the room. "I'll follow you wherever you go," the Chair went on. "And I'll tell you what: if you stay on here, I won't bother you much; but if you go traipsing off to Mississippi—well, you'll wish you hadn't."

Mr. Bell was scared and bothered, but he studied a while and screwed up his courage enough to ask the Witch why he couldn't live where he pleased. But there was no answer. He asked some more questions. But the Chair had lapsed into the habit of silence that chairs have.

Mary, Mr. Bell's daughter, was now old enough to argue with the old folks about things. She was pretty as a spotted puppy, they say, and had lots of spunk and took after her pa. She sided with him. Girls always like to be moving. So when the family got over its scare about the Chair they argued back and forth. But finally Mrs. Bell and what they remembered about the Witch got the upper hand. Mr. Bell and Mary gave up the idea of moving to Mississippi—for a while anyway.

And for a while the Witch eased up on them. It even did some good turns. One day Mr. Bell was talking of visiting a family across the creek where he had heard everybody was sick. "I have just come from there," said a Voice from the eight-day clock, and went on to tell how well everybody was and what everybody was doing. Later Mr. Bell met up with a member of the family and learned that everything the Witch said was so.

Maybe because she had taken side with him in the argument about going to Mississippi, the Witch was partial to Mrs. Bell. The old nigger woman said the ha'nt sided with her because she had stood up for the overseer when Mr. Bell wanted to fire him in North Carolina.

One Christmas time the family was invited to a taffy-pulling. Mrs. Bell was sick and couldn't go. They talked about whether they ought to go off and leave their mammy feeling poorly. Mr. Bell was invited too, and they needed him to do the driving; so Mary and the children begged him to take them. Mrs. Bell told them to go ahead, she didn't need them and could make out all right. So they all piled into the wagon and started.

But before they got far one of the wagon wheels flew off and let the axle down into the road with a bump. It looked like a common accident, and the old man climbed down and put the wheel back on the axle and stuck the linchpin in. He looked at all the other linchpins and saw they were on all right. Before long another wheel flew off. They looked on the ground for the linchpin but couldn't find it there. Mr. Bell whittled a new one, and when he went to put the wheel back on he found the old one in place. He fixed the wheel and drove off again, telling all of the children to watch all of the wheels. Soon they saw something like a streak of moonshine dart around the wagon, and all four wheels flew off, and the wagon dropped kersplash into a mud-hole. They put them back on, turned round, and drove back home, going quiet and easy, like sitting on eggs.

When they got there, they found their mammy sitting up by the Christmas tree eating a plate of fresh strawberries, and feeling lots better.

Other pranks were laid to the Witch. Often when the old man and the boys would go to the stable to catch the horses and mules for the day's plowing or a trip to town, the critters would back their ears and rare and kick and stomp like hornets or yellow-jackets were after them. Some morning they would be puny as chickens with the pip, and caked with sweat and mud, and their manes and tails tangled in witch-locks. The neighbors said that off and on they met an unbridled and bare-backed horse, and the horse would stop, and something on his back that they couldn't see would talk to them—but not long—they had business the other way.

Maybe because Mary had sided with her pa against her mammy and the Witch, the Witch was harder on her after the argument than anybody else. She would wake up in the middle of the night, screaming and crying that something cold and heavy had been sitting on her breast, sucking her breath and pressing the life out of her.

One time she was getting ready to go to a play-party. Some of the young sprouts were waiting for her in the front room. While she was combing her long, black hair, it suddenly was full of cuckleburs. She tugged and pulled and broke the comb to untangle it, and when she couldn't, she leaned on the bureau and cried.

"I put them in your hair," said the Witch from the looking-glass. "You've got no business going to the party. Stay here with me. I can say sweet things to you."

She screamed, and the young fellows rushed in the room, and when she told them about the Voice they shot at the glass with their pistols. But the glass didn't break. And the Witch caught every bullet and pitched it into their vest pockets and laughed. So they called it a draw and went out of there. And Mary stayed at home.

Mary was now mighty near grown. She had turned out to be a beautiful woman. She had lots of beaux. But whenever one of them screwed himself up to the point of popping the question he always found that the words stuck in his throat and his face and ears burned. For young fellows these were strange signs. But it was always that way. And none of

them seemed to be able to ask Mary the question. They laid it on the
Witch, and finally quit hitching their horses to the Bell fence.

All but one. His name was Gardner. He was a catch for any girl,
smart as a briar, good-looking, easy-going and open-hearted, and the owner
of rich bottom land, a passel of niggers, and a home as big as the courthouse, with columns as tall and white. He got all wrapped up in Mary,
and they say Mary was leaning to him.

The way of the Witch with him was different, more businesslike.
Maybe it was because the Witch realized this was the man Mary was
setting her heart on. One night when Gardner was walking up the row of
cedars in the Bell yard to see Mary, something he couldn't see reached
out from a big cedar and touched him on the shoulder, and a voice
said, "Wait a minute." Gardner was afraid to wait, but he was more afraid
to run. So he waited.

"You might as well understand, here and now, that you are not going
to have Mary Bell."

"Why not?" Gardner asked.

"You might have guessed from all that's happened round here. I'm
in love with her myself. It's going to be hard to get her consent, and it
may be harder to get the old man's. But she's not going to marry you. I'll
see to that. If you open your mouth about it to-night, you'll be dead
as a door-nail before morning."

Gardner studied a while and said, "If you'd only come out like a man."

The cedar tree stepped out and snatched his hat off and stomped it.

"Well, I reckon I'll have to lay off for a while," says Gardner. "But
I do love her, and I'd go to the end of the world for. . . ."

"Well, you don't have to go that far, and it wouldn't do you any
good if you did, and if you love her the only way you can keep her out
of hell is to get out yourself. If you keep on hanging round here, I'll
make it hell for you. Now this is how far you go. Pack up your traps
and get out of the country, hide and hair. Go any place you think the
Bells won't hear tell of you—and go before breakfast. If you slip out
quiet without raising any rookus I'll never pester you again. What's
more, on the day you get married I'll give you a pair of new boots you'll
be proud of all your life."

Gardner couldn't see why the Witch's promise of a pair of wedding
boots was in the same class as the threat of death before breakfast, but
he didn't split hairs, and he didn't argue any more. He picked up his
hat, sneaked back to his horse, and rode off.

He never said or wrote a thing to the Bells about what had happened,
part because he was scared, but more because he was ashamed of being
scared. He left the neighborhood before sunup and moved to the western
part of the state. He got somebody else to sell out for him. They say
the town of Gardner, where he settled, was named after him when he got
old and respected.

After he had been there a while he fell in love with a girl and got engaged to her. And they say that when he was dressing for the wedding he couldn't find his boots. He looked high and low, every place a pair of boots was liable to be and lots of places where they couldn't possibly be, but no boots could he find. He was about to give up and go to his wedding in his sock feet, when a Voice told him to crawl out from under the bed and look in the bed. And there between the sheets he found a pair of shiny new boots. He put them on and went his way rejoicing and thinking of how well a ghost kept his word, and wondering if the boots would ever wear out and if they were like the Seven-League boots he had read about in old McGuffey.

But they looked like natural boots. He told some of his friends how he had got them. They thought he was a liar. But they had to own up they were wrong. One day Gardner's house-boy made a mistake and carried them instead of another pair to a cobbler. The cobbler said they were in perfect shape, that they were not made by mortal hands, and that the soles were sewed on in a way that no man or man-made machine could have stitched them. And there is a lady in this neighborhood who has seen the boots.

While Gardner's mind was getting mossed over about Mary, Mr. Bell decided again to move to Mississippi. It looked like his move from North Carolina was jumping from the frying pan into the fire, but he figured maybe the skillet wouldn't be any hotter. Gardner's break-up with Mary and Mary not marrying hung heavy on his mind. Mrs. Bell raised up again, telling him about rolling stones. And the Witch horned in. By this time the family got used to the Witch and would talk free with him, but respectful. Every time the question came up there was a row between Mr. Bell and Mary on one side and Mrs. Bell and the Witch on the other. The old nigger woman told Mr. Bell the ha'nt didn't want him to move because he was afraid of witch hunters in Mississippi. She said there were powerful ones down there.

And so one winter after the crops had petered out on him again, he sold his place dirt cheap. But the old nigger woman told him to wait till spring to start. She said Easter was early that year and there would be plenty of time to pitch a crop. Good Friday would be a good day to leave, she said, for the ha'nt would have to go back to his grave and stay three days under the ground and would be puny-like several days more. While he was in good working order he could be in two or three places at once and be in any of them in the bat of an eye, but then he would have to lie low, and that would give them plenty of start. So Mr. Bell early on Good Friday stacked his furniture and duds in a couple of wagons, climbed into the front one with Mary, put the old nigger woman and his biggest boy into the hind one, and told Mrs. Bell, "Git in with old Patsy if you're a-comin', and don't forget the young-uns."

And that was the way the Bell family came to Mississippi. Mr. Bell bought him a little place in Panola County, ten miles east of Batesville on the Oxford road. He was all ready to begin life over again without supernatural interference.

But the Witch made a quick come-back, not before the family got there, but before they moved into their new home.

When Mr. Bell first got to Batesville, or Panola as they called it then, he left the family there and went out to look at the land he aimed to buy. When he got a place that suited him, he went back to town for his family and stuff. There was some sort of hitch, and the wagons did not get started till late in the evening. As the wagons moved slowly out of town, dark clouds began to roll up in the south and west, and before they had gone three miles the storm broke. Dark came on earlier than usual, for the clouds hid the sun. The rain beat down on the wagon covers. Every now and then the lightning flashes lit up the swaying trees on each side of the road, the draggle-tailed horses, and the road itself,—a long, muddy creek,—and then it was dark as a stack of black cats. The folks all stopped talking. There was nothing to listen to but the beating rain and the thunder and the suck of the horses' feet and the wheels in the mud.

All at once the hind wagon, with the family in it slid to the side of the road and sunk into the mud up to the bed. Mr. Bell saw it in a lightning flash and came back. It couldn't be moved; the horses had no foothold, and the wheels were in too deep. The fix they were in wasn't dangerous, but it was mighty uncomfortable.

And then the Witch took a hand.

"If you'll go back to your wagon and stop your cussin'," said the empty dark beside the wagon, "I'll get you out. Hump it back to your wagon now—light a shuck!"

Mr. Bell waded back and crawled in.

And then the horses and the wagon and the furniture and the family and the dog under the wagon and the calf tied behind and everything else but the mud on the wheels riz up about eight feet high and floated down the road till they were just behind the front wagon, and then they settled down easy and went on home without any trouble.

The family got settled down in their two-story double-loghouse amongst the cedars on the Oxford road.

A few nights later, the Witch spoke up from one of the andirons and told Mr. and Mrs. Bell he was in love with Mary. He said he wanted to marry her. Mr. Bell was shocked and surprised. He explained, respectful but emphatic like, that he could never dream of letting a daughter of his marry a ghost, not even so noble a ghost like the one he was talking with.

"I got a claim on you, John Bell," said the Witch. "I got a claim on you and yours. I got a claim." And his voice was deep and hollowlike.

This was a point Mr. Bell maybe didn't want to hear any more about. So he said, "Have you spoken to Mary?"

"No, not spoken."

"Well, how do you know she would have you?"

"I don't. But I haven't got any reason to believe she wouldn't love me. She's never seen me. She doesn't know whether she would or not. Maybe she would consider it an honor to be married to a ghost. Not many girls are, you know. Why, it would make her famous."

"I don't want any daughter of mine getting famous that way. And besides, what if you were to have children? What in the world do you reckon they'd be like? Like you or her? Maybe half good human meat and bone, and the other half sight unseen. Or maybe they'd be the vanishin' kind and goin' round here and raisin' hell invisible. Do you think I want a passel of soap-suds young-uns floatin' round here and poppin' up into puffs of wind every time I p'inted to the stovewood pile or sprouts on a ditch bank? Not on your life. I reckon plain flesh and blood's good enough for Mary."

"But, John Bell, I love Mary. And remember. Remember."

"So do I, and that's why I'm not a-goin' to let you marry her. Why, when she got old and hard-favored I reckon you'd quit her for some young hussy. You could do it easy enough. Mary'd have a hard time keepin' up with a stack of wind and a voice, and I'd have a hard time trackin' down and shootin' a low-down, no-count dust devil. When Mary marries, she marries a man that's solid and alive in body."

"I gather, John Bell, that you're opposed to me courting your daughter. But she's the one to say, and I'm going to talk to her about it. You'll be my father-in-law yet, or you'll be a-mourning, a-mourning."

"But what kind of wedding would it be like?" Mrs. Bell put in. "Think of it. Mary standing in front of the preacher and the preacher saying, 'Do you take this woman?' to a vase of flowers. And the ring floating down to Mary from the hanging-lamp maybe, or rising up from under a bench. I won't stand for it. I've stood for a lot of things, and you can't say I haven't been a friend to you. But I won't stand for Mary being a laughing-stock and disgrace to the family."

"If we're a-goin' to add to this family," Mr. Bell took up, "we're a-goin' to be able to see what we're addin'. I don't even know what shape you've got, if any."

"Oh, I can give you some idea what shape I have. I'll let you shake hands with me. But you must promise not to squeeze. We're very delicate, especially when we touch folks. Here, hold out your hand, and I'll put mine in it."

Mr. Bell held out his hand, felt something, and grabbed it. It was, he said later, the hand of a new-born baby—soft and crinkly and warm and just about the size of a new-born baby's hand.

"How big are you all over?" he asked.

"I can't tell you that."

"Well, there's one other thing I want to know. How do you get into this house any time you want to when every window and door is locked and barred? Do you ooze through the walls?"

"No. It's a lot easier than that. If you'll watch the corner of the ceiling up there, you'll see."

And all the rest of his life Mr. Bell swore to trustworthy witnesses that he saw the corner of the ceiling raised a good three feet and then let down again—all without the slightest racket.

"Do you mean to tell me that anything with a hand like that can h'ist the top off of the house that a-way?"

"Sure," came the answer. "But—about Mary. I'm going to talk to her right off."

"Don't," said Mr. Bell. "Do you want to drive her crazy?"

But the meeting was over, for there was no answer. And the fire had died down, and the andiron looked glum.

The story is kind of skimpy here. Nobody seems to know what the Witch said to Mary or what Mary said to the Witch.

But the family noticed next day that she was drooping and wasn't minding what was going on around her. For days she wandered about the house and up and down the yard under the gloomy old cedars, like somebody sleep-walking. And the color left her face, and deep in her wide-open black eyes was a far-away look, like she was trying to see something that ought to be but wasn't there. Every day she got up later and went to bed earlier.

And finally there came a day when she didn't get up at all. In the evening a screech-owl hollered in a cedar right by the gallery.

That night her fever was high, and by midnight she was raving. "We've put off seein' a doctor too long," said Mrs. Bell.

"The roads like they are, it'll take me two hours goin' and him and me two hours comin'," said Mr. Bell. "It'll be might' nigh daylight before we get back. But I reckon you're right, and I'll go as quick as I can saddle a horse."

"No use," said a Voice. "All the doctors and medicines in the world won't cure her. But if you want one, I'll get him, and get him a lot quicker than you can."

The doctor got there just as the old eight-day clock struck one. "I heard somebody hollering at my window about midnight, telling me to come out here right away. When I got to the door, nobody was there; but I thought I'd better come anyway." He was a young doctor just starting out. "Say, what kind of road overseer and gang do you fellows have out this way? Last time I came over this road, about Christmas, it was the the worst I ever saw. Why, I picked up a Stetson hat in the middle of a mud-hole near the four-mile board, and by George there was a man under it. 'You're in the middle of a bad fix, old man,' I said. 'Hell,' he said, 'that ain't nothin' to the fix this mule's in under me.' I had to lift up my feet half the way to keep them from dragging in the mud by the horse's belly. But to-night my horse skimmed over it in an hour. Well- who's sick out here?"

"It's her mind and nerves," he told them after he had questioned them and examined Mary. "I won't conceal from you, she's in pretty bad shape. And medicine won't do her any good. You've just got to be gentle and careful with her. Humor her and be patient with her. I'll give her something to put her to sleep when she gets like this. Watch her close and don't let her get lonesome. She's young and strong and ought to come round in time."

But she never did. For a month she lay there on the bed, looking at nothing and yet straining to see something. Something too far off. At night her pa and ma took turns sitting up. They didn't want the neighbors in. They called the doctor back a few times, but he shook his head and said he couldn't do any more. So they would watch and wait, wanting to do something, but helpless.

One night her ma was sitting there, holding Mary's hand and stroking the dark hair back from her forehead. Suddenly Mary pushed her mother away and sat up and looked across the foot of the bed, as if somebody was standing there.

"Mamma," she whispered, "Mamma . . . I see him . . . at last. . . . And I think . . . I think . . . I'm going . . . to love him."

And she died with the only expression of happiness they had seen on her face in months.

Some folks have tried to explain Mary's strange death. A few say the Witch tortured her continually and kept her in such constant terror that her mind was affected. Others have heard that a school teacher ventriloquist that was jealous of Gardner played tricks on her and the family, and then when she wouldn't have him tormented and frightened her to death. Some believe she was in love with the overseer from the first, and then when he was killed she was in love with the Witch and didn't want to live because she knew she would never be happy with him until she too became a ghost.

But she died, just the same. And they say that on the day of the funeral, when the coffin was carried from the house to a wagon a great black bird flew down from the sky and hung in the air just above the wagon. And around its neck was a bell that tolled in the mournfullest tone ever heard by the ear of man. And when the funeral procession began to move, the great bird floated just in front of it all the way to the graveyard and circled round and round the grave during the burial, the bell tolling all the while. And when the mound was rounded up, the bird swung high up in the air and flew away to the west and finally became just a little speck above the treetops and disappeared. But long after it was gone the mourning notes of the bell floated back to those who stood and watched.

The Leeds Devil

WITHIN recent times the Leeds Devil has ramped about the New Jersey pine region, between Freehold and Cape May, though it should have been "laid" many years ago. Its coming portends evil, for it appears before wars, fires, and great calamities.

Albeit a sober Quaker in appearance, Mother Leeds, of Burlington, New Jersey, was strongly suspected of witchcraft; and suspicion became certainty when, in 1735, a child was born to her. The old women who had assembled on that occasion, as they always do assemble wherever there is death or birth or marriage, reported that while it was like other human creatures at first, the child changed, under their very eyes. It began to lose its likeness to other babes, and grew long and brown; it presently took the shape of a dragon, with a snake-like body, a horse's head, a pig's feet, and a bat's wings. This dreadful being increased in strength as it gained in size, until it exceeded the bulk and might of a grown man, when it fell on the assemblage, beating all the members of the party, even its own mother, with its long, forked, leathery tail. This despite being wreaked, it arose through the chimney and vanished, its harsh cries mingling with the clamor of a storm that was raging out-of-doors.

That night several children disappeared: the dragon had eaten them. For several years thereafter it was glimpsed in the woods at nightfall, and it would wing its way heavily from farm to farm, though it seldom did much mischief after its first escape into the world. To sour the milk by breathing on it, to dry the cows, and to sear the corn were its usual errands. On a still night the farmers could follow its course, as they did with trembling, by the howling of dogs, the hoots of owls, and the squawks of poultry. It sometimes appeared on the coast, generally when a wreck impended, and was seen in the company of the spectres that haunt the shore: the golden-haired woman in white, the black-muzzled pirate, and the robber, whose head being cut off at Barnegat by Captain Kidd, stumps about the sands without it, guarding a treasure buried near. When it needed a change of diet the Leeds Devil would breathe upon the cedar swamps, and straightway the fish would die in the pools and creeks, their bodies, whitened and decayed by the poison, floating about in such numbers as to threaten illness to all the neighborhood. In 1740 the service of a clergyman was secured, who, by reason of his piety and exemplary life, had dominion over many of the fiends that plagued New Jersey, and had even prevailed in his congregation against applejack, which some declared to be a worse fiend than any other, if, indeed, it did not create some of those others. With candle, book, and bell the good man banned the creature for a hundred years, and, truly, the herds and henneries

From *American Myths and Legends*, by Charles M. Skinner, Vol. I, pp. 240–243. Copyright, 1903, by J. B. Lippincott Company. Philadelphia & London.

were not molested in all that time. The Leeds Devil had become a dim tradition when, in 1840, it burst its cerements, if such had been put about it; or, at all events, it broke through the clergyman's commandments, and went whiffling among the pines again, eating sheep and other animals, and making clutches at children that dared to sport about their dooryards in the twilight. From time to time it reappeared, its last raid occurring at Vincentown and Burrville in 1899, but it is said that its life has nearly run its course, and with the advent of the new century many worshipful commoners of Jersey dismissed, for good and all, the fear of this monster from their minds.

IV. GHOST TALES

"Why, I could tell ye a story'd make your har rise on eend, only I'm 'fraid of frightening boys when they're jist going to bed."
—HARRIET BEECHER STOWE

"REAL" ghost stories or accounts of individual experiences with hants and legends of haunted houses and other places belong to psychic research and local history rather than to folklore. To have fun with ghosts, as with witches, the story-teller must not take them too seriously. Fair game for such a story-teller are persons who accept a dare or a bet to spend the night in a haunted house, especially those who boast that they are not afraid of ghosts. Here practical jokes are a great temptation.

"The Half-Clad Ghost" is an amusing take-off on the ghost who returns for a missing object, already seen in "Tailypo" and "The Golden Arm"— a theme which is treated with gruesome effect in "Cap'n Santos' Leg." The familiar motifs of the spectral rider and the spectral bridegroom recur in "The Phantom Train of Marshall Pass" and "The Death Waltz." "High Walker and Bloody Bones" is a ghoulish danse macabre.

Four Black Cats and More

*   *   *   *   *

BIG JO JO BOLL WEEVIL JIM telling a tale, Little Tom Jim and Brown Boy Steve, and Tobe and Bob and Samuel, and twenty other black boys, pick and shovel bards, sprawling around, now jorreeing, now grumbling, now singing a snatch of song, now in ghost-story contest.

*   *   *   *   *

From *Cold Blue Moon, Black Ulysses Afar Off*, by Howard W. Odum, pp. 19–28. Copyright, 1931, by Howard W. Odum. Indianapolis: The Bobbs-Merrill Company, Publishers.

One time I was on trip in South Ca'lina and I got out of money, and it was in the fall of the year. And it was raining and very cool on my tramp, too. So I begin to hunt a place to rest for the night. And on the roadside I come to big white house. And so I goes up to this house and knocks on door. And a man come to the door. And I explain to him my condition. I told him I were a long ways from home, and I wanted to know if he would let me stay for the night in dog-house or barn or sumpin'.

So the man look at me and says he had house up on the hill an' I could stay there for the night. He told me I would find wood to make fire and bed to sleep in but no one was livin' there now. So now I felt satisfied. So I thanks him and tells him good night and off I goes up to that house on the hill.

I opens the door and goes in. Everything looks well and fine. So I strikes match and lit lamp. And also makes fire in fireplace. And I set down an' begin to dry and rest with ease, ease, my Lawd, settin' in the Kingdom jes' like John. Until all at once I heard some one say up-stairs, "I'm comin' down, I'm comin' down."

And just 'bout that time I look and there he was dress all in white between me an' the door, yes sir, Lawd, Lawd, between me an' the door. So out the window I had business.

I run 'bout seven miles down road and I met a preacher and he halt me and I stop. He said, "Young man, where are you going in such hurry?" I told him if he had seen what I seen he would be in a hurry too. So I explain to him what I had seen.

So he said, "My Brother, it is nothing to that."

I told him, "You don't tell me!"

So he says, "Listen, my friend, I'll prove that you are wrong."

I asks him, "How?"

He says then, "I'll go with you to the house." So then I asks him who was going to be with us an' he said the good Lord.

So off we went, I and he side by side. We kep' walkin', an' after so long time we come to the house. The light was still lit and fire was in fine shape. So he opens door and walks in. So I raises window and he sets down and opens his Bible an' begins to read. So I heard a voice sayin', "I'm comin' down, I'm comin' down." So there he was again. The preacher look at me and I look at him an' he look at me. So 'bout that time out the window I goes again, preacher in behind me. So after little ways we were side by side, 'cause he sho' wus runnin' for the Lord. So after we had run 'bout ten miles I asks old preacher if good Lord is with us now.

And preacher, he says, "Well, if He is, I be-dam' if He ain't traveling some!"

*   *   *   *   *

Well, that ain't no preacher ghost story at all. I heard tell 'bout preacher was offered so much money would he stay in ha'nted house all night. So he goes an' takes Bible an' sets down important like an' opens up Bible an' begins to read. 'Bout that time first ghost comes sneakin' in like hot air or maybe like cold breeze an' wet, look lak man only ain't got no head, 'scusin' if he have head ain't got no body, else if he have body ain't got no arms. So he says to preacher, "Is you gonna stay here till Whalem-Balem comes?"

Ole man so skeered he don't say nothin'. So nex' ghost come in he look lak mule, maybe old gray mule only he ain't got no head neither, 'scusin' if he got long-eared head, ain't got no body. So he says to preacher, "Is you gonna stay here till Whalem-Balem comes?"

Still the old man so skeered he don't know whut to do; thinks maybe he better be goin', neither can he move. So 'bout that time, third ghost comes in, look lak cat, only biggest cat anybody ever seen, got red eyes lak fire and spittin' and mewin' like red-hot stove or sumpin'. So he meows, "Is you gonna stay here till Whalem-Balem comes?"

'Bout that time old preacher ain't got no voice an' feel mighty sick at his stomach and decided maybe he better make him little coffee and fry some meat. So he does. 'Bout time he be ready to drink his hot flambotia strong, fo'th ghost comes in, look lak dog, only got big tushes lak boar. So he reaches down an' et up all meat an' lap up all coffee. He then snaps up at preacher with tushes all showin' an' like impudent snarl, maybe snappin' teeth together like wolf, "Is you gonna stay here till Whalem-Balem comes?"

So old preacher hollers, "Hell, no, I'm done gone."

> Singin' High-Stepper Lawd, you shall be free,
> Yes, when the Good Lawd sets you free;
> I'm on my way an' can't turn back,
> Lawd, I'm on my way an' can't turn back.

* * * * *

Well, I got better ghost story 'bout preacher an' cat, 'scusin' got so many don't know which ones to tell. Can't count 'em, so many take me till to-morrow night to name 'em. Wus one old preacher boastin' 'bout he ain't skeered of no ghosts. So sisters say, "You don't say. Ain't he brave man?" So they tells him 'bout big house ain't nobody never stayed all night in it since war.

So he goes over to house with Bible, gits down on his knees an' prays Lawd to keep him lak he kep' Daniel in lion's den. Jes' 'bout that time little bitty black kitty rubs 'gainst his leg. So he says, "Amen, Lawd, Amen." So he gits up an' sets down in cheer an' begins readin' Bible an' reaches down to rub kitten. Can't tech it. Howsomever, he sees it settin' down nex' to him.

So he goes on readin' till hears sumpin' else an' looks down. Settin' side of first kitten is 'nother black kitten little bigger, lookin' up at him an' lickin' his lips. So he tries to rub this kitten neither can he tech it.

'Bout that time 'nother black cat little bigger than other two wus settin' down side of other kittens. Howsomever, that ain't all cats he's gonna see. So 'nother one 'bout big as wildcat slips in, look lak he be laughin' at preacher. So 'bout that time one come in 'bout big as dog, then 'nother one 'bout big as calf. So preacher looks out of window an' up-stairs an' still cats keep comin', more an' bigger an' blacker. Then all black cats start meowin' and screamin' till old man jes' natchelly near 'bout skeered to death. Nobody never heard the like since they been born; little cats meowin', big cats growlin', screamin' and spittin', Lawd, Lawd, look like Jedgment day. Old man must 'a' fainted an' yelled, till somebody come by. Said they found Bible leaves layin' all over flo' and old man's hands all scratched up. So they took old man on home; thought he woke up groanin' an' singin'.

> Oh, Lord, I feel like feather in the air,
> Oh, Lord, feel like I never prayed a prayer.

*   *   *   *   *

Well, I heard 'bout black-cat ghost myself. One time fellow wus road hustlin' down that lonesome road. So when night ketches him he seen house. So he asks man to let him stay all night. "No," he says, "I got mo' chillun than I can bed, but there's house up 'bout mile nobody can stay in."

So he asks him why, an' he says it's ha'nted. "That ain't nothin'," fellow tells him, "I ain't skeered o' no ha'nts."

So he goes up 'bout dark, gits a lot o' light'ood an' wood, and built him big fire, roasted some 'taters, got box to set on, an' sholy wus feelin' lucky, 'cause started rainin' 'bout that time. So he dozed off to sleep. Long 'bout twelve o'clock wus woke up by sound, so he gits up lookin' fer ghost; got light'ood stick an' looks all through house. Eve'ything wus quiet an' wus nothin' he could see, so he says, "Well, this is fine." So thought he would pile down on flo' in front of fire an' go to sleep. So down he sot to pull off his old shoes. So he sot there bakin' his feet an' must 'a' nodded off 'cause all of sudden he felt wus company in room. So he looked an' do' wus shet, window wus shet, but still he look 'roun' and seen turr'blest thing he ever seen. Thing looked at him, he looked at thing, settin' right on end of box. Sholy wus settin' up, jes' bones, no skin, jes' bones, knees stickin' out an' techin' his leg. Oh, Lawd, creepin' feelin' all over fellow; wus shakin' so till thing jes' rattled self again an' grin at him.

So all of sudden this ghost turned into big black cat. 'Bout that time it ups an' says, "Seem like ain't nobody here but me an' you to-night." So this fellow says, "If I can jes' stand up little bit, won't be nobody here but you." So fellow gives mighty holler an' left through window an' run an' run, gettin' mo' skeerder ever' minute he run, till he jus' drop down in road. So big hollow voice meows at his elbow, "Sholy wus some race." Race, hell, that cat didn't know nuthin' 'bout race an' runnin'. Nex' time fellow didn't run, good God, he flew an' bu'st in white man's house what sent him up to old house. So this man says, "Hell, nigger, you skeered me 'bout to death; but whut you got on yo' neck?" So fellow look an' had brung whole blamed winder-sash clean all way from other house. So white man asks him if he wus going back after his shoes. Fellow tells him guess they can stay up there wid 'bout one hundred mo' pairs he seen settin' by fire.

Cap'n Santos' Leg

"You fellers wouldn't remember old Cap'n John Santos—feller that had his leg et off by a shark on the Western Banks. But I can remember him, back when I was a boy, and how proud he was of the new juryleg they rigged him up with. It was a sight, I tell you, to watch him dance a *chamarita* with that leg and not nick the floor once. Carried around furniture polish just like the doctor carries iodine, in case of a cut or scratch, and one time he copper-bottomed her to make sure the worms wouldn't get to him before his time.

"Well, you know once a man is chawed on by a shark, he's shark-jonahed for the rest of his life. Some day a shark's going to get the rest of that feller, if he keeps on going to sea. And Cap'n John kept on.

"The Cap'n's trawler, the *Hetty K*, was ten mile from the Race when the Portland Gale struck. That was November 27. On the 28th she come crippling round the Point under bare poles with two foot of harbor water over her lee rail. The crew said Cap'n John was washed overboard, along with two other men.

"The bodies of the other two drifted ashore; the Cap'n wasn't never found. But a couple of days after, Joe Barcia picked up the old man's wooden leg off the beach. He took it home to Mary Santos, the widow.

"Married thirty years, them two. When Joe Barcia brought back the leg, Mary took it into the house. She petted it and talked to it.

"Nothing more come of it till the night of November 26, a year later. That night, Mary said, she set up in bed, and there, standing straight as two yards of pump-water on his one leg, was old Cap'n John. He hopped over alongside the bed and canted over. Then he whispered to her.

" 'Barometer's falling, Mary,' he says, 'and the wind's no'theast. We're in for thick weather, and I'll want my store leg to keep me steady when she strikes.' He pinched her cheek, and Mary let out a yell. When she looked again, the Cap'n was gone.

"Next morning, Mary said, she had a little red spot on her cheek. And before she turned in that night, she took the skipper's leg out of the spice-cupboard and left it laid out for him in a corner near the fireplace.

From *Cape Cod Pilot,* by Jeremiah Digges, with Editorial and Research Assistance of the Members of the Federal Writers' Project, pp. 234–236. American Guide Series, Federal Writers' Project, Works Progress Administration for the State of Massachusetts. Sponsored by Poor Richard Associates. Copyright, 1937, by Poor Richard Associates. Modern Pilgrim Press and the Viking Press. Provincetown and New York.

"That night a breeze of wind come up, and in a couple of hours it turned into a living gale—from the no'theast. The willer tree outside howled like the yo-ho bird of every dead sailor in hell come there to roost. All of a sudden Mary hears a thump-thump-thump across the floor, down below, and then the door shut to. She stayed in bed.

"Next morning she went to look if the Cap'n's leg was still there. It was, but when she picked it up, it was wet.

"Well, it'd rained bad enough to come in by the chimney. But it gallied her so, the sight of that leg, with the water on it, that she got sick. She called in Doc Atwood. When he got through sounding, and didn't find nothing sprung, Doc said something was eating on her. Then she told him the whole story.

"When he'd went over the leg, he looked hard at the widow.

"'You say you left it by the fireplace all night and rain come in on it?' he asks. Then he sets the leg down, comes over to the widow, and tells her straight out. 'Mrs. Santos,' he says, 'I'm going to ask you to have one of the men take this thing out to sea, and weight it with netleads, and heave it overboard. I'm a doctor,' he says, 'and I don't listen to stories. But Mrs. Santos,' he says, 'I put my tongue to that wood. *It don't rain salt water!*'"

The Phantom Train of Marshall Pass

SOON after the rails were laid across Marshall Pass, Colorado, where they go over a height of twelve thousand feet above the sea, an old engineer named Nelson Edwards was assigned to a train. He had travelled the road with passengers behind him for a couple of months and met with no accident, but one night as he set off for the divide he fancied that the silence was deeper, the cañon darker, and the air frostier than usual. A defective rail and an unsafe bridge had been reported that morning, and he began the long ascent with some misgivings. As he left the first line of snow-sheds he heard a whistle echoing somewhere among the ice and rocks, and at the same time the gong in his cab sounded and he applied the brakes.

The conductor ran up and asked, "What did you stop for?"

"Why did you signal to stop?"

"I gave no signal. Pull her open and light out, for we've got to pass No. 19 at the switches, and there's a wild train climbing behind us."

Edwards drew the lever, sanded the track, and the heavy train got under way again; but the whistles behind grew nearer, sounding danger-signals, and in turning a curve he looked out and saw a train speeding after him at a rate that must bring it against the rear of his own train

From *Myths and Legends of Our Own Land*, by Charles M. Skinner, Vol. II, pp. 192–195. Copyright, 1896, by J. B. Lippincott Company. Philadelphia and London.

if something were not done. He broke into a sweat as he pulled the throttle wide open and lunged into a snow-bank. The cars lurched, but the snow was flung off and the train went roaring through another shed. Here was where the defective rail had been reported. No matter. A greater danger was pressing behind. The fireman piled on coal until his clothes were wet with perspiration, and fire belched from the smokestack. The passengers, too, having been warned of their peril, had dressed themselves and were anxiously watching at the windows, for talk went among them that a mad engineer was driving the train behind.

As Edwards crossed the summit he shut off steam and surrendered his train to the force of gravity. Looking back, he could see by the faint light from new snow that the driving-wheels on the rear engine were bigger than his own, and that a tall figure stood atop of the cars and gestured frantically. At a sharp turn in the track he found the other train but two hundred yards behind, and as he swept around the curve the engineer who was chasing him leaned from his window and laughed. His face was like dough. Snow was falling and had begun to drift in the hollows, but the trains flew on; bridges shook as they thundered across them; wind screamed in the ears of the passengers; the suspected bridge was reached; Edwards's heart was in his throat, but he seemed to clear the chasm by a bound. Now the switch was in sight, but No. 19 was not there, and as the brakes were freed the train shot by like a flash. Suddenly a red light appeared ahead, swinging to and fro on the track. As well be run into behind as to crash into an obstacle ahead. He heard the whistle of the pursuing locomotive yelp behind him, yet he reversed the lever and put on brakes, and for a few seconds lived in a hell of dread.

Hearing no sound, now, he glanced back and saw the wild train almost leap upon his own—yet just before it touched it the track seemed to spread, the engine toppled from the bank, the whole train rolled into the cañon and vanished. Edwards shuddered and listened. No cry of hurt men or hiss of steam came up—nothing but the groan of the wind as it rolled through the black depth. The lantern ahead, too, disappeared. Now another danger impended, and there was no time to linger, for No. 19 might be on its way ahead if he did not reach the second switch before it moved out. The mad run was resumed and the second switch was reached in time. As Edwards was finishing the run to Green River, which he reached in the morning ahead of schedule, he found written in the frost of his cab-window these words: "A frate train was recked as yu saw. Now that yu saw it yu will never make another run. The enjine was not ounder control and four sexshun men wor killed. If yu ever run on this road again yu will be recked." Edwards quit the road that morning, and returning to Denver found employment on the Union Pacific. No wreck was discovered next day in the cañon where he had seen it, nor has the phantom train been in chase of any engineer who has crossed the divide since that night.

The Death Waltz

YEARS ago, when all beyond the Missouri was a waste, the military post at Fort Union, New Mexico, was the only spot for miles around where any of the graces of social life could be discovered. Among the ladies at the post was a certain gay young woman, the sister-in-law of a captain, who enjoyed the variety and spice of adventure to be found there, and enjoyed, too, the homage that the young officers paid to her, for women who could be loved or liked were not many in that wild country. A young lieutenant proved especially susceptible to her charms, and devoted himself to her in the hope that he should ultimately win her hand. His experience with the world was not large enough to enable him to distinguish between the womanly woman and the coquette.

One day messengers came dashing into the fort with news of an Apache outbreak, and a detachment was ordered out to chase and punish the marauding Indians. The lieutenant was put in command of the expedition, but before starting he confided his love to the young woman, who not only acknowledged that she returned his affection, but promised that if the fortune of war deprived him of life she would never marry another. As he bade her good-by he was heard to say, "That is well. Nobody else shall have you. I will come back and make my claim."

In a few days the detachment came back, but the lieutenant was missing. It was noticed that the bride-elect grieved but little for him, and nobody was surprised when she announced her intention of marrying a young man from the East. The wedding-day arrived. All was gayety at the post, and in the evening the mess-room was decorated for a ball. As the dance was in full swing a door flew open with a bang, letting in a draught of air that made the candles burn dim, and a strange cry, unlike that of any human creature, sounded through the house. All eyes turned to the door. In it stood the swollen body of a dead man dressed in the stained uniform of an officer. The temple was marked by a hatchet-gash, the scalp was gone, the eyes were wide open and burned with a terrible light.

Walking to the bride the body drew her from the arms of her husband, who, like the rest of the company, stood as in a trance, without the power of motion, and clasping her to its bosom began a waltz. The musicians, who afterward declared that they did not know what they were doing, struck up a demoniac dance, and the couple spun around and around, the woman growing paler and paler, until at last the fallen jaw and staring eyes showed that life was also extinct in her. The dead man allowed her to sink to the floor, stood over her for a moment, wrung his hands as he sounded his fearful cry again, then vanished through the door. A few days after, a troop of soldiers who had been to the scene of the Apache encounter returned with the body of the lieutenant.

Ibid., pp. 208–210.

The Half-Clad Ghost

"I KNEW a' ole man once that alluz wo' two paiah o' draw's. But when he died his wife didn' lay out but one paiah foh 'im. Well, after de fune'l, he kep' a-comin' back an' a-comin' back. Evah night he'd come right in dat front do' o' her house. So she moved from dat place, but he jes' kep' a-comin' jes de same. She moved fo' o' five times, an' he jes' kep' on a-comin' back evah night o' de worl'. Finely she talked to some o' her frien's. They asked 'er why she don' talk to 'im. She say 'cause she scared to. But they say foh 'er to say, 'What in de name o' de Lawd do you want?' So dat night he come ag'in.

"This time she walk' right up an' met 'im an' say, 'What in de name o' de Lawd do you want?'

"He looked at 'er right study foh a long time, but she nevah move, an' she jes' stan' theah; an' finely he say, 'Honey, gimme 'nother paiah o' draw's, please.'

"She say, 'Aw right, I'll give 'em to you'; an' from dat day to this he nevah has come back no mo', she say. An' dat's de way it is: When you ask 'em what in de name o' de Lawd they want, an' then tell 'em you'll give it to 'em, they'll go 'way an' leave you alone."

High Walker and Bloody Bones

THIS wuz uh man. His name wuz High Walker. He walked into a boneyard with skull heads and other bones. So he would call them, "Rise up bloody bones and shake yo'self." And de bones would rise up and come together, and shake theirselves and part and lay back down. Then he would say to hisself, "High Walker," and de bones would say, "Be walkin'."

When he'd git off a little way he'd look back over his shoulder and shake hisself and say, "High Walker and bloodybones," and de bones would shake theirselves. Therefore he knowed he had power.

From "Dyin' Easy," by Martha Emmons, *Tone the Bell Easy*, Publications of the Texas Folk-Lore Society, edited by J. Frank Dobie, Number X, p. 59. Copyright, 1932, by the Texas Folk-Lore Society. Austin.

Elmira Johnson, of Waco, Texas, who gave the story to me, is a bright, vivacious Negro woman of some fifty or sixty years. She has a slight tendency to lisp, and a pronounced tendency to see the humor of things—even in ghost tales. Though very active and fairly supple, Elmira scorns dancing because "it's sinful." But she admits that sometimes "de Lawd jes' gits in my feet." Such must have been the case the morning she sang for us the song which is at the close of this paper. For she danced and skipped as she sang of being "done crossed over."—M. E.

From *Mules and Men*, by Zora Neale Hurston, pp. 219–220. Copyright, 1935, by Zora Neale Hurston. Philadelphia and London: J. B. Lippincott Company.

So uh man sold hisself to de high chief devil. He give 'im his whole soul and body tuh do ez he pleased wid it. He went out in uh drift uh woods and laid down flat on his back beyond all dese skull heads and bloody bones and said, "Go 'way Lawd, and come here Devil and do as you please wid me. Cause Ah want tuh do everything in de world dats wrong and never do nothing right."

And he dried up and died away on doin' wrong. His meat all left his bones and de bones all wuz separated.

And at dat time High Walker walked upon his skull head and kicked and kicked it on ahead of him a many and a many times and said tuh it, "Rise up and shake yo'self. High Walker is here."

Ole skull head wouldn't say nothin'. He looked back over his shoulder cause he heard some noises behind him and said, "Bloody bones you won't say nothin' yet. Rise tuh de power in de flesh."

Den de skull head said, "My mouf brought me here and if you don't mind, your'n will bring you here."

High Walker went on back to his white folks and told de white man dat a dry skull head wuz talkin' in de drift today. White man say he didn't believe it.

"Well, if you don't believe it, come go wid me and Ah'll prove it. And if it don't speak, you kin chop mah head off right where it at."

So de white man and High Walker went back in de drift tuh find dis ole skull head. So when he walked up tuh it, he begin tuh kick and kick de ole skull head, but it wouldn't say nothin'. High Walker looked at de white man and seen 'im whettin' his knife. Whettin' it hard and de sound of it said rick-de-rick, rick-de-rick! So High Walker kicked and kicked dat ole skull head and called it many and many uh time, but it never said nothin'. So de white man cut off High Walker's head.

And de ole dry skull head said, "See dat now! Ah told you dat mouf brought me here and if you didn't mind out it'd bring you here."

So de bloody bones riz up and shook they selves seben times and de white man got skeered and said, "What you mean by dis?"

De bloody bones say, "We got High Walker and we all bloody bones now in de drift together."

V. DEVIL TALES

"Here, take dis hot coal and g'wan off and start you a hell uh yo' own."—ZORA NEALE HURSTON

PEOPLE who traffic with the Devil for their own gain or pleasure generally end up by disappearing in smoke or turning into a jack-o-lantern or an African monkey. Sometimes the poor Devil is the victim, duped or discomfited by superior brain or brawn, as in "The Devil Marriage" (see also "Wiley and the Hairy Man") and "Samson and Satan." Slightly less familiar **are** the Devil's musical exploits. He not only loves singing but is a master of the violin, of which instrument of evil he is reputedly the inventor. By the same token he can give mastery of the violin, bartering infernal skill for the pupil's soul. These legends are related to the larger belief in the supernatural origin of musical skill and individual songs (e.g the fiddle tune, "The Devil's Dream").[1]

Stolen Fire

"WELL, long time ergo de debil he kim up ter de yeth, he did, an' went courtin' er gal."

"What's courtin'?" asked Fred.

"Talkin' putty, lack yo' Paw talk ter yo' Maw 'fore dey was married," said Mammy. "An' de gal was er mighty fine gal, wid long straight hair an' blue eyes, an' she could sing—laws er mussy! how dat gal could sing!

"Well, de debil ain't heared no singin' sence he was drapped in de bad place, an' dey guv 'im de keys, an' he was dat hongry fur singin', he mek dat gal sing all de time, an' he stan' by de pianny, he did, an' hide de foot dat got de hoof on hit. Yo' know by dis time, he done los' he tail, an' w'ar er tall stovepipe, 'case he hatter keep up wid whi' folks."

"How did he lose his tail?" asked both of the children at once.

"Mammy cain't tell yo' now 'bout dat, but he done los' hit. Anyway, he mek dat gal sing all day ter 'im, an' de gal she was peart an' lackly, an she sing twel her throat done plum dry, an' de debil he see hit were gittin' dark, an' he say hit were time fur him ter go home. He was 'feared 'case hit were so late, an' he herry, an' herry, clop-flop, clop-flop—de man's foot an' de hoof foot keep him back, fur de hoof foot mek two steps ter de man's one, an' when he git home, he find dat his fire were done plum out.

"Hit were er mighty sorry time fur de debil, 'case dar hain't nobody gwine give him none nor len' him none, an' he cain't steal hit hisse'f, on account er de hoof foot."

"Why didn't he buy some matches in town?" asked Fred.

"Didn't hab no matches den, honey, an' folkes hatter tote coals kivered wid ashes, fur miles an' miles, if dey let de fire go out."

" 'Count of the hoof foot," repeated Margie, coming back to the story.

" 'Count er de hoof foot," said Mammy, "so de debil castes 'roun' who he gwine git fur ter steal hit fur him.

"Fust he went ter de b'ar, an' stan' er long way off, 'case anybody kin beat de debil when his fire done out, an' he say: 'Please, Mister B'ar,

---

[1] Cf. "The Devil and the Fiddle," by Herbert Halpert, *Hoosier Folklore Bulletin*, Vol. II (December, 1943), No. 2, pp. 39–43. For the Texas legend of "The Devil and Strap Buckner," see *The Coming Empire or Two Thousand Miles in Texas on Horseback*, by H. F. McDanield and N. A. Taylor, (New York, 1877), pp. 49–73.

From *Devil Tales*, by Virginia Frazer Boyle, pp. 160–166. Copyright, 1900, by Harper & Brothers. New York and London.

won't yo' fetch me er coal fur ter light my pipe?' But de b'ar he growl, 'My hair's too thick, an' de fire's too hot, an' de road's too long, an' I 'feared I git het up, an' die.'

"Kimmin' back, he meet wid de rabbit, wid his mouf full er green, an' de debil he say: 'Hello, Mister Rabbit! won't yo' fetch me er coal fur ter light my pipe?' De rabbit he look meek an' sad, an' he 'low, 'I sorry, Mister Debil, but my baby chile's done got er awful cramp, an' I gwine fur ter mek him some catnip tea. Good-day, Mister Debil!' an' he lope right on, an' de debil mek er mark whar de rabbit cross his path, an' spit in hit.

"Den he kim an' knock at de tarrypin's door, but de tarrypin don't put more'n his nose outside, an' de debil he 'low, 'Please Mister Tarrypin, won't yo' fetch me er coal fur ter light my pipe?'

"De tarrypin he draw in his door er little more, an' 'low, 'Yo' knows I'd 'bleege yo', Mister Debil, but I goes so slow 'count er de mis'ry in de heart, dat de spark 'ud be out 'fore I could fetch hit! Good-day, Mister Debil!'

"De debil he 'low he must git dat fire somers, 'case dey was er needin' uv hit down dar, an' he 'pear ter meet up wid de fox, unbeknownst, an' he 'low ter be mighty cute, an' he say, 'Good-evenin', Mister Fox!' an' walk 'long side er him, lack dey was thick es peas in er pod, but Mister Fox he keep er poppin' uv his tail. Bime-by, Mister Debil he 'low, 'I got two fine segars in my ves' pocket—tek er smoke, Mister Fox?'

"But de fox he see de debil ain' got no light, an' he 'low, 'I sorry ter lose such good comp'ny es yo' is, but I gwine tek tea wid Misser Dominick Rooster. Good-evenin', Mister Debil!'

"So de debil he were hard up now, 'case dey keep er hollerin' fur fire down dar, so he ups an' goes ter de ole blue jay; de jay don' eben tek he head frum unner his wing. 'Go 'way, an' lemme 'lone,' say de jay—'I done been totin' wood fur yo' all dis Friday long, an' I'se tired an' I'se sleepy,' say de jay.

" 'Better kim down frum dar er I'll roas' yo'!' say de debil, gittin' mad.

" 'Hain't got no fire,' laugh de jay, an' he go back ter sleep ergin.

"Den de debil he go ter his nigger, de crow, an' he 'low, 'Go git me er coal er fire dis minute, 'fore I w'ar yo' des plum out!'

"De crow he git mighty sassy, 'case he know de debil cain't do nuffin' lessen he got er fire, an' he say: 'I done toted corn fur yo', Mister Debil, twel I'se got my wing des plum full er bird-shot; I cain't fetch yo' no fire!'

"Den de debil he 'low he 'bout ter gib hit up, twel he spy er worfless town nigger, er chawin' an' er spittin' at er chip in de moonshine, an' de debil he know he ain' got no call ter be keerful here, an' he up an' 'low, 'Say, boy! you want ter mek some money?'

"De town nigger plum keen, he don't keer how he git de money, so he git hit, an' de debil he say: 'Go git me er coal er fire—quick now—an' I'll gib yo' er dollar!'

"Well, de town nigger he light out an' ax two er three folks, but dey ain' got no fire ter spar', an' he go 'long twel he kim ter er po' widder 'oman, er blowin' on one po' little coal er fire ter mek er bed fur ter cook her hoe-cake, an' de nigger he 'low—'Lady, I'se hongry!'

"An' she say: 'I ain't cook supper yit—wait er while, an' I'll gib yo' er hoe-cake.' Den de nigger he move up closter, an' tell de 'oman how good she is, an' he stretch out his han's lack ter warm 'em, den all uv er suddent he retch an' snatch dat coal, an' go skootin' wid hit ter de debil."

Mammy paused to lay the last piece in the basket, but the children were too eager to wait.

"What did the devil do with him?" asked Fred.

"Skootin' to de devil," repeated Margie.

"Well," said Mammy, "de debil gib him de dollar in two halves so's de nigger could chink 'em; an' de nigger went 'long, chinkin' 'em, laughin' at how smart he were ter steal de coal fum de po' widder 'oman, an' it nebber cost him nuffin—when his lef' arm itch him, an' he feel dat hit were sproutin' hair, an' he fin' dat he were sproutin' hair all ober, an' he git skeered an' run, but de hair keep er sproutin' an' er sproutin', an' he keep er changin', an' er changin' so bimeby he des couldn't talk, an' bress goodness, honey! 'fore dat nigger git half-way home, he was er walkin' half on his han's an' half on his feet, an' wa'n't nuffin but er plum Afika monkey!"

Big Sixteen and the Devil

IT WAS slavery time, Zora, when Big Sixteen was a man. They called 'im Sixteen 'cause dat was de number of de shoe he wore. He was big and strong and Ole Massa looked to him to do everything.

One day Ole Massa said, "Big Sixteen, Ah b'lieve Ah want you to move dem sills Ah had hewed out down in de swamp."

"I yassuh, Massa."

Big Sixteen went down in de swamp and picked up dem 12×12's and brought 'em on up to de house and stack 'em. No one man ain't never toted a 12×12 befo' nor since.

So Ole Massa said one day, "Go fetch in de mules. Ah want to look 'em over."

Big Sixteen went on down to de pasture and caught dem mules by de bridle but they was contrary and balky and he tore de bridles to pieces pullin' on 'em, so he picked one of 'em up under each arm and brought 'em up to Ole Massa.

He says, "Big Sixteen, if you kin tote a pair of balky mules, you kin do anything. You kin ketch de Devil."

"Yassuh, Ah kin, if you git me a nine-pound hammer and a pick and shovel!"

From *Mules and Men*, by Zora Neale Hurston, pp. 207–208. Copyright, 1935, by Zora Neale Hurston. Philadelphia and London: J. B. Lippincott Company.

Ole Massa got Sixteen de things he ast for and tole 'im to go ahead and bring him de Devil.

Big Sixteen went out in front of de house and went to diggin'. He was diggin' nearly a month befo' he got where he wanted. Then he took his hammer and went and knocked on de Devil's door. Devil answered de door hisself.

"Who dat out dere?"

"It's Big Sixteen."

"What you want?"

"Wanta have a word wid you for a minute."

Soon as de Devil poked his head out de door, Sixteen lammed him over de head wid dat hammer and picked 'im up and carried 'im back to Ole Massa.

Ole Massa looked at de dead Devil and hollered, "Take dat ugly thing 'way from here, quick! Ah didn't think you'd ketch de Devil sho 'nuff."

So Sixteen picked up de Devil and throwed 'im back down de hole.

'Way after while, Big Sixteen died and went up to Heben. But Peter looked at him and tole 'im to g'wan 'way from dere. He was too powerful. He might git outa order and there wouldn't be nobody to handle 'im. But he had to go somewhere so he went on to hell.

Soon as he got to de gate de Devil's children was playin' in de yard and they seen 'im and run to de house, says, "Mama, mama! Dat man's out dere dat kilt papa!"

So she called 'im in de house and shet de door. When Sixteen got dere she handed 'im a li'l piece of fire and said, "You ain't comin' in here. Here, take dis hot coal and g'wan off and start you a hell uh yo' own."

So when you see a Jack O'Lantern in de woods at night you know it's Big Sixteen wid his piece of fire lookin' for a place to go.

Jack-O-My Lantern: A Maryland Version

ONE day wuz a man name Jack. He wuz a mighty weeked man, an' treat his wife an' chil'en like a dawg. He didn' do nuthin' but drink from mawin' tell night, an' twarn' no use to say nuthin' 'tall to 'im 'cause he wuz jus' es ambitious es a mad dawg. Well suh, he drink an' he drink tel whiskey couldn' mek 'im drunk; but et las' hit bu'n 'im up inside, an' den de Debble come fur 'im. When Jack see the Debble, he wuz so skeart he leetle mo'n er drapt in de flo'. Den he bague de Debble to let 'im off jes' a leetle while, but de Debble say:

"Naw, Jack, I ain' gwine wait no longer; my wife, Abbie Sheens, is speckin' yo'." So de Debble start off pretty bris' an' Jack wuz bleeged

From *Folk-Lore from Maryland,* collected by Annie Weston Whitney and Caroline Canfield Bullock, Memoirs of the American Folk-Lore Society, Volume XVIII, 1925, pp. 181–183. New York.

to foller tell dey come to a grog shop. "Mr. Debble," said Jack, "don' yo' wan' a drink?" "Well," said de Debble, "I b'leeve I does, but ain' got no small change; we don' keep no change down dyah." "Tell you wotcher do, Mr. Debble," said Jack, "I got one ten cent en my pocket; yo' change yo' sef inter'nurr ten cent, and we kin git two drinks, and den yo' kin change yo' sef back again." So de Debble change hisse'f inter a ten cent, and Jack pick 'im put, but 'stid o' gwine de grog shop, Jack clap de ten cent inter he pocket-book dat he hadn't took outen he pocket befo', 'cause he didn' wan' de Debble to see dat de ketch wuz in de shape ob a cross. He shet it tight, an' dyah he had de Debble, an' twarn' no use for 'im to struggle, 'cause he couldn' git by dat cross. Well suh; fus he swar and threat'n Jack wid wat he wuz going to do to 'im and den he begun to bague, but Jack jes' ta'n round an' start to go home. Den de Debble say:

"Jack, ef yo'll lemme out o' hyah, I'll let yo' off fur a whole year. I will, fur trufe. Lemme go, Jack, 'cause Abbie Sheens is too lazy to put the bresh on de fire, an' hit'll all go black out ef I ain' dyah fo' long ten' to it."

Den Jack say ter hisse'f, "I gret min' to let 'im go, 'cause in a whole year, I kin 'pent and git 'ligion, an' git shet in 'im dat er way."

Den he say, "Mr. Debble, I'll letcher out ef yo' 'clar fo' gracious yo' won't come after me fur tweel month."

Den de Debble promise befo' Jack undo de clasp, an' by de time Jack got the pocket-book open he wuz gone. Den Jack say to hisse'f, "Well, now I gwine to 'pent and git 'ligion sho'; but 'haint no use bein' in no hurry; de las' six mont' will be plenty o' time. Whar dat ten cent? Hyah it is. I gwine git me a drink." When de six mont' was gone, Jack 'lowed one mont' would be time 'nuff to 'pent, and when de las' mont' come, Jack 'lowed he gwine hab one mo' spree, and den he would have a week or ten days lef', and dat was plenty of time, 'cause 'e done hearn o' folks 'penting on dey death bade. Den he went on a spree for sho', and when de las' week come, Jack had 'lirium trimblins, and de fus' ting he knowed, dyah wuz de Debble at de do', and Jack had to git outen he bade and go 'long wid 'im. After a while dey pass a tree full o' gret big apples.

"Don' yo' want some apples, Mr. Debble?" said Jack.

"Yo' kin git some ef yo' wan' 'em," said de Debble and he stop and look up in de tree.

"How yo' 'spec' a man wid 'lirium trimblins to climb a tree?" said Jack. "Yo' catch hol' de bough, an' I'll push yer up in de crotch, an' den yo' kin git all yo' wants."

So Jack push 'im in de crotch, an' de Debble 'gin to feel de apples to git a meller one. While he wuz doin' dat, Jack, he whip he knife outen he pocket, an' cut a cross in de bark ob de tree jes' under de Debble, and de Debble holler, "Tzip! Sumpi' nurr heet me den. Wotcher doin' down dyah, Jack? I gwine cut yo' heart out."

But he couldn' git down while dat cross wuz dyah, an' Jack jes' sat down on de grass, an' watch 'im ragin' an' swarin' an' cussin'. Jack keep 'im dyah all night, tell 'twuz gret big day, an' de Debble change he chune an' he say:

"Jack, lemme git down hyah an' I'll gib yo' nurr year."

"Gimme nuttin'," said Jack, an' he stretch hisse'f out on de grass. After a while, 'bout sun up, de Debble say:

"Jack, cut dis ting offen hyah, an' lemme git down, an' I'll gib yo' ten year."

"Naw, surre," said Jack, "I won' letcher git down less yo' clar fo' gracious dat yo' won' never come arfter me no mo'."

When de Debble fin' Jack wuz es hard as rock, he 'greed, an' 'clared fo' gracious dat he wouldn' never come fur Jack agin, an' Jack cut de cross offen the tree, an' de Debble lef' widout a word. Arfter dat Jack never thought no mo' 'bout 'pentin', 'cause he warn' feared ob de Debble, an' he didn' wan' to go whar dey warn' no whiskey. Den he lib on tell he body war out, an he wuz bleeged to die. Fus' he went to de gate o' heaven but de angel jes' shake he hade. Den he went to de gate o' hell, but when it would come dat Jack wuz dyah, de Debble holler to de imps:

"Shet de do' an' don' let dat man come in hyah; he done treat me scan'lous. Tell 'im to go long back whar he come from."

Den Jack say:

"How I gwine fine my way back in de dark? Gimme a lantern."

Den de Debble tek a chunk outen de fire, an' say, "Hyah, tek dis, an' dontcher nuver come back hyah no mo'."

Samson and Satan

SATAN said to Samson, "They tell me that you are the strongest man in the world." Samson says, "Yes, I s'pose I am. Let us to-day try our strength." Satan said to Samson, "I will fus' try de hammer dat knock upon anvil." Samson says to Satan, "T'row dat hammer up, see how high you can t'row it." He t'rowed it seventy-five miles. Samson says, "Why, Satan, have you another hammer?" He says, "Why, yes!" He says, "What's the name of that hammer?"—"De one dat we wel's ahn (weld iron) with." He says, "How high can you t'row dat one?"—"Oh," he says, " 'bout a hundred miles."—"Oh," he says, "you can't t'row at all. I t'ought you was a man." He says, "Now, Satan, you stan' back! you ahn't a man at all." Samson steps an' takes up de anvil an' looks up ter de skies, an' said, "Michaei an' Rafeel an' all de holy angils," he says, "stan' back, because here comes de anvil!" An' when he swing de anvil twice, Satan said to Samson, he said, "Don' do that! Save heaven an' de hos'." He said, "If you knock 'em outer existence, what shall we do fe livin'?"

From "Folk-Tales Collected at Miami, Fla.," by Elsie Clews Parsons, *The Journal of American Folk-Lore*, Vol. XXX (April-June, 1917), No. CXVI, p. 223. Copyright, 1917, by the American Folk-Lore Society. New York.

The Devil Marriage

ONE time a lady said she was never goin' to marry a man unless he was dressed in gol'. Her father had a party,[1] en a man came dressed in gol'. Somebody at the gate. Man's son ran out, car'ed him to where the ol' people were. "Look as if you was havin' some to do here."—"Yes," said the man of the house, "you better go an' take part with them." Man's daughter took man dressed in gol' for her partner. Little boy about twelve noticed him, en said, "Sister, don't you notice his feet?"—"What's wrong? Why, no!"—"Why, sister, they ain't nothin' but nubbed.[2] Notice them when he get playin'. You ask moder what's the matter wi' his feet."—"Frien', what's de matter wi' your feet?"—"I fell in the fire when I was a little feller like you, en my feet got burned off." Now his hand burned too. He said he fell in the soap-pot when he was a small boy.[3] He fixed to be married. Dat night said he mus' go home. He kyar'ed dat man's daughter back with him. She says, "You let brother go with me. I'm goin' to a strange place. I like to have some of my people goin' with me." Little boy says, "Sister, don't you notice how he done? When he got up in his buggy, he throw out an aigg. He say, 'Hop en skip. Betty, go 'long.'" Betty des flew. He went until he came to where was a great big smoke. Girl said, "Mister, what sort of a big smoke? I can't go through dat smoke."—"Oh, dat my han's burnin' off new groun'. I go en lay that smoke."—"Sister, don't you take notice what he said. 'Hop, skip, Betty,' 'till we come to this smoke. He stop Betty, he lay this smoke. Is you willin' to go back home with me, sister? That ain't nothin' in de worl' but the Devil." Brother threw out an aigg, en said, "Wheel, Betty!" En Betty wheel. "Betty, go 'long! Hop en skip!" En Betty flew back home to her father. En behol'! next mornin' what should we see but the Devil comin'.[4] He went up to de gate. He says,[5]—

From "Tales from Guilford County, North Carolina," by Elsie Clews Parsons, *The Journal of American Folk-Lore,* Vol. XXX (April-June, 1917), No. CXVI, pp. 181-183. Copyright, 1917, by the American Folk-Lore Society. New York.

Informant, Carter Young. About 70. Father of Lulu, Nancy, and Katherine Young. Born in Guilford County; but he has lived in Alabama, Georgia, Mississippi. Heard by my informant at Macon, Ga. Compare Jones, XXXIV; MAFLS 2: 69; Parsons, XXIII; Pub. Folk-Lore Soc. 55:XXXIV, L.—E. C. P.

[1] *Variant:* Her father, the king, gave a big dance. This variant and the following were told me by Young's daughter Katherine, who had heard the tale only from her father.—E. C. P.

[2] *Variant:* Clubbed.—E. C. P.

[3] *Variant:* His father was making a plant-bed, and he ran through. His mother was making a pot o' lye, and he grabbed in it.—E. C. P.

[4] Ol' Betty turned an' went back to his master. That man know that Betty turn up to dat lady's house an' car'ed her home. He gettin' in his cheriot an' come back as hard as he could.—E. C. P.

[5] Young chanted the following. Obviously he had originally heard it sung.—E. C. P.

"Enbody here?
Enbody here?
Name Ma'y Brown
Genral Cling town." [1]

Ol' witch [2] says,—

"Somebody here,
Somebody here.
Name Ma'y Brown
Genral Cling town.

"What is whiter,
What is whiter,
Than any sheep's down
In Genral Cling town?

"Snow is whiter,
Snow is whiter,
Than any sheep's down
In Genral Cling town.

"What is greener,
What is greener,
Than any wheat growed
In Genral Cling town?

"Grass is greener,
Grass is greener,
Than any wheat growed
In Genral Cling town.

"What is bluer,
What is bluer,
Than anything down
In Genral Cling town?

"The sky is bluer,
The sky is bluer,
Than anything down
In Genral Cling town.

"What is louder,
What is louder,
Than any horns down
In Genral Cling town?

[1] That was hell.—E. C. P.

[2] *Variant:* The lady brother went an' got an ol' woman who could answer thav ul' man's questions. If that ol' woman couldn't have answered one of them questions, she'd [he'd] have got that girl.—E. C. P.

"Thunder is louder,
Thunder is louder,
Than any horns down
In Genral Cling town." [1]

Ol' Bad Man (ol' Scratch) said he won her soul. Ol' witch taken sole off shoe en throw at him. He jumped at it en took it down.[2]

Balaam Foster's Fiddle

BACK in de olden times all de music in dese parts was made by nigger fiddlers or banjo pickers or guitar players. Ever' plantation nuster have two or three real good ones to play for de white folks' dances an' parties. Hit was good pickin' for a man what hadn't been converted—co'se now, fiddlin' never was de thing for a man atter he bawned ag'in—but de fiddler boys would be give' a good dinner an' drinks an' ginally a han'ful of money too. Natchelly, mos' de young bucks want to be fiddlers.

Now dis hyah Balaam was as likely a boy as ever been raise in dis part de country, so I been tole. He six foot tall an' able to do a power o' work. All de 'oomans crazy 'bout him, but he ain' never stick to one un 'em mo'n a week at a time. All he care 'bout was dat fiddle of his'n. He fiddle from mawnin' till night, den fiddle right on atter de las' rooster crow. He could beat anybody else fiddlin', but he want to say satisfy. He say he gwine be de bes' fiddler in de whole worl', let 'lone de country. Everybody tell him 'tain't no nuse to try to git any better, 'cause he done able to outfiddle anybody else what had ever been hear tell of. He already playin' to all de white folks' dances an' totin' silver money in he pocket an' tu'nin' up he nose at de other niggers.

Well, one day he gone down by de creek wid he fiddle in he han' lak he allus use to tote it. He set down top of a stump an' he start studyin'. He say to hisse'f, "I shore wisht I could play dis here fiddle like I wanta play it. Co'se I know I got all dese here other niggers beat, but I want to show 'em some real fiddlin'!"

Wid dat he taken an' scrape a few sof' notes on he fiddle an' say, "Ole fiddle, you do very well now, but I aims to make you natchelly talk one dese days."

De words want out'n he mout' 'fo' a voice come right out de fiddle an' say, "If you wants me to talk, Balaam, I talkin' now. What you want me to say?"

When he hear dat voice in de fiddle, Balaam mos' drop it out'n he han',

---

[1] Compare JAFL 12:129, 130.—E. C. P. Also "Riddles Wisely Expounded" (Child, No. 1).

[2] *Variant:* He said, "Skip er light, Betty, an' go 'long."—E. C. P.

By Chapman J. Milling.

he so scared, but he git up 'nough strengt' to answer de voice back. "Ole fiddle," he say, "I'll tell you what I want. I want you to make us 'nough money to buy us freedom. Den you'n me'll go all over de country an' see all sorts of places an' have all de licker us wants."

"All right," say de fiddle, "but you cain't play good 'nough yet, Balaam. You jes startin' good. You shore is got to git better dan you is now."

"Why, I lowed I could play pretty good now," say Balaam.

"Pretty good ain't to say plum good," say de fiddle.

"What I hafta do to git plum good?" Balaam ax.

"Nuttin' much," say de voice. "All you got to do is to go to de cross-roads ever' night for nine nights an' make a crossmark in de middle o' de road. On de las' night you make de mark somebody'll be dar to tell you what to do nex'." Atter dis de fiddle ain't speak no mo'.

Balaam set an' he study, an' de longer he set de mo he study. Somep'm tell him dat if he follow dat voice out de fiddle he'll be los' in sin, but when he done 'bout 'cide not to go somep'm else 'suade him it ain' no harm nohow. So he set dar a rasslin' wid dem two notion' till dark catch him 'fo' he knowed it. Den he git up an' start for home still a-studyin'. He study so hard he ain't pay no min' whar he gwine, an' fus' news you know dar he been in de middle o' de crossroads. He git kinda frighten' when he fin' hisse'f dar, but he taken he fiddle an' he play a chune or two right dar in de middle o' de road, an' when he finish playin' he taken he foot an' mark a cross right whar de two roads meet. Jes as he make de mark he hear a noise an' when he look up dar been a great big ole rabbit a-settin' side de road in de moonlight, an' a-lookin' straight atter him. Balaam ain't like de looks o' dat rabbit, but he make out he ain't scared, so's he retch down an' heave a rock at him. De rock miss de rabbit an' jes as Balaam tu'n to leave hit seem like he hear dat rabbit say somep'm 'bout he'd fiddle better Friday atter nex'. Den he gone on home.

De nex' day Balaam ain't no good for work. He jes set 'roun' an' play chunes on he fiddle, mournful an' scary like. An' dat night he take an' ramble off, an' whar you reckon he win' up? De crossroads, you mought know!

When he git dar Balaam say to hisse'f, "Shorely can't be no harm makin' jes one mo' cross-mark. Maybe I'll go to de big meetin' nex' fall an' dat'll make it all right." So's he gone on an' taken he foot an' make 'nother cross-mark right whar he make de one de night befo'. An' jes as he turn 'roun' to go dar been dat same ole rabbit a settin' in de moonlight a-laughin' at him. But Balaam a bol' fellow, 'cause he taken an' throw another rock at him jes like he done de night befo', but it ain't do no good, 'cause he miss him ag'in. An' atter he throw de rock, he ain't sure, but seem like to Balaam dat de rabbit say de same thing as las' night 'bout he fiddlin'.

Dis here business kep' up for six mo' nights, an' Balaam study so much people think he gittin' mindless. Ever' night he slip out an' head for de crossroads, an' ever' time he git dar he make some 'scuse to go on an' make de cross-mark. An' ever' single time he make de mark he see dat same ole rabbit laughin' at him when he tu'n 'roun'.

De las' day Balaam study so much dat he mos' crazy sho nough. He play he fiddle all day long an' set 'roun' an' look 'way off. De Cap'm sen' for de doctor to fin' out what ail Balaam, but all he do was to gin him a big dose of physic salts. De Cap'm ax him what ail Balaam an' de doctor tell him ain't nuttin' ail him less'n he hoodooed. So de Cap'm think he all right an' gone on off an' lef' him 'lone.

Well, dat night Balaam slip off ag'in an' he head straight for de cross-roads dis time. He walk fas' an' when he git dar he make he cross-mark quick, so's he won't have time to change he min'. Atter he make de mark hit didn' look like nuttin' gwine happen an' Balaam begin to breave easy when he hear somebody call he name. He look up an' shore 'nough dar been dat same ole rabbit a-settin' right whar he allus set.

"I gwine to git you dis time," Balaam holler, an' wid dat he grab up a rock an' sail it at dat air rabbit hard as he could let her fly. But de rock sail right on th'oo dat rabbit. When he seen dat, Balaam gin a screech an' make a grab at 'nother rock, but he han' was strike to he side an' de rabbit jes disappear. In he place Balaam see a black cloud full of smoke an' sulphur, an he hear a fiddle comin' from de cloud an' a voice singin':

> "Munanee, munanee ho!
> Munanee, munanee ho!
> Munanee, munanee ho!
> Big pot o' mush I gwine to git dar."

Wid dat de cloud part in two an' out step de natchel ole Bugger Man hisse'f, lookin' jes like people say he look. He had a long tail wid a arrer pint, he hoofs was clove an' he tote a long, slim, narrer li'l pitch-fork. He look to be 'bout six foot tall an' he had on a black robe line wid red velvet on de inside. He step out an' bow perlite like white-folks an' he say,

"Evenin', Mister Foster, sho is a pretty fiddle you got dar. I hears dat you'd like to be able to play a li'l better dan you been a-playin'. Now you jes lemme hol' yo' fiddle a minute an' I'll show you some rale playin'. I de inventor of de fiddle, you know."

By dis time Balaam so scared he han' he fiddle right over to de Bugger Man. De ole Bugger Man take he fiddle an' bow low an' switch he tail sassy like, an' start in for to play. An' de chunes he didn't git out'n dat fiddle. He make de air natchelly ring like silver bells; he make hit soun' like all de mockin'-birds in de whole worl' a-bustin' dey th'oats at de same time. He make hit soun' like cow-bells late in de evenin' an' de song of little frogs down by de mill pon'. He make dat fiddle sob an' cry. Hit soun' like a 'ooman moanin' for her los' man. Hit soun' like people singin' acrost still water. Den he turnt 'roun' an' play dance chunes an' reels an' Balaam jes can't stan' it less'n he stomp an' pat he han'.

When de Bugger Man done playin' it want nuttin' Balaam wouldn't give to be able to play dat-a-way, an' when de Bugger Man ax him would he 'gree to whatever he say, Balaam say, "Sho I will!" So right den an' dar de Bugger Man make Balaam promise him he'd serve him all he life an' let him have he soul when he die. To bin' de promise, Balaam have to bow down to Satan an' receive de serpent mark on he lef' shoulder. He have to eat a moufful of powder Satan give him an' he have to swaller some of Satan' spit. When he do all dem things de Bugger Man han' him back he fiddle an' disappear right 'fo' he eyes th'oo a hole in de groun' what open up whar he standin'. When he drap outa sight a great smoke come out de hole an' flames belch fo'th an' Balaam smell sulphur an' brimstone.

Balaam so scared by dis time dat he mos' forgit he fiddle, but in a minute he 'member it an' he taken an' try a chune or so. He fin' when he done dat dat he could play jes as good as de Bugger Man. Dat make him so happy he git over bein' scared an' he gone on home an' gone to bed. De nex' day he take he fiddle up an' fin' he kin still play jes as good as de Bugger Man, an' dat make him so proud he glad of he bargain.

It want long 'fo' ever'body axin' for Balaam to play, an' dey jes wouldn' be satisfy less'n he come. He reppertation gone all over de country. De ole Cap'm glad 'nough to let him go, 'cause he got so he want no good nohow for nuttin' 'cep'n fiddlin'. By'mby Balaam had save 'nough money to buy he freedom. He kep' on playin' for ever' dance an' party he hear 'bout. Hit git so he gone fifty an' a hundred mile 'way f'um home to play. He live to be a ole man, but nemmine how ole he been, he play jes as good as ever.

One day, atter Balaam no tellin' how ole, he call he ole 'ooman an' all he chillun an' gran'chillun 'roun' him, an' tell 'em he gwine die. He ain't look sick, an' he say he ain't feel sick, but he sho he time done come. Dey want to sen' for de doctor right away, but Balaam tell 'em it want no nuse. He say, dough, dat he got somep'm to tell 'em, an' when dey been all gether 'roun', he 'splain to 'em 'bout what happen dat night to de crossroads. When he tell 'em dat, dey all start to cry an' moan an' car' on, but Balaam ax 'em not to do dat-a-way, 'cause it ain' gwine do no good. When dey sorta quiet'n down he tell 'em dat when he die dey mus' lay him out, an' atter he be lay out a clap o' thunder would come, an' when dey hear dat dey mought know he soul had enter Tarment. Atter he tell 'em dat, hit seem like he feel better, an' he git outa de bed an' fetch he fiddle out de trunk an' start to play "Turkey in de Straw."

He play so good dat de mourners couldn't he'p pattin' an' stompin' to save dey souls. When he finish playin' he take de fiddle over to de trunk, lock de lid, an' throw de key in de fire. Den he walk back to de bed, lie down, an' breave he las'.

De mourners all stay quiet for a minute, den dey make sho he gone for true, an' dey put de money on he eye an' sen' for de preacher.

But whilst dey all a-standin' 'roun' lookin' at de co'pse, de fiddle in de trunk commence to play. Hit play de lonesomes' chunes you ever hear, an' ever' note hit play soun' like hit was sayin', "Po' los' soul! Po' los' soul!"

De people in de house couldn' stan' no sicha doin's, an' dey all make a break for de door. Soon's dey git outside de house dey git bolder, an' one de mens grab up a ax an' say he gwine in dar an' bus open dat trunk an' smash dat fiddle. De res' o' de people back him up an' say for him to go on in, so he spit on he han's an' take holda de ax like he mean business an' gone on back in de house. Time he outa sight de people outside hear a voice comin' out de house 'long wid de music o' de fiddle an' hit soun' like hit say:

> "Munanee, munanee ho!
> Munanee, munanee ho!
> Munanee, munanee ho!
> Big pot o' mush I gwine to git dar."

Jes' as soon as dat song stop dar come a turrible peal o' thunder an' de whole house shake same as de Charleston yearthquake. De man wid de ax come a-flyin' out like a mule done kick 'im. De lamp inside was blowed out an' de whole place smell like smoke. Atter while some de mens git bol' 'nough to go in an' see what had happen. But soon as dey git inside de ones outside hear 'em holler, "Whar Balaam?"

Wid dat de res' of de mens gone on in an' dey fin' dat, sho nough, de co'pse done gone, an' whar he been a-lyin' all de bed-clothes was scorch black as de chimbly-flue. Atter dey see Balaam' co'pse done gone dey think 'bout de fiddle an' gone over to de trunk, but it want no nuse o' dat. Dat trunk got a hole burn out de top big as a nail kag, an' hit was all scorch on de inside an' dat fiddle was gone for keeps. So dat was de een o' Balaam Foster an' he conjured fiddle.

Tell me nuttin' 'bout no fiddlin! Dese days dey got fiddles in de chu'ches an' ever'whars else, but us ole people what know 'bout Balaam, us ain't got no nuse for fiddlin'.

The Devil and Tom Walker

A FEW miles from Boston in Massachusetts, there is a deep inlet, winding several miles into the interior of the country from Charles Bay, and terminating in a thickly-wooded swamp or morass. On one side of this inlet is a beautiful dark grove; on the opposite side the land rises abruptly from the water's edge into a high ridge, on which grow a few scattered oaks

From *Tales of a Traveller*, by Geoffrey Crayon, Gent.,[n] pp. 376–392. Entered . . . , 1849, by Washington Irving. The Works of Washington Irving, New Edition, Revised, Volume VII. New York: George P. Putnam.

of great age and immense size. Under one of these gigantic trees, according
to old stories, there was a great amount of treasure buried by Kidd the
pirate. The inlet allowed a facility to bring the money in a boat secretly
and at night to the very foot of the hill; the elevation of the place permitted a good look-out to be kept that no one was at hand; while the
remarkable trees formed good landmarks by which the place might easily be
found again. The old stories add, moreover, that the devil presided at
the hiding of the money, and took it under his guardianship; but this it is
well known he always does with buried treasure, particularly when it has
been ill-gotten. Be that as it may, Kidd never returned to recover his
wealth; being shortly after seized at Boston, sent out to England, and
there hanged for a pirate.

About the year 1727, just at the time that earthquakes were prevalent
in New-England, and shook many tall sinners down upon their knees, there
lived near this place a meagre, miserly fellow, of the name of Tom Walker.
He had a wife as miserly as himself: they were so miserly that they even
conspired to cheat each other. Whatever the woman could lay hands on,
she hid away; a hen could not cackle but she was on the alert to secure
the new-laid egg. Her husband was continually prying about to detect
her secret hoards, and many and fierce were the conflicts that took place
about what ought to have been common property. They lived in a forlorn-
looking house that stood alone, and had an air of starvation. A few
straggling savin-trees, emblems of sterility, grew near it; no smoke ever
curled from its chimney; no traveller stopped at its door. A miserable
horse, whose ribs were as articulate as the bars of a gridiron, stalked about
a field, where a thin carpet of moss, scarcely covering the ragged beds of
puddingstone, tantalized and balked his hunger; and sometimes he would
lean his head over the fence, look piteously at the passer-by, and seem to
petition deliverance from this land of famine.

The house and its inmates had altogether a bad name. Tom's wife was
a tall termagant, fierce of temper, loud of tongue, and strong of arm. Her
voice was often heard in wordy warfare with her husband; and his face
sometimes showed signs that their conflicts were not confined to words.
No one ventured, however, to interfere between them. The lonely wayfarer
shrunk within himself at the horrid clamor and clapper-clawing; eyed the
den of discord askance; and hurried on his way, rejoicing, if a bachelor,
in his celibacy.

One day that Tom Walker had been to a distant part of the neighborhood, he took what he considered a short cut homeward, through the
swamp. Like most short cuts, it was an ill-chosen route. The swamp was
thickly grown with great gloomy pines and hemlocks, some of them ninety
feet high, which made it dark at noonday, and a retreat for all the owls
of the neighborhood. It was full of pits and quagmires, partly covered
with weeds and mosses, where the green surface often betrayed the
traveller into a gulf of black, smothering mud: there were also dark and
stagnant pools, the abodes of the tadpole, the bull-frog, and the water-

snake; where the trunks of pines and hemlocks lay half-drowned, half-rotting, looking like alligators sleeping in the mire.

Tom had long been picking his way cautiously through this treacherous forest; stepping from tuft to tuft of rushes and roots, which afforded precarious footholds among deep sloughs; or pacing carefully, like a cat, along the prostrate trunks of trees; startled now and then by the sudden screaming of the bittern, or the quacking of a wild duck, rising on the wing from some solitary pool. At length he arrived at a piece of firm ground, which ran out like a peninsula into the deep bosom of the swamp. It had been one of the strong-holds of the Indians during their wars with the first colonists. Here they had thrown up a kind of fort, which they had looked upon as almost impregnable, and had used as a place of refuge for their squaws and children. Nothing remained of the old Indian fort but a few embankments, gradually sinking to the level of the surrounding earth, and already overgrown in part by oaks and other forest trees, the foliage of which formed a contrast to the dark pines and hemlocks of the swamp.

It was late in the dusk of evening when Tom Walker reached the old fort, and he paused there awhile to rest himself. Any one but he would have felt unwilling to linger in this lonely, melancholy place, for the common people had a bad opinion of it, from the stories handed down from the time of the Indian wars; when it was asserted that the savages held incantations here, and made sacrifices to the evil spirit.

Tom Walker, however, was not a man to be troubled with any fears of the kind. He reposed himself for some time on the trunk of a fallen hemlock, listening to the boding cry of the tree toad, and delving with his walking staff into a mound of black mould at his feet. As he turned up the soil unconsciously, his staff struck against something hard. He raked it out of the vegetable mould, and lo! a cloven skull, with an Indian tomahawk buried deep in it, lay before him. The rust on the weapon showed the time that had elapsed since this death-blow had been given. It was a dreary memento of the fierce struggle that had taken place in this last foothold of the Indian warriors.

"Humph!" said Tom Walker, as he gave it a kick to shake the dirt from it.

"Let that skull alone!" said a gruff voice. Tom lifted up his eyes, and beheld a great black man seated directly opposite him, on the stump of a tree. He was exceedingly surprised, having neither heard nor seen any one approach; and he was still more perplexed on observing, as well as the gathering gloom would permit, that the stranger was neither negro nor Indian. It is true he was dressed in a rude half-Indian garb, and had a red belt or sash swathed round his body; but his face was neither black nor copper-color, but swarthy and dingy, and begrimed with soot, as if he had been accustomed to toil among fires and forges. He had a shock of coarse black hair, that stood out from his head in all directions, and bore an axe on his shoulder.

He scowled for a moment at Tom with a pair of great red eyes.

"What are you doing on my grounds?" said the black man, with a hoarse growling voice.

"Your grounds!" said Tom with a sneer, "no more your grounds than mine; they belong to Deacon Peabody."

"Deacon Peabody be d—d," said the stranger, "as I flatter myself he will be, if he does not look more to his own sins and less to those of his neighbors. Look yonder, and see how Deacon Peabody is faring."

Tom looked in the direction that the stranger pointed, and beheld one of the great trees, fair and flourishing without, but .otten at the core, and saw that it had been nearly hewn through, so that the first high wind was likely to blow it down. On the bark of the tree was scored the name of Deacon Peabody, an eminent man, who had waxed wealthy by driving shrewd bargains with the Indians. He now looked round, and found most of the tall trees marked with the name of some great man of the colony, and all more or less scored by the axe. The one on which he had been seated, and which had evidently just been hewn down, bore the name of Crowninshield; and he recollected a mighty rich man of that name, who made a vulgar display of wealth, which it was whispered he had acquired by buccaneering.

"He's just ready for burning!" said the black man, with a growl of triumph. "You see I am likely to have a good stock of firewood for winter."

"But what right have you," said Tom, "to cut down Deacon Peabody's timber?"

"The right of a prior claim," said the other. "This woodland belonged to me long before one of your white-faced race put foot upon the soil."

"And pray, who are you, if I may be so bold?" said Tom.

"Oh, I go by various names. I am the wild huntsman in some countries; the black miner in others. In this neighborhood I am known by the name of the black woodsman. I am he to whom the red men consecrated this spot, and in honor of whom they now and then roasted a white man, by way of sweet-smelling sacrifice. Since the red men have been exterminated by you white savages, I amuse myself by presiding at the persecutions of Quakers and Anabaptists; I am the great patron and prompter of slave-dealers, and the grand-master of the Salem witches."

"The upshot of all which is, that, if I mistake not," said Tom, sturdily, "you are he commonly called Old Scratch."

"The same, at your service!" replied the black man, with a half-civil nod.

Such was the opening of this interview, according to the old story; though it has almost too familiar an air to be credited. One would think that to meet with such a singular personage, in this wild, lonely place, would have shaken any man's nerves; but Tom was a hard-minded fellow, not easily daunted, and he had lived so long with a termagant wife, that he did not even fear the devil.

It is said that after this commencement they had a long and earnest conversation together, as Tom returned homeward. The black man told him of great sums of money buried by Kidd the pirate, under the oak-trees on the high ridge, not far from the morass. All these were under his command, and protected by his power, so that none could find them but such as propitiated his favor. These he offered to place within Tom Walker's reach, having conceived an especial kindness for him; but they were to be had only on certain conditions. What these conditions were may easily be surmised, though Tom never disclosed them publicly. They must have been very hard, for he required time to think of them, and he was not a man to stick at trifles where money was in view. When they had reached the edge of the swamp, the stranger paused—"What proof have I that all you have been telling me is true?" said Tom. "There is my signature," said the black man, pressing his finger on Tom's forehead. So saying, he turned off among the thickets of the swamp, and seemed, as Tom said, to go down, down, down, into the earth, until nothing but his head and shoulders could be seen, and so on, until he totally disappeared.

When Tom reached home, he found the black print of a finger, burnt, as it were, into his forehead, which nothing could obliterate.

The first news his wife had to tell him was the sudden death of Absalom Crowninshield, the rich buccaneer. It was announced in the papers with the usual flourish, that "A great man had fallen in Israel."

Tom recollected the tree which his black friend had just hewn down, and which was ready for burning. "Let the freebooter roast," said Tom, "who cares!" He now felt convinced that all he had heard and seen was no illusion.

He was not prone to let his wife into his confidence; but as this was an uneasy secret, he willingly shared it with her. All her avarice was awakened at the mention of hidden gold, and she urged her husband to comply with the black man's terms, and secure what would make them wealthy for life. However Tom might have felt disposed to sell himself to the Devil, he was determined not to do so to oblige his wife; so he flatly refused, out of the mere spirit of contradiction. Many and bitter were the quarrels they had on the subject, but the more she talked, the more resolute was Tom not to be damned to please her.

At length she determined to drive the bargain on her own account, and if she succeeded, to keep all the gain to herself. Being of the same fearless temper as her husband, she set off for the old Indian fort towards the close of a summer's day. She was many hours absent. When she came back, she was reserved and sullen in her replies. She spoke something of a black man, whom she had met about twilight, hewing at the root of a tall tree. He was sulky, however, and would not come to terms: she was to go again with a propitiatory offering, but what it was she forbore to say.

The next evening she set off again for the swamp, with her apron heavily laden. Tom waited and waited for her, but in vain; midnight came, but she did not make her appearance: morning, noon, night returned, but still she did not come. Tom now grew uneasy for her safety, especially as he found she had carried off in her apron the silver teapot and spoons, and every portable article of value. Another night elapsed, another morning came; but no wife. In a word, she was never heard of more.

What was her real fate nobody knows, in consequence of so many pretending to know. It is one of those facts which have become confounded by a variety of historians. Some asserted that she lost her way among the tangled mazes of the swamp, and sank into some pit or slough; others, more uncharitable, hinted that she had eloped with the household booty, and made off to some other province; while others surmised that the tempter had decoyed her into a dismal quagmire, on the top of which her hat was found lying. In confirmation of this, it was said a great black man, with an axe on his shoulder, was seen late that very evening coming out of the swamp, carrying a bundle tied in a check apron, with an air of surly triumph.

The most current and probable story, however, observes, that Tom Walker grew so anxious about the fate of his wife and his property, that he set out at length to seek them both at the Indian fort. During a long summer's afternoon he searched about the gloomy place, but no wife was to be seen. He called her name repeatedly, but she was nowhere to be heard. The bittern alone responded to his voice, as he flew screaming by; or the bull-frog croaked dolefully from a neighborhood pool. At length, it is said, just in the brown hour of twilight, when the owls began to hoot, and the bats to flit about, his attention was attracted by the clamor of carrion crows hovering about a cypress-tree. He looked up, and beheld a bundle tied in a check apron, and hanging in the branches of the tree, with a great vulture perched hard by, as if keeping watch upon it. He leaped with joy; for he recognized his wife's apron, and supposed it to contain the household valuables.

"Let us get hold of the property," said he, consolingly to himself, "and we will endeavor to do without the woman."

As he scrambled up the tree, the vulture spread its wide wings, and sailed off screaming into the deep shadows of the forest. Tom seized the check apron, but woful sight! found nothing but a heart and liver tied up in it!

Such, according to the most authentic old story, was all that was to be found of Tom's wife. She had probably attempted to deal with the black man as she had been accustomed to deal with her husband; but though a female scold is generally considered a match for the devil, yet in this instance she appears to have had the worst of it. She must have died game, however; for it is said Tom noticed many prints of cloven feet deeply stamped about the tree, and found handfuls of hair, that looked as if they had been plucked from the coarse black shock of the woodman. Tom knew his wife's prowess by experience. He shrugged his shoulders, as he looked at the signs of a fierce clapper-clawing. "Egad," said he to himself, "Old Scratch must have had a tough time of it!"

Tom consoled himself for the loss of his property, with the loss of his wife, for he was a man of fortitude. He even felt something like gratitude towards the black woodman, who, he considered, had done him a kindness. He sought, therefore, to cultivate a further acquaintance with him, but for some time without success; the old black-legs played shy, for whatever people may think, he is not always to be had for calling for: he knows how to play his cards when pretty sure of his game.

At length, it is said, when delay had whetted Tom's eagerness to the quick, and prepared him to agree to any thing rather than not gain the promised treasure, he met the black man one evening in his usual woodman's dress, with his axe on his shoulder, sauntering along the swamp, and humming a tune. He affected to receive Tom's advances with great indifference, made brief replies, and went on humming his tune.

By degrees, however, Tom brought him to business, and they began to haggle about the terms on which the former was to have the pirate's treasure. There was one condition which need not be mentioned, being generally understood in all cases where the devil grants favors; but there were others about which, though of less importance, he was inflexibly obstinate. He insisted that the money found through his means should be employed in his service. He proposed, therefore, that Tom should employ it in the black traffick; that is to say, that he should fit out a slave-ship. This, however, Tom resolutely refused: he was bad enough in all conscience; but the devil himself could not tempt him to turn slave-trader.

Finding Tom so squeamish on this point, he did not insist upon it, but proposed, instead, that he should turn usurer; the devil being extremely anxious for the increase of usurers, looking upon them as his peculiar people.

To this no objections were made, for it was just to Tom's taste.

"You shall open a broker's shop in Boston next month," said the black man.

"I'll do it to-morrow, if you wish," said Tom Walker.

"You shall lend money at two per cent a month."

"Egad, I'll charge four!" replied Tom Walker.

"You shall extort bonds, foreclose mortgages, drive the merchant to bankruptcy—"

"I'll drive him to the d—l," cried Tom Walker.

"You are the usurer for my money!" said the black-legs with delight, "When will you want the rhino?"

"This very night."

"Done!" said the devil.

"Done!" said Tom Walker.—So they shook hands and struck a bargain.

A few days' time saw Tom Walker seated behind his desk in a counting-house in Boston.

His reputation for a ready-moneyed man, who would lend money out for a good consideration, soon spread abroad. Everybody remembers the time of Governor Belcher, when money was particularly scarce. It was a time of paper credit. The country had been deluged with government bills; the famous Land Bank had been established; there had been a rage for speculating; the people had run mad with schemes for new settlements; for building cities in the wilderness; land-jobbers went about with maps of grants, and townships, and Eldorados, lying nobody knew where, but which everybody was ready to purchase. In a word, the great speculating fever which breaks out every now and then in the country, had raged to an alarming degree, and everybody was dreaming of making sudden fortunes from nothing. As usual the fever had subsided; the dream had gone off, and the imaginary fortunes with it; the patients were left in doleful plight, and the whole country resounded with the consequent cry of "hard times."

At this propitious time of public distress did Tom Walker set up as usurer in Boston. His door was soon thronged by customers. The needy and adventurous; the gambling speculator; the dreaming land-jobber; the thriftless tradesman; the merchant with cracked credit; in short, every one driven to raise money by desperate means and desperate sacrifices, hurried to Tom Walker.

Thus Tom was the universal friend of the needy, and acted like a "friend in need"; that is to say, he always exacted good pay and good security. In proportion to the distress of the applicant was the hardness of his terms. He accumulated bonds and mortgages; gradually squeezed his customers closer and closer: and sent them at length, dry as a sponge, from his door.

In this way he made money hand over hand; became a rich and mighty man, and exalted his cocked hat upon 'Change. He built himself, as usual, a vast house, out of ostentation; but left the greater part of it unfinished and unfurnished, out of parsimony. He even set up a carriage in the fulness of his vainglory, though he nearly starved the horses which drew it; and as the ungreased wheels groaned and screeched on the axle-trees, you would have thought you heard the souls of the poor debtors he was squeezing.

As Tom waxed old, however, he grew thoughtful. Having secured the good things of this world, he began to feel anxious about those of the next. He thought with regret on the bargain he had made with his black friend, and set his wits to work to cheat him out of the conditions. He became, therefore, all of a sudden, a violent church-goer. He prayed loudly and strenuously, as if heaven were to be taken by force of lungs. Indeed, one might always tell when he had sinned most during the week, by the clamor of his Sunday devotion. The quiet Christians who had been modestly and steadfastly travelling Zionward, were struck with self-reproach at seeing themselves so suddenly outstripped in their career by this new-made convert. Tom was as rigid in religious as in money matters; he was a stern supervisor and censurer of his neighbors, and seemed to think every sin entered up to their account became a credit on his own side of the page. He even talked of the expediency of reviving the persecution of Quakers and Anabaptists. In a word, Tom's zeal became as notorious as his riches.

Still, in spite of all this strenuous attention to forms, Tom had a lurking dread that the devil, after all, would have his due. That he might not be taken unawares, therefore, it is said he always carried a small Bible in his coat-pocket. He had also a great folio Bible on his counting-house desk, and would frequently be found reading it when people called on business; on such occasions he would lay his green spectacles in the book, to mark the place, while he turned round to drive some usurious bargain.

Some say that Tom grew a little crack-brained in his old days, and that fancying his end approaching, he had his horse new shod, saddled and bridled, and buried with his feet uppermost; because he supposed that at the last day the world would be turned upside down; in which case he should find his horse standing ready for mounting, and he was determined at the worst to give his old friend a run for it. This, however, is probably a mere old wives' fable. If he really did take such a precaution, it was totally superfluous; at least so says the authentic old legend, which closes his story in the following manner.

One hot summer afternoon in the dog-days, just as a terrible black thundergust was coming up, Tom sat in his counting-house in his white linen cap and India silk morning-gown. He was on the point of foreclosing a mortgage, by which he would complete the ruin of an unlucky land speculator for whom he had professed the greatest friendship. The poor land-jobber begged him to grant a few months' indulgence. Tom had grown testy and irritated and refused another day.

"My family will be ruined and brought upon the parish," said the land-jobber. "Charity begins at home," replied Tom; "I must take care of myself in these hard times."

"You have made so much money out of me," said the speculator.

Tom lost his patience and his piety—"The devil take me," said he, "if I have made a farthing!"

Just then there were three loud knocks at the street door. He stepped out to see who was there. A black man was holding a black horse, which neighed and stamped with impatience.

"Tom, you're come for," said the black fellow, gruffly. Tom shrunk back, but too late. He had left his little Bible at the bottom of his coat-pocket, and his big Bible on the desk buried under the mortgage he was about to foreclose: never was sinner taken more unawares. The black man whisked him like a child into the saddle, gave the horse the lash, and away he galloped, with Tom on his back, in the midst of the thunderstorm. The clerks stuck their pens behind their ears, and stared after him from the windows. Away went Tom Walker, dashing down the streets; his white cap bobbing up and down; his morning-gown fluttering in the wind, and his steed striking fire out of the pavement at every bound. When the clerks turned to look for the black man he had disappeared.

Tom Walker never returned to foreclose the mortgage. A countryman who lived on the border of the swamp, reported that in the height of the thundergust he had heard a great clattering of hoofs and a howling along the road, and running to the window caught sight of a figure, such as I have described, on a horse that galloped like mad across the fields, over the hills and down into the black hemlock swamp towards the old Indian fort; and that shortly after a thunderbolt falling in that direction seemed to set the whole forest in a blaze.

The good people of Boston shook their heads and shrugged their shoulders, but had been so much accustomed to witches and goblins and tricks of the devil, in all kind of shapes from the first settlement of the colony, that they were not so much horror-struck as might have been expected. Trustees were appointed to take charge of Tom's effects. There was nothing, however, to administer upon. On searching his coffers all his bonds and mortgages were found reduced to cinders. In place of gold and silver his iron chest was filled with chips and shavings; two skeletons lay in his stable instead of his half-starved horses, and the very next day his great house took fire and was burnt to the ground.

Such was the end of Tom Walker and his ill-gotten wealth. Let all griping money-brokers lay this story to heart. The truth of it is not to be doubted. The very hole under the oak-trees, whence he dug Kidd's money, is to be seen to this day; and the neighboring swamp and old Indian fort are often haunted in stormy nights by a figure on horseback, in morning-gown and white cap, which is doubtless the troubled spirit of the usurer. In fact, the story has resolved itself into a proverb, and is the origin of that popular saying, so prevalent throughout New England, of "The Devil and Tom Walker."

Why Spuyten Duyvil Is So Named

THE tide-water creek that forms the upper boundary of Manhattan Island is known to dwellers in tenements round about as "Spittin' Divvle." The proper name of it is Spuyten Duyvil, and this, in turn, is the compression of a celebrated boast by Anthony Van Corlaer. This redoubtable gentleman, famous for fat, long wind, and long whiskers, was trumpeter for the garrison at New Amsterdam, which his countryman had just bought for twenty-four dollars, and he sounded the brass so sturdily that in the fight between the Dutch and Indians at the Dey Street peach orchard his blasts struck more terror into the red men's hearts than did the matchlocks of his comrades. William the Testy vowed that Anthony and his trumpet were garrison enough for all Manhattan Island, for he argued that no regiment of Yankees would approach near enough to be struck with lasting deafness, as must have happened if they came when Anthony was awake.

Peter Stuyvesant—Peter the Headstrong—showed his appreciation of

From *Myths and Legends of Our Own Land*, by Charles M. Skinner, Vol. I, pp. 51–52. Copyright, 1896, by J. B. Lippincott Company. Philadelphia and London.

Anthony's worth by making him his esquire, and when he got news of an English expedition on its way to seize his unoffending colony, he at once ordered Anthony to rouse the villages along the Hudson with a trumpet call to war. The esquire took a hurried leave of six or eight ladies, each of whom delighted to believe that his affections were lavished on her alone, and bravely started northward, his trumpet hanging on one side, a stone bottle, much heavier, depending from the other. It was a stormy evening when he arrived at the upper end of the island, and there was no ferryman in sight, so, after fuming up and down the shore, he swallowed a mighty draught of Dutch courage,—for he was as accomplished a performer on the horn as on the trumpet,—and swore with ornate and voluminous oaths that he would swim the stream "in spite of the devil" [En spuyt den Duyvil].

He plunged in, and had gone half-way across when the Evil One, not to be spited, appeared as a huge moss-bunker, vomiting boiling water and lashing a fiery tail. This dreadful fish seized Anthony by the leg; but the trumpeter was game, for, raising his instrument to his lips, he exhaled his last breath through it in a defiant blast that rang through the woods for miles and made the devil himself let go for a moment. Then he was dragged below, his nose shining through the water more and more faintly, until, at last, all sight of him was lost. The failure of his mission resulted in the downfall of the Dutch in America, for, soon after, the English won a bloodless victory, and St. George's cross flaunted from the ramparts where Anthony had so often saluted the setting sun. But it was years, even then, before he was hushed, for in stormy weather it was claimed that the shrill of his trumpet could be heard near the creek that he had named, sounding above the deeper roar of the blast.

VI. QUEER TALES

GHOSTLY and devilish adventures like those of Peter Rugg and Dowsabel Casselman and curious relations between people and animals as in the stories of "The Lobo Girl of Devil's River" and "Gretchen and the White Steed" carry over from folk tales to local legends. Many of the latter are adaptations of migratory legends. Thus "Peter Rugg, the Missing Man" is a landlubber version of the Flying Dutchman, and "The Lobo Girl of Devil's River" relates to the world-wide legend of wolf-children.

Approaching fiction in the individuality of their characterization and setting, tales like these stand out above the lovers'-leap type of local legend; and yet for all their bizarreness they do not, like many a literary treatment of legend, smell of the lamp. Recalling the saga (e.g., Dick Whittington) type of folk tale, they lend enchantment to history. Defoe might have written of Peter Rugg; Irving, of Dowsabel Casselman; and Frank Stockton, of the Lobo Girl.

Peter Rugg, the Missing Man

(From Jonathan Dunwell of New York to Mr. Herman Krauff)

SIR,—Agreeably to my promise, I now relate to you all the particulars of the lost man and child which I have been able to collect. It is entirely owing to the humane interest you seemed to take in the report that I have pursued the inquiry to the following result.

You may remember that business called me to Boston in the summer of 1820. I sailed in the packet to Providence; and when I arrived there, 1 learned that every seat in the stage was engaged. I was thus obliged either to wait a few hours, or accept a seat with the driver, who civilly offered me that accommodation. Accordingly I took my seat by his side, and soon found him intelligent and communicative. When we had travelled about ten miles, the horses suddenly threw their ears on their necks as flat as a hare's. Said the driver, "Have you a surtout with you?"

"No," said I; "why do you ask?"

"You will want one soon," said he. "Do you observe the ears of all the horses?"

"Yes"; and was just about to ask the reason.

"They see the storm-breeder, and we shall see him soon."

At this moment there was not a cloud visible in the firmament; soon after a small speck appeared in the road.

"There," said my companion, "comes the storm-breeder; he always leaves a Scotch mist behind him. By many a wet jacket do I remember him. I suppose the poor fellow suffers much himself—much more than is known to the world."

Presently a man with a child beside him, with a large black horse and a weather-beaten chair, once built for a chaise-body, passed in great haste, apparently at the rate of twelve miles an hour. He seemed to grasp the reins of his horse with firmness, and appeared to anticipate his speed. He seemed dejected, and looked anxiously at the passengers, particularly at the stage-driver and myself. In a moment after he passed us, the horses' ears were up, and bent themselves forward so that they nearly met.

"Who is that man?" said I; "he seems in great trouble."

"Nobody knows who he is; but his person and the child are familiar to me. I have met him more than a hundred times, and have been so often asked the way to Boston by that man, even when he was travelling directly from that town, that of late I have refused any communication with him; and that is the reason he gave me such a fixed look."

"But does he never stop anywhere?"

By William Austin. From *A Book of New England Legends and Folk Lore in Prose and Poetry*, by Samuel Adams Drake, pp. 90–105. Copyright, 1883, by Samuel Adams Drake. Boston: Roberts Brothers.

"I have never known him to stop anywhere longer than to inquire the way to Boston. And let him be where he may, he will tell you he cannot stay a moment, for he must reach Boston that night."

We were now ascending a high hill in Walpole; and as we had a fair view of the heavens, I was rather disposed to jeer the driver for thinking of his surtout, as not a cloud as big as a marble could be discerned.

"Do you look," said he, "in the direction whence the man came; that is the place to look. The storm never meets him, it follows him."

We presently approached another hill; and when at the height the driver pointed out in an eastern direction a little black speck about as big as a hat,—"There," said he, "is the seed storm; we may possibly reach Polley's before it reaches us, but the wanderer and his child will go to Providence through rain, thunder, and lightning."

And now the horses, as though taught by instinct, hastened with increased speed. The little black cloud came on rolling over the turnpike, and doubled and trebled itself in all directions. The appearance of this cloud attracted the notice of all the passengers; for after it had spread itself to a great bulk, it suddenly became more limited in circumference, grew more compact, dark, and consolidated. And now the successive flashes of chain lightning caused the whole cloud to appear like a sort of irregular network, and displayed a thousand fantastic images. The driver bespoke my attention to a remarkable configuration in the cloud; he said every flash of lightning near its centre discovered to him distinctly the form of a man sitting in an open carriage drawn by a black horse. But in truth I saw no such thing. The man's fancy was doubtless at fault. It is a very common thing for the imagination to paint for the senses, both in the visible and invisible world.

In the mean time the distant thunder gave notice of a shower at hand; and just as we reached Polley's tavern the rain poured down in torrents. It was soon over, the cloud passing in the direction of the turnpike toward Providence. In a few moments after, a respectable-looking man in a chaise stopped at the door. The man and child in the chair having excited some little sympathy among the passengers, the gentleman was asked if he had observed them. He said he had met them; that the man seemed bewildered, and inquired the way to Boston; that he was driving at great speed, as though he expected to outstrip the tempest; that the moment he had passed him, a thunder-clap broke directly over the man's head, and seemed to envelop both man and child, horse and carriage. "I stopped," said the gentleman, "supposing the lightning had struck him; but the horse only seemed to loom up and increase his speed; and as well as I could judge, he traveled just as fast as the thunder-cloud."

While this man was speaking, a pedlar with a cart of tin merchandise came up all dripping; and on being questioned, he said he had met that man and carriage, within a fortnight, in four different States; that at each time he had inquired the way to Boston, and that a thunder-shower, like the present, had each time deluged his wagon and his wares, setting his tinpots, etc., afloat, so that he had determined to get marine insurance done for the future. But that which excited his surprise most was the strange conduct of his horse; for that long before he could distinguish the man in the chair, his own horse stood still in the road, and flung back his ears. "In short," said the pedlar, "I wish never to see that man and horse again; they do not look to me as though they belonged to this world."

This was all I could learn at that time; and the occurrence soon after would have become with me "like one of those things which had never happened," had I not, as I stood recently on the doorstep of Bennett's Hotel in Hartford, heard a man say, "There goes Peter Rugg and his child! He looks wet and weary, and farther from Boston than ever." I was satisfied it was the same man I had seen more than three years before; for whoever has once seen Peter Rugg can never after be deceived as to his identity.

"Peter Rugg!" said I; "and who is Peter Rugg?"

"That," said the stranger, "is more than any one can tell exactly. He is a famous traveller, held in light esteem by all inn-holders, for he never stops to eat, drink, or sleep. I wonder why the Government does not employ him to carry the mail."

"Ay," said a bystander; "that is a thought bright only on one side. How long would it take in that case to send a letter to Boston?—for Peter has already, to my knowledge, been more than twenty years travelling to that place."

"But," said I, "does the man never stop anywhere? Does he never converse with any one? I saw the same man more than three years since near Providence, and I heard a strange story about him. Pray, sir, give me some account of this man."

"Sir," said the stranger, "those who know the most respecting that man say the least. I have heard it asserted that Heaven sometimes sets a mark on a man either for judgment or a trial. Under which Peter Rugg now labors, I cannot say; therefore I am rather inclined to pity than to judge."

"You speak like a humane man," said I; "and if you have known him so long, I pray you will give me some account of him. Has his appearance much altered in that time?"

"Why, yes; he looks as though he never ate, drank, or slept; and his child looks older than himself; and he looks like time broken off from eternity, and anxious to gain a resting-place."

"And how does his horse look?" said I.

"As for his horse, he looks fatter and gayer, and shows more animation and courage, than he did twenty years ago. The last time Rugg spoke to me he inquired how far it was to Boston. I told him just one hundred miles.

" 'Why,' said he, 'how can you deceive me so? It is cruel to mislead a traveller. I have lost my way; pray direct me the nearest way to Boston.'

"I repeated, it was one hundred miles.

"'How can you say so?' said he; 'I was told last evening it was but fifty, and I have travelled all night.'

"'But,' said I, 'you are now travelling from Boston. You must turn back.'

"'Alas!' said he, 'it is all turn back! Boston shifts with the wind, and plays all around the compass. One man tells me it is to the east, another to the west; and the guide-posts, too, they all point the wrong way.'

"'But will you not stop and rest?' said I; 'you seem wet and weary.'

"'Yes,' said he; 'it has been foul weather since I left home.'

"'Stop, then, and refresh yourself.'

"'I must not stop; I must reach home to-night, if possible; though I think you must be mistaken in the distance to Boston.'

"He then gave the reins to his horse, which he restrained with difficulty, and disappeared in a moment. A few days afterward I met the man a little this side of Claremont, winding around the hills in Unity, at the rate, I believe, of twelve miles an hour."

"Is Peter Rugg his real name, or has he accidentally gained that name?"

"I know not, but presume he will not deny his name; you can ask him—for see, he has turned his horse, and is passing this way."

In a moment a dark-colored, high-spirited horse approached, and would have passed without stopping; but I had resolved to speak to Peter Rugg, or whoever the man might be. Accordingly I stepped into the street, and as the horse approached, I made a feint of stopping him. The man immediately reined in his horse. "Sir," said I, "may I be so bold as to inquire if you are not Mr. Rugg?—for I think I have seen you before."

"My name is Peter Rugg," said he: "I have unfortunately lost my way. I am wet and weary, and will take it kindly of you to direct me to Boston."

"You live in Boston, do you?—and in what street?"

"In Middle Street."

"When did you leave Boston?"

"I cannot tell precisely; it seems a considerable time."

"But how did you and your child become so wet? It has not rained here to-day."

"It has just rained a heavy shower up the river. But I shall not reach Boston to-night if I tarry. Would you advise me to take the old road, or the turnpike?"

"Why, the old road is one hundred and seventeen miles, and the turnpike is ninety-seven."

"How can you say so? You impose on me! It is wrong to trifle with a traveller. You know it is but forty miles from Newburyport to Boston."

"But this is not Newburyport; this is Hartford."

"Do not deceive me, sir. Is not this town Newburyport, and the river that I have been following the Merrimac?"

"No, sir; this is Hartford, and the river the Connecticut."

He wrung his hands and looked incredulous.

"Have the rivers, too, changed their courses, as the cities have changed places? But see! the clouds are gathering in the south, and we shall have a rainy night. Ah, that fatal oath!"

He would tarry no longer. His impatient horse leaped off, his hind flanks rising like wings; he seemed to devour all before him, and to scorn all behind.

I had now, as I thought, discovered a clew to the history of Peter Rugg, and I determined, the next time my business called me to Boston, to make a further inquiry. Soon after, I was enabled to collect the following particulars from Mrs. Croft, an aged lady in Middle Street, who has resided in Boston during the last twenty years. Her narration is this:

The last summer, a person, just at twilight, stopped at the door of the late Mrs. Rugg. Mrs. Croft, on coming to the door, perceived a stranger, with a child by his side, in an old weather-beaten carriage, with a black horse. The stranger asked for Mrs. Rugg, and was informed that Mrs. Rugg had died in a good old age more than twenty years before that time.

The stranger replied, "How can you deceive me so? Do ask Mrs. Rugg to step to the door."

"Sir, I assure you Mrs. Rugg has not lived here these nineteen years; no one lives here but myself, and my name is Betsey Croft."

The stranger paused, and looked up and down the street, and said: "Though the painting is rather faded, this looks like my house."

"Yes," said the child; "that is the stone before the door that I used to sit on to eat my bread and milk."

"But," said the stranger, "it seems to be on the wrong side of the street. Indeed everything here seems to be misplaced. The streets are all changed, the people are all changed, the town seems changed; and, what is strangest of all, Catherine Rugg has deserted her husband and child. Pray," continued the stranger, "has John Foy come home from sea? He went a long voyage; he is my kinsman. If I could see him, he could give me some account of Mrs. Rugg."

"Sir," said Mrs. Croft, "I never heard of John Foy. Where did he live?"

"Just above here, in Orange Tree Lane."

"There is no such place in this neighborhood."

"What do you tell me? Are the streets gone? Orange Tree Lane is at the head of Hanover Street, near Pemberton's Hill."

"There is no such lane now."

"Madam! you cannot be serious. But you doubtless know my brother, William Rugg. He lives in Royal Exchange Lane, near King Street."

"I know of no such lane, and I am sure there is no such street as King Street in this town."

"No such street as King Street! Why, woman, you mock me! You may as well tell me there is no King George! However, madam, you see I am wet and weary; I must find a resting-place. I will go to Hart's tavern, near the market."

"Which market, sir?—for you seem perplexed; we have several markets."

"You know there is but one market,—near the Town dock."

"Oh, the old market; but no such person has kept there these twenty years."

Here the stranger seemed disconcerted, and uttered to himself quite audibly: "Strange mistake! How much this looks like the town of Boston! It certainly has a great resemblance to it; but I perceive my mistake now. Some other Mrs. Rugg, some other Middle Street."

"Then," said he, "madam, can you direct me to Boston?"

"Why, this is Boston, the city of Boston. I know of no other Boston."

"City of Boston it may be; but it is not the Boston where I live. I recollect now, I came over a bridge instead of a ferry. Pray what bridge is that I just came over?"

"It is Charles River Bridge."

"I perceive my mistake; there is a ferry between Boston and Charlestown; there is no bridge. Ah, I perceive my mistake. If I were in Boston my horse would carry me directly to my own door. But my horse shows by his impatience that he is in a strange place. Absurd, that I should have mistaken this place for the old town of Boston! It is a much finer city than the town of Boston. It has been built long since Boston. I fancy it must lie at a distance from this city, as the good woman seems ignorant of it."

At these words his horse began to chafe and strike the pavement with his fore-feet. The stranger seemed a little bewildered, and said, "No home to-night"; and giving the reins to his horse, passed up the street, and I saw no more of him.

It was evident that the generation to which Peter Rugg belonged had passed away.

This was all the account of Peter Rugg I could obtain from Mrs. Croft; but she directed me to an elderly man, Mr. James Felt, who lived near her, and who had kept a record of the principal occurrences for the last fifty years. At my request she sent for him; and after I had related to him the object of my inquiry, Mr. Felt told me he had known Rugg in his youth; that his disappearance had caused some surprise; but as it sometimes happens that men run away, sometimes to be rid of others, and sometimes to be rid of themselves; and Rugg took his child with him, and his own horse and chair; and as it did not appear that any creditors made a stir,—the occurrence soon mingled itself in the stream of oblivion, and Rugg and his child, horse and chair, were soon forgotten.

"It is true," said Mr. Felt, "sundry stories grew out of Rugg's affair,—whether true or false I cannot tell; but stranger things have happened in my day, without even a newspaper notice."

"Sir," said I, "Peter Rugg is now living; I have lately seen Peter Rugg and his child, horse, and chair. Therefore I pray you to relate to me all you know or ever heard of him."

"Why, my friend," said James Felt, "that Peter Rugg is now a living man, I will not deny; but that you have seen Peter Rugg and his child is impossible, if you mean a small child; for Jenny Rugg, if living, must be at least—let me see—Boston Massacre, 1770—Jenny Rugg was about ten years old. Why, sir, Jenny Rugg, if living, must be more than sixty years of age. That Peter Rugg is living, is highly probable, as he was only ten years older than myself, and I was only eighty last March; and I am as likely to live twenty years longer as any man."

Here I perceived that Mr. Felt was in his dotage; and I despaired of gaining any intelligence from him on which I could depend.

I took my leave of Mrs. Croft, and I proceeded to my lodgings at the Marlborough Hotel.

If Peter Rugg, thought I, has been travelling since the Boston Massacre, there is no reason why he should not travel to the end of time. If the present generation know little of him, the next will know less; and Peter and his child will have no hold on this world.

In the course of the evening I related my adventure in Middle Street.

"Ha!" said one of the company, smiling, "do you really think you have seen Peter Rugg? I have heard my grandfather speak of him as though he seriously believed his own story."

"Sir," said I, "pray let us compare your grandfather's story of Mr. Rugg with my own."

"Peter Rugg, sir, if my grandfather was worthy of credit, once lived in Middle Street, in this city. He was a man in comfortable circumstances, had a wife and one daughter, and was generally esteemed for his sober life and manners. But, unhappily, his temper at times was altogether ungovernable; and then his language was terrible. In these fits of passion, if a door stood in his way, he would never do less than kick a panel through. He would sometimes throw his heels over his head and come down on his feet, uttering oaths in a circle; and thus in a rage he was the first who performed a somerset, and did what others have since learned to do for merriment and money. Once Rugg was seen to bite a tenpenny nail in halves. In those days everybody, both men and boys, wore wigs; and Peter, at these moments of violent passion, would become so profane that his wig would rise up from his head. Some said it was on account of his terrible language; others accounted for it in a more philosophical way, and said it was caused by the expansion of his scalp,—as violent passion, we know, will swell the veins and expand the head. While these fits were on him Rugg had no respect for heaven or earth. Except this infirmity, all agreed that Rugg was a good sort of man; for when his fits were over, nobody was so ready to commend a placid temper as Peter.

"It was late in autumn, one morning, that Rugg, in his own chair, with a fine large bay horse, took his daughter and proceeded to Concord. On his return a violent storm overtook him. At dark he stopped in Menotomy, now West Cambridge, at the door of a Mr. Cutter, a friend of his, who urged him to tarry the night. On Rugg's declining to stop, Mr. Cutter urged him vehemently. 'Why, Mr. Rugg,' said Cutter, 'the storm is overwhelming you: the night is exceeding dark: your little daughter will perish: you are in an open chair, and the tempest is increasing.' '*Let the storm increase,*' said Rugg, with a fearful oath; '*I will see home to-night, in spite of the last tempest, or may I never see home!*' At these words he gave his whip to his high-spirited horse, and disappeared in a moment. But Peter Rugg did not reach home that night, or the next; nor, when he became a missing man, could he ever be traced beyond Mr. Cutter's in Menotomy.

"For a long time after, on every dark and stormy night, the wife of Peter Rugg would fancy she heard the crack of a whip, and the fleet tread of a horse, and the rattling of a carriage passing her door. The neighbors, too, heard the same noises; and some said they knew it was Rugg's horse, the tread on the pavement was perfectly familiar to them. This occurred so repeatedly, that at length the neighbors watched with lanterns, and saw the real Peter Rugg, with his own horse and chair, and child sitting beside him, pass directly before his own door, his head turned toward his house, and himself making every effort to stop his horse, but in vain.

"The next day the friends of Mrs. Rugg exerted themselves to find her husband and child. They inquired at every public-house and stable in town; but it did not appear that Rugg made any stay in Boston. No one, after Rugg had passed his own door, could give any account of him; though it was asserted by some that the clatter of Rugg's horse and carriage over the pavements shook the houses on both sides of the streets. And this is credible, if indeed Rugg's horse and carriage did pass on that night. For at this day, in many of the streets, a loaded truck or team in passing will shake the houses like an earthquake. However, Rugg's neighbors never afterward watched; some of them treated it all as a delusion, and thought no more of it. Others, of a different opinion, shook their heads and said nothing.

"Thus Rugg and his child, horse and chair, were soon forgotten, and probably many in the neighborhood never heard a word on the subject.

"There was, indeed, a rumor that Rugg afterward was seen in Connecticut, between Suffield and Hartford, passing through the country with headlong speed. This gave occasion to Rugg's friends to make further inquiry. But the more they inquired, the more they were baffled. If they heard of Rugg one day in Connecticut, the next day they heard of him winding round the hills in New Hampshire; and soon after, a man in a chair with a small child, exactly answering the description of Peter Rugg, would be seen in Rhode Island inquiring the way to Boston.

"But that which chiefly gave a color of mystery to the story of Peter Rugg was the affair at Charlestown Bridge. The toll-gatherer asserted that sometimes on the darkest and most stormy nights, when no object could be discerned, about the time Rugg was missing, a horse and wheel carriage, with a noise equal to a troop, would at midnight, in utter contempt of the rates of toll, pass over the bridge. This occurred so frequently, that the toll-gatherer resolved to attempt a discovery. Soon after, at the usual time, apparently the same horse and carriage approached the bridge from Charlestown Square. The toll-gatherer, prepared, took his stand as near the middle of the bridge as he dared, with a large three-legged stool in his hand. As the appearance passed, he threw the stool at the horse, but heard nothing, except the noise of the stool skipping across the bridge. The toll-gatherer, on the next day, asserted that the stool went directly through the body of the horse; and he persisted in that belief ever after. Whether Rugg, or whoever the person was, ever passed the bridge again, the toll-gatherer would never tell; and when questioned, seemed anxious to waive the subject. And thus Peter Rugg and his child, horse and carriage, remain a mystery to this day."

This, sir, is all that I could learn of Peter Rugg in Boston.

The Right Hand of Robber Lewis

IT WAS on a fine Monday morning in the early fall of 1820, and wash day. An old-time copper kettle on a spider was boiling water by the kitchen door of the tavern, which was on the side of the building on which was painted on the plastered wall the white horse of colossal proportions which gave the old inn its name. Rosanna Casselman, the innkeeper's bustling wife, was at work over the tubs on the side porch, and her young daughter Dowsabel was carrying buckets of water from the well to replenish the kettle. The girl, who was of amazing loveliness, was standing by the well box, and while the long pole with chain attached was dipped into the watery depths to replenish "the old oaken bucket," a horseman approached on the road which led from the south. The autumnal sun was clearing away the fogs and mist as he drew rein at the horse-trough which received the overflow from the fountain's copious source. The stranger was a young man of possibly thirty years of age, wearing a broad-brimmed black felt hat, in which was stuck the wing feather of a golden eagle, and pulled down over his eyes, almost hiding his regular features, and his handsome dark side-whiskers; he wore a cloak, or "Cardinal," as they were called in those days, which was loosened at the collar, as the exercise and growing warmth of the day had made it a trifle uncomfortable. He was mounted on a superb black horse, an entire, called Pulverhorn, said to be a son of old Topgallant, by a fugitive union with a Cumberland horse doctor's mare; the same Topgallant known as the "iron horse" which later won the great race against Whalebone at Baltimore, in three mile heats, when in his twenty-fourth year. Hiram Woodruff,

From *Two Pennsylvania Mountain Legends,* collected by Henry W. Shoemaker, pp. 2–11, Publications of The Pennsylvania Folk-Lore Society, Volume I, Number 4. Published by The Reading Eagle Press, Reading, Pa. 1928.

This is a story that an old lady, Mrs. Elmira Atkinson, born in 1828, and still living in her cabin in the foothills of the Alleghenies, in Clinton County, told to this writer. . . . The first scene of the story takes place at the White Horse Tavern, in Somerset County.—H. W. S.

the greatest of horse trainers, said of him: "His like was never seen before or since." Touching the brim of his hat, the rider asked the girl if she could hand him a can of water from the well, while his horse quenched his thirst at the trough, which was hewed from a solid log of original white pine. The girl looked at him boldly, and deciding to be polite, as she liked his appearance, she, after balancing the filled bucket on the coping of the well, ran to the waterbench on the porch to get a cup. Returning in a minute with a gourd, she filled it to the brim with the sparkling water, and handed it over the paling fence to the thirsty horseman, smiling at him in her pleasantest manner. This is how she impressed the stranger, who was a hardened citizen of the world, and a connoisseur of the fair sex.

Dowsabel Casselman was a Pennsylvania mountain beauty, typical of her medley of Continental ancestors, all except in the coloring, for her cropped curly hair, instead of being of raven blackness, was of coppery gold. It is strange that out of every thousand of the dark mountain girls of Pennsylvania there will be one or two red heads, and these will be of rarest loveliness. Her eyes, however, were dark, a hazel or amber, though her skin was fair, transparently white as alabaster. She was a little above the average height, smoothly and gracefully built, with a wonderful pair of legs, as her skirts, worn above the knees in the style of the Indian girls of those days, generously disclosed. Pleased with his reception, and promising to return shortly for a stay at the hotel, the handsome stranger resumed his way in the direction of Berlin, and Brunerstown, now called Somerset. Dowsabel, fascinated, day-dreamed watching after him, until her mother brought her back to earth by incessantly shouting, "Bring that water instanter, or I'll put a tin ear on you, you dulless slommach, standing out there grinning at that laddy-buck like a Cheshire cat." Several days later Dowsabel was again at the well drawing a bucket of water to fill the big pint Stiegel glasses which were placed on the table at dinner time, when outside the fence she noticed the small figure of an old, old man, whose head hardly came above the top of the horse-trough. The aged stranger wore a broad-brimmed soft black hat, adorned with an eagle's plume, and pulled down over his eyes, barely revealing his fine high nose and full blue eyes; the rest of his face was hidden by a huge beard, yellowish white and curly, which hung several inches below his waist. Naturally short, his big head seemed top-heavy even for his sturdy body to support, and seemed to rest on one of his shoulders. He wore a ragged great-coat that had once been brown. In one hand he carried a blackthorn cane with a branch curling around it like a grapevine, and in the other hand a small charcoal brazier, which he used partly to warm himself in the cold sheds and outbuildings where he generally slept, and partly to heat glue, for he was a traveling furniture-mender by occupation. Tipping his crumpled hat with old world politeness, he said: "Milady, would you be so kind as to fetch me a can so that I may have a drink of your good water." The handsome girl gazed at him a moment, contempt appearing in her flawless features, and, at length, replied in cutting tones: "Who do you think I am, old codger, to get your kind a cup; besides, I haven't got one, and if you're dry, the trough's in front of you."

The hardened old wayfarer was taken aback, but replied with spirit: "Young missy, if I was your lover, you would not have spoken that way to me, and would have broken your neck to get me a drink." The girl's pale face colored a little as she replied: "I have no lover, and you can see for yourself there is no cup." "Stuff and nonsense, Carrots," said the old man, as he turned to walk away, "you have had a dozen lovers already, and a thirteenth is on the way, and when he is finished you will be ready to lead an ape in hell. Au revoir, for I am sure that we will probably meet again a couple of times."

Dowsabel said nothing more, but filled her bucket and carried it to the house, for again her mother had her "dander up." "You goosesap," she shouted, "I've a notion to give you the worst ferricadouzer of your young life, shilly-shallying out there with that old chuckle-head." But the old man's remarks made an ugly impression on the girl's mind, and she was silent and moody the rest of the day.

Several days went by again, and the handsome stranger returned from Somerset and made a stay of nearly a week at the tavern, ostensibly to condition his horse, which he said had a "sidebone." While the steed rested the young man was tireless in pressing his suit with the lovely Dowsabel. It was an easy conquest, as he had the youth, the good looks, the smooth ways of the big world, which were the attributes that girls of Dowsabel's type most admired. When he went away the beautiful girl was in tears and begged him to return soon. "Quit your blubbering, kid, I'll be back soon enough," he said, as he mounted Pulverhorn and rode away.

Several weeks elapsed, and the stranger was at the White Horse again for a longer stay. This time he was put in the great east room, which commanded a glorious view from its long windows, the room that William Makepeace Thackeray occupied on his second American tour, when he sat on the broad window sill and wrote his name with a diamond on one of the small "lights" of home-made glass, and penned his immortal descriptions of Pennsylvania mountain scenery. He was laying his plans carefully for the coup that he had been planning ever since he first set eyes on the incomparably lovely girl at the well earlier in the autumn. He soon found out that she wasn't happy at home. He slept in the next room, and could hear her mother punishing her almost every night, and her cries of agony and outraged pride.

When he at last told her that he was leaving and might not return for a long time, if at all, Dowsabel again begged tearfully to be taken along. The stranger knew that his time had come, and in the chance meetings they had in the hallways, on the porch, in the yard, and in the harness room at the barn, gradually made clear to her who and what he was. He told her that while his real name was David Pevreferry, he was known on the roads as "Young Lewis," so much were his deeds and characteristics like the famous "David Lewis, the Robber," who had died a few months before in Bellefonte jail, having been mortally wounded by a sheriff's posse on the Driftwood Branch of Sinnemahoning, and buried in the jail yard of said prison on the night of July 13, 1820.

"I will take you along if you'll stop your didoes and can prove to me that you have the guts to stay with a dabster like myself." Dowsabel protested that there was no test or ordeal she would not undergo to prove her worthiness and fitness to be the companion of a man of the highroads, and be like Dally Sanry, the loveliest friend of David Lewis. "From the first time I laid eyes on you I would have put on boy's clothing and followed you to the ends of the earth," she protested over and over again. Then he explained to her that to prove this fitness she must secure for him what he most wanted, David Lewis' right hand, to be cut off the corpse which was now resting in the grave in the jail yard at Bellefonte.

It was a well-founded tradition on the roads in Europe, as well as in Pennsylvania and Maryland, that anyone possessing the right hand of a successful marauder, done to death for his crimes, exercised a spell over those he came in contact with, was able to put entire households to sleep and ransack premises at his leisure, and have nothing to fear in the way of annoyance, interference, apprehension or arrest. At the time of the wholesale hanging of highwaymen at Harper's Ferry in 1816, the only man who escaped had the right hand of an Indian murderer in his pocket, and thus equipped his horse could outrun any posse of pursuers on the road. But how was the hand to be secured from its grave inside the jail yard, with Dowsabel on the outside and guiltless of any offense making her eligible to be inside? "Young Lewis" then stated that as a prerequisite of her worthiness to be a second Dally Sanry she must help him decamp with her father's hooded gig, which was the old taverner's holiday and Battalion Day pride, also his best brass-mounted harness, and with these they would drive to the vicinity of Bellefonte, as far as Earlysburg. Then she must walk to Bellefonte, and put up at the Benner House, and wait there until bills announcing rewards for her capture as a runaway were posted at the hotel and she was recognized and taken up. These he would have printed at Lewistown while she was on her way to Bellefonte, and see that they were on view in every public house and every conspicuous post and pillar in the "village of the belles."

Dowsabel heard the plot with keen interest and could scarcely repress screaming with enthusiasm. On a dark night during the equinoctial rains "Young Lewis" drugged the girl's parents by putting the parings of finger nails in their wine, and made his departure with the gig and harness, driving off behind his black horse through a back lane to a point a mile down the Pike, where, under a clump of old white pines, Dowsabel awaited him, filled with loving excitement. She had slipped out of the house earlier in the evening and was not missed. The plucky steed, which had once been a lead horse in a stage-coach, was fit for the long drive ahead of him, carrying them at a break-neck pace through the muddy roads, on and on without stopping, over a succession of mountain ranges in the direction of Earlysburg. There were no telegraphs or other rapid means of communication, and only a few weekly newspapers in the back country in those days and news traveled slowly. By the time that John Caspar Peter Casselman recovered from his surprise and went to Brunerstown to advertise the loss of daughter, covered gig, brass-mounted harness and best whip with stock of mountain ash (to ward off highwaymen or evil eye), the wonderful-looking, copper-haired Dowsabel was comfortably ensconced at the spacious old Benner House at Bellefonte. There she was the object of admiration and consternation of the village sheiks who frequented the hostelry. Meanwhile the pseudo Lewis, Jr. had gotten bills struck off at Lewistown, which read approximately:

$100 REWARD IN GOLD COIN

Disappeared from "The White Horse," in Somerset County, Pa., on night of September 14, 1820, girl answering name of Dowsabel Urckart Casselman: She is aged eighteen years coming November 19, will weigh 120 lbs., 5:5 1/2 inches tall, red gold hair worn Indian style, jasper eyes, white complexion, wore white linsey woolsey jersey, dark green velvet skirt, black cotton stockings, low-cut shoes. All are asked to take her up on sight and communicate with Col. J. C. P. Casselman, Wellersburg, Pa.

Coming to the hotel at dinner time, "Lewis" tacked the bill below the face of the grandfather clock in the lobby, unobserved by anyone. He had arranged with the trusting belle that if she should be seized by too zealous claimants for the reward and hurried in the direction of Brunerstown without the formality of consigning her to jail, he would adopt desperate measures and waylay and rescue her at the rock once frequented by the genuine David Lewis, on top of the Seven Brothers (this rock was blasted away only a few months ago by State Highway engineers while reconstructing the Earlysburg-Milroy road), and he whispered to her that it might even be said that "she had been captured and carried off by Robber Lewis' ghost." But it was most likely that she would first be put in jail and her family notified, and kept there until they arrived to divide the rewards among those who gave information, the sheriff and jailers.

But the hardest ordeal of all was that she must exhume the right arm of Lewis, break the hand off at the wrist, and climb to freedom over the twenty-foot jail wall. If she couldn't scale the wall, the stranger would have to wait until she started for Brunerstown with her captors, when he would waylay and capture her in the place and manner previously stated. The landlord at the Benner House quickly recognized the girl described on the bill so mysteriously tacked up on the clock as his guest. The broadside was worded in a way to arouse most anyone's cupidity, and, despite her tears and protests, the beautiful Dowsabel was marched off to the gloomy precincts of Bellefonte jail. There were several graves of unfortunates in the central court-yard of the jail, and the rows of "cells" looked out on this enclosure. Some of the cells intended for robbers or hardened criminals were equipped with a grille of iron bars, over which doors were closed at night, while the rest were like boxstalls at a race track with oaken panelled doors and no gratings. There were small barred windows at the backs of all the cells. Young Lewis had given the girl a tiny saw to sever the bars, which she kept in the corsage of her dress, as, not being accused of any crime except truancy, she was not likely to be searched before her committal. She was not put in a cell, but in one of the "stalls" with an oaken door, and heavy lock and key. The approximate location of Lewis' grave had been explained to her by the stranger, but Dowsabel quickly verified it from her fellow-inmates of the jail. But there was another complication. A big dog, part wolf, which today would be called a "German police dog," had the run of the jailyard at night. "Lewis, Jr." had given the girl some pills to put to sleep the little penny dog at the White Horse (called Wasser, which meant that no hechs could ever take hold of him) the night of their joint escape, in reality nux vomica, which killed the poor little faithful watcher despite his mystic name. She had some of this poison left to use on the magnificent half-wild beast of the Seven Mountains. But Dietz, the wolf-dog, took an uncanny fancy to her, and as she was allowed the freedom of the jailyard, he attached himself to her like a shadow.

It was arranged that she should make her getaway on the second night, but before she was locked in her "box" for the night, the dog became so friendly that Nick Pankaloss, the old Greek from Aaronsburg, who acted as warder, allowed the animal to sleep by her spool bed. There were only three other prisoners in the jail at the time, all decrepit old men, "in" for variations of the more or less technical charge of vagrancy and beneath the dignity of the dog to guard. One of them happened to be Gaston Ythorrotz, the old furniture-mender whose request for a cup of water at the White Horse she had so insolently refused, but he chose not to notice her, and she pretended that she had never seen him before. However, his presence again made her nervous and melancholy. At eight o'clock on the appointed night a game of French ruff was in progress in the sheriff's parlor facing the main street, participated in by the high sheriff himself, his deputy, the turnkey and the old Greek, who, in his way, was a regular levanter, or card sharper. Dowsabel, inspired by great love, which gave her added strength to return to the man of her choice, and anxiety to be away from the old furniture-mender, cleverly broke off the old, rusty lock, and with the big dog licking at her hands, calmly walked out into the jail-yard. The other cell doors were shut tight, and none could see her even if there had been any light. It had been arranged that she was to be arrested during the dark of the moon, and this was a dreary night, cold, and a few snowdrops drifting about. There was a pick and shovel standing against the stone wall in a corner of the yard, and Dowsabel was soon at work digging open David Lewis' grave in the half-frozen ground.

The erstwhile robber chief had been buried three feet deep, but the quicklime had already gotten in its work. The darkness saved the girl from a gruesome sight, but she soon had a grip on the crumbling right arm, and dragged it forth, deftly twisting off the hand at the wrist, which caused such an odor of lime to arise that her eyes smarted. She covered the body again with the lime and clay, while Dietz lay beside her, flopping his tail against the hard ground as if to register satisfaction. Then, almost before the dog could realize what she was doing, the girl walked to the door of the warden's house, through the hall, and out into the street, holding all the while the ghastly but precious relic of David Lewis, which would forever keep her lover out of the toils of the law and make his horse show his heels to the fleetest of his foes, and which acted as a charm to her.

At the end of the steep road which leads out of town below the present site of the Academy, "Lewis, Jr." was waiting with the covered gig and the black horse resplendent in the brass-mounted harness. And they made a second getaway into the night, into a snowstorm which came out of the east and grew in velocity as they sped down Penn's Valley and almost engulfed them when they reached the Narrows.

After Dowsabel had gone, the wolf-dog began to run about and howl dismally, but he was given to such spells of melancholy restlessness. Besides, the jailers were too intent on French ruff and too much under the influence of "shrub" to recall that Dietz had been locked up with the girl. In the morning Dowsabel's "box" was found open; the $200 golden bird had flown. Snow had mercifully covered Lewis' rifled grave, and there were no signs but that it was still inviolate. None of the prisoners could have seen her escape, and they were not questioned. Five days later, before the hue and cry was scarcely beyond the borders of Centre County— in fact, the local authorities did not want the news to spread, in the hopes that they might recapture the fair jail-breaker and save the rewards for themselves—a hooded gig, drawn by a great black horse, drew up in front of the old stone tavern on the edge of Millerstown. Until the day before "Young Lewis" and Dowsabel had been only a few miles outside of Centre County, quietly "stowed away" in a resort frequented by counterfeiters and gamblers, near the easterly outlet of the dark, wooded narrows between Motz's Bank, now known as Woodward and Hartley Hall, now called Hartleton, in the shadow of Jones Mountain. The pattern of David Lewis ordered the girl, who was joyously glad to comply with his slightest wish, to go in the hotel to see if accommodations were to be had. As she hurried into the kitchen, the only room where there was any light, she noticed an old man seated on one of the courting blocks in the inglenook. When he saw her, he rose up, waving his heavy blackthorn staff and pointing at her, his eyes ablaze with surprise and rage. It was Gaston Ythorrotz, the old furniture-mender. "Bloody murder," he shouted, "here's that young huzzy that made the getaway from Bellefonte jail; there's reward of $100 in gold from her people in

Somerset County, and $100 more gold from Centre County. Boys, oh, boys, take her up quick!"

His cries literally "brought the whole house to the kitchen," to use an old expression. Dowsabel turned to escape, but the old man was already at the door blocking the way with his cane. There she was caught red-headed; she didn't have a chance. In fact, her screams for assistance only served as a warning to "Young Lewis," knight of the road, outside in the covered gig, who fancied that his new-found possession of the grisly right hand of David Lewis was quickly beginning to prove his lucky talisman. He laid the long whip with its stock of "quicken tree" over the black horse's flanks, and was gone like a spectre into the night, leaving his sweetie and slave in hostile hands, a prisoner for cash rewards.

Soon the sturdy Dutch landlord and his boys, acting under the old furniture-mender's instructions, tied her hand and foot. "She's cute as a pet fox, and quick as chain lightning," he said. They tossed her on a sofa in an alcove in a cold, empty room to await the morning. After she was placed in that helpless position like a sack of buckwheat, and the captors made ready to leave the room, the old man came close to her, holding aloft his old brazier, like a lantern, saying: "Now, my beauty, the tables have turned. When I saw you in Bellefonte jail I thought to myself, 'I will say nothing, my time is the third time we meet,' and I let you get away as neat as any hechs could have done it. Now I say, 'I am the law, the law of retribution.'"

After a further consultation with the landlord it was suggested that with $200 in gold at stake, a gigantic sum in those poverty stricken days, when the whole country was "flat" from the effects of the War of 1812–1815, someone should watch her all night, lest "Young Lewis" return and stage another "Bellefonte jail delivery." "That dressy off-scouring will not come back for her," said the old furniture-mender, "I've known him and his kind too well for more than fifty years. Yet I'll watch this tricky minx only too gladly, but I don't think she is overly anxious to go home." Then he drew a huge flint-lock pistol from his belt under his long coat, which he brandished in a menacing fashion. "All right, daddy, go at it, we know we're leaving her in good hands," said the landlord, as he left the room. The old man drew a deer horn stool out of the hall, and slouched down on it in a corner, with the smouldering brazier at his feet.

For a time he sat there, pistol in his lap, gazing at the gagged and helpless damsel in all the misery of her ignominious position. As soon as they were alone together, Dowsabel never allowed her dark Levantine eyes off his face, seeking to cast her glamor over him, as they say in the mountains. Gradually, under the effect of her dazzling beauty, as revealed to him by the red glow of the brazier, the old man began to review his past life, the man he might have been before the weight of human misery and injustice had borne him down, and he became less determined. Women had ill-used him in many lands, in war and in peace, and he had no kindly feeling for any of them except the one who gave him birth, yet he had never taken a mean advantage of any of them. Dowsabel's coppery beauty tantalized him as no other woman's had, cold as she was to him.

Looking at her with his squinty, bloodshot eyes that had beheld from afar many pulchritudinous women, he fancied that she must be fully as beautiful as that red-headed Dutch girl of Bruges, in honor of whom Duke Philip of Burgundy instituted the Order of the Golden Fleece. At last he whispered to her: "I am so very sorry that I let you into this mess, but my heart rebelled at the way you treated me at the 'White Horse.'" Dowsabel did not answer; it was as if she had known what was coming, the usual tribute to the power of her matchless loveliness. Rising up from the stool, the old man fumbled in his belt, under his long coat, drawing forth from its shabby sheath a schlor, or Gipsy dagger, made out of a single piece of steel, and sharp and glistening as a misericorde. With it he cut the gag, and the ropes which bound her lovely wrists and ankles. "Go," he continued, "I don't care where, back home to your mother, who'll whallop the lights out of you, to your lover, who'll deceive the heart out of you, or to lead an ape in hell, it's all the same to me."

Dowsabel straightened herself up, and on tiptoes vanished from the room, uttering not a word, partly because she was naturally wayward and partly as she knew that her real days of suffering were close in front of her. The old man put his schlor back in sheath, his pistol in his belt, settled down on the stool, and began warming his hands at the almost extinguished flame of his rusty brazier. As he gazed at the empty couch his brooding thoughts began to picture, while his great head nodded, an ideal kingdom of life where the obstacles of age, poverty and physical imperfection were but a state of mind that vanished, and he had but to fix his fancy on a person for his love to be requited. But those moments of sublime introspection were as near to human happiness as he would ever reach in his long span of earthly existence. Just before the tall clock in a corner of the kitchen, which had painted on the dial that strange Biscayan proverb, "Every hour wounds, the last one kills," struck three, and the Creeley roosters had begun to crow, he pulled himself together and slipped out a side door, fading into the fog which precedes the dawn along the Juniata. When, half an hour later, the landlord and his family came downstairs, they felt as if the previous evening's happenings had been some fantastic dream.

The Lobo Girl of Devil's River

IN THE fall of 1830 John Dent and Will Marlo went in partners to trap fur along the headwaters of Chickamauga River in Georgia. Pelts were plentiful, and they got along harmoniously enough until the spring of 1833, when they fell out over a division of the winter's catch.

By L. D. Bertillion. From *Straight Texas*, Publications of the Texas Folk-Lore Society, Number XIII, edited by J. Frank Dobie and Mody C. Boatright, pp. 79–85. Copyright, 1937, by the Texas Folk-Lore Society.

A woman was at the bottom of the quarrel. She was Mollie Pertul, daughter of a mountaineer. While trapping in the vicinity of the Pertul cabin, John Dent had fallen in love with her and the two had engaged to be married. In forming their partnership the two trappers had agreed to sell jointly all pelts they took and to divide the money equally. Through two seasons this agreement they had carried out, but now Dent insisted on taking half the hides and disposing of them in his own way. He had a notion that he could get more money, to start married life on, by selling his fur separately.

After a bitter quarrel the division was made as Dent wanted it. Immediately almost, Marlo began telling around that he had been cheated. The quarrel went on for about two weeks; then there was a fight in which Dent stabbed Marlo to death. Public opinion was against him, and there was nothing for him to do but skip the country. Before leaving, however, he managed to see his love and tell her that he was going to locate a place in which they could live together and that he would return and steal her away.

Months passed by and people began to lose interest in the matter. During all this time, presumably, Mollie Pertul heard nothing from her murderer lover. Then a little after sundown on April 13, 1834—just a year to the day after Marlo was stabbed—the mountaineer girl went to the cow lot to milk as was her daily custom. After she had been absent from the house an unusually long time, her parents decided to investigate and see if anything had gone wrong. They found the cows unmilked and in the empty milk pail a Bowie knife with dried blood caked about the hilt. It had a staghorn handle of peculiar design that made it easily identified, next day, as the knife with which Dent had killed Marlo.

In the darkness of the night the parents called and searched for Mollie, but in vain. As soon as daylight showed, a few mountaineers who had been summoned began looking for sign. They struck the tracks of a man and woman leading to the Chickamauga River. There they found in the bank a freshly driven stob to which, apparently, a small canoe had recently been moored. Mollie Pertul was gone without a word of explanation and without a moment's preparation. All she took with her were the clothes on her back.

Six months passed. Then old Mrs. Pertul received a letter postmarked Galveston, Texas. It read:

"Dear Mother,
   "The Devil has a river in Texas that is all his own and it is made only for those who are grown.
                    "Yours with love—
                           Mollie."

In those days the people of Georgia were not familiar with the streams of Texas and their names. Indeed, very few people in Texas itself knew anything about Devil's River, far to the west of San Antonio, the outpost of all settlements, its inhabitants almost exclusively Spanish-speaking. Mrs. Pertul and her husband and neighbors merely considered that some- where in Texas Dent had to himself a river on which to trap. They knew that Dent was a devil all right, though maybe they were a little surprised at Mollie's admitting it.

Now, one of the little known chapters in Texas history is of a small colony of English people who in 1834 settled on Devil's River, calling their settlement Dolores. It was short-lived. Indians killed most of the settlers. A few of them drifted into Mexico. The remainder, fourteen adults and three children, in attempting to get back east were attacked at Espantosa Lake, near what is now Carrizo Springs. After killing them all, the Comanches threw their bodies and the carts in which they were traveling into the lake. That is why to this day Mexicans consider the lake haunted, the name Espantosa meaning "frightful."

Dent and his bride had joined this English colony. Devil's River had plenty of beaver; so did the Rio Grande both above and below where Devil's River empties into it. We may be sure that Dent did not live in the group of Englishmen, but, like the lone wolf he was, off to one side. He, no doubt, had an agreement with the Indians. A considerable ride westward two or three Mexican families, more Indianized than anything else, raised a few goats on the Pecos Canyon.

About noon one day in May of the year 1835, a rider on a reeling horse drew up at one of these goat ranches. He told the Mexican *ranchero* and his wife that he was camped where Dry Creek runs into Devil's River. He said that his wife was giving birth to a baby and that they must have help. The Mexican woman agreed to go with her husband, who at once began saddling the horses. Meantime, one of those black electricity- charged clouds for which that part of the country is noted was coming up. A bolt of lightning struck the messenger dead.

This delayed the Mexicans considerably in getting off. From the description of his camp site given by the dead man the *ranchero* knew how to reach it, but night came on before he and his wife got over the divide to Devil's River. They did not find the camp until next morning. There, under an open brush arbor lay the woman dead, alone. Indications pointed to the fact that she had died while giving birth to a child. Yet no child was visible. No child could be found. No trace of it was evident any- where. Tracks thick around the brush arbor made the *ranchero* suspect that lobo wolves had devoured the infant.

In the scantily furnished brush cabin the Mexicans found a letter, which they took along to show the first person they might encounter who could read English. This letter, as it later developed, had been written by Mollie Pertul Dent to her mother in Georgia several weeks before her death. It served to identify her and her husband. Thus their romance ended.

Ten years passed. A wagon road that had been laid out across the new Republic of Texas to El Paso went by San Felipe Springs (now Del Rio), where there were a few Mexicans, and on across Devil's River, only twelve miles beyond, and then across the Pecos. Occasionally armed travelers passed over the road. In the year 1845 a boy living at San Felipe Springs reported that he had seen a pack of lobo wolves attacking a herd of goats and with them a creature, long hair half covering its features, that looked like a naked girl. Some passing Americans who heard the story quizzed him. But they seemed more interested in getting his description of what a naked girl looked like than in getting information about the strange creature he reported. The story was ridiculed, but it spread back among the settlements.

Not more than a year after this a Mexican woman at San Felipe declared she had seen two big lobos and a naked girl devouring a freshly killed goat. She got close to them, she said, before they saw her. Then they all three ran. The naked girl ran at first on all-fours, but then rose up and ran on two feet, keeping in company with the wolves. The woman was positive of what she had seen. The few people in the Devil's River country began to keep a sharp lookout for the girl. They recalled the disappearance of the dead Mollie Dent's infant amid lobo tracks. Men of the camp told how female wolves carried their cubs by the scruff of the neck without injuring them. Perhaps, they said, some lobo wolf in whom the mother instinct was strong had carried the new-born to her den and raised it. Indians reported having noted in sandy places along the river barefoot tracks, sometimes accompanied by hand prints.

A hunt was organized to capture the Lobo, or Wolf, Girl of the Devil's River, as she had now come to be called. It was made up mostly of wild-riding Mexican vaqueros. These people had doubtless never heard anything of the story of the wolf-suckled Romulus and Remus who founded Rome or of wolf-nursed children in India like Kipling's Mowgli, but far out on this isolated, stark border they had been confronted with unmistakable evidence of a human being reared by and running wild with lobo wolves.

On the third day of the hunt two of the riders jumped the girl near a side canyon. She was with a big lobo that cut off from her when she dodged into a crevice. Here the vaqueros cornered her. She cowered at first like a rabbit. Then she spat and hissed like a wildcat. She fought too, clawing and biting. While the vaqueros were tying her she began to belch forth pitiful, frightful, unearthly sounds described as resembling both the scream of a woman and the howl of a lobo but being neither. As she was howling forth this awful scream, a monster he-wolf, presumably the one from whom she had become separated, suddenly appeared rushing at her captors. The fact that one of them saw it coming before it got close enough to use its powerful jaws probably saved their lives. He shot it dead with a pistol. At that the wild girl sank into a silent faint.

The captured creature was now securely tied and could be examined more carefully. She was excessively hairy, but breasts of beautiful curvature and other features showed that she was a normally formed human female.

Her hands and arms were muscled in an extraordinary manner but not ill proportioned.

Having revived from her faint, she was placed on a horse and carried to the nearest ranch. There she was unbound and turned loose in an isolated room for the night. With gestures of kindness she was offered a covering for her body, food and water, but no eagle of the free air, no lion of the deep jungle, ever showed more distrust and fear of its captors than she. She backed into the darkest corner, and there she was left alone. The door to the room was closed. The only other opening was a little window across which a board had been nailed.

The ranch was but a two-roomed hovel, alone amid the desert wilderness. By dark four or five men were gathered at it, and now the wild and frantic being fastened up in the room began voicing forth the terrifying screamish howls. Through the log walls of many vents they carried far on the night air. Soon they were answered by the long drawn out, deep howls of lobos beyond. Lobos seemed to answer from all sides, and their dismal and far-carrying voices brought answers from farther and farther away. All the lobos of the western world seemed to be gathering. Rancheros who all their lives had heard lobos howl had never heard anything like this, either from such a number of wolves now assembling or in the sullen, doom-like quality of the long, deep howling. Nearer and more compactly the horde gathered. Now they would howl all in unison, a bass-throated chorus of ferocity and darkness and lost hopes such as no musician of the world ever dreamed of. Then they would be silent as if waiting for some answer, and the wild girl in the dark room there would answer back with her unearthly howling scream, a voice neither of woman nor of beast.

After a time the great pack made a rush for the corrals, attacking goats, milk cows and the saddle horses. The noises made by these domestic animals, especially the screams and neighs of the plunging kicking horses, brought the men to the rescue. Ordinarily no man at all familiar with lobo wolves would fear one. Now these rancheros kept together, shooting in the darkness and yelling as they advanced. The wolves retreated.

Meantime, in the pandemonium, the Lobo Girl somehow wrenched the cross plank from the window and got out. It was supposed that she immediately rejoined the wolves. Hardly another howl was heard that night, and the next day not a track of the girl could be found. For a long time the sight of a wolf in that particular region was very rare.

Nothing more was heard of the Wolf Girl of Devil's River for six years. Meantime, gold had been discovered in California and travel westward had greatly increased. Along in 1852 an exploring party of frontiersmen hunting a route to El Paso that would be better watered than the Chihuahua Trail, as the road used was called, rode down to the Rio Grande at a sharp bend far above the mouth of Devil's River.

They were almost upon the water before they saw it or could be seen from its edge. There, sitting on a sand bar, two young wolf whelps tugging at her full breasts, they at close range caught clear sight of a naked young woman. In an instant she was upon her feet, a whelp under each arm, dashing into the breaks at a rate no horse could follow. The creature could have been no other than the wild Lobo Girl of Devil's River.

So far as is known she was never glimpsed by man after this, though perhaps some of the old-time Apaches might have had a tale to tell could they have been asked. What the fate of the Lobo Girl—or woman—was, nobody probably will ever know. During the war of extermination that has been waged on lobos, the most predatory of animals that stockmen of America have known, in the border country, a wolf has occasionally been found with a marked human resemblance, and for many years now "human-faced" wolves, so called, have been considered the final culmination of a Georgia murder and elopement. If man can bear the "mark of the beast," why may not beast bear the mark of the man? Speaking only for myself, I will say that despite the fact that over a century has passed since the beginning of the incidents just related, yet during the past forty years I have in the western country met more than one wolf face strongly marked with human characteristics.

Gretchen and the White Steed

ALWAYS in the narratives of the soil the Pacing White Mustang is a generous, beneficent animal. Black Devil was the fighter, the slayer, and any report accusing the White Steed of manslaughter may be set down to the confused memories of people who had heard of the black murderer. A tale that illustrates the White Sultan's benignity and intelligence came to me from the late J. O. Dyer, of Galveston. He heard it in the seventies from an old woman who as a girl, about 1848, was among German colonists locating homes in Texas. Her name was Gretchen.

As the story goes, her family, in company with some other German immigrants, was moving up the Guadalupe River to locate on a wide spread of the valley. They traveled in wagons, single file. The family in the last wagon, Gretchen's family, had a very gentle old gray mare that followed along without rope or halter, stopping every once in a while to grab a mouthful of particularly lush grass. She was stupid and lazy and her ears flopped, but she was faithful. On her back she carried two big sacks of corn meal so arranged that they made a kind of platform.

The wagon was running over with such things as German settlers carried—beds and bedding, pots and pans, a heavy chest of drawers, a few pot plants, and a great many children. Gretchen, eight or nine years old, was the liveliest of these. One day she told her father that she wanted to get out and ride the old gray mare. He could see no harm in this; in fact, her absence might lessen the constant hubbub. So he lifted Gretchen

From "The White Steed of the Prairies," *Tales of the Mustang*, by J. Frank Dobie, pp. 58–64. Copyright, 1936, by J. Frank Dobie. Dallas: The Book Club of Texas.

up on the platform of corn meal sacks and tied her there with a rope in such a way that she would be comfortable and could not fall off. The old mare hardly batted an eye, and with Gretchen on her back continued as usual to walk and pick grass along behind the wagon.

That afternoon, however, one wheel of the wagon was wrenched in a buffalo wallow, and a halt had to be made for repairs. Gretchen was asleep at the time, firmly tied on her pillion of corn meal. She did not know when the old gray mare grazed out of sight down a mesquite draw. Her father was busy with the wheel; her mother, like the old woman who lived in a shoe, had so many children that she did not know what to do; and so neither of them noticed. It was only after the wagon was repaired and the other children were counted into it and the train started on, that little Gretchen was missed. Then the old gray mare could not be found. None of the German men, so new to the frontier, could follow her tracks in the maze of mustang tracks they now discovered. They struck camp to search. Night came and no little Gretchen; the next day came and passed and no little Gretchen. Then on the morning of the third day the old gray mare brought her in, and this is the explanation the little girl gave.

After dozing she knew not how long, she awoke with a start. The lazy old mare was lumbering along in a gallop after a prancing, neighing, pacing white horse with cream-colored mane and tail. She tried to stop the old mare, but she had neither bridle nor halter. She tried to jump off, but she was tied on and the knots of the rope were beyond her reach.

After they had trotted and galloped until nearly sundown, the white horse all the time pacing ahead "like a rocking chair," they came to a large bunch of mares. These were, though Gretchen then knew nothing of such matters, the White Steed's *manada*. They came out full of curiosity to greet their new sister, and they were very cordial in their greeting. Here I will say that no human beings can be more cordial towards each other than horses. I have seen a pair of horses that had been separated from each other and then allowed to get together again, rub each other's noses, caress each other's necks, nip each other fondly with their teeth, nicker, and otherwise show the most sincere affection and delighted cordiality in the world.

The wild mares seemed not to notice little Gretchen at all. They were so cordial in their nosings of the old gray mare that soon their muzzles were touching the meal sacks. Probably the sacking was salty; certainly some of the meal had sifted through so that it could be tasted. The mares tasted it. No matter if it was the first taste of corn they had ever had, they liked it.

They began to nip at the meal sacks so eagerly that they nipped Gretchen's bare legs. She screamed. She expected to be chewed up right away, even if the mares meant no harm. But at her scream the Pacing White Stallion was with one bound beside her. He was as considerate as he was intelligent. He drove the wild mares off. Then he chewed in two the ropes that bound Gretchen, took her gently by the collar of her dress, as a cat takes one of her kittens, and set her down upon the ground.

It was about dark now and the coyotes were beginning to howl. Little Gretchen howled too, but there was no danger. After a while she made a kind of nest in some tall fragrant grass near a mesquite bush and, having cried a while, fell asleep.

When she awoke, the sun was high and not a horse was within sight. She was hungry. She went down to a waterhole that she saw close by and drank water for breakfast. She had heard that a person lost on the prairies had better stay in one place until he "found himself" or until someone found him. She had no hope of finding herself, but she did hope that her papa would come. She remained near the waterhole.

Noon came and still no horse or person appeared within sight. Gretchen was hungrier than ever. It was the spring of the year, and she gathered some of the red agrito berries (called also wild currants) growing near, but the thorny leaves pricked her fingers so severely that she quit before she had eaten enough of them to satisfy her hunger. Evening fell and she was still alone. She gathered some sheep sorrel down in the bottom of the draw and drank some more water. Darkness came, the stars came out, the coyotes set up their lonely howling. Little Gretchen lay down in her nest again, and again cried herself to sleep.

When she awoke the next morning, there standing over her, sound asleep, ears flopped down and lower lip hanging shapeless like a bag of curd, was the old gray mare. Gretchen was as glad as the redbird singing over her head. She jumped up and, as soon as she had washed her face, ran to the mare and tried to get on her. But the old mare was too tall. Then Gretchen grasped her by the mane and tried to lead her to a log that lay near at hand. If she could get the old mare beside it, she could use it as a stepping block. But the stupid old mare would not budge. After vainly pulling, coaxing, and jumping about for a long time, Gretchen began to wail.

She was leaning against the shoulder of the old mare sobbing, when she heard swift hoofbeats, rhythmic and racking. She looked up and saw coming out of the bushes the beautiful White Steed. The sunshine was on his whiteness. He came arching his neck and pacing with all the fire of a mustang emperor, but there was something about him that prevented Gretchen from being in the least frightened. On the contrary, she stretched her arms towards him and gave a childish "oh" of welcome. He paced right up to where she stood, gently grasped the collar of her dress and the scruff of her neck in his teeth and lifted her upon the mare. Then he must have told the old gray mare to go home. At least she went—went with Gretchen but no corn meal.

Home was the camp by the buffalo wallow where the wagon had broken down. Gretchen's parents were so happy at having her restored to them that they did not mind the loss of the meal. After she had told her adventures, she showed the nipped places on her legs.

In after years she told the story many, many times. When she was an old woman and some of her grandchildren seemed doubtful of the facts, she would in a pet pull down her cotton stockings and show the small, faint scars on her legs where the wild mares had nipped her. Then the grandchildren would have to believe her. Coincidentally, almost at the very time little Gretchen's family was moving towards a homestead, the German scientist Ferdinand Roemer, in July, 1846, noted—as he soon thereafter set down in his *Texas*—between San Marcos and the Colorado River "a magnificent white stallion speeding away at the head of a herd of mustangs."

PART SIX

SONGS AND RHYMES

*There were games that everyone played; and when
there was music, everyone sang.*
—M. L. WILSON

I. PLAY RHYMES AND CATCH COLLOQUIES

Marezleetoats
Dozeleetoats
Dozeleetivytoo
(Mares will eat oats; does'll eat oats; does'll eat ivy too.)
— OLD RIDDLE

ONE of the most fascinating fields for the student of beliefs and customs as these enter into the vernacular poetry of folk rhymes is the jingles and doggerels of childhood. The persistence and diffusion of such rhymes in infinite variety and yet in much the same form all over the world offers conclusive evidence of the twin aspects of tradition, especially the tradition of children—its inventiveness and its conservatism.

Like popular jests and sayings in general, play rhymes and catches have their local and contemporary sources or applications, illustrating the principle that "The happiness of a witticism or of a taunt hangs on its relationship at some sort of angle to the customs and notions prevalent in a country."[1] The 1944 version of the old counting-out rhyme has it, in Washington, D. C.:

> Eenie, meenie, minie, mo,
> Catch a Jap by the toe.
> If he hollers, make him say:
> "I surrender, U. S. A."

In 1938, in the shadow of war and hunger, New York City children jingled this ironic bit of nonsense reminiscent of Old Dan Tucker:

> Haile Selassie was a kind old man,
> He lit the match to the frying pan.
> When all the people tasted the beef,
> They all trucked off to the home relief.

These "waifs and strays of folklore," remnants of ancient charms and rituals, are both trivia and curiosa, eloquent with nostalgia for the sidewalks and back-yards of one's play-time. Recited or chanted as a rhymed or rhythmic accompaniment to rope-skipping or ball-bouncing, as a formula for counting out, as a nominy or set speech, as a taunt, quip, or crank, they have social and poetic interest apart from their game or pastime usage.

Salt, vinegar, mustard, pie and
  [cayenne] PEPPER!

Harvey, jarvey, jig, jig, jig,
Went to buy a pig, pig, pig.
Went to France to learn to dance,
Harvey, jarvey, jig, jig, jig.

Engine, engine, number nine,
Running on Chicago Line.
If it's polished, it will shine,
Engine, engine, number nine.

Knife and fork!
Bottle and cork!
That's the way to
Spell New York!

----
[1] *Studies in Jocular Literature*, by W. C. Hazlitt (1890), p. 26.

——'s it
And caught [got] a fit,
And don't know how
To get out of [over] it!

Do you like jelly?
Punch in the belly!

Do you like gravy?
Punch in the navy [navel]!

Do you like bananners?
Go play the pianner!

Do you like cheese?
You big Japanese!

Do you know what?
What?
That's what!

New England Rhymes for Counting Out

There are various ways in which children decide who shall begin in a game, or, as the phrase is, be "it." When this position is an advantage, it is often determined by the simple process of "speaking first." So far as can be determined when all are shouting at once, the first speaker is then entitled to the best place. Otherwise it is the practice to draw straws, the shortest gaining; to "toss up" a coin, "heads or tails"; or to choose between the two hands, one of which holds a pebble.

The most interesting way of decision, however, is by employing the rhymes for "counting out." A child tells off with his finger one word of the rhyme for each of the group, and he on whom the last word falls is "out." This process of exclusion is continued until one only is left, who has the usually unpleasant duty of leading in the sport. All European nations possess such rhymes, and apply them in a like manner. These have the common peculiarity of having very little sense, being often mere jargons of unmeaning sounds. This does not prevent them from being very ancient. People of advanced years often wonder to find their grand-children using the same formulas, without the change of a word. The identity between American and English usage establishes the currency of some such for three centuries, since they must have been in common use at the time of the settlement of this country. We may be tolerably sure that Shakespeare and Sidney directed their childish sports by the very same rhymes which are still employed for the purpose. Furthermore, German and other languages, while they rarely exhibit the identical phrases, present us with types which resemble our own, and obviously have a common origin. Such a relation implies a very great antiquity; and it becomes a matter of no little curiosity to determine the origin of a practice which must have been consecrated by the childish usage of all the great names of modern history.

This origin is by no means clear; but we may make remarks which will at least clear away misconceptions. . . .

From *Games and Songs of American Children,* collected and compared by William Wells Newell, pp. 194–203. New and Enlarged Edition. Copyright, 1893, 1903, by Harper & Brothers. New York and London.

Respecting these rhymes, we observe, in the first place, that they are meaningless. We might suppose that they were originally otherwise; for example, we might presume that the first of the formulas given below had once been an imitation or parody of some list of saints, or of some charm or prayer. A wider view, however, shows that the rhymes are in fact a mere jargon of sound, and that such significance, where it appears to exist, has been interpreted into the lines. We observe, further, that in despite of the antiquity of some of these formulas, their liability to variation is so great that phrases totally different in sound and apparent sense may at any time be developed out of them.

These variations are effected chiefly in two ways—rhyme and alliteration. A change in the termination of a sound has often involved the introduction of a whole line to correspond; and in this manner a fragment of nursery song may be inserted which totally alters the character of the verse. Again, the desire for a quaint alliterative effect has similarly changed the initial letters of the words of the formulas, according as the whim of the moment suggested.

From the fact that neither rhyme nor alliteration is any guide to the relations of these formulas, but seem arbitrarily introduced, we might conclude that the original type had neither one nor the other of these characteristics. This view is confirmed by European forms in which they appear as mere lists of unconnected words, possessing some equality of tone. Rhythm is a more permanent quality in them than termination or initial. From these considerations it appears likely that the original form of the rhymes of which we speak was that of a comparatively brief list of dissyllabic or trisyllabic words.

Now, when we observe that the first word of all the rhymes of this class is obviously a form of the number one; that the second word appears to be *two*, or a euphonic modification of *two*, and that numbers are perpetually introducing themselves into the series, it is natural to suppose that these formulas may have arisen from simple numeration.

This supposition is made more probable by a related and very curious system of counting up to twenty (of which examples will be found below), first brought into notice by Mr. Alexander J. Ellis, vice-president of the Philological Society of Great Britain, and called by him the "Anglo-Cymric Score." Dr. J. Hammond Trumbull, of Hartford, Conn., noticing the correspondence of Mr. Ellis's score with numerals attributed to a tribe of Indians in Maine (the Wawenocs), was led to make inquiries, which have resulted in showing that the method of counting in question was really employed by Indians in dealing with the colonists, having been remembered in Rhode Island, Connecticut, Massachusetts, New Hampshire, and Ohio (where it passed for genuine Indian numeration), and in this way handed down to the present generation as a curiosity. Mr. Ellis has found this score to be still in use in parts of England—principally in Cumberland, Westmoreland, and Yorkshire, where it is employed by shepherds to count their sheep, by old women to enumerate the stitches of their knitting, by boys and girls for "counting out," or by nurses to amuse children. It is, therefore, apparent that this singular method of numeration must have been tolerably familiar in the mother-country in the seventeenth century, since the Indians evidently learned it from the early settlers of New England. It appears, indeed, that not only the score itself, but also its chief variations, must have been established at that time. Mr. Ellis, however, who has shown that the basis of these formulas is Welsh, is disposed "to regard them as a comparatively recent importation" into England. Be that as it may, we see that the elements of change we have described, alliteration and rhyme, have been busy with the series. While the score has preserved its identity as a list of numerals, the successive pairs of numbers have been altered beyond all recognition, and with perfect arbitrariness.

It is plain that our counting rhymes cannot have been formed from the ' Anglo-Cymric score," since the latter is only in use in parts of England, while the former are common to many European nations. Nothing, however, prevents the supposition that they owe their origin to a similar root. All that can be said is, that no modern language is responsible for the practice, which can hardly be supposed to have originated within the last thousand years.

*   *   *   *   *

Onery, uery, ickory, Ann,
Filisy, folasy, Nicholas John,
Queevy, quavy, Irish Mary,
Stingalum, stangalum, buck.[1]
—*New England.*

Onery, uery, ickory, a,
Hallibone, crackabone, ninery-lay,
Whisko, bango, poker my stick,
Mejoliky one leg!
—*Scituate, Mass.* (about 1800).

One's all, zuzall, titterall, tann,
Bobtailed vinegar, little Paul ran,
Harum scarum, merchant marum,
Nigger, turnpike, toll-house, out.
—*Salem, Mass.*[2]

Onery, uery, ickery, see,
Huckabone, crackabone, tillibonee;
Ram pang, muski dan,
Striddledum, straddledum, twenty-one.
—*Connecticut.*

---

[1] English *onery, twoery,* etc. The forms we give date back to about 1820, before the publication of the "Nursery Rhymes of England." There are numerous small variations. "*Virgin* Mary" we have from informants in the Middle States; "*Irish* Mary" was the common New England phrase.—W. W. N.

[2] Used by *boys* in the western part of the town, where were the toll-house and negro settlement.—W. W. N.

Eny, meny, mony, my,
Tusca, leina, bona, stry,
Kay bell, broken well,
We, wo, wack.
—*Massachusetts.*

Eny, meny, mony, mine,
Hasdy, pasky, daily, ine,
Agy, dagy, walk.
—*Connecticut.*

Ena, mena, mona, my,
Panalona, bona, stry,
Ee wee, fowl's neck,
Hallibone, crackabone, ten and eleven,
O-u-t spells out.

Intery, mintery, cutery corn,
Apple-seed and apple-thorn,
Wire, briar, limber lock,
Five mice in a flock;
Catch him Jack,
Hold him Tom,
Blow the bellows,
Old man out.
—*Massachusetts.*

Ikkamy, dukkamy, alligar, mole,
Dick slew alligar slum,
Hukka pukka, Peter's gum,
Francis.
—*Massachusetts.*

1. ane.	6. sother.	11. een dick.	16. een bumfrey.
2. tane.	7. lother.	12. teen dick.	17. teen bumfrey.
3. tother.	8. co.	13. tother dick.	18. tother bumfrey.
4. feather.	9. deffrey.	14. feather dick.	19. feather bumfrey.
5. fip.	10. dick.	15. bumfrey.	20. gig it.

1. een.	6. sother.	11. een dick.	16. een bumpit.
2. teen.	7. lother.	12. teen dick.	17. teen bumpit.
3. tuther.	8. porter.	13. tuther dick.	18. tuther bumpit.
4. futher.	9. dubber.	14. futher dick.	19. futher bumpit.
5. fip.	10. dick.	15. bumpit.	20. gig it.[1]

---

[1] These examples of the "Anglo-Cymric score" . . . were obtained, . . . from Mrs. Ellis Allen of West Newton, now ninety years of age, who was born at Scituate, Mass., where she learned the formula; and . . . of her daughter, who learned it from an Indian woman, *Mary Wolsomog,* of Natick. Though mother and daughter, neither had ever heard the other's version of the score. To illustrate the relation of this score with Welsh numerals, we add two examples from Mr. Ellis's paper ("reprinted for private circulation from the Transactions of the Philological Society for 1877–8–9," pp. 316–372), selected from his fifty-three versions; the first is from England, the second from Ireland:

1, 2, 3, 4,
Mary at the kitchen-door,
5, 6, 7, 8,
Mary at the garden-gate.
              —*Massachusetts* (1820)

1, 2, 3, 4, 5, 6, 7, 8,
Mary sat at the garden-gate,
Eating plums off a plate,
1, 2, 3, 4, 5, 6, 7, 8.

1, 2, 3, 4, 5, 6, 7,
All good children go to heaven.
              —*Massachusetts to Pennsylvania.*

1, 2, 3, 4, 5, 6, 7, 8
All bad children have to wait.
              —*Massachusetts.*

Monkey, monkey, bottle of beer,
How many monkeys are there here?
1, 2, 3,
You are he (she).
              —*Massachusetts to Georgia.*

Little man, driving cattle,
Don't you hear his money rattle?
One, two, three,
Out goes he (she).
              —*Massachusetts.*

1. aina.	6. ithy.	11. ain-a-dig.	16. ain-a-bumfit.
2. peina.	7. mithy.	12. pein-a-dig.	17. pein-a-bumfit.
3. para.	8. owera.	13. par-a-dig.	18. par-a-bumfit.
4. peddera.	9. lowera.	14. peddler-a-dig.	19. pedder-a-bumfit.
5. pimp.	10. dig.	15. bumfit.	20. giggy.

1. eina.	6. chester.	11. eina dickera.	16. eina pumpi.
2. mina.	7. nester.	12. mina dickera.	17. mina pumpi.
3. pera.	8. nera.	13. pera dickera.	18. pera pumpi.
4. peppera.	9. dickera.	14. peppera dickera.	19. peppera pumpi.
5. pinn.	10. nin.	15. pumpi.	20. ticket.

The modern Welsh numerals, as given by Mr. Ellis:

1. un.	6. chwech.	11. un ar deg.	16. un ar bymtheg.
2. dau.	7. saith.	12. deuddeg.	17. dau ar bymtheg.
3. tri.	8. wyth.	13. tri ar deg.	18. tri ar bymtheg.
4. pedwar.	9. nau.	14. pedwar ar deg.	19. pedwar ar bymtheg.
5. pump.	10. deg.	15. pymtheg.	20. ugain.

The numbers 4, 5, 15, and combinations 1+15, 2+15, 3+15, 4+15, seem to make
the connection unmistakable; but 2, 3, 6, 7, 8, 9 appear to have been arbitrarily
affected by rhyme and alliteration.—W. W. N.

Tricks and Catches

BOY: Now you say, "Just like me," every time I stop, and I'll tell you a story.

FRIEND: All right.

BOY: I went up one flight of stairs.

FRIEND: Just like me.

BOY: I went up two flights of stairs.

FRIEND: Just like me.

BOY: I went up three flights of stairs.

FRIEND: Just like me.

BOY: I went up four flights of stairs.

FRIEND: Just like me.

BOY: I went into a little room.

FRIEND: Just like me.

BOY: I looked out of a window.

FRIEND: Just like me.

BOY: And I saw a monkey.

FRIEND: Just like me.

BOY: Oh, ho, ho, ho! Just like *you!*

The friend collapses, and seeks another boy whom he can try the same on. The boy who knows the catch turns the tables by going through everything right but his final sentence. That he changes to "Just like *you!* Ha, ha, ha! You didn't get me that time!"

There are various rough tricks that have their outbreaks and periods of infliction among school-boys just like measles or whooping-cough. One of these is the making another fellow "walk Spanish." You catch him by the collar and the slack of his pants behind, and make him step along on the tips of his toes. The walker feels very awkward and helpless, and the other fellows are very much amused by his manner. This performance is also called "The Shirt-tail Run."

"The Dutch Whirl" is considered a very clever thing among the boys. Two of them catch a third between them, each with a grip on his coat-sleeve and "pant-leg," and turn him over and land him on his feet again. It makes the whirled one a little dizzy and disconcerted, but has no serious effect if his clothing holds.

Say the following over and over as fast as you can:—

1. Six gray geese in a green field grazing.

2. Six, slick, slim saplings.

3. Theophilus Thistledown, the successful thistle sifter, in sifting a sieve full of unsifted thistles, thrust three thousand thistles through the thick

---

From *What They Say in New England,* A Book of Signs, Sayings, and Superstitions, collected by Clifton Johnson, pp. 167–173. Copyright, 1896, by Lee and Shepard. Boston.

of his thumb. If, then, Theophilus Thistledown, the successful thistle sifter, in sifting a sieve full of unsifted thistles, thrust three thousand thistles through the thick of his thumb, see that thou, in sifting a sieve full of unsifted thistles, dost not get the thistles stuck in thy tongue.

4. Six, thick, thistle sticks.

5. A cup of coffee in a copper coffee-pot.

6. The cat ran up the ladder with a raw lump of liver in its mouth. This is likewise repeated in this form:—

The cat ran over the roof of the house with a lump of raw liver in her mouth.

7. Round and round the rugged rock the ragged rascal ran.

A boy asks a friend to play a number game with him. After he has given the friend the necessary rudimentary instruction, the game proceeds in the following dialogue:—

Boy: I one it.

Friend: I two it.

Boy: I three it.

Friend: I four it.

Boy: I five it.

Friend: I six it.

Boy: I seven it.

Friend: I eight it.

Boy: Oh, you *ate* the old dead horse! (or some other subject equally choice for eating purposes).

If the friend knows the trick, he, at the end, changes the final sentence to "*You* ate it."

Ancient Joke

First person: Did you ever notice that when you get up in the morning it is always your left foot that you dress last?

Second person: No; and I don't believe it is, either.

First person: Well, whichever foot you dress first, the other must be the *left* one, mustn't it?

When this point has been made, it is proper that the company should laugh.

A Chicken Question

Boy to companion: Which would you rather have, a rooster or a pullet?

If boy number two says "a rooster," boy number one goes behind him, and gives him a hoist with his knee.

If he says "a pullet," number one pulls number two's nose.

Number one considers himself very smart in either case.

A Present

Boy: Don't you want me to give you a little red box?
Companion: Yes.
The boy then gives the other a box on the ear.

The Arrest

Boy number one: You're going to be 'rested.
Boy number two: When?
Boy number one: When you go to bed to-night.

A Mother's Call

Boy to companion: Your mother calls you, Harry (or whatever the other fellow's name is).
Harry: What for?
Boy: Because that's your name.

A Serious Charge

Boy: You're going to be arrested.
Friend: What for?
Boy: For stealin' your grandpa's toenails.

Innuendo

When two boys in school go for a drink to the waterpail at the same time, number one hands the glass to number two and says, "Age before beauty." Number two takes it, and says, "Men before monkeys." Number one finishes the dialogue and keeps up his end by responding, "The dirt before the broom."

The Monkey at School

First Child: Do you want to see a monkey?
Second Child: Yes.
Then number one holds up a mirror before number two, or goes outside and holds a dark shawl up against the window-pane for number two to look into.

A Foreign Language

Hog Latin: "Igry knowgry somegry thinggry yougry don'tgry knowgry."
Translation: "I know something you don't know."
A conversation carried on in this language between two children is as blind to their uninitiated mates as real Latin. How the speakers can

make anything out of such outlandish grunting talk is a great puzzle. But children find it even more difficult than grown people to keep a secret, and this accomplishment is not long in becoming a common possession.

Catches and Riddles

Twenty-nine and one?
　　　　Thirty.
Your face is dirty.

April's gone, summer's come;
You're a fool and I'm none.

A flock of white sheep
　On a red hill,
Here they go, there they go,
　Now they stand still.

Tell story?
　Who?
My old shoe,
Dressed in blue,
That came walking down the avenue.

Red-headed sinner,
Come down to your dinner.

Red-headed fox,
Stole your mother's pigeon-box.

Reddy in the woods
Can't catch a butterfly.

Over latch, under latch,
It takes good kisses to make a match.

Where was little Moses when the light went out,
What was he adoing and what was he about?

I climbed up the apple tree
And all the apples fell on me.
Make a pudding, make a pie.
Did you ever tell a lie?
Yes, you did, you know you did,
You stole your mother's teapot lid.

From "Games of Washington Children," by W. H. Babcock, *The American Anthropologist,* Vol. I (July, 1888), No. 3, p. 271. Washington, D.C.: Judd & Detweiler, Printers.

Rhymes and Jingles

WHEN about to run a race or engage in a jumping-match, this rhyme is appropriate:—

> One to begin
> Two to show,
> Three to make ready,
> And four to go.

At the end of the race the one who came in last sometimes consoles himself by calling out:—

> First's the worst,
> Second's the same,
> Last's the best of all the game.

> QUESTION: What's your name?
> ANSWER: Pudden tame;
> Ask me again
> And I'll tell you the same.

Some of the boys give a much ruder answer to this question in these words:—

> John Brown,
> Ask me again and I'll knock you down.

Second form:—

> QUESTION: What's your name?
> ANSWER: Pudden tame.
> QUESTION: What's your natur'?
> ANSWER: Pudden tater.
> QUESTION: What's your will?
> ANSWER: Pudden swill.

Third form:—

> QUESTION: What's your name?
> ANSWER: Pudden tame.
> QUESTION: What's your other?
> ANSWER: Bread and butter.
> QUESTION: Where do you live?
> ANSWER: In a sieve.
> QUESTION: What's your number?
> ANSWER: Cucumber.

From *What They Say in New England*, A Book of Signs, Sayings, and Superstitions, collected by Clifton Johnson, pp. 174–197. Copyright, 1896, by Lee and Shepard. Boston.

> Crowing hens and jumping sheep
> Are the worst property a farmer can keep.

Boys often say it in this way:—

> Whistling girls and crowing hens
> Always come to some bad ends.

Another version is:—

> Whistling girls and blatting sheep
> Are the worst property a farmer can keep.

Still another way to say the same thing is:—

> Whistling girls and hens that crow
> Are always sure to get a blow.

The girl's response to this innuendo is, "That is not right. It's like this:—

> Whistling girls and merino sheep
> Are the *best* property a farmer can keep."

When a boy gets mad at another he will sometimes call out derisively:—

> Paady Whacker, chew tobacker,
> If he dies, it is no matter.

In the following, two children stand and take hold of hands, and swing their arms from side to side in time to the rhythm of the verse they repeat. With the final words, hands still clasped, they turn the arms on one side over their heads and at the same time turn around themselves. The verse runs as follows:—

> Wash your mother's dishes,
> Hang 'em on the bushes.
> When the bushes begin to crack,
> Hang 'em on the nigger's back.
> When the nigger begins to run,
> Shoot him with a leather gun.

The following is a programme for Thanksgiving week:—

> Monday—wash,
> Tuesday—scour,
> Wednesday—bake,
> Thursday—devour.

In a game of tag, it is the proper thing to shout out to the one in chase:—

> Fire on the mountain,
> Fire on the sea,
> You can't catch me.

A variation:—

> Fire on the mountain
> Run, boys, run;
> The cat's in the cream-pot,
> Run, girls, run!

A quick way of counting up to one hundred:—

> Ten, ten, double ten, forty-five, fifteen.

William Blake, William Austin, and William Bond all lived in the same town. This fact inspired some local poet with the following strains, that proved quite popular among the young people:—

> Bill Blake made the cake,
> Bill Austin made the frostin,
> And Bill Bond put it on.

Rhyme addressed to a person who has red hair:—

> Redny, redny, fire on top,
> All the rednys come flipperty flop.

When you are getting ready to jump, swing your arms and say this:—

> One, two, three,
> The bumble bee,
> The rooster crows,
> And away he goes.

> Lazy folks work the best
> When the sun is in the west.

This rhyme the women folks like to repeat to the men folks when the latter find it necessary to work in the evening.

A suitable address to a Frenchman is the following:—

> Frenchy baboo
> Lived in a shoe,
> Never got up till half-past two.

A French citizen can respond to the American in terms like these:—

> Yankee Doodle went to town,
> Stuck a feather in his crown,
> Called him Macaroni.

Another derisive rhyme employed against the French is this:—

> Pea-soup and Johnny-cake
> Make a Frenchman's belly ache.

There was a little man,
He had a little gun,
He put it in his pocket,
And away he did run.

Variation:—

There was a little man,
He had a little gun,
His bullets were made of lead,
And he went out to shoot the duck,
And shot him right in the head.
Then away he did run to old Granny Jones
Because there was a fire to make,
Saying, "Here is the duck I shot in the brook,
And now I'll go after the drake."

Little Dick,
He was so quick,
He tumbled over the timber,
He bent his bow,
To shoot a crow,
And shot the cat in the winder.

If a body meet a body in a bag of beans,
Can a body tell a body what a body means?

A Modern Mother Goose

The hero of this tale was probably very like many of the makers of the chance jingles that have caught the children's ears, and become immortal by much repetition.

He is said to have lived in Enfield, Conn. One morning, in schooltime, he wrote something on a slip of paper and passed it round among his fellows. It made a good deal of ill-concealed merriment, and the teacher was fortunate enough to capture the offending bit of paper and to ferret out its author. The words on the paper were:—

Three little mice ran up the stairs
To hear Miss Blodgett say her prayers.

The teacher realized that she was being made fun of, but was so impressed by the clever expression of the lines that she said, "John, I give you five minutes to make another two lines. If you fail, I shall punish you."

The boy scratched his head, and went to work. The result was as follows:—

When Miss Blodgett said "Amen,"
The three little mice ran down again.

One person says to another: —

> Adam and Eve and Pinchme
> Went out for a swim;
> Adam and Eve got drowned,
> Who was saved?

The second person answers, "Pinchme."
Number one responds by giving number two a pinch.

Old rhyme: —

> Said Aaron to Moses,
> "Let's cut off our noses,"
> Says Moses to Aaron,
> "It's the fashion to wear 'em."

Indian counting up to twenty: —

> Eeen, teen, tether, fether, fip,
> Satra, latra, co, tethery, dick,
> Eendick, teendick, tetherdick, fetherdick, bump,
> Eenbump, teenbump, tetherbump, fetherbump, jicket.

A boy ties another's stockings together, and then hollers as loud as he can: —

> "Charlo beef,
> The beef was tough,
> Poor little Charley
> Couldn't get enough."

The name in the third line is changed to suit the case in hand.

This stocking-tying is usually done by a boy's friends while he is in swimming, and the jokers try to tie such a knot that the owner can only untie it by using his teeth. The appropriate time to say the poetry is when the boy begins to work with his teeth on the knot.

Here is a variation: —

> Chew, chew—the beef.
> The beef is tough,
> If you don't chew hard,
> You'll never get enough.

If a boy has a friend named Joseph, he can entertain him by the following rhyme: —

> Joe, Joe,
> Broke his toe
> Riding on a buffalo.

If the friend's name is Frank, the following will suit:—

> Frank, Frank,
> Turned the crank,
> His mother come out and gave him a spank,
> And knocked him over the sandbank.

If his name is Bert the following is appropriate:—

> Bert, Bert, tore his shirt
> Riding on a lump of dirt.

If his name is Samuel, he will very likely be interested in this:—

> Sam, Sam,
> The dirty man,
> Washed his face in a frying-pan,
> Combed his hair with the back of a chair,
> And danced with the toothache in the air.

Something like the above ditty is appropriate for a boy named John. The accepted way to repeat the jingle is as follows:—

> My son John is a nice old man,
> Washed his face in a frying-pan,
> Combed his hair with a wagon-wheel,
> And died with the toothache in his heel.

Take the baby's foot in your hand, wiggle the toes one after the other, beginning with the big one, and recite:—

> This little pig says, "I go steal wheat";
> This little pig says, "Where'll you get it?"
> This little pig says, "In father's barn";
> This little pig says, "I go tell";
> And this little pig says, "Quee, quee, quee!"

A variation of this story is the following:—

> This little pig goes to market,
> This little pig stays home,
> This little pig has plenty to eat,
> This little pig has none,
> This little pig says, "Wee, wee, wee!"
>   all the way home.

One of close resemblance to the above is this:—

> This little pig says, "I want some corn";
> This little pig says, "Where'll you get it?"
> This little pig says, "In grandpa's barn";
> This little pig says, "It'll do no harm";
> This little pig says, "Quee, quee, quee,
>   I can't get over the barn door-sill!"

Another toe refrain is the following, which begins with the smallest of the five:—

> Little Pee,
> Penny Rue,
> Ludy Whistle,
> Mary Hustle,
> Great big Tom, gobble, gobble!

A burlesque:—

> The boy stood on the burning deck,
> Peeling potatoes by the peck.
> When all but he had fled,
> He cried aloud and said,
> "Say! father, say!
> Shall I throw the peels away?"

Second form:—

> The boy stood on the burning deck,
> Eating peanuts by the peck.
> His father called; he could not go,
> Because he did love peanuts so.

Third form:—

> The boy stood on the burning deck,
> Eating peanuts by the peck.
> A girl stood by all dressed in blue,
> And said, "I guess I'll have some too."

A verse for a small boy:—

> Fishy, fishy, in the brook,
> Papa catch him with a hook,
> Mama fry him in a pan,
> Georgy eat him fast's he can.

The last line sometimes ends, "Like a man."

The last two lines may also be changed to read:—

> Mama fry him in the spider,
> Georgie eat him like a tiger.

The boy's name can be varied to suit the speaker.

One way of counting to ten:—

> Onery, twoery, fithery, sithery, san,
> Wheelerbone, whackerbone, inery, ninery, tan.

A verse said by a boy who parts from his companion in the evening:—

> Good-night,
> Sleep tight,
> Don't let the bedbugs bite.

A political couplet shouted by schoolboys:—

> Republican rats, take off your hats,
> And make way for the Democrats.

A jingle to say when churning:—

> Come, butter, come,
> Peter's at the gate,
> Waiting for a patty cake.

This used to be said as a charm to make the butter come quickly.

The schoolhouse at the little Massachusetts village of Hockanum seventy-five years ago was far too small to accommodate the outpouring of the population on the momentous occasion of a "last day," and it was the custom to have the exercises in the long hall of "Granther" Lyman's tavern. The piece which created the greatest sensation on one of these last days was delivered before a crowded audience by a certain small boy in the following words:—

> A woodchuck lived far over the hills, a good way off,
> And died with the whooping-cough.

It bears every mark of being original poetry, and it was repeated and laughed over for a long time afterwards.

Whether this boy originated the idea and expression or not, there are at the present time extended variations of the tale. The best of these is the following:—

> Over the hills and a good way off,
> A woodchuck died with the whooping-cough.
> The thunders rolled, the lightnings flashed,
> And broke grandma's teapot all to smash—down cellar.

When you have the baby in your lap, you can amuse it by saying:—

> "Pat a cake, pat a cake, baker's man."
> "So I will, master, as fast as I can."
> "Roll it, roll it, roll it,
>   Prick it, prick it, prick it,
>   Toss it up in the oven and bake it."

You at the same time take the baby's hands in yours, and pat them together to suit the two first lines, rub them against each other to suit the third, take one finger and dig it into the palm of the other hand to suit the fourth, and toss both hands up, and the baby too if you choose, to suit the final line. Then, if the baby is anything like the babies used to be, it will crow and be very happy.

Here is a variation of the same theme:—

> Pat a cake, pat a cake, baker's man,
> Pat it and pat it as fast as you can,
> Pat it and prick it, and mark it with B,
> And toss it in the oven for baby and me.

This is acted out in the same way, and the letter B is marked with a finger on the child's palm. B, of course, stands for baby.

Jog the baby up and down on your knees, and say:—

> Trot, trot to Boston,
> To buy a loaf of bread.
> Trot, trot, home again,
> The old trot's dead.

Trot the baby on your knee, and say:—

> Seesaw, Jack in the hedge,
> Which is the way to London Bridge?

When you have the baby in your arms and are rocking it to sleep, say:—

> Bye baby bunting,
> Papa's gone a-hunting;
> Mother's gone to milk the cow;
> Sister's gone—*I* don't know how;
> Brother's gone to get a skin
> To wrap the baby bunting in.

Whether it is a nurse or one of the sisters of the infant that is supposed to say this is not quite clear.

Catch a grasshopper, and say to it:—

> Grasshopper, grasshopper, give me some molasses,
> Or I'll kill you today, and bury you to-morrow.

When you are asked to tell a story, or to furnish amusement of most any sort, you can say:—

> I'll tell you a story
> About old Mother Morey,
> And now my story's begun;
> I'll tell you another
> About her brother,
> And now my story is done.

Or you can put it in this form:—

> I'll tell you a story
> About Jack a Nory;
> And he had a calf,
> And that's half;
> And he threw it over the wall,
> And that's all.

Two children sit opposite each other with their palms on their knees. They say this rhyme together, and clap each other's hands in time to the metre:—

> Bean porridge hot,
> Bean porridge cold,
> Bean porridge's best
> When nine days old.

In the English version, it is pease porridge or pease pudding, but New Englanders are not acquainted with those dishes.

The child's hands in the following are put palm down on the table. Go over the fingers one word to each to the end of the incantation. The finger that has the final word is turned under. Go over the remaining nine with the same lingo, and turn under the one that comes last. Repeat the process till all are turned under.

> Intra, mintra, cute-ra corn,
> Apple-seed and apple-thorn,
> Wire, brier, limber lock,
> Six geese in a flock,
> Sit and sing by the spring
> O-u-t, out; up on yonder hill
> There sits old Father Wells;
> He has jewels, he has rings,
> He has many pretty things,
> Whip-jack, two nails, blow the bellows
>   out, old man.

This is also said as follows:—

> Intra, mintra, cute-ra, corn,
> Apple-seed, and apple-thorn,
> Wire, brier, limber lock,
> Six geese in a flock,
> Seven sit by the spring,
> O-u-t, out,
> Hang mother's dishcloth out,
> Fling, flang, flash it off.

THE WEEK

Wash on Monday,
Iron on Tuesday,
Bake on Wednesday,
Brew on Thursday,
Churn on Friday,
Mend on Saturday,
Go to meeting on Sunday.

A girl will sometimes make the following remarks to the new moon.
I have never heard that the revelation was made to her that she prayed
for—at any rate, not by the moon.

New moon, new moon, pray tell to me
Who my true lover is to be.—
The color of his hair,
The clothes he will wear,
And the day he'll be wedded to me.

If before April first one boy tries to fool another, boy number two
squelches the would-be fooler by saying:—

April fool's a-coming,
And you're the biggest fool a-running.

If the attempt is made after April first, he says:—

April fool is past,
And you're the biggest fool at last.

A rhyme that does service for both occasions is this:—

Up the ladder, and down the tree,
You're a bigger fool than me.

A JINGLE FOR THE BABY'S FEET

Shoe the old horse, shoe the old mare,
Drive a nail here, and drive a nail there;
But let the little nobby colt go bare.

When you say, "Shoe the old horse," pat the bottom of the baby's
right foot to imitate the driving of nails. When you say, "Shoe the old
mare," pat the left foot. Continue this process in the second line, first
the right foot, then the left. In the final line it is imagined that the little
nobby colt kicks up its heels, and you must catch the baby's ankles, and
give them a grand toss to suit this idea.

Boy number one inquires of boy number two, "What do you do when
your mother licks you?"

Boy number two replies:—

> "Ice-cream
> Made by steam,
> Sold by a donkey in a charcoal team."

At picnics you will sometimes hear the children say:—

> Lemonade,
> Made in the shade,
> Stirred with a spade,
> By an old maid.

The children at one time used to enjoy shouting at each other the following poem:—

> Oh, what is the use
> Of chewing tobacco,
> And spitting the juice?

Whether it was the rhythm and rhyme of the piece or its moral sentiment that was so pleasing to them is uncertain.

Here is one way to amuse a child. Clasp your hands with the fingers turned inward, and repeat the following ditty, which you illustrate by changing the position of your fingers and hands:—

> Here's a meeting-house, there's the steeple,
> Look inside and see all the people.
> Here's the singers going up-stairs,
> And here's the minister saying his prayers.

To make the steeple, elevate your forefingers with the tips joined. To suit the second line open your hands a little, and wiggle the ends of your clasped fingers. Illustrate the singers going up-stairs by making the fingers of your right hand walk up those of your left. Lastly, clinch your hands, put one fist on top of the other, and that is the minister.

When a schoolboy wishes to be humorous, he will sometimes call out to a companion:—

> "Can you read, can you write,
> Can you smoke your daddy's pipe?"

A small girl who wishes her companions to understand that she is overcome by ennui will sometimes sighingly remark:—

> "Oh, dear, bread and beer,
> If I was home I shouldn't be here!"

A FINGER POEM

Five little rabbits went out to walk;
They liked to boast as well as talk.
The first one said, "I hear a gun!"
The second one said, "I will not run!"
Two little ones said, "Let's sit in the shade."
The big one said, "I'm not afraid!"
Bang, bang! went a gun,
And the five little rabbits run.

The child holds up one of its hands while it repeats these lines. The fingers are the five rabbits. With his other hand he takes hold of each finger in turn as he speaks of the rabbit it represents. "The first one" is the thumb. "The second one" is the forefinger. "The two little ones" are the two final fingers. "The big one" is the middle finger.

A SCHOOLBOY JINGLE

"Fire, fire!"
Said Mrs. McGuire.
"Where, where?"
Said Mrs. Ware.
"Down town!"
Said Mrs. Brown.
"Oh, Lord save us!"
Said Mrs. Davis.

ANOTHER JINGLE

Two's a couple
Three's a crowd,
Four on the sidewalk
Is never allowed.

Pin Lore

See a pin and pick it up,
All that day you will have luck;
See a pin and let it lay,
You'll have bad luck all that day.

Needles and pins!
Needles and pins!
When a man's married
His trouble begins.

It is a sin to steal a pin,
It is a greater to steal a tater.

Rope-Skipping Rhymes

Cinderella dressed in yellow
Went uptown to meet her fellow.
How many kisses did he give **her?**
(Count until there is a miss.)

Johnny over the ocean,
Johnny over the sea,
Johnny broke a teacup
And blamed it on me.

I told Ma,
Ma told Pa;
Johnny got a lickin',
Hee, hee, haw!
Salt, vinegar,
Mustard, pepper!
(Gradual increase of speed.)

Standing on the corner
Chewing bubble gum,
Along came a beggar
And asked me for some.

O you dirty beggar,
O you dirty bum!
Ain't you ashamed
To ask me for gum?

I love coffee,
I love tea;
How many boys
Are stuck on me?
(Count until there is a miss.)

Teddy bear, teddy bear, turn around;
Teddy bear, teddy bear, touch the ground;
Teddy bear, teddy bear, tie your shoe;
Teddy bear, teddy bear, now skidoo!

From "Rope-Skipping, Counting-Out, and Other Rhymes of Children," by Paul G. Brewster, *Southern Folklore Quarterly*, Vol. III (September, 1939), No. 3, pp. 173–178. Gainesville: University of Florida.

Most of the rhymes presented here I obtained as long ago as 1934, at which time I was just beginning my search for folksongs still current in Indiana; some are part of a collection made during the past summer, when, with the aid of a grant from Indiana University, I was gathering folklore in the southern part of the state; still others were given me by some of my students here at the University of Missouri. —P. G. B.

Teddy bear, teddy bear, point to the sky;
Teddy bear, teddy bear, show your glass eye;
Teddy bear, teddy bear, pull your wig;
Teddy bear, teddy bear, dance a jig.

Down in the valley
Where the green grass grows
There sat *(girl's name)*
Sweet as a rose.
She sang, she sang,
She sang so sweet;
Along came *(boy's name)*
And kissed her cheek.
How many kisses did he give her?
(Count until there is a miss.)

Ice cream soda, lemonade pop;
Tell me the initials of your sweetheart.
(Call letters of the alphabet until there is a miss.)

Johnny gave me apples,
Johnny gave me pears,
Johnny gave me fifteen cents
And kissed me on the stairs.

I'd rather wash the dishes,
I'd rather scrub the floor,
I'd rather kiss a nigger boy
Behind the kitchen door.

Red, white, and yellow,
Went downtown to meet my fellow:
How many kisses did he give me?
(Count until there is a miss.)

Red, white, and yellow,
Have you any fellow?
("Yes," "no," "maybe so.")

Red, white, and green,
Have you any queen?
(Same as above—for boys.)

Grace, Grace, dressed in lace,
Went upstairs to powder her face.
How many boxes did she use?
(Count until there is a miss.)

Mabel, Mabel, set the table;
Don't forget the salt—and PEPPER!

Rooms for rent,
Inquire within;
When I move out,
Let —— move in.
(Used for "calling in.")

Charlie Chaplin sat on a fence
Trying to make a dollar out of fifteen cents.

Charlie Chaplin went to France
To teach the ladies how to dance;
First a heel and then a toe,
A skip and a hop and away you go!

Charlie Chaplin went to France
To teach the ladies how to dance;
First the heel and then the toe,
Spin around and out you go!

Old lady, old lady, touch the ground;
Old lady, old lady, turn around;
Old lady, old lady, point your shoe;
Old lady, old lady, 23 skidoo!

Miss, miss, little Miss, miss;
When she misses, she misses like this.

Rooms for rent; inquire within;
A lady got put out for drinking gin.
If she promises to drink no more,
Here's the key to *(boy's name)* door.

Last night and the night before
Twenty-four robbers came to my door,
And this is what they said:
"Buster, Buster, hands on head;
Buster, Buster, go to bed;
Buster, Buster, if you don't,
I'm afraid they'll find you dead."

Apples, peaches, creamery butter,
Here's the name of my true lover.
(Call letters of the alphabet.)

Old Man Lazy
Drives me crazy;
Up the ladder,
Down the ladder,
H-O-T spells hot!

Had a little girl dressed in blue;
She died last night at half-past two,
Did she go up or down?
("Up," "down," "up," "down," etc.)

Raspberry, raspberry, raspberry jam;
What are the initials of my young man?
   (Call letters of the alphabet.)

Teddy, teddy, teddy,
Turn around, 'round, 'round;
Teddy, teddy, teddy,
Touch the ground, ground, ground;

Teddy, teddy, teddy,
Show your shoe, shoe, shoe;
Teddy, teddy, teddy,
That's enough for you.

Betty, Betty, Betty Jo,
What are the initials of my best beau?
   (Call letters of the alphabet.)

Raspberry, strawberry, cherry pie;
You love them all and so do I.
      ("Yes," "no," "maybe so.")

Virginia had a baby;
She named it Tiny Tim;
She put it in the bath tub
To teach it how to swim.
It floated up the river;
It floated down the lake;
Now Virginia's baby
Has the stomach ache.

Fudge, fudge, tell the judge
Mother has a newborn baby;
It isn't a girl and it isn't a boy;
It's just a fair young lady.
Wrap it up in tissue paper
And send it up the elevator:
First floor, miss;
Second floor, miss;
Third floor, miss;
Fourth floor,
Kick it out the elevator door.

I went uptown to see Miss Brown;
She gave me a nickel and I bought a pickle;
The pickle was sour, so I bought a flower;
The flower was red, so I bought a thread;
The thread was thin, so I bought a pin;
[The pin was sharp, so I bought a harp;]
And on this harp I played;
I love coffee, I love tea;
How many boys are stuck on me?
            (Count until there is a miss.)

My mother and your mother live across the way;
Every night they have a fight, and this is what they say:
Icka backa, soda cracker, icka backa boo;
Icka backa, soda cracker, out goes you!

            One, two, buckle my shoe;
            Three, four, shut the door;
            Five, six, pick up sticks;
            Seven, eight, shut the gate;
            Nine, ten, begin again.

            Spanish dancer, do the split;
            Spanish dancer, give a high kick;
            Spanish dancer, turn around;
            Spanish dancer, get out of town.

Teacher, teacher, don't whip me;
Whip that nigger behind that tree;
He stole peaches, I stole none;
Put him in the calaboose just for fun.

            Johnny over the ocean,
            Johnny over the sea;
            If you can catch Johnny
            You can catch me.

            Johnny over the ocean,
            Johnny over the sea;
            You may catch Johnny,
            But you can't catch me.

Betty, Betty stumped her toe
On the way to Mexico;
On the way back she broke her back
Sliding on the railroad track.

Sidewalk Rhymes of New York

Roses are red,
Violets are blue,
I like pecans,
Nuts to you.

Roses are red,
Violets are blue,
Elephants are fat
And so are you.

Roses are red,
Violets are blue,
If I had your mug,
I'd join the zoo.

Roses are red,
Violets are blue,
Everybody stinks
And so do you.

Roses are red,
Violets are blue,
I use Lifebuoy.
Why don't you?

Looie, pooie,
You're full of hooey.

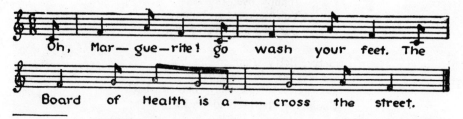

From "Songs of Innocence," by Dorothy Mills and Morris Bishop, *The New Yorker*, Vol. XIII (November 13, 1937), No. 39, pp. 32–42. Copyright, 1937, by the F-R Publishing Corporation. New York City. Tunes transcribed by Charles Seeger.

Marguerite,
Go wash your feet;
The Board of Health
Is 'cross the street.

Eight and eight are sixteen,
Stick your nose in kerosene,
Wipe it off with ice cream.

Tonight, tonight,
The pillow fight,
Tomorrow's the end of school;
Break the dishes, break the chairs,
Trip the teachers on the stairs.

Bouncy, bouncy ballie,
I lost the leg of my dollie;
My mother came out
And gave me a clout
That turned my petticoat
Inside out.

My mother, your mother, hanging out the clothes,
My mother gave your mother a punch in the nose.
What color did it turn?
Red, yellow, blue, green, violet, orange, etc.

Your mother, my mother, live across the way;
Every night they have a fight,
And this is what they say:
"Your old man is a dirty old man,
'Cause he washes his face in the frying pan,
He combs his hair
With the leg of a chair;
Your old man is a dirty old man."

I should worry, I should care,
I should marry a millionaire;
He should die, I should cry,
I should marry another guy.

I had a little brother,
His name was Tiny Tim;
I put him in the bathtub
To teach him how to swim.
He drank up all the water,
He ate up all the soap;
He died last night
With a bubble in his throat.

Mother, Mother, I am sick;
Send for the doctor, quick, quick, quick.
Doctor, Doctor, shall I die?
Yes, my darling, do not cry.
How many coaches shall I have?
Ten, twenty, thirty, etc.
       (Till the skipper misses.)

    Teddy on the railroad,
    Picking up stones;
    Along came an engine
    And broke Teddy's bones.
    "Oh," said Teddy,
    "That's no fair!"
    "Oh," said the engineer,
    "I don't care."

    Silence in the courtroom!
    The judge wants to spit.

Mother, Mother, Mother, pin a rose on me.
Two little girls [or boys] are after me;
One is blind and the other can't see;
Mother, Mother, Mother, pin a rose on me.

        Bless the meat,
        Damn the skin,
        Open your mouth
        And cram it in.

    Jesus, lover of my soul,
    Lead me to the sugar bowl.
    If the sugar bowl is empty,
    Lead me to my mamma's pantry.

        Up the river,
        Down the lake;
        The teacher's got
        The bellyache.

    Hot roasted peanuts,
    Tell the teacher she's nuts;
    If she asks you what's your name,
    Tell the teacher she's a pain.

        Up the ladder,
        Down the tree,
        You're a bigger
        Fool than me.

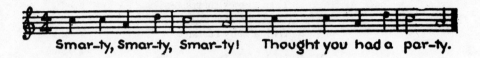

Smar-ty, Smar-ty, Smar-ty! Thought you had a par-ty.

> Smarty, smarty,
> Had a party,
> And nobody came
> But an old fat darky.[1]

> Mary's mad,
> And I am glad,
> And I know what will please her:
> A bottle of wine
> To make her shine,
> And a sweet little boy to squeeze her.

> Mary's mad,
> And I am glad,
> And I know what will please her:
> A bottle of ink
> To make her stink,
> And a little nigger to squeeze her.

I went down to Grandpa's farm,
The billygoat chased me all around the barn,
Chased me up in the sycamore tree,
And this is the song he sang to me:
"I love coffee, I love tea,
I love the boys and the boys love me."

> If you don't like my apples,
> Then don't shake my tree;
> I'm not after your boy friend,
> He's after me.

> Life is short,
> Death will come;
> Go it, Ruth,
> While you're young.

> When you get married,
> And your husband gets cross,
> Just pick up the broom
> And ask who's boss.

May your life be strewn with roses,
And your children have pug noses.

---

[1] Tune transcribed by Charles Seeger.

First comes love,
Then comes marriage;
Then comes Edith
With a baby carriage.

Buck, buck, you lousy muck,
How many fists have I got up,
One, two, or none?

Inty minty tibblety fig,
Deema dima doma nig,
Howchy powchy domi nowchy,
Hom tom tout,
Olligo bolliga boo,
Out goes YOU.

One-ery two-ery ickery Ann,
Fillicy fallacy Nicholas John,
Queever quaver Irish Mary,
Stinclum stanclum buck.

Ibbety bibbety gibbety goat,
Ibbety bibbety canalboat,
Dictionary,
Down the ferry,
Out goes YOU.

Minnie and a minnie and a ha, ha, ha,
Kissed her fellow in a trolley car;
I told Ma, Ma told Pa,
Minnie got a licking and a ha, ha, ha.

I went downtown
To meet Mrs. Brown;
She gave me a nickel
To buy me a pickle;
The pickle was sour,
She gave me a flower;
The flower was dead,
She gave me a thread;
The thread was thin,
She gave me a pin;
The pin was sharp,
She gave me a harp;
The harp began to sing:
Minnie and a minnie and a ha, ha, ha.

Cinderella, dressed in yellow,
Gone downtown to buy an umbrella;
On the way she met her fellow.
How many kisses did she receive?
Five, ten, fifteen, twenty, etc.

Cinderella, dressed in red,
Went downtown to buy some thread.
Along came a fellow whose name was Red,
And shot her with a bullet that was made of lead.

Judge, judge, tell the judge
Mamma has a baby.
It's a boy, full of joy,
Papa's going crazy.
Wrap it up in tissue paper,
Send it down the elevator.
How many pounds did it weigh?
One, two, three, etc.

I won't go to Macy's any more, more, more,
There's a big fat policeman at the door, door, door,
He grab me by the collar and he make me pay a dollar,
So I won't go to Macy's any more, more, more.

Ivory soap,
See it float
Down the river
Like a boat.

Roll, roll, Tootsie Roll,
Roll, marble, in the hole.

Floor to let,
Inquire within;
Lady put out
For drinking gin.
If she promises to drink no more,
Here's the key to her back door.

When Buster Brown was one,
He used to suck his thumb,
Thumb me over, thumb me over,
A, B, C.
When Buster Brown was two,
He used to buckle his shoe,
Shoe me over, shoe me over,
A, B, C, etc.

Happy Hooligan, number nine,
Hung his breeches on the line;
When the line began to swing,
Happy Hooligan began to sing:
"On the mountain stands a lady,
Who she is I do not know;
All she wants is gold and silver,
And a nice young man with whom to go."
Come in, my sister ——,
Go out, my sister ——.

Toots and Casper went to town,
Tootsie bought an evening gown,
Casper bought a pair of shoes,
Buttercup bought the *Daily News*.
How many pages did he read?
Five, ten, fifteen. twenty, etc.

Rin Tin Tin
Swallowed a pin,
He went to the doctor,
And the doctor wasn't in.
He went to the nurse,
And she said a curse,
And that was the end
Of Rin Tin Tin.

Rin Tin Tin
Swallowed a pin,
He went to the doctor,
And the doctor wasn't in.
He knocked on the door,
And fell on the floor;
Along came a nurse,
And hit him on the jaw.

Charlie Chaplin sat on a pin;
How many inches did it go in?
One, two, three, etc.

Charlie Chaplin went to war;
He pulled the trigger,
And shot a nigger,
And that was the end of the war.

One, two, three, four,
Charlie Chaplin went to war.
He taught the nurses how to dance,
And this is what he taught them:
Heel, toe, over we go,
Heel, toe, over we go;
Salute to the king,
And bow to the queen,
And turn your back
On the Kaiserine.

I scream,
You scream,
We all scream
For ice cream.

Annie bolanny,
Tillie annie, go sanny,
Tee-legged, tie-legged,
Bow-legged Annie.

I asked my mother for fifty cents
To see the elephant jump the fence;
He jumped so high,
He reached the sky,
And never came back till the Fourth of July.

Yellow-belly, yellow-belly, come and take a swim;
Yes, by golly, when the tide comes in.

II. SINGING AND PLAY-PARTY GAMES

*These amusements came into existence because they were adapted
to the conditions of early life; they pass away because those conditions are altered. The taste of other days sustained them; the
taste of our day abandons them.—W. W. NEWELL*

IN THE field of the game and dance, two distinctive American developments from British sources are the square dance, quadrille, or cotillion
(as distinguished from the English contra-dance or longways dance, which
still persists in New England) and the play-party.

In the United States the term square dance has come to stand for old-
time set dancing generally, whether of the square, longways, or circle
formation. Although the guitar and the banjo are used to accompany the
fiddle at dances, as well as to accompany the folk singer, the fiddle is the
American folk musical instrument par excellence. Its portability and
adaptability made it the musical voice of backwoods and frontier America
and the country fiddler one of the most picturesque of pioneer folk characters. Another minstrel type is the square-dance caller or prompter,
who, in a mixture of rhythmic prose and doggerel made up of "calls" interspersed with patter, intones and (in the Northeast and Southwest) sings
or half-sings the directions.

Because of religious prejudice against dancing and especially the fiddle,
as the instrument of the devil, the young people of rural America developed
the play-party as an alternative form of amusement, which substituted singing for instrumental accompaniment. A cross between dancing and the
traditional singing games of children, the play-party retains the best
features of both. To the courtship and other dramatic devices of the
game, such as choosing and stealing partners, the play-party adds certain
square dance movements and figures, in which, however, partners are
swung by the hands instead of by the waist. The leader combines the
functions of caller and floor-manager; and like the caller he is something
of a folk-poet, with the gift of improvisation.

A comparison of play-party games and singing games shows the former returning to the grown-up level from which the latter were originaliy descended. Whether or not singing games reflect, in their form and content, the traditional formations and formulae of ancient pagan ceremonials, they represent the survival, on the childhood level, of the rounds, reels, and carols of adults of an earlier day. In the process of "downward transmission," singing games have acquired many childish features, such as the "pleasures of motion" and "playing at work." Play-party games, on the other hand, have come of age, and make the most of realistic and satiric comment on the personalities of the players and incidents of the "swinging play" as well as on the customs, characters, objects, activities, and backgrounds of rural and frontier America.

These changes also illustrate the process of modernization and localization. Thus in an Oklahoma version of "Hog Drovers" (originally an Irish game played at wakes) cowboys and oil-drillers are among the rejected occupations. One of the largest collections of allusive stanzas, many of them interchangeable with other play-party songs, such as "Cindy" and "Liza Jane," has been attracted to "Old Joe Clark," which is a vigorously and fabulously vulgar comic epic of cards, chickens, courting, chains, coons, coon dogs, and other critters.

There She Stands, a Lovely Creature

THIS pretty song has been recited to us by informants of the most cultivated class, and, on the other hand, we have seen it played as a round by the very "Arabs of the street," in words identically the same. It is an old English song, which has been fitted for a ring-game by the composition of an additional verse, to allow the selection of a partner.

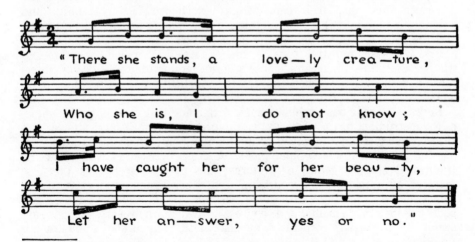

"There she stands, a love—ly crea—ture,
Who she is, I do not know;
I have caught her for her beau—ty,
Let her an—swer, yes or no."

From *Games and Songs of American Children*, collected and compared by William Wells Newell, pp. 55–56. Copyright, 1883, 1903, by Harper & Brothers. New York and London.

"There she stands, a lovely creature,
Who she is, I do not know;
I have caught her for her beauty,—
Let her answer, yes or no.

"Madam, I have gold and silver,
Lady, I have houses and lands,
Lady, I have ships on the ocean,
All I have is at thy command."

"What care I for your gold and silver,
What care I for your houses and lands,
What care I for your ships on the ocean—
All I want is a nice young man."
New York.

Do, Do, Pity My Case

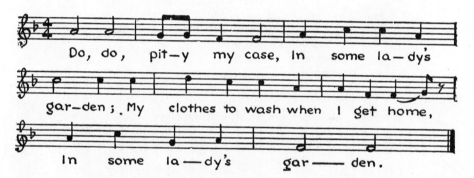

Do, do, pity my case,
In some lady's garden;
My clothes to wash when I get home,
In some lady's garden.

Do, do, pity my case,
In some lady's garden;
My clothes to iron when I get home,
In some lady's garden.

And so on, the performers lamenting the duty which lies upon them of
scrubbing their floors, baking their bread, etc.

Louisiana.

This pretty dance, with its idiomatic English, which comes to us from
the extreme South, is obviously not modern. The chorus refers, not to the
place of the labor, but to the locality of the dance: it may have been

Ibid., p. 87.

originally *in my lady's garden.* Our informant remembers the game as danced by Negro children, their scanty garments flying as the ring spun about the trunk of some large tree; but (though the naïve appeal to pity may seem characteristic of Southern indolence) this is evidently no Negro song.

Hunt the Squirrel (Itisket, Itasket)

A RING of players is formed, about the outside of which circles a child who carries a knotted handkerchief, with which he finally taps another on the shoulder, and starts to run around the ring. The child touched must pick up the handkerchief, and run in the opposite direction from the first. The two players, when they meet, must curtsey three times. The toucher endeavors to secure the other's place in the ring, failing which, he must begin again. As he goes about the circle, he recites the words:

> Hunt the squirrel through the wood,
> I lost him, I found him;
> I have a little dog at home,
> He won't bite you,
> He won't bite you,
> And he *will* bite you.
>
> *Cambridge, Mass.*

In Philadelphia, a corresponding rhyme begins:

> I carried water in my glove,
> I sent a letter to my love.

A variation from New York:

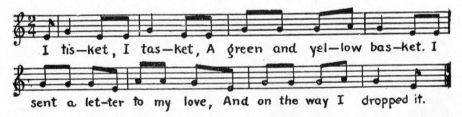

I tis—ket, I tas—ket, A green and yel—low bas—ket. I sent a let—ter to my love, And on the way I dropped it.

The name of the game in England is "Drop-glove."

Another and apparently older way of playing "Hunt the Squirrel" is a game in which the child touched follows the toucher until he has caught him, pursuing him both in and out of the ring, being obliged to enter and leave the circle at the same point as the latter.

A kissing-game, in which the player who makes the circuit taps another

---

Ibid., pp. 168–169.

on the shoulder, and then takes flight, while the person touched is entitled to a kiss if he can capture the fugitive before the latter has made the tour of the circle and gained the vacant place, is a favorite among the "Pennsylvania Dutch," under the name of "Hen-slauch" (Hand-slag), that is, striking with the hand. The game is there called "Ring," and has inspired certain verses of Harbach, the nearest approach to a poet which that unimaginative race has produced.[1]

In a similar game, formerly played in Massachusetts, the leader of the game touches one of the party on the shoulder, and asks, "Have you seen my sheep?" The first replies, "How was it dressed?" The toucher now describes the costume of some player, who, as soon as he recognizes the description of himself, must take flight, and endeavor to regain his place in safety.

Walking on the Green Grass

Walking on the green grass,
    Walking side by side,
Walking with a pretty girl,
    She shall be my bride.

And now we form a round ring,
    The girls are by our sides;
Dancing with the pretty girls
    Who shall be our brides.

And now the king upon the green
Shall choose a girl to be his queen;
    Shall lead her out his bride to be,
    And kiss her, one, two, three.
Now take her by the hand, this queen,
And swing her round and round the green.

Oh, now we'll go around the ring,
And ev'ry one we'll swing.
    Oh, swing the king and swing the queen,
    Oh, swing the king and swing the queen,
    Oh, swing 'em round and round the green.
    Oh, swing 'em round the green.

---

[1] See his "Schulhaus an dem Krik."—W. W. N.

Ibid., pp. 227–229.

Walk-ing on the green grass, Walk-ing side by side,

Walk-ing with a pret-ty girl, She shall be my bride. And

now we form a round ring, The girls are by our sides;

Danc-ing with the pret-ty girls Who shall be our brides. And

now the king up-on the green, Shall choose a girl to be his queen; Shall

lead her out his bride to be, And kiss her one, two, three.

Now take her by the hand, this queen, And

swing her round and round the green. Oh, now we'll go a —

round the ring, And ev'—ry one we'll swing.

Oh, swing the king and swing the queen, Oh,

swing the king and swing the queen, Oh, swing'em round and

round the green, Oh, swing 'em round the green.

This dance, belonging to young men and women as well as to children, is described by the recorder as follows:

The men select their partners as if for a dance, and, thus paired, promenade as in a school procession, singing the first verse, "Walking on the green grass." The procession then resolves itself into a ring, youths and maidens alternating, all singing: "And now we form a round ring." During the singing of this stanza the ring has kept moving. It is next broken into two lines, one of maidens, the other of youths, facing each other as for a reel. The song is resumed with the words, "And now the king upon the green," and each of the actions described in the verse is performed by the couple at the head of the lines. Having thus called out, saluted, and swung his partner, the man begins with the second woman, and thence down the line, swinging each of the women dancers in turn, the example being followed by his partner with the men, the song continuing, "Oh, now we'll go around the ring, and every one we'll swing." These words are sung over and over, if necessary, until all the dancers have been swung. Thereupon the king and queen take their places at the foot of the lines, and become the subjects of another couple, song and action beginning with the verse, "And now the king upon the green," etc. After all the couples have played at royalty, the promenade is resumed, and the game begun again, generally with change of partners.

This song is unrecorded in Great Britain; but its antiquity and status as a portion of a dance of which "Tread the Green Grass" is also a fragment seem to me sufficiently attested by correspondence with the third verse of the following rhyme, given by Mrs. Gomme:

> Here we come up the green grass,
>   Green grass, green grass,
> Here we come up the green grass,
>   Dusty, dusty, day.

> Fair maid, pretty maid,
>   Give your hand to me,
> I'll show you a blackbird,
>   A blackbird on the tree.

> We'll all go roving,
>   Roving side by side;
> I'll take my fairest ——,
>   I'll take her for a bride.

Sugar-Lump

MR. BABCOCK supplies a rude rhyme, obviously the reduction of this pretty dance [Walking on the Levy]. The play begins, "Bounce around, my sugar-lump," and proceeds, "Lower the window," "Hoist the window," "Don't miss a window," the player accosted being always addressed as "sugar-lump." The game seems to continue until a window is missed.

"Sugar-lump" is British also, but I have not elsewhere noticed as term of endearment "cinnamon," which occurs in a Florida dance resembling the "Virginia Reel." The first man leads his partner to the foot of the

Ibid., p. 231.

ladies' line, himself proceeds to the top of the men's line, and turns each lady, as his partner does each man, the couple themselves turning after each of the others, to the melody:

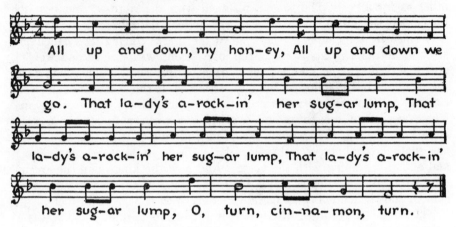

All up and down, my honey,
All up and down we go.
That lady's a-rockin' her sugar lump,
That lady's a-rockin' her sugar lump,
That lady's a-rockin' her sugar lump,
O, turn, cinnamon, turn.

Swine-Herders (Hog Drovers)

A.—"Hog-drivers, hog-drivers, hog-drivers we air,
A-courtin' yer darter so sweet and fair;
And kin we git lodgin' here, O here—
And kin we git lodgin' here?"

Ibid., pp. 232–233.

"Now this is my darter that sets by my side,
And no hog-driver can get 'er fer a bride;
And you kain't git lodgin' here, O here—
And you kain't git lodgin' here."

"Yer darter is pretty, yer ugly yerself,
So we'll travel on further and seek better wealth,
And we don't want lodgin' here, O here—
And we don't want lodgin' here."

"Now this is my darter that sets by my side,
And Mr. —— kin git 'er fer a bride,
And he kin git lodgin' here, O here—
And he kin git lodgin' here."

Come under, come under, My honey, my love, my heart's a-bove, Come under, come under, Be —— low Gal — i — lee.

Come under, come under,
   My honey, my love, my heart's above—
Come under, come under,
   Below Galilee.

We've caught you as a prisoner,
   My honey, my love, my heart's above—
We've caught you as a prisoner,
   Below Galilee.

Then hug 'er neat, and kiss 'er sweet,
   My honey, my love, my heart's above—
Then hug 'er nice, and kiss 'er twice,
   Below Galilee.

     *   *   *   *   *

From the communication of the recorder is given the following account of the manner of playing: A man, generally an older man, and a girl sit side by side on two chairs in the middle of a room, so placed as to face in opposite directions; another man and a girl walk around hand in hand, and sing, "Naow this is my darter," etc. The "Hog-drivers" retort with the second verse, after which the father sings the third verse, in which he names as partner of his daughter any man whom the girl selects. The latter and her chosen swain then join hands and withdraw, another girl sits beside the father, and the performance is repeated until all players are paired. Then the last girl and the father stand up, and by joining hands make a bridge; they sing, "Come under," etc., while the other couples pass through. On a second attempt at passage, the first couple is captured by the father and his companion, who sing, "We've caught you as a prisoner," etc. The imprisoned man kisses his partner twice, the two are released, and the game continues with another couple. In the Hickory Gap region, some twenty miles from Asheville, the game is popular with old and young. These mountaineers consider dancing immoral, but gather from far and wide whenever a "fuss" is on foot.

In regard to the music, the recorder remarks that none of the intervals are absolutely correct, and that the impression made on the hearer curiously resembles that caused by songs of North American Indians. The intervals could be accurately reproduced only by a violin, but in singing the effect may be gained by flatting the crossed intervals.

In the mountains the game would be designated as "comic," such appellation being bestowed on any song which cannot be termed "sacred."

North Carolina Mountains (near Asheville, N. C.).

Sailing at High Tide

Sail-ing in the boat when the tide runs high,
Sail-ing in the boat when the tide runs high,
Sail-ing in the boat when the tide runs high,
Wait-ing for the pret-ty girl to come by'm by.
Here she comes so fresh and fair, Sky—blue
eyes and curl-y hair, Ros-y in cheek, dim-ple in her
chin, Say, young men, but you can't come in.

Ibid., pp. 238–239.

Sailing in the boat when the tide runs high, [*thrice*]
Waiting for the pretty girl to come by'm by.
  Here she comes so fresh and fair.
  Sky-blue eyes and curly hair,
Rosy in cheek, dimple in her chin,
Say, young men, but you can't come in.

Rose in the garden for you, young man, [*twice*]
Rose in the garden, get it if you can,
But take care and don't choose a frost-bitten one.

Choose your partner, stay till day, [*thrice*]
Never mind what the old folks say.

Old folks say 'tis the very best way, [*thrice*]
To court all night and sleep all day.
Ashford, Conn. (1865).

The recorder [1] remarks concerning this game and others from the same
neighborhood that they were played as late as the year 1870, at the so-
called "Evening Party." About midnight were served refreshments, and
the singing and dancing kept up until about four o'clock in the morning,
when the young men huddled about the door, and as the girls came out
each offered his arm to the maid of his choice, with the words, "Can I
see you home?" After which they separated, and went in the dark, often
across fields, to their scattered homes, perhaps two miles away. At the
door of the fair one there was always a final hug and kiss. Of flirting
there was not much; when a girl had acquired the name of "liking the
boys" (which meant receiving questionable attentions from more than one)
she herself, and the young men who would "wait on her," were considered
as of doubtful character, and likely no more to be accepted as escor'
by those on whom no reproach rested.

Weevily Wheat

It's step her to your weev'ly wheat,
It's step her to your barley,
It's step her to your weev'ly wheat,
To bake a cake for Charley.

---

[1] Emma S. Backus, "Song-Games from Connecticut," *The Journal of American
Folk-Lore,* Vol. XIV, p. 296.—W. W. N.

From *The American Songbag,* by Carl Sandburg, p. 161. Copyright, 1927, by Harcourt, Brace & Company, Inc. New York.

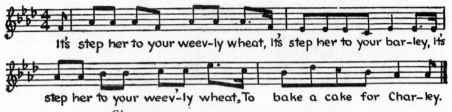

It's step her to your weev-ly wheat, It's step her to your bar-ley, It's step her to your weev-ly wheat, To bake a cake for Char-ley.

Chorus:

O Charley he's a fine young man,
O Charley he's a dandy,
He loves to hug and kiss the girls,
And feed 'em on good candy.

The higher up the cherry tree,
The riper grow the cherries,
The more you hug and kiss the girls,
The sooner they will marry.

Over the river to water the sheep,
To measure up the barley,
Over the river to water the sheep,
To bake a cake for Charley.

My pretty little Pink, I suppose you think,
I care but little about you,
But I'll let you know before you go
I cannot do without you.

Old Joe Clark [1]

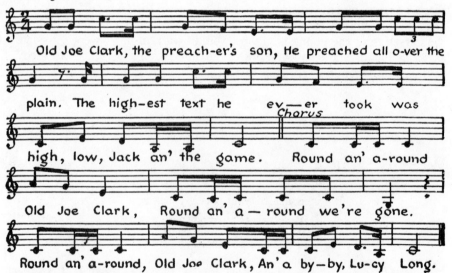

Old Joe Clark, the preach-er's son, He preached all o-ver the plain. The high-est text he ev — er took was high, low, Jack an' the game. *Chorus* Round an' a-round Old Joe Clark, Round an' a — round we're gone. Round an' a-round, Old Joe Clark, An' a by—by, Lu-cy Long.

From *The American Play-Party Song, With a Collection of Oklahoma Texts and Tunes*, by B. A. Botkin, pp. 272–285. Copyright, 1937, by B. A. Botkin. The University Studies of the University of Nebraska, Volume XXXVII, Nos. 1–4. Lincoln, Nebraska.

[1] Sung by Clayton Black, east of Noble, Cleveland County, Oklahoma.

Old Joe Clark, the preacher's son,
  He preached all over the plain.
The highest text he ever took
  Was high, low, Jack an' the game.

Chorus:
  Round an' around, Old Joe Clark,
    Round an' around we're gone.
  Round an' around, Old Joe Clark,
    An' a by-by, Lucy Long.

Old Joe Clark he had a dog,
  As blind as he could be.
Ran a redbug round a stump,
  And a coon up a holler tree.

If you see that girl of mine,
  Tell her if you please
Whenever she goes to roll that dough
  To roll up her dirty sleeves.

If you see that girl of mine,
  Tell her if you can
Whenever she goes to roll that dough
  To wash her dirty hands.

Variant and Additional Stanzas [1]

Old Joe Clark is dead and gone,
  Hope he is doing well.
Made me wear the ball and chain
  Till my old ankle swelled.

I went down to old Joe's house,
  He was sick in bed;
Rammed my finger down his throat
  And pulled out a chicken head.[2]

I went down to old Joe's house,
  He was eating supper.
Stumped my toe on the table leg
  And rammed my nose in the butter.

Old Joe Clark had a dog,
  He was as blind as he could be.
He chased a Negro round a stump,
  I believe that dog could see.

Some one stole my old coon dog,
  Wish they'd bring him back.
He chased the big hogs through the
  fence
And the little ones through the crack.

Old Joe Clark had a house,
  It was sixteen stories high,
And every room in that house
  Just smelled like chicken pie.[3]

Met a possum in the road,
  Blind as he could be,
Jumped the fence and whipped my dog
  And bristled up at me.

Chicken on a haystack,
  Hawk came flying by,
Grabbed the chicken by the neck
  And feathers began to fly.

Wouldn't marry a preacher gal,
  I'll tell you the reason why:
Her neck's so long and stringy,
  I'm afraid she'll never die.

Went down to Dinah's house,
  Saw her standin' in the door,
Shoes and stockin's in her hand
  And feet all over the floor.

Old Joe Clark had a horse,
  Name was Morgan Brown,
And everywhere he went
  He covered an acre of ground.

Well, I wish I had a nickel,
  I wish I had a dime,
I wish I had a pretty gal
  To kiss and call her mine.

Going down the lane,
  It was dark and hazy.
Every time I thought of my girl
  It nearly drove me crazy.

---

[1] For the names of informants and printed parallels, see *The American Play-Party Song.*

[2] Elsewhere this becomes a turkey, rabbit's, or pole-cat's head, and also a wagon bed. Sometimes it is "my girl" who is "sick abed."

[3] The number of stories in Old Joe Clark's house increases, in variants, to twenty, forty, fifty, and sixty; and the pie that fills or lines every story or every room may be pumpkin or apple, though chicken is preferred.

Driving an old mule team,
  Leading Old Gray behind,
Before I'll see my true love walk,
  I'll pull Old Nellie blind.

I had an old gray mule,
  As blind as he could be.
rode him under a chicken roost
  And pulled off ninety-three.

Joe Clark killed a man,
  Killed him with a knife.
I'm so glad he killed that man,
  Now I'll get his wife.

Wish I had a lariat rope,
  Long as I could throw.
Throw it around a pretty girl,
  And to Arkansaw I'd go.

You may ride the old gray horse,
  And I may ride the roan.
If you get there before I do,
  Leave my honey alone.

The higher up the cherry tree,
  The sweeter are the cherries.
Every pretty girl I meet
  I always want to marry.

The higher up the cherry tree,
  The riper grows the cherry.
The more you hug and kiss the girls,
  The sooner you'll get married.

I wish I had a needle and thread,
  As fine as I could sew.
I'd sew the girls to my coat-tail,
  And down the road I'd go.

Massa had an old gray horse,
  He rode him down in town.
Sold the horse for fifteen cents
  And even dollar down.

Massa had an old gray horse,
  Rode him down to town.
Before he got his trading done,
  The buzzards had him down.

Massa had a yellow girl,
  Brought her from the South.
Black eyes and curly hair—
  She could not shut her mouth.

He took her to the blacksmith shop
  To have her mouth made small.
She backed her ears and opened her
    mouth,
  And swallowed shop and all.

I wish I was in Arkansaw,
  Setting on a rail,
Sweet potato in my hand
  And a possum by the tail.

Now I ain't got much money,
  Ain't got no place to stay,
Ain't got no place to lay my head
  Till roosters crow for day.

When I see that girl of mine,
  I have a thing to tell her.
She need not fool her time away,
  But court some other feller.

Old Joe Clark is dead and gone,
  And I ain't goin'-a cry.
Can't get round his garden spot
  Without mashing down his rye.

Mushy had an old coon dog,
  Three-quarters hound.
Every tooth in that dog's head
  Was a mile and a quarter round.

Old Joe Clark he had a horse,
  His name was Morgan Brown.
And every tooth the old horse had
  Was fifteen inches round.

Peaches in the summertime,
  Apples in the fall.
If I can't get the girl I want,
  I won't have none at all.

I wouldn't marry a widow,
  I'll tell you the reason why.
She'd have so many children
  They'd make those biscuits fly.

I wouldn't marry a yellow gal,
  I'll tell you the reason why:
She'd eat a barrel of sauerkraut
  And drink the river dry.

I wish I had a lariat rope,
  As long as I could throw.
I'd throw it around my sweetheart's
    neck
  And around and around we'd go.

I wish I was a big red apple,
  Hanging on a tree,
And every girl that came along
  Would take a bite of me.

I will ride the old gray horse,
  And you will ride the roan.
I'll go see your sweetheart,
  And you'd better leave mine alone.

Old Joe Clark had a girl,
  She was as blind as she could be.
She caught a beau the other night,
  I swear I believe that girl can see.

An India-rubber overcoat,
  A gumbo lassie's shoe,
Old Joe writes a telegram,
  Trying to get the news.

Old Joe on the mountain top,
  Can see him very well.
Nigger in the watermelon patch,
  Giving them watermelons hell.

Joe wouldn't marry an old maid,
  I'll tell you the reason why:
Her nose was always dripping,
  And her chin was never dry.

Old Joe Clark he killed a man,
  And throwed him in the branch.
Old Joe Clark he's going to hang,
  There ain't no other chance.

There's a building in Noo Yawk
  That's sixteen stories high.
And every story in that house
  Is full of chicken pie.

He used to live in the country,
  But now he lives in town,
Living at the James Hotel,
  And sparking Betty Brown.

Old Joe Clark he had a wife,
  And she was seven feet tall.
She slept with her head in the kitchen,
  And her feet in the hall.

And that's the end of old Joe Clark,
  For he is dead and gone.
And that's the end of old Joe Clark,
  As well as Lucy Long.

Went down to Lexington,
  Didn't know the route,
Put me in the coffee pot
  And poured me out the spout.

Old Joe Clark had a dog,
  Blind as he could be,
And that dog on the darkest night
  Put a chigger up a tree.

Went down to see my girl,
  Never been there before.
Locked me in a chicken coop,
  Ain't going back no more.

I went upon a mountain top
  To give my horn a blow.
I thought I heard my true love say,
  "Yonder comes your Beau."

If I had a sweetheart,
  I'd set her upon a shelf,
And every time she'd grin at me,
  I'd get up there myself.

Old Joe Clark he had a hat,
  It didn't have any crown.
He put that hat upon his head
  And swore he'd take in the town.

Old Joe Clark he had a mule,
  Didn't have no ears.
Reminded me of a farmer
  Workin' on the shears.

Old Joe Clark is mad at me,
I'll tell you the reason why,
I ran all over the garden patch
And stomped down all his rye.

I wish I had a pig in a pen,
Corn to feed it on,
Pretty little girl to stay at home
To feed it while I'm gone.

Sixteen horses in my team,
The leaders had no line.
I whip them around a rocky road
To see that girl of mine.

I wouldn't marry a school teacher,
I'll tell you the reason why.
She blows her nose in yellow corn
bread
And calls it punkin pie.

I wish I had a candy box
To put my sweetheart in,
Take her out and kiss her twice
And put her back again.

If I had a needle and thread,
I tell you what I'd do.
I'd sew my true love to my side
And down the river I'd go.
Doggone!

III. BALLADS AND SONGS

It has often been pointed out that contemporary historians en-
deavor to chronicle the common man as well as the hero. . . .
Similarly, the interest of literary historians and of students and
readers has extended downward from the masterpiece till it em-
braces the humble and unrecorded literature of the folk.—
LOUISE POUND

FOLK song should properly be regarded as an activity, a functional activity of the group singing or playing for self-gratification or for power,
to attain the ends of social adjustment and human freedom, by lightening
labor, filling leisure, recording events, voicing praise or protest. Certain
"traditionalist" folk-song authorities like Cecil J. Sharp tend to stress
the "heritage" rather than the "participation" aspects of folk song and
the passive rather than the active rôle of the folk singer, making him
out to be a carrier of national culture, who sings to "forget himself and
everything that reminds him of his everyday life" and thus, by escaping
into an "imaginary world," to "enter into [his] racial inheritance."[1] The
"functionalists," on the other hand, such as Alan Lomax, stress the rôle
of folk song in America as "an expression of its democratic, interracial,
international character, as a function of its inchoate and turbulent many-
sided development." According to this view, people not only sing songs
in their own way but make their own songs as they begin to "examine
their problems self-consciously and comment on them with an objective
vigor and irony."[2] Taking issue with Sharp, John and Alan Lomax fling
down this challenge:

[1] *English Folk Songs from the Southern Appalachians,* collected by Cecil J. Sharp,
edited by Maud Karpeles (1932), Vol. I, "Introduction to the First Edition, 1917."
[2] "Songs of the American Folk," *Modern Music,* Vol. XVIII (January-February,
1941), No. 2, p. 138.

The American singer has been concerned with themes close to his everyday experience, with the emotions of ordinary men and women who were fighting for freedom and for a living in a violent new world.[1]

Accepting the latter interpretation, one comes to regard the difference between folk singers and art singers as not so much the difference between not having and having an audience as a difference in the relationship between the singer and his audience. In the case of folk singing, like folk story-telling, there is no sharp differentiation between performer and auditor. The rôles are interchangeable, and both participate in the performance as a shared experience, drawing upon the common stock of ideas and expressions and communicating chiefly by symbols, or signs which "bind value to value and man to man by bonds of common meaning and shared emotion."

Every folk song, of course, has an author; but his authorship is conceived in terms of the proverb's wit of one and wisdom of the many, and he is eventually forgotten as his song enters into the public domain. The folk singer, as truly as the professional singer, is an artist in his own right; but he is a people's artist, who sings from the heart and to the hearts of the people and whose distinguishing mark is a sense of the proper balance between remembering and inventing, between pattern and variation. In him the art of improvisation has been raised to high art. This is a matter not of "ad libbing" but of fitting new words to old tunes and old texts to changing circumstances. It is participation made spontaneous. It is rhythmic and poetic freedom akin to the freedom of interpolation and variation that belongs to the blues and jazz and the impromptu steps of the square dance.

The folk basis of the blues and jazz in Negro blues, work songs, hollers, and reels points to the existence of an urban as well as a rural folk music and to the fact that folk music is not a pure but a hybrid activity, which is a fusion of "folk," "art," and "popular" idioms and tastes. This very quality of mixed style and of a certain complex, plastic simplicity and collective individuality, rather than any other single trait, may be the hallmark of folk song as of all folk art. The exploitation of folk music for the purposes of commercial entertainment has resulted in cheapening and slicking up the product by means of hokum and "corn." But there is good "corn" as well as bad "corn," and even "hillbilly" has its place in the hierarchy of American folk styles.

The same mixed or hybrid character applies to types of folk song, and requires that we do not distinguish too sharply between them. For instance, the ballad, or story-telling song, has its lyric elements, as the folk-lyric has its narrative or dramatic elements. Although ballads are not something that we read in the newspapers, they deal with the same situations that make the headlines—wars, crimes, disasters, love tragedies, family feuds, and passion and violence generally. Just as ballad singers and hawkers of broadside ballads once performed a journalistic function, so spectacular and sensational events, such as wrecks, storms, floods, fires, and executions, still bring in their train the crude minstrelsy of local bards.

---

[1] *Our Singing Country,* collected and compiled by John A. Lomax and Alan Lomax (1941), p. xiii.

Here the line between fact and fantasy, the timely and the timeless, is a shifting one. History passes into legend and legend into history.

In the same way written and unwritten tradition, the academic and the commercial, mingle in the creation and diffusion of ballads and folk songs. In addition to broadsides, songsters, manuscript collections, and scrap-books, the stage, traveling troupes of singers, medicine and minstrel shows, camp and political meetings, and the like have served to keep folk songs alive and afloat. To-day the phonograph, the radio, the folk song archive, and the folk festival tend to perform the same function in folk song survival or revival. But for all these external aids folk song is still distinguished from popular and art song by the predominance of word-of-mouth transmission.

Perhaps the best example of the transitional, evolving nature of folk song as the product of an interim or backward stage of culture or society is afforded by Negro folk song—slave songs, spirituals, work songs, reels, and blues. With the displacement of hand by machine labor, work songs of the choral type, such as shanties, field songs, chopping songs, steel-driving songs, etc., tend to disappear. The last refuge of gang or group-hand-labor songs in the United States has been the Southern prison, which until recently provided a "pocket" for primitive labor conditions that have passed out of existence elsewhere. Cultural isolation, as in the Southern mountains, has also fostered the survival of traditional ballads and social songs. With the exception of sea shanties and cowboy songs, our white occupational songs, including lumberjack, canaller, and miners' songs, are social songs to accompany leisure rather than work, or songs of protest, akin to the "hard times" songs of the pioneer, or (more recently) industrial union songs.

Almost every phase or period of American life has left its record in the form of folk songs that describe, reflect, or evoke the time and the place, their conditions, customs, and characters. In this sense American folk song provides material for a social and cultural history of the United States which comes as near as anything we have to being a folk or people's history —a history of, by, and for the people, in which for the first time the people speak and are allowed to tell their own story, in their own way.

BALLADS

Bonny Barbara Allen

> It was upon a high, high hill,
> Two maidens chose their dwelling,
> And one was known both far and wide,
> Was known as Barb'ra Allen.

From *American Anthology of Old-World Ballads*, compiled and edited by Reed Smith, settings by Hilton Rufty, pp. 32–34. Copyright, 1937, by J. Fischer & Bro. New York.

It was up-on a high, high hill, Two maid-ens chose their dwell-ing, And one was known both far and wide, Was known as Bar——bra Al—len.

'Twas in the merry month of May,
All the flowers blooming,
A young man on his deathbed lay
For the love of Barb'ra Allen.

He sent a servant unto her
In the town where she was dwelling.
"Come, Miss, O Miss to my master dying
If your name be Barb'ra Allen!"

Slowly, slowly she got up,
And to his bedside going,
She drew the curtain to one side
And said, "Young man you're dying."

He stretched one pale hand to her
As though he would to touch her.
She hopped and skipped across the floor.
"Young man," says, "I won't have you."

"Remember, 'member in the town,
'Twas in the tavern drinking,
You drank a health to the ladies all
But you slighted Barb'ra Allen."

Of all the ballads in America "Barbara Allen" has more texts, more tunes, and wider geographical spread than any other. It is found all over the United States. Virginia, alone, for example, affords ninety-two variant texts and a dozen tunes. Six different tunes have been recorded in New England. Its wide American prevalence is not entirely due to oral tradition, for it has appeared in many old songbooks, first in *The American Songster* issued at Baltimore in 1830 and repeatedly since.

In Great Britain it was first printed in Allan Ramsay's *Tea-Table Miscellany*, 1740, and next in Percy's *Reliques*, 1765.—R. S.

He turned his face toward the wall,
His back upon his darling.
"I know I shall see you no more,
So goodbye, Barb'ra Allen."

As she was going to her home,
She heard the church bell tolling.
She looked to the east and looked to the west,
And saw the corpse a-coming.

"O hand me down that corpse of clay
That I may look upon it.
I might have saved that young man's life,
If I had done my duty.

"O mother, mother, make my bed;
O make it long and narrow.
Sweet William died for me today,
I shall die for him tomorrow."

Sweet William died on a Saturday night,
And Barb'ra Allen on a Sunday.
The old lady died for the love of them both,
She died on Easter morning.

Sweet William was buried in one graveyard,
Barb'ra Allen in another;
A rose grew on Sweet William's grave
And a brier on Barb'ra Allen's.

They grew and they grew to the steeple top,
And there they grew no higher;
And there they tied in a true-lover knot,
The rose clung 'round the brier.

The Hangsman's Tree

"Slack your rope, hangsaman,
O slack it for a while;
I think I see my father coming,
Riding many a mile.
O father have you brought me gold?
Or have you paid my fee?
Or have you come to see me hanging
On the gallows tree?"
"I have not brought you gold;
I have not paid your fee;
But I have come to see you hanging
On the gallows tree."

Ibid., pp. 37–38.

"The Hangsman's Tree" is one of the oldest and most interesting of the ballads.
Along with "Lady Isabel and the Elf Knight" and "Lord Randal" it has a remarkable

"Slack your rope, hangs-a-man, O slack it for a while; . I think I see my fa—ther com—ing, Rid—ing man—y a mile. O fa—ther have you brought me gold? Or have you paid my fee? Or have you come to see me hang—ing On the gal—lows tree?" "I have not brought you gold; I have not paid your fee; But I have come to see you hang—ing On the gal—lows tree."

"Slack your rope, hangsaman,
O slack it for a while;
I think I see my mother [1] coming," etc.

European spread. Versions are known not only in English and Scottish but also in Sicilian, Spanish, Faroese, Icelandic, Swedish, Danish, German, Esthonian, Wendish, Russian, Little-Russian, and Slavonian. Truly a remarkable distribution.

The story the ballad tells is clear: the girl has been condemned to die presumably for the loss (or theft) of a golden ball or key. In some of the non-English forms of the ballad the victim has fallen into the hands of corsairs or pirates, who demand ransom, but none of the English or American versions account for the situation in this way. . . .

Still persisting all over the Eastern half of America this ballad is especially common in the South, where many versions have been recorded. It is easily the favorite of all the traditional ballads among the Negroes, who relish the dramatic situation and fall in naturally with the easy method of telling the story in groups of three repetitive stanzas. The ballad drama has also become a child's game known as "The Golden Ball," and also exists as a *cante-fable* among the Negroes of the West Indies—R. S.

[1] And so on for brother, sister, aunt, uncle, cousin, etc.—R. S.

"Slack your rope, hangsaman,
O slack it for a while;
I think I see my true love coming," etc.
"Yes, I have brought you gold;
Yes, I have paid your fee;
Nor have I come to see you hanging
On the gallows tree."

The Little Mohee

As I went a-walking all by the seashore
The wind it did whistle, the water did roar.

As I sat a-musing, myself on the grass,
Oh, who did I spy but a young Indian lass.

She came and sat by me, took hold of my hand
And said "You're a stranger and in a strange land."

"But if you will follow you're welcome to come
And dwell in the cottage where call it my home."

The sun was past sinking far over the sea,
As I wandered along with my little Mohee.

Together we wandered, together we roam,
'Til I came to the little cottage where she called it her home.

She asked me to marry and offered her hand
Saying "My father's the chieftain all over this land."

"My father's a chieftain and ruler can be,
I'm his only daughter, my name is Mohee."

"O no, my dear maiden, that never can be,
I have a dear sweetheart in my own countree."

From *Lonesome Tunes,* Folk Songs from the Kentucky Mountains, the Words Collected and Edited by Loraine Wyman, the Pianoforte Accompaniment by Howard Brockway, pp. 52–54. Copyright, 1916, by the H. W. Gray Co. New York.

"I will not forsake her, I know she loves me,
Her heart is as true as any Mohee!"

"It was early one morning, Monday morning in May,
I broke her poor heart by the words I did say."

"I'm going to leave you, so fare you well, my dear,
My ship's spreads [sails] are now spreading, over home I must steer."

The last time I saw her she knelt on the stand,
Just as my boat passed her she waved me her hand.

Saying "When you get over with the girl that you love,
O remember the Mohee, in the cocoanut grove."

And when I had landed with the girl that I love,
Both friends and relations gathered round me once more.

I gazed all about me, not one did I see
That really did compare with my little Mohee.

And the girl I had trusted had proved untrue to me,
So I says "I'll turn my courses back over the sea."

"I'll turn my courses and backward I'll flee,
I'll go and spend my days with the little Mohee."

Young Charlotte

Young Charlotte lived by the mountainside
In a lone and dreary spot.
No dwelling there, for five miles round,
Except her father's cot;
But yet on many a winter's eve
Young swains would gather there,
For her father kept a social board
And she was very fair.

From *Vermont Folk-Songs & Ballads,* Edited by Helen Hartness Flanders and George Brown, pp. 35–38. The Green Mountain Series. Copyright, 1932, by Arthur Wallace Peach as Trustee for Committee on Vermont Traditions and Ideals. Brattleboro: Stephen Daye Press.

"Young Charlotte" was written by Seba Smith, best known as the author of the *Jack Downing Letters*. It was published by him in *The Rover* (1884), II, 225. He tells us it was based on an actual event reported in the papers; we have found the record in the *New York Observer*, February 8, 1840. . . . Accordingly, the place of William Lorenzo Carter, the blind Homer of Benson, Vermont, in the composition and diffusion of this ballad must now be reinvestigated. . . . The frequent occurrence of the ballad in the vicinity of early Mormon settlements in the West, where he is known to have been, since he was a Mormon himself . . . indicates that he must have had

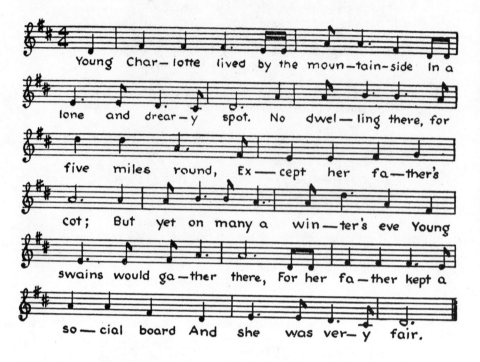

Young Char—lotte lived by the moun—tain-side In a
lone and drear—y spot. No dwel—ling there, for
five miles round, Ex——cept her fa—ther's
cot; But yet on many a win—ter's eve Young
swains would ga—ther there, For her fa—ther kept a
so——cial board And she was ver—y fair.

Her father loved to see her dressed
Fine as a city belle,
For she was the only child he had,
And he loved his daughter well.
'Twas New Year's Eve. The sun went down.
Wild looked her anxious eyes
Along the frosty window panes
To see the sleighs pass by.

At a village Inn, fifteen miles round,
There's a merry ball to-night.
The air is freezing cold above,
But the hearts are warm and light.
And while she looked with longing eyes,
Then a well-known voice she hears,
And dashing up to the cottage door
Young Charley's sleigh appears.

---

much to do with the early diffusion of it in the West. It is probable, though it cannot
be proved, that Carter wrote the additional stanzas of the ballad. . . . Moreover, it
seems safe to infer that it was Carter who associated the text with the *Western tune*,
a set of the air to "The False-Hearted Knight," Child 4. . . . The Eastern or woods
tune is the exceedingly popular "Fainne Geal an Lae" (The Bright Dawn of Day, or
The Dawning of the Day). . . .—Phillips Barry, *The New Green Mountain Songster*,
Traditional Folk Songs of Vermont, collected, transcribed, and edited by Helen Hartness Flanders, Elizabeth Flanders Ballard, George Brown, and Phillips Barry (1939),
pp. 112-113.

Her mother says, "My daughter dear,
This blanket around you fold,
For it is a dreadful night abroad,
You'll take your death of cold."
"Oh, no! oh, no!" young Charlotte said,
And she laughed like a gypsy queen,
"For to ride in blankets muffled up
I never could be seen.

"My silken cloak is quite enough.
'Tis lined, you know, throughout,
And then I have the silken scarf
To tie my face about."
Her gloves and bonnet being on,
She jumped into the sleigh
And away they ride o'er the mountainside
And o'er the hills away.

There's merry music in the bells
As o'er the hills they go,
For the creaking rake the runners make
As they bite the frozen snow.
Then o'er the hills and faster o'er
And by the cold starlight,
When Charles, in these few frozen words,
At last the silence broke:

"Such a night as this I never knew.
My reins I scarce can hold."
Young Charlotte said with a trembling voice,
"I am exceeding cold."
He cracked his whip which urged his steed
Much faster than before,
And then the other five miles round
In silence were rode o'er.

"How fast," says Charles, "the freezing ice
Is gathering on my brow."
Young Charlotte said with a feeble voice,
"I'm growing warmer now."
Then o'er the hills and faster o'er
And by the cold starlight
Until they reached the village inn
And the ballroom was in sight.

They reached the inn and Charles sprang out
And giving his hand to her,
"Why sit you like a monument
What has no power to stir?"
He called her once, he called her twice,
But yet she never stirred.
He called her name again and again,
But she answered not a word.

He took her hand in his. O God!
'Twas cold and hard as stone.
He tore the mantle from her brow
And the cold stars on her shone.
Then quickly to the lighted hall
Her lifeless form he bore,
For Charlotte was a frozen corpse
And a word spake never more.

He knelt himself down by her side
And bitter tears did flow,
For he said, "My young intended bride,
I never more shall know."
He flung his arms around her neck
And kissed her marble brow.
His thoughts went back to the place she said,
"I'm growing warmer now."

He bore her out into the sleigh
And with her he rode home,
And when they reached the cottage door
Oh, how her parents mourned!
They mourned for the loss of their daughter dear,
And Charles mourned o'er the gloom
When Charles' heart with grief did break.
They slumber in one tomb.

On Springfield Mountain

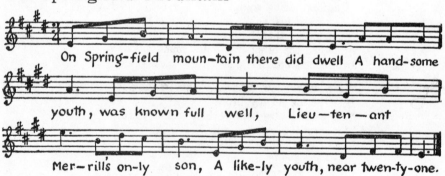

On Spring-field moun-tain there did dwell A hand-some youth, was known full well, Lieu-ten-ant Mer-rill's on-ly son, A like-ly youth, near twen-ty-one.

On Springfield mountain there did dwell
A handsome youth, was known full well,
Lieutenant Merrill's only son,
A likely youth, near twenty-one.

Ibid., pp. 15–16.
Recorded by Mr. Brown in Townshend, Vermont, from the singing of Mr. Josiah S. Kennison. Mr. Kennison's version of this truly New England folk-song differs from almost all others in that it is entirely serious, and without a trace of the caricature and clownishness that usually characterize the piece.—H. H. F.

On Friday morning he did go
Down to the meadows for to mow.
He mowed, he mowed all around the field
With a poisonous serpent at his heel.

When he received his deathly wound
He laid his scythe down on the ground.
For to return was his intent,
Calling aloud, long as he went.

His calls were heard both far and near
But no friend to him did appear.
They thought he did some workman call.
Alas, poor man, alone did fall!

Day being past, night coming on,
The father went to seek his son,
And there he found his only son
Cold as a stone, dead on the ground.

He took him up and he carried him home
And on the way did lament and mourn,
Saying, "I heard but did not come,
And now I'm left alone to mourn."

In the month of August, the twenty-first,
When this sad accident was done.
May this a warning be to all,
To be prepared when God shall call.

SONGS OF SAILORMEN AND RIVERMEN

Blow, Ye Winds

'Tis advertised in Boston, New York and Buffalo,
Five hundred brave Americans, a-whaling for to go, singing,

Chorus:
    Blow, ye winds in the morning,
    And blow, ye winds, high-o!
    Clear away your running gear,
    And blow, ye winds, high-o!

From *Songs of American Sailormen*, by Joanna C. Colcord, pp. 191–192. Copyright, 1938, by W. W. Norton & Company. New York.

The words were copied out of an old logbook in the New Bedford Public Library. No modern whaleman has been able to say what is meant by the reference to forty-four points in the whaler's compass. "Tonbas" was Tumbez, at the mouth of the Guayaquil River; the same well-known whaling rendezvous to which Admiral Porter took his fleet of captured British whalers after his South Pacific raid in 1812. "Tuckoona" was undoubtedly Talcahuano, on the Chilean coast, though the merchant sailor's pronunciation of this name was "Turkey'wanna." The tune is reminiscent of "You Gentlemen of England."—J. C. A forecastle song.

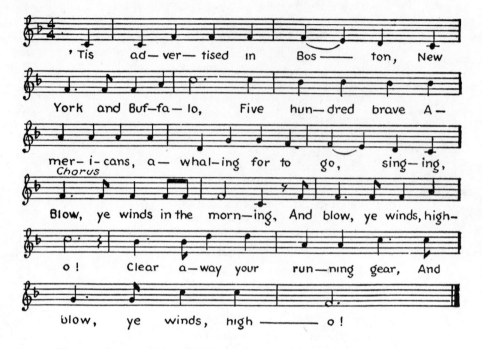

'Tis ad—ver—tised in Bos———ton, New York and Buf—fa—lo, Five hun—dred brave A—mer—i—cans, a— whal—ing for to go, sing—ing,

Chorus

Blow, ye winds in the morn—ing, And blow, ye winds, high—o! Clear a—way your run—ning gear, And blow, ye winds, high———o!

They send you to New Bedford, that famous whaling port,
And give you to some land-sharks to board and fit you out.

They send you to a boarding-house, there for a time to dwell;
The thieves they there are thicker than the other side of hell!

They tell you of the clipper-ships a-going in and out,
And say you'll take five hundred sperm before you're six months out.

It's now we're out to sea, my boys, the wind comes on to blow;
One half the watch is sick on deck, the other half below.

But as for the provisions, we don't get half enough;
A little piece of stinking beef and a blamed small bag of duff.

Now comes that damned old compass, it will grieve your heart full sore.
For theirs is two-and-thirty points and we have forty-four.

Next comes the running rigging, which you're all supposed to know;
'Tis "Lay aloft, you son-of-a-gun, or overboard you go!"

The cooper's at the vise-bench, a-making iron poles,
And the mate's upon the main hatch a-cursing all our souls.

The Skipper's on the quarter-deck a-squinting at the sails,
When up aloft the lookout sights a school of whales.

"Now clear away the boats, my boys, and after him we'll travel,
But if you get too near his fluke, he'll kick you to the devil!"

Now we have got him turned up, we tow him alongside;
We over with our blubber-hooks and rob him of his hide.

Now the boat-steerer overside the tackle overhauls,
The Skipper's in the main-chains, so loudly he does bawl!

Next comes the stowing down, my boys; 'twill take both night and day,
And you'll all have fifty cents apiece on the hundred and ninetieth lay.

Now we are bound into Tonbas, that blasted whaling port,
And if you run away, my boys, you surely will get caught.

Now we are bound into Tuckoona, full more in their power,
Where the skippers can buy the Consul up for half a barrel of flour!

But now that our old ship is full and we don't give a damn,
We'll bend on all our stu'nsails and sail for Yankee land.

When we get home, our ship made fast, and we get through our sailing,
A winding glass around we'll pass and damn this blubber whaling!

Boston

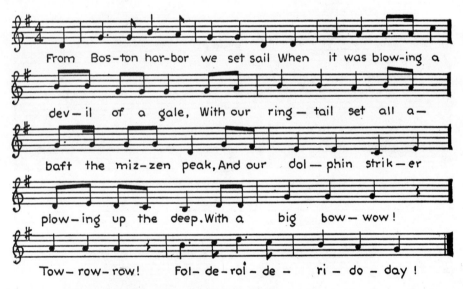

From Boston harbor we set sail
When it was blowing a devil of a gale,
With our ring-tail set all abaft the mizzen peak,
And our dolphin striker plowing up the deep.
With a big bow-wow! Tow-row-row!
Fol-de-rol-de-ri-do-day!

Ibid, pp. 168-169. A forecastle song.

Up comes the skipper from down below,
And he looks aloft and he looks alow,
And he looks alow and he looks aloft,
And it's "Coil up your ropes there, fore and aft."

Then down to his cabin he quickly crawls,
And unto his steward he loudly bawls,
"Go mix me a glass that will make me cough,
For it's better weather here than it is up aloft."

We poor sailors standing on the deck,
With the blasted rain all a-pouring down our necks;
Not a drop of grog would he to us afford,
But he damns our eyes with every other word.

And one thing which we have to crave
Is that he may have a watery grave,
So we'll heave him down into some dark hole,
Where the sharks'll have his body and the devil have his soul.

Greenland Fishery

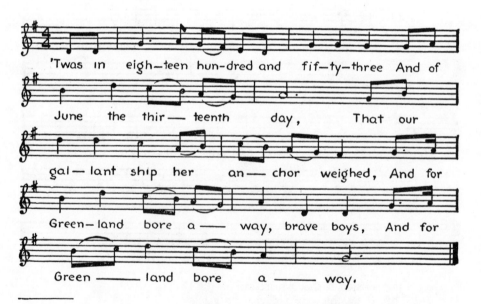

'Twas in eigh—teen hun-dred and fif—ty—three And of
June the thir— teenth day, That our
gal— lant ship her an— chor weighed, And for
Green—land bore a —— way, brave boys, And for
Green ——— land bore a —— way.

Ibid., pp. 151–152.

A forecastle song. Joanna Colcord notes: "'Greenland Fishery' or 'The Whale' was not more popular on whaling ships than in the ships of the merchant marine. It arose in the British, not the American, whaling trade, probably in the latter part of the eighteenth century, and in the earlier British versions the ship's name, the *Lion*, and the captain's, Speedicutt, are both preserved."

'Twas in eighteen hundred and fifty three
And of June the thirteenth day,
That our gallant ship her anchor weighed,
And for Greenland bore away, brave boys,
And for Greenland bore away.

The lookout in the crosstrees stood,
With his spyglass in his hand.
"There's a whale, there's a whale, there's a whalefish," he cried,
"And she blows at every span, brave boys,
And she blows at every span."

The captain stood on the quarter-deck,
And a fine little man was he.
"Overhaul! Overhaul! Let your davit-tackles fall,
And launch your boats for sea, brave boys,
And launch your boats for sea."

Now the boats were launched and the men aboard,
And the whale was in full view;
Resolv-ed was each seaman bold
To steer where the whalefish blew, brave boys,
To steer where the whalefish blew.

We struck that whale, the line paid out,
But she gave a flourish with her tail;
The boat capsized and four men were drowned,
And we never caught that whale, brave boys,
And we never caught that whale.

"To lose the whale," our captain said,
"It grieves my heart full sore;
But oh! to lose four gallant men,
It grieves me ten times more, brave boys,
It grieves me ten times more."

"The winter star doth now appear,
So, boys, we'll anchor weigh;
It's time to leave this cold country,
And homeward bear away, brave boys,
And homeward bear away."

Oh, Greenland is a dreadful place,
A land that's never green,
Where there's ice and snow, and the whalefishes blow,
And the daylight's seldom seen, brave boys,
And the daylight's seldom seen.

Stormalong

Solo: Old Stormy was a fine old man,
Chorus: To me way, O Stormalong!
Solo: Old Stormy was a fine old man,
Chorus: Way, hay, hay, Mister Stormalong!

Solo: Old Stormy was a fine old man,
Chorus: To me way, O Stormalong!
Solo: Old Stormy was a fine old man,
Chorus: Way, hay, hay, Mister Stormalong!

Old Stormy he is dead and gone,
Oh, poor old Stormy's dead and gone.

We'll dig his grave with a silver spade, *(twice)*

And lower him down with a golden chain. *(twice)*

I wish I was old Stormy's son;
I'd build me a ship of a thousand ton.

I'd sail this wide world round and round;
With plenty of money I'd be found.

I'd fill her up with New England rum,
And all my shellbacks they'd have some.

Oh, Stormy's dead and gone to rest;
Of all the sailors he was the best.

Ibid., pp. 88–89. This and the next two songs are windlass or capstan shanties.
Bullen says . . . : "It embodies all the admiration that a sailor used to feel for a
great seaman; gives it expression, as it were, though I have never been able to learn
who the antitype of Stormalong could have been. I suspect that he was just the
embodiment of all the prime seamen the sailor had ever known, and in the song he
voiced his heart's admiration."—J. C.

Santy Anna

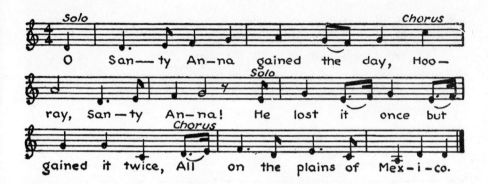

Solo: O Santy Anna gained the day,
Chorus: Hooray, Santy Anna!
Solo: He lost it once but gained it twice,
Chorus: All on the plains of Mexico!

And Gen'ral Taylor ran away,
He ran away at Monterey.

Oh, Santy Anna fought for fame,
And there's where Santy gained his name.

Oh, Santy Anna fought for gold,
And the deeds he done have oft been told.

And Santy Anna fought for his life,
But he gained his way in the terrible strife.

Oh, Santy Anna's day is o'er,
And Santy Anna will fight no more.

I thought I heard the Old Man say
He'd give us grog this very day.

Ibid., pp. 84–85.

It must have come into use shortly after our war with Mexico. No one has ever explained why this obscure Mexican general should be as dear to the heart of the sailor as the mighty "Boney" himself; nor why the roles of Santa Aña and General Taylor should have been exchanged in the shanty. The latter was of course the victor at Monterey, and General Santa Aña fled shortly afterward into exile.—J. C.

The Hog-Eye Man

Oh, the hog-eye man is the man for me,
He was raised way down in Tennisee,

Chorus:
　With a hog-eye!
　Row boat ashore with a hog-eye,
　Row boat ashore with a hog-eye,
　All she wants is a hog-eye man!

Oh, the hog-eye man is all the go
When he comes down to San Francisco.

Oh, go fetch me down my riding cane,
For I'm going to see my darling Jane.

Oh, who been here since I been gone?
Some big buck nigger wid his sea-boots on.

Oh, I won't wed a nigger, I'll be damned if I do,
He's got jiggers in his feet and he can't wear a shoe.

Ibid., p. 104.

Another Negro shanty which has no connection with the cotton trade is "The Hog-Eye Man," which dates from the days of the " 'forty-niners" in California. None of its versions can be printed in anything like their entirety. Whall derives the name from a type of barge used on the California coast called "hog-eye"; Terry hints at hidden obscenity in the name itself. . . .—J. C.

Raftsman Jim and His Songs

IF IN the face of the fairly eloquent testimony of the foregoing examples I continue to maintain that my rascals of the raft had sometimes a redeeming substratum of sentiment and poetry under their rowdyism, I may be judged merely eccentric. Yet I have reasons. I knew the floating raftsmen. Not many men now alive had first-hand knowledge of them. Besides, there were raftsmen and raftsmen. As to which, perpend.

To impressionable minds, of all the singular, mysterious spells that pertained to the Mississippi River the strongest came about the windless and cloudless sunset of a summer day. I do not believe there are such sunsets elsewhere in northern latitudes. not even on the Bay of Naples. Their only peers within my knowledge have been in the South Seas. The mirror of the river held the sky's burning and gorgeous colors, the unutterable bronzes and imperious reds, along with the Courbet green of the bluffs or of the willows on the tow heads; and there was an almost unearthly quiet abroad, a kind of competent and pervading self-sense of exaltation in so much beauty. The air was like glass; I could see a man in his shirt-sleeves leaning out of a window of Johnny Woods's house, across the river on the Illinois side, and hear the bell of the Port Byron Congregational church. In the midst of this idyllic and luminous quietude a great raft would come without a sound down the long Le Claire reach, drifting through the bronze, crimson, and dark-green without disturbing them by a single ripple; and then, of a sudden, there would float over the water the sounds of a fiddle, or maybe an accordion, playing "Buffalo Gals," and we could easily make out the crew sitting in a semicircle rapt upon the solitary musician.

From Princeton down to Le Claire, about five miles, the river ran almost straight, and if the rafts came slowly they came easily; but a mile below my grandfather's house the stream turned sharply to the west, and when a raft approached that point we could hear the queer, hoarse voice of the pilot booming weirdly through the stillness. "Forward oars, there!" and then came the creaking of the great oars upon the thole-pins, and the red and green bow lanterns upon the head of the raft would slowly go from sight around the point.

I brought my narrative in the first chapter to the place where I was sitting on a rock below my grandfather's house, listening to the singing and whooping of the wild men of Black River that went on all day.

It was not always hymnody of a kind to edify the youthful mind, but I am bound to say that, when there were children about, the raftsmen, if they happened to be sufficiently sober, would put some restraint upon both their language and their lyric offerings. They had a singular and absorbing passion for music—crude music, but still something approaching melody. Most rafts carried fiddlers as conscientiously as they carried cooks.

A few of the old songs and their tunes still run in my memory. Those that provided a chorus or an opportunity to dance a few steps between the stanzas were the favorites. "One-Eyed Riley" went like this:

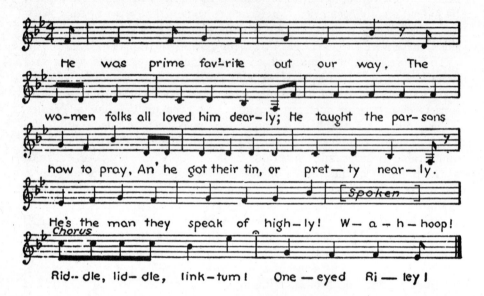

He was prime fav'rite out our way,
    The women folks all loved him dearly;
He taught the parsons how to pray,
    An' he got their tin, or pretty nearly.
He's the man they speak of highly!
    W-a-h-hoop!
    Riddle, liddle, linktum!
    [*Pause—then all together, fortissimo*]
    One-eyed Riley!

The music now goes on without stopping, the air is repeated, and they dance out the measure until they come to the chorus:

    W-a-h-hoop!!
Riddle, liddle, linktum!—[*pause*]
    One-eyed Riley!

When "tum" is reached, all the boot-soles must slap the floor together. Then the dancers remain rigid until the refrain, which they deliver with roaring enthusiasm, "One-eyed Riley!"

"The Big Maquoketa," flowerage of an undiscovered river laureate, was sung to an alteration of an air once a favorite in the politest circles

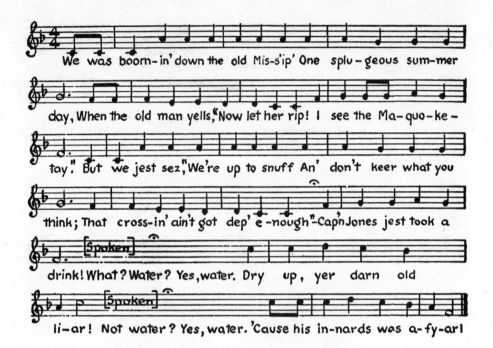

We was boomin' down the ole Miss'ip',
  One splugeous summer day,
When the old man yells, "Now let her rip!
  I see the Maquoketay!"
But we jest sez, "We're up to snuff
  An' don't keer what you think;
That crossin' ain't got dep' enough"—[*pause*]

Cap'n Jones jest took a drink!
          [*Spoken:*]
What? Water? Yes, water.
          [*Sung:*]
Dry up, yer darn old liar! [1]
          [*Spoken:*]
Not water? Yes, water.
          [*Sung:*]
'Cause his innards was a-fy-ar!

"Raftsman Jim" was a narrative of somewhat dubious adventures of a youth that embodied the ideals of gallantry and daring supposed to typify the calling. The air was pilfered. I can recall a few stanzas. One went thus:

---

[1] Liberal translation here.—C. E. R.

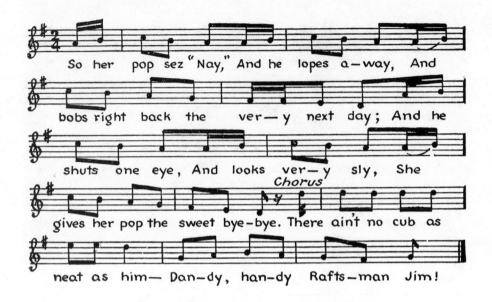

So her pop sez "Nay,"
And he lopes away,
And bobs right back the very next day;
And he shuts one eye,
And looks very sly,
She gives her pop the sweet bye-bye.

[*Chorus:*]
There ain't no cub as neat as him—
Dandy, handy Raftsman Jim!

As in the other instance, the air was repeated after a stanza, when everybody danced, ending with four slapping steps sounding in unison and the roaring of the refrain:

Dandy, handy Raftsman Jim!

But at all times the standard favorite was "Buffalo Gals." I have been told that this song originated on the old Erie Canal and landed early on the Mississippi in the keel-boat days, before the advent of steam. If so, it is the eldest of these lyrics, and certainly it had the widest vogue. From Pembina to New Orleans men sang it and danced to it; taken by its lively refrain and the pleasant alternations in its recurrent phrasing.

If the words had been twice as boshy—a thing that would not be in nature—that refrain would still have carried them. I offer the text with a sense of humiliation; and yet I have found this song on old Broadway programs as having been sung to audiences that ought to have known better, and there is evidence that East and West it was the darling of its times.

As I was lumb'ring down de street,
  Down de street,
  Down de street,
A handsome gal J chanced to meet—
Oh! she was fair to view.

[*Chorus:*]
Buffalo gals, can't you come out to-night?
  Can't you come out to-night,
  Can't you come out to-night;
Buffalo gals, can't you come out to-night,
And dance by the light ob de moon?

I ask'd her would she have some talk,
  Have some talk,
  Have some talk,
As she stood close to me. [*Chorus*]

I ask'd her would she have some dance,
  Have some dance,
  Have some dance.
I thought that I might get a chance
To shake a foot with her. [*Chorus*]

I'd like to make that gal my wife,
  Gal my wife,
  Gal my wife.
I'd be happy all my life
If I had her by me. [*Chorus*]

    *   *   *   *   *

Some attempts were made to improve upon this poor fustian, one of which for a peculiar reason came to celebrity.

A few miles below McGregor on the Iowa side an irascible old gentleman named Dee kept a wood-yard for steamboats; also an ever-ready rifle and a collection of dogs. He had a daughter, known all up and down the river as the Corn-Fed Girl, who was at once the dream and the despair of every batty poet from Pig Eye's Bar to Alton Slough. These, undergoing for her sake the pains of composition, caused the odd corners of many a local newspaper to echo with lame numbers. To win a sight of Mary Dee while the boat stopped for supplies at the wood-yard was a feat of distinction, usually achieved, if at all, at some risk from guns and dogs. Mr. Dee, I may say, was a retired riverman; it is likely that he knew what he was about when he kept his daughter secluded like a nun.

When a boat headed for the Dee yard, officers and passengers made bets on whether without being shot or bitten they would or would not succeed in getting a glimpse of the fair recluse, and the expedients resorted to made the basis of many a well-spun lie in the watches of the night. Sometimes ingenuity or persistence succeeded. A commercial traveler from St. Louis was supposed to have played the lowest trick on innocent womanhood. He had a suspicion that while Mary was locked up in the house she might be watching the visitors unobserved. He placed himself with his back to a window apparently engaged in most earnest conversation with Pop about the coming election and the state of the nation (Pop being an unconverted Copperhead), while he unfurled a copy of "Godey's Ladies' Book," and of course Mary came right out.

For myself, I may say that for a long time I heard these reports and sniffed at them. Rivermen were notorious for fervent imaginations about such world wonders; in their view anything that wore skirts was divine. Besides, there was, and for years had been, competition among Le Claire, La Crosse, and Dubuque on this subject, each asserting itself to have the prettiest girls and each advancing the claim on what seemed to the judicious mind but trifling warrant. But once when I was making trips on the old steamer *St. Croix* in a capacity something like that of a supercargo, we came one Monday morning unusually close around the point below the Dee place. The river was high, and Uncle Joe, the first pilot of the *St. Croix,* was hunting slack water. So we boomed unperceived upon the wood-yard, and there was Mary hanging out the washing with her sleeves above her elbows.

Well, there was no doubt that for once reputation was justified, a thing I have seldom observed since. She was a great beauty, and no mistake. She had the Irish deep-black hair, Irish blue eyes, a face of almost classical contour, a white skin set off with a delicate pink glow—all this away out here in the wilderness. I could understand, also, how she won her peculiar name. It was in right of her statuesque figure and her air of exceeding wholesomeness. After this, I suppose it will be needless to remark that I fell with the rest.

But about the addendum to "Buffalo Gals," I have spoken of my towny that had the amazing and fevered vision of our water-front as a diadem. He now produced some execrable verses about the invisible siren of Dee's Wood-Yard, and as he adapted them to the tune of "Buffalo Gals" (more or less), it became a habit of raftsmen to roar them out as a serenade when the raft hove in sight of the Dee place. A single sample will be enough:

> Oh, the Corn-Fed Girls, they are the best
> In all the West
> They are the best,
> And of all the tribe that I have seen,
> May Dee, she is the queen.

> [*Chorus:*]
> Corn-Fed Girl, see the moon shine bright,
> Ain't you coming out to-night?
> Ain't you coming out to-night?
> Oh, Corn-Fed Girl, ain't you walking out to-night
> With your hand laid in mine?

The rest of the story of the Corn-Fed Girl went at first as might have been expected. Yes—you are right; she eloped. It happened, however, contrary to form, that the man for whom she left the parental roof was not wholly unworthy, a circumstance to excite remark anywhere. When Mr. Dee's emotions had passed the dog and gun stage, he admitted that the joke was on him and turned in his blessing.

LUMBERJACK SONGS

The Bigler's Crew

> Come all my boys and listen, a song I'll sing to you.
> It's all about the Bigler and of her jolly crew.
> In Milwaukee last October I chanced to get a sight
> In the schooner called the Bigler belonging to Detroit.

> *Chorus:*
> Watch her, catch her, jump up on her juber-ju.
> Give her the sheet and let her slide, the boys will push her through.
> You ought to seen us howling, the winds were blowing free.
> On our passage down to Buffalo from Milwaukee.

> It was on a Sunday morning about the hour of ten,
> The Robert Emmet towed us out into Lake Michigan;
> We set sail where she left us in the middle of the fleet,
> And the wind being from the south'ard, oh, we had to give her sheet.

From *Ballads and Songs of the Shanty-Boy*, collected and edited by Franz Rickaby, pp. 168–172. Copyright, 1926, by Harvard University Press. Cambridge. Sung by Mr. M. C. Dean, Virginia, Minnesota.

Come all my boys and list-en, a song I'll sing to you. It's
all a-bout the Big—ler and of her jol—ly
crew. In Mil — wau — kee last Oc — to — ber I
chanced to get a sight In the schoo—ner called the
Big— ler be — long—ing to De — troit.

Chorus

Watch her, catch her, jump up on her ju-ber-ju.
Give her the sheet and let her slide, The boys will push her
through. You ought to seen us howl-ing, the winds were blow-ing
free, On our pas-sage down to Buf-fa-lo from Mil-wau-kee.

Then the wind chopped round to the sou'-sou'west and blew both fresh
    and strong,
But softly through Lake Michigan the Bigler she rolled on,
And far beyond her foaming bow the dashing waves did fling.
With every inch of canvas set, her course was wing and wing.

But the wind it came ahead before we reached the Manitous.
Three dollars and a half a day just suited the Bigler's crew.
From there unto the Beavers we steered her full and by,
And we kept her to the wind, my boys, as close as she would lie.

Through Skillagalee and Wabble Shanks, the entrance to the Straits,
We might have passed the big fleet there if they'd hove to and wait;
But we drove them on before us, the nicest you ever saw,
Out into Lake Huron from the Straits of Mackinaw.

We made Presque Isle Light, and then we boomed away,
The wind it being fair, for the Isle of Thunder Bay.
But when the wind it shifted, we hauled her on her starboard tack.
With a good lookout ahead for the Light of the Point Aubarques.

We made the Light and kept in sight of Michigan North Shore,
A-booming for the river as we'd ofttimes done before.
When right abreast Port Huron Light, our small anchor we let go
And the Sweepstakes came alongside and took the Bigler in tow.

The Sweepstakes took eight in tow and all of us fore and aft,
She towed us down to Lake St. Clare and stuck us on the flats.
She parted the Hunter's tow-line in trying to give relief,
And stem and stern went the Bigler into the boat called Maple Leaf.

The Sweepstakes then she towed us outside the River Light,
Lake Erie for to roam and the blustering winds to fight.
The wind being from the south'ard, we paddled our own canoe,
With her nose pointed for the Dummy she's hell bent for Buffalo.

We made the Oh and passed Long Point, the wind was blowing free.
We howled along the Canada shore, Port Colborne on our lee.
What is it that looms up ahead, so well known as we draw near?
For like a blazing star shone the light on Buffalo Pier.

And now we are safely landed in Buffalo Creek at last,
And under Riggs' elevator the Bigler she's made fast.
And in some lager beer saloon we'll let the bottle pass,
For we are jolly shipmates and we'll drink a social glass.

The Flying Cloud

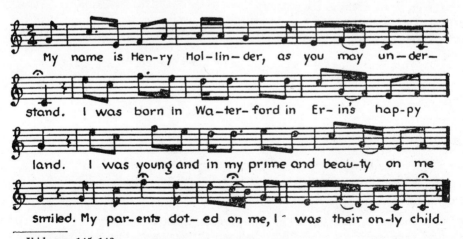

My name is Hen-ry Hol-lin-der, as you may un-der-
stand. I was born in Wa-ter-ford in Er-in's hap-py
land. I was young and in my prime and beau-ty on me
smiled. My par-ents dot-ed on me, I was their on-ly child.

Ibid., pp. 145–149.
Sung by Mr. Arthur C. Milloy, Omemee, North Dakota. This is the ballad of which
it was said that, in order to get a job in the Michigan camps, one had to be able to
sing it through from end to end!—F. R.

My name is Henry Hollinder, as you may understand.
I was born in Waterford in Erin's happy land.
I was young and in my prime and beauty on me smiled.
My parents doted on me, I was their only child.

My father bound me to a trade in Waterford's fair town.
He bound me to a cooper there by the name of William Brown.
I served my master faithfully for eighteen months or more,
And I stepped aboard the Ocean Queen bound for Belfraser's shore.

When I landed at Belfraser, I fell in with Captain More,
Commander of the Flyin' Cloud goin' out from Baltimore.
He asked me if I'd hire on a slavin' voyage to go
To the burning shores of Africa, where the sugar cane does grow.

The Flyin' Cloud was as fine a ship as ever sailed from shore.
She could easily sail round any craft going out from Baltimore.
Her sheets was as white as the driven snow and on them not one speck,
And forty-nine brass powder guns she carried on her deck.

In about three weeks sailing we reached the African shore.
We took five hundred Negro men to be slaves for evermore.
We made them march out on our plank and stowed them down below.
Scarcely eighteen inches to a man was all they had to go.

Next day we set sail again with our cargo of slaves.
It would have been better for those poor souls if they were in their graves.
The plague and fever came on board, swept half of them away.
We dragged their bodies across our decks and hove them in the sea.

In about six weeks after, we reached the Cuban shores,
And sold them to the planters there to be slaves for evermore,
To sow the rice and coffee seed and toil out in the sun,
And lead a hard and wretched life till their creear [1] was done.

When our money was all spent, brave boys, we put to sea again,
And Captain More he came on board and sayed unto his men,
"There's gold and silver to be had if with me you'll remain.
We'll hist aloft a pirate's flag and scour the Spanish main."

We all agreed but five brave lads. We told those boys to land.
Two of them were Boston boys, two more from Newfoundland.
The other was an Irish lad from the town of sweet Trymore.
I wish to God I'd joined those lads and gone with them on shore.

We robbed and plundered many's the ship down on the Spanish main.
We left many's the widow and orphan in sorrow to remain.
Their crews we made them walk our planks, gave them a watery grave.
The saying of our captain was that dead men tells no tales.

---

[1] Career.—F. R.

Pursued we were by many a ship, by liners and frigates too,

. . . .[1]

But 'twas always in our stern-ways their cannons roared aloud.
It was all in vain for them to try to catch the Flyin' Cloud.

At length the Spanish man-o'-war with vengeance hove in view.
They fired a shot across our decks, a signal to lay to.
We paid to them no answer, but flew before the wind,
When a chain-shot broke our mizzen-mast and then we fell behind.

We cleared our decks for action as they hove up 'longside,
And across our quarter decks, brave boys, they fired a crimson tide.
We fired till Captain More was shot and eighty of his men,
And a bomb-shell set our ship afire; we were forced to surrender then.

Fare ye well to the shady groves and the girl that I adore.
Her dark brown eyes and curly hair I'll never see no more.
I'll never kiss her ruby lips nor press her soft white hand,
For I must die a scornful death out in some foreign land.

It's next to —— [2] I was brought, bound down in iron chains,
For the robbing and plundering of ships we saw down on the Spanish main.
It was whiskey and bad company that made a rake of me.
So, youth, beware of my sad fate and shun bad company.

Gerry's Rocks

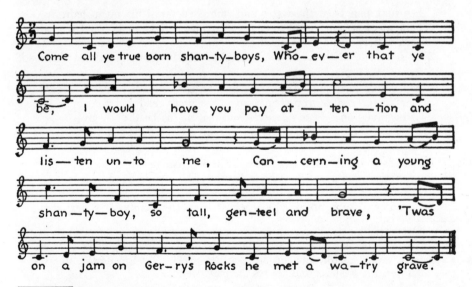

Come all ye true born shan-ty-boys, Who- ev — er that ye
be, I would have you pay at — ten —tion and
lis — ten un —to me, Con — cern—ing a young
shan —ty— boy, so tall, gen—teel and brave, 'Twas
on a jam on Ger—ry's Rocks he met a wa—try grave.

---

[1] The missing line reads: "But for to catch the Flyin' Cloud was a thing they
ne'er could do" [Dean].—F. R.
[2] New Gate [Dean]; Newgate [Colcord].—F. R.

Ibid., pp. 11–14.
This ballad, one of several celebrating death by that most spectacular of all hazards

Come all ye true born shanty-boys, whoever that ye be,
I would have you pay attention and listen unto me,
Concerning a young shanty-boy so tall, genteel, and brave,
'Twas on a jam on Gerry's Rocks he met a wat'ry grave.

It happened on a Sunday morn as you shall quickly hear.
Our logs were piled up mountain high, there being no one to keep them clear.
Our boss he cried, "Turn out, brave boys. Your hearts are void of fear.
We'll break that jam on Gerry's Rocks, and for Agonstown we'll steer."

Some of them were willing enough, but others they hung back.
'Twas for to work on Sabbath they did not think 'twas right.
But six of our brave Canadian boys did volunteer to go
And break the jam on Gerry's Rocks with their foreman, young Monroe.

They had not rolled off many logs when the boss to them did say,
"I'd have you be on your guard, brave boys. That jam will soon give way."
But scarce the warning had he spoke when the jam did break and go,
And it carried away these six brave youths and their foreman, young Monroe.

When the rest of the shanty-boys these sad tidings came to hear,
To search for their dead comrades to the river they did steer.
One of these a headless body found, to their sad grief and woe,
Lay cut and mangled on the beach the head of young Monroe.

They took him from the water and smoothed down his raven hair.
There was one fair form amongst them, her cries would rend the air.
There was one fair form amongst them, a maid from Saginaw town.
Her sighs and cries would rend the skies for her lover that was drowned.

They buried him quite decently, being on the seventh of May.
Come all the rest of you shanty-boys, for your dead comrade pray.
'Tis engraved on a little hemlock tree that at his head doth grow,
The name, the date, and the drowning of this hero, young Monroe.

Miss Clara was a noble girl, likewise the raftsman's friend.
Her mother was a widow woman lived at the river's bend.
The wages of her own true love the boss to her did pay,
And a liberal subscription she received from the shanty-boys next day.

---

in lumbering, the log jam, was easily the most widely current of all lumber woods songs. Some of the old fellows have told me that anyone starting *Gerry's Rocks* in the shanties was summarily shut off because the song was sung to death; others vow that of all songs it was ever and always the most welcome.

* * * * *

One of the most interesting elements in the story, one which appears in all versions, and happily one reflecting a well-authenticated shanty-boy habit, is the subscription presented to the bereaved sweetheart. In actual life this contribution was sent the wife or other dependent; but the practice was common.—F. R.

Miss Clara did not long survive her great misery and grief.
In less than three months afterwards death came to her relief.
In less than three months afterwards she was called to go,
And her last request was granted—to be laid by young Monroe.

Come all the rest of ye shanty-men who would like to go and see,
On a little mound by the river's bank there stands a hemlock tree.
The shanty-boys cut the woods all around. These lovers they lie low.
Here lies Miss Clara Dennison and her shanty-boy, Monroe.

The Little Brown Bulls

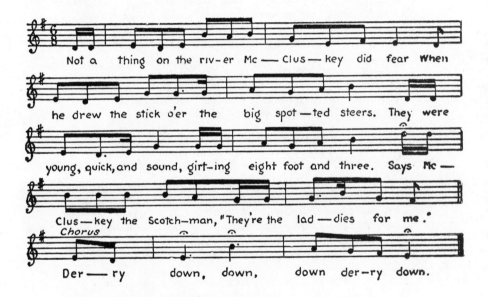

Not a thing on the river McClusky did fear When he drew the stick o'er the big spot—ted steers. They were young, quick, and sound, girt-ing eight foot and three. Says McClus—key the Scotch-man, "They're the lad—dies for me."

Chorus

Der — ry down, down, down der—ry down.

Not a thing on the river McCluskey did fear
When he drew the stick o'er the big spotted steers.
They were young, quick, and sound, girting eight foot and three.
Says McCluskey the Scotchman, "They're the laddies for me."

Ibid., pp. 65–68.

This is an old Wisconsin classic, dating from the days when oxen were used in the woods almost entirely. It resounds with that valorous spirit of the days when supremacy among men and animals was measured in terms of ability to do work, to stand physical exertion. Competition between camps, teams and even individual men, was a tremendous driving force. . . . One cannot help regretting the ballad "leap" between stanzas 9 and 10; for, although one gets from the ballad as it is a considerable reflection of the spirit in which the contest was waged, there is no word of the battle itself, which must have had its Homeric aspects.

According to Mr. Fred Bainter, the singer . . . , the ballad was composed in Mart Douglas's camp in northwestern Wisconsin in 1872 or 1873. It was in this camp and at this date, he said, that the contest between the big spotted steers and the little brown bulls was waged.—F. R.

Chorus:
  Derry down, down, down derry down.

Bull Gordon, the Yankee, on skidding was full,
As he cried "Whoa-*hush*" to the little brown bulls.
Short-legged and soggy, girt six foot and nine.
Says McCluskey the Scotchman, "Too light for our pine."

It's three to the thousand our contract did call.
Our hauling was good and the timber was tall.
McCluskey he swore he'd make the day full
And skid two to one of the little brown bulls.

"Oh no," says Bull Gordon; "that you cannot do,
Though it's well do we know you've the pets of the crew.
And mark you, my boy, you would have your hands full,
If you skid one more log than the little brown bulls."

The day was appointed and soon it drew nigh,
For twenty-five dollars their fortunes to try.
Both eager and anxious that morning were found,
And scalers and judges appeared on the ground.

With a whoop and a yell came McCluskey in view,
With the big spotted steers, the pets of the crew,
Both chewing their cuds—"O boys, keep your jaws full,
For you easily can beat them, the little brown bulls."

Then out came Bull Gordon with a pipe in his jaw,
The little brown bulls with their cuds in their mouths;
And little we think, when we seen them come down,
That a hundred and forty could they jerk around.

Then up spoke McCluskey: "Come stripped to the skin.
We'll dig them a hole and tumble them in.
We'll learn the d—d Yankee to face the bold Scot.
We'll mix them a dose and feed it red hot."

Said Gordon to Stebbin, with blood in his eye,
"Today we must conquer McCluskey or die."
Then up spoke bold Kennebec, "Boy, never fear,
For you ne'er shall be beat by the big spotted steers."

The sun had gone down when the foreman did say,
"Turn out, boys, turn out; you've enough for the day.
We have scaled them and counted, each man to his team,
And it's well do we know now which one kicks the beam."

After supper was over McCluskey appeared
With the belt ready made for the big spotted steers.
To form it he'd torn up his best mackinaw.
He was bound he'd conduct it according to law.

Then up spoke the scaler, "Hold on, you, a while.
The big spotted steers are behind just one mile.
For you have a hundred and ten and no more,
And Gordon has beat you by ten and a score."

The shanty did ring and McCluskey did swear.
He tore out by handfuls his long yellow hair.
Says he to Bull Gordon, "My colors I'll pull.
So here, take the belt for the little brown bulls."

Here's health to Bull Gordon and Kennebec John;
The biggest day's work on the river they done.
So fill up your glasses and fill them up full;
We'll drink to the health of the little brown bulls.

COWBOY SONGS

The Old Chisholm Trail

Come a-long boys and lis-ten to my tale, I'll
tell you of my trou-bles on the old Chis-holm trail, Come a
Refrain
ti yi yip—pee, come a ti yi yea, Come a
ti yi yip—pee, come a ti yi yea.

From *American Songs for American Children*, [edited by Alan Lomax, Charles Seeger, and Ruth Crawford Seeger], pp. 8-9. Chicago: Music Educators National Conference. 1942.

The Chisholm Trail once wound all the way from San Antonio to Montana, and old-time punchers say that if you laid all the stanzas of this ballad end to end, they would stretch all the way to the Canadian line.

This song is the cowboy folk-song par excellence, completely improvised and casual, and every man who ever sang it added his own verses. In fact, it's still growing to-day. Into it the cowboys poured the account of every movement, every accident of the day's work. If the foreman of an outfit drove his men too hard, he was sure to be made the butt of some satiric stanza of this cowboy epic. When a cowboy dashed away after an unruly steer to turn him back into the herd, he might shout out a new stanza to the rhythm of his galloping horse as he rode.

There are almost as many versions of the ballad as there are singers, but the tunes are all basically kin. All end with the "ti-yi-youpy" or the "ki-yi-yippy" refrain,

Come along boys and listen to my tale,
I'll tell you of my troubles on the old Chisholm trail.

Refrain:
　　Come a ti yi yippee, come a ti yi yea,
　　Come a ti yi yippee, come a ti yi yea.

Oh, a ten-dollar hoss and a forty-dollar saddle,
And I'm goin' to punchin' Texas cattle.

I wake in the mornin' afore daylight
And afore I sleep the moon shines bright.

It's cloudy in the west, a-lookin' like rain,
And my durned old slicker's in the wagon again.

No chaps, no slicker, and it's pourin' down rain,
And I swear, by gosh, I'll never night-herd again.

Feet in the stirrups and seat in the saddle,
I hung and rattled with them long-horn cattle.

The wind commenced to blow, and the rain began to fall,
Hit looked, by grab, like we was goin' to lose 'em all.

I don't give a darn if they never do stop;
I'll ride as long as an eight-day clock.

We rounded 'em up and put 'em on the cars,
And that was the last of the old Two Bars.

Oh, it's bacon and beans most every day,
I'd as soon be a-eatin' prairie hay.

I went to the boss to draw my roll,
He had it figgered out I was nine dollars in the hole.

Goin' back to town to draw my money,
Goin' back home to see my honey.

With my knees in the saddle and my seat in the sky,
I'll quit punchin' cows in the sweet by and by.

---

which may be an imitation of an Indian war-cry, for the Indians taught the Mexicans how to tame and ride the Western pony and the Mexican vaqueros taught the Texas cowboys. My father, John A. Lomax, says that this version is the one that was sung to the easy-pace gait of the cowpony—the gentle, rocking pace that devours miles and does not tire the rider.—A. L.

Git Along, Little Dogies

As I was a-walking one morning for pleasure,
I spied a young cowpuncher a-riding alone.
His hat was throwed back and his spurs was a-jingling,
As he approached me a-singing this song.

Chorus:
    Whoopee ti yi yo, git along, little dogies,
    It's your misfortune and none of my own,
    Whoopie ti yi yo, git along, little dogies,
    For you know Wyoming will be your new home.

Some fellows goes up the trail for pleasure,
But that's where they've got it most awfully wrong,
For you haven't an idea the trouble they give us,
As we go a-driving them dogies along.

From *Singing Cowboy,* A Book of Western Songs, collected and edited by Margaret Larkin, arranged for the piano by Helen Black, pp. 96–97. Copyright, 1931, by Alfred A. Knopf, Inc. New York.

Oh, you'll be soup for Uncle Sam's Injuns,
"It's beef, heap beef," I hear them cry.
Git along, git along, you lazy little mavericks,
You're going to be beef steers by and by.

The night's coming on, we'll hold them on the bedground,
These little dogies that roll on so slow.
Round up the herd and cut out the strays,
And roll the little dogies that never rolled before.

The Buffalo Skinners

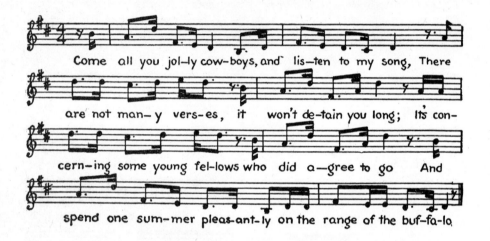

Come all you jolly cowboys, and listen to my song, There are not many verses, it won't detain you long; Its concerning some young fellows who did agree to go And spend one summer pleasantly on the range of the buffalo

Come all you jolly cowboys, and listen to my song,
There are not many verses, it won't detain you long;
It's concerning some young fellows who did agree to go
And spend one summer pleasantly on the range of the buffalo.

From Resettlement Song Sheets, [edited by Charles Seeger]. "Number 7 of a series of American songs to supplement popular collections." Washington, D. C.: Special Skills Division of the Resettlement Administration. [1936–1937.]
As sung by John A. Lomax.
In 1853, in Hudson, Maine (according to Mrs. F. H. Eckstorm), a lumberman named Ephraim Braley joined an expedition into Canada. He made a song upon it, set to the tune of a well-known English sea-song called "Canaday-I-O." It began:
> It happened late one season in the fall of fifty-three,
> A preacher of the gospel one morning came to me,
> Said he, "My jolly fellow, how would you like to go
> To spend one pleasant winter up in Canaday-I-O?"
Its appearance has been reported in Pennsylvania, Michigan ("I-O"), Texas, Idaho, and other parts of the West, where details of new events have been woven into the frame of the old Maine story. The tune also underwent changes. The town of Jacksboro, mentioned in this version, is in western Texas, where John A. Lomax heard the song in the early 1900's. It seems that he was the first to print, in his *Cowboy Songs,* what had become an undeniably American song.—C. S.

It happened in Jacksboro, in the spring of seventy-three,
A man by the name of Crego came stepping up to me;
Says, "How do you do, young fellow, and how would you like to go
And spend one summer pleasantly on the range of the buffalo?"

"It's me being out of employment," this to Crego I did say,
"This going out on the buffalo range depends upon the pay;
But if you will pay good wages, and transportation too,
I think, sir, I will go with you to the range of the buffalo."

"Yes, I will pay good wages, give transportation too,
Provided you will go with me and stay the summer through;
But if you should grow homesick, come back to Jacksboro,
I won't pay transportation from the range of the buffalo."

It's now we've crossed Pease River, boys, our troubles have begun.
The first damned tail I went to rip, gosh! how I cut my thumb!
While skinning the damned old stinkers our lives wasn't a show,
For the Indians watched to pick us off while skinning the buffalo.

Our meat it was buffalo rump and iron wedge bread,
And all we had to sleep on was a buffalo robe for a bed;
The fleas and graybacks worked on us, oh, boys, it was not slow,
I'll tell you there's no worse hell on earth than the range of the buffalo.

The season being near over, old Crego he did say
The crowd had been extravagant, was in debt to him that day.
We coaxed him and we begged him, and still it was no go—
We left his damned old bones to bleach on the range of the buffalo.

Oh, it's now we've crossed Pease River and homeward we are bound,
No more in that hell-fired country shall ever we be found.
Go home to our wives and sweethearts, tell others not to go,
For God's forsaken the buffalo range and the damned old buffalo.

Rye Whisky

I'll eat when I'm hungry, I'll drink when I'm dry;
If the hard times don't kill me, I'll live till I die.

Refrain:
Rye whisky, rye whisky, rye whisky, I cry,
If you don't give me rye whisky, I surely will die.

From *Cowboy Songs and Other Frontier Ballads,* collected by John A. Lomax and Alan Lomax, Revised and Enlarged, pp. 163–165. Copyright, 1910, 1916, 1938, by The Macmillan Company. New York. Copyright, 1938, by John A. Lomax.

I'll tune up my fiddle, and I'll rosin my bow,
And make myself welcome wherever I go.

Beefsteak when I'm hungry, red liquor when I'm dry,
Greenbacks when I'm hard up, and religion when I die.

They say I drink whisky; my money's my own,
All them that don't like me can leave me alone.

Sometimes I drink whisky, sometimes I drink rum,
Sometimes I drink brandy, at other times none.

But if I get boozy, my whisky's my own,
And them that don't like me can leave me alone.

Jack o' diamonds, jack o' diamonds, I know you of old,
You've robbed my poor pockets of silver and gold.

Oh, whisky, you villain, you've been my downfall;
You've kicked me, you've cuffed me, but I love you for all

If the ocean was whisky and I was a duck
I'd dive to the bottom and get one sweet suck.

But the ocean ain't whisky and I ain't a duck,
So we'll round up the cattle and then we'll get drunk.

Sweet milk when I'm hungry, rye whisky when I'm dry,
If a tree don't fall on me, I'll live till I die.

I'll buy my own whisky, I'll make my own stew;
If I get drunk. madam. it's nothing to you.

I'll drink my own whisky, I'll drink my own wine;
Some ten thousand bottles I've killed in my time.

I'll drink and I'll gamble, my money's my own,
And them that don't like me can leave me alone.

My foot in the stirrup, my bridle in my hand,
A-courting fair Mollie, to marry if I can.

My foot's in my stirrup, my bridle's in my hand;
I'm leaving sweet Mollie, the fairest in the land.

Ier parents don't like me, they say I'm too poor;
They say I'm unworthy to enter her door.

I've no wife to quarrel, no babies to bawl;
The best way of living is no wife at all.

Way up on Clinch Mountain I wander alone;
I'm as drunk as the devil. Oh, let me alone.

You may boast of your knowledge, and brag of your sense,
'Twill all be forgotten a hundred years hence.

I Ride an Old Paint

From *Singing Cowboy,* A Book of Western Songs, collected and edited by Margaret Larkin. Arranged for the piano by Helen Black, pp. 17–19. Copyright, 1931, by Alfred A. Knopf, Inc. New York City.

I ride an old paint, and I lead an old dam,
I'm going to Montana for to throw the houlihan.
They feed in the coulees and water in the draw;
Their tails are all matted, and their backs are all raw.
Chorus:

 Git along, you little dogies, git along there slow,
 For the fiery and the snuffy are a-r'aring to go!

Old Bill Jones had two daughters and a song,
One went to Denver and the other went wrong.
His wife she died in a pool room fight,
But still he sings from morning till night.

Oh, when I die take my saddle from the wall,
Put it on my pony, lead him out of his stall,
Tie my bones to his back, turn our faces to the West,
And we'll ride the prairies that we love best.
Chorus:

 Ride around the little dogies, ride around 'em slow,
 For the fiery and the snuffy are a-r'aring to go!

Trail to Mexico

 I made up my mind in the earl-y morn, To leave the
 home where I was born, To leave my
 na —— tive home for a while, And trav-el
 west for man—y a mile.

I made up my mind in the early morn,
To leave the home where I was born,
To leave my native home for a while,
And travel west for many a mile.

'Twas in the year of '83.
That A. J. Stinson he hired me,
He said, "Young man, I want you to go,
And follow my herd to Mexico."

Ibid., pp. 49–51.

'Twas in the springtime of the year,
I volunteered to drive the steers,
I'll tell you boys, 'twas a long hard go,
As the trail rolled on into Mexico.

When I arrived in Mexico,
I wanted my girl, but I could not go,
So I wrote a letter to my dear,
But not a word from her did I hear.

So I returned to my one time home,
Inquired for the girl whom I adore,
She said, "Young man, I've wed a richer life,
Therefore young fellow, go and get another wife."

"Oh curse your gold and your silver too,
Oh curse the girl who won't prove true,
I'll go right back to the Rio Grande,
And get me a job with a cowboy band."

"Oh, Buddy, oh, Buddy, oh, please don't go,
Oh, please don't go to Mexico,
If you've no girl more true than I,
Oh, please don't go where the bullets fly."

"If I've no girl more true than you,
If I've no girl who will prove true,
I'll go right back where the bullets fly,
And follow the cow trail till I die."

The Cowboy's Lament

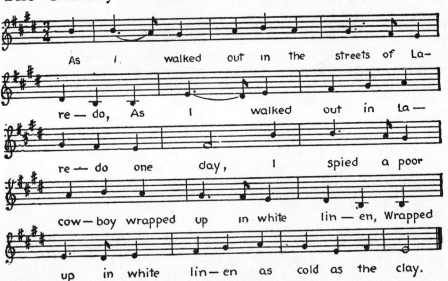

As I walked out in the streets of La-
re — do, As I walked out in La-
re — do one day, I spied a poor
cow — boy wrapped up in white lin — en, Wrapped
up in white lin — en as cold as the clay.

From *Cowboy Songs and Other Frontier Ballads*, collected by John A. Lomax and Alan Lomax, Revised and Enlarged, pp. 417–420. Copyright, 1910, 1916, 1938, by The Macmillan Company. New York. Copyright, 1938, by John A. Lomax.

As I walked out in the streets of Laredo,
As I walked out in Laredo one day,
I spied a poor cowboy wrapped up in white linen,
Wrapped up in white linen as cold as the clay.

"Oh, beat the drum slowly and play the fife lowly,
Play the dead march as you carry me along;
Take me to the green valley, there lay the sod o'er me,
For I'm a young cowboy and I know I've done wrong.

"I see by your outfit that you are a cowboy"—
These words he did say as I boldly stepped by.
"Come sit down beside me and hear my sad story;
I am shot in the breast and I know I must die.

"Let sixteen gamblers come handle my coffin,
Let sixteen cowboys come sing me a song.
Take me to the graveyard and lay the sod o'er me,
For I'm a poor cowboy and I know I've done wrong.

"My friends and relations they live in the Nation,
They know not where their boy has gone.
He first came to Texas and hired to a ranchman
Oh, I'm a young cowboy and I know I've done wrong.

"It was once in the saddle I used to go dashing,
It was once in the saddle I used to go gay;
First to the dram-house and then to the card-house;
Got shot in the breast and I am dying today.

"Get six jolly cowboys to carry my coffin;
Get six pretty maidens to bear up my pall.
Put bunches of roses all over my coffin,
Put roses to deaden the sods as they fall.

"Then swing your rope slowly and rattle your spurs lowly,
And give a wild whoop as you carry me along;
And in the grave throw me and roll the sod o'er me
For I'm a young cowboy and I know I've done wrong.

"Oh, bury beside me my knife and six-shooter,
My spurs on my heel, my rifle by my side,
And over my coffin put a bottle of brandy
That the cowboys may drink as they carry me along.

"Go bring me a cup, a cup of cold water,
To cool my parched lips," the cowboy then said;
Before I returned his soul had departed,
And gone to the round-up—the cowboy was dead.

We beat the drum slowly and played the fife lowly,
And bitterly wept as we bore him along;
For we all loved our comrade, so brave, young, and handsome,
We all loved our comrade although he'd done wrong.

MINERS' SONGS

What Was Your Name in the States?

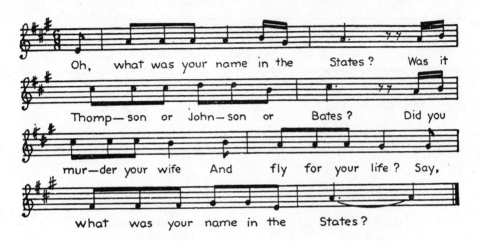

Oh, what was your name in the States? Was it
Thomp—son or John—son or Bates? Did you
mur—der your wife And fly for your life? Say,
what was your name in the States?

Oh, what was your name in the States?
Was it Thompson or Johnson or Bates?
Did you murder your wife
And fly for your life?
Say, what was your name in the States?

Sweet Betsey from Pike

Oh, don't you remember sweet Betsey from Pike,
Who crossed the big mountains with her lover Ike,
With two yoke of cattle, a large yellow dog,
A tall shanghai rooster and one spotted hog.

From *The American Songbag*, by Carl Sandburg, p. 106. Copyright, 1927, by Harcourt, Brace & Company, Inc.

From *Put's Golden Songster*, Containing the Largest and Most Popular Collection of California Songs Ever Published, by the Author of "Put's Original California Songster," pp. 50–52. Copyright, 1858, by John A. Stone. San Francisco: D. E. Appleton & Co.
The tune ("Villikins and His Dinah") and chorus are given as sung by John McCready at Groveland, Tuolumne Co., California, recorded by Sidney Robertson for the Archive of California Folk Music at the University of California, and published in *The Gold Rush Song Book*, compiled by Eleanora Black and Sidney Robertson (1940), pp. 10–11.

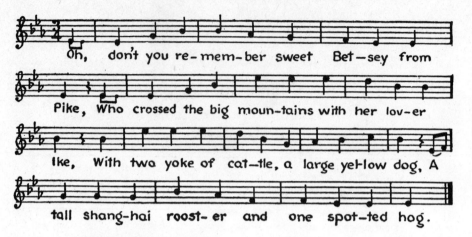

Oh, don't you re-mem-ber sweet Bet-sey from Pike, Who crossed the big moun-tains with her lov-er Ike, With two yoke of cat-tle, a large yel-low dog, A tall shang-hai roost-er and one spot-ted hog.

Chorus:

Singing tooral lal looral lal looral lal la,
Singing tooral lal looral lal looral lal la,
Sing tooral lal looral, sing tooral lal la,
Singing tooral lal looral lal looral lal la.

One evening quite early they camped on the Platte,
'Twas near by the road on a green shady flat,
Where Betsey, sore-footed, lay down to repose—
With wonder Ike gazed on that Pike County rose.

Their wagon broke down with a terrible crash,
And out on the prairie rolled all kinds of trash;
A few little baby clothes done up with care—
'Twas rather suspicious, though all on the *square.*

The shanghai ran off, and their cattle all died;
That morning the last piece of bacon was fried;
Poor Ike was discouraged, and Betsey got mad,
The dog drooped his tail and looked wondrously sad.

They stopped at Salt Lake to inquire the way,
When Brigham declared that sweet Betsey should stay;
But Betsey got frightened and ran like a deer,
While Brigham stood pawing the ground like a steer.

They soon reached the desert, where Betsey gave out,
And down in the sand she lay rolling about;
While Ike, half distracted, looked on with surprise,
Saying, "Betsey, get up, you'll get sand in your eyes."

Sweet Betsey got up in a great deal of pain,
Declared she'd go back to Pike County again;
But Ike gave a sigh, and they fondly embraced,
And they travelled along with his arm round her waist.

They suddenly stopped on a very high hill,
With wonder looked down upon old Placerville;
Ike sighed when he said, and he cast his eyes down,
"Sweet Betsey, my darling, we've got to Hangtown."

Long Ike and sweet Betsey attended a dance;
Ike wore a pair of his Pike County pants;
Sweet Betsey was covered with ribbons and rings;
Say Ike, "You're an angel, but where are your wings?"

A miner said, "Betsey, will you dance with me?"
"I will that, old hoss, if you don't make too free;
But don't dance me hard; do you want to know why?
Dog on you! I'm chock full of strong alkali!"

This Pike County couple got married of course,
And Ike became jealous—obtained a divorce;
Sweet Betsey, well satisfied, said with a shout,
"Good-by, you big lummox, I'm glad you've backed out!"

Lousy Miner

It's four long years since I reached this land, In search of gold a-mong the rocks and sand; And yet I'm poor when the truth is told. I'm a lous-y min-er, I'm a lous-y min—er in search of shin-ing gold.

From *The Gold Rush Song Book,* Comprising a Group of Twenty-Five Authentic Ballads as They Were Sung by the Men Who Dug for Gold in California during the Period of the Great Gold Rush of 1849, compiled by Eleanora Black and Sidney Robertson, pp. 24–25. Copyright, 1940, by the Colt Press. San Francisco, California.

Text from *Put's Original California Songster;* tune from the singing of Leon Ponce, Columbia, California.

It's four long years since I reached this land,
In search of gold among the rocks and sand;
And yet I'm poor when the truth is told.
I'm a lousy miner,
I'm a lousy miner in search of shining gold.

I've lived on swine till I grunt and squeal,
No one can tell how my bowels feel,
With slapjacks a-swimming round in bacon grease.
I'm a lousy miner,
I'm a lousy miner; when will my troubles cease?

I was covered with lice coming on the boat,
I threw away my fancy swallow-tailed coat,
And now they crawl up and down my back;
I'm a lousy miner,
I'm a lousy miner, a pile is all I lack.

My sweetheart vowed she'd wait for me
Till I returned; but don't you see
She's married now, sure, so I'm told,
Left her lousy miner,
Left her lousy miner, in search of shining gold.

Oh, land of gold, you did me deceive,
And I intend in thee my bones to leave;
So farewell, home, now my friends grow cold,
I'm a lousy miner,
I'm a lousy miner in search of shining gold.

My Sweetheart's the Mule in the Mines

My sweetheart's the mule in the mines,
I drive her without reins or lines,
On the bumper I sit,
I chew and I spit
All over my sweetheart's behind.

A bowdlerized version follows:

From *Minstrels of the Mine Patch,* Songs and Stories of the Anthracite Industry, by George Korson, pp. 122–123. Copyright, 1938, by the University of Pennsylvania Press. Philadelphia.
Air: "My Sweetheart's the Man in the Moon." Transcribed by Melvin LeMon.

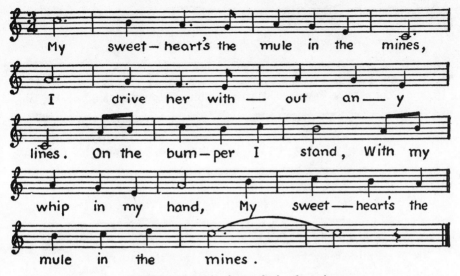

My sweetheart's the mule in the mines,
I drive her without any lines.
On the bumper I stand,
With my whip in my hand,
My sweetheart's the mule in the mines.

Me Johnny Mitchell Man

Oh, you know Joe Silovatsky,
Dat man my brudder;
Last night him come fer my shanty:
"John, I'm come un tell you fer,
I'm tell you fer tomorra,
Ev'nink dark like night;
Lotsa miners all, beeg un shmall,
Gonna have a shtrike.
Dunt be shcabby fella, John,
Dat's I'm tell you right."
I'm say, "No sir, Joe, come out on shtrike,
Me Johnny Mitchell man."

Ibid., pp. 234–236.

The union's [United Mine Workers of America] president, thirty-year-old John Mitchell, made his entrance in 1899. . . . The Slavs worried Mitchell. How would they stand up in this fight? Undisciplined, illiterate peasants, would they remain loyal to the union? When he first came into the region Mitchell saw clearly that if he were to succeed in his mission to organize the industry, racial and national barriers must first be broken down. He made this one of his first objectives. All races, creeds, and classes he addressed with this gospel: "The coal you dig is not Slavish coal, or Polish coal, or Irish coal, it is coal." At every opportunity he urged the Welsh and Irish miners to be tolerant toward their Slavic brothers. It took time and much persuasion to dissipate the mutual hatred and distrust existing between these groups. Gradually he accomplished his purpose, and Slavs mingled with English-

Oh, you know Joe Sil-o-vats-ky, Dat man my brud-der; Last
night him come fer my shan-ty: John, i'm come un tell you fer, I'm
tell you fer to-mor-ra, Ev'—nink dark like night; Lot-sa
min-ers all, beeg un shmall, Gon-na have a shtrike.
Dunt be shcab-by fel-la, John, Dat's I'm tell you right." I'm say,
"No sir, Joe, come out on shtrike, Me John-ny Mit-chell man."

Chorus

Vell, I dunt 'fraid fer not-tink, Dat's me nev-air shcare,
Com-in' shtrike to-mor-ra night? Dat's de biz-ness, I dunt care.
Right-a here I'm tell-a you, Me no shcab-by fel-la, Me
good un-ion cit-i-zen, Me John—ny Mit—chell man.

Chorus:

Vell, I dunt 'fraid fer nottink,
Dat's me nevair shcare,
Comin' shtrike tomorra night?
Dat's de bizness, I dunt care.
Righta here I'm tella you,
Me no shcabby fella,
Me good union citizen,
Me Johnny Mitchell man.

---

speaking fellow workers at mass meetings, picnics, and parades on terms of equality.
The Slavs grew to love Mitchell. When he finally issued the call to strike, there was
no doubt in his mind as to where they stood. The ballad, "Me Johnny Mitchell
Man," in the Slavic-American dialect, which was sung throughout the region, had
reassured him. It was composed by Con Carbon. . . . Jerry Byrne, Buck Run fireboss
and minstrel, sang Version B.—G. K., *ibid.*, pp. 214–216.

Vell, me belong fer union,
Me good citizen,
Seven, mebbe 'leven, year,
I'm vorkin' in beeg, beeg 'merica;
I'm vorkin' fer de Black Heat',
Down in Lytle shaft,
In de Pine Hill shaft, Pine Knot shaft,
Un every place like dat.
Me got lotsa money,
Nine hoondret, mebbe ten,
Un shtrike kin come, like son-of-a-gun,
Me Johnny Mitchell man.

Ah, son-of-a-gun, Mr. Truesdale,
Dat's a bugger, Mr. Baer,
He dunt vantsa gib it ten per zent,
Cripes a'mighty dat's no fair.
I'm vorkin' in a gangway,
Vorkin' in a breast,
I'm loadin' coal every day,
By jeez, me nevair rest.
Me got lotsa money,
Nine hoondret, mebbe ten,
Un shtrike kin come, like son-of-a-gun,
Me Johnny Mitchell man.

Down, Down, Down

"Down, Down, Down," another barroom ballad, relates the experiences of a miner reporting for work with a hangover. But it is more than the record of a tipsy worker's muddled thoughts. Rather is it a reflection of the anthracite miner's buffetings which gives it added significance.

"The material for 'Down, Down, Down,'" writes William Keating, its author, "was picked up between gangway roof falls, put together on a mine car bumper, penciled with car sprags, punctuated with mule kicks, tuned to the thunder and vibration of underground blasts and muted to the solitude of the mines, while this mule driver rhymester worked between drunks traveling in and out of the Buck Mountain counter gangway on the third level of Oak Hill shaft at Buckley's Gap, Duncott."

"Down, Down, Down," for a long time an exclusively barroom ballad, has become generally popular. Keating himself, with his resonant bass voice, is its best interpreter. The manner in which it was sung in the first years of its existence, and how he happened to compose it, are told by Keating as follows:

In the days when I was hittin' the booze the drinks would come up, up, up when I sang "Down, Down, Down." She was too long to sing straight through, so I broke her up into groups of verses corresponding to levels in a mine. When I got through singing one level, the boys alongside the bar would yell, "Time

Ibid., pp. 38–41, 48–53.

out for drinks." Then the drinks would go round and Billy Keating would have a drink on the house or on whoever was payin' at the time. As the ballad has about forty verses, you can imagine in what condition the singer and the customers were by the time I got to the end. The barroom floor was me stage for thirty years and, be jabers, I done it up brown when I was at it. But I'm off the hard stuff for life. I've got it licked now.

How did I happen to make up "Down, Down, Down"? Well, about twenty years ago I was drivin' a mule in the Oak Hill mine. Me and the mule were the only livin' things in the gangway unless you count the rats. It got kind o' lonesome, me sittin' there on the bumper with the cars rattlin' along the dark gangways and headin's. To break the loneliness and at the same time show Jerry, me mule, that I wasn't such a bad egg after all, I used to make up ditties out o' me head and sing them as we rode along. One of them was "Down, Down, Down."

"Down, Down, Down" circulated a long time by word of mouth before being set down on paper. Keating was unable to write until he was thirty-two years old and even after he had learned to write, putting things down on paper was too irksome for him. It was so much easier to make up a ballad out of his head and just sing it.

The incentive finally to write out "Down, Down, Down," came to him in the fall of 1927 under the following circumstances: He sang the ballad at a picnic of Oak Hill colliery employees at Duncott, Schuylkill County, and when he had finished, a mine boss named McGee, from the western part of the county, offered him five dollars for a copy of the ballad. This embarrassed Keating as there were no copies in existence, and he promised to make one. However, when he realized the momentous task ahead of him, he promptly forgot the promise.

Then, three weeks later, came a memorable after pay-day spree at Duncott in which the balladist and several butties indulged. Keating had bartered a ham for a quart of moonshine, and after the bottle had made the rounds it became empty. Powerful stuff, the moonshine knocked them out. Stretched out on the grass, they lay moaning and groaning and, even in their stupor, trying to find a way to obtain a refill of the bottle. Finally an idea emerged from the party.

"Say Bill," said one of the boys. "Did you ever write that copy of 'Down, Down, Down,' for that mine boss from the West End—remember, at the Oak Hill picnic he told you he'd give you five bucks for it?"

Keating was in no condition to do any writing, but slowly it penetrated his befogged mind that this was an opportunity to earn enough cash with which to purchase more moonshine.

"We'll go over to my place," he replied at length. "My woman'll raise hell with the whole of us, but I'll write that song, even if it takes me until midnight."

Keating describes the next scene as follows: "We went to my house. I borrowed several sheets of writing-paper from my nearest neighbor and, seated around our middle-room table, with the rest of the fellows helping me with the 'spelling' (while my wife RAVED!), I wrote 'Down, Down,

Down.' After several hours' (awful!) efforts, we finished a shamefully 'scribbled!' but possibly readable, copy of my song."

The next problem was to find the boss whose address Keating knew only vaguely as somewhere in the West End. The four booze-thirsty musketeers then got into a rickety automobile and rode to the West End looking for a McGee where the woods could not be seen for McGees. "Finally, after miles of back-tracking, after hootin', and tootin' the flivver's horn through nearly every town, village and 'Patch' in the western end of Schuylkill County without finding 'our' McGee," writes Keating, "we gave up, or rather, we took a different 'tack.' "

They stopped in front of a pool room speakeasy which made them feel at home. The sage behind the bar knew plenty of McGees but not the one the boys were hunting. While Keating poured out his story, the bartender kept his Irish blue eyes glued to the scribbled copy of "Down, Down, Down," smiling as he read. Presently he said, "Say, Butty, is this the only copy ye have of this song?" To which Keating replied, "It is, and it's only through the Mercy of God that I had strength enough in me hand to write that one this evenin'."

"Well," said the bartender, "ye needn't hunt any farther for any McGees. I'll give ye five dollars fer this song, and call your butties in. I'll give ye all a drink and thin ye'll sing this song till I learn the 'chune' av it if it takes from now till mornin'."

"The show was on," Keating adds. "We drank, I sang. We drank again, and I sang again—this song without end. Amen!"

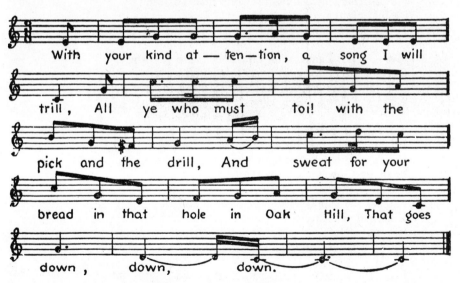

With your kind attention, a song I will trill,
All ye who must toil with the pick and the drill,
And sweat for your bread in that hole in Oak Hill,
That goes down, down, down.

When I was a boy says my daddy to me:
"Stay out of Oak Hill, take my warning," says he,
"Or with dust you'll be choked and a pauper you'll be,
Broken down, down, down."

But I went to Oak Hill and I asked for a job,
A mule for to drive or a gangway to rob.
The boss said, "Come out, Bill, and follow the mob
That goes down, down, down."

On the strength of the job and the tune of this rhyme,
I strolled into Tim's an' drank twenty-five shines;
Reported next morning, half dead but on time
To go down, down, down.

Says Pete McAvoy, "Here's Bill Keatin' the scamp."
Just back, Pete supposed, from a million-mile tramp.
Pete showed me the "windie" [1] where I'd get a lamp
To go down, down, down.

The lamp man he squints through the window at me,
"What's your name? What's your age? What's your number?" says he
"Bill Keatin', I'm thirty, number twenty-three,
Mark that down, down, down."

With a frown of disfavor, my joke it was met,
For an argument plainly, the lamp man was set.
He told me that divil a lamp would I get
To go down, down, down.

Says I, "Mr. Lamp Man, now don't l'ave us fight;
Can't ye see be me eyes I was boozin' all night?
Sure the mines will be dark and I'll have to have light
While I'm down, down, down."

With an old greasy apron, Jim polished his specks,
Declarin' the lamp house rules would be wrecked,
If he'd give out his lantherns 'thout gettin' brass checks
From us Clowns! Clowns! Clowns!

I found the supply clerk, of him I inquired
If he had any checks of the sort Jim desired.
He said: "Here's a check, if you lose it, you're fired,
Mark that down, down, down."

I had the precious lamp check that would pacify Jim,
Flip, into his window, I flung it to him
Sayin', "Now quit your grumbling, an' give me a glim
To go down, down, down."

---

[1] Window.—G. K.

A contraption Jim gave me, a hose on a box,
'Twas so heavy I thought it was loaded with rocks.
If a car jumped the track, you could use it for blocks
While you're down, down, down.

The box breaks the bones in the small of your back,
Wears the hide off your hips where it hangs be a strap;
Oh! the gawk that transported such lamps to the Gap
May go down, down, down.

When you ask for a lamp you commit an offense,
You'd imagine the lamp man stood all the expense;
While for lamps that won't light we pay sixty-five cents
While we're down, down, down.

We wait at Jim's window while winter winds stab,
While the lamp man unravels a lot of crank gab.
Did ye e'er meet a lamp man that wasn't a crab
In your rounds? Aren't they hounds?

Crabbed lamp lords, ye'll cringe for your cranks whin ye die,
For the way that ye bulldozed me butties [1] and I;
Me and Tracy'll be twanging this ballad on high
While you're down, down, down.

Then into the office I sauntered to Boss Sam.
With a cheery "Good mornin'," says I, "here I am,
With booze in me bottle and beer in me can
To go down, down, down."

"Well, Billy, me bucko, how are you today?"
"Outside of a headache," says I, "I'm O.K.
I've been samplin' the soda in every café
In the town, town, town.

"Sam, where is my job at?" I wanted to know.
"Was it in the new drift?" Sam shook his head, no.
"When you hit the fifth lift you'll have one more to go,
So get down, down, down."

I asked Sam what tools would I need in the place.
"Very few," said the boss with a grin on his face.
"One seven-size scoop in a coop-stoopy space
Away down, down, down."

With a note from the boss to the shaft I made haste,
Saluted the top-man and in line took me place
Sayin' "Gi' me a cage, for I've no time to waste,
Let me down, down, down."

---

[1] Fellow miners, especially one who works abreast in partnership with another miner.
A term used in English mining for two hundred years, and by soldiers in the World
War under its other form "buddy."—G. K.

"All aboard for the bottom!" the top-man did yell,
We stepped on the cage, he ding-donged a bell;
Through that hole in Oak Hill, like a bat out o' hell
We went down, down, down.

In wet or dry weather that shaft always rains,
There's a trembling of timbers and clanking of chains.
Just off of a spree, it flip-flopped me few brains
Going down, down, down.

It happened that something was wrong with the pump;
The water was up—we struck a wet bump.
But the cage kept descending and into the sump [1]
We went down, down, down.

I've been on the outside and inside before,
I fell into oceans and rivers galore,
But that dip in that deep dirty sump made me sore
Away down, down, down.

The fireboss he flagged me, fool questions to ask.
Was I married, or single and where I worked last.
Says I, "Lind me you pincil, me present and past
I'll write down, down, down."

Between the sump bath and headache I felt like a dope,
Going down in the gloom of the underground slope,
On a tricky man-truck and a rotten old rope,
Going down, down, down.

She was blocked from the dish to the knuckle with smoke,
The dust was so thick that I thought I would choke.
Says I to meself I guess here's where I croak
Away down, down, down.

Groped into the gangway they gave me a scoop,
The cut was just fired, muck heaped to the roof.
I stooped an' I scooped till me back looped-the-loop
Stoopin' down, down, down.

That first car we loaded held five tons I swore
And that Buck Mountain coal has the weight of iron ore.
We scooped seven cars but when they brought us one more
I laid down, down, down.

She was heaved on the bottom and cracked on the top
Ne'er a pole, ne'er a slab, ne'er a laggin', nor prop
Pretty soon I expect that Gap Mountain will drop
And come down, down, down.

[1] A basin at the bottom of a slope or shaft where water is collected to be pumped out.—G. K.

That journey each morning it near breaks me heart;
The steps in the mule-way is ten feet apart;
You must watch your brogans, for if you get a start
You'll roll down, down, down.

The Oak Hill officials are foxy galoots,
With company-store tyrants they're all in cahoots;
With the gangways a river, you're bound to buy boots,
While you're down, down, down.

On pay days I rave; Rube Tracy oft swore,
In fact 'twas enough to make both of us sore,
When our wives drag our wages all out in the store
While we're down, down, down.

But yet I'm in right, for I'm on the ground floor,
In deep in the wet and in deep in the store;
If they sink Oak Hill shaft six or seven lifts more
I'll go down, down, down.

It's a most cruel fate, but continue we must,
Delvin' deep for black diamonds, beneath the earth's crust,
Moil for mush and molasses and eating coal dust
Away down, down, down.

All I drew for a year was a dollar or three,
Those company-store thieves made a pauper of me,
But for ballads like this, I'd have starved for a spree
In the town, town, town.

Toil, you put early-gray on my poor daddy's head,
While he slaved in Oak Hill to provide us with bread;
How I wish I had heeded the warning he plead:
"Don't go down, down, down."

Now my back is toil-bent, my feet work-worn, slow.
Soon the hair on my head will be white as the snow.
Then I fear I'll be shipped to the Pogie below—
Broken down, a pauperized clown.

SONGS OF THE FARMER

Young Man Who Wouldn't Hoe Corn

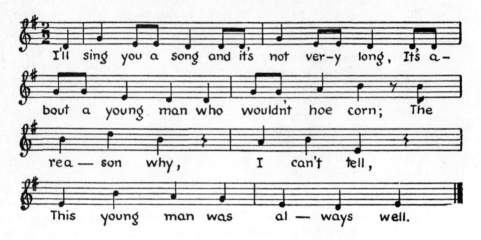

I'll sing you a song and it's not very long,
It's about a young man who wouldn't hoe corn;
The reason why, I can't tell,
This young man was always well.

He planted his corn in the month of June
And in July it was knee high;
First of September came a big frost
And all this young man's corn was lost.

He went to the fence and there peeped in,
The weeds and the grass came up to his chin;
The weeds and the grass they grew so high,
They caused this young man for to sigh.

So he went down to his neighbor's door,
Where he had often been before:
"Pretty little miss, will you marry me?
Pretty little miss, what do you say?"

"Here you are, a-wanting for to wed
And cannot make your own cornbread!
Single I am, single I'll remain,
A lazy man I'll not maintain."

From Resettlement Song Sheets, [edited by Charles Seeger]. "Number 3 of a series of American Songs rarely found in popular collections." Washington, D. C.: Special Skills Division of the Resettlement Administration. [1936–1937.]

"You go down to that pretty little widow
And I hope by heck that you don't get her."
She gave him the mitten, sure as you're born,
All because he wouldn't hoe corn.

The Dodger

Yes, the can-di-date's a dodg-er, yes, a well-known dodg-er; Yes, the can-di-date's a dodg-er, yes, and I'm a dodg-er too. He'll meet you and treat you and ask you for your vote, But look out, boys, he's a— dodg-ing for a note! *Chorus* Yes, we're all dodg—ing, a— dodg-ing, dodg-ing, dodg-ing. Yes, we're all dodg—ing out a way through the world.

Yes, the candidate's a dodger, yes, a well-known dodger;
Yes, the candidate's a dodger, yes, and I'm a dodger too.
He'll meet you and treat you and ask you for your vote,
But look out, boys, he's a-dodging for a note!

Chorus:
    Yes, we're all dodging, a-dodging, dodging, dodging,
    Yes, we're all dodging out a way through the world.

Yes, the lawyer he's a dodger, yes, a well-known dodger;
Yes, the lawyer he's a dodger, yes, and I'm a dodger too.
He'll plead you a case and claim you as a friend,
But look out, boys, he's easy for to bend!

Ibid. "Number 6 of a series of American songs to supplement popular collections."
Mrs. Emma Dusenbury, of Mena, Arkansas, sings "The Dodger" in this way. She
learned it in the 1880's when a farmer could still make a living, "just as sure as he
was born." —C. S.

Yes, the doctor he's a dodger, yes, a well-known dodger;
Yes, the doctor he's a dodger, yes, and I'm a dodger too.
He'll doctor you and cure you for half you possess,
But look out, boys, he's a-dodging for the rest!

Yes, the preacher he's a dodger, yes, a well-known dodger;
Yes, the preacher he's a dodger, yes, and I'm a dodger too.
He'll preach you a gospel and tell you of your crimes,
But look out, boys, he's a-dodging for your dimes!

Yes, the merchant he's a dodger, yes, a well-known dodger;
Yes, the merchant he's a dodger, yes, and I'm a dodger too.
He'll sell you the goods at double the price,
But when you go to pay him, you'll have to pay him twice!

Yes, the farmer he's a dodger, yes, a well-known dodger;
Yes, the farmer he's a dodger, yes, and I'm a dodger too.
He'll plow his cotton, he'll plow his corn,
He'll make a living just as sure as you're born!

Yes, the lover he's a dodger, yes, a well-known dodger;
Yes, the lover he's a dodger, yes, and I'm a dodger, too .
He'll hug you and kiss you and call you his bride,
But look out, girls, he's telling you a lie!

I'm A-Goin' down This Road Feelin' Bad

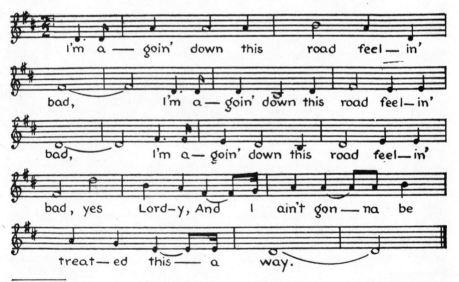

I'm a — goin' down this road feel—in' bad,
I'm a — goin' down this road feel—in' bad,
I'm a — goin' down this road feel—in' bad, yes Lord—y,
And I ain't gon—na be treat—ed this—a way.

From *A Treasury of American Song*, text by Olin Downes and Elie Siegmeister, music arranged by Elie Siegmeister, pp. 400–401. Second edition revised and enlarged, with a new introduction. Copyright, 1940, 1943, by Elie Siegmeister and Olin Downes. Alfred A. Knopf. New York. Words by Woody Guthrie.

I'm a-goin' down this road feelin' bad,
I'm a-goin' down this road feelin' bad,
I'm a-goin' down this road feelin' bad, yes Lordy,
And I ain't gonna be treated this-a way.

Yes, they fed me on cornbread and beans,
Yes, they fed me on cornbread and beans,
They fed me on cornbread and beans, yes Lordy,
And I ain't gonna be treated this-a way.

Got me way down in jail on my knees,
Got me way down in jail on my knees,
Got me way down in jail on my knees, yes Lordy,
And I ain't gonna be treated this-a way.

Takes a ten dollah shoe to fit my feet,
Takes a ten dollah shoe to fit my feet,
Takes a ten dollah shoe to fit my feet, yes Lordy,
And I ain't gonna be treated this-a way.

I'm a-goin' down where the climate suits my clothes,
I'm a-goin' down where the climate suits my clothes,
I'm a-goin' down where the climate suits my clothes,
And I ain't gonna be treated this-a way.

Seven-Cent Cotton and Forty-Cent Meat

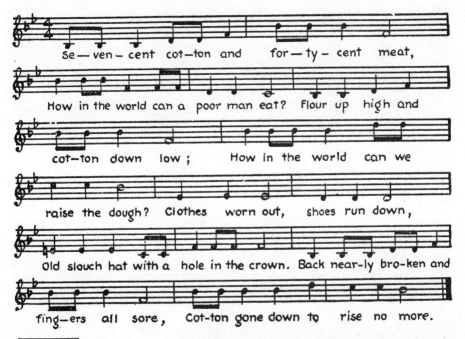

As sung by the Almanac Singers. Transcribed by the Almanac Singers. Copyright

Seven-cent cotton and forty-cent meat,
How in the world can a poor man eat?
Flour up high and cotton down low,
How in the world can we raise the dough?
Clothes worn out, shoes run down,
Old slouch hat with a hole in the crown.
Back nearly broken and fingers all sore,
Cotton gone down to rise no more.

Seven-cent cotton and eight-dollar pants,
Who in the world has got a chance?
We can't buy clothes and we can't buy meat;
Too much cotton and not enough to eat.
Can't help each other, what shall we do?
I can't explain it so it's up to you.
Seven-cent cotton and two-dollar hose,
Guess we'll have to do without any clothes.

Seven-cent cotton and forty-cent meat,
How in the world can a poor man eat?
Mules in the barn, no crops laid by,
Corn crib empty and the cow's gone dry.
Well water low, nearly out of sight,
Can't take a bath on Saturday night.
No use talking, any man is beat
With seven-cent cotton and forty-cent meat.

Seven-cent cotton and forty-cent meat,
How in the world can a poor man eat?
Poor getting poorer all around here;
Kids coming regular every year.
Fatten our hogs, take 'em to town,
All we get is six cents a pound.
Very next day we have to buy it back,
Forty cents a pound in a paper sack.

We'll raise our cotton, we'll raise our meat.
We'll raise everything we eat.
We'll raise our chickens, pigs, and corn;
We'll make a living just as sure as you're born.
Farmers getting stronger every year,
Babies getting fatter all around here.
No use talking, Roosevelt's the man,
To show the world that the farmer can.

The Farmer Comes to Town

When the farmer comes to town,
With his wagon broken down,
Oh, the farmer is the man who feeds them all.
If you'll only look and see,
I am sure you will agree
That the farmer is the man who feeds them all.

From *Resettlement Song Sheets*, [edited by Charles Seeger]. "Number 1 in a series of American songs rarely found in popular collections." Washington, D. C.: Special Skills Division of the Resettlement Administration. [1936–1937.]

In his *American Songbag*, Carl Sandburg says that he heard fragments of this song in Illinois in the early 1890's. "S. K. Barlow," he says, "a Galesburg milkman, who used to be a fiddler at dances near Galva, sang it for me as we washed eight- and two-gallon delivery cans and quart-measure cups on winter afternoons. W. W. Delaney said, 'As near as I can remember, that song came out in the 1860's just after the war.' "—C. S.

Chorus:
> The farmer is the man,
> The farmer is the man,
> Lives on credit till the fall;
> Then they take him by the hand
> And they lead him from the land,
> And the middleman's the man who gets it all.

When the lawyer hangs around,
While the butcher cuts a pound,
Oh, the farmer is the man who feeds them all.
And the preacher and the cook
Go a-strolling by the brook,
Oh, the farmer is the man who feeds them all.

Chorus:
> The farmer is the man,
> The farmer is the man,
> Lives on credit till the fall;
> With the int'rest rate so high,
> It's a wonder he don't die,
> For the mortgage man's the man who gets it all.

When the banker says he's broke,
And the merchant's up in smoke,
They forget that it's the farmer feeds them all.
It would put them to the test
If the farmer took a rest;
Then they'd know that it's the farmer feeds them all.

Chorus:
> The farmer is the man,
> The farmer is the man,
> Lives on credit till the fall;
> And his pants are wearing thin,
> His condition it's a sin;
> He's forgot that he's the man who feeds them all.

Wayfaring Stranger

A [1]

I'm just a poor wayfaring stranger, a-trav'ling through this world of woe;
But there's no sickness, toil nor danger in that bright world to which I go.
I'm going there to see my father, I'm going there no more to roam,
I'm just a-going over Jordan, I'm just a-going over home.

Ibid. "Number 9 of a series of American songs to supplement popular collections."

[1] L. L. McDowell, of Smithville, Tennessee, says that this is the tune and verse sung by the old settlers of DeKalb County, Tennessee. Additional stanzas were made by changing the words "father" and "mother" to "brother, " "sister," etc.
In his book, *White Spirituals in the Southern Uplands,* G. P. Jackson points out that the tune of the "Wayfaring Stranger" is almost identical to that of "Parting Friends," learned by J. G. McCurry, editor of the *Social Harp,* from Mrs. Catherine Penn in 1829.—C. S.

I'm just a poor wayfaring stranger, a-trav'ling through this world of woe;
But there's no sickness, toil nor danger in that bright world to which I go.
I'm going there to see my mother, I'm going there no more to roam,
I'm just a-going over Jordan, I'm just a-going over home.

B

The following modern verses from Virginia and Florida respectively
have been received:

Our fathers dear fought for our liberty,
Across the ocean they did roam,
They suffered pain and many hardships,
For in this land to build a home.

We've lived here many generations,
And many dear ones here have died,
But still our lives are filled with trouble,
In vain a helping hand we've cried.

I'm just a poor and lonesome traveler,
Behind a mule that's powerful slow,
A-creaking on to debt and worry,
The only place that I can go.

My father lived and died a farmer,
A-reaping less than he did sow;
And now I travel in his footsteps,
A-knowing less than he did know.

HOBO AND JAILHOUSE SONGS

Hallelujah, Bum Again

I

Oh, why don't I work like the other men do?
How the hell can I work when the skies are so blue?

Chorus:
    Hallelujah, I'm a bum!
    Hallelujah, bum again,
    Hallelujah! Bum a handout,
    Revive me again.

If I was to work and save all I earn,
I could buy me a bar and have whiskey to burn.

Oh, I love Jim Hill, he's an old friend of mine,
Up North I ride rattlers all over his line.

Oh, I ride box cars and I ride fast mails,
When it's cold in the winter I sleep in the jails.

I passed by a saloon and I hear someone snore,
And I found the bartender asleep on the floor.

I stayed there and drank till a fly-mug came in,
And he put me to sleep with a sap on the chin.

Next morning in court I was still in a haze,
When the judge looked at me, he said, "Thirty days!"

From *The Hobo's Hornbook,* A Repertory for a Gutter Jongleur, collected and annotated by George Milburn, pp. 97–101. Copyright, 1930, by George Milburn New York: Ives Washburn.

It is hardly safe to classify the following widely-sung ballad as a Wobbly song. There is some dispute as to its origin. Budd L. McKillips, who has himself written some first-rate hobo poetry, has given me the following notes on "Hallelujah, Bum Again's" history:

"A member of the I. W. W. is credited with having written the words to 'Hallelujah, I'm a Bum.' The question of authorship isn't worth an argument, but if anybody will take the trouble to do some investigating, he will find that 'Hallelujah, I'm a Bum' was a lilting, carefree song at least eight years before the I. W. W. came squalling into the industrial world. . . . The song was found scribbled on the wall of a Kansas City jail cell where an old hobo, known as 'One-Finger Ellis,' had spent the night, recovering from an overdose of rotgut whiskey."

The first version is that of One-Finger Ellis, as well as McKillips can recall it, and the second version is the song that the Wobblies sing today. Both songs are sung to the hymn tune, "Hallelujah, Thine the Glory."—G. M.

Some day a long train will run over my head,
And the sawbones will say, "Old One-Finger's dead!"

II

When springtime does come,
Oh, won't we have fun!
We'll all throw up our jobs
And we'll go on the bum.

Chorus:
   Hallelujah, I'm a bum,
   Hallelujah, bum again,
   Hallelujah, give us a handout
   To revive us again.

Oh, springtime has come,
And I'm just out of jail,
Ain't got no money,
It all went for bail.

I went up to a house
And I knocked on the door.
A lady came out, says,
"You been here before!"

I went up to a house,
Asked for some bread;
A lady came out, says,
"The baker is dead."

I went up to a house,
Asked for a pair of pants;
A lady came out, says,
"I don't clothe no tramps!"

I went into a saloon,
And I bummed him for a drink;
He give me a glass
And he showed me the sink.

Oh, I love my boss,
And my boss loves me;
That is the reason
I'm so hun-ga-ree!

"Why don't you go to work
Like all the other men do?"
"How the hell we going to work
When there ain't no work to do?"

The Big Rock Candy Mountains

One ev'ning as the sun went down
And the jungle fire was burning,
Down the track came a hobo, hamming,[1]
And he said, "Boys, I'm not turning.
I'm headed for a land that's far away,
Beside the crystal fountains.
. I'll see you all this coming fall
In the Big Rock Candy Mountains.

Refrain:
"In the Big Rock Candy Mountains,
There's a land that's fair and bright,
Where the handouts grow on bushes
And you sleep out ev'ry night,
Where the boxcars all are empty
And the sun shines ev'ry day—
Oh, the birds and the bees and the cigaret trees,
The rock-and-rye springs where the whangdoodle sings,
In the Big Rock Candy Mountains.

Ibid., pp. 86–89.

When the hobo bard smites his lyre and sings of Utopia, a rare spirit of burlesque
moves through his song. The following selection is very similar to that better known
hobo hymn, "The Dying Hobo," and a few of the lines are identical.—G. M.

[1] *Ham,* to walk across country. From the traditional ham actor whose company
gets stranded on the road, and who is forced to walk back to the city.—G. M.

One ev'-ning as the sun went down And the jun-gle fire was burn-ing, Down the track came a ho-bo, ham-ming, And he said, "Boys, I'm not turn-ing. I'm head-ed for a land that's far a-way, Be-side the crys-tal foun-tains. I'll see you all this com-ing fall In the *Refrain* Big Rock Can-dy Moun-tains. In the Big Rock Can-dy Moun-tains, There's a land that's fair and bright, Where the hand-outs grow on bush-es And you sleep out ev'-ry night, Where the box-cars all are emp-ty And the sun shines ev'-ry day— Oh, the birds and the bees and the cig-a-ret trees, The rock-and-rye springs where the whang— dood-le sings, In the Big Rock Can-dy Moun-tains."

"In the Big Rock Candy Mountains,
All the cops have wooden legs,
And the bulldogs all have rubber teeth,
And the hens lay softboiled eggs:
The farmers' trees are full of fruit,

And the barns are full of hay.
Oh, I'm bound to go where there ain't no snow,
Where the sleet don't fall and the wind don't blow,
In the Big Rock Candy Mountains.

"In the Big Rock Candy Mountains,
You never change your socks,
And the little streams of alkyhol
Come trickling down the rocks.
The shacks all have to tip their hats
And the railroad bulls are blind,
There's a lake of stew and of whisky, too,
You can paddle all around in a big canoe,
In the Big Rock Candy Mountains.

"In the Big Rock Candy Mountains,
The jails are made of tin,
And you can bust right out again
As soon as they put you in.
There ain't no shorthandled shovels,
No axes, saws or picks—
I'm a-going to stay where you sleep all day—
Oh, they boiled in oil the inventor of toil
In the Big Rock Candy Mountains.

"Oh, come with me, and we'll go see
The Big Rock Candy Mountains."

Pie in the Sky

Long-haired preachers come out ev'ry night,
Try to tell you what's wrong and what's right;
But when asked about something to eat,
They will answer in accents so sweet:

Chorus:
    You will eat bye and bye,
    In that glorious land above the sky.
                    (way up high)
    Work and pray, live on hay,
    You'll get pie in the sky when you die.
                    (that's no lie!)

Ibid., pp. 83–85.

At the missions where the hobo sometimes applies for food and shelter he hears and becomes familiarized with religious tunes. This, in part, accounts for the amazing popularity, among hoboes, of Joe Hill's parodies. One of the best known is "Pie in the Sky," which Hill adapted to the tune of "In the Sweet Bye and Bye." Its spirit is indicative of the hobo's resentful attitude toward organized religion and, very possibly, is a more genuine expression than the mission stiff's testimonials.—G. M.

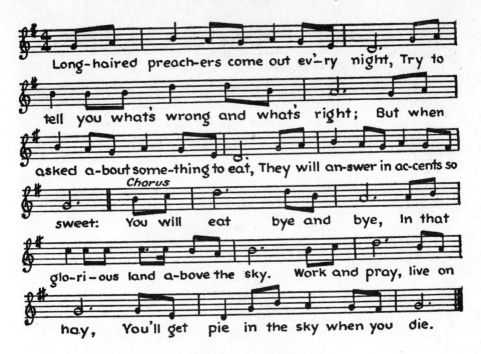

Long-haired preach-ers come out ev'-ry night, Try to
tell you what's wrong and what's right; But when
asked a-bout some-thing to eat, They will an-swer in ac-cents so

Chorus

sweet: You will eat bye and bye, In that
glo-ri-ous land a-bove the sky. Work and pray, live on
hay, You'll get pie in the sky when you die.

And the starvation army they play,
And they sing and they clap and they pray,
Till they get all your coin on the drum,
Then they'll tell you when you're on the bum:

Holy rollers and jumpers come out,
And they holler and jump and they shout,
But when eating time comes around they will say,
"You will eat on that glorious day."

Hard Times in Mount Holly Jail

When you go to Mount Holly, it's there where you're set,
It's whiskey and tobacco you get damned a bit.

From "Ballads and Folk Songs from New Jersey," by Herbert Halpert, *The Journal of American Folk-Lore*, Vol. 52, No. 203, pp. 67–68. Copyright, 1938, by The American Folk-Lore Society. New York.

Sung by Oliver Minney, near Cookstown, N. J., October 11, 1936, and several times thereafter. He did not sing the verses in the same order on different occasions.

In JAFL 48, p. 339, a song "It's Hard Times in Lancaster Jail" is given as a local product from New Hampshire. The Mount Holly text is so similar in a number of verses and in general attitude that I suggest both songs are based on some common original. See also Lomax, *American Ballads and Folk Songs*, pp. 138–143. Check for comparable material the references in Cox, p. 511 and Mackenzie, p 148.—H. H.

When you go to Mount Hol-ly, it's there where you're set, its whis-ky and to-bac-co you get damned a bit. And its hard times in Mount Hol-ly Jail, And its hard times in Mount Hol-ly Jail.

Chorus:
> And it's hard times in Mount Holly Jail,
> And it's hard times in Mount Holly Jail.

Your hands and your feet chained down to the floor,
God damn their old souls why can't they do more.

Soup that you get is not very neat,
It's full some scraps and some damned dirty meat.

Fetched from the kitchen in an old slop pail,
And that's the way they serve you in Mount Holly Jail.

Oh lice! Oh lice! as big as young quails,
You can't help get lousy in Mount Holly Jail.

There is High Sheriff Townsell, I almost forgot,
He's greatest old loafer was in the whole lot.

If he was tried and had his just due,
He'd been sent to state's prison 'count burglaries too.

There's Billy Reeves I almost forgot,
He's the damndest old loafer was in the whole lot.

Your pockets he'll pick and your clothes he will sell,
Get drunk on your money at Townsell's hotel.

There is Mr. Pitcher, he's a very nice man,
If you ask him for a favor, he'll do it if he can.

That ain't all I'd have you to know,
Every Sunday morning we have Holy Joe.

There he will stand and the truth he will tell,
To save the poor prisoners from going to hell.

The Roving Gambler

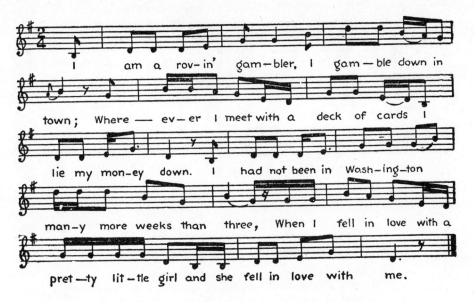

I am a rov-in' gam-bler, I gam-ble down in
town; Where — ev-er I meet with a deck of cards I
lie my mon-ey down. I had not been in Wash-ing-ton
man-y more weeks than three, When I fell in love with a
pret-ty lit-tle girl and she fell in love with me.

I am a rovin' gambler, I gamble down in town;
Wherever I meet with a deck of cards I lie my money down.
I had not been in Washington many more weeks than three,
When I fell in love with a pretty little girl and she fell in love with me.

She took me in her parlor, she cool me with her fan;
She whispered soft in her mother's ear, "I love this gambling man."
"O daughter, O dear daughter, why do you treat me so?
To leave your dear old mother and with a gambler go!"

"O mother, O dear mother, you know I love you well,
But the love I have for the gambling man no human tongue can tell."
I've gambled down in Washington, I've gambled down in Spain,
I'm goin' down to Georgia to gamble my last game.

I hear the train a-comin', a-comin' around the curve,
A-whistlin' and a-blowin', and strainin' every nerve.
"O mother, my dear mother, I'll tell you if I can
If you ever see me comin' back it'll be with a gambling man."

From Champion record, Number 45063 B ("Old Time Singin'"), sung with harmonica by Pie Plant Pete. Decca Records, Inc. New York. Transcribed by Peter Seeger.

Worried Man Blues

Chorus:

It takes a worried man to sing a worried song,
It takes a worried man to sing a worried song.
I'm worried now, but I won't be worried long.

I went across the river, and I lay down to sleep,
I went across the river, and I lay down to sleep,
When I woke up with the shackles on my feet.

Twenty-nine links of chain around my leg,
Twenty-nine links of chain around my leg,
And on each link is initial of my name.

I asked the judge what might be my fine,
I asked the judge what might be my fine.
"Twenty-one years on the R. C. Mountain line."

The train arrived, sixteen coaches long,
The train arrived, sixteen coaches long.
The girl I love is on that train and gone.

If any one asks you who composed this song,
If any one asks you who composed this song,
Tell him it was I and I sing it all day long.

From Perfect Record No. 7-05-55, sung by the Carter Family with autoharp and
guitar. Transcribed by Charles Seeger.

MOUNTAIN SONGS

Rowan County Troubles

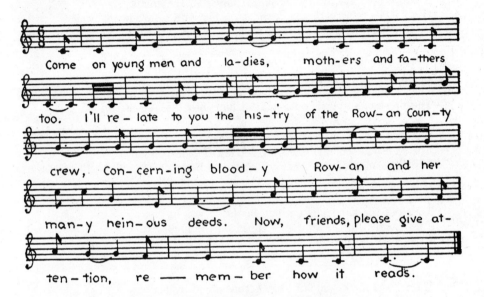

Come on young men and ladies, mothers and fathers too. I'll re-late to you the his-try of the Row-an Coun-ty crew, Con-cern-ing blood-y Row-an and her man-y hein-ous deeds. Now, friends, please give at-ten-tion, re — mem — ber how it reads.

Come on young men and ladies, mothers and fathers too.
I'll relate to you the hist'ry of the Rowan County crew,
Concerning bloody Rowan and her many heinous deeds.
Now, friends, please give attention, remember how it reads.

It was in the month of August upon election day,
John Martin he was wounded, they say by Johnny Day,
Martin could not believe it, he could not think it so;
He thought it was Floyd Tolliver that struck the fatal blow.

They shot and killed Sol Bradley, a sober innocent man,
He left his wife and loving children to do the best they can,
They wounded young Ad Sizemore; although his life was saved
He seemed to shun the grog shops since he stood so near the grave.

Martin did recover, some months had come and past,
In the town of Morehead those men both met at last;
Tolliver and a friend or two about the streets did walk,
He seemed to be uneasy and with no one wished to talk.

From *Ballad Makin' in the Mountains of Kentucky*, by Jean Thomas ("The Traipsin' Woman"), pp. 5–9. Copyright, 1939, by Henry Holt and Company, Inc. New York.

He walked in Judge Carey's grocery and stepped up to the bar,
But little did he think, dear friends, that he met the fatal hour;
The sting of death was near him, Martin rushed in at the door,
A few words passed between them concerning a row before.

The people soon were frightened, began to rush out of the room,
A ball from Martin's pistol laid Tolliver in the tomb.
His friends soon gathered round him, his wife to weep and wail;
Martin was arrested and soon confined in jail.

He was put in the jail of Rowan there to remain a while,
In the hands of law and justice to bravely stand his trial.
The people all talked of lynching him, at present though they failed,
The prisoner's friends soon moved him into the Winchester jail.

Some persons forged an order, their names I do not know,
The plan was soon agreed upon, for Martin they did go;
Martin seemed discouraged, he seemed to be in dread,
"They have sought a plan to kill me," to the jailer Martin said.

They put the handcuffs on him, his heart was in distress,
They hurried to the station, stepped on the night express.
Along the line she lumbered at her usual speed;
They were only two in numbers to commit the dreadful deed.

Martin was in the smoking car accompanied by his wife,
They did not want her present when they took her husband's life;
When they arrived at Farmers they had no time to lose,
A band approached the engineer and bid him not to move.

They stepped up to the prisoner with pistols in their hands,
In death he soon was sinking, he died in iron bands.
His wife soon heard the horrid sound; she was in another car,
She cried, "Oh Lord! they've killed him!" when she heard the pistol fire.

The death of these two men has caused great trouble in our land,
Caused men to leave their families and take the parting hand.
Retaliating, still at war they may never, never cease,
I would that I could only see my land once more in peace.

They killed the deputy sheriff, Baumgartner was his name,
They shot him from the bushes after taking deliberate aim;
The death of him was dreadful, it may never be forgot,
His body pierced and torn with thirty-three buckshot.

I compose this as a warning. Oh! beware, young men!
Your pistols may cause trouble, on this you may depend;
In the bottom of a whisky glass the lurking devils dwell,
It burns the breast of those who drink, it sends their souls to hell.

Groun'-Hog

Old Joe Dig-ger, Sam and Dave, Old Joe Dig-ger, Sam and Dave,

They went a-hog-hun-tin hard as they could stave. To-my-

rang - tang - a - whad - dle - link - y - dey !

Old Joe Digger, Sam and Dave,
Old Joe Digger, Sam and Dave,
They went a-'hog-huntin' hard as they could stave,
To-my-rang-tang-a-whaddle-linky-dey!
or To-my-whang-fol-doodle-daddy-dey!
or To-my-whack-fol-doodle-lol-dey!

Call up yer dog, O call up yer dog,
Le's go a-huntin' to ketch a groun'-hog.

Whistle up ye dog an' loaden up ye gun,
Away to the hills to have some fun.

Loaden up ye guns and whistle up ye dogs,
Away to the hills to ketch groun'-hogs.

Whet up ye knife an' whistle up ye dog,
We're goin' to the hills to hunt a groun'-hog.

Up the holler an' on each side,
We'll git ten cents fer the groun'-hog hide.

Too many rocks an' too many logs,
Too many rocks to ketch groun'-hogs.

They picked up their guns and went to the brash,
By dam, Joe, here's the hog sign fraish.

From "Cornstalk Fiddle and a Buckeye Bow," by Josiah H. Combs, in *Folk-Say,
A Regional Miscellany: 1930*, pp. 246–250. Copyright, 1930, by B. A. Botkin.
Norman: University of Oklahoma Press.
The story of a mighty chase after the lowly woodchuck. If it had transpired in the
"heroic age," it should to-day perhaps be standing alongside "The Battle of Otterburn"
and the others! Cf. Wyman and Brockway, p. 30; Cox, No. 176.—J. H. C.

Git away, Sam, an' lemme load my gun,
The groun'-hog hunt has jist begun.

He's in here, boys, the hole's wore slick.
Run here, Sam, with ye forked stick.

Git down, Sam, an' in there peep,
Fer I think I see him sound asleep.

Stand back, boys, an' le's be wise,
Fer I think I see his beaded eyes.

Hold them dogs, boys, don't let 'em howl,
I thought I heerd the groun'-hog growl.

Up jumped Sam with a ten-foot pole,
He roused it in that groun'-hog's hole.

Work, boys, work, jist as hard as ye can tear,
The meat'll do to eat an' the hide'll do to wear.

Work, boys, work for all you earn,
Skin 'im atter dark an' tan 'im in a churn.

Stand back, boys, and do it up fair,
The meat'll do to eat an' the hide'll do to wear.

Stand back, boys, an' lemme git my breath,
Ketchin' this groun'-hog's might' nigh death.

I heerd 'im give a whistle an' a wail,
I've wound my stick right in his tail.

Stand back, boys, an' gimme a little air,
I've got a little o' the groun'-hog's hair.

Git aroun', boys, on the other side,
When I pull 'im out, so he may not hide.

Up come Kate an' stood right there,
Till Berry twisted out some groun'-hog hair.

Kate an' Berry kept a-prizin' about,
Till at last they got that groun'-hog out.

Here he comes right in a whirl,
He's the biggest groun'-hog in this world.

Sam cocked his gun an' Dave pulled the trigger,
But the one killed the 'hog was old Joe Digger.

They took 'im by the tail an' wagged 'im to a log,
An' swore by Gosh! he's a hell-of-a-'hog!

Up stepped Sal with a snigger an' a grin,
Whatcha goin' a-do with the groun'-hog skin?"

Scrapes 'im down to his head an' feet,
By dam, Sam, here's a fine pile o' meat!

Listen, boys, it must be well dressed,
Er it won't sell well when we git out West.

They put 'im in the pot an' the chil'ren begin to smi
They eat that 'hog before he struck a bile.

Run here, mam, hit's bilin' hot,
Sam an' Dave's both eatin' out'n the pot.

The chil'ren screamed an' the chil'ren cried,
They love groun'-hog cooked an' fried.

Hello, mam, make Sam quit—
He's eatin' all the 'hog, I cain't git a bit.

Hello, boys, ain't it a sin,
Watch that gravy run down Sam's chin!

Oh, mam, look at Sam,
He's eat all the 'hog 'n' a-soppin' out the pan.

Watch 'im, boys, he's about to fall,
He's eat till his pants won't button at all.

Hello, boys, what ye think o' that,
Sam's eat 'hog till he's right slick-fat.

He eat that grease till it run to his nabel—
He'll eat no more 'hog until he's able.

Old Joe Digger's a smart old man,
He got that groun'-hog off on Sam.

Crawdad

Sit-tin' on the ice till my feet got cold, sug-ar-babe,

Sit-tin' on the ice till my feet got cold, sug-ar-babe,

Sit-tin' on the ice till my feet got cold, Watch-in' dat

craw-dad go to his hole, sug-ar-babe.

Sittin' on the ice till my feet got cold, sugar-babe,
Sittin' on the ice till my feet got cold, sugar-babe,
Sittin' on the ice till my feet got cold,
Watchin' that crawdad go to his hole, sugar-babe.

Crawdad, crawdad, you'd better dig deep, sugar-babe, *(twice)*
Crawdad, crawdad, you'd better dig deep,
For I'm a-goin' to ramble in my sleep, sugar-babe.

Sittin' on the ice till my feet got hot, sugar-babe, *(twice)*
Sittin' on the ice till my feet got hot,
Watchin' that crawdad rock and trot, sugar-babe.

Crawdad, crawdad, you'd better go to hole, sugar-babe, *(twice)*
Crawdad, crawdad, you'd better go to hole,
If I don't catch you, damn my soul, sugar-babe.

Sittin' on the ice till my feet got numb, sugar-babe, *(twice)*
Sittin' on the ice till my feet got numb,
Watchin' that crawdad back and come, sugar-babe.

Shoot your dice and roll 'em in the sand, sugar-babe, *(twice)*
Shoot your dice and roll 'em in the sand,
I ain't a-goin' to work for no damned man, sugar-babe.

Apple cider and cinnamon beer, sugar-babe, *(twice)*
Apple cider and cinnamon beer,
Cold hog's head and a nigger's ear, sugar-babe.

Ibid., pp. 245–246.
    The small, lobster-like crustacean. Also sometimes called "crawdaddy" by the
mountaineer. The song is doubtless of Negro origin.—J. H. C.

Sourwood Mountain

I got a girl in the head of the hollow,
Hey, diddledum dey.
She won't come and I won't call 'er,
Hey, diddledum dey,
Hey, diddledum dey,
Hey, diddledum dey.
She won't come and I won't call 'er,
Hey, diddledum dey.

She sits up with ole Si Hall,
Hey, diddledum dey.
Me and Jeff can't go there a-tall,
Hey, diddledum dey,
Hey, diddledum dey,
Hey, diddledum dey.
Me and Jeff can't go there a-tall,
Hey, diddledum dey.

From *30 and 1 Folksongs* (From the Southern Mountains), Compiled and Arranged by Bascom Lamar Lunsford and Lamar Stringfield, pp. 24–25. Copyright, 1929, by Carl Fischer, Inc. New York. International Copyright secured.
This song, which is also used as a fiddle tune, has many stanzas in addition to those given above. It is sung and played in the Carolinas, East Tennessee, and Kentucky.—B. L. L.

Some-a these days before very long,
Hey, diddledum dey,
I'll get that gal and a-home I'll run,
Hey, diddledum dey,
Hey, diddledum dey,
Hey, diddledum dey.
I'll get that gal and a-home I'll run,
Hey, diddledum dey.

Cripple Creek

I got a girl and she loves me,
She's as sweet as sweet can be.
She's got eyes of baby blue,
Makes my gun shoot straight and true.

Chorus:
   Goin' down Cripple Creek,
   Goin' in a run,
   Goin' down Cripple Creek
   To 'ave some fun.

Cripple Creek's wide and Cripple Creek's deep,
I'll wade ole Cripple Creek before I sleep.
Roll my breeches to my knees,
I wade ole Cripple Creek when I please.

Ibid., p. 53. Copyright, 1929, by Carl Fischer, Inc. New York. International Copyright secured.
This song takes its name from a wild mountain stream near Asheville, North Carolina. It is said that the Creek was named for the western mining town.—B. L. L.

I went down to Cripple Creek,
To see what them girls had to eat.
I got drunk and fell against the wall,
Ole corn likker was the cause of it all.

Cindy

I wish I was an ap—ple, A hang—in' in the
tree, And ev'—ry time my sweet—heart passed, She'd
take a bite of me. She told me that she
loved me, She called me su—gar plum, She
throwed 'er arms a—round me— I thought my time had
come. *Chorus* Git a—long home, Cin—dy, Cin—dy,
Git a—long home, Cin—dy, Cin—dy, Git a—long home,
Cin—dy, Cin—dy, I'll mar—ry you some time.

I wish I was an apple,
A-hangin' in the tree,
And ev'ry time my sweetheart passed,
She'd take a bite of me.
She told me that she loved me,
She called me sugar plum,
She throwed 'er arms around me—
I thought my time had come.

Ibid., pp. 42-43. Copyright, 1929, by Carl Fischer, Inc. New York. International
Copyright secured.
A "crackerjack" party tune, with countless stanzas. —B. L. L.

Chorus:
Git along home, Cindy, Cindy,
Git along home, Cindy, Cindy,
Git along home, Cindy, Cindy,
I'll marry you some time.

She took me to the parlor,
She cooled me with her fan,
She swore that I's the purtiest thing
In the shape of mortal man.
Oh where did you git your liquor,
Oh where did you git your dram,
I got it from a nigger
Away down in Rockinhar

Cindy got religion,
She had it once before,
When she heard my old banjo
She 'uz the first un on the floor.
I wish I had a needle,
As fine as I could sew,
I'd sew the girls to my coat tail,
And down the road I'd go.

I Wish I Wuz a Mole in the Ground

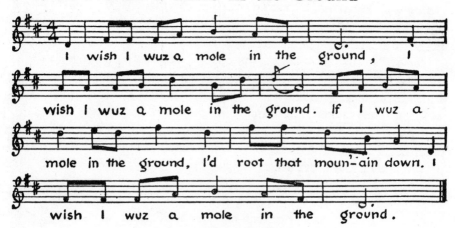

I wish I wuz a mole in the ground,
I wish I wuz a mole in the ground.
If I wuz a mole in the ground, I'd root that moun'ain down.
I wish I wuz a mole in the ground.

A typical product of the Pigeon River Valley [North Carolina].—B. L. L.

I've been in the bend so long,
I've been in the bend so long.
I've been in the bend with the rough and rowdy men,
It's baby where you been so long.

I don't like a railroad man,
No, I don't like a railroad man.
A railroad man will kill you when he can,
And drink up your blood like wine.

I wish I wuz a lizard in the spring.
Yes, I wish I wuz a lizard in the spring.
If I wuz a lizard in the spring, I could hear my darlin' sing,
I wish I wuz a lizard in the spring.

Careless Love

It's on this railroad bank I stand,
It's on this railroad bank I stand,
It's on this railroad bank I stand,
All for the love of a railroad man.
How I wish that train would come,
How I wish that train would come,
How I wish that train would come,
And take me back where I come from.

Chorus:
    Love, oh, love, oh, careless love,
    Love, oh, love, oh, careless love,
    Love, oh, love, oh, careless love,
    See what careless love has done.

When my apron string will bow,
When my apron string will bow,
When my apron string will bow,
You'll pass my door an' say "hello."
But when my apron string won't pin,
When my apron string won't pin,
When my apron string won't pin,
You'll pass my door an' won't come in.

It's caused me to weep, it's caused me to mourn,
It's caused me to weep, it's caused me to mourn,
It's caused me to weep, it's caused me to mourn,
It's caused me to leave my happy home.
What do you reckon my mama'll say,
What do you reckon my mama'll say,
What do you reckon my mama'll say,
When she hears I've gone astray.

Down in the Valley

Down in the val—ley, val—ley so low, Hang your head o—ver, hear the wind blow. Hear the wind blow, dear, hear the wind blow; Hang your head o—ver, hear the wind blow.

From Resettlement Song Sheets, [edited by Charles Seeger]. "Number 5 of a series of American songs to supplement popular collections." Washington, D. C.: Special

Down in the valley, valley so low,
Hang your head over, hear the wind blow.
Hear the wind blow, dear, hear the wind blow;
Hang your head over, hear the wind blow.

If you don't love me, love whom you please;
Throw your arms round me, give my heart ease.
Give my heart ease, dear, give my heart ease;
Throw your arms round me, give my heart ease.

Write me a letter, send it by mail;
And back it in care of Birmingham Jail.
Birmingham Jail, dear, Birmingham Jail,
And back it in care of Birmingham Jail.

Writing this letter, containing three lines,
Answer my question, "Will you be mine?"
Will you be mine, dear, will you be mine?
Answer my question, "Will you be mine?"

Go build me a castle, forty feet high,
So I can see her as she goes by.
As she goes by, dear, as she goes by,
So I can see her as she goes by.

Roses love sunshine, violets love dew;
Angels in heaven know I love you.
Know I love you, dear, know I love you,
Angels in heaven know I love you.

NEGRO SONGS

Massa Had a Yaller Gal

Massa had a yaller gal,
    He brought her from de South;
Her hair it curled so very tight
    She couldn't shut her mouth.

Skills Division of the Resettlement Administration. [1936–1937.]

This song is also widely known as "Birmingham Jail"; but the names of other cities are found in its stead, with, of course, a countless variety of verses: as "Barbourville Jail," in Kentucky; "Powder Mill Jail," in Tennessee, etc. Upon the San Francisco Bridge, in 1935, it was sung as "We're building bridges, bridges so low; Hang yourself over, feel the wind blow." Then there are the verses called "Little Willie":

Tree on the mountain, tree in full bloom;
Oh, Willie my darling, I've loved you too soon.
Your parents don't like me, so well do I know;
They say I'm not worthy to knock at your door.—C. S.

From *On the Trail of Negro Folk-Songs*, by Dorothy Scarborough, assisted by Ola Lee Gulledge, p. 68. Copyright, 1925, by Harvard University Press. Cambridge. From Louise Laurens, of Shelbyville, Kentucky.

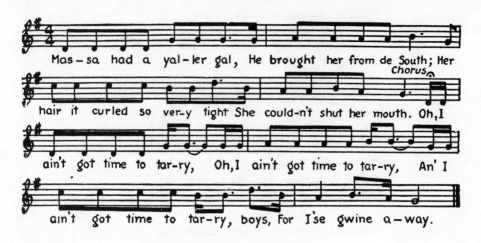

Mas-sa had a yal-ler gal, He brought her from de South; Her
hair it curled so ver-y tight She could-n't shut her mouth. Oh,I
ain't got time to tar-ry, Oh,I ain't got time to tar-ry, An' I
ain't got time to tar-ry, boys, For I'se gwine a—way.

Chorus:

> Oh, I ain't got time to tarry,
> Oh, I ain't got time to tarry,
> An' I ain't got time to tarry, boys,
> For I'se gwine away.

> He took her to de tailor,
>   To have her mouth made small.
> She swallowed up the tailor,
>   Tailorshop and all.

> Massa had no hooks nor nails
>   Nor anything like that;
> So on this darky's nose he used
>   To hang his coat and hat.

I'm Gwine to Alabamy

I'm gwine to A—la—ba—my, Oh.................................
For to see my mam—my, Ah.................................

From *Slave Songs of the United States,* by William Francis Allen, Charles Pickard Ware, Lucy McKim Garrison, p. 89. Copyright, 1867. Reprinted 1929. New York: Peter Smith.

A very good specimen, so far as notes can give one, of the strange barbaric songs that one hears upon the Western steamboats.—W. F. A., C. P. W., L. McK. G.

I'm gwine to Alabamy, — Oh,
For to see my mammy, — Ah.

She went from Ole Virginny, — Oh,
And I'm her pickaninny, — Ah.

She lives on the Tombigbee, — Oh,
I wish I had her wid me, — Ah.

Now I'm a good big nigger, — Oh,
I reckon I won't git bigger, — Ah.

But I'd like to see my mammy, — Oh,
Who lives in Alabamy, — Ah.

Charleston Gals

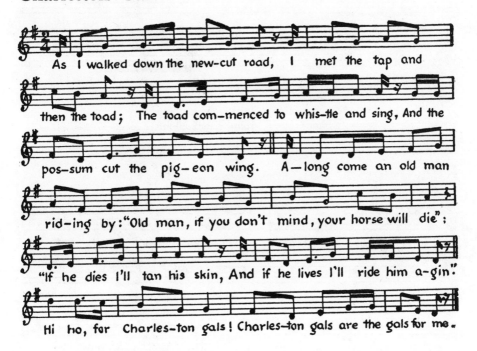

As I walked down the new-cut road,
I met the tap and then the toad;
The toad commenced to whistle and sing,
And the possum cut the pigeon wing.

Along come an old man riding by:
"Old man, if you don't mind, your horse will die";
"If he dies I'll tan his skin,
And if he lives I'll ride him agin."

Ibid., p. 88

Hi, ho, for Charleston gals!
Charleston gals are the gals for me.

As I went a-walking down the street,
Up steps Charleston gals to take a walk with me.
I kep' a-walking and they kep' a-talking,
I danced with a gal with a hole in her stocking.

Shock Along, John

Shock along, John, shock along.
Shock along, John, shock along.

Run, Nigger, Run!

O some tell me that a nigger won't steal,
But I've seen a nigger in my cornfield;
O run, nigger, run, for the patrol will catch you,
O run, nigger, run, for 'tis almost day.

Ibid., p. 67.
A corn-song, of which only the burden is remembered.—W. *F.* A., C. P. W.,
L. McK. G.

Ibid., p. 89.

The Grey Goose

Well, las' Mon-day morn-in', Lawd, Lawd, Lawd!, Well, las' Mon—day morn-in', Lawd, Lawd, Lawd!

Well, las' Monday mornin',
Lawd, Lawd, Lawd!
Well, las' Monday mornin',
Lawd, Lawd, Lawd!

My daddy went a-hunting.

Well, he carried along his zulu.

Well, along come a grey goose.

Well, he throwed it to his shoulder.

Well, he reared his hammer 'way back.

Well, he pulled on his trigger.

Well, a-down he come, windin'.

He was six weeks a-fallin'.

We was six weeks a-findin'.

And we put him on his wagon.

And we taken him to the white house.

He was six weeks a-pickin'.

Lordy, your wife and my wife.

Gonna give a feather-pickin'.

And we put him on to parboil.

He was six months a-parboil'.

As sung by Alan Lomax. Transcribed by Charles Seeger. The design of the song is the African leader-chorus form, and this version is used on the Texas prison farms 'or hoeing—a whole gang moving forward together, their hoes flashing together in the sun, across an irrigation ditch, thus:

Well, *las'* Monday *mornin'*,
Lawd, Lawd, *Lawd!*
—A. L.

And we put him on the table.

Now the forks couldn't stick him.

And the knife couldn't cut him.

And we threwed him in the hog-pen.

And he broke the belly's [1] jawbone.

And we taken him to the sawmill.

And he broke the saw's teeth out.

And the last time I seen him.

Well, he's flyin' across the ocean.

With a long string o' goslin's.

And he's goin' "Quank quink-quank!"

The Midnight Special

Well, you wake up in the mornin', hear the ding dong ring, You go a-marchin' to the ta—ble, see the same damn thing. Well, it's on-a one ta—ble, knife-a, fork, an' a pan, An' if you say an-y-thing a—bout it, you're in trou-ble with the man. Chorus let the Mid-night Spe-cial shine its light on me, Let the Mid-night Spe-cial shine its ev-er-lov-in' light on me.

[1] The sow's.—A. L.

As sung by Huddie ("Lead Belly") Ledbetter. Transcribed by Peter Seeger.

Well, you wake up in the mornin', hear the ding dong ring,
You go a-marchin' to the table, see the same damn thing.
Well, it's on-a one table, knife-a, fork, an' a pan,
An' if you say anything about it, you're in trouble with the man.

Chorus:
> Let the Midnight Special shine its light on me,
> Let the Midnight Special shine its ever-lovin' light on me.

If you go to Houston, you better walk right;
You better not stagger, you better not fight,
Or Sheriff Benson will arrest you, he will carry you down.
If the jury finds you guilty, you'll be penitentiary-bound.

Yonder comes li'l Rosie. How in the worl' do you know?
I can tell her by her apron and the dress she wo',
Umberella on her shoulder, piece o' paper in her han'.
Well, I heard her tell the captain: "I want my man."

I'm gwine away to leave you, an' my time ain't long.
The man is gonna call me an' I'm a-goin' home.
Then I'll be done all my grievin', whoopin', holl'in', an' a-cryin',
Then I'll be done all my studyin' 'bout my great long time.

Well, the biscuits on the table, just as hard as any rock.
If you try to swallow them, break a convict's heart.
My sister wrote a letter, my mother wrote a card—
"If you want to come an' see us, you'll have to ride the rods."

Po' Laz'us (Poor Lazarus)

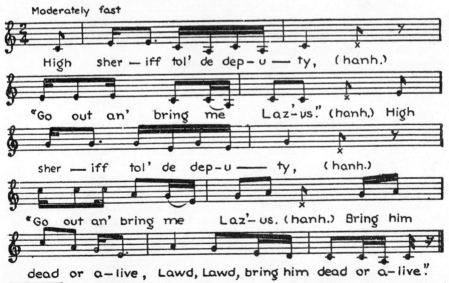

Moderately fast

High sher — iff tol' de dep-u — ty, (hanh.)
"Go out an' bring me Laz-us." (hanh.) High
sher — iff tol' de dep-u — ty, (hanh.)
"Go out an' bring me Laz'-us. (hanh.) Bring him
dead or a-live, Lawd, Lawd, bring him dead or a-live."

From *American Ballads and Folk Songs*, collected and compiled by John A. Lomax and Alan Lomax, pp. 91–93. Copyright, 1934, by The Macmillan Company. New York.

High sheriff tol' de deputy, *(hanh.)* "Go out an' bring me Laz'us." *(hanh.)*
High sheriff tol' de deputy, *(hanh.)* "Go out an' bring me Laz'us." *(hanh.)*
Bring him dead or alive, Lawd, Lawd, bring him dead or alive."

Oh, bad man Laz'us done broke in de commissary winder,
Oh, bad man Laz'us done broke in de commissary winder.
He been paid off, Lawd, Lawd, he been paid off.

Oh, de deputy 'gin to wonder, where in de worl' he could fin' him.
Oh, de deputy 'gin to wonder, where in de worl' he could fin' him.
Well, I don' know, Lawd, Lawd, I jes' don' know.

Oh, dey foun' po' Laz'us way out between two mountains,
Oh, dey foun' po' Laz'us way out between two mountains,
An' dey blowed him down, Lawd, Lawd, an' dey blowed him down.

Ol' Laz'us tol' de deputy he had never been arrested,
Ol' Laz'us tol' de deputy he had never been arrested,
By no one man, Lawd, Lawd, by no one man.

So dey shot po' Laz'us, shot him wid a great big number,
Dey shot po' Laz'us, shot him wid a great big number.
Number 45, Lawd, Lawd, number 45.

An' dey taken po' Laz'us an' dey laid him on de commissary county.
Dey taken po' Laz'us an' dey laid him on de commissary county,
An' dey walked away, Lawd, Lawd, an' dey walked away.

Laz'us tol' de deputy, "Please gimme a cool drink o' water."
Laz'us tol' de deputy, "Please gimme a cool drink o' water,
Jes' befo' I die, Lawd, Lawd, jes' befo' I die."

Laz'us' sister run an' tol' her mother,
Laz'us' sister run an' tol' her mother,
Dat po' Laz'us dead, Lawd, Lawd, po' Laz'us dead.

Laz'us' mother, she laid down her sewin',
Laz'us' mother, she laid down her sewin',
'Bout de trouble, Lawd, Lawd, she had wid Laz'us.

Laz'us' mother she come a-screamin' an' a-cryin',
Laz'us' mother she come a-screamin' an' a-cryin',
"Dat's my only son, Lawd, Lawd, dat's my only son."

Some of the verses of this ballad work song we have taken from *Negro Workaday Songs*. The rest of the words and the tune were recorded in Southern Prison camps.—J. A. L. and A. L.

Delia Holmes

De-lia, De-lia, Why did-nt you run? See dat des-per-a-do, Had a for-ty-fo' smoke-less gun, Cryin', 'All I had done gone."

Chorus

All I ·had done gone ! All I had done gone !

Good-by, Moth-er, friends and all; All I had done gone!

Delia, Delia,
Why didn't you run?
See dat desperado,
Had a forty-fo' smokeless gun,
Cryin', "All I had done gone."

Chorus:
All I had done gone!
All I had done gone!
Good-by, Mother, friends and all;
All I had done gone!

Now Coonie an' his little sweetheart
Settin' down talkin' low;
Axed her would she marry him,
She said, "Why sho'."

When the time come for marriage
She refuse' to go.
"If you don't marry me
You cannot live no mo'."

From "Delia Holmes—A Neglected Negro Ballad," by Chapman J. Milling, *Southern Folklore Quarterly*, Vol. I (December, 1937), No. 4, pp. 3–7.

. . . Will Winn [is] a most interesting colored troubador who has wandered all over the South and West, carrying a battered guitar and earning his meals and lodging by his song. Although bearing many outward indications of an unsheltered life, Will possesses personality and natural born showmanship. He states that "Delia" originated following a murder in Georgia, having been composed about 1900 by a white minstrel of Dallas, Texas, known as "Whistlin' Bill Ruff." The song, however, seems too typically Negroid to admit of this explanation.

Careful search among the most promising collections has failed to reveal anything approaching the story as rendered in Will's version. The tune could not be found at all. White, in *American Negro Folk Songs* (Cambridge, 1928), gives two brief variants of "Delia," one a mere fragment. Both of these are regarded by the compiler as variants of "Frankie and Johnny." The only other place I have been able to find the song is in Odum and Johnson's *The Negro and His Songs* (Chapel Hill, 1925). The authors here note that it is called "Pauly," "Frankie" or "Lilly," and list their version under the last name. It differs so little from "Frankie and Johnny" that I am forced to regard their variant as belonging to the latter, and better known, song.

I am deeply indebted to Mr. H. J. Martin, Columbia, S. C., for transcribing the music in connection with this article. The refrain line is repeated at the end of each stanza. The chorus is sung after every six or eight stanzas.—C. J. M.

Shot her with a pistol,
Number forty-fo'.
"You did not marry me,
You cannot live no mo'."

Turned po' Delia over
On her side very slow.
She was cryin', "Coonie,
Please don't shoot no mo'."

Death had proceeded,
It wasn't so very long
Till her mother come runnin'
With a bucket on her arm.

"Tell me, my darlin',
What have you done wrong,
Cause Coonie to shoot you
With that forty-fo' smokeless gun?"

"Some give a nickel
Some give a dime,
Help to bury
This body of mine."

Threw down his pistol
An' tried to get away.
Officers picked him up
In just a few days.

Placed him in the jail
Till his trial should come.
"Tell me now, officer,
What have I done?"

They axed him did he remember this,
"A girl that you were in love,
An' spoken things unto her
That instantly taken her nerve?"

"She moved closely beside of me
An' threw her arms around."
"Do you remember little Delia
    Holmes
And which you shot down?"

"Have I now any bond,
Or can I get one,
For the crime that I am charged,
I plead guilty I have done?"

The judge that tried him,
Handsome with the time,
Say, "Coonie, if I don't hang you
I'll give you ninety-nine."

Coonie went to Atlanta,
Drinkin' from a silver cup.
Po' li'l Delia's in the cemetery,
I hope to never wake up.

Delia's mother
Taken a trip out west,
Just to keep from hearin' the talk
Of po' li'l Delia's death.

Everywhere the train would stop
You could hear the people moan,
Singin' dat lonesome song,
"Po' Delia's dead an' gone."

Rubber tire' buggy,
Rubber tire' hack,
Take you to de cemetery,
Don't never bring you back.

Coonie wrote to the Governor,
Asked him, "Pardon me,
I was charged with murder
In the first degree.

"The judge was liberal
In givin' me my time;
Happened that he didn't hang me
But he give me ninety-nine.

"I am now a murderer,
Servin' a long, long time;
And if you will pardon me,
I'll not be guilty of another crime.

"This is Coonie in Atlanta,
Workin' 'mong the stone.
Have been here for forty-five years,
And I'm now needed at home."

Take This Hammer

Take this ham-mer, (huh!) car-ry it to the cap—tain, (huh!)

Take this ham-mer, (huh!) car-ry it to the cap—tain, (huh!)

Take this ham-mer, (huh!) car-ry it to the cap—tain, (huh!)

Tell him I'm gone, (huh) tell him I'm gone. (huh!)

Take this hammer, (*huh!*) carry it to the captain, (*huh!*)
Take this hammer, (*huh!*) carry it to the captain, (*huh!*)
Take this hammer, (*huh!*) carry it to the captain, (*huh!*)
Tell him I'm gone, (*huh!*) tell him I'm gone. (*huh!*)

Take this hammer, (*huh!*) carry it to the captain, (*huh!*)
Take this hammer, (*huh!*) carry it to the captain, (*huh!*)
Take this hammer, (*huh!*) carry it to the captain, (*huh!*)
Tell him I'm gone, (*huh!*) tell him I'm gone. (*huh!*)

If he ask you (*huh!*) was I runnin', (*huh!*)
Tell him I's flyin', (*huh!*) tell him I's flyin'. (*huh!*)

If he ask you (*huh!*) was I laughin', (*huh!*)
Tell him I's cryin', (*huh!*) tell him I's cryin'. (*huh!*)

Cap'n called me, (*huh!*) called me "a nappy-headed devil," (*huh!*)
That ain't my name, (*huh!*) that ain't my name. (*huh!*)

I don't want no (*huh!*) peas, cornbread, neither molasses, (*huh!*)
They hurt my pride, (*huh!*) they hurt my pride. (*huh!*)

I don't want no (*huh!*) cold iron shackles (*huh!*)
Around my leg, (*huh!*) around my leg. (*huh!*)

Cap'n got a big gun, (*huh!*) an' he try to play bad. (*huh!*)
Go'n' take it in the mornin' (*huh!*) if he make me mad. (*huh!*)

I'm go'n' make these (*huh!*) few days I started, (*huh!*)
Then I'm goin' home, (*huh!*) then I'm goin home, (*huh!*)

As sung by the Almanac Singers. Transcribed by Ruth Crawford Seeger.

Little Black Train Is A-Comin'

God tole Hezykiah
In a message from on high:
Go set yo' house in ordah,
For thou shalt sholy die.
He turned to the wall an' a-weepin',
Oh! see the King in tears;
He got his bus'ness fixed all right,
God spared him fifteen years.

Chorus:
    Little black train is a-comin',
    Get all yo' bus'ness right;
    Go set yo' house in ordah,
    For the train may be here tonight.

From *The Negro Sings a New Heaven,* by Mary Allen Grissom, pp. 10–11. Copyright, 1930, by the University of North Carolina Press. Chapel Hill.

Go tell that ball room lady,
All filled with worldly pride,
That little black train is a-comin',
Prepare to take a ride.
That little black train and engine
An' a little baggage car,
With idle thoughts and wicked deeds,
Must stop at the judgment bar.

There was a po' young man in darkness,
Cared not for the gospel light,
Suddenly a whistle blew
From a little black train in sight.
"Oh, death, will you not spare me?
I'm just in my wicked plight.
Have mercy, Lord, do hear me,
Pray come an' set me right."
But death had fixed his shackles
About his soul so tight,
Just befo' he got his bus'ness fixed,
The train rolled in that night.

Lord, Remember Me

From *Slave Songs of the United States*, by William Francis Allen, Charles Pickard Ware, Lucy McKim Garrison, p. 12. Copyright, 1867. Reprinted, 1929. New York: Peter Smith.

Oh, Deat' he is a little man,
  And he goes from do' to do'.
He kill some souls and he wounded some,
  And he lef' some souls to pray.

Oh,[1] Lord, remember me,
  Do, Lord, remember me;
Remember me [2] as de year roll round,
  Lord, remember me.

I want to die like-a Jesus die,
  And he die wid a free good will,
I lay out in de grave and I stretchee out e arms,
  Do, Lord, remember me.

Boll Weevil Song

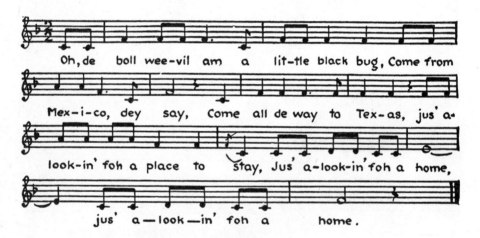

Oh, de boll wee-vil am a lit-tle black bug, Come from Mex-i-co, dey say, Come all de way to Tex-as, jus' a-look-in' foh a place to stay, Jus' a-look-in' foh a home, jus' a—look—in' foh a home.

Oh, de boll weevil am a little black bug,
  Come from Mexico, dey say,
Come all de way to Texas, jus' a-lookin' foh a place to stay,
  Jus' a-lookin' foh a home, jus' a-lookin' foh a home.

De first time I seen de boll weevil,
  He was a-settin' on de square.
De next time I seen de boll weevil, he had all of his family **dere,**
  Jus' a-lookin' foh a home, jus' a-lookin' foh a home.

---

[1] Do.—W. F. A., C. P. W., L. McK. G.
[2] I pray (cry) to de Lord.—W. F. A., C. P. W., L. McK. G.

From *The American Songbag*, by Carl Sandburg, pp. 8–10. Copyright, 1927, by Harcourt, Brace & Company. New York.

De farmer say to de weevil:
  "What make yo' head so red?"
De weevil say to de farmer, "It's a wondah I ain't dead,
  A-lookin' foh a home, jus' a-lookin' foh a home."

De farmer take de boll weevil,
  An' he put him in de hot san'.
De weevil say: "Dis is mighty hot, but I'll stan' it like a man,
  Dis'll be my home, it'll be my home."

De farmer take de boll weevil,
  An' he put him in a lump of ice;
De boll weevil say to de farmer: "Dis is mighty cool an' nice,
  It'll be my home, dis'll be my home."

De farmer take de boll weevil,
  An' he put him in de fire.
De boll weevil say to de farmer: "Here I are, here I are,
  Dis'll be my home, dis'll be my home."

De boll weevil say to de farmer:
  "You better leave me alone;
I done eat all yo' cotton, now I'm goin' to start on yo' corn,
  I'll have a home, I'll have a home."

De merchant got half de cotton,
  De boll weevil got de res'.
Didn't leave de farmer's wife but one old cotton dress,
  An' it's full of holes, it's full of holes.

De farmer say to de merchant:
  "We's in an awful fix;
De boll weevil et all de cotton up an' lef' us only sticks,
  We's got no home, we's got no home."

De farmer say to de merchant:
  "We ain't made but only one bale,
And befoh we'll give yo' dat one we'll fight an' go to jail,
  We'll have a home, we'll have a home."

As you increase the farm products you increase the insects that destroy them. You will pretty soon find out what my old Latin teacher told me about the meaning of ad infinitum. He said, "As you have learned in your entomology, you will find big bugs have little bugs on their backs to bite 'em, and the little bugs have smaller bugs and so ad infinitum." I fail to quote it accurately but you have the idea. . . .

My friends, the cotton boll weevil awakes in the spring, and by the first of September the generations coming from one pair will amount to 154,000,000, equal to the population of the Chinese Empire. What a blessing it would have been if a lark had been there to catch that pair in the beginning. (Laughter.)—*Speeches of William Henry Murray, Governor of Oklahoma* (1931), pp. 65–66.

De cap'n say to de missus:
 "What d' you t'ink o' dat?
De boll weevil done make a nes' in my bes' Sunday hat,
 Goin' to have a home, goin' to have a home."

And if anybody should ax you
 Who it was dat make dis song,
Jus' tell 'em 'twas a big buck niggah wid a paih o' blue duckin's on,
 Ain' got no home, ain' got no home.

INDEX OF AUTHORS, TITLES, AND
FIRST LINES OF SONGS

INDEX OF SUBJECTS AND NAMES